KARL MARX
FREDERICK ENGELS
COLLECTED WORKS
VOLUME
4

KARL MARX
FREDERICK ENGELS

COLLECTED
WORKS

INTERNATIONAL PUBLISHERS
NEW YORK

KARL MARX
FREDERICK ENGELS

Volume
4

MARX AND ENGELS: 1844-45

INTERNATIONAL PUBLISHERS
NEW YORK

This volume has been prepared jointly by Lawrence & Wishart Ltd., London, International Publishers Co. Inc., New York, and Progress Publishers, Moscow, in collaboration with the Institute of Marxism-Leninism, Moscow.

Library of Congress Cataloging in Publication Data

Karl Marx, 1818-1883

    Karl Marx, Frederick Engels, collected works.

      1. Socialism — Collected works.   2. Economics — Collected works.
I. Engels, Friedrich, 1820-1895.   Works. English. 1975   II. Title
HX39.5.A16 1975   335.4   73-84671
ISBN 0-7178-0455-0 (v. 4)

Editorial commissions:

GREAT BRITAIN: Jack Cohen, Maurice Cornforth, Maurice Dobb, E. J. Hobsbawm, James Klugmann, Margaret Mynatt.
USA: James S. Allen, Philip S. Foner, Dirk J. Struik, William W. Weinstone.
USSR: for Progress Publishers — N. P. Karmanova, V. N. Pavlov, M. K. Shcheglova, T. Y. Solovyova; for the Institute of Marxism-Leninism — P. N. Fedoseyev, L. I. Golman, A. I. Malysh, A. G. Yegorov, V. Y. Zevin.

College
HX
39.5
.A16
1975
v. 4

First printing 1975

Contents

Preface XV

K. Marx and F. Engels. **The Holy Family, or Critique of Critical Criticism.**
Against Bruno Bauer and Company 5

Foreword 7

C h a p t e r I. "Critical Criticism in the Form of a Master-Bookbinder", or Critical Criticism as Herr Reichardt (*by Engels*) 9

C h a p t e r II. "Critical Criticism" as a "Mill-Owner", or Critical Criticism as
Herr Jules Faucher (*by Engels*) 12

C h a p t e r III. "The Thoroughness of Critical Criticism", or Critical Criticism
as Herr J. (Junguitz?) (*by Engels*) 17

C h a p t e r IV. "Critical Criticism" as the Tranquillity of Knowledge, or "Critical
Criticism" as Herr Edgar 19

    1) Flora Tristan's *Union Ouvrière* (*by Engels*) 19
    2) Béraud on Prostitutes (*by Engels*) 20
    3) Love (*by Marx*) 20
    4) Proudhon (*by Marx*) 23

        Characterising Translation No. 1 24
        Critical Comment No. 1 31
        Critical Comment No. 2 34
        Characterising Translation No. 2 38
        Critical Comment No. 3 39
        Characterising Translation No. 3 43
        Critical Comment No. 4 48
        Characterising Translation No. 4 50
        Critical Comment No. 5 51

C h a p t e r V. "Critical Criticism" as a Mystery-Monger, or "Critical Criticism"
as Herr Szeliga (*by Marx*) 55

    1) "The Mystery of Degeneracy in Civilisation" and "The Mystery
of Rightlessness in the State" 56
    2) The Mystery of Speculative Construction 57

3) "The Mystery of Educated Society" 61
4) "The Mystery of Probity and Piety" 69
5) "Mystery, a Mockery" 72
6) Turtle-Dove (Rigolette) 75
7) The World System of the *Mysteries of Paris* 76

Chapter VI. Absolute Critical Criticism, or Critical Criticism as Herr Bruno   78

1) Absolute Criticism's First Campaign (*by Marx*) 78

a) "Spirit" and "Mass" 78
b) The Jewish Question No. 1. The Setting of the Questions 87
c) Hinrichs No. 1. Mysterious Hints on Politics, Socialism and Philosophy 90

2) Absolute Criticism's Second Campaign 92

a) Hinrichs No. 2. "Criticism" and "Feuerbach". Condemnation of Philosophy (*by Engels*)   92
b) The Jewish Question No. 2. Critical Discoveries on Socialism, Jurisprudence and Politics
   (Nationality) (*by Marx*) 94

3) Absolute Criticism's Third Campaign (*by Marx*) 99

a) Absolute Criticism's Self-Apology. Its "Political" Past 99
b) The Jewish Question No. 3 106
c) Critical Battle against the French Revolution 118
d) Critical Battle against French Materialism 124
e) Final Defeat of Socialism 134
f) The Speculative Cycle of Absolute Criticism and the Philosophy of Self-Consciousness 136

Chapter VII. Critical Criticism's Correspondence 144

1) The Critical Mass (*by Marx*) 144
2) The "Un-Critical Mass" and "Critical Criticism" 148

a) The "Obdurate Mass" and the "Unsatisfied Mass" (*by Marx*) 148
b) The "Soft-Hearted" Mass "Pining for Redemption" (*by Engels*) 151
c) Grace Bestowed on the Mass (*by Marx*) 154

3) The Un-Critically Critical Mass, or "Criticism" and the "Berlin
   Couleur" (*by Marx*) 154

Chapter VIII. The Earthly Course and Transfiguration of "Critical Criticism", or "Critical Criticism" as Rudolph, Prince of Geroldstein (*by Marx*) 162

1) Critical Transformation of a Butcher into a Dog, or Chourineur 163
2) Revelation of the Mystery of Critical Religion, or Fleur de Marie 166

a) The Speculative "Marguerite" 166
b) Fleur de Marie 168

3) Revelation of the Mysteries of Law 176

a) The *Maître d'école*, or the New Penal Theory. The Mystery of Solitary Confinement
   Revealed. Medical Mysteries 176
b) Reward and Punishment. Double Justice (*with a Table*) 188
c) Abolition of Degeneracy Within Civilisation and of Rightlessness in the State 190

4) The Revealed Mystery of the "Standpoint" 191
5) Revelation of the Mystery of the Utilisation of Human Impulses,
   or Clémence d'Harville 193
6) Revelation of the Mystery of the Emancipation of Women, or
   Louise Morel 195
7) Revelation of Political Economic Mysteries 196

a) Theoretical Revelation of Political Economic Mysteries 196
b) "The Bank for the Poor" 197
c) Model Farm at Bouqueval 199

8) Rudolph, "the Revealed Mystery of All Mysteries" 201

Chapter IX. The Critical Last Judgment (*by Marx*) 210
Historical Epilogue 211

F. Engels. Continental Socialism 212

F. Engels. Description of Recently Founded Communist Colonies Still
in Existence 214

F. Engels. Rapid Progress of Communism in Germany 229

F. Engels. Speeches in Elberfeld 243
 February 8, 1845 243
 February 15, 1845 256

K. Marx. Draft of an Article on Friedrich List's Book *Das nationale
System der politischen Oekonomie* 265
 I. General Characterisation of List 265
 II. The Theory of Productive Forces and the Theory of Exchange
  Values 277
 III. From Chapter Three. The Problem of Land Rent 286
 IV. Herr List and Ferrier 290

F. Engels. The Condition of the Working-Class in England. From Personal
Observation and Authentic Sources 295

To the Working-Classes of Great-Britain 297
 Preface 302
 Introduction 307
  The State of the Workers before the Industrial Revolution.— The
  Jenny.— Emergence of the Industrial and the Agricultural Proletariat.—
  The Throstle, the Mule, the Power-Loom, the Steam-Engine.— The
  Victory of Machine-Work over Hand-Work.— The Development of·
  Industrial Might.— The Cotton Industry.— The Hosiery Manufac-
  ture.— The Manufacture of Lace.— Dyeing, Bleaching, Printing.—
  The Manufacture of Wool.— The Linen Trade.— The Manufacture
  of Silk.— The Production and Manufacture of Iron.— Coal-Mining.—
  The Production of Pottery.— Agriculture.— Roadways, Canals, Rail-
  roads, Steamboats.— Summary.— The Emergence of the Proletariat
  as a Factor of National Importance.— The Middle-Class' View of the
  Workers.

The Industrial Proletariat 324
  Classification of the Proletariat.— Centralisation of Property.— The
  Levers of Modern Manufacture.— Centralisation of Population.

The Great Towns 328
  The Impression Produced by London.— The Social War and the
  System of General Plundering.— The Lot of the Poor.— General
  Description of the Slums.— In London: St. Giles and the Adjoin-
  ing Quarters.— Whitechapel.— The Interior of the Workers' Dwell-
  ings.— The Homeless in the Parks.— Night Refuges.— Dublin.—

Edinburgh.— Liverpool.— Factory Towns: Nottingham, Birmingham, Glasgow, Leeds, Bradford, Huddersfield.—Lancashire: General Description.— Bolton.—Stockport.— Ashton-under-Lyne.— Stalybridge.— Detailed Description of Manchester: the General System of Its Building.— The Old Town.— The New Town.— The Method of Construction of Working-Men's Quarters.— Courts and Side Streets.— Ancoats.—Little   Ireland.—Hulme.—Salford.—Summary.—Lodging-Houses.—Overcrowdedness of Population.—Cellar Dwellings.—The Clothing of the Workers.—Food.—Tainted Meat.—Adulteration of Provision.—False Weights, etc.—General Conclusion.

Competition 375

Competition among the Workers Determines the Minimum of Wages, Competition among the Property-Holding People Determines Their Maximum.— The Worker, the Slave of the Bourgeoisie, Is Forced to Sell Himself by the Day, and by the Hour.— Surplus Population.— Commercial Crises.— A Reserve Army of Workers.— The Hard Lot of This Reserve Army during the Crisis of 1842.

Irish Immigration 389

The Causes and Figures.— Description by Thomas Carlyle.— Lack of Cleanliness, Crudeness and Drunkenness among the Irishmen.— The Influence of Irish Competition and of the Contacts with the Irish upon the English Workers.

Results 393

Preliminary Remarks.— The Influence of the Above-Described Conditions on the Health of the Workers.— The Influence of Large Towns, Dwellings, Uncleanliness, etc.— The Facts.— Consumption.— Typhus, in Particular in London, Scotland and Ireland.— Digestive Troubles.— The Results of Drunkenness.— Quack Remedies.— "Godfrey's Cordial".—Mortality among Workers, Especially among Young Children.— Accusation of the Bourgeoisie of Social Murder.— Influence on the Mental and Moral Condition of the Workers.— Absence of the Necessary Conditions for Education.— Inadequacy of Evening and Sunday Schools.— Ignorance.— The Worker's Living Conditions Give Him a Sort of Practical Training.—Neglect of the Workers' Moral Training.— The Law as the Only Instructor in Morals. The Worker's Conditions of Life Tempt Him to Disregard Law and Morality.— The Influence of Poverty and Insecurity of Existence upon the Proletariat.—Forced Work.—The Centralisation of the Population.— Irish Immigration.— The Difference in Character between the Worker and the Bourgeois.—The Proletarian's Advantages over the Bourgeois.—The Unfavourable Sides of the Proletarian Character.—Drunkenness.—Sexual   Irregularities.—Neglect   of Family Duties.— Contempt for the Existing Social Order.— Crimes.— Description of the Social War.

Single Branches of Industry. *Factory Hands* 428

The Influence of Machinery.— Hand-Loom Weavers.— The Work of Men Being Superseded by Machinery.— Female Labour, the Dissolution of the Family.— The Reversal of All Relations within the Family.—

The Moral Consequences of the Mass Employment of Women in Factories.— *Jus Primae Noctis.*— The Work of Children.— The Apprentice System.— Subsequent Measures.— The Facts Related by the Factory Report.— Long Working-Day.— Night-Work.— Cripples.— Other Deformities.—The Nature of Factory-Work.—Relaxation of the Whole Organism.— Special Diseases.— Testimony of the Commissioners.— Premature Old Age.— The Specific Influence of Factory-Work upon the Female Physique.— Some Especially Injurious Branches.— Accidents.— The Bourgeoisie's Opinion of the Factory System.— Factory Laws and Agitation for the Ten Hours' Bill.— The Stupefying and Demoralising Nature of Factory-Work.— Slavery.— Factory Regulations.— The Truck-System.— The Cottage System.— The Comparison of the Serf of 1145 with the Free Working-Man of 1845.

The Remaining Branches of Industry 479

Stocking Weavers.—The Lace Industry.—Calico Printers.—Fustian Cutters.—Silk Weavers.—Metal-Wares.—Birmingham.—Staffordshire.—Sheffield.—Production of Machinery.—Potteries in the North of Staffordshire.—Manufacture of Glass.—Handicraftsmen.— Dressmakers and Sewing-Women.

Labour Movements· 501

Preliminary Remarks.— Crimes.— Revolts Against Machinery.— Associations, Strikes.—The Objects of the Unions and Strikes.— Excesses Connected with Them.— The General Character of the Struggle Waged by the English Proletariat against the Bourgeoisie.— The Battle in Manchester in May 1843.— Respect for the Law is Alien to the Proletariat.—Chartism.—The History of the Chartist Movement.—Insurrection of 1842.—The Decisive Separation of Proletarian Chartism from Bourgeois Radicalism.— The Social Nature of Chartism.— Socialism.— The Working-Men's Views.

The Mining Proletariat 530

Cornish Miners.— Alston Moor.— Coal and Iron Mines.— The Work of Grown-up Men, Women and Children.— Special Affections.— Work in Low Shafts.—Accidents, Explosions, etc.—Mental Education.—Morals. —Laws Relating to the Mining Industry.—Systematic Exploitation of the Coal-Miners.— The Beginning of the Workers' Movement.— The Union of Coal-Miners.— The Great Campaign of 1844 in the North of England.—Roberts and the Campaign against Justices of the Peace and the Truck-System.— The Results of the Struggle.

The Agricultural Proletariat 548

Historical Survey.—Pauperism in the Country.—The Condition of the Wage-Workers.— Incendiarisms.— Indifference to the Corn Laws.— Religious State of the Agricultural Labourers.— Wales: Small Tenants.— "Rebecca" Disturbances.—Ireland: Subdivision of the Land.—Pauperisation of the Irish Nation.—Crimes.—Agitation for the Repeal of the Union with England.

The Attitude of the Bourgeoisie Towards the Proletariat 562

> Demoralisation of the English Bourgeoisie.—Its Avarice.—Political
> Economy and Free Competition.—Pharisaic Charity.—The Hypocrisy
> of Political Economy and Politics in the Question of the Corn Laws.—
> Bourgeois Legislation and Justice.—The Bourgeoisie in Parliament.—
> A Bill Regulating the Relation of Master and Servant.—Malthus'
> Theory.—The Old Poor Law.—The New Poor Law.—Examples
> of the Brutal Treatment of the Poor in the Workhouses.—The Chances
> of the English Bourgeoisie.

F. Engels. Postscript to The Condition of the Working-Class in England.
An English Turnout 584

K. Marx. Peuchet: On Suicide 597

F. Engels. A Fragment of Fourier's on Trade 613

> I. 616
> II. Falseness of the Economic Principles of Circulation 620
> III. Hierarchy of Bankruptcy 624
> IV. Ascending Wing of Bankrupts 626
>   The Innocent.—The Honourable.—The Seductive
> V. Centre.—Grandiose Hues 630
>   The Tacticians.—The Manoeuvrers.—The Agitators
> VI. Descending Wing.—Dirty Hues 636
>   The Cunning Sneakers.—The Bunglers.—The False Brothers
> VII. Conclusion 640

F. Engels. The Late Butchery at Leipzig.—The German Working Men's
Movement. 645

F. Engels. Victoria's Visit.—The "Royals" at Loggerheads.—Row
Betwixt Vic and the German Bourgeoisie.—The Condemnation
of the Paris Carpenters 649

F. Engels. "Young Germany" in Switzerland. (Conspiracy against
Church and State) 651

F. Engels. Persecution and Expulsion of Communists 654

F. Engels. History of the English Corn Laws 656

FROM THE PREPARATORY MATERIALS

K. Marx. Hegel's Construction of the Phenomenology 665
K. Marx. Draft Plan for a Work on the Modern State 666
K. Marx. Plan of the "Library of the Best Foreign Socialist Writers" 667
K. Marx. From the Notebook 668

APPENDICES

To the Readers of and Contributors to the *Gesellschaftsspiegel* 671

Contract Between Marx and the Leske Publishers in Darmstadt on the
  Publication of *Kritik der Politik und Nationalökonomie. February 1, 1845* 675

Marx to Leopold I, King of Belgium, in Brussels. *February 7, 1845* 676

Marx's Undertaking Not to Publish Anything in Belgium on Current
  Politics. *March 22, 1845* 677

Marx to Chief Burgomaster Görtz in Trier. *October 17, 1845* 678

Marx to Chief Burgomaster Görtz in Trier. *November 10, 1845* 679

NOTES AND INDEXES

Notes 683
Name Index 723
Index of Quoted and Mentioned Literature 741
Index of Periodicals 757
Subject Index 763

ILLUSTRATIONS

Title-page of the first edition of *The Holy Family* by Marx and Engels 5

Reproduction of K. Hübner's painting, *Weavers Delivering Finished
  Cloth*. 1844 235-236

Cover of the first edition of Engels' *The Condition of the Working-Class in England* 299

First page of Engels' address *To the Working-Classes of Great-Britain* 305

A page from *The Condition of the Working-Class in England* (1845), with Edward
  Mead's poem, "The Steam King", translated by Engels 475

Map of Manchester 515

The covers of the journals to which Engels contributed 599-601

TRANSLATORS

JACK COHEN: Speeches in Elberfeld; Postscript to *The Condition of the Working-Class in England*. An English Turnout

RICHARD DIXON: To the Readers of and Contributors to the *Gesellschaftsspiegel*; Contract Between Marx and the Leske Publishers in Darmstadt on the Publication of *Kritik der Politik und Nationalökonomie*

RICHARD DIXON and CLEMENS DUTT: *The Holy Family, or Critique of Critical Criticism. Against Bruno Bauer and Company*; A Fragment of Fourier's on Trade

CLEMENS DUTT: Draft of an Article on Friedrich List's Book *Das nationale System der politischen Oekonomie*; History of the English Corn Laws; Hegel's Construction of the Phenomenology; Draft Plan for a Work on the Modern State; Plan of the "Library of the Best Foreign Socialist Writers"; From the Notebook; Marx to Leopold I, King of Belgium, in Brussels; Marx's Undertaking Not to Publish Anything in Belgium on Current Politics; Marx to Chief Burgomaster Görtz in Trier (two items)

BARBARA RUHEMANN: Peuchet: On Suicide.

CHRISTOPHER UPWARD: Description of Recently Founded Communist Colonies Still in Existence

FLORENCE KELLEY-WISCHNEWETZKY: *The Condition of the Working-Class in England*

Preface

The fourth volume of the *Collected Works* of Marx and Engels includes their works written from the time when their close friendship was first established (late August-early September 1844) to the autumn of 1845. Beginning with the present volume, works of both Marx and Engels will be published in this edition in the chronological order in which they were written.

The meeting of Marx and Engels in Paris in August 1844 inaugurated their lifelong partnership. Each of them had independently traversed a difficult path of intellectual development from idealism to materialism, from revolutionary democracy to communism. By the time they met in Paris each was a convinced revolutionary and Communist. With this shared standpoint, their work, while preserving the individual features of each, developed thereafter in a spirit of the unbreakable unity of two thinkers. At the same time, their creative co-operation opened up immediately a new stage in the development of their views. Not only did they go on to achieve, during the year that followed their meeting, greater concreteness in the dialectical and materialist principles both had advanced in their works of 1843 and 1844, but they broadened the whole range of their ideas and set themselves and tackled new problems of elaborating the theoretical foundations of the revolutionary world outlook of the proletariat.

Marx and Engels continued their study of existing philosophical, economic and socialist ideas, and their painstaking research into the actual social-economic reality and the working-class movement of the time. They maintained close contacts with democratic and socialist circles in Germany, France, Belgium and other countries, with representatives of the Chartist movement in England, and with members of the League of the Just. And all this increasingly convinced them that the practice of revolutionary struggle demanded profound and comprehensive theoretical work, the creation of an entirely new and self-consistent theory which would be of relevance in all the basic fields of human knowledge. It was to the fulfilment of this task that Marx and Engels together directed their efforts. They sought not only to establish the scientific basis for communism, but to spread communist ideas among the working class and revolutionary intellectuals of Europe. For them, the new revolutionary theory could be consolidated only in struggle against the various non-proletarian trends which had taken shape by that time, and by dissociating itself from them.

A primary task in the autumn of 1844 was to deal with the Young Hegelians, who had given up their former radical convictions and swung to the Right. Indeed, a campaign against socialism and communism was being mounted by the monthly *Allgemeine Literatur-Zeitung*, edited by the Bauer brothers.

What Marx had had to say in the *Deutsch-Französische Jahrbücher* about the proletariat's historical mission was declared "uncritical", and working people written off as an inert and passive "mass", a hindrance to social progress. The Bauer brothers and their fellow-thinkers announced that the sole active element in the world-historical process was their own theoretical activity, to which they gave the name of "Critical Criticism".

Marx had first expressed his intention to come out against the philosophical views of the Young Hegelians in 1843, in his articles *Contribution to the Critique of Hegel's Philosophy of Law. Introduction* and *On the Jewish Question* (see present edition, Vol. 3). And he returned to the idea in the summer of 1844, among other occasions in his conversations with Engels in Paris. The outcome was the decision by Marx and Engels to write a book together against the Young Hegelians. "A war has been declared," Engels wrote sometime later, "against those of the German philosophers, who refuse to draw from their mere theories practical inferences, and who contend that man has nothing to do but to speculate upon metaphysical questions" (see p. 240 of this volume).

This fourth volume of the *Collected Works* begins with the first joint work of Marx and Engels, *The Holy Family, or Critique of Critical Criticism. Against Bruno Bauer and Co.* Its idea and general plan were agreed upon by the two friends, but the major part of the text was in fact written by Marx. This work, mainly philosophical in content, occupies an important place in the formation of Marx's and Engels' philosophical and social-political views. It attacks from a consistently materialist standpoint both the subjectivist views of the Young Hegelians and Hegel's idealist philosophical system as a whole, on which they had based them. At the same time, it demonstrates in sharp polemic that the subjective idealism of the Young Hegelians was a step backward in comparison with Hegel's philosophy.

Marx and Engels had already in previous works begun to work out the principles of the materialist conception of history. In *The Holy Family* these were further developed. A new step forward was made, particularly as compared with Marx's "Economic and Philosophic Manuscripts of 1844", in clarifying the decisive role of material production in social development. Marx now saw in it the basis of the whole of mankind's historical progress. He wrote, in particular, that it was impossible to understand a single historical period "without knowing ... the industry of that period, the immediate mode of production of life itself" (see p. 150 of this volume).

Formulated in this work are very profound thoughts on the correspondence of the political system of a given society with the economic structure, their dialectical connection and mutual influence.

Closely connected with the exposition of the initial principles of the materialist conception of history is the clear statement in *The Holy Family* of the decisive role of the popular masses in historical development and the growth of this role as the development proceeds. Marx declared that mankind was facing the task of further profound social transformations, in the course of which "together with the thoroughness of the historical action, the size of the mass whose action it is will therefore increase" (see p. 82 of this volume).

In developing the idea of the world-historical role of the proletariat as the force destined to carry out the future socialist revolution, Marx shows in *The Holy Family* that this historical destiny of the working class is the inevitable result of its position in capitalist society. "The conditions of life of the proletariat," Marx writes, "sum up all the conditions of life of society today in their most inhuman form." The proletariat, as a class, by virtue of its historical existence "can and must emancipate itself" (see pp. 36-37 of this volume). Marx also declared that the social emancipation of the proletariat would mean the emancipation of the whole of society from exploitation. He therefore stressed the universal human significance, the genuinely humanistic meaning of the proletariat's class struggle. Thus the basic Marxist idea of the leading role of the proletariat in the anti-capitalist revolutionary and liberation movement was formulated for the first time in *The Holy Family*. Lenin later described it as a work containing "Marx's view — already almost fully developed — concerning the revolutionary role of the proletariat" (V. I. Lenin, *Collected Works*, Vol. 38, p. 26).

The Holy Family contains, moreover, Marx and Engels' materialist interpretation of the role of ideas in history. Analysing more deeply the conception of the transformation of theory into a material force which he had put forward in *A Contribution to the Critique of Hegel's Philosophy of Law*, Marx showed how ideas become an effective force of social development when they correspond to the requirements of real life by expressing the interests of progressive classes. He demonstrated this by taking as an example the history of philosophy from the seventeenth to the beginning of the nineteenth century. Analysing the struggle of the two basic trends, materialism and idealism, he reveals the significance of materialism as the progressive philosophy in social life, particularly in its having created the ideological prerequisites for the French bourgeois revolution at the end of the eighteenth century; he points out the organic link between the development of materialist ideas and the achievements of the natural sciences, and emphasises that further creative development of materialist philosophical thought must inevitably lead to communist conclusions.

While building on the progressive philosophical traditions of the past, Marx and Engels by no means intended to stop at the achievements of previous materialism. *The Holy Family* reflects the endeavour to develop and re-interpret in a materialist way the rational element in Hegel's philosophy — its dialectics — and organically to unite dialectics which, on the whole, previous materialist philosophers lacked, with materialism. The creative development of dialectics, the dialectical approach to both social-economic and ideological phenomena, the study in social and intellectual processes of the operation of the basic objective laws of dialectics, especially the law of the unity and struggle of opposites — these run through the whole content of *The Holy Family*.

Although it marks so significant a stage accomplished in the creation of the theoretical foundation of the proletarian world outlook, *The Holy Family* nevertheless belongs to the period when Marxism was still in formation and when the basic principles of the materialist conception of history and of scientific communism had not yet been fully stated. Marx and Engels had not yet completely crossed the divide between themselves and their ideological predecessors. In particular, they had not yet entirely and in all respects overcome the influence of the weaker aspects of Feuerbach's philosophy. It is true that in declaring themselves his followers, "real humanists", supporters of Feuerbach's "anthropological" materialism, Marx and Engels were actually coming out as revolutionary Communists and materialist dialecticians, and so filling his terminology with a new content. Their obvious dissatisfaction with the metaphysical character and inconsistency of all previous materialism soon developed, however, into an understanding of the fundamental difference between Feuerbach's speculative philosophy and the proletarian outlook that was taking shape. That is why, in April 1845, in his "Theses on Feuerbach", Marx came out so trenchantly against Feuerbachianism (these Theses, together with other works related to *The German Ideology*, will be included in the fifth volume of the present edition).

The fourth volume also contains Engels' fundamental work, *The Condition of the Working-Class in England*. This was the fruit of his careful study of and theoretical generalisation from vast factual data drawn from official documents, from both bourgeois and working-class newspapers, and from special investigations made by economists, sociologists, historians, etc. But above all, the book reflects (and this lends it its particular authenticity) the results of Engels' own observation of the working and living conditions of the workers during his almost two years' stay in Manchester.

In substance, this work of Engels continues his previous articles devoted to studying capitalist development in England (see present edition, Vols. 2 and 3). In the scale of the problems it deals with and the depth and thoroughness with which they are clarified, it considerably surpasses, however, his previous writings. As regards the ideas informing it, this work is close to *The Holy Family*. It shows by the whole of its content that in working out their revolutionary theory the founders of Marxism based themselves on a scientific concrete sociological analysis of the existing reality.

The Condition of the Working-Class in England provides evidence that Engels arrived, at the same time as Marx, at an understanding of the role of the economic factor in social development, and that he made his own independent contribution to the materialist analysis of social phenomena. One of the central features of this work is his study of the social-economic consequences of the industrial revolution in England. Engels brought out the decisive influence of changes in social production on the condition of whole classes and the entire life of society. And he came to the all-important conclusion that the industrial revolution in England had resulted in the formation of a new revolutionary class — the proletariat. The position of this class in modern capitalist society "is the real basis and point of departure of all social movements of the present because it is the highest and most unconcealed pinnacle of the social misery existing in our day" (see p. 302 of this volume).

Engels was able to deduce from the example of England, the most advanced country in the capitalist world at the time, the characteristic features of the capitalist system as a whole. He demonstrated the typical features of capitalist industrialisation, and its inevitable consequences — the ruin, and in England the almost complete disappearance, of the artisans and working peasantry, the pauperisation of the former small proprietors and the proletarianisation of a considerable part of the population. In what must rank as a classical characterisation, Engels drew his picture of the big towns as the offspring of capitalist industry, a focus of social evils, and at the same time as centres of the proletarian masses' resistance to oppression and exploitation. And he vividly depicted phenomena inherent in capitalism—the anarchy of production, the periodic crises, the deepening of class antagonisms, and the formation and growth of a reserve army of labour, or in other words, chronic unemployment. Engels' book is no specialist theoretical economic study, and yet it defines with deadly accuracy many aspects of the economic structure of capitalist society and its inherent laws and tendencies. Not without reason did Marx write later in the first volume of *Capital* that the author of *The Condition of the Working-Class in England* "completely understood the nature of the capitalist mode of production".

Engels' masterly picture of the condition of the English proletariat is an unanswerable indictment of the capitalist system as it then existed. But this is not the distinguishing feature of his book, the one which sets it apart from all other socialist writings of the time. Many utopian Socialists or authors who merely sympathised with the working people had already vividly described their unfortunate condition. But they had shown the working class only as a suffering mass, not as a revolutionary force. The enduring significance of *The Condition of the Working-Class in England* lies in the fact that, as Lenin noted, in it "Engels was the *first* to say that the proletariat is *not only* a suffering class; that it is, in fact, the disgraceful economic condition of the proletariat that drives it irresistibly forward and compels it to fight for its ultimate emancipation. And the fighting proletariat *will help itself*" (V. I. Lenin, *Collected Works*, Vol. 2, p. 22).

As in Marx's works of this time, the world-historical revolutionary role of the working class is deduced in Engels' book from the social conditions in capitalist society and the proletarians' position in it. There was evident, Engels concludes, an inexorable tendency towards the sharpening of the contradictions inherent in capitalism, towards polarisation of the class forces, and the transformation of the struggle between the proletariat and the bourgeoisie into the principal factor in the life of society. The social revolution to overthrow the existing system had become historically inevitable. The proletariat, the class in which "reposes the strength and the capacity of development of the nation" (see p. 529 of this volume), precisely by virtue of its position in capitalist society, has the historic mission of destroying it and accomplishing the socialist revolution.

For the first time in socialist literature, Engels systematically analysed the development of the proletariat's emancipation movement and showed the historical significance of this process, which, in the final account, will lead to the communist transformation of society. Engels demonstrated the regular and progressive character of the development of the working-class movement, the inevitability of the transition from primitive spontaneous forms of revolutionary protest to higher and more organised forms of struggle—from local and sporadic actions against individual employers to systematic resistance of the workers to the exploiters and to struggle against the capitalist system itself; from uniting the proletarian forces within the framework of separate trades to creating nationwide class organisations. He elucidated the role of strikes, and of the trade unions as schools of class struggle. At the same time, he stressed that only by taking the path of *political* struggle would the working class be able to deal the decisive blow against the rule of the capitalist class as a whole and achieve genuine emancipation. That was the reason he so much stressed and lavished such praise on the activity of the English Chartists, who transferred the struggle against the bourgeoisie to political ground and began a mass proletarian political movement. Engels saw in Chartism the concentrated form of working-class opposition to the bourgeoisie.

Yet Engels discerned at the same time the crucial weakness of the Chartist movement in its inability to understand the socialist aim of the working-class revolutionary struggle, which was reflected in a certain ideological narrow-mindedness on the part of its leaders. The English working-class movement, he concluded, must find the way to acquire socialist consciousness. The need was to unite the Chartist movement with socialism—not with Robert Owen's utopian socialism, divorced as it was from genuine class struggle, but with militant proletarian socialism.

The Condition of the Working-Class in England nevertheless reflects to a certain extent the fact that the scientific outlook of the proletariat had not yet been completely shaped. Engels himself later regarded this book as a stage in the "embryonic" development of scientific socialism, when there were still visible "traces" of its descent from German classical philosophy. As an example of such immaturity, reflecting the influence of the abstract humanism of Feuerbach and of utopian socialism, he pointed to the proposition that the bourgeoisie itself had an interest in the social advantages of the communist system. Such delusions, especially in respect of the German bourgeoisie, which was often alleged to be far more disinterested than the English, are also apparent in other works by Engels belonging to the same period (see p. 230 of this volume). And as he himself later admitted in the Preface to the second German edition (1892), his idea that England was not far from a socialist revolution was also much too optimistic.

Alongside the two big works of Marx and Engels already named, this volume includes a group of their journalistic works, with manuscript outlines, and so on. Nearly all these works were written by Marx in Brussels, after he had been obliged to move there early in February 1845, when the French authorities closed down the Paris newspaper *Vorwärts!* and deported a number of its contributors and editors. Until the beginning of the revolution in Europe in 1848, Marx pursued his theoretical and political work in the Belgian capital. Engels wrote some of his journalistic works at the same time as *The Condition of the Working-Class in England*—during his stay in Barmen from September 1844 to April 1845. He continued to contribute reports on the state of the revolutionary movement and of communist propaganda on the Continent from Barmen to the Owenites' *New Moral World*. Another group of articles and reports by Engels, including his contributions to the Chartist newspaper *The Northern Star*, which he resumed in the autumn of 1845, were written in Brussels, where he stayed for a time from April 1845.

The content of the articles and reports written by Marx and Engels in this period corresponded to the tasks they set themselves in the two major works. They were all devoted to exposing the capitalist system, passionately defending the interests of the working class, spreading revolutionary communist ideas, and criticising ideological trends hostile to the communist movement.

The socialist journals *Rheinische Jahrbücher zur gesellschaftlichen Reform, Deutsches Bürgerbuch, Gesellschaftsspiegel,* and *Das Westphälische Dampfboot,* which were published in Germany at that time and for which Marx and Engels intended many of their articles, were all to a greater or lesser extent mouthpieces for the ideas of petty-bourgeois "true socialism", alien to the revolutionary communist outlook. Attempts to influence the trend of some of these periodicals, in particular Engels' efforts to impart a revolutionary critical character to the *Gesellschaftsspiegel,* did not succeed. The collaboration of Marx and Engels with these publications could only be incidental and of short duration. They soon broke entirely with some, and wrote elsewhere in opposition to them. Nevertheless, their contributions, even in these publications, played no small part in formulating and spreading communist views and in the birth of the revolutionary proletarian trend in the socialist movement of the time, drawing the line between revolutionary communism and other, non-proletarian trends. A group of their first adherents already began to unite around Marx and Engels in Brussels.

Marx's article on the book *Das nationale System der politischen Oekonomie,* by the German economist Friedrich List, was intended for one of the above-named periodicals, but remained unpublished. The present volume includes a recently discovered draft of this article, which contains a trenchant criticism of the views held by List as an apologist of the German bourgeoisie, which was then seeking by protective tariffs to defend itself against competition from the more developed capitalist countries. Marx stresses that List's views reflected the physiognomy of the German bourgeois: his desire to cover up his greedy exploitation and lust for profit with pompous talk about the national interest, coupled with his abject servility towards the aristocracy. But Marx did not confine himself to merely criticising List's views. The draft published in this volume bears witness to his intense work in thinking over the theoretical problems, the materialist interpretation of basic economic and sociological categories such as "labour", "worker", "exchange value", "productive forces", and others. In the course of his analysis Marx reveals the difference in principle between the "human kernel" of factory and plant production which creates "the proletariat, and in the shape of the proletariat the power of a new world order", and its capitalist "dirty outer shell" which has to be broken to free the productive forces of society from their fetters (see p. 282 of this volume). The thoughts set forth by Marx in this draft were developed in his subsequent philosophical and economic works.

The article "Peuchet: On Suicide" provides proof that in criticising bourgeois society Marx sought not only to lay bare its economic contradictions, but also to expose bourgeois morality, customs and way of living. Making use of material on suicides and their motives, which he obtained from the memoirs of the police archives custodian in Paris, Marx showed that the bourgeois world is ruled by egoism, violation of the human personality, trampling on natural feelings, monstrous family relations.

Engels' articles published in this volume: "Continental Socialism", "Rapid Progress of Communism in Germany", "Speeches in Elberfeld", and others, belong to the Barmen period of his work. They present a picture of the social discontent in Germany in the forties, the growth of opposition to the feudal and absolutist system, and the social dissatisfaction of the working people reflected in the wide propagation of communist and socialist ideas. These articles contain remarkable biographical material and illustrate the mercurial enthusiasm with which young Engels set about his organisational, agitational and journalistic activity in the Rhine Province of Prussia.

In the "Speeches in Elberfeld", Engels pronounced a detailed condemnation of the capitalist system eroded by internal contradictions, and laid bare the economic roots of the class struggle, basing himself both on his experiences in England and a thorough study of conditions in Germany. He spoke of the "contradiction between a few rich people on the one hand, and many poor on the other", and foretold that it would go on deepening "as long as the present basis of society is retained". To the world of cruel exploitation, barbarous squandering of human resources, ruthless competition, war of all against all, Engels opposed a communist society, humanely and economically organised, in which "the interests of individuals are not opposed to one another but, on the contrary, are united" (see pp. 244, 246 of this volume). Engels likewise endeavoured to demonstrate the superiority of the communist system in the article "Description of Recently Founded Communist Colonies Still in Existence". He did not share the views of utopian Socialists who thought that the entire social system could be peacefully transformed by the diffusion of these experimental colonies; he saw their significance rather in their example, which proved that it was possible to organise social and economic relations more justly and rationally on a collective basis.

Among the works written by Engels in Brussels is his "A Fragment of Fourier's on Trade", which contains his translation of extracts from Fourier's work *Des trois unités externes* accompanied by an introduction and a conclusion written by himself. It was no accident that Engels took the trouble to translate this outstanding representative of utopian socialism. He placed a high value on Fourier's criticism of existing society, and intended to include his works in the "Library of the Best Foreign Socialist Writers", the publication of which he and Marx had planned (see p. 667 of this volume). The excerpts from Fourier's writings which he selected expose the cupidity, money-grubbing and deceit reigning in the sphere of finance and trade. This work of Engels was also the first public attack against petty-bourgeois "true socialism", which debased socialist teaching into something sentimental, eclectic, abstract and divorced from the requirements of revolutionary struggle.

Engels' article on Fourier and his intention to publish the works of other Socialists show that Marx and himself held their ideological forerunners in high respect. Criticism of the weaknesses of utopian socialism did not prevent them from seeing in it the rational elements appreciation of which would contribute to the workers' education and help them to acquire the revolutionary proletarian world outlook.

Close to the book *The Condition of the Working-Class in England* are Engels' articles "An English Turnout" and "History of the English Corn Laws". These articles throw additional light on the acute class struggle which had developed in England between the proletariat and the bourgeoisie. The second describes the workers' demonstrations in August 1842, and the provocative role played in these events by the bourgeois adherents of free trade united in the Anti-Corn Law League.

This volume also contains several articles by Engels published in September and October 1845 in *The Northern Star*. Engels informed his English Chartist readers that, in comparison with the middle-of-the-road and irresolute positions adopted by bourgeois liberal circles in Germany, the German working class was distinguished by greater radicalism and receptivity to revolutionary views. One of the basic ideas expounded in these reports was the need for ideological and political independence for the working class, "who have a movement of their own—a knife-and-fork movement" (see p. 648 of this volume).

In the section of this volume "From the Preparatory Materials" are published draft plans revealing the broad scope of Marx's intentions and the variety of fields which his searching mind explored (problems concerning the state, the history of the French Revolution, and so on). The Appendices include, besides other biographical documents, Marx's contract with the Leske publishing house for the publication of his projected work in two volumes *Kritik der Politik und Nationalökonomie*. It was out of this plan, which was partially implemented in the "Economic and Philosophic Manuscripts of 1844", that the idea of *Capital* later crystallised.

* * *

Some of the works included in this volume have been translated into English for the first time. Among these are such writings by Marx as "Draft of an Article on Friedrich List's Book *Das nationale System der politischen Oekonomie*", "Peuchet: On Suicide", "Plan of the Library of the Best Foreign Socialist Writers", and all the items contained in the Appendices.

Among the works of Engels the following articles have not been previously translated into English: "Description of Recently Founded Communist Colonies Stillin Existence", "Speeches in Elberfeld", "A Fragment of Fourier's on Trade", "History of the English Corn Laws", and the prospectus of the *Gesellschaftsspiegel* (published as an Appendix, since it was written in co-authorship with Hess). Reprinted for the first time in the language of the original are Engels' two articles from *The Northern Star*: " 'Young Germany' in Switzerland" and "Persecution and Expulsion of Communists". Engels' book *The Condition of the Working-Class in England* is published in the English translation by Florence Kelley-Wischnewetzky which Engels himself authorised in the 1880s. The most important differences between the original and the translation which affect the meaning are particularised in footnotes.

Those works which have previously been published in English are either rendered in new translations or previous translations have been checked with the original. The special features in the presentation of individual works, in particular manuscripts, are described in the Notes.

Most of the works published in this volume have been translated from the German. If the translation is from another language, or if the text was written by the authors in English, mention is made of this at the end of the particular work.

The volume was compiled and the preface and notes written by Tatyana Yeremeyeva and edited by Lev Golman (Institute of

Marxism-Leninism of the C.C., C.P.S.U.). Valentina Kholopova (Institute of Marxism-Leninism of the C.C., C.P.S.U.) prepared the Name Index, the Index of Quoted and Mentioned Literature and the Index of Periodicals, and Yevgenia Zastenker the Subject Index.

The new translations are by Jack Cohen, Richard Dixon, Clemens Dutt, Barbara Ruhemann and Christopher Upward, and edited by Margaret Mynatt, Pat Sloan and Alick West (Lawrence & Wishart), Richard Dixon, Yelena Chistyakova and Victor Schnittke (Progress Publishers) and Vladimir Mosolov, scientific editor (Institute of Marxism-Leninism of the C.C., C.P.S.U.).

The volume was prepared for the press by the editor Nadezhda Rudenko and the assistant-editor Tatyana Shimanovskaya, for Progress Publishers.

KARL MARX
and
FREDERICK ENGELS

WORKS

September 1844-November 1845

Karl Marx and Frederick Engels

THE HOLY FAMILY
OR
CRITIQUE OF CRITICAL CRITICISM

AGAINST BRUNO BAUER AND COMPANY [1]

Written in September-November 1844

First published as a separate book
in 1845 in Frankfurt am Main

Signed: *Frederick Engels* and *Karl Marx*

Translated from the German
edition of 1845

Die heilige Familie,

oder

Kritik

der

kritischen Kritik.

Gegen Bruno Bauer & Consorten.

Von

Friedrich Engels und Karl Marx.

Frankfurt a. M.
Literarische Anstalt.
(J. Rütten.)
1 8 4 5.

Title-page of the first edition of *The Holy Family*

Foreword

Real humanism has no more dangerous enemy in Germany than *spiritualism* or *speculative idealism*, which substitutes *"self-consciousness"* or the *"spirit"* for the *real individual man* and with the evangelist teaches: "It is the spirit that quickeneth; the flesh profiteth nothing." Needless to say, this incorporeal spirit is spiritual only in its imagination. What we are combating in *Bauer's* criticism is precisely *speculation* reproducing itself as a *caricature*. We see in it the most complete expression of the *Christian-Germanic* principle, which makes its last effort by transforming *"criticism"* itself into a transcendent power.

Our exposition deals first and foremost with *Bruno Bauer's Allgemeine Literatur-Zeitung*—the first eight numbers are here before us—because in it Bauer's criticism, and with it the nonsense of *German speculation in general,* has reached its peak. The more completely Critical Criticism (the criticism of the *Literatur-Zeitung*) distorts reality into an obvious comedy through philosophy, the more instructive it is.—For examples see *Faucher* and *Szeliga.*—The *Literatur-Zeitung* offers material by which even the broad public can be enlightened on the illusions of speculative philosophy. That is the aim of our book.

Our exposition is naturally determined by its *subject.* Critical Criticism is in all respects *below* the level already attained by German theoretical development. The nature of our subject therefore justifies our refraining *here* from further *discussion* of that development itself.

Critical Criticism makes it necessary rather to assert, in contrast to it, the already achieved results *as such.*

We therefore give this polemic as a preliminary to the independent works in which we—each of us for himself, of course—shall present our positive view and thereby our positive attitude to the more recent philosophical and social doctrines.

Paris, September 1844

Engels, Marx

Chapter I

"CRITICAL CRITICISM
IN THE FORM OF A MASTER-BOOKBINDER",
OR CRITICAL CRITICISM AS HERR REICHARDT

Critical Criticism, however superior to the mass it deems itself,
nevertheless has boundless pity for the mass. And Criticism so loved
the mass that it sent its only begotten son, that all who believe in him
may not be lost, but may have Critical life. Criticism was made mass
and dwells amongst us and we behold its glory, the glory of the only
begotten son of the father. In other words, Criticism becomes
socialistic and speaks of "works on pauperism".[2] It does not regard it
as a crime to be equal to God but alienates itself and takes the form of
a master-bookbinder and humiliates itself to the extent of nonsense — indeed even to Critical nonsense in foreign languages. It,
whose heavenly virginal purity shrinks from contact with the sinful
leprous mass, overcomes itself to the extent of taking notice of
"*Bodz*"[a] and "*all* original writers on pauperism" and "has for years
been following this evil of the present time step by step"; it scorns
writing for experts, it writes for the general public, banning all
outlandish expressions, all "Latin intricacies, all professional jargon". It bans all that from the works of *others,* for it would be too
much to expect Criticism itself to submit to "this administrative
regulation". And yet it does do so partly, renouncing with admirable
ease, if not the words themselves, at least their content. And who will
reproach it for using "the huge heap of unintelligible foreign words"
when it repeatedly proves that it does not understand those words
itself? Here are a few samples[3]:

---

[a] Reichardt's distortion of Charles Dickens' pseudonym: Boz.—*Ed.*

"That is why the *institutions of mendicancy* inspire them with horror."

"A doctrine of responsibility in which every motion *of human thought becomes an image of Lot's wife.*"

"On the keystone of this really *profound edifice of art.*"

"This is the main content of Stein's political testament, which the great statesman handed in even before retiring from the active service of the government *and from all its transactions.*"

"This people had *not yet any dimensions* at that time for such extensive freedom."

"By *palavering* with fair assurance at the end of his publicistic work that only confidence was still lacking."

"To the manly state-elevating understanding, rising above routine and pusillanimous fear, reared on history and nurtured with a live perception of foreign public state system."

"The education of general national welfare."

"Freedom lay dead *in the breast of the Prussian national mission* under the control of the authorities."

"*Popular-organic* publicism."

"The people to whom even Herr Brüggemann delivers the *baptismal certificate of its adulthood.*"

"A rather glaring contradiction to the other *certitudes* which are expressed in the work on the professional capacities of the people."

"Wretched self-interest quickly dispels all the *chimeras of the national will.*"

"Passion for great gains, etc., was the spirit that pervaded the whole of the Restoration period and which, with a *fair quantity of indifference, adhered* to the new age."

"The obscure idea of political significance to be found in the *Prussian countrymanship nationality rests on the memory of a great history.*"

"The antipathy disappeared and turned into a completely exalted condition."

"In this wonderful transition each one in his own way still *put forward in prospect* his own special *wish.*"

"A catechism with unctuous Solomon-like language the words of which rise gently like a dove—chirp! chirp!—to the regions of pathos and *thunder-like aspects.*"

"All the *dilettantism of thirty-five years of neglect.*"

"The *too sharp thundering* at the citizens by one of their former town authorities could have been suffered with the calmness of mind characteristic of our representatives if Benda's view of the Town Charter of 1808 had not laboured under a *Mussulman conceptual affliction* with regard to the essence and the application of the Town Charter."

In Herr Reichardt, the audacity of style always corresponds to the audacity of the thought. He makes transitions like the following:

"Herr Brüggemann ... 1843 ... state theory ... every upright man ... the great modesty of our Socialists ... natural marvels ... demands to be made on Germany ... supernatural marvels ... Abraham ... Philadelphia ... manna ... baker ... but *since* we are speaking of *marvels, Napoleon* brought," etc.

After these samples it is no wonder that Critical Criticism gives us a further "explanation" of a sentence which it itself describes as expressed in "popular language", for it "arms its eyes with organic power to penetrate chaos". And here it must be said that then even "popular language" cannot remain unintelligible to Critical Criticism. It is aware that the way of the writer must necessarily be a crooked one if the individual who sets out on it is not strong enough to make it straight; and therefore it naturally ascribes "mathematical operations" to the author.

It is self-evident—and history, which proves everything which is self-evident, also proves this—that Criticism does not become mass in order to remain mass, but in order to redeem the mass from its mass-like mass nature, that is, to raise the popular language of the mass to the critical language of Critical Criticism. It is the lowest grade of degradation for Criticism to learn the popular language of the mass and transfigure that vulgar jargon into the high-flown intricacy of the dialectics of Critical Criticism.

Chapter II

"CRITICAL CRITICISM" AS A "MILL-OWNER",
OR CRITICAL CRITICISM AS HERR JULES FAUCHER [4]

After rendering most substantial services to self-consciousness by humiliating itself to the extent of nonsense in foreign languages, and thereby at the same time freeing the world from pauperism, Criticism still further humiliates itself to the extent of *nonsense* in *practice* and *history*. It masters *"English questions of the day"* and gives us a genuinely *critical outline of the history of English industry*.

Criticism, which is self-sufficient, and complete and perfect in itself, naturally cannot recognise history as it really took place, for that would mean recognising the base Mass in all its mass-like mass nature, whereas the problem is precisely to redeem the Mass from its mass nature. History is therefore freed from its mass nature, and Criticism, which has a *free* attitude to its object, calls to history: *"You ought to have happened in such and such a way!"* All the laws of Criticism have *retrospective* force: *prior to* the decrees of Criticism, history behaved quite differently from how it did *after* them. Hence mass-type history, so-called *real* history, deviates considerably from *Critical* history, as it takes place in Heft VII of the *Literatur-Zeitung* from page 4 onwards.

In mass-type history there were *no factory towns* before there were *factories;* but in Critical history, in which, as already in *Hegel*, the son begets his father, *Manchester*, *Bolton* and *Preston* were flourishing factory towns before factories were even thought of. In real history the *cotton industry* was founded mainly on *Hargreaves' jenny* and *Arkwright's throstle*, *Crompton's mule* being only an improvement of the spinning jenny according to the new principle discovered by Arkwright. But Critical history knows how to make distinctions: it scorns the one-sidedness of the jenny and the throstle, and gives the crown to the mule as the speculative identity of the extremes. In reality, the invention of the throstle and the mule immediately made possible the *application of water-power* to those machines, but Critical Criticism sorts out the principles lumped together by crude history and makes this application come only later, as something quite special. In reality the invention of the steam-engine *preceded* all the above-mentioned inventions; according to Criticism it is the crown of them all and the *last*.

In reality the *business ties* between Liverpool and Manchester in their present scope were the result of the export of English goods; according to Criticism they are the *cause* of the export and both are the result of the proximity of the two towns. In reality nearly all goods from Manchester go to the Continent via *Hull,* according to Criticism via *Liverpool.*

In reality all *grades of wages* exist in English factories, from 1s 6d to 40s and more; but according to Criticism only *one* rate is paid — 11s. In reality the *machine* replaces *manual labour;* according to Criticism it replaces *thought.* In reality the *association* of workers for wage rises is allowed in *England,* but according to Criticism it is prohibited, for when the Mass wants to allow itself anything it must first ask Criticism. In reality *factory labour* is extremely *tiring* and gives rise to specific diseases — there are even special medical works on them; according to Criticism "excessive exertion cannot be a hindrance to work, for the power is provided by the machine". In reality the machine is a machine; according to Criticism it has a *will,* for as it does not rest, neither can the worker, and he is subordinated to an alien will.

But that is still nothing at all. Criticism cannot be content with the *mass-type parties* in England; it creates new ones, including a *"factory party",* for which history may be thankful to it. On the other hand, it lumps together the factory-owners and the factory workers in *one* massive heap — why bother about such trifles! — and decrees that the factory workers refused to contribute to the Anti-Corn-Law League[5] not out of ill-will or because of Chartism, as the stupid factory-owners maintain, but merely because they were poor. It further decrees that with the repeal of the English Corn Laws agricultural labourers will have to put up with a lowering of wages, in regard to which, however, we must most submissively remark that that destitute class cannot be deprived of another penny without being reduced to absolute starvation. It decrees that the working day in English factories is *sixteen* hours, although a silly un-Critical English law has fixed a maximum of twelve hours. It decrees that England is to become a huge workshop for the world, although the un-Critical mass of Americans, Germans and Belgians are ruining one market after another for the English by their competition. Lastly, it decrees that neither the propertied nor the non-propertied classes in England are aware of the *centralisation of property* and its consequences for the working classes, although the stupid Chartists think they are well aware of them; the *Socialists* maintain that they expounded those consequences in detail long ago, and even Tories and Whigs like *Carlyle, Alison* and *Gaskell* have proved their knowledge of them in their works.

Criticism decrees that Lord *Ashley's Ten Hour Bill*[6] is a half-hearted *juste-milieu* measure and Lord Ashley himself "a true illustration of constitutional action",[a] while the factory-owners, the Chartists, the landowners — in short, all that makes up the mass nature of England — have so far considered this measure as an expression, the mildest possible one admittedly, of a downright radical principle, since it would lay the axe at the root of foreign trade and thereby at the root of the factory system — nay, not merely lay the axe to it, but cut deeply into it. Critical Criticism knows better. It knows that the ten hour question was discussed before a "commission" of the Lower House, although the un-Critical newspapers try to make us believe that this "commission" was the *House itself, "a Committee of the Whole House"*[7]; but Criticism must needs do away with that eccentricity of the English Constitution.

Critical Criticism, which itself *begets* its *opposite,* the *stupidity of the Mass,* also produces the stupidity of Sir James Graham: by a Critical understanding of the English language it puts things in his mouth which the un-Critical Home Secretary never said, just to allow Critical wisdom to shine brighter in comparison with his stupidity. Graham, according to Criticism, says that the machines in the factories wear out in about twelve years whether they work ten hours a day or twelve, and that therefore a Ten Hour Bill would make it impossible for the capitalists to reproduce in twelve years through the work of their machines the capital laid out on them. Criticism proves that it has thus put a false conclusion in the mouth of Sir James Graham, for a machine that works one-sixth of the time less every day will naturally remain usable longer.

However correct this observation of Critical Criticism against its own false conclusion, it must, on the other hand, be conceded that

---

[a] Here and below the quotations are taken from the continuation of Faucher's article, published in the *Allgemeine Literatur-Zeitung*, Heft VIII, July 1844.— *Ed.*

Sir James Graham said that under a Ten Hour Bill the machine would have to work quicker in the proportion that its working time was reduced (Criticism itself quotes this in [Heft] VIII, page 32) and that in that case the time when it would be worn out would be the same—twelve years.[8] This must all the more be acknowledged as the acknowledgement contributes to the glory and exaltation of *"Criticism"*; for only Criticism both made the false conclusion and then refuted it. Criticism is just as magnanimous towards Lord *John Russell*, to whom it imputes the wish to change the political form of the state and the electoral system. From this we must conclude either that Criticism's urge to produce stupidities is uncommonly powerful or that Lord John Russell must have become a Critical Critic within the past week.

But Criticism only becomes truly magnificent in its fabrication of stupidities when it discovers that the English workers—who in April and May held meeting after meeting, drew up petition after petition, and all for the Ten Hour Bill, and displayed more agitation throughout the factory districts than at any time during the past two years—that those workers take only a *"partial interest"* in this question, although it is evident that "legislation limiting the working day has also occupied their attention". Criticism is truly magnificent when it finally makes the great, the glorious, the unheard-of discovery that

"the apparently more immediate help from the repeal of the Corn Laws absorbs most of the wishes of the workers and will do so until no longer doubtful realisation of those wishes practically proves the futility of the repeal"—

proves it to workers who drag Anti-Corn-Law agitators down from the platform at every public meeting, who have seen to it that the Anti-Corn-Law League no longer dares to hold a public meeting in any English industrial town, who consider the League to be their only enemy and who, during the debate of the Ten Hour Bill—as nearly always before in similar matters—had the support of the Tories. Criticism is superb, too, when it discovers that "the workers still let themselves be lured by the sweeping promises of the *Chartist movement"*, which is nothing but the political expression of public opinion among the workers. Criticism is superb, too, when it realises, in the depths of its Absolute Spirit, that

"the two party groupings, the political one and that of the landowners and mill-owners, *no longer* wish to merge or coincide".

It was so far not known that the party grouping of the landowners and the mill-owners, because of the numerical smallness of either class of owners and the equal political rights of each (with the exception of the few peers), was so comprehensive that it was completely identical with the political party groupings, and not their most consistent expression, their peak. Criticism is splendid when it suggests that the Anti-Corn-Law Leaguers do not know that, *ceteris paribus*,[a] a drop in the price of bread must be followed · by a drop in wages, so that all would remain as it was; whereas these people expect that, granted there is a drop in wages and a consequent lowering of production costs, the result will be an expansion of the market. This, they expect, would lead to a reduction of competition among the workers, and consequently wages would still be kept a little higher in comparison with the price of bread than they are now.

Freely creating its opposite — nonsense — and moving in artistic rapture, Criticism, which only two years ago exclaimed "Criticism speaks German, theology speaks Latin!",[b] has now learnt *English* and calls the estate-owners "*Landeigner*" (landowners), the factory-owners "*Mühleigner*" (mill-owners) — in English a mill means any factory with machinery driven by steam or water-power — and the workers "*Hände*" (hands). Instead of "*Einmischung*" it says *Interferenz* (interference); and in its infinite mercy for the English language, the sinful mass nature of which is abundantly evident, it condescends to improve it by doing away with the pedantry with which the English place the title "Sir" before the *Christian* name of knights and baronets. Where the Mass says "Sir James Graham", it says "Sir Graham".

That Criticism reforms *English* history and the *English* language out of *principle* and not out of *levity* will presently be proved by the *thoroughness* with which it treats the *history of Herr Nauwerck*.

---

[a] Other things remaining the same.—*Ed.*

[b] Bruno Bauer, *Die Gute Sache der Freiheit und meine eigene Angelegenheit*, Zürich u. Winterthur, 1842.—*Ed.*

Chapter III

"THE THOROUGHNESS OF CRITICAL CRITICISM",
OR CRITICAL CRITICISM AS HERR J. (JUNGNITZ?)[9]

Criticism cannot ignore Herr *Nauwerck's* infinitely important dispute with the Berlin Faculty of Philosophy. It has indeed had a similar experience and it must take Herr Nauwerck's fate as a background in order to put its own *dismissal from Bonn*[10] in sharper relief. Criticism, being accustomed to considering the Bonn affair as the event of the century, and having already written the "philosophy of the deposition of criticism", could be expected to give a similar detailed philosophical construction of the Berlin "collision". Criticism proves *a priori* that everything had to happen in such a way and no other. It proves:

1) Why the Faculty of Philosophy was bound to come into "collision" not with a logician or metaphysician, but with a philosopher of the state;

2) Why that collision could not be so sharp and decisive as Criticism's conflict with theology in Bonn;

3) Why that collision was, properly speaking, a stupid business, since Criticism had already concentrated all principles and all content in its Bonn collision, so that world history could only become a plagiarist of Criticism;

4) Why the Faculty of Philosophy considered attacks on the works of Herr Nauwerck as attacks on itself;

5) Why no other course remained for Herr N. but to retire of his own accord;

6) Why the Faculty had to defend Herr N. if it did not want to disavow itself;

7) Why the "inner split in the Faculty had necessarily to manifest itself in such a way" that the Faculty declared both N. and the Government right and wrong at the same time;

8) Why the Faculty finds in N.'s works no reason for dismissing him;

9) What determined the lack of clarity of the whole verdict;

10) Why the Faculty "deems itself (!) entitled (!) as a scientific authority (!) to examine the essence of the matter", and finally;

11) Why, nevertheless, the Faculty does not want to write in the same way as Herr N.

Criticism disposes of these important questions with rare thoroughness in four pages, proving by means of Hegel's logic why everything had to happen as it did and why no god could have prevented it. In another place Criticism says that there has not yet been full knowledge of a single epoch in history; modesty prevents it from saying that it has full knowledge of at least its own collision and Nauwerck's, which, although they are not epochs, appear to Criticism to be epoch-*making*.

Having "abolished" in itself the "element" of *thoroughness*, Critical Criticism becomes "*the tranquillity of knowledge*".[11]

Chapter IV

"CRITICAL CRITICISM" AS THE TRANQUILLITY OF KNOWLEDGE,

OR "CRITICAL CRITICISM" AS HERR EDGAR

1) FLORA TRISTAN'S *UNION OUVRIÈRE* [12]

The French Socialists maintain that the worker makes everything, produces everything and yet has no rights, no possessions, in short, nothing at all. Criticism answers in the words of Herr Edgar, the personification of the *tranquillity of knowledge*:

"To be able to create everything, a stronger consciousness is needed than that of the worker. Only the opposite of the above proposition would be true: the worker makes nothing, therefore he has nothing; but the reason why he makes nothing is that his work is always individual, having as its object his most personal needs, and is everyday work."

Here Criticism achieves a height of abstraction in which it regards only the creations of its own thought and generalities which contradict all reality as "something", indeed as "*everything*". The worker creates nothing because he creates only "individual", that is, perceptible, palpable, spiritless and un-Critical objects, which are an abomination in the eyes of pure Criticism. Everything that is real and living is un-Critical, of a mass nature, and therefore "nothing"; only the ideal, fantastic creatures of Critical Criticism are "*everything*".

The worker creates nothing, because his work remains individual, having only his individual needs as its object, that is, because in the present world system the individual interconnected branches of labour are separated from, and even opposed to, one another; in short, because labour is not *organised*. Criticism's own proposition, if taken in the only reasonable sense it can possibly have, demands the organisation of labour. Flora Tristan, in an assessment of whose work this great proposition appears, puts forward the same demand and is treated *en canaille*[a] for her insolence in anticipating Critical Criticism. Anyhow, the proposition that the

---

[a] Contemptuously.— *Ed.*

worker creates nothing is absolutely crazy except in the sense that the *individual* worker produces nothing *whole*, which is tautology. Critical Criticism creates nothing, the worker creates everything; and so much so that even his intellectual creations put the whole of Criticism to shame; the English and the French workers provide proof of this. The worker creates even *man*; the critic will never be anything but sub-human[a] though on the other hand, of course, he has the satisfaction of being a Critical critic.

> "Flora Tristan is an example of the feminine dogmatism which must have a formula and constructs it out of the categories of what exists."

Criticism does nothing but "construct formulae out of the categories of what exists", namely, out of the existing *Hegelian* philosophy and the existing social aspirations. Formulae, nothing but formulae. And despite all its invectives against dogmatism, it condemns itself to dogmatism and even to *feminine* dogmatism. It is and remains an old woman — faded, widowed *Hegelian* philosophy which paints and adorns its body, shrivelled into the most repulsive abstraction, and ogles all over Germany in search of a wooer.

2) BÉRAUD ON PROSTITUTES[13]

Herr Edgar, taking pity on social questions, meddles also in "*conditions of prostitutes*" (Heft V, p. 26).[b]

He criticises Paris Police Commissioner Béraud's book on prostitution because he is concerned with the "*point of view*" from which "Béraud considers the attitude of prostitutes to society". The "tranquillity of knowledge" is surprised to see that a policeman adopts the point of view of the police, and it gives the Mass to understand that that point of view is quite wrong. But it does not reveal its own point of view. Of course not! When Criticism takes up with prostitutes it cannot be expected to do so in public.

3) LOVE

In order to complete its transformation into the "tranquillity of knowledge", Critical Criticism must first seek to dispose of *love*. Love is a passion, and nothing is more dangerous for the

---

[a] In the German text there is a pun on the words "Mensch" (man) and "Unmensch" (brute).— *Ed.*

[b] *Allgemeine Literatur-Zeitung*, Heft V, April 1844.— *Ed.*

tranquillity of knowledge than passion. That is why, speaking of Madame von Paalzow's novels, which, he assures us, he has "thoroughly *studied*", Herr Edgar is amazed at "a *childish thing* like *so-called love*".[14] It is a horror and abomination and excites the wrath of Critical Criticism, makes it almost as bitter as gall, indeed, insane.

"Love ... is a cruel goddess, and like every deity she wishes to possess the whole of man and is not satisfied until he has surrendered to her not merely his soul, but his physical self. The worship of love is suffering, the peak of this worship is self-immolation, suicide."

In order to change love into "Moloch", the devil incarnate, Herr Edgar first changes it into a goddess. When love has become a goddess, i. e., a theological object, it is of course submitted to *theological criticism*; moreover, it is known that god and the devil are not far apart. Herr Edgar changes love into a "goddess", a "cruel goddess" at that, by changing *man who loves*, the love of *man*, into a man of *love*; by making "*love*" a being apart, separate from man and as such independent. By this simple process, by changing the predicate into the subject, all the attributes and manifestations of human nature can be Critically transformed into their *negation* and into *alienations* of human nature.[a] Thus, for example, Critical Criticism makes criticism, as a predicate and activity of man, into a subject apart, criticism which relates itself to itself and is therefore *Critical Criticism*: a "Moloch", the worship of which consists in the self-immolation, the suicide of man, and in particular of his *ability to think*.

"*Object*," exclaims the tranquillity of knowledge, "object is the right expression, for the beloved is important to the lover [*denn der Geliebte ist dem Liebenden*] (there is no feminine) only as *this external object* of the *emotion of his soul*, as the object in which he wishes to see his selfish feeling satisfied."

Object! Horrible! There is nothing more damnable, more profane, more mass-like than an *object*—*à bas*[b] the object! How could absolute subjectivity, the *actus purus*,[c] "*pure*" Criticism, not see in love its *bête noire*,[d] that Satan incarnate, in love, which first really teaches man to believe in the objective world outside himself,

---

[a] A pun in the original: "*alle Wesensbestimmungen und Wesensäusserungen des Menschen* (all the attributes and manifestations of human nature) are transformed into "*Unwesen*" (fantastic creatures, monsters) and into "*Wesensentäusserungen*" (alienations of human essence).—*Ed.*

[b] Down with.—*Ed.*

[c] Pure act.—*Ed.*

[d] Object of special detestation.—*Ed.*

which not only makes man into an object, but even the object into a man!

Love, continues the tranquillity of knowledge, beside itself, is not even content with turning man into the *category* of *"object"* for another man, it even makes him into a *definite, real* object, into *this* bad-individual (see Hegel's *Phänomenologie*[a] on the categories "This" and "That", where there is also a polemic against the bad *"This"*), *external* object, which does not remain internal, hidden in the brain, but is sensuously manifest.

Love
Lives not *only* in the *brain* immured.

No, the beloved is a *sensuous object,* and if Critical Criticism is to condescend to recognition of an object, it demands at the very least a *senseless* object. But love is an *un-Critical, unchristian materialist.*

Finally, love even makes one human being *"this external object of the emotion of the soul"* of another, the object in which the *selfish* feeling of the other finds its satisfaction, a *selfish* feeling because it *looks for its own essence* in the other, and that must not be. Critical Criticism is so *free* from all *selfishness* that for it the whole range of human essence is exhausted *by its own self.*

Herr Edgar, of course, does not tell us in what way the beloved differs from the other "external objects of the emotion of the soul in which the selfish feelings of men find their satisfaction". The spiritually profound, meaningful, highly expressive object of love means nothing to the tranquillity of knowledge but the abstract formula: "this external object of the emotion of the soul", much as the comet means nothing to the speculative natural philosopher but "negativity". By making man the external object of the emotion of his soul, man does in fact attach "importance" to him, Critical Criticism itself admits, but only *objective importance,* so to speak, while the importance which Criticism attaches to objects is none other than that which it attaches to itself. Hence this importance lies not in "bad *external being*", but in the *"Nothing"* of the Critically important object.

If the tranquillity of knowledge has no *object* in real man, it has, on the other hand, a *cause* in *humanity.* Critical love *"is careful* above all not to forget the *cause* behind the personality, for that cause is none other than the cause of humanity". Un-Critical love does not separate humanity from the personal, individual man.

---

[a] G. W. F. Hegel, *Phänomenologie des Geistes.—Ed.*

"Love itself, as an *abstract* passion, which comes we know not whence and goes we know not whither, is incapable of having an interest in *internal* development."

In the eyes of the tranquillity of knowledge, love is an abstract passion according to the *speculative* terminology in which the concrete is called abstract and the abstract concrete.

> The maid was not born in that valley,
> But where she came from, no one knew.
> And soon all trace of her did vanish
> Once she had bidden them adieu.[a]

For abstraction, love is "the maid from a foreign land" who has no dialectical passport and is therefore expelled from the country by the Critical police.

The passion of love is incapable of having an interest in *internal* development because it cannot be construed *a priori*, because its development is a real one which takes place in the world of the senses and between real individuals. But the main interest of speculative construction is the "Whence" and the "Whither". The "Whence" is the "*necessity* of a concept, its proof and deduction" (Hegel). The "Whither" is the determination "by which each individual link of the speculative circular course, as the animated content of the method, is at the same time the beginning of a new link" (Hegel). Hence, only if its "Whence" and its "Whither" could be construed *a priori* would love deserve the "interest" of speculative Criticism.

What Critical Criticism combats here is not merely love but everything living, everything which is immediate, every sensuous experience, any and every *real* experience, the "Whence" and the "Whither" of which one never *knows* beforehand.

By overcoming love, Herr Edgar has completely *asserted* himself as the "tranquillity of knowledge", and now by his treatment of *Proudhon*, he can show great virtuosity in knowledge, the "*object*" of which is no longer "*this external object*", and a still greater *lack of love* for the French language.

4) PROUDHON

It was not *Proudhon* himself, but "Proudhon's *point of view*", Critical Criticism informs us, that wrote *Qu'est-ce que la propriété?*

"I begin my exposition of Proudhon's point of view by characterising its" (the point of view's) "work, *Qu'est-ce que la propriété?*"[15]

As only the works of the Critical point of view possess a character of their own, the Critical characterisation necessarily

[a] From Schiller's *Das Mädchen aus der Fremde.*—Ed.

begins by giving a character to Proudhon's work. Herr Edgar gives this work a character by *translating* it. He naturally gives it a *bad* character, for he turns it into an *object* of "Criticism".

Proudhon's work, therefore, is subjected to a double attack by Herr Edgar—an *unspoken* one in his characterising translation and an *outspoken* one in his Critical comments. We shall see that Herr Edgar is more devastating when he translates than when he comments.

Characterising Translation No. 1

"I do not wish" (says the Critically translated Proudhon) "to give any system of the new; I wish for nothing but the abolition of privilege, the abolition of slavery.... Justice, nothing but justice, that is what I mean."

The characterised Proudhon confines himself to will and opinion, because "good will" and unscientific "opinion" are characteristic attributes of the un-Critical Mass. The characterised Proudhon behaves with the humility that is fitting for the Mass and subordinates what he wishes to what he does *not* wish. He does not presume to wish to give a system of the new, he wishes less, he even wishes for *nothing* but the abolition of privilege, etc. Besides this Critical subordination of the will he has to the will he has not, his very first word is marked by a characteristic lack of logic. A writer who begins his book by saying that he does not wish to give any system of the new, should then tell us what he does wish to give: whether it is a systematised old or an unsystematised new. But does the characterised Proudhon, who does not wish to *give* any system of the new, wish to give the abolition of privilege? No. He just *wishes* it.

The *real* Proudhon says: "*Je ne fais pas de système; je demande la fin du privilège*,"[a] etc. I make no system, I demand, etc., that is to say, the real Proudhon declares that he does not pursue any abstract scientific aims, but makes immediately practical demands on society. And the demand he makes is not an arbitrary one. It is motivated and justified by his whole argument and is the summary of that argument for, he says, "*justice, rien que justice; tel est le resumé de mon discours*."[b] With his "justice, nothing but justice, that is what I mean", the characterised Proudhon gets himself into a position which is all the more embarrassing as he means much more. According to Herr Edgar, for example, he *"means"* that philosophy has not been practical enough, he *"means"* to refute Charles Comte, and so forth.

---

[a] "I make no system, I demand an end of privilege."—*Ed.*

[b] "Justice, nothing but justice; that is the summary of what I say."—*Ed.*

The Critical Proudhon asks: "Ought *man* then always to be unhappy?" In other words, he asks whether unhappiness is man's moral destiny. The real Proudhon is a light-minded Frenchman and he asks whether unhappiness is a material necessity, a *must*. (*L'homme doit-il être éternellement malheureux?* [a])

The mass-type Proudhon says:

"Et, sans m'arrêter aux explications à toute fin des entrepreneurs de réformes, accusant de la détresse générale, ceux-ci la lâcheté et l'impéritie du pouvoir, ceux-là les conspirateurs et les émeutes, d'autres l'ignorance et la corruption générale", etc. [b]

The expression *"à toute fin"* being a bad mass-type expression that is not in the mass-type German dictionaries, the Critical Proudhon naturally omits this more exact definition of the "explanations". This term is taken from mass-type French juris-prudence, and *"explications à toute fin"* means explanations which preclude any objection. The Critical Proudhon censures the *"Reformists"*, a French Socialist Party [16]; the mass-type Proudhon censures the initiators of reforms. The mass-type Proudhon distinguishes various classes of *"entrepreneurs de réformes"*. These (*ceux-ci*) say *one thing*, those (*ceux-là*) say *another*, others (*d'autres*) a *third*. The Critical Proudhon, on the other hand, makes *the same reformists* "accuse now one, then another, then a third", which in any case is proof of their inconstancy. The real Proudhon, who follows mass-type French practice, speaks of *"les conspirateurs et les émeutes"*, i.e., first of the conspirators and then of their activity, revolts. The Critical Proudhon, on the other hand, who has lumped together the various classes of reformists, classifies the rebels and hence says: the conspirators and the *rebels*. The mass-type Proudhon speaks of *ignorance* and *"general corruption"*. The Critical Proudhon changes ignorance into stupidity, "corrup-tion" into "depravity", and finally, as a Critical critic, makes the stupidity *general*. He himself gives an immediate example of it by putting *"générale"* in the singular instead of the plural. He writes: *"l'ignorance et la corruption générale"* for general stupidity and depravity. According to un-Critical French grammar this should be: *l'ignorance et la corruption générales*.

The characterised Proudhon, who speaks and thinks otherwise than the mass-type one, necessarily went through quite a different

_____

[a] *Must* man for ever be unhappy?—*Ed.*

[b] "Without dwelling on the explanations precluding all objections given by the initiators of reforms, some of whom blame for the general distress the cowardice and incapacity of the government, others—conspirators and revolts, others again—ignorance and general corruption", etc.—*Ed.*

course of education. He "questioned the masters of science, read hundreds of volumes of philosophy and law, etc., and *at last*" he "realised that we have never yet grasped the meaning of the words Justice, Equity, Freedom". The real Proudhon thought he had realised *at first* (*je crus d'abord reconnaître*[a]) what the Critical Proudhon realised only *"at last"*. The Critical alteration of *d'abord* into *enfin* is necessary because the Mass may not think it realises anything "at first". The mass-type Proudhon tells explicitly how he was staggered by the unexpected result of his studies and distrusted it. Hence he decided to carry out a *"countertest"* and asked himself: "Is it possible that mankind has so long and so universally been mistaken over the principles of the application of morals? How and why was it mistaken?" etc. He made the correctness of his observations dependent on the solution of these questions. He found that in morals, as in all other branches of knowledge, errors *"are stages of science"*. The Critical Proudhon, on the other hand, immediately trusted the first impression that his studies of political economy, law and the like made upon him. Needless to say, the Mass cannot proceed in any *thorough* way; it is bound to raise the first results of its investigations to the level of indisputable truths. It has "reached the end before it has started, before it has measured itself with its opposite". Hence, "it is seen" later "that it is not yet at the beginning when it thinks it has reached the end".

The Critical Proudhon therefore continues his reasoning in the most untenable and incoherent way.

"Our knowledge of moral laws is not complete from the beginning; *thus* it can for some time suffice for social progress, but in the long run it will lead us on a false path."

The Critical Proudhon does not give any reason why incomplete knowledge of moral laws can suffice for social progress even for a single day. The real Proudhon, having asked himself whether and why mankind could universally and so long have been mistaken and having found as the solution that all errors are stages of science and that our most imperfect judgments contain a sum of truths sufficient for a certain number of inductions and for a certain area of practical life, beyond which number and which area they lead theoretically to the absurd and practically to decay, is in a position to say that even imperfect knowledge of moral laws can suffice for social progress for a time.

The Critical Proudhon says:

_____
[a] I thought *at first* I had recognised.— *Ed.*

"But if new knowledge has become necessary, a bitter struggle arises between the old prejudices and the new idea."

How can a struggle arise against an opponent who does *not yet* exist? Admitted, the Critical Proudhon has told us that a new idea has become necessary but he has not said that it has already *come into existence*.

The mass-type Proudhon says:

"Once higher knowledge has become indispensable it *is never lacking*", it is therefore ready at hand. *"It is then* that the struggle begins."

The Critical Proudhon asserts: "It is man's destiny to learn step by step", as if man did not have a quite different destiny, namely, that of being man, and as if that learning "step by step" necessarily brought him a step farther. I can go step by step and arrive at the very point from which I set out. The un-Critical Proudhon speaks, not of "destiny", but of the *condition* (*condition*) for man to learn not *step by step* (*pas à pas*), but *by degrees* (*par degrés*). The Critical Proudhon says to himself:

"Among the principles upon which society rests there is one which society does not understand, which is spoilt by society's ignorance and is the cause of all evil. Nevertheless, man honours *this* principle" and "wills it, for otherwise it would have no influence. Now this principle which is true in its *essence* but is false in the way we conceive it ... what is it?"

In the first sentence the Critical Proudhon says that the principle is spoilt, misunderstood by society, hence that it is correct in itself. In the second sentence he admits superfluously that it is true in its essence; nevertheless he reproaches society with willing and honouring "this principle". The mass-type Proudhon, on the other hand, reproaches society with willing and honouring not this principle, but this principle *as* falsified by our ignorance (*"Ce principe ... tel que notre ignorance l'a fait, est honoré."* [a]). The Critical Proudhon finds the *essence* of the principle in its untrue form *true*. The mass-type Proudhon finds that the essence of the falsified principle is our incorrect conception, but that it is true in its *object* (*objet*), just as the essence of alchemy and astrology is our imagination, but their objects — the movement of the heavenly bodies and the chemical properties of substances — are true.

The Critical Proudhon continues his monologue:

"The object of our investigation is the law, the definition of the social principle. Now the politicians, i.e., the men of social science, are a prey to complete lack of clarity ...; but as there is a reality at the basis of every error, in their books we shall find the truth, which they have brought into the world without knowing it."

---

[a] "This principle ... as our ignorance has made it, is honoured." — *Ed.*

The Critical Proudhon has a most fantastic way of reasoning. From the fact that the politicians are ignorant and unclear, he goes on in the most arbitrary fashion to say that a reality lies at the basis of every error, which can all the less be doubted as there is a reality at the basis of every error—in the person of the one who errs. From the fact that a reality lies *at the basis* of every error he goes on to conclude that truth is to be found *in the books* of politicians. And finally he even makes out that the politicians have brought this truth into the *world*. Had they brought it into the *world* we should not need to look for it in their *books*.

The mass-type Proudhon says:

"The politicians do not understand one another (*ne s'entendent pas*); their error is therefore a subjective one, having its origin in them (*donc c'est en eux qu'est l'erreur*)." Their mutual misunderstanding proves their one-sidedness. They confuse "their private opinion with common sense", and "as", according to the previous deduction, "every error has a true reality as its *object,* their books must contain the truth, which they unconsciously have put there"—i.e., in their books—"but have not brought into the world" (*dans leurs livres doit se trouver la vérité, qu'à leur insu ils y auront mise*).

The Critical Proudhon asks himself: "What is justice, what is its essence, its character, its meaning?" As if it had some meaning apart from its essence and character. The un-Critical Proudhon asks: What is its principle, its character and its formula (*formule*)? The formula is the principle as a principle of scientific reasoning. In the mass-type French language there is an essential difference between *formule* and *signification*. In the Critical French language there is none.

After his highly irrelevant disquisitions, the Critical Proudhon pulls himself together and exclaims:

"Let us try to get somewhat closer to our object."

The un-Critical Proudhon, on the other hand, who arrived at his object long ago, tries to attain more precise and more positive definitions of his object (*d'arriver à quelque chose de plus précis et de plus positif*).

For the Critical Proudhon "the law is a *definition* of what is right", for the un-Critical Proudhon it is a *"statement"* (*déclaration*) of it. The un-Critical Proudhon disputes the view that right is made by law. But a "definition of the law" can mean that the law is defined just as it can mean that it defines. Previously, the Critical Proudhon himself spoke about the definition of the social principle in this latter sense. To be sure, it is unseemly of the mass-type Proudhon to make such nice distinctions.

Considering these differences between the Critically character-

ised Proudhon and the real Proudhon, it is no wonder that
Proudhon No. 1 seeks to *prove* quite different things than
Proudhon No. 2.

The Critical Proudhon

> *"seeks to prove* by the *experience of history"* that "if the idea that we have of
> what is just and right is false, *evidently"* (he tries to prove it in spite of its evidence)
> "all its applications in law must be bad, all our institutions must be defective".

¨ The mass-type Proudhon is far from wishing to prove what is
evident. He says instead:

> "If the idea that we have of what is just and right were badly defined, if it were
> incomplete or even false, it is *evident* that all our legislative applications would be
> bad", etc.

What, then, does the un-Critical Proudhon wish to prove?

> "This hypothesis," he continues, "of the perversion of justice in our under-
> standing, and as a necessary consequence in our actions, would be an established
> fact if the opinions of men concerning the concept of justice and its applications
> had not remained constantly the same, if at different times they had undergone
> modifications; in a word, if there had been progress in ideas."

And precisely that inconstancy, that change, that progress "is
what *history* proves by the most striking testimonies". And the
un-Critical Proudhon quotes these striking testimonies of history.
His Critical double, who proves a completely different proposition
by the experience of history, also presents that experience itself in a
different way.

According to the real Proudhon, "the wise" (*les sages*), according
to the Critical Proudhon, "the philosophers", foresaw the fall of
the Roman Empire. The Critical Proudhon can of course consider
only philosophers to be wise men. According to the real
Proudhon, Roman "rights were consecrated by ten centuries of
law practice" or "administration of justice" (*ces droits consacrés par
une justice dix fois séculaire*); according to the Critical Proudhon,
Rome had "rights consecrated by ten centuries of *justice*".

According to the same Proudhon No. 1, the Romans reasoned
as follows:

> "Rome ... was victorious through its policy and its gods; any reform in worship
> or public spirit would be stupidity and profanation" (according to the Critical
> Proudhon, *sacrilège* means not the profanation or desecration of a holy thing, as in
> the mass-type French language, but just profanation). "Had it wished to free the
> peoples, it would thereby have renounced its right." "Rome had thus fact and right
> in its favour," Proudhon No. 1 adds.

According to the un-Critical Proudhon, the Romans reasoned
more logically. The *fact* was set out in detail:

> "The slaves are the most fertile source of its wealth; the freeing of the peoples
> would therefore be *the ruin of its finance*."

And the mass-type Proudhon adds, referring to law: "Rome's claims were justified by the law of nations (*droit des gens*)." This way of proving the right of subjugation was completely in keeping with the Roman view on law. See the mass-type pandects: *"jure gentium servitus invasit"* (Fr. 4. D. I. I).[a]

According to the Critical Proudhon, "idolatry, slavery and softness" were "the basis of Roman institutions", of all its institutions without exception. The real Proudhon says: "Idolatry in religion, slavery in the state and Epicureanism in private life" (*épicurisme* in the ordinary French language is not synonymous with *mollesse*, softness) "were the basis of the institutions." Within that Roman situation there "appeared", says the mystic Proudhon, "the Word of God", whereas according to the real, rationalistic Proudhon, it was "a man who *called* himself the Word of God". In the real Proudhon this man calls the priests "vipers" (*vipères*); in the Critical Proudhon he speaks more courteously with them and calls them "serpents". In the former he speaks in the Roman way of "advocates" [*Advokaten*], in the latter in the German way of "lawyers" [*Rechtsgelehrte*].

The Critical Proudhon calls the spirit of the French Revolution a spirit of contradiction, and adds:

"That is enough to realise that the new which replaced the old had on itself [*an sich*] nothing methodical and considered."

He cannot refrain from repeating mechanically the favourite categories of Critical Criticism, the "old" and the "new". He cannot refrain from the senseless demand that the "new" should have *on* itself [*an* sich] something methodical and considered, just as one might have a stain on oneself [an sich]. The real Proudhon says:

"That is enough to prove that the new order of things which was substituted for the old was *in* itself [*in* sich] without method or reflection."

Carried away by the memory of the French Revolution, the Critical Proudhon *revolutionises* the French language so much that he translates *un fait physique*[b] by "a fact of physics", and *un fait intellectuel*[c] by "a fact of the intellect". By this revolution in the French language the Critical Proudhon manages to put physics in possession of all the facts to be found in nature. Raising natural science unduly on one side, he debases it just as much on the

---

[a] "Slavery was spread *by the law of nations*." (*Corpus iuris civilis*, Vol. 1. Digesta[17]: Liber primus, titulus I, fragmentum 4.)—*Ed.*

[b] A physical fact.—*Ed.*

[c] An intellectual fact.—*Ed.*

other by depriving it of intellect and distinguishing between a fact of physics and a fact of the intellect. To the same extent he makes all further psychological and logical investigation unnecessary by raising the intellectual fact directly to the level of a fact of the intellect.

Since the Critical Proudhon, Proudhon No. 1, has not the slightest idea what the real Proudhon, Proudhon No. 2, wishes to prove by his historical deduction, neither does the real content of that deduction exist for him, namely, the proof of the change in the views on law and of the continuous *implementation* of justice by the *negation* of historical actual right.

"La société fut sauvée par la *négation* de ses ... principes ... et la *violation des droits* les plus sacrés."[a]

Thus the real Proudhon proves how the negation of Roman law led to the widening of right in the Christian *conception,* the negation of the right of conquest to the right of the communes and the negation of the whole feudal law by the French Revolution to the present more comprehensive system of law.

Critical Criticism could not possibly leave Proudhon the glory of having discovered the law of the implementation of a principle by its negation. In this conscious formulation, this idea was a real revelation for the French.

Critical Comment No. 1

As the first criticism of any science is necessarily influenced by the premises of the science it is fighting against, so Proudhon's treatise *Qu'est-ce que la propriété?* is the criticism of *political economy* from the standpoint of political economy. — We need not go more deeply into the juridical part of the book, which criticises law from the standpoint of law, for our main interest is the criticism of political economy. — Proudhon's treatise will therefore be scientifically superseded by a criticism of *political economy,* including Proudhon's conception of political economy. This work became possible only owing to the work of Proudhon himself, just as Proudhon's criticism has as its premise the criticism of the mercantile system by the physiocrats, Adam Smith's criticism of the physiocrats, Ricardo's criticism of Adam Smith, and the works of Fourier and Saint-Simon.

All treatises on political economy take *private property* for

---

[a] "Society was saved by the *negation* of its principles ... and the *violation* of the most sacred *rights.*" — *Ed.*

granted. This basic premise is for them an incontestable fact to which they devote no further investigation, indeed a fact which is spoken about only "*accidentellement*", as *Say* naively admits.[a] But Proudhon makes a critical investigation—the first resolute, ruthless, and at the same time scientific investigation—of the basis of political economy, *private property*. This is the great scientific advance he made, an advance which revolutionises political economy and for the first time makes a real science of political economy possible. Proudhon's treatise *Qu'est-ce que la propriété?* is as important for modern political economy as Sieyès' work *Qu'est-ce que le tiers état?*[b] for modern politics.

Proudhon does not consider the further creations of private property, e.g., wages, trade, value, price, money, etc., as forms of private property in themselves, as they are considered, for example, in the *Deutsch-Französische Jahrbücher* (see *Outlines of a Critique of Political Economy* by F. Engels[c]), but uses these economic premises in arguing against the political economists; this is fully in keeping with his historically justified standpoint to which we referred above.

Accepting the relationships of private property as human and rational, political economy operates in permanent contradiction to its basic premise, private property, a contradiction analogous to that of the theologian who continually gives a human interpretation to religious conceptions, and by that very fact comes into constant conflict with his basic premise, the superhuman character of religion. Thus in political economy wages appear at the beginning as the proportional share of the product due to labour. Wages and profit on capital stand in the most friendly, mutually stimulating, apparently most human relationship to each other. Afterwards it turns out that they stand in the most hostile relationship, in *inverse* proportion to each other. Value is determined at the beginning in an apparently rational way, by the cost of production of an object and by its social usefulness. Later it turns out that value is determined quite fortuitously and that it does not need to bear any relation to either the cost of production or social usefulness. The size of wages is determined at the beginning by *free* agreement between the free worker and the free capitalist. Later it turns out that the worker is compelled to allow the capitalist to determine it, just as the capitalist is compelled to

---

[a] J.-B. Say, *Traité d'économie politique*, t. II, p. 471.—*Ed.*
[b] *What Is the Third Estate?—Ed.*
[c] See present edition, Vol. 3, pp. 418-43.—*Ed.*

fix it as low as possible. *Freedom* of the contracting parties has been supplanted by *compulsion*. The same holds good of trade and all other economic relationships. The economists themselves occasionally feel these contradictions, the development of which is the main content of the conflict between them. When, however, the economists become conscious of these contradictions, *they themselves* attack *private property* in one or other *particular* form as the falsifier of what is in itself (i.e., in their imagination) rational wages, in itself rational value, in itself rational trade. Adam Smith, for instance, occasionally polemises against the capitalists, Destutt de Tracy against the money-changers, Simonde de Sismondi against the factory system, Ricardo against landed property, and nearly all modern economists against the *non-industrial* capitalists, among whom property appears as a mere *consumer.*

Thus, as an exception — when they attack some special abuse — the economists occasionally stress the semblance of humanity in economic relations, but sometimes, and as a rule, they take these relations precisely in their clearly pronounced *difference* from the human, in their strictly economic sense. They stagger about within this contradiction completely unaware of it.

Now *Proudhon* has put an end to this unconsciousness once for all. He takes the *human semblance* of the economic relations seriously and sharply opposes it to their *inhuman reality.* He forces them to be in reality what they imagine themselves to be, or rather to give up their own idea of themselves and confess their real inhumanity. He therefore consistently depicts as the falsifier of economic relations not this or that particular kind of private property, as other economists do, but private property as such and in its entirety. He has done all that criticism of political economy from the standpoint of political economy can do.

Herr Edgar, who wishes to *characterise* the *standpoint* of the treatise *Qu'est-ce que la propriété?*, naturally does not say a word either of political economy or of the distinctive character of this book, which is precisely that it has made the *essence of private property* the vital question of political economy and jurisprudence. This is all self-evident for Critical Criticism. Proudhon, it says, has done nothing new by his negation of private property. He has only let out a secret which Critical Criticism did not want to divulge.

"Proudhon," Herr Edgar continues immediately after his characterising translation, "therefore finds something absolute, an eternal foundation in history, a god that guides mankind — justice."

Proudhon's book, written in France in 1840, does not adopt the standpoint of German development in 1844. It is Proudhon's standpoint, a standpoint which is shared by countless diametrically opposed French writers, which therefore gives Critical Criticism the advantage of having characterised the most contradictory standpoints with a single stroke of the pen. Incidentally, to be relieved from this Absolute in history as well one has only to apply consistently the law formulated by Proudhon himself, that of the implementation of justice by its negation. If Proudhon does not carry consistency as far as that, it is only because he had the misfortune of being born a Frenchman, not a German.

For Herr Edgar, Proudhon has become a *theological* object by his Absolute in history, his belief in justice, and Critical Criticism, which is *ex professo* a criticism of theology, can now set to work on him in order to expatiate on "religious conceptions".

"It is a characteristic of every religious conception that it sets up as a dogma a situation in which at the end one of the opposites comes out victorious as the only truth."

We shall see how religious Critical Criticism sets up as a dogma a situation in which at the end one of the opposites, "*Criticism*", comes out victorious over the other, the "Mass", as the only truth. By seeing in mass-type justice an Absolute, a god of history, Proudhon committed an injustice that is all the greater because just Criticism has *explicitly* reserved for itself the role of that Absolute, that god in history.

Critical Comment No. 2

"The fact of misery, of poverty, makes Proudhon one-sided in his considerations; he sees in it a *contradiction* to equality and justice; it provides him with a weapon. Hence this fact becomes for him absolute and justified, whereas the fact of property becomes unjustified."

The tranquillity of knowledge tells us that Proudhon sees in the fact of poverty a contradiction to justice, that is to say, finds it unjustified; yet in the same breath it assures us that this fact becomes for him absolute and justified.

Hitherto political economy proceeded from *wealth*, which the movement of private property supposedly creates for the *nations*, to its considerations which are an apology for private property. Proudhon proceeds from the opposite side, which political economy sophistically conceals, from the poverty bred by the movement of private property to his considerations which negate private property. The first criticism of private property proceeds, of course, from the fact in which its contradictory essence appears in the form that is most perceptible and most glaring and most directly arouses man's indignation—from the fact of poverty, of misery.

"Criticism, on the other hand, joins the two facts, poverty and property, in a single unity, grasps the inner link between them and makes them a single whole, which it investigates as such to find the preconditions for its existence."

Criticism, which has hitherto understood nothing of the facts of property and of poverty, uses, "on the other hand", the deed which it has accomplished in its imagination as an argument against Proudhon's real deed. It unites the *two* facts in a *single* one, and having made *one* out of *two*, grasps the inner link between the *two*. Criticism cannot deny that Proudhon, too, is aware of an inner link between the facts of poverty and of property, since because of that very link he abolishes property in order to abolish poverty. Proudhon did even more. He proved in detail *how* the movement of capital produces poverty. But Critical Criticism does not bother with such trifles. It recognises that poverty and private property are *opposites*—a rather widespread recognition. It *makes* poverty and wealth *a single whole*, which it "investigates *as such* to find ·the preconditions for its existence"; an investigation which is all the more superfluous since it has just *made* "the whole as such" and therefore its *making* is in itself the precondition for the existence of this whole.

By investigating "the whole as such" to find the preconditions for its existence, Critical Criticism is searching in the genuine theological manner *outside* the "whole" for the preconditions for its existence. Critical speculation operates outside the object which it pretends to deal with. Whereas the *whole antithesis* is nothing but the *movement of both its sides*, and the precondition for the existence of the whole lies in the very nature of the two sides. But Critical Criticism dispenses with the study of this real movement which forms the whole in order to be able to declare that it, Critical Criticism as the tranquillity of knowledge, is above both extremes of the antithesis, and that its activity, which has made "the whole as such", is now alone in a position to abolish the abstraction of which it is the maker.

Proletariat and wealth are opposites; as such they form a single whole. They are both creations of the world of private property. The question is exactly what place each occupies in the antithesis. It is not sufficient to declare them two sides of a single whole.

Private property as private property, as wealth, is compelled to maintain *itself*, and thereby its opposite, the proletariat, in *existence*.

That is the *positive* side of the antithesis, self-satisfied private property.

The proletariat, on the contrary, is compelled as proletariat to abolish itself and thereby its opposite, private property, which determines its existence, and which makes it proletariat. It is the *negative* side of the antithesis, its restlessness within its very self, dissolved and self-dissolving private property.

The propertied class and the class of the proletariat present the same human self-estrangement. But the former class feels at ease and strengthened in this self-estrangement, it recognises estrangement as *its own power* and has in it the *semblance* of a human existence. The latter feels annihilated in estrangement; it sees in it its own powerlessness and the reality of an inhuman existence. It is, to use an expression of Hegel, in its abasement the *indignation* at that abasement, an indignation to which it is necessarily driven by the contradiction between its human *nature* and its condition of life, which is the outright, resolute and comprehensive negation of that nature.

Within this antithesis the private property-owner is therefore the *conservative* side, the proletarian the *destructive* side. From the former arises the action of preserving the antithesis, from the latter the action of annihilating it.

Indeed private property drives itself in its economic movement towards its own dissolution, but only through a development which does not depend on it, which is unconscious and which takes place against the will of private property by the very nature of things, only inasmuch as it produces the proletariat *as* proletariat, poverty which is conscious of its spiritual and physical poverty, dehumanisation which is conscious of its dehumanisation, and therefore self-abolishing. The proletariat executes the sentence that private property pronounces on itself by producing the proletariat, just as it executes the sentence that wage-labour pronounces on itself by producing wealth for others and poverty for itself. When the proletariat is victorious, it by no means becomes the absolute side of society, for it is victorious only by abolishing itself and its opposite. Then the proletariat disappears as well as the opposite which determines it, private property.

When socialist writers ascribe this world-historic role to the proletariat, it is not at all, as Critical Criticism pretends to believe, because they regard the proletarians as *gods*. Rather the contrary. Since in the fully-formed proletariat the abstraction of all humanity, even of the *semblance* of humanity, is practically complete; since the conditions of life of the proletariat sum up all the conditions of life of society today in their most inhuman form; since man has lost himself in the proletariat, yet at the same time has not only gained theoretical consciousness of that loss, but through urgent, no longer removable, no longer disguisable, absolutely imperative *need*—the practical expression of *necessity*—is driven directly to revolt against this inhumanity, it follows that the proletariat can and must emancipate itself. But it cannot emancipate itself without abolishing the conditions of its own life. It cannot abolish the conditions of its own life without abolishing *all* the inhuman conditions of life of society today which are summed up in its own situation. Not in vain does it go through the stern but steeling school of *labour*. It is not a question of what this or that proletarian, or even the whole proletariat, at the moment *regards* as its aim. It is a question of *what the proletariat is*, and what, in accordance with this *being*, it will historically be compelled to do. Its aim and historical action is visibly and irrevocably foreshadowed in its own life situation as well as in the whole organisation of bourgeois society today. There is no need to explain here that a large part of the English and French proletariat is already *conscious* of its historic task and is constantly working to develop that consciousness into complete clarity.

"Critical Criticism" can all the less admit this since it has proclaimed itself the exclusive creative element in history. To it belong the historical antitheses, to it belongs the task of abolishing them. That is why it issues the following *notification* through its incarnation, Edgar:

> "Education and lack of education, property and absence of property, these *antitheses*, if they are not to *be desecrated*, must *be wholly and entirely the concern* of Criticism."

Property and absence of property have received metaphysical consecration as Critical speculative antitheses. That is why only the hand of Critical Criticism can touch them without committing a sacrilege. Capitalists and workers must not interfere in their mutual relationship.

Far from having any idea that his Critical conception of antitheses could be touched, that this holy thing could be desecrated, Herr Edgar lets his opponent make an objection that he alone could make to himself.

> "Is it then possible," the imaginary opponent of Critical Criticism asks, "to use other concepts than those already existing—liberty, equality, etc.? I answer" (note Herr Edgar's answer) "that Greek and Latin perished as soon as the range of thoughts that they served to express was exhausted."

It is now clear why Critical Criticism does not give a single thought in *German*. The language of its thoughts has not yet come into being in spite of all that Herr Reichardt by his Critical handling of foreign words, Herr Faucher by his handling of English, and Herr Edgar by his handling of French, have done to prepare the *new Critical* language.

Characterising Translation No. 2

The Critical Proudhon says:

"The husbandmen divided the land among themselves; equality consecrated only possession; on this occasion it consecrated property."

The Critical Proudhon makes landed property arise simultaneously with the division of land. He effects the transition from possession to property by the expression "on this occasion".

The real Proudhon says:

"Husbandry was the basis of *possession of the land....* It was not enough to ensure for the tiller the fruit of his labour without ensuring for him at the same time the instruments of production. To guard the weaker against the encroachments of the stronger ... it was felt necessary to establish permanent demarcation lines between owners."

On this occasion, therefore, it is *possession* that equality consecrated in the first place.

"Every year saw the population increase and the greed of the settlers grow; it was thought ambition should be checked by new insuperable barriers. Thus the land became property owing to the need for equality ... doubtless the division was never geographically equal ... but the principle nevertheless remained the same; equality had consecrated possession, equality consecrated property."

According to the Critical Proudhon

"the ancient founders of property, absorbed with concern for their needs, overlooked the fact that to the right of property corresponded at the same time the right to alienate, to sell, to give away, to acquire and to lose, which destroyed the equality from which they started out."

According to the real Proudhon it was not that the founders of property overlooked this course of its development in their concern for their needs. It was rather that they did not foresee it; but even if they had been able to foresee it, their actual need would have gained the upper hand. Besides, the real Proudhon is too mass-minded to counterpose the right to alienate, sell, etc., to the *"right of property"*, i.e., to counterpose the varieties to the species. He contrasts the "right to *keep* one's heritage" to the "right to *alienate* it, etc.", which constitutes a real opposition and a real step forward.

Critical Comment No. 3

"On what then does Proudhon base his proof of the impossibility of property? Difficult as it is to believe it—on the same principle of equality!"

A short consideration would have sufficed to arouse the belief of Herr Edgar. He must be aware that Herr Bruno Bauer based all his arguments on "*infinite* self-consciousness" and that he also saw in this principle the creative principle of the gospels which, by their infinite unconsciousness, appear to be in direct contradiction to infinite self-consciousness. In the same way Proudhon conceives equality as the creative principle of private property, which is in direct contradiction to equality. If Herr Edgar compares French *equality* with German "self-consciousness" for an instant, he will see that the latter principle expresses *in German*, i.e., in abstract thought, what the former says *in French*, that is, in the language of politics and of thoughtful observation. Self-consciousness is man's equality with himself in pure thought. Equality is man's consciousness of himself in the element of practice, i.e., man's consciousness of other men as his equals and man's attitude to other men as his equals. Equality is the French expression for the unity of human essence, for man's consciousness of his species and his attitude towards his species, for the practical identity of man with man, i.e., for the social or human relation of man to man. Hence, just as destructive criticism in Germany, before it had progressed in *Feuerbach* to the consideration of *real man,* tried to resolve everything definite and existing by the principle of *self-consciousness,* destructive criticism in France tried to do the same by the principle of *equality.*

"Proudhon is angry with philosophy, for which, in itself, we cannot blame him. But why is he angry? Philosophy, he maintains, has not yet been practical enough; it has mounted the high horse of *speculation* and from up there *human beings* have seemed much too small. I think that philosophy is overpractical; i.e., it has so far been nothing but the abstract expression of the existing state of things; it has always been captive to the premises of the existing state of things, which it has accepted as absolute."

The opinion that philosophy is the abstract expression of the existing state of things does not belong originally to Herr Edgar. It belongs to *Feuerbach,* who was the first to describe philosophy as speculative and mystical empiricism and to prove it. But Herr Edgar manages to give this opinion an original, Critical twist. While Feuerbach concludes that philosophy must come down from the heaven of speculation to the depth of human misery, Herr Edgar, on the contrary, informs us that philosophy is overpractical. However, it seems rather that philosophy, precisely because it was only the transcendent, abstract expression of the actual state of things, by reason of its transcendentalism and abstraction, by reason of its *imaginary difference* from the world, must have imagined it had left the actual state of things and real human beings far below itself. On the other hand, it seems that because philosophy was not *really* different from the world it could not pronounce any *real judgment* on it, it could not bring any real differentiating force to bear on it and could therefore not interfere *practically*, but had to be satisfied at most with a practice *in abstracto*. Philosophy was overpractical only in the sense that it soared above practice. Critical Criticism, by lumping humanity together in a spiritless mass, gives the most striking proof how infinitely small real human beings seem to speculation. In this the old speculation agrees with Critical Criticism, as the following sentence out of Hegel's *Rechtsphilosophie* shows:

"From the standpoint of needs, it is the concrete object of the idea that is called *man*; therefore what we are concerned with here, and *properly speaking only* here, is man in this sense." [a]

In other cases in which speculation speaks of man it does not mean the *concrete*, but the *abstract*, the *idea*, the *spirit*, etc. The way in which philosophy expresses the actual state of things is strikingly exemplified by Herr Faucher in connection with the actual English situation and by Herr Edgar in connection with the actual situation of the French language.

"Thus Proudhon also is practical because, finding that the concept of equality is the basis of the proofs in favour of property, he argues from the same concept against property."

Proudhon here does exactly the same thing as the German critics who, finding that the proofs of the existence of God are based on the idea of man, argue from that idea against the existence of God.

"If the consequences of the principle of equality are more powerful than equality itself, how does Proudhon intend to help that principle to acquire its sudden power?"

Self-consciousness, according to Herr Bruno Bauer, lies at the basis of all religious ideas. It is, he says, the creative principle of the gospels. Why, then, were the consequences of the principle of self-consciousness more powerful than self-consciousness itself? Because, the answer comes after the German fashion, self-consciousness is indeed the creative principle of religious ideas,

---

[a] G.W.F. Hegel, *Grundlinien der Philosophie des Rechts*, § 190.— *Ed.*

but only as self-consciousness outside itself, in contradiction to itself, alienated and estranged. Self-consciousness that has come to itself, that understands itself, that apprehends its essence, therefore governs the creations of its self-alienation. Proudhon finds himself in exactly the same case, with the difference, of course, that he speaks French whereas we speak German, and he therefore expresses in a French way what we express in a German way.

Proudhon asks himself why equality, although as the creative principle of reason it underlies the institution of property and as the ultimate rational foundation is the basis of all arguments in favour of property, nevertheless does not exist, while its negation, private property, does. He accordingly considers the fact of property in itself. He proves "that, in truth, property, as an institution and a principle, is *impossible*" [a] (p. 34), i.e., that *it contradicts itself* and abolishes itself in all points; that, to put it in the German way, it is the existence of alienated, self-contradicting, self-estranged equality. The real state of things in France, like the recognition of this estrangement, suggests correctly to Proudhon the necessity of the real abolition of this estrangement.

While negating private property, Proudhon feels the need to justify the existence of private property *historically*. His argument, like all first arguments of this kind, is pragmatic, i.e., he assumes that earlier generations wished consciously and with reflection to realise in their institutions that equality which for him represents the human essence.

"We always come back to the same thing.... Proudhon writes in the interest of the proletarians."

He does not write in the interest of self-sufficient Criticism or out of any abstract, self-made interest, but out of a mass-type, real, historic interest, an interest that goes beyond *criticism*, that will go as far as a *crisis*. Not only does Proudhon write in the interest of the proletarians, he is himself a proletarian, an *ouvrier*.[b] His work is a scientific manifesto of the French proletariat and therefore has quite a different historical significance from that of the literary botch work of any Critical Critic.

"Proudhon writes in the interest of those who have nothing; to have and not to have are for him absolute categories. To have is for him the highest, because at the same time not to have is for him the highest object of thought. Every man ought to

---

[a] "*Est impossible, mathématiquement*" (Proudhon, *Qu'est-ce que la propriété?*, p. 34.)—*Ed.*

[b] A worker.—*Ed.*

have, but no more or less than another, Proudhon thinks. But one should bear in mind that of all I have, only what I have exclusively, or what I have more of than other people have, is interesting for me. With equality, both to have and equality itself will be a matter of indifference to me."

According to Herr Edgar, *having* and *not having* are for Proudhon absolute *categories*. Critical Criticism sees nothing but categories everywhere. Thus, according to Herr Edgar, having and not having, wages, salary, want and need, and work to satisfy that need, are nothing but categories.

If society had to free itself only from the *categories* of having and not having, how easy would the "overcoming" and "abolition" of those categories be made for it by any dialectician, even if he were weaker than Herr Edgar! Indeed, Herr Edgar considers this such a trifle that he does not think it worth the trouble to give even an *explanation* of the categories of having and not having as an argument against Proudhon. But not having is not a mere category, it is a most dismal reality; today the man who has nothing is nothing, for he is cut off from existence in general, and still more from a human existence, for the condition of not having is the condition of the complete separation of man from his objectivity. Therefore not having seems quite justified in being the highest object of thought for Proudhon; all the more since so little thought had been given to this subject prior to him and the socialist writers in general. Not having is the most despairing *spiritualism*, a complete unreality of the human being, a complete reality of the dehumanised being, a very positive having, a having of hunger, of cold, of disease, of crime, of debasement, of hebetude, of all inhumanity and abnormity. But every object which for the first time is made the object of thought with full consciousness of its importance is the *highest object of thought*.

Proudhon's wish to abolish not having and the old way of having is quite identical with his wish to abolish the practically estranged relation of man to his *objective essence* and the *economic* expression of human self-estrangement. But since his criticism of political economy is still captive to the premises of political economy, the re-appropriation of the objective world itself is still conceived in the economic form of *possession*.

Proudhon does not oppose having to not having, as Critical Criticism makes him do; he opposes *possession* to the old way of having, to *private property*. He proclaims possession to be a *"social function"*. What is "interesting" in a function, however, is not to "exclude" the other person, but to affirm and to realise the forces of my own being.

Proudhon did not succeed in giving this thought appropriate development. The idea of *"equal* possession" is the economic and therefore itself still estranged expression for the fact that the *object* as *being for man,* as the *objective being of man,* is at the same time the *existence of man for other men,* his *human relation to other men,* the *social behaviour of man to man.* Proudhon abolishes economic estrangement *within* economic estrangement.

Characterising Translation No. 3

The Critical Proudhon has a *Critical property-owner,* too, according to whose

"*own* admission those who had to work for him lost what he appropriated".

The mass-type Proudhon says to the mass-type property-owner:

"You have worked! Ought you never to have let others work for you? How, then, have they lost while working for you, what you were able to acquire while not working for them?"

By *"richesse naturelle",*[a] the Critical Proudhon makes Say understand "natural *possessions*" although Say, to preclude any error, states explicitly in the *Épitomé* to his *Traité d'économie politique*[b] that by *richesse* he understands neither property nor possession, but a "sum of values". Of course, the Critical Proudhon reforms Say just as he himself is reformed by Herr Edgar. He makes Say "infer immediately a right to take a field as property" because land is easier to appropriate than air or water. But Say, far from inferring from the greater possibility of appropriating land a property *right* to it, says instead quite explicitly:

"Les *droits* des propriétaires de terres—remontent à une *spoliation."*[c] (*Traité d'économie politique,* édition III, t. I., p. 136, Nota.)

That is why, in Say's opinion, there must be *"concours de la législation"*[d] and *"droit positif"*[e] to provide a basis for the *right* to landed property. The real Proudhon does not make Say "immediately" *infer* the right of landed property from the easier appropriation of land. He reproaches him with basing himself on possibility *instead of* right and *confusing* the question of possibility with the question of right:

---

[a] "Natural wealth."—*Ed.*
[b] Treatise of Political Economy.—*Ed.*
[c] "The *rights* of landed proprietors are to be traced to *plunder."*—*Ed.*
[d] "Co-operation of legislation."—*Ed.*
[e] "Positive right."—*Ed.*

"Say prend la possibilité *pour* le droit. On ne demande pas pourquoi la terre a été plutôt appropriée que la mer et les airs; on veut savoir, en vertu de quel *droit* l'homme s'est approprié cette richesse."[a]

The Critical Proudhon continues:

"The *only* remark to be made on this is that with the appropriation of a piece of land the other elements—air, water and fire—are also appropriated: *terra, aqua, aëre et igne interdicti sumus.*"[b]

Far from making "*only*" this remark, the real Proudhon says, on the contrary, that he draws "attention" to the appropriation of air and water incidentally (*en passant*). The Critical Proudhon makes an unaccountable use of the Roman formula of banishment. He forgets to say who the "*we*" are who have been banished. The real Proudhon addresses the non-property-owners:

"Proletarians ... property *excommunicates* us: *terra, etc. interdicti sumus.*"

The Critical Proudhon polemises against Charles Comte as follows:

"Charles Comte thinks that, in order to live, man needs air, food and clothing. Some of these things, like air and water, are inexhaustible and therefore always remain common property; but others are available in smaller quantities and become private property. Charles Comte therefore bases his proof on the concepts of limitedness and unlimitedness; he would perhaps have come to a different conclusion had he made the concepts of dispensability and indispensability his main categories."

How childish the Critical Proudhon's polemic is! He expects Charles Comte to give up the categories he uses for his proof and to jump over to others so as to come, not to his own conclusions, but "*perhaps*" to those of the Critical Proudhon.

The real Proudhon does not make any such demands on Charles Comte; he does not dispose of him with a "perhaps", but defeats him with his own categories.

Charles Comte, Proudhon says, proceeds from the indispensability of air, food, and, in certain climates, clothing, not in order to live, but in order not to stop living. Hence (according to Charles Comte) in order to maintain himself, man constantly needs to appropriate things of various kinds. These things do not all exist in the same proportion.

"The light of the heavenly bodies, air and water exist in such quantities that man can neither increase nor decrease them appreciably; hence everyone can

---

[a] "Say takes possibility *for* right. The question is not why land has been appropriated rather than sea or air, but by what *right* man has appropriated this wealth."—*Ed.*

[b] We are banished from land, water, air and fire.—*Ed.*

appropriate as much of them as his needs require, *without prejudice to the enjoyment of others*".[a]

Proudhon proceeds from Comte's own definitions. First of all he proves to him that land is also an object of primary necessity, the usufruct of which must therefore remain free to everyone, within the limits of Comte's clause, namely: "*without prejudice to the enjoyment of others.*" Why then has land become private property? Charles Comte answers: because it is *not unlimited*. He should have concluded, on the contrary, that because land is *limited* it may not be appropriated. The appropriation of air and water causes no prejudice to anybody because, as they are unlimited, there is always enough left. The arbitrary appropriation of land, on the other hand, prejudices the enjoyment of others precisely because the land is *limited*. The use of the land must therefore be regulated in the interests of *all*. Charles Comte's method of proving refutes his own thesis.

"Charles Comte, so Proudhon" (the Critical one, of course) "reasons, proceeds from the view that a nation can be the owner of a land; yet if property involves the right to use and misuse— *jus utendi et abutendi re sua*—even a nation cannot be adjudged the right to use and misuse a land."

The real Proudhon does not speak of *jus utendi et abutendi* that the right of property "*involves*". He is too mass-minded to speak of a right of property that the right of property involves. *Jus utendi et abutendi re sua* is, in fact, the right of property itself. Hence Proudhon directly refuses a people the right of property over its territory. To those who find that exaggerated, he replies that in all epochs the imagined right of national property gave rise to suzerainty, tribute, royal prerogatives, corvée, etc.

The real Proudhon reasons against Charles Comte as follows: Comte wishes to expound how property arises and he begins with the hypothesis of a nation as owner. He thus falls into a *petitio principii*.[b] He makes the state sell lands, he lets industrialists buy those estates, that is to say, he presupposes the *property* relations that he wishes to prove.

The Critical Proudhon scraps the French *decimal system*. He keeps the *franc* but replaces the *centime* by the "*Dreier*".[c]

"If I cede a piece of land, Proudhon" (the Critical one) "continues, I not only rob myself of one harvest; I deprive my children and children's children of a

---

[a] The quotation from Comte's *Traité de la propriété* is given according to Proudhon's *Qu'est-ce que la propriété?* p. 93.— *Ed.*

[b] The fallacy of seeking to prove a conclusion by presupposing it as the premise.— *Ed.*

[c] A small coin worth three pfennigs.— *Ed.*

lasting good. Land has value not only today, it has also the value of its capacity and its future."

The real Proudhon does not speak of the fact that land has value not only today but also tomorrow: he contrasts the full present value to the value of its capacity and its future, which depends on my skill in exploiting the land. He says:

"Destroy the land, or, what comes to the same thing for you, sell it; you not only deprive yourself of one, two or more harvests; you annihilate all the produce you could have obtained from it, you, your children and your children's children."

For Proudhon the question is not one of stressing the contrast between one harvest and the lasting good — the money I get for the field can, as capital, also become a "lasting good" — but the contrast between the present value and the value the land can acquire through continuous cultivation.

"The new value, Charles Comte says, that I give to a thing by my work is my property. Proudhon" (the Critical one) "thinks he can refute him in the following way: *Then* a man must cease to be a property-owner as soon as he ceases to work. Ownership of the product can by no means involve ownership of the material from which the product was made."

The real Proudhon says:

"Let the worker appropriate the products of his work, but I do not understand how ownership of the products involves ownership of the matter. Does the fisherman who manages to catch more fish than the others on the same bank become by this skill the owner of the place where he fishes? Was the skill of a hunter ever considered a title to ownership of the game in a canton? The same applies to agriculture. In order to transform *possession* into *property, another condition* is necessary besides work, or a man would cease to be a property-owner as soon as he ceased to be a worker."

Cessante causa cessat effectus. [a] When the owner is owner *only* as a worker, he ceases to be an owner as soon as he ceases to be a worker.

"According to *law*, it is *prescription* which creates ownership; *work* is only the perceptible sign, the material act by which occupation is *manifested*."
"The system of appropriation through work," Proudhon goes on, "is therefore *contrary* to *law*; and when the supporters of that system put it forward as an explanation of the laws they are *contradicting themselves*."

To say further, according to this opinion, that the cultivation of the land, for example, "creates full ownership of the same" is a *petitio principii*. It is a fact that a new productive capacity of the matter has been created. But what has to be proved is that ownership of the matter itself has thereby been created. Man has not created the matter itself. And he cannot even create any productive capacity if the matter does not exist beforehand.

---

[a] When the cause ceases, the effect ceases.— *Ed.*

The Critical Proudhon makes *Gracchus Babeuf* a partisan of *freedom,* but for the mass-minded Proudhon he is a partisan of *equality (partisan de l'égalité).*

The *Critical Proudhon,* who wanted to estimate *Homer's* fee for the *Iliad,* says:

"The fee which I pay Homer should be equal to what he *gives me.* But how is the value of what he gives to be determined?"

The Critical Proudhon is too superior to the trifles of political economy to know that the *value* of an object and what that object *gives* somebody else are two different things. The real Proudhon says:

"The fee of the poet should be equal to his *product:* what then is the value of that product?"

The real Proudhon supposes that the *Iliad* has an infinite *price* (or exchange value, *prix*), while the Critical Proudhon supposes that it has an infinite *value.* The real Proudhon counterposes the value of the *Iliad, its value* in the *economic* sense (*valeur intrinsèque*), to its exchange value (*valeur échangeable*); the Critical Proudhon counterposes its "value for exchange" to its "intrinsic value", i.e., its value as a poem.

The real Proudhon says:

"Between material reward and talent there is no common measure. In *this* respect the situation of all producers is the same. Consequently any comparison between them, any classification according to fortune is impossible." ("Entre une récompense matérielle et le talent il n'existe pas de commune mesure; sous *ce* rapport la condition de tous les producteurs est égale; conséquemment toute comparaison entre eux et toute distinction de fortunes est impossible.")

The Critical Proudhon says:

"*Relatively,* the position of all producers is the same. Talent cannot be weighed materially.... Any comparison of the producers among themselves, any *external distinction* is impossible."

In the Critical Proudhon we read that

"the man of science must *feel* himself *equal* in society, because his talent and his insight are *only* a product of the insight of society".

The real Proudhon does not speak anywhere about the feelings of talent. He says that talent must lower itself to the level of society. Nor does he at all assert that the man of talent is *only* a product of society. On the contrary, he says:

"The man of talent has contributed to produce in himself a useful instrument.... There exist in him a free worker *and* an accumulated social capital."

The Critical Proudhon goes on to say:

"Besides, he must be thankful to society for releasing him from other work so that he can apply himself to science."

The real Proudhon nowhere resorts to the gratitude of the man of talent. He says:

"The artist, the scientist, the poet, receive their just reward by the mere fact that society allows them to apply themselves exclusively to science and art."

Finally, the Critical Proudhon achieves the miracle of making a society of 150 workers able to maintain a "*marshal*" and, therefore, probably, an *army*. In the real Proudhon the marshal is a "*farrier*" (*maréchal*).

Critical Comment No. 4

"If he" (Proudhon) "retains the concept of wages, if he sees in society an institution that gives us work and pays us for it, he has all the less right to recognise time as the measure for payment as he but shortly before, agreeing with *Hugo Grotius,* professed that time has no bearing on the *validity* of an object."

This is the only point on which Critical Criticism attempts to solve its problem and to prove to Proudhon that from the standpoint of political economy he is arguing wrongly against political economy. Here Criticism *disgraces* itself in truly Critical fashion. Proudhon agrees with Hugo Grotius in arguing that *prescription* is no title to change *possession* into *property* or a "*legal principle*" into another principle, any more than time can change the truth that the three angles of a triangle are together equal to two right angles into the truth that they are equal to three right angles.

"Never," exclaims Proudhon, "will you succeed in making length of time, which of itself creates nothing, changes nothing, modifies nothing, able to *change* the *user* into a *proprietor*."

Herr Edgar's conclusion is: since Proudhon said that mere time cannot *change* one legal principle into another, that by itself it cannot change or modify anything, he is inconsistent when he makes *labour time* the measure of the economic *value* of the product of labour. Herr Edgar achieves this Critically Critical remark by translating "*valeur*" [a] by "*Geltung*" [b] so that he can use the word for validity of a legal principle in the same sense as for the commercial value of a product of labour. He achieves it by identifying empty length of time with time filled with labour. Had

---

[a] Value.—*Ed.*
[b] Validity.—*Ed.*

Proudhon said that time cannot change a fly into an elephant, Critical Criticism could have said with the same justification: he has therefore no right to make labour time the measure of wages.

Even Critical Criticism must be capable of grasping that the *labour time expended* on the production of an object is included in the *cost of production* of that object, that the *cost of production* of an object is what it *costs*, and therefore what it can be *sold* for, abstraction being made of the influence of *competition*. Besides the labour time and the material of labour, economists include in the cost of production the rent paid to the owner of the land, interest and the profit of the capitalist. The latter are excluded by Proudhon because he excludes private property. Hence there remain only the labour time and the expenses. By making labour time, the immediate existence of human activity as activity, the measure of wages and the determinant of the value of the product, Proudhon makes the human side the decisive factor. In old political economy, on the other hand, the decisive factor was the material power of capital and of landed property. In other words, Proudhon reinstates man in his rights, but still in an economic and therefore contradictory way. How right he is from the standpoint of political economy can be seen from the fact that *Adam Smith*, the founder of modern political economy, in the very first pages of his book, *An Inquiry into the Nature and Causes of the Wealth of Nations*, develops the idea that *before* the invention of private property, that is to say, presupposing the *non-existence of private property, labour time* was the measure of *wages* and of the *value of the product of labour*, which was not yet distinguished from wages.

But even let Critical Criticism suppose for an instant that Proudhon did not proceed from the premise of wages. Does it believe that the *time* which the production of an object requires will *ever* not be an essential factor in the *"validity"* of the object? Does it believe that time will lose its *costliness*?

As far as immediate material production is concerned, the decision whether an object is to be produced or not, i.e., the decision on the *value* of the object, will depend essentially on the labour time required for its production. For it depends on time whether society has time to develop in a human way.

And even as far as *intellectual* production is concerned, must I not, if I proceed reasonably in other respects, consider the time necessary for the production of an intellectual work when I determine its scope, its character and its plan? Otherwise I risk at least that the object that is in my idea will never become an object in reality, and can therefore acquire only the value of an imaginary object, i.e., an *imaginary value*.

The criticism of political economy from the standpoint of political economy recognises all the essential determinants of human activity, but only in an estranged, alienated form. Here, for example, it converts the importance of time for *human labour* into its importance for *wages*, for wage-labour.

Herr Edgar continues:

"In order to force talent to accept that measure, Proudhon *misuses* the concept of *free contract* and asserts that society and its individual members have the right to reject the products of talent."

Among the *followers of Fourier* and *Saint-Simon,* talent puts forward exaggerated *fee claims* on an economic basis and makes its imagined notion of its infinite value the measure of the *exchange value* of its products. Proudhon answers it in exactly the same way as political economy answers any claim for a price much higher than the so-called natural price, that is, higher than the cost of production of the object offered. He answers by freedom of contract. But Proudhon does not *misuse* this relation in the sense of political economy; on the contrary, he assumes that to be real which the economists consider to be only nominal and illusory— the *freedom* of the contracting parties.

Characterising Translation No. 4

The Critical Proudhon finally reforms *French society* by as deep a transformation of the French proletarians as of the French bourgeoisie.

He denies the French proletarians *"strength"* because the real Proudhon reproaches them with a lack of *virtue (vertu)*. He makes their *skill* in work problematic—"you are *perhaps* skilled in work"—because the real Proudhon unconditionally recognises it (*"prompts au travail vous êtes,"* [a] etc.). He converts the French bourgeoisie into *dull* burghers whereas the real Proudhon counterposes the ignoble bourgeois (*bourgeois ignobles*) to the blemished nobles (*nobles flétris*). He converts the bourgeois from happy-medium burghers (*bourgeois juste-milieu*) [18] into "our *good* burghers", for which the French bourgeoisie can be grateful. Hence, where the real Proudhon says the *"ill will"* of the French bourgeoisie (*la malveillance de nos bourgeois*) is growing, the Critical

---

[a] "You are smart at work."—*Ed.*

Proudhon consistently makes the *"carefreeness* of our burghers" grow. The real Proudhon's bourgeois is so far from being carefree that he calls out to himself: *"N'ayons pas peur! N'ayons pas peur!"* [a] Those are the words of a man who wishes to reason himself out of fear and worry.

By creating the Critical Proudhon through its translation of the real Proudhon, Critical Criticism has revealed to the Mass what a Critically perfect translation is. It has given directions for "translation as it ought to be". It is therefore rightly against bad, mass-type translations.

"The German public wants the booksellers' wares ridiculously cheap, so the publisher needs a cheap translation; the translator does not want to starve at his work, he cannot even perform it with mature reflection" (with all the tranquillity of knowledge) "because the publisher must anticipate rivals by quick delivery of translations; even the translator has to fear competition, has to fear that someone else will produce the ware cheaper and quicker; he therefore dictates his manuscript offhand to some poor scribe — as quickly as he can in order not to pay the scribe his hourly wage for nothing. He is more than happy when he can next day adequately satisfy the harassing type-setter. For the rest, the translations with which we are flooded are but a manifestation of the present-day *impotence* of German literature", etc. (*Allgemeine Literatur-Zeitung*, Heft VIII, p. 54.[19])

Critical Comment No. 5

"The proof of the impossibility of property that Proudhon draws from the fact that mankind ruins itself particularly by the interest and profit system and by the disproportion between consumption and production lacks its counterpart, namely, the proof that private property is historically possible."

Critical Criticism has - the fortunate instinct not to go into Proudhon's reasoning on the interest and profit system, etc., i.e., into the most important part of his argument. The reason is that on this point not even a semblance of criticism of Proudhon can be offered without absolutely positive knowledge of the movement of private property. Critical Criticism tries to make up for its impotence by observing that Proudhon has not proved the historical possibility of property. Why does Criticism, which has nothing but words to give, expect others to give it *everything*?

"Proudhon proves the impossibility of property by the fact that the worker cannot buy back the product of his work out of his wage. Proudhon does not give an exhaustive proof of this by expounding the essence of capital. The worker cannot buy back his product because it is always a joint product, whereas he is never anything but an individual paid man."

Herr Edgar, in contrast to Proudhon's deduction, could have expressed himself still more exhaustively to the effect that the

---

[a] "Let us not be afraid! Let us not be afraid!" — *Ed.*

worker can*not* buy back his product because in general he must *buy* it *back*. The definition of buying already implies that he regards his product as an object that is no longer his, an estranged object. Among other things, Herr Edgar's exhaustive argument does not exhaust the question why the capitalist, who himself is *nothing* but an *individual* man, and what is more, a man *paid* by profit and interest, can buy back not only the product of labour, but still more than this product. To explain this Herr Edgar would have to explain the relationship between labour and capital, that is, to expound the essence of capital.

The above quotation from Criticism shows most palpably how Critical Criticism immediately makes use of what it has learnt from a writer to pass it off as wisdom it has itself discovered and use it with a Critical twist against the same writer. For it is from Proudhon himself that Critical Criticism drew the argument that it says Proudhon did not give and that Herr Edgar did. Proudhon says:

> "*Divide et impera* ... separate the workers from one another, and it is quite possible that the daily wage paid to each one may exceed the value of each individual product; but that is not the point at issue.... Although you have paid for all the individual powers you have still not paid for the collective power."

Proudhon was the *first* to draw attention to the fact that the sum of the wages of the individual workers, even if each individual labour be paid for completely, does not pay for the collective power objectified in its product, that therefore the worker is not paid as a *part* of the *collective labour power* [*gemeinschaftlichen Arbeitskraft*]. Herr Edgar twists this into the assertion that the worker is nothing but an individual paid man. Critical Criticism thus opposes a *general* thought of Proudhon's to the further *concrete* development that Proudhon himself gives to the same thought. It takes possession of this thought after the fashion of Criticism and expresses the secret of *Critical socialism* in the following sentence:

> "The modern worker *thinks* only of himself, i.e., he allows himself to be paid only for his own person. It is he *himself* who fails to take into account the enormous, the immeasurable power which arises from his co-operation with other powers."

According to Critical Criticism, the whole evil lies only in the workers' "*thinking*". It is true that the English and French workers have formed associations in which they exchange opinions not only on their immediate needs as *workers*, but on their needs as *human beings*. In their associations, moreover, they show a very thorough and comprehensive consciousness of the "enormous" and "immeasurable" power which arises from their co-operation. But these *mass-minded,* communist workers, employed, for instance, in the Manchester or Lyons workshops, do not believe that by *"pure thinking"* they will be able to argue away their industrial masters and their own practical debasement. They are most painfully aware of the *difference* between *being* and *thinking,* between *consciousness* and *life.* They know that property, capital, money, wage-labour and the like are no ideal figments of the brain but very practical, very objective products of their self-estrangement and that therefore they must be abolished in a practical, objective way for man to become man not only in *thinking,* in *consciousness,* but in mass *being,* in life. Critical Criticism, on the contrary, teaches them that they cease in reality to be wageworkers if in thinking they abolish the thought of wage-labour; if in thinking they cease to regard themselves as wage-workers and, in accordance with that extravagant notion, no longer let themselves be paid for their person. As absolute idealists, as ethereal beings, they will then naturally be able to live on the ether of pure thought. Critical Criticism teaches them that they abolish real capital by overcoming in *thinking* the category Capital, that they *really* change and transform themselves into real human beings by changing their *"abstract ego"* in consciousness and scorning as an un-Critical operation all *real* change of their real existence, of the real conditions of their existence, that is to say, of their *real ego.* The *"spirit",* which sees in reality only categories, naturally reduces all human activity and practice to the dialectical process of thought of Critical Criticism. That is what distinguishes *its* socialism from *mass-type* socialism and communism.

After his great argumentation, Herr Edgar must, of course, declare Proudhon's criticism "devoid of consciousness".

"Proudhon, *however,* wishes to be *practical too."* "He thinks he has grasped." "And nevertheless," cries the tranquillity of knowledge triumphantly, "we cannot even now credit him with the *tranquillity of knowledge."* "We quote a few passages to show how little he has thought out his attitude to society."

Later we shall also quote a few passages from the works of Critical Criticism (see the *Bank for the Poor* and the *Model Farm*)[a] to show that it has not yet become acquainted with the most elementary economic relationships, let alone thought them out, and hence with its characteristic Critical tact has felt itself called upon to pass judgment on Proudhon.

---

[a] See pp. 197-200 of this volume.— *Ed.*

Now that Critical Criticism as the tranquillity of knowledge has *"made" all the mass-type "antitheses its concern"*, has mastered all reality in the form of categories and dissolved all human activity into speculative dialectics, we shall see it produce the world again out of speculative dialectics. It goes without saying that if the miracles of the Critically speculative creation of the world are not to be "desecrated", they can be presented to the profane Mass only in the form of *mysteries*. Critical Criticism therefore appears in the incarnation of Vishnu-Szeliga as a *mystery-monger*.

Chapter V

"CRITICAL CRITICISM" AS A MYSTERY-MONGER,
OR "CRITICAL CRITICISM" AS HERR SZELIGA [20]

"Critical Criticism" in its *Szeliga-Vishnu* incarnation provides an apotheosis of the *Mystères de Paris*. Eugène Sue is proclaimed a "Critical Critic". Hearing this, he may exclaim like Molière's *Bourgeois gentilhomme*:

"Par ma foi, il y a plus de quarante ans que je dis de la prose, sans que j'en susse rien: et je vous suis le plus obligé du monde de m'avoir appris cela." [a]

Herr Szeliga prefaces his criticism with an *aesthetic* prologue. "The aesthetic prologue" gives the following explanation of the general meaning of the "Critical" epic and in particular of the *Mystères de Paris*:

"The epic gives rise to the thought that the present in itself is nothing, and not only" (*nothing* and not only!) "the eternal *boundary* between *past* and *future*, but" (nothing, and not only, but) "but the *gap* that separates *immortality* from *transience* and *must* continually be *filled*.... Such is the *general meaning* of the *Mystères de Paris*."

The "aesthetic prologue" further asserts that "if the *Critic* wished he could also be a *poet*".

The whole of Herr Szeliga's criticism will prove that assertion. It is "*poetic fiction*" in every respect.

It is also a product of "*free art*" according to the definition of the latter given in the "aesthetic prologue"—it "invents *something quite new, something that absolutely never existed before*".

Finally, it is even a *Critical epic*, for it is "the gap that separates immortality"—Herr Szeliga's Critical Criticism—from "transience"—Eugène Sue's novel—and "must continually be filled".

---

[a] "Faith, I have been speaking prose for more than forty years without knowing it. I am infinitely grateful to you for telling me so." (Molière, *Bourgeois gentilhomme*, Act II, Scene 6.)—*Ed.*

1) "THE MYSTERY OF DEGENERACY IN CIVILISATION"
AND "THE MYSTERY OF RIGHTLESSNESS IN THE STATE"

Feuerbach, we know, conceived the Christian ideas of the Incarnation, the Trinity, Immortality, etc., as the mystery of the Incarnation, the mystery of the Trinity, the mystery of Immortality. Herr Szeliga conceives all present world conditions as mysteries. But whereas *Feuerbach* disclosed *real mysteries*, Herr *Szeliga* makes *mysteries* out of real *trivialities*. His art is not that of disclosing what is hidden, but of hiding what is disclosed.

Thus he proclaims as *mysteries* degeneracy (criminals) within civilisation and rightlessness and inequality in the state. This means that socialist literature, which has revealed these mysteries, is still a mystery to Herr Szeliga, or that he wants to convert the best-known findings of that literature into a private mystery of "Critical Criticism".

We therefore need not go more deeply into Herr Szeliga's discourse on these mysteries; we shall merely draw attention to a few of the most brilliant points.

"Before the law and the judge everything is *equal,* the high and the low, the rich and the poor. This proposition stands at the head of the credo of *the state.*"

Of the state? The credo of most states starts, on the contrary, by making the high and the low, the rich and the poor *unequal* before the *law.*

"The gem-cutter Morel in his naive probity most clearly expresses the mystery" (the mystery of the antithesis of poor and rich) "when he says: If only the rich knew! If only the rich knew! The misfortune is that they do not know what poverty is."

Herr Szeliga does not know that Eugène Sue commits an *anachronism* out of courtesy to the French bourgeoisie when he puts the motto of the burghers of Louis XIV's time *"Ah! si le roi le savait!"* [a] in a modified form: *"Ah! si le riche le savait!"* [b] into the mouth of the working man Morel who lived at the time of the *Charte vérité*.[21] In England and France, at least, this *naive* relation between rich and poor has ceased to exist. There the scientific representatives of wealth, the economists, have spread a very detailed understanding of the physical and moral misery of poverty. They have made up for that by proving that misery must remain because the present state of things must remain. In their solicitude they have even calculated the *proportions* in which the

---

[a] "Ah! if the king knew it!"—*Ed.*
[b] "Ah! if the rich knew it!"—*Ed.*

poor must be reduced in number by deaths for the good of the rich and for their own welfare.

If Eugène Sue depicts the taverns, hide-outs and language of *criminals*, Herr Szeliga discloses the *"mystery"* that what the "author" wanted was not to depict that language or those hide-outs, but

"to teach us the mystery of the mainsprings of evil, etc." "It is precisely in the most crowded places ... that criminals feel *at home.*"

What would a natural scientist say if one were to prove to him that the bee's cell does not interest him as a bee's cell, that it has no mystery for one who has not studied it, because the bee "feels at home precisely" in the open air and on the flower? The hide-outs of the criminals and their language reflect the character of the criminal, they are part of his existence, their description is part of his description just as the description of the *petite maison* is part of the description of the *femme galante*.

For Parisians in general and even for the Paris police the hide-outs of criminals are such a "mystery" that at this very moment broad light streets are being laid out in the *Cité* to give the police access to them.

Finally, Eugène Sue himself states that in the descriptions mentioned above he was counting *"sur la curiosité craintive"*[a] of his readers. M. Eugène Sue has counted on the timid curiosity of his readers in all his novels. It is sufficient to recall *Atar Gull, Salamandre, Plick and Plock*, etc.

2) THE MYSTERY OF SPECULATIVE CONSTRUCTION

The mystery of the Critical presentation of the *Mystères de Paris* is the mystery of *speculative,* of *Hegelian construction.* Once Herr Szeliga has proclaimed that "degeneracy within civilisation" and rightlessness in the state are "mysteries", i.e., has dissolved them in the category *"mystery"*, he lets "mystery" begin its *speculative career.* A few words will suffice to characterise speculative construction *in general.* Herr Szeliga's treatment of the *Mystères de Paris* will give the application *in detail.*

If from real apples, pears, strawberries and almonds I form the general idea *"Fruit"*, if I go further and *imagine* that my abstract idea *"Fruit"*, derived from real fruit, is an entity existing outside me, is indeed the *true* essence of the pear, the apple, etc., then—

---

[a] On the timid curiosity.—*Ed.*

in the *language of speculative* philosophy—I am declaring that "*Fruit*" is the "*Substance*" of the pear, the apple, the almond, etc. I am saying, therefore, that to be a pear is not essential to the pear, that to be an apple is not essential to the apple; that what is essential to these things is not their real existence, perceptible to the senses, but the essence that I have abstracted from them and then foisted on them, the essence of my idea—"*Fruit*". I therefore declare apples, pears, almonds, etc., to be mere forms of existence, *modi*, of "*Fruit*". My finite understanding supported by my senses does of course *distinguish* an apple from a pear and a pear from an almond, but my speculative reason declares these sensuous differences inessential and irrelevant. It sees in the apple *the same* as in the pear, and in the pear the same as in the almond, namely "*Fruit*". Particular real fruits are no more than *semblances* whose true essence is "*the* substance"—"*Fruit*".

By this method one attains no particular *wealth of definition*. The mineralogist whose whole science was limited to the statement that all minerals are really "*the* Mineral" would be a mineralogist only in *his imagination*. For every mineral the speculative mineralogist says "*the* Mineral", and his science is reduced to repeating this word as many times as there are real minerals.

Having reduced the different real fruits to the *one* "fruit" of abstraction— "*the* Fruit", speculation must, in order to attain some semblance of real content, try somehow to find its way back from "*the* Fruit", from the *Substance* to the *diverse*, ordinary real fruits, the pear, the apple, the almond, etc. It is as hard to produce real fruits from the abstract idea "*the* Fruit" as it is easy to produce this abstract idea from real fruits. Indeed, it is impossible to arrive at the *opposite* of an abstraction without *relinquishing* the abstraction.

The speculative philosopher therefore relinquishes the abstraction "*the* Fruit", but in a *speculative, mystical* fashion—with the appearance of *not* relinquishing it. Thus it is really only in appearance that he rises above his abstraction. He argues somewhat as follows:

If apples, pears, almonds and strawberries are really nothing but "*the* Substance", "*the* Fruit", the question arises: Why does "*the* Fruit" manifest itself to me sometimes as an apple, sometimes as a pear, sometimes as an almond? Why this *semblance of diversity* which so obviously contradicts my speculative conception of *Unity*, "*the* Substance", "*the* Fruit"?

This, answers the speculative philosopher, is because "*the* Fruit" is not dead, undifferentiated, motionless, but a living, self-differentiating, moving essence. The diversity of the ordinary fruits is significant not only for *my* sensuous understanding, but also for "*the* Fruit" itself and for speculative reason. The different ordinary fruits are different manifestations of the life of the "*one* Fruit"; they are crystallisations of "*the* Fruit" itself. Thus in the apple "*the* Fruit" gives itself an apple-like existence, in the pear a pear-like existence. We must therefore no longer say, as one might from the standpoint of the Substance: a pear is "*the* Fruit", an apple is "*the* Fruit", an almond is "*the* Fruit", but rather "*the* Fruit" presents itself as a pear, "*the* Fruit" presents itself as an apple, "*the* Fruit" presents itself as an almond; and the differences which distinguish apples, pears and almonds from one another are the self-differentiations of "*the Fruit*" and ,.make the particular fruits different members of the life-process of "*the* Fruit". Thus "*the* Fruit" is no longer an empty undifferentiated unity; it is oneness as *allness,* as "*totality*" of fruits, which constitute an "*organically linked series of members*". In every member of that series "*the* Fruit" gives itself a more developed, more explicit existence, until finally, as the "*summary*" of all fruits, it is at the same time the living *unity* which contains all those fruits dissolved in itself just as it produces them from within itself, just as, for instance, all the limbs of the body are constantly dissolved in and constantly produced out of the blood.

We see that if the Christian religion knows only *one* Incarnation of God, speculative philosophy has as many incarnations as there are things, just as it has here in every fruit an incarnation of the Substance, of the Absolute Fruit. The main interest for the speculative philosopher is therefore to produce the *existence* of the real ordinary fruits and to say in some mysterious way that there are apples, pears, almonds and raisins. But the apples, pears, almonds and raisins that we rediscover in the speculative world are nothing but *semblances* of apples, *semblances* of pears, *semblances* of almonds and *semblances* of raisins, for they are moments in the life of "*the* Fruit", this abstract *creation of the mind,* and therefore themselves abstract *creations of the mind.* Hence what is delightful in this speculation is to rediscover all the real fruits there, but as fruits which have a higher mystical significance, which have grown out of the ether of your brain and not out of the material earth, which are incarnations of "*the* Fruit", of the *Absolute Subject.* When you return from the abstraction, the *supernatural* creation of the mind, "*the* Fruit", to real *natural* fruits, you give on the contrary the natural fruits a supernatural significance and transform them into sheer abstractions. Your main interest is then to point out the unity of "*the* Fruit" in all the manifestations of its life—the apple, the pear, the almond—that is, to show the *mystical interconnection* between these fruits, how in each one of them "*the* Fruit" realises itself by *degrees* and *necessarily* progresses, for instance, from its existence as a raisin to its existence as an almond. Hence the value of the ordinary fruits *no longer* consists in their *natural* qualities, *but* in their *speculative* quality, which gives each of them a definite place in the life-process of "*the* Absolute Fruit".

The ordinary man does not think he is saying anything extraordinary when he states that there are apples and pears. But when the philosopher expresses their existence in the speculative way he says something *extraordinary*. He performs a *miracle* by producing the real *natural objects,* the apple, the pear, etc., out of the unreal *creation of the mind* "*the* Fruit", i.e., by *creating* those fruits out of his *own abstract reason*, which he considers as an Absolute Subject outside himself, represented here as "*the* Fruit". And in regard to every object the existence of which he expresses, he accomplishes an act of creation.

It goes without saying that the speculative philosopher accomplishes this continuous creation only by presenting universally known qualities of the apple, the pear, etc., which exist in reality, as determining features *invented* by him, by giving the *names* of the real things to what abstract reason alone can create, to abstract formulas of reason, finally, by declaring his *own* activity, by which *he passes* from the idea of an apple to the idea of a pear, to be the *self-activity* of the Absolute Subject, "*the* Fruit".

In the speculative way of speaking, this operation is called comprehending *Substance* as *Subject*, as an *inner process*, as an *Absolute Person,* and this comprehension constitutes the essential character of *Hegel's* method.

These preliminary remarks were necessary to make Herr Szeliga intelligible. Only now, after dissolving real relations, e.g., law and civilisation, in the category of mystery and thereby making "*Mystery*" into Substance, does he rise to the true speculative, *Hegelian* height and transforms "*Mystery*" into a self-existing Subject *incarnating* itself in real situations and persons so that the manifestations of its life are countesses, marquises, grisettes, porters, notaries, charlatans, and love intrigues, balls, wooden doors, etc. Having produced the category "*Mystery*" out of the real world, he produces the real world out of this category.

The mysteries of *speculative construction* in Herr Szeliga's presentation will be all the *more visibly* disclosed as he has an indisputable *double* advantage over *Hegel*. On the one hand, Hegel with masterly sophistry is able to present as a process of the imagined creation of the mind itself, of the Absolute Subject, the process by which the philosopher through sensory perception and imagination passes from one subject to another. On the other hand, however, Hegel very often gives a *real* presentation, embracing the *thing* itself, within the *speculative* presentation. This real development *within* the speculative development misleads the reader into considering the speculative development as real and the real as speculative.

With Herr Szeliga both these difficulties vanish. His dialectics have no hypocrisy or dissimulation. He performs his tricks with the most laudable honesty and the most ingenuous straightforwardness. But then he *nowhere* develops any *real content*, so that his speculative construction is free from all disturbing accessories, from all ambiguous disguises, and appeals to the eye in its naked beauty. In Herr Szeliga we also see a brilliant illustration of how speculation on the one hand apparently freely creates its object *a priori* out of itself and, on the other hand, precisely because it wishes to get rid by sophistry of the rational and natural dependence on the *object*, falls into the most irrational and unnatural *bondage* to the object, whose most accidental and most individual attributes it is obliged to construe as absolutely necessary and general.

3) "THE MYSTERY OF EDUCATED SOCIETY"

After leading us through the lowest strata of society, for example through the criminals' taverns, Eugène Sue transports us to "*haute volée*",[a] to a *ball* in the Quartier Saint-Germain.

This *transition* Herr Szeliga construes as follows:

"*Mystery* tries to evade examination by a ,... twist: so far it appeared as the absolutely enigmatic, elusive and negative, in contrast to the true, real and positive; now it withdraws into the latter as its *invisible content*. But by doing so it gives up the unconditional possibility[b] of becoming known."

"Mystery" which has so far appeared in contrast to the "true", the "real", the "positive", that is, to law and education, "now withdraws into the latter", that is, into the realm of education. It is certainly a *mystère for* Paris, if not *of* Paris, that "*haute volée*" is the exclusive realm of education. Herr Szeliga does not pass from the

---

[a] High society.—*Ed.*
[b] "Impossibility" in the *Allgemeine Literatur-Zeitung.*—*Ed.*

mysteries of the criminal world to those of aristocratic society; instead, *"Mystery"* becomes the "invisible content" of educated society, its *real essence*. It is *"not a new twist"* of Herr Szeliga's designed to enable him to proceed to further examination; *"Mystery"* itself takes this "new twist" in order to escape examination.

Before really following Eugène Sue where his heart leads him — to an aristocratic ball, Herr Szeliga resorts to the *hypocritical* twists of speculation which makes *a priori* constructions.

"One can *naturally foresee* what a solid shell 'Mystery' will *choose* to hide in; *it seems, in fact,* that it is of *insuperable impenetrability* ... that ... *hence* it may *be expected* that *in general* ... *nevertheless* a new attempt to pick out the kernel is *here indispensable*."

Enough. Herr Szeliga has gone so far that the

"*metaphysical* subject, *Mystery*, now steps forward, light, self-confident and jaunty".

In order now to change aristocratic society into a "mystery", Herr Szeliga gives us a few considerations on *"education"*. He presumes aristocratic society to have all sorts of qualities that no man would look for in it, in order later to find the "mystery" that it does not possess those qualities. Then he presents this discovery as the "mystery" of educated society. Herr Szeliga wonders, for example, whether *"general* reason" (does he mean speculative logic?) constitutes the content of its *"drawing-room talk"*, whether "the *rhythm* and *measure* of love *alone* makes" it a "harmonious whole", whether "what we call *general education* is the form of the *general*, the *eternal*, the *ideal"*, i.e., whether what we call education is a metaphysical illusion. It is not difficult for Herr Szeliga to prophesy *a priori* in answer to his questions:

"It is to be *expected, however* ... that the answer will be in the negative."

In Eugène Sue's novel, the transition from the low world to the aristocratic world is a normal transition for a novel. The *disguises of Rudolph*, Prince of Geroldstein, give him entry into the lower strata of society as his title gives him access to the highest circles. On his way to the aristocratic ball he is by no means engrossed in the contrasts of contemporary life; it is the contrasts of his *own* disguises that he finds *piquant*. He informs his obedient companions how extraordinarily interesting he finds himself in the various situations.

"Je trouve," he says, "assez de piquant dans ces contrastes: un jour peintre en éventails, m'établant dans un bouge de la rue aux Fèves; ce matin commis

marchand offrant un verre de cassis à Madame Pipelet, et ce soir ... un des
privilégiés par la grâce de dieu, qui règnent sur ce monde." [a]

When Critical Criticism is ushered into the ball-room, it sings:

> Sense and reason forsake me near,
> In the midst of the potentates here! [b]

It pours forth in *dithyrambs* as follows:

"Here magic brings the brilliance of the sun at night, the verdure of spring and
the splendour of summer in winter. We immediately feel in a mood to believe in
the miracle of the divine presence in the breast of man, especially when beauty and
grace uphold the conviction that we are in the immediate proximity of ideals." (!!!)

Inexperienced, credulous *Critical country parson*! Only your Critical ingenuousness can be raised by an elegant Parisian ball-room
"to a mood" in which you believe in "the miracle of the divine
presence in the breast of man", and see in Parisian lionesses
"immediate ideals" and angels corporeal!

In his *unctuous* naivety the Critical parson listens to the two
"most beautiful among the beautiful", Clémence d'Harville and
Countess Sarah MacGregor. One can guess what he wishes to
"*hear*" from them:

"In what way we can be the *blessing* of beloved children and the *fullness*
of happiness of a husband"!... "We hark ... we wonder ... we do not trust our
ears."

We secretly feel a malicious pleasure when the listening parson
is disappointed. The ladies converse neither about "blessing", nor
"fullness", nor "general reason", but about "an infidelity of
Madame d'Harville to her husband".

We get the following naive revelation about one of the ladies,
Countess MacGregor:

She was "*enterprising enough* to become *mother to a child as the result* of a secret
marriage".

Unpleasantly affected by the *enterprising spirit* of the Countess,
Herr Szeliga has sharp words for her:

"We find that all the strivings of the Countess are for her personal, selfish
advantage."

Indeed, he expects nothing good from the attainment of her
purpose — marriage to the Prince of Geroldstein:

---

[a] "I find these contrasts piquant enough: one day a painter of fans established
in a hovel in the *rue aux Fèves*; this morning a salesman offering a glass of black
currant wine to Madame Pipelet, and this evening ... one of the privileged by the
grace of God who reign over the world." — *Ed.*

[b] A paraphrase of a couplet from Goethe's *Faust*, Part I, Scene 6 (*The Witches'
Kitchen*). — *Ed.*

"concerning which we can *by no means* expect that she will avail herself of it for the *happiness* of the Prince of Geroldstein's *subjects*."

The puritan ends his admonitory sermon with "profound earnestness":

"Sarah" (the *enterprising* lady), "*incidentally, is hardly* an exception in this brilliant circle, *although* she is one of its *summits*."

Incidentally, hardly! Although! And is not the "summit" of a circle an exception?

Here is what we learn about the character of two other ideals, the Marquise d'Harville and the Duchess of Lucenay:

They "'lack satisfaction of the heart'. They have not found in marriage the object of love, so they seek it outside marriage. In marriage, love has remained a *mystery* for them, and the imperative urge of the heart drives them to unravel this mystery. *So* they give themselves up to *secret love*. These 'victims' of 'loveless marriage' are 'driven against their will to debase love to something external, to a so-called affair, and take the romantic, the *secrecy*, for the internal, the vivifying, the essential element of love'".

The merit of this dialectical reasoning is to be assessed all the higher as it is of more general application.

He, for example, who is not allowed to *drink* at home and yet feels the need to drink looks for the "object" of drinking "*outside*" the house, and "so" takes to *secret drinking*. Indeed, he will be driven to consider secrecy an essential ingredient of drinking, although he will not debase drink to a mere "external" indifferent thing, any more than those ladies did with love. For, according to Herr Szeliga himself, it is not love, but marriage without love, that they debase to what it really is, to something external, to a so-called affair.

Herr Szeliga goes on to ask: "What is the '*mystery*' of love?"

We have just had the speculative construction that "mystery" is the "*essence*" of this kind of love. How is it that we now come to be looking for the mystery of the mystery, the essence of the essence?

"Not the shady paths in the thickets," declaims the parson, "not the *natural* semi-obscurity of moonlight night nor the artificial semi-obscurity of costly curtains and draperies; not the soft and enrapturing notes of the harps and the organs, not the attraction of what is forbidden...."

Curtains *and* draperies! Soft *and* enrapturing notes! Even the *organ*! Let the reverend parson stop thinking of *church*! Who would bring an organ to a love tryst?

"All this" (curtains, draperies and organs) "is only the *mysterious*."

And is not the *mysterious* the "mystery" of mysterious love? By no means:

"The mysterious in it is what excites, what intoxicates, what enraptures, the *power of sensuality.*"

In the "soft and *enrapturing*" notes, the parson already had what enraptures. Had he brought turtle soup and champagne to his love tryst instead of curtains and organs, the "*exciting* and *intoxicating*" would have been present too.

"It is true we do not like to admit," the reverend gentleman argues, "the power of sensuality; but it has such tremendous power over us only because we cast it out of us and will not recognise it as our own nature, which we should then be in a position to dominate if it tried to assert itself at the expense of reason, of true love and of will-power."

The parson advises us, after the fashion of speculative theology, to *recognise* sensuality as our *own* nature, in order afterwards to be able to *dominate* it, i.e., to retract recognition of it. True, he wishes to dominate it only when it tries to assert itself at the expense of *Reason*—will-power and love as *opposed* to sensuality are only the will-power and love of *Reason.* The unspeculative Christian also recognises *sensuality* as long as it does not assert itself at the expense of true reason, i.e., of faith, of true love, i.e., of love of God, of true will-power, i.e., of will in Christ.

The parson immediately betrays his real meaning when he continues:

"If then love ceases to be the essential element of marriage and of morality in general, *sensuality* becomes the mystery of love, of morality, of educated society—sensuality both in its *narrow* meaning, in which it is a *trembling in the nerves* and a *burning stream* in the veins, and in the broader meaning, in which it is elevated to a *semblance* of spiritual power, to lust for power, ambition, craving for glory.... Countess MacGregor represents" the latter meaning "of sensuality as the mystery of educated society."

The parson hits the nail on the head. To overcome *sensuality* he must first of all overcome the *nerve currents* and the quick *circulation of the blood.*— Herr Szeliga believes in the "narrow" meaning that greater warmth in the body comes from the heat of the blood in the veins; he does not know that *warm-blooded animals* are so called because the temperature of their blood, apart from slight modifications, always remains at a constant level.— As soon as there is no more nerve current and the blood in the veins is no longer hot, the *sinful body*, this seat of sensual lust, becomes a *corpse* and the souls can converse unhindered about "general reason", "true love", and "pure morals". The parson debases sensuality to such an extent that he abolishes the very elements of sensual love which inspire it—the rapid circulation of the blood, which proves that man does not love by insensitive phlegm; the nerve currents which connect the organ that is the main seat of sensuality with the brain. He reduces true sensual love to the *mechanical secretio seminis* and lisps with a notorious German theologian:

"Not for the sake of sensual love, not for the lust of the flesh, but because the Lord said: Increase and multiply."

Let us now compare the speculative construction with Eugène Sue's novel. It is not *sensuality* which is presented as the secret of love, but mysteries, adventures, obstacles, fears, dangers, and especially the attraction of what is forbidden.

"Pourquoi," says Eugène Sue, "beaucoup de femmes prennent-elles pourtant des hommes qui ne valent pas leurs maris? Parce que le *plus grand charme de l'amour* est l'attrait affriandant *du fruit défendu* ... avancez que, en retranchant de cet amour les craintes, les angoisses, les difficultés, les mystères, les dangers, il ne reste rien ou peu de chose, c'est-à-dire, l'amant ... dans sa simplicité première ... en un mot, ce serait toujours plus ou moins l'aventure de cet homme à qui l'on disait: 'Pourquoi n'épousez-vous donc pas cette veuve, votre maîtresse?'—'Hélas, j'y ai bien pensé'—répondit-il'—'mais alors je ne saurais plus où aller passer mes soirées.'"[a]

Whereas Herr Szeliga says explicitly that the mystery of love is not in the *attraction of what is forbidden,* Eugène Sue says just as explicitly that it is the "greatest charm of love" and the reason for all love adventures *extra muros.*

"La prohibition et la contrebande sont inséparables en amour comme en marchandise."[b]

Eugène Sue similarly maintains, contrary to his speculative commentator, that

"the propensity to pretence and craft, the liking for mysteries and intrigues, is an essential quality, a natural propensity and an imperative instinct of woman's nature".

The only thing which embarrasses Eugène Sue is that this propensity and this liking are directed against *marriage.* He would like to give the instincts of woman's nature a more harmless, more useful application.

Herr Szeliga makes Countess MacGregor a representative of the kind of *sensuality* which "is elevated to a semblance of spiritual

---

[a] "Why do many women take as lovers men who are of less worth than their husbands? Because the *greatest charm of love* is the tempting attraction of the *forbidden fruit....* Grant that if the fears, anxieties, difficulties, mysteries and dangers are taken away from that love nothing or very little remains, that is to say, the lover ... in his original simplicity ... in a word, it would always be more or less the adventure of the man who was asked, 'Why do you not marry that widow, your mistress?' 'Alas, I have thought a good deal about that,' he answered, 'but then I would not know where to spend my evenings.'"—*Ed.*

[b] "Prohibition and smuggling are as inseparable in love as in trade."—*Ed.*

power", but in Eugène Sue she is a *person of abstract reason*. Her "ambition" and her "pride", far from being forms of sensuality, are born of an abstract reason which is completely independent of sensuality. That is why Eugène Sue explicitly notes that

"the fiery impulses of love could never make her *icy* breast heave; *no* surprise of the *heart* or the *senses* could upset the pitiless calculations of this crafty, selfish, ambitious woman".

This woman's essential character lies in the egoism of abstract *reason* that never suffers from the sympathetic senses and on which the blood has no influence. Her soul is therefore described as "dry and hard", her mind as "artfully wicked", her character as "treacherous" and—what is very typical of a person of abstract reason—as "absolute", her dissimulation as "profound".— It is to be noted incidentally that Eugène Sue motivates the career of the Countess just as stupidly as that of most of his characters. An old nurse gives her the idea that she must become a "crowned head". Convinced of this, she undertakes journeys to capture a crown through marriage. Finally she commits the inconsistency of considering a petty German "*Serenissimus*"[a] as a "crowned head".

After his outpourings against *sensuality*, our Critical saint deems it necessary to show why Eugène Sue introduces us to *haute volée* at a ball, a method which is used by nearly all French novelists, whereas the *English* do so more often at the chase or in a country mansion.

"For this" (i.e., Herr Szeliga's) "conception it cannot be indifferent there" (in Herr Szeliga's construction) "and merely accidental that Eugène Sue introduces us to high society at a ball."

Now the horse has been given a free rein and it trots briskly towards the necessary end through a series of conclusions reminding one of the late Wolff.

"*Dancing* is the most common manifestation of *sensuality as a mystery*. The immediate *contact*, the embracing of the two sexes" (?) "necessary to form a couple are allowed in dancing because, in spite of appearances, and the really" (really, Mr. Parson?) "perceptible pleasant sensation, it is not considered as *sensual* contact and embracing" (but probably as connected with universal reason?).

And then comes a closing sentence which at best staggers rather than dances:

"*For* if it were *in actual fact* considered *as such it would be impossible to understand why* society is so lenient only as regards dancing *while it, on the contrary*, so severely condemns *that which*, if exhibited with similar freedom *elsewhere*, incurs branding and merciless casting out as a most unpardonable offence against morals and modesty."

The reverend parson speaks here neither of the *cancan* nor of the *polka*, but of *dancing* in general, of the *category* Dancing, which

---

[a] The title for a German prince.— *Ed.*

is not performed anywhere except in his Critical cranium. Let him see a dance at the Chaumière in Paris, and his Christian-German soul would be outraged by the boldness, the frankness, the graceful petulance and the music of that most sensual movement. His own "really perceptible pleasant sensation" would make it "perceptible" to him that "in actual fact it would be impossible to understand why the dancers themselves, while on the contrary they" give the spectator the uplifting impression of frank human sensuality—"which, if exhibited in the same way elsewhere"—namely in Germany—"would be severely condemned as an unpardonable offence", etc., etc.—why those dancers, at least so to speak in their own eyes, not only should not and may not, but of necessity canot and must not be frankly sensual human beings!!

The Critic introduces us to the *ball* for the sake of the *essence of dancing*. He encounters a great difficulty. True, there is dancing at this ball, but only in imagination. The fact is that Eugène Sue does not say a word describing the dancing. He does not mix among the throng of dancers. He makes use of the ball only as an opportunity for bringing together his characters from the upper aristocracy. In despair, "Criticism" comes to help out and *supplement* the author, and its own "fancy" easily provides a description of ball incidents, etc. If, as prescribed by Criticism, Eugène Sue was not directly interested in the criminals' hide-outs and language when he described them, the dance, on the other hand, which *not he* but his "fanciful" Critic describes, necessarily interests him infinitely.

Let us continue.

> "*Actually*, the secret of sociable tone and tact—the secret of that extremely unnatural thing—is the longing to return to nature. That is why the appearance of a person like *Cecily* in educated society has such an electrifying effect and is crowned with such extraordinary success. She grew up a slave among slaves, without any education, and the only source of life she has to rely upon is her nature. Suddenly transported to a court and subjected to its constraint and customs, she soon learns to see through the secret of the latter.... In this sphere, which she can undoubtedly hold in sway because her power, the power of her nature, has an enigmatic magic, Cecily must necessarily stray into losing all sense of measure, whereas formerly, when she was still a slave, the same nature taught her to resist any unworthy demand of the powerful master and to remain true to her love. *Cecily* is the *mystery of educated society disclosed*. The scorned senses finally break down the barriers and surge forth completely uncurbed", etc.

Those of Herr Szeliga's readers who have not read Sue's novel will certainly think that Cecily is the lioness of the ball that is described. In the novel she is in a German gaol while the dancing goes on in Paris.

Cecily, as a slave, remains true to the Negro doctor David

because she loves him "passionately" and because her owner, Mr. Willis, is *"brutal"* in courting her. The reason for her change to a dissolute life is a very simple one. Transported into the "European world", she "blushes" at being "married to a Negro". On arriving in Germany she is *"at once"* seduced by a wicked man and her "Indian blood" comes into its own. This the hypocritical M. Sue, for the sake of *douce morale*[a] and *doux commerce,*[b] is bound to describe as *"perversité naturelle"*.[c]

The secret of Cecily is that she is a *half-breed.* The secret of her sensuality is the *heat of the tropics.* Parny sang praises of the half-breed in his beautiful lines to Eleonore.[d] Over a hundred sea-faring tales tell us how dangerous she is to sailors.

"Cecily était le type incarné de la sensualité brûlante, qui ne s'allume qu'au feu des tropiques.... Tout le monde a entendu parler de ces filles de couleur, pour ainsi dire mortelles aux Européens, de ces vampyrs enchanteurs, qui, enivrant leurs victimes de séductions terribles ... ne lui laissent, selon l'énergique expression du pays, que ses larmes à boire, que son coeur à ronger."[e]

Cecily was far from producing such a magical effect precisely on people aristocratically educated, *blasé...*

"les femmes de l'espèce de Cecily exercent une action soudaine, une omnipotence magique sur les hommes de *sensualité brutale* tels que *Jacques Ferrand*".[f]

Since when have men like Jacques Ferrand been representative of fine society? But Critical Criticism must speculatively make *Cecily* a factor in the life-process of Absolute Mystery.

4) "THE MYSTERY OF PROBITY AND PIETY"

"Mystery, as *that* of educated society, withdraws, *it is true,* from the *antithesis* into the *inner* sphere. *Nevertheless,* high society *once again* has exclusively *its own* circles in which it preserves the holy. It is, *as it were,* the chapel for this holy of holies. *But* for people in the forecourt, the chapel itself is the *mystery.* Education, *therefore,* in its exclusive position is the same thing for the people ... as vulgarity is for the educated."

It is true, nevertheless, once again, as it were, but, therefore—those are the magic hooks which hold together the links of the *chain of*

---

[a] Sweet morality.—*Ed.*
[b] Tender commerce.—*Ed.*
[c] "Natural perversity."—*Ed.*
[d] E. D. Parny, *Poésies érotiques.*—*Ed.*
[e] "Cecily was the incarnation of the burning sensuality which only the heat of the tropics can kindle.... Everybody has heard of those coloured girls who are fatal, so to speak, to Europeans; of those charming vampires who intoxicate their victim with terrible seductions ... and leave him nothing, as the forceful expression of the country says, but his tears to drink and his heart to gnaw."—*Ed.*
[f] "Women of the type of Cecily have a sudden effect, a magic omnipotence over men of *brutal sensuality* like *Jacques Ferrand.*"—*Ed.*

speculative reasoning. Herr Szeliga has made *Mystery* withdraw from the world of criminals into high society. Now he has to construct the mystery that high society has its *exclusive* circles and that the mysteries of those circles are mysteries for the people. Besides the magic hooks already mentioned, this construction requires the transformation of a *circle* into a *chapel* and the transformation of non-aristocratic society into a *forecourt* of that chapel. Again it is a mystery *for* Paris that all the spheres of bourgeois society are only a forecourt of the chapel of high society.

Herr Szeliga pursues two aims. Firstly, *Mystery* which has become incarnate in the exclusive circle of high society must be declared *"common property of the world".* Secondly, the *notary Jacques Ferrand* must be construed as a link in the life of Mystery. Here is the way Herr Szeliga reasons:

"Education as yet is unable and unwilling to bring all estates and distinctions into its circle. Only *Christianity* and *morality* are able to found universal kingdoms on earth."

Herr Szeliga identifies education, civilisation, with *aristocratic* education. That is why he cannot see that *industry and trade* found universal kingdoms quite different from Christianity and morality, domestic happiness and civic welfare. But how do we come to the *notary Jacques Ferrand?* Quite simply!

Herr Szeliga transforms *Christianity* into an *individual* quality, *"piety",* and *morality* into another *individual* quality, *"probity".* He combines these two qualities in *one* individual whom he christens *Jacques Ferrand,* because Jacques Ferrand does not possess these two qualities but only pretends to. Thus Jacques Ferrand becomes the "mystery of probity and piety". His "testament", on the other hand, is "the mystery of *seeming* piety and probity", and therefore no longer of piety and probity themselves. If Critical Criticism had wanted speculatively to construe this testament as a mystery, it should have declared the seeming probity and piety to be the mystery of this testament, and not the other way round, this testament as the mystery of the seeming probity.

Whereas the Paris college of notaries considered Jacques Ferrand as a malicious libel against itself and through the theatrical censorship had this character removed from the stage performance of the *Mystères de Paris,* Critical Criticism, at the very time when it *"polemises against the airy kingdom of conceptions",* sees in a Paris notary not a Paris notary but religion and morality, probity and piety. The trial of the notary *Lehon* ought to have taught it better. The position held by the *notary* in Eugène Sue's novel is closely connected with his official position.

"Les notaires sont au temporel ce qu'au spirituel sont les curés; ils sont les *dépositaires de nos secrets*"[a] (Monteil, *Hist[oire] des français des div[ers] états,"* etc. t. ix, p. 37).

The notary is the secular confessor. He is a *puritan* by profession, and "honesty", Shakespeare says, is "no Puritan".[b] He is at the same time the go-between for all possible purposes, the manager of all civil intrigues and plots.

With the notary Ferrand, whose whole mystery consists in his hypocrisy and his profession, we do not seem to have made a single step forward yet. But listen:

"If for the notary hypocrisy is a matter of the most complete consciousness, and for Madame Roland it is, *as it were*, instinct, *then* between them there is the great mass of those who cannot get to the bottom of the mystery and yet involuntarily feel a desire to do so. It is therefore not superstition that leads the high and the low to the sombre dwelling of the charlatan Bradamanti (Abbé Polidori); no, it is the search for *Mystery*, to justify themselves to the world."

"The high and the low" flock to Polidori not to find out a definite mystery which is justified to the whole world, but to look for *Mystery* in general, Mystery as the Absolute Subject, *in order to* justify themselves to the world; as if to chop wood one looked, not for an axe, but for *the* Instrument *in abstracto*.

All the mysteries that Polidori possesses are limited to a means for abortion and a poison for murder.— In a speculative frenzy Herr Szeliga makes the *"murderer"* resort to Polidori's poison "because he wants to be not a murderer, but respected, loved and honoured". As if in an act of murder it was a question of respect, love or honour and not of one's *neck!* But the *Critical* murderer does not bother about his neck, but only about *"Mystery"*.— As not everyone commits murder or becomes pregnant illegitimately, how is Polidori to put *everyone* in the desired possession of Mystery? Herr Szeliga probably confuses the charlatan Polidori with the scholar *Polydore Virgil* who lived in the sixteenth century and who, although he did not discover any mysteries, tried to make the history of those who did, the *inventors*, the "common property of the world" (see *Polidori Virgilii liber de rerum inventoribus*, Lugduni MDCCVI).

Mystery, Absolute Mystery, as it has finally established itself as the "common property of the world", consists therefore in the mystery of abortion and poisoning. *Mystery* could not make itself

---

[a] "Notaries are in the temporal realm what priests are in the spiritual: they are the *depositories of our secrets*."— *Ed.*

[b] Shakespeare, *All's Well that Ends Well*, Act I, Scene 3.— *Ed.*

"the common property of the world" more skilfully than by turning itself into mysteries which are mysteries to no one.

5) "MYSTERY, A MOCKERY"

"*Mystery* has *now* become common property, the mystery of the whole world and of every individual. Either it is my art or my instinct, or I can buy it as a purchasable commodity."

What mystery has now become the common property of the world? Is it the mystery of rightlessness in the state, or the mystery of educated society, or the mystery of adulterating wares, or the mystery of making eau-de-cologne, or the mystery of "Critical Criticism"? None of all these, but *Mystery in abstracto*, the category Mystery!

Herr Szeliga intends to depict the *servants* and the *porter Pipelet and his wife* as the incarnation of Absolute Mystery. He wants speculatively to construct the *servant* and the porter of "*Mystery*". How does he manage to make the headlong descent from *pure category* down to the "*servant*" who "*spies at a locked door*", from *Mystery as the Absolute Subject*, which is enthroned above the *roof* in the cloudy heavens of abstraction, down to the ground floor where the porter's lodge is situated?

First he subjects the category Mystery to a speculative process. When by the aid of means for abortion and poisoning Mystery has become the common property of the world, it is

"*therefore by no means any longer concealment* and *inaccessibility itself*, but *it conceals itself*, or better still" (always better!) "I conceal it, *I make it inaccessible*".

With this transformation of Absolute Mystery from *essence* into *concept*, from the *objective* stage, in which it is concealment itself, into the *subjective* stage, in which it conceals itself, or better still, in which *I* conceal *it*, we have not made a single step forward. On the contrary, the difficulty seems to grow, for a mystery in man's head or breast is more inaccessible and concealed than at the bottom of the sea. That is why Herr Szeliga comes to the aid of his *speculative* progress *directly* by means of an *empirical* progress.

"*It is behind locked doors*"—hark! hark!—"that *henceforth*"—henceforth!—"*Mystery*, is hatched, brewed and perpetrated."

Herr Szeliga has "*henceforth*" changed the speculative *ego* of Mystery into a very empirical, very *wooden* reality—a *door*.

"*But with that*"—i.e., with the locked door, not with the transition from the closed essence to the concept—"there exists *also the possibility* of my overhearing, eavesdropping, and spying on it."

It is not *Herr Szeliga* who discovered the "mystery" that one can eavesdrop at locked doors. The mass-type proverb even says that walls have ears. On the other hand it is a quite Critical speculative mystery that only "*henceforth*", after the descent into the hell of the criminals' hide-outs and the ascent into the heaven of educated society, and after Polidori's miracles, mysteries can be brewed *behind* locked doors and overheard *through* closed doors. It is just as great a Critical mystery that locked doors are a *categorical necessity* for hatching, brewing and perpetrating mysteries — how many mysteries are hatched, brewed, and perpetrated behind bushes! — as well as for spying them out.

After this brilliant dialectical feat of arms, Herr Szeliga naturally goes on from *spying* itself to the *reasons for spying*. Here he reveals the mystery that *malicious gloating* is the reason for it. From malicious gloating he goes on to the *reason for malicious gloating*.

"Everyone wishes to be better than the others," he says, "because he keeps secret the mainsprings not only of his good actions, but of his bad ones too, which he tries to hide in impenetrable darkness."

The sentence should be the other way round: Everyone not only keeps the mainsprings of his good actions secret, but tries to conceal his bad ones in impenetrable darkness because he wishes to be better than the others.

Thus it seems we have gone from *Mystery that conceals itself* to the *ego* that conceals it, from the *ego* to the *locked door*, from the *locked door* to *spying*, from *spying* to the *reason for spying*, malicious gloating; from *malicious gloating* to the *reason for malicious gloating*, the *desire to be better than the others*. We shall soon have the pleasure of seeing the *servant* standing at the locked door. For the general desire to be better than the others leads us directly to this: that "everyone is inclined to find out the mysteries of another", and this is followed easily by the witty remark:

"In this respect *servants* have the *best opportunity*."

Had Herr Szeliga read the records from the Paris police archives, Vidocq's memoirs, the *Livre noir*[a] and the like, he would know that in this respect the *police* has still greater opportunity than the "best opportunity" that servants have; that it uses servants only for crude jobs, that it does not stop at the door or where the masters are in *negligé*, but creeps under their sheets next to their naked body in the shape of a *femme galante* or even of a legitimate wife. In Sue's novel the police spy *"Bras rouge"* plays a leading part in the story.

---

[a] Black book.— *Ed.*

What "henceforth" annoys Herr Szeliga in servants is that they are not *"disinterested"* enough. This *Critical misgiving* leads him to the *porter Pipelet and his wife.*

"The porter's position, on the other hand, gives him relative independence so that he can pour out free, disinterested, although vulgar and injurious, mockery on the mysteries of the house."

At first this speculative construction of the porter is put into a great difficulty because in many Paris houses the servant and the porter are one and the same person for some of the tenants.

The following facts will enable the reader to form an opinion of the Critical fantasy concerning the relatively independent, disinterested position of the porter. The porter in Paris is the representative and spy of the landlord. He is generally paid not by the landlord but by the tenants. Because of that precarious position he often combines the functions of commission agent with his official duties. During the Terror, the Empire and the Restoration, the porter was one of the main agents of the secret police. General Foy, for instance, was watched by his porter, who took all the letters addressed to the general to be read by a police agent not far away (see Froment, *La police dévoilée*). As a result *"portier"*[a] and *"épicier"*[b] are considered insulting names and the porter prefers to be called *"concierge"*.[c]

Far from being depicted as "disinterested" and harmless, Eugène Sue's Madame Pipelet immediately cheats Rudolph when giving him his change; she recommends to him the dishonest money-lender living in the house and describes Rigolette to him as an acquaintance who may be pleasant to him. She teases the major because he pays her badly and haggles with her — in her vexation she calls him a *"commandant de deux liards"*[d] — *"ca t'apprendra à ne donner que douze francs par mois pour ton ménage."* [e] — and because he has the *"petitesse"*[f] as to keep a check on his firewood, etc. She herself gives the reason for her "independent" behaviour: the major only pays her twelve francs a month.

According to Herr Szeliga, "Anastasia Pipelet has, *to some extent,* to declare a small war on *Mystery*".

---

[a] Porter.— *Ed.*

[b] Grocer.— *Ed.*

[c] Caretaker.— *Ed.*

[d] A twopenny major.— *Ed.*

[e] That'll teach you to give only twelve francs a month for your house-keeping.— *Ed.*

[f] Pettiness.— *Ed.*

According to Eugène Sue, Anastasia Pipelet is a typical *Paris Portière*. He wants "to dramatise the *Portière*, whom Henri Monier portrayed with such mastery". But Herr Szeliga feels bound to transform one of Madame Pipelet's qualities— "*médisance*"[a]—into a separate being and then to make her a representative of that being.

"The husband," Herr Szeliga continues, "the porter Alfred Pipelet, helps her, but with less luck."

To console him for this bad luck, Herr Szeliga makes him also into an *allegory*. He represents the *"objective"* side of Mystery, *"Mystery as Mockery"*.

"The mystery which defeats him is a mockery, a joke, that is played on him."

Indeed, in its infinite pity divine dialectic makes the "unhappy, old, childish man" a *"strong man"* in the *metaphysical sense*, by making him represent a very worthy, very happy and very decisive factor in the life-process of Absolute Mystery. The victory over Pipelet is

"*Mystery's most decisive defeat.*" "A cleverer, courageous man would not let himself be duped by a *joke.*"

6) TURTLE-DOVE (RIGOLETTE)

"There is still one step left. Through *its own consistent development*, Mystery, as we saw in Pipelet and Cabrion, is driven to debase itself to mere clowning. The *one* thing necessary *now* is that the individual should no longer agree to play that silly comedy. *Turtle-dove* takes that step in the most nonchalant way in the world."

Anyone in two minutes can see through the mystery of this speculative clowning and learn to practise it himself. We will give brief directions in this respect.

Problem. You must give me the speculative construction showing how man becomes master over animals.

Speculative solution. Given are half a dozen animals, such as the lion, the shark, the snake, the bull, the horse and the pug. From these six animals abstract the category: *the* "Animal". Imagine *the* "Animal" to be an independent being. Regard the lion, the shark, the snake, etc., as disguises, incarnations, of *the* "Animal". Just as you made your imagination, *the* "Animal" of your abstraction, into a real being, now make the real animals into beings of abstraction, of your imagination. You see that the "Animal", which in the *lion* tears man to pieces, in the *shark* swallows him up, in the *snake* stings him with venom, in the *bull* tosses him with its horns and in the *horse* kicks him, only barks at him when it presents itself as a

---

[a] Backbiting.—*Ed.*

pug, and converts the fight against man into the mere *semblance of a fight.* Through its *own consistent development, the* "Animal" is driven, as we have seen in the *pug,* to debase itself to a *mere clown.* When a child or a childish man runs away from a pug, the only thing is for the individual no longer to agree to play the silly comedy. The individual X takes this step in the most nonchalant way in the world by using his bamboo cane on the pug. You see how *"Man",* through the agency of the individual X and the pug, has become master over *the* "Animal", and consequently over animals, and in the *Animal as a pug* has defeated the *lion as an animal.*

Similarly Herr Szeliga's "turtle-dove" defeats the mysteries of the present state of the world through the intermediary of Pipelet and Cabrion. More than that! She is herself a manifestation of the category *"Mystery".*

"She herself is not yet conscious of her high moral value, therefore she is still a mystery to herself."

The mystery of *non-*speculative Rigolette is revealed in Eugène Sue's book by Murph. She is *"une fort jolie grisette".*[a] Eugène Sue described in her the lovely human character of the Paris *grisette.* Only owing to his devotion to the bourgeoisie and his own tendency to high-flown exaggeration, he had to idealise the *grisette morally.* He had to gloss over the essential point of her situation in life and her character, to be precise, her disregard for the form of marriage, her naive attachment to the Etudiant[b] or the Ouvrier.[c] It is precisely in that attachment that she constitutes a really human contrast to the hypocritical, narrow-hearted, self-seeking wife of the bourgeois, to the whole circle of the bourgeoisie, that is, to the official circle.

7) THE WORLD SYSTEM OF THE MYSTERIES OF PARIS

"This world of mysteries is *now* the general world system, in which the individual action of the *Mysteries of Paris* is set."

Before, "however", Herr Szeliga "passes on to the *philosophical reproduction* of the epic event", he must "assemble in a general picture the sketches previously jotted down separately".

It must be considered as a real confession, a revelation of Herr

---

[a] A very pretty *grisette.— Ed.*
[b] Student.— *Ed.*
[c] Worker.— *Ed.*

Szeliga's Critical Mystery, when he says that he wishes to pass on to the "philosophical reproduction" of the epic event. He has so far been "philosophically reproducing" the world system.

Herr Szeliga continues his confession:

"From our presentation it appears that the individual mysteries dealt with have not their value in themselves, each separate from the others, and are in no way magnificent novelties for gossip, but that their value consists in their constituting an *organically linked sequence*, the *totality* of which is "*Mystery*".

In his mood of sincerity, Herr Szeliga goes still further. He admits that the "*speculative sequence*" is not the *real* sequence of the *Mystères de Paris*.

"Granted, the mysteries do not appear in our epic in the relationship of this *self-knowing sequence*" (to cost prices?). "*But* we are *not* dealing with the *logical, obvious, free organism of criticism*, but with a *mysterious vegetable existence*."

We shall pass over Herr Szeliga's summary and go on immediately to the point that constitutes the "transition". In Pipelet we saw the "self-mockery of Mystery".

"In self-mockery, Mystery passes judgment on itself. *Thereby* the mysteries, annihilating themselves in their final consequence, challenge every strong character to independent examination."

Rudolph, Prince of Geroldstein, *the man of "pure Criticism"*, is destined to carry out this examination and the "*disclosure of the mysteries.*"

If we deal with Rudolph and his deeds only later, after diverting our attention from Herr Szeliga for some time,[a] it can already be foreseen, and to a certain degree the reader can sense, indeed even surmise without presumption, that instead of treating him as a "*mysterious vegetable existence*", which he is in the Critical *Literatur-Zeitung*, we shall make him a "*logical, obvious, free link*" in the "*organism of Critical Criticism.*"

---

[a] See pp. 162-209 of this volume.—*Ed.*

Chapter VI

ABSOLUTE CRITICAL CRITICISM,
OR CRITICAL CRITICISM AS HERR BRUNO

1) ABSOLUTE CRITICISM'S FIRST CAMPAIGN

a) "Spirit" and "Mass"

So far Critical Criticism has seemed to deal more or less with the Critical treatment of various *mass*-type objects. We now find it dealing with the absolutely Critical object, *with itself*. So far it has derived its relative glory from Critical debasement, rejection and transformation of *definite* mass-type objects and persons. It now derives its *absolute* glory from the Critical debasement, rejection and transformation of the Mass in general. Relative Criticism was faced with relative limits. Absolute Criticism is faced with an absolute limit, the limit of the Mass, the Mass as limit. Relative Criticism in its opposition to definite limits was itself necessarily a *limited* individual. Absolute Criticism, in its opposition to the *general* limit, to limit in general, is necessarily an *absolute* individual. As the various mass-type objects and persons have merged in the *impure* pulp of the "*Mass*", so has still seemingly objective and personal Criticism changed into "*pure Criticism*". So far Criticism has appeared to be more or less a *quality* of the Critical individuals: Reichardt, Edgar, Faucher, etc. Now it is the *Subject* and Herr Bruno is its incarnation.

So far *mass character* has seemed to be more or less the quality of the objects and persons criticised; now objects and persons have become the "*Mass*", and the "*Mass*" has become object and person. All previous Critical attitudes have been dissolved in the attitude of absolute Critical wisdom to absolute mass-type stupidity. This *basic attitude* appears as the *meaning*, the *tendency* and the *keyword* of Criticism's previous deeds and struggles.

In accordance with its absolute character, "pure" Criticism, as soon as it appears, will pronounce the differentiating "*cue*"; nevertheless, as Absolute Spirit it must go through a dialectical process. Only at the end of its heavenly motion will its original concept be truly realised (see Hegel, *Enzyklopädie*).

"Only a few months ago," Absolute Criticism announces, "the Mass believed itself to be of gigantic strength and destined to world mastery within a time that it could count on its fingers."

It was precisely Herr *Bruno Bauer,* in *Die gute Sache der Freiheit*[a] (his *"own"* cause, of course), in *Die Judenfrage,*[22] etc., who counted on his fingers the time until the approaching world mastery, although he admitted he could not give the exact date. To the record of the sins of the Mass he adds the mass of his own sins.

"The Mass thought itself in possession of so many truths which seemed obvious to it." "But one *possesses a truth* completely only ... when one follows it through *its* proofs."

For Herr Bauer, as for Hegel, truth is an *automaton* that proves itself. Man must *follow* it. As in Hegel, the result of real development is nothing but the *truth proven,* i.e., brought to *consciousness.* Absolute Criticism may therefore ask with the most narrow-minded theologian:

"*What* would be the purpose of *history* if its task were not precisely to *prove* these simplest of all truths (such as the movement of the earth round the sun)?"

Just as, according to the earlier teleologists, plants exist to be eaten by animals, and animals to be eaten by men, history exists in order to serve as the act of consumption of theoretical eating—*proving.* Man exists so that history may exist, and history exists so that the *proof of truths* exists. In this *Critically* trivialised form is repeated the speculative wisdom that man exists, and history exists, so that *truth* may arrive at *self-consciousness.*

That is why *history,* like *truth,* becomes a person apart, a metaphysical subject of which the real human individuals are merely the bearers. That is why Absolute Criticism uses phrases like these:

"*History* does not allow itself to be mocked at ... *History* has exerted *its* greatest efforts to ... *History* has been engaged ... what would be the purpose of History?... *History* provides the explicit proof ... *History* puts forward truths," etc.

If, as Absolute Criticism asserts, history has so far been occupied with only a *few* such truths—the simplest of all—which in the end are self-evident, this inadequacy to which Absolute Criticism reduces previous human experiences proves first of all only its *own* inadequacy. From the un-Critical standpoint the result of history is, on the contrary, that the most complicated truth, the quintessence of all truth, *man,* is self-evident in the end.

---

[a] *The Good Cause of Freedom.*—*Ed.*

"But truths," Absolute Criticism continues to argue, "which *seem* to the mass to be so crystal-clear that they are self-evident *from the start* ... and that the mass regards proof of them as superfluous, are not worth history supplying explicit proof of them; they are in general no part of the problem which history is engaged in solving."

In its holy zeal against the mass, Absolute Criticism pays it the finest compliment. If a truth is *crystal-clear* because it *seems* crystal-clear to the mass; if history's *attitude* to truths *depends* on the *opinion* of the mass, then the verdict of the mass is absolute, infallible, the *law* of history, and history proves only what does *not* seem crystal-clear to the mass, and therefore needs proof. It is the mass, then, that prescribes history's "task" and "occupation".

Absolute Criticism speaks of "truths which are self-evident *from the start*". In its Critical naivety it invents an absolute "*from the start*" and an abstract, immutable " *nass*". There is just as little difference, in the eyes of Absolute Criticism, between the "from the start" of the sixteenth-century mass and the "from the start" of the nineteenth-century mass as there is between those masses themselves. It is precisely the characteristic feature of a truth which has become *true* and *obvious* and is self-evident that it is "self-evident *from the start*". Absolute Criticism's polemic against truths which are self-evident from the start is a polemic against truths which are "self-evident" in general.

A truth which is self-evident has lost its savour, its meaning, its *value* for Absolute Criticism as it has for divine *dialectic.* It has become flat, like stale water. On the one hand, therefore, Absolute Criticism proves everything which is self-evident and, in addition, many things which have the luck to be incomprehensible and therefore will never be self-evident. On the other hand, it considers as self-evident everything which needs some elaboration. Why? Because it is *self*-evident that *real problems* are *not* self-evident.

Since, the "Truth", like history, is an ethereal subject separate from the material mass, it addresses itself not to the empirical man but to the "*innermost depths of the soul*"; in order to be "*truly apprehended*" it does not act on his *vulgar body,* which may live deep down in an English cellar or at the top of a French block of flats; it "stretches" "from end to end" through his idealistic intestines. Absolute Criticism does certify that "the mass" has so far in its own way, i.e., superficially, been affected by the truths that history has been so gracious as to "put forward"; but at the same time it prophesies that

"the *attitude* of the *mass* to *historical progress* will "*completely change*".

It will not be long before the mysterious meaning of this Critical prophecy becomes "crystal-clear" to us.

"All great actions of previous history," we are told, "were failures *from the start* and had no effective success because the mass became *interested* in and *enthusiastic* over them—or, they were bound to come to a pitiful end because the idea underlying them was such that it had to be content with a superficial comprehension and therefore to rely on the approval of the mass."

It seems that the comprehension which suffices for, and therefore corresponds to, an idea ceases to be superficial. It is only for *appearance's sake* that Herr Bruno brings out a *relation* between an *idea* and its *comprehension,* just as it is only for *appearance's sake* that he brings out a *relation* between unsuccessful historical *action* and the *mass.* If, therefore, Absolute Criticism condemns something as "superficial", it is simply previous history, the actions and ideas of which were those of the "masses". It rejects *mass-type* history to replace it by *Critical* history (see Herr Jules Faucher on English problems of the day).[a] According to previous *un-Critical* history, i.e., history not conceived in the sense of Absolute Criticism, it must further be precisely distinguished to what extent the *mass* was "*interested*" in aims and to what extent it was "*enthusiastic*" over them. The "*idea*" always disgraced itself insofar as it differed from the "*interest*". On the other hand, it is easy to understand that every mass-type "*interest*" that asserts itself historically goes far beyond its real limits in the "*idea*" or "*imagination*" when it first comes on the scene and is confused with *human* interest in general. This *illusion* constitutes what *Fourier* calls the *tone* of each historical epoch. The *interest* of the bourgeoisie in the 1789 Revolution, far from having been a "*failure*", "*won*" everything and had "*most effective success*", however much its "*pathos*" has evaporated and the "*enthusiastic*" flowers with which that interest adorned its cradle have faded. That *interest* was so powerful that it was victorious over the pen of Marat, the guillotine of the Terror and the sword of Napoleon as well as the crucifix and the blue blood of the Bourbons. The Revolution was a "failure" only for the mass which did not have in the *political* "idea" the idea of its real "*interest*", i.e., whose true life-principle did not coincide with the life-principle of the Revolution, the mass whose real conditions for emancipation were essentially different from the conditions within which the bourgeoisie could emancipate itself and society. If the Revolution, which can exemplify all great historical "actions", was a failure, it was so because the mass within whose living conditions it

---

[a] See pp. 12-16 of this volume.—*Ed.*

essentially came to a stop, was an *exclusive, limited* mass, not an all-embracing one. If the Revolution was a failure it was not because the mass was *"enthusiastic"* over it and *"interested"* in it, but because the most numerous part of the mass, the part distinct from the bourgeoisie, did not have its *real* interest in the principle of the Revolution, did not have a revolutionary principle of its *own*, but *only* an *"idea"*, and hence only an object of momentary *enthusiasm* and only seeming *uplift*.

Together with the thoroughness of the historical action, the size of the mass whose action it is will therefore increase. In Critical history, according to which in historical actions it is not a matter of the acting masses, of empirical action, or of the empirical *interest* of this action, but instead is only "a matter of an *idea in them*", things must naturally take a different course.

"*In the mass*," Criticism teaches us, "*not somewhere else*, as its former liberal spokesmen believed, *is the true enemy of the spirit to be found*."

The enemies of progress *outside* the mass are precisely those *products* of *self-debasement, self-rejection* and *self-alienation* of the *mass* which have been endowed with independent being and a life of their *own*. The mass therefore turns against its *own* deficiency when it turns against the independently existing *products* of its *self-debasement*, just as man, turning against the existence of God, turns against his *own religiosity*. But as those *practical* self-alienations of the mass exist in the real world in an outward way, the mass must fight them in an *outward* way. It must by no means hold these products of its self-alienation for mere *ideal* fantasies, mere *alienations of self-consciousness*, and must not wish to abolish *material* estrangement by purely *inward spiritual* action. As early as 1789 Loustalot's journal bore the motto:

Les grands ne nous paraissent grands
Que parce que nous sommes à genoux
—— Levons nous! ——[a]

But to rise it is not enough to do so in *thought* and to leave hanging over one's *real sensuously perceptible* head the *real sensuously perceptible* yoke that cannot be subtilised away with ideas. Yet *Absolute Criticism* has learnt from Hegel's *Phänomenologie* at least *the* art of converting *real objective* chains that exist *outside me* into *merely ideal,* merely *subjective* chains, existing merely *in me* and thus

[a] The great appear great in our eyes
Only because we are kneeling.
Let us rise!—*Ed.*

of converting all *external* sensuously perceptible struggles into pure struggles of thought.

This Critical transformation is the basis of the *pre-established harmony* between *Critical Criticism* and the *censorship.* From the Critical point of view, the writer's fight against the censor is not a fight of "man against man". The censor is nothing but *my own tact personified* for me by the solicitous police, my own tact struggling against my tactlessness and un-Criticalness. The struggle of the writer with the censor is only seemingly, only in the eyes of wicked sensuousness, anything else than the *inner* struggle of the writer *with himself. Insofar as* the censor is *really individually different* from myself, a *police executioner* who mishandles the product of my mind by applying an external standard alien to the matter in question, he is a mere *mass-type* fantasy, an *un-Critical figment of the brain.* When Feuerbach's *Thesen zur Reform der Philosophie*[23] were prohibited by the censorship, it was not the official barbarity of the censorship that was to blame but the uncultured character of Feuerbach's *Thesen.* "*Pure*" Criticism, unsullied by mass or matter, too, has in the censor a purely "ethereal" form, divorced from all mass-type reality.

Absolute Criticism has declared the "*Mass*" to be the *true enemy of the Spirit.* It develops this in more detail as follows:

"The Spirit now knows where to *look* for *its* only *adversary*—in the self-deception and the pithlessness of the Mass."

Absolute Criticism proceeds from the *dogma* of the absolute competency of *the "Spirit".* Furthermore, it proceeds from the *dogma* of the *extramundane* existence of the Spirit, i.e., of its existence outside the mass of humanity. Finally, it transforms "*the* Spirit", "*Progress*", on the one hand, and "*the Mass*", on the other, into *fixed* entities, into concepts, and then relates them to one another as such given rigid extremes. It does not occur to Absolute Criticism to investigate *the "Spirit"* itself, to find out whether it is not in its spiritualistic nature, in its airy pretensions, that the "phrase", "self-deception" and "pithlessness" are rooted. No, the Spirit is *absolute,* but unfortunately at the same time it continually turns into *spiritlessness;* it continually reckons without its host. Hence it must necessarily have an *adversary* that intrigues against it. That *adversary* is the Mass.

The position is the same with "*Progress*". In spite of the pretensions of "*Progress*", continual *retrogressions* and *circular movements* occur. Far from suspecting that the category "*Progress*" is completely empty and abstract, Absolute Criticism is so profound as to recognise *"Progress"* as being absolute, so as to explain retrogression by assuming a *"personal adversary"* of Progress, *the Mass*. As *"the Mass"* is nothing but the *"opposite of the Spirit"*, of *Progress*, of *"Criticism"*,[a] it can accordingly be defined only by this imaginary opposition; apart from that opposition all that Criticism can say about the *meaning* and the existence of the Mass is only something *meaningless*, because completely undefined:

"The Mass, in *that sense* in which the *'word'* also embraces the *so-called* educated world."

"Also" and "so-called" suffice for a Critical definition. *The* "Mass" is therefore distinct from the *real* masses and exists as *the* *"Mass"* only for *"Criticism"*.

All communist and socialist writers proceeded from the observation that, on the one hand, even the most favourably brilliant deeds seemed to remain without brilliant results, to end in trivialities, and, on the other, *all progress of the Spirit* had so far been *progress against the mass of mankind*, driving it into an ever more *dehumanised* situation. They therefore declared *"progress"* (see *Fourier*) to be an inadequate, abstract *phrase*; they assumed (see *Owen* among others) a fundamental flaw in the civilised world; that is why they subjected the *real* foundations of contemporary society to incisive *criticism*. This communist criticism had practically at once as its counterpart the movement of the *great mass*, in opposition to which history had been developing so far. One must know the studiousness, the craving for knowledge, the moral energy and the unceasing urge for development of the French and English workers to be able to form an idea of the *human* nobility of this movement.

How infinitely *profound* then is "Absolute Criticism", which, in face of these intellectual and practical facts, sees in a one-sided way only *one* aspect of the relationship, the continual foundering of the Spirit, and, vexed at this, seeks in addition an *adversary* of *the* "Spirit", which it finds in *the* "Mass"! In the end this great Critical *discovery* amounts to a *tautology*. According to Criticism, *the* Spirit has so far had a limit, an obstacle, in other words, an *adversary, because* it has had an *adversary*. Who, then, is the adversary of the *Spirit*? *Spiritlessness*. For the Mass is defined only as the "opposite" of the Spirit, as *spiritlessness* or, to take the more precise definitions of spiritlessness, as "indolence", "superficiali-

---

[a] In the German text: *des* Fortschritts *der* "Kritik" (the Progress of Criticism)— probably a misprint.—*Ed.*

ty", "self-complacency". What a fundamental superiority over the communist writers it is not to have traced spiritlessness, indolence, superficiality and self-complacency to their places of origin, but to have denounced them *morally* and *exposed* them as the opposite of the Spirit, of Progress! If these qualities are proclaimed qualities of *the* Mass, as of a *subject* still distinct from them, that distinction is nothing but a "Critical" *semblance* of distinction. Only in *appearance* has Absolute Criticism a *definite* concrete subject besides the abstract qualities of spiritlessness, indolence, etc., for "*the Mass*" in the Critical conception is *nothing* but those abstract qualities, another *word* for them, a *fantastic personification* of them.

The relation between "Spirit and Mass" has, however, also a *hidden* meaning which will be completely revealed in the course of the reasoning. We only indicate it here. That relation *discovered* by Herr Bruno is, in fact, nothing but a *Critically caricatured consummation of Hegel's conception of history*, which, in turn, is nothing but the *speculative* expression of the *Christian-Germanic* dogma of the antithesis between *Spirit* and *Matter*, between *God* and the *world*. This antithesis finds expression in history, in the human world itself in such a way that a few chosen *individuals* as the *active* Spirit are counterposed to the rest of mankind, as the *spiritless Mass*, as *Matter*.

Hegel's conception of history presupposes an *Abstract* or *Absolute Spirit* which develops in such a way that mankind is a mere *mass* that bears the Spirit with a varying degree of consciousness or unconsciousness. Within *empirical*, exoteric history, therefore, Hegel makes a speculative, esoteric history, develop. The history of mankind becomes the history of the *Abstract Spirit* of mankind, hence a *spirit far removed* from the real man.

Parallel with this doctrine of Hegel's there developed in France the theory of the *doctrinaires*[24] proclaiming the *sovereignty of reason* in opposition to the *sovereignty of the people*, in order to exclude the masses and rule *alone*. This was quite consistent. If the activity of *real* mankind is nothing but the activity of a *mass* of human individuals, then *abstract generality*, *Reason*, the *Spirit*, on the contrary, must have an abstract expression restricted to a few individuals. It then depends on the situation and imaginative power of each individual whether he will claim to be this representative of "*the* Spirit".

Already in *Hegel* the *Absolute Spirit* of history has its material in the *Mass* and finds its appropriate expression only in *philosophy*. *The* philosopher, however, is only the organ through which the maker of history, the Absolute Spirit, arrives at self-consciousness *retrospectively* after the movement has ended. The participation of the philosopher in history is reduced to this retrospective consciousness, for the real movement is accomplished by the Absolute Spirit *unconsciously.* Hence the philosopher appears on the scene *post festum.*[a]

Hegel is guilty of being doubly half-hearted: firstly in that, while declaring that philosophy is the mode of existence of the Absolute Spirit, he refuses to recognise the *actual philosophical individual* as the *Absolute* Spirit; secondly, in that he lets the Absolute Spirit as Absolute Spirit make history only *in appearance.* For since the Absolute Spirit becomes *conscious* of itself as the creative World Spirit only *post festum* in the philosopher, its making of history exists only in the consciousness, in the opinion and conception of the philosopher, i.e., only in the speculative imagination. Herr Bruno Bauer overcomes Hegel's half-heartedness.

Firstly, he proclaims *Criticism* to be the Absolute Spirit and *himself* to be *Criticism.* Just as the element of Criticism is banished from the Mass, so the element of the Mass is banished from Criticism. Therefore *Criticism* sees itself incarnate not in a *mass,* but exclusively in a *handful* of chosen men, in Herr *Bauer* and his disciples.

Herr Bauer furthermore overcomes Hegel's other half-heartedness. No longer, like the Hegelian Spirit, does he make history *post festum* and in imagination. He *consciously* plays the part of the *World Spirit* in opposition to the mass of the rest of mankind; he enters into a contemporary *dramatic* relation with that mass; he invents and executes history with a purpose and after mature reflection.

On the one side is the Mass as the passive, spiritless, unhistorical, *material* element of history. On the other is *the* Spirit, *Criticism,* Herr Bruno and Co. as the active element from which all *historical* action proceeds. The act of transforming society is reduced to the *cerebral activity* of Critical Criticism.

Indeed, the relation of Criticism, and hence of Criticism incarnate, Herr Bruno and Co., to the Mass is in truth the *only* historical relation of the present time. The whole of present-day history is reduced to the movement of these two sides against each other. All antitheses have been dissolved in this *Critical* antithesis.

Critical Criticism, which becomes *objective* to itself only in relation to its antithesis, to the Mass, to *stupidity,* is consequently obliged continually *to produce* this antithesis for itself, and Herren

---

[a] After the event.— *Ed.*

Faucher, Edgar and Szeliga have supplied sufficient proof of their virtuosity in their speciality, the *mass stupefaction* of persons and things.

Let us now accompany Absolute Criticism in its *campaigns* against the *Mass*.

b) The Jewish Question No. 1.
The Setting of the Questions

The "Spirit", contrary to the Mass, behaves from the outset in a *Critical* way by considering its own narrow-minded work, Bruno Bauer's *Die Judenfrage,* as absolute, and only the opponents of that work as sinners. In Reply No. 1[25] to attacks on that treatise, he does not show any inkling of its defects; on the contrary, he declares he has set forth the "true", "*general*" (!) significance of the Jewish question. In later replies we shall see him obliged to admit his "*oversights*".[a]

> "The reception my book has had is the *beginning* of the proof that the very ones who so far have advocated freedom, and still advocate it, must rise against the Spirit more than any others; the defence of my book which I am now going to undertake will supply further proof how thoughtless the *spokesmen of the Mass* are; they have God knows what a great opinion of themselves for supporting emancipation and the dogma of the '*rights of man*'."

On the occasion of a treatise by Absolute Criticism, the "Mass" must necessarily have *begun* to prove its antithesis to the Spirit; for it is its antithesis to Absolute Criticism that *determines* and *proves* its very *existence*.

The polemic of a few liberal and rationalist Jews against Herr Bruno's *Die Judenfrage* has naturally a Critical meaning quite different from that of the mass-type polemic of the liberals against philosophy and of the rationalists against Strauss. Incidentally, the originality of the above-quoted remark can be judged by the following passage from *Hegel*:

> "We can here note the particular form of bad conscience manifest in the kind of eloquence with which that shallowness" (of the liberals) "plumes itself, and first of all in the fact that it speaks most of *Spirit* where its speech has the *least spirit*, and uses the word *life*", etc., "where it is most dead and withered."[b]

As for the "*rights of man*", it has been proved to Herr Bruno ("On the Jewish Question", *Deutsch-Französische Jahrbücher*[c]) that it

---

[a] See pp. 95-96, 106-07 of this volume.—*Ed.*

[b] G.W.F. Hegel, *Grundlinien der Philosophie des Rechts. Vorrede.*—*Ed.*

[c] See present edition, Vol. 3, pp. 146-74.—*Ed.*

is "*he himself*", not the *spokesmen of the Mass*, who has misunderstood and dogmatically mishandled the essence of those rights. Compared to his discovery that the rights of man are not "*inborn*"—a discovery which has been made innumerable times in England during the last 40-odd years—Fourier's assertion that the right to fish, to hunt, etc., are inborn rights of men is one of genius.

We give only a few examples of Herr Bruno's fight against *Philippson, Hirsch* and others. Even such poor opponents as these are not disposed of by Absolute Criticism. It is by no means preposterous of Herr *Philippson*, as Absolute Criticism maintains, to say:

"Bauer conceives a peculiar kind of state ... a *philosophical ideal* of a *state*."

Herr Bruno, who confuses the state with humanity, the rights of man with man and political emancipation with human emancipation, was bound, if not to conceive, at least to imagine a peculiar kind of state, a philosophical ideal of a state.

"Instead of writing his laboured statement, the rhetorician" (Herr Hirsch) "would have done better to refute my proof that the *Christian state*, having as its vital principle a definite religion, cannot allow adherents of another particular religion ... complete equality with its own social estates."

Had the rhetorician *Hirsch* really refuted Herr Bruno's proof and shown, as is done in the *Deutsch-Französische Jahrbücher*, that the state of social estates and of exclusive Christianity is not only an incomplete state but an incomplete *Christian* state, Herr Bruno would have answered as he does to that refutation:

"Objections in this matter are meaningless." [26]

Herr Hirsch is quite correct when in answer to Herr Bruno's statement:

"By pressure against the mainsprings of history the Jews provoked counter-pressure",

he recalls:

"Then they must have counted for something in the making of history, and if Bauer himself asserts this, he has no right to assert, on the other hand, that they did not contribute anything to the making of modern times."

Herr Bruno answers:

"An eyesore is something too—does that mean it contributes to develop my eyesight?"

Something which has been an eyesore to me from birth, as the Jews have been to the Christian world, and which persists and develops with the eye is not an ordinary sore, but a wonderful one, one that really belongs to my eye and must even contribute to a highly original development of my eyesight. The Critical "*eyesore*" does not therefore hurt the rhetorician "*Hirsch*". Incidentally, the criticism quoted above revealed to Herr Bruno the significance of Jewry in "the *making* of modern times".

The theological mind of Absolute Criticism feels so offended by a *deputy of the Rhenish Landtag* stating that "the Jews are *queer* in their own Jewish way, not in our so-called Christian way", that it is still "calling him *to order* for using that argument".

Concerning the assertion of another deputy that "*civil* equality of the Jews can be implemented only where Jewry no longer exists", Herr Bruno comments:

> "Correct! That is correct if Criticism's other proposition, which I put forward in my treatise, is not omitted", namely the proposition that Christianity also must have ceased to exist.

We see that in its Reply No. 1 to the attacks upon *Die Judenfrage*, Absolute Criticism still regards the abolition of religion, atheism, as the condition for *civil* equality. In its first stage it has therefore not *yet* acquired any deeper insight into the essence of the state than into the "*oversights*" of its "*work*".

Absolute Criticism feels offended when one of its *intended* "latest" scientific discoveries is betrayed as something already generally recognised. A Rhenish deputy remarks:

> "No one has yet maintained that France and Belgium were distinguished by particular clarity in recognising principles in the organisation of their political affairs."

Absolute Criticism could have objected that that assertion transferred the present into the past by representing as traditional the now trivial view of the inadequacy of French political principles. Such a relevant objection would not be profitable for Absolute Criticism. On the contrary, it must assert the obsolete view to be that at present prevailing, and proclaim the now prevailing view a Critical mystery which *its* investigation still has to reveal to the Mass. Hence it must say:

> "It" (the antiquated prejudice) "has been asserted *by very many*" (of the Mass): "*but a thorough investigation* of history *will* provide the proof that *even* after the great work done by France to comprehend the principles, *much still remains to be achieved*."

That means that a thorough investigation of history will not itself "*achieve*" the comprehension of the principles. It will only *prove* in its thoroughness that "*much still remains to be achieved*". A great achievement, especially after the works of the Socialists! Nevertheless Herr Bruno *already* achieves *much* for the comprehension of the present social state of things by his remark:

"The *certainty* prevailing at present is *uncertainty*."

If Hegel says that the prevailing *Chinese* certainty is "Being", that the prevailing *Indian* certainty is "Nothing", etc., Absolute Criticism joins him in the "pure" way when it resolves the character of the present time in the logical category "*Uncertainty*", and all the purer since "Uncertainty", like "Being" and "Nothing", belongs to the first chapter of speculative logic, the chapter on "*Quality*".

We cannot leave No. 1 of *Die Judenfrage* without a general remark.

One of the chief pursuits of Absolute Criticism consists in first bringing all questions of the day into their *right setting*. For it does not answer the *real* questions — it substitutes *quite different* ones. As it makes everything, it must also first *make* the "questions of the day", make them *its own* questions, questions of Critical Criticism. If it were a question of the Code Napoléon, it would prove that it is *properly* a question of the *Pentateuch*.[27] Its *setting* of "questions of the day" is Critical *distortion* and *misrepresentation* of them. It thus distorted the "Jewish question", too, in such a way that it did not need to investigate *political emancipation*, which is the subject-matter of that question, but could instead confine itself to a criticism of the Jewish religion and a description of the Christian-Germanic state.

This method, too, like all Absolute Criticism's originalities, is the repetition of a *speculative* verbal trick. *Speculative* philosophy, namely, *Hegel's* philosophy, had to transpose all questions from the form of common sense to the form of speculative reason and convert the real question into a *speculative* one to be able to answer it. Having distorted *my* question on my lips and, like the catechism, put *its own* question into my mouth, it could, of course, like the catechism, have its ready answer to all my questions.

c) Hinrichs No. 1. Mysterious Hints on Politics, Socialism and Philosophy

"*Political!*" Absolute Criticism is literally horrified at the presence of this word in Professor *Hinrichs'* lectures.[28]

"Whoever has followed the development of modern times and knows history will *also* know that the political movements at present taking place have a significance *quite different*" (!) "from a *political* one: at their base" (at their base! ... now for basic wisdom) "they have a *social*" (!) "significance, which, as we know" (!) "is such" (!) "that *all* political interests appear *insignificant*" (!) "in comparison with it."

A few months before the Critical *Literatur-Zeitung* began to be published, there appeared, *as we know* (!), Herr Bruno's fantastic political treatise: *Staat, Religion und Parthei*!

If *political* movements *have social significance,* how can political interests appear *"insignificant"* in comparison with their own social significance?

"Herr Hinrichs does not know his way about either in his own house or anywhere else in the world.... He could not be at home anywhere *because* ... *because* Criticism, which in the last four years has begun and carried on its *by no means* 'political' but 'social'" (!) "work, has remained *completely*" (!) "unknown to him."

Criticism, which according to the opinion of the Mass carried on "by no means *political*" but "in *all* respects *theological*" work, is still content with the *word* "*social*", even now when it has uttered this *word* for the first time, not just in the last four years, but since its literary birth.

Since socialist writings spread in Germany the recognition that *all* human aspirations and actions without exception have *social* significance, Herr Bruno can call his theological works *social* too. But what a *Critical* demand it is that Professor Hinrichs should have derived socialism from an *acquaintance* with *Bauer's* works, considering that all Bruno Bauer's works published up to the appearance of Hinrichs' lectures, when they do draw practical conclusions, draw *political* ones! It was impossible, un-Critically speaking, for Professor Hinrichs to supplement Herr Bruno's published works with his as yet unpublished ones. From the Critical point of view, the Mass is, of course, obliged to interpret all Absolute Criticism's mass-type "movements", as well as "political" ones, from the angle of the future and of Absolute Progress! But in order that Herr Hinrichs, after becoming acquainted with the *Literatur-Zeitung,* may never again forget the word "*social*" or fail to recognise the "*social*" character of *Criticism, Criticism* prohibits the word "*political*" for the third time before the whole world and solemnly repeats the word "*social*" for the third time.

"If the *true* tendency of modern history is considered it is *no longer a question of political, but*—but of *social* significance", etc.

Just as Professor Hinrichs is the scapegoat for the former "political" movements, so is he also for the "*Hegelian*" movements and expressions which Absolute Criticism used intentionally up to the publication of the *Literatur-Zeitung,* and continues to use unintentionally in it.

Once "*real Hegelian*" and twice "*Hegelian philosopher*" are thrown in Hinrichs' face as catchwords. Herr Bruno even "*hopes*" that the "banal expressions so tiresomely circulated in all the books of the *Hegelian* school" (in particular in his own books) will, *in view of* their great *"exhaustion"* as seen in Professor Hinrichs' lectures, soon reach the end of their journey. From the *"exhaustion" of Professor Hinrichs,* Herr Bruno hopes for the dissolution of *Hegel's philosophy* and thereby *his own redemption* from it.

Thus in its *first campaign* Absolute Criticism overthrows its own long-worshipped gods, *"Politics"* and *"Philosophy",* declaring them idols of Professor Hinrichs.

Glorious first campaign!

2) ABSOLUTE CRITICISM'S SECOND CAMPAIGN

a) Hinrichs No. 2. "Criticism" and "Feuerbach". Condemnation of Philosophy

As the result of its first campaign, *Absolute Criticism* can regard *"philosophy"* as having been dealt with and term it outright an ally of the *"Mass".*

"*Philosophers* were predestined to fulfil the heart's desires of the '*Mass*'". For "the Mass *wants* simple concepts, in order to have nothing to do with the thing itself, shibboleths, so as to have finished with everything from the start, phrases by which *Criticism* can be done away with."[29]

And "philosophy" fulfils this longing of the "Mass"!

Dizzy after its victories, Absolute Criticism breaks out in *Pythian* frenzy against philosophy. *Feuerbach's Philosophie der Zukunft*[a] is the concealed cauldron[b] whose fumes inspire the frenzy of Absolute Criticism's victory-intoxicated head. It read Feuerbach's work in March. The fruit of that reading, and at the same time the criterion of the earnestness with which it was undertaken, is Article No. 2 against Professor Hinrichs.

In this article Absolute Criticism, which has never freed itself from the cage of the Hegelian way of viewing things, storms at the iron bars and walls of its prison. The "simple concept", the terminology, the whole mode of thought of philosophy, indeed, the whole of philosophy, is rejected with disgust. In its place we suddenly find the *"real wealth of human relations",* the *"immense content of history",* the *"significance of man",* etc. *"The mystery of the system"* is declared *"revealed".*

---

[a] L. Feuerbach, *Grundsätze der Philosophie der Zukunft.—Ed.*
[b] Engels here makes a pun on *"Feuerbach"* (literally stream of fire) and '*Feuerkessel*' (boiler).—*Ed.*

But who, then, revealed the mystery of the "system"? *Feuerbach*. Who annihilated the dialectics of concepts, the war of the gods that was known to the philosophers alone? *Feuerbach*. Who substituted for the old lumber and for "infinite self-consciousness" if not, indeed, *"the significance of man"* — as though man had another significance than that of being man! — at any rate *"Man"*? *Feuerbach*, and only *Feuerbach*. And he did more. Long ago he did away with the very categories with which *"Criticism"* now operates — the "real wealth of human relations, the immense content of history, the struggle of history, the fight of the Mass against the Spirit", etc., etc.

Once man is recognised as the essence, the basis of all human activity and situations, only *"Criticism"* can invent *new categories* and transform *man* himself into a category and into the principle of a whole series of categories, as it is doing now. It is true that in so doing it takes the only road to salvation that has remained for frightened and persecuted *theological* inhumanity. *History* does *nothing*, it "possesses *no* immense wealth", it "wages *no* battles". It is *man*, real, living man who does all that, who possesses and fights; "history" is not, as it were, a person apart, using man as a means to achieve *its own* aims; history is *nothing but* the activity of man pursuing his aims. If *Absolute* Criticism, after *Feuerbach's* brilliant expositions, still dares to reproduce all the old trash in a new form, at the same time abusing it as *"mass-type"* trash — which it has all the less right to do as it never stirred a finger to dissolve philosophy — that fact alone is sufficient to bring the *"mystery"* of *Criticism* to light and to assess the Critical naivety with which it says the following to Professor Hinrichs, whose *"exhaustion"* once did it such a great service:

"The *damage* is to those who have not gone through any development and therefore *could not alter themselves even if they wished to,* and at most to the *new* principle — but no! The new *cannot* be made *into a phrase, separate turns of speech cannot be borrowed from it."*

Absolute Criticism prides itself that, in contrast to Professor Hinrichs, it has solved *"the mystery of the faculty sciences"*. Has it then solved the "mystery" of philosophy, jurisprudence, politics, medicine, political economy and so forth? Not at all! It has — be it noted! — shown in *Die gute Sache der Freiheit* that science as a source of livelihood and free science, freedom of teaching and faculty statutes, contradict each other.

If "Absolute Criticism" were honest it would have admitted where its pretended illumination on the "Mystery of Philosophy" comes from. It is a good thing all the same that it does not put into *Feuerbach*'s mouth such nonsense as the misunderstood and distorted propositions that it borrowed from him, as it has done with other people. By the way, it is characteristic of "Absolute Criticism's" *theological* viewpoint that, whereas the German philistines are now beginning to understand *Feuerbach* and to adopt his conclusions, it is unable to grasp a single sentence of his correctly or to use it properly.

Criticism achieves a real advance over its feats of the first campaign when it "defines" the struggle of "*the Mass*" against the "*Spirit*" as "*the aim*" of all previous history, when it declares that "*the Mass*" is the "*pure nothing*" of "misery"; when it calls the Mass purely and simply "*Matter*" and contrasts "*the Spirit*" as truth to "Matter". Is not Absolute Criticism therefore *genuinely Christian-Germanic?* After the old antithesis between spiritualism and materialism has been fought out on all sides and overcome once for all by *Feuerbach*, "*Criticism*" again makes a basic dogma of it in its most loathsome form and gives the victory to the "*Christian-Germanic spirit*".

Finally, it must be considered as a development of Criticism's mystery concealed in its first campaign when it now identifies the antithesis between *Spirit* and *Mass* with the antithesis between "*Criticism*" and the Mass. Later it will go on to identify *itself* with "*Criticism*" and therefore to represent itself as "*the Spirit*", the Absolute and Infinite, and the Mass, on the other hand, as finite, coarse, brutal, dead and inorganic—for that is what "*Criticism*" understands by matter.

How immense is the wealth of history that is exhausted in the relationship of humanity to *Herr Bauer!*

b) The Jewish Question No. 2
Critical Discoveries on Socialism, Jurisprudence and Politics (Nationality)

To the material, mass-type Jews is preached the *Christian* doctrine of *freedom of the Spirit, freedom in theory,* that *spiritualistic* freedom which *imagines* itself to be free even in chains, and whose soul is satisfied with "*the idea*" and only embarrassed by any mass-type existence.

"The Jews are *emancipated* to the extent they have now reached in *theory*, they are *free* to the extent that they *wish to be free*." [30]

From this proposition one can immediately measure the Critical gap which separates *mass-type*, profane communism and socialism from *absolute* socialism. The first proposition of profane socialism rejects emancipation *in mere theory* as an illusion and for *real* freedom it demands besides the idealistic *"will"* very tangible, very material conditions. How low *"the* Mass" is in comparison with holy Criticism, the Mass which considers material, practical up-heavals necessary even to win the time and means required merely to occupy itself with *"theory"*!

Let us leave purely spiritual socialism an instant for *politics!*

Herr *Riesser* maintains against Bruno Bauer that *his* state (i.e., the *Critical* state) must exclude "Jews" and "Christians". Herr Riesser is right. Since Herr Bauer confuses *political* emancipation with *human* emancipation, since the state can react to antagonistic elements — and Christianity and Judaism are described as treason-able elements in *Die Judenfrage* — only by forcible exclusion of the *persons* representing them (as the Terror, for instance, wished to do away with hoarding by guillotining the hoarders [31]), Herr Bauer must have both Jews and Christians hanged in his "Critical state". Having confused political emancipation with human emancipation, he had to be consistent and confuse the *political means* of emancipation with the *human means.* But as soon as Absolute Criticism is told the *definite* meaning of its deductions, it gives the answer that *Schelling* once gave to all his opponents who substi-tuted *real* thoughts for his phrases:

> *"Criticism's* opponents are its opponents because they not only measure it with their *dogmatic* yardstick but regard Criticism itself as *dogmatic;* they oppose Criticism because it does not recognise their dogmatic distinctions, definitions and evasions."

It is, of course, to adopt a dogmatic attitude to Absolute Criticism, as also to Herr *Schelling,* if one assumes it to have *definite,* real meaning, thoughts and views. In order to be accom-modating and to prove to Herr Riesser its humanity, *"Criticism",* however, decides to resort to dogmatic distinctions, definitions and especially to *"evasions".*

Thus we read:

> "Had I in that work" (*Die Judenfrage*) "had the *will* or the *right* to go *beyond*· criticism, I *ought*" (!) "to *have spoken*" (!) "not of the *state,* but of *'society',* which excludes no one but from which only those exclude themselves who not wish to take part in its development."

Here Absolute Criticism makes a *dogmatic distinction* between what it ought to have done, if it had not done the contrary, and what it actually did. It explains the narrowness of its work *Die Judenfrage* by the *"dogmatic evasions"* of having the *will* and the *right* which prohibited it from going "*beyond criticism*". What? "*Criticism*" should go *beyond* "*criticism*"? This quite *mass-type* notion occurs to Absolute Criticism because of the dogmatic necessity for, on the one hand, asserting its conception of the Jewish question as absolute, as "*Criticism*", and on the other hand, admitting the possibility of a more comprehensive conception.

The *mystery* of its "*not having the will*" and "*not having the right*" will later be revealed as the Critical *dogma* according to which all apparent limitations of "Criticism" are nothing but necessary *adaptations* to the powers of comprehension of the Mass.

It had not the *will!* It *had* not the *right* to go beyond its narrow conception of the Jewish question! But what would it have done *had* it *had* the *will* or the *right?* — It would have given a *dogmatic definition.* It would have spoken of "*society*" instead of the "*state*", that is to say, it would not have studied the *real* relation of Jewry to *present-day civil* society! It would have given a *dogmatic definition* of "*society*" as distinct from the "*state*", in the sense that if the *state* excludes, on the other hand *they exclude* themselves from society who do not wish to take part in its development!

Society behaves just as exclusively as the state, only in a more polite form: it does not throw you out, but it makes it so uncomfortable for you that you go out of your own will.

Basically, the state does not behave otherwise, for it does not exclude anybody who complies with all *its* demands and orders and *its* development. In its *perfection* it even closes its eyes and declares *real* contradictions to be *non-political* contradictions which do not disturb it. Besides, Absolute Criticism itself has argued that the state excludes Jews because and in so far as the Jews exclude the state and hence exclude *themselves* from the state. If this reciprocal relationship has a more polite, a more hypocritical, a more insidious form in *Critical* "society", this only proves that "*Critical*" "*society*" is more hypocritical and less developed.

Let us follow Absolute Criticism deeper in its "dogmatic distinctions" and "definitions", and, in particular, in its "*evasions*".

Herr Riesser, for example, demands of the critic "that he *distinguish* what belongs to the domain of law" from "what is beyond its sphere".

The Critic is indignant at the impertinence of this *juridical* demand.

"So far, *however*," he retorts, "both feeling and conscience have interfered in law, always supplemented it, and because of its character, based on its *dogmatic form*" (not, therefore, on its dogmatic *essence?*), "have always had to supplement it."

The Critic forgets only that *law*, on the other hand, *distinguishes itself* quite explicitly from "feeling and conscience", that this distinction is based on the one-sided *essence* of *law* as well as on its dogmatic *form*, and is even one of the *main dogmas* of law; that, finally, the practical implementation of that distinction is just as much the peak of the *development of law* as the separation of religion from all profane content makes it *abstract, absolute* religion. The fact that "feeling and conscience" interfere in law is sufficient reason for the "Critic" to speak of feeling and conscience when it is a matter of *law*, and of *theological* dogmatism when it is a matter of *juridical* dogmatism.

The "definitions and distinctions of Absolute Criticism" have prepared us sufficiently to hear its latest *"discoveries"* on *"society"* and *"law"*.

"The world form that *Criticism* is preparing, and the *thought* of which it is *even only* just preparing, is not a *merely legal* form but" (collect yourself, reader) "a *social* one, about which *at least* this much" (this little?) "*can* be said: whoever has not made his contribution to its development and does not live with his conscience and feeling in it, cannot feel at home in it or take part in its history."

The world form that *"Criticism"* is preparing is defined as *not merely* legal, *but* social. This definition can be interpreted in two ways. The sentence quoted may be taken as *"not legal but social"* or as "not merely legal, but *also* social". Let us consider its content according to both readings, beginning with the first. Earlier, Absolute Criticism defined the new "world form" distinct from the *"state"* as "society". Now it defines the noun *"society"* by the adjective *"social"*. If Herr Hinrichs was three times given the *word* *"social"* in contrast to his *"political"*, Herr Riesser is now given *social society* in contrast to his *"legal"* society. If the *Critical* explanations for Herr Hinrichs reduced themselves to the formula "social" + "social" + "social" = 3a, Absolute Criticism in its second campaign passes from *addition* to *multiplication* and Herr Riesser is referred to society multiplied by itself, society to the *second* power, social society = a^2. In order to complete its deductions on society, all that now remains for Absolute Criticism to do is to go on to fractions, to extract the *square root* of society, and so forth.

If, on the other hand, we take the second reading: the *"not merely* legal, *but also* social" world form, this hybrid world form is nothing but the *world form* existing *today*, the world form of *present-day society*. It is a great, a meritorious *Critical miracle* that *"Criticism"* in its pre-world thinking is only just *preparing* the *future* existence of the world form which *exists today*. But however

matters stand with "not merely legal but social society", *Criticism*
can for the time being say no more about it than "*fabula docet*",[a]
the *moral* application. Those who do not live in that society with
their feeling and their conscience will "not *feel* at home" in it. In
the end, no one will live in that society except "pure feeling"
and "pure conscience", that is, "the Spirit", "*Criticism*" and its
supporters. The *Mass* will be excluded from it in one way or
another so that "mass-type society" will exist outside "social
society".

In a word, this society is nothing but the *Critical heaven* from
which the real world is excluded as being the *un-Critical hell*. In its
pure thinking, Absolute Criticism is preparing this transfigured
world form of the contradiction between "*Mass*" and "*Spirit*".

Of the same *Critical* depth as these explanations on "*society*" are
the explanations Herr Riesser is given on the destiny of *nations*.

The Jews' desire for emancipation and the desire of the
Christian states to "classify" the Jews in "their government
scheme" — as though the Jews had not long ago been classified in
the Christian government scheme! — lead Absolute Criticism to
prophecies on the *decay of nationalities*. See by what a complicated
detour Absolute Criticism arrives at the present historical movement — namely, by the *detour of theology*. The following illuminat-
ing oracle shows us what great results Criticism achieves in this
way:

"The *future* of all nationalities— is — very— obscure!"

But let the future of nationalities be as obscure as it may be, for
Criticism's sake. The one essential thing is *clear*: the *future* is the
work of Criticism.

"*Destiny*," it exclaims, "may decide as it will: we now know that it is *our work*."

As God leaves *his creation,* man, *his own will,* so *Criticism* leaves
destiny, which is *its creation,* its *own will. Criticism,* of which destiny
is the work, is, like God, *almighty.* Even the "resistance" which it
"*finds*" outside itself is its own work. "*Criticism makes* its adver-
saries." The "*mass indignation*" against it is therefore "dangerous"
only for "the Mass" itself.

But if Criticism, like God, is *almighty,* it is also, like God, *all-wise*
and is capable of combining its almightiness with the *freedom,* the
will and the *natural determination* of human individuals.

---

[a] The fable teaches.— *Ed.*

"It would not be the *epoch-making* force if it did not have the effect of *making each one* what he *wills* to be and showing each one irrevocably the standpoint *corresponding to his nature* and *his will.*"

Leibniz could not have given a happier presentation of the pre-established harmony between the almightiness of God and the freedom and natural determination of man.

If *"Criticism"* seems to clash with psychology by *not distinguishing* between the *will* to be something and the *ability* to be something, it must be borne in mind that it has decisive grounds to declare this *"distinction"* *"dogmatic"*.

Let us steel ourselves for the third campaign! Let us recall once more that *"Criticism makes* its adversary"! But how could it make its adversary, the *"phrase"*, if it were not a phrase-monger?

3) ABSOLUTE CRITICISM'S THIRD CAMPAIGN

a) Absolute Criticism's Self-Apology.
Its "Political" Past

Absolute Criticism begins its third campaign against the *"Mass"* with the question:

"What is now the object of criticism?" [32]

In the same number of the *Literatur-Zeitung* we find the information:

"Criticism wishes *nothing* but to know *things."*

According to this, all things are the *object* of Criticism. It would be senseless to inquire about some particular, definite object peculiar to Criticism. The contradiction is easily resolved when one remembers that all things "merge" into Critical things and all Critical things into *the Mass*, as the *"Object"* of *"Absolute Criticism"*.

First of all, Herr Bruno describes his *infinite pity* for the *"Mass."* He makes *"the gap* that separates him from the *crowd"* an object of *"persevering study."* He wants *"to find out the significance of that gap for the future"* (this is what above was called knowing *"all"* things) and at the same time *"to abolish it"*. In truth he therefore already knows the *significance* of that gap. It consists in being *abolished* by him.

As each man's self is nearest to him, *"Criticism"* first sets about abolishing its *own mass nature*, like the Christian ascetics who begin the campaign of the spirit against the flesh with the mortification of their *own* flesh. The *"flesh"* of Absolute Criticism is its *really massive* literary *past*, amounting to 20-30 volumes. Herr Bauer must therefore free the literary biography of *"Criticism"* — which coincides exactly with his own literary biography — from its *mass-like appearance*; he must retrospectively *improve* and *explain* it and by this *apologetic* commentary *"place its earlier works in safety"*.

He begins by explaining by a double cause the error of the *Mass*, which until the end of the *Deutsche Jahrbücher* and the *Rheinische Zeitung*[33] regarded Herr Bauer as one of *its* supporters. Firstly the mistake was made of regarding the literary movement as *not "purely literary"*. At the same time the opposite mistake was made, that of regarding the literary movement as "a merely" or "purely" *literary* movement. There is no doubt that the "Mass" was mistaken in any case, if only because it made two mutually incompatible errors *at the same time*.

Absolute Criticism takes this opportunity of exclaiming to those who ridiculed the "German nation" as a *"blue stocking"*:

"Name even a single historical epoch which was not authoritatively *outlined beforehand by the 'pen'* and had not to allow itself to be shattered by a stroke of the pen."

In his Critical naivety Herr Bruno separates *"the pen"* from the *subject who writes*, and the subject who writes as "abstract *writer*" from the living *historical man* who wrote. This allows him to go into ecstasy over the *wonder-working* power of the *"pen"*. He might just as well have demanded to be told of a historical movement which was not outlined beforehand by "poultry" or the "goose girl".

Later we shall be told by the same Herr Bruno that so far not one historical epoch, not a single one, has become known. How could the *"pen"*, which so far has been unable to *outline "any single"* historical epoch *after* the event, have been able to *outline them all beforehand*?

Nevertheless, Herr Bruno proves the correctness of his view by *deeds*, by himself *"outlining beforehand"* his own *"past"* with *apologetic "strokes of the pen"*.

Criticism, which was involved on all sides not only in the *general* limitation of the world and of the epoch, but in quite particular and personal limitations, and which nevertheless assures us that it has been *"absolute, perfect and pure"* Criticism in all its works for as long as man can think, has only *accommodated* itself to the *prejudices* and *power of comprehension* of the Mass, as God is wont to do in his revelations to man.

"It was bound to come," Absolute Criticism informs us, "to a breach of *Theory* with its *seeming ally*."

But because *Criticism,* here called *Theory* for a change, comes to *nothing,* but everything, on the contrary, comes from it; because it develops not inside but *outside* the world, and has predestined everything in its divine immutable consciousness, the *breach* with its former ally was a "*new* turn" only in *appearance,* only for others, not in itself and not for *Criticism* itself.

"But this turn '*properly speaking*' was not even new. *Theory* had continually worked on *criticism of itself*" (we know how much effort has been expended on it to force it to criticise itself); "it had never flattered the Mass" (but itself all the more); "it had always *taken care* not to get itself ensnared in the premises of its opponent."

"The Christian theologian must tread *cautiously.*" (Bruno Bauer, *Das entdeckte Christenthum,* p. 99.) How did it happen that "cautious" Criticism nevertheless did get ensnared and did not already at that time express its "proper" meaning clearly and audibly? Why did it not speak out bluntly? Why did it let the illusion of its brotherhood with the Mass persist?

"'Why hast thou done this to me?' said Pharaoh to Abraham as he restored to him Sarah his wife. 'Why didst thou say she was thy sister?'" (*Das entdeckte Christenthum* by Bruno Bauer, p. 100.)

"'Away with reason and language!' says the theologian, 'for otherwise Abraham would be a liar. It would be a mortal insult to Revelation!'" (loc. cit.)

"Away with reason and language!" says the Critic. For had Herr Bauer *really* and not just apparently been ensnared with the Mass, Absolute Criticism would not be absolute in its revelations, it would be mortally insulted.

"It is *only,*" Absolute Criticism continues, "that its" (Absolute Criticism's) "efforts *had not been noticed,* and *there was moreover* a stage of Criticism when it was *forced sincerely* to consider its opponent's premises and to take them seriously for an instant; a stage, in short, when it was *not yet fully* capable of taking away from the Mass the latter's conviction that it had the same cause and the same interest as Criticism."

"*Criticism*'s efforts had just not been noticed; therefore the Mass was to blame. On the other hand, Criticism admits that its efforts *could* not be noticed because it itself was not yet "*capable*" *of making* them *noticeable.* Criticism *therefore appears* to be to blame.

God help us! *Criticism* was "forced"—violence was used against it—"sincerely to consider its opponent's premises and to take them seriously for an instant". A fine sincerity, a truly theological sincerity, which does not really take a thing seriously but only "*takes it* seriously *for an instant*"; which has always, therefore *every instant,* been careful not to get itself ensnared in its opponent's premises, and nevertheless, "for *an instant*" "sincerely" takes these very premises into consideration. Its "sincerity" is still greater in the closing part of the sentence. It was in the same instant when

Criticism "sincerely took into consideration the premises of the Mass" that it "was not yet fully *capable*" of destroying the illusion about the unity of *its* cause and the cause of the *Mass*. It was *not yet capable,* but it already had the *will* and the *thought* of it. It *could* not yet *outwardly* break with the Mass but the break was already *complete inside it,* in its *mind*—complete in the same instant when it *sincerely* sympathised with the Mass!

In its involvement with the prejudices of the Mass, Criticism was not *really* involved in *them*; on the contrary, it was, *properly speaking,* free from its own limitation and was only *"not yet completely* capable" of informing the Mass of this. Hence all the limitation of "Criticism" was pure *appearance*; an appearance which without the limitation of the Mass would have been superfluous and would therefore not have existed at all. It is therefore *again* the Mass that is to blame.

Insofar as this *appearance,* however, was supported by "the inability", "the impotence" of Criticism to express its thought, Criticism itself was *imperfect.* This it admits in its own way, which is as sincere as it is apologetic.

> "In spite of having subjected liberalism itself to devastating criticism, it" (Criticism) "could *still* be regarded as a peculiar kind of liberalism, *perhaps* as its extreme form; *in spite of* its true and decisive arguments having gone beyond politics, it *nevertheless* was *still* bound to give an *appearance* of *engaging in politics,* and this *incomplete appearance* won it most of the friends mentioned above."

Criticism won its friends through its *incomplete appearance* of engaging in politics. Had it *completely appeared* to engage in politics, it would inevitably have lost its *political* friends. In its *apologetic anxiety* to wash itself free of all sin, it accuses the *false appearance* of having been an *incomplete false appearance,* not a *complete false one.* By substituting one appearance for the other, "Criticism" can console itself with the thought that if it had the "complete appearance" of wishing to engage in politics, it does not have, on the other hand, even the "incomplete appearance" of anywhere or at any time having dissolved politics.

Not completely satisfied with the "incomplete appearance", Absolute Criticism again asks itself:

> "How did it happen that *Criticism* at that time became involved in 'mass-linked, political' interests; that *it—even*" (!)—"*was obliged*" (!)—"*to engage in politics*" (!).

Bauer the *theologian* takes it *as a matter of course* that *Criticism* had to indulge endlessly in *speculative theology* for he, "Criticism", is indeed a theologian *ex professo.* But to *engage in politics*? That must be motivated by very special, political, personal circumstances!

Why, then, had "*Criticism*" to *engage* even in *politics*? "It was accused — *that is the answer to the question.*" At least the "mystery" of "*Bauer's politics*" is thereby disclosed; at least the *appearance*, which in Bruno Bauer's *Die gute Sache der Freiheit* und *meine eigene Sache* links *its* "*own* cause" to the *mass-linked* "cause of freedom" by means of an "*and*", cannot be called *non-political.* But if Criticism pursued not its "*own cause*" in the *interest of politics*, but *politics* in the *interest of its own cause*, it must be admitted that not Criticism was taken in by politics, but politics by Criticism.

So Bruno Bauer was to be dismissed from his chair of theology[34]: he was *accused*; "*Criticism*" had to engage in politics, that is to say, to *conduct* "*its*", i.e., Bruno Bauer's, suit. Herr Bauer did not conduct Criticism's suit, "*Criticism*" conducted Herr Bauer's suit. Why did "Criticism" *have* to conduct its suit?

"In order to justify itself!" *It may well be*; only "*Criticism*" is far from limiting itself to such a personal, vulgar reason. It may well be; but *not solely* for that reason, "*but mainly* in order to bring out the contradictions of its opponents", and, Criticism could add, in order to have bound together in a single *book* old essays against various theologians — see among other things the wordy bickering with *Planck*,[35] that family affair between "Bauer-theology" and Strauss-theology.

Having got a load off its heart by admitting the real interest of its "*politics*", Absolute Criticism remembers its "*suit*" and again chews the old *Hegelian* cud (see the struggle between Enlightenment and faith[36] in the *Phänomenologie*, see *the whole of* the *Phänomenologie*) that "the old which resists the new is no longer really the old", the cud which it has already chewed over at length in *Die gute Sache der Freiheit.* Critical Criticism is a ruminant animal. It keeps on warming up a few crumbs dropped by Hegel, like the above-quoted proposition about the "old" and the "new", or again that about the "development of the extreme out of its opposite extreme", and the like, without ever feeling the need to deal with "*speculative dialectic*" in any other way than by the exhaustion of Professor Hinrichs. Hegel, on the contrary, it continually transcends "Critically" by repeating him. For example:

"Criticism, by appearing and giving the investigation a new form, i.e., giving it *the* form which is *no longer* susceptible of being *transformed* into an *external limitation,*" etc.

When I *transform* something I make it something essentially different. Since every form is also an "*external limitation*", *no* form is "susceptible" of being *transformed* into an "external limitation"

any more than an apple of being "transformed" into an apple.
Admittedly, the form which "Criticism" gives to the investigation
is not susceptible of being transformed into any "external limitation" for quite *another* reason. Beyond every "external limitation"
it is blurred into an ash-grey, dark-blue vapour of nonsense.

"It" (the struggle between the old and the new) "would, *however, be quite
impossible even then*" (namely at the moment when Criticism "gives" the investigation "the new form") "if the old were to deal with the question of compatibility or
incompatibility ... *theoretically.*"

But why does not the old deal with this question theoretically?
Because "this, *however*, is *least of all* possible for it in the beginning,
since at *the moment of surprise*" (i.e., in the beginning) it "knows
neither itself nor the new", i.e., it deals *theoretically* neither with
itself nor with the new. It would be quite impossible if "impossibility", unfortunately, were not impossible!

When *the* "Critic" from the theological faculty further "admits
that he erred *intentionally,* that he committed the mistake deliberately and after mature reflection" (all that Criticism has experienced, learnt, and done *is transformed* for it into a free, pure and
intentional product of its reflection) this confession of the Critic
has only an "incomplete appearance" of truth. Since the *Kritik der
Synoptiker*[a] has a completely *theological* foundation, since it is
through and through *theological* criticism, Herr Bauer, university
lecturer in theology, could write and teach it "without mistake or
error". The mistake and error were rather on the part of the
theological faculties, which did not realise how strictly Herr Bauer
had kept his promise, the promise he gave in *Kritik der Synoptiker,*
Bd. I, Foreword, p. xxiii.

"If the *negation* may appear still too sharp and far-reaching in this first volume
too, we must remember that the truly *positive* can be born only if the negation has
been serious and general.... *In the end* it will be seen that only the most devastating
criticism of the world can teach us the creative *power of Jesus* and of his *principle.*"

Herr Bauer intentionally separates the Lord "Jesus" and his
"principle" in order to free the *positive* meaning of his promise
from all semblance of ambiguity. And Herr Bauer has really made
the "*creative*" power of the Lord Jesus and of his principle so
evident that his "*infinite self-consciousness*" and the "*Spirit*" are
nothing but *creations* of Christianity.

If Critical Criticism's dispute with the Bonn theological faculty
explained so well its "politics" at that time, why did Critical

---

[a] B. Bauer, *Kritik der evangelischen Geschichte der Synoptiker.—Ed.*

Criticism continue to engage in politics after the dispute had been settled? Listen to this:

> "At this point 'Criticism' *should have* either *come to a halt* or immediately *proceeded further* to examine the essence of politics and depict it as its adversary;—if only it had been possible for it to be able to come to a halt in the struggle at that time and if, on the *other* hand, there had not been a far too strict historical law that when a principle measures itself for the first time with its opposite it must let itself be repressed by it...."

What a delightful apologetic phrase! "Criticism *should have* come to a halt" if only it had been possible ... "to be able to come to a halt"! Who "*should*" come to a halt? And who should have done what "it would not have been possible ... to be able to do"? On the other hand! Criticism should have proceeded "if *only*, on the other hand, there had *not* been a far *too* strict historical law," etc. Historical laws are also "*far too strict*" with Absolute Criticism! If *only* they did *not* stand on the *opposite* side to Critical Criticism, how brilliantly the latter would proceed! But *à la guerre comme à la guerre*! In history, Critical Criticism must allow itself to be made a sorry "story" of!

> "If Criticism" (still Herr Bauer) "had to ... it will *at the same time* be *admitted* that it always felt *uncertain* when it gave in to demands of this" (political) "kind, and that as a result of these demands it came into contradiction with its *true elements*, a contradiction that had *already* found its *solution* in those *elements*."

Criticism was forced into political weaknesses by the all too strict laws of history, but—it entreats—*it will at the same time be admitted* that it was above those weaknesses, if not in reality, at least *in itself*. Firstly, it had overcome them, "*in feeling*", for "it always felt uncertain in its demands"; it felt *ill at ease* in politics, it could not make out what was the matter with it. More than that! It came into contradiction with its *true elements*. And finally the greatest thing of all! The contradiction with its true *elements* into which it came found its solution not in the course of Criticism's *development*, but "*had*", on the contrary, "*already*" found its solution in Criticism's true *elements* existing independently of the contradiction! These Critical elements can claim with pride: before Abraham was, we were. Before the opposite to us was produced by development, it lay yet *unborn* in our chaotic womb, dissolved, dead, ruined. But since Criticism's contradiction with its true elements "had *already* found its solution" in the true elements of Criticism, and since a *solved* contradiction is *not* a contradiction, it found itself, to be precise, in *no* contradiction with its true elements, in *no* contradiction with itself, and—the general aim of self-apology seems attained.

Absolute Criticism's self-apology has a whole *apologetical* dictionary at its disposal:

"not even properly speaking", "only not noticed", "there was besides", "not yet complete", "although—nevertheless", "not only—but mainly", "just as much, properly speaking, only", "Criticism should have if only it had been possible and if on the other hand", "*if* ... it will *at the same time* be admitted", "was it not natural, was it not inevitable", "neither ..." etc.

Not so very long ago Absolute Criticism said the following about apologetic phrases of this kind:

"'Although' and 'nevertheless', 'indeed' and 'but', a heavenly 'Nay', and an earthly 'Yea', are the main pillars of modern theology, the stilts on which it strides along, the artifice to which its whole wisdom is reduced, the phrase which recurs in all its phrases, its alpha and omega" (*Das entdeckte Christenthum,* p. 102).

b) The Jewish Question No. 3

"Absolute Criticism" does not stop at proving by its autobiography its own singular almightiness which "*properly speaking, first creates the old,* just as much as the *new*". It does not stop at writing *in person* the apology of its past. It now sets third persons, the rest of the secular world, the Absolute "Task", the "task which is *much more* important *now*", the *apologia* for Bauer's deeds and "works".

The *Deutsch-Französische Jahrbücher* published a criticism of Herr Bauer's *Die Judenfrage.*[a] His basic error, the confusion of "*political*" with "*human* emancipation", was revealed. True, the old Jewish question was not first brought into its "*correct setting*"; the "Jewish question" was rather dealt with and solved in the setting which recent developments have given to *old questions of the day*, and as a result of which the latter have become "questions" of the present instead of "questions" of the past.

Absolute Criticism's *third* campaign, it seems, is intended to reply to the *Deutsch-Französische Jahrbücher*. First of all, Absolute Criticism *admits*:

"In *Die Judenfrage* the same '*oversight*' was made—that of identifying the *human* with the *political* essence."

Criticism remarks:

"it would be too late to *reproach* criticism for the stand which it still maintained partially *two* years ago." "*The question is rather to explain* why *criticism* ... even had to engage in politics."

---

[a] K. Marx, *On the Jewish Question.* See present edition, Vol. 3.—*Ed.*

"*Two* years ago?" We must reckon according to the *absolute* chronology, from the *birth* of the Critical Redeemer of the world, Bauer's *Literatur-Zeitung*! The Critical world redeemer was born anno *1843.* In the same year the second, enlarged edition of *Die Judenfrage* was published. The "Critical" treatment of the "Jewish question" in *Einundzwanzig Bogen aus der Schweiz* appeared later in the same year, 1843 old style.[37] *After the end* of the *Deutsche Jahrbücher* and the *Rheinische Zeitung,* in the same momentous year 1843 old style, or anno 1 of the Critical era, appeared Herr Bauer's fantastic-political work *Staat, Religion und Parthei,* which exactly repeated his old errors on the "*political* essence". The apologist is forced to falsify *chronology.*

The "*explanation*" why Herr Bauer "*even had to*" engage in politics is a matter of general interest only under certain conditions. If the infallibility, purity and absoluteness of Critical Criticism are assumed as *basic dogma,* then, of course, the facts contradicting that dogma turn into riddles which are just as difficult, profound and mysterious as the apparently ungodly deeds of God are for theologians.

If, on the other hand, "*the Critic*" is considered as a finite individual, if he is not separated from the *limitations* of his time, one does not have to answer the question *why he* had to develop *even* within the world, because the *question* itself does not exist.

If, however, Absolute Criticism insists on its demand, one can offer to provide a little scholastic treatise dealing with the following "*questions of the times*":

"Why had the Virgin Mary's conception by the Holy Ghost to be proved by no other than Herr Bruno Bauer?" "Why had Herr Bauer to prove that the angel that appeared to Abraham was a *real* emanation of God, an emanation which, nevertheless, lacked the consistency necessary to *digest food*?" "Why had Herr Bauer to provide an apologia for the Prussian royal house and to raise the Prussian state to the rank of *absolute* state?" "Why had Herr Bauer, in his *Kritik der Synoptiker*, to substitute '*infinite self-consciousness*' for *man*?" "Why had Herr Bauer in his *Das entdeckte Christenthum* to repeat the *Christian theory of creation* in a Hegelian form?" "Why had Herr Bauer to demand of himself and others an '*explanation*' of the miracle that he was bound to be mistaken?"

While waiting for proofs of these necessities, which are just as "Critical" as they are "Absolute", let us listen once more to "*Criticism's*" apologetic evasions.

"The Jewish question ... had ... first to be brought into its *correct* setting, as a *religious* and *theological* and as a *political* question." "As to the treatment and solution of both these questions, *Criticism* is *neither religious nor political*."

The point is that the *Deutsch-Französische Jahrbücher* declares Bauer's treatment of the "Jewish question" to be *really* theological and *fantastic*-political.

First, "*Criticism*" replies to the "reproach" of *theological* limitation.

"The Jewish question *is* a *religious* question. The *Enlightenment* claimed to solve it by describing the *religious contradiction* as *insignificant* or even by denying it. *Criticism*, on the contrary, had to present it in its purity."

When we come to the *political* part of the Jewish question we shall see that in politics, too, Herr Bauer the theologian is not concerned with politics but with theology.

But when the *Deutsch-Französische Jahrbücher* attacked his treatment of the Jewish question as "*purely religious*", it was concerned especially with his article in *Einundzwanzig Bogen,* the title of which was:

"*Die Fähigkeit der heutigen Juden und Christen, frei zu werden*".[a]

This article has nothing to do with the old "Enlightenment". It contains Herr Bauer's *positive* view on the ability of the present-day Jews to be emancipated, that is, on the possibility of their emancipation.

"Criticism" says:

"The Jewish question is a *religious* question."

The question is: *What is* a *religious* question? and, in particular, *what is* a religious question today?

The *theologian* will judge by *appearances* and see a *religious* question in a *religious* question. But "Criticism" must remember the explanation it gave Professor *Hinrichs* that the *political* interests of the present time have *social* significance, that it is "*no longer* a question" of *political interests*.[b]

The *Deutsch-Französische Jahrbücher* with equal right said to Criticism: *Religious* questions of the day have at the present time a *social* significance. It is no longer a question of *religious* interests as *such*. Only the *theologian* can believe it is a question of religion as religion. Granted, the *Jahrbücher* committed the *error* of not stopping at the *word* "*social*". It characterised the *real* position of the Jews in civil society today. Once Jewry was stripped bare of the

---

[a] "The Ability of Present-Day Jews and Christians to Obtain Freedom."—*Ed.*
[b] See pp. 90-91 of this volume.—*Ed.*

religious shell and its empirical, worldly, practical kernel was revealed, the practical, *really social* way in which this kernel is to be abolished could be indicated. Herr Bauer was content with a "religious question" being a "religious question".

It was by no means denied, as Herr Bauer *makes out*, that the Jewish question is also a *religious* question. On the contrary, it was shown that Herr Bauer grasps *only the religious* essence of Jewry, but not the *secular, real basis* of that religious essence. He combats *religious consciousness* as if it were something independent. Herr Bauer therefore explains the *real* Jews by the *Jewish religion*, instead of explaining the mystery of the Jewish religion by the *real Jews*. Herr Bauer therefore understands the Jew only insofar as he is an immediate object of *theology* or a *theologian*.

Consequently Herr Bauer has no inkling that real *secular* Jewry, and hence *religious* Jewry *too*, is being continually produced by the *present-day civil life* and finds its final development in the *money system*. He could not have any inkling of this because he did not know Jewry as a part of the real world but only as a part of *his* world, *theology*; because he, a pious, godly man, considers not the active *everyday Jew* but the hypocritical *Jew of the Sabbath* to be the *real* Jew. For Herr Bauer, as a theologian of the *Christian faith*, the *world-historic* significance of Jewry had to cease the *moment* Christianity was *born*. Hence he had to repeat the old orthodox view that it has maintained itself *in spite* of history; and the old theological superstition that Jewry exists only as a *confirmation* of the divine curse, as a *tangible proof* of the Christian revelation had to recur with him in the *Critical-theological* form that it exists and has existed only as *crude religious doubt* about the supernatural origin of Christianity, i.e., as a *tangible proof* against Christian revelation.

On the other hand, it was proved that Jewry has maintained itself and developed *through* history, *in* and *with* history, and that this development is to be perceived not by the eye of the theologian, but only by the eye of the man of the world, because it is to be found, not in *religious theory*, but only in *commercial* and *industrial practice*. It was explained *why* practical Jewry attains its full development only in the fully developed *Christian* world, why indeed it is the fully developed *practice* of the *Christian world itself*. The existence of the *present-day* Jew was not explained by his religion — as though this religion were something apart, independently existing — but the tenacious survival of the Jewish religion was explained by practical features of civil society which are *fantastically* reflected in that religion. The emancipation of the Jews into human beings, or the human emancipation of Jewry, was therefore not conceived, as by Herr Bauer, as the special task of the Jews, but as a general practical task of the present-day world, which is *Jewish* to the core. It was proved that the task of abolishing the essence of Jewry is actually the task of abolishing the *Jewish character of civil society*, abolishing the inhumanity of the present-day practice of life, the most extreme expression of which is the *money system*.

Herr Bauer, as a *genuine*, although *Critical, theologian* or *theological* Critic, could not get beyond the *religious contradiction*. In the attitude of the Jews to the Christian world he could see *only* the attitude of the *Jewish religion* to the *Christian religion*. He even had to restore the religious contradiction in a *Critical way*—in the *antithesis* between the attitudes of the Jew and the Christian to *Critical* religion—*atheism*, the last stage of *theism*, the *negative* recognition of God. Finally, in his *theological fanaticism* he had to *restrict* the ability of the "present-day Jews and Christians", i.c., of the present-day world, "to obtain freedom" to their ability to grasp "the Criticism" of theology and apply it themselves. For the orthodox theologian the whole world is dissolved in "religion and theology". (He could just as well dissolve it in politics, political economy, etc., and call *theology* heavenly *political economy*, for example, since it is the theory of the production, distribution, exchange and consumption of "*spiritual wealth*" and of the treasures of heaven!) Similarly, for the radical, Critical theologian, the *ability* of the world to achieve freedom, is dissolved in the *single* abstract ability to criticise "religion and theology" as "religion and theology". The only struggle he knows is the struggle against the *religious* limitations of self-consciousness, whose Critical "*purity*" and "*infinity*" is just as much a theological limitation.

Herr Bauer, therefore, dealt with the *religious* and *theological* question in the *religious* and *theological* way, if only because he saw in the "religious" question of the time a "*purely religious*" question. His "*correct setting* of the question" set the question "correctly" only in respect of his "*own ability*"—to answer!

Let us now go on to the political part of the *Jewish question*.

The *Jews* (like the Christians) *are* fully *politically emancipated* in various states. Both Jews and Christians are far from being *humanly* emancipated. Hence there must be a *difference* between *political* and *human* emancipation. The essence of *political* emancipation, i.e., of the developed, modern state, must therefore be studied. On the other hand, states which cannot yet *politically* emancipate the Jews must be rated by comparison with the perfected political state and shown to be under-developed states.

That is the point of view from which the "*political* emancipation" of the Jews should have been dealt with and is dealt with in the *Deutsch-Französische Jahrbücher.*

Herr Bauer offers the following defence of "Criticism's" *Die Judenfrage.*

"The Jews were shown that they laboured under an illusion about *the system* from which they demanded freedom."

Herr Bauer did show that the illusion of *the German* Jews was to demand the right to partake in the political community life in a land where there was no political community and to demand *political rights* where only political privileges existed. On the other hand, Herr Bauer was shown that he himself, no less than the Jews, laboured under "illusions" about the "German political system". For he explained the position of the Jews in the German states as being due to the inability of "*the Christian state*" to emancipate the Jews politically. Flying in the face of the facts, he depicted the state of *privilege*, the *Christian-Germanic* state, as the Absolute Christian state. It was proved to him, on the contrary, that the politically perfected, modern state that knows no religious privileges is also the fully developed *Christian* state, and that therefore the fully developed Christian state, not only *can* emancipate the Jews but has emancipated them and by its very nature must emancipate them.

"The Jews are shown ... that they are under the greatest illusion about themselves when they think they are demanding *freedom* and the recognition of *free humanity*, whereas for them it is, and can be, only a question of a special *privilege.*"

Freedom! Recognition of free humanity! Special privilege! Edifying words by which to by-pass certain questions apologetically!

Freedom? It was a question of *political* freedom. Herr Bauer was shown that when the Jew demands freedom and nevertheless refuses to renounce his religion, he "*is engaging in politics*" and sets no condition that is contrary to *political* freedom. Herr Bauer was shown that it is by no means contrary to political emancipation to *divide* man into the non-religious *citizen* and the religious *private individual.* He was shown that just as the state emancipates itself from religion by emancipating itself from *state religion* and leaving religion to itself within civil society, so the individual emancipates himself *politically* from religion by regarding it no longer as a *public* matter but as a *private matter.* Finally, it was shown that the *terroristic* attitude of the French *Revolution* to *religion*, far from refuting this conception, bears it out.

Instead of studying the real attitude of the *modern* state to religion, Herr Bauer thought it necessary to imagine a *Critical* state, a state which is nothing but the *Critic of theology inflated into a state* in Herr Bauer's imagination. If Herr Bauer is caught up in *politics* he continually makes politics a prisoner of his faith, *Critical* faith. Insofar as he deals with the state he always makes out of it an *argument* against "*the* adversary", *un-Critical* religion and theology. The state acts as executor of *Critical-theological* cherished desires.

When Herr Bauer had first freed himself from *orthodox*, un-Critical *theology*, *political authority* took for him the place of *religious authority*. His faith in Jehovah changed into faith in the Prussian state. In Bruno Bauer's work *Die evangelische Landeskirche*,[a] not only the Prussian state, but, quite consistently, the Prussian royal house too, was made into an *absolute*. In reality Herr Bauer had no *political* interest in that state; its merit, in the eyes of "Criticism", was rather that it abolished dogmas by means of the *Unified* Church[38] and suppressed the dissenting sects with the help of the police.

The political movement that began in the year 1840 redeemed Herr Bauer from *his conservative politics* and raised him for a moment to *liberal* politics. But here again politics was in reality only a *pretext* for theology. In his work *Die gute Sache der Freiheit und meine eigene Angelegenheit*, the free state is the Critic of the theological faculty in Bonn and an argument against religion. In *Die Judenfrage* the contradiction between state and religion is the main interest, so that the criticism of political emancipation changes into a criticism of the Jewish religion. In his latest political work, *Staat, Religion und Parthei*, the most secret cherished desire of the Critic inflated into a state is at last expressed. *Religion* is *sacrificed* to *the state* or rather the state is only the *means* by which the opponent of "*Criticism*", un-Critical religion and theology, is done to death. Finally, after *Criticism* has been redeemed, if only apparently, from all politics by the socialist ideas, which have been spreading in Germany from 1843 onwards, in the same way as it was redeemed from its conservative politics by the political movement after 1840, it is finally able to proclaim its writings against *un-Critical* theology to be social and to indulge unhindered in its own *Critical* theology, the contrasting of Spirit and Mass, as the annunciation of the Critical Saviour and Redeemer of the world.

Let us return to our subject!

---

[a] [B. Bauer,] *Die evangelische Landeskirche Preussens und die Wissenschaft.—Ed.*

Recognition of free humanity? "Free humanity", recognition of which the Jews did not merely think they wanted, but really did want, is. the same "free humanity" which found *classic* recognition in the so-called universal *rights of man.* Herr Bauer himself explicitly treated the Jews' efforts for recognition of their free humanity as their efforts to obtain the universal *rights of man.*

In the *Deutsch-Französische Jahrbücher* it was demonstrated to Herr Bauer that this "free humanity" and the "recognition" of it are nothing but the recognition of the *egoistic civil individual* and of the *unrestrained* movement of the spiritual and material elements which are the content of his life situation, the content of *present-day* civil life; that the *rights of man* do not, therefore, free man from religion, but give him *freedom of religion*; that they do not free him from property, but procure for him *freedom of property*; that they do not free him from the filth of gain, but rather give him *freedom of gainful occupation.*

It was shown that the *recognition of the rights of man* by the *modern state* has no other meaning than the *recognition of slavery* by the *state of antiquity* had. In other words, just as the ancient state had slavery as its *natural basis,* the *modern state* has as its *natural basis* civil society and the *man* of civil society, i.e., the independent man linked with other men only by the ties of private interest and *unconscious* natural necessity, the *slave* of labour for gain and of his own as well as other men's *selfish* need. The modern state has recognised this its natural basis as such in the *universal rights of man.* It did not create it. As it was the product of civil society driven beyond the old political bonds by its own development, the modern state, for its part, now recognised the womb from which it sprang and its basis by the *declaration* of the *rights of man.* Hence, the *political* emancipation of the Jews and the granting to them of the *"rights of man"* is an act the two sides of which are mutually dependent. Herr *Riesser* correctly expresses the meaning of the Jews' desire for recognition of their free humanity when he demands, among other things, the freedom of movement, sojourn, travel, earning one's living, etc. These manifestations of *"free humanity"* are explicitly recognised as such in the French Declaration of the Rights of Man. The Jew has all the more right to the recognition of his "free humanity" as "free civil society" is of a thoroughly commercial and Jewish nature, and the Jew is a necessary member of it. The *Deutsch-Französische Jahrbücher* further demonstrated why the member of civil society is called, *par excellence,* "Man" and why the rights of man are called "inborn rights".

The only Critical thing *Criticism* could say about the rights of man was that they are *not* inborn but arose in the course of history. That much *Hegel* had already told us. Finally, to its assertion that both Jews and Christians, in order to grant or receive the universal rights of man, *must sacrifice the privilege of faith*—the Critical theologian supposes his *one* fixed idea at the basis of all things—there was specially counterposed the fact contained in all un-Critical declarations of the rights of man that the *right* to believe what one wishes, the right to practise any religion, is explicitly recognised as a *universal right of man*. Besides, "*Criticism*" should have known that Hébert's party in particular was defeated on the pretext that it attacked the rights of man by attacking *freedom of religion*,[39] and that similarly the rights of man were invoked later when freedom of worship was restored.[40]

"As far as *political* essence is concerned, *Criticism* followed its contradictions to the point where the *contradiction between theory and practice* had been most thoroughly elaborated during the past fifty years—to the *French representative system*, in which the freedom of theory is disavowed by practice and the freedom of practical life seeks in vain its expression in theory.

"Now that the basic illusion has been done away with, *the contradiction* proved in the *debates in the French Chamber*, the contradiction between *free theory* and the *practical validity of privileges*, between the legal validity of privileges and a *public system* in which the *egoism of the pure individual* tries to dominate the *exclusivity of the privileged*, should be conceived as a *general contradiction* in this sphere."

The contradiction that *Criticism* proved in the debates in the French Chamber was nothing but a contradiction of *constitutionalism*. Had Criticism grasped it as a *general* contradiction it would have grasped the general contradiction of constitutionalism. Had it gone still further than in its opinion it "should have" gone, had it, to be precise, gone as far as the *abolition* of this general contradiction, it would have proceeded correctly from constitutional *monarchy* to arrive at the *democratic representative state*, the perfected modern state. Far from having criticised the essence of political emancipation and proved its definite relation to the essence of man, it would have arrived only at the *fact* of political emancipation, at the fully developed modern state, that is to say, only at the point where the existence of the modern state conforms to its essence and where, therefore, not only the relative, but the absolute *imperfections*, those which constitute its very essence, can be observed and described.

The above-quoted "Critical" passage is all the more valuable as it proves beyond any doubt that at the very moment when *Criticism* sees the "*political essence*" far below itself, it is, on the contrary, far below the political essence; it still needs to find in the latter the solution of *its own* contradictions and it still persists in not giving a thought to the *modern principle of the state*.

To *"free theory"* Criticism contrasts the *"practical validity of privileges"*; to the *"legal validity of privileges"* it contrasts the *"public system"*.

In order not to misinterpret the opinion of *Criticism*, let us recall the contradiction it proved in the debates in the French Chamber, the very contradiction which "should have been conceived" as a *general* one. One of the questions dealt with was the fixing of a day in the week on which children would be freed from work. *Sunday* was suggested. One deputy moved to leave out mention of Sunday in the law as being unconstitutional. The Minister Martin (du Nord) saw in this motion an attempt to proclaim that Christianity had ceased to exist. Monsieur Crémieux declared on behalf of the French Jews that the Jews, out of respect for the religion of the great majority of Frenchmen, did not object to Sunday being mentioned. Now, according to free theory, Jews and Christians are equal, but according to this practice Christians have a privilege over Jews; for otherwise how could the Sunday of the Christians have a place in a law made for all Frenchmen? Should not the Jewish Sabbath have the same right, etc.? Or in the practical life of the French too, the Jew is not really oppressed by Christian privileges; but the law does not dare to express this practical equality. All the contradictions in the political essence expounded by Herr Bauer in *Die Judenfrage* are of this kind — contradictions of *constitutionalism*, which is, in general, the contradiction between the modern representative state and the old state of privileges.

Herr Bauer is committing a very serious oversight when he thinks he is rising from the *political* to the *human* essence by conceiving and criticising this contradiction as a "general" one. He would thus only rise from partial political emancipation to full political emancipation, from the constitutional state to the democratic representative state.

Herr Bauer thinks that by the abolition of *privilege* the *object* of privilege is also abolished. Concerning the statement of Monsieur Martin (du Nord), he says:

> *"There is no longer any religion* when *there is no longer any privileged religion.* Take from religion its exclusive power and it will no longer exist."[a]

Just as *industrial activity* is not abolished when the *privileges of the*

---

[a] This passage from B. Bauer's *Die Judenfrage* (p. 66) is quoted by Marx in his article "On the Jewish Question" (see present edition, Vol. 3, p. 149).—*Ed.*

trades, guilds and corporations are abolished, but, on the contrary, real *industry* begins only after the abolition of these privileges; just as *ownership of the land* is not abolished when *privileged* land-ownership is abolished, but, on the contrary, begins its universal movement only with the abolition of privileges and with the free division and free sale of land; just as *trade* is not abolished by the abolition of *trade privileges,* but finds its true realisation in free trade; so religion develops in its *practical* universality only where there is no *privileged* religion (cf. the North American States).

The modern *"public system",* the developed modern state, is not based, as *Criticism* thinks, on a society of privileges, but on a society in which *privileges have been abolished* and *dissolved,* on developed *civil society* in which the vital elements which were still politically bound under the privilege system have been set free. Here *no "privileged exclusivity,"* stands opposed either to any other exclusivity or to the public system. Free industry and free trade abolish privileged exclusivity and thereby the struggle between the privileged exclusivities. They replace exclusivity with man freed from privilege — which isolates from the general totality but at the same time unites in a smaller exclusive totality — man no longer bound to other men even by the *semblance* of a common bond. Thus they produce the universal struggle of man against man, individual against individual. In the same way *civil society* as a whole is this war against one another of all individuals, who are no longer isolated from one another by anything but their *individuality,* and the universal unrestrained movement of the elementary forces of life freed from the fetters of privilege. The contradiction between the *democratic representative state* and *civil society* is the completion of the *classic* contradiction between public *commonweal* and *slavery.* In the modern world each person is *at the same time* a member of slave society and of the public commonweal. Precisely the *slavery of civil society* is *in appearance* the greatest *freedom* because it is in appearance the fully developed *independence* of the individual, who considers as his *own* freedom the uncurbed movement, no longer bound by a common bond or by man, of the estranged elements of his life, such as property, industry, religion, etc., whereas actually this is his fully developed slavery and inhumanity. *Law* has here taken the place of *privilege.*

It is therefore only here, where we find no contradiction between free theory and the practical validity of privilege, but, on the contrary, the practical abolition of privilege, *free* industry, *free* trade, etc., conform to "free theory", where the public system is *not* opposed by any privileged exclusivity, where the contradiction expounded by Criticism is *abolished*—only here is the *fully developed modern state to be found.*

Here also reigns the *reverse* of the law which Herr Bauer, on the occasion of the debates in the French Chamber, formulated in perfect agreement with Monsieur Martin (du Nord):

"Just as M. Martin (du Nord) saw the proposal to omit mention of *Sunday* in the law as a motion to declare that Christianity has ceased to exist, with equal reason (*and this reason is very well founded*)—the declaration that the *law of the Sabbath* is no longer binding on the Jews would be *a proclamation abolishing Judaism.*" [a]

It is just *the opposite* in the developed modern state. The state declares that religion, like the other elements of civil life, only *begins* to exist in its full scope when the state declares it to be *non-political* and therefore leaves it to itself. To the dissolution of the *political* existence of these elements, as for example, the dissolution of *property* by the abolition of the *property qualification for electors,* the dissolution of *religion* by the abolition of the *state church,* to this proclamation of their civil death corresponds their most vigorous life, which henceforth obeys its own laws undisturbed and develops to its full scope.

Anarchy is the law of civil society emancipated from divisive privileges, and the *anarchy of civil society* is the basis of the modern *public system,* just as the public system in its turn is the guarantee of that anarchy. To the same great extent that the two are opposed to each other they also determine each other.

It is clear how capable *Criticism* is of assimilating the "new". But if we remain within the bounds of "pure Criticism", the question arises: Why did Criticism not conceive as a *universal* contradiction the contradiction which it disclosed in connection with the debates in the French Chamber, although in its own opinion that is what "*should have*" been done?

"That step *was*, however, then *impossible*—not only because ... not only because ... *but also* because without that *last remnant* of inner involvement with its opposite Criticism *was impossible* and *could not have come to the point* from which only *one step* remained to be taken." [b]

It was impossible ... because ... it was impossible! *Criticism* assures us, moreover, that the fateful "*one step*" necessary "to come to the point from which only *one step* remained to be taken"

---

[a] This passage from B. Bauer's *Die Judenfrage* (p. 71) is quoted by Marx in his article "On the Jewish Question" (see present edition, Vol. 3, p. 149).—*Ed.*

[b] Here and below quotations are taken from the article "*Was ist jetzt der Gegenstand der Kritik?*" (*Allgemeine Literatur-Zeitung,* Heft VIII).—*Ed.*

was impossible. Who will dispute that? In order to be able to come to a point from which only *"one step"* remains to be taken, it is absolutely impossible to take that *"one step"* more which leads over the point beyond which still *"one step"* remains to be taken.

All's well that ends well! At the end of the encounter with the *Mass*, which is hostile to Criticism's *Die Judenfrage*, *"Criticism"* admits that *its* conception of the *"rights of man"*, *its*

"appraisal of religion in the French Revolution", the "free political essence *it* pointed to occasionally *at the conclusion of its* considerations", in short, the whole "period of the French Revolution, was for *Criticism* neither more nor less than a symbol—that is to say, not the period of the revolutionary efforts of the French in the exact and prosaic sense—a symbol and therefore only a fantastic expression of the shapes which it saw at the end".

We shall not deprive *Criticism* of the consolation that when it sinned politically it did so only at the "conclusion" and at the "end" of its works. A notorious drunkard used to console himself with the thought that he was never drunk before midnight.

In the sphere of the "Jewish question", *Criticism* has indisputably been winning more and more ground from *the* Enemy. In No. 1 of the "Jewish question", the treatise of *"Criticism"* defended by Herr Bauer was still absolute and revealed the *"true"* and *"general"* significance of the "Jewish question". In No. 2 *Criticism* had neither the *"will"* nor the *"right"* to go beyond *Criticism*. In No. 3 it *had* still to take *"one step"*, but that step was "impossible"—because it was—"impossible". It was not its "will or right" but its involvement in its "opposite" that prevented it from taking that *"one step"*. It would very much have liked to clear the last obstacle, but unfortunately a *last remnant* of *Mass* stuck to its Critical seven-league boots.

c) Critical Battle Against the French Revolution

The *narrow-mindedness of the Mass* forced *the* "Spirit", *Criticism*, Herr Bauer, to consider the *French Revolution* not as the time of the revolutionary efforts of the French in the *"prosaic* sense" but *"only"* as the *"symbol* and *fantastic expression"* of the Critical figments of his own brain. *Criticism* does *penance* for its *"oversight"* by submitting the *Revolution* to a *fresh examination*. At the same time it punishes the seducer of its innocence—"the Mass"—by communicating to it the results of this "fresh examination".

"The *French Revolution* was an experiment which still belonged entirely to the eighteenth century."

The chronological truth that an experiment of the eighteenth century like the French Revolution is still entirely an experiment of the eighteenth century, and not, for example, an experiment of the nineteenth, seems "still entirely" to be one of those truths which "are self-evident from the start". But in the terminology of *Criticism*, which is very prejudiced against "crystal-clear" truths, a truth like that is called an "*examination*" and therefore naturally has its place in a "fresh examination of the Revolution".

"The ideas to which the French Revolution gave rise did not, however, lead beyond the *order of things* that it wanted to abolish by force."

Ideas can never lead beyond an old world order but only beyond the ideas of the old world order. Ideas *cannot carry out anything* at all. In order to carry out ideas men are needed who can exert practical force. In its literal *sense* the Critical sentence is therefore another truth that is self-evident, and therefore another "*examination*".

Undeterred by this examination, the French Revolution gave rise to ideas which led beyond the *ideas* of the entire old world order. The revolutionary movement which began in 1789 in the *Cercle social*,[41] which in the middle of its course had as its chief representatives *Leclerc* and *Roux*, and which finally with *Babeuf*'s conspiracy was temporarily defeated, gave rise to the *communist* idea which *Babeuf*'s friend *Buonarroti* re-introduced in France after the Revolution of 1830. This idea, consistently developed, is the *idea* of the *new world order*.

"After the Revolution had therefore" (!) "abolished the feudal barriers in the life of the people, it was compelled to satisfy and even to inflame the pure egoism of the nation and, on the other hand, to curb it by its necessary complement, the recognition of a supreme being, by this higher confirmation of the general state system, which has to hold together the individual self-seeking atoms."

The egoism of the nation is the natural egoism of the general state system, as opposed to the egoism of the feudal classes. The supreme being is the higher confirmation of the general state system, and hence also of the nation. Nevertheless, the supreme being is supposed to *curb* the egoism of the nation, that is, of the general state system! A really Critical task, to curb egoism by means of its confirmation and even of its *religious* confirmation, i.e., by recognising that it is of a superhuman nature and therefore free of human restraint! The creators of the supreme being were not aware of this, their Critical intention.

Monsieur *Buchez*, who bases national fanaticism on religious fanaticism, understands his hero *Robespierre* better.[42]

Nationalism [*Nationalität*] led to the downfall of Rome and Greece. *Criticism* therefore says nothing specific about the French Revolution when it maintains that nationalism caused its downfall, and it says just as little about the nation when it defines its egoism as *pure*. This pure egoism appears rather to be a very dark, spontaneous egoism, combined with flesh and blood, when compared, for example, with the pure egoism of *Fichte*'s "*ego*". But if, in contrast to the egoism of the feudal classes, its purity is only relative, no "fresh examination of the revolution" was needed to see that the egoism which has a nation as its content is more general or purer than that which has as its content a particular social class or a particular corporation.

Criticism's explanations about the general state system are no less instructive. They are confined to saying that the general state system must hold together the individual self-seeking atoms.

Speaking exactly and in the prosaic sense, the members of civil society are not *atoms*. The *specific property* of the atom is that it has *no* properties and is therefore not connected with beings outside it by any relationship determined by its own *natural necessity*. The atom *has no needs*, it is *self-sufficient*; the world outside it is an absolute *vacuum*, i.e., is contentless, senseless, meaningless, just because the atom has *all fullness* in itself. The egoistic individual in civil society may in his non-sensuous imagination and lifeless abstraction inflate himself into an *atom*, i.e., into an unrelated, self-sufficient, wantless, *absolutely full*, blessed being. Unblessed *sensuous reality* does not bother about his imagination, each of his senses compels him to believe in the existence[a] of the world and of individuals outside him, and even his *profane* stomach reminds him every day that the world *outside* him is not *empty*, but is what really *fills*. Every activity and property of his being, every one of his vital urges, becomes a *need*, a *necessity*, which his *self-seeking* transforms into seeking for other things and human beings outside him. But since the need of one individual has no self-evident meaning for another egoistic individual capable of satisfying that need, and therefore no direct connection with its satisfaction, each individual has to create this connection; it thus becomes the intermediary between the need of another and the objects of this need. Therefore, it is *natural necessity*, the *essential human properties* however estranged they may seem to be, and *interest* that hold the members of civil society together; *civil*, not *political* life is their *real*

---

[a] There is evidently an error in the original: "an den Sinn" instead of "an das Sein".— *Ed*.

tie. It is therefore not the state that holds the atoms of civil society together, but the fact that they are atoms only in imagination, in the heaven of their fancy, but in reality beings tremendously different from atoms, in other words, not divine egoists, but egoistic human beings. Only political superstition still imagines today that civil life must be held together by the state, whereas in reality, on the contrary, the state is held together by civil life.

"Robespierre's and Saint-Just's tremendous idea of making a 'free people' which would live only according to the rules of justice and virtue—see, for example, Saint-Just's report on Danton's crimes and his other report on the general police—could be maintained for a certain time only by terror and was a contradiction against which the vulgar, self-seeking elements of the popular community reacted in the cowardly and insidious way that was only to be expected from them."

This phrase of Absolute Criticism, which describes a "free people" as a "contradiction" against which the elements of the "popular community" are bound to react, is absolutely hollow, for according to Robespierre and Saint-Just liberty, justice and virtue could, on the contrary, be only manifestations of the life of the "people" and only properties of the "popular community". Robespierre and Saint-Just spoke explicitly of "liberty, justice and virtue" of ancient times, belonging only to the "popular community". Spartans, Athenians and Romans at the time of their greatness were "free, just and virtuous peoples".

"What," asks Robespierre in his speech on the principles of public morals (sitting of the Convention on February 5, 1794), "is the fundamental principle of democratic or popular government? It is virtue, I mean public virtue, which worked such miracles in Greece and Rome and which will work still greater ones in republican France; virtue which is nothing but love of one's country and its laws." [43]

Robespierre then explicitly calls the Athenians and Spartans "peuples libres".[a] He continually recalls the ancient popular community and quotes its heroes as well as its corrupters—Lycurgus, Demosthenes, Miltiades, Aristides, Brutus and Catilina, Caesar, Clodius and Piso.

In his report on Danton's arrest (referred to by Criticism) Saint-Just says explicitly:

"The world has been empty since the Romans, and only their memory fills it and still prophesies liberty." [44]

His accusation is composed in the ancient style and directed against Danton as against Catilina.

In Saint-Just's other report, the one on the general police,[45] the

---

[a] Free peoples.—Ed.

republican is described exactly in the *ancient* sense, as *inflexible, modest, simple* and so on. The *police* should be an institution of the same nature as the Roman *censorship.*—He does not fail to mention Codrus, Lycurgus, Caesar, Cato, Catilina, Brutus, Antonius, and Cassius. Finally, *Saint-Just* describes the "*liberty,* justice and virtue" that he demands in *a single word* when he says:

"Que les hommes révolutionnaires soient des *Romains.*"[a]

Robespierre, Saint-Just and their party fell because they confused the ancient, *realistic-democratic commonweal* based on *real slavery* with the *modern spiritualistic-democratic representative state,* which is based on *emancipated slavery, bourgeois society.* What a terrible illusion it is to have to recognise and sanction in the *rights of man* modern bourgeois society, the society of industry, of universal competition, of private interest freely pursuing its aims, of anarchy, of self-estranged natural and spiritual individuality, and at the same time to want afterwards to annul the *manifestations of the life* of this society in particular individuals and simultaneously to want to model the *political head* of that society in the manner of *antiquity!*

The illusion appears tragic when Saint-Just, on the day of his execution, pointed to the large table of the *Rights of Man* hanging in the hall of the *Conciergerie* and said with proud dignity: "*C'est pourtant moi qui ai fait cela.*"[b] It was just this table that proclaimed the *right* of a *man* who cannot be the man of the ancient commonweal any more than his *economic* and *industrial* conditions are those of *ancient* times.

This is not the place to vindicate the illusion of the *Terrorists* historically.

"After the fall of Robespierre the *political enlightenment* and *movement* hastened to the point where they became the prey of *Napoleon* who, shortly after 18 Brumaire, could say: 'With my prefects, gendarmes and priests I can do what I like with France.'"

Profane history, on the other hand, reports: After the fall of Robespierre, the *political* enlightenment, which formerly had been *overreaching* itself and had been *extravagant,* began for the first time to develop *prosaically.* Under the government of the *Directory,*[46] *bourgeois society,* freed by the Revolution itself from the trammels of feudalism and officially recognised in spite of the *Terror's* wish to sacrifice it to an ancient form of political life,

---

[a] "Let revolutionary men be *Romans.*"—*Ed.*
[b] "Yet it was I who made that."—*Ed.*

broke out in powerful streams of life. A storm and stress of commercial enterprise, a passion for enrichment, the exuberance of the new bourgeois life, whose first self-enjoyment is pert, light-hearted, frivolous and intoxicating; a *real* enlightenment of the *land* of France, the feudal structure of which had been smashed by the hammer of the Revolution and which, by the first feverish efforts of the numerous new owners, had become the object of all-round cultivation; the first moves of industry that had now become free—these were some of the signs of life of the newly emerged bourgeois society. *Bourgeois society* is *positively* represented by the *bourgeoisie*. The bourgeoisie, therefore, *begins* its rule. The *rights of man* cease to exist *merely* in *theory.*

It was not the revolutionary movement as a whole that became the prey of Napoleon on 18 Brumaire, as *Criticism* in its faith in a Herr von Rotteck or Welcker believes[47]; it was the *liberal bourgeoisie*. One only needs to read the speeches of the legislators of the time to be convinced of this. One has the impression of coming from the National Convention into a modern Chamber of Deputies.

Napoleon represented the last battle of *revolutionary terror* against the *bourgeois society* which had been proclaimed by this same Revolution, and against its policy. Napoleon, of course, already discerned the essence of the *modern state;* he understood that it is based on the unhampered development of bourgeois society, on the free movement of private interest, etc. He decided to recognise and protect this basis. He was no terrorist with his head in the clouds. Yet at the same time he still regarded the *state* as an *end in itself* and civil life only as a treasurer and his *subordinate* which must have no *will of its own.* He *perfected* the *Terror* by *substituting permanent war* for *permanent revolution.* He fed the egoism of the French nation to complete satiety but demanded also the sacrifice of bourgeois business, enjoyments, wealth, etc., whenever this was required by the political aim of conquest. If he despotically suppressed the liberalism of bourgeois society—the political idealism of its daily practice—he showed no more consideration for its essential *material* interests, trade and industry, whenever they conflicted with his political interests. His scorn of industrial *hommes d'affaires* was the complement to his scorn of *ideologists.* In his home policy, too, he combated bourgeois society as the opponent of the state which in his own person he still held to be an absolute aim in itself. Thus he declared in the State Council that he would not suffer the owner of extensive estates to cultivate them or not as he pleased. Thus, too, he conceived the plan of subordinating

trade to the state by appropriation of *roulage.*[a] French businessmen took steps to anticipate the event that first shook Napoleon's
power. Paris exchange brokers forced him by means of an
artificially created famine to delay the opening of the Russian
campaign by nearly two months and thus to launch it too late in
the year.

Just as the liberal bourgeoisie was opposed once more by
revolutionary terror in the person of Napoleon, so it was opposed
once more by counter-revolution in the Restoration in the person
of the Bourbons. Finally, in 1830 the bourgeoisie put into effect its
wishes of the year 1789, with the only difference that its *political
enlightenment* was now *completed,* that it no longer considered the
constitutional representative state as a means for achieving the
ideal of the state, the welfare of the world and universal human
aims but, on the contrary, had acknowledged it as the *official*
expression of its own *exclusive* power and the *political* recognition
of its own *special* interests.

The history of the French Revolution, which dates from 1789,
did not come to an end in 1830 with the victory of one of its
components enriched by the consciousness of its own *social*
importance.

d) Critical Battle Against French Materialism

"*Spinozism* dominated the eighteenth century both in its later French variety,
which made matter into substance, and in deism, which conferred on matter a
more spiritual name.... *Spinoza's French school* and the supporters of deism were but
two sects disputing over the true meaning of *his system*.... The simple fate of this
Enlightenment was its decline in *romanticism* after being obliged to surrender to the
reaction which began after the French movement."

That is what *Criticism* says.

To the Critical history of French materialism we shall oppose a
brief outline of its ordinary, mass-type history. We shall acknowledge with due respect the abyss between history as it really
happened and history as it takes place according to the decree of
"*Absolute Criticism*", the creator equally of the old and of the new.
And finally, obeying the prescriptions of *Criticism*, we shall make
the "Why?", "Whence?" and "Whither?" of Critical history the
"object of a persevering study".

"Speaking *exactly* and in the *prosaic sense*", the French Enlightenment of the eighteenth century, and in particular *French*

---

[a] Road haulage.— *Ed.*

materialism, was not only a struggle against the existing political institutions and the existing religion and theology; it was just as much an *open, clearly expressed* struggle against the *metaphysics of the seventeenth century,* and against *all metaphysics,* in particular that of *Descartes, Malebranche, Spinoza* and *Leibniz. Philosophy* was counterposed to *metaphysics,* just as *Feuerbach,* in his first resolute attack on *Hegel,* counterposed *sober philosophy* to *wild speculation.* Seventeenth century *metaphysics,* driven from the field by the French Enlightenment, notably, by *French materialism* of the eighteenth century, experienced a *victorious and substantial restoration* in *German philosophy,* particularly in the *speculative German philosophy* of the nineteenth century. After *Hegel* linked it in a masterly fashion with all subsequent metaphysics and with German idealism and founded a metaphysical universal kingdom, the attack on theology again corresponded, as in the eighteenth century, to an attack on *speculative metaphysics* and *metaphysics in general.* It will be defeated for ever by *materialism,* which has now been perfected by the work of *speculation* itself and coincides with *humanism.* But just as *Feuerbach* is the representative of *materialism* coinciding with *humanism* in the *theoretical* domain, French and English *socialism* and *communism* represent *materialism* coinciding with *humanism* in the *practical* domain.

"Speaking *exactly* and in the *prosaic sense"*, there are *two trends* in *French materialism;* one traces its origin to *Descartes,* the other to *Locke.* The latter is *mainly* a *French* development and leads directly to *socialism.* The former, *mechanical* materialism, merges with French *natural science* proper. The two trends intersect in the course of development. We have no need here to go more deeply into the French materialism that derives directly from *Descartes,* any more than into the French school of *Newton* and the development of French natural science in general.

We shall therefore merely say the following:

Descartes in his *physics* endowed *matter* with self-creative power and conceived *mechanical* motion as the manifestation of its life. He completely separated his *physics* from his *metaphysics. Within* his physics, *matter* is the sole *substance,* the sole basis of being and of knowledge.

Mechanical French materialism adopted *Descartes' physics* in opposition to his metaphysics. His followers were by profession *anti-metaphysicians,* i.e., *physicists.*

This school begins with the *physician Le Roy,* reaches its zenith with the physician *Cabanis,* and the physician *La Mettrie* is its centre. Descartes was still living when Le Roy, like *La Mettrie* in the eighteenth century, transposed the Cartesian structure of the *animal* to the human soul and declared that the soul is a *modus of the body* and *ideas* are *mechanical motions*. Le Roy even thought Descartes had kept his real opinion secret. Descartes protested. At the end of the eighteenth century *Cabanis* perfected Cartesian materialism in his treatise: *Rapports du physique et du moral de l'homme.* [48]

Cartesian materialism still exists today in France. It has achieved great successes in *mechanical natural science* which, "speaking *exactly* and in the *prosaic sense*", will be least of all reproached with *romanticism.*

The *metaphysics* of the seventeenth century, represented in France by *Descartes,* had *materialism* as its *antagonist* from its very birth. The latter's opposition to Descartes was personified by *Gassendi,* the restorer of *Epicurean* materialism. French and English materialism was always closely related to *Democritus* and *Epicurus.* Cartesian metaphysics had another opponent in the *English* materialist *Hobbes.* Gassendi and Hobbes triumphed over their opponent long after their death at the very time when metaphysics was already officially dominant in all French schools.

Voltaire pointed out that the indifference of the French of the eighteenth century to the disputes between the Jesuits and the Jansenists[49] was due less to philosophy than to *Law's* financial speculations. So the downfall of seventeenth-century metaphysics can be explained by the materialistic theory of the eighteenth century only in so far as this theoretical movement itself is explained by the practical nature of French life at that time. This life was turned to the immediate present, to worldly enjoyment and worldly interests, to the *earthly* world. Its anti-theological, anti-metaphysical, materialistic practice demanded corresponding anti-theological, anti-metaphysical, materialistic theories. Metaphysics had *in practice* lost all credit. Here we have only to indicate briefly the *theoretical* course of events.

In the seventeenth century metaphysics (cf. Descartes, Leibniz, and others) still contained a *positive,* secular element. It made discoveries in mathematics, physics and other exact sciences which seemed to come within its scope. This semblance was done away with as early as the beginning of the eighteenth century. The positive sciences broke away from metaphysics and marked out their independent fields. The whole wealth of metaphysics now consisted only of beings of thought and heavenly things, at the very time when real beings and earthly things began to be the centre of all interest. Metaphysics had become insipid. In the very year in which Malebranche and Arnauld, the last great French metaphysicians of the seventeenth century, died, *Helvétius* and *Condillac* were born.

The man who deprived seventeenth-century metaphysics and metaphysics in general of all *credit* in the domain of *theory* was *Pierre Bayle*. His weapon was *scepticism*, which he forged out of metaphysics' own magic formulas. He himself proceeded at first from Cartesian metaphysics. Just as *Feuerbach* by combating speculative theology was driven further to combat *speculative philosophy*, precisely because he recognised in speculation the last prop of theology, because he had to force theology to retreat from pseudo-science to *crude*, repulsive *faith*, so Bayle too was driven by religious doubt to doubt about the metaphysics which was the prop of that faith. He therefore critically investigated metaphysics in its entire historical development. He became its historian in order to write the history of its death. He refuted chiefly *Spinoza* and *Leibniz*.

Pierre Bayle not only prepared the reception of materialism and of the philosophy of common sense in France by shattering metaphysics with his scepticism. He heralded the *atheistic society* which was soon to come into existence by *proving* that a society consisting only of atheists is *possible*, that an atheist *can* be a man worthy of respect, and that it is not by atheism but by superstition and idolatry that man debases himself.

To quote a French writer, *Pierre Bayle* was *"the last metaphysician in the sense of the seventeenth century and the first philosopher in the sense of the eighteenth century"*.

Besides the negative refutation of seventeenth-century theology and metaphysics, a *positive, anti-metaphysical* system was required. A book was needed which would systematise and theoretically substantiate the life practice of that time. *Locke's* treatise *An Essay Concerning Humane Understanding* came from across the Channel as if in answer to a call. It was welcomed enthusiastically like a long-awaited guest.

The question arises: Is *Locke* perhaps a disciple of *Spinoza*? "Profane" history can answer:

Materialism is the *natural-born* son of *Great Britain*. [50] Already the British schoolman, *Duns Scotus*, asked, *"whether it was impossible for matter to think?"*

In order to effect this miracle, he took refuge in God's omnipotence, i.e., he made *theology* preach *materialism*. Moreover, he was a *nominalist*.[51] Nominalism, the *first form* of materialism, is chiefly found among the *English* schoolmen.

The real progenitor of *English materialism* and all *modern experimental* science is *Bacon*. To him natural philosophy is the only true philosophy, and *physics* based upon the experience of the senses is the chiefest part of natural philosophy. *Anaxagoras* and his *homoeomeriae*[52], *Democritus* and his atoms, he often quotes as his authorities. According to him the *senses* are infallible and the *source* of all knowledge. All science is based on *experience*, and consists in subjecting the data furnished by the senses to a *rational method* of investigation. Induction, analysis, comparison, observation, experiment, are the principal forms of such a rational method. Among the qualities inherent in *matter, motion* is the first and foremost, not only in the form of *mechanical* and *mathematical* motion, but chiefly in the form of an *impulse*, a *vital spirit, a tension*—or a '*Qual*',[52a] to use a term of Jakob Böhme's—of matter. The primary forms of matter are the living, individualising *forces of being* inherent in it and producing the distinctions between the species.

In *Bacon,* its first creator, materialism still holds back within itself in a naive way the germs of a many-sided development. On the one hand, matter, surrounded by a sensuous, poetic glamour, seems to attract man's whole entity by winning smiles. On the other, the aphoristically formulated doctrine pullulates with inconsistencies imported from theology.

In its further evolution, materialism becomes *one-sided. Hobbes* is the man who *systematises Baconian* materialism. Knowledge based upon the senses loses its poetic blossom, it passes into the abstract experience of the *geometrician*. *Physical* motion is sacrificed to *mechanical* or *mathematical* motion; *geometry* is proclaimed as the queen of sciences. Materialism takes to *misanthropy*. If it is to overcome its opponent, *misanthropic, fleshless* spiritualism, and that on the latter's own ground, materialism has to chastise its own flesh and turn *ascetic*. Thus it passes into an *intellectual entity;* but thus, too, it evolves all the consistency, regardless of consequences, characteristic of the intellect.

Hobbes, as Bacon's continuator, argues thus: if all human knowledge is furnished by the senses, then our concepts, notions, and ideas are but the phantoms of the real world, more or less divested of its sensual form. Philosophy can but give names to these phantoms. One name may be applied to more than one of them. There may even be names of names. But it would imply a contradiction if, on the one hand, we maintained that all ideas had their origin in the world of sensation, and, on the other, that a word was more than a word; that besides the beings known to us by our senses, beings which are one and all individuals, there existed also beings of a general, not individual, nature. An *unbodily substance* is the same absurdity as an *unbodily body*. Body, being, substance, are but different terms for the same *reality*. It is impossible to separate thought from matter *that* thinks. This matter is the substratum of all changes going on in the world. The word *infinite* is *meaningless*, unless it states that our mind is capable of performing an endless process of addition. Only material things being perceptible, knowable to us, we cannot know *anything* about the existence of God. My own existence alone is certain. Every human passion is a mechanical movement which has a beginning and an end. The objects of impulse are what we call good. Man is subject to the same laws as nature. Power and freedom are identical.

Hobbes had systematised Bacon without, however, furnishing a proof for Bacon's fundamental principle, the origin of all human knowledge and ideas from the world of sensation.

It was *Locke* who, in his *Essay on the Humane Understanding*, supplied this proof.

Hobbes had shattered the *theistic* prejudices of Baconian materialism; Collins, Dodwell, Coward, Hartley, Priestley, similarly shattered the last theological bars that still hemmed in Locke's sensationalism. At all events, for materialists, deism is but an easy-going way of getting rid of religion.

We have already mentioned how opportune Locke's work was for the French. Locke founded the philosophy of *bon sens*, of common sense; i.e., he said indirectly that there cannot be any philosophy at variance with the healthy human senses and reason based on them.

Locke's *immediate* pupil, *Condillac*, who translated him into *French*, at once applied Locke's sensualism against seventeenth-century *metaphysics*. He proved that the French had rightly rejected this metaphysics as a mere botch work of fancy and theological prejudice. He published a refutation of the systems of *Descartes*, *Spinoza*, *Leibniz* and *Malebranche*.

In his *Essai sur l'origine des connaissances humaines* he expounded Locke's ideas and proved that not only the soul, but the senses too, not only the art of creating ideas, but also the art of sensuous perception, are matters of *experience* and *habit*. The whole development of man therefore depends on *education* and *external circumstances*. It was only by *eclectic* philosophy that Condillac was ousted from the French schools.

The difference between *French* and *English* materialism reflects the difference between the two nations. The French imparted to English materialism wit, flesh and blood, and eloquence. They gave it the temperament and grace that it lacked. They *civilised* it. In *Helvétius,* who also based himself on Locke, materialism assumed a really French character. Helvétius conceived it immediately in its application to social life (Helvétius, *De l'homme*).[53] The sensory qualities and self-love, enjoyment and correctly understood personal interest are the basis of all morality. The natural equality of human intelligences, the unity of progress of reason and progress of industry, the natural goodness of man, and the omnipotence of education, are the main features in his system.

In *La Mettrie*'s works we find a synthesis of Cartesian and English materialism. He makes use of Descartes' physics in detail. His *L'homme machine* is a treatise after the model of Descartes' animal-machine. The physical part of Holbach's *Système de la nature* is also a result of the combination of French and English materialism, while the moral part is based essentially on the morality of Helvétius.[54] *Robinet* (*De la nature*), the French materialist who had the most connection with metaphysics and was therefore praised by Hegel, refers explicitly to *Leibniz*.

We need not dwell on Volney, Dupuis, Diderot and others, any more than on the physiocrats, after we have proved the dual origin of French materialism from Descartes' physics and English materialism, and the opposition of French materialism to seventeenth-century *metaphysics,* to the metaphysics of Descartes, Spinoza, Malebranche, and Leibniz. This opposition only became evident to the Germans after they themselves had come into opposition to *speculative metaphysics*.

Just as *Cartesian* materialism passes into *natural science proper,* the other trend of French materialism leads directly to *socialism* and *communism.*

There is no need for any great penetration to see from the teaching of materialism on the original goodness and equal intellectual endowment of men, the omnipotence of experience, habit and education, and the influence of environment on man, the great significance of industry, the justification of enjoyment, etc., how necessarily materialism is connected with communism and socialism. If man draws all his knowledge, sensation, etc., from the world of the senses and the experience gained in it, then what has to be done is to arrange the empirical world in such a way that man experiences and becomes accustomed to what is truly human in it and that he becomes aware of himself as man. If correctly understood interest is the principle of all morality, man's private interest must be made to coincide with the interest of humanity. If man is unfree in the materialistic sense, i.e., is free not through the negative power to avoid this or that, but through the positive power to assert his true individuality, crime must not be punished in the individual, but the anti-social sources of crime must be destroyed, and each man must be given social scope for the vital manifestation of his being. If man is shaped by environment, his environment must be made human. If man is social by nature, he will develop his true nature only in society, and the power of his nature must be measured not by the power of the separate individual but by the power of society.

These and similar propositions are to be found almost literally even in the oldest French materialists. This is not the place to assess them. The apologia of vices by *Mandeville*, one of Locke's early English followers, is typical of the socialist tendencies of materialism. He proves that in *modern* society vice is *indispensable* and *useful*.ᵃ This was by no means an apologia for modern society.

Fourier proceeds directly from the teaching of the French materialists. The *Babouvists* were crude, uncivilised materialists, but developed communism, too, derives *directly* from *French materialism*. The latter returned to its mother-country, *England*, in the form *Helvétius* gave it. *Bentham* based his system of *correctly understood interest* on Helvétius' morality, and *Owen* proceeded from *Bentham's* system to found English communism. Exiled to England, the Frenchman *Cabet* came under the influence of communist ideas there and on his return to France became the most popular, if the most superficial, representative of communism. Like Owen, the more scientific French Communists, *Dézamy, Gay* and others, developed the teaching of *materialism* as the teaching of *real humanism* and the *logical* basis of *communism*.

Where, then, did Herr Bauer or, *Criticism*, manage to acquire the documents for the Critical history of French materialism?

1) Hegel's *Geschichte der Philosophie* ᵇ presents French materialism as the *realisation* of the Substance of Spinoza, which at any rate is far more comprehensible than "the French school of Spinoza".

2) Herr *Bauer* read Hegel's *Geschichte der Philosophie* as saying that French materialism was the *school* of Spinoza. Then, as he found in another of Hegel's works that deism and materialism are *two parties* representing *one and the same* basic principle, he

---

ᵃ Bernard de Mandeville, *The Fable of the Bees: or, Private Vices, Publick Benefits.— Ed.*

ᵇ G. W. F. Hegel, *Vorlesungen über die Geschichte der Philosophie.— Ed.*

concluded that Spinoza had *two* schools which disputed over the meaning of his system. Herr Bauer could have found the supposed explanation in Hegel's *Phänomenologie*, where it is said:

"Regarding that Absolute Being, *Enlightenment* itself falls out with itself ... and is divided between the views of *two parties*.... The one ... calls *Absolute Being* that predicateless Absolute ... the other calls it *matter* .... Both are entirely the *same* notion—the distinction lies not in the objective fact, but purely in the diversity of starting-point adopted by the two developments" (Hegel, *Phänomenologie*, pp. 420, 421, 422).[a]

3) Finally Herr Bauer could find, again in Hegel, that when Substance does not develop into a concept and self-consciousness, it degenerates into "romanticism". The journal *Hallische Jahrbücher* at one time developed a similar theory.

But at all costs the *"Spirit"* had to decree a *"foolish destiny"* for its *"adversary"*, materialism.

———

Note. French materialism's connection with Descartes and Locke and the opposition of eighteenth-century philosophy to seventeenth-century metaphysics are presented in detail in most recent *French* histories of philosophy. In this respect, we had only to repeat against Critical Criticism what was already known. But the connection of eighteenth-century materialism with English and French *communism* of the nineteenth century still needs to be presented in detail. We confine ourselves here to quoting a few typical passages from Helvétius, Holbach and Bentham.

1) *Helvétius.* "Man is not wicked, but he is subordinate to his interests. One must not therefore complain of the wickedness of man but of the ignorance of the legislators, who have always placed the particular interest in opposition to the general interest." — "The moralists have so far had no success because we have to dig into legislation to pull out the roots which create vice. In New Orleans women have the right to repudiate their husbands as soon as they are tired of them. In countries like that women are not faithless, because they have no interest in being so." — "Morality is but a frivolous science when not combined with politics and legislation." — "The hypocritical moralists can be recognised on the one hand by the equanimity with which they consider vices which undermine the state, and on the other by the fury with which they condemn private vice." — "Human beings are born neither good nor bad but ready to become one or the other according as a common interest unites or divides them." — "If citizens could not achieve their own particular good without achieving the general good, there would be no vicious people except fools" (*De l'esprit*, t. I, Paris, 1822,[55] pp. 117, 240, 241, 249, 251, 369 and 339).

———

[a] English text taken from the translation by J. B. Baille, published by Allen and Unwin, 1931, pp. 591, 592, 593.— *Ed.*

As, according to Helvétius, it is education, by which he means (cf. loc. cit., p. 390) not only education in the ordinary sense but the totality of the individual's conditions of life, which forms man, if a reform is necessary to abolish the contradiction between particular interests and those of society, so, on the other hand, a transformation of consciousness is necessary to carry out such a reform:

"Great reforms can be implemented only by weakening the stupid respect of the peoples for old laws and customs" (loc. cit., p. 260)

or, as he says elsewhere, by abolishing ignorance.

2) *Holbach.* "Ce n'est que lui-même que l'homme peut aimer dans les objets qu'il aime: ce n'est que lui-même qu'il peut affectionner dans les êtres de son espèce." "L'homme ne peut jamais se séparer de lui-même dans aucun instant de sa vie; il ne peut se perdre de vue." "C'est toujours notre utilité, notre intérêt ... qui nous fait haïr ou aimer les objets".[a] (*Système social,* t. 1, Paris, 1822,[56] pp. 80, 112), but "L'homme pour son propre intérêt doit aimer les autres hommes puisqu'ils sont nécessaires à son bien-être... La morale lui prouve, que de tous les êtres le *plus nécessaire à l'homme c'est l'homme*".[b] (p. 76). "La vraie morale, ainsi que la vraie politique, est celle qui cherche à approcher les hommes, afin de les faire travailler par des efforts réunis à leur bonheur mutuel. Toute morale qui sépare *nos intérêts de ceux de nos associés* est fausse, insensée, contraire à la nature"[c] (p. 116). "Aimer les autres ... c'est *confondre nos intérêts avec ceux de nos associés,* afin de travailler à *l'utilité commune... La vertu* n'est que *l'utilité des hommes réunis en société*[d] (p. 77). "Un homme sans passions ou sans désirs cesserait d'être un homme... Parfaitement détaché de lui-même, comment pourrait-on le déterminer à s'attacher à d'autres? Un homme, indifférent pour tout, privé de passions, qui se suffirait à lui-même, ne serait plus un être sociable... La vertu n'est que la *communication du bien*"[e] (loc. cit., p. 118). "La morale religieuse ne servit jamais à rendre les mortels plus sociables"[f] (loc. cit., p. 36).

---

[a] "Man can only love himself in the objects he loves: he can have affection only for himself in the other beings of his kind." "Man can never separate himself from himself for a single instant in his life; he cannot lose sight of himself." "It is always our convenience, our interest ... that makes us hate or love things."—*Ed.*

[b] "In his own interest man must love other men, because they are necessary to his welfare.... Morality proves to him that of all beings the *most necessary to man is man."—Ed.*

[c] "True morality, and true politics as well, is that which seeks to bring men nearer to one another to make them work by united efforts for their common happiness. Any morality which separates *our interests from those of our associates,* is false, senseless, unnatural."—*Ed.*

[d] "To love others ... is to *merge our interests with those of our associates,* to work *for the common benefit.... Virtue* is but *the usefulness of men united in society."—Ed.*

[e] "A man without desires or passions would cease to be a man.... Perfectly detached from himself, how could one make him decide to attach himself to others? A man indifferent to everything and having no passions, sufficient to himself, would cease to be a social being.... Virtue is but the *communication of good."—Ed.*

[f] "Religious morality never served to make mortals more sociable."—*Ed.*

3) *Bentham.* We only quote one passage from Bentham in which he opposes "*intérêt général* in the political sense". "L'intérêt des individus ... doit céder à l'intérêt public. Mais ... qu'est-ce que cela signifie? Chaque individu n'est-il pas partie du public autant que chaque autre? Cet intérêt public, que vous personnifiez, n'est qu'un terme abstrait: il ne représente que la masse des intérêts individuels... S'il était bon de sacrifier la fortune d'un individu pour augmenter celle des autres, il serait encore mieux d'en sacrifier un second, un troisième, sans qu'on puisse assigner aucune limite.... Les intérêts individuels sont les seuls intérêts réels"[a] (Bentham, *Théorie des peines et des récompenses,* Paris, 1826, 3ᵉᵐᵉ éd., II, p. [229], 230).

e) Final Defeat of Socialism

"The French set up a series of *systems* of *how* the *mass* should be *organised,* but they had to resort to *fantasy* because they considered the mass, as it is, to be usable material."

Actually, the French and the English have proved, and proved in great detail, that the present social system organises the "mass *as it is*" and is therefore its *organisation. Criticism,* following the example of the *Allgemeine Zeitung,* disposes of all socialist and communist systems by means of the *fundamental* word "*fantasy*".[57]

Having thus shattered foreign socialism and communism, *Criticism* transfers its war-like operations to Germany.

"When the *German Enlighteners* suddenly found themselves disappointed in their hopes of 1842 and, in their embarrassment, did not know *what to do, news* of the recent *French* systems came in the nick of time. They were henceforth able to speak of raising the lower classes of the people and at that price they were able to dispense with the question whether they did not themselves belong to the mass, which is to be found not only in the lowest strata."

Criticism has obviously so exhausted its entire provision of well meaning motives in the apologia for Bauer's literary past that it can find no other explanation for the German socialist movement than the "embarrassment" of the Enlighteners in 1842. "Fortunately they received news of the recent *French* systems." Why not of the *English?* For the decisive *Critical* reason that Herr Bauer received no news of the recent English systems through *Stein's* book: *Der Communismus und Socialismus des heutigen Frankreichs.* This is also the decisive reason why only *French systems* ever exist for *Criticism* in all its talk about socialist systems.

The German Enlighteners, Criticism goes on to explain, commit-

[a] "The interest of individuals ... must give way to the public interest. But .... what does that mean? Is not each individual part of the public as much as any other? This public interest that you personify is but an abstract term: it represents but the mass of individual interests.... If it were good to sacrifice the fortune of one individual to increase that of others, it would be better to sacrifice that of a second, a third, and so on ad infinitum.... Individual interests. are the only real interests."—*Ed.*

ted a sin against the Holy Ghost. They busied themselves with the "lower classes of the people", already in existence in 1842, in order to *get rid of* the question, which did *not* yet exist then, as to what rank they were destined to occupy in the *Critical world system* that was to be instituted in anno 1843: sheep or goat, Critical Critic or impure Mass, *Spirit* or *Matter*. But above all they should have thought seriously of the Critical *salvation of their own souls*, for of what profit is it to me if I gain the whole world, including the lower classes of the people, and suffer the loss of my own soul?

"But a spiritual being cannot be raised to a higher level unless it is altered, and it cannot be altered before it has experienced extreme resistance."

Were *Criticism* better acquainted with the movement of the lower classes of the people it would know that the extreme resistance that they have experienced from practical life is changing them every day. Modern prose and poetry emanating in England and France from the lower classes of the people would show it that the lower classes of the people know how to raise themselves spiritually even without being directly *overshadowed* by the *Holy Ghost of Critical Criticism*.

"They," Absolute Criticism continues to indulge in fancy, "whose *whole wealth* is the word '*organisation of the mass*'", etc.

A lot has been said about "organisation of labour", although even this "catchword" came not from the Socialists themselves but from the politically radical party in France, which tried to be an intermediary between politics and socialism.[58] But nobody before Critical Criticism spoke of "organisation of the mass" as of a question yet to be solved. It was proved, on the contrary, that *bourgeois society*, the dissolution of the old *feudal* society, *is* this organisation of the mass.

Criticism puts its discovery in quotation marks [*Gänsefüsse*[a]]. The goose that cackled to Herr Bauer the watchword for saving the Capitol[59] is none but his *own goose, Critical Criticism*. It organised the mass anew by speculatively constructing it as the Absolute Opponent of *the* Spirit. The antithesis between spirit and mass is the Critical "organisation of society", in which *the* Spirit, or *Criticism*, represents the organising *work*, the mass—the *raw material*, and history—the *product*.

After Absolute Criticism's great victories over revolution, materialism and socialism in its third campaign, we may ask: What is the *final result* of these Herculean feats? Only that these

---

[a] *Gänsefüsse* (=goose-feet) is a German word for quotation marks.—*Ed.*

movements *perished* without any result because they were still *criticism adulterated by mass* or *spirit adulterated by matter*. Even in Herr Bauer's own literary past *Criticism* discovered manifold adulterations of *criticism* by the mass. But *here* it writes an apologia instead of a criticism, "*places in safety*" instead of *surrendering*; instead of seeing in the *adulteration of the spirit* by the *flesh* the death of the spirit too, it reverses the case and finds in the adulteration of the *flesh by the spirit* the life even of *Bauer's* flesh. On the other hand, it is all the more ruthless and decisively *terroristic* as soon as imperfect criticism still adulterated by mass is no longer the *work* of Herr Bauer but of whole peoples and of a number of ordinary Frenchmen and Englishmen; as soon as imperfect criticism is no longer entitled *Die Judenfrage*, or *Die gute Sache der Freiheit*, or *Staat, Religion und Parthei*, but revolution, materialism, socialism or communism. Thus *Criticism* did away with the adulteration of spirit by matter and of criticism by mass by sparing its own flesh and crucifying the flesh of others.

One way or the other, the "spirit adulterated by flesh" or "Criticism adulterated by mass" has been cleared out of the way. Instead of this un-Critical adulteration, there appears absolutely Critical *disintegration* of spirit and flesh, criticism and mass, their pure opposition. This opposition in its *world-historic* form in which it constitutes the true historical interest of the present time, is the opposition of Herr Bauer and Co., or *the* Spirit, to the rest of the human race as Matter.

Revolution, materialism and communism *therefore* have fulfilled their historic mission. By their *downfall* they have prepared the way for the Critical *Lord*. Hosanna!

f) The Speculative Cycle of Absolute Criticism and the Philosophy of Self-Consciousness

Criticism, having supposedly attained *perfection* and purity in *one* domain, *therefore* committed only one *oversight*, "only" one "inconsistency", that of not being "pure" and "perfect" in *all* domains. The "one" Critical domain is none other than that of *theology*. The *pure* area of this domain extends from the *Kritik der Synoptiker* by Bruno Bauer to *Das entdeckte Christenthum* by Bruno Bauer, as the farthest frontier post.

"Modern Criticism," we are told, "had finally dealt with Spinozism; it was therefore inconsistent of it naively to presuppose *Substance* in one domain, even if only in individual, falsely expounded points."

Criticism's earlier admission that it had been involved in *political* prejudice was immediately followed by the extenuating circumstance that this involvement had been *"basically so slight!"* Now the admission of *inconsistency* is tempered by the parenthesis that it was committed only in *individual, falsely expounded points.* It was not Herr Bauer who was to blame, but the *false points* which *ran away with Criticism* like recalcitrant mounts.

A few quotations will show that by overcoming *Spinozism Criticism* ended up in *Hegelian idealism,* that from "*Substance*" it arrived at another *metaphysical monster, the "Subject", "Substance as a process", "infinite self-consciousness",* and that the final result of "perfect" and "pure" Criticism is the *restoration of the Christian theory of creation* in a *speculative, Hegelian* form.

Let us first open the *Kritik der Synoptiker.*

"Strauss remains true to the view that *Substance* is the Absolute. Tradition in this form of universality, which has not yet attained the real and rational certitude of universality, that certitude which can be attained only in *self-consciousness,* in the *oneness* and *infinity* of self-consciousness, is nothing but *Substance* which has emerged from its logical simplicity and has assumed a definite form of existence as the *power of the community*" (*Kritik der Synoptiker,* Vol. I, Preface, pp. vi [-vii]).

Let us leave to their fate *"the* universality which attains certitude", the "oneness and infinity" (the Hegelian *Notion*).— Instead of saying that the view put forward in *Strauss'* theory on the "power of the community" and "tradition" has its *abstract* expression, its logical and metaphysical *hieroglyphic,* in the Spinozist conception of *Substance,* Herr Bauer makes *"Substance emerge* from its *logical simplicity* and assume a definite form of existence in the power of the community". He applies the *Hegelian* miracle apparatus by which the *"metaphysical categories"* — abstractions extracted out of *reality*— emerge from *logic,* where they are dissolved in the *"simplicity"* of thought, and assume "a definite form" of physical or human existence; he makes them become incarnate. Help, *Hinrichs!*

"Mysterious," *Criticism* continues its argument against Strauss, "mysterious is this view because whenever it wishes to explain and make visible the process to which the gospel history owes its origin, it can only bring out the *semblance* of a process [...] The sentence: 'The gospel history has its source and origin in tradition', posits the same thing *twice*—'tradition' and the 'gospel history'; admittedly it does posit a relation between them, but it does not tell us to what *internal process of Substance* the development and exposition owe their origin."[a]

According to *Hegel, Substance* must be conceived as an *internal*

---

[a] This is also a quotation from B. Bauer's book *Kritik der evangelischen Geschichte der Synoptiker.—Ed.*

process. He characterises *development* from the viewpoint of Substance as follows:

> "But if we look more closely at this *expansion*, we find that it has not come about by one and the same principle taking shape in diverse ways; it is only the shapeless *repetition of one and the same thing* ... keeping up a tedious *semblance* of diversity" (*Phänomenologie*, Preface, p. 12).

Help, Hinrichs!

"Criticism," Herr Bauer continues, "according to this, must turn against itself and look for the solution of the *mysterious substantiality* ... in what the *development of Substance itself* leads to, in the universality and certitude of the idea and its real existence, in *infinite self-consciousness*."

Hegel's criticism of the substantiality view continues:

> "The compact solidity of Substance is to be opened up and Substance raised to *self-consciousness*" (loc. cit., p. 7).

Bauer's *self-consciousness*, too, is *Substance raised* to self-consciousness or *self-consciousness* as *Substance*; self-consciousness is transformed from an *attribute of man* into a *self-existing subject*. This is the *metaphysical-theological* caricature of man in his *severance* from nature. The *being* of this self-consciousness is therefore not *man*, but *the idea* of which self-consciousness is the *real existence*. It is the idea *become man*, and therefore it is *infinite*. All *human* qualities are thus transformed in a *mysterious way* into qualities of imaginary "*infinite self-consciousness*". Hence, Herr Bauer says *expressly* that *everything* has its *origin* and its *explanation* in this "infinite self-consciousness", i.e., finds in it the *basis* of its *existence*. Help, *Hinrichs!*

Herr Bauer continues:

> "The power of the *substantiality relation* lies in its impulse, which leads us to the concept, the idea and self-consciousness."

Hegel says:

> "Thus the *concept* is the *truth* of the substance." "The transition of the *substantiality relation* takes place through its own immanent necessity and consists in this only, that *the* concept is the truth of the substance." "The *idea* is the adequate concept." "The concept ... having achieved *free* existence ... is nothing but the *ego* or *pure self-consciousness*" (*Logik*, Hegel's *Werke*, 2nd ed., Vol. 5, pp. 6, 9, 229, 13).

Help, *Hinrichs!*

It seems comic in the extreme when Herr Bauer says in his *Literatur-Zeitung*:

> "*Strauss* came to grief because he was unable to *complete the criticism of Hegel's system*, although he proved by his half-way criticism the necessity for its completion", etc.[60]

It was not a *complete criticism* of Hegel's system that Herr Bauer himself thought he was giving in his *Kritik der Synoptiker* but at the most the *completion of Hegel's system*, at least in its application to theology.

He describes his criticism (*Kritik der Synoptiker*, Preface, p. xxi) as "the last act of a definite system", which is no other than *Hegel's* system.

The dispute between *Strauss* and *Bauer* over *Substance* and *Self-Consciousness* is a dispute *within* Hegelian speculation. In *Hegel* there are *three* elements, *Spinoza's Substance, Fichte's Self-Consciousness* and *Hegel's* necessarily antagonistic *unity* of the two, the *Absolute Spirit.* The first element is metaphysically disguised *nature separated* from man; the second is metaphysically disguised *spirit separated* from nature; the third is the metaphysically disguised *unity* of both, *real man* and the real *human species.*

Within the domain of theology, *Strauss* expounds *Hegel* from *Spinoza's point of view*, and Bauer does so from *Fichte's point of view*, both quite consistently. They both *criticised* Hegel insofar as with him each of the two elements was *falsified* by the other, whereas they carried each of these elements to its *one-sided* and hence consistent development.— Both of them therefore go *beyond* Hegel in their criticism, but both also remain *within* his speculation and each represents only *one* side of his system. *Feuerbach*, who completed and criticised *Hegel from Hegel's point of view* by resolving the metaphysical *Absolute* Spirit into "*real man on the basis of nature*", was the first to complete the *criticism of religion* by sketching in a grand and masterly manner the *basic features* of the *criticism of Hegel's speculation* and hence *of all metaphysics.*

With Herr Bauer it is, admittedly, no longer the *Holy Ghost*, but nevertheless *infinite self-consciousness* that dictates the writings of the evangelist.

"We ought not any longer to conceal the fact that the correct conception of the gospel history also has its *philosophical basis, namely, the philosophy of self-consciousness*" (Bruno Bauer, *Kritik der Synoptiker*, Preface, p. xv).

This philosophy of Herr Bauer, the *philosophy of self-consciousness*, like the *results* he achieved by his criticism of theology, must be characterised by a few extracts from *Das entdeckte Christenthum*, his *last* work on the philosophy of religion.

Speaking of the *French materialists*, he says:

"When the *truth* of materialism, the *philosophy of self-consciousness*, is revealed and *self-consciousness* is recognised as the *Universe*, as the solution of the riddle of Spinoza's *substance* and as the true *causa sui*[a] ..., what is the purpose of *the Spirit?*

_____

[a] Cause of itself.— *Ed.*

What is the purpose of self-consciousness? As if *self-consciousness*, by positing the *world*, did not posit *distinction*, and did not produce *itself* in all it produces, since it does away again with *the distinction of what it produced from itself*, and since, consequently it is itself only in production and in movement—as if self-consciousness in this movement, which is itself, had not its purpose and did not possess itself!" (*Das entdeckte Christenthum*, p. 113.)

"The French materialists did, indeed, conceive the movement of self-consciousness as the movement of the universal being, matter, but they could *not yet* see that the *movement of the universe* became *real* for itself and achieved unity with itself *only* as the *movement of self-consciousness*" (l. c., pp. [114-] 115).

Help, *Hinrichs*!

In plain language the *first* extract means: the truth of *materialism* is the *opposite* of materialism, *absolute*, i.e., exclusive, unmitigated *idealism*. Self-consciousness, *the Spirit*, is the *Universe*. Outside of it there is *nothing*. "Self-consciousness", "*the Spirit*", is the almighty creator of the world, of heaven and earth. The *world* is a manifestation of the life of self-consciousness which has to *alienate* itself and take on *the form of a slave*, but the difference between the world and self-consciousness is only an *apparent difference*. Self-consciousness distinguishes *nothing real* from itself. The world is, rather, only a metaphysical *distinction*, a phantom of its ethereal brain and an *imaginary* product of the latter. Hence self-consciousness does away again with the appearance, which it conceded for a moment, that something exists outside of it, and it recognises in what it has "produced" no real object, i.e., no object which in reality is distinct from it. By this movement, however, *self-consciousness* first produces itself as absolute, for the *absolute* idealist, in order to be an absolute idealist, must necessarily constantly go through the *sophistical process* of first transforming the world *outside himself* into an *appearance*, a mere fancy of *his* brain, and afterwards declaring this *fantasy* to be what it really is, i.e., a mere fantasy, so as finally to be able to proclaim his sole, exclusive existence, which is no longer disturbed even by the semblance of an external world.

In plain language the *second* extract means: The French materialists did, of course, conceive the movements of matter as movements involving spirit, but they were not yet able to see that they are not *material*, but *ideal* movements, movements of self-consciousness, consequently pure movements of thought. They were not yet able to see that the real movement of the universe became true and real only as the *ideal* movement of self-consciousness free and freed from *matter*, that is, from *reality*; in other words, that a *material* movement distinct from ideal brain movement exists only *in appearance*. Help, *Hinrichs*!

This speculative *theory of creation* is almost word for word in *Hegel*; it can be found in his *first* work, his *Phänomenologie*.

"The alienation *of self-consciousness* itself establishes *thinghood*.... In this alienation self-consciousness establishes itself as *object*, or sets up the object as *itself*. On the other hand, there is also this other moment in the process that it has just as much *abolished* this *alienation* and *objectification* and resumed them into itself.... This is the *movement of consciousness*" (Hegel, *Phänomenologie*, pp. 574-75).

"Self-consciousness has a *content*, which it distinguishes *from itself*.... This content in its *distinction* is itself the *ego*, for it is the *movement* of superseding itself.... More precisely stated, this content is nothing but the *very movement just spoken of*; for the content is *the Spirit* which traverses the whole range of its own being, and does this *for itself* as *Spirit*" (loc. cit., pp. [582-] 583).[a]

Referring to this theory of creation of Hegel's, *Feuerbach* observes:

"Matter is the self-alienation of the spirit. Thereby matter itself acquires spirit and reason—but at the same time it is assumed as a *nothingness*, an *unreal* being, inasmuch as being producing itself from this alienation, i.e., being divesting itself of matter, of sensuousness, is pronounced to be being in its perfection, in its true shape and form. Therefore the natural, the material, the sensuous, is what is to be *negated* here too, as *nature poisoned by original sin* is in theology" (*Philosophie der Zukunft*, p. 35).[b]

Herr Bauer therefore defends materialism against *un-Critical theology*, at the same time as he reproaches it with "not yet" being *Critical theology, theology of reason, Hegelian speculation. Hinrichs! Hinrichs!*

Herr Bauer, who in *all* domains carries through *his* opposition to *Substance, his philosophy of self-consciousness* or of *the* Spirit, must therefore in all domains have only the *figments* of his own *brain* to deal with. In his hands, *Criticism* is the instrument to sublimate into mere *appearance* and *pure* thought all that affirms a *finite* material existence *outside infinite self-consciousness.* What he combats in Substance is not the *metaphysical illusion* but its *mundane* kernel—*nature*; nature both as it exists *outside* man and as man's nature. Not to presume *Substance* in any domain—he still uses this language—means therefore for him not to recognise any *being* distinct from thought, any *natural energy* distinct from the *spontaneity of the spirit*, any *power of human nature* distinct from *reason*, any *passivity* distinct from *activity*, any *influence of others* distinct from *one's own action*, any *feeling* or *willing* distinct from *knowing*, any *heart* distinct from the *head*, any *object* distinct from the *subject*, any *practice* distinct from *theory*, any *man* distinct from the *Critic*, any

---

[a] See the English edition of Hegel's *Works*, pp. 789, 790.—*Ed.*
[b] Ludwig Feuerbach, *Grundsätze der Philosophie der Zukunft.—Ed.*

real community distinct from *abstract generality,* any *Thou* distinct from *I.* Herr Bauer is therefore consistent when he goes on to identify *himself* with *infinite self-consciousness,* with the *Spirit,* i.e., to replace these creations of his by their creator. He is just as consistent in rejecting as *stubborn mass* and *matter* the *rest of the world* which obstinately insists on being something *distinct* from what *he,* Herr Bauer, has produced. And so he hopes:

> It will not be long
> Before all bodies perish.[a]

His *own* ill-humour at so far being unable to master "the *something* of this *clumsy* world" he interprets equally consistently as the *self-discontent* of this world, and the indignation of his Criticism at the development of mankind as the *mass-type* indignation of mankind against *his* Criticism, against *the* Spirit, against Herr Bruno Bauer and Co.

Herr Bauer was a *theologian* from the very beginning, but no ordinary one; he was a *Critical theologian* or a *theological Critic.* While still the extreme representative of *old Hegelian* orthodoxy who put in a speculative form all *religious* and *theological nonsense,* he constantly proclaimed *Criticism* his *private domain.* At that time he called *Strauss'* criticism *human* criticism and *expressly* asserted the right of *divine* criticism in opposition to it. He later stripped the great *self-reliance* or *self-consciousness,* which was the hidden kernel of this divinity, of its religious shell, made it self-existing as an independent being, and raised it, under the trade-mark *"Infinite Self-consciousness",* to the rank of the principle of Criticism. Then he accomplished in his *own* movement the movement that the "philosophy of self-consciousness" describes as the absolute act of life. He abolished anew the "distinction" between "the product", *infinite self-consciousness,* and the producer, *himself,* and acknowledged that infinite self-consciousness in its movement *"was only he himself",* and that therefore the movement of the universe only becomes *true* and *real* in his ideal self-movement.

Divine criticism in its *return into itself* is restored in a rational, conscious, Critical way; *being in-itself* is transformed into *being in-and-for-itself* and only at the *end* does the fulfilled, realised, revealed *beginning* take place. *Divine* criticism, as *distinct* from *human* criticism, reveals itself as *Criticism, pure Criticism, Critical Criticism.* The apologia for the Old and the New Testament is replaced by the apologia for the old and new works of Herr

---

[a] J. W. Goethe, *Faust,* Part I, Scene 3 ("Faust's Study").—*Ed.*

Bauer. The *theological* antithesis of God and man, spirit and flesh, infinity and finiteness is transformed into the *Critical-theological* antithesis *of the Spirit, Criticism*, or Herr *Bauer*, and the *matter* of the *mass*, or the secular world. The theological antithesis of faith and reason has been resolved into the Critical-theological antithesis of *common sense* and pure Critical thought. The *Zeitschrift für spekulative Theologie* has been transformed into the Critical *Literatur-Zeitung. The religious redeemer of the world* has finally become a reality in the *Critical redeemer of the world*, Herr *Bauer*.

Herr Bauer's last stage is not an anomaly in his development; it is the *return* of his development *into* itself from its *alienation*. Naturally, the point at which *divine* Criticism *alienated* itself and came out of itself coincided with the point at which it became partly untrue to itself and created something *human*.

Returning to its starting-point, *Absolute Criticism* has ended the *speculative cycle* and thereby its own *life's career*. Its further movement is *pure*, lofty *circling within itself*, above all interest of a *mass nature* and therefore devoid of any further interest for the Mass.

Chapter VII

CRITICAL CRITICISM'S CORRESPONDENCE

1) THE CRITICAL MASS

> Où peut-on être mieux
> Qu'au sein de sa famille?[a]

In its *Absolute* existence as Herr *Bruno*, Critical Criticism has declared the *mass* of mankind, the whole of mankind that is not Critical Criticism, to be its *opposite*, its *essential object*; *essential*, because the Mass exists *ad majorem gloriam dei*,[b] the glory of *Criticism*, of *the* Spirit; *its object*, because it is only the *matter* on which Critical Criticism operates. Critical Criticism has proclaimed its relationship to the Mass as the *world-historic relationship* of the present time.

No *world-historic opposition* is formed, however, by the statement that one is in opposition to the whole world. One can imagine that one is a stumbling-block for the world because one is clumsy enough to stumble everywhere. But for a world-historic opposition it is not enough for me to declare the world *my* opposite; the *world* for its part must declare me to be its essential opposite, and must treat and *recognise* me as such. Critical Criticism ensures itself this recognition by its *correspondence*, which is called upon to *bear witness* before the world to Criticism's function of redeemer and equally to the general *irritation* of the world at the Critical gospel. Critical Criticism is its own object as the *object of the world*. The correspondence is intended to *show it as such*, as the *world interest* of the present time.

Critical Criticism is in its own eyes the *Absolute Subject*. The Absolute Subject requires a cult. A *real* cult requires other believing individuals. The *Holy Family of Charlottenburg* therefore receives from its correspondents the cult due to it. The correspondents tell it *what* it *is* and what its adversary, the Mass, *is not.*

---

[a] Where can one feel better than in the bosom of one's family? (From J. F. Marmontel's one-act comedy *Lucile*, Scene 4.)—*Ed.*

[b] For the greater glory of God.—*Ed.*

However, Criticism falls into an inconsistency by thus having its opinion of itself represented as the opinion of the world and by its *concept* being converted into *reality*. *Within Criticism itself* a sort of *Mass* is forming, a Critical Mass whose simple function is untiringly to echo the stock phrases of Criticism. For consistency's sake this inconsistency may be forgiven. Not feeling at home in the sinful world, Critical Criticism must set up a sinful world in its own home.

The path of Critical Criticism's correspondent, a member of the Critical Mass, is not a rosy one. It is a difficult, thorny path, a Critical path. Critical Criticism is a spiritualistic lord, pure spontaneity, *actus purus*, intolerant of any influence *from without*. The correspondent can therefore be a *subject* only *in appearance*, can only *seem* to behave *independently* towards Critical Criticism, can only *seemingly* want to communicate something new and of his own to it. In *reality* he is Critical Criticism's own *product*, its perception of its own voice made for an instant *objective* and self-existing.

That is why the correspondents do not fail to assert incessantly that Critical Criticism itself *knows, realises, understands, grasps*; and *experiences* what at the same moment is being communicated to it for *appearance*'s sake.[61] Thus *Zerrleder*, for instance, uses the expressions: "Do you grasp it? You know. You know for the second and third time. You have probably heard enough to be able to see for yourself."

So too the Breslau correspondent *Fleischhammer* says: "But the fact," etc., "will be as little of a puzzle to you as to me." Or the Zurich correspondent *Hirzel*: "You will probably find out for yourself." The Critical correspondent has such anxious respect for the absolute understanding of *Critical Criticism* that he attributes understanding to it even where there is absolutely nothing to understand. For example, *Fleischhammer* says:

"You will *perfectly* [!] *understand* [!] me when I tell you that one can hardly go out without meeting young Catholic priests in their long black cowls and cloaks."

Indeed, in their *fear* the correspondents *hear* Critical Criticism *saying, answering, exclaiming, deriding*!

Zerrleder, for example, says: "But—you *say*. Well, then, listen." And *Fleischhammer*: "Yes, I hear what *you say*—I *only* mean that...." And *Hirzel*: "Good for you, you *will exclaim*!" And a Tübingen correspondent: "*Do not laugh at* me!"

The correspondents, therefore, also express themselves as though they were communicating *facts* to Critical Criticism and expect from it the *spiritual interpretation*; they provide it with *premises* and leave the *conclusion* to it, or they even *apologise* for repeating things Criticism has known for a long time.

Zerrleder, for example, says:

"Your correspondent can only give a picture, a description of the facts. The *Spirit* which animates these things is *certainly* not unknown to *you*." Or again: "Now you will *surely* draw the *conclusion for yourself*."

And *Hirzel* says:

"*I shall not presume* to entertain you with the speculative proposition that every creation arises out of its extreme opposite."

Sometimes, too, the *experiences* of the correspondents are merely the *fulfilment* and *confirmation* of Criticism's *prophecies*.

Fleischhammer, for example, says:

"Your *prediction* has come true."

And *Zerrleder*:

"Far from being disastrous, the tendencies that I have described to you as gaining ever greater scope in Switzerland, are very *fortunate*; they *only confirm* the *thought you* have already often expressed," etc.

Critical Criticism sometimes feels urged to express the condescension involved by its participation in the correspondence and motivates this condescension by the fact that the correspondent has successfully carried out some *task*. Thus Herr Bruno writes to the Tübingen correspondent:

"It is really inconsistent on my part to answer your letter.— On the other hand, you have again ... made such an *apt remark* that I ... *cannot refuse* the explanation you request." [62]

Critical Criticism has letters written to it *from the provinces*; not the provinces in the political sense, which, as we know, do not exist anywhere in Germany, but from the *Critical provinces* of which· Berlin is the capital, *Berlin*, the seat of the Critical patriarchs and of the Holy Critical Family, whereas the provinces are where the Critical Mass resides. The *Critical provincials* dare not engage the attention of the *supreme Critical authority* without bows and apologies.

Thus, someone writes anonymously to Herr *Edgar*, who, being a member of the Holy Family, is also an eminent personage:

"Honourable Sir, I hope you will *excuse* these lines on the grounds that young people like to unite in common strivings (there is not more than two years' *difference* in our *ages*)."

The coeval of Herr Edgar describes *himself* incidentally as *the essence of modern philosophy*. Is it not in the nature of things that *Criticism* should correspond with *the essence* of philosophy? If Herr

Edgar's coeval affirms that he has already lost his *teeth*, that is only an allusion to his *allegorical* essence. This "essence of modern philosophy" has "learned from *Feuerbach* to set the factor of education in objective view". It at once gives a sample of its *education* and *views* by assuring Herr Edgar that it has acquired a "*complete view* of his short story", "Es leben feste Grundsätze!"[a] At the same time it openly admits that Herr Edgar's point of view is by no means quite clear to it, and finally invalidates the assurance concerning the complete view by the question: "Or have I *completely misunderstood* you?" After this sample it will be found quite normal that the essence of modern philosophy, referring to the Mass, should say:

"*We* must at least once *condescend* to examine and untie the magic knot which bars *common human reason* from access to the *unrestricted flood of thought*."

In order to get a complete view of the Critical Mass one should read the *correspondence* of Herr *Hirzel* from Zurich (Heft V). This unfortunate man memorises the stock phrases of Criticism with really touching docility and praiseworthy power of recall, not omitting Herr Bruno's favourite phrases about the battles he has waged and the campaigns he has planned and led. But Herr *Hirzel* exercises his profession as a member of the Critical Mass especially by raging against the *profane Mass* and its attitude to *Critical Criticism*.

He speaks of the Mass claiming a part in history, "of the pure Mass", of "pure Criticism", of the "purity of this contradiction"—"a contradiction purer than any that history has provided"—of the "*discontented being*", of the "perfect emptiness, ill humour, dejection, heartlessness, timidity, fury and bitterness of the Mass towards Criticism"; of "the Mass which only exists in order by its resistance to make Criticism sharper and more vigilant". He speaks of "creation from the extreme opposite", of how Criticism is above *hate* and similar profane sentiments. The whole of Herr *Hirzel*'s contribution to the *Literatur-Zeitung* is confined to this profusion of Critical stock phrases. While reproaching the *Mass* for being satisfied with mere "disposition", "good will", "the phrase", "faith", etc., he himself, as a member of the *Critical Mass*, is content with phrases, expressions of his "Critical disposition", his "Critical faith", his "Critical good will" and leaves "action, work, struggle" and "works" to Herr Bruno and Co.

Despite the terrible picture of the world-historic tension between

---

[a] "Long live firm principles!" A. Weill und E. Bauer, *Berliner Novellen.*—*Ed.*

the profane world and "Critical Criticism" which the members of the "Critical Mass" outline, for the non-believer at least not even the fact of the matter is stated, the factual existence of this *world-historic* tension. The obliging and un-Critical repetition of Criticism's "imaginations" and "pretensions" by the correspondents only proves that the fixed ideas of the master are the fixed ideas of the servant as well. It is true that one of the Critical correspondents[a] makes an attempt at a proof based on *fact*.

"You see," he writes to the Holy Family, "that the *Literatur-Zeitung* is fulfilling its purpose, i.e., that it meets with *no approval*. It could meet with approval only if it sounded in unison with the general thoughtlessness, if you strode proudly before it with the jingling of hackneyed phrases of a whole janissary band of current categories."

The jingling of hackneyed phrases of a whole janissary band of current categories! It is evident that the Critical correspondent does his best to keep pace with non-"current" hackneyed phrases. But his explanation of the fact that the *Literatur-Zeitung* meets with no approval must be rejected as purely *apologetic*. This fact could be better explained in just the opposite way by saying that Critical Criticism is in *unison* with the great *mass*, to be precise, the great mass of scribblers who meet with *no* approval.

It is therefore not enough for the *Critical* correspondent to address Critical hackneyed phrases to the Holy Family as "prayers" and at the same time to the Mass as "anathemas". *Un-Critical, mass-type* correspondents, *real* delegates of the *Mass* to Critical Criticism, are needed to show the *real* tension between the Mass and Criticism.

That is why Critical Criticism also assigns a place to the *un-Critical Mass*. It makes unbiased *representatives* of the latter *correspond* with it, acknowledge the opposition to itself, Criticism, as important and absolute, and utter a *fearful cry* for redemption from this opposition.

2) THE "UN-CRITICAL MASS" AND "CRITICAL CRITICISM"

a) The "Obdurate Mass" and the "Unsatisfied Mass"

The hardness of heart, the obduracy and blind unbelief of "the Mass" has one rather determined representative. This representa-

---

[a] The reference is to the author of an anonymous report published in the *Allgemeine Literatur-Zeitung*, Heft VI, May 1844, in the section "Correspondenz aus der Provinz".— *Ed.*

tive speaks of the exclusively "Hegelian philosophical education of the Berlin Couleur".[63]

"The only true progress that we can make," he says, "lies in the acknowledgement of reality. But we learn from you that our knowledge was not knowledge of reality but of something unreal."

He calls "natural science" the basis of philosophy.

"A good naturalist stands in the same relation to the philosopher as the philosopher to the theologian."

Further he comments as follows on the "Berlin Couleur".

"I do not think it would be exaggerating to try to explain the state of these people by saying that, although they have gone through a process of spiritual moulting, they have not yet altogether got rid of their old skin in order to be able to absorb the elements of renovation and rejuvenation." "We must yet assimilate this" (natural-scientific and industrial) "knowledge". "The knowledge of the world and of man, which we need most of all, cannot be acquired only by acuity of thought; all the senses must collaborate and all the aptitudes of man must be applied as indispensable instruments; otherwise contemplation and knowledge will always remain defective—and will lead to *moral death*."

This correspondent, however, sweetens the pill that he hands out to Critical Criticism. He "makes *Bauer's words* find their correct application", he has "followed *Bauer's thoughts*", he agrees that "*Bauer has spoken* the truth" and in the end he seems to polemise, not against *Criticism* itself, but against a "Berlin Couleur" which is distinct from it.

Critical Criticism, feeling itself hit and, moreover, being as sensitive as an old maid in all *matters of faith*, is not taken in by these distinctions and this semi-homage.

"You are *mistaken*," it answers, "if you have taken the party you described at the beginning of your letter for *your opponent*. Rather *admit*" (and now comes the crushing sentence of excommunication) "that *you are an opponent of Criticism itself!*"

The miserable wretch! The man of the Mass! An opponent of *Criticism itself*! But as far as the content of that *mass-type* polemic is concerned, Critical Criticism declares its *respect* for its critical attitude to *natural science* and *industry*.

"*All respect for natural science! All respect* for James Watt and" (a really noble turn!) "no respect at all for the millions that he made for his relatives."

All respect for the respect of Critical Criticism! In the same letter in which Critical Criticism reproaches the above-mentioned *Berlin Couleur* with too easily disposing of thorough and solid works without studying them and having *finished* with a work when they have merely remarked that it is epoch-making, etc.— in that same letter *Criticism itself disposes* of the whole of natural science and *industry* by merely declaring its respect for them. The clause which it appends to its declaration of respect for *natural science* reminds one of the first fulminations of the deceased knight *Krug* against natural philosophy.

"Nature is not the only reality *because we eat and drink it in its individual products.*"

Critical Criticism knows this much about the *individual products* of nature that "we *eat and drink* them". All respect for the natural science of Critical Criticism!

Criticism is consistent in countering the embarrassingly importunate demand to study "nature" and "industry" with the following indisputably witty rhetorical exclamation:

"Or" (!) "do you think that the knowledge of *historical* reality is *already complete*? Or" (!) "do you know of any single period in history which is already *actually* known?"

Or does Critical Criticism believe that it has reached even the *beginning* of a knowledge of historical reality so long as it excludes *from* the historical movement the theoretical and practical relation of man to nature, i.e., natural science and industry? Or does it think that it actually knows any period without knowing, for example, the industry of that period, the immediate mode of production of life itself? Of course, spiritualistic, *theological* Critical Criticism only knows (at least it imagines it knows) the main political, literary and theological acts of history. Just as it separates thinking from the senses, the soul from the body and itself from the world, it separates history from natural science and industry and sees the origin of history not in vulgar *material* production on the earth but in vaporous clouds in the heavens.

The representative of the "obdurate" and "hard-hearted" Mass with his trenchant reproofs and counsels is disposed of as a *mass-type materialist.* Another correspondent, not so malicious or mass-like, who places his hopes in Critical Criticism but finds them unsatisfied, fares no better. The representative of the "*unsatisfied*" Mass writes:

"I must, however, admit that the first number of your paper was *by no means satisfying.* We expected something else."

The *Critical patriarch* answers in person:

"I knew beforehand that it would not satisfy expectations, because I could rather easily imagine those expectations. One is so exhausted that one wishes to have *everything at once.* Everything? No! If possible everything and nothing at the same time. An everything that costs no trouble, an everything that one can absorb without going through any development, an everything that is contained in a single word."

In his vexation at the undue demands of the "Mass", which demands *something*, indeed *everything*, from Criticism, which by principle and disposition *"gives nothing"*, the Critical patriarch relates an *anecdote* in the way that old men do. Not long ago a Berlin *acquaintance* complained bitterly of the verbosity and profusion of detail of his works — Herr Bruno is known to make a bulky work out of the tiniest semblance of a thought. He was consoled with the promise of being sent the ink necessary for the printing of the book in a small pellet so that he could easily absorb it. The patriarch explains the length of his "works" by the bad spreading of the ink, as he explains the nothingness of his *Literatur-Zeitung* by the emptiness of the "profane Mass", which, in order to be full, wants to swallow everything and nothing at the same time.

Just as it is difficult to deny the importance of what has so far been related, it is equally difficult to see a *world-historic contradiction* in the fact that a mass-type acquaintance of Critical Criticism considers Criticism empty, while Criticism, for its part, declares him to be un-Critical; that a second acquaintance does not find that the *Literatur-Zeitung* satisfies his expectations, and that a *third* acquaintance and friend of the family finds Criticism's works too bulky. However, acquaintance No. 2, who entertains expectations, and friend of the family No. 3, who wishes at least to find out the secrets of Critical Criticism, constitute the transition to a *more substantial* and tenser relationship between Criticism and the "un-Critical Mass". Cruel as *Criticism* is to the "hard-hearted" Mass which has only "common human reason", we shall find it condescending to the Mass that is pining for *redemption* from contradiction. The Mass which approaches Criticism with a contrite heart, a spirit of repentance and a humble mind will be rewarded for its honest striving with many a *wise, prophetic and outspoken* word.

b) The "Soft-Hearted" Mass "Pining for Redemption"

The representative of the *sentimental, soft-hearted Mass pining for redemption* cringes and implores Critical Criticism for a kind word with effusions of the heart, deep bows and rolling of the eyes, as follows:

"Why am I writing this to you? Why am I justifying myself before you? Because I *respect* you and therefore *desire* your *respect*; because I owe you deepest *thanks* for my development and therefore *love* you. My *heart* impels me to *justify myself* before you ... who have upbraided me.... *Far be it* from me to *obtrude* upon you; judging *by myself,* I thought you *might be pleased* to have proof of *sympathy* from a man who is still little known to you. I *make no claim whatsoever* that you should answer my letter: I wish *neither* to take up your time, of which you can make better use, *nor* to be irksome to you, *nor* to expose myself to the mortification of seeing something that I hoped for remain *unfulfilled.* You *may* interpret my letter as *sentimentality, importunity* or *vanity*" (!) "or whatever you like; you may answer me or not, I cannot resist the *impulse* to send it and I only hope that you will realise the *friendly feeling* which inspired it" (!!).

Just as from the beginning God has had mercy on the *poor in spirit,* this mass-like but humble correspondent, too, who whimpers for mercy from Critical Criticism, has his wish *fulfilled.* Critical Criticism gives him a kind answer. More than that! It gives him *most profound* explanations on the objects of his curiousity.

"Two years ago," Critical Criticism teaches, "it was opportune to remember the Enlightenment of the French in the eighteenth century in order to be able to make use of those *light troops,* too, at a place in the battle that was then being waged. The situation is now *quite different.* Truths now change very quickly. What was then *opportune* is now an *oversight.*"

Of course it was only "an *oversight*" then too, but an *"opportune"* one, when the Absolute Critical All-high itself (cf. *Anekdota,* Book II, p. 89)[a] called those *light troops* "our saints", our "prophets", "patriarchs", etc. Who would call *light troops* a troop of "patriarchs"? It was an "opportune" oversight when it spoke with enthusiasm of the self-denial, moral energy and inspiration with which these *light* troops "thought, worked—and studied—throughout their lives for the truth". It was an "oversight" when, in the preface to *Das entdeckte Christenthum,* it was stated that these "light" troops "seemed invincible and *any one well-informed* would have wagered that they would *put the world out of joint*" and that "it seemed beyond doubt that they would succeed in giving *the world a new shape*". *Those light troops?*

Critical Criticism continues to teach the inquisitive representative of the "*cordial* Mass":

"Although it was a *new* historical merit of the French to attempt to set up a social theory, they are *none the less now exhausted;* their new theory was not yet *pure,* their social fantasies and their *peaceful democracy* are by no means free from the assumptions of the old state of things."

Criticism is talking here about *Fourierism*—if it is talking about anything—and in particular of the Fourierism of *La Démocratie pacifique.* But this is far from being the "social theory" of the French. The French have *social theories,* but not *a* social theory; the

---

[a] B. Bauer, "Leiden und Freuden des theologischen Bewusstseins". *Anekdota zur neuesten deutschen Philosophie und Publicistik,* Bd. 2.—*Ed.*

diluted Fourierism that *La Démocratie pacifique* preaches is nothing but the social doctrine of a section of the philanthropic bourgeoisie. The people is *communistic*, and, as a matter of fact, split into a multitude of different groups; the true movement and the elaboration of these different social shades is not only not *exhausted*, it is really only *beginning*. But it will not end in pure, i.e., abstract, *theory* as Critical Criticism would like it to; it will end in a quite *practical practice* that will not bother at all about the categorical categories of Criticism.

> "No nation," Criticism chatters on, "has *so far* any advantage over another. If one can succeed in winning some spiritual superiority over the others, it will be the one which is in a position to criticise itself and the others and to discover the causes of the universal decay."

Every nation has *so far some advantage* over another. But if the Critical prophecy is right, no nation *will* have any advantage over another, because all the civilised peoples of Europe — the English, the Germans, the French — now "*criticise* themselves and others" and "are in a position to discover the causes of the universal decay". Finally, it is high-sounding *tautology* to say that "criticising", "discovering", i.e., *spiritual* activities, give a *spiritual superiority*, and Criticism, which in its infinite self-consciousness places itself above the nations and expects them to kneel at its feet and implore it for enlightenment, only shows by this caricatured Christian-Germanic idealism that it is still up to its neck in the mire of *German nationalism*.

The criticism of the French and the English is not an abstract, preternatural personality outside mankind; it is the *real human activity* of individuals who are active members of society and who suffer, feel, think and act as human beings. That is why their criticism is at the same time practical, their communism a socialism in which they give practical, concrete measures, and in which they not only think but even more act, it is the living, real criticism of existing society, the recognition of the causes of "the decay".

After Critical Criticism's explanations for the inquisitive member of the Mass, it is entitled to say of its *Literatur-Zeitung*:

> "Here Criticism that is *pure*, graphic, relevant and adds nothing is practised."

Here "*nothing self-existing* is given"; here *nothing* at all *is given* except *criticism that gives nothing*, that is, criticism which culminates in extreme non-criticism. *Criticism* has underlined passages printed and reaches its full bloom in *excerpts*. *Wolfgang Menzel* and *Bruno Bauer* stretch a brotherly hand to each other and Critical Criticism stands where the *philosophy of identity* stood at the beginning of this century, when *Schelling* protested against the mass-like supposition that he wanted to give something, anything except *pure, entirely philosophical* philosophy.[64]

c) Grace Bestowed on the Mass

The soft-hearted correspondent whose instruction we have just witnessed stood in a *comfortable* relationship to Criticism. In his case there was only an idyllic hint of the tension between the *Mass* and *Criticism*. Both sides of the *world-historic* contradiction behaved *kindly* and *politely*, and therefore *exoterically*, to each other.

Critical Criticism, in its *unhealthy*, soul-shattering effect on the Mass, is seen first in regard to a correspondent who has one foot already in Criticism and the other still in the profane world. He represents the "Mass" in its *inner* struggle with Criticism.

At times it seems to him "that Herr Bruno and his friends do not understand *mankind*", that "they are the ones who are really blinded". Then he immediately corrects himself:

"Yes, it is *as clear as daylight* to me that you are right and that your thoughts are correct; but *excuse* me, the people is *not* wrong either.... Oh *yes!* The people is right.... I cannot deny that you are right.... I really do not know what it will all lead to: you will say ... well, stay at home.... *Alas*, I can no longer stand it.... *Alas!* One might otherwise go *mad* in the end.... *Kindly* accept... Believe me, the knowledge one has acquired sometimes makes one feel as *stupid* as if a mill-wheel were turning in one's head."

Another correspondent, too, writes that he "is *occasionally disconcerted*". One can see that *Critical grace* is about *to be bestowed* on this mass-type correspondent. The poor wretch! The sinful Mass is tugging at him on one side and Critical Criticism on the other. It is not the knowledge he has acquired that reduces this pupil of Critical Criticism to a state of stupor; it is the question of *faith* and *conscience*; Critical Christ or the people, God or the world, Bruno Bauer and his friends or the profane Mass! But just as bestowal of *divine* grace is preceded by extreme wretchedness of the sinner, *Critical* grace is preceded by a crushing *stupefaction*. And when it is at last bestowed, the chosen one loses not stupidity but the *consciousness of stupidity*.

3) THE UN-CRITICALLY CRITICAL MASS OR "CRITICISM" AND THE "BERLIN COULEUR"

Critical Criticism has not succeeded in depicting itself as the *essential opposite*, and hence at the same time as the *essential object*, of the mass of humanity. Apart from the representatives of the *obdurate* Mass which reproaches Critical Criticism for its *objectlessness* and gives it to understand in the most courteous possible way that it has not yet gone through the *process* of its spiritual *"moult"* and must first of all acquire solid knowledge, there is the *soft-hearted* correspondent. He is no *opposite* at all, but then the actual reason for his approach to Critical Criticism is a *purely personal* one. As we can see a little further on in his letter, he really only wants to reconcile his devotion to Herr Arnold Ruge with his devotion to Herr *Bruno Bauer*. This attempt at reconciliation does credit to his kind heart, but it in no way constitutes an *interest of a mass nature*. Finally, the last correspondent to appear was no longer a *real* member of the Mass, he was only a catechumen of Critical Criticism.

In general, the *Mass* is an *indefinite* object, and therefore can neither carry out a definite action nor enter into a definite relationship. *The* Mass, as the object of Critical Criticism, has nothing in common with the *real* masses who, for their part, form among themselves oppositions of a pronounced mass nature. *Critical Criticism's* mass is "made" by Criticism itself, as would be the case if a naturalist, instead of speaking of definite classes, contrasted *the* Class to himself.

Hence, in order to have an opposite of a really mass nature, *Critical Criticism* needs, besides this *abstract* Mass which is the figment of its own brain, a *definite Mass* that can be empirically demonstrated and not just conjured up. This Mass must see in Critical Criticism both its *essence* and *the annihilation of its essence*. It must *wish* to be Critical Criticism, non-Mass, without *being able to*. This Critically un-Critical Mass is the above-mentioned *"Berlin Couleur"*. The *mass* of humanity which is seriously concerned with Critical Criticism is confined to a Berlin Couleur.

The "Berlin Couleur", the *"essential object"* of Critical Criticism, of which it is always thinking and which, Critical Criticism imagines, is always thinking of Critical Criticism, consists, as far as we know, of a few *ci-devant*[a] *Young Hegelians* in whom Critical Criticism claims to inspire partly a *horror vacui*[b] and partly a feeling of *futility*. We are not investigating the actual state of affairs, we rely on what *Criticism* says.

The *Correspondence* is mainly intended to expound *at length* to the public this *world-historic* relation of *Criticism* to the "Berlin Couleur", to reveal its profound significance, to show why Criti-

---

[a] Former.—*Ed.*

[b] Horror of emptiness.—*Ed.*

cism must necessarily be cruel towards this "Mass", and finally to make it appear that *the whole world* is in fearful agitation over this opposition, expressing itself now in favour of, and then against the actions of *Criticism*. For example, *Absolute* Criticism writes to a correspondent who sides with the "Berlin Couleur":

> "I have *already* heard things like that *so often* that I have made up my mind not to take any more notice of them."

The world has no idea how often it has dealt with Critical things *like that*.

Let us now hear what a member of the *Critical* Mass reports on the Berlin Couleur:

> "'If anyone recognises the Bauers'" (the Holy Family must always be recognised *pêle-mêle*) "began his answer[a]—'*I* am the one. But the *Literatur-Zeitung!* Let us be quite fair!'* It was interesting for me to hear what one of those radicals, those clever men of *anno* 42, thought of you...."

The correspondent goes on to report that the unfortunate man had all sorts of reproaches to make to the *Literatur-Zeitung*.

Herr Edgar's short story, *Die drei Biedermänner*,[b] he found lacking in polish and exaggerated. He could not understand that *censorship* is not so much a fight of man against man, an external fight, as an internal one. They do not take the trouble to bethink themselves and to replace the *phrase the censor objects to* by a *cleverly* expressed and thoroughly developed *Critical thought*. He found Herr Edgar's essay on Béraud[c] lacking in thoroughness. The Critical reporter thinks it was thorough. True he admitted himself: "I have *not* read Béraud's book." But he *believes* that Herr Edgar has *succeeded*, etc., and belief, we know, is bliss. "In general," the Critical believer continues, "he" (the one from the Berlin Couleur) "is *not at all satisfied* with Herr Edgar's works." He also finds that "*Proudhon* is not dealt with *thoroughly* enough".[d] And here the reporter gives Herr Edgar a testimonial:

> "*It is true*" (!?) "*that I am acquainted with* Proudhon. I *know* that Edgar's presentation took the *characteristic* points from him and set them out clearly."

The only reason why Herr Edgar's *excellent* criticism of Proudhon is not liked, the reporter says, can only be that Herr Edgar does *not fulminate* against property. And just imagine it, the opponent

---

[a] The reference is to the answer given by an adherent to the Berlin Couleur to one of the authors of the anonymous report "Aus der Provinz" published in the *Allgemeine Literatur-Zeitung*, Heft VI, May 1844.— *Ed.*

[b] Published in the *Allgemeine Literatur-Zeitung*, Heft III-V.— *Ed.*

[c] See p. 20 of this volume.—*Ed.*

[d] See pp. 23-54 of this volume.— *Ed.*

finds Herr Edgar's essay on the *"Union ouvrière"*[a] *unimportant.*
To console Herr Edgar the reporter says:

"Of course, it does not give anything *independent,* and these people have really
gone back to *Gruppe's* point of view, which, to be sure, they have *always maintained.*
Criticism must give, give and *give!"*

As though Criticism had not given quite new linguistic, historical, philosophical, economic, and juridical discoveries! And it is so
modest as to let itself be told that it has not given anything
independent! Even our Critical correspondent gave mechanics something that it had not hitherto known when he made people *go back
to the same* point of view which they had always *maintained.* It is
clumsy to recall *Gruppe's* point of view. In his pamphlet, which is
otherwise miserable and not worth mentioning, Gruppe asked
Herr Bruno what criticism he could give on *speculative logic.*[65]
Herr Bruno referred him to future generations and—

"a fool is waiting for an answer".[b]

As God punished the unbelieving Pharaoh by hardening his
heart and did *not think* him *worthy* of being enlightened, so the
reporter assures us:

"They are therefore *not at all worthy* of seeing or knowing the contents of your
Literatur-Zeitung."

And instead of advising his friend Edgar to acquire thoughts
and knowledge he gives him the following advice:

"Let Edgar get a *bag of phrases* and draw blindly out of it when he writes essays
in future, in order to acquire a style in harmony with the public."

Besides assurances of "a certain fury, ill-favour, emptiness,
thoughtlessness, an inkling of something which they are not able
to fathom, and a feeling of nullity" (all these epithets apply, of
course, to the Berlin Couleur), eulogies like the following are
made of the Holy Family:

"Lightness of treatment penetrating the matter, command of the categories,
insight acquired by study, in a word, *command* of *the* Objects. He" (of the Berlin
Couleur) "takes an easy attitude to the thing, you make the thing easy." Or: "Your
criticism in the *Literatur-Zeitung* is pure, graphic and relevant."

Finally it is stated:

"I have written it all to you at such length because I know that I shall give you
pleasure by reporting the opinions of my friend. From this you can see that the
Literatur-Zeitung is fulfilling its purpose."

Its purpose is opposition to the Berlin Couleur. Having just

---

[a] See pp. 19-20 of this volume.—*Ed.*
[b] H. Heine, *Die Nordsee* (second cycle "Fragen").—*Ed.*

witnessed the *Berlin Couleur*'s *polemic* against Critical Criticism and the reproof it received for that polemic, we are now given a double picture of its efforts to obtain mercy from Critical Criticism.

One correspondent writes:

"My acquaintances in Berlin told me when I was there at the beginning of the year that you repel all and keep all at a distance; that you keep yourself to yourself and let nobody approach you, assiduously avoiding all intercourse. I, of course, cannot tell which side is to blame."

Absolute Criticism replies:

"Criticism does *not* form any *party* and will have no party of its own; it is *solitary* because it is engrossed in *its*" (!) "*object* and opposes itself to it. It *isolates itself from everything*."

Critical Criticism thinks it rises above all dogmatic antitheses by substituting for the real antitheses the imaginary antithesis between *itself and the world*, between the *Holy Ghost* and the *profane Mass*. In the same way it thinks it rises *above parties* by falling *below the party point of view*, by counterposing itself as a *party* to the rest of mankind and concentrating all interest in the personality of Herr Bruno and Co. The truth of Criticism's *admission* that it sits enthroned in the solitude of *abstraction*, that even when it seems to be occupied with some *object* it does not come out of its objectless solitude into a truly *social* relation to a *real object*, because *its object* is only the object of *its imagination*, only an imaginary object — the truth of this Critical *admission* is proved by the whole of our exposition. Equally correctly Criticism defines its *abstraction* as *absolute* abstraction, in the sense that "it *isolates* itself *from everything*", and precisely this isolation of *nothing from everything*, from *all* thought, contemplation, etc., is *absolute nonsense*. Incidentally, the solitude which it achieves by isolating and abstracting itself from *everything* is no more free from the object from which it abstracts itself than *Origen* was from the *genital organ* that he *isolated* from himself.

Another correspondent begins by describing *one* of the members of the "Berlin Couleur", whom he saw and spoke with, as "gloomy", "depressed", "no longer able to open his mouth" (although he was formerly always "ready with a quite *impudent* word"), and "despondent". This member of the "Berlin Couleur" related the following to the correspondent, who in turn reported it to Criticism:

"He cannot grasp how people like you two, who formerly respected the principle of humanity, can behave in such an aloof, repelling, indeed arrogant manner." He does not know "why there are some people who, it seems, intentionally cause a split. Have we not all the same point of view? Do we not all *pay homage* to the extreme, to Criticism? Are we not all capable, if not of producing, at least of grasping and applying an extreme thought?" He "finds that this split is motivated by no other principle than egoism and arrogance".

Then the correspondent puts in a good word:

"Have not at least some of our friends grasped *Criticism,* or perhaps *the good will of Criticism* ... '*ut desint vires, tamen est laudanda voluntas*'." [a]

Criticism replies with the following *antitheses* between itself and the Berlin Couleur:

"There are *various* standpoints on criticism." The members of the Berlin Couleur "thought they had criticism in their pocket", but Criticism "really knows and applies the force of criticism", i.e., does not keep it in its pocket. For the former, criticism is pure form, whereas for Criticism, on the other hand, it is the "*most substantial* or rather the only *substantial thing*". Just as Absolute Thought considers itself the whole of reality, *so* does Critical Criticism. That is why it sees no content *outside itself* and is therefore not the criticism of *real* objects existing outside the Critical subject; on the contrary, it *makes* the object, it is the Absolute *Subject-Object*. Further! "The former kind of criticism disposes of everything, of the investigation of things, by means of phrases. The latter isolates itself *from everything* by means of phrases." The former is *"clever in ignorance"*, the latter is "learning". The latter, at any rate, is not clever, it learns *par ça, par là,*[b] but only in appearance, only in order to be able to fling what it has superficially learnt from the Mass back at the Mass in the form of a "catchword", as wisdom that it itself has discovered, and to resolve it into the nonsense of Critical Criticism.

"For the former, words such as 'extreme', 'proceed', 'not go far enough' are of importance and highly revered categories; the latter *investigates the standpoints* and does not apply to them the *measures* of those abstract categories."

The exclamations of Criticism No. 2 that it is no longer a question of politics, that philosophy is done away with, and its dismissal of social systems and developments by means of words like "fantastic", "utopian", etc.— what is all that if not a *Critically revised* version of "proceeding" and "not going far enough"? And are not its "measures", such as "*History*", "*Criticism*", "summing up of objects", "the old and the new", "Criticism and Mass", "investigation of standpoints"—in a word, are not all its catch-

---

[a] "The strength may be lacking, but the will is praiseworthy."—*Ed*.
[b] Here and there.—*Ed*.

words *categorical measures* and abstractly categorical ones at that!?

"The former is theological, spiteful, envious, petty, presumptuous, the latter is the *opposite* of all that."

After thus praising itself a dozen times in one breath and ascribing to itself all that the Berlin Couleur lacks, just as God *is* all that *man is not, Criticism* bears witness to itself that:

"It has achieved a clarity, a thirst for learning, a tranquillity in which it is *unassailable* and *invincible*."

Hence it can "at the most treat" its opponent, the Berlin Couleur, "with *Olympic laughter*". This *laughter*—it explains with its customary thoroughness what it is and what it is not—"this laughter is not arrogance". By no means! It is the negation of the negation. It is "*only the process* that *the Critic must apply* in all ease and equanimity against a *subordinate standpoint* which *thinks* itself *equal* to him" (what conceit!). When *the* Critic laughs, therefore, he is *applying a process!* And "in all equanimity" he applies the *process of laughter* not against *persons*, but against a *standpoint!* Even *laughter* is a *category* which he applies and even *must* apply!

Extramundane Criticism is not an *essential activity* of the *human subject* who is *real* and therefore lives and suffers in *present-day* society, sharing in its pains and pleasures. The *real* individual is only an *accidental feature*, an earthly vessel of *Critical Criticism*, which reveals itself in it as *eternal Substance*. The subject is not the human individual's criticism, but the *non-human individual of Criticism*. Criticism is not a *manifestation of man*, but man is an *alienation of Criticism*, and that is why the Critic lives completely outside society.

"Can the Critic live in the society which he criticises?"

It should be asked instead: Must he not live in that society? Must he not himself be a manifestation of the life of that society? Why does the Critic *sell* the products of his mind, for thereby he makes the worst law of present-day society his own law?

"*The* Critic must not even dare to mix *personally* with society."

That is why he creates for himself a *Holy Family*, just as the solitary God endeavours in the Holy Family to end his tedious isolation from society. If the Critic *wants to free himself* from *bad society* he must first of all free himself from *his own society*.

"Thus the Critic dispenses with *all the pleasures of society*, but *its sufferings*, too, stay remote from him. He knows neither *friendship*" (except that of Critical friends) "nor love" (except *self-love*) "but on the other hand calumny is powerless against him; nothing can offend him; no hatred, no envy can affect him; vexation and grief are *feelings unknown* to him."

In short, the Critic is free from all *human passions*, he is a *divine person*; he can apply to himself the song of the nun.

> I think not of a lover,
> I think not of a spouse.
> I think of God the Father
> For he my life endows.[a]

Criticism cannot write a single passage without contradicting itself. Thus it tells us finally:

"The Philistinism that stones the Critic" (he has to be stoned by analogy with the Bible), "that misjudges him and ascribes *impure* motives to him" (ascribes *impure* motives to *pure* Criticism!) "in order to make *him equal to itself*" (the conceit of equality reproved above!), "is *not laughed at* by him, because it is not worth it, but is seen through and calmly relegated to its own insignificant significance."

Earlier the Critic *had to* apply the *process of laughter* to the "subordinate standpoint that thought itself equal to him". Critical Criticism's unclarity about its mode of procedure with the godless "Mass" seems almost to indicate an interior irritation, a sort of bile to which "feelings" are not "unknown".

However, there should be no misunderstanding. Having waged a Herculean struggle *to free* itself from the un-Critical "profane Mass" and "everything", Critical Criticism has at last succeeded in achieving its *solitary, god-like, self-sufficient, absolute* existence. If in its first pronouncement in this, its "new phase", the old world of *sinful feelings* seems still to have some power over it, we shall now see Criticism find aesthetic relaxation and *transfiguration* in an "*artistic form*" and complete its *penance* so it can finally as a second triumphant *Christ* accomplish the *Critical last judgment* and after its victory over the dragon ascend calmly to heaven.

---

[a] From the German folk-song *Die Nonne* published in the book by F. K. Freiherr von Erlach, *Die Volkslieder der Deutschen*, Bd. IV.— *Ed.*

Chapter VIII

THE EARTHLY COURSE AND TRANSFIGURATION OF "CRITICAL CRITICISM", OR "CRITICAL CRITICISM" AS RUDOLPH, PRINCE OF GEROLDSTEIN[a]

Rudolph, Prince of Geroldstein, *does penance* in his *earthly course* for a *double* crime: his *personal* crime and that of *Critical Criticism.* In a furious dialogue he drew his sword against his father; Critical Criticism, also in a furious dialogue, let itself be carried away by sinful·feelings against the Mass. Critical Criticism did *not* reveal *a single* mystery. Rudolph does penance for that and reveals *all* mysteries.

Rudolph, Herr Szeliga informs us, is the *first* servant of the *state* of humanity (the *Humanitätsstaat* of the Swabian *Egidius.* See *Konstitutionelle Jahrbücher* by Dr. Karl Weil, 1844, Bd. 2[66]).

For *the world not to be destroyed,* Herr Szeliga asserts, it is necessary that

"men of ruthless criticism appear.... Rudolph is *such* a man.... Rudolph grasps the thought of *pure criticism.* And that thought is more fruitful for him and mankind than *all* the experiences of the latter in its *history,* than *all* the knowledge that Rudolph, guided even by the most reliable teacher, was able to derive from that history.... The impartial judgment by which Rudolph perpetuates his *earthly course* is, *in fact,* nothing but

the revelation of the mysteries of society."
He is: *"the revealed mystery of all mysteries."*

Rudolph has far more *external* means at his disposal than the other men of Critical Criticism. But the latter consoles itself:

"Unattainable for those less favoured by destiny are Rudolph's *results*" (!), "not unattainable is the splendid goal (!)."

---

[a] In this chapter Marx continues his criticism of Szeliga's article "Eugène Sue: Die Geheimnisse von Paris" (see pp. 55-77 of this volume).— *Ed.*

That is why Criticism leaves the *realisation* of its own *thoughts* to Rudolph, who is so favoured by destiny. It sings to him:

> *Hahnemann, go on ahead.*
> *You've waders on, you won't get wet!*[a]

Let us accompany Rudolph in his Critical earthly course, which "is *more fruitful* for *mankind* than *all the experiences* of the latter in its history, than *all the knowledge*" etc., and which *twice* saves the world from *destruction*.

1) CRITICAL TRANSFORMATION OF A BUTCHER INTO A DOG, OR CHOURINEUR[b]

Chourineur was a butcher by trade. Owing to a concourse of circumstances, this mighty son of nature becomes a murderer. Rudolph comes across him accidentally just when he is molesting Fleur de Marie. Rudolph gives the dexterous brawler a few impressive, masterly punches on the head, and thus wins his respect. Later, in the tavern frequented by criminals, Chourineur's kind-hearted disposition is revealed. "You still have heart and honour," Rudolph says to him. By these words he instils in Chourineur respect for himself. Chourineur is reformed or, as Herr Szeliga says, is transformed into a *"moral being"*. Rudolph takes him under his protection. Let us follow the course of Chourineur's education under the guidance of Rudolph.

1st Stage. The first lesson Chourineur receives is a lesson in hypocrisy, faithlessness, craft and *dissimulation*. Rudolph uses the reformed Chourineur in exactly the same way as *Vidocq* used the criminals he had reformed, i.e., he makes him a *mouchard*[c] and *agent provocateur*. He advises him to *"pretend"* to the *"maître d'école"*[d] that he has altered his *"principle of not stealing"* and to suggest a robbery so as to lure him into a trap set by Rudolph. Chourineur feels that he is being made a fool of. He protests against the suggestion of playing the role of *mouchard* and *agent provocateur*. Rudolph easily convinces the son of nature by the *"pure"* *casuistry* of Critical Criticism that a foul trick is not foul when it is done for *"good, moral"* reasons. Chourineur, as an *agent provocateur* and under the pretence of friendship and confidence, lures his former companion to destruction. For the *first time* in his life he commits an act of *infamy*.

---

[a] From the German folk-tale *Sieben Schwaben* published in *Volksbücher*, hrsg. v. G. O. Marbach.— *Ed.*

[b] *Chourineur* is French thieves' slang for a murderous ruffian.— *Ed.*

[c] *Police spy.*— *Ed.*

[d] The "maître d'école", a nickname given by his fellow criminals.— *Ed.*

2nd Stage. We next find Chourineur acting as *garde-malade*[a] to Rudolph, whom he has saved from mortal danger.

Chourineur has become such a *respectable moral* being that he rejects the Negro doctor David's suggestion to sit on the floor, for fear of dirtying the carpet. He is indeed too *shy* to sit on a chair. He first lays the chair on its back and then sits on the front legs. He never fails to apologise when he addresses Rudolph, whom he saved from a mortal danger, as "friend" or "*Monsieur*" instead of "*Monseigneur*".

What a wonderful training of the ruthless son of nature! Chourineur expresses the innermost secret of his Critical transformation when he admits to Rudolph that he has the same attachment for him as a *bulldog* for its master: "Je me sens pour vous, comme qui dirait *l'attachement* d'un *bouledogue* pour *son maître.*" The former butcher is transformed into a dog. Henceforth all his virtues will be reduced to the virtue of a dog, pure "*dévouement*" to its master. His independence, his individuality will disappear completely. But just as bad painters have to label their pictures to say what they are supposed to represent, Eugène Sue has to put a label on "*bulldog*" Chourineur, who constantly affirms: "The two words, 'You still have heart and honour', made a *man* out of me." Until his very last breath, Chourineur will find the motive for his actions, not in his human individuality, but in that label. As proof of his moral reformation he will often reflect on his own excellence and the wickedness of other individuals. And every time he throws out moral sentences, Rudolph will say to him: "I like to hear you *speak* like that." Chourineur has not become an ordinary *bulldog* but a *moral one.*

3rd Stage. We have already admired the *petty-bourgeois respectability* which has taken the place of Chourineur's *coarse* but *daring* unceremoniousness. We now learn that, as befits a "*moral being*", he has also adopted the gait and demeanour of the *petty bourgeois.*

"A le voir marcher—on l'eût pris pour le *bourgeois* le plus inoffensif du monde."[b]

Still sadder than this form is the content that Rudolph gives his Critically reformed life. He sends him to Africa "to serve as a living and salutary example of repentance to the world of unbelievers". In future, he will have to represent, not his own human nature, but a Christian dogma.

---

[a] Sick attendant.—*Ed.*

[b] "To see him walk you would have taken him for the most harmless *bourgeois* in the world."—*Ed.*

4th Stage. The Critically moral transformation has made Chourineur a quiet, cautious man who behaves according to the rules of fear and worldly wisdom.

"Le Chourineur", reports Murph, who in his indiscreet simplicity continually tells tales out of school "n'a pas dit un mot de l'exécution du maître d'école, de *peur* de *se* trouver compromis." [a]

So Chourineur knows that the punishment of the *maître d'école* was an illegal act. But he does not talk about it for fear of compromising himself. *Wise* Chourineur!

5th Stage. Chourineur has carried his moral education to such perfection that he gives his *dog-like* attitude to Rudolph a civilised form — he becomes conscious of it. After saving *Germain* from a mortal danger he says to him:

"I have a protector who is to me what *God* is to *priests* — he is such as to make one kneel before him."

And in imagination he kneels before his God.

"Monsieur Rudolph," he says to Germain, "protects you. I say '*Monsieur*' though I should say '*Monseigneur*'. But I am used to calling him '*Monsieur* Rudolph', and he allows me to."

"Magnificent awakening and flowering!" exclaims Szeliga in Critical delight.

6th Stage. Chourineur worthily ends his career of pure *dévouement*, or moral bulldogishness, by finally letting himself be stabbed to death for his gracious lord. At the moment when Squelette threatens the prince with his knife, Chourineur stays the murderer's arm. Squelette stabs him. But, dying, Chourineur says to Rudolph:

"I was right when I said that a *lump of earth*" (a bulldog) "like me can sometimes be useful to a *great and gracious master* like you."

To this dog-like utterance, which sums up the whole of Chourineur's Critical life like *an* epigram, the label put in his mouth adds:

"We are quits, Monsieur Rudolph. You told me that I had heart and honour."

Herr Szeliga cries as loud as he can:

"What a merit it was for Rudolph to have restored the *Schurimann*[b]" (?) "to *mankind* (?)!"

---

[a] "Chourineur said nothing of the punishment meted out to the *maître d'école* for fear of compromising himself." — *Ed.*

[b] Schurimann is a Germanised form of Chourineur. — *Ed.*

2) REVELATION OF THE MYSTERY OF CRITICAL RELIGION, OR FLEUR DE MARIE

a) The Speculative "Marguerite" [a]

A word more about Herr Szeliga's speculative "Marguerite" before we go on to Eugène Sue's Fleur de Marie.

The speculative "Marguerite" is above all a *correction*. The fact is that the reader could conclude from Herr Szeliga's construction that Eugène Sue had

"separated the presentation of the objective basis" (of the "world system") "from the development of the acting individual forces which can be understood only against that background".

Besides the task of correcting this erroneous conjecture that the reader may have made from Herr Szeliga's presentation, Marguerite has also a metaphysical mission in our, or rather Herr Szeliga's, "epic".

"The *world system* and an epic event *would still not be* artistically united in a really *single* whole if they were only interspersed in a motley mixture — now here a bit of world system and then there some stage play. If *real unity* is to result, both things, the mysteries of this prejudiced *world* and the clarity, frankness and confidence with which *Rudolph* penetrates and reveals them, must clash in a *single* individual.... This is the task of Marguerite."

Herr Szeliga speculatively constructs Marguerite by analogy with *Bauer's* construction of the *Mother of God*.

On one side is the "*divine element*" (*Rudolph*) to which "all power and freedom" are attributed, the only *active* principle. On the other side is the passive "*world system*" and the human beings belonging to it. The world system is the "ground of reality". If this ground is not to be "entirely abandoned" or "the last remnant of the natural condition is not to be abolished"; if the world itself is to have some share in the "principle of development" that Rudolph, in contrast to the world, concentrates in himself; if "the human element is not to be represented simply as unfree and inactive", Herr Szeliga is bound to fall into the "contradiction of religious consciousness". Although he tears apart the world system and its activity as the dualism of a dead Mass and Criticism (Rudolph), he is nevertheless obliged to concede some attributes of divinity to the world system and the mass and to give in Marguerite a speculative construction of the unity of the two, Rudolph and the world (see *Kritik der Synoptiker*, Band I, p. 39).

---

[a] "Fleur de Marie" is translated by the authors into German as "Marien-Blume" which means Marguerite.— *Ed.*

Besides the real relations of the *house-owner*, the acting "individual force", to his *house* (the "objective basis"), mystical speculation, and speculative aesthetics too, need a third *concrete, speculative unity*, a *Subject-Object* which is the house and the house-owner in *one*. As speculation does not like natural mediations in their extensive circumstantiality, it does not realise that the same "bit of world system", the house, for example, which for one, the house-owner, for example, is an "objective basis", is for the other, the builder of the house, an "epic event". In order to get a "really single whole" and "real unity", Critical Criticism, which reproaches "romantic art" with the "dogma of unity", replaces the natural and human connection between the world system and world events by a fantastic connection, a mystical Subject-Object, just as *Hegel replaces* the real connection between man and nature by an absolute Subject-Object which is at one and the same time the whole of nature and the whole of humanity, the *Absolute Spirit*.

In the Critical Marguerite "the universal guilt of the time, the guilt of mystery", becomes the *"mystery of guilt"*, just as the universal debt[a] of mystery becomes the *mystery of debts* in the indebted *Epicier*.[b]

According to the Mother-of-God construction, Marguerite should *really* have been the *mother of Rudolph*, the redeemer of the world. Herr Szeliga expressly says:

"According to the *logical sequence*, Rudolph should have been the *son* of Marguerite."

Since, however, he is not her son, but her father, Herr Szeliga finds in this "the new mystery that the present often bears in its womb the long departed past instead of the future". He even reveals another mystery, a still greater one, a mystery which directly contradicts mass-type statistics, the mystery that

"a child, if it does not, in its turn, become a father or mother, but goes to its grave pure and innocent, is ... *essentially* ... a *daughter*".

Herr Szeliga faithfully follows Hegel's speculation when, according to the *"logical* sequence", he regards the daughter as the mother of her father. In Hegel's philosophy of history, as in his philosophy of nature, the son engenders the mother, the spirit nature, the Christian religion paganism, the result the beginning.

After proving that according to the *"logical* sequence" Marguerite ought to have been Rudolph's mother, Herr Szeliga proves the opposite:

---

[a] Here the authors have a pun on the word "*Schuld*" which means "guilt" and "debt".— *Ed.*

[b] Grocer.— *Ed.*

"in order to conform fully to the *idea* she embodies in *our* epic, she *must never become a mother*".

This shows at least that the idea of our epic and Herr Szeliga's logical sequence are mutually contradictory.

The speculative Marguerite is nothing but the "*embodiment of an idea*". But what idea?

"She has the task of representing, *as it were,* the last tear of grief that the past sheds prior to its final passing away."

She is the representation of an allegorical tear, and even this little that she is, *is* only "*as it were*".

We shall not follow Herr Szeliga in his further description of Marguerite. We shall leave her the satisfaction, according to Herr Szeliga's prescription, of "constituting *the most decisive* antithesis to *everyone*", a mysterious antithesis, as mysterious as the attributes of God.

Neither shall we delve into the "*true mystery*" that is "deposited *by God* in the breast of man" and at which the speculative Marguerite "as it were" hints. We shall pass from Herr Szeliga's Marguerite to Eugène Sue's Fleur de Marie and to the Critical miraculous cures Rudolph accomplishes on her.

b) Fleur de Marie

We meet Marie surrounded by criminals, as a prostitute in bondage to the proprietress of the criminals' tavern. In this debasement she preserves a human nobleness of soul, a human unaffectedness and a human beauty that impress those around her, raise her to the level of a poetical flower of the criminal world and win for her the name of Fleur de Marie.

We must observe Fleur de Marie attentively from her first appearance in order to be able to compare her *original form* with her *Critical transformation*.

In spite of her frailty, Fleur de Marie at once gives proof of vitality, energy, cheerfulness, resilience of character — qualities which alone explain her human development in her *inhuman* situation.

When Chourineur ill-treats her, she defends herself with her scissors. That is the situation in which we first find her. She does not appear as a defenceless lamb who surrenders without any resistance to overwhelming brutality; she is a girl who can vindicate her rights and put up a fight.

In the criminals' tavern in the Rue aux Fèves she tells Chourineur and Rudolph the story of her life. As she does so she *laughs* at Chourineur's wit. She blames herself because on being released from prison she spent the 300 francs she had earned there on amusements instead of looking for work. "But," she said, "I had no one to advise me." The memory of the catastrophe of her life — her selling herself to the proprietress of the criminals' tavern — puts her in a melancholy mood. It is the first time since her childhood that she has recalled these events.

"Le fait est, que ça me chagrine de regarder ainsi derrière moi ... ça doit être bien bon d'être honnête." [a]

When Chourineur makes fun of her and tells her she must become honest, she exclaims:

"Honnête, mon dieu! et avec quoi donc veux-tu que je sois honnête?" [b]

She insists that she is not one "to have fits of tears": "*Je ne suis pas pleurnicheuse*" [c]; but her position in life is sad —"*Ça n'est pas gai.*" [d] Finally, contrary to Christian *repentance*, she pronounces on the past the human sentence, at once *Stoic* and *Epicurean*, of a free and strong nature:

"*Enfin ce qui est fait, est fait.*" [e]

Let us accompany Fleur de Marie on her first outing with Rudolph.

"The consciousness of your terrible situation has probably often distressed you," Rudolph says, itching to moralise.

"Yes," she replies, "more than once I looked over the embankment of the Seine; but then I would gaze at the flowers and the sun and say to myself: the river will always be there and I am not yet seventeen years old. Who can say? Dans ces moments-là il me semblait que mon sort n'était pas mérité, qu'il y avait en moi quelque chose de bon. Je me disais, on m'a bien tourmenté, mais au moins je n'ai jamais fait de mal à personne." [f]

Fleur de Marie considers her situation not as one she has freely created, not as the expression of her own personality, but as a fate she has not deserved. Her bad fortune can change. She is still young.

Good and *evil*, as Marie conceives them, are not the *moral abstractions* of good and evil. She is *good* because she has never caused *suffering* to anyone, she has always been *human* towards her

---

[a] "The fact is that it grieves me when I look back in this way ... it must be lovely to be honest."—*Ed.*

[b] "Honest! My God! What do you want me to be honest with?"—*Ed.*

[c] "I am no crybaby."—*Ed.*

[d] "It isn't a happy one."—*Ed.*

[e] "Well, what is done is done."—*Ed.*

[f] "On such occasions it seemed to me that I had not deserved my fate, that I had something good in me. People have tormented me enough, I used to say to myself, but at least I have never done any harm to anyone."—*Ed.*

inhuman surroundings. She is *good* because the sun and the flowers reveal to her her own sunny and blossoming nature. She is *good* because she is still *young*, full of hope and vitality. Her situation is *not good*, because it puts an unnatural constraint on her, because it is not the expression of her human impulses, not the fulfilment of her human desires; because it is full of torment and without joy. She measures her situation in life by her *own individuality*, her *essential nature*, not by the *ideal of what is good*.

In *natural* surroundings, where the chains of bourgeois life fall away and she can freely manifest her own nature, Fleur de Marie bubbles over with love of life, with a wealth of feeling, with human joy at the beauty of nature; these show that her social position has only grazed the surface of her and is a mere misfortune, that she herself is neither good nor bad, but *human*.

"Monsieur Rodolphe, quel bonheur ... de l'herbe, des champs! Si vous vouliez me permettre de descendre, il fait si beau ... j'aimerais tant à courir dans ces prairies!"[a]

Alighting from the carriage, she plucks flowers for Rudolph, "can hardly speak for joy", etc., etc.

Rudolph tells her that he is going to take her to *Madame George's farm*. There she can see dove-cotes, cow-stalls and so forth; there they have milk, butter, fruit, etc. Those are real *blessings* for this child. She will be *merry*, that is her main thought. "*C'est à n'y pas croire ... comme je veux m'amuser!*"[b] She explains to Rudolph in the most unaffected way her own *share* of responsibility for her misfortune. "*Tout mon sort est venu de ce que je n'ai pas économisé mon argent!*"[c] She therefore advises him to be thrifty and to put money in the savings-bank. Her fancy runs wild in the castles in the air that Rudolph builds for her. She becomes sad only because she

"has forgotten the *present*" and "the contrast of that present with the dream of a joyous and laughing existence reminds her of the cruelty of her situation".

So far we have seen Fleur de Marie in her original un-Critical form. Eugène Sue has risen above the horizon of his narrow world outlook. He has slapped bourgeois prejudice in the face. He will hand over Fleur de Marie to the hero Rudolph to atone for his temerity and to reap applause from all old men and women, from the whole of the Paris police, from the current religion and from "Critical Criticism".

[a] "Monsieur Rudolph, what happiness! ... grass, fields! If you would allow me to get out, the weather is so fine ... I should love so much to run about in these meadows."—*Ed.*

[b] "You can't believe how I am longing for some fun!"—*Ed.*

[c] "My whole fate is due to the fact that I did not save up my money."—*Ed.*

Madame George, to whom Rudolph entrusts Fleur de Marie, is an unhappy, hypochondriacal religious woman. She immediately welcomes the child with the unctuous words: "*God* blesses those who love and fear him, who have been unhappy and who *repent*." Rudolph, the man of "pure Criticism", has the wretched priest *Laporte*, whose hair has greyed in superstition, called in. He has the mission of accomplishing Fleur de Marie's Critical reform.

Joyfully and unaffectedly Marie approaches the old priest. In his Christian brutality, *Eugène Sue* makes a "marvellous instinct" at once whisper in her ear that "*shame* ends where *repentance* and *penance* begin", that is, in the church, which alone saves. He forgets the unconstrained merriness of the outing, a merriness which nature's grace and Rudolph's friendly sympathy had produced, and which was troubled only by the thought of having to go back to the criminals' landlady.

The priest Laporte immediately adopts a *supermundane* attitude. His first words are:

"*God's* mercy is infinite, my dear child! He has proved it to you by not abandoning you in your severe trials.... The magnanimous man who saved you fulfilled the *word of the Scriptures*" (note—the word of the Scriptures, not a human purpose!): "Verily the Lord is nigh to those who invoke him; he will fulfil their desires ... he will hear their voice and will save them ... the Lord will accomplish *his* work."

Marie cannot yet understand the *evil* meaning of the priest's exhortations. She answers:

"I shall pray for those who pitied me and brought me back to God."

Her first thought is *not* for God, it is for her *human* saviour and she wants to pray for *him*, not for her *own* absolution. She attributes to her prayer some influence on the salvation of others. Indeed, she is still so naive that she supposes she has *already been brought back* to God. The priest feels it is his duty to destroy this unorthodox illusion.

"Soon," he says, interrupting her, "soon you will deserve absolution, absolution from your great errors ... for, to quote the prophet once more, the Lord holdeth up those who are on the brink of falling."

One should not fail to see the inhuman expressions the priest uses. Soon you will deserve absolution. Your sins are *not yet forgiven.*

As Laporte, when he receives the girl, bestows on her the *consciousness of her sins*, so Rudolph, when he leaves her, presents her with a gold *cross*, the symbol of the *Christian crucifixion* awaiting her.

Marie has already been living for some time on Madame

George's farm. Let us first listen to a dialogue between the old priest Laporte and Madame George.

> He considers "marriage" out of the question for Marie "because no man, in spite of the priest's guarantee, will have the courage to face the past that has soiled her youth". He adds: "she has great errors to atone for, her moral sense ought to have kept her upright."

He proves, as the commonest of bourgeois would, that she could have remained good: "There are many virtuous people in Paris today." The hypocritical priest knows quite well that at any hour of the day, in the busiest streets, those virtuous people of Paris pass indifferently by little girls of seven or eight years who sell *allumettes*[a] and the like until about midnight as Marie herself used to do and who, almost without exception, will have the same fate as Marie.

The priest has made up his mind concerning Marie's *penance*; in his own mind he has already *condemned* her. Let us follow Marie when she is accompanying Laporte home in the evening.

> "See, my child," he begins with unctuous eloquence, "the boundless horizon the limits of which are no longer visible" (for it is evening), "it seems to me that the calm and the vastness almost give us an idea of eternity.... I am telling you this, Marie, because you are sensitive to the beauties of creation.... I have often been moved by the religious admiration which they inspire in you — you who for so long were deprived of religious feeling."

The priest has already succeeded in changing Marie's immediate naive pleasure in the beauties of nature into a *religious* admiration. For her, *nature* has already become devout, *Christianised* nature, debased to *creation*. The transparent sea of space is desecrated and turned into the dark symbol of stagnant *eternity*. She has already learnt that all human manifestations of her being were "*profane*", devoid of religion, of real consecration, that they were impious and godless. The priest must soil her in her own eyes, he must trample underfoot her natural, spiritual resources and means of grace, in order to make her receptive to the supernatural means of grace he promises her, *baptism*.

When Marie wants to make a confession to him and asks him to be lenient he answers:

> "The *Lord* has shown you that he is merciful."

In the clemency which she is shown Marie must not see a natural, self-evident attitude of a related human being to her, another human being. She must see in it an extravagant, supernatural,

---

[a] Matches.— *Ed.*

superhuman mercy and condescension; in *human leniency* she must see *divine mercy.* She must transcendentalise all human and natural relationships by making them *relationships to God.* The way Fleur de Marie in her answer accepts the priest's chatter about divine mercy shows how far she has already been spoilt by religious doctrine.

As soon as she entered upon her improved situation, she said, she had felt only her *new happiness.*

> "Every instant I thought of Monsieur Rudolph. I often raised my eyes to heaven, to look there, not for God, but for Monsieur Rudolph, and to thank him. Yes, *I confess,* Father, *I thought more* of him than of God; for *he* did for me what God alone could have done.... I was *happy,* as happy as someone who has escaped a great danger for ever."

Fleur de Marie already finds it wrong that she took a new happy situation in life simply for what it *really* was, that she felt it as a new happiness, that her attitude to it was a natural, not a supernatural one. She accuses herself of seeing in the man who rescued her what he *really* was, her rescuer, instead of supposing some imaginary saviour, *God,* in his place. She is already caught in religious hypocrisy, which takes away from *another man* what he has deserved in respect of me in order to give it to God, and which in general regards everything human in man as alien to him and everything inhuman in him as *really* belonging to him.

Marie tells us that the *religious transformation* of her thoughts, her sentiments, her attitude to life was effected by Madame George and Laporte.

> "When Rudolph took me away from the *Cité,* I already had a vague consciousness of my degradation. But the education, the advice and examples I got from you and Madame George made me understand ... that I had been more guilty than unfortunate.... You and Madame George made me *realise the infinite depth of my damnation.*"

That is to say she owes to the priest Laporte and Madame George the replacement of the human and therefore bearable consciousness of her degradation by the Christian and hence unbearable consciousness of eternal damnation. The priest and the bigot have taught her to judge herself from the *Christian point of view.*

Marie feels the depth of the spiritual misfortune into which she has been cast. She says:

> "Since the consciousness of good and evil had to be so frightful for me, why was I not left to my wretched lot?... Had I not been snatched away from infamy, misery and blows would soon have killed me. At least I should have died in ignorance of a purity that I shall always wish for in vain."

The heartless priest replies:

"Even the most noble nature, were it to be plunged only for a day in the filth from which you have been saved, would be *indelibly branded.* That is the *immutability of divine justice!*"

Deeply wounded by this *priestly curse* uttered in such honeyed tones, Fleur de Marie exclaims:

"You see therefore, I must despair!"

The grey-headed slave of religion answers:

"You must renounce hope of effacing this desolate page from your life, but you must trust in the *infinite mercy of God.* Here *below,* my poor child, you will have tears, remorse and penance, but one day *up above,* forgiveness and *eternal bliss!*"

Marie is not yet stupid enough to be satisfied with eternal bliss and forgiveness up above.

"Pity, pity, my God!" she cries. "I am so young.... *Malheur à moi!*"[a]

Then the hypocritical sophistry of the priest reaches its peak:

"On the contrary, happiness for you, Marie; happiness for you to whom the Lord sends this bitter but saving remorse! It shows the *religious* susceptibility of your soul.... Each of your sufferings is counted up above. Believe me, God left you awhile on the path of evil only to reserve for you the *glory of repentance* and the eternal reward due to *atonement.*"

From this moment Marie is *enslaved by the consciousness of sin.* In her former most unhappy situation in life she was able to develop a lovable, human individuality; in her outward debasement she was conscious that *her human* essence was *her true essence.* Now the filth of modern society, which has touched her externally, becomes her innermost being, and continual hypochondriacal self-torture because of that filth becomes her duty, the task of her life appointed by God himself, the self-purpose of her existence. Formerly she said of herself "*Je ne suis pas pleurnicheuse*" and knew that "*ce qui est fait, est fait*". Now self-torment will be her *good* and remorse will be her *glory.*

It turns out later that Fleur de Marie is Rudolph's daughter. We come across her again as Princess of Geroldstein. We overhear a conversation she has with her father:

"En vain je prie Dieu de me délivrer de ces obsessions, de remplir uniquement mon cœur de son pieux amour, de ses saintes espérances, de me prendre enfin toute entière, puisque je veux me donner toute entière à lui ... il n'exauce pas mes vœux—sans doute, parce que mes préoccupations *terrestres* me rendent indigne d'entrer en commun avec lui."[b]

---

[a] "Woe unto me!"—*Ed.*

[b] "In vain I pray to God to deliver me from these obsessions, to fill my heart solely with his pious love and his holy hopes; in a word, to take me entirely,

When man has realised that his transgressions are *infinite* crimes against God he can be sure of *salvation* and *mercy* only if he gives himself *wholly* to God and becomes *wholly* dead to the world and worldly concerns. When Fleur de Marie realises that her delivery from her inhuman situation in life was a miracle of *God* she *herself* has to become a *saint* in order to be worthy of such a *miracle.* Her human love must be transformed into religious love, the striving for happiness into striving for eternal bliss, worldly satisfaction into holy hope, communion with people into communion with God. God must take her entirely. She herself reveals to us why he does not take her entirely. She has not yet *given* herself entirely to him, her heart is still preoccupied and engaged with earthly affairs. This is the last flickering of her strong nature. She gives herself entirely up to God by becoming wholly dead to the world and entering a *convent.*

> A monastery is no place for him
> Who has no stock of sins laid in,
> So numerous and great
> That be it early, be it late
> He may not miss the sweet delight
> Of penance for a heart contrite.
>
> (Goethe)[a]

In the convent Fleur de Marie is promoted to *abbess* through the intrigues of Rudolph. At first she refuses to accept this appointment because she feels unworthy. The old abbess persuades her:

"Je vous dirai plus, ma chère fille, avant d'entrer au bercail, votre existence aurait été aussi égarée, qu'elle a été au contraire pure et louable ... que les *vertus évangéliques*, dont vous avez donné l'exemple depuis votre séjour ici, expieraient et rachèteraient encore aux yeux du Seigneur un passé si coupable qu'il fût."[b]

From what the abbess says, we see that Fleur de Marie's earthly virtues have changed into evangelical virtues, or rather that her real virtues can no longer appear otherwise than as evangelical caricatures.

Marie answers the abbess:

"Sainte mère — je crois maintenant pouvoir accepter."[c]

---

because I wish to give myself entirely to him ... he does not grant my wishes, doubtless because my *earthly* preoccupations make me unworthy of communion with him."—*Ed.*

[a] J. W. Goethe, *Zahme Xenien*, IX.—*Ed.*

[b] "I shall say more, my dear daughter: if before entering the fold your life had been as full of error as, on the contrary, it was pure and praiseworthy ... the *evangelical virtues* of which you have given an example since you have been here would have atoned for and redeemed your past in the eyes of the Lord, no matter how sinful it was."—*Ed.*

[c] "Holy Mother, I now believe that I can accept."—*Ed.*

Convent life does not suit Marie's individuality — she dies. Christianity consoles her only in imagination, or rather her Christian consolation is precisely the annihilation of her real life and essence — her death.

So Rudolph first changed Fleur de Marie into a repentant sinner, then the repentant sinner into a nun and finally the nun into a corpse. At her funeral not only the Catholic priest, but also the *Critical* priest Szeliga preaches a sermon over her grave.

Her *"innocent"* existence he calls her *"transient"* existence, opposing it to "eternal and unforgettable guilt". He praises the fact that her *"last breath"* was a "prayer for forgiveness and pardon". But just as the protestant Minister, after expounding the necessity of the Lord's mercy, the participation of the deceased in universal original sin and the intensity of his consciousness of sin, must praise the virtues of the departed in *earthly* terms, so, too, Herr Szeliga uses the expression:

"And yet *personally*, she has nothing to ask forgiveness for."

Finally he throws on Marie's grave the most faded flower of pulpit eloquence:

"Inwardly pure as human beings seldom are, she has closed her eyes to this world."

Amen!

3) REVELATION OF THE MYSTERIES OF LAW

a) The *Maître d'école*, or the New Penal Theory. The Mystery of Solitary Confinement Revealed. Medical Mysteries

The *maître d'école* is a criminal of Herculean strength and great intellectual vigour. He was brought up an educated and well-schooled man. This passionate athlete comes into conflict with the laws and customs of bourgeois society, whose universal yardstick is mediocrity, delicate morals and quiet trade. He becomes a murderer and abandons himself to all the excesses of a violent temperament that can nowhere find a fitting human occupation.

Rudolph captures this criminal. He wants to reform him critically and set him up as an example for the world of *law*. He quarrels with the world of law not over *"punishment"* itself, but over *kinds and methods* of punishment. He invents, as the Negro doctor David aptly expresses it, a penal theory which would be

worthy of the "*greatest German criminal expert*", and which has since
had the good fortune to be defended by a German criminal expert
with German earnestness and German thoroughness. Rudolph has
not the slightest idea that one can rise *above* criminal experts: his
ambition is to be "*the greatest criminal expert*", *primus inter pares*.[a] He
has the *maître d'école* blinded by the Negro doctor David.

At first Rudolph repeats all the trivial objections to capital
punishment: that it has no effect on the criminal and no effect on
the people, for whom it seems to be an entertaining spectacle.

Further Rudolph establishes a difference between the *maître
d'école* and the *soul* of the *maître d'école*. It is not the man, not the
real maître d'école whom he wishes to save; he wants the *spiritual
salvation* of his *soul*.

"The salvation of a soul," he teaches, "is something holy.... Every crime can be
atoned for and redeemed, the Saviour said, but only if the criminal earnestly desires
to repent and *atone*. The transition from the court to the scaffold is too short....
You" (the *maître d'école*) "have criminally misused your *strength*. I shall *paralyse*
your strength ... you will tremble before the weakest, your punishment will be
equal to your crime ... but this terrible punishment will at least leave you the
boundless horizon of *atonement*.... I shall cut you off only from the outer world in
order to plunge you into impenetrable night and leave you *alone* with the memory
of your ignominious deeds.... You will be forced to look into yourself ... your
intelligence, which you have degraded, will be roused and will lead you to
atonement."

Since Rudolph regards the *soul* as *holy* and man's *body* as *profane,*
since he thus considers only the soul to be the true essence,
because — according to Herr Szeliga's Critical description of humanity — it belongs to heaven, the body and the strength of the
maître d'école do not belong to humanity, the manifestation of their
essence cannot be given human form or claimed for humanity and
cannot be treated as essentially human. The *maître d'école* has
misused his strength; Rudolph paralyses, lames, destroys that
strength. There is no more *Critical* means of getting rid of the
perverse manifestations of a human essential strength than the
destruction of this essential strength. This is the Christian means
— plucking out the eye if it offends or cutting off the hand if it
offends, in a word, killing the body if the body gives offence; for
the eye, the hand, the body are really only superfluous sinful
appendages of man. Human nature must be killed in order to heal
its ailments. Mass-type jurisprudence, too, in agreement here with
the Critical, sees in the *laming* and paralysing of human strength
the antidote to the objectionable manifestations of that strength.

---

[a] The first among equals.— *Ed.*

What Rudolph, the man of pure Criticism, objects to in profane criminal justice is the too swift transition from the court to the scaffold. He, on the other hand, wants to link *vengeance* on the criminal with *penance* and *consciousness of sin* in the criminal, corporal punishment with spiritual punishment, sensuous torture with the non-sensuous torture of remorse. Profane punishment must at the same time be a means of Christian moral education.

This penal theory, which links *jurisprudence* with *theology,* this "revealed mystery of the mystery", is no other than the penal theory of the *Catholic* Church, as already expounded at length by *Bentham* in his work *Punishments and Rewards.*[a] In that book Bentham also proved the moral futility of the punishments of today. He calls legal penalties "*legal parodies*".

The punishment that Rudolph imposed on the *maître d'école* is the same as that which Origen imposed on himself. He *emasculates* him, robs him of a *productive organ,* the eye. "The eye is the light of the body."[b] It does great credit to Rudolph's religious instinct that he should hit, of all things, upon the idea of *blinding.* This punishment was current in the thoroughly Christian empire of Byzantium and came to full flower in the vigorous youthful period of the Christian-Germanic states of England and France. Cutting man off from the perceptible outer world, throwing him back into his abstract inner nature in order to correct him — blinding — is a necessary consequence of the Christian doctrine according to which the consummation of this cutting off, the pure isolation of man in his spiritualistic "*ego*", is *good itself.* If Rudolph does not shut the *maître d'école* up in a real monastery, as was the case in Byzantium and in Franconia, he at least shuts him up in an ideal monastery, in the cloister of an impenetrable night which the light of the outer world cannot pierce, the cloister of an idle conscience and consciousness of sin filled with nothing but the phantoms of memory.

A certain speculative bashfulness prevents Herr Szeliga from discussing openly the penal theory of his hero Rudolph that worldly punishment must be linked with Christian repentance and atonement. Instead he imputes to him — naturally as a mystery which is only just being revealed to the world — the theory that punishment must make the criminal the "*judge*" of his "*own*" crime.

---

[a] *Théorie des peines et des récompenses.—Ed.*
[b] *New Testament,* Matthew, 6:22.— *Ed.*

The mystery of this revealed mystery is *Hegel*'s penal theory. According to Hegel, the criminal in his punishment passes sentence on himself. *Gans* developed this theory at greater length. In Hegel this is the *speculative disguise* of the old *jus talionis*,[a] which *Kant* expounded as the *only juridical* penal theory. For Hegel, self-judgment of the criminal remains a mere *"Idea"*, a mere speculative interpretation of the *current empirical punishments for criminals*. He thus leaves the mode of application to the respective stage of development of the state, i.e., he leaves punishment as it is. Precisely in that he shows himself more critical than his Critical echo. A *penal* theory which at the same time sees in the criminal the *man* can do so only in *abstraction*, in imagination, precisely because *punishment, coercion*, is contrary to *human* conduct. Moreover, this would be impossible to carry out. Purely subjective arbitrariness would take the place of the abstract law because it would always depend on the official, "honourable and decent" men to adapt the penalty to the individuality of the criminal. Plato long ago realised that the *law* must be one-sided and *take no account* of the individual. On the other hand, under *human* conditions punishment will *really* be nothing but the sentence passed by the culprit on himself. No one will want to convince him that *violence* from *without*, done to him by others, is violence which he had done to himself. On the contrary, he will see in *other* men his natural saviours from the punishment which he has imposed on himself; in other words, the relation will be reversed.

Rudolph expresses his innermost thought—the purpose of blinding the *maître d'école*—when he says to him:

"Chacune de tes paroles sera une prière."[b]

He wants to teach him to *pray*. He wants to convert the Herculean robber into a *monk* whose only work is prayer. Compared with this Christian cruelty, how humane is the ordinary penal theory that just chops a man's head off when it wants to destroy him. Finally, it goes without saying that whenever real mass-type legislation was seriously concerned with improving the criminal it acted incomparably more sensibly and humanely than the German Harun al-Rashid. The four Dutch agricultural colonies and the Ostwald penal colony in Alsace are truly human attempts in comparison with the blinding of the *maître d'école*. Just as

---

[a] The right of retaliation—an eye for an eye.—*Ed.*
[b] "Every word you say will be a prayer." —*Ed.*

Rudolph kills Fleur de Marie by handing her over to the priest and consciousness of sin, just as he kills Chourineur by robbing him of his human independence and degrading him into a bulldog, so he kills the *maître d'école* by having his eyes gouged out in order that he can learn to *"pray"*.

This is, of course, the way in which all reality emerges *"simply"* out of *"pure Criticism"*, namely, as a distortion and *senseless abstraction* of reality.

Immediately after the blinding of the *maître d'école* Herr Szeliga causes a *moral miracle* to take place.

"The terrible *maître d'école*," he reports, "*suddenly* recognises the power of honesty and decency and says to Schurimann: '*Yes, I can trust you, you have never stolen anything*'."

Unfortunately Eugène Sue recorded a statement of the *maître d'école* about Chourineur which contains the same recognition and cannot be the effect of his having been blinded, since it was made *earlier*. In talking to Rudolph alone, the *maître d'école* said about Chourineur:

"Du reste il n'est pas capable de vendre un ami. Non: il a du bon ... il a toujours eu des idées singulières." [a]

This would seem to do away with Herr Szeliga's moral miracle. Now we shall see the *real* results of Rudolph's *Critical* cure.

We next meet the *maître d'école* as he is going with a woman called Chouette to Bouqueval farm to play a foul trick on Fleur de Marie. The thought that dominates him is, of course, the thought of *revenge* on Rudolph. But the only way he knows of wreaking vengeance on him is metaphysically, by thinking and hatching *"evil"* to spite him.

"Il m'a ôté la vue, il ne m'a pás ôté la pensée du mal." [b]

He tells Chouette why he had sent for her:

"I was *bored* all alone with those honest people."

When Eugène Sue satisfies his monkish, bestial lust in the *self-humiliation* of man to the extent of making the *maître d'école* implore on his knees the old hag Chouette and the little imp Tortillard not to abandon him, the great moralist forgets that that

---

[a] "Besides, he is not capable of betraying a friend. No, there's something good in him ... he has always had strange ideas."—*Ed.*

[b] "He has taken away my sight but not the thought of evil."—*Ed.*

is the height of diabolical satisfaction for Chouette. Just as
Rudolph, precisely by the *violent act* of *blinding* the criminal,
proved to him the power of *physical force*, which he wants to show
him is insignificant, so Eugène Sue now teaches the *maître d'école*
really to recognise the *full* power of the *senses*. He teaches him to
understand that without it man is *unmanned* and becomes a
helpless object of mockery for children. He convinces him that the
world deserved his crimes, for he had only to lose his sight to be
ill-treated by it. He robs him of his last human illusion, for so far
the *maître d'école* believed in Chouette's attachment to him. He had
said to Rudolph: "She would let herself be thrown into the fire
for me." Eugène Sue, on the other hand, has the satisfaction of hearing the *maître d'école* cry out in the depths of
despair:

> *"Mon dieu! Mon dieu! Mon dieu!"*

He has learnt to *"pray"*! In this "*appel involontaire de la
commisération divine*," Eugène Sue sees "*quelque chose de providen-
tiel*".[a]

The first result of Rudolph's Criticism is this *spontaneous prayer*. It is
followed immediately by an *involuntary atonement* at Bouqueval farm,
where the ghosts of those whom the *maître d'école* murdered appear
to him in a dream.

We shall not give a detailed description of this dream. We next
find the Critically reformed *maître d'école* fettered in the cellar of
the "Bras rouge", half devoured by rats, half starving and half
insane as a result of being tortured by Chouette and Tortillard,
and roaring like a beast. Tortillard had delivered Chouette to him.
Let us watch the treatment he inflicts on her. He *copies* the hero
Rudolph not only outwardly, by scratching out Chouette's *eyes*, but
morally too by repeating Rudolph's hypocrisy and embellishing his
cruel treatment with pious phrases. As soon as the *maître d'école* has
Chouette in his power he gives vent to "*une joie effrayante*"[b] and his
voice trembles with rage.

> "Tu sens bien," he says, "que je ne veux pas en finir tout de suite ... torture pour
> torture ... il faut que je te parle longuement avant de te tuer ... ca va être affreux pour
> toi. D'abord, vois-tu ... depuis ce rêve de la ferme de Bouqueval, qui m'a remis sous les
> yeux tous nos crimes, depuis ce rêve, qui a manqué de me rendre fou ... qui me rendra
> fou ... il s'est passé en moi un changement étrange ... J'ai eu horreur de ma férocité
> passée ... d'abord je ne t'ai pas permis de martyriser la goualeuse, cela n'était rien
> encore ... en m'entraînant ici dans cette cave, en m'y faisant souffrir le froid et la faim
> ... tu m'as laissé tout à l'épouvante de mes réflexions ... Oh! tu ne sais pas ce que c'est

---

[a] "*Spontaneous* appeal for divine mercy ... something providential." —*Ed.*

[b] "A terrifying joy." —*Ed.*

que d'être seul ... l'isolement m'a purifié. Je ne l'aurais pas cru possible ... une preuve que je suis peut-être moins scélérat qu'autrefois ... ce que j'éprouve une joie infinie à te tenir là ... monstre ... non pour me venger, mais ... mais pour venger nos victimes ... oui, j'aurai accompli un devoir quand de ma propre main j'aurai puni ma complice ... j'ai maintenant horreur de mes meurtres passés, et pourtant ... trouves-tu pas cela bizarre? c'est sans crainte, c'est avec sécurité que je vais commettre sur toi un meurtre affreux avec des raffinements affreux ... dis ... dis ... conçois-tu cela?"[a]

In those few words the *maître d'école* goes through a whole gamut of *moral casuistry*.

His first words are a *frank* expression of his desire for vengeance. He wants to give torture for torture. He wants to murder Chouette and he wants to prolong her agony by a long sermon. And—delightful sophistry!—the speech with which he tortures her is a *sermon on morals*. He asserts that his dream at Bouqueval has improved him. At the same time he reveals the real effect of the dream by admitting that it almost drove him mad and that it will actually do so. He gives as a proof of his reform that he prevented Fleur de Marie from being tortured. Eugène Sue's personages—earlier Chourineur and now the *maître d'école*—must express, as the result of *their* thoughts, as the conscious. motive of their actions, his own intention as a writer, which causes him to make them behave in a certain way and no other. They must continually say: I have reformed myself in this, in that, etc. Since their life has no real content, their words must give vigorous tones to insignificant features like the protection of Fleur de Marie.

Having reported the *salutary* effect of his Bouqueval dream, the *maître d'école* must explain why Eugène Sue had him locked up in a cellar. He must find the novelist's procedure reasonable. He

---

[a] "You realise that I do not want to get it over at once.... Torture for torture.... I must have a long talk with you before killing you.... It is going to be terrible for you. First of all, you see ... since that dream at Bouqueval farm which brought all our crimes back before me, since that dream which nearly drove me mad ... and which will drive me mad ... a strange change has come over me.... I have become horrified at my past cruelty.... At first I would not let you torture the songstress [Fleur de Marie], but that was nothing.... By bringing me to this cellar and making me suffer cold and hunger.... you left me to the terror of my own thoughts.... Oh, you don't know what it is to be alone.... Isolation purified me. I should not have thought it possible ... a proof that I am perhaps less of a blackguard than before ... what an infinite joy I feel to have you in my power, you monster ... not in order to revenge myself but ... to avenge our victims.... Yes, I shall have done my duty when I have punished my accomplice with my own hand.... I am now horrified at my past murders, and yet ... don't you find it strange? ... it is without fear and quite calmly that I am going to commit a terrible murder on you, with terrible refinements ... tell me, tell me ... do you understand that?"—*Ed.*

must say to Chouette: by locking me up in a cellar, causing me to
be gnawed by rats and to suffer hunger and thirst, you have
completed my reform. Solitude has *purified* me.

The beastly roar, the wild fury, the terrible lust for vengeance
with which the *maître d'école* welcomes Chouette are in complete
contradiction to this moralising talk. They betray what kind of
thoughts occupied him in his dungeon.

The *maître d'école* himself seems to realise this, but being
a *Critical moralist*, he will know how to reconcile the contradictions.

He declares that the "infinite joy" of having Chouette in his
power is precisely a sign of his reform, for his lust for vengeance
is not a *natural* one but a *moral* one. He wants to avenge, not
himself, but the common *victims* of Chouette and himself. If he
murders her, he does not commit *murder*, he fulfils a *duty*. He does
not *avenge* himself on her, he *punishes* his accomplice like an
impartial judge. He shudders at his past murders and, nevertheless, marvelling at his own casuistry, he asks Chouette: "Don't you
find it strange? Without fear and quite calmly I am going to kill
you." On moral grounds that he does not reveal, he gloats at the
same time over the picture of the murder that he is going to
commit, as being a *meurtre affreux*, a *meurtre avec des raffinements
affreux*.[a]

It is in accord with the character of the *maître d'école* that he
should murder Chouette, especially after the cruelty with which
she treated him. But that he should commit murder on moral
grounds, that he should give a moral interpretation to his savage
pleasure in the *meurtre affreux* and the *raffinements affreux*, that he
should show his remorse for the past murders precisely by
committing a fresh one, that from a simple murderer he should
become *a murderer in a double sense*, a *moral murderer*— all this is the
glorious result of Rudolph's Critical cure.

Chouette tries to get away from the *maître d'école*. He notices it
and holds her fast.

"Tiens-toi donc, la chouette, il faut que je finisse de t'expliquer comment peu à
peu j'en suis venu à me repentir ... cette révélation te sera odieuse ... et elle te
prouvera aussi combien je dois être impitoyable dans la vengeance, que je veux
exercer sur toi au nom de nos victimes ... Il faut que je me hâte ... la joie de te
tenir là me fait boudir le sang ... j'aurai le temps de te rendre les approches de la
mort effroyables en te forçant de m'entendre ... Je suis aveugle ... et ma pensée
prend une forme, un corps pour me représenter incessamment d'une manière
visible, presque palpable ... les traits de mes victimes ... les idées s'imagent presque

---

[a] Terrible murder ... murder with terrible refinements.—*Ed.*

matériellement dans le cerveau. Quand au repentir se joint une expiation d'une effrayante sévérité ... une expiation qui change notre vie en une longue insomnie remplie d'hallucinations vengeresses ou de réflexions désespérées ... peut-être alors le pardon des hommes succède au remords et à l'expiation."[a]

The *maître d'école* continues with his hypocrisy which every minute betrays itself as such. Chouette must hear how he came by degrees to repentance. This revelation will be hateful to her, for it will prove that it is his *duty* to take a pitiless revenge on her, not in his own name, but in the name of their common victims. Suddenly the *maître d'école* interrupts his didactic lecture. He must, he says, "hurry" with his lecture, for the pleasure of having her in his hands makes the blood pound in his veins; that is a moral reason for cutting the lecture short! Then he calms his blood again. The long time that he takes in preaching her a moral sermon is not wasted for his revenge. It will "make the approach of death terrifying" for her. That is a different moral reason, one for protracting his sermon! And having such moral reasons he can safely resume his moral text where he left off.

The *maître d'école* describes correctly the condition to which isolation from the outer world reduces a man. For one to whom the *sensuously perceptible world* becomes a *mere idea,* for him mere ideas are transformed into *sensuously perceptible beings.* The figments of his brain assume corporeal form. A world of tangible, palpable ghosts is begotten within his mind. That is the secret of all pious visions and at the same time it is the general form of insanity. When the *maître d'école* repeats Rudolph's words about the "power of repentance and atonement linked with terrible torments", he does so in a state of semi-madness, thus proving in fact the connection between Christian consciousness of sin and insanity. Similarly, when the *maître d'école* considers the transformation of *life* into a *night of dream* filled with ghosts as the real result of repentance and atonement, he is expressing the

---

[a] "Keep still, Chouette, I must finish explaining to you how I gradually came to repentance.... This revelation will be hateful to you ... and it will also show you how pitiless I must be in the vengeance I want to wreak on you in the name of our victims.... I must hurry.... The joy of having you here in my hands makes the blood pound in my veins.... I shall have time to make the approach of your death terrifying to you by forcing you to listen to me.... I am blind ... and my thoughts take a shape, a body, such that they incessantly present to me visibly, almost palpably ... the features of my victims.... The ideas are reflected almost materially in my brain. When repentance is linked with an atonement of terrifying severity, an atonement that changes our life into a long sleeplessness filled with hallucinations of revenge or desperate reflections ... then, perhaps, the pardon of men follows remorse and atonement."—*Ed.*

true mystery of pure Criticism and of Christian reform, which consists in changing man into a ghost and his life into a *life of dream.*

At this point Eugène Sue realises how the *salutary thoughts* which he makes the blind robber prate after Rudolph will be made ridiculous by the robber's treatment of Chouette. That is why he makes the *maître d'école* say:

"La salutaire influence de ces pensées est telle que ma fureur s'apaise." [a]

So the *maître d'école* now admits that his *moral wrath* was nothing but *profane rage.*

"Le courage ... la force ... la volonté me manquent pour te tuer ... non, ce n'est pas à moi de verser ton sang ... ce serait ... un *meurtre*" (he calls things by their names) ... "meurtre excusable peut-être ... mais ce serait toujours un meurtre." [b]

Chouette wounds the *maître d'école* with a dagger just in time. Eugène Sue can now let him kill her without any further moral casuistry.

"Il poussa un cri de douleur ... les ardeurs féroces de sa vengeance, de ses rages, ses instincts sanguinaires, brusquement réveillés et exaspérés par cette attaque, firent une explosion soudaine, terrible, où s'abîma sa raison déjà fortement ébranlée ... Ah vipère! ... j'ai senti ta dent ... tu seras comme moi *sans yeux.*" [c]

And he scratches her eyes out.

When the nature of the *maître d'école,* which has been only hypocritically, sophistically disguised, only ascetically repressed by Rudolph's cure, breaks out, the *outburst* is all the more violent and terrifying. We must be grateful to Eugène Sue for his admission that the reason of the *maître d'école* was badly shaken by all the events which Rudolph has prepared.

"The last spark of his reason was extinguished in that cry of terror, in that cry of a damned soul" (he sees the ghosts of his murdered victims) "... the *maître d'école* rages and roars like a *frenzied beast....* He tortures Chouette to death."

Herr Szeliga mutters under his breath:

---

[a] "The salutary influence of these thoughts is such that my rage is appeased."—*Ed.*

[b] "I lack courage ... strength ... will to kill you.... No, it is not for me to shed your blood ... it would be ... *murder....* Excusable murder, perhaps, but murder all the same."—*Ed.*

[c] "He uttered a cry of pain ... his fierce passion of vengeance, of rage and of bloodthirsty instinct, suddenly aroused and exacerbated by this attack, had a sudden and terrible outburst in which his already badly shaken reason was shattered.... Viper! I have felt your fang ... you will be *sightless* as I am."—*Ed.*

"With the *maître d'école* there cannot be such a *swift*" (!) "and *fortunate*" (!) "*transformation*" (!) "as with *Schurimann*."

Just as Rudolph sends Fleur de Marie into a convent, he makes the *maître d'école* an inmate of the *Bicêtre* asylum. He has paralysed his *spiritual* as well as his physical strength. And rightly. For the *maître d'école* sinned with his spiritual as well as his physical strength, and according to Rudolph's penal theory the *sinning forces* must be annihilated.

But Eugène Sue has not yet consummated the "repentance and atonement linked with a terrible revenge". The *maître d'école* recovers his reason, but fearing to be delivered to justice he remains in Bicêtre and *pretends* to be mad. Monsieur Sue forgets that "every word he said was to be a *prayer*", whereas finally it is much more like the inarticulate howling and raving of a madman. Or does Monsieur Sue perhaps ironically put these manifestations of life on the *same* level as praying?

The idea underlying the punishment that Rudolph carried out in blinding the *maître d'école*—the isolation of the man and his soul from the outer world, the combination of legal punishment with theological torture—finds its ultimate expression in *solitary confinement*. That is why Monsieur Sue glorifies this system.

"How many centuries had to pass before it was realised that there is *only one* means of overcoming the rapidly spreading leprosy" (i.e., the corruption of morals in prisons) "which is threatening the body of society: isolation."

Monsieur Sue shares the opinion of the worthy people who explain the spread of crime by the organisation of prisons. To remove the criminal from bad society he is left to his own society.

Eugène Sue says:

"I should consider myself lucky if my weak voice could be heard among all those which so rightly and so insistently demand the *complete* and *absolute* application of solitary confinement."

Monsieur Sue's wish has been only *partially* fulfilled. In the debates on solitary confinement in the Chamber of Deputies this year, even the official supporters of that system had to acknowledge that it leads sooner or later to insanity in the criminal. All sentences of imprisonment for more than ten years had therefore to be converted into deportation.

Had Messieurs Tocqueville and Beaumont studied Eugène Sue's novel thoroughly they would certainly have secured complete and absolute application of solitary confinement.

If Eugène Sue deprives criminals with a sane mind of society in order to make them insane, he gives insane persons society to make them sane.

"L'expérience prouve que pour les aliénés l'isolement est aussi funeste qu'il est salutaire pour les détenus criminels."[a]

If Monsieur Sue and his Critical hero Rudolph have not made *law* poorer by any mystery, whether through the *Catholic penal theory* or the *Methodist solitary confinement*, they have, on the other hand, enriched medicine with new mysteries, and after all, it is just as much of a service to *discover new* mysteries as to *disclose old* ones. In its report on the blinding of the *maître d'école*, Critical Criticism fully agrees with Monsieur Sue:

"When he is told he is deprived of the light of his eyes he does not even believe it."

The *maître d'école* could not believe in the loss of his sight because in reality he could still see. Monsieur Sue is describing a new kind of cataract and is reporting a real mystery for mass-type, un-Critical *ophthalmology*.

The *pupil* is *white* after the operation, so it is a case of *cataract of the crystalline lens*. So far, this could, of course, be caused by injury to the envelope of the lens without causing much pain, though not entirely without pain. But as doctors achieve this result only by *natural,* not by *Critical* means, the only resort was to wait until inflammation set in after the injury and the exudation dimmed the lens.

A still greater *miracle* and greater *mystery* befall the *maître d'école* in the third chapter of the third book.

The man who has been blinded *sees* again.

"La Chouette, le maître d'école et Tortillard *virent* le prêtre et Fleur de Marie."[b]

If we do not interpret this restoration of the *maître d'école*'s ability to see as an *author's miracle* after the method of the *Kritik der Synoptiker,* the *maître d'école* must have had his cataract operated on again. Later he is blind again. So he used his eyes too soon and the irritation of the light caused inflammation which ended in paralysis of the *retina* and incurable *amaurosis*. It is another *mystery* for un-Critical ophthalmology that this process takes place here in a *single* second.

---

[a] "Experience proves that isolation is as fatal for the insane as it is salutary for imprisoned criminals."—*Ed.*

[b] "Chouette, the *maître d'école* and Tortillard *saw* the priest and Fleur de Marie."—*Ed.*

b) Reward and Punishment. Double Justice
(with a Table)

The hero Rudolph reveals a new theory to keep society upright by *rewarding the good* and *punishing the wicked*. Un-Critically considered, this theory is nothing but the theory of society as it is today. How little lacking it is in rewards for the good and punishments for the wicked! Compared with this revealed mystery, how un-Critical is the mass-type Communist *Owen*, who sees in punishment and reward the consecration of differences in social rank and the complete expression of a servile abasement.

It could be considered as a *new* revelation that Eugène Sue makes rewards derive from the judiciary—from a new appendix to the Penal Code—and not satisfied with *one* jurisdiction he invents a *second*. Unfortunately this revealed mystery, too, is the repetition of an old theory expounded in detail by *Bentham* in his work already mentioned.[a] On the other hand, we cannot deny Monsieur Eugène Sue the honour of having motivated and developed Bentham's suggestion in an incomparably more Critical way than the latter. Whereas the mass-type Englishman keeps his feet on the ground, Sue's deduction rises to the Critical region of the heavens. His argument is as follows:

"The supposed effects of heavenly wrath are materialised to deter the wicked. Why should not the effect of the divine reward of the good be similarly materialised and anticipated on earth?"

In the *un-Critical* view it is the other way round: the heavenly criminal theory has only idealised the earthly theory, just as divine reward is only an idealisation of human wage service. It is absolutely necessary that society should not reward all good people so that divine justice will have some advantage over human justice.

In depicting his Critical rewarding justice, Monsieur Sue gives "an example of the *feminine dogmatism* that must have a formula and forms it according to the categories of *what exists*",[b] dogmatism which was censured with all the "tranquillity of knowledge" by Herr Edgar in Flora Tristan. For each point of the present *penal code*, which he retains, Monsieur Sue projects the addition of a counterpart in a *reward code* copied from it to the last detail. For easier survey we shall give his description of the complementary pairs in tabular form:

---

[a] *Théorie des peines et des récompenses.—Ed.*
[b] See pp. 19-20 of this volume.— *Ed.*

Table of Critically Complete Justice

Existing Justice	Critically Supplementing Justice
Name: Justice *Criminelle*[a]	Name: Justice *Vertueuse*[b]
Description: holds in its hand a *sword* to shorten the wicked by a head.	*Description*: holds in its hand a *crown* to raise the good by a head.
Purpose: Punishment of the wicked—imprisonment, infamy, deprivation of life. The people is notified of the terrible chastisements for the wicked.	*Purpose*: Reward of the good, free board, honour, maintenance of life. The people is notified of the brilliant triumphs for the good.
Means of discovering the wicked: Police spying, *mouchards*, to keep watch over the wicked.	*Means of discovering the good*: *Espionnage de vertu*, *mouchards*[c] to keep watch over the virtuous.
Method of ascertaining whether someone is wicked: *Les assises du crime*, criminal assizes. The public ministry points out and indicts the crimes of the accused for public vengeance.	*Method of ascertaining whether someone is good*: *Assises de la vertu*, virtue assizes. The public ministry points out and proclaims the noble deeds of the accused for public recognition.
Condition of the criminal after sentence: Under *surveillance de la haute police*.[d] Is fed in prison. The state defrays expenses.	*Condition of the virtuous after sentence*: Under *surveillance de la haute charité morale*.[e] Is fed at home. The state defrays expenses.
Execution: The criminal stands on the scaffold.	*Execution*: Immediately opposite the scaffold of the criminal a *pedestal* is erected on which the *grand homme de bien*[f] stands.—*A pillory of virtue*.

[a] *Criminal* justice.—*Ed.*
[b] *Virtuous* justice.—*Ed.*
[c] Spying out virtue, informers.—*Ed.*
[d] Supervision of the supreme police.—*Ed.*
[e] Supervision of supreme moral charity.—*Ed.*
[f] Man of great virtue.—*Ed.*

Moved by the sight of this picture, Monsieur Sue exclaims:

"Hélas, c'est une utopie, mais supposez qu'une société soit *organisée* de telle sorte!"[a]

That would be the *Critical organisation of society*. We must defend this organisation against Eugène Sue's reproach that up to now it has remained a utopia. Sue has again forgotten the "*Virtue Prize*" which is awarded every year in Paris and which he himself mentions. This prize is even organised in duplicate: the material *prix Montyon* for noble acts of men and women, and the *prix rosière* for girls of highest morality. There is even the *wreath* of roses demanded by Eugène Sue.

As far as *espionnage de vertu* and the *surveillance de haute charité morale* are concerned, they were organised long ago by the Jesuits. Moreover, the *Journal des Débats, Siècle, Petites affiches de Paris*, etc., point out and proclaim the virtues, noble acts and merits of all the Paris stockjobbers[b] daily and at cost price not counting the pointing out and proclamation of political noble acts, for which each party has its own organ.

Old Voss remarked long ago that Homer is better than his gods. The "revealed mystery of all mysteries", Rudolph, can therefore be made responsible for Eugène Sue's ideas.

In addition, Herr *Szeliga* reports:

"Besides, the passages in which Eugène Sue interrupts the narration and introduces or concludes episodes are very numerous, and all are *Critical*."

c) Abolition of Degeneracy Within Civilisation and of Rightlessness in the State

The juridical *preventive means* for the abolition of crime and hence of degeneracy within civilisation consists in the

"protective guardianship assumed by the state over the children of executed criminals or of those condemned to a life sentence".

Sue wants to organise the subdivision of crime in a more liberal way. No family should any longer have a hereditary privilege to crime; free competition in crime should triumph over monopoly.

Monsieur Sue abolishes "rightlessness in the state" by reforming the section of the *Code pénal* on *abus de confiance*,[c] and especially by the institution of *paid lawyers for the poor*. He finds that in

---

[a] Alas! It is a utopia! But suppose a society were *organised* in this way!
[b] This word is in English in the original.—*Ed.*
[c] Breach of trust.—*Ed.*

Piedmont, Holland, etc., where there are lawyers for the poor, rightlessness in the state has been abolished. The only failing of French legislation is that it does not provide for payment of lawyers for the poor, has no lawyers restricted to serving the poor, and makes the legal limits of poverty too narrow. As if rightlessness did not begin in the very *lawsuit* itself, and as if it had not already been known for a long time in France that the *law* gives nothing, but only sanctions what exists. The already trivial differentiation between *droit* and *fait* seems still to be a *mystère de Paris* for the Critical novelist.

If we add to the Critical revelation of the mysteries of law the great reforms which Eugène Sue wants to institute in respect of *huissiers*,[a] we shall understand the Paris journal *Satan*. There we see the residents of a district in the city write to the *"grand réformateur à tant la ligne"*[b] that there is no gaslight yet in their streets. Monsieur Sue replies that he will deal with this shortcoming in the sixth volume of his *Juif errant*.[c] Another part of the city complains of the shortcomings of preliminary education. He promises a preliminary education reform for that district of the city in the tenth volume of *Juif errant*.

4) THE REVEALED MYSTERY OF THE "STANDPOINT"

"Rudolph does not remain at his lofty" (!) *"standpoint ...* he does not shirk the trouble of adopting by free choice the *standpoints* on the right and on the left, above and below" (*Szeliga*).

One of the principal mysteries of Critical Criticism is the *"standpoint"* and *judgment from the standpoint of the standpoint*. For Criticism every man, like every product of the spirit, is turned into a standpoint.

Nothing is easier than to see through the mystery of the standpoint when one has seen through the general mystery of Critical Criticism, that of warming up old speculative trash.

First of all, let *Criticism* itself expound its theory of the "standpoint" in the words of its patriarch, Herr *Bruno Bauer*.

"Science ... *never* deals with a *given single individual* or a *given definite standpoint*.... It will not fail, of course, *to do away with the limitations of a standpoint* if it is worth the trouble and if these limitations have really general human significance; but it conceives them as *pure category and determinateness of self-consciousness* and accordingly speaks only for those who have the courage to rise to

---

[a] Bailiffs.—*Ed.*
[b] "Great reformer at so much a line."—*Ed.*
[c] *The Wandering Jew.*—*Ed.*

the *generality of self-consciousness*, i.e., who do not wish with all their strength to remain within those limitations" (*Anekdota*, t. II, p. 127).[a]

The *mystery* of this courage of Bauer's is *Hegel's Phänomenologie*. Because Hegel here substitutes *self-consciousness* for *man*, the *most varied* manifestations of human reality appear only as *definite* forms, as *determinateness of self-consciousness*. But mere determinateness of self-consciousness is a *"pure category"*, a mere "thought", which I can consequently also transcend in "pure" thought and overcome through pure thought. In Hegel's *Phänomenologie* the *material, sensuously perceptible, objective* foundations of the various estranged forms of human self-consciousness are allowed to remain. The whole destructive work results in the *most conservative philosophy* because it thinks it has overcome the *objective world*, the sensuously perceptible real world, by transforming it into a "Thing of Thought", a mere *determinateness of self-consciousness*, and can therefore also dissolve its opponent, which has become *ethereal*, in the *"ether of pure thought"*. The *Phänomenologie* is therefore quite consistent in that it ends by replacing human reality by *"absolute knowledge"* — *knowledge*, because this is the only mode of existence of self-consciousness, and because self-consciousness is considered the only mode of existence of man — *absolute* knowledge for the very reason that self-consciousness knows *only itself* and is no longer disturbed by any objective world. Hegel makes man the *man of self-consciousness* instead of making self-consciousness the *self-consciousness of man*, of real man, i.e., of man living also in a real, objective world and determined by that world. He stands the world *on its head* and can therefore *in his head* also dissolve all limitations, which nevertheless remain in existence *for bad sensuousness*, for *real* man. Moreover, everything that betrays the *limitations of general self-consciousness* — all sensuousness, reality, individuality of men and of their world — is necessarily held by him to be a limit. The whole of the *Phänomenologie* is intended to prove that *self-consciousness* is the *only reality* and *all reality*.

Herr Bauer has recently re-christened absolute knowledge *Criticism*, and given the more profane sounding name *standpoint* to the determinateness of self-consciousness. In the *Anekdota* both names are still to be found side by side, and standpoint is still explained as the determinateness of self-consciousness.

Since the *"religious world as such"* exists only as the world of *self-consciousness*, the Critical Critic — the theologian *ex profes-*

---

[a] B. Bauer, *Leiden und Freuden des theologischen Bewusstseins.—Ed.*

so—cannot by any means entertain the thought that there is a world in which *consciousness* and *being* are distinct; a world which continues to exist when I merely abolish its existence in thought, its existence as a category or as a standpoint; i.e., when I modify my own subjective consciousness without altering the objective reality in a really objective way, that is to say, without altering my own *objective* reality and that of other men. Hence the speculative *mystical identity* of *being* and *thinking* is repeated in Criticism as the equally mystical identity of *practice* and *theory*. That is why Criticism is so vexed with practice which wants to be something distinct from theory, and with theory which wants to be something other than the dissolution of a definite *category* in the "*boundless generality of self-consciousness*". Its own theory is confined to stating that everything determinate is an opposite of the boundless generality of self-consciousness and is, therefore, of no significance; for example, the state, private property, etc. It must be shown, on the contrary, how the state, private property, etc., turn human beings into abstractions, or are products of *abstract* man, instead of being the reality of individual, concrete human beings.

Finally, it goes without saying that whereas Hegel's *Phänomenologie*, in spite of its speculative original sin, gives in many instances the elements of a true description of human relations, Herr Bruno and Co., on the other hand, provide only an empty caricature, a caricature which is satisfied with deriving any determinateness out of a product of the spirit or even out of real relations and movements, changing this determinateness into a determinateness of thought, into a *category*, and making out that this category is the *standpoint* of the product, of the relation and the movement, in order then to be able to look down on this determinateness triumphantly with old-man's wisdom from the standpoint of abstraction, of the general category and of general self-consciousness.

Just as in Rudolph's opinion all human beings maintain the standpoint of good or bad and are judged by these two immutable conceptions, so for Herr Bauer and Co. all human beings adopt the standpoint of *Criticism* or that of the *Mass*. But both turn *real human beings* into *abstract standpoints*.

5) REVELATION OF THE MYSTERY OF THE UTILISATION OF HUMAN IMPULSES, OR CLEMENCE D'HARVILLE

So far Rudolph has been unable to do more than reward the good and punish the wicked in his own way. We shall now see an example of how he makes the *passions* useful and "gives the good natural disposition of Clémence d'Harville an appropriate development".

"Rudolph," says Herr Szeliga, "draws her attention to the *entertaining* aspect of *charity*, a thought which testifies to a knowledge of human beings that can *only* arise in the soul of Rudolph after it has been through trial."

The expressions which Rudolph uses in his conversation with Clémence:

"*faire attrayant*", "*utiliser le goût naturel*", "*régler l'intrigue*", "*utiliser les penchants à la dissimulation et à la ruse*", "changer en qualités généreuses des instincts impérieux, inexorables" [a] *etc.*,

these expressions just as much as the *impulses* themselves, which are mostly attributed here to woman's nature, *betray* the secret source of Rudolph's wisdom — *Fourier*. He has come across some popular presentation of Fourier's theory.

The *application* is again just as much Rudolph's Critical own as is the exposition of Bentham's theory given above.

It is not in charity *as such* that the young marquise is to find the satisfaction of her essential human nature, a human content and purpose of her activity, and hence entertainment. Charity offers rather only the external occasion, only the *pretext*, only the *material*, for a kind of entertainment that could just as well use any other material as its content. Misery is exploited consciously to procure the charitable person "the piquancy of a novel, the satisfaction of curiosity, adventure, disguise, enjoyment of his or her own excellence, violent nervous excitement", and the like.

Rudolph has thereby unconsciously expressed the mystery which was revealed long ago, that human misery itself, the infinite abjectness which is obliged to receive alms, must serve the aristocracy of money and education as a *plaything* to satisfy its self-love, tickle its arrogance and amuse it.

The numerous charitable associations in Germany, the numerous charitable societies in France and the great number of charitable quixotic societies in England, the concerts, balls, plays, meals for the poor, and even the public subscriptions for victims of accidents, have no other object. It seems then that along these lines charity, too, has long been *organised* as entertainment.

The sudden, unmotivated transformation of the marquise at the mere word *"amusant"* makes us doubt the durability of her cure;

---

[a] "To make *attractive*", "*to utilise natural taste*", "*to regulate intrigue*", "*to utilise the propensity to dissimulation and craft*", "to change imperious, inexorable instincts into noble qualities".— *Ed.*

or rather this transformation is sudden and unmotivated only in appearance and is caused only in appearance by the description of *charité* as an amusement. The marquise *loves* Rudolph and Rudolph wants to disguise himself *along with her*, to intrigue and to indulge in charitable adventures. Later, when the marquise pays a charity visit to the prison of Saint-Lazare, her jealousy of Fleur de Marie becomes apparent and out of charity towards her jealousy she conceals from Rudolph the fact of Marie's detention. At the best, Rudolph has succeeded in teaching an unhappy woman to play a silly comedy with unhappy beings. The mystery of the *philanthropy* he has hatched is betrayed by the Paris fop who invites his partner to supper after the dance in the following words:

> "Ah, Madame! ce n'est pas assez d'avoir dansé au bénéfice des ces pauvres Polonais ... soyons philanthropes jusqu'au bout ... allons *souper* maintenant au *profit des pauvres!*" [a]

6) REVELATION OF THE MYSTERY OF THE EMANCIPATION OF WOMEN, OR LOUISE MOREL

On the occasion of the arrest of *Louise Morel*, Rudolph indulges in reflections which he sums up as follows:

> "The master often ruins the maid, either by fear, surprise or other use of the opportunities provided by the ·nature of *the servants' condition*. He reduces her to misery, shame and crime. The *law is not concerned* with this.... The criminal who has in fact driven a girl to infanticide is not *punished*."

Rudolph's reflections do not go so far as to make the *servants' condition* the object of his most gracious Criticism. Being a *petty* ruler, he is a *great* patroniser of servants' conditions. Still less does he go so far as to understand that the general position of women in modern society is inhuman. Faithful in all respects to his previous theory, he deplores only that there is no *law which punishes* a seducer and links repentance and atonement with terrible chastisement.

Rudolph has only to take a look at the existing legislation in other countries. *English* laws fulfil all his wishes. In their delicacy, which *Blackstone* so highly praises, they go so far as to declare it a *felony* to seduce even a prostitute.

Herr Szeliga exclaims with a *flourish*:

---

[a] "Ah, Madame, it is not enough to have danced for the benefit of these poor Poles.... Let us be philanthropic to the end.... Let us have *supper* now for the *benefit of the poor!*"—*Ed*.

"So" (!)— *"thinks"* (!) — *"Rudolph"* (!)— "and now compare *these thoughts* with your *fantasies* about the *emancipation of woman*. The act of this emancipation can be *almost* physically grasped from them, but you are much too practical to start with, and that is why your attempts have failed so often."

In any case we must thank Herr Szeliga for revealing the mystery that an act can be almost physically grasped from thoughts. As for his ridiculous comparison of Rudolph with men who taught the emancipation of woman, compare Rudolph's *thoughts* with the following "fantasies" of *Fourier*:

"Adultery, seduction, are a credit to the seducer, are good tone.... But, poor girl! Infanticide! What a crime! If she prizes her honour she must efface all traces of dishonour. But if she sacrifices her child to the prejudices of the world her ignominy is all the greater and she is a victim of the prejudices of the law.... That is the *vicious circle* which every civilised mechanism describes."

"Is not the young daughter a ware held up for sale to the first bidder who wishes to obtain exclusive ownership of her?... De même qu'en grammaire deux négations valent une affirmation, l'on peut dire qu'en *négoce conjugal deux prostitutions valent une vertu*." [a]

"The change in a historical epoch can always be determined by women's progress towards freedom, because here, in the relation of woman to man, of the weak to the strong, the victory of human nature over brutality is most evident. The degree of emancipation of woman is the natural measure of general emancipation."

"The humiliation of the female sex is an essential feature of civilisation as well as of barbarism. The only difference is that the civilised system raises every vice that barbarism practises in a simple form to a compound, equivocal, ambiguous, hypocritical mode of existence.... No one is punished more severely for keeping woman in slavery than man himself" (*Fourier*).[67]

It is superfluous to contrast Rudolph's thoughts with Fourier's masterly characterisation of *marriage*, or with the works of the materialist section of French communism.[68]

The most pitiful off-scourings of socialist literature, a sample of which is to be found in this novelist, reveal "mysteries" still unknown to Critical Criticism.

7) REVELATION OF POLITICAL ECONOMIC MYSTERIES

a) Theoretical Revelation of Political Economic Mysteries

First revelation: Wealth often leads to waste, waste to ruin.

Second revelation: The above-mentioned effects of wealth arise from a lack of instruction in rich youth.

Third revelation: *Inheritance* and *private property* are and *must* be inviolable and sacred.

---

[a] "Just as in grammar two negations are the equivalent of an affirmation, we can say that in the *marriage trade two prostitutions are the equivalent of virtue*." — *Ed.*

Fourth revelation: The rich man is *morally* responsible to the workers for the way he uses his fortune. A large fortune is a hereditary deposit—a *feudal tenement* —entrusted to clever, firm, skilful and magnanimous hands, which are at the same time charged with making it fruitful and using it in such a way that everything which has the *good luck* to be within the range of the dazzling and wholesome radiation of that large fortune is fructified, vitalised and improved.

Fifth revelation: The state must give inexperienced rich youth the *rudiments* of *individual economy*. It must give a moral character to riches.

Sixth revelation: Finally, the state must tackle the vast question of *organisation of labour*. It must give the wholesome example of the *association of capitals and labour*, of an association which is honest, intelligent and fair, which ensures the well-being of the *worker without* prejudice to the *fortune of the rich*, which establishes *links* of sympathy and gratitude *between* these *two classes* and thus ensures tranquillity in the state *for ever*.

Since the state at present does not yet accept this theory *Rudolph* himself gives some practical examples. They reveal the mystery that the most generally known *economic relations* are still "mysteries" for Monsieur Sue, Monsieur Rudolph and Critical Criticism.

b) "The Bank for the Poor"

Rudolph institutes a *Bank for the Poor*. The statute of this *Critical Bank for the Poor* is as follows:

It must give support during periods of unemployment to honest workers with families. It must replace alms and pawnshops. It has at its disposal an annual income of 12,000 francs and distributes interest-free assistance loans of 20 to 40 francs. At first it extends its activity only to the *seventh arrondissement* of Paris, where most of the workers live. Working men and women applying for relief must have a certificate from their last employer vouching for their good behaviour and giving the cause and date of the interruption of work. These loans are to be paid off in monthly instalments of one-sixth or one-twelfth of the sum at the choice of the borrower, counting from the day on which he finds employment again. The loan is guaranteed by the borrower's word of honour. Moreover, the latter's *parole jurée*[a] must be guaranteed by two other workers.

---

[a] Sworn word.— *Ed*.

As the Critical purpose of the Bank for the Poor is to remedy one of the most grievous misfortunes in the life of the worker—*interruption in employment*—assistance would be given only to unemployed manual workers. Monsieur Germain, the manager of this institution, draws a yearly salary of 10,000 francs.

Let us now cast a mass-type glance at the practice of Critical political economy. The annual income is 12,000 francs. The amount loaned per person is from 20 to 40 francs, hence an average of 30 francs. The number of workers in the seventh *arrondissement* who are officially recognised as "needy" is at least 4,000. Hence, in a year only 400, or one-tenth, of the neediest workers in the seventh *arrondissement* can receive relief. If we estimate the *average length* of unemployment in Paris at 4 months, i.e., 16 weeks, we shall be considerably below the actual figure. Thirty francs divided over 16 weeks gives somewhat less than 37 sous and 3 centimes a week, not even 27 centimes a day. The daily expense on *one prisoner* in France is on the average a little over 47 centimes, somewhat over 30 centimes being spent on food alone. But the worker to whom Monsieur Rudolph pays relief has a family. Let us take the average family as consisting of man, wife and only two children; that means that 27 centimes must be divided among four persons. From this we must deduct rent—a minimum of 15 centimes a day—so that 12 centimes remain. The average amount of *bread* eaten by a *single* prisoner costs about 14 centimes. Therefore, even disregarding all other needs, the worker and his family will not be able to buy even a quarter of the bread they need with the help obtained from the Critical Bank for the Poor. They will certainly starve if they do not resort to the means that the bank is intended to obviate—the pawnshop, begging, thieving and prostitution.

The manager of the Bank for the Poor, on the other hand, is all the more brilliantly provided for by the man of ruthless Criticism. The income he administers is 12,000 francs, his salary is 10,000. The management therefore costs 85 per cent of the total, nearly three times as much as the mass-type administration of poor relief in Paris, which costs about 17 per cent of the total.

Let us suppose for a moment that the assistance that the Bank for the Poor provides is real, not just illusory. In that case the institution of the revealed mystery of all mysteries rests on the illusion that only a different *distribution* of wages is required to enable the workers to live through the year.

Speaking in the prosaic sense, the income of 7,500,000 French workers averages no more than 91 francs per head, that of another 7,500,000 is only 120 francs per head; hence for at least 15,000,000 it is less than is absolutely necessary for life.

The idea of the Critical Bank for the Poor, if it is rationally conceived, amounts to this: during the time the worker is employed as much will be deducted from his wages as he needs for his living during unemployment. It comes to the same thing whether I advance him a certain sum during his unemployment and he gives it back when he has employment, or he gives up a certain sum when he has employment and I give it back to him when he is unemployed. In either case he gives me when he is working what he gets from me when he is unemployed.

Thus, the "pure" *Bank for the Poor* differs from the mass-type *savings-banks* only in two very original, very Critical qualities. The first is that the Bank for the Poor lends money *"à fonds perdus"*[a] on the senseless assumption that the worker could pay back if he wanted to and that he would always want to pay back if he could. The second is that it pays no *interest* on the sum put aside by the worker. As this sum is given the form of an advance, the Bank for the Poor thinks it is doing the worker a favour by not charging him any interest.

The difference between the Critical Bank for the Poor and the mass-type savings-banks is therefore that the worker loses his interest and the Bank its capital.

c) Model Farm at Bouqueval

Rudolph founds a *model farm* at *Bouqueval.* The choice of the place is all the more fortunate as it preserves memories of feudal times, namely of a *château seigneurial.*[b]

Each of the six men employed on this farm is paid 150 écus, or 450 francs a year, while the women get 60 écus, or 180 francs. Moreover they get board and lodging free. The ordinary daily fare of the people at Bouqueval consists of a "formidable" plate of ham, an equally formidable plate of mutton and, finally, a no less massive piece of veal supplemented by two kinds of winter salad, two large cheeses, potatoes, cider, etc. Each of the six men does *twice* the work of the ordinary French agricultural labourer.

As the total annual income produced by France, if divided equally, would come to no more than 93 francs per person, and as the total number of inhabitants employed directly in agriculture is

---

[a] Not to be repaid.—*Ed.*

[b] A feudal manor.—*Ed.*

two-thirds of the population of France, it will be seen what a revolution the general imitation of the German caliph's model farm would cause not only in the distribution, but also in the production of the national wealth.

According to what has been said, Rudolph achieved this enormous increase in production solely by making each labourer work twice as much and eat six times as much as before.

Since the French peasant is very industrious, labourers who work *twice* as much must be *superhuman athletes*, as the "formidable" meat dishes also seem to indicate. Hence we may assume that each of the six men eats at least a pound of meat a day.

If all the meat produced in France were distributed equally there would not be even a quarter of a pound per person per day. It is therefore obvious what a revolution Rudolph's example would cause in this respect too. The agricultural population *alone* would consume more meat than is produced in France, so that as a result of this Critical reform France would be left without any livestock.

The fifth part of the gross product which Rudolph, according to the report of the manager of Bouqueval, Father Chatelain, allows the labourers, in addition to the high wage and sumptuous board, is nothing else than his *rent*. It is assumed that, on the average, after deduction of all production costs and profit on the working capital, one-fifth of the gross product remains for the French landowner, that is to say, the ratio of the rent to the gross product is one to five. Although it is beyond doubt that Rudolph decreases the profit on his working capital beyond all proportion by increasing the expenditure for the labourers beyond all proportion—according to Chaptal (*De l'industrie française*, t. I, p. 239) the average yearly income of the French agricultural labourer is 120 francs—although Rudolph gives his whole rent away to the labourers, Father Chatelain nevertheless reports that the prince thereby increases his revenue and thus inspires un-Critical landowners to farm in the same way.

The Bouqueval model farm is nothing but a fantastic illusion; its *hidden fund* is not the *natural* land of the Bouqueval estate, it is a magic purse of Fortunatus that Rudolph has!

In this connection Critical Criticism exultantly declares:

"You can see from the *whole* plan at a *first glance* that it is *not a utopia*."

Only Critical Criticism can see at a first glance at a *Fortunatus'* *purse* that it is not a utopia. The first glance of Criticism is—the glance of "the evil eye"!

8) RUDOLPH,
"THE REVEALED MYSTERY OF ALL MYSTERIES"

The miraculous means by which Rudolph accomplishes all his redemptions and miracle cures is not his fine words but his *ready money*. That is what the moralists are like, says Fourier. You must be a millionaire to be able to imitate their heroes.

Morality is *"impuissance mise en action"*.[a] Every time it fights a vice it is defeated. And Rudolph does not even rise to the standpoint of independent morality, which is based at least on the consciousness of *human dignity*. His morality, on the contrary, is based on the consciousness of *human weakness*. His is the *theological* morality. We have investigated in detail the heroic feats that he accomplished with his *fixed, Christian* ideas, by which he measures the world, with his *"charité"*, *"dévouement"*, *"abnégation"*, *"repentir"*, *"bons"* and *"méchants"*, *"récompense"* and *"punition"*, *"châtiments terribles"*, *"isolement"*, *"salut de l'âme"*,[b] etc. We have proved that they are mere Eulenspiegel tricks. All that we still have to deal with here is the *personal* character of Rudolph, the "revealed mystery of all mysteries" or the revealed mystery of *"pure* Criticism".

The antithesis of "good" and "evil" confronts the Critical Hercules when he is still a youth in two personifications, *Murph* and *Polidori*, both of them Rudolph's teachers. The former educates him in good and is "the *Good One"*. The latter educates him in evil and is "the *Evil One"*. So that this conception should by no means be inferior in triviality to similar conceptions in other novels, Murph, the personification of *"the good"*, cannot be *"savant"* or "particularly endowed intellectually". But he is *honest, simple*, and *laconic*; he feels himself great when he applies to evil such monosyllabic words as *"foul"* or *"vile"*, and he has a *horreur* of anything which is *base*. To use Hegel's expression, he honestly sets the melody of the good and the true in an equality of tones, i.e., on *one note*.

Polidori, on the contrary, is a prodigy of cleverness, knowledge and education, and at the same time of the "most dangerous immorality", having, in particular, what Eugène Sue, as a member of the young pious French bourgeoisie, could not forget— *"le plus*

---

[a] *"Impotence in action."* Ch. Fourier, *Théorie des quatre mouvements et des destinées générales*, Part II, Epilogue.—*Ed.*

[b] *"Charity"*, *"devotion"*, *"self-denial"*, *"repentance"*, the *"good"* and the *"wicked"* people, *"reward"* and *"punishment"*, *"terrible chastisements"*, *"isolation"*, *"salvation of the soul"*.—*Ed.*

effrayant scepticisme".[a] We can judge the spiritual energy and education of Eugène Sue and his hero by their panic fear of *scepticism*.

"Murph," says Herr Szeliga, "is at the same time the perpetuated guilt of January 13[b] and the perpetual redemption of that guilt by his incomparable love and self-sacrifice for the person of Rudolph."

Just as Rudolph is the *deus ex machina* and the mediator of the world, so Murph, for his part, is the personal *deus ex machina* and mediator of Rudolph.

"Rudolph and the salvation of mankind, Rudolph and the realisation of man's essential perfections, are for Murph an inseparable unity, a unity to which he dedicates himself not with the stupid dog-like devotion of the slave, but knowingly and independently."

So Murph is an enlightened, knowing and independent slave. Like every prince's valet, he sees in his master the salvation of mankind personified. *Graun* flatters Murph with the words: "*intrépide garde du corps*".[c] Rudolph himself calls him *modèle d'un valet*[d] and truly he is a *model servant*. Eugène Sue tells us that Murph scrupulously addresses Rudolph as "Monseigneur" when alone with him. In the presence of others he calls him *Monsieur* with his lips to keep his incognito, but "Monseigneur" with his heart.

"Murph helps to raise the veil from the mysteries, but only for Rudolph's sake. He helps in the work of destroying the power of mystery."

The denseness of the veil which conceals the simplest conditions of the world from Murph can be seen from his conversation with the envoy Graun. From the legal right of self-defence in case of emergency he concludes that Rudolph, as *judge of the secret court*, was entitled to blind the *maître d'école*, although the latter was in chains and "defenceless". His description of how Rudolph will tell of his "noble" actions before the assizes, will make a display of eloquent phrases, and will let his great heart pour forth, is worthy of a grammar-school boy who has just read Schiller's *Raüber*. The only mystery which Murph lets the world solve is whether he blacked his face with coal-dust or black paint when he played the *charbonnier*.[e]

---

[a] "*The most frightful scepticism*".— Ed.

[b] On this day, Rudolph, in a fit of anger, made an attempt on the life of his father, but repented and gave the word to do good.— Ed.

[c] "*Fearless bodyguard*".— Ed.

[d] A model servant.— Ed.

[e] Coal-man.— Ed.

"The angels shall come forth and sever the wicked from among the just" (Mat. 13:49). "Tribulation and anguish, upon every soul of man that doeth evil...; But glory, honour, and peace, to every man that worketh good" (Rom. 2:9-10).

Rudolph makes himself one of those *angels*. He goes forth into the world to sever the wicked from among the just, to punish the wicked and reward the good. The conception of good and evil has sunk so deep into his weak brain that he really believes in a corporeal Satan and wants to catch the devil alive, as at one time Professor *Sack* wanted to in Bonn.[69] On the other hand, he tries to copy on a small scale the opposite of the devil, *God*. He likes "*de jouer un peu le rôle de la providence*".[a] Just as in *reality all* differences become merged more and more in the difference between *poor* and *rich*, so *all* aristocratic differences become dissolved in *idea* in the opposition between *good* and *evil*. This distinction is the last form that the aristocrat gives to his prejudices. Rudolph regards himself as a good man and thinks that the wicked exist to afford him the self-satisfaction of his own excellence. Let us consider this personification of "the good" a little more closely.

Herr Rudolph indulges in charity and extravagance like the Caliph of Baghdad in the Arabian Nights. He cannot possibly lead that kind of life without sucking the blood out of his little principality in Germany to the last drop like a vampire. As Monsieur Sue tells us, he would have been one of the mediatised German princes[70] had he not been saved from involuntary abdication by the protection of a French *marquis*. This gives us an idea of the size of his territory. We can form a further idea of how *Critically* Rudolph appraises *his own situation* by the fact that he, a minor German *Serenissimus*, thinks it necessary to live semi-incognito in Paris in order not to attract attention. He specially takes with him one of his *chancellors* for the Critical purpose of the latter representing for him "*le côté théâtral et puéril du pouvoir souverain*"[b] as though a minor German *Serenissimus* needed another representative of the theatrical and childish side of sovereign power besides himself and his mirror. Rudolph has succeeded in imposing on his suite the same *Critical self-delusion*. Thus his servant *Murph* and his envoy *Graun* do not notice that the Parisian *homme d'affaires*,[c] Monsieur *Badinot*, makes fun of them when he pretends to take their private instructions as matters of state and sarcastically chatters about

---

[a] "To play the role of Providence a little".—*Ed.*
[b] "The theatrical and childish side of sovereign power".—*Ed.*
[c] Household manager.—*Ed.*

"rapports occultes qui peuvent exister entre les intérêts les plus divers et les *destinés des empires*".[a] "Yes," says Rudolph's envoy, "he has the impudence to say to me sometimes: 'How many complications unknown to the people there are in the government of a state! Who would think, Herr Baron, that the notes which I deliver to you doubtless have their influence on the course of *European affairs?*'"

The envoy and Murph do not find it impudent that influence on European affairs is ascribed to them, but that Badinot idealises his lowly occupation in such a way.

Let us first recall a scene from *Rudolph*'s domestic life. Rudolph tells Murph "he was having moments of pride and bliss". Immediately afterwards he becomes furious because Murph will not answer a question of his. "*Je vous ordonne de parler.*"[b] Murph will not let himself be ordered. Rudolph says: "*Je n'aime pas les réticences.*"[c] He forgets himself so far as to be base enough to remind Murph that he *pays* him for all his services. He will not be calmed until Murph reminds him of January 13. Murph's servile nature reasserts itself after its momentary abeyance. He tears out his "hair", which he luckily has not got, and is desperate at having been somewhat rude to his exalted master who calls him "a model servant", "his good old faithful Murph".

After these samples of evil in him, Rudolph repeats his fixed ideas on "good" and "evil" and reports the progress he is making in regard to the good. He calls alms and compassion the chaste and pious consolers of *his* wounded soul. It would be horrible, impious, a *sacrilege*, to prostitute them to abject, unworthy beings. Of course alms and compassion are the consolers of *his* soul. That is why it would be a sacrilege to desecrate them. It would be "to inspire doubt in God, and he who gives must make people believe in Him". To give alms to one abject is unthinkable!

Rudolph considers every motion of his soul as infinitely important. That is why he constantly observes and appraises them. Thus the simpleton consoles himself as far as his outburst against Murph is concerned by the fact that he was moved by Fleur de Marie. "I was moved to tears, and I am accused of being *blasé*, hard and inflexible!" After thus proving *his own goodness*, he waxes furious over "*evil*", over the wickedness of Marie's unknown mother, and says with the greatest possible solemnity to Murph:

---

[a] "Occult relations that can exist between the most varying interests and the destinies of empires".—*Ed.*

[b] "I order you to speak."—*Ed.*

[c] "I do not like reticences."—*Ed.*

"*Tu le sais—certaines vengeances me sont bien chères, certaines souffrances bien* précieuses".[a]

In speaking, he makes such diabolical grimaces that his faithful servant cries out in fear: "Hélas, Monseigneur!" This great lord is like the members of *Young England*,[71] who also wish to reform the world, perform noble deeds, and are subject to similar hysterical fits.

The explanation of the adventures and situations in which Rudolph finds himself involved is to be found above all in Rudolph's *adventurous disposition*. He loves "the piquancy of novels, distractions, adventures, disguise"; his "curiosity" is "insatiable", he feels a "need for vigorous, stimulating sensations", he is "eager for *violent nervous excitement*".

This disposition of Rudolph is reinforced by his craze for *playing the role of Providence* and arranging the world according to his fixed ideas.

His attitude to other persons is determined either by an abstract fixed idea or by quite personal, fortuitous motives.

He frees the Negro doctor David and his beloved, for example, not because of the direct human sympathy which they inspire, not to free *them*, but to play *Providence* to the slave-owner Willis and to punish him for *not believing in God*. In the same way the *maître d'école* seems to him a godsent opportunity for *applying* the penal theory that he invented so long ago. Murph's conversation with the envoy Graun enables us from another aspect to see deeply into the purely personal motives that determine Rudolph's noble acts.

The prince's interest in Fleur de Marie is based, as Murph says, "apart from" the pity which the poor girl inspires, on the fact that the daughter whose loss caused him such bitter grief would now be of the same age. Rudolph's sympathy for the Marquise d'Harville has, "apart from" his philanthropic idiosyncrasies, the personal ground that without the old Marquise d'Harville and his friendship with the Emperor Alexander, Rudolph's father would have been deleted from the line of German sovereigns.

His kindness towards Madame George and his interest in Germain, her son, have the same motive. Madame George belongs to the d'Harville family.

"C'est non moins à ses malheurs et à ses vertus qu'à *cette parenté* que la pauvre Madame George a dû les incessantes bontés de son Altesse."[b]

---

[a] "You know—some vengeances are very dear to me, some sufferings very precious."—*Ed.*

[b] "It is no less to her misfortunes and her virtues than *to this relationship* that poor Madame George owes the ceaseless kindness of His Highness."—*Ed.*

The apologist Murph tries to gloss over the ambiguity of Rudolph's motives by such expressions as: "*surtout, à part, non moins que*".[a]

The whole of Rudolph's character is finally summed up in the "*pure*" *hypocrisy* by which he manages to see and make others see the *outbursts of his evil passions* as *outbursts against the passions of the wicked*, in a way similar to that in which Critical Criticism represents *its own stupidities* as the *stupidities* of the *Mass*, its spiteful rancour at the progress of the world outside itself as the rancour of the world outside itself at progress, and finally its egoism, which thinks it has absorbed all Spirit in itself, as the egoistic opposition of the Mass to the Spirit.

We shall prove *Rudolph's* "pure" hypocrisy in his attitude to the *maître d'école*, to Countess *Sarah MacGregor* and to the notary *Jacques Ferrand*.

In order to lure the *maître d'école* into a trap and seize him, Rudolph persuades him to break into his apartment. The interest he has in this is a purely personal one, not a general human one. The fact is that the *maître d'école* has a *portfolio* belonging to *Countess MacGregor*, and Rudolph is greatly interested in gaining possession of *it*. Speaking of Rudolph's *tête-à-tête* with the *maître d'école*, the author says explicitly:

"Rodolphe se trouvait dans une anxiété cruelle; s'il laissait *échapper cette occasion de s'emparer du maître d'école*, il ne la retrouverait sans doute jamais; ce brigand *emporterait les secrets* que Rodolphe avait tant d'intérêt a savoir."[b]

With the *maître d'école*, Rudolph obtains possession of Countess MacGregor's *portfolio*; he *seizes* the *maître d'école* out of purely personal interest; he has him *blinded* out of personal passion.

When Chourineur tells Rudolph of the struggle of the *maître d'école* with Murph and gives as the reason for his resistance the fact that he knew what was in store for him, Rudolph replies: "He did not know", and he says it "*d'un air sombre, les traits contractés par cette expression presque féroce, dont nous avons parlé.*"[c] The thought of vengeance flashes across his mind, he anticipates the savage pleasure that the barbarous punishment of the *maître d'école* will afford him.

---

[a] "Above all", "apart from" and "no less than".—*Ed.*

[b] "Rudolph was cruelly anxious; if he *let slip this opportunity of seizing the maître d'école*, he would probably never have another; the brigand would *carry away the secrets* that Rudolph was so keen to find out."—*Ed.*

[c] "With a sombre mien, his features contracted by the almost ferocious expression of which we have spoken".—*Ed.*

On the entrance of the Negro doctor David, whom he intends to make the instrument of his *revenge*, Rudolph cries out:

> "'*Vengeance!*... Vengeance!' s'écria Rodolphe avec une *fureur froide* et concentrée."[a]

A cold and concentrated fury is seething in him. Then he whispers his plan in the doctor's ear, and when the latter recoils at it, he immediately finds a "pure" theoretical motive to substitute for *personal vengeance*. It is only a case, he says, of "*applying an idea*" that has often flashed across his noble mind, and he does not forget to add unctuously: "He will still have before him the boundless horizon of atonement." He follows the example of the Spanish Inquisition which, when handing over to civil justice the victim condemned to be burnt at the stake, added a hypocritical request for mercy for the repentant sinner.

Of course, when the interrogation and sentencing of the *maître d'école* is to take place, His Highness is seated in a most comfortable study in a long, deep black dressing-gown, his features impressively pale, and in order to copy the court of justice more faithfully, he is sitting at a long table on which are the exhibits of the case. He must now discard the expression of rage and revenge with which he told Chourineur and the doctor of his plan for blinding the *maître d'école*. He must show himself "calm, sad and composed", and display the extremely comic, solemn attitude of a self-styled world judge.

In order to leave no doubt as to the "pure" motive of the blinding, the silly *Murph* admits to the envoy Graun:

> "The cruel punishment of the *maître d'école* was intended *chiefly* to give me my *revenge* against the *assassin*."

In a *tête-à-tête* with Murph, Rudolph says:

> "Ma haine des méchants... est devenue plus vivace, mon aversion pour *Sarah* augmente en raison sans doute du chagrin que me cause la mort de ma fille."[b]

Rudolph tells us how much stronger his hatred of the wicked has become. Needless to say, his hatred is a Critical, pure, moral hatred—hatred of the wicked *because* they are wicked. That is why he regards this hatred as his own progress in the good.

---

[a] "'*Revenge!* ... Revenge!' Rudolph cries out with *cold* and *concentrated fury*."—*Ed.*

[b] "My hatred of the wicked ... has become stronger, my aversion for *Sarah* increases, doubtless because of the grief caused by the death of my daughter."—*Ed.*

At the same time, however, he betrays that this growth of moral hatred is nothing but a *hypocritical justification* to excuse the growth of his *personal aversion* for Sarah. The vague moral idea of his increasing hatred of the wicked is only a mask for the definite immoral fact of his increased aversion for Sarah. This aversion has a very natural and a very personal basis, his personal grief, which is also the measure of his aversion. *Sans doute!*[a]

Still more repugnant is the hypocrisy to be seen in Rudolph's meeting with the dying Countess MacGregor.

After the revelation of the mystery that Fleur de Marie is the daughter of Rudolph and the Countess, Rudolph goes up to her "*l'air menaçant, impitoyable*".[b] She begs for mercy.

"Pas de grâce," he replies, "malédiction sur vous ... vous ... mon mauvais génie et celui de ma race."[c]

So it is his "race" that he wishes to avenge. He goes on to inform the Countess how, to atone for his attempted murder of his father, he has taken upon himself a world crusade for the reward of the good and the punishment of the wicked. He tortures the Countess, he abandons himself to his *rage,* but in his *own* eyes he is only carrying out the task which he took upon himself after January 13, of "*poursuivre le mal*".[d]

As he is leaving, Sarah cries out:

"'Pitié! Je meurs!' 'Mourez donc, maudite!' dit Rodolphe effrayant de fureur".[e]

The last words "*effrayant de fureur*" betray the pure, Critical and moral motives of his actions. It was the same rage that made him draw his sword against his father, his *blessed* father, as Herr Szeliga calls him. Instead of fighting this evil in himself he fights it, like a pure Critic, in others.

In the end, Rudolph himself discards his Catholic penal theory. He wanted to abolish capital punishment, to change punishment into penance, but only as long as the murderer murdered strangers and spared members of Rudolph's family. He adopts the death penalty as soon as one of his kin is murdered; he needs a double set of laws, one for his own person and one for ordinary persons.

---

[a] Doubtless!—*Ed.*

[b] "Looking threatening and pitiless."—*Ed.*

[c] "No mercy. A curse on you ... you ... my evil genius and the evil genius of my race."—*Ed.*

[d] "Prosecuting evil."—*Ed.*

[e] "'Have pity! I am dying!' 'Die then, accursed one!' replies Rudolph, terrible in his rage."—*Ed.*

He learns from Sarah that Jacques Ferrand was the cause of the death of Fleur de Marie. He says to himself:

"No, it is not enough!... What a burning desire for revenge!... What a thirst for blood!... What calm, deliberate rage!... *Until I knew* that *one* of the monster's victims was *my child* I said to myself: this man's death would be fruitless.... Life without money, life without satisfaction of his frenzied sensuality will be a long and double torture.... *But it is my daughter!*... I shall *kill* this man!"

And he rushes out to kill him, but finds him in a state which makes murder superfluous.

The "good" Rudolph! Burning with desire for revenge, thirsting for blood, with calm, deliberate rage, with a hypocrisy which excuses every evil impulse with its casuistry, he has all the *evil* passions for which he gouges out the eyes of others. Only accidental strokes of luck, money and rank in society save this "*good*" man from the *penitentiary*.

"The *power of Criticism*", to compensate for the otherwise complete nullity of this Don Quixote, makes him "bon locataire", "bon voisin", "bon ami", "bon père", "bon bourgeois", "bon citoyen", "bon prince",[a] and so on, according to Herr Szeliga's gamut of eulogy. *That is more than all the results* that "*mankind* in its *entire history*" has achieved. That is enough for Rudolph to *save* "the *world*" twice from "*downfall*"!

---

[a] A "good tenant", a "good neighbour", a "good friend", a "good father", a "good bourgeois", a "good citizen", a "good prince".—*Ed.*

Chapter IX

THE CRITICAL LAST JUDGMENT

Through *Rudolph*, Critical Criticism has twice saved the world from downfall, but only that it may now *itself* decree the *end of the world.*

And I saw and heard a mighty angel, Herr *Hirzel*, flying from Zurich across the heavens. And he had in his hand a little book open like the fifth number of the *Allgemeine Literatur-Zeitung*; and he set his right foot upon the Mass and his left foot upon Charlottenburg; and he cried with a loud voice as when a lion roareth, and his words rose like a dove—chirp! chirp!—to the regions of pathos and thunder-like aspects of the *Critical Last Judgment.*

"When, finally, *all* is united against Criticism and—*verily, verily I say unto you*[a]—this time is no longer far off—when the whole world in dissolution—*to it it was given to fight against the Holy*—groups around Criticism for the last onslaught; then the courage of Criticism and its significance will have found the greatest recognition. We can have no fear of the outcome. It will all end by our settling accounts with the various groups—*and we shall separate them from one another as the shepherd separateth the sheep from the goats; and we shall set the sheep on our right hand and the goats on our left*—and we shall give a general certificate of poverty to the hostile knights—*they are spirits of the devil, they go out into the breadth of the world and they gather to fight on the great day of God the Almighty*—and all who dwell on earth will wonder."

And when the angel had cried, seven thunders uttered their voices:

---

[a] The words in italics between dashes are Marx's ironical insertions.—*Ed.*

Dies irae, dies illa
Solvet saeclum in favilla.
Judex ergo cum sedebit,
Quidquid latet, adparebit,
Nil inultum remanebit.
Quid sum, miser, tunc dicturus? etc.[a]

Ye shall hear of wars and rumours of wars. All this must first of all come to pass. For there shall rise false Christs and false prophets, Messieurs *Buchez* and *Roux* from Paris, Herr *Friedrich Rohmer* and *Theodor Rohmer* from Zurich, and they will say: Here is Christ! But then the sign of the *Bauer* brothers will appear in Criticism and the words of the Scripture on *Bauer's work*[b] will be accomplished:

Quand les bœufs vont deux à deux
Le. *labourage* en va mieux![c]

HISTORICAL EPILOGUE

As we learned later, it was not the world, but the Critical *Literatur-Zeitung* that came to an end.

---

[a] That day of wrath
Will reduce the world to ashes.
When the judge takes his seat
All that is hidden will come to light,
Nothing will remain unpunished.
What shall I, wretch, say then?—*Ed.*

[b] The author says "*Bauernwerk*", which literally means "peasant's work".—*Ed.*

[c] With the oxen paired together.
Ploughing goes much better!
(From a French drinking song.)—*Ed.*

THE

NEW MORAL WORLD:

AND

GAZETTE OF THE RATIONAL SOCIETY.

Enrolled under Acts of Parliament, 10 Geo. IV. c. 56, and 4, 5, Will. IV. c. 40.

"ANY GENERAL CHARACTER, FROM THE BEST TO THE WORST, FROM THE MOST IGNORANT TO THE MOST ENLIGHTENED, MAY BE GIVEN TO ANY COMMUNITY, EVEN TO THE WORLD AT LARGE, BY THE APPLICATION OF PROPER MEANS, WHICH MEANS ARE TO A GREAT EXTENT AT THE COMMAND AND UNDER THE CONTROL OF THOSE WHO HAVE INFLUENCE IN THE AFFAIRS OF MEN."—ROBERT OWEN.

W. JOHNSTON, PRINTER, LITTLE RED LION COURT, CHARTERHOUSE LANE, LONDON.

No. 15. VOL. VI *Third Series.*   SATURDAY, OCTOBER 5, 1844.   PRICE 2d.

Frederick Engels

[CONTINENTAL SOCIALISM] [72]

Continental Socialism seems to deserve and to obtain a considerable portion of public attention at present. I forward you a few extracts from a letter addressed me from Barmen in Prussia, by a former contributor to the *New Moral World.*

"In Paris, on my way home, I visited a Communist Club of the mystic school. I was introduced by a Russian who speaks French and German perfectly,[a] and who very cleverly opposed Feuerbach's reasoning,* to them. They mean just as much by the term God as the Ham Common folks [73] by *Love-Spirit.* They however declared this a secondary question, and to all practical intents agreed with us, and said, *"enfin, l'athéisme c'est votre religion"*:—In the end, atheism is your religion. Religion, in French, means *conviction, feeling*, not worship. They affirmed, that the noise and hubbub of the *Bourgeois*, or middle class, against England, is all nonsense; and they were very anxious to convince us, that they had not the slightest national prejudice, that the working men of France care nothing about Morocco,[74] but know that the *ouvriers*, workers, of all countries are allies, having the same interests. The French middle class are quite as egotistical, as avaricious, and quite as insupportable in society as the English, but the French *ouvriers* are fine fellows. We have made much progress among the Russians at Paris. There are three or four noblemen and proprietors of serfs now at Paris who are radical Communists and Atheists. We have in Paris a German Communist Paper, the

---

* The resolution of the God idea into man.— *Note by Engels.*

[a] Evidently, by M. A. Bakunin.— *Ed.*

Vorwärts!, published twice-a-week. In Belgium there is an active Communist agitation going on, and a paper, the *Débat Social*, published at Brussels. In Paris there are about half-a-dozen Communist papers. *Socialiste, Socialitaire*, are very fashionable names in France; and Louis Philippe, the arch-*bourgeois*, supports the *Démocratie Pacifique* with money and protection. The religious exterior of the French Socialists is mostly hypocritical; the people are thoroughly irreligious, and the first victims of the next revolution will be the parsons. The Cologne folks have made enormous progress. When we assembled in a public house we filled a good room with our company, mostly lawyers, medical men, artists etc., also three or four lieutenants in the artillery, one of whom is a very clever fellow. In Düsseldorf we have a few men, amongst them a very talented poet. In Elberfeld, about half-a-dozen of my friends and some others are Communists. In fact there is scarcely a town in Northern Germany where we have not some radical Anti-Proprietarians and Atheists. Edgar Bauer, of Berlin, has just been sentenced to three years imprisonment for his last book." [a]

Thinking the above facts would be interesting to your readers, I forward them for insertion in your paper.

Written about September 20, 1844

First published in the newspaper
The New Moral World No. 15,
October 5, 1844
Signed: *Anglo-German*

Printed according to the newspaper

---

[a] E. Bauer, *Der Streit der Kritik mit Kirche und Staat.—Ed.*

Frederick Engels

DESCRIPTION OF RECENTLY FOUNDED COMMUNIST COLONIES STILL IN EXISTENCE [75]

When one talks to people about socialism or communism, one very frequently finds that they entirely agree with one regarding the substance of the matter and declare communism to be a very fine thing; "but", they then say, "it is impossible ever to put such things into practice in real life". One encounters this objection so frequently that it seems to the writer both useful and necessary to reply to it with a few facts which are still very little known in Germany and which completely and utterly dispose of this objection. For communism, social existence and activity based on community of goods, is not only possible but has actually already been realised in many communities in America and in one place in England, with the greatest success, as we shall see.

Incidentally, if one goes into this objection somewhat more deeply, one finds that it is made up of two further objections; these are, firstly: no workers would be prepared to carry out the menial and unpleasant manual tasks; and secondly, with everyone having an equal claim to the communal possessions, people would quarrel about these possessions, and in this way the community would break up again. The first objection is overcome very simply, as follows: these tasks, being now within the community, are no longer menial; and furthermore they can be almost entirely dispensed with by improved facilities, machines and so forth. For instance, in a large hotel in New York, the boots are cleaned by steam, and in the communist colony at Harmony in England (see below) not merely are the water-closets, which are so conveniently fitted out in the English fashion, cleaned automatically, but they are also provided with pipes which take the waste directly to the great dung-pit.— Regarding the second objection, however, all communist colonies so far have become so enormously rich after ten or fifteen years that they have everything they can desire in greater abundance than they can consume, so that no grounds for dispute exist.

The reader will discover that most of the colonies that will be described in this article had their origins in all kinds of religious sects most of which have quite absurd and irrational views on various issues; the author just wants to point out briefly that these views have nothing whatsoever to do with communism. It is in any case obviously a matter of indifference whether those who prove by their actions the practicability of communal living believe in *one* God, in twenty or in none at all; if they have an irrational religion, this is an obstacle in the way of communal living, and if communal living is successful in real life despite this, how much more feasible must it be with others who are free of such inanities. Of the more recent colonies, almost all are in any case quite free of religious nonsense, and nearly all the English Socialists are despite their great tolerance quite without religion, for which very reason they are particularly ill-spoken of and slandered in sanctimonious England. However, when it comes to providing proof, even their opponents have to admit that there is no foundation for all the evil things that are said of them.

The first people to set up a society on the basis of community of goods in America, indeed in the whole world, were the so-called Shakers. These people are a distinct sect who have the strangest religious beliefs, do not marry and allow no intercourse between the sexes, and these are not their only peculiarities of this kind. But this does not concern us here. The sect of the Shakers originated some seventy years ago. Its founders were poor people who united in order to live together in brotherly love and community of goods and to worship their God in their own way. Although their religious views and particularly the prohibition on marriage deterred many, they nevertheless attracted support and now have *ten large communities*, each of which is between three and eight hundred members strong. Each of these communities is a fine, well laid-out town, with dwelling houses, factories, workshops, assembly buildings and barns; they have flower and vegetable gardens, fruit trees, woods, vineyards, meadows and arable land in abundance; then, livestock of all kinds, horses and beef-cattle, sheep, pigs and poultry, in excess of their needs, and of the very best breeds. Their granaries are always full of corn, their store-rooms full of clothing materials, so that an English traveller who visited them said he could not understand why these people still worked, when after all they possessed an abundance of everything; unless it was that they worked simply as a pastime, having nothing else to do. Amongst these people no one is obliged to work against his will, and no one seeks work in vain. They have no poor-houses and infirmaries, having not a single person poor and destitute, nor any abandoned widows and orphans; all their needs are met and they need fear no want. In their ten towns there is not a single gendarme or police officer, no judge, lawyer or soldier, no prison or penitentiary; and yet there is proper order in all their affairs. The laws of the land are not for them and as far as they are concerned could just as well be abolished and nobody would notice any difference for they are the most peaceable citizens and *have never yielded a single criminal for the prisons.* They enjoy, as we said, the most absolute community of goods and have no trade and no money among themselves. One of these towns, Pleasant Hill near Lexington in the State of Kentucky, was visited last year by an English traveller named Finch, who gives the following description of it.

"Pleasant Hill consists of a great number of large, handsome hewn stone and brick houses, manufactories, workshops, farm buildings, all in the neatest order, some of the best in Kentucky; the Shaker farm-land was easily known by the fine stone wall fences by which it was enclosed, and by its superior cultivation; a great number of fat cows and sheep were grazing in the fields, and numerous fat swine were picking up fallen fruit in the orchards. The Shakers possess nearly four thousand acres of land here, of which about two-thirds is under cultivation. This colony was commenced by a single family about the year 1806; others joined afterwards and they gradually increased in numbers; some brought a little capital and others none at all. They had many difficulties to contend with, and suffered many privations at the first, being generally very poor persons; but by diligence, economy and temperance, they have overcome all and now have a great abundance of everything and owe nothing to any man. This Society consists at present of about three hundred individuals, out of which some fifty to sixty are children under sixteen years of age. They have no masters—no servants; far less do they have slaves; they are free, wealthy and happy. They have two schools, a Boys' and a Girls' School, in which are taught reading, writing, arithmetic, grammar and the principles of their religion; they do not teach science to the children as they believe science is not necessary to salvation. As they tolerate no marriages, they would inevitably die out, if new members were not always joining them; but although the prohibition on marriage deters many thousands and many of their best members leave again for that reason, so many new members nevertheless still come that their number constantly increases. They rear livestock and variously cultivate the fields, and themselves produce flax, wool and silk, spinning and weaving them in their own manufactories. What they produce in excess of their needs they sell or exchange amongst their neighbours. They generally labour from sunrise to sunset.

The board of trustees keeps all the books and accounts in a public office, and the books are open for all members to see, as often as they choose. They do not know themselves how wealthy they are, as they never take account of their stock; they are satisfied to know that all they have is their own, for they are in debt to no one. All they do is to make out a list of the debts their neighbours have with them once a year.

"The Church is divided into five families (divisions) of from forty to eighty in each; each family has a separate domestic establishment and lives together in a large, handsome mansion; and *all get every article required, and as much as they want from the common stores of the Society, and without any payment.* A deacon is appointed to each family, whose business is to see that all are provided with every thing they want, and to anticipate their wants as far as possible. They all clothe in Quaker-fashion — plain, clean and neat; they have *a great variety* of articles of food and all of the very *best description.* If a new member seeks admission, he must, according to the laws of the Society, give up every thing he has to the community and is never allowed to claim it back, even if he leaves; nevertheless it is their practice to give back to each as much as he brought in. If a person leaves who has brought in no capital, he is not allowed by the laws to claim any thing for services either, as he has been fed and clothed at general expense whilst he was working; nevertheless it is their custom in this case too to make parting presents to every person if they leave in a kind and proper manner.

"Their government is established in the manner of the first Christians. There is a male and a female minister in each Society, and each has an assistant. These four ministers are the highest power in the whole Society and decide all cases of contention. There are also two elders in each family of the Society, with two assistants and a deacon or administrator. The property of the Society is vested in the board of trustees, which consists of three persons, oversees the whole establishment, directs labour and carries on transactions with neighbours. They have no power to buy or sell any land without the consent of the Society. There are of course also foremen and managers in each department of labour; however they have made it a rule *that no commands are ever given by any one, but all are to be persuaded by kindness.*"[a]

Another colony of Shakers, New Lebanon in the State of New York, was visited by a second English traveller, by the name of *Pitkeithly*, in the year 1842. Mr. Pitkeithly most thoroughly inspected the whole town, which numbers some eight hundred inhabitants and owns between seven and eight thousand acres of land, he examined its workshops and factories, its tanneries, sawmills and so on, and declares the whole arrangement to be *perfect.* He too is surprised at the wealth of these people who began with nothing and are now becoming richer with each passing year, and he says:

"They are happy and gay among themselves; there is no quarrelling but on the contrary friendliness and love prevail throughout their habitation, in every part of which reigns an orderliness and regularity which have not their equal."[76]

So much regarding the Shakers. As we said, they enjoy complete

---

[a] Finch, Letter V, *The New Moral World,* Feb. 10, 1844.—*Ed.*

community of goods and have ten such communities in the United States of North America.

Apart from the Shakers, however, there are other settlements in America based on community of goods. In particular the *Rappites* are to be mentioned here. *Rapp* is a minister from *Württemberg* who in about 1790 dissociated himself and his congregation from the Lutheran Church and, being persecuted by the government, went to America in 1802. His followers went after him in 1804, and thus he settled in Pennsylvania with about one hundred families. Their combined fortune amounted to about 25,000 dollars, and with this they bought land and tools. Their land was uncultivated virgin forest and cost them their total fortune; however they only paid for it in stages. They now joined together in community of goods [*Gütergemeinschaft*], and made the following agreement:

1) Each member surrenders all his possessions to the community, without gaining any privileges from this. All are equal within the community.

2) The laws and regulations of the society are equally binding on all.

3) Each member works only for the benefit of the whole society and not each for himself alone.

4) Whoever leaves the society has no claim to compensation for his work, but is given back everything he put in; and those who have put nothing in and depart in peace and friendship receive a parting gratuity.

5) In exchange the community undertakes to provide each member and his family with the necessities of life and the necessary care in sickness and old age, and if the parents die or withdraw, leaving their children behind, the community will bring up these children.

In the first years of their communal life, when they had to put a wilderness under the plough and also pay off some 7,000 dollars of the purchase price of the land each year, times were naturally hard for them. Several of the more wealthy were deterred by this, withdrew and took out their money, which much aggravated the colonists' troubles. But most held out faithfully and in this way had paid off all their debts in 1810, within just five years. In 1815 for various reasons they sold up their whole colony and once more bought twenty thousand acres of virgin forest in the State of Indiana. Here they built the fine town of *New Harmony* after a few years and put most of the land under the plough, established vineyards and corn-fields, built a wool- and cotton-mill, and became richer with each passing day. In 1825 they sold up their whole colony to Mr. Robert Owen for twice one hundred thousand dollars and set off for the third time into the virgin forest. This time they settled by the great river Ohio and built the town of *Economy*, which is larger and more handsome than any in which they had previously lived. In 1831 Count Leon came to America with a company of some thirty Germans to join them. They received these new arrivals gladly, but the Count stirred up some of the members against Rapp, and for this reason it was decided at a meeting of the whole community that Leon and his followers should leave. Those remaining behind paid those who were dissatisfied more than *one hundred and twenty thousand dollars*, and with this money Leon founded a second colony, which failed, however, on account of mismanagement; its members dispersed and *Count Leon* died shortly afterwards as a *tramp* in Texas. *Rapp's* settlement, on the other hand, has flourished to the present day. The above-mentioned traveller Finch reports about its present circumstances:

"The town of *Economy* consists of three long wide streets and five equally broad streets that cross these three at right angles; it has a church, a public hotel, a woollen factory, a cotton factory, and a silk-mill, a cocoonery for rearing silkworms, public stores for selling to strangers and for the supply of the members, a museum of natural curiosities, workshops for the various trades, agricultural buildings and large, handsome houses for the various families, with a large garden by each house. The farm-land belonging to it is about six miles in length and about one mile wide, contains large vineyards, an orchard of thirty-seven acres, and grain and pasture lands. The number of members is about four hundred and fifty, all well clothed, well fed and splendidly lodged, cheerful, contented, happy, and moral people who for many years have not known want.

"For a time marriage was greatly discouraged among them too, but they now marry and have families and are very desirous of increasing the number of members if proper persons would present themselves. Their religion is the New Testament, but *they have no special creed and do not interfere with the opinions of the members,* so long as they let the others be and abstain from sowing dissension on matters of faith. They call themselves *Harmonists.* They have no paid priests; Mr. Rapp, who is above eighty years of age, acts both as priest and governor. They like to make music and occasionally have concerts and music-meetings in the evenings. They commenced their harvest the day before my arrival with a grand concert in the fields. In their schools they teach reading, writing, arithmetic and grammar; but, like the Shakers, they do not teach any of the sciences. They labour much longer than they need, from sunrise till sunset all the year; all labour and those who cannot work in the factories in winter find employment with threshing and feeding cattle, etc. They have 75 milking cows, large flocks of sheep, and great numbers of horses, hogs and poultry, and from what they have saved, they have lent large sums to businessmen and bankers; through bankruptcies they have lost a great deal that they lent, but they have still a great amount of *useless money* which is constantly increasing.

"Their endeavour was always to make themselves every article they required so that they should need to buy from others as little as they could and eventually made more than they needed; later they acquired a flock of 100 merino sheep to improve the strain of their sheep, paying fifteen thousand dollars for them. They were among the first in establishing the woollen manufacture in America. Then they began to plant the vine, grow flax, erect a cotton factory and rear silkworms for manufacture. However in all things they first take care to abundantly supply their own wants before they sell anything.

"They live in families of from twenty to forty individuals, each of which has a separate house and domestic establishment. The family gets its supplies as much as it requires from the common stores. *They have an abundance for all and they get as much as they wish without charge.* When they need clothing, they apply to the head tailor, the head seamstress or shoemaker and are furnished with it made to their taste. Flesh meat and the other foods are divided among the families according to the number of individuals in each, and they have everything *in abundance and plenitude.*" [a]

Another settlement enjoying community of goods was established at *Zoar* in the State of Ohio. These people are also *Separatists from Württemberg* who detached themselves from the Lutheran Church at the same time as Rapp and, after being persecuted for ten years by it and by the government, likewise emigrated. They were very poor and were only able to reach their destination with the support of philanthropic Quakers in London and America. Led by their minister, *Bäumler,* they arrived in Philadelphia in the autumn of 1817 and bought from a Quaker the land which they still own today and which is seven thousand acres in area. The purchase price, which amounted to some six thousand dollars, was to be paid off gradually. When they arrived at the site and counted their money, they found that they had just six dollars per person. That was all; not a penny of the purchase price of the land had yet been paid, and out of these few dollars they had to buy seed-corn, farm-tools and provisions until the next harvest. They were confronted with a forest with a few log cabins, and this they had to put under the plough; but they set to work with a will, soon had their fields ready for ploughing and in the very next year built a corn-mill. *Initially they divided their land into fairly small pieces*, each of which was farmed by one family on its own account and as its *private property. But they soon saw that this would not do,* because since each one was only working *for himself,* they could not clear the forest fast enough and put it under the plough, they could give each other no *proper assistance* at all, and in this way many got into debt and *were in danger of becoming quite impoverished.* After a year and a half therefore, in April 1819, *they joined together in community of goods,* worked out a constitution and unanimously chose

[a] Finch, Letters VI and VII. *The New Moral World,* Feb. 17 and Feb. 24, 1844.—*Ed.*

their minister, Bäumler, as Director. They then paid all the members' debts, were allowed two years extension on the purchase price of the land and worked with redoubled enthusiasm and united efforts. With this new arrangement they did so well that they had paid off the whole purchase price of their land together with the interest four whole years before the appointed time, and how they are faring in other respects, the following description of two eyewitnesses will show:

An American businessman who comes to Zoar very frequently portrays the place as a perfect model of cleanliness, order and beauty, with a splendid inn, a mansion for the aged Bäumler to live in, a fine public garden of two acres, with a large greenhouse, and fine, well-built houses and gardens. He portrays the people as very happy and contented, industrious and respectable. His description was published in the Pittsburg (Ohio) newspaper (*Pittsburg Daily Advocate and Advertiser*, July 17th 1843).[a]

Finch, whom we have mentioned several times, declares this settlement to be the most perfectly organised of all those living in community of goods in America. He gives a long list of their wealth, and says that they have a flax-spinning mill and a woollen-mill, a tannery, iron-foundries, two corn-mills, two sawmills, two threshing-machines and a host of workshops for every conceivable trade. He also says that their arable land is better farmed than anything else he had seen in America. The *Pfennig Magazin* estimates the Separatists' property at between one hundred and seventy and one hundred and eighty thousand dollars, all of which has been earned in twenty-five years, since they began with nothing at all except six dollars a head. There are about two hundred of them. They too had prohibited marriages for a time, but like the Rappites they have gone back on that and now they do marry.

Finch reproduces the Constitution of these Separatists, which consists principally in the following:

All the Society's officers are elected, in fact by all its members who are above twenty-one years of age, from amongst their own number. These officers comprise:

1) *Three managers*, one of whom is re-elected each year, and who may be dismissed by the Society at any time. They administer all the property of the Society and provide the members with the necessities of life, dwelling, clothing and food, as well as circumstances permit

---

[a] Here and below in the description of the Separatists' colony, use is made of Finch, Letters VIII and IX. *The New Moral World*. March 2 and 9, 1844.— *Ed.*

and without favour for anyone. They appoint assistant managers for
the different kinds of work, settle small disputes and may, jointly
with the Council of the Society, promulgate new regulations, which,
however, must never conflict with the Constitution.

2) The *Director,* who remains in office as long as he enjoys the
confidence of the Society and manages all business as chief officer.
He has the right to buy and sell, and to conclude contracts, but in all
matters of importance he can only act with the consent of the three
managers.

3) The *Council of the Society,* which consists of five members, one of
whom resigns each year, and which enjoys the highest power in the
Society, promulgates laws with the Managers and the Director,
supervises the other officers and settles disputes when the parties are
not satisfied with the Managers' decision; and

4) The *Paymaster,* who is elected for four years and who alone of
all the members and officers has the right to have *money* in his
keeping.

Besides this, the Constitution decrees that an educational establishment shall be set up, that all members shall surrender all their
possessions to the community for ever and can never demand them
back, that new members may only be accepted after they have lived
with the Society for a year and if all the members vote for them, and
the Constitution can only be altered if two-thirds of the members are
in favour.

These descriptions could easily be much expanded, for almost all
the travellers who go into the American interior visit one or other of
the above-mentioned colonies, and *almost all accounts of these journeys*
describe them. But *not even a single one* has been able to report any ill
of these people, on the contrary, they all have only praise for them
and the most they can find to criticise are the religious prejudices,
especially of the Shakers, which, however, clearly have nothing to do
with the ideal of community of goods. I could thus also quote the
works of Miss Martineau, Messrs. Melish and Buckingham and many
others; but as sufficient has been said above and these people anyway
all tell the same tale, this is not necessary.

The success enjoyed by the Shakers, Harmonists and Separatists,
and also the general urge for a new order in human society and the
efforts of the Socialists and Communists that this has given rise to,
have caused many other people in America to undertake similar
experiments in recent years. Thus Herr *Ginal,* a *German minister* in
Philadelphia, has founded a society which has bought 37,000 acres of
forest in the State of Philadelphia, built more than 80 houses there
and already settled some five hundred people, *mostly Germans,* there.

They have a large tannery and pottery, many workshops and storehouses, and they are really thriving. It goes without saying that they live in *community of goods,* as is the case with all the following examples. A Mr. *Hizby,* an ironmaster of Pittsburg (Ohio) has set up in his native town a similar society which last year bought some 4,000 acres of land in the vicinity of the town and is planning to establish a settlement there based on community of goods.— In addition there is a similar settlement in the State of New York at *Skaneateles* which was founded by *J. A. Collins,* an English Socialist, in the spring of 1843[a] with thirty members; then at *Minden* in the State of Massachusetts, where about a hundred people have been settled since 1842; then *two* in *Pike County* in the State of Pennsylvania, which were also recently set up; then one at *Brook Farm,* Massachusetts, where fifty members and thirty pupils live on about two hundred acres and have set up an excellent school under the leadership of the Unitarian[77] minister *G. Ripley;* and then one at Northampton, in the same State, which has been in existence since 1842 and provides work for one hundred and twenty members on five hundred acres of land, in arable and livestock farming as well as in sawmills, silk-mills and dyeing, and finally a colony of emigrant English Socialists at *Equality* near *Milwaukee* in the State of *Wisconsin,* which was started last year by *Thomas Hunt* and is making rapid progress. Apart from these, several other communities are said to have been founded recently, but there is as yet no news of them.— This much is however certain: the Americans, and particularly the poor workers in the large towns of New York, Philadelphia, Boston, etc., have taken the matter to their hearts and founded a large number of societies for the establishment of such colonies, and all the time new communities are being set up. The Americans are tired of continuing as the slaves of the few rich men who feed on the labour of the people; and it is obvious that with the great energy and endurance of this nation, community of goods will soon be introduced over a significant part of their country.

However, it is not just in America but in England too that attempts have been made to realise community of goods. Here the philanthropist *Robert Owen* has been preaching this ideal for thirty years, he has sunk the whole of his large fortune in it and given everything he had in order to found the present colony at *Harmony* in *Hampshire.* After he had founded a society with this aim, the latter bought up an estate of 1,200 acres and established a

---

[a] In the original: 1813 (probably a misprint).— *Ed.*

community there based on Owen's suggestions. It now numbers over one hundred members, who all live together in a large building and have been mainly engaged so far in arable farming. As it was to be set up from the start as a perfect model for the new order of society, considerable capital was required for this, and up to now some two hundred thousand talers have already been put into it. Some of this money was borrowed and had to be paid back from time to time, with the result that many difficulties ensued from this, and for lack of money many of the installations could not be completed and made profitable. And as the members of the community were not the sole owners of the establishment, but were governed by the Directors of the Society of Socialists, to whom the establishment belongs, misunderstandings and dissatisfaction arose at intervals from this too. But despite all this, the matter is proceeding on its course, the members get on exceedingly well with each other, as every visitor testifies, help each other on, and for all the difficulties, the existence of the establishment is nevertheless now secured. The main thing is that all the difficulties arise not from within the community but from the fact that the community has not yet been fully realised. For if it were, the members would not have to use all their earnings to pay off interest and borrowed money but could use them to finish equipping the establishment and run it better; and then they would elect their managers themselves as well and not be always dependent on the Directors of the Society.

The following description of the establishment itself is given by a practising economist who has travelled the length and breadth of England to acquaint himself with the state of agriculture and report on it to the London newspaper *Morning Chronicle*, signing as "One who has whistled at the Plough" [a] (*Morning Chronicle*, Dec. 13th, 1842).

After passing through a very poorly cultivated district, where more weeds than corn were growing, in a nearby village he heard speak for the first time in his life of the Socialists at Harmony. A prosperous man there told him that they were farming a large estate, and doing it very well too, that all the lying rumours spread about them were untrue, that it would be very much to the credit of the parish if but half of its inhabitants would conduct themselves with as much propriety as these Socialists and that it would be equally desirable that the big landowners of the

---

[a] Pseudonym of Alexander Somerville.— *Ed.*

neighbourhood would give the poor as much and as beneficial employment as these people. They had their own views on property, but for all that they conducted themselves very well and set the whole neighbourhood a good example. He added: Their religious opinions vary: some go to this and others to that church, and they never speak about religion or politics with the people of the village. Two of them replied to my inquiries that there was no specific religious opinion among them and each man could believe what he wished. We were all very disturbed when we heard they were coming here; but now we find that they are very good neighbours, set our people a good example of morality, employ many of our poor, and as they never try to impose their opinions on us, we have no cause to be dissatisfied with them. They are all distinguished by respectable and well-bred behaviour, and no one here in the neighbourhood would dare criticise their moral conduct.

Our reporter heard the same from others too, and then went to Harmony. After once more passing through poorly cultivated fields, he came across a very well farmed turnip field with an abundant, fine crop, and said to his friend, a local tenant-farmer: If those are socialist turnips, they promise well. Shortly after, he encountered seven hundred socialist sheep, which were likewise in splendid condition, and then came to the large, handsome and solid dwelling-house. However, everything was still unfinished, bricks and timber, half-completed walls and the ground undug. They entered, were received in a courteous and friendly manner, and shown round the building. On the ground-floor there was a large dining-hall and the kitchen, from which the full dishes were taken by a machine to the dining-hall and the empty ones back to the kitchen. Some children showed the strangers this machine, and they were noticeable for clean, neat clothing, healthy appearance and proper behaviour. The women in the kitchen likewise looked very tidy and decent, and the visitor was most surprised that amid all the unwashed dishes — the midday meal was just over — they could still look so smart and clean. The fittings in the kitchen itself were finer than words could describe, and the London master-builder who had made it declared that even in London very few kitchens were so perfectly and expensively fitted, a remark with which our visitor concurs. Next to the kitchen were convenient washhouses, baths, cellars, and separate rooms where each member could wash on returning from work.

On the next floor was a large ball-room and above that the bedrooms, all very comfortably furnished.

The garden, twenty-seven acres in extent, was in perfect condition, and in general there was great activity to be observed on every side. Bricks were being made, lime burnt, builders were at work and roads were being laid down; a hundred acres of wheat had already been sown, and still more land was to be put under wheat; a pond to take liquid manure was being dug, and from the copse situated on the estate, humus was being gathered for spreading as fertiliser; in short, everything was done to increase the fertility of the soil.

Our visitor concludes:

"I believe their land to be well worth £3" (twenty-one talers) "per acre of rent, and they only pay 15s." (five talers). "They have an excellent bargain, if they manage it well; and whatever may be said of their social crotchets, it must be said of them that their style of farming is of a superior kind."

Let us add to this description something about the domestic arrangements of this community. The members live together in a large house, each with a separate bedroom, which is most comfortably furnished; the housekeeping is done for all of them together by some of the women, and this of course saves a great deal of expense, time and trouble, which would be wasted with a large number of small homes, and allows for many comforts which are quite impossible in small households. For example, the kitchen fire heats all the rooms in the building simultaneously with warm air, and there are pipes taking warm and cold water to each room, and other such agreeable and practical features which are only possible in a communal institution. The children are sent to the school which is connected with the establishment and educated there at communal expense. The parents can see them when they wish and the education is designed both for physical and intellectual development and for life in the community. The children are not tormented with religious and theological controversies, nor with Greek and Latin; instead they become the better acquainted with nature, their own bodies and their intellectual capacities, and in the fields they relax from the small amount of sitting that is expected of them; for the classes are held as often in the open air as in enclosed rooms, and work is part of their education. Their moral education is restricted to the application of the one principle: Do not do to others what you would not háve them do to you, in other words, the practice of complete equality and brotherly love.

As we said, the colony is under the management of the President and Directors of the Society of Socialists; these directors are chosen annually by the congress, to which each local Society sends a member, and they have full, unrestricted powers within the Statutes of the Society, and are responsible to the congress. The community is thus governed by people who live outside it, and in these circumstances there cannot fail to be misunderstandings and irritations; but even if the experiment at Harmony were to fail in consequence of this and of financial problems, which however is not in the slightest degree in prospect, this would only be one further argument for community of goods, as these two difficulties have their cause only in the fact that the community has not yet been fully realised. But despite all this the existence of the colony is assured, and even if it cannot progress and reach completion very rapidly, at least the opponents of the community will not enjoy the triumph of seeing it collapse.

We see then that community of goods is by no means an impossibility but that on the contrary all these experiments have been entirely successful. We also see that the people who are living communally live better with less work, have more leisure for the development of their minds, and that they are better, more moral people than their neighbours who have retained private property. And all this has already been acknowledged by the Americans, British, French and Belgians and by a large number of Germans. In every country there are a number of people who are busy spreading the ideal and have already taken up the communal cause.

If this question is important for everyone, it is most particularly so for the poor workers who own nothing, who tomorrow consume the wage they earn today and may at any time become destitute through unforeseen and unavoidable contingencies. To them it offers the prospect of an independent, secure existence without anxiety, of complete equality of rights with those who can now through their wealth turn the worker into their slave. These workers are the ones to whom the question matters most. In other countries the workers form the core of the party which is demanding community of goods, and it is the duty of the German workers also to take the question seriously to their hearts.

If the workers are united among themselves, hold together and pursue *one* purpose, they are infinitely stronger than the rich. And if, moreover, they have set their sights upon such a rational purpose, and one which desires the best for all mankind, as community of goods, it is self-evident that the better and more intelligent among the rich will declare themselves in agreement with the workers and support them. And there are already many prosperous and educated people in all parts of Germany who have openly declared for community of goods and defend the people's claims to the good things of this earth which have been appropriated by the wealthy class.

Written in mid-October 1844

First published in *Deutsches Bürgerbuch für 1845*, Darmstadt 1845

Printed according to the journal

Published in English for the first time

Frederick Engels

RAPID PROGRESS OF COMMUNISM IN GERMANY[78]

I

[*The New Moral World* No. 25, December 13, 1844]

Hoping, as I do, that your countrymen will be glad to hear something on the progress of our common cause on this side of the channel, I send you a few lines for your paper.[a] At the same time, I rejoice in being able to show that the German people, though, as usual, rather late in mooting the question of Social Reform, are now exerting themselves to make up for lost time. Indeed, the rapidity with which Socialism has progressed in this country is quite miraculous. Two years ago, there were but two solitary individuals who cared at all about Social questions; a year ago, the first Socialist publication was printed.[b] It is true, there were some hundreds of German Communists in foreign countries; but being working men, they had little influence, and could not get their publications circulated among the "upper classes". Besides, the obstacles in the way of Socialism were enormous; the censorship of the press, no right of public meeting, no right of association, and despotic laws and secret courts of law, with paid judges to punish every one who in any way dared to set the people about thinking. And notwithstanding all this, what is the state of things in Germany now? Instead of the two poor devils who wrote about Socialism to a public no ways acquainted with, or interested in the question, we have dozens of clever writers preaching the new gospel to thousands who are anxious to hear everything connected with the subject; we have several papers as radically Socialist as the censorship will allow, principally the *Trier'sche Zeitung* (Gazette of Trier), and the *Sprecher* (Speaker) of

[a] *The New Moral World.—Ed.*
[b] *Deutsch-Französische Jahrbücher.—Ed.*

Wesel; we have a paper published under the free press of Paris,[a] and there is no periodical, save those under the immediate influence of the governments, but comments every day, and in very creditable terms, upon Socialism and the Socialists. Our very opponents want the moral courage to speak their full minds against us. Even the governments are obliged to favour all *legal* movements in the direction towards Socialism. Societies are forming everywhere for ameliorating the condition of the working people, as well as for giving them the means to cultivate their minds, and some of the highest officers of the Prussian Government have taken an active part in those associations. In short, Socialism is the question of the day in Germany, and in the space of a year, a strong Socialist party has grown up, which already now commands the respect of all political parties, and is principally courted by the liberals of this country. Up to the present time our stronghold is the middle class, a fact which will perhaps astonish the English reader, if he do not know that this class in Germany is far more disinterested, impartial, and intelligent, than in England, and for the very simple reason, because it is poorer. We, however, hope to be in a short time supported by the working classes, who always, and everywhere, must form the strength and body of the Socialist party, and who have been aroused from their lethargy by misery, oppression, and want of employment, as well as by the manufacturing riots in Silesia and Bohemia.[79] Let me on this occasion mention a painting by one of the best German painters, Hübner, which has made a more effectual Socialist agitation than a hundred pamphlets might have done. It represents some Silesian weavers bringing linen cloth to the manufacturer, and contrasts very strikingly cold-hearted wealth on one side, and despairing poverty on the other. The well-fed manufacturer is represented with a face as red and unfeeling as brass, rejecting a piece of cloth which belongs to a woman; the woman, seeing no chance of selling the cloth, is sinking down and fainting, surrounded by her two little children, and hardly kept up by an old man; a clerk is looking over a piece, the owners of which are with painful anxiety waiting for the result; a young man shows to his desponding mother the scanty wages he has received for his labour; an old man, a girl, and a boy, are sitting on a stone bench, and waiting for their turn; and two men, each with a piece of rejected cloth on his back, are just leaving the room, one of whom is clenching his fist in rage, whilst the other, putting his hand on

---

[a] *Vorwärts!—Ed.*

Reproduction of K. Hübner's painting,
Weavers Delivering Finished Cloth. 1844

his neighbour's arm, points up towards heaven, as if saying: be quiet, there is a judge to punish him. This whole scene is going on in a cold and unhomely-looking lobby, with a stone floor: only the manufacturer stands upon a piece of carpeting; whilst on the other side of the painting, behind a bar, a view is opened into a luxuriously furnished counting-house, with splendid curtains and looking-glasses, where some clerks are writing, undisturbed by what is passing behind them, and where the manufacturer's son, a young, dandy-like gentleman, is leaning over the bar, with a horsewhip in his hand, smoking a cigar, and coolly looking at the distressed weavers. The painting has been exhibited in several towns of Germany, and, of course, prepared a good many minds for Social ideas. At the same time, we have had the triumph of seeing the first historical painter of this country, Charles Lessing, become a convert to Socialism. In fact, Socialism occupies at this moment already a ten times prouder position in Germany than it does in England. This very morning, I read an article in a liberal paper, the *Cologne Journal*,[a] the author of which had for some reasons been attacked by the Socialists, and in which article he gives his defence[80]; and to what amounts it? He professes himself a Socialist, with the only difference that he wants political reforms to begin with, whilst we want to get all at once. And this *Cologne Journal* is the second newspaper of Germany in influence and circulation. It is curious, but, at least in the north of Germany, you cannot go on board a steamer, or into a railway-carriage, or mail-coach, without meeting somebody who has imbibed at least some Social idea, and who agrees with you, that something must be done to reorganise society. I am just returning from a trip to some neighbouring towns, and there was not a single place where I did not find at least half-a-dozen or a dozen of out-and-out Socialists. Among my own family—and it is a very pious and loyal one—I count six or more, each of which has been converted without being influenced by the remainder. We have partisans among all sorts of men—commercial men, manufacturers, lawyers, officers of the government and of the army, physicians, editors of newspapers, farmers, etc., a great many of our publications are in the press, though hardly three or four have as yet appeared; and if we make as much progress during the next four or five years as we have done in the past twelve months, we shall be able to erect forthwith a Community. You see, we German theorists are getting practical men of business. In fact, one of our

---

[a] *Kölnische Zeitung.—Ed.*

number has been invited to draw up a plan of organisation and regulations for a practical Community, with reference to the plans of Owen, Fourier, etc., and profiting of the experience gained by the American Communities and your own experiment at Harmony,[a] which I hope goes on prosperously. This plan will be discussed by the various localities and printed with the amendments. The most active literary characters among the German Socialists are:— Dr. Charles Marx, at Paris; Dr. M. Hess, at present at Cologne; Dr. Ch. Grün, at Paris; Frederick Engels, at Barmen (Rhenan Prussia); Dr. O. Lüning, Rheda, Westphalia; Dr. H. Püttmann, Cologne; and several others. Besides those, Henry Heine, the most eminent of all living German poets, has joined our ranks, and published a volume of political poetry, which contains also some pieces preaching Socialism. He is the author of the celebrated *Song of the Silesian Weavers*, of which I give you a prosaic translation, but which, I am afraid, will be considered blasphemy in England. At any rate, I will give it you, and only remark, that it refers to the battle-cry of the Prussians in 1813:—"With God for King and fatherland!" which has been ever since a favourite saying of the loyal party. But for the song, here it is[81]:—

> Without a tear in their grim eyes,
> They sit at the loom, the rage of despair in their faces;
> "We have suffered and hunger'd long enough;
> Old Germany, we are weaving a shroud for thee
> And weaving it with a triple curse.
>   "We are weaving, weaving!
>
> "The first curse to the God, the blind and deaf god
> Upon whom we relied, as children on their father;
> In whom we hoped and trusted withal,
> He has mocked us, he has cheated us nevertheless.
>   "We are weaving, weaving!
>
> "The second curse for the King of the rich,
> Whom our distress could not soften nor touch;
> The King, who extorts the last penny from us,
> And sends his soldiers, to shoot us like dogs.
>   "We are weaving, weaving!
>
> "A curse to the false fatherland,
> That has nothing for us but distress and shame,
> Where we suffered hunger and misery—
> We are weaving thy shroud, Old Germany!
>   "We are weaving, weaving!"

---

[a] See pp. 223-27 of this volume.—*Ed.*

With this song, which in its German original is one of the most powerful poems I know of, I take leave from you for this time, hoping soon to be able to report on our further progress and social literature.

Yours sincerely,

An old friend of yours in Germany

[*The New Moral World* No. 37, March 8, 1845]

Barmen, Feb. 2nd, 1845[82]

Since I last addressed you, the cause of Communism has been making the same rapid progress as during the latter part of the year 1844. A short time ago I visited several towns on the Rhine, and everywhere I found that our ideas had gained, and were daily gaining more vantage ground than when I last left those places. Everywhere I found fresh proselytes, displaying as much energy in discussing and spreading the idea of Communism as could possibly be desired. A great many public meetings have been held in all the towns of Prussia, for the purpose of forming associations to counteract the growing pauperism, ignorance and crime among the great mass of the population.[83] These meetings, at first supported, but when becoming too independent, checked by the Government, have, nevertheless, forced the Social question upon the public attention, and have done a great deal towards the dissemination of our principles. The meeting at Cologne was struck so much by the speeches of the leading Communists, that a committee for drawing up the rules of the association was elected, the majority of which consisted of thorough Communists. The abstract of rules was, of course, founded upon Communist principles; organisation of labour, protection of labour against the power of capital, &c., and those rules were adopted almost unanimously by the meeting. Of course the sanction of Government, which is necessary in this country for all associations, has been refused; but since those meetings have been held, the question of communities has been discussed everywhere throughout Cologne. At Elberfeld, it was pronounced as the fundamental principle of the association, *that all men had an equal right to education, and ought to participate in the fruits of science*. The rules of the association, however, have not yet been confirmed by the Government, and in all probability they will share in the lot of the Cologne rules, as the parsons got up an association of their own as soon as their plan, to make the Society a branch of the town mission, had been rejected by the meeting. The liberal association will be prohibited, and the parsons' association will be supported by Government. This, however, is of the little importance as the question having been mooted once, is now generally discussed throughout the town. Other associations have been formed at Munster, Cleve, Düsseldorf, etc., and it remains to be seen what the results will be. As to Communist literature, a collection of papers relating to this subject has been published by H. Püttmann, of Cologne, containing among the rest, an account of the American communities, as well as of your own Hampshire Establishment, which has done very much towards annihilating the prejudice of the impracticability of our ideas.[84] Mr. Püttmann, at the same time, has issued the prospectus of a quarterly review,[85] the first number of which he intends issuing in May next, and which will be exclusively dedicated to the promulgation of our ideas. Another monthly periodical[86] will be commenced by Messrs. Hess of Cologne, and Engels of Barmen, the first number to be published on the first of April next; this periodical will contain *facts* only, showing the state of civilised society, and preaching the necessity of a radical reform by the eloquence of facts. A new work by Dr. Marx, containing a review of the principles of Political Economy, and politics in general, will be published shortly. Dr. Marx himself has been forced by the French Conservative Government, to quit his abode at Paris.[87] He intends to go to Belgium, and if the vengeance of the Prussian Government (which has induced the French Ministers to expel Marx) follows him even there, he must go to England. But the most important fact which has come to my knowledge since my last, is, that Dr. Feuerbach, the most eminent philosophical genius in Germany at the present time, has declared himself a Communist. A friend of ours lately visited him in his retired country seat, in a remote corner of Bavaria, and to him he declared his full conviction that Communism was only a necessary consequence of the principles he had proclaimed, and that Communism was, in fact, only the *practice* of what he had proclaimed long before theoretically. Feuerbach said, he had never been delighted so much with any other book, as with the first part of Weitling's *Guarantees*.[a] I never dedicated, he said, a book to anybody, but I feel much inclined to dedicate to Weitling my next work. Thus the union between the German philosophers, of whom Feuerbach is the most eminent representative, and the German working men represented by Weitling, an union which, a year ago, had been predicted by Dr. Marx,[b] is all but accomplished. With the philosophers to think, and the working men to fight for us, will any earthly power be strong enough to resist our progress?

An old friend of yours in Germany

---

[a] W. Weitling, *Garantien der Harmonie und Freiheit.—Ed.*

[b] K. Marx, *Contribution to the Critique of Hegel's Philosophy of Law. Introduction* (see present edition, Vol. 3, pp. 175-87).—*Ed.*

III

[*The New Moral World* No. 46, May 10, 1845]

Dear sir,

Having been unable, for a time, from certain causes, to write you on the state of affairs in Germany, I now continue my reports, hoping that they will interest your readers, and follow each other more uninterruptedly than heretofore. I am glad of being enabled to tell you that we are making the same rapid and steady progress which we made up to my last report. Since I wrote to you last, the Prussian Government have found it unsafe to continue their support to the "Associations for the Benefit of the Working Classes". They have found that everywhere these associations became infected with something like Communism, and therefore they have done everything in their power to suppress, or at least obstruct, the progress of these associations. On the other hand, the majorities of the members of those societies, being composed of middle-class men, were totally at a loss with regard to the steps they might take to benefit the working people. All their measures—savings-banks, premiums and prizes for the best workers, and such like,—were instantly proved by the Communists to be good for nothing, and held up to public laughter. Thus the intention of the middle classes, to dupe the working classes, by hypocrisy and sham philanthropy, has been totally frustrated; while to us it gave an opportunity which is rather rare in a country of patriarchal police government: thus the trouble of the matter has been with the Government and the moneyed men, while we have had all the profit.

But not only these meetings were taken profit of for Communist agitation: at Elberfeld, the centre of the manufacturing district of

Rhenan Prussia, regular Communist meetings were held. The Communists of this town were invited by some of the most respectable citizens to discuss their principles with them. The first of these meetings took place in February, and was more of a private character. About forty or fifty individuals assisted, including the attorney-general of the district, and other members of the courts of law, as well as representatives of almost all the leading commercial and manufacturing firms. Dr. Hess, whose name I have had more than once an opportunity of mentioning in your columns, opened the proceedings by proposing Mr. Koettgen, a Communist, as chairman, to which no opposition was made. Dr. Hess then read a lecture on the present state of society, and the necessity of abandoning the old system of competition, which he called a system of downright robbery. The lecture was received with much applause (the majority of the audience being Communists); after which Mr. Frederick Engels (who some time ago had some papers on Continental Communism[a] printed in your columns) spoke at some length on the practicability and the advantages of the Community system.[b] He also gave some particulars of the American colonies and your own establishment at Harmony in proof of his assertions. After which a very animated discussion took place, in which the Communist side was advocated by the foregoing speakers and several others; while the opposition was maintained by the attorney-general, by Dr. Benedix, a literary character, and some others. The proceedings, which commenced about nine o'clock in the evening, were continued until one in the morning.

The second meeting took place a week after, in the large room of the first hotel in the town. The room was filled with the "respectables" of the place. Mr. Koettgen, chairman of the former meeting, read some remarks on the future state and prospects of society, as imagined by the Communists, after which Mr. Engels delivered a speech[c] in which he proved (as may be concluded from the fact, that not a word was offered in reply), that the present state of Germany was such as could not but produce in a very short time a social revolution; that this imminent revolution was not to be averted by any possible measures for promoting commerce and manufacturing industry; and that the only means

---

[a] F. Engels, *Progress of Social Reform on the Continent* (see present edition, Vol. 3, pp. 392-408).— *Ed.*

[b] See pp. 243-55 of this volume.— *Ed.*

[c] See pp. 256-64 of this volume.— *Ed.*

to prevent such a revolution—a revolution more terrible than any of the mere subversions of past history—was the introduction of, and the preparation for, the Community system. The discussion, in which some gentlemen of the profession of the bar, who had come from Cologne and Düsseldorf for the purpose, took part on the Communist side, was again very animated, and prolonged till after midnight. Some Communist poems, by Dr. Müller of Düsseldorf, who was present, were also read.

A week afterwards a third meeting took place in which Dr. Hess again lectured, and besides, some particulars about the American communities were read from a printed paper.[a] The discussion was repeated before the close of the meeting.

Some days afterwards a rumour was spread through the town that the next meeting was to be dispersed by the police, and the speakers to be arrested. The mayor of Elberfeld, indeed, went to the hotel-keeper, and threatened to withdraw the licence, if any such meetings in future should be allowed to take place in his house. The Communists instantly communicated with the mayor about the matter, and received, the day before the next meeting, a circular directed to Messrs. Hess, Engels and Koettgen, by which the provincial Government, with a tremendous amount of quotations from ancient and written laws, declared such meetings to be illegal, and threatened to put a stop to them by force, if they should not be abandoned. The meeting took place next Saturday,[b] the mayor and the attorney-general (who after the first meeting had absented himself) were present, supported by a troop of armed police, who had been sent by railroad from Düsseldorf. Of course, under such circumstances, no public addresses were delivered: the meeting occupied themselves with beef-steaks and wine, and gave the police no handle for interference.

These measures, however, could not but serve our cause: those who had not yet heard of the matter were now induced to ask for information about it from the importance ascribed to it by the Government; and a great many of those who had come to the discussion ignorant or scoffing at our proposals, went home with a greater respect for Communism. This respect was also partially produced by the respectable manner in which our party was represented; nearly every patrician and moneyed family of the town had one of its members or relatives present at the large table occupied by the Communists. In short the effect produced by these meetings upon the public mind of the whole manufacturing

[a] See pp. 214-28 of this volume.—*Ed.*

[b] March 1, 1845.—*Ed.*

district was truly wonderful; and in a few days afterwards those who had publicly advocated our cause were overrun by numbers of people who asked for books and papers from which they might get a view of the whole system. We understand that the whole proceedings will shortly be published.

As to Communist literature, there has been exhibited a great activity in this branch of agitation. The public literally long for information: they devour every book published in this line. Dr. Püttmann has published a collection of essays,[a] containing an excellent paper by Dr. Hess, on the distress of modern society, and the means of redressing it[b]; a detailed description of the distressing state of the working people of Silesia, with a history of the riots of last spring; some other articles descriptive of the state of society in Germany; and, finally, an account of the American and Harmony communities (from Mr. Finch's letters and that of "One who has whistled at the Plough"[c]), by F. Engels. The book, though prosecuted by the Prussian Government, met with a rapid sale in all quarters. A number of monthly periodicals have been established: the *Westphalian Steamboat*,[d] published at Bielefeld, by Lüning, containing popular essays on Socialism and reports on the state of the working people; the *People's Journal*,[e] at Cologne, with a more decided Socialist tendency; and the *Gesellschaftsspiegel* (Mirror of Society), at Elberfeld, by Dr. Hess, founded expressly for the publication of facts characteristic of the present state of society, and for the advocacy of the rights of the working classes. A quarterly review, the *Rheinische Jahrbücher* (Rhenish Annals), by Dr. Püttmann, has also been established; the first number is now in the press and will shortly be published.

On the other hand, a war has been declared against those of the German philosophers, who refuse to draw from their mere theories practical inferences, and who contend that man has nothing to do but to speculate upon metaphysical questions. Messrs. Marx and Engels have published a detailed refutation of the principles advocated by B. Bauer[f]; and Messrs. Hess and Bürgers are engaged in refuting the theory of M. Stirner:—Bauer

---

[a] *Deutsches Bürgerbuch für 1845.—Ed.*

[b] M. Hess, *Über die Noth in unserer Gesellschaft und deren Abhülfe.—Ed.*

[c] See pp. 214-28 of this volume. "One who has whistled at the Plough" is Alexander Somerville's pseudonym.—*Ed.*

[d] *Das Westphälische Dampfboot.—Ed.*

[e] *Allgemeines Volksblatt.—Ed.*

[f] See pp. 7-211 of this volume.—*Ed.*

and Stirner being the representatives of the ultimate consequences of *abstract* German philosophy, and therefore the only important philosophical opponents of Socialism — or rather Communism, as in this country the word Socialism means nothing but the different vague, undefined, and undefinable imaginations of those who see that something must be done, and who yet cannot make up their minds to go the whole length of the Community system.

In the press are also — Dr. Marx's *Review of Politics and Political Economy*; Mr. F. Engels' *Condition of the Working Classes of Great-Britain*[a]; *Anecdota, or a Collection of Papers on Communism*[88]; and in a few days will be commenced a translation of the best French and English works on the subject of Social Reform.[89]

In consequence of the miserable political state of Germany, and the arbitrary proceedings of her patriarchal governments, there is hardly a chance of any but a literary connection between the Communists of the different localities. The periodicals, principally the *Rhenish Annals*, offer a centre for those who, by the press, advocate Communism. Some connection is kept up by travellers, but this is all. Associations are illegal, and even correspondence is unsafe, as the "secret offices"[90] of late have displayed an unusual activity. Thus it is only by the newspapers that we have received the news of the existence of two Communist associations in Posen and the Silesian mountains. It is reported that at Posen, the capital of Prussian Poland, a number of young men had formed themselves into a secret society, founded upon Communist principles, and with the intention of taking possession of the town; that the plot was discovered, and its execution prevented: this is all we know about the matter. This much, however, is certain, that a great many young men of aristocratic and wealthy Polish families, have been arrested; that since (more than two months) all watch posts are doubled and provided with ball cartridge; and that two youths (of 12 and 19 years respectively), the brothers Rymar-kiewicz, have absconded, and not yet been got hold of by the authorities. A great number of the prisoners are youths of from 12 to 20 years. The other so-called conspiracy, in the Silesian mountains, is said to have been very extensive, and also for a Communist purpose: they are reported to have intended to take the fortress of Schweidnitz, to occupy the whole range of mountains, and to appeal from thence to the suffering workpeople of all Germany. How far this may be true, nobody is able to judge; but in this unfortunate district, also, arrests have taken place on the

---

[a] See pp. 295-583 of this volume.— *Ed.*

depositions of a police spy; and a wealthy manufacturer, Mr. Schlöffel, has been transported to Berlin, where he is now under trial, as the supposed head of the conspiracy.

The associations of German Communists of the working classes in Switzerland, France and England continue to be very active; though in France, and some parts of Switzerland, they have much to suffer from the police. The papers announce that about sixty members of the Communist association of Geneva have been expelled from the town and canton. A. Becker, one of the cleverest of the Swiss Communists, has published a lecture delivered at Lausanne, entitled, "What do the Communists Want?"[a] which belongs to the best and most spirited things of the sort we know of. I dare say it would merit an English translation, and I should be glad if any of your readers were acquainted enough with the German language to undertake it. It is, of course, only a small pamphlet.

I expect to continue my reports from time to time, and remain, etc.

An old friend of yours in Germany

Written between November 9, 1844, and   Printed according to the news-
April 5, 1845   paper

Published in *The New Moral World*
Nos. 25, 37 and 46, December 13, 1844,
March 8 and May 10, 1845

---

[a] A. Becker, "Was wollen die Kommunisten?"—*Ed.*

Frederick Engels

SPEECHES IN ELBERFELD [91]

FEBRUARY 8, 1845

Gentlemen!

As you have just heard and as, moreover, I may assume it to be generally known, we live in a world of free competition. Let us then look a little closer at this free competition and at the world order to which it has given rise. In our present-day society, each man works on his own, each strives for his own enrichment and is not in the least concerned with what the rest are doing; rational organisation, or distribution of jobs, is out of the question; on the contrary, each seeks to get the better of the other, seeks to exploit any favourable opportunity for his own private advantage and has neither time nor inclination to think about the fact that, at bottom, his own interests coincide with those of all other people. The individual capitalist is involved in struggle with all the other capitalists; the individual worker with all the other workers; all capitalists fight against the workers just as the mass of workers in their turn have, of necessity, to fight against the mass of capitalists. In this war of all against all, in this general confusion and mutual exploitation, the essence of present-day bourgeois society is to be found. But, gentlemen, such an unregulated economic system must, in the long run, lead to the most disastrous results for society; the disorder which lies at its basis, the disregard for the real, general well-being must sooner or later make itself felt in the most striking fashion. The ruin of the small middle class, that estate which constituted the main foundation of states during the last century, is the first result of this struggle. Daily we see how this class in society is crushed by the power of capital, how, for example, the individual master tailors and cabinet-makers lose their best customers to shops selling ready-made clothes and furniture and from being small capitalists, members of the *propertied* class, are transformed into dependent proletarians working for others, into members of the *propertyless* class. The ruin of the middle class is a much deplored consequence of our much lauded freedom of occupation, it is a necessary result of the advantages which the big capitalist has over his less affluent competitors; it is the most vigorous living expression of capital's tendency to become concentrated in a few hands. This tendency is likewise widely recognised; there is general lamentation about the fact that property is being accumulated daily in fewer hands and that on the contrary the great majority of the nation is becoming more and more impoverished. Thus there arises the glaring contradiction between a few rich people on the one hand, and many poor on the other; a contradiction which has already risen to a menacing point in England and France and is daily growing sharper in our country too. And as long as the present basis of society is retained, so long will it be impossible to halt the progressing enrichment of a few individuals and the impoverishment of the great majority: the contradiction will develop more and more sharply until finally necessity compels society to reorganise itself on more rational principles.

But these, gentlemen, are far from being all the consequences of free competition. Since each man produces and consumes on his own without concerning himself much about what others are producing and consuming, a crying disproportion between production and consumption must, of necessity, quickly develop. Since present-day society entrusts the distribution of the goods produced to merchants, speculators and shopkeepers, each one of whom has only his own advantage in mind, similarly in the distribution — even apart from the fact that it is impossible for the propertyless man to secure for himself a sufficient share — similarly in the distribution of the products the same disproportion will arise. How is the manufacturer to discover how much of his products are needed in this or that market, and even if he could discover this, how could he get to know how much his competitors are sending to each of these markets? How can he — who in most cases does not even know where the goods he is just producing will go — possibly know how much his foreign competitors will send to each of the markets in question? He knows nothing about all this; like his competitors, he manufactures at haphazard and consoles himself with the thought that the others must do likewise. He has no other guide than the constantly fluctuating level of prices which, in the case of distant markets, is quite different at the moment when he dispatches his goods from what it was when the letter informing him about it was written, and which again is different at the time the goods arrive from what it was when they were despatched. Where you have such irregularity of production it is also quite natural that at every moment there are interruptions to trade, which naturally must be all the more serious the more advanced the industry and trade of a given country is. In this regard England — the country with the most developed industry — provides us with the most striking examples. Due to the expansion of trade, to the many speculators and commission agents who have forced themselves in between the producing manufacturer and the actual consumers, it is becoming much more difficult for the English than for the German manufacturer to obtain even the remotest idea of the relationship between the stocks available and production on the one hand and consumption on the other; in addition he has to supply nearly all the markets in the world, but in hardly a single case does he know where his goods go and thus, with the gigantic productive power of British industry, it very frequently happens that all the markets are suddenly glutted. Trade comes to a standstill, factories work half-time or stop altogether; a series of bankruptcies begins, stocks must be sold off at ridiculously low prices and a great part of the capital, accumulated with great effort, is lost again as a result of this kind of trade crisis. We have had a whole series of such trade crises in England since the beginning of this century, and one every five or six years in the last twenty years.[92] The last two, gentlemen, those of 1837 and 1842, will still be vividly remembered by most of you. And if our industry were as big, our sales as extensive as the industry and trade of England, then we would experience the same results, whereas at present the effect of competition in industry and in trade is making itself felt here in a general, continuous depression in all branches of business, in a miserable half-way position between a definite boom and complete decline, in a situation of mild stagnation, i.e., of stability.

Gentlemen, what is the real reason of this deplorable state of affairs? What gives rise to the ruin of the middle class, to the glaring contradiction between rich and poor, to stagnation in trade and the waste of capital resulting therefrom? Nothing else than the divergence of interests. All of us work each for his own advantage, unconcerned about the welfare of others and, after all, it is an obvious, self-evident truth that the interest, the well-being, the happiness of every individual is inseparably bound up with that of his fellow-men. We must all acknowledge that we cannot do without our fellow-men, that our interests, if nothing else, bind us all to one another, and yet by our actions we fly in the face of this truth: and yet we arrange our society as if our interests were not identical but completely and utterly opposed. We have seen what the results of this fundamental mistake were; if we want to eliminate these unpleasant consequences then we must correct this fundamental mistake, and that is precisely the aim of communism.

In communist society, where the interests of individuals are not opposed to one another but, on the contrary, are united, competition is eliminated. As is self-evident, there can no longer be any question of the ruin of particular classes, nor of the very existence of classes such as the rich and the poor nowadays. As soon as private gain, the aim of the individual to enrich himself on his own, disappears from the production and distribution of the goods necessary to life, trade crises will also disappear of themselves. In communist society it will be easy to be informed about both production and consumption. Since we know how much, on the average, a person needs, it is easy to calculate how much is needed by a given number of individuals, and since production is no longer in the hands of private producers but in those of the community and its administrative bodies, it is a trifling matter *to regulate production according to needs.*

Thus we see how the main evils of the present social situation disappear under communist organisation. If, however, we go into a little more detail, we will find that the advantages of such a social organisation are not limited to this but also include the elimination of a host of other defects. I shall only touch today on a few of the economic drawbacks. From the economic point of view the present arrangement of society is surely the most irrational and unpractical we can possibly conceive. The opposition of interests results in a great amount of labour power being utilised in a way from which society gains nothing, and in a substantial amount of capital being unnecessarily lost without reproducing itself. We already see this in the commercial crises; we see how masses of goods, all of which men have produced with great effort, are thrown away at prices which cause loss to the sellers; we see how masses of capital, accumulated with great effort, disappear before the very eyes of their owners as a result of bankruptcies. Let us, however, discuss present-day trade in a little more detail. Consider through how many hands every product must go before it reaches the actual consumer. Consider, gentlemen, how many speculating, swindling superfluous middlemen have now forced themselves in between the producer and the consumer! Let us take, for example, a bale of cotton produced in North America. The bale passes from the hands of the planter into those of the agent on some station or other on the Mississippi and travels down the river to New Orleans. Here it is sold—for a second time, for the agent has already bought it from the planter—sold, it might well be, to the speculator, who sells it once again, to the exporter. The bale now travels to Liverpool where, once again, a greedy speculator stretches out his hands towards it and grabs it. This man then trades it to a commission agent who, let us assume, is a buyer for a German house. So the bale travels to Rotterdam, up the Rhine, through another dozen hands of forwarding agents, being unloaded and loaded a dozen times, and only then does it arrive in the hands, not of the consumer, but of the manufacturer, who first makes it into an article of consumption, and who perhaps sells his yarn to a weaver, who disposes of what he has woven to the textile printer, who then does business with the wholesaler, who then deals with the retailer, who finally sells the commodity to the consumer. And all these millions of intermediary swindlers, speculators, agents, exporters, commission agents, forwarding agents, wholesalers and retailers, who actually contribute nothing to the commodity itself—they all want to live and make a profit—and they do make it too, on the average, otherwise they could not subsist. Gentlemen, is there no simpler, cheaper way of bringing a bale of cotton from America to Germany and of getting the product manufactured from it into the hands of the real consumer than this complicated business of ten times selling and a hundred times loading, unloading and transporting it from one warehouse to another? Is this not a striking example of the manifold waste of labour power brought about by the divergence of interests? Such a complicated way of transport is out of the question in a rationally organised society. To keep to our example, just as one can easily know how much cotton or manufactured cotton goods an individual colony needs, it will be equally easy for the central authority to determine how much all the villages and townships in the country need. Once such statistics have been worked out—which can easily be done in a year or two—average annual consumption will only change in proportion to the increasing population; it is therefore easy at the appropriate time to determine in advance what amount of each particular article the people will need—the entire great amount will be ordered direct from the source of supply; it will then be possible to procure it directly, without middlemen, without more delay and unloading than is really required by the nature of the journey, that is, with a great saving of labour power; it will not be necessary to pay the speculators, the dealers large and small, their rake-off. But this is still not all—in this way these middlemen are not only made harmless to society, they are, in fact, made useful to it. Whereas they now perform to the disadvantage of everyone else a kind of work which is, at best, superfluous but which, nevertheless, provides them with a living, indeed, in many cases even with great riches, whereas they are thus at present directly prejudicial to the general good, they will then become free to engage in useful labour and to take up an occupation in which they can prove themselves as actual members, not merely apparent, sham members, of human society, and as participants in its activity as a whole.

Present-day society, which breeds hostility between the individual man and everyone else, thus produces a social war of all against all which inevitably in individual cases, notably among uneducated people, assumes a brutal, barbarously violent form—that of crime. In order to protect itself against crime, against direct acts of violence, society requires an extensive, complicated system of administrative and judicial bodies which requires an immense labour force. In communist society this would likewise be vastly simplified, and precisely because—strange though it may sound—precisely because the administrative body in this society would have to manage not merely individual aspects of social life, but the whole of social life, in all its various activities, in all its aspects. We eliminate the contradiction between the individual man and all others, we counterpose social peace to social war, we put the axe to the *root* of crime—and thereby render the greatest, by far the greatest, part of the present activity of the administrative and judicial bodies superfluous. Even now crimes of passion are becoming fewer and fewer in comparison with calculated crimes, crimes of interest—crimes against *persons* are declining, crimes against *property* are on the increase. Advancing civilisation moderates violent outbreaks of passion even in our present-day society, which is on a war footing; how much more will this be the case in communist, peaceful society! Crimes against property cease of their own accord where everyone receives what he needs to satisfy his natural and his spiritual urges, where social gradations and distinctions cease to exist. Justice concerned with criminal cases ceases of itself, that dealing with civil cases, which are almost all rooted in the property relations or at least in such relations as arise from the situation of social war, likewise disappears; conflicts can then be only rare exceptions, whereas they are now the natural result of general hostility, and will be easily settled by arbitrators. The activities of the administrative bodies at present have likewise their source in the continual social war—the police and the entire administration do nothing else but see to it that the war remains concealed and indirect and does not erupt into open violence, into crimes. But if it is infinitely easier to maintain peace than to keep war within certain limits, so it is vastly more easy to administer a communist community rather than a competitive one. And if civilisation has already taught men to seek their interest in the maintenance of public order, public security, and the public interest, and therefore to make the police, administration and justice as superfluous as possible, how much more will this be the case in a society in which community of interests has become the basic principle, and in which the public interest is no longer distinct from that of each individual! What already exists now, *in spite of* the social organisation, how much more will it exist when it is no longer hindered, but supported by the social institutions! We may thus also in this regard count on a considerable increase in the labour force through that part of the labour force of which society is deprived by the present social condition.

One of the most expensive institutions which present-day society cannot dispense with are the standing armies, by which the nation is deprived of the most vigorous and useful section of the population and compelled to feed it since it thereby becomes unproductive. We know from our own budget what the standing army costs—twenty-four million a year and the withdrawal from production of twice one hundred thousand of the most muscular arms. In communist society it would not occur to anyone to have a standing army. What for, anyhow? To maintain peace in the country? As we saw above, it will not occur to anyone to disturb internal peace. Fear of revolutions is, of course, the consequence only of the opposition of interests; where the interests of all coincide, such fears are out of the question.— For aggressive wars? But how could a communist society conceive the idea of undertaking an aggressive war?—this society which is perfectly well aware that in war it will only lose men and capital while the most it could gain would be a couple of recalcitrant provinces, which would as a consequence be disruptive of social order.— For a war of defence? For that there is no need of a standing army, as it will be easy to train every fit member of society, in addition to his other occupations, in real, not barrack-square handling of arms to the degree necessary for the defence of the country. And, gentlemen, consider this, that in the event of a war, which anyway could *only*

be waged against anti-communist nations, the member of such a
society has a *real* Fatherland, a *real* hearth and home to defend, so
that he will fight with an enthusiasm, endurance and bravery
before which the mechanically trained soldiers of a modern army
must be scattered like chaff. Consider what wonders were worked
by the enthusiasm of the revolutionary armies from 1792 to 1799,
which only fought for an *illusion*, for the *semblance of a Fatherland*,
and you will be bound to realise how powerful an army must be
which fights, not for an illusion, but for a tangible reality. Thus
these immense masses of labour power of which the civilised
nations are now deprived by the armies, would be returned to
labour in a communist society; they would not only produce as
much as they consume, but would be able to supply to the public
storehouses a great many more products than those necessary for
their own sustenance.

An even worse wastage of labour power is to be seen in our
existing society in the way the rich exploit their social position. I
will say nothing of all the useless and quite ridiculous luxury
which arises only from the passion for display and occupies a great
deal of labour power. But, gentlemen, just go into the house, the
inmost sanctuary, of a rich man and tell me if it is not the most
senseless waste of labour power when you have a number of
people waiting on one single individual, spending their time in
idleness or, at best, in work which results from the isolation of a
single man inside his own four walls? This crowd of maids, cooks,
lackeys, coachmen, domestic servants, gardeners and whatever
they are called, what do they really do? For how *few moments*
during the day they are occupied in making the lives of their
masters *really* pleasant, in facilitating the free development and
exercise of their human nature and inborn capacities—and *how
many hours* during the day they are occupied in tasks which arise
only from the bad arrangement of our social relations—standing
at the back of the carriage, serving their employers' every whim,
carrying lap-dogs, and other absurdities. In a rationally organised
society, where everyone will be in a position to live without
pandering to the whims of the rich and without lapsing into any
such whims himself—in such a society, the labour power now thus
wasted on the provision of luxury can naturally be used to the
advantage of all and to its own.

A further waste of labour power occurs in our present society
quite directly as a result of competition, for this creates a large
number of destitute workers who *would* gladly work, but *cannot* get
any work. Since society is not by any means arranged so as to be

able to pay attention to the real utilisation of the labour force, since it is left to every individual to look for a source of gain, it is quite natural that when really or apparently useful work is being distributed, a number of workers are left without any. This is all the more the case as the competitive struggle compels everyone to strain his power to the utmost, to utilise all available advantages, to replace dearer labour by cheaper for which advancing civilisation provides more and more means or, in other words, everyone has to work at making others destitute, at displacing other people's labour by one means or another. Thus in every civilised society there are large numbers of unemployed people who would gladly work but cannot find work and their number is larger than is commonly believed. And so we find these people *prostituting* themselves in one way or another, begging, sweeping the streets, standing on corners, only barely keeping body and soul together by occasional small jobs, hawking and peddling all manner of petty wares or, as we saw a couple of poor girls doing this evening, going from place to place with a guitar, playing and singing for money, compelled to put up with all kinds of shameless talk, every insulting suggestion in order to earn a couple of *groschen.* How many finally fall victims to *real* prostitution! Gentlemen, the number of these destitute people who have no other course open but to prostitute themselves in one way or another is very large — our Poor Relief authorities can tell you all about this — and don't forget that society nevertheless feeds these people in one way or another despite their uselessness. If, then, society has to bear the cost of their maintenance, it should also make it possible for these unemployed to earn their keep *honourably.* But the present competitive society *cannot* do this.

If you think about all this, gentlemen — and I could have given you many other examples of how our present society wastes its labour force — if you think about this, you will find that human society has an abundance of productive forces at its disposal which only await a rational organisation, regulated distribution, in order to go into operation to the greatest benefit for all. After this you will be able to judge how totally unfounded is the fear that, given a just distribution of social activity, individuals would have to bear such a load of labour as would make it impossible for them to engage in anything else. On the contrary, we can assume that given this kind of organisation, the present customary labour time of the individual will be reduced by half simply by making use of the labour which is either not used at all or used disadvantageously.

However, the benefits which communist organisation offers through the *utilisation of wasted labour power* are *not yet the most significant*. The greatest saving of labour power lies in the *fusing of the individual powers* into social collective power and in the kind of organisation which is based on this concentration of powers hitherto opposed to one another. Here I should like to subscribe to the proposals of *Robert Owen*, the English Socialist, since these are the most practical and most fully worked out. Owen proposes that instead of the present towns and villages with their separate individual houses standing in each other's way, we should construct large palaces which, built in the form of a square some 1,650 feet in length and breadth, would enclose a large garden and comfortably accommodate from two to three thousand people. It is obvious that such a building, while providing its occupants with the amenities of the best contemporary housing, is far cheaper and easier to erect than the generally worse individual dwellings required under the present system for the same number of people. The many rooms which now remain empty in almost every decent house, or are only used once or twice a year, disappear without any inconvenience; the saving in space for store-rooms, cellars, etc., is also very great.—But it is only when we go into domestic economy in detail that we will really grasp the advantages of community housing. What an amount of labour and material is squandered under the present system of separate housing—in heating for example! Every room needs to have a separate stove, every stove has to be specially heated, kept alight, supervised, the fuel for heating has to be brought to all the different places, the ashes removed; how much simpler and cheaper it would be to install, instead of the present separate heating, large-scale central heating with, for example, steam pipes and a single, central heating unit, as is already done in big public buildings, factories, churches, etc. Gaslighting, again, is expensive at present because even the thinner pipes have to be laid underground and owing to the large areas to be illuminated in our towns the pipes have to be disproportionately long, whereas under the proposed arrangement everything would be concentrated in an area of a 1,650 foot square and the number of gas burners would nevertheless be as great, so that the result would be at least as beneficial as in a moderately-sized town. And then the preparation of meals—what a waste of space, ingredients, labour, is involved in the present, separate households, where every family cooks its little bit of food on its own, has its own supply of crockery, employs its own cook, must fetch its own supplies separately from the market, from the garden, from the butcher and the baker! One can safely assume that under a communal system of preparing and serving meals, two-thirds of the labour force now engaged in this work will be saved, and the remaining third will nevertheless be able to perform it better and more attentively than is the case at present. And finally, the housework itself! Will not such a building be infinitely easier to keep clean and in good condition when, as is possible, this kind of work also is organised and regularly shared out, than the two to three hundred separate houses which would be the equivalent under the present housing system?

These, gentlemen, are a few of the innumerable economic advantages which are bound to result from the communist organisation of human society. It is not possible for us in a couple of hours and in a few words to elucidate our principle and duly substantiate it from all points of view. Nor is this by any means our intention. All we can and want to do is to shed light on a few points and to induce those to whom the matter is still strange to study it. And we hope at least that we have made it clear this evening that communism is not contrary to human nature, reason, or the human heart, and that it is not a theory which, taking no account whatever of reality, is rooted in pure fantasy.

People ask how this theory is to be translated into reality, what measures we propose to prepare its introduction. There are various ways to this end; the English will probably begin by setting up a number of colonies and leaving it to every individual whether to join or not; the French, on the other hand, will be likely to prepare and implement communism on a national basis. Not much can be said about how the Germans will start since the social movement in Germany is new. Meanwhile, among the many possible ways of preparing, I would like to mention only one which has recently been much discussed—the carrying through of three measures which are bound to result in practical communism.

The first would be the *general education* of all children without exception at the expense of the state—an education which is equal for all and continues until the individual is capable of emerging as an independent member of society. This measure would be only an act of justice to our destitute fellow creatures, for clearly, every man has the right to the full development of his abilities and society wrongs individuals twice over when it makes ignorance a necessary consequence of poverty. It is obvious that society gains more from educated than from ignorant, uncultured members, and while, as may be well expected, an educated proletariat will not be disposed to remain in the oppressed condition in which our present proletariat finds itself, the calm and composure necessary for the peaceful transformation of society can also be expected only from an *educated* working class. But that the *uneducated* proletariat likewise has no wish to remain in its present condition is proved also for Germany—not to speak of other peoples—by the disorders in Silesia and Bohemia.[93]

The second measure would be a complete *reorganisation of the Poor Relief System*, so that all destitute citizens would be housed in colonies where they would be employed in agriculture and industry and their work organised for the benefit of the whole colony. Poor Relief capital has, up to now, been lent out at interest, thus providing the rich with new means for exploiting the propertyless. Let this capital at last work for the benefit of the poor, let the whole yield of this capital, not simply its 3 per cent interest, be used for the poor, and thus give a splendid example of the association of capital and labour! In this way, the labour power of all destitute people would be utilised for the benefit of society and the destitute themselves transformed from demoralised, oppressed paupers into moral, independent, active people whose condition would very soon come to be regarded as enviable by isolated workers and would prepare a thoroughgoing reorganisation of society.

Both these measures require money. In order to raise it and at the same time replace all the present, unjustly distributed taxes, the present reform plan proposes a general, progressive tax on capital, at a rate increasing with the size of the capital. In this way, the burden of public administration would be shared by everyone according to his ability and would no longer fall mainly on the shoulders of those least able to bear it, as has hitherto been the case in all countries. For the principle of taxation is, after all, a purely communist one, since the right to levy taxes is derived in all countries from so-called national property. For either private property is sacrosanct, in which case there is no such thing as national property and the state has no right to levy taxes, or the state has this right, in which case private property is not sacrosanct, national property stands above private property, and the state is the true owner. This latter principle is the one generally accepted—well then, gentlemen; for the present we demand only that this principle be taken seriously, that the state proclaim itself the common owner and, as such, administer public property for the public good, and that as the first step, it introduce a system of taxation based solely on each individual's ability to pay taxes and on the real public good.

So you see, gentlemen, that it is not intended to introduce common ownership [*Gütergemeinschaft*] overnight and against the will of the nation, but that it is only a matter of establishing the *aim* and the *ways* and *means* of advancing towards it. But that the communist principle will be that of the future is attested by the course of development of all civilised nations, it is attested by the swiftly advancing dissolution of all hitherto existing social institutions; it is attested by common sense and, above all, by the human heart.

Gentlemen!

At our last meeting I was accused of taking my examples and illustrations almost exclusively from foreign countries, namely from England. It was said that England and France were of no concern to us, we lived in Germany and it was our business to prove the necessity and advantages of communism for Germany. We were likewise accused of not having sufficiently demonstrated the historical necessity of communism in general. This is quite correct and it was not possible to do otherwise. A historical necessity cannot be demonstrated in as short a time as the congruence of two triangles. It can only be done by study and inquiry into all kinds of far-reaching presuppositions. I will, however, today do my best to answer these two accusations. I will try to show that communism is, if not a historical, at any rate *an economic necessity* for *Germany*.

Let us, first of all, consider the present social situation in Germany. It is known that a great deal of poverty exists among us. Silesia and Bohemia have spoken for themselves. The *Rheinische Zeitung* had much to tell us about the poverty existing in the Mosel and Eifel areas.[a] Large-scale and continuous poverty has prevailed in the Erzgebirge from time immemorial. It is no better in the Senne and in the Westphalian linen districts. There are complaints from all parts of Germany and nothing else is to be expected. Our proletariat is numerous and must be so, as we must realise from the most superficial examination of our social situation. It is in the

---

[a] Karl Marx, "Justification of the Correspondent from the Mosel" (see present edition, Vol. 1, pp. 332-58).—*Ed.*

nature of things that there should be a numerous proletariat in the *industrial districts*. Industry cannot exist without a large number of workers who are wholly at its disposal, work exclusively for it and renounce every other way of making a living. Under conditions of competition, industrial employment makes any other employment impossible. For this reason we find in all industrial districts a proletariat too numerous and too obvious for its existence to be denied.— But in the *agricultural districts*, on the other hand, many people assert, no proletariat exists. But how is this possible? In areas where big landownership prevails such a proletariat is necessary; the big farms need farm-hands and servant girls and cannot exist without proletarians. In areas where the land has been parcelled out the rise of a propertyless class cannot be avoided either; the estates are divided up to a certain point, then the division comes to an end; and as then only one member of the family can take over the farm the others must, of course, become proletarians, propertyless workers. This dividing up usually proceeds until the farm becomes too small to feed a family and so a class of people comes into existence which, like the small middle class in the towns, is in transition from the possessing to the non-possessing class, and which is prevented by its property from taking up any other occupation, and yet cannot live on it. In this class, too, great poverty prevails.

That this proletariat is bound steadily to increase in numbers is guaranteed by the increasing impoverishment of the middle classes of which I spoke in detail last week, and by the tendency of capital to become concentrated in a few hands. I do not need to return to these points today, and will only remark that these causes which continually produce and multiply the proletariat will remain the same and will have the same consequences as long as there is competition. The proletariat must under all circumstances not only continue to exist but also enlarge itself continually, become an ever more threatening power in our society as long as we continue to produce each on his own and in opposition to everyone else. But one day the proletariat will attain a level of power and of insight at which it will no longer tolerate the pressure of the entire social structure always bearing down on its shoulders, when it will demand a more even distribution of social burdens and rights; and then — unless human nature has changed by that time — a social revolution will be inevitable.

This is a question which our economists have not as yet gone into at all. They do not concern themselves with the distribution but only with the production of the national wealth. However, let us leave aside for the moment the fact that, as we have just demonstrated, a social revolution is the consequence of competition; let us consider the individual forms in which competition appears, the different economic possibilities for Germany, and see what the consequences of each must be.

Germany—or the German Customs Union,[94] to be more precise—has a *juste-milieu* customs tariff at the moment. Our duties are too low to constitute a real protective tariff and too high for free trade. So three things are possible. Either we go over to free trade completely, or we protect our industry by adequate tariffs, or we retain the existing system. Let us examine each of these possibilities.

If we proclaim *free trade* and do away with our tariffs, then our whole industry with the exception of a few branches will be ruined. There can *then* be no question whatsoever of cotton spinning, of mechanised weaving, of most branches of the cotton and woollen industry, of important branches of the silk industry, of almost all production and processing of iron. The workers suddenly made destitute in all these branches would be hurled in masses into agriculture and the debris of industry, pauperism would grow out of the very ground everywhere, the centralisation of property in the hands of a few would be speeded up by such a crisis and, judging by the events in Silesia, the result of this crisis would of necessity be a social revolution.

Or we provide ourselves with *protective tariffs*. These have lately become the darlings of most of our industrialists and therefore deserve closer examination. Herr *List* has brought the wishes of our capitalists into a system[a] and I should like to deal for a little while with this system, now almost generally adopted by them as a credo. Herr List proposes gradually increasing protective tariffs which are finally to become high enough to guarantee the home market for the manufacturers; they should then remain at that level for a time and then be gradually reduced again so that finally, after a number of years, all tariffs are abolished. Let us assume for a moment that this plan is adopted and increasing protective tariffs are decreed. Industry will expand, idle capital will rush into industrial undertakings, the demand for workers will increase and so will wages along with it, the poor-houses will empty, and to all appearances everything will be in a most flourishing state. This will continue until our industry has suffi-

---

[a] Friedrich List, *Das nationale System der politischen Oekonomie* (for a detailed analysis of this work see Marx's article on pp. 265-93 of this volume).—*Ed.*

ciently expanded to supply the home market. It cannot expand any further, for since it cannot maintain its hold on the *home* market without protection it will be even less able to do anything against foreign competition in neutral markets. But, says Herr List, by then home industry will be strong enough to require less protection and the reduction of tariffs can commence. Let us agree with this for a moment. The tariffs are reduced. Protection is decreased to such an extent — if not by the first reduction then certainly by the second or third — that foreign, let us say right away, English, industry can compete with our own in the German market. Herr List himself wishes this. But what will be the result of all this? From then on, German industry will have to endure, along with the English, all the fluctuations, all the crises, of the latter. As soon as the overseas markets are glutted with English goods, the English will throw the whole of their surplus stocks on the German market, the nearest one available, just as they are doing now, and as Herr List reports with great emotion, and so transform the German Customs Union into their "second-hand shop" once more. Then English industry will soon rise again because it has the whole world for its market, because the whole world cannot do without it, while German industry is not indispensable even for its own market and has to fear English competition in its own house and is labouring under a profusion of English goods thrown to its customers during the crisis. Then our industry will have to taste to the dregs all the bad times experienced by the English industry while being able to have only a modest share in the latter's boom periods — in short, we shall be in exactly the same position as we are now. And to come straightaway to the final result, there will then ensue the same depression in which our half-protected industries now find themselves, then one establishment after another will go under without new ones arising, then our machines will become obsolete without our being able to replace them with new and better ones, then the standstill will be transformed into retrogression and, according to Herr List's own assertion, one industry after another will decay and finally collapse altogether. But then we shall have a numerous proletariat which will have been created by industry and will now have no food, no work; and then, gentlemen, this proletariat will confront the propertied class with the demand to be given work and to be fed.

This is what will happen if the protective tariffs are reduced. Let us now assume that they are not reduced but remain in operation and that it is proposed to wait until competition between the home manufacturers makes them illusory and then to reduce them. The result of this will be that as soon as German industry is in a position to supply the German market completely it will stand still. New establishments will not be needed since the existing ones suffice for the market and, as has been said above, new markets are out of the question so long as protection is needed at all. But an industry which does not *expand* cannot *improve* itself. It remains stationary both internally and externally. For it there is no such thing as improving the machinery. The old machines cannot just be scrapped, and there are no new establishments which could make use of new ones. Meanwhile other nations go forward, and the standstill in our industry again becomes retrogression. The English, as a result of their advance, will soon be in a position to produce so cheaply that they can compete with our backward industry in our own market *despite* the protective tariffs, and since in competition as in every other kind of struggle victory always goes to the strongest, our ultimate defeat is certain. The same situation then arises about which I have just been speaking: the artificially created proletariat will demand from the property-owners something which, so long as they wish to remain exclusive owners, they are unable to provide, and social revolution begins.

There is yet another possibility, namely, the very improbable one that we Germans will be able owing to protective tariffs to bring our industry to a point at which it can compete with the English without protection. Let us assume that this is so, what would be the result? As soon as we begin to compete with the English in foreign, neutral markets, a life-and-death struggle will arise between our industry and that of the English. They will muster all their strength to keep us out of the markets they have supplied hitherto; they will have to do so because now they will be attacked at their life's source, at the most dangerous spot. And with all the means at their disposal, with all the advantages of a hundred-year-old industry, they will succeed in defeating us. They will keep our industry limited to our own market and thus make it stationary—and then the same situation will arise which has already been outlined; we shall remain stationary, the English will stride forward, and our industry, in view of its unavoidable decay, will not be in a position to feed the proletariat it will have artificially created—the social revolution begins.

But assuming that we could beat the English even in neutral markets, that we were to win from them one trade outlet after another—what would we have gained in this well-nigh impossible case? At best we should repeat the industrial development which

England went through before us, and sooner or later we should arrive at the point which England has now reached — namely the eve of the social revolution. But in all probability it would not take as long as that. As a result of the continual victories of German industry that of the English would necessarily be ruined and this would only speed up the mass uprising of the proletariat against the propertied classes, which is imminent in England in any case. Rapidly spreading destitution would drive the English workers to revolution, and as things stand now, such a social revolution would have enormous repercussions in the continental countries, notably in France and Germany, which must be all the greater the more a proletariat is artificially produced by forcing the pace of industrial development in Germany. Such a revolution would immediately become a European one and would violently upset our manufacturers' dreams of a German industrial monopoly. And that German and English industry should exist peacefully side by side is made impossible if only by competition. I repeat, every industry must advance in order not to lag behind and go under; it must expand, conquer new markets, become enlarged by the addition of new establishments in order to be able to advance. But as no new markets are being won since the opening up of China,[95] and only better exploitation of the existing markets is possible, and as the expansion of industry will therefore proceed more slowly in future than it has done up to now, England can tolerate a competitor even less now than it could in the past. It must hold down the industry of all other countries in order to protect its own industry from ruin. For England the maintenance of industrial monopoly is no longer merely a question of a greater or lesser profit, it has become *a question of life or death*. The competitive struggle between nations is, in any case, much fiercer, much more decisive than that between individuals, because it is a more concentrated struggle, a struggle between masses, which can only be ended by the decisive victory of one side and the decisive defeat of the other. And for this reason, such a struggle between us and the English, no matter what the outcome, would be of no benefit either to our or to the English industrialists but, as I have shown, would only bring a social revolution in its train.

We have thus seen, gentlemen, what Germany can expect in all possible cases both from free trade and from protection. We still have, however, one economic possibility open to us, namely, that we continue with the *juste-milieu* tariffs now in operation. But we have already seen what the results would be. One branch of our industry after another would collapse, the industrial workers would become destitute, and when the destitution reached a certain point they would explode into a revolution against the propertied classes.

So you see, gentlemen, substantiated also in detail what in the beginning, proceeding from competition in general, I set out in general terms—namely, that the unavoidable result of our existing social relations, under all circumstances, and in all cases, will be a *social revolution*. With the same certainty with which we can develop from given mathematical principles a new mathematical proposition, with the same certainty we can deduce from the existing economic relations and the principles of political economy the imminence of social revolution. Let us, however, look at this upheaval a little closer; what form will it take, what will be its results, in what ways will it differ from the previous violent upheavals? A social revolution, gentlemen, is something quite different from the political revolutions which have taken place so far. It is not directed, as these have been, against the property of monopoly, but against the monopoly of property; a social revolution, gentlemen, is *the open war of the poor against the rich*. And such a struggle, in which all the mainsprings and causes, which in previous historical conflicts lay dark and hidden at the bottom, operate openly and without concealment, such a struggle, to be sure, threatens to be far fiercer and bloodier than all those that preceded it. The result of this struggle can be twofold. Either the rebellious party only attacks the appearance, not the essence, only the form, not the thing itself, or it goes for the thing itself, grasps the evil itself by the root. In the first case private property will be allowed to continue and will only be distributed differently, so that the causes which have led to the present situation remain in operation and must sooner or later bring about a similar situation and another revolution. But, gentlemen, is this possible? Has there been a revolution which did not really carry out what it was out for? The English revolution realised both the religious and the political principles whose suppression by Charles I caused it to break out; the French bourgeoisie in its fight against the aristocracy and the old monarchy achieved everything that it aimed for, made an end to all the abuses which drove it to insurrection. And should the insurrection of the poor cease before poverty and its causes have been eliminated? It is not possible, gentlemen; it would be flying in the face of all historical experience to suppose such a thing. Furthermore, the level of education of the workers, especially in England and France, forbids us to consider this possible. There only remains, then, the other alternative, namely, that the future social revolution will deal with the real causes of want and poverty, of ignorance and crime, that it will therefore carry through a real social reform. And this can only happen by the proclamation of the principles of communism. Just consider, gentlemen, the ideas which actuate the worker in those countries where the worker too thinks. Look at France, at the different sections of the labour movement, whether they are not *all* communistic; go to England and listen to the kind of proposals being made to the workers for the improvement of their position — are they not *all* based on the principle of common property; study the different systems of social reform and how many will you find that are not communistic? Of all the systems which are still of any importance today, the only one which is not communistic is that of Fourier, who devoted more attention to the social organisation of human activity than to the distribution of its products. All these facts justify the conclusion that a future social revolution will end with the implementation of the principles of communism and hardly permit any other possibility.

If, gentlemen, these conclusions are correct, if the social revolution and practical communism are the necessary result of our existing conditions — then we will have to concern ourselves above all with the measures by which we can avoid a violent and bloody overthrow of the social conditions. And there is only *one* means, namely, the peaceful introduction or at least preparation of communism. If we do not want the *bloody* solution of the social problem, if we do not want to permit the daily growing contradiction between the education and the condition of our proletarians to come to a head, which, according to all our experience of human nature, will mean that this contradiction will be solved by brute force, desperation and thirst for revenge, then, gentlemen, we must apply ourselves seriously and without prejudice to the social problem; then we must make it our business to contribute our share towards humanising the condition of the modern helots. And if it should perhaps appear to some of you that the raising of the hitherto abased classes will not be possible without an abasement of your own condition, then you ought to bear in mind that what is involved is to create for *all people* such a condition that everyone can freely develop his human nature and live in a human relationship with his neighbours, and has no need to fear any violent shattering of his condition; it must be borne in mind that what some individuals have to sacrifice is not their real human enjoyment of life, but only the semblance of this enjoyment produced by our bad conditions, something which conflicts

with the reason and the heart of those who now enjoy these
apparent advantages. Far from wishing to destroy real human life
with all its requirements and needs, we wish on the contrary really
to bring it into being. And if, even apart from this, you will only
seriously consider for a moment what the consequences of our
present situation are bound to be, into what labyrinths of contradictions and disorders it is leading us — then, gentlemen, you
will certainly find it worth the trouble to study the social question
seriously and thoroughly. And if I can induce you to do this, I
shall have achieved the purpose of my talk.

Delivered in Elberfeld
on February 8 and 15, 1845

Published in *Rheinische Jahrbücher zur
gesellschaftlichen Reform*, 1845, Bd. I

Printed according to the journal

Published in English for the first
time

Karl Marx

DRAFT OF AN ARTICLE ON FRIEDRICH LIST'S BOOK
DAS NATIONALE SYSTEM
DER POLITISCHEN OEKONOMIE[96]

[*1. General Characterisation of List*]

... [2] that awareness of the death of the bourgeoisie has already penetrated the consciousness even of the German bourgeois, so the German bourgeois is naive enough himself to admit this "sad fact".

"For this reason also it is *so sad* that the evils which in our day accompany industry are advanced as a reason for rejecting industry itself. There exist far greater evils than a social estate [Stand] of *proletarians*: an empty exchequer—national impotence—national slavery—national death" (p. LXVII).

It is truly sadder that the proletariat already exists and already advances claims, and already inspires fear, before the German bourgeois has yet achieved the development of industry. As far as the proletarian himself is concerned, he will certainly find his social situation [Stand] a happy one when the ruling bourgeoisie has a full exchequer and national might. Herr List only speaks about what is *sadder* for the bourgeois. And we admit that for him it is very sad that he wants to establish the domination of industry precisely at the unsuitable moment when the slavery of the majority resulting from this domination has become a generally known fact. The German bourgeois is the *knight of the rueful countenance*, who wanted to introduce knight-errantry just when the police and money had come to the fore.

3. A great inconvenience (obstacle)[97] affecting the German bourgeois in his striving for industrial wealth is his *idealism* professed hitherto. How is it that this nation of the *"spirit"* suddenly comes to find the supreme blessings of mankind in calico, knitting yarn, the self-acting mule, in a mass of factory slaves, in the materialism of machinery, in the full money-bags of

Messrs. the factory-owners? The empty, shallow, sentimental idealism of the German bourgeois, beneath which lies hidden (is
concealed) the pettiest, dirtiest and most cowardly shopkeeper's
spirit (soul), has arrived at the epoch when this bourgeois is
inevitably compelled to divulge his secret. But again he divulges it
in a truly German, highflown manner. He divulges it with an
idealistic-Christian sense of shame. He disavows wealth while
striving for it. He clothes spiritless materialism in an idealistic
disguise and only then ventures to pursue it.

The whole theoretical part of List's system is nothing but a
[. . . . . .]ᵃ disguising of the industrial materialism of frank
political economy in idealistic phrases. Everywhere he allows the
thing to remain in existence but idealises the expression of it. We
shall trace this in detail. It is just this empty idealistic phraseology
that enables him to ignore the *real* barriers standing in the way of
his pious wishes and to indulge in the most absurd fantasies (what
would have become of the English and French bourgeoisie if it
had first to ask a high-ranking nobility, an esteemed bureaucracy
and the ancient ruling dynasties for permission to give "industry"
the "force of law"?).

The German bourgeois is religious even when he is an industrialist. He shrinks from speaking about the nasty exchange values
which he covets and speaks about productive forces [von Produktiv-
kräften]; he shrinks from speaking about competition and speaks
of a national confederation of national productive forces; he
shrinks from speaking of his private interest and speaks about the
national interest. When one looks at the frank, classic cynicism
with which the English and French bourgeoisie, as represented by
its first—at least at the beginning of its domination—scientific
spokesmen of political economy, elevated wealth into a god and
ruthlessly sacrificed everything else to it, to this Moloch, in science
as well, and when, on the other hand, one looks at the idealising,
phrase-mongering, bombastic manner of Herr List, who in the
midst of political economy despises the wealth of "righteous
men" and knows loftier aims, one is bound to find it "also sad"
that the present day is no longer a day for wealth.

Herr List always speaks in Molossus metre.⁹⁸ He continually
shows off in a clumsy and verbose rhetoric, the troubled waters of
which always drive him in the end on to a sandbank, and the
essence of which consists of constant repetitions about protective

---

ᵃ There are three illegible words in the manuscript here, apparently meaning
"fallen in front of him".—*Ed.*

tariffs and true German ["teutsche"] factories. He is continually sensuously supersensuous.

The German idealising philistine who wants to become wealthy must, of course, first create for himself a new theory of wealth, one which makes wealth worthy of his striving for it. The bourgeois in France and England see the approach of the storm which will destroy in practice the *real* life of what has hitherto been called wealth, but the German bourgeois, who has not yet arrived at this inferior wealth, tries to give a new, "spiritualistic" interpretation of it. He creates for himself an "idealising" political economy, which has nothing in common with profane French and English political economy, in order to justify to himself and the world that he, too, wants to become wealthy. The German bourgeois begins his creation of wealth with the creation of a highflown hypocritically idealising political economy.

3.[99] How Herr List interprets history and what attitude he adopts towards Smith and his school.

Humble as is Herr List's attitude to the nobility, the ancient ruling dynasties and the bureaucracy, he is to the same degree "audacious" in opposing French and English political economy, of which Smith is the protagonist, and which has cynically betrayed the *secret* of "wealth" and made impossible all illusions about its nature, tendency and movement. Herr List lumps them all together by calling them "the School". For since the German bourgeois is concerned with protective tariffs, the whole development of political economy since Smith has, of course, no meaning for him, because all its most outstanding representatives presuppose the present-day bourgeois society of competition and free trade.

The German philistine here reveals his "national" character in many ways.

1) In the whole of political economy, he sees only systems concocted in academic study rooms. That the development of a science such as political economy is connected with the real movement of society, or is only its theoretical [3] expression, Herr List, of course, does not suspect. A German theoretician.

2) Since his own work (theory) conceals a secret aim, he suspects secret aims everywhere.

Being a true German philistine, Herr List, instead of studying real history, looks for the secret, bad aims of individuals, and, owing to his cunning, he is very well able to discover them (puzzle them out). He makes great discoveries, such as that Adam Smith wanted to deceive the world by his theory, and that the whole world let itself be deceived by him until the great Herr List woke it from its dream, rather in the way that a certain Düsseldorf Counsellor of Justice made out that Roman history had been invented by medieval monks in order to justify the domination of Rome.

But just as the German bourgeois knows no better way of opposing his enemy than by casting a moral slur on him, casting aspersions on his frame of mind, and seeking bad motives for his actions, in short, by bringing him into *bad repute* and making him personally an object of suspicion, so Herr List also casts aspersions on the English and French economists, and retails gossip about them. And just as the German philistine does not disdain the pettiest profit-making and swindling in trade, so Herr List does not disdain to juggle with words from the quotations he gives in order to make them profitable. He does not disdain to stick the trade-mark of his rival on to his own bad products, in order to bring his rival's products into disrepute by falsifying them, or even to invent downright lies about his competitor in order to discredit him.

We shall give a few samples of Herr List's mode of procedure.

It is well known that the German priests believed they could inflict no more deadly blow on the Enlightenment than by telling us the stupid anecdote and lie that on his death-bed Voltaire had renounced his views. Herr List, too, takes us to Adam Smith's death-bed and informs us that it turned out that Smith had not been sincere in his teaching. However, listen to Herr List himself and his further verdict on Smith. We put alongside List's words the source of his wisdom.

List:

[*National System of Political Economy, Vol. I: International Trade, Trade Policy and the German Customs Union.* Stuttgart and Tübingen, 1841:]

"I recalled from the biography by Dugald Stewart how this great mind [Adam Smith] could not die in peace before all his manuscripts had been burned, by which I wanted to make it understood how serious is the suspicion that these papers contained proofs against his sincerity" (p. LVIII). "I showed that the English Ministers [...] made use of his theory in order to throw dust into the eyes of other nations for the benefit of England" (loc.

Ferrier, F.L.A., *Du gouvernement considéré dans ses rapports avec le commerce*, Paris, 1805:

"Is it possible that Smith was sincere in heaping up so many false arguments in favour of free trade?... Smith had as his secret aim to spread in Europe principles the adoption of which he knew very well would give his country the world market" (pp. 385, 386). "One is even justified in assuming that Smith did not always propound one and the same doctrine; and how otherwise is one to explain the torment he suffered on his death-bed because of the fear

cit.). "As regards its relation to national and international conditions, Adam Smith's theory is a mere continuation of the physiocratic system. Like the latter, it ignores the nature of the nations [...] and presupposes eternal peace and universal union as already in existence" (p. 475).

that the manuscripts of his lectures would survive him" (p. 386). He [Ferrier] loc. cit. (p. 388) reproaches Smith for having been a *commissaire des douanes*.[a] "Smith almost always argued like the economists" (physiocrats), "without taking into account the divergence between the interests of the different nations, and on the assumption of a situation where there would be only one society in the world" (p. 381). "Let us set aside all these projects of union" (p. 15).

(Monsieur Ferrier was an *inspecteur des douanes*[b] under Napoleon and loved his profession.)

J.-B. Say's political economy is interpreted by Herr List as an unsuccessful speculation. We shall give below in full his categorical verdict on the life of Say. But before doing so, one more example of the way in which List copies from other authors and in copying falsifies them in order to hit at his opponents.

List:

"*Say* and *McCulloch* seem not to have seen or read more than the title of this book" (that of Antonio Serra from Naples); "both loftily throw it aside with the remark: it treats only of money, and the title by itself proves that the author laboured under the delusion that the precious metals were the sole objects of wealth. If they had read on further," etc. (p. 456).

Count *Pecchio, History of Political Economy in Italy, etc.* Paris, 1830[c]:

"Foreigners tried to rob Serra of the merit of having been the first founder of the principles of this science" (political economy). "What I have just said cannot be applied at all to Monsieur *Say,* who while always reproaching Serra for having regarded only the materials of gold and silver as wealth, nevertheless allowed him the glory of having been the first to make known the productive power of industry.... My reproach is addressed to Mr. McCulloch.... If Mr. McCulloch had read a little more than the title [of Serra's book]", etc. (pp. 76, 77).

One sees how Herr List *deliberately* falsifies Pecchio, from whom he copies, in order to discredit Monsieur Say. No less false is the biographical information given about Say.

---

[a] Customs officer.— *Ed.*

[b] Customs inspector.— *Ed.*

[c] Pecchio, J. (comte), *Histoire de l'économie politique en Italie,* Paris, 1830. (In the manuscript the title of the book is given in German.)— *Ed.*

Herr List says about him:

"First a merchant, then a factory-owner, then an unsuccessful politician, Say took up political economy, as people take up some new enterprise when the old one no longer succeeds.... Hatred of the Continental System, which ruined his factory, and of the originator of this system, who drove him out of the Tribunate, caused him to come out in support of absolute freedom of trade" (pp. 488, 489).

So Say supported the system of free trade *because* his factory was ruined by the Continental System! But what if he had written his *Traité d'économie politique*[a] *before* he owned a factory? Say became a supporter of the system of free trade because Napoleon drove him out of the Tribunate![100] But what if he had written his book *while he was a tribune*? What if Say, who according to Herr List was an unsuccessful businessman who saw in literature only a branch of business, had from his early youth played a part in the French literary world?

Where did Herr List obtain his new information? From the *Historical Note on the Life and Works of J.-B. Say* by *Charles Comte*,[101] which was published as an introduction to Say's *Cours complet d'économie politique*. What does this note tell us? It contains the opposite of all List's statements. Listen:

"J.-B. Say was intended by his father, who was a merchant, [4] to engage in trade. However, his inclination drew him to literature. In 1789 he published a pamphlet in behalf of freedom of the press. From the outset of the revolution he contributed to the newspaper *Courrier de Provence*, published by Mirabeau. He also worked in the office of the Minister Clavière. His penchant 'for the moral and political sciences', as also his father's bankruptcy, caused him to give up trade completely and to make scientific activity his sole occupation. In 1794 he became editor-in-chief of the *Décade philosophique, littéraire et politique*. In 1799 Napoleon appointed him a member of the Tribunate. The spare time left him from his function as tribune he used to work on his *Traité politique*, which he published in 1803. He was dismissed from the Tribunate because he belonged to the few who dared to be in opposition. He was offered a lucrative post in the finance department, but he refused although *chargé de six enfants et n'ayant presque point de fortune*[b]..., since he would not have been able to carry out the duties of the post offered him without taking part in implementing a system which he had condemned as being disastrous for France. He preferred to start up a cotton-spinning mill, etc."

If the slur which Herr List here casts on J.-B. Say owes its origin to falsification, this is no less the case with the praise List bestows on the brother, Louis Say. To prove that *Louis Say* shares the crafty [*listig*][c] view, List falsifies a passage from this author.

Herr List says on p. 484:

---

[a] Published in 1803.—*Ed.*
[b] Burdened with six children and having almost no fortune.—*Ed.*
[c] A pun: "listig" means crafty, but could also be an adjective from "List".—*Ed.*

"In his" (Louis Say's) "opinion, the wealth of nations consists not in material goods and their exchange value, but in the *ability continually to produce these goods*."

According to Herr List, the following are Louis Say's own words:

The Louis Say of Herr List:	The real Louis Say:
"La richesse ne consiste pas dans les choses qui satisfont nos besoins ou nos goûts, mais dans le pouvoir d'en jouir annuellement" (*Études sur la richesse des nations*, p. 10).[a]	"Quoique la richesse ne consiste pas dans les choses qui satisfont nos besoins ou nos goûts, mais dans *le revenu ou* dans le pouvoir d'en jouir annuellement."[b]

Thus, Say is not speaking of the ability to produce, but of the ability to enjoy, of the ability which provides the "income" (*revenu*) of a nation. From the disproportion between the growing productive force and the income of the nation as a whole, and of all its classes in particular, there arose precisely the theories most inimical to Herr List as, for example, those of Sismondi and Cherbuliez.

Let us now give an example of Herr List's ignorance in his verdict on the "School". He says about Ricardo (List on productive forces):

"In general, since Adam Smith, the School has been unfortunate in its researches into the nature of rent. Ricardo, and following him Mill, McCulloch and others, hold that rent is paid for the natural productivity inherent in plots of land. Ricardo based a whole system on this view.... Since he considered only English conditions, he was misled into the erroneous view that these English ploughed fields and meadows, for the apparently natural productivity of which such fine rent is paid at the present time, have been the very same ploughed fields and meadows at all times" (p. 360).

Ricardo says:

"If the surplus produce which land affords in the form of rent be an advantage, it is desirable that, every year, the machinery newly constructed should be less efficient than the old, as that would undoubtedly give a greater exchangeable value to the goods manufactured ... in the kingdom; and a rent would be paid to all those who possessed the most productive machinery." "Rent increases most rapidly, as the disposable land decreases in its productive powers. Wealth increases most rapidly in those countries ... where through agricultural improvements, productions can be multiplied without any increase in the proportional quantity of labour, and where consequently the progress of rent is slow." (Ricardo, *Principles of Political Economy*, etc. Paris, 1835, Vol. I, pp. 77 and 80-82.)[c]

---

[a] "Wealth consists not in the objects which satisfy our requirements or our tastes, but in the possibility of enjoying them annually." (*Researches into the Wealth of Nations*, p. 10.)—*Ed.*

[b] "Although wealth consists not in the objects which satisfy our requirements or our tastes, but in *income*, or in the possibility of enjoying it annually."—*Ed.*

[c] David Ricardo, *Des principes de l'économie politique et de l'impôt*. Traduit de l'anglais par Constancio. In the manuscript Marx gives an abridged German translation of the title.—*Ed.*

According to Ricardo's theory, rent, far from being the consequence of the natural productivity inherent in the soil, is rather a
consequence of the constantly increasing *unproductiveness* of the
soil, a consequence of civilisation and the increasing population.
According to Ricardo, as long as the most fertile land is still
available in an unlimited amount, there is still no land rent. Hence
rent is determined by the ratio of the population to the amount of
available land.

Ricardo's theory, which serves as the theoretical basis for the
whole Anti-Corn-Law League[a] in England and the anti-rent
movement in the free states of North America,[102] had to be
falsified by Herr List — assuming he had more than hearsay
knowledge of it — if only because it proves how little the "free,
mighty and wealthy bourgeois" are inclined to work "diligently"
for [the increase of] "land rents" and to bring them [the landowners]
honey from the hive.[103] Ricardo's theory of land rent is nothing
but the economic expression of a life-and-death struggle of the
industrial bourgeois against the landowners.

Herr List instructs us further about Ricardo as follows:

"At the present time the theory of exchange value has fallen into such
impotence ... that Ricardo ... could say: 'to determine the laws by which the yield
from land is distributed between landowners, tenant-farmers and workers is the
chief task of political economy'" (p. 493).

The necessary observations on this are to be made in the
appropriate place.[b]

[5] Herr List reaches the height of infamy in his verdict on
Sismondi.

List:	*Sismondi:*
"He" (Sismondi) "wants, for example, the spirit of inventiveness to be curbed and bridled" (p. xxix).	"My objections are not to machines, not to inventions, not to civilisation, but only to *the modern organisation of society*, which deprives the working man of any property other than his hands, and gives him no guarantee against competition, of which he will inevitably become a victim. Suppose that all people share equally in the product of the labour in which they have participated, then every technical invention will in all possible cases be a blessing for all of them" (*Nouveaux principes d'économie politique*, Paris, 1827, t. II, p. 433).

[a] Here and below Marx gives the name of the League in English.—*Ed*.
[b] See pp. 284-88 of this volume.—*Ed*.

Whereas Herr List casts moral aspersions on Smith and Say he can only explain the theory of Monsieur Sismondi from the latter's *bodily* defects. He says:

"Monsieur de Sismondi sees with his bodily eyes everything red as black; it seems that his spiritual sight in matters of political economy suffers from the same defect" (p. xxix).

In order to appreciate to the full the vileness of this outburst, one must know the passage from which Herr List derived his remark. Sismondi says in his *Études sur l'économie politique*, where he speaks of the devastation of the Roman Campagna:

"The rich tints of the Roman Campagna ... even entirely escape our eyes, for which the red ray is non-existent" (p. 6). Brussels reprint, 1838 [Vol. II].

Sismondi explains this by saying: "the charm which attracts all other travellers to Rome" is destroyed for him and he "therefore has eyes that are all the more open to see the real, miserable condition of the inhabitants of the Campagna."

If de Sismondi did not see the rosy tints of the sky which magically illumine the whole (factory) industry for Herr List, he did see the *red cock* on the gables (roofs) of these factories. We shall have an opportunity later[a] [to examine] List's verdict that

"Monsieur de Sismondi's writings on international trade and trade policy are without any value" [p. xxix].

Whereas Herr List explains Smith's system from the latter's personal vanity (p. 476) and the hidden English shopkeeper's mentality, and Say's system from a desire for revenge and as a business enterprise, in regard to Sismondi he descends so low as to explain Sismondi's system from the defects of his bodily constitution.

[5] 4. Herr List's Originality

It is highly characteristic of Herr List that, despite all his boasting, he has put forward *not a single proposition* that had not been advanced long before him not only by the defenders of the prohibitive system, but even by writers of the "School" invented by Herr List—if Adam Smith is the theoretical starting-point of political economy, then its real point of departure, its real school, is "civil society" [*die bürgerliche Gesellschaft*], of which the different phases of development can be accurately traced in political economy. Only the illusions and idealising language (phrases)

---

[a] Apparently, the reference is to a part of the manuscript which is missing.—*Ed.*

belong to Herr List. We consider it important to give detailed proof of this to the reader and must claim his attention for this tedious labour. He will derive from it the conviction that the German bourgeois comes on the scene *post festum*, that it is just as impossible for him to advance further the political economy exhaustively developed by the English and French as it would probably be for them to contribute anything new to the development of philosophy in Germany. The German bourgeois can only add his illusions and phrases to the French and English reality. But little possible as it is for him to give a new development to political economy, it is still more impossible for him to achieve in practice a further advance of industry, of the by now almost exhausted development on the present foundations of society.

5. We therefore restrict our criticism to the theoretical part of List's book, and in fact only to his main discoveries.

What are the main propositions which Herr List has to prove? Let us inquire into the aim he wants to achieve.

1) The bourgeois wants protective tariffs from the state in order to lay his hands on state power and wealth. But since [in Germany], unlike in England and France, he does not have state power at his disposal and therefore cannot arbitrarily guide it as he likes, but has to resort to requests, it is necessary for him in relation to the state, the activity (mode of action) of which he wants to control for his own benefit, to depict his demand from it as a *concession* that he makes to the state, whereas [in reality] he demands *concessions* from the state. Therefore, through the medium of Herr List, he [the German bourgeois] proves to the state that his theory differs from all others in that he allows the state to interfere in and control industry, in that he has the highest opinion of the economic wisdom of the state, and only asks it to give full scope for its wisdom, on condition, of course, that this wisdom is limited to providing "strong" protective tariffs. His demand that the state should act in accordance with his interests is depicted by him as recognition of the state, recognition that the state has the right to interfere in the sphere of civil society.

2) The bourgeois [Bürger] wants to become *rich*, to make money; but at the same time he must come to terms with the present idealism of the German public and with his own conscience. Therefore he tries to prove that he does not strive for unrighteous material goods, but for a *spiritual essence*, for an infinite *productive force*, instead of bad, finite *exchange values*. Of course, this spiritual essence involves the circumstance that the "citizen" ["*Bürger*"] takes this opportunity to fill his own pockets with worldly exchange values.

[6]ᵃ Since the bourgeois now hopes to become rich mainly through "protective tariffs", and since protective tariffs can enrich him only insofar as no longer Englishmen, but the German bourgeois himself, will *exploit* his *fellow-countrymen*, indeed exploit them even *more* than they were exploited from abroad, and since protective tariffs demand a sacrifice of exchange values from the consumers (chiefly from the workers who are to be superseded by machines, from all those who draw a fixed income, such as officials, recipients of land rent, etc.), the industrial bourgeois has therefore to prove that, far from hankering after material goods, he wants nothing else but the sacrifice of exchange values, material goods, for a spiritual essence. Fundamentally, therefore, it is solely a matter of *self-sacrifice*, of *asceticism*, of Christian *grandeur of the soul*. It is pure accident that A makes the sacrifice, but B puts the sacrifice in his pocket. The German bourgeois is much too unselfish to think in this connection of his private gain, which accidentally proves to be linked with this *sacrifice*. But if it should turn out that a class whose permission the German bourgeois thinks he requires for his emancipation, cannot go along with this spiritual theory, then this theory must be abandoned and, in opposition to the School [which advocates freedom of trade], precisely the theory of exchange values be brought into play.

3) Since the whole desire of the bourgeoisie amounts, in essence, to bringing the factory system to the level of "English" prosperity and making industrialism the regulator of society, i.e., to bringing about the disorganisation of society, the bourgeois has to prove that he is only concerned for the harmonisation of all social production, and for the organisation of society. He restricts foreign trade by means of protective tariffs, while agriculture, he maintains, will rapidly attain its highest prosperity owing to manufacturing industry. The organisation of society, therefore, is summed up in the factories. They are the organisers of society, and the system of competition which they bring into being is the finest confederation of society.¹⁰⁴ The organisation of society which the factory system creates is the *true organisation of society*.

The bourgeoisie is certainly right in conceiving in general its interests as identical interests, just as the *wolf* as a *wolf* has an identical interest with his fellow wolves, however much it is to the interest of each individual wolf that he and not another should pounce on the prey.

6. Finally, it is characteristic of Herr List's theory, as also of the

---

ᵃ The manuscript here has a new sheet marked 2.—*Ed.*

entire German bourgeoisie, that in order to defend their desires to exploit they are compelled everywhere to resort to "socialist" phrases and thus forcibly to maintain a deception that has long been refuted. We shall show in various passages[a] that Herr List's phrases, if the consequences are drawn from them, are *communistic*. We, of course, are far from accusing someone like Herr List and his German bourgeoisie of communism, but this affords us fresh proof of the internal weakness, falsity and infamous hypocrisy of the "good-natured", "idealistic" bourgeois. It proves to us that his idealism in practice is nothing but the unscrupulous, unthinking disguise of a repulsive materialism.

Finally, it is characteristic that the German bourgeoisie begins with the lie with which the French and English bourgeoisie *ends*,— after reaching a position where it is compelled to apologise for itself, to offer excuses for its existence.

---

7. Since Herr List distinguishes the present, ostensibly cosmopolitan, political economy from his own (national-political) economy by the former being based on exchange values and the latter on productive forces, we have to start with this theory. Furthermore, since the confederation of productive forces is supposed to represent the nation in its unity, we have also to examine this theory prior to the above-mentioned distinction. These two theories form the *real* basis of [List's] national economy as distinct from political economy.[b]

* * *

It can never occur to Herr List that the real organisation of society is a soulless materialism, an individual spiritualism, individualism. It can never occur to him that the political economists have only given this social state of affairs a corresponding theoretical expression. Otherwise, he would have to direct his criticism against the present *organisation of society* instead of against the political economists. He accuses them of not having found any

---

[a] The reference is to parts of the manuscript which either were not written or have not been found.—*Ed.*

[b] This paragraph is followed in the manuscript by an incomplete third of the third page of the sixth sheet and a blank whole page (the fourth of the sixth sheet). The first chapter, which ends here, is followed immediately by a separate unnumbered sheet containing a small fragment to which the author has given no title and which is placed in this edition after three asterisks inserted by the editors.—*Ed.*

embellishing expression for a cheerless reality. Hence he wants to leave this reality everywhere just as it is and only change the expression of it. Nowhere does he criticise real society, but like a true German, he criticises the theoretical expression of this society and reproaches it for expressing the real thing and not an imaginary notion of the real thing.

The factory is transformed into a goddess, the goddess of manufacturing power.

The factory-owner is the priest of this power.[a]

[7] II. The Theory of Productive Forces and the Theory of Exchange Values

1) ⟨ Herr List's theory of "productive forces" is limited to the following main propositions:

a) The *causes* of wealth are something quite different from wealth itself; the force capable of creating wealth is infinitely more important than wealth itself [p. 201];⟩

⟨ b) List is far from rejecting the theory of cosmopolitan economy; he is merely of the opinion that political economy also should be scientifically developed [p. 187];

c) What then is the cause of labour?..., what impels these minds and these arms and hands to undertake production and what gives efficacy to these efforts? What else can it be but the *spirit* which animates the individuals, the social system which makes their activity fruitful, the natural forces the use of which is at their disposal? [p. 205].⟩

⟨ 6) Smith "went astray by explaining spiritual forces from material conditions" [p. 207].⟩

⟨ 7) "That science which teaches how *productive forces* are aroused and cultivated and how they are suppressed or destroyed" (ibid.).⟩

8) An example [of the distinction] between two fathers of families, Christian religion, monogamy,[105] etc. [pp. 208-209].

⟨9) "One can establish the concepts of value and capital, profit, wages, land rent, resolve them into their component parts, and speculate about what could influence their rise and fall, etc., without in so doing taking into account the political conditions of the nations" [p. 211].⟩

Transition.

10) Workshops and factories are the mothers and children of scientific (civic) freedom [p. 212].[106]

11) The theory of productive and non-productive classes. The former produce exchange values, the latter produce productive forces [p. 215].

12) Foreign trade must not be judged solely from the standpoint of the theory of values [p. 216].

13) The nation must sacrifice material forces in order to acquire spiritual or social forces. Protective tariffs for raising manufacturing power [pp. 216-217].

14) "If therefore a sacrifice of *values* is made owing to protective tariffs, that sacrifice is compensated by the acquisition of productive forces, and this not only

---

[a] Here this fragment written on a separate unnumbered sheet breaks off.—*Ed.*

ensures the nation an infinitely greater sum of material goods for the future, but also industrial independence in the event of war" [p. 217].

15) "In all these respects, however, the chief thing depends on the state of the society in which the individual takes shape, on whether crafts and sciences flourish" (p. 206).

2) Herr List is so much a prey to the economic prejudices of the old political economy—more so, as we shall see, than other economists of the "School"—that for him "material goods" and "exchange values" completely coincide. But exchange value is entirely independent of the specific nature of the "material goods". It is independent of both the quality and the quantity of material goods. Exchange value falls when the quantity of material goods rises, although both before and afterwards these bear the same relation to human needs. Exchange value is not connected with quality. The most useful things, such as knowledge, have no exchange value. Herr List therefore ought to have understood that the conversion of material goods into exchange values is a result of the existing social system, of the society of developed private property. The *abolition of exchange value* is the *abolition* of *private property* and of *private acquisition*. Herr List, on the other hand, is so naive as to admit that by means of the theory of exchange values

"one can establish the concepts of value and capital, profit, wages, land rent, resolve them into their component parts, and speculate about what could influence their rise and fall, etc., without in so doing taking into account the political conditions of the nations" (p. 211).

Hence, without taking into account the "theory of productive forces" and the "political conditions of the nations", all this can be "established". What is established thereby? Reality. What is established, for example, by wages? The life of the worker. Furthermore, it is established thereby that the worker is the slave of capital, that he is a "*commodity*", an exchange value, the higher or lower level of which, the rise or fall of which, depends on competition, on supply and demand; it is established thereby that his activity is not a free manifestation of his human life, that it is, rather, a huckstering sale of his forces, an alienation (sale) to capital of his one-sidedly developed abilities, in a word, that it is "*labour*". One is supposed to forget this. "*Labour*" is the living basis of private property, it is private property as the creative source of itself. Private property is nothing but *objectified* labour. If it is desired to strike a mortal blow at private property, one must attack it not only as a *material state of affairs*, but also as *activity*, as *labour*. It is one of the greatest misapprehensions to speak of free, human, social labour, of labour without private property. "Labour" by its very nature is unfree, unhuman, unsocial activity, determined by private property and creating private property. Hence the abolition of private property will become a reality only when it is conceived as the abolition of "*labour*" (an abolition which, of course, has become possible only as a result of labour itself, that is to say, has become possible as a result of the material activity of society and which should on no account be conceived as the replacement of one category by another).[107] An "organisation of labour", therefore, is a contradiction. *The* best organisation that labour can be given is the present organisation, free competition, the dissolution of all its previous apparently "social" organisation.

Thus, if wages can be "established" according to the theory of values, if it is thereby "established" that man himself is an exchange value, that the overwhelming majority of people in the nations constitutes a *commodity*, which can be determined without taking "the political conditions of the nations" into account, what does all this prove but that this overwhelming majority of people in the nations does not have to take "political conditions" into account, that these are for it a sheer *illusion*, that a theory which in reality sinks to this sordid materialism of making the majority of people in the nations into a "commodity", into an "exchange value", and of subjecting this majority to the wholly material conditions of exchange value, is an infamous hypocrisy and idealistic eye-wash (embellishment), when in relation to other nations it looks down contemptuously on the bad "materialism" of "exchange values", and is itself ostensibly only concerned with "productive forces"? Furthermore, if the conditions of capital, land rent, etc., can be "established" without taking the "political conditions" of the nations into account, what does this prove but that the industrial capitalist and the recipient of land rent are guided in their actions in real life by profit, exchange values, and not by considerations about "political conditions" and "productive forces", and that their talk about civilisation and productive forces is only an embellishment of narrow-minded egoistic tendencies?

The bourgeois says: Of course, the theory of exchange values should not be undermined within the country, the majority of the nation should remain a mere "exchange value", a "commodity", one which must find its own buyer, one which is not sold, but which sells itself. In relation to you proletarians, and even in our mutual relations, we regard ourselves as exchange values, here the law of universal *huckstering* holds good. But in relation to other nations we must interrupt the operation of this law. As a nation we cannot huckster ourselves to other nations. Since the majority of people in the nations has become subject to the laws of huckstering "without taking into account" the "political conditions of the nations", that proposition has no other meaning than the following: We German bourgeois do not want to be exploited by the English bourgeois in the way that you German proletarians are exploited by us and that we exploit one another. We do not want to subject ourselves to the same laws of exchange value as those to which we subject you. We do not want any longer to 'recognise outside the country the economic laws which we recognise inside the country.

. [8] What then does the German philistine want? He wants to be a *bourgeois*, an exploiter, inside the country, but he wants also not to be exploited outside the country. He puffs himself up into being the "nation" in relation to foreign countries and says: I do not submit to the laws of competition; that is contrary to my national dignity; as the nation I am a being superior to huckstering.

The nationality of the worker is neither French, nor English, nor German, it is *labour, free slavery, self-huckstering*. His government is neither French, nor English, nor German, it is *capital*. His native air is neither French, nor German, nor English, it is *factory air*. The land belonging to him is neither French, nor English, nor German, it lies a few feet *below the ground*. Within the country, money is the fatherland of the industrialist. Thus, the German philistine wants the laws of competition, of exchange value, of huckstering, to lose their power at the frontier barriers of his country! He is willing to recognise the power of bourgeois society only in so far as it is in accord with *his interests*, the interests of his class! He does not want to fall victim to a power to which he wants to *sacrifice* others, and to which he sacrifices himself inside his own country! Outside the country he wants to show himself and be treated as a different being from what he is within the country and how he himself behaves within the country! He wants to leave the *cause* in existence and to abolish one of its *effects*! We shall prove to him that selling oneself out inside the country has as its necessary consequence selling out outside, that competition, which gives him his power inside the country, cannot prevent him from becoming powerless outside the country; that the state, which he subordinates to bourgeois society inside the country, cannot protect him from the action of bourgeois society outside the country.

However much the individual bourgeois fights against the others, as a *class* the bourgeois have a common interest, and this community of interest, which is directed against the proletariat inside the country, is directed against the bourgeois of other nations outside the country. This the bourgeois calls his *nationality*.

2)[a] It is possible, of course, to regard industry from a completely different point of view than that of sordid huckstering interest, from which it is nowadays regarded not only by the individual merchant and the individual manufacturer, but also by the manufacturing nations and the trading nations. Industry can be regarded as a great workshop in which man first takes possession of his own forces and the forces of nature, objectifies himself and creates for himself the conditions for a human existence. When industry is regarded in this way, one *abstracts* from the *circumstances* in which it operates today, and in which it exists *as industry*; one's standpoint is *not* from within the industrial epoch, but *above* it; industry is regarded not by what it is for *man* today, but by what present-day man is for *human history*, what he is historically; it is not its present-day *existence* (not *industry* as such) that is recognised, but rather the power which industry has without knowing or willing it and which *destroys* it and creates the basis for a *human* existence. (To hold that every nation goes through this development internally would be as absurd as the idea that every nation is bound to go through the political development of France or the philosophical development of Germany. What the nations have done as nations, they have done for human society; their whole value consists only in the fact that each single nation has accomplished for the benefit of other nations one of the main historical aspects (one of the main determinations) in the framework of which mankind has accomplished its development, and therefore after industry in England, politics in France 'and philosophy in Germany have been developed, they have been developed for the world, and their world-historic significance, as also that of these nations, has thereby come to an end.)

This assessment of industry is then at the same time the recognition that the hour has come for it to be done away with, or for the abolition of the material and social conditions in which mankind has had to develop its abilities as a slave. For as soon as industry is no longer regarded as a huckstering interest, but as the development of man, man, instead of huckstering interest, is made

---

[a] In the manuscript point 2 occurs twice in this chapter.—*Ed.*

the principle and what in industry could develop only in contradiction with industry itself is given the basis which is in harmony with that which is to be developed.

But the wretched individual who [in his ideas] remains within the present system, who desires only to raise it to a level which it has not yet reached in his own country, and who looks with greedy envy on another nation that has reached this level—has this wretched individual the right to see in industry anything else but huckstering interest? Has he the right to say that he is concerned only for the development of man's abilities and man's mastery of the forces of nature? For this is just as *vile* as if a slave-driver were to boast that he flourished his whip over his slaves in order that the slaves should have the pleasure of exercising their *muscular power*. The German philistine is the slave-driver who flourishes the whip of protective tariffs in order to instil in his nation the spirit of "industrial education" [108] and teach it to exercise its muscular powers.

The *Saint-Simon* school has given us an instructive example of what it leads to if the *productive force* that industry creates unconsciously and against its will is put to the credit of present-day industry and the two are confused: *industry* and the *forces* which industry brings into being unconsciously and without its will, but which will only become human forces, man's power, when industry is abolished. This is as much an absurdity as if the bourgeois wanted to take the credit for *his* industry creating the proletariat, and in the shape of the proletariat the power of a new world order. The forces of nature and the social forces which industry brings into being (conjures up), stand in the same relation to it as the proletariat. Today they are still the slaves of the bourgeois, and in them he sees nothing but the instruments (the bearers) of his dirty (selfish) lust for profit; tomorrow they will break their chains and reveal themselves as the bearers of human development which will blow him sky-high together with his industry, which assumes the dirty outer shell—which he regards as its essence—only until the human kernel has gained sufficient strength to burst this shell and appear in its own shape. Tomorrow they will burst the chains by which the bourgeois separates them from man and so distorts (transforms) them from a real social bond into fetters of society.

The Saint-Simon school glorified in dithyrambs the productive power of industry. The forces which industry calls into being it lumped together with industry itself, that is to say, with the present-day conditions of existence that industry gives to these forces. We are of course far from putting the Saint-Simonists on the same level as someone like List or the German philistine. The first step towards breaking the spell cast on industry was to abstract from the conditions, the money fetters, in which the forces of industry operate today and to examine these forces in themselves. This was the first call to the people to emancipate their industry from huckstering and to understand present-day industry as a transitional epoch. The Saint-Simonists, moreover, did *not stop* at this interpretation. They went further — to attack exchange value, private property, the organisation of present-day society. They put forward association in place of competition. But they were punished for their original error. Not only did the above-mentioned confusion lead them further into the illusion of seeing the dirty bourgeois as a priest, but it also caused them [9], after the first external struggles, to fall back into the old illusion (confusion) — but now hypocritically, because precisely in the course of the struggle the contradiction of the two forces which they had confused became manifest. Their glorification of industry (of the productive forces of industry) became a glorification of the bourgeoisie, and Monsieur Michel Chevalier, Monsieur Duveyrier, Monsieur Dunoyer have pilloried themselves and the bourgeoisie in the eyes of the whole of Europe — after which the rotten eggs that history throws in their faces became transformed by the magic of the bourgeoisie into golden eggs — since the first of those named above has retained the old phrases but has endowed them with the content of the present-day bourgeois regime, the second is himself engaged in huckstering on a wholesale scale and presides over the selling-out of French newspapers, while the third has become the most rabid apologist for the present state of affairs and surpasses in inhumanity (in shamelessness) all previous English and French economists. — The German bourgeois and Herr List begin where the Saint-Simon school left off — with *hypocrisy, deception* and *phrase-mongering*.

England's industrial tyranny over the world is the domination of industry over the world. England dominates us because industry dominates us. We can free ourselves from England abroad only if we free ourselves from industry at home. We shall be able to put an end to England's domination in the sphere of competition only if we overcome competition within our borders. England has power over us because we have made industry into a power over us.

3) That the industrial social order is the best world for the bourgeois, the order most suitable for developing his "abilities" as

a bourgeois and the ability to exploit both people and nature—who will dispute this *tautology*? Who will dispute that all that
is nowadays called "virtue", individual or social virtue, is a source
of profit for the bourgeois? Who will dispute that political power
is a means for his enrichment, that even science and intellectual
pleasures are his slaves? Who will dispute it? That for him
everything is excellently [adapted[a]]? That for him everything has
become a means of wealth, a "productive force of wealth"?

4) Modern political economy starts out from the social system of
competition. Free labour, that is to say, indirect slavery which
offers itself for sale, is its principle. Its primary propositions are
division of labour and the machine. And this can be given its
highest development only in the factories, as modern political
economy itself admits. Thus political economy today starts out
from the factories as its creative principle. It presupposes present-
day social conditions. Hence it does not need to expatiate on
"manufacturing force".[109]

If the "School" made no *"scientific elaboration"*[110] of the theory
of productive forces *alongside* and *separately* from the theory of
exchange values, it acted in this way because such a separation is
an arbitrary abstraction, because it is impossible and cannot go
beyond general phrases.

5) "The causes of wealth are something quite different from wealth itself. The
force capable of creating wealth is infinitely more important than wealth itself"
[List, op. cit., p. 201].

Productive force appears as an entity infinitely superior to
exchange value. This force claims the position of inner essence,
whereas exchange value claims that of a transient phenomenon.
The force appears as infinite, exchange value as finite, the former
as non-material, the latter as material—and we find all these
antitheses in Herr List. Hence the supernatural world of forces
takes the place of the material world of exchange values. Whereas
the baseness of a nation sacrificing itself for exchange values, of
people being sacrificed for things, is quite obvious, forces, on the
other hand, appear to be independent spiritual essences—phantoms—and pure personifications, deities, and after all one may
very well demand of the German people that it should sacrifice
the bad exchange values for phantoms! An exchange value,
money, always seems to be an external aim, but productive force
seems to be an aim which arises from my very nature, a self-aim.
Thus, what I sacrifice in the form of exchange values is

---

[a] There are one or two illegible words in the manuscript here.—*Ed.*

something external to me; what I gain in the form of productive forces is my self-acquisition.— That is how it *seems* if one is satisfied with a word or, like an idealising German, does not worry about the dirty reality which lies behind this grandiloquent word.

In order to destroy the mystical radiance which transfigures "productive force", one has only to consult any book of statistics. There one reads about water-power, steam-power, manpower, horse-power. All these are "productive forces". Is it a high appreciation of man for him to figure as a "force" alongside horses, steam and water?

Under the present system, if a crooked spine, twisted limbs, a one-sided development and strengthening of certain muscles, etc., make you more capable of working (more productive), then your crooked spine, your twisted limbs, your one-sided muscular movement are a productive force. If your intellectual vacuity is more productive than your abundant intellectual activity, then your intellectual vacuity is a productive force, etc., etc. If the monotony of an occupation makes you better suited for that occupation, then monotony is a productive force.

Is the bourgeois, the factory-owner, at all concerned for the worker developing all his abilities, exercising his productive capacities, fulfilling himself as a human being, and thereby at the same time fulfilling his human nature?

We will leave it to the English *Pindar* of the factory system, Mr. Ure, to reply to this question:

"It is, in fact, the constant aim and tendency of every improvement in machinery to supersede human labour altogether, or to diminish its cost, by substituting the industry of women and children for that of men; or that of ordinary labourers, for trained artisans" (*Philosophie des manufactures, etc.*, Paris, 1836, t. I, p. 34). "By the infirmity of human nature it happens, that the more skilful the workman, the more self-willed and intractable he is apt to become, and, of course, the less fit a component of a *mechanical* system ... therefore [the main point] of the modern manufacturer is, through the union of capital and science, to reduce the task of his work-people to the exercise of vigilance and dexterity, etc." (loc. cit., t. I, p. 30).

Force, Productive Force, Causes

"The causes of wealth are something quite different from wealth itself."

But if the effect is different from the cause, must not the nature of the effect be contained already in the cause? The cause must already carry with it the determining feature that is manifested later in the effect. Herr List's philosophy goes as far as knowing that cause and effect are "something quite different".

["The force capable of creating wealth is infinitely more important than wealth itself."]

It is a fine recognition of man that degrades him to a *"force"* capable of creating wealth! The bourgeois sees in the proletarian not a *human being*, but a *force* capable of creating wealth, a force which moreover he can then compare with other productive forces—an animal, a machine—and if the comparison proves unfavourable to man, the force of which man is the bearer must give place to the force of which the bearer is an animal or a machine, although in that case man still has (enjoys) the honour of figuring as a "productive force".

If I characterise man as an "exchange value", this expression already implies that social conditions have transformed him into a "thing". If I treat him as a "productive force", I am putting in the place of the real subject a different subject, I am substituting another person for him, and he now exists only as a cause of wealth.

The whole of human society becomes merely a machine for the creation of wealth.

The cause is in no way superior to the *effect*. The effect is merely the openly *manifested* cause.

List pretends that he is everywhere interested in productive forces for their own sake, quite apart from bad exchange values.

Some light is already thrown for us on the essence of the present-day "productive forces" by the fact that in the present state of affairs productive force consists not only in, for instance, making man's labour more efficient or natural and social forces more effective, but just as much in making labour cheaper or *more unproductive* for the worker. Hence productive force is from the outset determined by exchange value. It is just as much an increase of....[a]

[*III. From Chapter Three*]
[The Problem of Land Rent]

...[22] land rent disappears. These higher grain prices—since the worker always consumes a certain amount of grain, however dear it may be, and therefore his nominal wage increases even when in reality it decreases—must be deducted from the profits of Messrs. the industrialists; Ricardo is wise enough to assume that

---

[a] Here the text occupying the fourth page of the ninth manuscript sheet ends. Sheets 10-21 have not come down to us. These missing sheets should contain the end of Chapter II and the beginning of Chapter III.—*Ed.*

wages cannot be depressed further. Hence, when there is a rise in the price of grain, there follows a reduction in profits and an increase in wages, without the latter increasing in reality. However, the increase in the price of grain raises the production costs of the industrialists, thereby making accumulation and competition more difficult for them, in a word, cripples the *productive force* of the country. Therefore the bad "exchange value", which falls in the form of land rent into the pockets of the landowners without *any advantage* (to the greatest detriment) to the country's productive force, must in one way or another be *sacrificed* to the general good—by free trade in grain, by shifting all taxes on to land rent, or by outright appropriation of land rent, i.e. of landed property, by the state (this conclusion has been drawn by, among others, [James] Mill, Hilditch and Cherbuliez).

Herr List, of course, did not dare to tell the German landed aristocracy of this frightening consequence of industrial productive force for landed property. Hence he berates Ricardo, who disclosed such unpleasant truths, and ascribes to him the opposite view, that of the physiocrats, according to which land rent is nothing but a proof of the natural productive force of land, and falsifies him.

List:

"In general, since Adam Smith, the School has been unfortunate in its researches into the nature of rent. Ricardo, and following him Mill, McCulloch and others, hold that rent is paid for the *natural productivity* inherent in plots of land. Ricardo based a whole system on this view.... Since he considered only English conditions, he was misled into the erroneous view that these English ploughed fields and meadows, for the apparently natural productivity of which such fine rent is paid at the present time, have been the very same ploughed fields and meadows at all times" (p. 360).

Ricardo:

"If the surplus produce which land affords in the form of rent be an advantage, it is desirable that, every year, the machinery newly constructed should be *less efficient* than the old, as that would undoubtedly give a greater exchangeable value to the goods manufactured ... in the kingdom; and a rent would be paid to all those who possessed the most productive machinery" (*Des principes de l'économie politique,* etc., Paris, 1835, t. I, p. 77).

"Wealth increases most rapidly in those countries ... where through agricultural *improvements,* productions can be multiplied without any increase in the proportional quantity of labour, and where consequently the progress of rent is only gradual" (p. 81 et seq.).[a]

---

[a] Marx quoted these passages from List and Ricardo above (see pp. 12-13). In repeating the quotation from Ricardo, Marx translated the end differently.—*Ed.*

Hence, in relation to the higher nobility, Herr List does not dare to keep up his shadow play with "productive forces". He wants to lure this nobility with "exchange values" and therefore slanders the School of Ricardo, who neither judges land rent from the standpoint of productive force, nor judges the latter from the standpoint of the modern large-scale factory system.

Thus Herr List is doubly a liar. Nevertheless we must not do Herr List an injustice in this matter. In one large Württemberg factory (Köchlin, if we are not mistaken) the King of Württemberg[a] himself participates, having invested a large sum in it. In the Württemberg factories, and to a greater or lesser extent in those of Baden as well, the landed nobility plays an important role by holding shares. Here, therefore, the nobility participates monetarily in the "manufacturing force", not as landowners but as bourgeois and manufacturers themselves, and[b]...

...[24] "productive forces" and the "continuity and permanence of production" of a whole generation arises—the disguised Communist List teaches this as well—and is therefore also a hereditary feature of the generation *and not* of Messrs. the industrialists (see, for example, Bray[111]).

In England, high land rents were ensured for the landlords only through ruining the tenant-farmers and reducing the farm labourers to the level (of real beggars) of an Irish poverty. All this in spite of the various Corn Laws, and apart from the fact that the landlords in receipt of rent were often compelled to allow the tenant-farmers a remission of one-third to one-half of the rent. Since 1815, three various Corn Laws have been passed to improve the position of the tenant-farmers and encourage them. During this period, five parliamentary committees were appointed to establish the existence of the distressed state of agriculture and to investigate its causes. The continual ruin of the tenant-farmers, on the one hand, in spite of the total (full) exploitation of the farm labourers and the utmost possible reduction of their wages, and, on the other hand, the frequent necessity for the landowners to forego part of the rent, are themselves proof that not even in England—in spite of all its manufacturing industry—have high land rents been produced. For, from the economic point of view, it cannot be regarded as land rent when part of the costs of production,[112] by means of agreements and other circumstances lying outside the sphere of economics, is drawn into the pocket

---

[a] The reference is to Wilhelm I, King of Württemberg.—*Ed.*

[b] The text breaks off here, as the 23rd manuscript sheet is missing.—*Ed.*

of the landlord instead of that of the tenant-farmer. If the landowner himself cultivated his land, he would certainly take care not to enter part of the ordinary profit of working capital under the heading "land rent".

Writers of the 16th, 17th and even the first two-thirds of the 18th century, still regarded the export of grain by England as the main source of its wealth. The old English industry—the main branch of which was the woollen industry, and the less important branches of which processed mostly materials supplied by the main branch itself—was wholly *subordinated* to agriculture. Its chief raw material was the product of English agriculture. As a matter of course, therefore, this industry promoted agriculture. Later, when the factory system proper developed, already in a short space of time the necessity for customs duties on corn began to be felt. But they remained nominal. The rapid growth of the population, the abundance of fertile land which had yet to be made cultivable, the inventions, at first, of course, raised also the level of agriculture. It especially profited from the war against Napoleon, which established a regular system of prohibition for it. But 1815 revealed how little the "productive force" of agriculture had really increased. A general outcry arose among landowners and tenant-farmers, and the present Corn Laws were enacted.[113] It is in the nature of modern factory industry, firstly, to estrange industry from the native soil since it processes mainly raw materials from abroad and bases itself on foreign trade. It is in the nature of this industry [secondly] to cause the population to grow in a ratio which, under the system of private property, does not correspond to the exploitation of the soil. It is furthermore in its nature, if it gives rise to Corn Laws, as it has always done in Europe up to now, to convert the peasants into the very poorest proletarians through high rents and factory methods of exploiting landed property. If, on the other hand, it succeeds in preventing the passing of Corn Laws, it puts a mass of land out of cultivation, subjects the price of grain to external contingencies, and completely alienates the country [*entäussert das Land völlig*] by making its most essential means of subsistence dependent on trade, which undermines *landed property* as an independent source of property. This last feature is the aim of the Anti-Corn-Law League in England and the anti-rent movement in North America, for *land rent* is the economic expression of *landed property*. Therefore the Tories continually draw attention to the danger of England being made dependent for its means of subsistence on, for example, *Russia*.

Large-scale factory industry—of course, countries like North America which have a huge amount of land still to be brought under cultivation (and protective duties by no means increase the amount of land) do not count here—certainly has a tendency to *paralyse* the productive force of the soil, as soon as its exploitation has reached a certain level, just as, on the other hand, the conduct of agriculture on factory lines has a tendency to oust people and to convert all the land—of course, within certain limits—into pasture, so that cattle take the place of people.

Ricardo's theory of land rent, in a few words, amounts to the following:

Land rent adds nothing to the productivity of land. On the contrary, rising land rent is proof that the productive force of land is falling. It is in fact determined by the relation of the area of land suitable for cultivation to the number of the population and to the level of civilisation in general. The price of grain is determined by the cost of production on the least fertile land that has to be cultivated because of the needs of the population. If land of a poorer quality has to be resorted to, or if amounts of capital have to be applied with a lesser yield to the same piece of land, then the owner of the most fertile land sells his product as dearly as the peasant who has the worst. He pockets the difference between the cost of production on the best land and that on the most infertile. Thus, the less productive the land that is put into cultivation, or the less the yield from second and third amounts of capital applied to the same piece of land, in short, the more the relative productive force of the land decreases, the higher the land rent rises. The land made fruitful everywhere....[a]

IV. Herr List and Ferrier[b]

The book by *Ferrier, sous-inspecteur des douanes*[c] under Napoleon, *Du gouvernement considéré dans ses rapports avec le commerce*, Paris, 1805, is the work from which Herr List copied. In List's book there is not a single basic idea that has not been stated, and better stated, in Ferrier's book.

Ferrier was one of Napoleon's officials. He defended the Continental System. He does not speak about the *system of protection*

---

[a] The text of the fourth page of the last numbered sheet in Marx's manuscript breaks off here.—*Ed.*

[b] This chapter of the manuscript occupies four pages of an unnumbered sheet.—*Ed.*

[c] Sub-inspector of customs.—*Ed.*

but about the *prohibitive system*. He is far from making phrases about a *union* of all nations or *eternal peace* within the country. Nor, of course, has he any socialist phrases yet. We shall give a short extract from his book in order to throw light on this secret source of List's wisdom. Whereas Herr List falsifies *Louis Say* so as to be able to present him as his ally, nowhere, on the other hand, does he quote Ferrier, whom he has copied out everywhere. He wanted to lead the reader on a false trail.

———

We have already quoted Ferrier's judgment on Smith.[a] Ferrier still adheres to the old prohibitive system, but more honestly.

State Intervention. The Thrift of Nations

"There is a thrift and an extravagance (*prodigalité*) of nations, but a nation is extravagant or thrifty only in its relations with *other* peoples" (p. 143).

"It is untrue that the most profitable use of capital for the person who owns it is necessarily also the most profitable for industry.... The interest of the capitalists, far from coinciding with the general interest, is almost always in opposition to it" (pp. 168, 169).

"There is a thrift of nations, but it is very different from Smith's.... It consists in buying foreign products only in so far as they can be paid for by one's own products. Sometimes it consists in completely foregoing them" (pp. [174], 175).

Productive Forces and Exchange Value

"The principles of the thrift of nations which Smith laid down (set) are all based on the distinction between productive and unproductive labour.... This distinction is essentially incorrect. There is no unproductive labour" (p. 141).

"He" (Garnier) "saw in *silver* only the *value* of the silver, without thinking about its *property*, as silver, to make *circulation* more active and, consequently, to multiply the products of labour" (p. 18). "Therefore, when governments seek to prevent the outflow of money ... this is not on account of its *value* ..., but because the *value* that is received in exchange for it cannot have the same effect in circulation ..., because it cannot cause a new creation at each transition" (pp. 22, 23). "The word 'wealth', as applied to money that circulates as money, must be understood from the acts of reproduction that it facilitates ..., and in this sense a country enriches itself when it increases the quantity of its money, because with this increase of money all the *productive forces* of labour increase" (p. 71). "When it is said that a country can lay out (expend) an income of two milliards, ... what is meant is that the country has the *means*, with the aid of these two milliards, to support a circulation 10, 20, 30 times greater in values or, what is the same thing, that it can *produce* these values. It is these *means of production*, which the country owes to money, that are called wealth" (p. 22).

You see: Ferrier distinguishes the *exchange value* possessed by money from the *productive force* of money. Apart from the fact that

———

[a] See pp. 268-69 of this volume.—*Ed.*

in general he calls the means of production wealth, there was in any case nothing easier than to apply to all capital the distinction which he drew between the *value* and the *productive force* of money.

But Ferrier goes still farther, he defends the prohibitive system, in general on the grounds that it safeguards for the nations their *means of production*:

"Thus prohibitions are useful whenever they make it easier for nations to acquire the *means* to satisfy their needs.... I compare a nation which with its money buys abroad commodities it can make itself, although of poorer quality, with a gardener who, dissatisfied with the fruit he gathers, would buy juicier fruits from his neighbours, giving them his gardening tools in exchange" (p. 288). "Foreign trade is always profitable when it endeavours to enlarge *productive capital*. It is unprofitable when instead of multiplying capital it demands its alienation" (pp. 395-96).

Agriculture, Manufacture, Trade

"Should a government promote trade and factories in preference to agriculture? This question is still one of those on which governments and writers cannot agree" (p. 73).

"The progress of industry and trade is bound up with that of civilisation, the arts, the sciences, and shipping. A government, which can do almost nothing for agriculture, can do almost everything for industry. If a nation has habits or tastes capable of holding back its development, the government must use all its means to combat them" (p. 84).

"The true means of encouraging agriculture is the encouragement of manufactures" (p. 225). "Its domain" (that of industry, by which M. Ferrier means manufacturing industry) "is not limited, whether in its successes or in its means of improvement.... Far-reaching like imagination, and like imagination mobile and fruitful, its creative power has no limits other than those of the human mind itself, from which it daily receives fresh *eclat*" (p. 85).

"The true source of wealth for an agricultural-manufacturing nation is *reproduction* and labour. It must apply its capital to this end and be concerned to transport and sell its own commodities before it can engage in transporting and selling those of other nations" (p. 186). "This growth of man's wealth is to be ascribed primarily to internal trade, which long preceded the exchange of nation with nation" (p. 145). "According to Smith himself, of two capitals, one of which is invested in home trade and the other in foreign trade, the first gives the country's industry 24 times greater support and encouragement" (p. [145]-146).

But M. Ferrier at least understands that home trade cannot exist without foreign trade (loc. cit.).

"If some private persons import from England 50,000 pieces of velvet, they will make a great deal of money by this transaction and will be very well able to market their wares. But they reduce the home industry and put 10,000 workers out of work" (p. 170; cf. pp. 155, 156).

Like List, M. Ferrier draws attention to the difference between towns engaged in manufacture and trade and towns which only consume (p. 91), but in so doing he is at least honest enough to refer to Smith himself. He refers to the *Methuen Treaty*,[114] so dear to Herr List, and the subtlety of Smith's judgment of that treaty (p. 159). We have already seen how in general his judgment of Smith coincides almost word for word with List's. See also on *carrying trade* (p. 186 et passim).

The difference between Ferrier and List is that the former writes in support of an undertaking of world-historic importance—the Continental System, whereas the latter writes in support of a petty, weak-minded bourgeoisie.

The reader will admit that the whole of Herr List is contained in *nuce* in the extracts quoted from Ferrier. If, moreover, one adds the phrases he borrows from the development of political economy since Ferrier, then all that remains as his share is empty *idealising*, the productive force of which consists in words — and the clever hypocrisy of the German bourgeois striving for domination.

Written in March 1845

First published in Russian translation in the magazine *Voprosy Istorii K.P.S.S.* No. 12, 1971

Published from the manuscript

Published in English for the first time

congenial (p. 91), but in so judging he is at least modest enough to refer to Smith himself. He refers to the *Wealth of Nations*, as do we to Herr List and the similarity of Smith's judgment of List (note p. 129). We have already seen how in general his treatment of Smith coincides almost word for word with List's. See also on passing trade (p. 186 et passim).

The difference between Ferrier and Smith is that List is a former writer in support of an, and making of, world literate importance—the Continental System, whereas the latter writes in support of a petty weak-minded bourgeoisie.

The reader will admit that the whole of Herr List's economical man can the extracts quoted from Ferrier. If, moreover one adds the phrases he borrows from the development of political economy since Ferrier, then all that remains as his share is entirely excluding the productive forms of which consists in words—and the clever hypocrisy of the German bourgeois striving for domination.

Written in March 1845.

First published in human translation in the magazine Poverty from P.S.S. Nov 24, 1971

Published from the manuscript

Published in English for the first time

Frederick Engels

THE CONDITION
OF THE WORKING-CLASS
IN ENGLAND

FROM PERSONAL OBSERVATION
AND AUTHENTIC SOURCES[115]

Written September 1844 to March 1845

Published in Leipzig in 1845

Signed: *Frederick Engels*

Printed according to the text of the authorised English edition of 1892, checked with the German editions of 1845 and 1892

TO THE WORKING-CLASSES OF GREAT-BRITAIN [116]

Working Men!

To you I dedicate a work, in which I have tried to lay before my German Countrymen a faithful picture of your condition, of your sufferings and struggles, of your hopes and prospects. I have lived long enough amidst you to know something about your circumstances; I have devoted to their knowledge my most serious attention, I have studied the various official and non-official documents as far as I was able to get hold of them — I have not been satisfied with this, I wanted more than a mere *abstract* knowledge of·my subject, I wanted to see you in your own homes, to observe you in your every-day life, to chat with you on your condition and grievances, to witness your struggles against the social and political power of your oppressors. I have done so: I forsook the company and the dinner-parties, the port-wine and champaign of the middle-classes, and devoted my leisure-hours almost exclusively to the intercourse with plain Working-Men; I am both glad and proud of having done so. Glad, because thus I was induced to spend many a happy hour in obtaining a knowledge of the realities of life — many an hour, which else would have been wasted in fashionable talk and tiresome etiquette; proud, because thus I got an opportunity of doing justice to an oppressed and calumniated class of men who with all their faults and under all the disadvantages of their situation, yet command the respect of every one but an English money-monger; proud, too, because thus I was placed in a position to save the English people from the growing contempt which on the Continent has been the necessary consequence of the brutally selfish policy and general behaviour of your ruling middle-class.

Having, at the same time, ample opportunity to watch the middle-classes, your opponents, I soon came to the conclusion that you are right, perfectly right in expecting no support whatever from them. Their interest is diametrically opposed to yours, though they always will try to maintain the contrary and to make you believe in their most hearty sympathy with your fates. Their doings give them the lie. I hope to have collected more than sufficient evidence of the fact, that — be their words what they please — the middle-classes intend in reality nothing else but to enrich themselves by your labour while they can sell its produce, and to abandon you to starvation as soon as they cannot make a profit by this indirect trade in human flesh. What have they done to prove their professed good-will towards you? Have they ever paid any serious attention to your grievances? Have they done more than paying the expenses of half-a-dozen commissions of inquiry, whose voluminous reports are damned to ever-lasting slumber among heaps of waste paper on the shelves of the Home Office? Have they even done as much as to compile from those rotting blue-books a single readable book from which everybody might easily get some information on the condition of the great majority of "free-born Britons"? Not they indeed, those are things they do not like to speak of — they have left it to a foreigner to inform the civilised world of the degrading situation you have to live in.

A foreigner to *them*, not to *you*, I hope. Though my English may not be pure, yet, I hope, you will find it *plain* English. No working-man in England — nor in France either, by-the-by — ever treated me as a foreigner. With the greatest pleasure I observed you to be free from that blasting curse, national prejudice and national pride, which after all means nothing but *wholesale selfishness* — I observed you to sympathise with every one who earnestly applies his powers to human progress — may he be an Englishman or not — to admire every thing great and good, whether nursed on your native soil or not — I found you to be more than mere *English*men, members of a single, isolated nation, I found you to be *Men*, members of the great and universal family of Mankind, who know their interest and that of all the human race to be the same. And as such, as members of this Family of "One and Indivisible" Mankind, as Human Beings in the most emphatical meaning of the word, as such I, and many others on the Continent, hail your progress in every direction and wish you speedy success.

Die Lage

der

arbeitenden Klasse

in

England.

Nach eigner Anschauung und authentischen Quellen

von

Friedrich Engels.

Leipzig.
Druck und Verlag von Otto Wigand.
1845.

Cover of the first edition of *The Condition of the Working-Class in England*

Go on then, as you have done hitherto. Much remains to be undergone; be firm, be undaunted — your success is certain, and no step you will have to take in your onward march, will be lost to our common cause, the cause of Humanity!

Barmen (Rhenan Prussia)
March 15th, 1845

Frederick Engels

Preface[117]

The book prefaced by the following pages treats of a subject which I originally intended to deal with in a single chapter of a more comprehensive work on the social history of England.[118] However, the importance of that subject soon made it necessary for me to investigate it separately.

The condition of the working-class is the real basis and point of departure of all social movements of the present because it is the highest and most unconcealed pinnacle of the social misery existing in our day. French and German working-class Communism are its direct, Fourierism and English Socialism, as well as the Communism of the German educated bourgeoisie, are its indirect products. A knowledge of proletarian conditions is absolutely necessary to be able to provide solid ground for socialist theories, on the one hand, and for judgments about their right to exist, on the other; and to put an end to all sentimental dreams and fancies pro and con. But proletarian conditions exist in their *classical form,* in their perfection, only in the British Empire, particularly in England proper. Besides, only in England has the necessary material been so completely collected and put on record by official enquiries as is essential for any in the least exhaustive presentation of the subject.

Twenty-one months I had the opportunity to become acquainted with the English proletariat, its strivings, its sorrows and its joys, to see them from near, from personal observation and personal intercourse, and at the same time to supplement my observations by recourse to the requisite authentic sources. What I have seen, heard and read has been worked up in the present book. I am prepared to see not only my standpoint attacked in many quarters but also the facts I have cited, particularly when the book gets into the hands of the English. I know equally well that here and there I may be proved wrong in some particular of no importance, something that in view of the comprehensive nature of the subject and its far-reaching assumptions even an Englishman might be unable to avoid; so much the more so since even in England there exists as yet not a single piece of writing which, like mine, takes up *all* the workers. But without a moment's hesitation I challenge the English bourgeoisie to prove that even in a single instance of any consequence for the exposition of my point of view as a whole I have been guilty of any inaccuracy, and to prove it by data as authentic as mine.

A description of the classical form which the conditions of existence of the proletariat have assumed in Britain is very important, particularly for Germany and precisely at the present moment. German Socialism and Communism have proceeded, more than any other, from theoretical premises; we German theoreticians still knew much too little of the real world to be driven directly by the real relations to reforms of this "bad reality". At any rate almost none of the avowed champions of such reforms arrived at Communism otherwise than by way of the Feuerbachian dissolution of Hegelian speculation. The real conditions of the life of the proletariat are so little known among us that even the well-meaning "societies for the uplift of the working-classes",[119] in which our bourgeoisie is now mistreating the social question, constantly start out from the most ridiculous and preposterous judgments concerning the condition of the workers. We Germans more than anybody else stand in need of a knowledge of the facts concerning this question. And while the conditions of existence of Germany's proletariat have not assumed the classical form that they have in England, we nevertheless have, at bottom, the same social order, which sooner or later must necessarily reach the same degree of acuteness as it has already attained across the North Sea, unless the intelligence of the nation brings about in time the adoption of measures that will provide a new basis for the whole social system. The root-causes whose effect in England has been the misery and oppression of the proletariat exist also in Germany and in the long run must engender the same results. In the meantime, however, the established fact of wretched conditions in *England* will impel us to establish also the fact of wretched conditions in *Germany* and will provide us with a yardstick wherewith to measure their extent and the magnitude of the danger — brought to light by the Silesian and Bohemian disturbances[120]—which directly threatens the tranquillity of Germany from that quarter.

Finally, there are still two remarks I wish to make. Firstly, that I have used the word *Mittelklasse* all along in the sense of the English word middle-class (or middle-classes, as is said almost always). Like the French word *bourgeoisie* it means the possessing class, specifically that possessing class which is differentiated from the so-called aristocracy—the class which in France and England is directly and in Germany, figuring as "public opinion", indirectly in possession of political power. Similarly, I have continually used the expressions working-men (*Arbeiter*) and proletarians, working-class, propertyless class and proletariat as equivalents. Secondly, that in the case of most of the quotations I have indicated the party to which the respective authors belong, because in nearly every instance the Liberals try to emphasise the distress in the rural areas and to argue away that which exists in the factory districts, while the Conservatives, conversely, acknowledge the misery in the factory districts but disclaim any knowledge of it in the agricultural areas. For the same reason, whenever I lacked official documents for describing the condition of the industrial workers, I always preferred to present proof from *Liberal* sources in order to defeat the liberal bourgeoisie by casting their own words in their teeth. I cited Tories or Chartists in my support only when I could confirm their correctness from personal observation or was convinced of the truthfulness of the facts quoted because of the personal or literary reputation of the authorities I referred to.

Barmen, March 15, 1845

F. Engels

TO THE WORKING CLASSES

OF

GREAT-BRITAIN.

Working Men!

To you I dedicate a work, in which I have tried to lay before my German Countrymen a faithful picture of your condition, of your sufferings and struggles, of your hopes and prospects. I have lived long enough amidst you to know something about your circumstances; I have devoted to their knowledge my most serious attention, I have studied the various official and non-official documents as far as I was able to get hold of them — I have not been satisfied with this, I wanted more than a mere *abstract* knowledge of my subject, I wanted to see you in your own homes, to observe you in your every-day life, to chat with you on your condition and grievances, to witness your struggles against the social and political power of your oppressors. I have done so: I forsook the company and the dinner-parties, the port-wine and champaign of the middle-classes, and devoted my leisure-hours almost exclusively to the intercourse with plain Working Men; I am both glad and proud of having done so. Glad, because thus I was induced to spend many a happy hour in obtaining a knowledge of the realities of life — many an hour,

First page of Engels' address
To the Working-Classes of Great-Britain

INTRODUCTION

The history of the proletariat[a] in England begins with the second half of the last century, with the invention of the steam-engine and of machinery for working cotton. These inventions gave rise, as is well known, to an industrial revolution, a revolution which altered the whole civil society; one, the historical importance of which is only now beginning to be recognised. England is the classic soil of this transformation, which was all the mightier, the more silently it proceeded; and England is, therefore, the classic land of its chief product also, the proletariat. Only in England can the proletariat be studied in all its relations and from all sides.

We have not, here and now, to deal with the history of this revolution, nor with its vast importance for the present and the future. Such a delineation must be reserved for a future, more comprehensive work. For the moment, we must limit ourselves to the little that is necessary for understanding the facts that follow, for comprehending the present state of the English proletariat.

Before the introduction of machinery, the spinning and weaving of raw materials was carried on in the working-man's home. Wife and daughter spun the yarn that the father wove or that they sold, if he did not work it up himself. These weaver families lived in the country in the neighbourhood of the towns, and could get on fairly well with their wages, because the home market was almost the only one,[b] and the crushing power of competition that came

---

[a] The German editions of 1845 and 1892 have "the working-class".—*Ed.*

[b] The German editions of 1845 and 1892 enlarge on this phrase: "because the home market was still the decisive one as regards the demand for fabrics and almost the only one."—*Ed.*

later, with the conquest of foreign markets and the extension of trade, did not yet press upon wages. There was, further, a constant increase in the demand for the home market, keeping pace with the slow increase in population and employing all the workers; and there was also- the impossibility of vigorous competition of the workers among themselves, consequent upon the rural dispersion of their homes. So it was that the weaver was usually in a position to lay by something, and rent a little piece of land, that he cultivated in his leisure hours, of which he had as many as he chose to take, since he could weave whenever and as long as he pleased. True, he was a bad farmer and managed his land inefficiently, often obtaining but poor crops; nevertheless, he was no proletarian, he had a stake in the country, he was permanently settled, and stood one step higher in society than the English workman of today.

So the workers vegetated throughout a passably comfortable existence, leading a righteous and peaceful life in all piety and probity; and their material position was far better than that of their successors. They did not need to overwork; they did no more than they chose to do, and yet earned what they needed. They had leisure for healthful work in garden or field, work which, in itself, was recreation for them, and they could take part besides in the recreations and games of their neighbours, and all these games—bowling, cricket,[a] football, etc., contributed to their physical health and vigour. They were, for the most part, strong, well-built people, in whose physique little or no difference from that of their peasant neighbours was discoverable. Their children grew up in the fresh country air, and, if they could help their parents at work, it was only occasionally; while of eight or twelve hours work for them there was no question.

What the moral and intellectual character of this class was may be guessed. Shut off from the towns, which they never entered, their yarn and woven stuff being delivered to travelling agents for payment of wages—so shut off that old people who lived quite in the neighbourhood of the town never went thither until they were robbed of their trade by the introduction of machinery and obliged to look about them in the towns for work—the weavers stood upon the moral and intellectual plane of the yeomen with whom they were usually immediately connected through their little holdings. They regarded their squire, the greatest landholder of

---

[a] The word "cricket" does not occur in the German editions of 1845 and 1892.—*Ed.*

the region, as their natural superior; they asked advice of him, laid their small disputes before him for settlement, and gave him all honour, as this patriarchal relation involved. They were "respectable" people, good husbands and fathers, led moral lives because they had no temptation to be immoral, there being no groggeries or low houses in their vicinity, and because the host, at whose inn they now and then quenched their thirst, was also a respectable man, usually a large tenant-farmer who took pride in his good order, good beer, and early hours. They had their children the whole day at home, and brought them up in obedience and the fear of God; the patriarchal relationship remained undisturbed so long as the children were unmarried. The young people grew up in idyllic simplicity and intimacy with their playmates until they married; and even though sexual intercourse before marriage almost unfailingly took place, this happened only when the moral obligation of marriage was recognised on both sides, and a subsequent wedding made everything good. In short, the English industrial workers of those days lived and thought after the fashion still to be found here and there in Germany, in retirement and seclusion, without mental activity and without violent fluctuations in their position in life. They could rarely read and far more rarely write; went regularly to church, never talked politics, never conspired, never thought, delighted in physical exercises, listened with inherited reverence when the Bible was read, and were, in their unquestioning humility, exceedingly well-disposed towards the "superior" classes. But intellectually, they were dead; lived only for their petty, private interest, for their looms and gardens, and knew nothing of the mighty movement which, beyond their horizon, was sweeping through mankind. They were comfortable in their silent vegetation, and but for the industrial revolution they would never have emerged from this existence, which, cosily romantic as it was, was nevertheless not worthy of human beings. In truth, they were not human beings; they were merely toiling machines in the service of the few aristocrats who had guided history down to that time. The industrial revolution has simply carried this out to its logical end by making the workers machines pure and simple, taking from them the last trace of independent activity, and so forcing them to think and demand a position worthy of men. As in France politics, so in England manufacture and the movement of civil society in general drew into the whirl of history the last classes which had remained sunk in apathetic indifference to the universal interests of mankind.

The first invention which gave rise to a radical change in the state of the English workers was the jenny, invented in the year 1764 by a weaver, James Hargreaves, of Stanhill,[a] near Blackburn, in North Lancashire. This machine was the rough beginning of the later invented mule, and was moved by hand. Instead of one spindle like the ordinary spinning-wheel, it carried sixteen or eighteen manipulated by a single workman. This invention made it possible to deliver more yarn than heretofore. Whereas, though one weaver had employed three spinners, there had never been enough yarn, and the weaver had often been obliged to wait for it, there was now more yarn to be had than could be woven by the available workers. The demand for woven goods, already increasing, rose yet more in consequence of the cheapness of these goods, which cheapness, in turn, was the outcome of the diminished cost of producing the yarn. More weavers were needed, and weavers' wages rose. Now that the weaver could earn more at his loom, he gradually abandoned his farming, and gave his whole time to weaving. At that time a family of four grown persons and two children (who were set to spooling) could earn, with eight[b] hours' daily work, four pounds sterling[c] in a week, and often more if trade was good and work pressed. It happened often enough that a single weaver earned two pounds a week at his loom. By degrees the class of farming weavers wholly disappeared, and was merged in the newly arising class of weavers who lived wholly upon wages, had no property whatever, not even the pretended property of a holding, and so became working-men,[d] proletarians. Moreover, the old relation between spinner and weaver was destroyed. Hitherto, so far as this had been possible, yarn had been spun and woven under one roof. Now that the jenny as well as the loom required a strong hand, men began to spin, and whole families lived by spinning, while others laid the antiquated, superseded spinning-wheel aside; and, if they had not means of purchasing a jenny, were forced to live upon the wages of the father alone. Thus began with spinning and weaving that division of labour which has since been so infinitely perfected.

---

[a] In the editions which appeared during Engels' lifetime the name of this place was given wrongly as Standhill (as in Ure's book *The Cotton Manufacture of Great Britain*).— *Ed*.

[b] The German editions of 1845 and 1892 have "ten".— *Ed*.

[c] After this the German editions of 1845 and 1892 have "(28 Prussian talers)."— *Ed*.

[d] The German editions of 1845 and 1892 give this word in English in brackets after the word "proletarians".— *Ed*.

While the industrial proletariat was thus developing with the first still very imperfect machine, the same machine gave rise to the agricultural proletariat. There had, hitherto, been a vast number of small landowners, yeomen, who had vegetated in the same unthinking quiet as their neighbours, the farming weavers. They cultivated their scraps of land quite after the ancient and inefficient fashion of their ancestors, and opposed every change with the obstinacy peculiar to such creatures of habit, after remaining stationary from generation to generation. Among them were many small holders also, not tenants in the present sense of the word, but people who had their land handed down from their fathers, either by hereditary lease, or by force of ancient custom, and had hitherto held it as securely as if it had actually been their own property. When the industrial workers withdrew from agriculture, a great number of small holdings fell idle, and upon these the new class of large tenants established themselves, tenants-at-will,[a] holding fifty, one hundred, two hundred or more acres,[b] liable to be turned out at the end of the year, but able by improved tillage and larger farming to increase the yield of the land. They could sell their produce more cheaply than the yeoman, for whom nothing remained when his farm no longer supported him but to sell it, procure a jenny or a loom, or take service as an agricultural labourer in the employ of a large farmer. His inherited slowness and the inefficient methods of cultivation bequeathed by his ancestors, and above which he could not rise, left him no alternative when forced to compete with men who managed their holdings on sounder principles and with all the advantages bestowed by farming on a large scale and the investment of capital for the improvement of the soil.

Meanwhile, the industrial movement did not stop here. Single capitalists began to set up spinning jennies in great buildings and to use water-power for driving them, so placing themselves in a position to diminish the number of workers, and sell their yarn more cheaply than single spinners could do who moved their own machines by hand. There were constant improvements in the jenny, so that machines continually became antiquated, and must be altered or even laid aside; and though the capitalists could hold out by the application of water-power even with the old machinery, for the single spinner this was impossible. And the factory

---

[a] The German editions of 1845 and 1892 have this expression in English.—*Ed*.

[b] The German editions of 1845 and 1892 have "Morgen" instead of "acres". One Morgen is rather less than 2/3 of an acre.—*Ed*.

system, the beginning of which was thus made, received a fresh extension in 1767, through the spinning throstle invented by Richard Arkwright, a barber, in Preston, in North Lancashire. After the steam-engine, this is the most important mechanical invention of the 18th century.[a] It was calculated from the beginning for mechanical motive power, and was based upon wholly new principles. By the combination of the peculiarities of the jenny and throstle, Samuel Crompton, of Firwood, Lancashire, contrived the mule in 1785,[b] and as Arkwright invented the carding engine, and preparatory ("slubbing and roving")[c] frames about the same time, the factory system became the prevailing one for the spinning of cotton. By means of trifling modifications these machines were gradually adapted to the spinning[d] of flax, and so to the superseding of hand-work here, too. But even then, the end was not yet. In the closing years of the last century, Dr. Cartwright, a country parson, had invented the power-loom, and about 1804 had so far perfected it, that it could successfully compete with the hand-weaver; and all this machinery was made doubly important by James Watt's steam-engine, invented in 1764 and used for supplying motive power for spinning since 1785.

With these inventions, since improved from year to year, the victory of machine-work over hand-work in the chief branches of English industry was won; and the history of the latter from that time forward simply relates how the hand-workers have been driven by machinery from one position after another. The consequences of this were, on the one hand, a rapid fall in price of all manufactured commodities, prosperity of commerce and manufacture, the conquest of nearly all the unprotected foreign markets, the sudden multiplication of capital and national wealth; on the other hand, a still more rapid multiplication of the proletariat, the destruction of all property-holding and of all security of employment for the working-class, demoralisation, political excitement, and all those facts so highly repugnant to Englishmen in comfortable circumstances, which we shall have to consider in the following pages. Having already seen what a transformation in the social condition of the lower classes a single

----

[a] The German editions of 1845 and 1892 have here "usually called Kettenstuhl in German" to explain the word spinning throstle given above in English.—*Ed*.

[b] 1779 according to more precise data.—*Ed*.

[c] The German editions of 1845 and 1892 have no words given in brackets.—*Ed*.

[d] The German editions of 1845 and 1892 have "of wool and later (in the first decade of the present century) also" after "to the spinning".—*Ed*.

such clumsy machine as the jenny had wrought, there is no cause for surprise as to that which a complete and interdependent system of finely adjusted machinery has brought about, machinery which receives raw material and turns out woven goods.

Meanwhile, let us trace the development of English manufacture* somewhat more minutely, beginning with[a] the cotton industry. In the years 1771-1775, there were annually imported into England rather less than 5,000,000 pounds of raw cotton; in the year 1841 there were imported 528,000,000 pounds, and the import for 1844 will reach at least 600,000,000 pounds. In 1834 England exported 556,000,000 yards of woven cotton goods, 76,500,000 pounds of cotton yarn, and cotton hosiery to the value of £1,200,000. In the same year over 8,000,000 mule spindles were at work, 110,000 power and 250,000 hand-looms, throstle spindles not included, in the service of the cotton industry; and, according to McCulloch's reckoning,[b] nearly a million and a half human beings were supported by this branch,[c] of whom but 220,000 worked in the mills; the power used in these mills was steam, equivalent to 33,000 horse-power, and water, equivalent to 11,000 horse-power. At present these figures are far from adequate, and it may be safely assumed that, in the year 1845, the power and number of the machines and the number of the workers is greater by one-half than it was in 1834. The chief centre of this industry is Lancashire, where it originated; it has thoroughly revolutionised this county, converting it from an obscure, ill-cultivated swamp into a busy, lively region, multiplying its population tenfold in eighty years, and causing giant cities such as Liverpool and Manchester, containing together 700,000 inhabitants, and their neighbouring towns, Bolton with 60,000, Rochdale with 75,000, Oldham with 50,000, Preston with 60,000, Ashton and Stalybridge with 40,000, and a whole list of other manufacturing towns to spring up as if by a magic touch. The history of South Lancashire contains some of the greatest marvels of modern

---

* According to Porter's *Progress of the Nation*, London, 1836, Vol. I; 1838, Vol. II; 1843, Vol. III (official data), and other sources, chiefly official.— *Note by Engels*.

(1892) The historical outline of the industrial revolution given above is not exact in certain details; but in 1843-44 no better sources were available.— *Added by Engels in the German edition of 1892*.

---

[a] Here the German editions of 1845 and 1892 have "its main branch".—*Ed.*
[b] J. R. McCulloch, *A   Dictionary of Commerce.—Ed.*
[c] The German editions of 1845 and 1892 have here "directly or indirectly".—*Ed.*

times, yet no one ever mentions them and all these miracles are the product of the cotton industry. Glasgow, too, the centre[a] for the cotton district of Scotland, for Lanarkshire and Renfrewshire, has increased in population from 30,000 to 300,000 since the introduction of the industry. The hosiery manufacture of Nottingham and Derby also received one fresh impulse from the lower price of yarn, and a second one from an improvement of the stocking loom, by means of which two stockings could be woven at once. The manufacture of lace, too, became an important branch of industry after the invention of the lace machine in 1777; soon after that date Lindley invented the point-net machine, and in 1809 Heathcoat invented the bobbin-net machine, in consequence of which the production of lace was greatly simplified, and the demand increased proportionately in consequence of the diminished cost, so that now, at least 200,000 persons are supported by this industry. Its chief centres are Nottingham, Leicester, and the West of England, Wiltshire, Devonshire, etc. A corresponding extension has taken place in the branches dependent upon the cotton industry, in dyeing, bleaching, and printing. Bleaching by the application of chlorine in place of the oxygen of the atmosphere, dyeing and printing by the rapid development of chemistry, and printing by a series of most brilliant mechanical inventions, received a yet greater advance which, with the extension of these branches caused by the growth of the cotton industry, raised them to a previously unknown degree of prosperity.

The same activity manifested itself in the manufacture of wool. This had hitherto been the leading department of English industry, but the quantities formerly produced are as nothing in comparison with that which is now manufactured. In 1782 the whole wool crop of the preceding three years lay unused for want of workers, and would have continued so to lie if the newly invented machinery had not come to its assistance and spun it. The adaptation of this machinery to the spinning of wool was most successfully accomplished. Then began the same sudden development in the wool districts which we have already seen in the cotton districts. In 1738 there were 75,000 pieces of woollen cloth produced in the West Riding of Yorkshire; in 1817 there were 490,000 pieces, and so rapid was the extension of the industry that in 1834, 450,000 more pieces were produced[b] than

---

[a] The German editions of 1845 and 1892 have "a second centre".—*Ed.*

[b] The German editions of 1845 and 1892 have "exported" instead of "produced".—*Ed.*

in 1825. In 1801, 101,000,000 pounds of wool (7,000,000 pounds of. it imported) were worked up; in 1835, 180,000,000 pounds were worked up, of which 42,000,000 pounds were imported. The principal centre of this industry is the West Riding of Yorkshire, where, especially at Bradford, long English wool is converted into worsted yarns, etc., while in the other cities, Leeds, Halifax, Huddersfield, etc., short wool is converted into hard-spun yarn and cloth. Then come the adjacent part of Lancashire, the region of Rochdale, where in addition to the cotton industry much flannel is produced, and the West of England, which supplies the finest cloths. Here also the growth of population is worthy of observation:

		in 1801	and	in 1831	
Bradford	contained	29,000,	„	77,000	inhabitants
Halifax	„	63,000,	„	110,000	„
Huddersfield	„	15,000,	„	34,000	„
Leeds	„	53,000,	„	123,000	„
And the whole West Riding	„	564,000,	„	980,000	„

A population which, since 1831, must have increased at least 20 to 25 per cent further. In 1835 the spinning of wool employed in the United Kingdom 1,313 mills, with 71,300 workers, these last being but a small portion of the multitude who are supported directly or indirectly by the manufacture of wool, and excluding nearly all weavers.

Progress in the linen trade developed later, because the nature of the raw material made the application of spinning machinery very difficult. Attempts had been made in the last years of the last century in Scotland, but the Frenchman Girard, who introduced flax spinning in 1810, was the first who succeeded practically, and even Girard's machines first attained on British soil the importance they deserved by means of improvements which they underwent in England, and of their universal application in Leeds, Dundee, and Belfast. From this time' the British linen trade rapidly extended. In 1814, 3,000 tons* of flax were imported[a]; in 1833, nearly 19,000 tons of flax and 3,400 tons of hemp. The export of Irish linen to Great Britain rose from 32,000,000 yards in 1800 to 53,000,000 in 1825, of which a large part was

* The English ton weighs 2,240 English pounds, almost 1,000 kilogrammes.—*Note by Engels to the 1845 German edition* (the last three words being. added in the 1892 German edition—*Ed.*).

[a] The German editions of 1845 and 1892 have here "to Dundee".—*Ed.*

re-exported. The export of English and Scotch woven linen goods rose from 24,000,000 yards in 1820 to 51,000,000 yards in 1833. The number of flax spinning establishments in 1835 was 347, employing 33,000 workers, of which one-half were in the South of Scotland, more than 60 in the West Riding of Yorkshire, Leeds, and its environs, 25 in Belfast, Ireland, and the rest in Dorset and Lancashire. Weaving is carried on in the South of Scotland, here and there in England, but principally in Ireland.

With like success did the English turn their attention to the manufacture of silk. Raw material was imported from Southern Europe and Asia ready spun, and the chief labour lay in the twisting of fine threads.[a] Until 1824 the heavy import duty, four shillings per pound on raw material, greatly retarded the development of the English silk industry, while only the markets of England and the Colonies were protected for it. In that year the duty was reduced to one penny, and the number of mills at once largely increased. In a single year the number of throwing spindles rose from 780,000 to 1,180,000; and, although the commercial crisis of 1825 crippled this branch of industry for the moment, yet in 1827 more was produced than ever, the mechanical skill and experience of the English having secured their twisting machinery the supremacy over the awkward devices of their competitors. In 1835 the British Empire possessed 263 twisting mills, employing 30,000 workers, located chiefly in Cheshire, in Macclesfield, Congleton, and the surrounding districts, and in Manchester and Somersetshire. Besides these, there are numerous mills for working up waste, from which a peculiar article known as spun silk[b] is manufactured, with which the English supply even the Paris and Lyons weavers. The weaving of the silk so twisted and spun is carried on in Paisley and elsewhere in Scotland, and in Spitalfields, London, but also in Manchester and elsewhere.

Nor is the gigantic advance achieved in English manufacture since 1760 restricted to the production of clothing materials. The impulse, once given, was communicated to all branches of industrial activity, and a multitude of inventions wholly unrelated to those here cited received double importance from the fact that they were made in the midst of the universal movement. But as soon as

---

[a] The German editions of 1845 and 1892 have here in brackets the German word "*Tramieren*".—*Ed.*

[b] The German editions of 1845 and 1892 give this English term in brackets.—*Ed.*

the immeasurable importance of mechanical power was practically demonstrated, every energy was concentrated in the effort to exploit this power in all directions, and to exploit it in the interest of individual inventors and manufacturers; and the demand for machinery, fuel, and materials called a mass of workers and a number of trades into redoubled activity. The steam-engine first gave importance to the broad coal-fields of England; the production of machinery began now for the first time, and with it arose a new interest in the iron mines which supplied raw material for it. The increased consumption of wool stimulated English sheep breeding, and the growing importation of wool, flax, and silk called forth an extension of the British ocean carrying trade. Greatest of all was the growth of production of iron. The rich iron deposits of the English hills had hitherto been little developed; iron had always been smelted by means of charcoal, which became gradually more expensive[a] as agriculture improved and forests were cut away. The beginning of the use of coke[b] in iron smelting had been made in the last century, and in 1780 a new method was invented of converting into available wrought-iron coke-smelted iron, which up to that time had been convertible into cast-iron only. This process, known as "puddling", consisted in withdrawing the carbon which had mixed with the iron during the process of smelting, and opened a wholly new field for the production of English iron. Smelting furnaces were built fifty times larger than before, the process of smelting was simplified by the introduction of hot blasts, and iron could thus be produced so cheaply that a multitude of objects which had before been made of stone or wood were now made of iron.

In 1788, Thomas Paine, the famous democrat, built in Yorkshire the first iron bridge,[121] which was followed by a great number of others, so that now nearly all bridges, especially for railroad traffic, are built of cast-iron, while in London itself a bridge across the Thames, the Southwark bridge, has been built of this material. Iron pillars, supports for machinery, etc., are universally used, and since the introduction of gas-lighting and railroads, new outlets for English iron products are opened. Nails and screws gradually came to be made by machinery. Huntsman, a Sheffielder, discovered in 1740 a method for casting steel, by which much labour was saved, and the production of wholly new

---

[a] The German editions of 1845 and 1892 have here "and scarce".—*Ed.*
[b] The German editions of 1845 and 1892 have the English word in brackets after its German equivalent.—*Ed.*

cheap goods rendered practicable; and through the greater purity of the material placed at its disposal, and the more perfect tools, new machinery and minute division of labour, the metal trade of England now first attained importance. The population of Birmingham grew from 73,000 in 1801 to 200,000 in 1844; that of Sheffield from 46,000 in 1801 to 110,000 in 1844, and the consumption of coal in the latter city alone reached in 1836, 515,000 tons. In 1805 there were exported 4,300 tons of iron products and 4,600 tons of pig-iron; in 1834, 16,200 tons of iron products and 107,000 tons of pig-iron, while the whole iron product, reaching in 1740 but 17,000 tons, had risen in 1834 to nearly 700,000 tons. The smelting of pig-iron alone consumes yearly more than 3,000,000 tons of coal,[122] and the importance which coal-mining has attained in the course of the last 60 years can scarcely be conceived. All the English and Scotch deposits are now worked, and the mines of Northumberland and Durham alone yield annually more than 5,000,000 tons for shipping, and employ from 40 to 50,000 men. According to the *Durham Chronicle*, there were worked in these two counties:

In 1753, 14 mines; in 1800, 40 mines; in 1836, 76 mines; in 1843, 130 mines.

Moreover, all mines are now much more energetically worked than formerly. A similarly increased activity was applied to the working of tin, copper, and lead, and alongside of the extension of glass manufacture arose a new branch of industry in the production of pottery, rendered important by the efforts of Josiah Wedgwood, about 1763. This inventor placed the whole manufacture of stoneware on a scientific basis, introduced better taste, and founded the potteries of North Staffordshire, a district of eight English miles square, which, formerly a desert waste, is now sown with works and dwellings, and supports more than 60,000 people.

Into this universal whirl of activity everything was drawn. Agriculture made a corresponding advance. Not only did landed property pass, as we have already seen, into the hands of new owners and cultivators, agriculture was affected in still another way. The great holders applied capital to the improvement of the soil, tore down needless fences, drained, manured, employed better tools, and applied a rotation of crops.[a] The progress of science came to their assistance also; Sir Humphry Davy applied chemistry to agriculture with success, and the development of

---

[a] The German editions of 1845 and 1892 have in brackets the English term "cropping by rotation" after the corresponding German term.—*Ed.*

mechanical science bestowed a multitude of advantages upon the large farmer. Further, in consequence of the increase of population, the demand for agricultural products increased in such measure that from 1760 to 1834, 6,840,540 acres of waste land were reclaimed; and, in spite of this, England was transformed from a grain exporting to a grain importing country.

The same activity was developed in the establishment of communication. From 1818 to 1829, there were built in England and Wales, 1,000 English miles of roadway of the width prescribed by law, 60 feet, and nearly all the old roads were reconstructed on the new system of McAdam. In Scotland, the Department of Public Works built since 1803 nearly 900 miles of roadway and more than 1,000 bridges, by which the population of the Highlands was suddenly placed within reach of civilisation. The Highlanders had hitherto been chiefly poachers and smugglers; they now became farmers[a] and hand-workers. And, though Gaelic schools were organised for the purpose of maintaining the Gaelic language, yet Gaelic-Celtic customs and speech are rapidly vanishing before the approach of English civilisation. So, too, in Ireland; between the counties of Cork, Limerick, and Kerry, lay hitherto a wilderness wholly without passable roads, and serving, by reason of its inaccessibility, as the refuge of all criminals and the chief protection of the Celtic Irish nationality in the South of Ireland. It has now been cut through by public roads, and civilisation has thus gained admission even to this savage region. The whole British Empire, and especially England, which, sixty years ago, had as bad roads as Germany or France then had, is now covered by a network of the finest roadways; and these, too, like almost everything else in England, are the work of private enterprise, the State having done very little in this direction.

Before 1755 England possessed almost no canals. In that year a canal was built in Lancashire from Sankey Brook to St. Helen's; and in 1759, James Brindley built the first important one, the Duke of Bridgewater's Canal from Manchester and the coal-mines of the district to the mouth of the Mersey passing, near Barton, by aqueduct, over the river Irwell. From this achievement dates the canal building of England, to which Brindley first gave importance. Canals were now built, and rivers made navigable in all directions. In England alone, there are 2,200 miles of canals and 1,800 miles of navigable river. In Scotland, the Caledonian Canal was cut directly across the country, and in Ireland several canals

---

[a] The German editions of 1845 and 1892 have "industrious farmers".—*Ed.*

were built. These improvements, too, like the railroads and roadways, are nearly all the work of private individuals and companies.

The railroads have been only recently built. The first great one was opened from Liverpool to Manchester in 1830, since which all the great cities have been connected by rail. London with Southampton, Brighton, Dover, Colchester, Exeter,[a] and Birmingham; Birmingham with Gloucester, Liverpool, Lancaster (via Newton and Wigan, and via Manchester and Bolton); also with Leeds (via Manchester and Halifax, and via Leicester, Derby, and Sheffield); Leeds with Hull and Newcastle (via York). There are also many minor lines building or projected, which will soon make it possible to travel from Edinburgh to London in one day.

As it had transformed the means of communication by land, so did the introduction of steam revolutionise travel by sea. The first steamboat was launched in 1807, in the Hudson, in North America; the first in the British Empire, in 1811, on the Clyde. Since then, more than 600 have been built in England; and in 1836 more than 500 were plying to and from British ports.

Such, in brief, is the history of English industrial development in the past sixty years, a history which has no counterpart in the annals of humanity. Sixty, eighty years ago, England was a country like every other, with small towns, few and simple industries, and a thin but *proportionally* large agricultural population. Today it is a country like *no* other, with a capital of two and a half million inhabitants; with vast manufacturing cities; with an industry that supplies the world, and produces almost everything by means of the most complex machinery; with an industrious, intelligent, dense population, of which two-thirds are employed in trade and commerce,[b] and composed of classes wholly different; forming, in fact, with other customs and other needs, a different nation from the England of those days. The industrial revolution is of the same importance for England as the political revolution for France, and the philosophical revolution for Germany; and the difference between England in 1760 and in 1844 is at least as great as that between France under the *ancien régime* and during the revolution of July. But the mightiest result of this industrial transformation is the English proletariat.

---

[a] The German editions of 1845 and 1892 have "Colchester, Cambridge, Exeter (via Bristol)".— *Ed*.

[b] In the German editions of 1845 and 1892 the words "and commerce" do not occur.— *Ed*.

We have already seen how the proletariat was called into
existence by the introduction of machinery. The rapid extension
of manufacture demanded hands, wages rose, and troops of
workmen migrated from the agricultural districts to the towns.
Population multiplied enormously, and nearly all the increase took
place in the proletariat. Further, Ireland had entered upon an
orderly development only since the beginning of the eighteenth
century. There, too, the population, more than decimated by
English cruelty in earlier disturbances, now rapidly multiplied,
especially after the advance in manufacture began to draw masses
of Irishmen towards England. Thus arose the great manufacturing
and commercial cities of the British Empire, in which at least
three-fourths of the population belong to the working-class, while
the lower middle-class consists only of small shop-keepers, and
very very few handicraftsmen. For, though the rising manufacture
first attained importance by transforming tools into machines,
work-rooms into factories, and consequently, the toiling lower
middle-class into the toiling proletariat, and the former large
merchants into manufacturers, though the lower middle-class was
thus early crushed out, and the population reduced to the two
opposing elements, workers and capitalists, this happened outside
of the domain of manufacture proper, in the province of handicraft and retail trade as well. In the place of the former masters
and apprentices, came great capitalists and working-men who had
no prospect of rising above their class. Hand-work was carried on
after the fashion of factory work, the division of labour was strictly
applied, and small employers who could not compete with great
establishments were forced down into the proletariat. At the same
time the destruction of the former organisation of hand-work, and
the disappearance of the lower middle-class deprived the working-
man of all possibility of rising into the middle-class himself.
Hitherto he had always had the prospect of establishing himself
somewhere as master artificer, perhaps employing journeymen
and apprentices; but now, when master artificers were crowded
out by manufacturers, when large capital had become necessary
for carrying on work independently, the working-class became, for
the first time, an integral, permanent class of the population,
whereas it had formerly often been merely a transition leading to
the bourgeoisie. Now, he who was born to toil had no other
prospect than that of remaining a toiler all his life. Now, for the
first time, therefore, the proletariat was in a position to undertake
an independent movement.

In this way were brought together those vast masses of working-men who now fill the whole British Empire, whose social condition forces itself every day more and more upon the attention of the civilised world.

The condition of the working-class is the condition of the vast majority of the English people. The question: What is to become of those destitute millions, who consume today what they earned yesterday; who have created the greatness of England by their inventions and their toil; who become with every passing day more conscious of their might, and demand, with daily increasing urgency, their share of the advantages of society?—This, since the Reform Bill,[123] has become the national question. All Parliamentary debates, of any importance, may be reduced to this; and, though the English middle-class will not as yet admit it, though they try to evade this great question, and to represent their own particular interests as the truly national ones, their action is utterly useless. With every session of Parliament the working-class gains ground, the interests of the middle-class diminish in importance; and, in spite of the fact that the middle-class is the chief, in fact, the only power in Parliament, the last session of 1844 was a continuous debate upon subjects affecting the working-class, the Poor Relief Bill, the Factory Act, the Masters' and Servants' Act[a]; and Thomas Duncombe, the representative of the working-men in the House of Commons, was the great man of the session; while the Liberal middle-class with its motion for repealing the Corn Laws, and the Radical middle-class with its resolution for refusing the taxes, played pitiable rôles. Even the debates about Ireland were at bottom debates about the Irish proletariat, and the means of coming to its assistance. It is high time, too, for the English middle-class to make some concessions to the working-men who no longer plead but threaten[b]; for in a short time it may be too late.

In spite of all this, the English middle-class, especially the manufacturing class, which is enriched directly by means of the poverty of the workers, persists in ignoring this poverty. This class, feeling itself the mighty representative class of the nation, is ashamed to lay the sore spot of England bare before the eyes of the world; will not confess, even to itself, that the workers are in distress, because it, the property-holding, manufacturing class, must bear the moral responsibility for this distress. Hence the

---

[a] Concerning the Parliamentary Session of 1844 see below, pp. 464-65, 569-70, 578.—*Ed.*

[b] The German editions of 1845 and 1892 have here "threaten and demand".—*Ed.*

scornful smile which intelligent Englishmen (and they, the middle-class, alone are known on the Continent) assume when any one begins to speak of the condition of the working-class; hence the utter ignorance on the part of the whole middle-class of everything which concerns the workers; hence the ridiculous blunders which men of this class, in and out of Parliament, make when the position of the proletariat comes under discussion; hence the absurd freedom from anxiety, with which the middle-class dwells upon a soil that is honeycombed, and may any day collapse, the speedy collapse of which is as certain as a mathematical or mechanical demonstration; hence the miracle that the English have as yet no single book upon the condition of their workers, although they have been examining and mending the old state of things no one knows how many years. Hence also the deep wrath of the whole working-class, from Glasgow to London, against the rich, by whom they are systematically plundered and mercilessly left to their fate, a wrath which before too long a time goes by, a time almost within the power of man to predict,[a] must break out into a revolution in comparison with which the French Revolution, and the year 1794, will prove to have been child's play.

---

[a] The German editions of 1845 and 1892 have "calculate" instead of "predict".— *Ed*.

THE INDUSTRIAL PROLETARIAT

The order of our investigation of the different sections of the proletariat follows naturally from the foregoing history. of its rise. The first proletarians were connected with manufacture, were engendered by it, and accordingly, those employed in manufacture, in the working up of raw materials, will first claim our attention. The production of raw materials and of fuel for manufacture attained importance only in consequence of the industrial change, and engendered a new proletariat, the coal and metal miners. Then, in the third place, manufacture influenced agriculture, and in the fourth, the condition of Ireland; and the fractions of the proletariat belonging to each, will find their place accordingly. We shall find, too, that with the possible exception of the Irish, the degree of intelligence of the various workers is in direct proportion to their relation to manufacture; and that the factory-hands are most enlightened as to their own interests, the miners somewhat less so, the agricultural labourers scarcely at all. We shall find the same order again among the industrial workers, and shall see how the factory-hands, eldest children of the industrial revolution, have from the beginning to the present day formed the nucleus of the Labour Movement, and how the others have joined this movement just in proportion as their handicraft has been invaded by the progress of machinery.[a] We shall thus learn from the example which England offers, from the equal

---

[a] The German editions of 1845 and 1892 have "the industrial revolution" instead of "the progress of machinery".— Ed.

pace which the Labour Movement has kept with the movement of industrial development, the historical significance of manufacture.

Since, however, at the present moment, pretty much the whole industrial proletariat is involved in the movement, and the condition of the separate sections has much in common, because they all are industrial, we shall have first to examine the condition of the industrial proletariat as a whole, in order later to notice more particularly each separate division with its own peculiarities.

It has been already suggested that manufacture centralises property in the hands of the few. It requires large capital with which to erect the colossal establishments that ruin the petty trading bourgeoisie and with which to press into its service the forces of Nature, so driving the hand-labour of the independent workman out of the market. The division of labour, the application of water and especially steam, and the application of machinery, are the three great levers with which manufacture, since the middle of the last century, has been busy putting the world out of joint. Manufacture, on a small scale, created the middle-class; on a large scale, it created the working-class, and raised the elect of the middle-class to the throne, but only to overthrow them the more surely when the time comes. Meanwhile, it is an undenied and easily explained fact that the numerous petty middle-class of the "good old times" has been annihilated by manufacture, and resolved into rich capitalists on the one hand and poor workers on the other.*

The centralising tendency of manufacture does not, however, stop here. Population becomes centralised just as capital does; and, very naturally, since the human being, the worker, is regarded in manufacture simply as a piece of capital for the use of which the manufacturer pays interest under the name of wages. A manufacturing establishment[a] requires many workers employed together in a single building, living near each other and forming a village of themselves in the case of a good-sized factory. They have needs for satisfying which other people are necessary; handicraftsmen, shoemakers, tailors, bakers, carpenters, stonemasons, settle at

* Compare on this point my "Outlines of a Critique of Political Economy" in the *Deutsch-Französische Jahrbücher*. In this essay "free competition" is the starting-point; but industry is only the practice of free competition and the latter is only the principle on which industry is based.— *Note by Engels*. (The American and English authorised editions give only the first sentence of this footnote. See present edition, Vol. 3.—*Ed.*)

---

[a] The German editions of 1845 and 1892 have "A big manufacturing establishment".—*Ed.*

hand. The inhabitants of the village, especially the younger generation, accustom themselves to factory work, grow skilful in it, and when[a] the first mill can no longer employ them all, wages fall, and the immigration of fresh manufacturers is the consequence. So the village grows into a small town, and the small town into a large one. The greater the town, the greater its advantages. It offers roads, railroads, canals; the choice of skilled labour increases constantly, new establishments can be built more cheaply, because of the competition among builders and machinists who are at hand, than in remote country districts, whither timber, machinery, builders, and operatives must be brought; it offers a market[b] to which buyers crowd, and direct communication with the markets supplying raw material or demanding finished goods. Hence the marvellously rapid growth of the great manufacturing towns. The country, on the other hand, had the advantage that wages are usually lower than in town, and so town and country are in constant competition; and, if the advantage is on the side of the town today, wages sink so low in the country tomorrow that new investments are most profitably made there. But the centralising tendency of manufacture continues in full force, and every new factory built in the country bears in it the germ of a manufacturing town. If it were possible for this mad rush of manufacture to go on at this rate for another century, every manufacturing district of England would be one great manufacturing town, and Manchester and Liverpool would meet at Warrington or Newton; for in commerce, too, this centralisation of the population works in precisely the same way, and hence it is that one or two great harbours, such as Hull and Liverpool, Bristol and London, monopolise almost the whole maritime commerce of Great Britain.

Since commerce and manufacture attain their most complete development in these great towns, their influence upon the proletariat is also most clearly observable here. Here the centralisation of property has reached the highest point; here the morals and customs of the good old times are most completely obliterated; here it has gone so far that the name Merry Old England[c] conveys no meaning, for Old England itself is unknown to memory and to the tales of our grandfathers. Hence, too, there exist here only a rich and a poor class, for the lower middle-class vanishes more completely with every passing day. Thus the class

---

[a] The German editions of 1845 and 1892 have here "as is natural".—*Ed.*

[b] The German editions of 1845 and 1892 have here "a stock exchange".—*Ed.*

[c] Given in English in the German editions of 1845 and 1892.—*Ed.*

formerly most stable has become the most restless one. It consists today of a few remnants of a past time, and a number of people eager to make fortunes, industrial Micawbers[a] and speculators of whom one may amass a fortune, while ninety-nine become insolvent, and more than half of the ninety-nine live by perpetually repeated failure.

But in these towns the proletarians are the infinite majority, and how they fare, what influence the great town exercises upon them, we have now to investigate.

---

[a] Instead of "Micawbers" (from *David Copperfield* by Ch. Dickens) the German editions of 1845 and 1892 have "knights of industry".—*Ed.*

THE GREAT TOWNS

A town, such as London, where a man may wander for hours together without reaching the beginning of the end, without meeting the slightest hint which could lead to the inference that there is open country within reach, is a strange thing. This colossal centralisation, this heaping together of two and a half millions of human beings at one point, has multiplied the power of this two and a half millions a hundredfold; has raised London to the commercial capital of the world, created the giant docks and assembled the thousand vessels that continually cover the Thames. I know nothing more imposing than the view which the Thames offers during the ascent from the sea to London Bridge. The masses of buildings, the wharves on both sides, especially from Woolwich upwards, the countless ships along both shores, crowding ever closer and closer together, until, at last, only a narrow passage remains in the middle of the river, a passage through which hundreds of steamers shoot by one another; all this is so vast, so impressive, that a man cannot collect himself, but is lost in the marvel of England's greatness before he sets foot upon English soil.*

But the sacrifices which all this has cost become apparent later. After roaming the streets of the capital a day or two, making

* This applies to the time of sailing vessels. The Thames now is a dreary collection of ugly steamers.—F. E.—*Note by Engels to the American edition of 1887* (reproduced in the English edition of 1892—*Ed.*).

(1892) This was written nearly fifty years ago, in the days of the picturesque sailing vessels. In so far as such ships still ply to and from London they are now to be found only in the docks, while the river itself is covered with ugly, sooty steamers.—*Note by Engels to the German edition of 1892.*

headway with difficulty through the human turmoil and the endless lines of vehicles, after visiting the slums of the metropolis, one realises for the first time that these Londoners have been forced to sacrifice the best qualities of their human nature, to bring to pass all the marvels of civilisation which crowd their city; that a hundred powers which slumbered within them have remained inactive, have been suppressed in order that a few might be developed more fully and multiply through union with those of others. The very turmoil of the streets has something repulsive, something against which human nature rebels. The hundreds of thousands of all classes and ranks crowding past each other, are they not all human beings with the same qualities and powers, and with the same interest in being happy? And have they not, in the end, to seek happiness in the same way, by the same means? And still they crowd by one another as though they had nothing in common, nothing to do with one another, and their only agreement is the tacit one, that each keep to his own side[a] of the pavement, so as not to delay the opposing streams of the crowd, while it occurs to no man to honour another with so much as a glance. The brutal indifference, the unfeeling isolation of each in his private interest, becomes the more repellent and offensive, the more these individuals are crowded together, within a limited space. And, however much one may be aware that this isolation of the individual, this narrow self-seeking, is the fundamental principle of our society everywhere, it is nowhere so shamelessly barefaced, so self-conscious as just here in the crowding of the great city. The dissolution of mankind into monads, of which each one has a separate principle,[b] the world of atoms, is here carried out to its utmost extreme.

Hence it comes, too, that the social war, the war of each against all, is here openly declared. Just as in Stirner's recent book,[c] people regard each other only as useful objects; each exploits the other, and the end of it all is that the stronger treads the weaker under foot; and that the powerful few, the capitalists, seize everything for themselves, while to the weak many, the poor, scarcely a bare existence remains.

What is true of London, is true of Manchester, Birmingham, Leeds, is true of all great towns. Everywhere barbarous indiffer-

---

[a] The German editions of 1845 and 1892 have "to the right side".—*Ed.*
[b] The German editions of 1845 and 1892 have "and a separate purpose".—*Ed.*
[c] Max Stirner, *Der Einzige und sein Eigenthum.*—*Ed.*

ence, hard egotism on one hand, and nameless misery on the other, everywhere social warfare, every man's house in a state of siege, everywhere reciprocal plundering under the protection of the law, and all so shameless, so openly avowed that one shrinks before the consequences of our social state as they manifest themselves here undisguised, and can only wonder that the whole crazy fabric still hangs together.

Since capital, the direct or indirect control of the means of subsistence and production, is the weapon with which this social warfare is carried on, it is clear that all the disadvantages of such a state must fall upon the poor. For him no man has the slightest concern. Cast into the whirlpool, he must struggle through as well as he can. If he is so happy as to find work, i.e., if the bourgeoisie does him the favour to enrich itself by means of him, wages await him which scarcely suffice to keep body and soul together; if he can get no work he may steal, if he is not afraid of the police, or starve, in which case the police will take care that he does so in a quiet and inoffensive manner.[a] During my residence in England, at least twenty or thirty persons have died of simple starvation under the most revolting circumstances, and a jury has rarely been found possessed of the courage to speak the plain truth in the matter. Let the testimony of the witnesses be never so clear and unequivocal, the bourgeoisie, from which the jury is selected, always finds some backdoor through which to escape the frightful verdict, death from starvation. The bourgeoisie dare not speak the truth in these cases, for it would speak its own condemnation. But indirectly, far more than directly, many have died of starvation, where long-continued want of proper nourishment has called forth fatal illness,[b] when it has produced such debility that causes which might otherwise have remained inoperative brought on severe illness and death. The English working-men call this "social murder", and accuse our whole society of perpetrating this crime perpetually. Are they wrong?

True, it is only individuals who starve, but what security has the working-man that it may not be his turn tomorrow? Who assures him employment, who vouches for it that, if for any reason or no reason his lord and master discharges him tomorrow, he can struggle along with those dependent upon him, until he may find

---

[a] The German editions of 1845 and 1892 have here "without offending the bourgeoisie".—Ed.

[b] The German editions of 1845 and 1892 have here "and thus snatched away its victim".—Ed.

some one else "to give him bread"? Who guarantees that willing-
ness to work shall suffice to obtain work, that uprightness,
industry, thrift, and the rest of the virtues recommended by the
bourgeoisie, are really his road to happiness? No one. He knows
that he has something today and that it does not depend upon
himself whether he shall have something tomorrow. He knows
that every breeze that blows, every whim of his employer, every
bad turn of trade may hurl him back into the fierce whirlpool
from which he has temporarily saved himself, and in which it is
hard and often impossible to keep his head above water. He
knows that, though he may have the means of living today, it is
very uncertain whether he shall tomorrow.

Meanwhile, let us proceed to a more detailed investigation of
the position in which the social war has placed the non-possessing
class. Let us see what pay for his work society does give the
working-man in the form of dwelling, clothing, food, what sort of
subsistence it grants those who contribute most to the maintenance
of society; and, first, let us consider the dwellings.

Every great city has one or more slums, where the working-class
is crowded together. True, poverty often dwells in hidden alleys
close to the palaces of the rich; but, in general, a separate territory
has been assigned to it, where, removed from the sight of the
happier classes, it may struggle along as it can. These slums are
pretty equally arranged in all the great towns of England, the
worst houses in the worst quarters of the towns; usually one- or
two-storied cottages[a] in long rows, perhaps with cellars used as
dwellings, almost always irregularly built. These houses of three or
four rooms and a kitchen[b] form, throughout England, some parts
of London excepted, the general dwellings of the working-class.
The streets are generally unpaved, rough, dirty, filled with
vegetable and animal refuse, without sewers or gutters, but
supplied with foul, stagnant pools instead. Moreover, ventilation is
impeded by the bad, confused method of building of the whole
quarter, and since many human beings here live crowded into a
small space, the atmosphere that prevails in these working-men's
quarters may readily be imagined. Further, the streets serve as
drying grounds in fine weather; lines are stretched across from
house to house, and hung with wet clothing.

---

[a] The German editions of 1845 and 1892 have "brick buildings" instead of
"cottages".—*Ed.*

[b] The German editions of 1845 and 1892 have here "are called cottages
and".—*Ed.*

Let us investigate some of the slums in their order. London comes first,* and in London the famous rookery[a] of St. Giles which is now, at last, about to be penetrated by a couple of broad streets.[b] St. Giles is in the midst of the most populous part of the town, surrounded by broad, splendid avenues in which the gay world of London idles about, in the immediate neighbourhood of Oxford Street, Regent Street, of Trafalgar Square and the Strand. It is a disorderly collection of tall, three- or four-storied houses, with narrow, crooked, filthy streets, in which there is quite as much life as in the great thoroughfares of the town, except that, here, people of the working-class only are to be seen. A vegetable market is held in the street, baskets with vegetables and fruits, naturally all bad and hardly fit to use obstruct the sidewalk still further, and from these, as well as from the fish-dealers' stalls, arises a horrible smell. The houses are occupied from cellar to garret, filthy within and without, and their appearance is such that no human being could possibly wish to live in them. But all this is nothing in comparison with the dwellings in the narrow courts and alleys between the streets, entered by covered passages between the houses, in which the filth and tottering ruin surpass all description. Scarcely a whole window-pane can be found, the walls are crumbling, door-posts and window-frames loose and broken, doors of old boards nailed together, or altogether wanting in this thieves' quarter, where no doors are needed, there being nothing to steal. Heaps of garbage and ashes lie in all directions, and the foul liquids emptied before the doors gather in stinking pools. Here live the poorest of the poor, the worst paid workers with thieves and the victims of prostitution[c] indiscriminately huddled together, the majority Irish, or of Irish extraction, and those who have not yet sunk in the whirlpool of moral ruin which surrounds

* The description given below had already been written when I came across an article in the *Illuminated Magazine* (October 1844) dealing with the working-class districts in London which coincides — in many places almost literally and everywhere in general tenor — with what I had said. The article was entitled "The Dwellings of the Poor, from the notebook of an M.D." — *Note by Engels*. (This note is reproduced in the German edition of 1892 but is missing in the American edition of 1887 and the English edition of 1892.— *Ed*.)

---

[a] In the German editions of 1845 and 1892 this English word is given in brackets after the corresponding German word.— *Ed*.

[b] The German editions of 1845 and 1892 have here "and thus done away with".— *Ed*.

[c] The German editions of 1845 and 1892 have "with thieves, rogues and victims of prostitution".— *Ed*.

them, sinking daily deeper, losing daily more and more of their power to resist the demoralising influence of want, filth, and evil surroundings.

Nor is St. Giles the only London slum. In the immense tangle of streets, there are hundreds and thousands of alleys and courts lined with houses too bad for anyone to live in, who can still spend anything whatsoever upon a dwelling fit for human beings. Close to the splendid houses of the rich such a lurking-place of the bitterest poverty may often be found. So, a short time ago, on the occasion of a coroner's inquest, a region close to Portman Square, one of the very respectable squares, was characterised as an abode "of a multitude of Irish demoralised by poverty and filth". So, too, may be found in streets, such as Long Acre and others, which, though not fashionable, are yet "respectable", a great number of cellar dwellings out of which puny children and half-starved, ragged women emerge into the light of day. In the immediate neighbourhood of Drury Lane Theatre, the second in London, are some of the worst streets of the whole metropolis, Charles, King, and Park Streets, in which the houses are inhabited from cellar to garret exclusively by poor families. In the parishes of St. John and St. Margaret[a] there lived in 1840, according to the *Journal of the Statistical Society*, 5,366 working-men's families in 5,294 "dwellings" (if they deserve the name!), men, women, and children thrown together without distinction of age or sex, 26,830 persons all told; and of these families three-fourths possessed but one room. In the aristocratic parish of St. George, Hanover Square, there lived, according to the same authority, 1,465 working-men's families, nearly 6,000 persons, under similar conditions, and here, too, more than two-thirds of the whole number crowded together at the rate of one family in one room. And how the poverty of these unfortunates, among whom even thieves find nothing to steal, is exploited by the property-holding class in lawful ways! The abominable dwellings in Drury Lane, just mentioned, bring in the following rents: two cellar dwellings, 3s.[b]; one room, ground-floor, 4s.; second-storey, 4s. 6d.; third-floor, 4s.; garret-room, 3s. weekly, so that the starving occupants of Charles Street alone, pay the house-owners a yearly tribute of £2,000,[c] and the 5,366 families above mentioned in Westminster, a yearly rent of £40,000.[124]

---

[a] The German editions of 1845 and 1892 have here "in Westminster".—*Ed.*

[b] The German editions of 1845 and 1892 here give "1 taler" in brackets.—*Ed.*

[c] The German editions of 1845 and 1892 give in brackets 14,000 taler after £2,000 and 270,000 taler after £40,000.—*Ed.*

The most extensive working-people's district lies east of the Tower in Whitechapel and Bethnal Green, where the greatest masses of London working-people live. Let us hear Mr. G. Alston, preacher of St. Philip's, Bethnal Green, on the condition of his parish. He says:

"It contains 1,400 houses, inhabited by 2,795 families, comprising a population of 12,000. The space within which this large amount of population are living is less than 400 yards square (1,200 feet), and it is no uncommon thing for a man and his wife, with four or five children, and sometimes the grandfather and grandmother, to be found living in a room from ten to twelve feet square, and which serves them for eating and working in. I believe that till the Bishop of London called the attention of the public to the state of Bethnal Green, about as little was known at the West-end of the town of this most destitute parish as the wilds of Australia or the islands of the South Seas. If we really desire to find out the most destitute and deserving, we must lift the latch of their doors, and find them at their scanty meal; we must see them when suffering from sickness and want of work; and if we do this from day to day in such a neighbourhood as Bethnal Green, we shall become acquainted with a mass of wretchedness and misery such as a nation like our own ought to be ashamed to permit. I was Curate of a parish near Huddersfield during the three years of the greatest manufacturing distress; but I never witnessed such a thorough prostration of the poor as I have seen since I have been in Bethnal Green. There is not one father of a family in ten throughout the entire district that possesses any clothes but his working dress, and that too commonly in the worst tattered condition; and with many this wretched clothing forms their only covering at night, with nothing better than a bag of straw or shavings to lie upon."[125]

The foregoing description furnishes an idea of the aspect of the interior of the dwellings. But let us follow the English officials, who occasionally stray thither, into one or two of these working-men's homes.

On the occasion of an inquest held Nov. 16th, 1843, by Mr. Carter, coroner for Surrey, upon the body of Ann Galway, aged 45 years, the newspapers related the following particulars concerning the deceased[126]: She had lived at No. 3 White Lion Court, Bermondsey Street, London, with her husband and a nineteen-year-old son in a little room, in which neither a bedstead nor any other furniture was to be seen. She lay dead beside her son upon a heap of feathers which were scattered over her almost naked body, there being neither sheet nor coverlet. The feathers stuck so fast over the whole body that the physician could not examine the corpse until it was cleansed, and then found it starved and scarred from the bites of vermin. Part of the floor of the room was torn up, and the hole used by the family as a privy.

On Monday, Jan. 15th, 1844, two boys were brought before the police magistrate[a] because, being in a starving condition, they had stolen and immediately devoured a half-cooked calf's foot from a shop. The magistrate felt called upon to investigate the case further, and received the following details from the policeman: The mother of the two boys was the widow of an ex-soldier, afterwards policeman, and had had a very hard time since the death of her husband, to provide for her nine children. She lived at No. 2 Pool's Place, Quaker Court, Spitalfields, in the utmost poverty. When the policeman came to her, he found her with six of her children literally huddled together in a little back room, with no furniture but two old rush-bottomed chairs with the seats gone, a small table with two legs broken, a broken cup, and a small dish. On the hearth was scarcely a spark of fire, and in one corner lay as many old rags as would fill a woman's apron, which served the whole family as a bed. For bed clothing they had only their scanty day clothing. The poor woman told him that she had been forced to sell her bedstead the year before to buy food. Her bedding she had pawned with the victualler for food. In short, everything had gone for food. The magistrate ordered the woman a considerable provision from the poor-box.

In February, 1844, Theresa Bishop, a widow 60 years old, was recommended, with her sick daughter, aged 26, to the compassion of the police magistrate in Marlborough Street. She lived at No. 5 Brown Street, Grosvenor Square, in a small back room no larger than a closet, in which there was not one single piece of furniture. In one corner lay some rags upon which both slept; a chest served as table and chair. The mother earned a little by charring. The owner of the house said that they had lived in this way since May, 1843, had gradually sold or pawned everything that they had, and had still never paid any rent. The magistrate assigned them £1 from the poor-box.[127]

I am far from asserting that *all* London working-people live in such want as the foregoing three families. I know very well that ten are somewhat better off, where one is so totally trodden under foot by society; but I assert that thousands of industrious and worthy people—far worthier and more to be respected than all the rich of London—do find themselves in a condition unworthy of human beings; and that every proletarian, everyone, without exception, is exposed to a similar fate without any fault of his own and in spite of every possible effort.

---

[a] The German editions of 1845 and 1892 have here "in Worship Street, London".—*Ed.*

But in spite of all this, they who have some kind of a shelter are fortunate, fortunate in comparison with the utterly homeless. In London fifty thousand human beings get up every morning, not knowing where they are to lay their heads at night. The luckiest of this multitude, those who succeed in keeping a penny or two until evening, enter a lodging-house, such as abound in every great city, where they find a bed. But what a bed! These houses are filled with beds from cellar to garret, four, five, six beds in a room; as many as can be crowded in. Into every bed four, five, or six human beings are piled, as many as can be packed in, sick and well, young and old, drunk and sober, men and women, just as they come, indiscriminately. Then come strife, blows, wounds, or, if these bedfellows agree, so much the worse; thefts are arranged and things done which our language, grown more humane than our deeds, refuses to record. And those who cannot pay for such a refuge? They sleep where they find a place, in passages, arcades, in corners where the police and the owners leave them undisturbed. A few individuals find their way to the refuges which are managed, here and there, by private charity, others sleep on the benches in the parks close under the windows of Queen Victoria. Let us hear the London *Times*:

"It appears from the report of the proceedings at Marlborough Street Police Court in our columns of yesterday, that there is an average number of 50 human beings of all ages, who huddle together in the parks every night, having no other shelter than what is supplied by the trees and a few hollows of the embankment. Of these, the majority are young girls who have been seduced from the country by the soldiers and turned loose on the world in all the destitution of friendless penury, and all the recklessness of early vice.

"This is truly horrible! Poor there must be everywhere. Indigence will find its way and set up its hideous state in the heart of a great and luxurious city. Amid the thousand narrow lanes and by-streets of a populous metropolis there must always, we fear, be much suffering — much that offends the eye — much that lurks unseen.

"But that within the precincts of wealth, gaiety, and fashion, nigh the regal grandeur of St. James, close on the palatial splendour of Bayswater, on the confines of the old and new aristocratic quarters, in a district where the cautious refinement of modern design has refrained from creating one single tenement for poverty; which seems, as it were, dedicated to the exclusive enjoyment of wealth, that *there* want, and famine, and disease, and vice should stalk in all their kindred horrors, consuming body by body, soul by soul!

"It is indeed a monstrous state of things! Enjoyment the most absolute, that bodily ease, intellectual excitement, or the more innocent pleasures of sense can supply to man's craving, brought in close contact with the most unmitigated misery! Wealth, from its bright saloons, laughing — an insolently heedless laugh — at the unknown wounds of want! Pleasure, cruelly but unconsciously mocking the pain that moans below! All contrary things mocking one another — all contrary, save the vice which tempts and the vice which is tempted!

"But let all men remember this—that within the most courtly precincts of the richest city of God's earth, there may be found, night after night, winter after winter, women—young in years—old in sin and suffering—outcasts from society—ROTTING FROM FAMINE, FILTH, AND DISEASE. Let them remember this, and learn not to theorise but to act. God knows, there is much room for action nowadays."*

I have referred to the refuges for the homeless. How greatly overcrowded these are, two examples may show. A newly erected Refuge for the Houseless[a] in Upper Ogle Street, that can shelter three hundred persons every night, has received since its opening, January 27th to March 17th, 1844, 2,740 persons for one or more nights; and, although the season was growing more favourable, the number of applicants in this, as well as in the asylums of Whitecross Street and Wapping, was strongly on the increase, and a crowd of the homeless had to be sent away every night for want of room. In another refuge, the Central Asylum in Playhouse Yard, there were supplied on an average 460 beds nightly, during the first three months of the year 1844, 6,681 persons being sheltered, and 96,141 portions of bread were distributed. Yet the committee of directors declare this institution began to meet the pressure of the needy to a limited extent only when the Eastern Asylum also was opened.[128]

Let us leave London and examine the other great cities of the three kingdoms in their order. Let us take Dublin first, a city the approach to which from the sea is as charming as that of London is imposing. The Bay of Dublin is the most beautiful of the whole British Island Kingdom, and is even compared by the Irish with the Bay of Naples. The city, too, possesses great attractions, and its aristocratic districts are better and more tastefully laid out than those of any other British city. By way of compensation, however, the poorer districts of Dublin are among the most hideous and repulsive to be seen in the world. True, the Irish character, which, under some circumstances, is comfortable only in the dirt, has some share in this; but as we find thousands of Irish in every great city in England and Scotland, and as every poor population must gradually sink into the same uncleanliness, the wretchedness of Dublin is nothing specific, nothing peculiar to Dublin, but something common to all great towns. The poor quarters of Dublin are extremely extensive, and the filth, the uninhabitable-

* *Times*, Oct. 12th, 1843.—*Note by Engels to the American edition of 1887 and the English edition of 1892.* (The German editions of 1845 and 1892 refer, before this citation, to the *Times*, October 1843, without any date.—*Ed.*)

[a] The German editions of 1845 and 1892 give this in English.—*Ed.*

ness of the houses and the neglect of the streets surpass all
description. Some idea of the manner in which the poor are here
crowded together may be formed from the fact that, in 1817,
according to the report of the Inspector of Workhouses,* 1,318
persons lived in 52 houses with 390 rooms in Barrack Street, and
1,997 persons in 71 houses with 393 rooms in and near Church
Street; that:

"foul lanes, courts, and yards, are interposed between this and the adjoining
streets.... There are many cellars which have no light but from the door.... In some
of these cellars the inhabitants sleep on the floors which are all earthen; but in
general, they have bedsteads.... Nicholson's Court ... contains 151 persons in 28
small apartments ... their state is very miserable, there being only two bedsteads
and two blankets in the whole court."

The poverty is so great in Dublin, that a single benevolent
institution, the Mendicity Association,[a] gives relief to 2,500 persons
or one per cent of the population daily, receiving and feeding
them for the day and dismissing them at night.

Dr. Alison describes a similar state of things in Edinburgh,
whose superb situation, which has won it the title of the modern
Athens, and whose brilliant aristocratic quarter in the New Town,
contrast strongly with the foul wretchedness of the poor in the
Old Town. Alison asserts that this extensive quarter is as filthy and
horrible as the worst districts of Dublin, while the Mendicity
Association would have as great a proportion of needy persons to
assist in Edinburgh as in the Irish capital. He asserts, indeed, that
the poor in Scotland, especially in Edinburgh and Glasgow, are
worse off than in any other region of the three kingdoms, and
that the poorest are not Irish, but Scotch. The preacher of the Old
Church of Edinburgh, Dr. Lee, testified in 1836, before the
Commission of Religious Instruction, that:

"I have never seen such a concentration of misery as in this parish," where the
people are without furniture, without everything. "I frequently see the same room
occupied by two married couples. I have been in one day in seven houses where
there was no bed, in some of them not even straw. I found people of eighty years
of age lying on the boards. Many sleep in the same clothes which they wear
during the day. I may mention the case of two Scotch families living in a cellar, who
had come from the country within a few months.... Since they came they had had

* Quoted by Dr. W. P. Alison, F.R.S.E., Fellow and late President of the
Royal College of Physicians, etc., etc. *Observations on the Management of the Poor in
Scotland and its Effects on the Health of Great Towns*, Edinburgh, 1840. The author is
a religious Tory, brother of the historian, Archibald Alison.— *Note by Engels.*

[a] Here and below the name of this association is given in English in the
German original.— *Ed.*

two children dead, and another apparently dying. There was a little bundle of dirty straw in one corner, for one family, and in another for the other. In the place they inhabit it is impossible at noonday to distinguish the features of the human face without artificial light. An ass stood in one corner.—It would almost make a heart of adamant bleed to see such an accumulation of misery in a country like this."

In the *Edinburgh Medical and Surgical Journal*,[a] Dr. Hennen reports a similar state of things. From a Parliamentary Report,* it is evident that in the dwellings of the poor of Edinburgh a want of cleanliness reigns, such as must be expected under these conditions. On the bed-posts chickens roost at night, dogs and horses share the dwellings of human beings, and the natural consequence is a shocking stench, with filth and swarms of vermin. The prevailing construction of Edinburgh favours these atrocious conditions as far as possible. The Old Town is built upon both slopes of a hill, along the crest of which runs the High Street. Out of the High Street there open downwards multitudes of narrow, crooked alleys, called wynds[b] from their many turnings, and these wynds form the proletarian district of the city. The houses of the Scotch cities, in general, are five or six-storied buildings, like those of Paris, and in contrast with England where, so far as possible, each family has a separate house.[c] The crowding of human beings upon a limited area is thus intensified.

"...the houses," says an English journal in an article upon the sanitary condition of the working-people in cities,** "are often so close together, that persons may step from the window of one house to that of the house opposite—so high, piled story after story, that the light can scarcely penetrate to the court beneath. In this part of the town there are neither sewers nor any private conveniences whatever belonging to the dwellings; and hence the excrementitious and other refuse of at least 50,000 persons is, during the night, thrown into the gutters, causing (in spite of the scavengers' daily labours) an amount of solid filth and foetid exhalation disgusting

* *Report to the Home Secretary from the Poor-Law Commissioner, on an Inquiry into the Sanitary Condition of the Labouring Classes in Great Britain, with Appendix.* Presented to both Houses of Parliament in July, 1842, 3 vols. Folio. Assembled and arranged from medical reports by Edwin Chadwick, Secretary of the Poor-Law Commissioners.—*Note by Engels.* (The last sentence is omitted in the American edition of 1887 and in the English edition of 1892.—*Ed.*)

** *The Artisan*, October, 1843. A monthly journal.—*Note by Engels.* ("A monthly journal" is omitted in the American edition of 1887 and the English edition of 1892.—*Ed.*)

[a] Vol. 14, 1818.—*Ed.*

[b] This word is in English in the German original.—*Ed.*

[c] In the German editions of 1845 and 1892 the end of the sentence reads: "and in contrast with England, where, as far as possible, each family has a separate house, are occupied by a number of families".—*Ed.*

to both sight and smell, as well as exceedingly prejudicial to health. Can it be wondered that, in such localities, health, morals, and common decency should be at once neglected? No; all who know the private condition of the inhabitants will bear testimony to the immense amount of their disease, misery, and demoralisation. Society in these quarters has sunk to a state indescribably vile and wretched.... The dwellings of the poorer classes are generally very filthy, apparently never subjected to any cleaning process whatever, consisting, in most cases, of a single room, ill-ventilated and yet cold, owing to broken, ill-fitting windows, sometimes damp and partially under ground, and always scantily furnished and altogether comfortless, heaps of straw often serving for beds, in which a whole family—male and female, young and old, are huddled together in revolting confusion. The supplies of water are obtained only from the public pumps, and the trouble of procuring it of course favours the accumulation of all kinds of abominations."

In the other great seaport towns the prospect is no better. Liverpool, with all its commerce, wealth, and grandeur yet treats its workers with the same barbarity. A full fifth of the population, more than 45,000 human beings, live in narrow, dark, damp, badly-ventilated cellar dwellings, of which there are 7,862 in the city. Besides these cellar dwellings there are 2,270 courts, small spaces built up on all four sides and having but one entrance, a narrow, covered passage-way,[a] the whole ordinarily very dirty and inhabited exclusively by proletarians. Of such courts we shall have more to say when we come to Manchester. In Bristol, on one occasion, 2,800 families were visited,[129] of whom 46 per cent occupied but one room each.

Precisely the same state of things prevails in the factory towns. In Nottingham there are in all 11,000 houses, of which between 7,000 and 8,000 are built back to back with a rear party-wall so that no through ventilation is possible, while a single privy usually serves for several houses. During an investigation made a short time since, many rows of houses were found to have been built over shallow drains covered only by the boards of the ground-floor. In Leicester, Derby, and Sheffield, it is no better. Of Birmingham, the article above cited from the *Artisan* states:

"In the older parts of the town there are many inferior streets and courts, which are dirty and neglected, filled with stagnant water and heaps of refuse. The courts of Birmingham are very numerous in every direction, exceeding 2,000, and comprising the residence of a large portion of the working-classes. They are for the most part narrow, filthy, ill-ventilated, and badly drained, containing from eight to twenty houses each, the houses being built against some other tenement and the end of the courts being pretty constantly occupied by ashpits, etc., the filth of which would defy description. It is but just, however, to remark that the courts of more modern date are built in a more rational manner, and kept tolerably respectable;

---

[a] The German editions of 1845 and 1892 have here "allowing *no* ventilation at all".— *Ed.*

and the cottages, even in old courts, are far less crowded than in Manchester and Liverpool, the result of which is, that the inhabitants, in epidemic seasons, have been much less visited by death than those of Wolverhampton, Dudley, and Bilston, at only a few miles distance. Cellar residences, also, are unknown in Birmingham, though some few are, very improperly, used as workshops. The low lodging-houses are pretty numerous (somewhat exceeding 400), chiefly in courts near the centre of the town; they are almost always loathsomely filthy and close, the resorts of beggars, trampers,[a] thieves and prostitutes, who here, regardless alike of decency or comfort, eat, drink, smoke and sleep in an atmosphere unendurable by all except the degraded, besotted inmates."

Glasgow is in many respects similar to Edinburgh, possessing the same wynds, the same tall houses. Of this city the *Artisan* observes:

The working-class forms here some 78 per cent of the whole population (about 300,000), and lives in parts of the city "which, in abject wretchedness, exceed the lowest purlieus of St. Giles' or Whitechapel, the liberties of Dublin, or the wynds of Edinburgh. Such localities exist most abundantly in the heart of the city—south of the Trongate and west of the Saltmarket, as well as in the Calton, off the High Street, etc.—endless labyrinths of narrow lanes or wynds, into which almost at every step debouche courts or closes formed by old, ill-ventilated, towering houses crumbling to decay, destitute of water and crowded with inhabitants, comprising three or four families (perhaps twenty persons) on each flat, and sometimes each flat let out in lodgings that confine—we dare not say accommodate—from fifteen to twenty persons in a single room. These districts are occupied by the poorest, most depraved, and most worthless portion of the population, and they may be considered as the fruitful source of those pestilential fevers which thence spread their destructive ravages over the whole of Glasgow."

Let us hear how J. C. Symons, Government Commissioner for the investigation of the condition of the hand-weavers, describes these portions of the city*:

"I have seen human degradation in some of its worst phases, both in England and abroad, but I did not believe until I visited the wynds of Glasgow, that so large an amount of filth, crime, misery, and disease existed in any civilised country. In the lower lodging-houses ten, twelve, and sometimes twenty persons of both sexes and all ages sleep promiscuously on the floor in different degrees of nakedness. These places are, generally, as regards dirt, damp and decay, such as no person would stable his horse in." [130]

And in another place:

"The wynds of Glasgow house a fluctuating population of between 15,000 and 30,000 persons. This district is composed of many narrow streets and square courts and in the middle of each court there is a dung-hill. Although the outward appearance of these places was revolting, I was nevertheless quite unprepared for

___

* *Arts and Artisans at Home and Abroad*, by J. C. Symons, Edinburgh, 1839. The author, as it seems, himself a Scotchman, is a Liberal, and consequently fanatically opposed to every independent movement of working-men. The passages here cited are to be found p. 116 *et seq.—Note by Engels.*

___

[a] In the German editions of 1845 and 1892 the quotation is broken by the author's remark "(concerning the exact meaning of this word see below)".—*Ed.*

the filth and misery that were to be found inside. In some of these bedrooms we [i.e. Police Superintendent Captain Miller and Symons] visited at night we found a whole mass of humanity stretched out on the floor. There were often 15 to 20 men and women huddled together, some being clothed and others naked. Their bed was a heap of musty straw mixed with rags. There was hardly any furniture there and the only thing which gave these holes the appearance of a dwelling was fire burning on the hearth. Thieving and prostitution are the main sources of income of these people. No one seems to have taken the trouble to clean out these Augean stables, this pandemonium, this nucleus of crime, filth and pestilence in the second city of the empire. A detailed investigation of the most wretched slums of other towns has never revealed anything half so bad as this concentration of moral iniquity, physical degradation and gross overcrowding.... In this part of Glasgow most of the houses have been condemned by the Court of Guild as dilapidated and uninhabitable—but it is just these dwellings which are filled to overflowing, because, by law no rent can be charged on them."

The great manufacturing district in the centre of the British Islands, the thickly peopled stretch of West Yorkshire and South Lancashire, with its numerous factory towns, yields nothing to the other great manufacturing centres. The wool district of the West Riding of Yorkshire is a charming region, a beautiful green hill country, whose elevations grow more rugged towards the west until they reach their highest point in the bold ridge of Blackstone Edge, the watershed between the Irish Sea and the German Ocean. The valleys of the Aire, along which stretches Leeds, and of the Calder, through which the Manchester-Leeds railway runs, are among the most attractive in England, and are strewn in all directions with the factories, villages, and towns. The houses of rough grey stone look so neat and clean in comparison with the blackened brick buildings of Lancashire, that it is a pleasure to look at them. But on coming into the towns themselves, one finds little to rejoice over. Leeds lies, as the *Artisan* describes it,[a] and as I found confirmed upon examination:

"on a slope running down towards the river Aire, which meanders about a-mile-and-a-half* through the town, and is liable to overflows during thaws or after heavy rains. The higher or western districts are clean for so large a town, but the lower parts contiguous to the river and its becks or rivulets are dirty, confined, and, in themselves, sufficient to shorten life, especially infant life; add to this the disgusting state of the lower parts of the town about Kirk-gate, March-lane, Cross-street and Richmond-road, principally owing to a general want of paving and draining, irregularity of building, the abundance of courts and blind alleys, as well

---

* Whenever miles are mentioned in the text the author refers—unless otherwise specified—to English miles; $69^1/2$ of these correspond to one degree of the Equator, hence 5 English miles roughly equal one German mile.—*Note by Engels*. (This note is omitted from the American edition of 1887 and the English edition of 1892.—*Ed.*)

[a] The German editions of 1845 and 1892 have here in brackets: "elsewhere".—*Ed.*

as the almost total absence of the commonest means for promoting cleanliness, and we have then quite sufficient data to account for the surplus mortality in these unhappy regions of filth and misery.... In consequence of the floods from the Aire" (which, it must be added, like all other rivers in the service of manufacture, flows into the city at one end clear and transparent, and flows out at the other end thick, black, and foul, smelling of all possible refuse), "the dwelling-houses and cellars are not infrequently so inundated that the water has to be pumped out by hand-pumps, on to the surface of the streets; and at such times, even where there are sewers, the water rises through them into the cellars,* creating miasmatic exhalations, strongly charged with sulphuretted hydrogen, and leaving offensive refuse, exceedingly prejudicial to human health. Indeed, during a season of inundation in the spring of 1839, so fatal were the effects of such an engorgement of the sewers, that the registrar of the North district made a report, that during that quarter there were, in that neighbourhood, two births to three deaths, whilst in all the other districts there were three to two deaths." Other populous districts are wholly without sewers, or so inadequately provided as to derive no advantage therefrom. "In some rows of houses, the cellar dwellings are seldom dry"; in certain districts there are several streets covered with soft mud a foot deep. "The inhabitants have from time to time vainly attempted to repair these streets with shovelfuls of ashes; and soil, refuse-water, etc., stand in every hole, there to remain until absorbed by wind or sun....** An ordinary cottage, in Leeds, extends over no more than about five yards square, and consists usually of a cellar, a sitting-room, and a sleeping chamber. This small size of the houses crammed with human beings both day and night, is another point dangerous alike to the morals and the health of the inhabitants."

And how greatly these cottages are crowded, the Report on the Health of the Working-Classes, quoted above,[a] bears testimony:

"In Leeds, brothers and sisters, and lodgers of both sexes, are found occupying the same sleeping-room with the parents, and consequences occur which humanity shudders to contemplate."

So, too, Bradford, which, but seven miles from Leeds at the junction of several valleys, lies upon the banks of a small, coal-black, foul-smelling stream. On week-days the town is enveloped in a grey cloud of coal smoke, but on a fine Sunday it offers a superb picture, when viewed from the surrounding heights. Yet within reigns the same filth and discomfort as in Leeds. The older portions of the town are built upon steep hillsides, and are narrow and irregular. In the lanes, alleys, and courts lie filth and *débris* in heaps; the houses are ruinous, dirty, and miserable, and in the immediate vicinity of the river and the valley bottom I found many a one whose ground-floor, half-buried

* It must be borne in mind that these cellars are not mere storing-rooms for rubbish, but dwellings of human beings.—*Note by Engels.*

** Compare Report of the Town Council in the *Statistical Journal*, Vol. 2, p. 404.—*Note by Engels.* (In the German editions of 1845 and 1892 this reference is given in the text as an author's remark.—*Ed.*)

[a] See p. 339 of this volume.—*Ed.*

in the hillside, was totally abandoned. In general, the portions of the valley bottom in which working-men's cottages have crowded between the tall factories, are among the worst-built and dirtiest districts of the whole town. In the newer portions of this, as of every other factory town, the cottages are more regular, being built in rows, but they share here, too, all the evils incident to the customary method of providing working-men's dwellings, evils of which we shall have occasions to speak more particularly in discussing Manchester. The same is true of the remaining towns of the West Riding, especially of Barnsley, Halifax, and Huddersfield. The last named, the handsomest by far of all the factory towns of Yorkshire and Lancashire by reason of its charming situation and modern architecture, has yet its bad quarter; for a committee appointed by a meeting of citizens to survey the town reported August 5th, 1844:

"It is notorious that there are whole streets in the town of Huddersfield, and many courts and alleys, which are neither flagged, paved, sewered, nor drained; where garbage and filth of every description are left on the surface to ferment and rot; where pools of stagnant water are almost constant, where the dwellings adjoining are thus necessarily caused to be of an inferior and even filthy description; thus where disease is engendered, and the health of the whole town perilled." [131]

If we cross Blackstone Edge or penetrate it with the railroad, we enter upon that classic soil on which English manufacture has achieved its masterwork and from which all labour movements emanate, namely, South Lancashire with its central city Manchester. Again we have beautiful hill country, sloping gently from the watershed westwards towards the Irish Sea, with the charming green valleys of the Ribble, the Irwell, the Mersey, and their tributaries, a country which, a hundred years ago chiefly swamp land, thinly populated, is now sown with towns and villages, and is the most densely populated strip of country in England. In Lancashire, and especially in Manchester, English manufacture finds at once its starting-point and its centre. The Manchester Exchange is the thermometer for all the fluctuations of trade. The modern art of manufacture has reached its perfection in Manchester. In the cotton industry of South Lancashire, the application of the forces of Nature, the superseding of hand-labour by machinery (especially by the power-loom and the self-acting mule), and the division of labour, are seen at the highest point; and, if we recognise in these three elements that which is characteristic of modern manufacture, we must confess that the cotton industry has remained in advance of all other branches of industry from the beginning down to the present day. The effects of modern manufacture upon the working-class must necessarily develop here most freely and perfectly, and the manufacturing proletariat present itself in its fullest classic perfection. The degradation to which the application of steam-power, machinery and the division of labour reduce the working-man, and the attempts of the proletariat to rise above this abasement, must likewise be carried to the highest point and with the fullest consciousness. Hence because Manchester is the classic type of a modern manufacturing town, and because I know it as intimately as my own native town, more intimately than most of its residents know it, we shall make a longer stay here.

The towns surrounding Manchester vary little from the central city, so far as the working-people's quarters are concerned, except that the working-class forms, if possible, a larger proportion of their population. These towns are purely industrial and conduct all their business through Manchester upon which they are in every respect dependent, whence they are inhabited only by working-men and petty tradesmen, while Manchester has a very considerable commercial population, especially of commission and "respectable" retail dealers. Hence Bolton, Preston, Wigan, Bury, Rochdale, Middleton, Heywood, Oldham, Ashton, Stalybridge, Stockport, etc., though nearly all towns of thirty, fifty, seventy to ninety thousand inhabitants, are almost wholly working-people's districts, interspersed only with factories, a few thoroughfares lined with shops, and a few lanes along which the gardens and houses of the manufacturers are scattered like villas. The towns themselves are badly and irregularly built with foul courts, lanes, and back alleys, reeking of coal smoke, and especially dingy from the originally bright red brick, turned black with time, which is here the universal building material. Cellar dwellings are general here; wherever it is in any way possible, these subterranean dens are constructed, and a very considerable portion of the population dwells in them.

Among the worst of these towns after Preston and Oldham is Bolton, eleven miles north-west of Manchester. It has, so far as I have been able to observe in my repeated visits, but one main street, a very dirty one, Deansgate, which serves as a market, and is even in the finest weather a dark, unattractive hole in spite of the fact that, except for the factories, its sides are formed by low one and two-storied houses. Here, as everywhere, the older part of the town is especially ruinous and miserable. A dark-coloured body of water, which leaves the beholder in doubt whether it is a brook or a long string of stagnant puddles, flows through the town and contributes its share to the total pollution of the air, by no means pure without it.

There is Stockport, too, which lies on the Cheshire side of the Mersey, but belongs nevertheless to the manufacturing district of Manchester. It lies in a narrow valley along the Mersey, so that the streets slope down a steep hill on one side and up an equally steep one on the other, while the railway from Manchester to Birmingham passes over a high viaduct above the city and the whole valley. Stockport is renowned throughout the entire district as one of the duskiest, smokiest holes, and looks, indeed, especially when viewed from the viaduct, excessively repellent. But far more repulsive are the cottages and cellar dwellings of the working-class, which stretch in long rows through all parts of the town from the valley bottom to the crest of the hill. I do not remember to have seen so many cellars used as dwellings in any other town of this district.

A few miles north-east of Stockport is Ashton-under-Lyne, one of the newest factory towns of this region. It stands on the slope of a hill at the foot of which are the canal and the river Tame, and is, in general, built on the newer, more regular plan. Five or six parallel streets stretch along the hill, intersected at right angles by others leading down into the valley. By this method, the factories would be excluded from the town proper, even if the proximity of the river and the canal-way did not draw them all into the valley where they stand thickly crowded, belching forth black smoke from their chimneys. To this arrangement Ashton owes a much more attractive appearance than that of most factory towns; the streets are broader and cleaner, the cottages look new, bright red, and comfortable. But the modern system of building cottages for working-men has its own disadvantages; every street has its concealed back lane to which a narrow paved path leads, and which is all the dirtier. And, although I saw no buildings, except a few on entering, which could have been more than fifty years old, there are even in Ashton streets in which the cottages are getting bad, where the bricks in the house-corners are no longer firm but shift about, in which the walls have cracks and will not hold the chalk whitewash inside; streets, whose dirty, smoke-begrimed aspect is nowise different from that of the other towns of the district, except that in Ashton this is the exception, not the rule.

A mile eastward lies Stalybridge, also on the Tame. In coming over the hill from Ashton, the traveller has, at the top, both right and left, fine large gardens with superb villa-like houses in their midst, built usually in the Elizabethan style, which is to the Gothic precisely what the Anglican Church is to the Apostolic Roman

Catholic. A hundred paces farther and Stalybridge shows itself in the valley, in sharp contrast with the beautiful country seats, in sharp contrast even with the modest cottages of Ashton! Stalybridge lies in a narrow, crooked ravine, much narrower even than the valley at Stockport, and both sides of this ravine are occupied by an irregular group of cottages, houses, and mills. On entering, the very first cottages are narrow, smoke-begrimed, old and ruinous; and as the first houses, so the whole town. A few streets lie in the narrow valley bottom, most of them run criss-cross, pell-mell, up hill and down, and in nearly all the houses, by reason of this sloping situation, the ground-floor is half-buried in the earth; and what multitudes of courts, back lanes, and remote nooks arise out of this confused way of building may be seen from the hills, whence one has the town, here and there, in a bird's-eye view almost at one's feet. Add to this the shocking filth, and the repulsive effect of Stalybridge, in spite of its pretty surroundings, may be readily imagined.

But enough of these little towns. Each has its own peculiarities, but in general, the working-people live in them just as in Manchester. Hence I have especially sketched only their peculiar construction, and would observe that all more general observations as to the condition of the labouring population in Manchester are fully applicable to these surrounding towns as well.[a]

Manchester lies at the foot of the southern slope of a range of hills, which stretch hither from Oldham,[b] their last peak, Kersall-moor, being at once the racecourse and the Mons Sacer of Manchester.[132] Manchester proper lies on the left bank of the Irwell, between that stream and the two smaller ones, the Irk and the Medlock, which here empty into the Irwell. On the right bank of the Irwell, bounded by a sharp curve of the river, lies Salford, and farther westward Pendleton; northward from the Irwell lie Upper and Lower Broughton; northward of the Irk, Cheetham Hill; south of the Medlock lies Hulme; farther east Chorlton on Medlock; still farther, pretty well to the east of Manchester, Ardwick. The whole assemblage of buildings is commonly called Manchester, and contains about four hundred thousand inhabitants, rather more than less. The town itself is peculiarly built, so that a person may live in it for years, and go in and out daily without coming into contact with a working-people's quarter or

---

[a] The German editions of 1845 and 1892 have here one more sentence: "We now turn our attention to the principal town."—Ed.

[b] The German editions of 1845 and 1892 have here "between the valleys of the Irwell and the Medlock".—Ed.

even with workers, that is, so long as he confines himself to his
business or to pleasure walks. This arises chiefly from the fact,
that by unconscious tacit agreement, as well as with outspoken
conscious determination, the working-people's quarters are sharply
separated from the sections of the city reserved for the middle-
class; or, if this does not succeed, they are concealed with the cloak
of charity. Manchester contains, at its heart, a rather extended
commercial district, perhaps half a mile long and about as broad,
and consisting almost wholly of offices and warehouses. Nearly the
whole district is abandoned by dwellers, and is lonely and deserted
at night; only watchmen and policemen traverse its narrow lanes
with their dark lanterns. This district is cut through by certain
main thoroughfares upon which the vast traffic concentrates, and
in which the ground level is lined with brilliant shops. In these
streets the upper floors are occupied, here and there, and there is
a good deal of life upon them until late at night. With the
exception of this commercial district, all Manchester proper, all
Salford and Hulme, a great part of Pendleton and Chorlton,
two-thirds of Ardwick, and single stretches of Cheetham Hill and
Broughton are all unmixed working-people's quarters, stretching
like a girdle, averaging a mile and a half in breadth, around the
commercial district. Outside, beyond this girdle, lives the upper
and middle bourgeoisie, the middle bourgeoisie in regularly laid
out streets in the vicinity of the working quarters, especially in
Chorlton and the lower lying portions of Cheetham Hill; the
upper bourgeoisie in remoter villas with gardens in Chorlton and
Ardwick, or on the breezy heights of Cheetham Hill, Broughton,
and Pendleton, in free, wholesome country air, in fine, comfortable homes, passed once every half or quarter hour by omnibuses
going into the city. And the finest part of the arrangement is this,
that the members of this money aristocracy can take the shortest
road through the middle of all the labouring districts to their
places of business without ever seeing that they are in the midst of
the grimy misery that lurks to the right and the left. For the
thoroughfares leading from the Exchange in all directions out of
the city are lined, on both sides, with an almost unbroken series of
shops, and are so kept in the hands of the middle and lower
bourgeoisie, which, out of self-interest, cares for a decent and
cleanly external appearance and *can* care for it. True, these shops
bear some relation to the districts which lie behind them, and are
more elegant in the commercial and residential quarters than
when they hide grimy working-men's dwellings; but they suffice to
conceal from the eyes of the wealthy men and women of strong

stomachs and weak nerves the misery and grime which form the complement of their wealth.[a] So, for instance, Deansgate, which leads from the Old Church directly southward, is lined first with mills and warehouses, then with second-rate shops and alehouses; farther south, when it leaves the commercial district, with less inviting shops, which grow dirtier and more interrupted by beerhouses and gin-palaces the farther one goes, until at the southern end the appearance of the shops leaves no doubt that workers and workers only are their customers. So Market Street running south-east from the Exchange; at first brilliant shops of the best sort, with counting-houses or warehouses above; in the continuation, Piccadilly, immense hotels and warehouses; in the farther continuation, London Road, in the neighbourhood of the Medlock, factories, beerhouses, shops for the humbler bourgeoisie and the working population[b]; and from this point onward, large gardens and villas of the wealthier merchants and manufacturers. In this way any one who knows Manchester can infer the adjoining districts from the appearance of the thoroughfare, but one is seldom in a position to catch from the street a glimpse of the real labouring districts. I know very well that this hypocritical plan is more or less common to all great cities; I know, too, that the retail dealers are forced by the nature of their business to take possession of the great highways; I know that there are more good buildings than bad ones upon such streets everywhere, and that the value of land is greater near them than in remoter districts; but at the same time I have never seen so systematic a shutting out of the working-class from the thoroughfares, so tender a conceal-ment of everything which might affront the eye and the nerves of the bourgeoisie, as in Manchester. And yet, in other respects, Manchester is less built according to a plan, after official[c] regulations, is more an outgrowth of accident than any other city; and when I consider in this connection the eager assurances of the middle-class, that the working-class is doing famously, I cannot help feeling that the Liberal manufacturers, the "Big Wigs"[d] of Manchester, are not so innocent after all, in the matter of this shameful method of construction.

---

[a] The German editions of 1845 and 1892 have "wealth and luxury".—*Ed.*

[b] The German editions of 1845 and 1892 have here "then along Ardwick Green are houses for the higher and middle bourgeoisie".—*Ed.*

[c] The German editions of 1845 and 1892 have "police" instead of "offi-cial".—*Ed.*

[d] The German editions of 1845 and 1892 have these two words in English.—*Ed.*

I may mention just here that the mills almost all adjoin the rivers or the different canals that ramify throughout the city, before I proceed at once to describe the labouring quarters. First of all, there is the Old Town of Manchester, which lies between the northern boundary of the commercial district and the Irk. Here the streets, even the better ones, are narrow and winding, as Todd Street, Long Millgate, Withy Grove, and Shude Hill, the houses

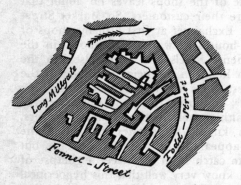

dirty, old, and tumble-down, and the construction of the side streets utterly horrible. Going from the Old Church to Long Millgate, the stroller has at once a row of old-fashioned houses at the right, of which not one has kept its original level; these are remnants of the old pre-manufacturing Manchester, whose former inhabitants

have removed with their descendants into better-built districts, and have left the houses, which were not good enough for them, to a population strongly mixed with Irish blood. Here one is in an almost undisguised working-men's quarter, for even the shops and beerhouses hardly take the trouble to exhibit a trifling degree of cleanliness. But all this is nothing in comparison with the courts and lanes which lie behind, to which access can be gained only through covered passages, in which no two human beings can pass at the same time. Of the irregular cramming together of dwellings in ways which defy all rational plan, of the tangle in which they are crowded literally one upon the other, it is impossible to convey an idea. And it is not the buildings surviving from the old times of Manchester which are to blame for this; the confusion has only recently reached its height when every scrap of space left by the old way of building has been filled up and patched over until not a foot of land is left to be further occupied.

To confirm my statement I have drawn here a small section of the plan of Manchester—not the worst spot and not one-tenth of the whole Old Town.[a]

---

[a] The drawings reproduced in the book as well as the relevant texts here and below are taken from the German editions of 1845 and 1892. In the American edition of 1887 and the English edition of 1892 they are omitted.—*Ed.*

This drawing will suffice to characterise the irrational manner in which the entire district was built, particularly the part near the Irk.

The south bank of the Irk is here very steep and between fifteen and thirty feet high. On this declivitous hillside there are planted three rows of houses, of which the lowest rise directly out of the river, while the front walls of the highest stand on the crest of the hill in Long Millgate. Among them are mills on the river, in short, the method of construction is as crowded and disorderly here as in the lower part of Long Millgate. Right and left a multitude of covered passages lead from the main street into numerous courts, and he who turns in thither gets into a filth and disgusting grime, the equal of which is not to be found—especially in the courts which lead down to the Irk, and which contain unqualifiedly the most horrible dwellings which I have yet beheld. In one of these courts there stands directly at the entrance, at the end of the covered passage, a privy without a door, so dirty that the inhabitants can pass into and out of the court only by passing through foul pools of stagnant urine and excrement. This is the first court on the Irk above Ducie Bridge—in case any one should care to look into it. Below it on the river there are several tanneries which fill the whole neighbourhood with the stench of animal putrefaction. Below Ducie Bridge the only entrance to most of the houses is by means of narrow, dirty stairs and over heaps of refuse and filth. The first court below Ducie Bridge, known as Allen's Court, was in such a state at the time of the cholera that the sanitary police ordered it evacuated, swept, and disinfected with chloride of lime. Dr. Kay gives a terrible description of the state of this court at that time.* Since then, it seems to have been partially torn away and rebuilt; at least looking down from Ducie Bridge, the passer-by sees several ruined walls and heaps of *débris* with some newer houses. The view from this bridge, mercifully concealed from mortals of small stature by a parapet as high as a man, is characteristic for the whole district. At the bottom flows, or rather stagnates, the Irk, a narrow, coal-black, foul-smelling stream, full of *débris* and refuse, which it deposits on the shallower right bank. In dry weather, a long string of the most disgusting, blackish-green, slime pools are left standing on this

* *The Moral and Physical Condition of the Working Classes employed in the Cotton Manufacture in Manchester.* By James Ph. Kay, M.D. 2nd Ed. 1832.

Dr. Kay confuses the working-class in general with the factory workers, otherwise an excellent pamphlet.—*Note by Engels.*

bank, from the depths of which bubbles of miasmatic gas constantly arise and give forth a stench unendurable even on the bridge forty or fifty feet above the surface of the stream. But besides this, the stream itself is checked every few paces by high weirs, behind which slime and refuse accumulate and rot in thick masses. Above the bridge are tanneries,[a] bonemills, and gasworks, from which all drains and refuse find their way into the Irk, which receives further the contents of all the neighbouring sewers and privies. It may be easily imagined, therefore, what sort of residue the stream deposits. Below the bridge you look upon the piles of *débris*, the refuse, filth, and offal from the courts on the steep left bank; here each house is packed close behind its neighbour and a piece of each is visible, all black, smoky, crumbling, ancient, with broken panes and window-frames. The background is furnished by old barrack-like factory buildings. On tne lower right bank stands a long row of houses and mills; the second house being a ruin without a roof, piled with *débris*; the third stands so low that the lowest floor is uninhabitable, and therefore without windows or doors. Here the background embraces the pauper burial-ground, the station of the Liverpool and Leeds railway, and, in the rear of this, the Workhouse, the "Poor-Law Bastille" of Manchester, which, like a citadel, looks threateningly down from behind its high walls and parapets on the hilltop, upon the working-people's quarter below.

Above Ducie Bridge, the left bank grows more flat and the right bank steeper, but the condition of the dwellings on both banks grows worse rather than better. He who turns to the left here from the main street, Long Millgate, is lost; he wanders from one court to another, turns countless corners, passes nothing but narrow, filthy nooks and alleys, until after a few minutes he has lost all clue, and knows not whither to turn. Everywhere half or wholly ruined buildings, some of them actually uninhabited, which means a great deal here; rarely a wooden or stone floor to be seen in the houses, almost uniformly broken, ill-fitting windows and doors, and a state of filth! Everywhere heaps of *débris*, refuse, and offal; standing pools for gutters, and a stench which alone would make it impossible for a human being in any degree civilised to live in such a district. The newly built extension of the Leeds railway, which crosses the Irk here, has swept away some of these courts and lanes, laying others completely open to view. Immediately

---

[a] The German editions of 1845 and 1892 have "dye-works" after "tanneries".— *Ed.*

under the railway bridge there stands a court, the filth and horrors of which surpass all the others by far, just because it was hitherto so shut off, so secluded that the way to it could not be found without a good deal of trouble. I should never have discovered it myself, without the breaks made by the railway, though I thought I knew this whole region thoroughly. Passing along a rough bank, among stakes and washing-lines, one penetrates into this chaos of small one-storied, one-roomed huts, in most of which there is no artificial floor; kitchen, living and sleeping-room all in one. In such a hole, scarcely five feet long by six broad, I found two beds—and such bedsteads and beds! —which, with a staircase and chimney-place, exactly filled the room. In several others I found absolutely nothing, while the door stood open, and the inhabitants leaned against it. Everywhere before the doors refuse and offal; that any sort of pavement lay underneath could not be seen but only felt, here and there, with the feet. This whole collection of cattle-sheds for human beings was surrounded on two sides by houses and a factory, and on the third by the river, and besides the narrow stair up the bank, a narrow doorway alone led out into another almost equally ill-built, ill-kept labyrinth of dwellings.

Enough! The whole side of the Irk is built in this way, a planless, knotted chaos of houses, more or less on the verge of uninhabitableness, whose unclean interiors fully correspond with their filthy external surroundings. And how could the people be clean with no proper opportunity for satisfying the most natural and ordinary wants? Privies are so rare here that they are either filled up every day, or are too remote for most of the inhabitants to use. How can people wash when they have only the dirty Irk water at hand, while pumps and water pipes can be found in decent parts of the city alone? In truth, it cannot be charged to the account of these helots of modern society if their dwellings are not more cleanly than the pig-sties which are here and there to be seen among them. The landlords are not ashamed to let dwellings like the six or seven cellars on the quay directly below Scotland Bridge, the floors of which stand at least two feet below the low-water level of the Irk that flows not six feet away from them; or like the upper floor of the corner-house on the opposite shore directly above the bridge, where the ground-floor, utterly uninhabitable, stands deprived of all fittings for doors and windows, a case by no means rare in this region, when this open ground-floor is used as a privy by the whole neighbourhood for want of other facilities!

If we leave the Irk and penetrate once more on the opposite side from Long Millgate into the midst of the working-men's dwellings, we shall come into a somewhat newer quarter, which stretches from St. Michael's Church to Withy Grove and Shude Hill. Here there is somewhat better order. In place of the chaos of buildings, we find at least long straight lanes and alleys or courts, built according to a plan and usually square. But if, in the former case, every house was built according to caprice, here each lane and court is so built, without reference to the situation of the adjoining ones. The lanes run now in this direction, now in that, while every two minutes the wanderer gets into a blind alley, or, on turning a corner, finds himself back where he started from; certainly no one who has not lived a considerable time in this labyrinth can find his way through it.

If I may use the word at all in speaking of this district, the ventilation of these streets and courts is, in consequence of this confusion, quite as imperfect as in the Irk region; and if this quarter may, nevertheless, be said to have some advantage over that of the Irk, the houses being newer and the streets occasionally having gutters, nearly every house has, on the other hand, a cellar dwelling, which is rarely found in the Irk district, by reason of the greater age and more careless construction of the houses. As for the rest, the filth, *débris*, and offal heaps, and the pools in the streets are common to both quarters, and in the district now under discussion, another feature most injurious to the cleanliness of the inhabitants, is the multitude of pigs walking about in all the alleys, rooting into the offal heaps, or kept imprisoned in small pens. Here, as in most of the working-men's quarters of Manchester, the pork-raisers rent the courts and build pig-pens in them. In almost every court one or even several such pens may be found, into which the inhabitants of the court throw all refuse and offal, whence the swine grow fat; and the atmosphere, confined on all four sides, is utterly corrupted by putrefying animal and vegetable substances. Through this quarter, a broad and measurably decent street has been cut, Millers Street, and the background has been pretty successfully concealed. But if any one should be led by curiosity to pass through one of the numerous passages which lead into the courts, he will find this piggery repeated at every twenty paces.

Such is the Old Town of Manchester, and on re-reading my description, I am forced to admit that instead of being exaggerated, it is far from black enough to convey a true impression of the filth, ruin, and uninhabitableness, the defiance of all considerations of cleanliness, ventilation, and health which characterise the construction of this single district, containing at least twenty to thirty thousand inhabitants. And such a district exists in the heart of the second city of England, the first manufacturing city of the world. If any one wishes to see in how little space a human being can move, how little air — and *such* air! — he can breathe, how little of civilisation he may share and yet live, it is only necessary to travel hither. True, this is the *Old* Town, and the people of Manchester emphasise the fact whenever any one mentions to them the frightful condition of this Hell upon Earth; but what does that prove? Everything which here arouses horror and indignation is of recent origin, belongs to the *industrial epoch* The couple of hundred houses, which belong to old Manchester, have been long since abandoned by their original inhabitants; the industrial epoch alone has crammed into them the swarms of workers whom they now shelter; the industrial epoch alone has built up every spot between these old houses to win a covering for the masses whom it has conjured hither from the agricultural districts and from Ireland; the industrial epoch alone enables the owners of these cattlesheds to rent them for high prices to human beings, to plunder the poverty of the workers, to undermine the health of thousands, in order that they *alone*, the owners, may grow rich. In the industrial epoch alone has it become possible that the worker scarcely freed from feudal servitude could be used as mere material, a mere chattel; that he must let himself be crowded into a dwelling too bad for every other, which he for his hard-earned wages buys the right to let go utterly to ruin. This manufacture has achieved, which, without these workers, this poverty, this slavery could not have lived. True, the original construction of this quarter was bad, little good could have been made out of it; but, have the landowners, has the municipality done anything to improve it when rebuilding? On the contrary, wherever a nook or corner was free, a house has been run up; where a superfluous passage remained, it has been built up; the value of land rose with the blossoming out of manufacture, and the more it rose, the more madly was the work of building up carried on, without reference to the health or comfort of the inhabitants, with sole reference to the highest possible profit on the principle that *no hole is so bad but that some poor creature must take it who can pay for nothing better.* However, it is the Old Town, and with this reflection the bourgeoisie is comforted. Let us see, therefore, how much better it is in the *New Town.*

The *New Town*, known also as Irish Town, stretches up a hill of clay, beyond the Old Town, between the Irk and St. George's Road. Here all the features of a city are lost. Single rows of houses or groups of streets stand, here and there, like little villages on the naked, not even grass-grown clay soil; the houses, or rather cottages, are in bad order, never repaired, filthy, with damp, unclean, cellar dwellings; the lanes are neither paved nor supplied with sewers, but harbour numerous colonies of swine penned in small sties or yards, or wandering unrestrained through the neighbourhood. The mud in the streets is so deep that there is never a chance, except in the dryest weather, of walking without sinking into it ankle deep at every step. In the vicinity of St. George's Road, the separate groups of buildings approach each other more closely, ending in a continuation of lanes, blind alleys, back lanes and courts, which grow more and more crowded and irregular the nearer they approach the heart of the town. True, they are here oftener paved or supplied with paved sidewalks and gutters; but the filth, the bad order of the houses, and especially of the cellars, remain the same.

It may not be out of place to make some general observations just here as to the customary construction of working-men's quarters in Manchester. We have seen how in the Old Town pure accident determined the grouping of the houses in general. Every house is built without reference to any other, and the scraps of space between them are called courts for want of another name.

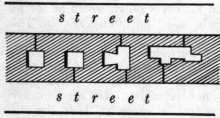

In the somewhat newer portions of the same quarter, and in other working-men's quarters, dating from the early days of industrial activity, a somewhat more orderly arrangement may be found. The space between two streets is divided into more regular, usually square courts.

These courts were built in this way from the beginning,[a] and communicate with the streets by means of covered passages. If the totally planless construction is injurious to the health of the workers by preventing ventilation, this method of shutting them up in courts surrounded on all sides by buildings is far more so. The air simply cannot escape; the chimneys of the houses are the

---

[a] The accompanying drawing is reproduced according to the German editions of 1845 and 1892.—*Ed.*

sole drains for the imprisoned atmosphere of the courts, and they serve the purpose only so long as fire is kept burning.* Moreover, the houses surrounding such courts are usually built back to back, having the rear wall in common; and this alone suffices to prevent any sufficient through ventilation. And, as the police charged with care of the streets does not trouble itself about the condition of these courts, as everything quietly lies where it is thrown, there is no cause for wonder at the filth and heaps of ashes and offal to be found here. I have been in courts, in Millers Street, at least half a foot below the level of the thoroughfare, and without the slightest drainage for the water that accumulates in them in rainy weather!

More recently another different method of building was adopted, and has now become general. Working-men's cottages are almost never built singly, but always by the dozen or score; a single contractor building up one or two streets at a time. These are then arranged as follows: One front is formed of cottages of the best class, so fortunate as to possess a back door and small court, and these command the highest rent. In the rear of these cottages runs a narrow alley, the back street, built up at both ends, into which either a narrow roadway or a covered passage leads from one side. The cottages which face this back street command least rent, and are most neglected. These have their rear walls in common with the third row of cottages, which face a second street and command less rent than the first row and more than the second. The streets are laid out somewhat in the following manner: [a]

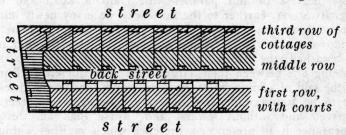

* And yet an English Liberal wiseacre asserts, in the *Report of the Children's Employment Commission,* that these courts are the masterpiece of municipal architecture, because, like a multitude of little parks, they improve ventilation, the circulation of air! Certainly, if each court had two or four broad open entrances facing each other, through which the air could pour; but they never have two, rarely one, and usually only a narrow covered passage.— *Note by Engels.* (The reference is to Grainger's assertion concerning Birmingham courts.— *Ed.*)

[a] The drawing and the words referring to it are reproduced according to the German editions of 1845 and 1892.—*Ed.*

By this method of construction, comparatively good ventilation can be obtained for the first row of cottages, and the third row is no worse off than in the former method. The middle row, on the other hand, is at least as badly ventilated as the houses in the courts, and the 'back street is always in the same filthy, disgusting condition as they. The contractors prefer this method because it saves them space, and furnishes the means of fleecing better-paid workers through the higher rents of the cottages in the first and third rows.

These three different forms of cottage building are found all over Manchester and throughout Lancashire and Yorkshire, often mixed up together, but usually separate enough to indicate the relative age of parts of towns. The third system, that of the back alleys, prevails largely in the great working-men's district east of St. George's Road and Ancoats Street,[a] and is the one most often found in the other working-men's quarters of Manchester and its suburbs.

In the last-mentioned broad district included under the name Ancoats, stand the largest mills of Manchester lining the canals, colossal six and seven-storied buildings towering with their slender chimneys far above the low cottages of the workers. The population of the district consists, therefore, chiefly of mill-hands, and in the worst streets, of hand-weavers. The streets nearest the heart of the town are the oldest, and consequently the worst; they are, however, paved, and supplied with drains. Among them I include those nearest to and parallel with Oldham Road and Great Ancoats Street. Farther to the north-east lie many newly built-up streets; here the cottages look neat and cleanly, doors and windows are new and freshly painted, the rooms within newly whitewashed; the streets themselves are better aired, the vacant building lots between them larger and more numerous. But this can be said of a minority of the houses only, while cellar dwellings are to be found under almost every cottage; many streets are unpaved and without sewers; and, worse than all, this neat appearance is all pretence, a pretence which vanishes within the first ten years. For the construction of the cottages individually is no less to be condemned than the plan of the streets. All such cottages look neat and substantial at first; their massive brick walls deceive the eye, and, on passing through a *newly built* working-men's street, without remembering the back alleys and the con-

---

[a] The German editions of 1845 and 1892 read as follows: "east of St. George's Road on both sides of Oldham Road and Great Ancoats Street".— *Ed.*

struction of the houses themselves, one is inclined to agree with the assertion of the Liberal manufacturers that the working population is nowhere so well housed as in England. But on closer examination, it becomes evident that the walls of these cottages are as thin as it is possible to make them. The outer walls, those of the cellar, which bear the weight of the ground-floor and roof, are one whole brick thick at most, the bricks lying with their long sides touching (▯▯▯▯); but I have seen many a cottage of the same height, some in process of building, whose outer walls were but one-half brick thick, the bricks lying not sidewise but lengthwise, their narrow ends touching (▭▭▭▭).[a] The object of this is to spare material, but there is also another reason for it; namely, the fact that the contractors never own the land but lease it, according to the English custom, for twenty, thirty, forty, fifty, or ninety-nine years, at the expiration of which time it falls, with everything upon it, back into the possession of the original holder, who pays nothing in return for improvements upon it. The improvements are therefore so calculated by the lessee as to be worth as little as possible at the expiration of the stipulated term. And as such cottages are often built but twenty or thirty years before the expiration of the term, it may easily be imagined that the contractors make no unnecessary expenditures upon them. Moreover, these contractors, usually carpenters and builders, or manufacturers, spend little or nothing in repairs, partly to avoid diminishing their rent receipts, and partly in view of the approaching surrender of the improvement to the landowner; while in consequence of commercial crises and the loss of work that follows them, whole streets often stand empty, the cottages falling rapidly into ruin and uninhabitableness. It is calculated in general that working-men's cottages last only forty years on the average. This sounds strangely enough when one sees the beautiful, massive walls of newly built ones, which seem to give promise of lasting a couple of centuries; but the fact remains that the niggardliness of the original expenditure, the neglect of all repairs, the frequent periods of emptiness, the constant change of inhabitants, and the destruction carried on by the dwellers during the final ten years, usually Irish families, who do not hesitate to use the wooden portions for firewood — all this, taken together, accomplishes the complete ruin of the cottages by the end of forty years. Hence it comes that Ancoats, built chiefly since the sudden

---

[a] The drawings are reproduced according to the German editions of 1845 and 1892.—Ed.

growth of manufacture, chiefly indeed within the present century, contains a vast number of ruinous houses, most of them being, in fact, in the last stages of inhabitableness. I will not dwell upon the amount of capital thus wasted, the small additional expenditure upon the original improvement and upon repairs which would suffice to keep this whole district clean, decent, and inhabitable for years together. I have to deal here with the state of the houses and their inhabitants, and it must be admitted that no more injurious and demoralising method of housing the workers has yet been discovered than precisely this. The working-man is constrained to occupy such ruinous dwellings because he cannot pay for others, and because there are no others[a] in the vicinity of his mill; perhaps, too, because they belong to the employer, who engages him only on condition of his taking such a cottage. The calculation with reference to the forty years' duration of the cottage is, of course, not always perfectly strict; for, if the dwellings are in a thickly built-up portion of the town, and there is a good prospect of finding steady occupants for them, while the ground-rent is high, the contractors do a little something to keep the cottages inhabitable after the expiration of the forty years. They never do anything more, however, than is absolutely unavoidable, and the dwellings so repaired are the worst of all. Occasionally when an epidemic threatens, the otherwise sleepy conscience of the sanitary police is a little stirred, raids are made into the working-men's districts, whole rows of cellars and cottages are closed, as happened in the case of several lanes near Oldham Road; but this does not last long: the condemned cottages soon find occupants again, the owners are much better off by letting them, and the sanitary police won't come again so soon. These east and north-east sides of Manchester are the only ones on which the bourgeoisie has not built, because ten or eleven months of the year the west and south-west wind drives the smoke of all the factories hither,[b] and that the working-people alone may breathe.

Southward from Great Ancoats Street, lies a great, straggling, working-men's quarter, a hilly, barren stretch of land, occupied by detached, irregularly built rows of houses or squares, between these, empty building lots, uneven, clayey, without grass and scarcely passable in wet weather. The cottages are all filthy and

---

[a] The German editions of 1845 and 1892 have "no better ones" instead of "no others".—Ed.

[b] The German editions of 1845 and 1892 have "—and there is plenty of it—".—Ed.

old,[a] and recall the New Town to mind. The stretch cut through
by the Birmingham railway is the most thickly built-up and the
worst. Here flows the Medlock with countless windings through a
valley, which is, in places, on a level with the valley of the Irk.
Along both sides of the stream, which is coal-black, stagnant and
foul,[b] stretches a broad belt of factories and working-men's dwellings, the latter all in the worst condition. The bank is chiefly
declivitous and is built over to the water's edge, just as we saw
along the Irk; while the houses are equally bad, whether built on
the Manchester side or in Ardwick, Chorlton, or Hulme. But the
most horrible spot (if I should describe all the separate spots in
detail I should never come to the end) lies on the Manchester side,
immediately south-west of Oxford Road, and is known as Little
Ireland. In a rather deep hole, in a curve of the Medlock and
surrounded on all four sides by tall factories and high embank-
ments, covered with buildings, stand two groups of about two
hundred cottages, built chiefly back to back, in which live about
four thousand human beings, most of them Irish. The cottages are
old, dirty, and of the smallest sort, the streets uneven, fallen into
ruts and in part without drains or pavement; masses of refuse,
offal and sickening filth lie among standing pools in all directions;
the atmosphere is poisoned by the effluvia from these, and laden
and darkened by the smoke of a dozen tall factory chimneys. A
horde of ragged women and children swarm about here, as filthy
as the swine that thrive upon the garbage heaps and in the
puddles. In short, the whole rookery furnishes such a hateful and
repulsive spectacle as can hardly be equalled in the worst court on
the Irk. The race that lives in these ruinous cottages, behind broken
windows, mended with oilskin, sprung doors, and rotten door-
posts, or in dark, wet cellars, in measureless filth and stench, in
this atmosphere penned in as if with a purpose, this race must
really have reached the lowest stage of humanity. This is the
impression and the line of thought which the exterior of this
district forces upon the beholder. But what must one think when
he hears that in each of these pens, containing at most two rooms,
a garret and perhaps a cellar, on the average twenty human beings
live; that in the whole region, for each one hundred and twenty
persons, one usually inaccessible privy is provided; and that in

---

[a] The German editions of 1845 and 1892 have here "often lie in hollows".— *Ed.*

[b] The German editions of 1845 and 1892 have "from where it enters the town
until it joins the Irwell".— *Ed.*

spite of all the preachings of the physicians, in spite of the excitement into which the cholera epidemic plunged the sanitary police by reason of the condition of Little Ireland, in spite of everything, in this year of grace 1844, it is in almost the same state as in 1831! Dr. Kay asserts* that not only the cellars but the first floors of all the houses in this district are damp; that a number of cellars once filled up with earth have now been emptied and are occupied once more by Irish people; that in one cellar the water constantly wells up through a hole stopped with clay, the cellar lying below the river level, so that its occupant, a hand-loom weaver, had to bale out the water from his dwelling every morning and pour it into the street!

Farther down, on the left side of the Medlock, lies Hulme, which properly speaking, is one great working-people's district, the condition of which coincides almost exactly with that of Ancoats; the more thickly built-up regions chiefly bad and approaching ruin, the less populous of more modern structure, but generally sunk in filth.ᵃ On the other side of the Medlock, in Manchester proper, lies a second great working-men's district which stretches on both sides of Deansgate as far as the business quarter, and in certain parts rivals the Old Town. Especially in the immediate vicinity of the business quarter, between Bridge and Quay Streets, Princess and Peter Streets, the crowded construction exceeds in places the narrowest courts of the Old Town. Here are long, narrow lanes between which run contracted, crooked courts and passages, the entrances to which are so irregular that the explorer is caught in a blind alley at every few steps, or comes out where he least expects to, unless he knows every court and every alley exactly and separately. According to Dr. Kay, the most demoralised class of all Manchester lived in these ruinous and filthy districts, people whose occupations are thieving and prostitution; and, to all appearances, his assertion is still true at the present moment. When the sanitary police made its expedition hither in 1831, it found the uncleanness as great as in Little Ireland or along the Irk (that it is not much better today, I can testify); and, among other items, they found in Parliament Street for three

---

* Dr. Kay, loc. cit.—*Note by Engels.* (It is omitted in the English and American editions.—*Ed.*)

ᵃ In the German editions of 1845 and 1892 the end of the sentence reads as follows: "of more modern structure, better ventilated, but generally sunk in filth". Then follows one more sentence omitted in the authorised American and English editions: "In both places the site of the cottages is damp and the type of building includes back alleys and cellar dwellings".—*Ed.*

hundred and eighty persons, and in Parliament Passage for thirty thickly populated houses, but a single privy.

If we cross the Irwell to Salford, we find on a peninsula formed by the river a town of eighty thousand inhabitants, which, properly speaking, is one large working-men's quarter, penetrated by a single wide avenue. Salford, once more important than Manchester, was then the leading town of the surrounding district to which it still gives its name, Salford Hundred. Hence it is that an old and therefore very unwholesome, dirty, and ruinous locality is to be found here, lying opposite the Old Church of Manchester, and in as bad a condition as the Old Town on the other side of the Irwell. Farther away from the river lies the newer portion, which is, however, already beyond the limit of its forty years of cottage life,[a] and therefore ruinous enough. All Salford is built in courts or narrow lanes, so narrow, that they remind me of the narrowest I have ever seen, the little lanes of Genoa. The average construction of Salford is in this respect much worse than that of Manchester, and so, too, in respect to cleanliness. If, in Manchester, the police, from time to time, every six or ten years, makes a raid upon the working-people's districts, closes the worst dwellings, and causes the filthiest spots in these Augean stables to be cleansed, in Salford it seems to have done absolutely nothing. The narrow side lanes and courts of Chapel Street, Greengate, and Gravel Lane have certainly never been cleansed since they were built. Of late, the Liverpool railway has been carried through the middle of them, over a high viaduct, and has abolished many of the filthiest nooks; but what does that avail? Whoever passes over this viaduct and looks down, sees filth and wretchedness enough; and, if any one takes the trouble to pass through these lanes and glance through the open doors and windows into the houses and cellars, he can convince himself afresh with every step that the workers of Salford live in dwellings in which cleanliness and comfort are impossible. Exactly the same state of affairs is found in the more distant regions of Salford, in Islington, along Regent Road, and back of the Bolton railway. The working-men's dwellings between Oldfield Road and Cross Lane, where[b] a mass of courts and alleys are to be found in the worst possible state, vie with the dwellings of the Old Town in filth and overcrowding. In this district I found a man, apparently about sixty years old, living

---

[a] In the German editions of 1845 and 1892 the words "of cottage life" do not occur.—*Ed.*

[b] The German editions of 1845 and 1892 have here "on both sides of Hope Street".—*Ed.*

in a cow-stable. He had constructed a sort of chimney for his square pen, which had neither windows, floor, nor ceiling, had obtained a bedstead and lived there, though the rain dripped through his rotten roof. This man was too old and weak for regular work, and supported himself by removing manure with a hand-cart; the dung-heaps lay next door to his palace!

Such are the various working-people's quarters of Manchester as I had occasion to observe them personally during twenty months. If we briefly formulate the result of our wanderings, we must admit that 350,000 working-people of Manchester and its environs live, almost all of them, in wretched, damp, filthy cottages, that the streets which surround them are usually in the most miserable and filthy condition, laid out without the slightest reference to ventilation, with reference solely to the profit secured by the contractor. In a word, we must confess that in the working-men's dwellings of Manchester, no cleanliness, no convenience, and consequently no comfortable family life is possible; that in such dwellings only a physically degenerate race, robbed of all humanity, degraded, reduced morally and physically[a] to bestiality, could feel comfortable and at home. And I am not alone in making this assertion. We have seen that Dr. Kay gives precisely the same description; and, though it is superfluous, I quote further the words of a Liberal, recognised and highly valued as an authority by the manufacturers, and a fanatical opponent of all independent movements of the workers*:

"But when I went through their [i.e., the Manchester operatives'] habitations in Irish Town, and Ancoats, and Little Ireland, my only wonder was that tolerable health could be maintained by the inmates of such houses. These towns, for such they are in extent and population, have been erected by small speculators with an utter disregard to everything except immediate profit. A carpenter and a bricklayer club to buy a patch of ground [i.e., they lease it for a number of years], and cover it with what they call houses. In one place we saw a whole street following the course of a ditch, in order to have deeper cellars (cellars for people, not for lumber) without the expense of excavations. *Not a house in this street escaped cholera.*[b] And generally speaking, throughout these suburbs the streets are unpaved, with a dung-hill or a pond in the middle; the houses built back to back, without ventilation or drainage; and whole families occupy a corner of a cellar or of a garret."

---

* Nassau W. Senior, *Letters on the Factory Act to the Rt. Hon., the President of the Board of Trade* (Chas. Poulett Thomson, Esq.), London, 1837, p. 24.—*Note by Engels.*

---

[a] The German editions of 1845 and 1892 have "intellectually" instead of "physically".—*Ed.*

[b] Italics by Engels.—*Ed.*

I have already referred to the unusual activity which the sanitary police manifested during the cholera visitation. When the epidemic was approaching, a universal terror seized the bourgeoisie of the city. People remembered the unwholesome dwellings of the poor, and trembled before the certainty that each of these slums would become a centre for the plague, whence it would spread desolation in all directions through the houses of the propertied class. A Health Commission was appointed at once to investigate these districts, and report upon their condition to the Town Council. Dr. Kay, himself a member of this Commission, who visited in person every separate police district except one, the eleventh, quotes extracts from their reports: There were inspected, in all, 6,951 houses — naturally in Manchester proper alone, Salford and the other suburbs being excluded. Of these, 2,565 urgently needed whitewashing within; 960 were out of repair[a]; 939 had insufficient drains; 1,435 were damp; 452 were badly ventilated; 2,221 were without privies. Of the 687 streets inspected, 248 were unpaved, 53 but partially paved, 112 ill-ventilated, 352 containing standing pools, heaps of *débris*, refuse, etc. To cleanse such an Augean stable before the arrival of the cholera was, of course, out of the question. A few of the worst nooks were therefore cleansed, and everything else left as before..In the cleansed spots, as Little Ireland proves, the old filthy condition was naturally restored in a couple of months. As to the internal condition of these houses, the same Commission reports a state of things similar to that which we have already met with in London, Edinburgh, and other cities.*

"A whole Irish family is often accommodated on a single bed, and sometimes a heap of filthy straw and a covering of old sacking hide them in one undistinguished heap, debased alike by penury, want of economy and dissolute habits. Frequently the inspectors found two families crowded into one small house, containing only two apartments, one in which they slept, and another in which they eat; and often more than one family lived in a damp cellar, containing only one room, in whose pestilential atmosphere from twelve to sixteen persons were crowded. To these fertile sources of disease were sometimes added the keeping of the pigs and other animals in the house, with other nuisances of the most revolting character."

We must add that many families, who had but one room for themselves, receive boarders and lodgers in it, that such lodgers of

* Kay, loc. cit., p. 32.—*Note by Engels.* (The word "Irish" in the quotation below was added by Engels.—*Ed.*)

---

[a] The German editions of 1845 and 1892 give the English expression "were out of repair" in brackets.—*Ed.*

both sexes by no means rarely sleep in the same bed with the married couple; and that the single case of a man and his wife and his adult sister-in-law sleeping in one bed was found, according to the "Report on the Sanitary Condition of the Labouring Population", six times repeated in Manchester. Common lodging-houses, too, are very numerous; Dr. Kay gives their number in 1831 as 267 in Manchester proper, and they must have increased greatly since then. Each of these receives from twenty to thirty guests, so that they shelter all told, nightly, from five to seven thousand human beings. The character of the houses and their guests is the same as in other cities. Five to seven beds in each room lie on the floor — without bedsteads, and on these sleep, mixed indiscriminately, as many persons as apply. What physical and moral atmosphere reigns in these holes I need not state. Each of these houses is a focus of crime, the scene of deeds against which human nature revolts, which would perhaps never have been executed but for this forced centralisation of vice. Gaskell* gives the number of persons living in cellars in Manchester proper as 20,000. The *Weekly Dispatch* gives the number, "according to official reports", as twelve per cent of the working-class, which agrees with Gaskell's number; the workers being estimated at 175,000, 21,000 would form twelve per cent of it.[133] The cellar dwellings in the suburbs are at least as numerous, so that the number of persons living in cellars in Manchester — using its name in the broader sense — is not less than forty to fifty thousand. So much for the dwellings of the workers in the largest cities and towns. The manner in which the need of a shelter is satisfied furnishes a standard for the manner in which all other necessities are supplied. That in these filthy holes a ragged, ill-fed population alone can dwell is a safe conclusion, and such is the fact. The clothing of the working-people, in the majority of cases, is in a

---

* P. Gaskell, *The Manufacturing Population of England: its Moral, Social and Physical Condition, and the Changes which have arisen from the Use of Steam Machinery; with an Examination of Infant Labour. Fiat Justitia,* 1833.— Depicting chiefly the state of the working-class in Lancashire. The author is a Liberal, but wrote at a time when it was not a feature of Liberalism to chant the happiness of the workers. He is therefore unprejudiced, and can afford to have eyes for the evils of the present state of things, and especially for the factory system. On the other hand, he wrote before the Factories Enquiry Commission, and adopts from untrustworthy sources many assertions afterwards refuted by the report of the Commission. This work, although on the whole a valuable one, can therefore only be used with discretion, especially as the author, like Kay, confuses the whole working-class with the mill-hands. The history of the development of the proletariat contained in the introduction to the present work, is chiefly taken from this work of Gaskell's.— *Note by Engels.*

very bad condition. The material used for it is not of the best adapted. Wool and linen have almost vanished from the wardrobe of both sexes, and cotton has taken their place. Shirts are made of bleached or coloured cotton goods; the dresses of the women are chiefly of cotton print goods, and woollen petticoats are rarely to be seen on the washline. The men wear chiefly trousers of fustian or other heavy cotton goods, and jackets or coats of the same. Fustian has become the proverbial costume of the working-men, who are called "fustian jackets",[a] and call themselves so in contrast to the gentlemen who wear broadcloth, which latter words are used as characteristic for the middle-class. When Feargus O'Connor, the Chartist leader, came to Manchester during the insurrection of 1842,[b] he appeared, amidst the deafening applause of the working-men, in a fustian suit of clothing. Hats are the universal head-covering in England, even for working-men, hats of the most diverse forms, round, high, broad-brimmed, narrow-brimmed, or without brims—only the younger men in factory towns wearing caps. Any one who does not own a hat folds himself a low, square paper cap.

The whole clothing of the working-class, even assuming it to be in good condition, is little adapted to the climate. The damp air of England, with its sudden changes of temperature, more calculated than any other to give rise to colds, obliges almost the whole middle-class to wear flannel next to the skin, about the body, and flannel scarfs and shirts are in almost universal use. Not only is the working-class deprived of this precaution, it is scarcely ever in a position to use a thread of woollen clothing; and the heavy cotton goods, though thicker, stiffer, and heavier than woollen clothes, afford much less protection against cold and wet, remain damp much longer because of their thickness and the nature of the stuff, and have nothing of the compact density of fulled woollen cloths. And, if a working-man once buys himself a woollen coat for Sunday, he must get it from one of the "cheap shops" where he finds bad, so-called "Devil's-dust"[c] cloth, manufactured for sale and not for use, and liable to tear or grow threadbare in a fortnight, or he must buy of an old clothes'-dealer a half-worn coat which has seen its best days, and lasts but a few weeks.

---

[a] In the German editions of 1845 and 1892 this expression is given in English; the word "broadcloth" is given in brackets after its German equivalent.—*Ed.*

[b] See below, pp. 508, 512-14, 520-22.—*Ed.*

[c] In the German editions of 1845 and 1892 this expression is given in English.—*Ed.*

Moreover, the working-man's clothing is, in most cases, in bad condition, and there is the oft-recurring necessity for placing the best pieces in the pawnbroker's shop. But among very large numbers, especially among the Irish, the prevailing clothing consists of perfect rags often beyond all mending, or so patched that the original colour can no longer be detected. Yet the English and Anglo-Irish go on patching, and have carried this art to a remarkable pitch, putting wool or bagging on fustian, or the reverse—it's all the same to them. But the true, transplanted Irish hardly ever patch except in the extremest necessity, when the garment would otherwise fall apart. Ordinarily the rags of the shirt protrude through the rents in the coat or trousers. They wear, as Thomas Carlyle says,—*

"a suit of tatters, the getting on or off which is said to be a difficult operation, transacted only in festivals and the high tides of the calendar."

The Irish have introduced, too, the custom, previously unknown in England, of going barefoot. In every manufacturing town there is now to be seen a multitude of people, especially women and children, going about barefoot, and their example is gradually being adopted by the poorer English.

As with clothing, so with food. The workers get what is too bad for the property-holding class. In the great towns of England everything may be had of the best, but it costs money; and the workman, who must keep house on a couple of pence, cannot afford much expense. Moreover, he usually receives his wages on Saturday evening, for, although a beginning has been made in the payment of wages on Friday, this excellent arrangement is by no means universal; and so he comes to market at five or even seven o'clock,[a] while the buyers of the middle-class have had the first choice during the morning, when the market teems with the best of everything. But when the workers reach it, the best has vanished, and, if it was still there, they would probably not be able to buy it. The potatoes which the workers buy are usually poor, the vegetables wilted, the cheese old and of poor quality, the bacon rancid, the meat lean, tough, taken from old, often diseased, cattle, or such as have died a natural death, and not fresh even then, often half decayed. The sellers are usually small

---

* Thomas Carlyle, *Chartism*, London, 1840, p. 28. Concerning Thomas Carlyle see below.—*Note by Engels*. (In the American edition of 1887 and the English edition of 1892 the last phrase is omitted.—*Ed.*)

---

[a] The German editions of 1845 and 1892 have here "at four, five or even seven o'clock".—*Ed.*

hucksters who buy up inferior goods, and can sell them cheaply by reason of their badness. The poorest workers are forced to use still another device to get together the things they need with their few pence. As nothing can be sold on Sunday, and all shops must be closed at twelve o'clock on Saturday night, such things as would not keep until Monday are sold at any price between ten o'clock and midnight. But nine-tenths of what is sold at ten o'clock is past using by Sunday morning, yet these are precisely the provisions which make up the Sunday dinner of the poorest class. The meat which the workers buy is very often past using; but having bought it, they must eat it. On the 6th of January, 1844 (if I am not greatly mistaken), a court leet[a] was held in Manchester, when eleven meat-sellers were fined for having sold tainted meat. Each of them had a whole ox or pig, or several sheep, or from fifty to sixty pounds of meat, which were all confiscated in a tainted condition. In one case, fifty-four stuffed Christmas geese were seized which had proved unsaleable in Liverpool, and had been forwarded to Manchester, where they were brought to market foul and rotten. All the particulars, with names and fines, were published at the time in the *Manchester Guardian*.[134] In the six weeks, from July lst to August 14th [1844], the same sheet reported three similar cases. According to the *Guardian* for July 3rd, a pig, weighing 200 pounds, which had been found dead and decayed, was cut up and exposed for sale by a butcher at Heywood, and was then seized. According to the number for July 31st, two butchers at Wigan, of whom one had previously been convicted of the same offence, were fined £2 and £4 respectively, for exposing tainted meat for sale; and, according to the number for August 10th, twenty-six tainted hams seized at a dealer's in Bolton, were publicly burnt, and the dealer fined twenty shillings. But these are by no means all the cases; they do not even form a fair average for a period of six weeks, according to which to form an average for the year. There are often seasons in which every number of the semi-weekly *Guardian* mentions a similar case found in Manchester or its vicinity. And when one reflects upon the many cases which must escape detection in the extensive markets that stretch along the front of every main street, under the slender supervision of the market inspectors—and how else can one explain the boldness with which whole animals are exposed for sale?—when one considers how great the temptation

---

[a] In the German editions of 1845 and 1892 this English term is given in brackets.—*Ed.*

must be, in view of the incomprehensibly small fines mentioned in the foregoing cases; when one reflects what condition a piece of meat must have reached to be seized by the inspectors, it is impossible to believe that the workers obtain good and nourishing meat as a usual thing. But they are victimised in yet another way by the money-greed of the middle-class. Dealers and manufacturers adulterate all kinds of provisions in an atrocious manner, and without the slightest regard to the health of the consumers. We have heard the *Manchester Guardian* upon this subject, let us hear another organ of the middle-class—I delight in the testimony of my opponents—let us hear the *Liverpool Mercury*:

"Salt butter is moulded into the form of pounds of fresh butter, and cased over with fresh. In other instances a pound of fresh is conspicuously placed to be tasted; but that pound is not sold; and in other instances salt butter, washed, is moulded and sold as fresh.... Pounded rice and other cheap materials are mixed in sugar, and sold at full monopoly price. A chemical substance—the refuse of the soap manufactories—is also mixed with other substances and sold as sugar.... Chicory is mixed in good coffee. Chicory, or some similarly cheap substance, is skilfully moulded into the form of the coffee berry, and is mixed with the bulk very liberally.... Cocoa is extensively adulterated with fine brown earth, wrought up with mutton fat, so as to amalgamate with portions of the real article.... The leaves of tea are mingled with sloe leaves and other abominations. Used leaves are also re-dried, and re-coloured on hot copper plates, and sold as tea. Pepper is adulterated with dust from husks etc.; port wine is altogether manufactured" (from spirits, dyes, etc.) "it being notorious that more port wine is drunk in this country than is made in Portugal. Nasty things of all sorts are mixed with the weed tobacco in all its manufactured forms".[135]

I can add that several of the most respected tobacco dealers in Manchester announced publicly last summer, that, by reason of the universal adulteration of tobacco, no firm could carry on business without adulteration, and that no cigar costing less than threepence is made wholly from tobacco. These frauds are naturally not restricted to articles of food, though I could mention a dozen more, the villainy of mixing gypsum or chalk with flour among them. Fraud is practised in the sale of articles of every sort: flannel, stockings, etc., are stretched, and shrink after the first washing; narrow cloth is sold as being from one and a half to three inches broader than it actually is; stoneware is so thinly glazed that the glazing is good for nothing and cracks at once, and a hundred other rascalities, *tout comme chez nous*. But the lion's share of the evil results of these frauds falls to the workers. The rich are less deceived, because they can pay the high prices of the large shops which have a reputation to lose, and would injure themselves more than their customers if they kept poor or adulterated wares; the rich are spoiled, too, by habitual good eating, and detect adulteration more easily with their sensitive palates. But the poor, the working-people, to whom a couple of farthings are important, who must buy many things with little money, who cannot afford to inquire too closely into the quality of their purchases, and cannot do so in any case because they have had no opportunity of cultivating their taste—to their share fall all the adulterated, poisoned provisions. They must deal with the small retailers, must buy perhaps on credit, and these small retail dealers who cannot sell even the same quality of goods so cheaply as the largest retailers, because of their small capital and the large proportional expenses of their business, must knowingly or unknowingly buy adulterated goods in order to sell at the lower prices required, and to meet the competition of the others. Further, a large retail dealer who has extensive capital invested in his business is ruined with his ruined credit if detected in a fraudulent practice; but what harm does it do a small grocer, who has customers in a single street only, if frauds are proved against him? If no one trusts him in Ancoats, he moves to Chorlton or Hulme, where no one knows him, and where he continues to defraud as before; while legal penalties attach to very few adulterations unless they involve revenue frauds. Not in the quality alone, but in the quantity of his goods as well, is the English working-man defrauded. The small dealers usually have false weights and measures, and an incredible number of convictions for such offences may be read in the police reports. How universal this form of fraud is in the manufacturing districts, a couple of extracts from the *Manchester Guardian* may serve to show. They cover only a short period, and, even here, I have not all the numbers at hand:

Guardian, June 15, 1844, Rochdale Sessions.—Four dealers fined five to ten shillings for using light weights. Stockport Sessions.—Two dealers fined one shilling, one of them having seven light weights and a false scale, and both having been warned.

Guardian, June 19, Rochdale Sessions.—One dealer fined five, and two farmers ten shillings.

Guardian, June 22, Manchester Justices of the Peace.—Nineteen dealers fined two shillings and sixpence to two pounds.

Guardian, June 26, Ashton Sessions.—Fourteen dealers and farmers fined two shillings and sixpence to one pound. Hyde Petty Sessions.—Nine farmers and dealers condemned to pay costs and five shillings fines.

Guardian, July 6, Manchester.—Sixteen dealers condemned to pay costs and fines not exceeding ten shillings.

Guardian, July 13, Manchester.—Nine dealers fined from two shillings and sixpence to twenty shillings.

Guardian, July 24, Rochdale.—Four dealers fined ten to twenty shillings.

Guardian, July 27, Bolton.—Twelve dealers and innkeepers condemned to pay costs.

Guardian, August 3, Bolton.—Three dealers fined two shillings and sixpence, and five shillings.

Guardian, August 10, Bolton.—One dealer fined five shillings.

And the same causes which make the working-class the chief sufferers from frauds in the quality of goods make them the usual victims of frauds in the question of quantity too.

The habitual food of the individual working-man naturally varies according to his wages. The better-paid workers, especially those in whose families every member is able to earn something, have good food as long as this state of things lasts; meat daily and bacon and cheese for supper. Where wages are less, meat is used only two or three times a week,[a] and the proportion of bread and potatoes increases. Descending gradually, we find the animal food reduced to a small piece of bacon cut up with the potatoes; lower still, even this disappears, and there remain only bread, cheese, porridge, and potatoes, until on the lowest round of the ladder, among the Irish, potatoes form the sole food. As an accompaniment, weak tea, with perhaps a little sugar, milk, or spirits, is universally drunk. Tea is regarded in England, and even in Ireland, as quite as indispensable as coffee in Germany, and where no tea is used, the bitterest poverty reigns. But all this presupposes that the workman has work. When he has none, he is wholly at the mercy of accident, and eats what is given him, what he can beg or steal. And, if he gets nothing, he simply starves, as we have seen. The quantity of food varies, of course, like its quality, according to the rate of wages, so that among ill-paid workers, even if they have no large families,[b] hunger prevails in spite of full and regular work; and the number of the ill-paid is very large. Especially in London, where the competition of the workers rises with the increase of population, this class is very numerous, but it is to be found in other towns as well. In these cases all sorts of devices are

---

[a] The German editions of 1845 and 1892 have "on Sundays or two or three times a week".—*Ed.*

[b] The German editions of 1845 and 1892 have "especially if they have large families".—*Ed.*

used; potato parings, vegetable refuse, and rotten vegetables* are eaten for want of other food, and everything greedily gathered up which may possibly contain an atom of nourishment. And, if the week's wages are used up before the end of the week, it often enough happens that in the closing days the family gets only as much food, if any, as is barely sufficient to keep off starvation. Of course such a way of living unavoidably engenders a multitude of diseases, and when these appear, when the father from whose work the family is chiefly supported, whose physical exertion most demands nourishment, and who therefore first succumbs—when the father is utterly disabled, then misery reaches its height, and then the brutality with which society abandons its members, just when their need is greatest, comes out fully into the light of day.

To sum up briefly the facts thus far cited. The great towns are chiefly inhabited by working-people, since in the best case there is one bourgeois for two workers, often for three, here and there for four; these workers have no property whatsoever of their own, and live wholly upon wages, which usually go from hand to mouth. Society, composed wholly of atoms, does not trouble itself about them; leaves them to care for themselves and their families, yet supplies them no means of doing this in an efficient and permanent manner. Every working-man, even the best, is there-fore constantly exposed to loss of work and food, that is to death by starvation, and many perish in this way. The dwellings of the workers are everywhere badly planned, badly built, and kept in the worst condition, badly ventilated, damp, and unwholesome. The inhabitants are confined to the smallest possible space, and at least one family usually sleeps in each room. The interior arrangement of the dwellings is poverty-stricken in various de-grees, down to the utter absence of even the most necessary furniture. The clothing of the workers, too, is generally scanty, and that of great multitudes is in rags. The food is, in general, bad; often almost unfit for use, and in many cases, at least at times, insufficient in quantity, so that, in extreme cases, death by starvation results. Thus the working-class of the great cities offers a graduated scale of conditions in life, in the best cases a temporarily endurable existence for hard work and good wages,[a]

---

* *Weekly Dispatch*, April or May, 1844, according to a report by Dr. Southwood Smith on the condition of the poor in London.—*Note by Engels*. (In the American edition of 1887 and in the English edition of 1892 this note is omitted.—*Ed.*)

---

[a] The German editions of 1845 and 1892 have here "good housing and generally good food".—*Ed.*

good and endurable, that is, from the worker's standpoint; in the worst cases, bitter want, reaching even homelessness and death by starvation. The average is much nearer the worst case than the best. And this series does not fall into fixed classes, so that one can say, this fraction of the working-class is well off,[a] has always been so, and remains so. If that is the case here and there, if single branches of work have in general an advantage over others, yet the condition of the workers in each branch is subject to such great fluctuations that a single working-man may be so placed as to pass through the whole range from comparative comfort to the extremest need, even to death by starvation, while almost every English working-man can tell a tale of marked changes of fortune. Let us examine the causes of this somewhat more closely.

---

[a] The German editions of 1845 and 1892 have "and that fraction is badly off".—*Ed.*

COMPETITION

   We have seen in the introduction how competition created the
proletariat at the very beginning of the industrial movement by
increasing the wages of weavers in consequence of the increased
demand for woven goods, so inducing the weaving peasants to
abandon their farms and earn more money by devoting themselves to their looms. We have seen how it crowded out the small
farmers by means of the large farm system, reduced them to the
rank of proletarians, and attracted them in part into the towns;
how it further ruined the small bourgeoisie in great measure and
reduced its members also to the ranks of the proletariat; how it
centralised capital in the hands of the few, and population in the
great towns. Such are the various ways and means by which
competition, as it reached its full manifestation and free development in modern industry, created and extended the proletariat.
We shall now have to observe its influence on the working-class
already created. And here we must begin by tracing the results of
competition of single workers with one another.
   Competition is the completest expression of the battle of all
against all which rules in modern civil society. This battle, a battle
for life, for existence, for everything, in case of need a battle of
life and death, is fought not between the different classes of
society only, but also between the individual members of these
classes. Each is in the way of the other, and each seeks to crowd
out all who are in his way, and to put himself in their place. The
workers are in constant competition among themselves as the
members of the bourgeoisie among themselves. The power-loom
weaver is in competition with the hand-loom weaver, the unem-

ployed or ill-paid hand-loom weaver with him who has work or is better paid, each trying to supplant the other. But this competition of the workers among themselves is the worst side of the present state of things in its effect upon the worker, the sharpest weapon against the proletariat in the hands of the bourgeoisie. Hence the effort of the workers to nullify this competition by associations, hence the hatred of the bourgeoisie towards these associations, and its triumph in every defeat which befalls them.

The proletarian is helpless; left to himself, he cannot live a single day. The bourgeoisie has gained a monopoly of all means of existence in the broadest sense of the word. What the proletarian needs, he can obtain only from this bourgeoisie, which is protected in its monopoly by the power of the state. The proletarian is, therefore, in law and in fact, the slave of the bourgeoisie, which can decree his life or death. It offers him the means of living, but only for an "equivalent", for his work. It even lets him have the appearance of acting from a free choice, of making a contract with free, unconstrained consent, as a responsible agent who has attained his majority.

Fine freedom, where the proletarian has no other choice than that of either accepting the conditions which the bourgeoisie offers him, or of starving, of freezing to death, of sleeping naked among the beasts of the forests! A fine "equivalent" valued at pleasure by the bourgeoisie! And if one proletarian is such a fool as to starve rather than agree to the "equitable" propositions of the bourgeoisie, his "natural superiors",* another is easily found in his place; there are proletarians enough in the world, and not all so insane as to prefer dying to living.

Here we have the competition of the workers among themselves. If *all* the proletarians announced their determination to starve rather than work for the bourgeoisie, the latter would have to surrender its monopoly. But this is not the case — is, indeed, a rather impossible case — so that the bourgeoisie still thrives. To this competition of the workers there is but one limit; no worker will work for less than he needs to subsist. If he must starve, he will prefer to starve in idleness rather than in toil. True, this limit is relative; one needs more than another, one is accustomed to more comfort than another; the Englishman, who is still somewhat civilised, needs more than the Irishman, who goes in rags, eats

---

* A favourite expression of the English manufacturers.—*Note by Engels*. (In the American edition of 1887 and the English edition of 1892 this note is omitted.—*Ed*.)

potatoes, and sleeps in a pig-sty. But that does not hinder the Irishman's competing with the Englishman, and gradually forcing the rate of wages, and with it the Englishman's level of civilisation, down to the Irishman's level. Certain kinds of work require a certain grade of civilisation, and to these belong almost all forms of industrial occupation; hence the interest of the bourgeoisie requires in this case that wages should be high enough to enable the workman to keep himself upon the required plane.

The newly immigrated Irishman, encamped in the first stable that offers, or[a] turned out in the street after a week because he spends everything upon drink and cannot pay rent, would be a poor mill-hand. The mill-hand must, therefore, have wages enough to enable him to bring up his children to regular work; but no more, lest he should be able to get on without the wages of his children, and so make something else of them than mere working-men. Here, too, the limit, the minimum wage, is relative. When every member of the family works, the individual worker can get on with proportionately less, and the bourgeoisie has made the most of the opportunity of employing and making profitable the labour of women and children afforded by machine-work. Of course it is not in every family that every member can be set to work, and those in which the case is otherwise would be in a bad way if obliged to exist upon the minimum wage possible to a wholly employed family. Hence the usual wages form an average according to which a fully employed family gets on pretty well, and one which embraces few members able to work, pretty badly. But in the worst case, every working-man prefers surrendering the trifling luxury to which he was accustomed to not living at all; prefers a pig-pen to no roof, wears rags in preference to going naked, confines himself to a potato diet in preference to starvation. He contents himself with half-pay and the hope of better times rather than be driven into the street to perish before the eyes of the world, as so many have done who had no work whatever. This trifle, therefore, this something more than nothing, is the minimum of wages. And if there are more workers at hand than the bourgeoisie thinks well to employ — if at the end of the battle of competition there yet remain workers who find nothing to do, they must simply starve; for the bourgeois will hardly give them work if he cannot sell the produce of their labour at a profit.

---

[a] The German editions of 1845 and 1892 have here: "or, even if he has a tolerable dwelling, is turned" etc.—*Ed.*

From this it is evident what the minimum of wages is. The maximum is determined by the competition of the bourgeoisie among themselves; for we have seen how they, too, must compete with each other. The bourgeois can increase his capital only in commerce and manufacture, and in both cases he needs workers. Even if he invests his capital at interest, he needs them indirectly; for without commerce and manufacture, no one would pay him interest upon his capital, no one could use it. So the bourgeois certainly needs workers, not indeed for his immediate living, for at need he could consume his capital, but as we need an article of trade or a beast of burden — as a means of profit. The proletarian produces the goods which the bourgeois sells with advantage. When, therefore, the demand for these goods increases so that all the competing working-men are employed, and a few more might perhaps be useful, the competition among the workers falls away, and the bourgeoisie begin to compete among themselves. The capitalist in search of workmen knows very well that his profits increase as prices rise in consequence of the increased demand for his goods, and pays a trifle higher wages rather than let the whole profit escape him. He sends the butter to fetch the cheese, and getting the latter, leaves the butter ungrudgingly to the workers.[a] So one capitalist after another goes in chase of workers, and wages rise; but only as high as the increasing demand permits. If the capitalist, who willingly sacrificed a part of his extraordinary profit, runs into danger of sacrificing any part of his ordinary average profit, he takes very good care not to pay more than average wages.

From this we can determine the average rate of wages. Under average circumstances, when neither workers nor capitalists have reason to compete, especially among themselves, when there are just as many workers at hand as can be employed in producing precisely the goods that are demanded, wages stand a little above the minimum. How far they rise above the minimum will depend upon the average needs and the grade of civilisation of the workers. If the workers are accustomed to eat meat several times in the week, the capitalists must reconcile themselves to paying wages enough to make this food attainable; not less, because the workers are not competing among themselves and have no occasion to content themselves with less; not more, because the

---

[a] The German editions of 1845 and 1892 have instead of this sentence: "He gives the worker the butter to make profits sooner, and when he gets them he ungrudgingly leaves the worker the butter."—*Ed.*

capitalists, in the absence of competition among themselves, have no occasion to attract working-men by extraordinary favours.

This standard of the average needs and the average civilisation of the workers has become very complicated by reason of the complications of English industry, and is different for different sorts of workers, as has been pointed out. Most industrial occupations demand a certain skill and regularity, and for these qualities, which involve a certain grade of civilisation, the rate of wages[a] must be such as to induce the worker to acquire such skill and subject himself to such regularity. Hence it is that the average wages of industrial workers are higher than those of mere porters, day-labourers, etc., higher especially than those of agricultural labourers, a fact to which the additional cost of the necessities of life in cities contributes somewhat. In other words, the worker is, in law and in fact, the slave of the property-holding class,[b] so effectually a slave that he is sold like a piece of goods, rises and falls in value like a commodity. If the demand for workers increases, the price of workers rises; if it falls, their price falls. If it falls so greatly that a number of them become unsaleable, if they are left in stock, they are simply left idle; and as they cannot live upon that, they die of starvation. For, to speak in the words of the economists, the expense incurred in maintaining them would not be reproduced, would be money thrown away, and to this end no man advances capital; and, so far, Malthus was perfectly right in his theory of population. The only difference as compared with the old, outspoken slavery is this, that the worker of today seems to be free because he is not sold once for all, but piecemeal by the day, the week, the year, and because no one owner sells him to another, but he is forced to sell himself in this way instead, being the slave of no particular person, but of the whole property-holding class. For him the matter is unchanged at bottom, and if this semblance of liberty necessarily gives him some real freedom on the one hand, it entails on the other the disadvantage that no one guarantees him a subsistence, he is in danger of being repudiated at any moment by his master, the bourgeoisie, and left to die of starvation, if the bourgeoisie ceases to have an interest in his employment, his existence. The bourgeoisie, on the other hand, is far better off under the present arrangement than under the old slave system; it can dismiss its employees at discretion

---

[a] The German editions of 1845 and 1892 have "average wages" instead of "rate of wages".—*Ed.*

[b] The German editions of 1845 and 1892 have "the bourgeoisie" after "class".—*Ed.*

without sacrificing invested capital, and gets its work done much more cheaply than is possible with slave labour, as Adam Smith comfortingly pointed out.*

Hence it follows, too, that Adam Smith was perfectly right in making the assertion:

"That the demand for men, like that for any *other commodity*, necessarily regulates the production of men, quickens it when it goes on too slowly, and stops it when it advances too fast."

Just as in the case of any other commodity! If there are too few labourers on hand, prices, i.e., wages, rise, the workers are more prosperous, marriages multiply, more children are born and more live to grow up, until a sufficient number of labourers has been secured. If there are too many on hand, prices fall, want of work, poverty, and starvation, and consequent diseases arise, and the "surplus population" is put out of the way. And Malthus, who carried the foregoing proposition of Smith farther, was also right, in his way, in asserting that there is always a "surplus population"; that there are always too many people in the world; he is wrong only when he asserts that there are more people on hand than can be maintained from the available means of subsistence.[a] Surplus population is engendered rather by the competition of the workers among themselves, which forces each separate worker to labour as much each day as his strength can possibly admit. If a manufacturer can employ ten hands nine hours daily, he can employ nine if each works ten hours, and the tenth goes hungry. And if a manufacturer can force the nine hands to work an extra hour

---

* Adam Smith, *Wealth of Nations*, I., McCulloch's edition in one volume, sect. 8, p. 36: "The wear and tear of a slave, it has been said, is at the expense of his master, but that of a free servant is at his own expense. The wear and tear of the latter, however, is, in reality, as much at the expense of his master as that of the former. The wages paid to journeymen and servants of every kind, must be such as may enable them, one with another, to continue the race of journeymen and servants, according as the increasing, diminishing, or stationary demand of the society may happen to require. But though the wear and tear of a free servant be equally at the expense of his master, it generally costs him much less than that of a slave. The fund for replacing or repairing, if I may say so, the wear and tear of the slave, is commonly managed by the negligent master or careless overseer."—*Note by Engels.* (The German editions of 1845 and 1892 give this quotation according to the four-volume edition of 1828, Vol. I, p. 134.—*Ed.*)

---

[a] This sentence is given according to the German editions of 1845 and 1892. In the American and English editions it is given abridged: "And Malthus, who carried the foregoing proposition of Smith farther, was also right, in his way, in asserting that there are always more people on hand than can be maintained from the available means of subsistence."—*Ed.*

daily[a] for the same wages by threatening to discharge them at a time when the demand for hands is not very great, he discharges the tenth and saves so much wages. This is the process on a small scale, which goes on in a nation on a large one. The productiveness of each hand raised to the highest pitch by the competition of the workers among themselves, the division of labour, the introduction of machinery, the subjugation of the forces of Nature, deprive a multitude of workers of bread. These starving workers are then removed from the market, they can buy nothing, and the quantity of articles of consumption previously required by them is no longer in demand, need no longer be produced; the workers previously employed in producing them are therefore driven out of work, and are also removed from the market, and so it goes on, always the same old round, or rather, so it would go if other circumstances did not intervene. The introduction of the industrial forces already referred to for increasing production leads, in the course of time, to a reduction of prices of the articles produced and to consequent increased consumption, so that a large part of the displaced workers finally, after long suffering, find work again.[b] If, in addition to this, the conquest of foreign markets constantly and rapidly increases the demand for manufactured goods, as has been the case in England during the past sixty years, the demand for hands increases, and, in proportion to it, the population. Thus, instead of diminishing, the population of the British Empire has increased with extraordinary rapidity, and is still increasing. Yet, in spite of the extension of industry, in spite of the demand for working-men which, in general, has increased, there is, according to the confession of all the official political parties (Tory, Whig, and Radical), permanent surplus, superfluous population; the competition among the workers is constantly greater than the competition to secure workers.

Whence comes this incongruity? It lies in the nature of industrial competition and the commercial crises which arise from it. In the present unregulated production and distribution of the means of subsistence, which is carried on not directly for the sake of supplying needs, but for profit, in the system under which every one works for himself to enrich himself, disturbances inevitably arise at every moment. For example, England supplies a number of countries with most diverse goods. Now, although the manufac-

---

[a] The German editions of 1845 and 1892 have after this "i.e., in our example, ten hours".—*Ed.*

[b] The German editions of 1845 and 1892 have after this "in new branches of labour".—*Ed.*

turer may know how much of each article is consumed in each
country annually, he cannot know how much is on hand at every
given moment, much less can he know how much his competitors
export thither. He can only draw most uncertain inferences from
the perpetual fluctuations in prices, as to the quantities on hand
and the needs of the moment. He must trust to luck in exporting
his goods. Everything is done blindly, as guess-work, more or less
at the mercy of accident. Upon the slightest favourable report,
each one exports what he can, and before long such a market is
glutted, sales stop, capital remains inactive, prices fall, and English
manufacture has no further employment for its hands. In the
beginning of the development of manufacture, these checks were
limited to single branches and single markets; but the centralising
tendency of competition, which drives the hands thrown out of
one branch into such other branches as are most easily accessible,
and transfers the goods which cannot be disposed of in one
market to other markets, has gradually brought the single minor
crises nearer together and united them into one periodically
recurring crisis. Such a crisis usually recurs once in five years after
a brief period of activity and general prosperity[136]; the home
market, like all foreign ones, is glutted with English goods, which
it can only slowly absorb, the industrial movement comes to a
standstill in almost every branch, the small manufacturers and
merchants who cannot survive a prolonged inactivity of their
invested capital fail, the larger ones suspend business during the
worst season, close their mills[a] or work short time, perhaps half
the day; wages fall by reason of the competition of the unemployed, the diminution of working-time and the lack of profitable
sales; want becomes universal among the workers, the small
savings, which individuals may have made, are rapidly consumed,
the philanthropic institutions are overburdened, the poor-rates are
doubled, trebled, and still insufficient, the number of the starving
increases, and the whole multitude of "surplus" population presses
in terrific numbers into the foreground. This continues for a
time; the "surplus" exist as best they may, or perish; philanthropy
and the Poor Law help many of them to a painful prolongation of
their existence. Others find scant means of subsistence here and
there in such kinds of work as have been least open to competition, are most remote from manufacture. And with how little can
a human being keep body and soul together for a time! Gradually
the state of things improves; the accumulations of goods are

---

[a] The German editions of 1845 and 1892 have "stop their machines" instead of
"close their mills".—*Ed.*

consumed, the general depression among the men of commerce and manufacture prevents a too hasty replenishing of the markets, and at last rising prices and favourable reports from all directions restore activity. Most of the markets are distant ones; demand increases and prices rise constantly while the first exports are arriving; people struggle for the first goods, the first sales enliven trade still more, the prospective ones promise still higher prices; expecting a further rise, merchants begin to buy upon speculation, and so to withdraw from consumption the articles intended for it, just when they are most needed. Speculation forces prices still higher, by inspiring others to purchase, and appropriating new importations at once. All this is reported to England, manufacturers begin to produce with a will, new mills are built, every means is employed to make the most of the favourable moment. Speculation arises here, too, exerting the same influence as upon foreign markets, raising prices, withdrawing goods from consumption, spurring manufacture in both ways to the highest pitch of effort. Then come the daring speculators working with fictitious capital, living upon credit, ruined if they cannot speedily sell; they hurl themselves into this universal, disorderly race for profits, multiply the disorder and haste by their unbridled passion, which drives prices and production to madness. It is a frantic struggle, which carries away even the most experienced and phlegmatic; goods are spun, woven, hammered, as if all mankind were to be newly equipped, as though two thousand million new consumers had been discovered in the moon. All at once the shaky speculators abroad, who must have money, begin to sell, below market price, of course, for their need is urgent; one sale is followed by others, prices fluctuate, speculators throw their goods upon the market in terror, the market is disordered, credit shaken, one house after another stops payments, bankruptcy follows bankruptcy, and the discovery is made that three times more goods are on hand or under way than can be consumed. The news reaches England, where production has been going on at full speed meanwhile, panic seizes all hands, failures abroad cause others in England, the panic crushes a number of firms, all reserves are thrown upon the market here, too, in the moment of anxiety, and the alarm is still further exaggerated. This is the beginning of the crisis, which then takes precisely the same course as its predecessor, and gives place in turn to a season of prosperity. So it goes on perpetually,—prosperity, crisis, prosperity, crisis, and this perennial round in which English industry moves is, as has been before observed, usually completed once in five or six years.

From this it is clear that English manufacture must have, at all times save the brief periods of highest prosperity, an unemployed reserve army of workers, in order to be able to produce the masses of goods required by the market in the liveliest months. This reserve army is larger or smaller, according as the state of the market occasions the employment of a larger or smaller proportion of its members. And if at the moment of highest activity of the market the agricultural districts and the branches least affected by the general prosperity[a] temporarily supply to manufacture a number of workers, these are a mere minority, and these too belong to the reserve army, with the single difference that the prosperity of the moment was required to reveal their connection with it. When they enter upon the more active branches of work, their former employers draw in somewhat, in order to feel the loss less, work longer hours, employ women and younger workers, and when the wanderers discharged at the beginning of the crisis return, they find their places filled and themselves superfluous—at least in the majority of cases. This reserve army, which embraces an immense multitude during the crisis and a large number during the period which may be regarded as the average between the highest prosperity and the crisis, is the "surplus population" of England, which keeps body and soul together by begging, stealing, street-sweeping, collecting manure, pushing hand-carts, driving donkeys, peddling, or performing occasional small jobs. In every great town a multitude of such people may be found.[b] It is astonishing in what devices this "surplus population" takes refuge. The London crossing-sweepers are known all over the world; but hitherto the principal streets in all the great cities, as well as the crossings, have been swept by people out of other work, and employed by the Poor Law guardians or the municipal authorities for the purpose. Now, however, a machine has been invented which rattles through the streets daily, and has spoiled this source of income for the unemployed. Along the great highways leading into the cities, on which there is a great deal of waggon traffic, a large number of people may be seen with small carts, gathering fresh horse-dung at the risk of their lives among the passing coaches and omnibuses, often paying a couple of shillings a week to the authorities for the

---

[a] The German editions of 1845 and 1892 have here "the agricultural districts, Ireland and the branches least affected by the general prosperity".—*Ed.*

[b] The German editions of 1845 and 1892 have after this "who keep body and soul together," as the English say, "by performing small occasional jobs".—*Ed.*

privilege. But this occupation is forbidden in many places, because the ordinary street-sweepings thus impoverished cannot be sold as manure. Happy are such of the "surplus" as can obtain a push-cart and go about with it. Happier still those to whom it is vouchsafed to possess an ass in addition to the cart. The ass must get his own food or is given a little gathered refuse, and can yet bring in a trifle of money.

Most of the "surplus" betake themselves to huckstering. On Saturday afternoons, especially, when the whole working popula-tion is on the streets, the crowd who live from huckstering and peddling may be seen. Shoe and corset laces, braces, twine, cakes, oranges, every kind of small articles are offered by men, women, and children; and at other times also, such peddlers are always to be seen standing at the street corners, or going about with cakes and ginger-beer or nettle-beer.* Matches and such things, sealing-wax, and patent mixtures for lighting fires are further resources of such vendors. Others, so-called jobbers,ᵃ go about the streets seeking small jobs. Many of these succeed in getting a day's work, many are not so fortunate.

"At the gates of each of the [London] docks," says the Rev. W. Champneys, preacher of the East End, "hundreds of poor men may be seen before day-break waiting for the opening of the gates in the hope of obtaining a day's work; and when the youngest and most able-bodied, and those best known, have been engaged, hundreds still may be seen returning to their destitute families with that sickness of heart which arises from hope deferred."[137]

When these people find no work and will not rebel against society, what remains for them but to beg? And surely no one can wonder at the great army of beggars, most of them able-bodied men, with whom the police carries on perpetual war. But the beggary of these men has a peculiar character. Such a man usually goes about with his family singing a pleading song in the streets or appealing, in a speech, to the benevolence of the passers-by. And it is a striking fact that these beggars are seen almost exclusively in the working-people's districts, that it is almost exclusively the gifts of the poor from which they live. Or the family takes up its position in a busy street, and without uttering a word, lets the mere sight of its helplessness plead for it. In this case, too, they reckon upon the sympathy of the workers alone, who know from

---

* Two cooling effervescent drinks, the former made of water, sugar and some ginger, the latter of water, sugar and nettles. They are much liked by the workers, especially the teetotallers.—*Note by Engels.* (This note is omitted in the American and English editions.—*Ed.*)

ᵃ In the German editions of 1845 and 1892 this word is given in English.—*Ed.*

experience how it feels 'to be hungry, and are liable to find themselves in the same situation at any moment; for this dumb, yet most moving appeal, is met with almost solely in such streets as are frequented by working-men, and at such hours as working-men pass by; but especially on summer[a] evenings, when the "secrets" of the working-people's quarters are generally revealed,[b] and the middle-class withdraws as far as possible from the district thus polluted. And he among the "surplus" who has courage and passion enough openly to resist society, to reply with declared war upon the bourgeoisie to the disguised war which the bourgeoisie wages upon him, goes forth to rob, plunder, murder, and burn![c]

Of this surplus population there are, according to the reports of the Poor Law commissioners, on an average, a million and a half in England and Wales; in Scotland the number cannot be ascertained for want of Poor Law regulations, and with Ireland we shall deal separately. Moreover, this million and a half includes only those who actually apply to the parish for relief; the great multitude who struggle on without recourse to this most hated expedient, it does not embrace. On the other hand, a good part of the number belongs to the agricultural districts, and does not enter into the present discussion. During a crisis this number naturally increases markedly, and want reaches its highest pitch. Take, for instance, the crisis of 1842, which, being the latest, was the most violent; for the intensity of the crisis increases with each repetition, and the next, which may be expected not later than 1847,* will probably be still more violent and lasting. During this crisis the poor-rates rose in every town to a hitherto unknown height. In Stockport, among other towns, for every pound paid in house-rent, eight shillings of poor-rate had to be paid, so that the rate alone formed forty per cent of the house-rent. Moreover, whole streets stood vacant, so that there were at least twenty thousand fewer inhabitants than usual, and on the doors of the empty houses might be read: "Stockport to let."[d] In Bolton,

---

* And it came in 1847.—*Note by Engels to the American edition of 1887 and the English edition of 1892.*

---

[a] The German editions of 1845 and 1892 have "on Saturday evenings".—*Ed.*
[b] The German editions of 1845 and 1892 have here "in the main streets".—*Ed.*
[c] The words "and burn" do not occur in the German editions of 1845 and 1892.—*Ed.*
[d] In the German editions of 1845 and 1892 these words are given in English and in German.—*Ed.*

where, in ordinary years, the rents from which rates are paid average £86,000, they sank to £36,000. The number of the poor to be supported rose, on the other hand, to 14,000, or more than twenty per cent of the whole number of inhabitants. In Leeds, the Poor Law guardians had a reserve fund of £10,000. This, with a contribution of £7,000, was wholly exhausted before the crisis reached its height. So it was everywhere. A report drawn up in January, 1843, by a committee of the Anti-Corn Law League, on the condition of the industrial districts in 1842, which was based upon detailed statements of the manufacturers, asserts that the poor-rate was, taking the average, twice as high as in 1839, and that the number of persons requiring relief has trebled, even quintupled, since that time; that a multitude of applicants belong to a class which had never before solicited relief; that the working-class commands more than two-thirds less of the means of subsistence than from 1834-1836; that the consumption of meat had been decidedly less, in some places twenty per cent, in others reaching sixty per cent less; that even handicraftsmen, smiths, bricklayers, and others, who usually have full employment in the most depressed periods, now suffered greatly from want of work and reduction of wages; and that, even now, in January, 1843, wages are still steadily falling. And these are the reports of manufacturers!

The starving workmen, whose mills were idle, whose employers could give them no work, stood in the streets in all directions, begged singly or in crowds, besieged the sidewalks in armies, and appealed to the passers-by for help; they begged, not cringing like ordinary beggars, but threatening by their numbers, their gestures, and their words. Such was the state of things in all the industrial districts, from Leicester to Leeds, and from Manchester to Birmingham. Here and there disturbances arose, as in the Staffordshire potteries,[a] in July. The most frightful excitement prevailed among the workers until the general insurrection broke out throughout the manufacturing districts in August. When I came to Manchester in November, 1842, there were crowds of unemployed working-men at every street corner, and many mills were still standing idle. In the following months these unwilling corner loafers gradually vanished, and the factories came into activity once more.

---

[a] The German editions of 1845 and 1892 have "potteries of North Stafford-shire".—*Ed.*

To what extent want and suffering prevail among these unemployed during such a crisis, I need not describe. The poor-rates
are insufficient, vastly insufficient; the philanthropy of the rich is
a rain-drop in the ocean, lost in the moment of falling, beggary
can support but few among the crowds. If the small dealers did
not sell to the working-people on credit at such times as long as
possible — paying themselves liberally afterwards, it must be con-
fessed — and if the working-people did not help each other, every
crisis would remove a multitude of the surplus through death by
starvation. Since, however, the most depressed period is brief,
lasting, at worst, but one, two, or two and a half years, most of
them emerge from it with their lives after dire privations. But
indirectly by disease, etc., every crisis finds a multitude of victims,
as we shall see. First, however, let us turn to another cause of
abasement to which the English worker is exposed, a cause
permanently active in forcing the whole class downwards.

IRISH IMMIGRATION

We have already referred several times in passing to the Irish who have immigrated into England; and we shall now have to investigate more closely the causes and results of this immigration.

The rapid extension of English industry could not have taken place if England had not possessed in the numerous and impoverished population of Ireland a reserve at command. The Irish had nothing to lose at home, and much to gain in England; and from the time when it became known in Ireland that the east side of St. George's Channel offered steady work and good pay for strong arms, every year has brought armies of the Irish hither. It has been calculated that more than a million have already immigrated, and not far from fifty thousand still come every year, nearly all of whom enter the industrial districts, especially the great cities, and there form the lowest class of the population. Thus there are in London, 120,000; in Manchester, 40,000; in Liverpool, 34,000; Bristol, 24,000; Glasgow, 40,000; Edinburgh, 29,000, poor Irish people.* These people having grown up almost without civilisation, accustomed from youth to every sort of privation, rough, intemperate, and improvident, bring all their brutal habits with them among a class of the English population which has, in truth, little inducement to cultivate education and morality. Let us hear Thomas Carlyle upon this subject**:

* Archibald Alison, *The Principles of Population, and their Connection with Human Happiness*, two vols., 1840. This Alison is the historian of the French Revolution, and, like his brother, Dr. W. P. Alison, a religious Tory.—*Note by Engels.*

** *Chartism*, pp. 28, 31, etc.—*Note by Engels.*

"The wild Milesian* features, looking false ingenuity, restlessness, unreason, misery, and mockery, salute you on all highways and byways. The English coachman, as he whirls past, lashes the Milesian with his whip, curses him with his tongue; the Milesian is holding out his hat to beg. He is the sorest evil this country has to strive with. In his rags and laughing savagery, he is there to undertake all work that can be done by mere strength of hand and back—for wages that will purchase him potatoes. He needs only salt for condiment, he lodges to his mind in any pig-hutch or dog-hutch, roosts in outhouses, and wears a suit of tatters, the getting on and off of which is said to be a difficult operation, transacted only in festivals and the high tides of the calendar. The Saxon-man, if he cannot work on these terms, finds no work. The uncivilised Irishman, not by his strength, but by the opposite of strength, drives the Saxon native out, takes possession in his room. There abides he, in his squalor and unreason, in his falsity and drunken violence, as the ready-made nucleus of degradation and disorder. Whoever struggles, swimming with difficulty, may now find an example how the human being can exist not swimming, but sunk.... That the condition of the lower multitude of English labourers approximates more and more to that of the Irish, competing with them in all the markets: that whatsoever labour, to which mere strength with little skill will suffice, is to be done, will be done not at the English price, but at an approximation to the Irish price; at a price superior as yet to the Irish, that is, superior to scarcity of potatoes for thirty weeks yearly; superior, yet hourly, with the arrival of every new steamboat, sinking nearer to an equality with that."

If we except his exaggerated and one-sided condemnation of the Irish national character, Carlyle is perfectly right. These Irishmen who migrate for fourpence[a] to England, on the deck of a steamship on which they are often packed like cattle, insinuate themselves everywhere. The worst dwellings are good enough for them; their clothing causes them little trouble, so long as it holds together by a single thread; shoes they know not; their food consists of potatoes and potatoes only; whatever they earn beyond these needs they spend upon drink. What does such a race want with high wages? The worst quarters of all the large towns are inhabited by Irishmen. Whenever a district is distinguished for especial filth and especial ruinousness, the explorer may safely count upon meeting chiefly those Celtic faces which one recognises at the first glance as different from the Saxon physiognomy of the native, and the singing, aspirate brogue which the true Irishman never loses. I have occasionally heard the Irish-Celtic language spoken in the most thickly populated parts of Manchester. The majority of the families who live in cellars are almost everywhere of Irish origin. In short, the Irish have, as Dr. Kay says,

* Milesian—the name of an ancient family of Celtic kings of Ireland.—*Note by Engels* (omitted in the American and English editions—*Ed.*).

[a] The German editions of 1845 and 1892 have here "$3^{1}/_{3}$ silver groschen" in brackets.—*Ed.*

discovered the minimum of the necessities of life, and are now making the English workers acquainted with it. Filth and drunkenness, too, they have brought with them. The lack of cleanliness, which is not so injurious in the country, where population is scattered, and which is the Irishman's second nature, becomes terrifying and gravely dangerous through its concentration here in the great cities. The Milesian deposits all garbage and filth before his house door here, as he was accustomed to do at home, and so accumulates the pools and dirt-heaps which disfigure the working-people's quarters and poison the air. He builds a pig-sty against the house wall as he did at home, and if he is prevented from doing this, he lets the pig sleep in the room with himself. This new and unnatural method of cattle-raising in cities is wholly of Irish origin. The Irishman loves his pig as the Arab his horse, with the difference that he sells it when it is fat enough to kill. Otherwise, he eats and sleeps with it, his children play with it, ride upon it, roll in the dirt with it, as any one may see a thousand times repeated in all the great towns of England. The filth and comfortlessness that prevail in the houses themselves it is impossible to describe. The Irishman is unaccustomed to the presence of furniture; a heap of straw, a few rags, utterly beyond use as clothing, suffice for his nightly couch. A piece of wood, a broken chair, an old chest for a table, more he needs not; a tea-kettle, a few pots and dishes, equip his kitchen, which is also his sleeping and living room. When he is in want of fuel, everything combustible within his reach, chairs, door-posts, mouldings, flooring, finds its way up the chimney. Moreover, why should he need much room? At home in his mud-cabin there was only one room for all domestic purposes; more than one room his family does not need in England. So the custom of crowding many persons into a single room, now so universal, has been chiefly implanted by the Irish immigration. And since the poor devil must have one enjoyment, and society has shut him out of all others, he betakes himself to the drinking of spirits. Drink is the only thing which makes the Irishman's life worth having, drink and his cheery care-free temperament; so he revels in drink to the point of the most bestial drunkenness. The southern facile character of the Irishman, his crudity, which places him but little above the savage, his contempt for all humane enjoyments, in which his very crudeness makes him incapable of sharing, his filth and poverty, all favour drunkenness. The temptation is great, he cannot resist it, and so when he has money he gets rid of it down his throat. What else should he do? How can society blame him when it places him in a position in which he almost of necessity becomes a drunkard; when it leaves him to himself, to his savagery?

With such a competitor the English working-man has to struggle, with a competitor upon the lowest plane possible in a civilised country, who for this very reason requires less wages than any other. Nothing else is therefore possible than that, as Carlyle says, the wages of English working-man should be forced down further and further in every branch in which the Irish compete with him. And these branches are many. All such as demand little or no skill are open to the Irish. For work which requires long training or regular, pertinacious application, the dissolute, unsteady, drunken Irishman is on too low a plane. To become a mechanic,[a] a mill-hand, he would have to adopt the English civilisation, the English customs, become, in the main, an Englishman. But for all simple, less exact work, wherever it is a question more of strength than skill, the Irishman is as good as the Englishman. Such occupations are therefore especially overcrowded with Irishmen: hand-weavers, bricklayers, porters, jobbers, and such workers, count hordes of Irishmen among their number, and the pressure of this race has done much to depress wages and lower the working-class. And even if the Irish, who have forced their way into other occupations, should become more civilised, enough of the old habits would cling to them to have a strong, degrading influence upon their English companions in toil, especially in view of the general effect of being surrounded by the Irish. For when, in almost every great city, a fifth or a quarter of the workers are Irish, or children of Irish parents, who have grown up among Irish filth, no one can wonder if the life, habits, intelligence, moral status—in short, the whole character of the working-class assimilates a great part of the Irish characteristics. On the contrary, it is easy to understand how the degrading position of the English workers, engendered by our modern history,[b] and its immediate consequences, has been still more degraded by the presence of Irish competition.

---

[a] The German editions of 1845 and 1892 have here in brackets: "a mechanic is the name given in England to any worker engaged in producing machinery".—*Ed.*
[b] The German editions of 1845 and 1892 have here "industry" instead of "history".—*Ed.*

RESULTS

Having now investigated, somewhat in detail, the conditions under which the English working-class lives,[a] it is time to draw some further inferences from the facts presented, and then to compare our inferences with the actual state of things. Let us see what the workers themselves have become under the given circumstances, what sort of people they are, what their physical, mental, and moral status.

When one individual inflicts bodily injury upon another such injury that death results, we call the deed manslaughter; when the assailant knew in advance that the injury would be fatal, we call his deed murder. But when society* places hundreds of pro-

* When as here and elsewhere I speak of society as a responsible whole, having rights and duties, I mean, of course, the ruling power of society, the class which at present holds social and political control, and bears, therefore, the responsibility for the condition of those to whom it grants no share in such control. This ruling class in England, as in all other civilised countries, is the bourgeoisie. But that this society, and especially the bourgeoisie, is charged with the duty of protecting every member of society, at least, in his life, to see to it, for example, that no one starves, I need not now prove to my *German* readers. If I were writing for the English bourgeoisie, the case would be different.—*Note by Engels to the German edition of 1845.*

And so it is now in Germany. Our German capitalists are fully up to the English level, in this respect at least, in the year of grace, 1886.—*Added by Engels to the American edition of 1887* (reproduced in the English edition of 1892—*Ed.*).

(1892) How things have changed in the last fifty years! Today there are members of the English middle-classes who recognise that society has duties to the individual citizen—but as for the German middle-classes?!?—*Added by Engels to the German edition of 1892.*

---

[a] The German editions of 1845 and 1892 have "the English urban factory workers".—*Ed.*

letarians in such a position that they inevitably meet a too early and an unnatural death, one which is quite as much a death by violence as that by the sword or bullet; when it deprives thousands of the necessaries of life, places them under conditions in which they *cannot* live — forces them, through the strong arm of the law, to remain in such conditions until that death ensues which is the inevitable consequence — knows that these thousands of victims must perish, and yet permits these conditions to remain, its deed is murder just as surely as the deed of the single individual; disguised, malicious murder, murder against which none can defend himself, which does not seem what it is, because no man sees the murderer,[a] because the death of the victim seems a natural one, since the offence is more one of omission than of commission. But murder it remains. I have now to prove that society in England daily and hourly commits what the working-men's organs, with perfect correctness, characterise as social murder, that it has placed the workers under conditions in which they can neither retain health nor live long; that it undermines the vital force of these workers gradually, little by little, and so hurries them to the grave before their time. I have further to prove that society knows how injurious such conditions are to the health and the life of the workers, and yet does nothing to improve these conditions. That it *knows* the consequences of its deeds; that its act is, therefore, not mere manslaughter, but murder, I shall have proved, when I cite official documents, reports of Parliament and of the Government, in substantiation of my charge.

That a class which lives under the conditions already sketched and is so ill-provided with the most necessary means of subsistence, cannot be healthy and can reach no advanced age, is self-evident. Let us review the circumstances once more with especial reference to the health of the workers. The centralisation of population in great cities exercises of itself an unfavourable influence; the atmosphere of London can never be so pure, so rich in oxygen, as the air of the country; two and a half million pairs of lungs, two hundred and fifty thousand fires, crowded upon an area three to four miles square,[b] consume an enormous amount of oxygen, which is replaced with difficulty, because the method of building cities in itself impedes ventilation. The

---

[a] The German editions of 1845 and 1892 have here "because everyone is responsible for the murder and yet no one is responsible".—*Ed.*

[b] The German editions of 1845 and 1892 have "geographical square miles" (the German mile is 7.42 km, or 4.64 English miles).—*Ed.*

carbonic acid gas, engendered by respiration and fire, remains in the streets by reason of its specific gravity, and the chief air current passes over the roofs of the city. The lungs of the inhabitants fail to receive the due supply of oxygen, and the consequence is mental and physical lassitude and low vitality. For this reason, the dwellers in cities are far less exposed to acute, and especially to inflammatory, affections than rural populations, who live in a free, normal atmosphere; but they suffer the more from chronic affections. And if life in large cities is, in itself, injurious to health, how great must be the harmful influence of an abnormal atmosphere in the working-people's quarters, where, as we have seen, everything combines to poison the air. In the country, it may, perhaps, be comparatively innoxious to keep a dung-heap adjoining one's dwelling, because the air has free ingress from all sides; but in the midst of a large town, among closely built lanes and courts that shut out all movement of the atmosphere, the case is different. All putrefying vegetable and animal substances give off gases decidedly injurious to health, and if these gases have no free way of escape, they inevitably poison the atmosphere. The filth and stagnant pools of the working-people's quarters in the great cities have, therefore, the worst effect upon the public health, because they produce precisely those gases which engender disease; so, too, the exhalations from contaminated streams. But this is by no means all. The manner in which the great multitude of the poor is treated by society today is revolting. They are drawn into the large cities where they breathe a poorer atmosphere than in the country; they are relegated to districts which, by reason of the method of construction, are worse ventilated than any others; they are deprived of all means of cleanliness, of water itself, since pipes are laid only when paid for, and the rivers so polluted that they are useless for such purposes; they are obliged to throw all offal and garbage, all dirty water, often all disgusting drainage and excrement into the streets, being without other means of disposing of them; they are thus compelled to infect the region of their own dwellings. Nor is this enough. All conceivable evils are heaped upon the heads of the poor. If the population of great cities is too dense in general, it is they in particular who are packed into the least space. As though the vitiated atmosphere of the streets were not enough, they are penned in dozens into single rooms, so that the air which they breathe at night is enough in itself to stifle them. They are given damp dwellings, cellar dens that are not waterproof from below, or garrets that leak from above. Their houses are so built that the

clammy air cannot escape. They are supplied bad, tattered, or
rotten clothing, adulterated and indigestible food. They are
exposed to the most exciting changes of mental condition, the
most violent vibrations between hope and fear; they are hunted
like game, and not permitted to attain peace of mind and quiet
enjoyment of life. They are deprived of all enjoyments except that
of sexual indulgence and drunkenness, are worked every day to
the point of complete exhaustion of their mental and physical
energies, and are thus constantly spurred on to the maddest excess
in the only two enjoyments at their command. And if they
surmount all this,[a] they fall victims to want of work in a crisis
when all the little is taken from them that had hitherto been
vouchsafed them.

How is it possible, under such conditions, for the lower class to
be healthy and long lived? What else can be expected than an
excessive mortality, an unbroken series of epidemics, a progressive
deterioration in the physique of the working population? Let us
see how the facts stand.

That the dwellings of the workers in the worst portions of the
cities, together with the other conditions of life of this class,
engender numerous diseases, is attested on all sides. The article
already quoted from the *Artisan* asserts with perfect truth, that
lung diseases must be the inevitable consequence of such conditions, and that, indeed, cases of this kind are disproportionately
frequent in this class. That the bad air of London, and especially
of the working-people's districts, is in the highest degree favourable to the development of consumption, the hectic appearance of
great numbers of persons sufficiently indicates. If one roams the
streets a little in the early morning, when the multitudes are on
their way to their work, one is amazed at the number of persons
who look wholly or half-consumptive. Even in Manchester the
people have not the same appearance; these pale, lank, narrow-
chested, hollow-eyed ghosts, whom one passes at every step, these
languid, flabby faces, incapable of the slightest energetic expression, I have seen in such startling numbers only in London,
though consumption carries off a horde of victims annually in the
factory towns of the North. In competition with consumption
stands typhus, to say nothing of scarlet fever,[b] a disease which
brings most frightful devastation into the ranks of the working-

---

[a] The German editions of 1845 and 1892 have "And if this is not enough,
if they survive all this".—*Ed.*

[b] The German editions of 1845 and 1892 have "to say nothing of other lung
diseases and scarlet fever".—*Ed.*

class. Typhus, that universally diffused affliction, is attributed by the official report on the sanitary condition of the working-class, directly to the bad state of the dwellings in the matters of ventilation, drainage, and cleanliness. This report compiled, it must not be forgotten, by the leading physicians of England from the testimony of other physicians, asserts that a single ill-ventilated court, a single blind alley without drainage, is enough to engender fever, and usually does engender it[138] especially if the inhabitants are greatly crowded.[a] This fever has the same character almost everywhere, and develops in nearly every case into specific typhus. It is to be found in the working-people's quarters of all great towns and cities, and in single ill-built, ill-kept streets of smaller places,[b] though it naturally seeks out single victims in better districts also. In London it has now prevailed for a considerable time; its extraordinary violence in the year 1837 gave rise to the report already referred to. According to the annual report of Dr. *Southwood Smith* on the London Fever Hospital, the number of patients in 1843 was 1,462, or 418 more than in any previous year.[139] In the damp, dirty regions of the north, south, and east districts of London, this disease raged with extraordinary violence. Many of the patients were working-people from the country, who had endured the severest privation while migrating, and, after their arrival, had slept hungry and half-naked in the streets, and so fallen victims to the fever. These people were brought into the hospital in such a state of weakness, that unusual quantities of wine, cognac, and preparations of ammonia and other stimulants were required for their treatment; $16^1/_2$ per cent of all patients died. This malignant fever is to be found in Manchester; in the worst quarters of the Old Town, Ancoats, Little Ireland, etc., it is rarely extinct; though here, as in the *English* towns generally, it prevails to a less extent than might be expected. In Scotland and Ireland, on the other hand, it rages with a violence that surpasses all conception. In Edinburgh and Glasgow it broke out in 1817, after the famine,[c] and in 1826 and 1837 with especial violence, after the commercial crisis, subsiding somewhat each time after having raged about

---

[a] The German editions of 1845 and 1892 have "and if organic refuse is allowed to decay there".—*Ed.*

[b] The German editions of 1845 and 1892 have here "where its effects are, of course, felt most severely".—*Ed.*

[c] The German editions of 1845 and 1892 have "during the period of dearth" instead of "after the famine".—*Ed.*

three years. In Edinburgh about 6,000 persons were attacked by the fever during the epidemic of 1817, and about 10,000 in that of 1837, and not only the number of persons attacked but the violence of the disease[a] increased with each repetition.*

But the fury of the epidemic in all former periods seems to have been child's play in comparison with its ravages after the crisis of 1842. One-sixth of the whole indigent population of Scotland was seized by the fever, and the infection was carried by wandering beggars with fearful rapidity from one locality to another. It did not reach the middle and upper classes of the population, yet in two months there were more fever cases than in twelve years before. In Glasgow, twelve per cent of the population were seized in the year 1843; 32,000 persons, of whom thirty-two per cent perished, while this mortality in Manchester and Liverpool does not ordinarily exceed eight per cent. The illness reached a crisis on the seventh and fifteenth days; on the latter, the patient usually became yellow, which our authority regards as an indication that the cause of the malady was to be sought in mental excitement and anxiety.** In Ireland, too, these fever epidemics have become domesticated. During twenty-one months of the years 1817-1818, 39,000 fever patients passed through the Dublin hospital; and in a more recent year, according to Sheriff Alison, 60,000.*** In Cork the fever hospital received one-seventh of the population in 1817-1818, in Limerick in the same time one-fourth, and in the bad quarter of Waterford, nineteen-twentieths of the whole population were ill of the fever at one time.****

When one remembers under what conditions the working-people live, when one thinks how crowded their dwellings are, how every nook and corner swarms with human beings, how sick and well sleep in the same room, in the same bed, the only wonder is that a contagious disease like this fever does not spread

---

* Dr. Alison, *Management of the Poor in Scotland.—Note by Engels.*

** Dr. Alison in an article read before the British Association for the Advancement of Science. October, 1844, in York.—*Note by Engels.*

*** Alison, *Principles of Population*, vol. ii.—*Note by Engels to the American edition of 1887* (reproduced in the English edition of 1892; in the German editions of 1845 and 1892 the reference is given in the text—*Ed.*).

**** Dr. Alison, *Management of the Poor in Scotland.—Note by Engels.* (This note is not given in the 1887 American and 1892 English editions.—*Ed.*)

---

[a] The German editions of 1845 and 1892 have here "and the mortality rate".—*Ed.*

yet farther. And when one reflects how little medical assistance the sick have at command, how many are without any medical advice whatsoever, and ignorant of the most ordinary precautionary measures,[a] the mortality seems actually small. Dr. Alison, who has made a careful study of this disease, attributes it directly to the want and the wretched condition of the poor, as in the report already quoted. He asserts that privations and the insufficient satisfaction of vital needs are what prepare the frame for contagion and make the epidemic widespread and terrible. He proves that a period of privation, a commercial crisis or a bad harvest, has each time produced the typhus epidemic in Ireland as in Scotland, and that the fury of the plague has fallen almost exclusively on the working-class. It is a noteworthy fact, that according to his testimony, the majority of persons who perish by typhus are fathers of families, precisely the persons who can least be spared by those dependent upon them; and several Irish physicians whom he quotes bear the same testimony.

Another category of diseases arises directly from the food rather than the dwellings of the workers. The food of the labourer, indigestible enough in itself, is utterly unfit for young children, and he has neither means nor time to get his children more suitable food. Moreover, the custom of giving children spirits, and even opium, is very general; and these two influences, with the rest of the conditions of life prejudicial to bodily development, give rise to the most diverse affections of the digestive organs, leaving life-long traces behind them. Nearly all workers have stomachs more or less weak, and are yet forced to adhere to the diet which is the root of the evil. How should they know what is to blame for it? And if they knew, how could they obtain a more suitable regimen so long as they cannot adopt a different way of living and are not better educated? But new disease arises during childhood from impaired digestion. Scrofula is almost universal among the working-class, and scrofulous parents have scrofulous children, especially when the original influences continue in full force to operate upon the inherited tendency of the children. A second consequence of this insufficient bodily nourishment, during the years of growth and development, is rachitis,[b] which is

---

[a] The German editions of 1845 and 1892 have "rules of diet" instead of "precautionary measures".—Ed.

[b] The German editions of 1845 and 1892 have here in brackets: "The English disease: knotty excrescences on the joints".—Ed.

extremely common among the children of the working-class. The hardening of the bones is delayed, the development of the skeleton in general is restricted, and deformities of the legs and spinal column are frequent, in addition to the usual rachitic affections. How greatly all these evils are increased by the changes to which the workers are subject in consequence of fluctuations in trade, want of work, and the scanty wages in time of crisis, it is not necessary to dwell upon. Temporary want of sufficient food, to which almost every working-man is exposed at least once in the course of his life, only contributes to intensify the effects of his usually sufficient but bad diet. Children who are half-starved, just when they most need ample and nutritious food — and how many such there are during every crisis and even when trade is at its best — must inevitably become weak, scrofulous and rachitic in a high degree. And that they do become so, their appearance amply shows. The neglect to which the great mass of working-men's children are condemned leaves ineradicable traces and brings the enfeeblement of the whole race of workers with it. Add to this the unsuitable clothing of this class, the impossibility of precautions against colds, the necessity of toiling so long as health permits, want made more dire when sickness appears, and the only too common lack of all medical assistance; and we have a rough idea of the sanitary condition of the English working-class. The injurious effects peculiar to single employments as now conducted, I shall not deal with here.

Besides these, there are other influences which enfeeble the health of a great number of workers, intemperance most of all. All possible temptations, all allurements combine to bring the workers to drunkenness. Liquor is almost their only source of pleasure, and all things conspire to make it accessible to them. The working-man comes from his work tired, exhausted, finds his home comfortless, damp, dirty, repulsive; he has urgent need of recreation, he *must* have something to make work worth his trouble, to make the prospect of the next day endurable. His unnerved, uncomfortable, hypochondriac state of mind and body arising from his unhealthy condition, and especially from indigestion, is aggravated beyond endurance by the general conditions of his life, the uncertainty of his existence, his dependence upon all possible accidents and chances, and his inability to do anything towards gaining an assured position. His enfeebled frame, weakened by bad air and bad food, violently demands some external stimulus; his social need can be gratified only in the public-house, he has absolutely no other place where he can meet his friends. How can he be expected to resist the temptation?[a] It is morally and physically inevitable that, under such circumstances, a very large number of working-men should fall into intemperance. And apart from the chiefly physical influences which drive the working-man into drunkenness, there is the example of the great mass, the neglected education, the impossibility of protecting the young from temptation, in many cases the direct influence of intemperate parents, who give their own children liquor, the certainty of forgetting for an hour or two the wretchedness and burden of life, and a hundred other circumstances so mighty that the workers can, in truth, hardly be blamed for yielding to such overwhelming pressure. Drunkenness has here ceased to be a vice, for which the vicious can be held responsible; it becomes a phenomenon, the necessary, inevitable effect of certain conditions upon an object possessed of no volition in relation to those conditions. They who have degraded the working-man to a mere object have the responsibility to bear. But as inevitably as a great number of working-men fall a prey to drink, just so inevitably does it manifest its ruinous influence upon the body and mind of its victims. All the tendencies to disease arising from the conditions of life of the workers are promoted by it, it stimulates in the highest degree the development of lung and digestive troubles, the rise and spread of typhus epidemics.

Another source of physical mischief to the working-class lies in the impossibility of employing skilled physicians in cases of illness. It is true that a number of charitable institutions strive to supply this want, that the infirmary in Manchester, for instance, receives or gives advice and medicine to 22,000 patients annually. But what is that in a city in which, according to Gaskell's calculation,* three-fourths of the population need medical aid every year? English doctors charge high fees, and working-men are not in a position to pay them. They can therefore do nothing, or are compelled to call in cheap charlatans, and use quack remedies, which do more harm than good. An immense number of such quacks thrive in every English town, securing their *clientèle* among the poor by means of advertisements, posters, and other such

---

* *The Manufacturing Population of England*, ch. 8.—*Note by Engels.*

---

[a] The German editions of 1845 and 1892 have instead of this sentence: "How can the worker be expected not to have the strongest temptation of intemperance, to be able to resist the attraction of drink?"—*Ed.*

devices. Besides these, vast quantities of patent medicines[a] are sold, for all conceivable ailments: Morrison's Pills, Parr's Life Pills, Dr. Mainwaring's Pills, and a thousand other pills, essences, and balsams, all of which have the property of curing all the ills that flesh is heir to. These medicines rarely contain actually injurious substances, but, when taken freely and often, they affect the system prejudicially; and as the unwary purchasers are always recommended to take as much as possible, it is not to be wondered at that they swallow them wholesale whether wanted or not.

It is by no means unusual for the manufacturer of Parr's Life Pills to sell twenty to twenty-five thousand boxes of these salutary pills in a week, and they are taken for constipation by this one, for diarrhoea by that one, for fever, weakness, and all possible ailments. As our German peasants are cupped or bled at certain seasons, so do the English working-people now consume patent medicines to their own injury and the great profit of the manufacturer. One of the most injurious of these patent medicines is a drink prepared with opiates, chiefly laudanum, under the name Godfrey's Cordial.[b] Women who work at home, and have their own and other people's children to take care of, give them this drink to keep them quiet, and, as many believe, to strengthen them. They often begin to give this medicine to newly born children, and continue, without knowing the effects of this "heart's-ease", until the children die. The less susceptible the child's system to the action of the opium, the greater the quantities administered. When the cordial ceases to act, laudanum alone is given, often to the extent of fifteen to twenty drops at a dose. The Coroner of Nottingham testified before a Parliamentary Commission* that one apothecary had, according to his own statement,

---

* Report of Commission of Inquiry into the Employment of Children and Young Persons in Mines and Collieries and in the Trades and Manufactures in which numbers of them work together, not being included under the terms of the Factories' Regulation Act. First and Second Reports, Grainger's Report. Second Report, usually cited as Children's Employment Commission's Report, is one of the best official reports of its kind and contains an immense quantity of evidence which is both valuable and horrifying. First Report, 1841; Second Report, 1843.—Note by Engels. (The assessment of the report is omitted in the American edition of 1887 and the English edition of 1892.—Ed.)

---

[a] In the German editions of 1845 and 1892 the words "patent medicines" are given in brackets.—Ed.

[b] In the German editions of 1845 and 1892 the name of the medicine is given in English.—Ed.

used thirteen hundredweight of treacle in one year in the preparation of Godfrey's Cordial. The effects upon the children so treated may be readily imagined. They are pale, feeble, wilted, and usually die before completing the second year. The use of this cordial is very extensive in all great towns and industrial districts in the kingdom.

The result of all these influences is a general enfeeblement of the frame in the working-class. There are few vigorous, well-built, healthy persons among the workers, i.e. among the factory operatives, who are employed in confined rooms, and we are here discussing these only. They are almost all weakly, of angular but not powerful build, lean, pale, and of relaxed fibre, with the exception of the muscles especially exercised in their work. Nearly all suffer from indigestion, and consequently from a more or less hypochondriac, melancholy, irritable, nervous condition.[a] Their enfeebled constitutions are unable to resist disease, and are therefore seized by it on every occasion. Hence they age prematurely, and die early. On this point the mortality statistics supply unquestionable testimony.

According to the Report of Registrar-General Graham, the annual death-rate of all England and Wales is something less than $2^1/_4$ per cent. That is to say, out of forty-five persons, one dies every year.* This was the average for the year 1839-40. In 1840-41 the mortality diminished somewhat, and the death-rate was but one in forty-six. But in the great cities the proportion is wholly different. I have before me official tables of mortality (*Manchester Guardian*, July 31st, 1844[140]), according to which the death-rate of several large towns is as follows:—In Manchester, including Chorlton and Salford, one in 32.72; and excluding Chorlton and Salford, one in 30.75. In Liverpool, including West Derby (suburb), 31.90, and excluding West Derby, 29.90; while the average of all the districts of Cheshire, Lancashire, and Yorkshire cited, including a number of wholly or partially rural districts and many small towns, with a total population of 2,172,506 for the whole, is one death in 39.80 persons. How unfavourably the workers are placed in the great cities, the mortality for Prescott in Lancashire shows: a district inhabited by miners, and showing a lower sanitary

---

* *Fifth Annual Report of the Reg. Gen. of Births, Deaths, and Marriages.—Note by Engels.*

---

[a] In the German editions of 1845 and 1892 the second part of this sentence reads: "and consequently are more or less hypochondriac and of a gloomy, uneasy disposition".—*Ed.*

condition than that of the agricultural districts, mining being by no means a healthful occupation. But these miners live in the country, and the death-rate among them is but one in 47.54, or nearly two-and-a-half per cent better than that for all England. All these statements are based upon the mortality tables for 1843. Still higher is the death-rate in the Scotch cities; in Edinburgh, in 1838-39, one in 29; in 1831, in the Old Town alone, one in 22. In Glasgow, according to Dr. Cowan,* the average has been, since 1830, one in 30; and in single years, one in 22 to 24. That this enormous shortening of life falls chiefly upon the working-class, that the general average is improved by the smaller mortality of the upper and middle-classes, is attested upon all sides. One of the most recent depositions is that of a physician, Dr. P. H. Holland, in Manchester, who investigated Chorlton-on-Medlock, a suburb of Manchester, under official commission. He divided the houses and streets into three classes each, and ascertained the following variations in the death-rate:

First	class	of streets.	Houses	I. class.	Mortality	one	in	51
"	"	"	"	II. "	"	"	"	45
"	"	"	"	III. "	"	"	"	36
Second	"	"	"	I. "	"	"	"	55
"	"	"	"	II. "	"	"	"	38
"	"	"	"	III. "	"	"	"	35
Third	"	"	"	I. "	Wanting	—	"	—
"	"	"	"	II. "	Mortality	"	"	35
"	"	"	"	III. "	"	"	"	25

It is clear from other tables given by Holland that the mortality in the *streets* of the second class is 18 per cent greater, and in the streets of the third class 68 per cent greater than in those of the first class; that the mortality in the *houses* of the second class is 31 per cent greater, and in the third class 78 per cent greater than in those of the first class; that the mortality in those bad streets which were improved, decreased 25 per cent. He closes with the remark, very frank for an English bourgeois**:

"When we find the rate of mortality four times as high in some streets as in others, and twice as high in whole classes of streets as in other classes, and further find that it is all but invariably high in those streets which are in bad condition, and

---

* Dr. Cowan, *Vital Statistics of Glasgow.*[141]—*Note by Engels to the American edition of 1887* (reproduced in the English edition of 1892; in the German editions of 1845 and 1892 the reference is given in the text—*Ed.*).

** *Report of Commission of Inquiry into the State of Large Towns and Populous Districts.* First Report, 1844. Appendix.—*Note by Engels.*

almost invariably low in those whose condition is good, we cannot resist the conclusion that multitudes of our fellow-creatures, *hundreds of our immediate neighbours,* are annually destroyed for want of the most evident precautions."

The Report on the Sanitary Condition of the Working-Class contains information which attests the same fact. In Liverpool, in 1840, the average longevity of the upper classes, gentry, professional men, etc., was thirty-five years; that of the business men and better-placed handicraftsmen, twenty-two years; and that of the operatives, day-labourers, and serviceable class in general, but fifteen years. The Parliamentary reports contain a mass of similar facts.

The death-rate is kept so high chiefly by the heavy mortality among young children in the working-class. The tender frame of a child is least able to withstand the unfavourable influences of an inferior lot in life; the neglect to which they are often subjected, when both parents work or one is dead, avenges itself promptly, and no one need wonder that in Manchester, according to the report last quoted, more than fifty-seven per cent of the children of the working-class perish before the fifth year, while but twenty per cent of the children of the higher classes, and not quite. thirty-two per cent of the children of all classes in the country die under five years of age.* The article of the *Artisan,* already several times referred to, furnishes exacter information on this point, by comparing the city death-rate in single diseases of children with the country death-rate, thus demonstrating that, in general, epidemics in Manchester and Liverpool are three times more fatal than in country districts; that affections of the nervous system are quintupled, and stomach troubles trebled,[a] while deaths from affections of the lungs in cities are to those in the country as $2^1/_2$ to 1. Fatal cases of small-pox, measles, scarlet fever, and whooping cough, among small children, are four times more frequent; those of water on the brain are trebled, and convulsions ten times more frequent. To quote another acknowledged authority, I append the following table. Out of 10,000 persons, there die—**

* *Factories' Inquiry Commission's Reports,* 3rd vol. Report of Dr. Hawkins on Lancashire, in which Dr. Roberton is cited—the "Chief Authority for Statistics in Manchester".—*Note by Engels.*

** Quoted by Dr. Wade from the Report of the Parliamentary Factories' Commission of 1832, in his *History of the Middle and Working-Classes,* London, 1835, 3rd ed.—*Note by Engels to the American edition of 1887* (reproduced in the English edition of 1892; the German editions of 1845 and 1892 give the reference in the text—*Ed.*).

---

[a] The German editions of 1845 and 1892 have "doubled".—*Ed.*

	Under 5 years,	5-19,	20-39,	40-59,	60-69,	70-79,	80-89,	90-99,	100 x
In Ruthlandshire, a healthy agricultural district	2,865	891	1,275	1,299	1,189	1,428	938	112	3
Essex, marshy agricultural district	3,159	1,110	1,526	1,413	963	1,019	630	77	3
Town of Carlisle, 1779-1787, before introduction of mills	4,408	911	1,006	1,201	940	826	533	153	22
Town of Carlisle, after the introduction of mills	4,738	930	1,261	1,134	677	727	452	80	1
Preston, factory town	4,947	1,136	1,379	1,114	553	532	298	38	3
Leeds, factory town...	5,286	927	1,228	1,198	593	512	225	29	2

Apart from the diverse diseases which are the necessary consequence of the present neglect and oppression of the poorer classes, there are other influences which contribute to increase the mortality among small children. In many families the wife, like the husband, has to work away from home, and the consequence is the total neglect of the children, who are either locked up or given out to be taken care of. It is, therefore, not to be wondered at if hundreds of them perish through all manner of accidents. Nowhere are so many children run over, nowhere are so many killed by falling, drowning, or burning, as in the great cities and towns of England. Deaths from burns and scalds are especially frequent, such a case occurring nearly every week during the winter months in Manchester, and very frequently in London, though little mention is made of them in the papers. I have at hand a copy of the *Weekly Dispatch* of December 15th, 1844, according to which, in the week from December 1st to December 7th inclusive, *six* such cases occurred. These unhappy children, perishing in this terrible way, are victims of our social disorder, and of the property-holding classes interested in maintaining and prolonging this disorder. Yet one is left in doubt whether even this terribly torturing death is not a blessing for the children in rescuing them from a long life of toil and wretchedness, rich in suffering and poor in enjoyment. So far has it gone in England; and the bourgeoisie reads these things every day in the newspapers and takes no further trouble in the matter. But it cannot complain if, after the official and non-official testimony here cited which must be known to it, I broadly accuse it of social murder. Let the ruling class see to it that these frightful conditions are ameliorated, or let it surrender the administration of the common interests to the labouring-class. To the latter course it is by no means inclined; for the former task, so long as it remains the bourgeoisie crippled by bourgeois prejudice, it has not the needed power. For if, at last, after hundreds of thousands of victims have perished, it manifests some little anxiety for the future, passing a "Metropolitan Buildings Act",[142] under which the most unscrupulous overcrowding of dwellings is to be, at least in some slight degree, restricted; if it points with pride to measures which, far from attacking the root of the evil, do not by any means meet the demands of the commonest sanitary police, it cannot thus vindicate itself from the accusation. The English bourgeoisie has but one choice, either to continue its rule under the unanswerable charge of murder and in spite of this charge, or to abdicate in favour of the labouring-class. Hitherto it has chosen the former course.

Let us turn from the physical to the mental state of the workers. Since the bourgeoisie vouchsafes them only so much of life as is absolutely necessary, we need not wonder that it bestows upon them only so much education as lies in the interest of the bourgeoisie; and that, in truth, is not much. The means of education in England are restricted out of all proportion to the population. The few day schools at the command of the working-class are available only for the smallest minority, and are bad besides. The teachers, worn-out workers, and other unsuitable persons who only turn to teaching in order to live, are usually without the indispensable elementary knowledge, without the moral discipline so needful for the teacher, and relieved of all public supervision. Here, too, free competition rules, and, as usual, the rich profit by it, and the poor, for whom competition is *not* free, who have not the knowledge needed to enable them to form a correct judgment, have the evil consequences to bear. Compulsory school attendance does not exist. In the mills it is, as we shall see, purely nominal; and when in the session of 1843 the Ministry was disposed to make this nominal compulsion effective, the manufacturing bourgeoisie opposed the measure with all its might, though the working-class was outspokenly in favour of compulsory school attendance. Moreover, a mass of children work the whole week through in the mills or at home, and therefore cannot attend school. The evening schools, supposed to be attended by children who are employed during the day, are almost abandoned or attended without benefit. It is asking too much, that young workers, who have been using themselves up twelve hours in the day, should go to school from eight to ten at night. And those who try it usually fall asleep, as is testified by hundreds of witnesses in the Children's Employment Commission's Report. Sunday schools have been founded, it is true, but they, too, are most scantily supplied with teachers, and can be of use to those only who have already learnt something in the day schools. The interval from one Sunday to the next is too long for an ignorant child to remember in the second sitting what it learned in the first, a week before. The Children's Employment Commission's Report furnishes a hundred proofs, and the Commission itself most emphatically expresses the opinion, that neither the week-day nor the Sunday schools, in the least degree, meet the needs of the nation. This Report gives evidence of ignorance in the working-class of England, such as could hardly be expected in Spain or Italy. It cannot be otherwise; the bourgeoisie has little to hope, and much to fear, from the education of the working-class. The Ministry, in its whole enormous budget of £55,000,000, has only the single trifling item of £40,000 for public education, and, but for the fanaticism of the religious sects which does at least as much harm as good, the means of education would be yet more scanty. As it is, the State Church manages its national schools[a] and the various sects their sectarian[b] schools for the sole purpose of keeping the children of the brethren of the faith within the congregation, and of winning away a poor childish soul here and there from some other sect. The consequence is that religion, and precisely the most unprofitable side of religion, polemical discussion, is made the principal subject of instruction, and the memory of the children overburdened with incomprehensible dogmas and theological distinctions; that sectarian hatred and bigotry are awakened as early as possible, and all rational mental and moral training shamefully neglected. The working-class has repeatedly demanded of Parliament a system of strictly secular public education, leaving religion to the ministers of the sects; but, thus far, no

---

[a] In the German editions of 1845 and 1892 the words "national schools" are given in English.—*Ed.*

[b] The word "sectarian" does not occur in the German editions of 1845 and 1892.—*Ed.*

Ministry has been induced to grant it. The Minister is the obedient servant of the bourgeoisie, and the bourgeoisie is divided into countless sects; but each would gladly grant the workers the otherwise dangerous education on the sole condition of their accepting, as an antidote, the dogmas peculiar to the especial sect in question. And as these sects are still quarrelling among themselves for supremacy, the workers remain for the present without education. It is true that the manufacturers boast of having enabled the majority to read, but the quality of the reading is appropriate to the source of the instruction, as the Children's Employment Commission proves. According to this report, he who knows his letters can read enough to satisfy the conscience of the manufacturers. And when one reflects upon the confused orthography of the English language which makes reading one of the arts, learned only under long instruction, this ignorance is readily understood. Very few working-people write readily; and writing orthographically is beyond the powers even of many "educated" persons. The Sunday schools of the State Church, of the Quakers, and, I think, of several other sects, do not teach writing, "because it is too worldly an employment for Sunday". The quality of the instruction offered the workers in other directions may be judged from a specimen or two, taken from the Children's Employment Commission's Report, which unfortunately does not embrace mill-work proper [143]:

In Birmingham, says Commissioner Grainger, the children examined by me are, as a whole, utterly wanting in all that could be in the remotest degree called a useful education. Although in almost all the schools religious instruction alone is furnished, the profoundest ignorance even upon that subject prevailed.— In Wolverhampton, says Commissioner Horne, I found, among others, the following example: A girl of eleven years who had attended both day and Sunday school "had never learnt of another world, nor of heaven, nor of another life". A boy, seventeen years old, "did not know how many two and two made, nor how many farthings[a] there were in twopence, even when the money was placed in his hand". Several boys had never heard of London nor of Willenhall, though the latter was but an hour's walk from their homes, and in the closest relations with Wolverhampton. Several had never heard the name of the Queen nor other names, such as Nelson, Wellington, Bonaparte; but it was noteworthy that those who had never heard even of St. Paul, Moses, or Solomon, were very well instructed as to the life, deeds, and character of Dick Turpin, and especially of Jack Sheppard.[b] A youth of sixteen did not know "how many twice two make", nor "how much money four farthings make". A youth of seventeen asserted that "ten

---

[a] In the German editions of 1845 and 1892 the word "farthings" is given in English, followed in brackets by the explanation "1/4 penny".—*Ed.*

[b] The German editions of 1845 and 1892 have "the highwayman" after Dick Turpin and "the thief and gaol-breaker" after Jack Sheppard.—*Ed.*

farthings make ten halfpence"; a third, seventeen years old, answered several very simple questions with the brief statement, that "he was ne jedge o' nothin'."* These children, who are crammed with religious doctrines for four or five years at a stretch, know as little at the end as at the beginning. One child had "attended a Sunday school regularly for five years; does not know who Jesus Christ was, but has heard the name. Never heard of the twelve apostles. Never heard of Samson, nor of Moses, nor Aaron, etc." ** Another "attended a Sunday school regularly six years. Knows who Jesus Christ was, he died on the cross to shed his blood, to save our Saviour. Never heard of St. Peter or St. Paul." *** A third, "attended the Sunday schools of different kinds about seven years; can read, only in the thin books, easy words of one syllable; has heard of the apostles, does not know if St. Peter was one, nor if St. John was one, unless it was St. John Wesley." **** To the question who Christ was, Horne received, among others, the following answers, "Yes, Adam," "He was an apostle," "He was the Saviour's Lord's Son,"[a] and from a youth of sixteen: "Jesus Christ was a king of London a long time ago." In Sheffield, Commissioner Symons let the children from the Sunday school read aloud; they could not tell what they had read, or what sort of people the apostles were, of whom they had just been reading. After he had asked them all one after the other about the apostles without securing a single correct answer, one sly-looking little fellow, with great glee, called out: "Please sir, they were the lepers!" ***** From the pottery districts and from Lancashire the reports are similar.

This is what the bourgeoisie and the State are doing for the education and improvement of the working-class. Fortunately the conditions under which this class lives are such as give it a sort of practical training, which not only replaces school cramming, but renders harmless the confused religious notions connected with it, and even places the workers in the vanguard of the national movement of England. Necessity is the mother of invention, and what is still more important, of thought and action. The English working-man who can scarcely read and still less write, nevertheless knows very well where his own interest and that of the nation lies. He knows, too, what the especial interest of the bourgeoisie is, and what he has to expect of that bourgeoisie. If he cannot write

---

* *Children's Employment Commission's Report*. App. Part II. Q. 18, Nos. 216, 217, 226, 233, etc. Horne.—*Note by Engels to the American edition of 1887*. (This and other notes to this passage are reproduced in the English edition of 1892; in the German editions of 1845 and 1892 all these references are given in the text.—*Ed*.)

** Ibid., evidence, pp. 9, 39; 133.—*Note by Engels to the American edition of 1887*.

*** Ibid., pp. 9, 36; 146.—*Note by Engels to the American edition of 1887*.

**** Ibid., pp. 34; 158.—*Note by Engels to the American edition of 1887*. (The German editions of 1845 and 1892 have "founder of the Methodists" in brackets.—*Ed*.)

***** *Symons' Rep*. App. Part I, pp. E, 22, *et seq.*—*Note by Engels to the American edition of 1887*.

---

[a] The German editions of 1845 and 1892 give this answer in English in brackets.—*Ed*.

he can speak, and speak in public; if he has no arithmetic, he can, nevertheless, reckon with the Political Economists enough to see through a Corn-Law-repealing bourgeois, and to get the better of him in argument; if celestial matters remain very mixed for him in spite of all the effort of the preachers, he sees all the more clearly into terrestrial, political, and social questions. We shall have occasion to refer again to this point; and pass now to the moral characteristics of our workers.

It is sufficiently clear that the instruction in morals can have no better effect than the religious teaching, with which in all English schools it is mixed up. The simple principles which, for plain human beings, regulate the relations of man to man, brought into the direst confusion by our social state, our war of each against all, necessarily remain confused and foreign to the working-man when mixed with incomprehensible dogmas, and preached in the religious form of an arbitrary and dogmatic commandment. The schools contribute, according to the confession of all authorities, and especially of the Children's Employment Commission, almost nothing to the morality of the working-class. So short-sighted, so stupidly narrow-minded is the English bourgeoisie in its egotism, that it does not even take the trouble to impress upon the workers the morality of the day, which the bourgeoisie has patched together in its own interest for its own protection! Even this precautionary measure is too great an effort for the enfeebled and sluggish bourgeoisie. A time must come when it will repent its neglect, too late. But it has no right to complain that the workers know nothing of its system of morals, and do not act in accordance with it.

Thus are the workers cast out and ignored by the class in power, morally as well as physically and mentally. The only provision made for them is the law, which fastens upon them when they become obnoxious to the bourgeoisie. Like the dullest of the brutes, they are treated to but one form of education, the whip, in the shape of force, not convincing but intimidating. There is, therefore, no cause for surprise if the workers, treated as brutes, actually become such; or if they can maintain their consciousness of manhood only by cherishing the most glowing hatred, the most unbroken inward rebellion against the bourgeoisie in power. They are men so long only as they burn with wrath against the reigning class. They become brutes the moment they bend in patience under the yoke, and merely strive to make life endurable while abandoning the effort to break the yoke.

This, then, is all that the bourgeoisie has done for the education of the proletariat—and when we take into consideration all the circumstances in which this class lives, we shall not think the worse of it for the resentment which it cherishes against the ruling class. The moral training which is not given to the worker in school is not supplied by the other conditions of his life; that moral training, at least, which alone has worth in the eyes of the bourgeoisie; his whole position and environment involves the strongest temptation to immorality. He is poor, life offers him no charm, almost every enjoyment is denied him, the penalties of the law have no further terrors for him; why should he restrain his desires, why leave to the rich the enjoyment of his birthright,[a] why not seize a part of it for himself? What inducement has the proletarian not to steal? It is all very pretty and very agreeable to the ear of the bourgeois to hear the "sacredness of property" asserted; but for him who has none, the sacredness of property dies out of itself. Money is the god of this world; the bourgeois takes the proletarian's money from him and so makes a practical atheist of him. No wonder, then, if the proletarian retains his atheism and no longer respects the sacredness and power of the earthly God. And when the poverty of the proletarian is intensified to the point of actual lack of the barest necessaries of life, to want and hunger, the temptation to disregard all social order does but gain power. This the bourgeoisie for the most part recognises. Symons * observes that poverty exercises the same ruinous influence upon the mind which drunkenness exercises upon the body; and Dr. Alison explains to property-holding readers, with the greatest exactness, what the consequences of social oppression must be for the working-class.** Want leaves the working-man the choice between starving slowly, killing himself speedily, or taking what he needs where he finds it—in plain English, stealing. And there is no cause for surprise that most of them prefer stealing to starvation and suicide.

True, there are, within the working-class, numbers too moral to steal even when reduced to the utmost extremity, and these starve or commit suicide. For suicide, formerly the enviable privilege of the upper classes, has become fashionable among the English workers, and numbers of the poor kill themselves to avoid the misery from which they see no other means of escape.

But far more demoralising than his poverty in its influence

* *Arts and Artisans.—Note by Engels.*
** *Principles of Population, vol. ii, pp. 196, 197.—Note by Engels.*

[a] The German editions of 1845 and 1892 have "the enjoyment of his riches" instead of "the enjoyment of his birthright".—*Ed.*

upon the English working-man is the insecurity of his position, the necessity of living upon wages from hand to mouth, that in short which makes a proletarian of him. The smaller peasants in Germany are usually poor, and often suffer want, but they are less at the mercy of accident, they have at least something secure. The proletarian, who has nothing but his two hands, who consumes today what he earned yesterday, who is subject to every possible chance, and has not the slightest guarantee for being able to earn the barest necessities of life, whom every crisis, every whim of his employer may deprive of bread, this proletarian is placed in the most revolting, inhuman position conceivable for a human being. The slave is assured of a bare livelihood by the self-interest of his master, the serf has at least a scrap of land on which to live; each has at worst a guarantee for life itself. But the proletarian must depend upon himself alone, and is yet prevented from so applying his abilities as to be able to rely upon them. Everything that the proletarian can do to improve his position is but a drop in the ocean compared with the floods of varying chances to which he is exposed, over which he has not the slightest control. He is the passive subject of all possible combinations of circumstances, and must count himself fortunate when he has saved his life even for a short time; and his character and way of living are naturally shaped by these conditions. Either he seeks to keep his head above water in this whirlpool, to rescue his manhood, and this he can do solely in rebellion * against the class which plunders him so mercilessly and then abandons him to his fate, which strives to hold him in this position so demoralising to a human being; or he gives up the struggle against his fate as hopeless, and strives to profit, so far as he can, by the most favourable moment. To save is unavailing, for at the utmost he cannot save more than suffices to sustain life for a short time, while if he falls out of work, it is for no brief period. To accumulate lasting property for himself is impossible; and if it were not, he would only cease to be a working-man and another would take his place. What better thing can he do, then, when he gets high wages, than live well upon them? The English bourgeoisie is violently scandalised at the extravagant living of the workers when wages are high; yet it is not only very natural but very sensible of them to enjoy life when they can, instead of laying up treasures which are of no lasting use

* We shall see later how the rebellion of the working-class against the bourgeoisie in England is legalised by the right of coalition.— *Note by Engels*. (In the German editions of 1845 and 1892 this passage reads: "in rebellion against the bourgeoisie, against the class", etc.—*Ed.*)

to them, and which in the end moth and rust (i.e., the bourgeoisie) get possession of. Yet such a life is demoralising beyond all others. What Carlyle says of the cotton spinners is true of all English industrial workers *:

> "Their trade, now in plethoric prosperity, anon extenuated into inanition and 'short time', is of the nature of gambling; they live by it like gamblers, now in luxurious superfluity, now in starvation. Black, mutinous discontent devours them; simply the miserablest feeling that can inhabit the heart of man. English commerce, with its world-wide, convulsive fluctuations, with its immeasurable Proteus Steam demon, makes all paths uncertain for them, all life a bewilderment; sobriety, steadfastness, peaceable continuance, the first blessings of man are not theirs.— This world is for them no home, but a dingy prison-house, of reckless unthrift, rebellion, rancour, indignation against themselves and against all men. Is it a green, flowery world, with azure everlasting sky stretched over it, the work and government of a God; or a murky, simmering Tophet, of copperas fumes, cotton fuzz, gin riot, wrath and toil, created by a Demon, governed by a Demon?"

And elsewhere**:

> "Injustice, infidelity to truth and fact and Nature's order, being properly the one evil under the sun, and the feeling of injustice the one intolerable pain under the sun, our grand question as to the condition of these working-men would be: Is it just? And, first of all, what belief have they themselves formed about the justice of it? The words they promulgate are notable by way of answer; their actions are still more notable. Revolt, sullen, revengeful humour of revolt against the upper classes, decreasing respect for what their temporal superiors command, decreasing faith for what their spiritual superiors teach, is more and more the universal spirit of the lower classes. Such spirit may be blamed, may be vindicated, but all men must recognise it as extant there, all may know that it is mournful, that unless altered it will be fatal."

Carlyle is perfectly right as to the facts and wrong only in censuring the wild rage of the workers against the higher classes. This rage, this passion, is rather the proof that the workers feel the inhumanity of their position, that they refuse to be degraded to the level of brutes, and that they will one day free themselves from servitude to the bourgeoisie. This may be seen in the case of those who do not share this wrath; they either bow humbly before the fate that overtakes them, live a respectful private life as well as they can, do not concern themselves as to the course of public affairs, help the bourgeoisie to forge the chains of the workers yet more securely and stand upon the plane of intellectual nullity that prevailed before the industrial period began; or they are tossed about by fate, lose their moral hold upon themselves as they have already lost their economic hold, live along from day to day, drink

---

* *Chartism*, p. 34, *et seq.—Note by Engels.*

** Ibid., p. 40.—*Note by Engels to the American edition of 1887* (reproduced in the English edition of 1892; in the German editions of 1845 and 1892 the reference is given in the text—*Ed.*).

and fall into licentiousness; and in both cases they are brutes. The last-named class contributes chiefly to the "rapid increase of vice", at which the bourgeoisie[a] is so horrified after itself setting in motion the causes which give rise to it.

Another source of demoralisation among the workers is their being condemned to work. As voluntary, productive activity is the highest enjoyment known to us, so is compulsory toil the most cruel, degrading punishment. Nothing is more terrible than being constrained to do some one thing every day from morning until night against one's will. And the more a man the worker feels himself, the more hateful must his work be to him, because he feels the constraint, the aimlessness of it for himself. Why does he work? For love of work? From a natural impulse? Not at all! He works for money, for a thing which has nothing whatsoever to do with the work itself[b]; and he works so long, moreover, and in such unbroken monotony, that this alone must make his work a torture in the first weeks if he has the least human feeling left. The division of labour has multiplied the brutalising influences of forced work. In most branches the worker's activity is reduced to some paltry, purely mechanical manipulation, repeated minute after minute, unchanged year after year.* How much human feeling, what abilities can a man retain in his thirtieth year, who has made needle points or filed toothed wheels twelve hours every day from his early childhood, living all the time under the conditions forced upon the English proletarian? It is still the same thing since the introduction of steam.[c] The worker's activity is made easy, muscular effort is saved, but the work itself becomes unmeaning and monotonous to the last degree. It offers no field for mental activity, and claims just enough of his attention to keep him from thinking of anything else.[d] And a sentence to such work, to work which takes his whole time for itself, leaving him scarcely time to eat and sleep, none for physical exercise in the open air,

---

* Shall I call bourgeois witnesses to bear testimony for me here, too? I select one only, whom every one may read, namely, Adam Smith, *Wealth of Nations* (McCulloch's four volume edition), vol. iii, book 5, chap. 1, p. 297.—*Note by Engels.*

---

[a] The German editions of 1845 and 1892 have "the sentimental bourgeoisie".—*Ed.*
[b] The German editions of 1845 and 1892 have here "he works because he has to work".—*Ed.*
[c] The German editions of 1845 and 1892 have here "and machinery".—*Ed.*
[d] The German editions of 1845 and 1892 have here "if he wants to do it properly".—*Ed.*

or the enjoyment of Nature, much less for mental activity, how can such a sentence help degrading a human being to the level of a brute? Once more the worker must choose, must either surrender himself to his fate, become a "good" workman, heed "faithfully" the interest of the bourgeoisie, in which case he most certainly becomes a brute, or else he must rebel, fight for his manhood to the last, and this he can only do in the fight against the bourgeoisie.

And when all these conditions have engendered vast demoralisation among the workers, a new influence is added to the old, to spread this degradation more widely and carry it to the extremest point. This influence is the centralisation of the population. The writers of the English bourgeoisie are crying murder at the demoralising tendency of the great cities; like perverted Jeremiahs, they sing dirges, not over the destruction, but the growth of the cities. Sheriff Alison attributes almost everything, and Dr. Vaughan, author of *The Age of Great Cities,* still more to this influence. And this is natural, for the propertied class has too direct an interest in the other conditions which tend to destroy the worker body and soul. If they should admit that poverty, insecurity, overwork, forced work, are the chief ruinous influences, they would have to draw the conclusion, then let us give the poor property, guarantee their subsistence, make laws against overwork, and this the bourgeoisie dare not formulate. But the great cities have grown up so spontaneously, the population has moved into them so wholly of its own motion, and the inference that manufacture and the middle-class which profits from it alone have created the cities is so remote, that it is extremely convenient for the ruling class to ascribe all the evil to this apparently unavoidable source; whereas the great cities really only secure a more rapid and certain development for evils already existing in the germ. Alison is humane enough to admit this; he is no thoroughbred Liberal manufacturer, but only a half developed Tory bourgeois, and he has, therefore, an open eye, now and then, where the full-fledged bourgeois is still stone blind. Let us hear him.*

It is in the great cities that "vice has spread her temptations, and pleasure her seductions, and folly her allurements; that guilt is encouraged by the hope of impunity, and idleness fostered by the frequency of example. It is to these great marts of human corruption that the base and the profligate resort from the simplicity of country life; it is here that they find victims whereon to practise their iniquity, and gains to reward the dangers that attend them. Virtue is here depressed from the obscurity in which it is involved. Guilt is matured from the difficulty of its detection; licentiousness is rewarded by the immediate enjoyment

* *Principles of Population*, vol. ii, p. 76, *et seq.*, p. 82, p. 135.—*Note by Engels* (in the German editions of 1845 and 1892 these quotations are abridged—*Ed.*).

which it promises. If any person will walk through St. Giles's, the crowded alleys of Dublin, or the poorer quarters of Glasgow by night, he will meet with ample proof of these observations; he will no longer wonder at the disorderly habits and profligate enjoyments of the lower orders; his astonishment will be, not that there is so much, but that there is so little crime in the world. The great cause of human corruption in these crowded situations is the contagious nature of bad example and the extreme difficulty of avoiding the seductions of vice when they are brought into close and daily proximity with the younger part of the people. Whatever we may think of the strength of virtue, experience proves that the higher orders are indebted for their exemption from atrocious crime or disorderly habits chiefly to their fortunate removal from the scene of temptation; and that where they are exposed to the seductions which assail their inferiors, they are noways behind them in yielding to their influence. It is the peculiar misfortune of the poor in great cities that they cannot fly from these irresistible temptations, but that, turn where they will, they are met by the alluring forms of vice, or the seductions of guilty enjoyment. It is the experienced impossibility of concealing the attractions of vice from the younger part of the poor in great cities which exposes them to so many causes of demoralisation.[a] All this proceeds not from any unwonted or extraordinary depravity in the character of these victims of licentiousness, but from the almost irresistible nature of the temptations to which the poor are exposed. The rich, who censure their conduct, would in all probability yield as rapidly as they have done to the influence of similar causes. There is a certain degree of misery, a certain proximity to sin, which virtue is rarely able to withstand, and which the young, in particular, are generally unable to resist. The progress of vice in such circumstances is almost as certain and often nearly as rapid as that of physical contagion."

And elsewhere:

"When the higher orders for their own profit have drawn the labouring-classes in great numbers into a small space, the contagion of guilt becomes rapid and unavoidable. The lower orders, situated as they are in so far as regards moral or religious instruction, are frequently hardly more to be blamed for yielding to the temptations which surround them than for falling victims to the typhus fever."

Enough! The half-bourgeois Alison betrays to us, however narrow his manner of expressing himself, the evil effect of the great cities upon the moral development of the workers. Another, a bourgeois *pur sang*,[b] a man after the heart of the Anti-Corn Law League, Dr. Andrew Ure,* betrays the other side. He tells us that life in great cities facilitates cabals among the workers and confers power on the Plebs. If here the workers are not educated (i.e., to obedience to the bourgeoisie), they may view matters one-sidedly, from the standpoint of a sinister selfishness, and may readily permit themselves to be hoodwinked by sly demagogues; nay, they

* *Philosophy of Manufactures*, London, 1835, p. 406, *et seq.* We shall have occasion to refer further to this reputable work.—*Note by Engels*.

---

[a] In the German editions of 1845 and 1892 the quotation is interrupted with a sentence by Engels "After a long description of morals, the author continues".—*Ed*.

[b] Pure-blooded.—*Ed*.

might even be capable of viewing their greatest benefactors, the frugal and enterprising capitalists, with a jealous and hostile eye. Here proper training alone can avail, or national bankruptcy and other horrors must follow, since a revolution of the workers could hardly fail to occur. And our bourgeois is perfectly justified in his fears. If the centralisation of population stimulates and develops the property-holding class, it forces the development of the workers yet more rapidly. The workers begin to feel as a class, as a whole; they begin to perceive that, though feeble as individuals, they form a power united; their separation from the bourgeoisie, the development of views peculiar to the workers and corresponding to their position in life, is fostered, the consciousness of oppression awakens, and the workers attain social and political importance. The great cities are the birthplaces of labour movements; in them the workers first began to reflect upon their own condition, and to struggle against it; in them the opposition between proletariat and bourgeoisie first made itself manifest; from them proceeded the Trades Unions, Chartism, and Socialism. The great cities have transformed the disease of the social body, which appears in chronic form in the country, into an acute one, and so made manifest its real nature and the means of curing it. Without the great cities and their forcing influence upon the popular intelligence, the working-class would be far less advanced than it is. Moreover, they have destroyed the last remnant of the patriarchal relation between working-men and employers, a result to which manufacture on a large scale has contributed by multiplying the employees dependent upon a single employer. The bourgeoisie deplores all this, it is true, and has good reason to do so; for, under the old conditions, the bourgeois was comparatively secure against a revolt on the part of his hands. He could tyrannise over them and plunder them to his heart's content, and yet receive obedience, gratitude, and assent from these stupid people by bestowing a trifle of patronising friendliness which cost him nothing, and perhaps some paltry present, all apparently out of pure, self-sacrificing, uncalled-for goodness of heart, but really not one-tenth part of his duty. As an individual bourgeois, placed under conditions which he had not himself created, he might do his duty at least in part; but, as a member of the ruling class, which, by the mere fact of its ruling, is responsible for the condition of the whole nation,[a] he did nothing of what his position

---

[a] The German editions of 1845 and 1892 have here "and undertakes to ensure the general interest".—Ed.

involved. On the contrary, he plundered the whole nation for his own individual advantage. In the patriarchal relation that hypocritically concealed the slavery of the worker, the latter must have remained an intellectual zero, totally ignorant of his own interest, a mere private individual. Only when estranged from his employer, when convinced that the sole bond between employer and employee is the bond of pecuniary profit, when the sentimental bond between them, which stood not the slightest test, had wholly fallen away, then only did the worker begin to recognise his own interests and develop independently; then only did he cease to be the slave of the bourgeoisie in his thoughts, feelings, and the expression of his will. And to this end manufacture on a grand scale and in great cities has most largely contributed.

Another influence of great moment in forming the character of the English workers is the Irish immigration already referred to. On the one hand it has, as we have seen, degraded the English workers, removed them from civilisation, and aggravated the hardship of their lot; but, on the other hand, it has thereby deepened the chasm between workers and bourgeoisie, and hastened the approaching crisis. For the course of the social disease from which England is suffering is the same as the course of a physical disease; it develops according to certain laws, has its own crises, the last and most violent of which determines the fate of the patient. And as the English nation cannot succumb under the final crisis, but must go forth from it, born again, rejuvenated, we can but rejoice over everything which accelerates the course of the disease. And to this the Irish immigration further contributes by reason of the passionate, mercurial Irish temperament, which it imports into England and into the English working-class. The Irish and English are to each other much as the French and the Germans; and the mixing of the more facile, excitable, fiery Irish temperament with the stable, reasoning, persevering English must, in the long run, be productive only of good for both. The rough egotism of the English bourgeoisie would have kept its hold upon the working-class much more firmly if the Irish nature, generous to a fault, and ruled primarily by sentiment, had not intervened, and softened the cold, rational English character in part by a mixture of the races, and in part by the ordinary contact of life.

In view of all this, it is not surprising that the working-class has gradually become a race wholly apart from the English bourgeoisie. The bourgeoisie has more in common with every other nation of the earth than with the workers in whose midst it lives. The workers speak other dialects, have other thoughts and ideals, other customs and moral principles, a different religion and other politics than those of the bourgeoisie. Thus they are two radically dissimilar nations, as unlike as difference of race could make them, of whom we on the Continent have known but one, the bourgeoisie. Yet it is precisely the other, the people, the proletariat, which is by far the more important for the future of England.*

Of the public character of the English working-man, as it finds expression in associations and political principles, we·shall have occasion to speak later; let us here consider the results of the influences cited above, as they affect the private character of the worker. The workman is far more humane in ordinary life than the bourgeois. I have already mentioned the fact that the beggars are accustomed to turn almost exclusively to the workers, and that, in general, more is done by the workers than by the bourgeoisie for the maintenance of the poor. This fact, which any one may prove for himself any day, is confirmed, among others, by Dr. Parkinson, Canon of Manchester, who says**:

> "The poor give more to each other than the rich give to the poor. I am confirmed in this assertion by the testimony of one of our oldest, most learned, and most observant physicians Dr. Bardsley, whose humanity is as conspicuous as his learning and talent, and who has often publicly declared that the aggregate sum given in each year by the poor to each other exceeds that contributed by the rich in the same period."

In other ways, too, the humanity of the workers is constantly manifesting itself pleasantly. They have experienced hard times themselves, and can therefore feel for those in trouble,[a] whence they are more approachable, friendlier, and less greedy for money, though they need it far more than the property-holding class. For them money is worth only what it will buy, whereas for the bourgeois it has an especial inherent value, the value of a god, and makes the bourgeois the mean, low money-grubber that he is. The working-man who knows nothing of this feeling of reverence for money is therefore less grasping than the bourgeois, whose whole activity is for the purpose of gain, who sees in the accumulations of his money-bags the end and aim of life. Hence

---

* (1892) The idea that large-scale industry has split the English into two different nations has, as is well known, been carried out about the same time also by Disraeli in his novel, *Sybil, or the Two Nations.—Note by Engels to the German edition of 1892.*

** *On the Present Condition of the Labouring Poor in Manchester*, etc. By the Rev. Rd. Parkinson, Canon of Manchester, 3rd ed., London and Manchester, 1841. Pamphlet.—*Note by Engels.*

[a] The German editions of 1845 and 1892 have here "to them every person is a human being, while the worker is less than a human being to the bourgeois".—*Ed.*

the workman is much less prejudiced, has a clearer eye for facts as they are than the bourgeois, and does not look at everything through the spectacles of personal selfishness. His faulty education saves him from religious prepossessions, he does not understand religious questions, does not trouble himself about them, knows nothing of the fanaticism that holds the bourgeoisie bound; and if he chances to have any religion, he has it only in name, not even in theory. Practically he lives for this world, and strives to make himself at home in it. All the writers of the bourgeoisie are unanimous on this point, that the workers are not religious, and do not attend church. From the general statement are to be excepted the Irish, a few elderly people, and the half-bourgeois, the overlookers, foremen, and the like. But among the masses there prevails almost universally a total indifference to religion, or at the utmost, some trace of Deism too undeveloped to amount to more than mere words, or a vague dread of the words infidel, atheist, etc. The clergy of all sects is in very bad odour with the working-men, though the loss of its influence is recent. At present, however, the mere cry: "He's a parson!"[a] is often enough to drive one of the clergy from the platform of a public meeting. And like the rest of the conditions under which he lives, his want of religious and other culture contributes to keep the working-man more unconstrained, freer from inherited stable tenets and cut-and-dried opinions, than the bourgeois who is saturated with the class prejudices poured into him from his earliest youth. There is nothing to be done with the bourgeois; he is essentially conservative in however liberal a guise, his interest is bound up with that of the property-holding class,[b] he is dead to all active movement; he is losing his position in the forefront of England's historical development. The workers are taking his place, in rightful claim first, then in fact.

All this, together with the correspondent public action of the workers, with which we shall deal later, forms the favourable side of the character of this class; the unfavourable one may be quite as briefly summed up, and follows quite as naturally out of the given causes. Drunkenness, sexual irregularities, brutality, and disregard for the rights of property are the chief points with which the bourgeois charges them. That they drink heavily is to be expected. Sheriff Alison asserts that in Glasgow some thirty thousand

---

[a] The German editions of 1845 and 1892 have "infidel" and "He's a parson" in English, followed by the German translation.—*Ed.*

[b] The German editions of 1845 and 1892 have "the existing system" instead of "the property-holding class".—*Ed.*

working-men get drunk every Saturday night, and the estimate is certainly not exaggerated; and that in that city in 1830, one house in twelve, and in 1840, one house in ten, was a public-house; that in Scotland, in 1823, excise was paid upon 2,300,000 gallons; in 1837, upon 6,620,000 gallons; in England, in 1823, upon 1,976,000 gallons, and in 1837, upon 7,875,000 gallons of spirits.* The Beer Act of 1830, which facilitated the opening of beerhouses (jerry-shops), whose keepers are licensed to sell beer to be drunk on the premises, facilitated the spread of intemperance by bringing a beerhouse, so to say, to everybody's door. In nearly every street there are several such beerhouses, and among two or three neighbouring houses in the country one is sure to be a jerry-shop. Besides these, there are hush-shops[a] in multitudes, i.e., secret drinking-places which are not licensed, and quite as many secret distilleries which produce great quantities of spirits in retired spots, rarely visited by the police, in the great cities. Gaskell estimates these secret distilleries in Manchester alone at more than a hundred, and their product at 156,000 gallons at the least. In Manchester there are, besides, more than a thousand public-houses selling all sorts of alcoholic drinks,[b] or quite as many in proportion to the number of inhabitants as in Glasgow. In all other great towns, the state of things is the same. And when one considers, apart from the usual consequences of intemperance, that men and women, even children, often mothers with babies in their arms, come into contact in these places with the most degraded victims of the bourgeois regime, with thieves, swindlers, and prostitutes; when one reflects that many a mother gives the baby on her arm gin to drink, the demoralising effects of frequenting such places cannot be denied.

On Saturday evenings, especially when wages are paid and work stops somewhat earlier than usual, when the whole working-class pours from its own poor quarters into the main thoroughfares, intemperance may be seen in all its brutality. I have rarely come out of Manchester on such an evening without meeting numbers of people staggering and seeing others lying in the gutter. On Sunday evening the same scene is usually repeated, only less

---

* *Principles of Population,* passim.—*Note by Engels.* (This note is not given in the English and American editions.—*Ed.*)

---

[a] The German editions of 1845 and 1892 give "a jerry-shop" and "hush-shops" in English.—*Ed.*

[b] The words "selling all sorts of alcoholic drinks" are not in the German editions of 1845 and 1892.—*Ed.*

noisily. And when their money is spent, the drunkards go to the nearest pawnshop, of which there are plenty in every city—over sixty in Manchester, and ten or twelve in a single street of Salford, Chapel Street—and pawn whatever they possess. Furniture, Sunday clothes where such exist, kitchen utensils in masses are fetched from the pawnbrokers on Saturday night only to wander back, almost without fail, before the next Wednesday, until at last some accident makes the final redemption impossible, and one article after another falls into the clutches of the usurer, or until he refuses to give a single farthing more upon the battered, used up pledge. When one has seen the extent of intemperance among the workers in England, one readily believes Lord Ashley's statement* that this class annually expends something like twenty-five million pounds sterling upon intoxicating liquor; and the deterioration in external conditions, the frightful shattering of mental and physical health, the ruin of all domestic relations which follow may readily be imagined. True, the temperance societies have done much, but what are a few thousand teetotallers[a] among the millions of workers? When Father Mathew, the Irish apostle of temperance, passes through the English cities, from thirty to sixty thousand workers take the pledge[b]; but most of them break it again within a month. If one counts up the immense numbers who have taken the pledge in the last three or four years in Manchester, the total is greater than the whole population of the town—and still it is by no means evident that intemperance is diminishing.

Next to intemperance in the enjoyment of intoxicating liquors, one of the principal faults of English working-men is sexual licence. But this, too, follows with relentless logic, with inevitable necessity out of the position of a class left to itself, with no means of making fitting use of its freedom. The bourgeoisie has left the working-class only these two pleasures, while imposing upon it a multitude of labours and hardships, and the consequence is that the working-men, in order to get something from life, concentrate their whole energy upon these two enjoyments, carry them to excess, surrender to them in the most unbridled manner. When people are placed under conditions which appeal to the brute only, what remains to them but to rebel or to succumb to utter

---

* Sitting of the Lower House on Feb. 28, 1843.—*Note by Engels.* (Omitted in the American and English editions.—*Ed.*)

---

[a] The German editions of 1845 and 1892 give this word in English.—*Ed.*
[b] The German editions of 1845 and 1892 give this word in English, followed by the German translation.—*Ed.*

brutality? And when, moreover, the bourgeoisie does its full share in maintaining prostitution—and how many of the 40,000 prostitutes who fill the streets of London* every evening live upon the virtuous bourgeoisie! How many of them owe it to the seduction of a bourgeois, that they must offer their bodies to the passers-by in order to live?—surely it has least of all a right to reproach the workers with their sexual brutality.

The failings of the workers in general may be traced to an unbridled thirst for pleasure, to want of providence, and of flexibility in fitting into the social order, to the general inability to sacrifice the pleasure of the moment to a remoter advantage. But is that to be wondered at? When a class can purchase few and only the most sensual pleasures by its wearying toil, must it not give itself over blindly and madly to those pleasures? A class about whose education no one troubles himself, which is a playball to a thousand chances, knows no security in life—what incentives has such a class to providence, to "respectability", to sacrifice the pleasure of the moment for a remoter enjoyment, most uncertain precisely by reason of the perpetually varying, shifting conditions under which the proletariat lives? A class which bears all the disadvantages of the social order without enjoying its advantages, one to which the social system appears in purely hostile aspects—who can demand that such a class respect this social order? Verily that is asking much! But the working-man cannot escape the present arrangement of society so long as it exists, and when the individual worker resists it, the greatest injury falls upon himself.

Thus the social order makes family life almost impossible for the worker. In a comfortless, filthy house, hardly good enough for mere nightly shelter, ill-furnished, often neither rain-tight nor warm, a foul atmosphere filling rooms overcrowded with human beings, no domestic comfort is possible. The husband works the whole day through, perhaps the wife also and the elder children, all in different places; they meet night and morning only, all under perpetual temptation to drink; what family life is possible under such conditions? Yet the working-man cannot escape from the family, must live in the family, and the consequence is a perpetual succession of family troubles, domestic quarrels, most demoralising for parents and children alike. Neglect of all domestic duties, neglect of the children, especially, is only too common

---

* Sheriff Alison, *Principles of Population*, vol. ii.—*Note by Engels*. (Omitted in the American and English editions.—*Ed.*)

among the English working-people, and only too vigorously fostered by the existing institutions of society. And children growing up in this savage way, amidst these demoralising influences,[a] are expected to turn out goody-goody and moral in the end! Verily the requirements are naïve, which the self-satisfied bourgeois makes upon the working-man!

The contempt for the existing social order is most conspicuous in its extreme form — that of offences against the law. If the influences demoralising to the working-man act more powerfully, more concentratedly than usual, he becomes an offender as certainly as water abandons the fluid for the vaporous state at 80 degrees, Réaumur. Under the brutal and brutalising treatment of the bourgeoisie, the working-man becomes precisely as much a thing without volition as water, and is subject to the laws of Nature with precisely the same necessity; at a certain · point all freedom ceases. Hence with the extension of the proletariat, crime has increased in England, and the British nation has become the most criminal in the world. From the annual criminal tables of the Home Secretary, it is evident that the increase of crime in England has proceeded with incomprehensible rapidity. The numbers of arrests for *criminal* offences reached in the years: 1805, 4,605; 1810, 5,146; 1815, 7,818; 1820, 13,710; 1825, 14,437; 1830, 18,107; 1835, 20,731; 1840, 27,187; 1841, 27,760; 1842, 31,309 in England and Wales alone.[144] That is to say, they increased sevenfold in thirty-seven years. Of these arrests, in 1842, 4,497 were made in Lancashire alone, or more than 14 per ·cent of the whole; and 4,094 in Middlesex, including London, or more than 13 per cent. So that two districts which include great cities with large proletarian populations, produced one-fourth[b] of the total amount of crime, though their population is far from forming one-fourth of the whole. Moreover, the criminal tables prove directly that nearly all crime arises within the proletariat; for, in 1842, taking the average, out of 100 criminals, 32.35 could neither read nor write; 58.32 read and wrote imperfectly; 6.77 could read and write well; 0.22 had enjoyed a higher education, while the degree of education of 2.34 could not be ascertained. In Scotland, crime has increased yet more rapidly. There were but 89 arrests for criminal offences in 1819, and as early as 1837 the number had risen to 3,126, and in 1842 to 4,189. In Lanarkshire, where

---

[a] The German editions of 1845 and 1892 have here "including often enough the parents themselves".—*Ed.*

[b] The German editions of 1845 and 1892 have "over one-fourth".—*Ed.*

Sheriff Alison himself made out the official report, population has doubled once in thirty years, and crime once in five and a half, or six times more rapidly than the population. The offences, as in all civilised countries, are, in the great majority of cases, against property, and have, therefore, arisen from want in some form; for what a man has, he does not steal. The proportion of offences against property to the population, which in the Netherlands is as 1:7,140, and in France, as 1:1,804, was in England, when Gaskell wrote, as 1:799. The proportion of offences against persons to the population is, in the Netherlands, 1:28,904; in France, 1:17,573; in England, 1:23,395; that of crimes in general to the population in the agricultural districts, as 1:1,043; in the manufacturing districts as 1:840.* In the whole of England today the proportion is 1:660 **; though it is scarcely ten years since Gaskell's book appeared!

These facts are certainly more than sufficient to bring any one, even a bourgeois, to pause and reflect upon the consequences of such a state of things. If demoralisation and crime multiply twenty years longer in this proportion (and if English manufacture in these twenty years should be less prosperous than heretofore, the progressive multiplication of crime can only continue the more rapidly), what will the result be? Society is already in a state of visible dissolution; it is impossible to pick up a newspaper without seeing the most striking evidence of the giving way of all social ties. I look at random into a heap of English journals lying before me; there is the *Manchester Guardian* for October 30, 1844, which reports for three days. It no longer takes the trouble to give exact details as to Manchester, and merely relates the most interesting cases: that the workers in a mill have struck for higher wages without giving notice, and been condemned by a Justice of the Peace to resume work; that in Salford a couple of boys had been caught stealing, and a bankrupt tradesman tried to cheat his creditors. From the neighbouring towns the reports are more detailed: in Ashton, two thefts, one burglary, one suicide; in Bury, one theft; in Bolton, two thefts, one revenue fraud; in Leigh, one theft; in Oldham, one strike for wages, one theft, one fight between Irish women, one non-Union hatter assaulted by Union men, one mother beaten by her son,[a] one attack upon the police,

---

* *The Manufacturing Population of England*, chap. 10.— Note by Engels.
** The total of population, about fifteen millions, divided by the number of *convicted* criminals (22,733).—*Note by Engels.*

---

[a] The German editions of 1845 and 1892 have here "in Rochdale a number of fights".—*Ed.*

one robbery of a church; in Stockport, discontent of working-men with wages, one theft, one fraud, one fight, one wife beaten by her husband; in Warrington, one theft, one fight; in Wigan, one theft, and one robbery of a church. The reports of the London papers are much worse; frauds, thefts, assaults, family quarrels crowd one another. A *Times* of September 12, 1844, falls into my hand, which gives a report of a single day, including a theft, an attack upon the police, a sentence upon a father requiring him to support his illegitimate son, the abandonment of a child by its parents, and the poisoning of a man by his wife. Similar reports are to be found in all the English papers. In this country, social war is under full headway, every one stands for himself, and fights for himself against all comers, and whether or not he shall injure all the others who are his declared foes, depends upon a cynical calculation as to what is most advantageous for himself. It no longer occurs to any one to come to a peaceful understanding with his fellow-man; all differences are settled by threats violence, or in a law-court. In short, every one sees in his neighbour an enemy to be got out of the way, or, at best, a tool to be used for his own advantage. And this war grows from year to year, as the criminal tables show, more violent, passionate, irreconcilable. The enemies are dividing gradually into two great camps[a]—the bourgeoisie on the one hand, the workers on the other. This war of each against all, of the bourgeoisie against the proletariat, need cause us no surprise, for it is only the logical sequel of the principle involved in free competition. But it may very well surprise us that the bourgeoisie remains so quiet and composed in the face of the rapidly gathering storm-clouds, that it can read all these things daily in the papers without, we will not say indignation at such a social condition, but fear of its consequences, of a universal outburst of that which manifests itself symptomatically from day to day in the form of crime. But then it is the bourgeoisie, and from its standpoint cannot even see the facts, much less perceive their consequences. One thing only is astounding, that class prejudice and preconceived opinions can hold a whole class of human beings in such perfect, I might almost say, such mad blindness. Meanwhile, the development of the nation goes its way whether the bourgeoisie has eyes for it or not, and will surprise the property-holding class one day with things not dreamed of in its philosophy.

---

[a] The German editions of 1845 and 1892 have "two great camps fighting each other".—*Ed.*

SINGLE BRANCHES OF INDUSTRY

FACTORY-HANDS[a]

In dealing now with the more important branches of the English manufacturing proletariat, we shall begin, according to the principle already laid down,[b] with the factory-workers, i.e., those who are comprised under the Factory Act. This law regulates the length of the working-day in mills in which wool, silk, cotton, and flax are spun or woven by means of water or steam-power, and embraces, therefore, the more important branches of English manufacture. The class employed by them is the most intelligent and energetic of all the English workers, and, therefore, the most restless and most hated by the bourgeoisie. It stands as a whole, and the cotton-workers pre-eminently stand, at the head of the labour movement, as their masters the manufacturers, especially those of Lancashire, take the lead of the bourgeois agitation.

We have already seen in the introduction how the population employed in working up the textile materials were first torn from their former way of life.[c] It is, therefore, not surprising that the progress of mechanical invention in later years also affected precisely these workers most deeply and permanently. The history

---

[a] The German editions of 1845 and 1892 have "factory-hands in the narrower sense".—*Ed.*

[b] The German editions of 1845 and 1892 give the reference to the page on which the chapter "The Industrial Proletariat" begins (see p. 324 of this volume). Concerning the Factory Laws see pp. 442, 459, 461, 464 of this volume.—*Ed.*

[c] The German editions of 1845 and 1892 have here "through the new machinery".—*Ed.*

of cotton manufacture as related by Ure,* Baines,** and others is the story of improvements in every direction, most of which have become domesticated in the other branches of industry as well. Hand-work is superseded by machine-work almost universally, nearly all manipulations are conducted by the aid of steam or water, and every year is bringing further improvements.

In a well-ordered state of society, such improvements could only be a source of rejoicing; in a war of all against all, individuals seize the benefit for themselves, and so deprive the majority of the means of subsistence. Every improvement in machinery throws workers out of employment, and the greater the advance, the more numerous the unemployed; each great improvement produces, therefore, upon a number of workers the effect of a commercial crisis, creates want, wretchedness, and crime. Take a few examples. The very first invention, the jenny, worked by one man, produced at least sixfold what the spinning-wheel had yielded in the same time; thus every new jenny threw five spinners out of employment. The throstle, which, in turn, produced much more than the jenny, and, like it, was worked by one man, threw still more people out of employment. The mule, which required yet fewer hands in proportion to the product, had the same effect, and every improvement in the mule, every multiplication of its spindles, diminished still further the number of workers employed. But this increase of the number of spindles in the mule is so great that whole armies of workers have been thrown out of employment by it. For, whereas one spinner, with a couple of children for piecers, formerly set six hundred spindles in motion, he could now manage fourteen hundred to two thousand spindles upon two mules, so that two adult spinners and a part of the piecers whom they employed were thrown out. And since self-acting mules have been introduced into a very large number of spinning-mills, the spinners' work is wholly performed by the machine. There lies before me a book from the pen of James Leach,*** one of the recognised leaders of the Chartists in Manchester. The author has worked for years in various branches of industry, in mills and coal-mines, and is known to me

* *The Cotton Manufacture of Great Britain*, by Dr. A. Ure, 1836.—*Note by Engels.*

** *History of the Cotton Manufacture of Great Britain* by E. Baines, Esq.—*Note by Engels.*

*** *Stubborn Facts from the Factories by a Manchester Operative.* Published and dedicated to the working-classes, by Wm. Rashleigh, M. P., London, Ollivier, 1844, p. 28, *et seq.*—*Note by Engels.*

personally as an honest, trustworthy, and capable man. In consequence of his political position, he had at command extensive
detailed information as to the different factories, collected by the
workers themselves, and he publishes tables from which it is clear
that in 1841, in 35 factories, 1,083 fewer mule spinners were
employed than in 1829, though the number of spindles in these
35 factories had increased by 99,429. He cites five factories in
which no spinners whatever are employed, self-actors only being
used. While the number of spindles increased by 10 per cent, the
number of spinners diminished more than 60 per cent. And Leach
adds that since 1841, so many improvements have been introduced by double-decking[a] and other means, that in some of the
factories named, half the operatives have been discharged. In one
factory alone, where eighty spinners were employed a short time
ago, there are now but twenty left; the others having been
discharged or set at children's work for children's wages. Of
Stockport Leach tells a similar story, that in 1835, 800 spinners
were employed, and in 1843 but 140, though the manufacture of
Stockport has greatly increased during the last eight or nine years.
Similar improvements have now been made in carding-frames, by
which one-half the operatives have been thrown out of employment. In one factory improved frames have been set up, which
have thrown four hands out of eight out of work, besides which
the employer reduced the wages of the four retained from eight
shillings to seven. The same process has gone on in the weaving
industry; the power-loom has taken possession of one branch of
hand-weaving after another, and since it produces much more
than the hand-loom, while one weaver can work two looms, it has
superseded a multitude of working-people. And in all sorts of
manufacture, in flax and wool-spinning, in silk-twisting, the case is
the same. The power-loom, too, is beginning to appropriate one
branch after another of wool and linen-weaving; in Rochdale
alone, there are more power than hand-looms in flannel and other
wool-weaving branches. The bourgeoisie usually replies to this,
that improvements in machinery, by decreasing the cost of
production, supply finished goods at lower prices, and that these
reduced prices cause such an increase in consumption that the
unemployed operatives soon find full employment in newly

---

[a] The German editions of 1845 and 1892 give the English terms "double-decking", "spinners", "self-actors" and "doffers" in English, sometimes in brackets, after
their German equivalents.—Ed.

founded factories.* The bourgeoisie is so far correct that under certain conditions favourable for the general development of manufacture, every reduction in price of goods *in which the raw material is cheap*, greatly increases consumption, and gives rise to the building of new factories; but every further word of the assertion is a lie. The bourgeoisie ignores the fact that it takes years for these results of the decrease in price to follow and for new factories to be built; it is silent upon the point that every improvement in machinery throws the real work, the expenditure of force, more and more upon the machine, and so transforms the work of full-grown men into mere supervision, which a feeble woman or even a child can do quite as well, and does for half or two-thirds wages; that, therefore, grown men are constantly more and more supplanted and *not re-employed* by the increase in manufacture; it conceals the fact that whole branches of industry fall away, or are so changed that they must be learned afresh; and it takes good care not to confess what it usually harps upon, whenever the question of forbidding the work of children is broached, that factory-work must be learned in earliest youth[a] in order to be learned properly. It does not mention the fact that the process of improvement goes steadily on, and that as soon as the operative has succeeded in making himself at home in a new branch, if he actually does succeed in so doing, this, too, is taken from him, and with it the last remnant of security which remained to him for winning his bread. But the bourgeoisie gets the benefit of the improvements in machinery; it has a capital opportunity for piling up money during the first years while many old machines are still in use, and the improvement not yet universally introduced; and it would be too much to ask that it should have an open eye for the disadvantages inseparable from these improvements.

The fact that improved machinery reduces wages has also been as violently disputed by the bourgeoisie, as it is constantly reiterated by the working-men. The bourgeoisie insists that although the price of piece-work has been reduced, yet the total of wages for the week's work has rather risen than fallen, and the condition of the operatives rather improved than deteriorated. It is hard to get to the bottom of the matter, for the operatives

---

* Compare Factories' Inquiry Commission's Report.—*Note by Engels to the American edition of 1887* (reproduced in the English edition of 1892; the German editions of 1845 and 1892 give the reference in the text below—*Ed.*).

---

[a] The German editions of 1845 and 1892 have "indeed before the age of ten" and a reference to the Factories' Inquiry Commission's Report.—*Ed.*

usually dwell upon the price of piece-work. But it is certain that the weekly wage, also, has, in many branches of work, been reduced by the improvement of machinery. The so-called fine spinners (who spin fine mule yarn), for instance, do receive high wages, .thirty to forty shillings a week, because they have a powerful association for keeping wages up, and their craft requires long training; but the coarse spinners who have to compete against self-actors (which are not as yet adapted for fine spinning), and whose association was broken down by the introduction of these machines, receive very low wages. A mule spinner told me that he does not earn more than fourteen shillings a week, and his statement agrees with that of Leach, that in various factories the coarse spinners earn less than sixteen shillings and sixpence a week, and that a spinner, who years ago[a] earned thirty shillings, can now hardly scrape up twelve and a half, and had not earned more on an average in the past year. The wages of women and children may perhaps have fallen less, but only because they were not high from the beginning. I know several women, widows with children, who have trouble enough to earn eight to nine shillings a week; and that they and their families cannot live decently upon that sum, every one must admit who knows the price of the barest necessaries of life in England. That wages in general have been reduced by the improvement of machinery is the unanimous testimony of the operatives. The bourgeois assertion that the condition of the working-class has been improved by machinery is most vigorously proclaimed a falsehood in every meeting of working-men in the factory districts. And even if it were true that the relative wage, the price of piece-work only, has fallen, while the absolute wage, the sum to be earned in the week, remained unchanged, what would follow? That the operatives have had quietly to look on while the manufacturers filled their purses from every improvement without giving the hands the smallest share in the gain. The bourgeois forgets, in fighting the working-man, the most ordinary principles of his own Political Economy. He who at other times swears by Malthus, cries out in his anxiety before the workers: "Where could the millions by which the population of England has increased find work, without the improvements in machinery?"* As though the bourgeois did not know well enough

* This is the question posed by J. C. Symons, in *Arts and Artisans.*—*Note by Engels.* (In the German editions of 1845 and 1892, this question is followed by: "Nonsense!"—*Ed.*)

[a] The German editions of 1845 and 1892 have "who three years ago".—*Ed.*

that without machinery and the expansion of industry which it produced, these "millions" would never have been brought into the world and grown up! The service which machinery has rendered the workers is simply this: that it has brought home to their minds the necessity of a social reform by means of which machinery shall no longer work against but for them. Let the wise bourgeois ask the people who sweep the streets in Manchester and elsewhere (though even this is past now, since machines for the purpose have been invented and introduced), or sell salt, matches, oranges, and shoe-strings on the streets, or even beg, what they were formerly, and he will see how many will answer: Mill-hands thrown out of work by machinery. The consequences of improvement in machinery under our present social conditions are, for the working-man, solely injurious, and often in the highest degree oppressive. Every new advance brings with it loss of employment, want, and suffering, and in a country like England where, without that, there is usually a "surplus population", to be discharged from work is the worst that can befall the operative. And what a dispiriting, unnerving influence this uncertainty of his position in life, consequent upon the unceasing progress of machinery,[a] must exercise upon the worker, whose lot is precarious enough without it! To escape despair, there are but two ways open to him; either inward and outward revolt against the bourgeoisie or drunkenness and general demoralisation. And the English operatives are accustomed to take refuge in both. The history of the English proletariat relates hundreds of uprisings against machinery and the bourgeoisie; we have already spoken of the moral dissolution which, in itself, is only another form of despair.

The worst situation is that of those workers who have to compete against a machine that is making its way. The price of the goods which they produce adapts itself to the price of the kindred product of the machine, and as the latter works more cheaply, its human competitor has but the lowest wages. The same thing happens to every operative employed upon an old machine in competition with later improvements. And who else is there to bear the hardship? The manufacturer will not throw out his old apparatus, nor will he sustain the loss upon it; out of the dead mechanism he can make nothing, so he fastens upon the living worker, the universal scapegoat of society. Of all the workers in competition with machinery, the most ill-used are the hand-loom cotton weavers. They receive the most trifling wages, and, with full

[a] The German editions of 1845 and 1892 have here "and the unemployment resulting from it".—*Ed.*

work, are not in a position to earn more than ten shillings a week. One class of woven goods after another is annexed by the power-loom, and hand-weaving is the last refuge of workers thrown out of employment in other branches, so that the trade is always overcrowded. Hence it comes that, in average seasons, the hand-weaver counts himself fortunate if he can earn six or seven shillings a week, while to reach this sum he must sit at his loom fourteen to eighteen hours a day. Most woven goods require moreover a damp weaving-room, to keep the weft from snapping, and in part for this reason, in part because of their poverty, which prevents them from paying for better dwellings, the work-rooms of these weavers are usually without wooden or paved floors. I have been in many dwellings of such weavers, in remote, vile courts and alleys, usually in cellars. Often half-a-dozen of these hand-loom weavers, several of them married, live together in a cottage with one or two work-rooms, and one large sleeping-room. Their food consists almost exclusively of potatoes, with perhaps oatmeal porridge, rarely milk, and scarcely ever meat. Great numbers of them are Irish or of Irish descent. And these poor hand-loom weavers, first to suffer from every crisis, and last to be relieved from it, must serve the bourgeoisie as a handle in meeting attacks upon the factory system. See, cries the bourgeois, triumphantly, see how these poor creatures must famish, while the mill operatives are thriving, and *then* judge the factory system!* As though it were not precise y the factory system and the machinery belonging to it which had so shamefully crushed the hand-loom weavers, and as though the bourgeoisie did not know this quite as well as ourselves! But the bourgeoisie has interests at stake, and so a falsehood or two and a bit of hypocrisy won't matter much.

Let us examine somewhat more closely the fact that machinery more and more supersedes the work of men. The human labour, involved in both spinning and weaving, consists chiefly in piecing broken threads, as the machine does all the rest. This work requires no muscular strength, but only flexibility of finger. Men are, therefore, not only not needed for it, but actually, by reason of the greater muscular development of the hand, less fit for it than women and children, and are, therefore, naturally almost superseded by them. Hence, the more the use of the arms, the expenditure of strength, can be transferred[a] to steam or water-

---

* See Dr. Ure in *The Philosophy of Manufactures.—Note by Engels.*

[a] The German editions of 1845 and 1892 have here "through the introduction of machinery".—*Ed.*

power, the fewer men need be employed; and as women and children work more cheaply, and in these branches better than men, they take their places. In the spinning-mills women and girls are to be found in almost exclusive possession of the throstles; among the mules one man, an adult spinner (with self-actors, he, too, becomes superfluous), and several piecers for tying the threads, usually children or women, sometimes young men of from eighteen to twenty years, here and there an old spinner* thrown out of other employment. At the power-looms women, from fifteen to twenty years, are chiefly employed, and a few men; these, however, rarely remain at this trade after their twenty-first year. Among the preparatory machinery, too, women alone are to be found, with here and there a man to clean and sharpen the carding-frames. Besides all these, the factories employ numbers of children—doffers—for mounting and taking down bobbins, and a few men as overlookers, a mechanic and an engineer for the steam-engines, carpenters, porters, etc.; but the actual work of the mills is done by women and children. This the manufacturers deny.

They published last year elaborate tables to prove that machinery does not supersede adult male operatives. According to these tables, rather more than half of all the factory-workers employed, viz., 52 per cent, were females and 48 per cent males, and of these operatives more than half were over eighteen years old.[145] So far, so good. But the manufacturers are very careful not to tell us, how many of the adults were men and how many women. And this is just the point. Besides this, they have evidently counted the mechanics, engineers, carpenters, all the men employed in any way in the factories, perhaps even the clerks, and still they have not the courage to tell the whole truth. These publications teem generally with falsehoods, perversions, crooked statements, with calculations of averages, that prove a great deal for the uninitiated reader and nothing for the initiated, and with suppressions of facts bearing on the most important points; and they prove only the selfish blindness and want of uprightness of the manufacturers concerned. Let us take some of the statements of a speech with which Lord Ashley introduced the Ten Hours' Bill, March 15th, 1844, into the House of Commons. Here he gives some data as to

* Report of Factory Inspector, L. Horner. October, 1843: "There is at present a very anomalous state of things in regard to wages in some departments of cotton mills in Lancashire; for there are hundreds of young men, between 20 and 30 years of age, employed as piecers and otherwise, who are receiving not more than eight or nine shillings a week; while under the same roof, children of 13 years of age are getting five shillings, and young women between 16 and 20 are getting from ten to twelve shillings a week."—Note by Engels.

the relations of sex and age of the operatives, not yet refuted by the manufacturers, whose statements, as quoted above, cover moreover only a part of the manufacturing industry of England. Of 419,590 factory operatives of the British Empire in 1839, 192,887, or nearly half, were under eighteen years of age, and 242,296 of the female sex, of whom 112,192 were less than eighteen years old. There remain, therefore, 80,695 male operatives under eighteen years, and 96,599 adult male operatives, *or not one full quarter*[a] of the whole number. In the cotton factories, $56^1/_4$ per cent; in the woollen mills, $69^1/_2$ per cent; in the silk mills, $70^1/_2$ per cent; in the flax-spinning mills, $70^1/_2$ per cent of all operatives are of the female sex. These numbers suffice to prove the crowding out of adult males. But you have only to go into the nearest mill to see the fact confirmed. Hence follows of necessity that inversion of the existing social order which, being forced upon them, has the most ruinous consequences for the workers. The employment of women at once breaks up the family; for when the wife spends twelve or thirteen hours every day in the mill, and the husband works the same length of time there or elsewhere, what becomes of the children? They grow up like wild weeds; they are put out to nurse for a shilling or eighteenpence a week, and how they are treated may be imagined. Hence the accidents to which little children fall victims[b] multiply in the factory districts to a terrible extent. The lists of the Coroner of Manchester* showed for nine months: 69 deaths from burning, 56 from drowning, 23 from falling, 67 from other causes, or a total of 215 deaths from accidents,** while in non-manufacturing Liverpool during twelve months there were but 146 fatal accidents. The mining accidents are excluded in both cases; and since the Coroner of Manchester has no authority in Salford, the population of both places mentioned in the comparison is about the same. The *Manchester Guardian* reports one or more deaths by

* Report of Factories' Inquiry Commission. Testimony of Dr. Hawkins, p. 3.— *Note by Engels to the American edition of 1887* (reproduced in the English edition of 1892; the German editions of 1845 and 1892 give this reference in the text— *Ed.*).

** In 1842, among the accidents brought to the Infirmary in Manchester, one hundred and eighty-nine were from burning. How many were fatal is not stated. *Note by Engels.* (The last sentence is omitted in the authorised English edition.—*Ed.*)

[a] The German editions of 1845 and 1892 have here "or 23 per cent, i.e., *not one full quarter*".—*Ed.*

[b] The German editions of 1845 and 1892 have here "due to lack of supervision".—*Ed.*

burning in almost every number. That the general mortality among young children must be increased by the employment of the mothers is self-evident, and is placed beyond all doubt by notorious facts. Women often return to the mill three or four days after confinement, leaving the baby, of course; in the dinner-hour they must hurry home to feed the child and eat something, and what sort of suckling that can be is also evident. Lord Ashley repeats the testimony of several workwomen:

"M. H., twenty years old, has two children, the youngest a baby that is tended by the other, a little older. The mother goes to the mill shortly after five o'clock in the morning, and comes home at eight at night; all day the milk pours from her breasts, so that her clothing drips with it." "H. W. has three children, goes away Monday morning at five o'clock, and comes back Saturday evening; has so much to do for the children then that she cannot get to bed before three o'clock in the morning; often wet through to the skin, and obliged to work in that state." She said: "My breasts have given me the most frightful pain, and I have been dripping wet with milk."[146]

The use of narcotics to keep the children still is fostered by this infamous system, and has reached a great extent in the factory districts. Dr. Johns, Registrar in Chief for Manchester, is of opinion that this custom is the chief source of the many deaths from convulsions. The employment of the wife dissolves the family utterly and of necessity, and this dissolution, in our present society, which is based upon the family, brings the most demoralising consequences for parents as well as children. A mother who has no time to trouble herself about her child, to perform the most ordinary loving services for it during its first year, who scarcely indeed sees it, can be no real mother to the child, must inevitably grow indifferent to it, treat it unlovingly like a stranger. The children who grow up under such conditions are utterly ruined for later family life, can never feel at home in the family which they themselves found, because they have always been accustomed to isolation, and they contribute therefore to the already general undermining of the family in the working-class. A similar dissolution of the family is brought about by the employment of the children. When they get on far enough to earn more than they cost their parents from week to week, they begin to pay the parents a fixed sum for board and lodging, and keep the rest for themselves. This often happens from the fourteenth or fifteenth year.* In a word, the children emancipate themselves,

* Factories' Inquiry Commission's Report, Power's Report on Leeds, passim; Tufnell Report on Manchester, p. 17, etc.—*Note by Engels to the American edition of 1887* (reproduced in the English edition of 1892; the German editions of 1845 and 1892 give the reference in the text—*Ed.*).

and regard the paternal dwelling as a lodging-house, which they often exchange for another, as suits them.

In many cases the family is not wholly dissolved by the employment of the wife, but turned upside down. The wife supports the family, the husband sits at home, tends the children, sweeps the room and cooks. This case happens very frequently; in Manchester alone, many hundred such men could be cited, condemned to domestic occupations. It is easy to imagine the wrath aroused among the working-men by this reversal of all relations within the family,[a] while the other social conditions remain unchanged. There lies before me a letter from an English working-man, Robert Pounder, Baron's Buildings, Woodhouse, Moorside, in Leeds (the bourgeoisie may hunt him up there; I give the exact address for the purpose), written by him to Oastler.*

He relates how another working-man, being on tramp, came to St. Helens, in Lancashire, and there looked up an old friend. He found him in a miserable, damp cellar, scarcely furnished.

"And when my poor friend went in, there sat poor Jack near the fire, and what did he, think you? Why he sat and mended his wife's stockings with the bodkin; and as soon as he saw his old friend at the door-post, he tried to hide them. But Joe, that is my friend's name, had seen it, and said: 'Jack, what the devil art thou doing? Where is the missus? Why, is that thy work?' and poor Jack was ashamed, and said: 'No, I know this is not my work, but my poor missus is i' th' factory; she has to leave at half-past five and works till eight at night, and then she is so knocked up that she cannot do aught when she gets home, so I have to do everything for her what I can, for I have no work, nor had any for more nor three years, and I shall never have any more work while I live;' and then he wept a big tear. Jack again said: 'There is work enough for women folks and childer hereabouts, but none for men: thou mayest sooner find a hundred pound on the road than work for men—but I should never have believed that either thou or any one else would have seen me mending my wife's stockings, for it is bad work. But she can hardly stand on her feet; I am afraid she will be laid up, and then I don't know what is to become of us, for it's a good bit that she has been the man in the house and I the woman; it is bad work, Joe;' and he cried bitterly, and said, 'It has not been always so.' 'No,' said Joe; 'but when thou hadn't no work, how hast thou not shifted?' 'I'll tell thee, Joe, as well as I can, but it was bad enough; thou knowest when I got married I had work plenty, and thou knows I was not lazy.' 'No, that thou wert not.' 'And we had

---

* This letter is re-translated from the German, no attempt being made to reproduce either the spelling or the original Yorkshire dialect.— *Note by Engels to the American edition of 1887 and the English edition of 1892.* (After "written bv him to Oastler" the German editions of 1845 and 1892 have: "and the naivety of which I can only partly render. The spelling can, if need be, but the Yorkshire dialect in no way, be imitated in German." The contents of the beginning of the letter are given in greater detail in the German version.— *Ed.*)

[a] The German editions of 1845 and 1892 have here "the just wrath aroused among the working-men by this virtual castration, and the reversal of all relations within the family".—*Ed.*

a good furnished house, and Mary need not go to work. I could work for the two of us; but now the world is upside down. Mary has to work and I have to stop at home, mind the childer, sweep and wash, bake and mend; and, when the poor woman comes home at night, she is knocked up. Thou knows, Joe, it's hard for one that was used different.' 'Yes, boy, it is hard.' And then Jack began to cry again, and he wished he had never married, and that he had never been born; but he had never thought, when he wed Mary, that it would come to this. 'I have often cried over it,' said Jack. Now when Joe heard this, he told me that he had cursed and damned the factories, and the masters, and the Government, with all the curses that he had learned while he was in the factory from a child."[147]

Can any one imagine a more insane state of things than that described in this letter? And yet this condition, which unsexes the man and takes from the woman all womanliness without being able to bestow upon the man true womanliness, or the woman true manliness — this condition which degrades, in the most shameful way, both sexes, and, through them, Humanity, is the last result of our much-praised civilisation, the final achievement of all the efforts and struggles of hundreds of generations to improve their own situation and that of their posterity. We must either despair of mankind, and its aims and efforts, when we see all our labour and toil result in such a mockery, or we must admit that human society has hitherto sought salvation in a false direction; we must admit that so total a reversal of the position of the sexes can have come to pass only because the sexes have been placed in a false position from the beginning. If the reign of the wife over the husband, as inevitably brought about by the factory system, is inhuman, the pristine rule of the husband over the wife must have been inhuman too. If the wife can now base her supremacy[a] upon the fact that she supplies the greater part, nay, the whole of the common possession, the necessary inference is that this community of possession is no true and rational one, since one member of the family boasts offensively of contributing the greater share. If the family of our present society is being thus dissolved, this dissolution merely shows that, at bottom, the binding tie of this family was not family affection, but private interest lurking under the cloak of a pretended community of possessions.* The same

* How numerous married women are in the factories is seen from information furnished by a manufacturer.[148] In 412 factories in Lancashire, 10,721 of them were employed; of the husbands of these women, but 5,314 were also employed in the factories, 3,927 were otherwise employed, 821 were unemployed, and information was wanting as to 659; or two, if not three men for each factory, are supported by the work of their wives.— *Note by Engels.*

[a] The German editions of 1845 and 1892 have here "as the husband did formerly".—*Ed.*

relation exists on the part of those children who support unemployed parents when they do not directly pay board as already referred to. Dr. Hawkins testified in the Factories' Inquiry Commission's Report that this relation is common enough, and in Manchester it is notorious. In this case the children are the masters in the house, as the wife was in the former case, and Lord Ashley gives an example of this in his speech*: A man berated his two daughters for going to the public-house, and they answered that they were tired of being ordered about, saying, "Damn you, we have to keep you."ᵃ Determined to keep the proceeds of their work for themselves, they left the family dwelling, and abandoned their parents to their fate.

The unmarried women, who have grown up in mills, are no better off than the married ones. It is self-evident that a girl who has worked in a mill from her ninth year is in no position to understand domestic work, whence it follows that female operatives prove wholly inexperienced and unfit as housekeepers. They cannot knit or sew, cook or wash, are unacquainted with the most ordinary duties of a housekeeper, and when they have young children to take care of, have not the vaguest idea how to set about it. The Factories' Inquiry Commission's Report gives dozens of examples of this, and Dr. Hawkins, Commissioner for Lancashire, expresses his opinion as follows**:

A girl marries early and recklessly; "she has had no time, no means, no opportunities of learning the common duties of domestic life; and even if she had acquired the knowledge she has still no time to practise them.... There is the young mother absent from her child above twelve hours daily. Who has the charge of the infant in her absence? Usually some little girl or aged woman, who is hired for a trifle and whose services are equivalent to the reward. Too often the dwelling of the factory family is no home; it sometimes is a cellar, which includes no cooking, no washing, no making, no mending, no decencies of life, no invitations to the fireside. I cannot help on these and on other grounds, especially for the better preservation of infant life, expressing my hope that a period may arrive when married women shall be rarely employed in a factory.***

* House of Commons, March 15th, 1844.—*Note by Engels to the American edition of 1887.* (This reference, like the others in this chapter, are reproduced in the English edition of 1892; the German editions of 1845 and 1892 give them in the text.—*Ed.*)

**Factories' Inquiry Commission's Report, p. 4.—*Note by Engels to the American edition of 1887.*

*** For further examples and information compare Factories' Inquiry Commission's Report. Cowell Evidence, pp. 37, 38, 39, 72, 77, 82; Tufnell Evidence, pp. 9, 15, 45, 54, etc.—*Note by Engels to the American edition of 1887.*

ᵃ The German editions of 1845 and 1892 give the words in quotes in English.—*Ed.*

But that is the least of the evil. The moral consequences of the employment of women in factories are even worse. The collecting of persons of both sexes and all ages in a single work-room, the inevitable contact, the crowding into a small space of people, to whom neither mental nor moral education has been given, is not calculated for the favourable development of the female character. The manufacturer, if he pays any attention to the matter, can interfere only when something scandalous actually happens; the permanent, less conspicuous influence of persons of dissolute character upon the more moral, and especially upon the younger ones, he cannot ascertain, and consequently cannot prevent. But precisely this influence is the injurious. The language used in the mills is characterised by many witnesses in the report of 1833, as "indecent", "bad", "filthy", etc.* It is the same process upon a small scale which we have already witnessed upon a large one in the great cities. The centralisation of population has the same influence upon the same persons, whether it affects them in a great city or a small factory. The smaller the mill the closer the packing, and the more unavoidable the contact; and the consequences are not wanting. A witness in Leicester said that he would rather let his daughter beg than go into a factory; that they are perfect gates of hell; that most of the prostitutes of the town had their employment in the mills to thank for their present situation.** Another, in Manchester, "did not hesitate to assert that three-fourths of the young factory employees, from fourteen to twenty years of age, were unchaste".*** Commissioner Cowell expresses it as his opinion, that the morality of the factory operatives is somewhat below the average of that of the working-class in general.**** And Dr. Hawkins***** says:

"An estimate of sexual morality is scarcely possible to be reduced into figures; but if I may trust my own observations, and the general opinion of those with whom I have conversed, and the spirit of our evidence, then a most discouraging view of the influence of the factory life upon the morality of female youth obtrudes itself."

It is, besides, a matter of course that factory servitude, like any other, and to an even higher degree, confers the *jus primae noctis* upon the master. In this respect also the employer is sovereign

---

* Cowell Evidence, pp. 35, 37, and elsewhere.— *Note by Engels to the American edition of 1887.*

** Power Evidence, p. 8.— *Note by Engels to the American edition of 1887.*

*** Cowell Evidence, p. 57.— *Note by Engels to the American edition of 1887.*

**** Cowell Evidence, p. 82.— *Note by Engels to the American edition of 1887.*

***** Factories Inquiry Commissions Report, p. 4, Hawkins.—*Note by Engels to the American edition of 1887.*

over the persons and charms of his employees. The threat of
discharge suffices to overcome all resistance in nine cases out of
ten, if not in ninety-nine out of a hundred, in girls who, in any
case, have no strong inducements to chastity. If the master is mean
enough, and the official report mentions several such cases, his
mill is also his harem; and the fact that not all manufacturers use
their power, does not in the least change the position of the girls.
In the beginning of manufacturing industry, when most of the
employers were upstarts without education or consideration for
the hypocrisy of society, they let nothing interfere with the
exercise of their vested rights.

To form a correct judgment of the influence of factory-work
upon the health of the female sex, it is necessary first to consider
the work of children, and then the nature of the work itself. From
the beginning of manufacturing industry, children have been
employed in mills, at first almost exclusively by reason of the
smallness of the machines, which were later enlarged. Even
children from the workhouses were employed in multitudes, being
rented out for a number of years to the manufacturers as
apprentices. They were lodged, fed, and clothed in common, and
were, of course, completely the slaves of their masters, by whom
they were treated with the utmost recklessness and barbarity. As
early as 1796, the public objection to this revolting system found
such vigorous expression through Dr. Percival and Sir Robert Peel
(father of the Cabinet Minister, and himself a cotton manufacturer), that in 1802 Parliament passed an Apprentices' Bill,[a] by
which the most crying evils were removed.[149] Gradually the
increasing competition of free workpeople crowded out the whole
apprentice system; factories were built in cities, machinery was
constructed on a larger scale, and work-rooms were made more
airy and wholesome; gradually, too, more work was found for
adults and young persons. The number of children in the mills diminished somewhat, and the age at which they began to work rose
a little; few children under eight or nine years were now employed.
Later, as we shall see, the power of the state intervened several
times to protect them from the money-greed of the bourgeoisie.

The great mortality among children of the working-class, and
especially among those of the factory operatives, is proof enough
of the unwholesome conditions under which they pass their first
years. These influences are at work, of course, among the children

---

[a] The German editions of 1845 and 1892 give the title of the Bill in
English.—Ed.

who survive, but not quite so powerfully as upon those who succumb. The result in the most favourable case is a tendency to disease, or some check in development, and consequent less than normal vigour of the constitution. A nine years old child of a factory operative that has grown up in want, privation, and changing conditions, in cold and damp, with insufficient clothing and unwholesome dwellings, is far from having the working force of a child brought up under healthier conditions. At nine years of age it is sent into the mill to work $6^1/_2$ hours (formerly 8, earlier still, 12 to 14, even 16 hours) daily, until the thirteenth year; then twelve hours until the eighteenth year. The old enfeebling influences continue, while the work is added to them. It is not to be denied that a child of nine years, even an operative's child, can hold out through $6^1/_2$ hours' daily work, without any one being able to trace visible bad results in its development directly to this cause; but in no case can its presence in the damp, heavy air of the factory, often at once warm and wet, contribute to good health; and, in any case, it is unpardonable to sacrifice to the greed of an unfeeling bourgeoisie the time of children which should be devoted solely to their physical and mental development, withdraw them from school and the fresh air, in order to wear them for the benefit of the manufacturers. The bourgeoisie says: If we do not employ the children in the mills, they only remain under conditions unfavourable to their development; and this is true on the whole. But what does this mean if it is not a confession that the bourgeoisie first places the children of the working-class under unfavourable conditions, and then exploits these bad conditions for its own benefit, appeals to that which is as much its own fault as the factory system, excuses the sin of today with the sin of yesterday? And if the Factory Act did not in some measure fetter their hands, how this "humane", this "benevolent" bourgeoisie, which has built its factories solely for the good of the working-class, would take care of the interests of these workers! Let us hear how they acted before the factory inspector was at their heels. Their own admitted testimony shall convict them in the Report of the Factories' Inquiry Commission of 1833.

The report of the Central Commission relates that the manufacturers began to employ children rarely of five years, often of six, very often of seven, usually of eight to nine years; that the working-day often lasted fourteen to sixteen hours, exclusive of meals and intervals; that the manufacturers permitted overlookers to flog and maltreat children, and often took an active part in so doing themselves. One case is related of a Scotch manufacturer, who rode after a sixteen years old runaway, forced him to return, running after[a] the employer as fast as the master's horse trotted, and beat him the whole way with a long whip.* In the large towns where the operatives resisted more vigorously, such things naturally happened less often. But even this long working-day failed to satisfy the greed of the capitalists. Their aim was to make the capital invested in the building and machinery produce the highest return, by every available means, to make it work as actively as possible. Hence the manufacturers introduced the shameful system of night-work. Some of them employed two sets of operatives, each numerous enough to fill the whole mill, and let one set work the twelve hours of the day, and the other the twelve hours of the night. It is needless to picture the effect upon the frames of young children, and even upon the health of young persons and adults, produced by permanent loss of sleep at night, which cannot be made good by any amount of sleep during the day. Irritation of the whole nervous system, with general lassitude and enfeeblement of the entire frame, were the inevitable results, with the fostering of temptation to drunkenness and unbridled sexual indulgence. One manufacturer testifies** that during the two years in which night-work was carried on in his factory, the number of illegitimate children born was doubled, and such general demoralisation prevailed that he was obliged to give up night-work. Other manufacturers were yet more barbarous, requiring many hands to work thirty to forty hours at a stretch, several times a week, letting them get a couple of hours sleep only, because the night-shift was not complete, but calculated to replace a part of the operatives only.

The reports of the Commission touching this barbarism surpass everything that is known to me in this line. Such infamies, as are here related, are nowhere else to be found — yet we shall see that the bourgeoisie constantly appeals to the testimony of the Commission as being in its own favour. The consequences of these cruelties became evident quickly enough. The Commissioners mention a crowd of cripples who appeared before them, who clearly owed their distortion to the long working-hours. This distortion usually consists of a curving of the spinal column and

---

* Stuart Evidence, p. 35.—*Note by Engels to the American edition of 1887.*
** Tufnell Evidence, p. 91.—*Note by Engels to the American edition of 1887.*

---

[a] The German editions of 1845 and 1892 have "in front of" instead of "after".—*Ed.*

legs, and is described as follows by Francis Sharp, M.R.C.S., of Leeds*:

"Before I came to Leeds, I had never seen the peculiar twisting of the ends of the lower part of the thigh bone. At first I considered it might be rickets, but from the numbers which presented themselves, particularly at an age beyond the time when rickets attack children (between 8 and 14), and finding that they had commenced since they began work at the factory I soon began to change my opinion. I now may have seen of such cases nearly 100, and I can most decidedly state they were the result of too much labour. So far as I know they all belong to factories, and have attributed their disease to this cause themselves." "Of distortions of the spine, which were evidently owing to the long standing at their labour, perhaps the number of cases might not be less than 300."

Precisely similar is the testimony of Dr. Hey, for eighteen years physician in the hospital in Leeds**:

"Diseases of the spine amongst people employed in factories presented themselves very frequently. Some were the result of pure labour; others were the result of labour on a constitution perhaps congenitally weak, or rendered feeble by bad food. The deformities of the limbs appear to be more frequent than the spinal diseases... the bending in of the knees, relaxation of the ligaments of the ankles was very frequent, and the bending of the large bones. The heads of the large bones have especially been increased and twisted to a considerable extent; and these cases I have found to have come from those mills and factories where long hours have been said to be common."

Surgeons Beaumont and Sharp, of Bradford, bear the same testimony. The reports of Drinkwater, Power, and Dr. Loudon contain a multitude of examples of such distortions, and those of Tufnell and Sir David Barry, which are less directed to this point, give single examples.*** The Commissioners for Lancashire, Cowell, Tufnell, and Hawkins, have almost wholly neglected this aspect of the physiological results of the factory system, though this district rivals Yorkshire in the number of cripples. I have seldom traversed Manchester without meeting three or four of them, suffering from ·precisely the same distortions of the spinal columns and legs as that described, and I have often been able to observe them closely. I know one personally who corresponds exactly with

* Dr. Loudon Evidence, pp. 12, 13.—*Note by Engels to the American edition of 1887.*

** Dr. Loudon Evidence, p. 16.—*Note by Engels to the American edition of 1887.*

*** Drinkwater Evidence, pp. 72, 80, 146, 148, 150 (two brothers); 69 (two brothers); 155, and many others.

Power Evidence, pp. 63, 66, 67 (two cases); 68 (three cases); 69 (two cases); in Leeds, pp. 29, 31, 40, 43, 53, *et seq.*

Loudon Evidence, pp. 4, 7 (four cases); 8 (several cases), etc.

Sir D. Barry Evidence, pp. 6, 8, 13, 21, 22, 44, 55 (three cases), etc.

Tufnell Evidence, pp. 5, 6, 16, etc.—*Note by Engels to the American edition of 1887.*

the foregoing description of Dr. Hey, and who got into this condition in Mr. Douglas' factory in Pendleton, an establishment which enjoys an unenviable notoriety among the operatives by reason of the former long working periods continued night after night. It is evident, at a glance, whence the distortions of these cripples come; they all look exactly alike. The knees are bent inward and backwards,[a] the ankles deformed and thick, and the spinal column often bent forwards or to one side. But the crown belongs to the philanthropic manufacturers of the Macclesfield silk district. They employed the youngest children of all, even from five to six years of age. In the supplementary testimony of Commissioner Tufnell, I find the statement of a certain, factory manager Wright, both of whose sisters were most shamefully crippled, and who had once counted the cripples in several streets, some of them the cleanest and neatest streets of Macclesfield. He found in Townley Street ten, George Street five, Charlotte Street four, Watercots fifteen, Bank Top three, Lord Street seven, Mill Lane twelve, Great George Street two, in the workhouse two, Park Green one, Peckford Street two, whose families all unanimously declared that the cripples had become such in consequence of overwork in the silk-twisting mills. One boy is mentioned so crippled as not to be able to go upstairs, and girls deformed in back and hips.

Other deformities also have proceeded from this overwork, especially flattening of the foot, which Sir D. Barry* frequently observed, as did the physicians and surgeons in Leeds.** In cases, in which a stronger constitution, better food, and other more favourable circumstances enabled the young operative to resist this effect of a barbarous exploitation, we find, at least, pain in the back, hips, and legs, swollen joints, varicose veins, and large, persistent ulcers in the thighs and calves. These affections are almost universal among the operatives. The reports of Stuart, Mackintosh, and Sir D. Barry contain hundreds of examples; indeed, they know almost no operative who did not suffer from some of these affections; and in the remaining reports, the occurrence of the same phenomena is attested by many physicians.

---

* Factories' Inquiry Commission's Report, 1833; Sir D. Barry Evidence, p. 21 (two cases).—*Note by Engels to the American edition of 1887.*

** Factories' Inquiry Commission's Report, 1833, Loudon Evidence, pp. 13, 16, etc.—*Note by Engels to the American edition of 1887.*

---

[a] The German editions of 1845 and 1892 have here "the feet bent inwards".—*Ed.*

The reports covering Scotland place it beyond all doubt, that a working-day of thirteen hours, even for men and women from eighteen to twenty-two years of age, produces at least these consequences, both in the flax-spinning mills of Dundee and Dunfermline, and in the cotton mills of Glasgow and Lanark.

All these affections are easily explained by the nature of factory-work, which is, as the manufacturers say, very "light", and precisely by reason of its lightness, more enervating than any other. The operatives have little to do, but must stand the whole time.[a] Any one who sits down, say upon a window-ledge or a basket, is fined, and this perpetual upright position, this constant mechanical pressure of the upper portions of the body upon spinal column, hips, and legs, inevitably produces the results mentioned. This standing is not required by the work itself, and at Nottingham chairs have been introduced,[b] with the result that these affections disappeared, and the operatives ceased to object to the length of the working-day. But in a factory where the operative works solely for the bourgeois, and has small interest in doing his work well, he would probably use the seats more than would be agreeable and profitable to the manufacturer; and in order that somewhat less raw material may be spoiled for the bourgeois, the operative must sacrifice health and strength.* This long protracted upright position, with the bad atmosphere prevalent in the mills, entails, besides the deformities mentioned, a marked relaxation of all vital energies, and, in consequence, all sorts of other affections general rather than local. The atmosphere of the factories is, as a rule, at once damp and warm, usually warmer than is necessary, and, when the ventilation is not *very* good, impure, heavy, deficient in oxygen, filled with dust and the smell of the machine oil, which almost everywhere smears the floor, sinks into it, and becomes rancid. The operatives are lightly clad by reason of the warmth, and would readily take cold in case of irregularity of the temperature; a draught is distasteful to them, the general enervation which gradually takes possession of all the physical functions diminishes the animal warmth: this must be replaced from without, and nothing is therefore more agreeable to

* In the spinning-room of a mill at Leeds, too, chairs had been introduced. Drinkwater Evidence, p. 85.— *Note by Engels.*

---

[a] The German editions of 1845 and 1892 have here "and cannot sit down".—*Ed.*

[b] The German editions of 1845 and 1892 have here "in the carding-rooms at least".—*Ed.*

the operative than to have all the doors and windows closed, and to stay in his warm factory air. Then comes the sudden change of temperature on going out into the cold and wet or frosty atmosphere, without the means of protection from the rain, or of changing wet clothing for dry, a circumstance which perpetually produces colds. And when one reflects that, with all this, not one single muscle of the body is really exercised, really called into activity, except perhaps those of the legs; that nothing whatsoever counteracts the enervating, relaxing tendency of all these conditions; that every influence is wanting which might give the muscles strength, the fibres elasticity and consistency; that from youth up, the operative is deprived of all fresh-air recreation, it is impossible to wonder at the almost unanimous testimony of the physicians in the Factories' Report, that they find a great lack of ability to resist disease, a general depression in vital activity, a constant relaxation of the mental and physical powers. Let us hear Sir D. Barry first*:

The unfavourable influences of mill-work upon the hands are the following: "(1) The indispensable necessity of forcing both their mental and bodily exertions to keep exact pace with the motions of machinery propelled by an unvarying, unceasing power. (2) The continuance of an erect posture for periods unnaturally prolonged and too quickly repeated. (3) The privation of sleep" (in consequence of too long working-hours, pain in the legs, and general physical derangement). "To these causes are often added low, crowded, dusty, or damp rooms; impure air, heated atmospheres, constant perspiration. Hence it is that male children particularly, after they have worked some time in mills lose—with very few exceptions indeed—the rosy chubbiness of boyhood, and become paler and thinner than boys not so employed generally are. Even the draw-boy who stands with his bare feet on the earthen floor of his master's shop preserves his appearance much better than the mill-boys," because he occasionally goes into the fresh air for a time. "But the mill-worker never has a moment's respite except at meals, and never gets into the open air except when he is going to look for them. All the adult male spinners are pale and thin; they are subject to capricious appetite and dyspepsia; all the spinners have been brought up in the mills from their very childhood, it is fair to conclude that their mode of life is not favourable to the development of the manly forms, seeing that few, or none of them are tall athletic men. Females are much less deteriorated in their appearance by mill-work than males." (Very naturally. But we shall see that they have their own diseases.)

So, too, Power**:

"I can have no hesitation in stating my belief that a large mass of deformity has been produced at Bradford by the factory system.... The effect of long and continuous work upon the frame and limbs is not indicated by actual deformity alone; a more common indication of it is found in a stunted growth, relaxed muscles, and slender conformation."

* General report by Sir D. Barry.—*Note by Engels to the American edition of 1887.*
** Power Report, p. 74.—*Note by Engels to the American edition of 1887.*

So, too, F. Sharp, in Leeds, the surgeon* already quoted:

When I moved from Scarborough to Leeds, "the general appearance of the children in Leeds immediately struck me as much more pallid, and also the firmness of the fibre as much inferior as what I had seen in Scarborough and the adjacent country. Observed also many to be more diminutive for their age.... Innumerable cases of scrofula, affections of the lungs, mesenteric diseases, and dyspepsia, have also occurred, which I have no doubt, as a professional man, were owing to the same cause", the mill-work. "The nervous energy of the body I consider to be weakened by the very long hours, and a foundation laid for many diseases. Were it not for the individuals who join the mills from the country, the factory people would soon be deteriorated."

So, too, Beaumont, surgeon in Bradford:

"I also consider the system of working in the factories in and around here induces for the most part a peculiar laxity of the whole system, rendering the children highly susceptible of either prevailing epidemics or casual medical disorders.... I certainly consider the want of wholesome regulations in the most of the factories, whether as to ventilation or cleanliness, to be productive in a great measure of that peculiar tendency or susceptibility of morbid affections of which my own practice affords ample experience."

Similar testimony is borne by Dr. Hey:

(1) "I have had an opportunity of observing the effect of the factory system in the health of children under the most advantageous circumstances" (in Wood's mill, in Bradford, the best arranged of the district, in which he was factory surgeon). (2) "This effect is decidedly, and, to a great extent, injurious, even under those favourable circumstances. (3) During the year 1832, three-fifths of all the children employed in Wood's mill had medical assistance from me; (4) The most injurious effect is not in the prevalence of deformed bodies, but debilitated and diseased constitutions." (5) All this is greatly improved since the working-hours of children have been reduced at Wood's to ten.

The Commissioner, Dr. Loudon himself, who sites these witnesses, says:

"I think it has been clearly proved that children have been worked a most unreasonable and cruel length of time daily, and that even adults have been expected to do a certain quantity of labour which scarcely any human being is able to endure. The result of this has been, that many have met with a premature death; many have been affected constitutionally for life; and the idea of a posterity being injured from the shattered frames of the survivors is, physiologically speaking, but too well founded."

And, finally, Dr. Hawkins, in speaking of Manchester:

"I believe that most travellers are struck by the lowness of stature, the leanness, and the paleness which present themselves so commonly to the eye at Manchester,

---

* The surgeons in England are scientifically educated as well as the physicians, and have, in general, medical as well as surgical practice. They are, in general, for various reasons, preferred to the physicians.—*Note by Engels*. (In the German editions of 1845 and 1892 the words "surgeons" and "physicians" are given in English in brackets.—*Ed.*)

and above all, among the factory classes. I have never been in any town in Great Britain nor in Europe in which degeneracy of form and colour from the national standard has been so obvious. The married women fall remarkably short of the usual characteristics of the English wife.... I cannot help remarking, that the boys and girls whom I examined from the Manchester factories very generally exhibited a depressed look, and a pallid complexion; none of the alacrity, activity, and hilarity of early life shone on their countenances and gestures. A large number of both, in reply to my questions, declared that they had no wish to play about on the Saturday afternoon and on the Sunday, but that they preferred remaining quiet."

I add, at once, another passage of Hawkins' report, which only half belongs here, but may be quoted here as well as anywhere else:

"Intemperance, debauchery and improvidence are the chief blemishes on the character of the factory workpeople, and those evils may easily be traced to habits formed under the present system, and springing from it almost inevitably. On all sides it is admitted that indigestion, hypochondriasis and languor affect this class of the population very widely. After twelve hours of monotonous labour, it is but too natural to seek for stimulants of one kind or another; but when we superadd the morbid states above alluded to, the transition to spirits is rapid and perpetual."

For all this testimony of the physicians and commissioners, the report itself offers hundreds of cases of proof. That the growth of young operatives is stunted, by their work, hundreds of statements testify; among others, Cowell gives the weight of 46 youths of 17 years of age, from one Sunday school, of whom 26 employed in mills, averaged 104.5 pounds, and 20 not employed in mills,[a] 117.7 pounds. One of the largest manufacturers of Manchester, leader of the opposition against the working-men, I think Robert Hyde Greg himself, said, on one occasion, that if things went on as at present, the operatives of Lancashire would soon be a race of pigmies.* A recruiting officer** testified that operatives are little adapted for military service, looked thin and nervous, and were frequently rejected by the surgeons as unfit. In Manchester he could hardly get men of five feet eight inches; they were usually only five feet six to seven, whereas in the agricultural districts, most of the recruits were five feet eight.[b]

The men wear out very early in consequence of the conditions

* This statement is not taken from the report.[150]—Note by Engels.
** Tufnell, p. 59.—Note by Engels to the American edition of 1887.

[a] The German editions of 1845 and 1892 have here "but belonging to the working-class".—Ed.

[b] The German editions of 1845 and 1892 have here in brackets: "the difference between English and Prussian measures is about 2 inches for 5 feet, the English measure being shorter."—Ed.

under which they live and work. Most of them are unfit for work at forty years, a few hold out to forty-five, almost none to fifty years of age. This is caused not only by the general enfeeblement of the frame, but also very often by a failure of the sight, which is a result of mule-spinning, in which the operative is obliged to fix his gaze upon a long row of fine, parallel threads, and so greatly to strain the sight.

Of 1,600 operatives employed in several factories in Harpur and Lanark, but 10 were over 45 years of age; of 22,094 operatives in diverse factories in Stockport and Manchester, but 143 were over 45 years old. Of these 143, 16 were retained as a special favour, and one was doing the work of a child. A list of 131 spinners contained but seven over 45 years, and yet the whole 131 were rejected by the manufacturers, to whom they applied for work, as "too old",[a] and were without means of support by reason of old age! Mr. Ashworth, a large manufacturer, admits in a letter to Lord Ashley, that, towards the fortieth year, the spinners can no longer prepare the required quantity of yarn, and are therefore "sometimes" discharged; he calls operatives forty years of age "old people"!* Commissioner Mackintosh expresses himself in the same way in the report of 1833:

"Although prepared by seeing childhood occupied in such a manner, it is very difficult to believe the ages of the men advanced in years as given by themselves, so complete is their premature old age."

Surgeon Smellie of Glasgow, who treated operatives chiefly, says that forty years is old age for them.** And similar evidence may be found elsewhere.*** In Manchester, this premature old age among the operatives is so universal that almost every man of forty would be taken for ten to fifteen years older, while the prosperous classes, men as well as women, preserve their appearance exceedingly well if they do not drink too heavily.

---

* All taken from Lord Ashley's speech (sitting of Lower House, March 15, 1844).— *Note by Engels* (omitted in the American and English editions—*Ed.*).

** Stuart Evidence, p. 101.—*Note by Engels to the American edition of 1887.* (In the German editions of 1845 and 1892 the words "old age" are given in English in brackets.—*Ed.*)

*** Tufnell Evidence, pp. 3, 6, 15; Hawkins Report, p. 4; Evidence, p. 11, etc., etc.—*Note by Engels to the American edition of 1887.*

---

[a] In the German editions of 1845 and 1892 the sentence follows: "Of fifty worked-out spinners in Bolton only two were over 50 and the rest did not yet average 40 —and all were" etc.—*Ed.*

The influence of factory-work upon the female physique also is marked and peculiar. The deformities entailed by long hours of work are much more serious among women. Protracted work frequently causes deformities of the pelvis, partly in the shape of abnormal position and development of the hip bones, partly of malformation of the lower portion of the spinal column.

"Although," says Dr. Loudon in his report, "no cases presented themselves of deformed pelvis, and some others of the diseases which have been described, yet their ailments are such as every medical man must expect to be the probable consequences" of such working-hours for young people, "and they are recorded by men of the highest professional and moral character".

That factory operatives undergo more difficult confinement than other women is testified to by several midwives and accoucheurs, and also that they are more liable to miscarriage.* Moreover, they suffer from the general enfeeblement common to all operatives, and, when pregnant, continue to work in the factory up to the hour of delivery, because otherwise they lose their wages and are made to fear that they may be replaced if they stop away too soon. It frequently happens that women are at work one evening and delivered the next morning, and the case is none too rare of their being delivered in the factory among the machinery. And if the gentlemen of the bourgeoisie find nothing particularly shocking in this, their wives will perhaps admit that it is a piece of cruelty, an infamous act of barbarism, indirectly to force a pregnant woman to work twelve or thirteen hours daily (formerly still longer), up to the day of her delivery, in a standing position, with frequent stoopings. But this is not all. If these women are not obliged to resume work within two weeks, they are thankful, and count themselves fortunate. Many come back to the factory after eight, and even after three to four days, to resume full work. I once heard a manufacturer ask an overlooker: "Is so and so not back yet?" "No." "How long since she was confined?" "A week." "She might surely have been back long ago. That one over there only stays three days." Naturally, fear of being discharged, dread of starvation drives her to the factory in spite of her weakness, in defiance of her pain. The interest of the manufacturer will not brook that his employees stay at home by reason of illness; they must not be ill, they must not venture to lie still through a long confinement, or he must stop his machinery or trouble his supreme head with a temporary change of arrangements; and

* Hawkins Evidence, pp. 11, 13.—*Note by Engels to the American edition of 1887.*

rather than do this, he discharges his people when they begin to be ill. Listen*:

A girl feels very ill, can scarcely do her work. "Why don't you ask for leave to stay away?" "Well, sir, the master is queer at letting us off; if we are off a quarter of a day we stand a chance of being turned away."

Or Sir D. Barry**:

Thomas McDurt, workman, has slight fever. "Cannot venture to be off work more than four days, for fear of losing his work."

And so it goes on in almost all the factories. The employment of young girls produces all sorts of irregularities during the period of development. In some, especially those who are better fed, the heat of the factories hastens this process, so that in single cases, girls of thirteen and fourteen[a] are wholly mature. Roberton, whom I have already cited (mentioned in the Factories' Inquiry Commission's Report as the "eminent" gynaecologist of Manchester), relates in the *North of England Medical and Surgical Journal,* that he had seen a girl of eleven years who was not only a wholly developed woman, but pregnant, and that it was by no means rare in Manchester for women to be confined at fifteen years of age).[151] In such cases, the influence of the warmth of the factories is the same as that of a tropical climate, and, as in such climates, the abnormally early development revenges itself by correspondingly premature age and debility. On the other hand, retarded development of the female constitution occurs, the breasts mature late or not at all.*** Menstruation first appears in the seventeenth or eighteenth, sometimes in the twentieth year, and is often wholly wanting.**** Irregular menstruation, coupled with great pain and numerous affections, especially with anaemia, is very frequent, as the medical reports unanimously state.

Children of such mothers, particularly of those who are obliged to work during pregnancy, cannot be vigorous. They are, on the contrary, described in the report, especially in Manchester, as very feeble; and Barry alone asserts that they are healthy, but says further, that in Scotland, where his inspection lay, almost no married women worked in factories. Moreover, most of the factories there are in the country (with the exception of Glasgow),

---

   * Cowell Evidence, p. 77.— *Note by Engels to the American edition of 1887.*
   ** Sir D. Barry Evidence, p. 44.— *Note by Engels to the American edition of 1887.*
   *** Cowell, p. 35.— *Note by Engels to the American edition of 1887.*
   **** Dr. Hawkins Evidence, p. 11; Dr. Loudon, p. 14, etc.; Sir D. Barry, p. 5, etc.— *Note by Engels to the American edition of 1887.*

---

   [a] The German editions of 1845 and 1892 have here "of twelve to fourteen".— *Ed.*

a circumstance which contributes greatly to the invigoration of the children. The operatives' children in the neighbourhood of Manchester are nearly all thriving and rosy, while those within the city look pale and scrofulous; but with the ninth year the colour vanishes suddenly, because all are then sent into the factories, when it soon becomes impossible to distinguish the country from the city children.

But besides all this, there are some branches of factory-work which have an especially injurious effect. In many rooms of the cotton and flax-spinning mills, the air is filled with fibrous dust, which produces chest affections, especially among workers in the carding and combing-rooms. Some constitutions can bear it, some cannot; but the operative has no choice. He must take the room in which he finds work, whether his chest is sound or not. The most common effects of this breathing of dust are blood-spitting, hard, noisy breathing, pains in the chest, coughs, sleeplessness — in short, all the symptoms of asthma ending in the worst cases in consumption.* Especially unwholesome is the wet spinning of linen-yarn which is carried on by young girls and boys. The water spirts over them from the spindle, so that the front of their clothing is constantly wet through to the skin; and there is always water standing on the floor. This is the case to a less degree in the doubling-rooms of the cotton mills, and the result is a constant succession of colds and affections of the chest. A hoarse, rough voice is common to all operatives, but especially to wet spinners and doublers. Stuart, Mackintosh, and Sir D. Barry express themselves in the most vigorous terms as to the unwholesomeness of this work, and the small consideration shown by most of the manufacturers for the health of the girls who do it. Another effect of flax-spinning is a peculiar deformity of the shoulder, especially a projection of the right shoulder-blade, consequent upon the nature of the work. This sort of spinning and the throstle-spinning of cotton frequently produce diseases of the knee-pan, which is used to check the spindle during the joining of broken threads. The frequent stooping and the bending to the low machines common to both these branches of work have, in general, a stunting effect upon the growth of the operative. In the throstle-room of the cotton mill at Manchester, in which I was employed, I do not remember to have seen one single tall,

---

* Compare Stuart, pp. 13, 70, 101; Mackintosh, p. 24, etc.; Power Report on Nottingham, on Leeds; Cowell, p. 33, etc.; Barry, p. 12 (five cases in one factory), pp. 17, 44, 52, 60, etc.; Loudon, p. 13.— *Note by Engels to the American edition of 1887.*

well-built girl; they were all short, dumpy, and badly-formed, decidedly ugly in the whole development of the figure. But apart from all these diseases and malformations, the limbs of the operatives suffer in still another way. The work between the machinery gives rise to multitudes of accidents of more or less serious nature, which have for the operative the secondary effect of unfitting him for his work more or less completely. The most common accident is the squeezing off of a single joint of a finger, somewhat less common the loss of the whole finger, half or a whole hand, an arm, etc., in the machinery. Lockjaw very often follows, even upon the lesser among these injuries, and brings death with it. Besides the deformed persons, a great number of maimed ones may be seen going about in Manchester; this one has lost an arm or a part of one, that one a foot, the third half a leg; it is like living in the midst of an army just returned from a campaign. But the most dangerous portion of the machinery is the strapping which conveys motive power from the shaft to the separate machines, especially if it contains buckles, which, however, are rarely used now. Whoever is seized by the strap is carried up with lightning speed, thrown against the ceiling above and floor below with such force that there is rarely a whole bone left in the body, and death follows instantly. Between June 12th and August 3rd, 1844, the *Manchester Guardian* reported the following serious accidents (the trifling ones it does not notice): June 12th, a boy died in Manchester of lockjaw, caused by his hand being crushed between wheels. June 15th, a youth in Saddleworth seized by a wheel and carried away with it; died, utterly mangled. June 29th, a young man at Green Acres Moor, near Manchester, at work in a machine shop, fell under the grindstone, which broke two of his ribs and lacerated him terribly. July 24th, a girl in Oldham died, carried around fifty times by a strap; no bone unbroken. July 27th, a girl in Manchester seized by the blower (the first machine that receives the raw cotton), and died of injuries received. August 3rd, a bobbins turner died in Dukenfield, caught in a strap, every rib broken. In the year 1842, the Manchester Infirmary treated 962 cases of wounds and mutilations caused by machinery, while the number of all other accidents within the district of the hospital was 2,426, so that for five accidents from all other causes, two were caused by machinery. The accidents which happened in Salford are not included here, nor those treated by surgeons in private practice. In such cases, whether or not the accident unfits the victim for further work, the employer, at best, pays the doctor, or, in very exceptional cases, he may pay wages during treatment; what becomes of the operative afterwards, in case he cannot work, is no concern of the employer.

The Factory Report says on this subject, that employers must be made responsible for all cases, since children cannot take care, and adults will take care in their own interest. But the gentlemen who write the report are bourgeois, and so they must contradict themselves and bring up later all sorts of bosh on the subject of the culpable temerity of the operatives.[a]

The state of the case is this: If children cannot take care, the employment of children must be forbidden. If adults are reckless, they must be mere overgrown children on a plane of intelligence which does not enable them to appreciate the danger in its full scope; and who is to blame for this but the bourgeoisie which keeps them in a condition in which their intelligence cannot develop? Or the machinery is ill-arranged, and must be surrounded with fencing, to supply which falls to the share of the bourgeoisie. Or the operative is under inducements which outweigh the threatened danger; he must work rapidly to earn his wages, has no time to take care, and for this, too, the bourgeoisie is to blame. Many accidents happen, for instance, while the operatives are cleaning machinery in motion. Why? Because the bourgeois would otherwise oblige the worker to clean the machinery during the free hours while it is not going, and the worker naturally is not disposed to sacrifice any part of his free time. Every free hour is so precious to the worker that he often risks his life twice a week rather than sacrifice one of them to the bourgeois. Let the employer take from working-hours the time required for cleaning the machinery, and it will never again occur to an operative to clean machinery in motion. In short, from whatever point of view, the blame falls ultimately on the manufacturer, and of him should be required, at the very least, life-long support of the incapacitated operative, and support of the victim's family in case death follows the accident. In the earliest period of manufacture, the accidents were much more numerous in proportion than now, for the machinery was inferior, smaller, more crowded, and almost never fenced. But the number is still large enough, as the foregoing cases prove, to arouse the grave question as to a state of things which permits so many deformities and mutilations for the benefit of a single class, and plunges so many

---

[a] The German editions of 1845 and 1892 have here "But it makes no difference", and give the words "culpable temerity" in English in brackets.—*Ed.*

industrious working-people into want and starvation by reason of injuries undergone in the service and through the fault of the bourgeoisie.

A pretty list of diseases engendered purely by the hateful money-greed of the manufacturers! Women made unfit for child-bearing, children deformed, men enfeebled, limbs crushed, whole generations wrecked, afflicted with disease and infirmity, purely to fill the purses of the bourgeoisie. And when one reads of the barbarism of single cases, how children are seized naked in bed by the overlookers, and driven with blows and kicks to the factory, their clothing over their arms,* how their sleepiness is driven off with blows, how they fall asleep over their work nevertheless, how one poor child sprang up, still asleep, at the call of the overlooker, and mechanically went through the operations of its work after its machine was stopped; when one reads how children, too tired to go home, hide away in the wool in the drying-room to sleep there, and could only be driven out of the factory with straps; how many hundreds came home so tired every night, that they could eat no supper for sleepiness and want of appetite, that their parents found them kneeling by the bedside, where they had fallen asleep during their prayers; when one reads all this and a hundred other villainies and infamies in this one report, all testified to on oath, confirmed by several witnesses, deposed by men whom the commissioners themselves declare trustworthy; when one reflects that this is a Liberal report, a bourgeois report, made for the purpose of reversing the previous Tory report, and rehabilitating the pureness of heart of the manufacturers, that the commissioners themselves are on the side of the bourgeoisie, and report all these things against their own will, how can one be otherwise than filled with wrath and resentment against a class which boasts of philanthropy and self-sacrifice, while its one object is to fill its purse à tout prix? Meanwhile, let us listen to the bourgeoisie speaking through the mouth of its chosen apostle,[a] Dr. Ure, who relates in his *Philosophy of Manufactures*** that the workers have been told that their wages bore no proportion to their sacrifices, the good understanding between masters and men being thus disturbed. Instead of this,

---

* Stuart, p. 39.—*Note by Engels to the American edition of 1887.*
** *Philosophy of Manufactures,* by Dr. Andrew Ure, p. 277, *et seq.*—*Note by Engels to the American edition of 1887.*

---

[a] The German editions of 1845 and 1892 have "lackey" instead of "apostle".—*Ed.*

the working-men should have striven to recommend themselves by attention and industry, and should have rejoiced in the prosperity of their masters. They would then become overseers, superintendents, and finally partners, and would thus — (Oh! Wisdom, thou speakest as the dove!) — "have increased at the same time the demand for their companions' labour in the market!"

"Had it not been for the violent collisions and interruptions resulting from erroneous views among the operatives, the factory system would have been developed still more rapidly and beneficially."*

Hereupon follows a long Jeremiad upon the spirit of resistance of the operatives, and on the occasion of a strike of the best-paid workers, the fine spinners, the following naive observation**

"In fact, it was their high wages which enabled them to maintain a stipendiary committee in affluence, and to pamper themselves into nervous ailments, by a diet too rich and exciting for their indoor employments."

Let us hear how the bourgeois describes the work of children***:

"I have visited many factories, both in Manchester and in the surrounding districts, during a period of several months, entering the spinning-rooms unexpectedly, and often alone, at different times of the day, and I never saw a single instance of corporal chastisement inflicted on a child; nor, indeed, did I ever see children in ill-humour. They seemed to be always cheerful and alert; taking pleasure in the light play of their muscles, enjoying the mobility natural to their age. The scene of industry, so far from exciting sad emotions, in my mind, was always exhilarating. It was delightful to observe the nimbleness with which they pieced broken ends, as the mule carriage began to recede from the fixed roller beam, and to see them at leisure, after a few seconds' exercise of their tiny fingers, to amuse themselves in any attitude they chose, till the stretch and winding on were once more completed. The work of these lively elves seemed to resemble a sport, in which habit gave them a pleasing dexterity. Conscious of their skill, they were delighted to show it off to any stranger. As to exhaustion by the day's work, they evinced no trace of it on emerging from the mill in the evening; for they immediately began to skip about any neighbouring play-ground, and to commence their little games with the same alacrity as boys issuing from a school."

Naturally! As though the immediate movement of every muscle were not an urgent necessity for frames grown at once stiff and relaxed! But Ure should have waited to see whether this momentary excitement had not subsided after a couple of minutes. And

* Ibid., p. 277.— *Note by Engels to the American edition of 1887.*
** Ibid., p. 298.— *Note by Engels to the American edition of 1887.*
*** Ibid., p. 301.— *Note by Engels to the American edition of 1887.* (The German editions of 1845 and 1892 give this quotation abridged, with the words "cheerful", "taking pleasure", "delightful" and "lively" in brackets in English after their German equivalents.—*Ed.*)

besides, Ure could see this whole performance only in the afternoon after five or six hours' work, but not in the evening! As to the health of the operatives, the bourgeois has the boundless impudence to cite the report of 1833 just quoted in a thousand places, as testimony for the excellent health of these people; to try to prove by detached and garbled quotations that no trace of scrofula can be found among them, and, what is quite true, that the factory system frees them from all acute diseases (that they have every variety of chronic affection instead he naturally conceals). To explain the impudence with which our friend Ure palms off the grossest falsehoods upon the English public, it must be known that the report consists of three large folio volumes, which it never occurs to a well-fed English bourgeois to study through. Let us hear further how he expresses himself as to the Factory Act of 1833, passed by the Liberal bourgeoisie, and imposing only the most meagre limitations upon the manufacturers, as we shall see. This law, especially its compulsory education clause, he calls an absurd and despotic measure directed against the manufacturers, through which all children under twelve years of age have been thrown out of employment; and with what results? The children thus discharged from their light and useful occupation receive no education whatsoever; cast out from the warm spinning-room into a cold world, they subsist only by begging and stealing, a life in sad contrast with their steadily improving condition in the factory and in Sunday school. Under the mask of philanthropy, this law intensifies the sufferings of the poor, and will greatly restrict the conscientious manufacturer in his useful work, if, indeed, it does not wholly stop him.*

The ruinous influence of the factory system began at an early day to attract general attention. We have already alluded to the Apprentices' Act of 1802. Later, towards 1817, Robert Owen, then a manufacturer in New Lanark, in Scotland, afterwards founder of English Socialism, began to call the attention of the Government, by memorials and petitions, to the necessity of legislative guarantees for the health of the operatives, and especially of children. The late Sir Robert Peel and other philanthropists united with him, and gradually secured the Factory Acts of 1819, 1825, and 1831, of which the first two were never enforced,[152] and the last only here and there. This law of 1831, based upon the motion of Sir J. C. Hobhouse, provided that in cotton mills no one under

---

* Dr. Andrew Ure, *Philosophy of Manufactures,* pp. 405, 406, *et seq.— Note by Engels to the American edition of 1887.*

twenty-one should be employed between half-past seven at night
and half-past five in the morning; and that in all factories young
persons under eighteen should work no longer than twelve hours
daily, and nine hours on Saturday. But since operatives could not
testify against their masters without being discharged, this law
helped matters very little. In the great cities, where the operatives
were more restive, the larger manufacturers came to an agreement
among themselves to obey the law; but even there, there were
many who, like the employers in the country, did not trouble
themselves about it. Meanwhile, the demand for a ten hours' law
had become lively among the operatives; that is, for a law which
should forbid all operatives under eighteen years of age to work
longer than ten hours daily; the Trades Unions, by their agitation,
made this demand general throughout the manufacturing population; the philanthropic section of the Tory party, then led by
Michael Sadler, seized upon the plan, and brought it before
Parliament. Sadler obtained a parliamentary committee for the
investigation of the factory system, and this committee reported in
1832.[153] Its report was emphatically partisan, composed by strong
enemies of the factory system, for party ends. Sadler permitted
himself to be betrayed by his noble enthusiasm into the most
distorted and erroneous statements, drew from his witnesses by
the very form of his questions, answers which contained the truth,
but truth in a perverted form. The manufacturers themselves,
incensed at a report which represented them as monsters, now
demanded an official investigation; they knew that an exact report
must, in this case, be advantageous to them; they knew that Whigs,
genuine bourgeois, were at the helm, with whom they were upon
good terms, whose principles were opposed to any restriction
upon manufacture. They obtained a commission, in due order,
composed of Liberal bourgeois, whose report I have so often cited.
This comes somewhat nearer the truth than Sadler's, but its
deviations therefrom are in the opposite direction. On every page
it betrays sympathy with the manufacturers, distrust of the Sadler
report, repugnance to the working-men agitating independently
and the supporters of the Ten Hours' Bill. It nowhere recognises
the right of the working-man to a life worthy of a human being, to
independent activity, and opinions of his own. It reproaches the
operatives that in sustaining the Ten Hours' Bill they thought, not
of the children only, but of themselves as well; it calls the
working-men engaged in the agitation demagogues, ill-intentioned,
malicious, etc., is written, in short, on the side of the bourgeoisie;
and still it cannot whitewash the manufacturers, and still it leaves

such a mass of infamies upon the shoulders of the employers, that even after this report, the agitation for the Ten Hours' Bill, the hatred against the manufacturers, and the committee's severest epithets applied to them are all fully justified. But there was the one difference, that whereas the Sadler report accuses the manufacturers of open, undisguised brutality, it now became evident that this brutality was chiefly carried on under the mask of civilisation and humanity. Yet Dr. Hawkins, the medical commissioner for Lancashire, expresses himself decidedly in favour of the Ten Hours' Bill in the opening lines of his report, and Commissioner Mackintosh explains that his own report does not contain the whole truth, because it is very difficult to induce the operatives to testify against their employers, and because the manufacturers, besides being forced into greater concessions towards their operatives by the excitement among the latter, are often prepared for the inspection of the factories, have them swept, the speed of the machinery reduced, etc. In Lancashire especially they resorted to the device of bringing the overlookers of work-rooms before the commissioners, and letting them testify as working-men to the humanity of the employers, the wholesome effects of the work, and the indifference, if not the hostility of the operatives, towards the Ten Hours' Bill. But these are not genuine working-men; they are deserters from their class, who have entered the service of the bourgeoisie for better pay, and fight in the interests of the capitalists against the workers. Their interest is that of the capitalists, and they are, therefore, almost more hated by the workers than the manufacturers themselves.

And yet this report suffices wholly to exhibit the most shameful recklessness of the manufacturing bourgeoisie towards its employees, the whole infamy of the industrial exploiting system in its full inhumanity. Nothing is more revolting than to compare the long register of diseases and deformities engendered by overwork, in this report, with the cold, calculating political economy of the manufacturers, by which they try to prove that they, and with them all England, must go to ruin, if they should be forbidden to cripple so and so many children every year. The language of Dr. Ure alone, which I have quoted, would be yet more revolting if it were not so preposterous.

The result of this report was the Factory Act of 1833, which forbade the employment of children under nine years of age (except in silk mills), limited the working-hours of children between 9-13 years to 48 per week, or 9 hours in any one day at the utmost; that of young persons from 14-18 years of age to 69

per week, or 12 on any one day as the maximum, provided for an
hour and a half as the minimum interval for meals, and repeated
the total prohibition of night-work for persons under eighteen
years of age. Compulsory school attendance two hours daily was
prescribed for all children under fourteen years, and the manufacturer declared punishable in case of employing children without a
certificate of age from the factory surgeon, and a certificate of
school attendance from the teacher. As recompense, the employer
was permitted to withdraw one penny from the child's weekly
earnings to pay the teacher. Further, surgeons and inspectors were
appointed to visit the factories at all times, take testimony of
operatives on oath, and enforce the law by prosecution before a
Justice of the Peace. This is the law against which Dr. Ure inveighs
in such unmeasured terms!

The consequence of this law, and especially of the appointment
of inspectors, was the reduction of working-hours to an average of
twelve to thirteen, and the superseding of children as far as
possible. Hereupon some of the most crying evils disappeared
almost wholly. Deformities arose now only in cases of weak
constitution, and the effects of overwork became much less
conspicuous. Nevertheless, enough testimony remains to be found
in the Factory Report, that the lesser evils, swelling of the ankles,
weakness and pain in the legs, hips, and back, varicose veins,
ulcers on the lower extremities, general weakness, especially of the
pelvic region, nausea, want of appetite alternating with unnatural
hunger, indigestion, hypochondria, affections of the chest in
consequence of the dust and foul atmosphere of the factories, etc.,
etc., all occur among employees subject to the provisions of Sir J.
C. Hobhouse's Law (of 1831), which prescribes twelve to thirteen
hours as the maximum. The reports from Glasgow and Manchester are especially worthy of attention in this respect. These evils
remained too, after the law of 1833, and continue to undermine
the health of the working-class to this day. Care has been taken to
give the brutal profit-greed of the bourgeoisie a hypocritical,
civilised form, to restrain the manufacturers through the arm of
the law from too conspicuous villainies, and thus to give them a
pretext for self-complacently parading their sham philanthropy.
That is all. If a new commission were appointed today, it would
find things pretty much as before. As to the extemporised
compulsory attendance at school, it remained wholly a dead letter,
since the Government failed to provide good schools. The manufacturers employed as teachers worn-out operatives, to whom
they sent the children two hours daily, thus complying with the

letter of the law; but the children learned nothing. And even the reports of the factory inspectors, which are limited to the scope of the inspector's duties, i.e., the enforcement of the Factory Act, give data enough to justify the conclusion that the old evils inevitably remain. Inspectors Horner and Saunders,[154] in their reports for October and December, 1843, state that, in a number of branches in which the employment of children can be dispensed with or superseded by that of adults,[a] the working-day is still fourteen to sixteen hours, or even longer. Among the operatives in these branches they found numbers of young people who had just outgrown the provisions of the law. Many employers disregard the law, shorten the meal times, work children longer than is permitted, and risk prosecution, knowing that the possible fines are trifling in comparison with the certain profits derivable from the offence. Just at present especially, while business is exceptionally brisk, they are under great temptation in this respect.

Meanwhile the agitation for the Ten Hours' Bill by no means died out among the operatives; in 1839 it was under full headway once more, and Sadler's place, he having died, was filled in the House of Commons by Lord Ashley[*] and[b] Richard Oastler, both Tories. Oastler especially, who carried on a constant agitation in the factory districts, and had been active in the same way during Sadler's life, was the particular favourite of the working-men. They called him their "good old king", "the king of the factory children", and there is not a child in the factory districts that does not know and revere him, that does not join the procession which moves to welcome him when he enters a town. Oastler vigorously opposed the New Poor Law also, and was therefore imprisoned for debt by a Mr. Thornhill,[c] on whose estate he was employed as agent, and to whom he owed money. The Whigs offered repeatedly to pay his debt and confer other favours upon him if he would

---

[*] Afterwards Earl of Shaftesbury, died 1885.— *Note by Engels to the American edition of 1887* (reproduced in the English edition of 1892 but omitted in the German edition of 1892— *Ed.*).

---

[a] The German editions of 1845 and 1892 have here "who were otherwise unemployed".— *Ed.*

[b] The German editions of 1845 and 1892 have here "and, outside the House, by Richard Oastler".— *Ed.*

[c] The German editions of 1845 and 1892 have "Mr. Thornhill, a Whig". Concerning the New Poor Law, see below, pp. 571-73.— *Ed.*

only give up his agitation against the Poor Law. But in vain; he remained in prison, whence he published his Fleet Papers against the factory system and the Poor Law.

The Tory Government of 1841 turned its attention once more to the Factory Acts. The Home Secretary, Sir James Graham, proposed, in 1843, a bill restricting the working-hours of children to six and one-half, and making the enactments for compulsory school attendance more effective, the principal point in this connection being a provision for better schools. This bill was, however, wrecked by the jealousy of the dissenters [155]; for, although compulsory religious instruction was not extended to the children of dissenters, the schools provided for were to be placed under the general supervision of the Established Church, and the Bible made the general reading-book, religion being thus made the foundation of all instruction, whence the dissenters felt themselves threatened. The manufacturers and the Liberals generally united with them, the working-men were divided by the Church question, and therefore inactive. The opponents of the bill, though outweighed in the great manufacturing towns, such as Salford and Stockport, and able in others, such as Manchester, to attack certain of its points only, for fear of the working-men, collected nevertheless nearly two million signatures for a petition against it, and Graham allowed himself to be so far intimidated as to withdraw the whole bill. The next year he omitted the school clauses, and proposed that, instead of the previous provisions, children between eight and thirteen years should be restricted to six and one-half hours, and so employed as to have either the whole morning or the whole afternoon free; that young people between thirteen and eighteen years, and all females, should be limited to twelve hours; and that the hitherto frequent evasions of the law should be prevented. Hardly had he proposed this bill, when the ten hours' agitation was begun again more vigorously than ever. Oastler had just then regained his liberty; a number of his friends and a collection among the workers had paid his debt, and he threw himself into the movement with all his might. The defenders of the Ten Hours' Bill in the House of Commons had increased in numbers, the masses of petitions supporting it which poured in from all sides brought them allies, and on March 19th, 1844, Lord Ashley carried, with a majority of 179 to 170, a resolution that the word "Night" in the Factory Act should express the time from six at night to six in the morning, whereby the prohibition of night-work came to mean the limitation of working-hours to twelve, including free hours, or ten hours of actual work a day. But the Ministry did not agree to this. Sir James Graham began to threaten resignation from the Cabinet, and at the next vote on the bill the House rejected by a small majority both ten and twelve hours. Graham and Peel now announced that they should introduce a new bill, and that if this failed to pass they should resign. The new bill was exactly the old Twelve Hours' Bill with some changes of form, and the same House of Commons which had rejected the principal points of this bill in March, now[a] swallowed it whole. The reason of this was that most of the supporters of the Ten Hours' Bill were Tories who let fall the bill rather than the Ministry; but be the motives what they may, the House of Commons by its votes upon this subject, each vote reversing the last, has brought itself into the greatest contempt among all the workers, and proved most brilliantly the Chartists' assertion of the necessity of its reform. Three members, who had formerly voted against the Ministry, afterwards voted for it and rescued it. In all the divisions, the bulk of the opposition voted *for* and the bulk of its own party *against* the Ministry.* The foregoing propositions of Graham touching the employment of children six and one-half and of all other operatives twelve hours[b] are now legislative provisions, and by them and by the limitation of overwork for making up time lost through breakdown of machinery or insufficient water-power by reason of frost or drought,[c] a working-day of more than twelve hours has been made well-nigh impossible. There remains, however, no doubt that, in a very short time, the Ten Hours' Bill will really be adopted.[157] The manufacturers are naturally all against it; there are perhaps not ten who are for it; they have used every honourable and dishonourable means against this dreaded measure, but with no other result than that of drawing down upon them the ever-deepening hatred of the working-men. The bill will pass. What the working-men will do they can do, and that they will have this bill they proved last spring. The economic arguments of the manufacturers that a Ten Hours' Bill would increase the cost

---

* It is notorious that the House of Commons made itself ridiculous a second time in the same session in the same way on the Sugar Question,[156] when it first voted against the Ministry and then for it, after an application of the ministerial whip.— *Note by Engels.*

---

[a] The German editions of 1845 and 1892 have here "in May".— *Ed.*

[b] The German editions of 1845 and 1892 have "concerning a $6^1/_2$-and 12-hour working-day respectively for the two categories of workers".— *Ed.*

[c] The German editions of 1845 and 1892 have here "and other less important limitations".— *Ed.*

of production and incapacitate the English producers for competition in foreign markets, and that wages must fall, are all *half* true; but they prove nothing except this, that the industrial greatness of England can be maintained only through the barbarous treatment of the operatives, the destruction of their health, the social, physical, and mental decay of whole generations. Naturally, if the Ten Hours' Bill were a final measure, it must ruin England; but since it must inevitably bring with it other measures which must draw England into a path wholly different from that hitherto followed, it can only prove an advance.

Let us turn to another side of the factory system which cannot be remedied by legislative provisions so easily as the diseases now engendered by it. We have already alluded in a general way to the nature of the employment, and enough in detail to be able to draw certain inferences from the facts given. The supervision of machinery, the joining of broken threads, is no activity which claims the operative's thinking powers, yet it is of a sort which prevents him from occupying his mind with other things. We have seen, too, that this work affords the muscles no opportunity for physical activity. Thus it is, properly speaking, not work, but tedium, the most deadening, wearing process conceivable. The operative is condemned to let his physical and mental powers decay in this utter monotony, it is his mission to be bored every day and all day long from his eighth year. Moreover, he must not take a moment's rest; the engine moves unceasingly; the wheels, the straps, the spindles hum and rattle in his ears without a pause, and if he tries to snatch one instant, there is the overlooker at his back with the book of fines. This condemnation to be buried alive in the mill, to give constant attention to the tireless machine is felt as the keenest torture by the operatives, and its action upon mind and body is in the long run stunting in the highest degree. There is no better means of inducing stupefaction than a period of factory-work, and if the operatives have, nevertheless, not only rescued their intelligence, but cultivated and sharpened it more than other working-men, they have found this possible only in rebellion against their fate and against the bourgeoisie, the sole subject on which under all circumstances they can think and feel while at work. Or, if this indignation against the bourgeoisie does not become the supreme passion of the working-man, the inevitable consequence is drunkenness and all that is generally called demoralisation. The physical enervation and the sickness, universal in consequence of the factory system, were enough to induce Commissioner Hawkins to attribute this demoralisation thereto as inevitable; how much more when mental lassitude is added to them, and when the influences already mentioned which tempt every working-man to demoralisation, make themselves felt here too! There is no cause for surprise, therefore, that in the manufacturing towns especially, drunkenness and sexual excesses have reached the pitch which I have already described.*

Further, the slavery in which the bourgeoisie holds the proletariat chained, is nowhere more conspicuous than in the factory system. Here ends all freedom in law and in fact. The operative must be in the mill at half-past five in the morning; if he comes a couple of minutes too late, he is fined; if he comes ten minutes too late, he is not let in until breakfast is over, and a quarter of the day's wages is withheld, though he loses only two and one-half hours' work out of twelve. He must eat, drink, and sleep at command. For satisfying the most imperative needs, he is vouchsafed the least possible time absolutely required by them. Whether his dwelling is a half-hour or a whole one removed from the factory does not concern his employer. The despotic bell calls him from his bed, his breakfast, his dinner.

What a time he has of it, too, inside the factory! Here the employer is absolute law-giver; he makes regulations at will, changes and adds to his codex at pleasure, and even, if he inserts the craziest stuff, the courts say to the working-man:

"You were your own master, no one forced you to agree to such a contract if you did not wish to; but now, when you have freely entered into it, you must be bound by it."

And so the working-man only gets into the bargain the mockery of the Justice of the Peace who is a bourgeois himself, and of the law which is made by the bourgeoisie. Such decisions have been

---

* Let us hear another competent judge: "When this example [i.e., of the Irish] is considered in connexion with the unremitted labour of the whole population engaged in the various branches of the cotton manufacture, our wonder will be less excited by their fatal demoralisation. Prolonged and exhausting labour, continued from day to day, and from year to year, is not calculated to develop the intellectual or moral faculties of man. The dull routine of a ceaseless drudgery, in which the same mechanical process is incessantly repeated, resembles the torment of Sisyphus — the toil, like the rock, recoils perpetually on the wearied operative. The mind gathers neither stores nor strength from the constant extension and retraction of the same muscles. The intellect slumbers in supine inertness; but the grosser parts of our nature attain a rank development. To condemn man to such severity of toil is, in some measure, to cultivate in him the habits of an animal. He becomes reckless. He disregards the distinguishing appetites and habits of his species. He neglects the comforts and delicacies of life. He lives in squalid wretchedness, on meagre food, and expends his superfluous gains in debauchery."— Dr. J. Kay.—*Note by Engels*.

given often enough. In October, 1844, the operatives of Kennedy's mill, in Manchester, struck. Kennedy prosecuted them on the strength of a regulation placarded in the mill, that at no time more than two operatives in one room may quit work at once. And the court decided in his favour, giving the working-men the explanation cited above.* And such rules as these usually are! For instance: 1. The doors are closed ten minutes after work begins, and thereafter no one is admitted until the breakfast hour; whoever is absent during this time forfeits 3d. per loom. 2. Every power-loom weaver detected absenting himself at another time, while the machinery is in motion, forfeits for each hour and each loom, 3d. Every person who leaves the room during working-hours, without obtaining permission from the overlooker, forfeits 3d. 3. Weavers who fail to supply themselves with scissors forfeit, per day, 1d. 4. All broken shuttles, brushes, oil-cans, wheels, window-panes, etc., must be paid for by the weaver. 5. No weaver to stop work without giving a week's notice. The manufacturer may dismiss any employee without notice for bad work or improper behaviour. 6. Every operative detected speaking to another, singing or whistling, will be fined 6d.; for leaving his place during working-hours, 6d. Another copy of factory regulations lies before me, according to which every operative who comes three minutes too late, forfeits the wages for a quarter of an hour, and every one who comes twenty minutes too late, for a quarter of a day. Every one who remains absent until breakfast forfeits a shilling on Monday, and sixpence every other day of the week, etc., etc. This last is the regulation of the Phoenix Works in Jersey Street, Manchester.** It may be said that such rules are necessary in a great, complicated factory, in order to insure the harmonious working of the different parts; it may be asserted that such a severe discipline is as necessary here as in an army. This may be so, but what sort of a social order is it which cannot be maintained without such shameful tyranny? Either the end sanctifies the means, or the inference of the badness of the end from the badness of the means is justified. Every one who has served as a soldier knows what it is to be subjected even for a short time to military discipline. But these operatives are condemned from their ninth year to their death to live under the sword, physically and mentally. They are worse slaves than the Negroes in America, for

---

    * *Manchester Guardian*, October 30th.—*Note by Engels to the American edition of 1887.*
    ** *Stubborn Facts*, p. 9 *et seq.*— *Note by Engels.*

they are more sharply watched, and yet it is demanded of them that they shall live like human beings, shall think and feel like men! Verily, this they can do only under glowing hatred towards their oppressors, and towards that order of things which places them in such a position, which degrades them to machines. But it is far more shameful yet, that according to the universal testimony of the operatives, numbers of manufacturers collect the fines imposed upon the operatives with the most heartless severity, and for the purpose of piling up extra profits out of the farthings thus extorted from the impoverished proletarians. Leach asserts, too, that the operatives often find the factory clock moved forward a quarter of an hour and the doors shut, while the clerk moves about with the fines-book inside, noting the many names of the absentees. Leach claims to have counted ninety-five operatives thus shut out, standing before a factory, whose clock was a quarter of an hour slower than the town clocks at night, and a quarter of an hour faster in the morning. The Factory Report relates similar facts. In one factory the clock was set back during working-hours, so that the operatives worked overtime without extra pay; in another, a whole quarter of an hour overtime was worked; in a third, there were two clocks, an ordinary one and a machine clock, which registered the revolutions of the main shaft; if the machinery went slowly, working-hours were measured by the machine clock until the number of revolutions due in twelve hours was reached; if work went well, so that the number was reached before the usual working-hours were ended, the operatives were forced to toil on to the end of the twelfth hour. The witness adds that he had known girls who had good work, and who had worked overtime, who, nevertheless, betook themselves to a life of prostitution rather than submit to this tyranny.* To return to the fines, Leach relates having repeatedly seen women in the last period of pregnancy fined 6d. for the offence of sitting down a moment to rest. Fines for bad work are wholly arbitrary; the goods are examined in the wareroom, and the supervisor charges the fines upon a list without even summoning the operative, who only learns that he has been fined when the overlooker pays his wages, and the goods have perhaps been sold, or certainly been placed beyond his reach. Leach has in his possession such a fines list, ten feet long, and amounting to £35 17s. 10d. He relates that in the factory where this list was made, a new supervisor was dismissed for fining too little, and so bringing in five pounds too little

---

* Drinkwater Evidence, p. 80.— *Note by Engels to the American edition of 1887.*

weekly.* And I repeat that I know Leach to be a thoroughly trustworthy man incapable of a falsehood.

But the operative is his employer's slave in still other respects. If his wife or daughter finds favour in the eyes of the master, a command, a hint suffices, and she must place herself at his disposal. When the employer wishes to supply with signatures a petition in favour of bourgeois interests, he need only send it to his mill. If he wishes to decide a Parliamentary election, he sends his enfranchised operatives in rank and file to the polls, and they vote for the bourgeois candidate whether they will or no. If he desires a majority in a public meeting, he dismisses them half-an-hour earlier than usual, and secures them places close to the platform, where he can watch them to his satisfaction.

Two further arrangements contribute especially to force the operative under the dominion of the manufacturer; the Truck system and the Cottage system.[a] The truck system, the payment of the operatives in goods, was formerly universal in England. The manufacturer opens a shop, "for the convenience of the operatives, and to protect them from the high prices of the petty dealers". Here goods of all sorts are sold to them on credit[b]; and to keep the operatives from going to the shops where they could get their goods more cheaply — the "Tommy shops" usually charging twenty-five to thirty per cent more than others — wages are paid in requisitions on the shop instead of money. The general indignation against this infamous system led to the passage of the Truck Act in 1831, by which, for most employees, payment in truck orders was declared void and illegal, and was made punishable by fine; but, like most other English laws, this has been enforced only here and there. In the towns it is carried out comparatively efficiently; but in the country, the truck system, disguised or undisguised, flourishes. In the town of Leicester, too, it is very common. There lie before me nearly a dozen convictions for this offence, dating from the period between November, 1843, and June, 1844, and reported, in part, in the *Manchester Guardian* and, in part, in the *Northern Star*. The system is, of course, less openly

---

* *Stubborn Facts*, pp. 13-17.—*Note by Engels to the American edition of 1887.* (The German editions of 1845 and 1892 have after "five pounds" the German equivalent "34 talers" in brackets.—*Ed.*)

---

[a] The German editions of 1845 and 1892 give the terms "Truck system", "Cottage system", "Tommy-shops" and "Truck Act" in English.—*Ed.*

[b] The German editions of 1845 and 1892 have "on his account" instead of "on credit".—*Ed.*

carried on at present; wages are usually paid in cash, but the employer still has means enough at command to force him to purchase his wares in the truck shop and nowhere else. Hence it is difficult to combat the truck system, because it can now be carried on under cover of the law,[a] provided only that the operative receives his wages in money. The *Northern Star* of April 27th, 1844, publishes a letter from an operative of Holmfirth, near Huddersfield, in Yorkshire, which refers to a manufacturer of the name of Bowers, as follows:

"It is almost strainge to see that the accursed truck sistim should exist to the enormoust extent that it dose in Holmfirth, and no one to be found to have the moral courage to attempt to put a stop to it. Thaire are a greate many honest handloome weavers that is suffering by that accurssed sistim. This is one specimen. Out of the many of that precious freetraid crew,* thaire is one manufacturer that as the curse of the whole neighbourhood upon im, for is baseness towards is weavers. When they finnish a warp, which comes to £1 14s, or £1 16s, he gives them £1, and the rest in goods, wearing apparel, at 40 or 50 per sent dearer then at the regular shopkeeppers, and many a time the goods are rotton. But as the Free-Trade *Mercury*** says by the factory labour, 'they are not bound to take it; its quite optional'. O, yes; but thay must eather take it or starve. If thay whant any more than the £1 os od, thay must wait of a warp a week or a fortnight; but if thay take the £1, os od and the goods, thaire is always a warp for them. This is free traidism. Lord Brougham says 'we should lay something by in our young days, that we may be independent in our old age of parochial relief'. Must we lay by these rotton goods? If this did not come from a lord, thay would think is brains wear as rotton as the goods wee got for our labour. When the unstampt newspapers wear in circulation thaire wear no lack of informers in Holmfirth. Thaire wear the Blyths, the Estwoods, &,; but wear are they now? O, but this is quite different. Our truckster is one of the free trading pious crew. He goes to the church twise every Sunday, and repeats after the parson very fervently: 'we have left undone those things wich we hought to have done; we have done those things wich we hought not to have done; and thaire is no help in us; but spare us, good Lord.'"[b] "Yes, spare us wile morning, and we will pay our weavers wages in rotton goods again."

The Cottage system looks much more innocent and arose in a much more harmless way, though it has the same enslaving influence upon the employee. In the neighbourhood of the mills in the country, there is often a lack of dwelling accommodation

---

* Supporters of the Anti-Corn Law League.— *Note by Engels* (omitted in the authorised English edition—*Ed.*).

** *Leeds Mercury*, a radical bourgeois newspaper.— *Note by Engels* (omitted in the authorised English edition—*Ed.*).

---

[a] The German editions of 1845 and 1892 have, instead of the foregoing sentence: "Hence it is rarely possible to get at the manufacturers who practise the Truck system, since they can now pursue their infamous practices under cover of the law."—*Ed.*

[b] In the German editions of 1845 and 1892 the author explains that these words are taken from the Anglican litany.—*Ed.*

for the operatives. The manufacturer is frequently obliged to build such dwellings and does so gladly, as they yield great advantages, besides the interest upon the capital invested.[a] If any owner of working-men's dwellings averages about six per cent on his invested capital, it is safe to calculate that the manufacturer's cottages yield twice this rate; for so long as his factory does not stand perfectly idle he is sure of occupants, and of occupants who pay punctually. He is therefore spared the two chief disadvantages under which other house-owners labour; his cottages never stand empty, and he runs no risk. But the rent of the cottages is as high as though these disadvantages were in full force, and by obtaining the same rent as the ordinary house-owner, the manufacturer, at cost of the operatives, makes a brilliant investment at twelve to fourteen per cent. For it is clearly unjust that he should make twice as much profit as other competing house-owners, who at the same time are excluded from competing with him. But it implies a double wrong, when he draws his fixed profit from the pockets of the non-possessing class, which must consider the expenditure of every penny. He is used to that, however, he whose whole wealth is gained at the cost of his employees. But this injustice becomes an infamy when the manufacturer, as often happens, forces his operatives, who must occupy his houses on pain of dismissal, to pay a higher rent than the ordinary one, or even to pay rent for houses in which they do not live! The *Halifax Guardian,* quoted by the Liberal *Sun,** asserts that hundreds of operatives in Ashton-under-Lyne, Oldham, and Rochdale, etc., are forced by their employers to pay house-rent whether they occupy the house or not.[158] The cottage system is universal in the country districts; it has created whole villages, and the manufacturer usually has little or no competition against his houses, so that he can fix his price regardless of any market rate, indeed at his pleasure. And what power does the cottage system give the employer over his operatives in disagreements between master and men? If the latter strike, he need only give them notice to quit his premises, and the notice need only be a week; after that time the operative is not only without bread but without a shelter, a vagabond at the mercy of the law which sends him, without fail, to the treadmill.[b]

---

* *Sun,* a London daily; end of November, 1843.—*Note by Engels.*

---

[a] In the German editions of 1845 and 1892 the end of the sentence reads as follows: "since they bring him a good profit upon the capital he has invested".—*Ed.*

[b] The German editions of 1845 and 1892 have "to the treadmill "for a month".—*Ed.*

Such is the factory system sketched as fully as my space permits, and with as little partisan spirit as the heroic deeds of the bourgeoisie against the defenceless workers permit—deeds towards which it is impossible to remain indifferent, towards which indifference were a crime. Let us compare the condition of the free Englishman of 1845 with the Saxon serf under the lash of the Norman barons of 1145. The serf was *glebae adscriptus,* bound to the soil, so is the free working-man through the cottage system. The serf owed his master the *jus primae noctis,* the right of the first night—the free working-man must, on demand, surrender to his master not only that, but the right of *every* night. The serf could acquire no property; everything that he gained, his master could take from him; the free working-man has no property, can gain none by reason of the pressure of competition, and what even the Norman baron did not do, the modern manufacturer does. Through the truck system, he assumes every day the administration in detail of the things which the worker requires for his immediate necessities. The relation of the lord of the soil to the serf was regulated by the prevailing customs and by laws which were obeyed, because they corresponded to them.[a] The free working-man's relation to his master is regulated by laws which are *not* obeyed, because they correspond neither with the interests of the employer nor with the prevailing customs. The lord of the soil could not separate the serf from the land, nor sell him apart from it, and since almost all the land was fief and there was no capital, practically could not sell him at all. The modern bourgeois forces the working-man to sell himself. The serf was the slave of the piece of land on which he was born, the working-man is the slave of his own necessaries of life and of the money with which he has to buy them—both are *slaves of a thing*. The serf had a guarantee for the means of subsistence in the feudal order of society in which every member had his own place. The free working-man has no guarantee whatsoever, because he has a place in society only when the bourgeoisie can make use of him; in all other cases he is ignored, treated as non-existent. The serf sacrificed himself for his master in war, the factory operative in peace. The lord of the serf was a barbarian who regarded his villain as a head of cattle; the employer of operatives is civilised and regards his "hand" as a machine. In short, the position of the two is not far

---

[a] In the German editions of 1845 and 1892 this sentence reads as follows: "The relation of the serf to the lord of the soil was regulated by laws, which were obeyed because they corresponded to the customs, and by the customs themselves."—*Ed*.

from equal, and if either is at a disadvantage, it is the free working-man. Slaves they both are, with the single difference that the slavery of the one is undissembled, open, honest; that of the other cunning, sly, disguised, deceitfully concealed from himself and every one else, a hypocritical[a] servitude worse than the old. The philanthropic Tories were right when they gave the operatives the name white slaves. But the hypocritical disguised slavery recognises the right to freedom, at least in outward form; bows before a freedom-loving public opinion, and herein lies the historic progress as compared with the old servitude, that the *principle* of freedom is affirmed, and the oppressed will one day see to it that this principle is carried out.[b]

At the close a few stanzas of a poem which voices the sentiments of the workers themselves about the factory system. Written by Edward P. Mead of Birmingham, it is a correct expression of the views prevailing among them.[159]

> There is a King, and a ruthless King;
> Not a King of the poet's dream;
> But a tyrant fell, white slaves know well,
> And that ruthless King is Steam.
>
> > He hath an arm, an iron arm,
> > And tho' he hath but one,
> > In that mighty arm there is a charm,
> > That millions hath undone.
>
> Like the ancient Moloch grim, his sire
> In Himmon's vale that stood,
> His bowels are of living fire,
> And children are his food.
>
> > His priesthood are a hungry band,
> > Blood-thirsty, proud, and bold;
> > 'Tis they direct his giant hand,
> > In turning blood to gold.
>
> For filthy gain in their servile chain
> All nature's rights they bind;
> They mock at lovely woman's pain,
> And to manly tears are blind.

---

[a] The German editions of 1845 and 1892 have "theological" instead of "hypocritical". Lower "white slaves" is given in English, followed by the German equivalent.— *Ed.*

[b] The following paragraph and the poem were omitted from the 1887 American and 1892 English editions, which, however, included the Author's note to this passage.— *Ed.*

Ein König lebt, ein zorniger Fürst,
Nicht des Dichters geträumtes Königsbild,
Ein Tyrann, den der weiße Sklave kennt,
Und der Dampf ist der König wild.

Er hat einen Arm, einen eisernen Arm,
Und obgleich er nur Einen trägt;
In dem Arme schafft eine Zauberkraft,
Die Millionen schlägt.

Wie der Moloch grimm, sein Ahn, der einst
Im Thale Himmon saß,
Ist Feuersgluth sein Eingeweid',
Und Kinder sind sein Fraß.

Seine Priesterschaar, der Menschheit bar,
Voll Blutdurst, Stolz und Wuth,
Sie lenken — o Schand'! — seine Riesenhand
Und zaubern Gold aus Blut.

Sie treten in Staub das Menschenrecht
Für das schnöde Gold, ihren Gott,
Des Weibes Schmerz ist ihnen Scherz,
Des Mannes Thrän' ihr Spott.

Musik ist ihrem Ohr das Schrei'n
Des Armen im Todeskampf;
Skelette von Jungfraun und Knaben füll'n
Die Höllen des König Dampf.

Die Höll'n auf Erd'! sie verbreiten Tod,
Seit der Dampf herrscht, rings im Reich,
Denn des Menschen Leib und Seele wird
Gemordet drin zugleich.

Drum nieder den Dampf, den Moloch wild,
Arbeitende Tausende, all',
Bind't ihm die Hand, oder unser Land
Bringt er über Nacht zu Fall!

Und seine Vögte grimm, die Mill-Lords stolz,
Goldstrotzend und blutigroth,
Stürzen muß sie des Volkes Zorn,
Wie das Scheusal, ihren Gott! *)

---

*) Ich habe weder Zeit noch Raum, mich weitläufig auf die Entgegnungen der

15*

A page from
The Condition of the Working-Class in England (1845),
with Edward Mead's poem "The Steam King"
translated by Engels

The sighs and groans of Labour's sons
Are music in their ear,
And the skeleton shades, of lads and maids,
In the Steam King's hell appear.

Those hells upon earth, since the Steam King's birth,
Have scatter'd around despair;
For the human mind for Heav'n design'd,
With the body, is murdered there.

Then down with the King, the Moloch King,
Ye working millions all;
O chain his hand, or our native land
Is destin'd by him to fall.

And his Satraps abhor'd, each proud Mill Lord,
Now gorg'd with gold and blood,
Must be put down by the nation's frown,
As well as their monster God.*

* I have neither time nor space to deal in detail with the replies of the manufacturers to the charges made against them for twelve years past. These men will not learn because their supposed interest blinds them. As, moreover, many of their objections have been met in the foregoing, the following is all that it is necessary for me to add:

You come to Manchester, you wish to make yourself acquainted with the state of affairs in England. You naturally have good introductions to respectable people. You drop a remark or two as to the condition of the workers. You are made acquainted with a couple of the first Liberal manufacturers, Robert Hyde Greg, perhaps, Edmund Ashworth, Thomas Ashton, or others. They are told of your wishes. The manufacturer understands you, knows what he has to do. He accompanies you to his factory in the country; Mr. Greg to Quarrybank in Cheshire, Mr. Ashworth to Turton near Bolton, Mr. Ashton to Hyde. He leads you through a superb, admirably arranged building, perhaps supplied with ventilators, he calls your attention to the lofty, airy rooms, the fine machinery, here and there a healthy-looking operative. He gives you an excellent lunch, and proposes to you to visit the operatives' homes; he conducts you to the cottages, which look new, clean and neat, and goes with you into this one and that one, naturally only to overlookers, mechanics, etc., so that you may see "families who live wholly from the factory". Among other families you might find that only wife and children work, and the husband darns stockings. The presence of the employer keeps you from asking indiscreet questions; you find every one well-paid, comfortable, comparatively healthy by reason of the country air; you begin to be converted from your exaggerated ideas of misery and starvation. But, that the cottage system makes slaves of the operatives, that there may be a truck shop in the neighbourhood, that the people hate the manufacturer, this they do not point out to you, because he is present. He has built a school, church, reading-room, etc. That he uses the school to train children to subordination, that he tolerates in the reading-room such prints only as represent the interests of the bourgeoisie, that he dismisses his employees if they read Chartist or Socialist papers or books, this is all concealed from you. You see an easy, patriarchal relation, you see the life of the overlookers, you see what the bourgeoisie *promises* the workers if they become its slaves, mentally and morally. This "country manufacture" has always been what the employers like to show, because in it the disadvantages of the factory system, especially from the point of view of health, are, in part, done away with by the free air and surroundings, and because the patriarchal servitude of the workers can here be longest maintained. Dr. Ure sings a dithyramb upon the theme. But woe to the operatives to whom it occurs to think for themselves and become Chartists! For them the paternal affection of the manufacturer comes to a sudden end. Further, if you should wish to be accompanied through the working-people's quarters of Manchester, if you should desire to see the development of the factory system in a factory town, you may wait long before these rich bourgeoisie will help you! These gentlemen do not know in what condition their employees are nor what they want, and they dare not know things which would make them uneasy or even oblige them to act in opposition to their own interests. But, fortunately, that is of no consequence: what the working-men have to carry out, they carry out for themselves.— *Note by Engels.*

THE REMAINING BRANCHES
OF INDUSTRY

We were compelled to deal with the factory system somewhat at length, as it is an entirely novel creation of the industrial period; we shall be able to treat the other workers the more briefly, because what has been said either of the industrial proletariat in general, or of the factory system in particular, will wholly, or in part, apply to them. We shall, therefore, merely have to record how far the factory system has succeeded in forcing its way into each branch of industry, and what other peculiarities these may reveal.

The four branches comprised under the Factory Act are engaged in the production of clothing stuffs. We shall do best if we deal next with those workers who receive their materials from these factories; and, first of all, with the stocking weavers of Nottingham, Derby, and Leicester. Touching these workers, the Children's Employment Commission reports that the long working-hours, imposed by low wages, with a sedentary life and the strain upon the eyes involved in the nature of the employment, usually enfeeble the whole frame, and especially the eyes. Work at night is impossible without a very powerful light produced by concentrating the rays of the lamp, making them pass through glass globes, which is most injurious to the sight. At forty years of age, nearly all wear spectacles. The children employed at spooling and hemming usually suffer grave injuries to the health and constitution. They work from the sixth, seventh, or eighth year ten to twelve hours daily in small, close rooms. It is not uncommon for them to faint at their work, to become too feeble for the most ordinary household occupation, and so near-sighted as to be obliged to wear glasses during childhood. Many were found by the commissioners to exhibit all the symptoms of a scrofulous constitu-

tion, and the manufacturers usually refuse to employ girls who
have worked in this way as being too weak. The condition of these
children is characterised as "a disgrace to a Christian country",
and the wish expressed for legislative interference.* The Factory
Report adds that the stocking weavers are the worst paid workers
in Leicester, earning six, or with great effort, seven shillings a
week, for sixteen to eighteen hours' daily work. Formerly they
earned twenty to twenty-one shillings, but the introduction of
enlarged frames has ruined their business; the great majority still
work with old, small, single frames, and compete with difficulty
with the progress of machinery. Here, too, every progress is a
disadvantage for the workers. Nevertheless, Commissioner Power
speaks of the pride of the stocking weavers that they are free, and
have no factory bell to measure out the time for their eating,
sleeping, and working. Their position today is no better than in
1833, when the Factory Commission made the foregoing statements; the competition of the Saxon stocking weavers, who have
scarcely anything to eat, takes care of that. This competition is too
strong for the English in nearly all foreign markets, and for the
lower qualities of goods even in the English market. It must be a
source of rejoicing for the patriotic German stocking weaver that
his starvation wages force his English brother to starve too! And,
verily, will he not starve on, proud and happy, for the greater
glory of German industry, since the honour of the Fatherland
demands that his table should be bare, his dish half-empty? Ah! it
is a noble thing this competition, this "race of the nations". In the
Morning Chronicle, another Liberal sheet, the organ of the
bourgeoisie par excellence, there were published[a] some letters
from a stocking weaver in Hinckley, describing the condition of
his fellow-workers. Among other things, he reports 50 families,
321 persons, who were supported by 109 frames; each frame
yielded on an average $5^{1}/_{2}$ shillings; each family earned an average
of 11s. 4d. weekly. Out of this there was required for house rent,
frame rent, fuel, light, soap, and needles, together 5s. 10d., so that
there remained for food, per head daily, $1^{1}/_{2}$d.,[b] and for clothing
nothing.

* Grainger Report. Appendix, Part I, p. F 15, sect. 132-142.—*Note by Engels to the
American edition of 1887* (reproduced in the English edition of 1892; the German
editions of 1845 and 1892 give this and similar references in the text—*Ed.*).

    [a] The German editions of 1845 and 1892 have here "in December 1843".—*Ed.*
    [b] The German editions of 1845 and 1892 have here in German "15 Prussian
pfennigs".—*Ed.*

"Eye hath not seen," says the stocking weaver, "ear hath not heard, the heart cannot conceive the half of the suffering endured by this poverty-stricken people."[160]

Beds were wanting either wholly or in part, the children ran about ragged and barefoot; the men said, with tears in their eyes: "We never tasted meat this many a day" — "We have almost forgotten its taste"; and, finally, some of them worked on Sunday, though public opinion pardons anything else more readily than this, and the rattling noise of the frame is audible throughout the neighbourhood.

"Look at my children," said one of them, "and ask no more. It is because my poverty compels me; I cannot and will not hear my children cry for bread without taking the only means honestly to get it. Last Monday morning I rose at two o'clock and worked till near midnight. I rose at six o'clock each succeeding morning and worked until between eleven and twelve each night. I cannot do it longer. I shall go to an untimely grave if I do; I will therefore end my labours at ten o'clock each night and make up the time lost by labouring on the Sunday."

Neither in Leicester, Nottingham, nor Derby have wages risen since 1833; and the worst of it is that in Leicester the truck system prevails to a great extent, as I have mentioned. It is, therefore, not to be wondered at that the weavers of this region take a very active part in all working-men's movements, the more active and effective because the frames are worked chiefly by men.

In this stocking weavers' district the lace industry also has its headquarters. In the three counties mentioned there are in all 2,760 lace frames in use, while in all the rest of England there are but 787. The manufacture of lace is greatly complicated by a rigid division of labour, and embraces a multitude of branches. The yarn is first spooled by girls fourteen years of age and upwards, winders[a]; then the spools are set up on the frames by boys, eight years old and upwards, threaders, who pass the thread through fine openings, of which each machine has an average of 1,800, and bring it towards its destination; then the weaver weaves the lace which comes out of the machine like a broad piece of cloth and is taken apart by very little children who draw out the connecting threads. This is called running or drawing lace, and the children themselves lace-runners. The lace is then made ready for sale. The winders, like the threaders, have no specified working-time, being called upon whenever the spools on a frame are empty, and are liable, since the weavers work at night, to be required at any time in the factory or work-room. This irregulari-

---

[a] The German editions of 1845 and 1892 give brackets the English names of this and the other occupations mentioned here.— *Ed.*

ty, the frequent night-work, the disorderly way of living consequent upon it, engender a multitude of physical and moral ills,
especially early and unbridled sexual licence, upon which point all
witnesses are unanimous. The work is very bad for the eyes, and
although a permanent injury in the case of the threaders is not
universally observable, inflammations of the eye, pain, tears, and
momentary uncertainty of vision during the act of threading are
engendered. For the winders, however, it is certain that their work
seriously affects the eye, and produces, besides the frequent
inflammations of the cornea, many cases of amaurosis and
cataract. The work of the weavers themselves is very difficult, as
the frames have constantly been made wider, until those now in
use are almost all worked by three men in turn, each[a] working
eight hours, and the frame being kept in use the whole twenty-
four. Hence it is that the winders and threaders are so often called
upon during the night, and must work to prevent the frame from
standing idle. The filling in of 1,800 openings with thread
occupies three children at least two hours. Many frames are
moved by steam-power, and the work of men thus superseded;
and, as the Children's Employment Commission's Report mentions
only lace factories to which the children are summoned, it seems
to follow either that the work of the weavers has been removed to
great factory rooms of late, or that steam-weaving has become
pretty general; a forward movement of the factory system in
either case. Most unwholesome of all is the work of the runners,
who are usually children of seven, and even of five and four, years
old. Commissioner Grainger actually found one child of two years
old employed at this work. Following a thread which is to be
withdrawn by a needle from an intricate texture, is very bad for
the eyes, especially when, as is usually the case, the work is
continued fourteen to sixteen hours. In the least unfavourable
case, aggravated near-sightedness follows; in the worst case, which
is frequent enough, incurable blindness from amaurosis. But,
apart from that, the children, in consequence of sitting perpetually
bent up, become feeble, narrow-chested, and scrofulous from bad
digestion. Disordered functions of the uterus are almost universal
among the girls, and curvature of the spine also, so that "all the
runners may be recognised from their gait". The same consequences for the eyes and the whole constitution are produced by the

---

[a] The German editions of 1845 and 1892 have here "each of whom is relieved
after four hours, so that all together they work twenty-four, each eight hours a
day".— Ed.

embroidery of lace. Medical witnesses are unanimously of the opinion that the health of all children employed in the production of lace suffers seriously, that they are pale, weak, delicate, undersized, and much less able than other children to resist disease. The affections from which they usually suffer are general debility, frequent fainting, pains in the head, sides, back, and hips, palpitation of the heart, nausea, vomiting and want of appetite, curvature of the spine, scrofula, and consumption. The health of the female lace-makers especially, is constantly and deeply undermined; complaints are universal of anaemia, difficult child-birth, and miscarriage.* The same subordinate official of the Children's Employment Commission reports further that the children are very often ill-clothed and ragged, and receive insufficient food, usually only bread and tea, often no meat for months together. As to their moral condition, he reports:**

"In the town of Nottingham all parties, police, clergy, manufacturers, work-people, and parents of the children agree that the present system of labour is a most fertile source of immorality. The threaders, who are usually boys, and the winders, who are generally girls, are called out of their parents' houses at all hours of the night, and as it is quite uncertain how long they may be required, a ready and unanswerable excuse for staying out is furnished and they have every facility for forming improper connections. This must have contributed, in no slight degree, to the immorality which, according to the opinion universally expressed, prevails to a most awful extent in Nottingham. In addition to the immediate evils to the children themselves, the domestic peace and comfort of the families to which they are members are sacrificed to this most unnatural state of things."

Another branch of lace-making, bobbin-lacework, is carried on in the agricultural shires of Northampton, Oxford, and Bedford,ᵃ chiefly by children and young persons, who complain universally of bad food, and rarely taste meat. The employment itself is most unwholesome. The children work in small, ill-ventilated, damp rooms, sitting always bent over the lace cushion. To support the body in this wearying position, the girls wear stays with a wooden busk, which, at the tender age of most of them, when the bones are still very soft, wholly displace the ribs, and make narrow chests universal. They usually die of consumption after suffering the severest forms of digestive disorders, brought on by sedentary work in a bad atmosphere. They are almost wholly without education, least of all do they receive moral training. They love finery,

* Grainger's whole Report.— *Note by Engels to the American edition of 1887.*

** Grainger Children's Employment Commission's Report.— *Note by Engels to the American edition of 1887.*

ᵃ The German editions of 1845 and 1892 have here "and Buckingham".— *Ed.*

and in consequence of these two influences their moral condition is most deplorable, and prostitution almost epidemic among them.*

This is the price at which society purchases for the fine ladies of the bourgeoisie the pleasure of wearing lace; a reasonable price truly! Only a few thousand blind working-men, some consumptive labourers' daughters, a sickly generation of the vile multitude bequeathing its debility to its equally "vile" children and children's children. But what does that come to? Nothing, nothing whatsoever! Our English bourgeoisie will lay the report of the Government Commission aside indifferently, and wives and daughters will deck themselves with lace as before. It is a beautiful thing, the composure of an English bourgeois.

A great number of operatives are employed in the cotton-printing establishments of Lancashire, Derbyshire, and the West of Scotland. In no branch of English industry has mechanical ingenuity produced such brilliant results as here, but in no other has it so crushed the workers. The application of engraved cylinders driven by steam-power, and the discovery of a method of printing four to six colours at once with such cylinders, has as completely superseded hand-work as did the application of machinery to the spinning and weaving of cotton, and these new arrangements in the printing-works have superseded the hand-workers much more than was the case in the production of the fabrics. One man, with the assistance of one child, now does with a machine the work done formerly by 200 block printers; a single machine yields 28 yards [a] of printed cloth per minute. The calico printers are in a very bad way in consequence; the shires of Lancaster, Derby, and Chester produced (according to a petition of the printers to the House of Commons), in the year 1842, 11,000,000 pieces of printed cotton goods: of these, 100,000 were printed by hand exclusively, 900,000 in part with machinery and in part by hand, and 10,000,000 by machinery alone, with four to six colours. [b] As the machinery is chiefly new and undergoes constant improvement, the number of hand-printers is far too great for the available quantity of work, and many of them are therefore starving; the petition puts the number at one-quarter of the whole, while the rest are employed but one or two, in the best

---

* Burns, Children's Employment Commission's Report.— *Note by Engels to the American edition of 1887.*

---

[a] The German editions of 1845 and 1892 have here in brackets "80 feet".— *Ed.*
[b] The German editions of 1845 and 1892 have "from one to six colours".— *Ed.*

case three days in the week, and are ill-paid. Leach * asserts of one print-works (Deeply Dale, near Bury, in Lancashire), that the hand-printers did not earn on an average more than five shillings, though he knows that the machine-printers were pretty well paid. The print-works are thus wholly affiliated with the factory system, but without being subject to the legislative restrictions placed upon it. They produce an article subject to fashion, and have therefore no regular work. If they have small orders, they work half-time; if they make a hit with a pattern, and business is brisk, they work twelve hours, perhaps all night.[a] In the neighbourhood of my home, near Manchester, there was a print-works that was often lighted when I returned late at night; and I have heard that the children were obliged at times to work so long there, that they would try to catch a moment's rest and sleep on the stone steps and in the corners of the lobby. I have no legal proof of the truth of the statement, or I should name the firm. The Report of the Children's Employment Commission is very cursory upon this subject, stating merely that in England, at least, the children are mostly pretty well clothed and fed (relatively, according to the wages of the parents), that they receive no education whatsoever, and are morally on a low plane. It is only necessary to remember that these children are subject to the factory system, and then, referring the reader to what has already been said of that, we can pass on.

Of the remaining workers employed in the manufacture of clothing stuffs little remains to be said; the bleachers' work is very unwholesome, obliging them to breathe chlorine, a gas injurious to the lungs. The work of the dyers is in many cases very healthful,[b] since it requires the exertion of the whole body; how these workers are paid is little known, and this is ground enough for the inference that they do not receive less than the average wages, otherwise they would make complaint. The fustian cutters, who, in consequence of the large consumption of cotton velvet, are comparatively numerous, being estimated at from 3,000 to 4,000, have suffered very severely, indirectly, from the influence of the factory system. The goods formerly woven with hand-looms, were not perfectly uniform, and required a practised hand in cutting

---

* Leach, *Stubborn Facts from the Factories*, p. 47.— *Note by Engels to the American edition of 1887.*

---

[a] The German editions of 1845 and 1892 have "they work till ten or twelve, even the whole night".— *Ed.*

[b] In the German editions of 1845 and 1892 this sentence reads: "The work of the dyers is healthier, in many cases very healthful", etc.— *Ed.*

the single rows of threads. Since power-looms have been used, the rows run regularly; each thread of the weft is exactly parallel with the preceding one, and cutting is no longer an art. The workers thrown out of employment by the introduction of machinery turn to fustian cutting, and force down wages by their competition; the manufacturers discovered that they could employ women and children, and the wages sank to the rate paid them, while hundreds of men were thrown out of employment. The manufacturers found that they could get the work done in the factory itself more cheaply than in the cutters' work-room, for which they indirectly paid the rent. Since this discovery, the low upper-storey cutters' rooms stand empty in many a cottage, or are let for dwellings, while the cutter has lost his freedom of choice of his working-hours, and is brought under the dominion of the factory bell. A cutter of perhaps forty-five years of age told me that he could remember a time when he had received 8d. a yard for work, for which he now received 1d.; true, he can cut the more regular texture more quickly than the old, but he can by no means do twice as much in an hour as formerly, so that his wages have sunk to less than a quarter of what they were. Leach * gives a list of wages paid in 1827 and in 1843 for various goods, from which it appears that articles paid in 1827 at the rate of 4d., $2^{1}/_{4}$d., $2^{3}/_{4}$d., and 1d. per yard, were paid in 1843 at the rate of $1^{1}/_{2}$d., 1d., $^{3}/_{4}$d., and $^{3}/_{8}$d. per yard, cutters' wages. The average weekly wage, according to Leach, was as follows: 1827, £1 6s. 6d.; £1 2s. 6d.; £1; £1 6s. 6d.; and for the same goods in 1843, 10s.; 7s.; 6s. 8d.; 10s.; while there are hundreds of workers who cannot find employment even at these last-named rates. Of the hand-weavers of the cotton industry we have already spoken; the other woven fabrics are almost exclusively produced on hand-looms. Here most of the workers have suffered as the weavers[a] have done from the crowding in of competitors displaced by machinery, and are, moreover, subject like the factory operatives to a severe fine system for bad work. Take, for instance, the silk weavers. Mr. Brocklehurst, one of the largest silk manufacturers in all England laid before a committee of Members of Parliament lists taken from his books, from which it appears that for goods for which he paid wages in 1821 at the rate of 30s., 14s.; $3^{1}/_{2}$s., $^{3}/_{4}$s., $1^{1}/_{10}$s., 10s.; he paid in 1831 but 9s., $7^{1}/_{2}$s., $2^{1}/_{4}$s., $^{1}/_{3}$s., $^{1}/_{2}$s., $6^{1}/_{4}$s., while in this case

---

* Leach, *Stubborn Facts from the Factories*, p. 35.— *Note by Engels to the American edition of 1887.*

---

[a] The German editions of 1845 and 1892 have "fustian cutters".—*Ed.*

no improvement in the machinery has taken place. But what Mr. Brocklehurst does may very well be taken as a standard for all. From the same lists it appears that the average weekly wage of his weavers, after all deductions, was, in 1821, $16^1/_2$s., and, in 1831, but 6s. Since that time wages have fallen still further. Goods which brought in 4d.[a] weavers' wages in 1831, bring in but $2^1/_2$d. in 1843 (single sarsnets[b]), and a great number of weavers in the country can get work only when they undertake these goods at $1^1/_2$d.-2d. Moreover, they are subject to arbitrary deductions from their wages. Every weaver who receives materials is given a card, on which is usually to be read that the work is to be returned at a specified hour of the day; that a weaver who cannot work by reason of illness must make the fact known at the office within three days, or sickness will not be regarded as an excuse; that it will not be regarded as a sufficient excuse if the weaver claims to have been obliged to wait for yarn; that for certain faults in the work (if, for example, more weft-threads are found within a given space than are prescribed), not less than half the wages will be deducted; and that if the goods should not be ready at the time specified, one penny will be deducted for every yard returned. The deductions in accordance with these cards are so considerable that, for instance, a man who comes twice a week to Leigh, in Lancashire, to gather up woven goods, brings his employer at least £15[c] fines every time. He asserts this himself, and he is regarded as one of the most lenient. Such things were formerly settled by arbitration; but as the workers were usually dismissed if they insisted upon that, the custom has been almost wholly abandoned, and the manufacturer acts arbitrarily as prosecutor, witness, judge, law-giver, and executive in one person. And if the workman goes to a Justice of the Peace, the answer is: "When you accepted your card you entered upon a contract, and you must abide by it." The case is the same as that of the factory operatives. Besides, the employer obliges the workman to sign a document in which he declares that he agrees to the deductions made. And if a workman rebels, all the manufacturers in the town know at once that he is a man who, as Leach says,*

* Leach, *Stubborn Facts from the Factories*, pp. 37-40.—*Note by Engels to the American edition of 1887.*

---

[a] The German editions of 1845 and 1892 give "$^1/_3$ s. or 4 d.".—*Ed.*

[b] The German editions of 1845 and 1892 give this term in English.—*Ed.*

[c] The German editions of 1845 and 1892 give in brackets the German equivalent "100 Prussian talers".—*Ed.*

"is an enemy to all ticket-made law and social order and has the impudence to dispute the wisdom of those whom he ought to know are his superiors in society."

Naturally, the workers are perfectly free; the manufacturer does not force them to take his materials and his cards, but he says to them what Leach translates into plain English with the words:

"If you don't like to be frizzled in my frying-pan, you can take a walk into the fire."[a]

The silk weavers of London, and especially of Spitalfields, have lived in periodic distress for a long time, and that they still have no cause to be satisfied with their lot is proved by their taking a most active part in English labour movements in general, and in London ones in particular. The distress prevailing among them gave rise to the fever which broke out in East London, and called forth the Commission for Investigating the Sanitary Condition of the Labouring Class. But the last report of the London Fever Hospital shows that this disease is still raging.

After the textile fabrics, by far the most important products of English industry are the metal-wares. This trade has its headquarters at Birmingham, where the finer metal goods of all sorts are produced, at Sheffield for cutlery, and in Staffordshire, especially at Wolverhampton, where the coarser articles, locks, nails, etc., are manufactured. In describing the position of the workers employed in these trades, let us begin with Birmingham. The disposition of the work has retained in Birmingham, as in most places where metals are wrought, something of the old handicraft character; the small employers are still to be found, who work with their apprentices in the shop at home, or when they need steam-power, in great factory buildings which are divided into little shops, each rented to a small employer, and supplied with a shaft moved by the engine, and furnishing motive power for the machinery. Léon Faucher, author of a series of articles[b] in the Revue des deux Mondes, which at least betray study, and are better than what has hitherto been written upon the subject by Englishmen or Germans,[161] characterises this relation in contrast with the manufacture of Lancashire as Démocratie industrielle, and observes that it produces no very favourable results for master or men. This observation is perfectly correct, for the many small employers cannot well

---

[a] The German editions of 1845 and 1892 give this sentence in German and the original English in brackets.— Ed.

[b] The German editions of 1845 and 1892 have here "concerning working-class conditions in England".— Ed.

subsist on the profit divided amongst them, determined by competition, a profit under other circumstances absorbed by a single manufacturer. The centralising tendency of capital holds them down. For one who grows rich ten are ruined, and a hundred placed at greater disadvantage than ever, by the pressure of the one upstart who can afford to sell more cheaply than they. And in the cases where they have to compete from the beginning against great capitalists, it is self-evident that they can only toil along with the greatest difficulty. The apprentices are, as we shall see, quite as badly off under the small employers as under the manufacturers, with the single difference that they, in turn, may become small employers, and so attain a certain independence — that is to say, they are at best less directly exploited by the bourgeoisie than under the factory system. Thus these small employers are neither genuine proletarians, since they live in part upon the work of their apprentices,[a] nor genuine bourgeois, since their principal means of support is their own work. This peculiar midway position of the Birmingham iron-workers is to blame for their having so rarely joined wholly and unreservedly in the English labour movements. Birmingham is a politically radical, but not a Chartist, town. There are, however, numerous larger factories belonging to capitalists; and in these the factory system reigns supreme. The division of labour, which is here carried out to the last detail (in the needle industry, for example), and the use of steam-power, admit of the employment of a great multitude of women and children, and we find here* precisely the same features reappearing which the Factories' Report presented,— the work of women up to the hour of confinement, incapacity as housekeepers, neglect of home and children, indifference, actual dislike to family life, and demoralisation; further, the crowding out of men from employment, the constant improvement of machinery, early emancipation of children, husbands supported by their wives and children, etc., etc. The children are described as half-starved and ragged, the half of them are said not to know what it is to have enough to eat, many of them get nothing to eat before the midday meal, or even live the whole day upon a pen-

* Children's Employment Commission's Report.— *Note by Engels to the American edition of 1887.*

[a] The German editions of 1845 and 1892 have here: "and sell not the labour itself, but the ready product." Mention of the sale of labour was perhaps omitted in the American edition of 1887 and the English edition of 1892 in connection with the later opinion of Marxist political economy that the worker sells his labour-power, and not his labour, to the capitalist.— *Ed.*

nyworth[a] of bread for a noonday meal—there were actually cases in which children received no food from eight in the morning until seven at night. Their clothing is very often scarcely sufficient to cover their nakedness, many are barefoot even in winter. Hence they are all small and weak for their age, and rarely develop with any degree of vigour. And when we reflect that with these insufficient means of reproducing the physical forces, hard and protracted work in close rooms is required of them, we cannot wonder that there are few adults in Birmingham fit for military service.

The working-men, says a recruiting surgeon, "are shorter, more puny, and altogether inferior in their physical powers. Many of the men presented for examinations, are distorted in the spine and chest."

According to the assertion of a recruiting sergeant, the people of Birmingham are smaller than those anywhere else, being usually 5 feet 4 to 5 inches tall; out of 613 recruits, but 238 were found fit for service. As to education, a series of depositions and specimens taken from the metal districts have already been given,[b] to which the reader is referred. It appears further, from the Children's Employment Commission's Report, that in Birmingham more than half the children, between five and fifteen years attend no school whatsoever, that those who do are constantly changing, so that it is impossible to give them any training of an enduring kind, and that they are all withdrawn from school very early and set to work. The report makes it clear what sort of teachers are employed. One teacher, in answer to the question whether she gave moral instruction, said, No, for threepence a week school fees that was too much to require, but that she took a great deal of trouble to instil good principles into the children.[c] (And she made a decided slip in her English in saying it.) In the schools the commissioner found constant noise and disorder. The moral state of the children is in the highest degree deplorable. Half of all the criminals are children under fifteen, and in a single year ninety ten-years'-old offenders, among them forty-four serious criminal

---

[a] The German editions of 1845 and 1892 have here in brackets "10 Prussian pfennigs".—Ed.

[b] The American edition of 1887 and the English edition of 1892 give reference to the respective pages. (See pp. 408-10 of this volume.)—Ed.

[c] In the German editions of 1845 and 1892 this passage reads as follows: "One teacher, in answer to the question whether she gave moral instruction, said, No, for threepence a week school fees that was too much to require; several others did not even understand this question and still others did not consider this part of their duty. One of the teachers said that she gave no moral instruction but that she took a great deal of trouble to instil good principles into the children."—Ed.

cases, were sentenced. Unbridled sexual intercourse seems, according to the opinion of the commissioner, almost universal, and that at a very early age.*

In the iron district of Staffordshire the state of things is still worse. For the coarse wares made here neither much division of labour (with certain exceptions) nor steam-power or machinery can be applied. In Wolverhampton, Willenhall, Bilston, Sedgeley, Wednesfield, Darlaston, Dudley, Walsall, Wednesbury, etc., there are, therefore, fewer factories. But chiefly single forges, where the small masters work alone, or with one or more apprentices, who serve them until reaching the twenty-first year. The small employers are in about the same situation as those of Birmingham; but the apprentices, as a rule, are much worse off. They get almost exclusively meat from diseased animals or such as have died a natural death, or tainted meat, or fish to eat, with veal from calves killed too young, and pork from swine smothered during transportation, and such food is furnished not by small employers only, but by large manufacturers, who employ from thirty to forty apprentices. The custom seems to be universal in Wolverhampton, and its natural consequence is frequent bowel complaints and other diseases. Moreover, the children usually do not get enough to eat, and have rarely other clothing than their working rags, for which reason, if for no other, they cannot go to Sunday school. The dwellings are bad and filthy, often so much so that they give rise to disease; and in spite of the not materially unhealthy work, the children are puny,[a] weak, and, in many cases, severely crippled. In Willenhall, for instance, there are countless persons who have, from perpetually filing at the lathe, crooked backs and one leg crooked, "hind-leg" as they call it, so that the two legs have the form of a K; while it is said that more than one-third of the working-men there are ruptured. Here, as well as in Wolverhampton, numberless cases were found of retarded puberty among girls (for girls, too, work at the forges), as well as among boys, extending even to the nineteenth year. In Sedgeley and its surrounding district, where nails form almost the sole product, the nailers live and work in the most wretched stable-like huts, which for filth can scarcely be equalled. Girls and boys work from the tenth or twelfth year, and are accounted fully skilled only when they make a thousand nails a day. For twelve hundred nails the

---

* Grainger Report and Evidence.— *Note by Engels to the American edition of 1887.*

---

[a] The German editions of 1845 and 1892 have, instead of "puny", "small, badly built". Below, "hind-leg" is given in English.— *Ed.*

pay is $5^3/_4$d.[a] Every nail receives twelve blows, and since the hammer weighs $1^1/_4$ pounds, the nailer must lift 18,000 pounds to earn this miserable pay. With this hard work and insufficient food, the children inevitably develop ill-formed, undersized frames, and the commissioners' depositions confirm this. As to the state of education in this district, data have already been furnished in the foregoing chapters. It is upon an incredibly low plane; half the children do not even go to Sunday school, and the other half go irregularly; very few, in comparison with the other districts, can read, and in the matter of writing the case is much worse. Naturally, for between the seventh and tenth years, just when they are beginning to get some good out of going to school, they are set to work, and the Sunday school teachers, smiths or miners, frequently cannot read, and write their names with difficulty. The prevailing morals correspond with these means of education. In Willenhall, Commissioner Horne asserts, and supplies ample proofs of his assertion, that there exists absolutely no moral sense among the workers. In general, he found that the children neither recognised duties to their parents nor felt any affection for them. They were so little capable of thinking of what they said, so stolid, so hopelessly stupid, that they often asserted that they were well treated, were coming on famously, when they were forced to work twelve to fourteen hours, were clad in rags, did not get enough to eat, and were beaten so that they felt it several days afterwards. They knew nothing of a different kind of life than that in which they toil from morning until they are allowed to stop at night, and did not even understand the question never heard before, whether they were tired.*

In Sheffield wages are better, and the external state of the workers also. On the other hand, certain branches of work are to be noticed here, because of their extraordinarily injurious influence upon health. Certain operations require the constant pressure of tools against the chest, and engender consumption in many cases; others, file-cutting among them, retard the general development of the body and produce digestive disorders; bone-cutting for knife handles brings with it headache, biliousness, and among girls, of whom many are employed, anaemia. By far the most unwholesome work is the grinding of knife-blades and forks, which, especially when done with a dry stone, entails certain early death. The unwholesomeness of this work lies in part in the bent

---

* Horne Report and Evidence.— *Note by Engels to the American edition of 1887.*

[a] The German editions of 1845 and 1892 have here the explanation "or not quite 5 silver groschen".— *Ed.*

posture, in which chest and stomach are cramped; but especially in the quantity of sharp-edged metal dust particles freed in the cutting, which fill the atmosphere, and are necessarily inhaled. The dry grinders' average life is hardly thirty-five years, the wet grinders' rarely exceeds forty-five. Dr. Knight, in Sheffield, says*:

> I can convey some idea of the injuriousness of this occupation only by asserting that "the greatest drinkers among the grinders are sometimes the longest lived, owing to their more frequent absence from their work". Altogether the grinders in Sheffield "amount to about two thousand five hundred, of this number about one hundred and fifty, viz. eighty men and seventy boys, are fork grinders—these die from twenty-eight to thirty-two years of age. The razor grinders, grind both wet, and dry, and they die from forty to forty-five years of age. The table-knife grinders work on wet stones, and they live to betwixt forty and fifty years of age."

The same physician gives the following description of the course of the disease called grinders' asthma:

> "Those who are to be brought up grinders, usually begin to work when they are about fourteen years old. Grinders, who have good constitutions seldom experience much inconvenience from their trade until they arrive at about twenty years of age: about that time the symptoms of their peculiar complaint begin to steal upon them, their breathing becomes more than usually embarrassed on slight exertions, particularly on going upstairs or ascending a hill; their shoulders are elevated in order to relieve their constant and increasing dyspnoea; they stoop forward, and appear to breathe the most comfortably in that posture in which they are accustomed to sit at their work. Their complexions assume a muddy, dirty appearance; their countenance indicates anxiety; they complain of a sense of tightness across the chest; their voice is rough, and hoarse; their cough loud, and as if the air were drawn through wooden tubes; they occasionally expectorate considerable quantities of dust, sometimes mixed up with mucus, at other times in globular or cylindrical masses enveloped in a thin film of mucus. Haemoptysis, inability to lie down, night sweats, colignative diarrhoea, extreme emaciation, together with all the usual symptoms of pulmonary consumption at length carry them off; but not until they have lingered through months, and even years of suffering, incapable of working so as to support either themselves or their families." I must add that "all the attempts which have hitherto been made, to prevent or to cure the grinders' asthma, have utterly failed."

All this Knight wrote ten years ago[162]; since then the number of grinders and the violence of the disease have increased, though attempts have been made to prevent it by covered grindstones and carrying off the dust by artificial draught. These methods have been at least partially successful, but the grinders do not desire their adoption, and have even destroyed the contrivance here and there, in the belief that more workers may be attracted to the business and wages thus reduced; they are for a short life and a merry one. Dr. Knight has often told grinders who came to him with the first symptoms of asthma that a return to grinding means

* Dr. Knight, Sheffield.— *Note by Engels to the American edition of 1887.*

certain death, but with no avail. He who is once a grinder falls into despair, as though he had sold himself to the devil. Education in Sheffield is upon a very low plane; a clergyman, who had occupied himself largely with the statistics of education, was of the opinion that of 16,500 children of the working-class who are in a position to attend school, scarcely 6,500 can read. This comes of the fact that the children are taken from school in the seventh, and, at the very latest, in the twelfth year, and that the teachers are good for nothing; one was a convicted thief who found no other way of supporting himself after being released from jail than teaching school! Immorality among young people seems to be more prevalent in Sheffield than anywhere else. It is hard to tell which town ought to have the prize, and in reading the report one believes of each one that this certainly deserves it! The younger generation spend the whole of Sunday lying in the street tossing coins or fighting dogs, go regularly to the gin palace, where they sit with their sweethearts until late at night, when they take walks in solitary couples. In an ale-house which the commissioner visited, there sat forty to fifty young people of both sexes, nearly all under seventeen years of age, and each lad beside his lass. Here and there cards were played, at other places dancing was going on, and everywhere drinking. Among the company were openly avowed professional prostitutes. No wonder, then, that, as all the witnesses testify, early, unbridled sexual intercourse, youthful prostitution, beginning with persons of fourteen to fifteen years, is extraordinarily frequent in Sheffield. Crimes of a savage and desperate sort are of common occurrence; one year before the commissioner's visit, a band, consisting chiefly of young persons, was arrested when about to set fire to the town, being fully equipped with lances and inflammable substances. We shall see later that the labour movement in Sheffield has this same savage character.*

Besides these two main centres of the metal industry, there are needle factories in Warrington, Lancashire, where great want, immorality, and ignorance prevail among the workers, and especially among the children; and a number of nail forges in the neighbourhood of Wigan, in Lancashire, and in the east of Scotland. The reports from these latter districts tell almost precisely the same story as those of Staffordshire. There is one more branch of this industry carried on in the factory districts, especially in Lancashire, the essential peculiarity of which is the production of machinery by machinery, whereby the workers,

---

* Symons Report and Evidence.— *Note by Engels to the American edition of 1887.*

crowded out elsewhere, are deprived of their last refuge, the creation of the very enemy which supersedes them. Machinery for planing and boring, cutting screws, wheels, nuts, etc., with power lathes, has thrown out of employment a multitude of men who formerly found regular work at good wages; and whoever wishes to do so may see crowds of them in Manchester.

North of the iron district of Staffordshire lies an industrial region to which we shall now turn our attention, the Potteries,[a] whose headquarters are in the borough of Stoke, embracing Henley, Burslem, Lane End, Lane Delph, Etruria, Coleridge, Langport, Tunstall, and Golden Hill, containing together 70,000 inhabitants. The Children's Employment Commission reports upon this subject that in some branches of this industry, in the production of stoneware, the children have light employment in warm, airy rooms; in others, on the contrary, hard, wearing labour is required, while they receive neither sufficient food nor good clothing. Many children complain: "Don't get enough to eat, get mostly potatoes with salt, never meat, never bread, don't go to school, haven't got no clothes." "Haven't got nothin' to eat today for dinner, don't never have dinner at home, get mostly potatoes and salt, sometimes bread." "This is all the clothes I have, no Sunday suit at home." Among the children whose work is especially injurious are the mould-runners, who have to carry the moulded article with the form to the drying-room, and afterwards bring back the empty form, when the article is properly dried. Thus they must go to and fro the whole day, carrying burdens heavy in proportion to their age, while the high temperature in which they have to do this increases very considerably the exhaustiveness of the work. These children, with scarcely a single exception, are lean, pale, feeble, stunted; nearly all suffer from stomach troubles, nausea, want of appetite, and many of them die of consumption. Almost as delicate are the boys called "jiggers", from the "jigger" wheel which they turn. But by far the most injurious is the work of those who dip the finished article into a fluid containing great quantities of lead, and often of arsenic, or have to take the freshly dipped article up with the hand. The hands and clothing of these workers, adults and children, are always wet with this fluid, the skin softens and falls off under the constant contact with rough objects, so that the fingers often bleed, and are constantly in a state most favourable for the absorption of this dangerous substance. The consequence is violent pain,

[a] The German editions of 1845 and 1892 give the name Potteries and below "mould-runners" and "jiggers" in English.—Ed.

and serious disease of the stomach and intestines, obstinate constipation, colic, sometimes consumption, and, most common of all, epilepsy among children. Among men, partial paralysis of the hand muscles, colica pictorum,[a] and paralysis of whole limbs are ordinary phenomena. One witness relates that two children who worked with him died of convulsions at their work; another who had helped with the dipping two years while a boy, relates that he had violent pains in the bowels at first, then convulsions, in consequence of which he was confined to his bed two months, since when the attacks of convulsions have increased in frequency, are now daily, accompanied often by ten to twenty epileptic fits, his right arm is paralysed, and the physicians tell him that he can never regain the use of his limbs. In one factory were found in the dipping-house four men, all epileptic and afflicted with severe colic, and eleven boys, several of whom were already epileptic. In short, this frightful disease follows this occupation universally: and that, too, to the greater pecuniary profit of the bourgeoisie! In the rooms in which the stoneware is scoured, the atmosphere is filled with pulverised flint, the breathing of which is as injurious as that of the steel dust among the Sheffield grinders. The workers lose breath, cannot lie down, suffer from sore throat and violent coughing, and come to have so feeble a voice that they can scarcely be heard. They, too, all die of consumption. In the Potteries district, the schools are said to be comparatively numerous, and to offer the children opportunities for instruction; but as the latter are so early set to work for twelve hours and often more per day, they are not in a position to avail themselves of the schools, so that three-fourths of the children examined by the commissioner could neither read nor write, while the whole district is plunged in the deepest ignorance. Children who have attended Sunday school for years could not tell one letter from another, and the moral and religious education, as well as the intellectual, is on a very low plane.*

In the manufacture of glass, too, work occurs which seems little injurious to men, but cannot be endured by children. The hard labour, the irregularity of the hours, the frequent night-work, and especially the great heat of the working place (100 to 130 Fahrenheit), engender in children general debility and disease, stunted growth, and especially affections of the eye, bowel complaint, and rheumatic and bronchial affections. Many of the

---

* Scriven Report and Evidence.— *Note by Engels to the American edition of 1887.*

[a] A professional disease of dyers.— *Ed.*

children are pale, have red eyes, often blind for weeks at a time, suffer from violent nausea, vomiting, coughs, colds, and rheumatism. When the glass is withdrawn from the fire, the children must often go into such heat that the boards on which they stand catch fire under their feet. The glass-blowers usually die young of debility and chest affections.*

As a whole, this report testifies to the gradual but sure introduction of the factory system into all branches of industry, recognisable especially by the employment of women and children. I have not thought it necessary to trace in every case the progress of machinery and the superseding of men as workers. Every one who is in any degree acquainted with the nature of manufacture can fill this out for himself, while space fails me to describe in detail an aspect of our present system of production, the result of which I have already sketched in dealing with the factory system. In all directions machinery is being introduced, and the last trace of the working-man's independence thus destroyed. In all directions the family is being dissolved by the labour of wife and children, or inverted by the husband's being thrown out of employment and made dependent upon them for bread[a]; everywhere inevitable machinery bestows upon the great capitalist command of trade and of the workers with it. The centralisation of capital[b] strides forward without interruption, the division of society into great capitalists and non-possessing workers is sharper every day, the industrial development of the nation advances with giant strides towards the inevitable crisis.

I have already stated that in the handicrafts the power of capital, and in some cases the division of labour too, has produced the same results, crushed the small tradesmen, and put great capitalists and non-possessing workers in their place. As to these handicraftsmen there is little to be said, since all that relates to them has already found its place where the proletariat in general[c] was under discussion. There has been but little change here in the

---

* Leifchild Report Append., Part II., p. L 2, ss. 11, 12; Franks Report Append., Part II., p. K 7, s. 48; Tancred Evid. Append., Part II., p. I 76, etc. } Children's Employment Commission's Rep't.
Note by Engels to the American edition of 1887.

[a] The German editions of 1845 and 1892 do not have the phrase "and made dependent upon them for bread".—*Ed.*

[b] The German editions of 1845 and 1892 have "property" instead of "capital".—*Ed.*

[c] The German editions of 1845 and 1892 have "the industrial proletariat in general".—*Ed.*

nature of the work and its influence upon health since the beginning of the industrial movement. But the constant contact with the factory operatives, the pressure of the great capitalists, which is much more felt than that of the small employer to whom the apprentice still stood in a more or less personal relation, the influences of life in towns, and the fall of wages, have made nearly all the handicraftsmen active participators in labour movements. We shall soon have more to say on this point, and turn meanwhile to one section of workers in London who deserve our attention by reason of the extraordinary barbarity with which they are exploited by the money-greed of the bourgeoisie. I mean the dress-makers and sewing-women.

It is a curious fact that the production of precisely those articles which serve the personal adornment of the ladies of the bourgeoisie involves the saddest consequences for the health of the workers. We have already seen this in the case of the lace-makers, and come now to the dress-making establishments of London for further proof. They employ a mass of young girls — there are said to be 15,000 of them in all — who sleep and eat on the premises, come usually from the country, and are therefore absolutely the slaves of their employers. During the fashionable season, which lasts some four months, working-hours, even in the best establishments, are fifteen, and, in very pressing cases, eighteen a day; but in most shops work goes on at these times without any set regulation, so that the girls never have more than six, often not more than three or four, sometimes, indeed, not more than two hours in the twenty-four, for rest and sleep, working nineteen to twenty-two hours, if not the whole night through, as frequently happens! The only limit set to their work is the absolute physical inability to hold the needle another minute. Cases have occurred in which these helpless creatures did not undress during nine consecutive days and nights, and could only rest a moment or two here and there upon a mattress, where food was served them ready cut up in order to require the least possible time for swallowing. In short, these unfortunate girls are kept by means of the moral whip of the modern slave-driver,[a] the threat of discharge, to such long and unbroken toil as no strong man, much less a delicate girl of fourteen to twenty years, can endure. In addition to this, the foul air of the work-room and sleeping-places, the bent posture, the often bad and indigestible food, all these causes,[b]

---

[a] The German editions of 1845 and 1892 have "the moral slave-driver's whip".— Ed.

[b] The German editions of 1845 and 1892 have here "but above all the long hours of work".— Ed.

combined with almost total exclusion from fresh air, entail the saddest consequences for the health of the girls. Enervation, exhaustion, debility, loss of appetite, pains in the shoulders, back, and hips, but especially headache, begin very soon; then follow curvatures of the spine, high, deformed shoulders, leanness, swelled, weeping, and smarting eyes, which soon become short-sighted; coughs, narrow chests, and shortness of breath, and all manner of disorders in the development of the female organism. In many cases the eyes suffer so severely that incurable blindness[a] follows; but if the sight remains strong enough to make continued work possible, consumption usually soon ends the sad life of these milliners and dress-makers. Even those who leave this work at an early age retain permanently injured health, a broken constitution; and, when married, bring feeble and sickly children into the world. All the medical men interrogated by the commissioner[b] agreed that no method of life could be invented better calculated to destroy health and induce early death.

With the same cruelty, though somewhat more indirectly, the rest of the needle-women of London are exploited. The girls employed in stay-making have a hard, wearing occupation, trying to the eyes. And what wages do they get? I do not know; but this I know, that the middleman who has to give security for the material delivered, and who distributes the work among the needle-women, receives $1^1/_2$d.[c] per piece. From this he deducts his own pay, at least $^1/_2$d., so that 1d. at most reaches the pocket of the girl. The girls who sew neckties must bind themselves to work sixteen hours a day, and receive $4^1/_2$s. a week.* But the shirt-makers' lot is the worst. They receive for an ordinary shirt $1^1/_2$d., formerly 2d.-3d.; but since the workhouse of St. Pancras, which is administered by a Radical board of guardians, began to undertake work at $1^1/_2$d., the poor women outside have been compelled to do the same. For fine, fancy shirts, which can be made in one day of eighteen hours, 6d. is paid.[d] The weekly wage of these sewing-

---

* See *Weekly Dispatch*, March 17th, 1844.—*Note by Engels*. (The German editions of 1845 and 1892 have "i.e., $1^1/_2$ Prussian talers, but this sum can buy no more than 20 silver groschen can in the most expensive German town."—*Ed.*)

---

[a] The German editions of 1845 and 1892 also have here "complete disablement of the eye".—*Ed.*

[b] The German editions of 1845 and 1892 give here in brackets "Ch. Empl. Comm.".—*Ed.*

[c] The German editions of 1845 and 1892 have here "i.e., 15 Prussian pfennigs".—*Ed.*

[d] The German editions of 1845 and 1892 have "i.e., 5 silver groschen".—*Ed.*

women according to this and according to testimony from many sides, including both needle-women and employers, is 2s. 6d. to 3s. for most strained work continued far into the night. And what crowns this shameful barbarism is the fact that the women must give a money deposit for a part of the materials entrusted to them, which they naturally cannot do unless they pawn a part of them (as the employers very well know), redeeming them at a loss; or if they cannot redeem the materials, they must appear before a Justice of the Peace, as happened to a sewing-woman in November, 1843. A poor girl who got into this strait and did not know what to do next, drowned herself in a canal in 1844.[a] These women usually live in little garret rooms in the utmost distress, where as many crowd together as the space can possibly admit, and where, in winter, the animal warmth of the workers is the only heat obtainable. Here they sit bent over their work, sewing from four or five in the morning until midnight, destroying their health in a year or two and ending in an early grave; without being able to obtain the poorest necessities of life meanwhile.* And below them roll the brilliant equipages of the upper bourgeoisie, and perhaps ten steps away some pitiable dandy loses more money in one evening at faro than they can earn in a year.

* * *

Such is the condition of the English manufacturing proletariat. In all directions, whithersoever we may turn, we find want and disease permanent or temporary, and demoralisation arising from the condition of the workers[b]; in all directions slow but sure undermining, and final destruction of the human being physically as well as mentally. Is this a state of things which can last? It cannot and will not last. The workers, the great majority of the nation, will not endure it. Let us see what they say of it.

---

* Thomas Hood, the most talented of all the English humorists now living, and, like all humorists, full of human feeling, but wanting in mental energy, published at the beginning of 1844 a beautiful poem, *The Song of the Shirt*, which drew sympathetic but unavailing tears from the eyes of the daughters of the bourgeoisie. Originally published in *Punch*, it made the round of all the papers. As discussions of the condition of the sewing-women filled all the papers at the time, special extracts are needless.—*Note by Engels.* (The German editions of 1845 and 1892 have "when accounts of the distress among the sewing-women filled all the papers" after "at the beginning of 1844" and "I have not sufficient space to reproduce the poem here" after "the daughters of the bourgeoisie".—*Ed.*)

---

[a] The German editions of 1845 and 1892 have "in August 1844".—*Ed.*
[b] The German editions of 1845 and 1892 have here "we find want, permanent or temporary, disease caused by their condition or their work, demoralisation".—*Ed.*

LABOUR MOVEMENTS

It must be admitted, even if I had not proved it so often in detail, that the English workers cannot feel happy in this condition; that theirs is not a state in which a man or a whole class of men can think, feel, and live as human beings. The workers must therefore strive to escape from this brutalising condition, to secure for themselves a better, more human position; and this they cannot do without attacking the interest of the bourgeoisie which consists in exploiting them. But the bourgeoisie defends its interests with all the power placed at its disposal by wealth and the might of the State. In proportion as the working-man determines to alter the present state of things, the bourgeois becomes his avowed enemy.

Moreover, the working-man is made to feel at every moment that the bourgeoisie treats him as a chattel, as its property, and for this reason, if for no other, he must come forward as its enemy. I have shown in a hundred ways in the foregoing pages, and could have shown in a hundred others, that, in our present society, he can save his manhood only in hatred and rebellion against the bourgeoisie. And he can protest with most violent passion against the tyranny of the propertied class, thanks to his education, or rather want of education, and to the abundance of hot Irish blood that flows in the veins of the English working-class. The English working-man is no Englishman nowadays; no calculating money-grubber like his wealthy neighbour. He possesses more fully developed feelings, his native northern coldness is overborne by the unrestrained development of his passions and their control over him. The cultivation of the understanding which so greatly strengthens the selfish tendency of the English bourgeois, which has made selfishness his predominant trait and concentrated all his emotional power upon the single point of money-greed, is wanting in the working-man, whose passions are therefore strong and mighty as those of the foreigner. English nationality is annihilated in the working-man.

Since, as we have seen, no single field for the exercise of his manhood is left him, save his opposition to the whole conditions of his life, it is natural that exactly in this opposition he should be most manly, noblest, most worthy of sympathy. We shall see that all the energy, all the activity of the working-men is directed to this point, and that even their attempts to attain general education all stand in direct connection with this. True, we shall have single acts of violence and even of brutality to report, but it must always be kept in mind that the social war is avowedly raging in England; and that, whereas it is in the interest of the bourgeoisie to conduct this war hypocritically, under the disguise of peace and even of philanthropy, the only help for the working-men consists in laying bare the true state of things and destroying this hypocrisy; that the most violent attacks of the workers upon the bourgeoisie and its servants are only the open, undisguised expression of that which the bourgeoisie perpetrates secretly, treacherously against the workers.

The revolt of the workers began soon after the first industrial development, and has passed through several phases. The investigation of their importance in the history of the English people I must reserve for separate treatment,[163] limiting myself meanwhile to such bare facts as serve to characterise the condition of the English proletariat.

The earliest, crudest, and least fruitful form of this rebellion was that of crime. The working-man lived in poverty and want, and saw that others were better off than he. It was not clear to his mind why he, who did more for society than the rich idler, should be the one to suffer under these conditions. Want conquered his inherited respect for the sacredness of property, and he stole. We have seen how crime increased with the extension of manufacture; how the yearly number of arrests bore a constant relation to the number of bales of cotton annually consumed.

The workers soon realised that crime did not help matters. The criminal could protest against the existing order of society only singly, as one individual; the whole might of society was brought to bear upon each criminal, and crushed him with its immense superiority. Besides, theft was the most primitive[a] form of

---

[a] The German editions of 1845 and 1892 have "and the most instinctive".— Ed.

protest, and for this reason, if for no other, it never became the universal expression of the public opinion of the working-men, however much they might approve of it in silence. As a class, they first manifested opposition to the bourgeoisie when they resisted the introduction of machinery at the very beginning of the industrial period. The first inventors, Arkwright and others, were persecuted in this way and their machines destroyed. Later, there took place a number of revolts against machinery, in which the occurrences were almost precisely the same as those of the printers' disturbances in Bohemia in 1844[164]; factories were demolished and machinery destroyed.

This form of opposition also was isolated, restricted to certain localities, and directed against one feature only of our present social arrangements. When the momentary end was attained, the whole weight of social power fell upon the unprotected evil-doers and punished them to its heart's content, while the machinery was introduced none the less. A new form of opposition had to be found.

At this point help came in the shape of a law enacted by the old, unreformed, oligarchic-Tory Parliament, a law which never could have passed the House of Commons later, when the Reform Bill had legally sanctioned the distinction between bourgeoisie and proletariat, and made the bourgeoisie the ruling class. This was enacted in 1824, and repealed all laws by which coalitions between working-men for labour purposes had hitherto been forbidden. The working-men obtained a right previously restricted to the aristocracy and bourgeoisie, the right of free association. Secret coalitions had, it is true, previously existed, but could never achieve great results. In Glasgow[a] as Symons* relates, a general strike of weavers had taken place in 1812, which was brought about by a secret association. It was repeated in 1822, and on this occasion vitriol was thrown into the faces of the two working-men who would not join the association, and were therefore regarded by the members as traitors to their class. Both the assaulted lost the use of their eyes in consequence of the injury. So, too, in 1818, the association of Scottish miners was powerful enough to carry on a general strike. These associations required their

---

* *Arts and Artisans*, p. 137, *et seq.*— *Note by Engels to the American edition of 1887* (reproduced in the English edition of 1892; in the German editions of 1845 and 1892 this and similar references are, generally, given in the text—*Ed.*).

---

[a] The German editions of 1845 and 1892 have "In Scotland".—*Ed.*

members to take an oath of fidelity and secrecy, had regular lists, treasurers, book-keepers, and local branches. But the secrecy with which everything was conducted crippled their growth. When, on the other hand, the working-men received in 1824 the right of free association, these combinations were very soon spread over all England and attained great power. In all branches of industry Trades Unions[a] were formed with the outspoken intention of protecting the single working-man against the tyranny and neglect of the bourgeoisie. Their objects were to deal,[b] *en masse*, as a power, with the employers; to regulate the rate of wages according to the profit of the latter, to raise it when opportunity offered, and to keep it uniform in each trade throughout the country. Hence they tried to settle with the capitalists a scale of wages to be universally adhered to, and ordered out on strike the employees of such individuals as refused to accept the scale. They aimed further to keep up the demand for labour by limiting the number of apprentices, and so to keep wages high; to counteract, as far as possible, the indirect wages reductions which the manufacturers brought about by means of new tools and machinery; and finally, to assist unemployed working-men financially. This they do either directly or by means of a card to legitimate the bearer as a "society man", and with which the working-man wanders from place to place, supported by his fellow-workers, and instructed as to the best opportunity for finding employment. This is tramping, and the wanderer a tramp. To attain these ends, a President and Secretary are engaged at a salary (since it is to be expected that no manufacturer will employ such persons), and a committee collects the weekly contributions and watches over their expenditure for the purposes of the association. When it proved possible and advantageous, the various trades of single districts united in a federation and held delegate conventions at set times. The attempt has been made in single cases to unite the workers of one branch over all England in one great Union; and several times (in 1830 for the first time) to form one universal trades association for the whole United Kingdom, with a separate organisation for each trade. These associations, however, never held together long, and were seldom realised even for the moment, since an exceptionally

---

[a] The German editions of 1845 and 1892 give the words: "Trades Unions", "the tramp", "strike", "turnout", "knobsticks" "thugs", etc., in English, often in brackets after the German equivalents.— *Ed*.

[b] The German edition of 1845 and 1892 have here: "Their objects were to fix wages and to deal", etc.— *Ed*.

universal excitement is necessary to make such a federation possible and effective.

The means usually employed by these Unions for attaining their ends are the following: If one or more employers refuse to pay the wage specified by the Union, a deputation is sent or a petition forwarded (the working-men, you see, know how to recognise the absolute power of the lord of the factory in his little State); if this proves unavailing, the Union commands the employees to stop work, and all hands go home. This strike is either partial when one or several, or general when all employers in the trade refuse to regulate wages according to the proposals of the Union. So far go the lawful means of the Union, assuming the strike to take effect after the expiration of the legal notice, which is not always the case. But these lawful means are very weak when there are workers outside the Union, or when members separate from it for the sake of the momentary advantage offered by the bourgeoisie. Especially in the case of partial strikes can the manufacturer readily secure recruits from these black sheep (who are known as knobsticks), and render fruitless the efforts of the united workers. Knobsticks are usually threatened, insulted, beaten, or otherwise maltreated by the members of the Union; intimidated, in short, in every way. Prosecution follows, and as the law-abiding bourgeoisie has the power in its own hands, the force of the Union is broken almost every time by the first unlawful act, the first judicial procedure against its members.

The history of these Unions is a long series of defeats of the working-men, interrupted by a few isolated victories. All these efforts naturally cannot alter the economic law according to which wages are determined by the relation between supply and demand in the labour market. Hence the Unions remain powerless against all *great* forces which influence this relation. In a commercial crisis the Union itself must reduce wages or dissolve wholly; and in a time of considerable increase in the demand for labour, it cannot fix the rate of wages higher than would be reached spontaneously by the competition of the capitalists among themselves. But in dealing with minor, single influences they are powerful. If the employer had no concentrated, collective opposition to expect, he would in his own interest gradually reduce wages to a lower and lower point; indeed, the battle of competition which he has to wage against his fellow-manufacturers would force him to do so, and wages would soon reach the minimum. But this competition of the manufacturers among themselves is, *under average conditions,* somewhat restricted by the opposition of the working-men.

Every manufacturer knows that the consequence of a reduction not justified by conditions to which his competitors also are subjected, would be a strike, which would most certainly injure him, because his capital would be idle as long as the strike lasted, and his machinery would be rusting, whereas it is very doubtful whether he could, in such a case, enforce his reduction. Then he has the certainty that if he should succeed, his competitors would follow him, reducing the price of the goods so produced, and thus depriving him of the benefit of his policy. Then, too, the Unions often bring about a more rapid increase of wages after a crisis than would otherwise follow. For the manufacturer's interest is to delay raising wages until forced by competition, but now the working-men demand an increased wage as soon as the market improves, and they can carry their point by reason of the smaller supply of workers at his command under such circumstances. But, for resistance to more considerable forces which influence the labour market, the Unions are powerless. In such cases hunger gradually drives the strikers to resume work on any terms, and when once a few have begun, the force of the Union is broken, because these few knobsticks, with the reserve supplies of goods in the market, enable the bourgeoisie to overcome the worst effects of the interruption of business. The funds of the Union are soon exhausted by the great numbers requiring relief, the credit which the shopkeepers give at high interest is withdrawn after a time, and want compels the working-man to place himself once more under the yoke of the bourgeoisie. But strikes end disastrously for the workers mostly, because the manufacturers, in their own interest (which has, be it said, become their interest only through the resistance of the workers), are obliged to avoid all useless reductions, while the workers feel in every reduction imposed by the state of trade a deterioration of their condition, against which they must defend themselves as far as in them lies.

It will be asked, "Why, then, do the workers strike in such cases, when the uselessness of such measures is so evident?" Simply because they *must* protest against every reduction, even if dictated by necessity; because they feel bound to proclaim that they, as human beings, shall not be made to bow to social circumstances, but social conditions ought to yield to them as human beings; because silence on their part would be a recognition of these social conditions, an admission of the right of the bourgeoisie to exploit the workers in good times and let them starve in bad ones. Against this the working-men must rebel so long as they have not lost all human feeling, and that they protest in this way and no other, comes of their being practical English people, who express themselves in *action*, and do not, like German theorists, go to sleep as soon as their protest is properly registered and placed *ad acta*, there to sleep as quietly as the protesters themselves. The active resistance of the English working-men has its effect in holding the money-greed of the bourgeoisie within certain limits, and keeping alive the opposition of the workers to the social and political omnipotence of the bourgeoisie, while it compels the admission that something more is needed than Trades Unions and strikes to break the power of the ruling class. But what gives these Unions and the strikes arising from them their real importance is this, that they are the first attempt of the workers to abolish competition. They imply the recognition of the fact that the supremacy of the bourgeoisie is based wholly upon the competition of the workers among themselves; i.e., upon their want of cohesion.[a] And precisely because the Unions direct themselves against the vital nerve of the present social order,[b] however one-sidedly, in however narrow a way, are they so dangerous to this social order. The working-men cannot attack the bourgeoisie, and with it the whole existing order of society, at any sorer point than this. If the competition of the workers among themselves is destroyed, if all determine not to be further exploited by the bourgeoisie, the rule of property is at an end. Wages depend upon the relation of demand to supply, upon the accidental state of the labour market, simply because the workers have hitherto been content to be treated as chattels, to be bought and sold. The moment the workers resolve to be bought and sold no longer, when, in the determination of the value of labour, they take the part of men possessed of a will as well as of working-power, at that moment the whole Political Economy of today is at an end.[c]

The laws determining the rate of wages would, indeed, come into force again in the long run, if the working-men did not go beyond this step of abolishing competition among themselves. But they must go beyond that unless they are prepared to recede again and to allow competition among themselves to reappear. Thus once advanced so far, necessity compels them to go farther; to abolish not only one kind of competition, but competition itself altogether, and that they will do.

---

[a] The German editions of 1845 and 1892 have "and "the setting of individual workers against one another".—*Ed.*

[b] The German editions of 1845 and 1892 have here "against competition, against the vital nerve", etc.—*Ed.*

[c] The German editions of 1845 and 1892 have "the whole Political Economy of today and the laws determining wages are at an end".—*Ed.*

The workers are coming to perceive more clearly with every day how competition affects them; they see far more clearly than the bourgeois that competition of the capitalists among themselves presses upon the workers too, by bringing on commercial crises, and that this kind of competition, too, must be abolished. They will soon learn *how* they have to go about it.

That these Unions contribute greatly to nourish the bitter hatred of the workers against the property-holding class need hardly be said. From them proceed, therefore, with or without the connivance of the leading members, in times of unusual excitement, individual actions which can be explained only by hatred wrought to the pitch of despair, by a wild passion overwhelming all restraints. Of this sort are the attacks with vitriol mentioned in the foregoing pages, and a series of others, of which I shall cite several. In 1831, during a violent labour movement, young Ashton, a manufacturer in Hyde, near Manchester, was shot one evening when crossing a field, and no trace of the assassin discovered. There is no doubt that this was a deed of vengeance of the working-men.[165] Incendiarisms and attempted explosions are very common. On Friday, September 29th, 1843, an attempt was made to blow up the saw-works of Padgin, in Howard Street, Sheffield. A closed iron tube filled with powder was the means employed, and the damage was considerable. On the following day, a similar attempt was made in Ibbetson's knife and file works at Shales Moor, near Sheffield. Mr. Ibbetson had made himself obnoxious by an active participation in bourgeois movements, by low wages, the exclusive employment of knobsticks, and the exploitation of the Poor Law for his own benefit. He had reported, during the crisis of 1842, such operatives as refused to accept reduced wages, as persons who could find work but would not take it, and were, therefore, not deserving of relief, so compelling the acceptance of a reduction. Considerable damage was inflicted by the explosion, and all the working-men who came to view it regretted only "that the whole concern was not blown into the air". On Friday, October 6th, 1843, an attempt to set fire to the factory of Ainsworth and Crompton, at Bolton, did no damage; it was the third or fourth attempt in the same factory within a very short time. In the meeting of the Town Council of Sheffield, on Wednesday, January 10th, 1844, the Commissioner of Police exhibited a cast-iron machine, made for the express purpose of producing an explosion, and found filled with four pounds of powder, and a fuse which had been lighted but had not taken effect, in the works of Mr. Kitchen, Earl Street, Sheffield.

On Sunday, January 21st, 1844, an explosion caused by a package of powder took place in the sawmill of Bentley & White, at Bury, in Lancashire, and produced considerable damage. On Thursday, February 1st, 1844, the Soho Wheel Works, in Sheffield, were set on fire and burnt up.

Here are six such cases in four months, all of which have their sole origin in the embitterment of the working-men against the employers. What sort of a social state it must be in which such things are possible I need hardly say. These facts are proof enough that in England, even in good business years, such as 1843, the social war is avowed and openly carried on, and still the English bourgeoisie does not stop to reflect! But the case which speaks most loudly is that of the Glasgow Thugs,* which came up before the Assizes from the 3rd to the 11th of January, 1838. It appears from the proceedings that the Cotton-Spinners' Union, which existed here from the year 1816, possessed rare organisation and power. The members were bound by an oath to adhere to the decision of the majority, and had during every turnout a secret committee which was unknown to the mass of the members, and controlled the funds of the Union absolutely. This committee fixed a price upon the heads of knobsticks and obnoxious manufacturers and upon incendiarisms in mills. A mill was thus set on fire in which female knobsticks were employed in spinning in the place of men; a Mrs. M'Pherson, mother of one of these girls, was murdered, and both murderers sent to America at the expense of the association. As early as 1820, a knobstick named M'Quarry was shot at and wounded, for which deed the doer received twenty pounds from the Union, but was discovered and transported for life.[a] Finally, in 1837, in May, disturbances occurred in consequence of a turnout in the Oatbank and Mile End factories, in which perhaps a dozen knobsticks were maltreated. In July, of the same year, the disturbances still continued, and a certain Smith, a knobstick, was so maltreated that he died. The committee was now arrested, an investigation begun, and the leading members found guilty of participation in conspiracies, maltreatment of knobsticks, and incendiarism in the mill of James

---

* So called from the East Indian tribe, whose only trade is the murder of all the strangers who fall into its hands.— Note by Engels.

---

[a] In the German editions of 1845 and 1892 this passage reads: "for which the doer received fifteen pounds from the Union. Later a certain Graham was shot at; the doer received twenty pounds, but was discovered and transported for life."— Ed.

and Francis Wood, and they were transported for seven years.
What do our good Germans say to this story?*

The property-holding class, and especially the manufacturing
portion of it which comes into direct contact with the working-men,
declaims with the greatest violence against these Unions, and is
constantly trying to prove their uselessness to the working-men
upon grounds which are economically perfectly correct, but for
that very reason partially mistaken, and for the working-man's
understanding totally without effect. The very zeal of the
bourgeoisie shows that it is not disinterested in the matter; and
apart from the direct loss involved in a turnout, the state of the
case is such that whatever goes into the pockets of the manufacturers comes of necessity out of those of the worker. So that even if
the working-men did not know that the Unions hold the emulation of their masters in the reduction of wages, at least in a
measure, in check, they would still stand by the Unions, simply to
the injury of their enemies, the manufacturers. In war the injury
of one party is the benefit of the other, and since the working-
men are on a war footing towards their employers, they do merely
what the great potentates do when they get into a quarrel. Beyond
all other bourgeois is our friend Dr. Ure, the most furious enemy
of the Unions. He foams with indignation at the "secret tribunals"
of the cotton-spinners, the most powerful section of the workers,
tribunals which boast their ability to paralyse every disobedient
manufacturer,** "and so bring ruin on the man who had given
them profitable employment for many a year". He speaks of a
time*** "when the inventive head and the sustaining heart of
trade were held in bondage by the unruly lower members". A pity
that the English working-men will not let themselves be pacified so
easily with thy fable as the Roman Plebs, thou modern Menenius
Agrippa! [166] Finally, he relates the following: At one time the

* "What kind of wild justice must it be in the hearts of these men that
prompts them, with cold deliberation, in conclave assembled, to doom their brother
workman, as the deserter of his order and his order's cause, to die as a traitor and
deserter; and have him executed, since not by any public judge and hangman, then
by a private one; — like your old Chivalry *Femgericht*, and Secret-Tribunal,
suddenly in this strange guise become new; suddenly rising once more on the
astonished eye, dressed now not in mail-shirts, but in fustian jackets, meeting not in
Westphalian forests but in the paved Gallowgate of Glasgow!... Such temper must
be widespread, virulent among the many, when even in its worst acme, it can take
such a form in a few."—Carlyle, *Chartism*, p. 40.— *Note by Engels.*

** Dr. Ure, *Philosophy of Manufactures*, p. 282.— *Note by Engels to the American
edition of 1887.*

*** Ibid., p. 282.— *Note by Engels to the American edition of 1887.*

coarse mule-spinners had misused their power beyond all endurance. High wages, instead of awakening thankfulness towards the manufacturers and leading to intellectual improvement (in harmless study of sciences useful to the bourgeoisie, of course), in many cases produced pride and supplied funds for supporting rebellious spirits in strikes, with which a number of manufacturers were visited one after the other in a purely arbitrary manner. During an unhappy disturbance of this sort in Hyde, Dukinfield, and the surrounding neighbourhood, the manufacturers of the district, anxious lest they should be driven from the market by the French, Belgians, and Americans, addressed themselves to the machine-works of Sharp, Roberts & Co., and requested Mr. Sharp to turn his inventive mind to the construction of an automatic mule in order "to emancipate the trade from galling slavery and impending ruin".*

"He produced in the course of a few months, a machine apparently instinct with the thought, feeling, and tact of the experienced workman — which even in its infancy displayed a new principle of regulation, ready in its mature state to fulfil the functions of a finished spinner.[a] Thus, the Iron Man, as the operatives fitly call it, sprang out of the hands of our modern Prometheus at the bidding of Minerva — a creation destined to restore order among the industrious classes, and to confirm to Great Britain the empire of art. The news of this Herculean prodigy spread dismay through the Union, and even long before it left its cradle, so to speak, it strangled the Hydra of misrule."**

Ure proves further that the invention of the machine, with which four and five colours are printed at once, was a result of the disturbances among the calico printers; that the refractoriness of the yarn-dressers in the power-loom weaving mills gave rise to a new and perfected machine for warp-dressing, and mentions several other such cases. A few pages earlier this same Ure gives himself a great deal of trouble to prove in detail that machinery is beneficial to the workers! But Ure is not the only one; in the Factory Report, Mr. Ashworth, the manufacturer, and many another, lose no opportunity to express their wrath against the Unions. These wise bourgeois, like certain governments, trace every movement which they do not understand to the influence of ill-intentioned agitators, demagogues, traitors, spouting idiots, and

* Dr. Ure, *Philosophy of Manufactures*, p. 367.— Note by Engels to the American edition of 1887.
** Ibid., p. 366, *et seq.*—Note by Engels to the American edition of 1887. (In the German editions this footnote is given to the words "several other such cases".—*Ed.*)

[a] The German editions give the quotation abridged, the part of the sentence following the dash being omitted.— *Ed.*

ill-balanced youth.[a] They declare that the paid agents of the Unions are interested in the agitation because they live upon it, as though the necessity for this payment were not forced upon them by the bourgeois, who will give such men no employment!

The incredible frequency of these strikes proves best of all to what extent the social war has broken out all over England. No week passes, scarcely a day, indeed, in which there is not a strike in some direction, now against a reduction, then against a refusal to raise the rate of wages, again by reason of the employment of knobsticks or the continuance of abuses, sometimes against new machinery, or for a hundred other reasons. These strikes, at first skirmishes, sometimes result in weighty struggles; they decide nothing, it is true, but they are the strongest proof that the decisive battle between bourgeoisie and proletariat is approaching. They are the military school of the working-men in which they prepare themselves for the great struggle which cannot be avoided; they are the pronunciamentos of single branches of industry that these too have joined the labour movement. And when one examines a year's file of the *Northern Star,* the only sheet which reports all the movements of the proletariat, one finds that all the proletarians of the towns and of country manufacture have united in associations, and have protested from time to time, by means of a general strike, against the supremacy of the bourgeoisie. And as schools of war, the Unions are unexcelled. In them is developed the peculiar courage of the English. It is said on the Continent that the English, and especially the working-men, are cowardly, that they cannot carry out a revolution because, unlike the French, they do not riot at intervals, because they apparently accept the bourgeois *régime* so quietly. This is a complete mistake. The English working-men are second to none in courage; they are quite as restless as the French, but they fight differently. The French, who are by nature political, struggle against social evils with political weapons; the English, for whom politics exist only as a matter of interest, solely in the interest of bourgeois society, fight, not against the Government, but directly against the bourgeoisie; and for the time, this can be done only in a peaceful manner. Stagnation in business, and the want consequent upon it, engendered the revolt at Lyons, in 1834, in favour of the Republic: in 1842, at Manchester, a similar cause gave rise to a universal turnout for the Charter and higher wages. That

---

[a] The German editions of 1845 and 1892 have "to the influence of ill-intentioned agitators, malefactors, demagogues, spouting idiots and young people".— *Ed.*

courage is required for a turnout, often indeed much loftier courage, much bolder, firmer determination than for an insurrection, is self-evident. It is, in truth, no trifle for a working-man who knows want from experience, to face it with wife and children, to endure hunger and wretchedness for months together, and stand firm and unshaken through it all. What is death, what the galleys which await the French revolutionist, in comparison with gradual starvation, with the daily sight of a starving family, with the certainty of future revenge on the part of the bourgeoisie, all of which the English working-man chooses in preference to subjection under the yoke of the property-holding class? We shall meet later an example of this obstinate, unconquerable courage of men who surrender to force only when all resistance would be aimless and unmeaning. And precisely in this quiet perseverance, in this lasting determination which undergoes a hundred tests every day, the English working-man develops that side of his character which commands most respect. People who endure so much to bend one single bourgeois will be able to break the power of the whole bourgeoisie.

But apart from that, the English working-man has proved his courage often enough. That the turnout of 1842 had no further results came from the fact that the men were in part forced into it by the bourgeoisie, in part neither clear nor united as to its object. But aside from this, they have shown their courage often enough when the matter in question was a specific social one. Not to mention the Welsh insurrection of 1839, a complete battle was waged in Manchester in May, 1843, during my residence there.[167] Pauling & Henfrey, a brick firm, had increased the size of the bricks without raising wages, and sold the bricks, of course, at a higher price. The workers, to whom higher wages were refused, struck work, and the Brickmakers' Union declared war upon the firm. The firm, meanwhile, succeeded with great difficulty in securing hands from the neighbourhood, and among the knobsticks, against whom in the beginning intimidation was used; the proprietors set twelve men to guard the yard, all ex-soldiers and policemen, armed with guns. When intimidation proved unavailing, the brick-yard, which lay scarcely four hundred paces from an infantry barracks, was stormed at ten o'clock one night by a crowd of brickmakers, who advanced in military order, the first ranks armed with guns.* They forced their way in, fired upon the

---

* At the corner of Cross Lane and Regent Road. See map of Manchester.— *Note by Engels* (not given in the American and English editions—*Ed*.).

watchmen as soon as they saw them, stamped out the wet bricks spread out to dry, tore down the piled-up rows of those already dry, demolished everything which came in their way, pressed into a building, where they destroyed the furniture and maltreated the wife of the overlooker who was living there. The watchmen, meanwhile, had placed themselves behind a hedge, whence they could fire safely and without interruption. The assailants stood before a burning brick-kiln, which threw a bright light upon them, so that every ball of their enemies struck home, while every one of their own shots missed its mark. Nevertheless, the firing lasted half-an-hour, until the ammunition was exhausted, and the object of the visit—the demolition of all the destructible objects in the yard—was attained. Then the military approached, and the brickmakers withdrew to Eccles, three miles from Manchester. A short time before reaching Eccles they held roll-call, and each man was called according to his number in the section when they separated, only to fall the more certainly into the hands of the police, who were approaching from all sides. The number of the wounded must have been very considerable, but those only could be counted who were arrested. One of these had received three bullets (in the thigh, the calf, and the shoulder), and had travelled in spite of them more than four miles on foot. These people have proved that they, too, possess revolutionary courage, and do not shun a rain of bullets. And when an unarmed multitude, without a precise aim common to them all, are held in check in a shut-off market-place, whose outlets are guarded by a couple of policemen and dragoons, as happened in 1842, this by no means proves a want of courage. On the contrary, the multitude would have stirred quite as little if the servants of public (i.e., of the bourgeois) order had not been present. Where the working-people have a specific end in view, they show courage enough; as, for instance, in the attack upon Birley's mill, which had later to be protected by artillery.[168]

In this connection, a word or two as to the respect for the law in England. True, the law is sacred to the bourgeois, for it is his own composition, enacted with his consent, and for his benefit and protection. He knows that, even if an individual law should injure him, the whole fabric protects his interests; and more than all, the sanctity of the law, the sacredness of order as established by the active will of one part of society, and the passive acceptance of the other, is the strongest support of his social position. Because the English bourgeois finds himself reproduced in his law, as he does in his God, the policeman's truncheon which, in a certain measure,

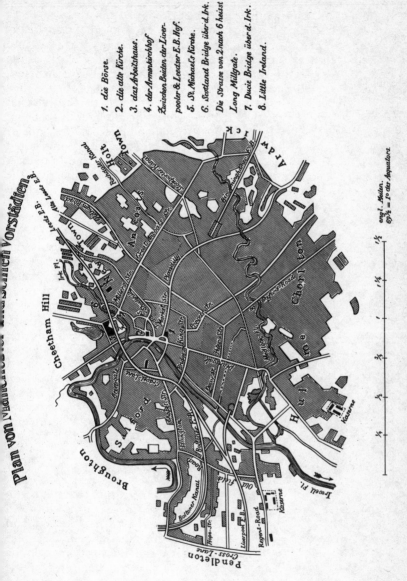

Map of Manchester

is his own club, has for him a wonderfully soothing power. But for the working-man quite otherwise! The working-man knows too well, has learned from too oft-repeated experience, that the law is a rod which the bourgeois has prepared for him; and when he is not compelled to do so, he never appeals to the law. It is ridiculous to assert that the English working-man fears the police, when every week in Manchester policemen are beaten, and last year an attempt was made to storm a station-house secured by iron doors and shutters. The power of the police in the turnout of 1842 lay, as I have already said, in the want of a clearly defined object on the part of the working-men themselves.[a]

Since the working-men do not respect the law, but simply submit to its power when they cannot change it, it is most natural that they should at least propose alterations in it, that they should wish to put a proletarian law in the place of the legal fabric of the bourgeoisie. This proposed law is the People's Charter,[b] which in form is purely political, and demands a democratic basis for the House of Commons. Chartism is the compact form of their opposition to the bourgeoisie. In the Unions and turnouts opposition always remained isolated: it was single working-men or sections who fought a single bourgeois. If the fight became general, this was scarcely by the intention of the working-men; or, when it did happen intentionally, Chartism was at the bottom of it. But in Chartism it is the whole working-class which arises against the bourgeoisie, and attacks, first of all, the political power, the legislative rampart with which the bourgeoisie has surrounded itself. Chartism has proceeded from the Democratic party which arose between 1780 and 1790 with and in the proletariat, gained strength during the French Revolution, and came forth after the peace as the Radical party. It had its headquarters then in Birmingham and Manchester, and later[c] in London; extorted the Reform Bill from the Oligarchs of the old Parliament by a union with the Liberal bourgeoisie, and has steadily consolidated itself, since then, as a more and more pronounced working-men's party in opposition to the bourgeoisie. In 1838 a committee of the General Working-men's Association of London,[169] with William

---

[a] The German editions of 1845 and 1892 have "in the helplessness of the workers themselves".—*Ed.*

[b] The German editions of 1845 and 1892 give such terms and expressions as the "People's Charter", "Working-men's Association", "a fair day's wages for a fair day's work", "universal suffrage", "complete suffrage", etc. in English in brackets, following their German equivalents.—*Ed.*

[c] The German editions of 1845 and 1892 have "earlier".—*Ed.*

Lovett at its head, drew up the People's Charter, whose six points are as follows: (1) Universal suffrage for every man who is of age, sane and unconvicted of crime; (2) Annual Parliaments; (3) Payment of members of Parliament, to enable poor men to stand for election; (4) Voting by ballot to prevent bribery and intimidation by the bourgeoisie; (5) Equal electoral districts to secure equal representation; and (6) Abolition of the even now merely nominal property qualification of £300 in land for candidates in order to make every voter eligible.[170] These six points, which are all limited to the reconstitution of the House of Commons, harmless as they seem, are sufficient to overthrow the whole English Constitution, Queen and Lords included. The so-called monarchical and aristocratic elements of the Constitution can maintain themselves only because the bourgeoisie has an interest in the continuance of their sham existence; and more than a sham existence neither possesses today. But as soon as real public opinion in its totality backs the House of Commons, as soon as the House of Commons incorporates the will, not of the bourgeoisie alone, but of the whole nation, it will absorb the whole power so completely that the last halo must fall from the head of the monarch and the aristocracy. The English working-man respects neither Lords nor Queen. The bourgeois, while in reality allowing them but little influence, yet offers to them personally a sham worship. The English Chartist is politically a republican, though he rarely or never mentions the word, while he sympathises with the republican parties of all countries, and calls himself in preference a democrat. But he is more than a mere republican, his democracy is not simply political.

Chartism was from the beginning of 1835 chiefly a movement among the working-men, though not yet sharply separated from the bourgeoisie.[a] The Radicalism of the workers went hand in hand with the Radicalism of the bourgeoisie; the Charter was the shibboleth of both. They held their National Convention every year in common, seeming to be one party. The lower middle-class was just then in a very bellicose and violent state of mind in consequence of the disappointment over the Reform Bill and of the bad business years of 1837-1839, and viewed the boisterous Chartist agitation with a very favourable eye. Of the vehemence of this agitation no one in Germany has any idea. The people were called upon to arm themselves, were frequently urged to revolt; pikes were got ready, as in the French Revolution, and in 1838,

---

[a] The German editions of 1845 and 1892 have here "the radical petty-bourgeoisie".—Ed.

one Stephens, a Methodist parson, said to the assembled working-people of Manchester:

"You have no need to fear the power of Government, the soldiers, bayonets, and cannon that are at the disposal of your oppressors; you have a weapon that is far mightier than all these, a weapon against which bayonets and cannon are powerless, and a child of ten years can wield it. You have only to take a couple of matches and a bundle of straw dipped in pitch, and I will see what the Government and its hundreds of thousands of soldiers will do against this one weapon if it is used boldly." *

As early as that year the peculiarly social character of the working-men's Chartism manifested itself. The same Stephens said, in a meeting of 200,000 men on Kersall Moor, the Mons Sacer of Manchester:

"Chartism, my friends, is no political movement, where the main point is your getting the ballot. Chartism is a knife and fork question: the Charter means a good house, good food and drink, prosperity, and short working-hours." [171]

The movements against the New Poor Law and for the Ten Hours' Bill were already in the closest relation to Chartism. In all the meetings of that time the Tory Oastler was active, and hundreds of petitions for improvements of the social conditions of the workers were circulated along with the national petition for the People's Charter adopted in Birmingham. In 1839 the agitation continued as vigorously as ever, and when it began to relax somewhat at the end of the year, Bussey, Taylor, and Frost hastened to call forth uprisings simultaneously in the North of England, in Yorkshire, and Wales. Frost's plan being betrayed, he was obliged to open hostilities prematurely.[a] Those in the North heard of the failure of his attempt in time to withdraw. Two months later, in January, 1840, several so-called spy outbreaks[b] took place in Sheffield and Bradford, in Yorkshire, and the excitement gradually subsided.[172] Meanwhile the bourgeoisie turned its attention to more practical projects, more profitable for itself, namely the Corn Laws. The Anti-Corn-Law Association was formed in Manchester, and the consequence was a relaxation of the tie between the Radical bourgeoisie and the proletariat. The working-men soon perceived that for them the abolition of the Corn Laws could be of little use, while very advantageous to the bourgeoisie; and they could therefore not be won for the project.

* We have seen that the workers took this advice seriously.— *Note by Engels* (not given in the American and English editions —*Ed.*).

---

[a] The German editions of 1845 and 1892 have "and therefore suffered a defeat".—*Ed.*

[b] The German editions of 1845 and 1892 give this English term in brackets.—*Ed.*

The crisis of 1842 came on. Agitation was once more as vigorous as in 1839. But this time the rich manufacturing bourgeoisie, which was suffering severely under this particular crisis, took part in it. The Anti-Corn Law League, as it was now called, assumed a decidedly revolutionary tone. Its journals and agitators used undisguisedly revolutionary language, one very good reason for which was the fact that the Conservative party had been in power since 1841. As the Chartists had previously done, these bourgeois leaders called upon the people to rebel; and the working-men who had most to suffer from the crisis were not inactive, as the year's national petition for the Charter with its three and a half million signatures proves. In short, if the two Radical parties had been somewhat estranged, they allied themselves once more. At a meeting of Liberals and Chartists held in Manchester, February 14th, 1842, a petition urging the repeal of the Corn Laws and the adoption of the Charter was drawn up. The next day it was adopted by both parties. The spring and summer passed amidst violent agitation and increasing distress. The bourgeoisie was determined to carry the repeal of the Corn Laws with the help of the crisis, the want which it entailed, and the general excitement. At this time, the Conservatives being in power, the Liberal bourgeoisie half abandoned their law-abiding habits; they wished to bring about a revolution with the help of the workers. The working-men were to take the chestnuts from the fire to save the bourgeoisie from burning their own fingers. The old idea of a "holy month", a general strike, broached in 1839 by the Chartists, was revived. This time, however, it was not the working-men who wished to quit work, but the manufacturers who wished to close their mills and send the operatives into the country parishes upon the property of the aristocracy, thus forcing the Tory Parliament and the Tory Ministry to repeal the Corn Laws. A revolt would naturally have followed, but the bourgeoisie stood safely in the background and could await the result without compromising itself if the worst came to the worst. At the end of July business began to improve; it was high time. In order not to lose the opportunity, three firms in Staleybridge reduced wages in spite of the improvement.* Whether they did so of their own motion or in agreement with other manufacturers, especially those of the League, I do not know. Two withdrew after a time, but the third, William Bailey & Brothers, stood firm, and told the

* Compare Report of Chambers of Commerce of Manchester and Leeds at the end of July and beginning of August.— *Note by Engels to the American edition of 1887.*

objecting operatives that "if this did not please them, they had better go and play a bit". This contemptuous answer the hands received with jeers. They left the mill, paraded through the town, and called upon all their fellows to quit work. In a few hours every mill stood idle, and the operatives marched to Mottram Moor to hold a meeting. This was on August 5th. August 8th they proceeded to Ashton and Hyde five thousand strong, closed all the mills and coal-pits, and held meetings, in which, however, the question discussed was not, as the bourgeoisie had hoped, the repeal of the Corn Laws, but, "a fair day's wages for a fair day's work". August 9th they proceeded to Manchester, unresisted by the authorities (all Liberals), and closed the mills; on the 11th they were in Stockport, where they met with the first resistance as they were storming the workhouse, the favourite child of the bourgeoisie. On the same day there was a general strike and disturbance in Bolton, to which the authorities here, too, made no resistance. Soon the uprising spread throughout the whole manufacturing district, and all employments, except harvesting and the production of food, came to a standstill. But the rebellious operatives were quiet. They were driven into this revolt without wishing it. The manufacturers, with the single exception of the Tory Birley, in Manchester, had, *contrary to their custom*, not opposed it. The thing had begun without the working-men's having any distinct end in view, for which reason they were all united in the determination not to be shot at for the benefit of the Corn Law repealing bourgeoisie. For the rest, some wanted to carry the Charter, others who thought this premature wished merely to secure the wages rate of 1840. On this point the whole insurrection was wrecked. If it had been from the beginning an intentional, determined working-men's insurrection, it would surely have carried its point; but these crowds who had been driven into the streets by their masters, against their own will, and with no definite purpose, could do nothing. Meanwhile the bourgeoisie, which had not moved a finger to carry the alliance of February 15th into effect, soon perceived that the working-men did not propose to become its tools, and that the illogical manner in which it had abandoned its law-abiding standpoint threatened danger. It therefore resumed its law-abiding attitude, and placed itself upon the side of Government as against the working-men.[a]

It swore in trusty retainers as special constables (the German

[a] The German editions of 1845 and 1892 have here "whom it had itself provoked and later forced to revolt".—*Ed*.

merchants in Manchester took part in this ceremony, and marched in an entirely superfluous manner through the city with their cigars in their mouths and thick truncheons in their hands). It gave the command to fire upon the crowd in Preston, so that the unintentional revolt of the people stood all at once face to face, not only with the whole military power of the Government, but with the whole property-holding class as well. The working-men, who had no especial aim, separated gradually, and the insurrection came to an end without evil results. Later, the bourgeoisie was guilty of one shameful act after another, tried to whitewash itself by expressing a horror of popular violence by no means consistent with its own revolutionary language of the spring; laid the blame of insurrection upon Chartist instigators, whereas it had itself done more than all of them together to bring about the uprising; and resumed its old attitude of sanctifying the name of the law with a shamelessness perfectly unequalled. The Chartists, who were all but innocent of bringing about this uprising, who simply did what the bourgeoisie meant to do when they made the most of their opportunity, were prosecuted and convicted, while the bourgeoisie escaped without loss, and had, besides, sold off its old stock of goods with advantage during the pause in work.

The fruit' of the uprising was the decisive separation of the proletariat from the bourgeoisie. The Chartists had not hitherto concealed their determination to carry the Charter at all costs, even that of a revolution; the bourgeoisie, which now perceived, all at once, the danger with which any violent change threatened its position, refused to hear anything further of physical force, and proposed to attain its end by moral force, as though this were anything else than the direct or indirect threat of physical force. This was one point of dissension, though even this was removed later by the assertion of the Chartists (who are at least as worthy of being believed as the bourgeoisie[a]) that they, too, refrained from appealing to physical force. The second point of dissension and the main one, which brought Chartism to light in its purity, was the repeal of the Corn Laws. In this the bourgeoisie[b] was directly interested, the proletariat not. The Chartists therefore divided into two parties whose political programmes agreed literally, but which were nevertheless thoroughly different and incapable of union. At the Birmingham National Convention, in January, 1843, Sturge, the representative of the Radical bourgeoisie, proposed that the

---

[a] The German editions of 1845 and 1892 have "liberal bourgeoisie".—*Ed*.
[b] The German editions of 1845 and 1892 have "radical bourgeoisie".—*Ed*

name of the Charter be omitted from the rules of the Chartist Association,[173] nominally because this name had become connected with recollections of violence during the insurrection, a connection, by the way, which had existed for years, and against which Mr. Sturge had hitherto advanced no objection. The working-men refused to drop the name, and when Mr. Sturge was outvoted, that worthy Quaker suddenly became loyal, betook himself out of the hall, and founded a "Complete Suffrage Association" within the Radical bourgeoisie. So repugnant had these recollections become to the Jacobinical bourgeoisie, that he altered even the name Universal Suffrage into the ridiculous title, Complete Suffrage. The working-men laughed at him and quietly went their way.

From this moment Chartism was purely a working-men's cause freed from all bourgeois elements. The "Complete" journals, the *Weekly Dispatch, Weekly Chronicle, Examiner*, etc., fell gradually into the sleepy tone of the other Liberal sheets, espoused the cause of Free Trade, attacked the Ten Hours' Bill and all exclusively working-men's demands, and let their Radicalism as a whole fall rather into the background. The Radical bourgeoisie joined hands with the Liberals against the working-men in every collision, and in general made the Corn Law question, which for the English is the Free Trade question,[a] their main business. They thereby fell under the dominion of the Liberal bourgeoisie, and now play a most pitiful role.

The Chartist working-men, on the contrary, espoused with redoubled zeal all the struggles of the proletariat against the bourgeoisie. Free competition has caused the workers suffering enough to be hated by them; its apostles, the bourgeoisie, are their declared enemies. The working-man has only disadvantages to await from the complete freedom of competition. The demands hitherto made by him, the Ten Hours' Bill, protection of the workers against the capitalist, good wages, a guaranteed position, repeal of the New Poor Law, all of the things which belong to Chartism quite as essentially as the "Six Points", are directly opposed to free competition and Free Trade. No wonder, then, that the working-men will not hear of Free Trade and the repeal of the Corn Laws (a fact incomprehensible to the whole English bourgeoisie), and while at least wholly indifferent to the Corn Law question, are most deeply embittered against its advocates. This

---

[a] The German editions of 1845 and 1892 have "a question of free competition".—*Ed.*

question is precisely the point at which the proletariat separates from the bourgeoisie, Chartism from Radicalism; and the bourgeois understanding cannot comprehend this, because it cannot comprehend the proletariat.

Therein lies the difference between Chartist democracy and all previous political bourgeois democracy. Chartism is of an essentially social nature, a class movement.[a] The "Six Points" which for the Radical bourgeois are the beginning and end of the matter, which are meant, at the utmost, to call forth certain further reforms of the Constitution, are for the proletarian a mere means to further ends.[b] "Political power our means, social happiness our end", is now the clearly formulated war-cry of the Chartists. The "knife and fork question" of the preacher Stephens was a truth for a part of the Chartists only, in 1838; it is a truth for all of them in 1845. There is no longer a mere politician among the Chartists, and even though their Socialism is very little developed, though their chief remedy for poverty has hitherto consisted in the land-allotment system, which was superseded* by the introduction of manufacture,[174] though their chief practical propositions[c] are apparently of a reactionary nature, yet these very measures involve the alternative that they must either succumb to the power of competition once more and restore the old state of things, or they must themselves entirely overcome competition and abolish it. On the other hand, the present indefinite state of Chartism, the separation from the purely political party, involves that precisely the characteristic feature, its social aspect, will have to be further developed. The approach to Socialism cannot fail, especially when the next crisis directs the working-men by force of sheer want to social instead of political remedies. And a crisis must follow the present active state of industry and commerce in 1847** at the latest, and probably in 1846; one, too, which will far exceed in extent and violence all former crises. The working-men will carry their Charter, naturally; but meanwhile they will learn to see

---

* See Introduction.—*Note by Engels to the American edition of 1887.*

** (1892) This prophecy has been exactly fulfilled.—*Note by Engels to the German edition of 1892.*

---

[a] The German editions of 1845 and 1892 do not have the words "a class movement".—*Ed.*

[b] The German editions of 1845 and 1892 do not have the words "to further ends".—*Ed.*

[c] The German editions of 1845 and 1892 have in brackets "protection for the worker, etc.".—*Ed.*

clearly with regard to many points which they can make by means of it and of which they now know very little.

Meanwhile the Socialist agitation also goes forward. English Socialism comes under our consideration so far only as it affects the working-class. The English Socialists demand the gradual introduction of possession in common in home colonies [175] embracing two to three thousand persons who shall carry on both agriculture and manufacture and enjoy equal rights and equal education. They demand greater facility of obtaining divorce, the establishment of a rational government, with complete freedom of conscience and the abolition of punishment, the same to be replaced by a rational treatment of the offender. These are their practical measures, their theoretical principles do not concern us here. English Socialism arose with Owen, a manufacturer, and proceeds therefore with great consideration toward the bourgeoisie and great injustice toward the proletariat in its methods, although it culminates in demanding the abolition of the class antagonism between bourgeoisie and proletariat.[a]

The Socialists are thoroughly tame and peaceable, accept our existing order, bad as it is, so far as to reject all other methods but that of winning public opinion. Yet they are so dogmatic[b] that success by this method is for them, and for their principles as at present formulated, utterly hopeless. While bemoaning the demoralisation of the lower classes, they are blind to the element of progress in this dissolution of the old social order, and refuse to acknowledge that the corruption wrought by private interests and hypocrisy in the property-holding class is much greater. They acknowledge no historic development, and wish to place the nation in a state of Communism at once, overnight,[c] not by the unavoidable march of its political development up to the point at which this transition becomes both possible and necessary. They understand, it is true, why the working-man is resentful against the bourgeois, but regard as unfruitful this class hatred, which is, after all, the only moral incentive by which the worker can be brought nearer the goal. They preach instead, a philanthropy and universal love

---

[a] The German editions of 1845 and 1892 have here "although essentially it goes beyond the framework of the antagonism between the bourgeoisie and the proletariat".—*Ed.*

[b] The German editions of 1845 and 1892 have "abstract" instead of "dogmatic".—*Ed.*

[c] The German editions of 1845 and 1892 give the end of this sentence as follows: "overnight, without pursuing the political struggle to the end, at which it dissolves itself [*sich selbst auflöst*]."—*Ed.*

far 'more unfruitful for the present state of England. They acknowledge only a psychological development, a development of man in the abstract, out of all relation to the Past, whereas the whole world rests upon that Past, the individual man included. Hence they are too abstract, too metaphysical, and accomplish little. They are recruited in part from the working-class, of which they have enlisted but a very small fraction representing, however, its most educated and solid elements. In its present form, Socialism can never become the common creed of the working-class; it must condescend to return for a moment to the Chartist standpoint. But the true proletarian Socialism having passed through Chartism, purified of its bourgeois elements, assuming the form which it has already reached in the minds of many Socialists and Chartist leaders (who are nearly all Socialists*), must, within a short time, play a weighty part in the history of the development of the English people. English Socialism, the basis of which is much more ample than that of the French, is behind it in theoretical[a] development, will have to recede for a moment to the French standpoint in order to proceed beyond it later. Meanwhile the French, too, will develop farther. English Socialism affords the most pronounced expression of the prevailing absence of religion among the working-men, an expression so pronounced indeed that the mass of the working-men, being unconsciously and merely practically irreligious, often draw back before it. But here, too, necessity will force the working-men to abandon the remnants of a belief which, as they will more and more clearly perceive, serves only to make them weak and resigned to their fate, obedient and faithful to the vampire property-holding class.

Hence it is evident that the working-men's movement is divided into two sections, the Chartists and the Socialists. The Chartists are theoretically[b] the more backward, the less developed, but they are genuine proletarians all over, the representatives of their class. The Socialists are more far-seeing, propose practical remedies against distress, but, proceeding originally from the bourgeoisie, are for this reason unable to amalgamate completely with the

---

* (1892) Socialists, naturally, in the general, not the specifically Owenistic sense.— *Note by Engels to the German edition of 1892.*

---

[a] The German editions of 1845 and 1892 do not have the word "theoretical", and above, instead of "than that of the French" they have "than French Communism".— *Ed.*

[b] The German editions of 1845 and 1892 do not have the word "theoretically".— *Ed.*

working-class. The union of Socialism with Chartism, the reproduction of French Communism in an English manner, will be the next step, and has already begun. Then only, when this has been achieved, will the working-class be the true intellectual[a] leader of England. Meanwhile, political and social development will proceed, and will foster this new party, this new departure of Chartism.

These different sections of working-men, often united, often separated, Trades Unionists, Chartists, and Socialists, have founded on their own hook numbers of schools and reading-rooms for the advancement of education. Every Socialist, and almost every Chartist institution, has such a place, and so too have many trades. Here the children receive a purely proletarian education, free from all the influences of the bourgeoisie; and, in the reading-rooms, proletarian journals and books alone, or almost alone, are to be found. These arrangements are very dangerous for the bourgeoisie, which has succeeded in withdrawing several such institutes, "Mechanics' Institutes",[176] from proletarian influences, and making them organs for the dissemination of the sciences useful to the bourgeoisie. Here the natural sciences are now taught, which may draw the working-men away from the opposition to the bourgeoisie, and perhaps place in their hands the means of making inventions which bring in money for the bourgeoisie; while for the working-man the acquaintance with the natural sciences is utterly useless *now* when it too often happens that he never gets the slightest glimpse of Nature in his large town with his long working-hours. Here Political Economy is preached, whose idol is free competition, and whose sum and substance for the working-man is this, that he cannot do anything more rational than resign himself to starvation. Here all education is tame, flabby, subservient to the ruling politics and religion, so that for the working-man it is merely a constant sermon upon quiet obedience, passivity, and resignation to his fate.

The mass of working-men naturally have nothing to do with these institutes, and betake themselves to the proletarian reading-rooms and to the discussion of matters which directly concern their own interests, whereupon the self-sufficient bourgeoisie says its *Dixi et salvavi*,[b] and turns with contempt from a class which "prefers the angry ranting of ill-meaning demagogues to the advantages of solid education". That, however, the working-men

---

[a] The German editions of 1845 and 1892 do not have the word "intellectual".—*Ed*.

[b] *Dixi et salvavi (animam meam)*: I have spoken and saved (my soul).—*Ed*.

appreciate solid education when they can get it unmixed with the interested cant of the bourgeoisie, the frequent lectures upon scientific, aesthetic, and economic subjects prove which are delivered especially in the Socialist institutes,[a] and very well attended. I have often heard working-men, whose fustian jackets scarcely held together, speak upon geological, astronomical, and other subjects, with more knowledge than most "cultivated" bourgeois in Germany possess. And in how great a measure the English proletariat has succeeded in attaining independent education is shown especially by the fact that the epoch-making products of modern philosophical, political, and poetical literature are read by working-men almost exclusively. The bourgeois, enslaved by social conditions and the prejudices involved in them, trembles, blesses, and crosses himself before everything which really paves the way for progress; the proletarian has open eyes for it, and studies it with pleasure and success. In this respect the Socialists, especially, have done wonders for the education of the proletariat. They have translated the French materialists, Helvétius, Holbach, Diderot, etc., and disseminated them, with the best English works, in cheap editions.[177] Strauss' *Life of Jesus* and Proudhon's *Property* also circulate among the working-men only.[178] Shelley, the genius, the prophet, Shelley, and Byron, with his glowing sensuality and his bitter satire upon our existing society, find most of their readers in the proletariat; the bourgeoisie owns only castrated editions, family editions, cut down in accordance with the hypocritical morality of today. The two great practical philosophers of latest date, Bentham and Godwin, are, especially the latter, almost exclusively the property of the proletariat; for though Bentham has a school within the Radical bourgeoisie, it is only the proletariat and the Socialists who have succeeded in developing his teachings a step forward. The proletariat has formed upon this basis a literature, which consists chiefly of journals and pamphlets, and is far in advance of the whole bourgeois literature in intrinsic worth. On this point more later.[179]

One more point remains to be noticed. The factory operatives, and especially those of the cotton district, form the nucleus of the labour movement. Lancashire, and especially Manchester, is the seat of the most powerful Unions, the central point of Chartism, the place which numbers most Socialists. The more the factory system has taken possession of a branch of industry, the more the

---

[a] The German editions of 1845 and 1892 have here "in all proletarian institutes, especially the socialist ones".—*Ed.*

working-men employed in it participate in the labour movement; the sharper the opposition between working-men and capitalists, the clearer the proletarian consciousness in the working-men. The small masters of Birmingham, though they suffer from the crises, still stand upon an unhappy middle ground between proletarian Chartism and shopkeepers' Radicalism. But, in general, all the workers employed in manufacture are won for one form or the other of resistance to capital and bourgeoisie; and all are united upon this point, that they, as working-men,[a] a title of which they are proud, and which is the usual form of address in Chartist meetings, form a separate class, with separate interests and principles, with a separate way of looking at things in contrast with that of all property-owners; and that in this class reposes the strength and the capacity of development of the nation.

---

[a] The German editions of 1845 and 1892 give the word "working-men" in English.— *Ed.*

THE MINING PROLETARIAT

The production of raw materials and fuel for a manufacture so colossal as that of England requires a considerable number of workers. But of all the materials needed for its industries (except wool, which belongs to the agricultural districts), England produces only the minerals: the metals and the coal. While Cornwall possesses rich copper, tin, zinc, and lead mines, Staffordshire, Wales,[a] and other districts yield great quantities of iron, and almost the whole North and West of England, central Scotland, and certain districts of Ireland, produce a superabundance of coal.*

* According to the census of 1841, the number of working-men employed in mines in Great Britain, without Ireland, was:

	Men over 20 years	Men under 20 years	Women over 20 years	Women under 20 years	Together
Coal-mines	83,408	32,475	1,185	1,165	118,233
Copper mines	9,866	3,428	913	1,200	15,407
Lead „	9,427	1,932	40	20	11,419
Iron „	7,773	2,679	424	73	10,949
Tin „	4,602	1,349	68	82	6,101
Various the mineral not specified	24,162	6,591	472	491	31,716
Total	139,238	48,454	3,102	3,031	193,825

As the coal and iron mines are usually worked by the same people, a part of the miners attributed to the coal-mines, and a very considerable part of those mentioned under the last heading are to be attributed to the iron mines.—Note by Engels.

---

[a] The German editions of 1845 and 1892 have "North Wales".—Ed.

In the Cornish mines about 19,000 men, and 11,000 women and children are employed, in part above and in part below ground. Within the mines below ground, men and boys above twelve years old are employed almost exclusively. The condition of these workers seems, according to the Children's Employment Commission's Report, to be comparatively endurable, materially, and the English often enough boast of their strong, bold miners, who follow the veins of mineral below the bottom of the very sea. But in the matter of the health of these workers, this same Children's Employment Commission's Report judges differently. It shows in Dr. Barham's intelligent report how the inhalation of an atmosphere containing little oxygen, and mixed with dust and the smoke of blasting powder, such as prevails in the mines, seriously affects the lungs, disturbs the action of the heart, and diminishes the activity of the digestive organs; that wearing toil, and especially the climbing up and down of ladders, upon which even vigorous young men have to spend in some mines more than an hour a day, and which precedes and follows daily work, contributes greatly to the development of these evils, so that men who begin this work in early youth are far from reaching the stature of women who work above ground; that many die young of galloping consumption, and most miners at middle age of slow consumption; that they age prematurely and become unfit for work between the thirty-fifth and forty-fifth years; that many are attacked by acute inflammations of the respiratory organs when exposed to the sudden change from the warm air of the shaft (after climbing the ladder in profuse perspiration) to the cold wind above ground; and that these acute inflammations are very frequently fatal. Work above ground, breaking and sorting the ore, is done by girls and children, and is described as very wholesome, being done in the open air.

In the North of England, on the borders of Northumberland and Durham, are the extensive lead-mines of Alston Moor. The reports from this district* agree almost wholly with those from Cornwall. Here, too, there are complaints of want of oxygen, excessive dust, powder smoke, carbonic acid gas, and sulphur, in the atmosphere of the workings. In consequence, the miners here, as in Cornwall, are small of stature, and nearly all suffer from the thirtieth year throughout life from chest affections, which end,

---

* Also found in the Children's Employment Commission's Report; Commissioner Mitchell's Report.—*Note by Engels to the American edition of 1887.* (In the German editions of 1845 and 1892 the reference is given in the text.—*Ed.*)

especially when this work is persisted in, as is almost always the case, in consumption, so greatly shortening the average of life of these people. If the miners of this district are somewhat longer lived than those of Cornwall, this is the case, because they do not enter the mines before reaching the nineteenth year, while in Cornwall, as we have seen, this work is begun in the twelfth year. Nevertheless, the majority die here, too, between forty and fifty years of age, according to medical testimony. Of 79 miners, whose death was entered upon the public register of the district, and who attained an average of 45 years, 37 had died of consumption and 6 of asthma. In the surrounding districts, Allendale, Stanhope, and Middleton, the average length of life was 49, 48, and 47 years respectively, and the deaths from chest affections composed 48, 54, and 56 per cent of the whole number.[a] Let us compare these figures with the so-called Swedish tables, detailed tables of mortality embracing all the inhabitants of Sweden, and recognised in England as the most correct standard hitherto attainable for the average length of life of the British working-class. According to them, male persons who survive the nineteenth year attain an average of $57^{1}/_{2}$ years; but, according to this, the North of England miners are robbed by their work of an average of ten years of life. Yet the Swedish tables are accepted as the standard of longevity of the *workers*, and present, therefore, the average chances of life as affected by the unfavourable conditions in which the proletariat lives, a standard of longevity less than the normal one. In this district we find again the lodging-houses and sleeping-places with which we have already become acquainted in the towns, and in quite as filthy, disgusting, and overcrowded a state as there. Commissioner Mitchell visited one such sleeping barrack, 18 feet long, 15 feet wide, and arranged for the reception of 42 men and 14 boys, or 56 persons altogether, one-half of whom slept above the other in berths as on shipboard.[b] There was no opening for the escape of the foul air; and, although no one had slept in this pen for three nights preceding the visit, the smell and the atmosphere were such that Commissioner Mitchell could not endure it a moment. What must it be through a hot summer night, with fifty-six occupants? And this is not the steerage of an American slave ship, it is the dwelling of free-born Britons!

---

[a] The German editions of 1845 and 1892 have here: "It must be borne in mind that all the data refer only to miners who did not begin to work *until they were nineteen years old*."—*Ed.*

[b] The German editions of 1845 and 1892 have "56 persons in 14 berths, half of them *above* the others as in ships".—*Ed.*

Let us turn now to the most important branch of British mining, the iron and coal-mines, which the Children's Employment Commission treats in common, and with all the detail which the importance of the subject demands. Nearly the whole of the first part of this report is devoted to the condition of the workers employed in these mines. After the detailed description which I have furnished of the state of the industrial workers, I shall, however, be able to be as brief in dealing with this subject as the scope of the present work requires.

In the coal and iron mines which are worked in pretty much the same way, children of four, five, and seven years are employed.[a] They are set to transporting the ore or coal loosened by the miner from its place to the horse-path or the main shaft, and to opening and shutting the doors (which separate the divisions of the mine and regulate its ventilation[b]) for the passage of workers and material. For watching the doors the smallest children are usually employed, who thus pass twelve hours daily, in the dark, alone, sitting usually in damp passages without even having work enough to save them from the stupefying, brutalising tedium of doing nothing. The transport of coal and iron-stone, on the other hand, is very hard labour, the stuff being shoved in large tubs, without wheels, over the uneven floor of the mine; often over moist clay, or through water, and frequently up steep inclines and through paths so low-roofed that the workers are forced to creep on hands and knees. For this more wearing labour, therefore, older children and half-grown girls are employed. One man or two boys per tub are employed, according to circumstances; and, if two boys, one pushes and the other pulls. The loosening of the ore or coal, which is done by men or strong youths of sixteen years or more, is also very weary work. The usual working-day is eleven to twelve hours, often longer; in Scotland it reaches fourteen hours, and double time is frequent, when all the employees are at work below ground twenty-four, and even thirty-six hours at a stretch. Set times for meals are almost unknown, so that these people eat when hunger and time permit.

The standard of living of the miners is in general described as fairly good and their wages high in comparison with those of the agricultural labourers surrounding them (who, however, live at

---

[a] The German editions of 1845 and 1892 have here "but most of them are over eight".—*Ed.*

[b] The words "and regulate its ventilation" do not occur in the German editions of 1845 and 1892.—*Ed.*

starvation rates), except in certain parts of Scotland and in the Irish mines, where great misery prevails. We shall have occasion to return later to this statement, which, by the way, is merely relative, implying comparison to the poorest class in all England. Meanwhile, we shall consider the evils which arise from the present method of mining, and the reader may judge whether any pay in money can indemnify the miner for such suffering.

The children and young people who are employed in transporting coal and iron-stone all complain of being overtired. Even in the most recklessly conducted industrial establishments there is no such universal and exaggerated overwork. The whole report proves this, with a number of examples on every page. It is constantly happening that children throw themselves down on the stone hearth or the floor as soon as they reach home, fall asleep at once without being able to take a bite of food, and have to be washed and put to bed while asleep; it even happens that they lie down on the way home, and are found by their parents late at night asleep on the road. It seems to be a universal practice among these children to spend Sunday in bed to recover in some degree from the overexertion of the week. Church and school are visited by but few, and even of these the teachers complain of their great sleepiness and the want of all eagerness to learn. The same thing is true of the elder girls and women. They are overworked in the most brutal manner. This weariness, which is almost always carried to a most painful pitch, cannot fail to affect the constitution. The first result of such overexertion is the diversion of vitality to the one-sided development of the muscles, so that those especially of the arms, legs, and back, of the shoulders and chest, which are chiefly called into activity in pushing and pulling, attain an uncommonly vigorous development, while all the rest of the body suffers and is atrophied from want of nourishment. More than all else the stature suffers, being stunted and retarded; nearly all miners are short, except those of Leicestershire and Warwickshire, who work under exceptionally favourable conditions. Further, among boys as well as girls, puberty is retarded, among the former often until the eighteenth year; indeed, a nineteen years old boy appeared before Commissioner Symons, showing no evidence beyond that of the teeth, that he was more than eleven or twelve years old. This prolongation of the period of childhood is at bottom nothing more than a sign of checked development, which does not fail to bear fruit in later years. Distortions of the legs, knees bent inwards and feet bent outwards, deformities of the spinal column and other malformations, appear the more readily in constitutions thus weakened, in consequence of the almost universally constrained position during work; and they are so frequent that in Yorkshire and Lancashire, as in Northumberland and Durham, the assertion is made by many witnesses, not only by physicians, that a miner may be recognised by his shape among a hundred other persons. The women seem to suffer especially from this work, and are seldom, if ever, as straight as other women. There is testimony here, too, to the fact that deformities of the pelvis and consequent difficult, even fatal, child-bearing arise from the work of women in the mines. But apart from these local deformities, the coal-miners suffer from a number of special affections[a] easily explained by the nature of the work. Diseases of the digestive organs are first in order; want of appetite, pains in the stomach, nausea, and vomiting, are most frequent, with violent thirst, which can be quenched only with the dirty, lukewarm water of the mine; the digestion is checked and all the other affections are thus invited. Diseases of the heart, especially hypertrophy, inflammation of the heart and pericardium, contraction of the auriculo-ventricular communications and the entrance of the aorta are also mentioned repeatedly as diseases of the miners, and are readily explained by overwork; and the same is true of the almost universal rupture which is a direct consequence of protracted overexertion. In part from the same cause and in part from the bad, dust-filled atmosphere mixed with carbonic acid and hydrocarbon gas, which might so readily be avoided, there arise numerous painful and dangerous affections of the lungs, especially asthma, which in some districts appears in the fortieth, in others in the thirtieth year in most of the miners, and makes them unfit for work in a short time. Among those employed in wet workings the oppression in the chest naturally appears much earlier; in some districts of Scotland between the twentieth and thirtieth years, during which time the affected lungs are especially susceptible to inflammations and diseases of a feverish nature. The peculiar disease of workers of this sort is "black spittle",[b] which arises from the saturation of the whole lung with coal particles, and manifests itself in general debility, headache, oppression of the chest, and thick, black mucous expectoration. In some districts this disease appears in a mild form; in others, on the contrary, it is wholly incurable,

---

[a] The German editions of 1845 and 1892 have here "which are the same as those of other miners and are", etc.—Ed.

[b] In the German editions of 1845 and 1892 this English term is given in brackets.—Ed.

especially in Scotland. Here, besides the symptoms just mentioned, which appear in an intensified form, short, wheezing breathing, rapid pulse (exceeding 100 per minute), and abrupt coughing, with increasing leanness and debility, speedily make the patient unfit for work. Every case of this disease ends fatally. Dr. Mackellar, in Pencaitland, East Lothian, testified that in all the coal-mines which are properly ventilated this disease is unknown, while it frequently happens that miners who go from well- to ill-ventilated mines are seized by it. The profit-greed of mine owners which prevents the use of ventilators is therefore responsible for the fact that this working-men's disease exists at all. Rheumatism, too, is, with the exception of the Warwick and Leicestershire workers, a universal disease of the coal-miners, and arises especially from the frequently damp working-places. The consequence of all these diseases is that, in all districts *without exception*, the coal-miners age early and become unfit for work soon after the fortieth year, though this is different in different places. A coal-miner who can follow his calling after the 45th or 50th year is a very great rarity indeed. It is universally recognised that such workers enter upon old age at forty. This applies to those who loosen the coal from the bed; the loaders, who have constantly to lift heavy blocks of coal into the tubs, age with the twenty-eighth or thirtieth year, so that it is proverbial in the coal-mining districts that the loaders are old before they are young. That this premature old age is followed by the early death of the colliers is a matter of course, and a man who reaches sixty is a great exception among them. Even in South Staffordshire, where the mines are comparatively wholesome, few men reach their fifty-first year. Along with this early superannuation of the workers we naturally find, just as in the case of the mills, frequent lack of employment of the elder men, who are often supported by very young children. If we sum up briefly the results of the work in coal-mines, we find, as Dr. Southwood Smith, one of the commissioners, does, that through prolonged childhood on the one hand and premature age on the other, that period of life in which the human being is in full possession of his powers, the period of manhood, is greatly shortened, while the length of life in general is below the average. This, too, on the debit side of the bourgeoisie's reckoning!

All this deals only with the average of the English coal-mines. But there are many in which the state of things is much worse, those, namely, in which thin seams of coal are worked. The coal would be too expensive if a part of the adjacent sand and clay were removed; so the mine owners permit only the seams to be worked; whereby the passages which elsewhere are four or five feet high and more are here kept so low that to stand upright in them is not to be thought of. The working-man lies on his side and loosens the coal with his pick; resting upon his elbow as a pivot, whence follow inflammations of the joint, and in cases where he is forced to kneel, of the knee also. The women and children who have to transport the coal crawl upon their hands and knees, fastened to the tub by a harness and chain (which frequently passes between the legs), while a man behind pushes with hands and head. The pushing with the head engenders local irritations, painful swellings, and ulcers. In many cases, too, the shafts are wet, so that these workers have to crawl through dirty or salt water several inches deep, being thus exposed to a special irritation of the skin. It can be readily imagined how greatly the diseases already peculiar to the miners are fostered by this especially frightful, slavish toil.

But these are not all the evils which descend upon the head of the coal-miner. In the whole British Empire there is no occupation in which a man may meet his end in so many diverse ways as in this one. The coal-mine is the scene of a multitude of the most terrifying calamities, and these come directly from the selfishness of the bourgeoisie. The hydrocarbon gas which develops so freely in these mines, forms, when combined with atmospheric air, an explosive which takes fire upon coming into contact with a flame, and kills every one within its reach. Such explosions take place, in one mine or another, nearly every day; on September 28th, 1844, one killed 96 men in Haswell Colliery, Durham. The carbonic acid gas, which also develops in great quantities, accumulates in the deeper parts of the mine, frequently reaching the height of a man, and suffocates every one who gets into it. The doors which separate the sections of the mines are meant to prevent the propagation of explosions and the movement of the gases; but since they are entrusted to small children, who often fall asleep or neglect them, this means of prevention is illusory. A proper ventilation of the mines by means of fresh air-shafts could almost entirely remove the injurious effects of both these gases. But for this purpose the bourgeoisie has no money to spare, preferring to command the working-men to use the Davy lamp, which is wholly useless because of its dull light, and is, therefore, usually replaced by a candle. If an explosion occurs, the recklessness of the miner is blamed, though the bourgeois might have made the explosion well-nigh impossible by supplying good ventilation.

Further, every few days the roof of a working falls in, and buries
or mangles the workers employed in it. It is the interest of the
bourgeois to have the seams worked out as completely as possible,
and hence the accidents of this sort. Then, too, the ropes by which
the men descend into the mines are often rotten, and break, so
that the unfortunates fall, and are crushed. All these accidents,
and I have no room for special cases, carry off yearly, according to
the *Mining Journal,* some fourteen hundred human beings.[180] The
Manchester Guardian reports at least two or three accidents every
week for Lancashire alone. In nearly all mining districts the
people composing the coroner's juries are, in almost all cases,
dependent upon the mine owners, and where this is not the case,
immemorial custom insures that the verdict shall be: "Accidental
Death". Besides, the jury takes very little interest in the state of
the mine, because it does not understand anything about the
matter. But the Children's Employment Commission does not
hesitate to make the mine owners directly responsible for the
greater number of these cases.

As to the education and morals of the mining population, they
are, according to the Children's Employment Commission, pretty
good in Cornwall, and excellent in Alston Moor; in the coal
districts, in general, they are, on the contrary, reported as on an
excessively low plane. The workers live in the country in neglected
regions, and if they do their weary work, no human being outside
the police force troubles himself about them. Hence, and from the
tender age at which children are put to work, it follows that their
mental education is wholly neglected. The day schools are not
within their reach, the evening and Sunday schools mere shams,
the teachers worthless. Hence, few can read and still fewer write.
The only point upon which their eyes are as yet open is the fact
that their wages are far too low for their hateful and dangerous
work. To church they go seldom or never; all the clergy complain
of their irreligion as beyond comparison. As a matter of fact, their
ignorance of religious and of secular things, alike, is such that the
ignorance of the factory operatives, shown in numerous examples
in the foregoing pages, is trifling in comparison with it. The
categories of religion are known to them only from the terms of
their oaths. Their morality is destroyed by their work itself. That
the overwork of all miners must engender drunkenness is self-
evident. As to their sexual relations, men, women, and children
work in the mines, in many cases, wholly naked, and in most cases,
nearly so, by reason of the prevailing heat, and the consequences
in the dark, lonely mines may be imagined. The number of

illegitimate children is here disproportionately large, and indicates what goes on among the half-savage population below ground; but proves too, that the illegitimate intercourse of the sexes has not here, as in the great cities, sunk to the level of prostitution. The labour of women entails the same consequences as in the factories, dissolves the family, and makes the mother totally incapable of household work.

When the Children's Employment Commission's Report was laid before Parliament, Lord Ashley hastened to bring in a bill wholly forbidding the work of women in the mines, and greatly limiting that of children. The bill was adopted,[181] but has remained a dead letter in most districts, because no mine inspectors were appointed to watch over its being carried into effect. The evasion of the law is very easy in the country districts in which the mines are situated; and no one need be surprised that the Miners' Union laid before the Home Secretary an official notice, last year, that in the Duke of Hamilton's coal-mines in Scotland, more than sixty women were at work; or that the *Manchester Guardian* reported that a girl perished in an explosion in a mine near Wigan, and no one troubled himself further about the fact that an infringement of the law was thus revealed. In single cases the employment of women may have been discontinued, but in general the old state of things remains as before.

These are, however, not all the afflictions known to the coal-miners. The bourgeoisie, not content with ruining the health of these people, keeping them in danger of sudden loss of life, robbing them of all opportunity for education, plunders them in other directions in the most shameless manner. The truck system is here the rule, not the exception, and is carried on in the most direct and undisguised manner. The cottage system, likewise, is universal, and here almost a necessity; but it is used here, too, for the better plundering of the workers. To these means of oppression must be added all sorts of direct cheating.[a] While coal is sold by weight, the worker's wages are reckoned chiefly by measure; and when his tub is not perfectly full he receives no pay whatever, while he gets not a farthing for overmeasure. If there is more than a specified quantity of dust in the tub, a matter which depends much less upon the miner than upon the nature of the seam, he not only loses his whole wage but is fined besides. The fine system in general is so highly perfected in the coal-mines, that

---

[a] In the German editions of 1845 and 1892 this sentence reads "To these must be added various other forms of fraud."—*Ed.*

a poor devil who has worked the whole week and comes for his wages, sometimes learns from the overseer, who fines at discretion and without summoning the workers, that he not only has no wages but must pay so and so much in fines extra! The overseer has, in general, absolute power over wages; he notes the work done, and can please himself as to what he pays the worker, who is forced to take his word. In some mines, where the pay is according to weight, false decimal scales are used, whose weights are not subject to the inspection of the authorities; in one coal-mine there was actually a regulation that any workman who intended to complain of the falseness of the scales *must give notice to the overseer three weeks in advance!* In many districts, especially in the North of England, it is customary to engage the workers by the year; they pledge themselves to work for no other employer during that time, but the mine owner by no means pledges himself to give them work, so that they are often without it for months together, and if they seek elsewhere, they are sent to the treadmill for six weeks for breach of contract. In other contracts, work to the amount of 26s. every 14 days, is promised the miners, but not furnished; in others still, the employers advance the miners small sums to be worked out afterwards, thus binding the debtors to themselves. In the North, the custom is general of keeping the payment of wages one week behindhand, chaining the miners in this way to their work. And to complete the slavery of these enthralled workers, nearly all the Justices of the Peace in the coal districts are mine owners themselves, or relatives or friends of mine owners, and possess almost unlimited power in these poor, uncivilised regions where there are few newspapers, these few in the service of the ruling class, and but little other agitation.[a] It is almost beyond conception how these poor coal-miners have been plundered and tyrannised over by Justices of the Peace acting as judges in their own cause.

So it went on for a long time. The workers did not know any better than that they were there for the purpose of being swindled out of their very lives. But gradually, even among them, and especially in the factory districts, where contact with the more intelligent operatives could not fail of its effect, there arose a spirit of opposition to the shameless oppression of the "coal kings". The men began to form Unions and strike from time to time. In civilised districts they joined the Chartists body and soul. The great coal district of the North of England, shut off from all

---

[a] The German editions of 1845 and 1892 have "political agitation".—*Ed.*

industrial intercourse, remained backward until, after many efforts, partly of the Chartists and partly of the more intelligent miners themselves, a general spirit of opposition arose in 1843. Such a movement seized the workers of Northumberland and Durham that they placed themselves at the forefront of a general Union of coal-miners throughout the kingdom, and appointed W. P. Roberts, a Chartist solicitor, of Bristol, their "Attorney General", he having distinguished himself in earlier Chartist trials. The Union soon spread over a great majority of the districts; agents were appointed in all directions, who held meetings everywhere and secured new members; at the first conference of delegates, in Manchester, in 1844,[a] there were 60,000 members represented, and at Glasgow, six months later, at the second conference, 100,000. Here all the affairs of the coal-miners were discussed and decisions as to the greater strikes arrived at. Several journals were founded, especially the *Miner's Advocate*,[b] at Newcastle-upon-Tyne, for defending the rights of the miners. On March 31st, 1844, the contracts of all the miners of Northumberland and Durham expired. Roberts was empowered to draw up a new agreement, in which the men demanded: (1) Payment by weight instead of measure; (2) Determination of weight by means of ordinary scales subject to the public inspectors; (3) Half-yearly renewal of contracts; (4) Abolition of the fines system and payment according to work actually done; (5) The employers to guarantee to miners in their exclusive service at least four days' work per week, or wages for the same. This agreement was submitted to the "coal kings", and a deputation appointed to negotiate with them; they answered, however, that for them the Union did not exist, that they had to deal with single workmen only, and should never recognise the Union. They also submitted an agreement of their own which ignored all the foregoing points, and was, naturally, refused by the miners. War was thus declared. On March 31st, 1844, 40,000 miners laid down their picks, and every mine in the county stood empty. The funds of the Union were so considerable that for several months a weekly contribution of 2s. 6d. could be assured to each family. While the miners were thus putting the patience of their masters to the test, Roberts organised with incomparable perseverance both strike and agitation, arranged for the holding of meetings, traversed England from one end to the

---

[a] The German editions of 1845 and 1892 have "in January 1844".—*Ed.*
[b] The German editions of 1845 and 1892 here have "the monthly *Miner's Advocate*".—*Ed.*

other,[a] preached peaceful and legal agitation, and carried on a crusade against the despotic Justices of the Peace and truck masters, such as had never been known in England. This he had begun at the beginning of the year. Wherever a miner had been condemned by a Justice of the Peace, he obtained a *habeas corpus* from the Court of Queen's bench, brought his client to London, and always secured an acquittal.[182] Thus, January 13th, Judge Williams of Queen's bench acquitted three miners condemned by the Justices of the Peace of Bilston, South Staffordshire; the offence of these people was that they refused to work in a place which threatened to cave in, and had actually caved in before their return! On an earlier occasion, Judge Patteson had acquitted six working-men, so that the name Roberts began to be a terror to the mine owners.[b] In Preston four of his clients were in jail. In the first week of January[c] he proceeded thither to investigate the case on the spot, but found, when he arrived, the condemned all released before the expiration of the sentence. In Manchester there were seven in jail; Roberts obtained a *habeas corpus* and acquittal for all from Judge Wightman. In Prescott nine coal-miners were in jail, accused of creating a disturbance in St. Helens, South Lancashire, and awaiting trial; when Roberts arrived upon the spot, they were released at once. All this took place in the first half of February. In April, Roberts released a miner from jail in Derby, four in Wakefield,[d] and four in Leicester. So it went on for a time until these Dogberries[e] came to have some respect for the miners. The truck system shared the same fate. One after another Roberts brought the disreputable mine owners before the courts, and compelled the reluctant Justices of the Peace to condemn them; such dread of this "lightning" "Attorney General" who seemed to be everywhere at once spread among them, that at Belper,[f] for instance, upon Roberts' arrival, a truck firm published the following notice:

---

[a] The German editions of 1845 and 1892 have here "made collections in aid of the strikers", etc.—*Ed.*

[b] The German editions of 1845 and 1892 have here "who were Justices of the Peace".—*Ed.*

[c] The German editions of 1845 and 1892 give "February".—*Ed.*

[d] The German editions of 1845 and 1892 give "Yorkshire" in brackets.—*Ed.*

[e] The German editions of 1845 and 1892 have here "as these Justices of the Peace were called after the famous character in Shakespeare's *Much Ado About Nothing*", etc.—*Ed.*

[f] The German editions of 1845 and 1892 have "at Belper, near Derby".—*Ed.*

NOTICE!
"Pentrich Colliery

"Messrs. Haslam think it right (to prevent mistake), to give notice that all men employed at their colliery will receive their wages wholly in money, and be at liberty to spend it where they like. If they buy at Messrs. Haslam's shop they will be supplied (as heretofore) at wholesale prices; but they are not expected to buy there, and will have the same work and wages whether they go to that shop or any other."

This triumph aroused the greatest jubilation throughout the English working-class, and brought the Union a mass of new members. Meanwhile the strike in the North was proceeding. Not a hand stirred, and Newcastle, the chief coal port, was so stripped of its commodity that coal had to be brought from the Scotch coast, in spite of the proverb.[a] At first, while the Union's funds held out, all went well, but towards summer the struggle became much more painful for the miners. The greatest want prevailed among them; they had no money, for the contributions of the workers of all branches of industry in England availed little among the vast number of strikers, who were forced to borrow from the small shop-keepers at a heavy loss. The whole press, with the single exception of the few proletarian journals, was against them; the bourgeois, even the few among them who might have had enough sense of justice to support the miners, learnt from the corrupt Liberal and Conservative sheets only lies about them. A deputation of twelve miners who went to London received a sum from the proletariat there, but this, too, availed little among the mass who needed support. Yet, in spite of all this, the miners remained steadfast, and what is even more significant, were quiet and peaceable in the face of all the hostilities and provocation of the mine owners and their faithful servants. No act of revenge was carried out, not a renegade was maltreated, not one single theft committed. Thus the strike had continued well on towards four months, and the mine owners still had no prospect of getting the upper hand. One way was, however, still open to them. They remembered the cottage system; it occurred to them that the houses of the rebellious spirits were THEIR property. In July, notice to quit was served the workers, and, in a week, the whole forty thousand were put out of doors. This measure was carried out with revolting cruelty. The sick, the feeble, old men and little

---

[a] In the German text the last phrase is expanded as follows: "although in English 'to carry coals to Newcastle' means the same as in Greek 'to carry owls to Athens', namely, to do something entirely superfluous".—*Ed.*

children, even women in child-birth, were mercilessly turned from their beds and cast into the roadside ditches. One agent dragged by the hair from her bed, and into the street, a woman in the pangs of child-birth. Soldiers and police in crowds were present, ready to fire at the first symptom of resistance, on the slightest hint of the Justices of the Peace, who had brought about the whole brutal procedure. This, too, the working-men endured without resistance. The hope had been that the men would use violence; they were spurred on with all force to infringements of the laws, to furnish an excuse for making an end of the strike by the intervention of the military. The homeless miners, remembering the warnings of their Attorney General, remained unmoved, set up their household goods upon the moors or the harvested fields, and held out. Some, who had no other place, encamped on the roadsides and in ditches, others upon land belonging to other people, whereupon they were prosecuted, and, having caused "damage of the value of a halfpenny", were fined a pound, and, being unable to pay it, worked it out on the treadmill. Thus they lived eight weeks and more of the wet fag-end of last[a] summer under the open sky with their families, with no further shelter for themselves and their little ones than the calico curtains of their beds; with no other help than the scanty allowances of their Union and the fast shrinking credit with the small dealers. Hereupon Lord Londonderry, who owns considerable mines in Durham, threatened the small tradesmen in "his" town of Seaham with his most high displeasure if they should continue to give credit to "his" rebellious workers. This "noble" lord made himself the first clown of the turnout in consequence of the ridiculous, pompous, ungrammatical ukases addressed to the workers, which he published from time to time, with no other result than the merriment of the nation.* When none of their efforts produced any effect, the mine owners imported, at great expense, hands from Ireland and such remote parts of Wales as have as yet no labour movement. And when the competition of workers against workers was thus restored, the strength of the strikers collapsed. The mine owners obliged them to renounce the Union, abandon Roberts, and accept the conditions laid down by the employers. Thus ended at the close[b] of September the great five months' battle of

---

* (1892) Nothing new under the sun, at least in Germany. Our "König Stumm" are only copies of long-past English originals which are now impossible in their native country.— *Note by Engels to the German edition of 1892.*

---

[a] The German editions of 1845 and 1892 give "1844" in brackets.—*Ed.*
[b] The German editions of 1845 and 1892 have "at the beginning".—*Ed.*

the coal-miners against the mine owners, a battle fought on the part of the oppressed with an endurance, courage, intelligence, and coolness which demands the highest admiration. What a degree of true human culture, of enthusiasm and strength of character, such a battle implies on the part of men[a] who, as we have seen in the Children's Employment Commission's Report, were described as late as 1840, as being thoroughly brutal and wanting in moral sense! But how hard, too, must have been the pressure which brought these forty thousand colliers to rise as one man and to fight out the battle like an army not only well-disciplined but enthusiastic, an army possessed of one single determination, with the greatest coolness and composure, to a point beyond which further resistance would have been madness. And what a battle! Not against visible, mortal enemies, but against hunger, want, misery, and homelessness, against their own passions provoked to madness by the brutality of wealth. If they had revolted with violence, they, the unarmed and defenceless, would have been shot down, and a day or two would have decided the victory of the owners. This law-abiding reserve was no fear of the constable's staff, it was the result of deliberation, the best proof of the intelligence and self-control of the working-men.

Thus were the working-men forced once more, in spite of their unexampled endurance, to succumb to the might of capital. But the fight had not been in vain. First of all, this nineteen weeks' strike had torn the miners of the North of England forever from the intellectual death in which they had hitherto lain; they have left their sleep, are alert to defend their interests, and have entered the movement of civilisation, and especially the movement of the workers. The strike, which first brought to light the whole cruelty of the owners, has established the opposition of the workers here, forever, and made at least two-thirds of them Chartists; and the acquisition of thirty thousand such determined, experienced men is certainly of great value to the Chartists. Then, too, the endurance and law-abiding which characterised the whole strike, coupled with the active agitation which accompanied it, has fixed public attention upon the miners. On the occasion of the debate upon the export duty on coal, Thomas Duncombe, the only decidedly Chartist member of the House of Commons, brought up the condition of the coal-miners, had their petition read, and by his speech forced the bourgeois journals to publish, at least in their reports of Parliamentary proceedings, a correct statement of

---

[a] The German editions of 1845 and 1892 have "a mass of 40,000 men".—*Ed.*

the case.[183] Immediately after the strike, occurred the explosion at Haswell; Roberts went to London, demanded an audience with Peel, insisted as representative of the miners upon a thorough investigation of the case, and succeeded in having the first geological and chemical notabilities of England, Professors Lyell and Faraday, commissioned to visit the spot. As several other explosions followed in quick succession, and Roberts again laid the details before the Prime Minister, the latter promised to propose the necessary measures for the protection of the workers, if possible, in the next session of Parliament, i. e., the present one of 1845. All this would not have been accomplished if these workers had not, by means of the strike, proved themselves freedom-loving men worthy of all respect, and if they had not engaged Roberts as their counsel.

Scarcely had it become known that the coal-miners of the North had been forced to renounce the Union and discharge Roberts, when the miners of Lancashire formed a Union of some ten thousand men, and guaranteed their Attorney General a salary of £1,200 a year. In the autumn of last year they collected more than £700, rather more than £200 of which they expended upon salaries and judicial expenses, and the rest chiefly in support of men out of work, either through want of employment or through dissensions with their employers. Thus the working-men are constantly coming to see more clearly that, united, they too are a respectable power, and can, in the last extremity, defy even the might of the bourgeoisie. And this insight, the gain of all labour movements, has been won for all the miners of England by the Union and the strike of 1844. In a very short time the difference of intelligence and energy which now exists in favour of the factory operatives will have vanished, and the miners of the kingdom will be able to stand abreast of them in every respect. Thus one piece of standing ground after another is undermined beneath the feet of the bourgeoisie; and how long will it be before their whole social and political edifice collapses with the basis upon which it rests?*

But the bourgeoisie will not take warning. The resistance of the miners does but embitter it the more. Instead of appreciating this forward step in the general movement of the workers,[a] the

---

* The coal-miners have at this moment, 1886, six of their body sitting in the House of Commons.— *Note by Engels to the American edition of 1887* (reproduced in the English edition of 1892—*Ed.*).

---

[a] The German editions of 1845 and 1892 have here "instead of being brought to their senses by this movement", etc.—*Ed.*

property-holding class saw in it only a source of rage against a class of people who are fools enough to declare themselves no longer submissive to the treatment they had hitherto received. It saw in the just demands of the non-possessing workers only impertinent discontent, mad rebellion against "Divine and human order", and, in the best case, a success (to be resisted by the bourgeoisie with all its might) won by "ill-intentioned demagogues who live by agitation and are too lazy to work". It sought, of course, without success, to represent to the workers that Roberts and the Union's agents, whom the Union very naturally had to pay, were insolent swindlers, who drew the last farthing from the working-men's pockets. When such insanity prevails in the property-holding class, when it is so blinded by its momentary profit that it no longer has eyes for the most conspicuous signs of the times, surely all hope of a peaceful solution of the social question for England must be abandoned. The only possible solution is a violent revolution, which cannot fail to take place.

THE AGRICULTURAL PROLETARIAT

We have seen in the introduction how, simultaneously with the small bourgeoisie and the modest independence of the former workers, the small peasantry also was ruined when the former Union of industrial and agricultural work was dissolved, the abandoned fields thrown together into large farms, and the small peasants superseded by the overwhelming competition of the large farmers. Instead of being landowners or leaseholders, as they had been hitherto, they were now obliged[a] to hire themselves as labourers to the large farmers or the landlords. For a time this position was endurable, though a deterioration in comparison with their former one. The extension of industry kept pace with the increase of population until the progress of manufacture began to assume a slower pace, and the perpetual improvement of machinery made it impossible for manufacture to absorb the whole surplus of the agricultural population. From this time forward, the distress which had hitherto existed only in the manufacturing districts, and then only at times, appeared in the agricultural districts too. The twenty-five years' struggle with France came to an end at about the same time[184]; the diminished production at the various seats of the wars, the shutting off of imports, and the necessity of providing for the British army in Spain, had given English agriculture an artificial prosperity, and had besides withdrawn to the army vast numbers of workers from their ordinary occupations. This check upon the import trade, the opportunity

---

[a] The German editions of 1845 and 1892 have "obliged to give up their own farms and".— Ed.

for exportation, and the military demand for workers, now suddenly came to an end; and the necessary consequence was what the English call agricultural distress.[a] The farmers had to sell their corn at low prices, and could, therefore, pay only low wages. In 1815, in order to keep up prices, the Corn Laws were passed, prohibiting the importation of corn so long as the price of wheat continued less than 80 shillings per quarter. These naturally ineffective laws were several times modified, but did not succeed in ameliorating the distress in the agricultural districts. All that they did was to change the disease, which, under free competition from abroad, would have assumed an acute form, culminating in a series of crises, into a chronic one which bore heavily but uniformly upon the farm labourers.

For a time after the rise of the agricultural proletariat, the patriarchal relation between master and man, which was being destroyed for manufacture, developed here the same relation of the farmer to his hands which still exists almost everywhere in Germany. So long as this lasted, the poverty of the farm-hands was less conspicuous; they shared the fate of the farmer, and were discharged only in cases of the direst necessity. But now all this is changed. The farm-hands have become day-labourers almost everywhere, are employed only when needed by the farmers, and, therefore, often have no work for weeks together, especially in winter. In the patriarchal time, the hands and their families lived on the farm, and their children grew up there, the farmer trying to find occupation on the spot for the oncoming generation; day-labourers, then, were the exception, not the rule. Thus there was, on every farm, a larger number of hands than were strictly necessary. It became, therefore, the interest of the farmers to dissolve this relation, drive the farm-hand from the farm, and transform him into a day-labourer. This took place pretty generally towards the year 1830,[b] and the consequence was that the hitherto latent[c] over-population was set free, the rate of wages forced down, and the poor-rate enormously increased. From this time the agricultural districts became the headquarters of permanent, as the manufacturing districts had long been of periodic,

---

[a] The German editions of 1845 and 1892 give "agricultural distress" in English, followed by the German equivalent.—*Ed.*

[b] The German editions of 1845 and 1892 have "towards the end of the twenties of the present century".—*Ed.*

[c] The German editions of 1845 and 1892 have "to use an expression from physics".—*Ed.*

pauperism[a]; and the modification of the Poor Law was the first measure which the State was obliged to apply to the daily increasing impoverishment of the country parishes. Moreover, the constant extension of farming on a large scale, the introduction of threshing and other machines, and the employment of women and children (which is now so general that its effects have recently been investigated by a special official commission), threw a large number of men out of employment. It is manifest, therefore, that here, too, the system of industrial production has made its entrance, by means of farming on a large scale, by the abolition of the patriarchal relation, which is of the greatest importance just here, by the introduction of machinery, steam, and the labour of women and children. In so doing, it has swept the last and most stationary portion of working humanity into the revolutionary movement. But the longer agriculture had remained stationary, the heavier now became the burden upon the worker, the more violently broke forth the results of the disorganisation of the old social fabric. The "over-population" came to light all at once, and could not, as in the manufacturing districts, be absorbed by the needs of an increasing production. New factories could always be built, if there were consumers for their products, but new land could not be created. The cultivation of waste common land was too daring a speculation for the bad times following the conclusion of peace.[b] The necessary consequence was that the competition of the workers among each other reached the highest point of intensity, and wages fell to the minimum. So long as the Old Poor Law existed, the workers received relief from the rates; wages naturally fell still lower, because the farmers forced the largest possible number of labourers to claim relief. The higher poor-rate, necessitated by the surplus population, was only increased by this measure, and the New Poor Law, of which we shall have more to say later, was now enacted as a remedy. But this did not improve matters. Wages did not rise, the surplus population could not be got rid of, and the cruelty of the new law did but serve to embitter the people to the utmost. Even the poor-rate, which diminished at first after the passage of the new law, attained its old height after a few years. Its only effect was that whereas previously three to

---

[a] In the German editions of 1845 and 1892 this sentence reads: "From this time the agricultural districts became the main seats of *permanent*, as the manufacturing districts of *periodic, pauperism*."—*Ed.*

[b] In the German editions of 1845 and 1892, this sentence reads: "The cultivation of waste common land was too risky a speculation for big capital to be invested in it following the conclusion of peace."—*Ed.*

four million half-paupers had existed, a million of total paupers now appeared, and the rest, still half-paupers, merely went without relief. The poverty in the agricultural districts has increased every year. The people live in the greatest want, whole families must struggle along with 6, 7, or 8 shillings a week, and at times have nothing. Let us hear a description of this population given by a Liberal member of Parliament as early as 1830*:

"That is an English peasant or pauper; for the words are synonymous. His sire was a pauper, and his mother's milk wanted nourishment. From infancy his food has been bad as well as insufficient; and he now feels the pains of unsatisfied hunger nearly whenever he is awake. But half-clothed, and never supplied with more warmth than suffices to cook his scanty meals, cold and wet come to him, and stay by him with the weather. He is married, but he has not tasted the highest joys of husband and father. His partner, and little ones being, like himself, often hungry, seldom warm, sometimes sick without aid, and always sorrowful without hope, are greedy, selfish, and vexing; so, to use his own expression, he 'hates the sight of them', and resorts to his hovel, only because a hedge affords less shelter from the wind and rain." He must support his family, though he cannot do so. "This brings begging, trickery, and quarrelling; and ends in settled craft. Though he have the inclination, he wants the courage to become, like more energetic men of his class, a poacher or smuggler on a large scale; but he pilfers occasionally, and teaches his children to lie and steal. His subdued and slavish manner towards his great neighbours shows that they treat him with suspicion and harshness. Consequently, he at once dreads and hates them; but he will never harm them by violent means. Too degraded to be desperate, he is thoroughly depraved. His miserable career will be short; rheumatism and asthma are conducting him to the workhouse, where he will breathe his last without one pleasant recollection, and so make room for another wretch who may live and die in the same way."[a]

Our author adds that besides this class of agricultural labourers, there is still another, somewhat more energetic and better endowed physically, mentally, and morally; those, namely, who live as wretchedly, but were not born to this condition. These he represents as better in their family life, but smugglers and poachers who get into frequent bloody conflicts with the gamekeepers and revenue officers of the coast, become more embittered against society during the prison life which they often undergo, and so stand abreast of the first class in their hatred of the property-holders.

* E. G. Wakefield, M. P., *Swing Unmasked; or, the Causes of Rural Incendiarism*, London, 1831. Pamphlet. The foregoing extracts may be found pp. 9-13, the passages dealing in the original with the then still existing Old Poor Law being here omitted.— *Note by Engels.*

[a] After the words "English peasant" at the beginning of the quotation the German editions of 1845 and 1892 have in brackets "i.e., agricultural labourer"; the words "hates the sight of them" are given in brackets after the German equivalent. —*Ed.*

"By courtesy," he says, in closing, "the entire body is called 'the bold peasantry of England'."[a]

Down to the present time, this description applies to the greater portion of the agricultural labourers of England. In June, 1844, the *Times* sent a correspondent into the agricultural districts to report upon the condition of this class, and the report which he furnished agreed wholly with the foregoing.[185] In certain districts wages were not more than six shillings a week; not more, that is, than in many districts in Germany, while the prices of all the necessaries of life are at least twice as high. What sort of life these people lead may be imagined; their food scanty and bad, their clothing ragged, their dwellings cramped and desolate, small, wretched huts, with no comforts whatsoever; and, for young people, lodging-houses, where men and women are scarcely separated, and illegitimate intercourse thus provoked. One or two days without work in the course of a month must inevitably plunge such people into the direst want. Moreover, they cannot combine to raise wages, because they are scattered, and if one alone refuses to work for low wages, there are dozens out of work, or supported by the rates,[b] who are thankful for the most trifling offer, while to him who declines work, every other form of relief than the hated workhouse is refused by the Poor Law guardians as to a lazy vagabond; for the guardians are the very farmers from whom or from whose neighbours and acquaintances alone he can get work. And not from one or two special districts of England do such reports come. On the contrary, the distress is general, equally great in the North and South, the East and West. The condition of the labourers in Suffolk and Norfolk corresponds with that of Devonshire, Hampshire, and Sussex. Wages are as low in Dorsetshire and Oxfordshire as in Kent and Surrey, Buckinghamshire and Cambridgeshire.

One especially barbaric cruelty against the working-class[c] is embodied in the Game Laws, which are more stringent[d] than in

---

[a] In the German editions of 1845 and 1892 the words "by courtesy" and "the bold peasantry of England" are given in English in brackets after their German equivalents. Engels attributed the phrase "the bold peasantry of England" to Shakespeare, an inaccuracy which was corrected in the American and English editions. In fact, the phrase "a bold peasantry, their country's pride" appears in Goldsmith's *The Deserted Village.—Ed*.

[b] The German editions of 1845 and 1892 have here "out of work and workhouse inmates".— *Ed*.

[c] The German editions of 1845 and 1892 have "agricultural proletariat" instead of the "working-class".— *Ed*.

[d] The German editions of 1845 and 1892 have here "in England".— *Ed*.

any other country, while the game is plentiful beyond all conception. The English peasant who, according to the old English custom and tradition, sees in poaching only a natural and noble expression of 'courage and daring, is stimulated still further by the contrast between his own poverty and the *car tel est notre plaisir*[a] of the lord, who preserves thousands of hares and game birds for his private enjoyment. The labourer lays snares, or shoots here and there a piece of game. It does not injure the landlord as a matter of fact, for he has a vast superfluity, and it brings the poacher a meal for himself and his starving family. But if he is caught he goes to jail, and for a second offence receives at the least seven years' transportation. From the severity of these laws arise the frequent bloody conflicts with the gamekeepers, which lead to a number of murders every year. Hence the post of gamekeeper is not only dangerous, but of ill-repute and despised. Last year, in two cases, gamekeepers shot themselves rather than continue their work. Such is the moderate price at which the landed aristocracy purchases the noble sport of shooting; but what does it matter to the lords of the soil[b]? Whether one or two more or less of the "surplus" live or die matters nothing, and even if in consequence of the Game Laws half the surplus population could be put out of the way, it would be all the better for the other half—according to the philanthropy of the English landlords.

Although the conditions of life in the country, the isolated dwellings, the stability of the surroundings and occupations, and consequently of the thoughts, are decidedly unfavourable to all development, yet poverty and want bear their fruits even here. The manufacturing and mining proletariat emerged early from the first stage of resistance to our social order, the direct rebellion of the individual by the perpetration of crime; but the peasants are still in this stage at the present time. Their favourite method of social warfare is incendiarism. In the winter which followed the Revolution of July, in 1830-31, these incendiarisms first became general. Disturbances had taken place, and the whole region of Sussex and the adjacent counties had been brought into a state of excitement in October, in consequence of an increase of the coastguard (which made smuggling much more difficult and "ruined the coast"—in the words of a farmer), changes in the Poor Law, low wages, and the introduction of machinery. In the

---

[a] For such is our pleasure.—*Ed*.

[b] In the German editions of 1845 and 1892 this expression is given in English.—*Ed*.

winter the farmers' hay and corn-stacks were burnt in the fields, and the very barns and stables under their windows. Nearly every night a couple of such fires blazed up, and spread terror among the farmers and landlords. The offenders were rarely discovered, and the workers attributed the incendiarism to a mythical person whom they named "Swing". Men puzzled their brains to discover who this Swing could be and whence this rage among the poor of the country districts. Of the great motive power, Want, Oppression, only a single person here and there thought, and certainly no one in the agricultural districts. Since that year the incendiarisms have been repeated every winter, with each recurring unemployed season of the agricultural labourers. In the winter of 1843-44, they were once more extraordinarily frequent. There lies before me a series of numbers of the *Northern Star* of that time, each one of which contains a report of several incendiarisms, stating in each case its authority. The numbers[a] wanting in the following list I have not at hand; but they, too, doubtless contain a number of cases. Moreover, such a sheet cannot possibly ascertain all the cases which occur. November 25th, 1843, two cases; several earlier ones are discussed. December 16th, in Bedfordshire, general excitement for a fortnight past in consequence of frequent incendiarisms, of which several take place every night. Two great farm-houses burnt down within the last few days; in Cambridgeshire four great farm-houses, Hertfordshire one, and besides these, fifteen other incendiarisms in different districts. December 30th, in Norfolk one, Suffolk two, Essex two, Cheshire one, Lancashire one, Derby, Lincoln, and the South twelve. January 6th, 1844, in all ten. January 13th, seven. January 20th, four incendiarisms. From this time forward, three of four incendiarisms per week are reported, and not as formerly until the spring only, but far into July and August. And that crimes of this sort are expected to increase in the approaching hard season of 1844-45, the English papers already indicate.[b]

What do my readers think of such a state of things in the quiet, idyllic country districts of England? Is this social war, or is it not? Is it a natural state of things which can last? Yet here the landlords and farmers are as dull and stupefied, as blind to

---

[a] The German editions of 1845 and 1892 have here "of this weekly".—*Ed.*

[b] In the German editions of 1845 and 1892 this sentence reads: "The English papers I have received since then and the reports in German papers prove that crimes of this sort increased with the approach of the hard season of 1844-45."—*Ed.*

everything which does not directly put money into their pockets, as the manufacturers and the bourgeoisie in general in the manufacturing districts. If the latter promise their employees salvation through the repeal of the Corn Laws, the landlords and a great part of the farmers promise theirs Heaven upon earth from the maintenance of the same laws. But in neither case do the property-holders succeed in winning the workers to the support of their pet hobby. Like the operatives, the agricultural labourers are thoroughly indifferent to the repeal or non-repeal of the Corn Laws. Yet the question is an important one for both. That is to say — by the repeal of the Corn Laws, free competition, the present social economy is carried to its extreme point; all further development within the present order comes to an end, and the only possible step farther is a radical transformation of the social order.* For the agricultural labourers the question has, further, the following important bearing: Free importation of corn involves (how, I cannot explain *here*) the emancipation of the farmers from the landlords, their transformation into Liberals. Towards this consummation the Anti-Corn Law League has already largely contributed, and this is its only real service. When the farmers become Liberals, i.e., conscious bourgeois, the agricultural labourers will inevitably become Chartists and Socialists[a]; the first change involves the second. And that a new movement is already beginning among the agricultural labourers is proved by a meeting which Earl Radnor, a Liberal landlord, caused to be held in October, 1844, near Highworth, where his estates lie, to pass resolutions against the Corn Laws. At this meeting, the labourers, perfectly indifferent as to these laws, demanded something wholly different, namely small holdings, at low rent, for themselves, telling Earl Radnor all sorts of bitter truths to his face. Thus the movement of the working-class is finding its way into the remote, stationary, mentally dead agricultural districts; and, thanks to the general distress, will soon be as firmly rooted and energetic as in the manufacturing districts.**

* This has been literally fulfilled. After a period of unexampled extension of trade, Free Trade has landed England in a crisis, which began in 1878, and is still increasing in energy in 1886.— *Note by Engels to the American edition of 1887* (reproduced in the English edition of 1892—*Ed.*).

** The agricultural labourers have now a Trade's Union; their most energetic representative, Joseph Arch, was elected M. P. in 1885.— *Note by Engels to the American edition of 1887* (reproduced in the English edition of 1892—*Ed.*).

[a] The German editions of 1845 and 1892 have here "i.e., conscious proletarians".—*Ed.*

As to the religious state of the agricultural labourers, they are, it is true, more pious than the manufacturing operatives; but they, too, are greatly at odds with the Church—for in these districts members of the Established Church almost exclusively are to be found. A correspondent of the *Morning Chronicle,* who, over the signature, "One who has whistled at the plough",[a] reports his tour through the agricultural districts, relates, among other things, the following conversation with some labourers after service:

"I inquired if the clergyman who had preached was the one who usually ministered there? 'Yes, blast him! he be our own parson sure enough—he be always a-begging; he be always, sin' ever I knowed him.'" (The sermon had been upon a mission to the heathen.) "'And sin' I knowed him,' said another, 'I never knowed a parson as wasn't a-begging for summat or tother.' 'Ah!' says a woman who came just out of the church: 'And look at wages a comin' down, look at them rich wagerbonds as the parsons hunt and dine and drink with! So help me God, we bes more fitter to be taken into the union and starved, than pay for parsons to go abroad.' 'Why don't they,' said another, 'send them parsons as be chantering every day in Salisbury Cathedral to nobody but the bare stones, why don't *they* go?' '*They* don't go,' said the old man who spoke first, 'because they be so rich as to have so much land all over, they wants the money to send away the poor uns; I knows what they want; I been knowing them too long not to know that.' 'But my good friends,' said I, 'you surely don't go to church always and come out of it with such bitter dislike to the parsons. If you do, why go at all?' 'Why go at all?' said the woman, 'we be like to go, and we wouldn't lose everything, work and all; we be like to go.' I learned later that they 'could get a few privileges in regard to fuel and ground for potatoes' (to be paid for!) if they went to church."

After describing their poverty and ignorance, the correspondent closes by saying:

"Now I assert fearlessly that the condition of these people, their poverty, their hatred of the churches, their outward compliance with, but inward bitterness towards, its dignitaries, is the rule throughout rural England; and that anything to the contrary is the exception."[186]

If the peasantry of England shows the consequences which a numerous agricultural proletariat in connection with large farming involves for the country districts, Wales illustrates the ruin of the small holders. If the English country parishes reproduce the antagonism between capitalist and proletarian, the state of the Welsh peasantry corresponds to the progressive ruin of the small bourgeoisie in the towns. In Wales are to be found, almost exclusively, small holders, who cannot with like profit sell their products as cheaply as the larger, more favourably situated English farmers, with whom, however, they are obliged to compete. Moreover, in some places the quality of the land admits of

---

[a] The pen-name of Alexander Somerville.—*Ed.*

the raising of livestock only, which is but slightly profitable. Then, too, these Welsh farmers, by reason of their separate nationality, which they retain pertinaciously, are much more stationary than the English farmers. But the competition among themselves and with their English neighbours (and the increased mortgages upon their land consequent upon this) has reduced them to such a state that they can scarcely live at all; and because they have not recognised the true cause of their wretched condition, they attribute it to all sorts of small causes, such as high tolls, etc., which do check the development of agriculture and commerce, but are taken into account as standing charges by every one who takes a holding, and are therefore really ultimately paid by the landlord. Here, too, the New Poor Law is cordially hated by the tenants, who hover in perpetual danger of coming under its sway. In 1843,[a] the famous "Rebecca" disturbances broke out among the Welsh peasantry; the men dressed in women's clothing, blackened their faces, and fell in armed crowds upon the toll-gates, destroyed them amidst great rejoicing and firing of guns, demolished the toll-keepers' houses, wrote threatening letters in the name of the imaginary "Rebecca", and once went so far as to storm the workhouse of Carmarthen. Later, when the militia was called out and the police strengthened, the peasants drew them off with wonderful skill upon false scents, demolished toll-gates at one point while the militia, lured by false signal bugles, was marching in some opposite direction; and betook themselves finally, when the police was too thoroughly reinforced, to single incendiarisms and attempts at murder. As usual, these greater crimes were the end of the movement. Many withdrew from disapproval, others from fear, and peace was restored of itself. The Government appointed a commission to investigate the affair and its causes, and there was an end of the matter. The poverty of the peasantry continues, however, and will one day, since it cannot under existing circumstances grow less, but must go on intensifying, produce more serious manifestations than these humorous Rebecca masquerades.

If England illustrates the results of the system of farming on a large scale and Wales on a small one, Ireland exhibits the consequences of overdividing the soil. The great mass of the population of Ireland consists of small tenants who occupy a sorry hut without partitions, and a potato patch just large enough to

---

[a] The German editions of 1845 and 1892 have here "In February 1843".—*Ed.*

supply them most scantily with potatoes through the winter. In consequence of the great competition which prevails among these small tenants, the rent has reached an unheard-of height, double, treble, and quadruple that paid in England. For every agricultural labourer seeks to become a tenant-farmer, and though the division of land has gone so far, there still remain numbers of labourers in competition for plots. Although in Great Britain 34,000,000 acres of land are cultivated, and in Ireland but 14,000,000; although Great Britain produces[a] agricultural products to the value of £150,000,000, and Ireland of but £36,000,000, there are in Ireland 75,000 agricultural proletarians *more* than in the neighbouring island.* How great the competition for land in Ireland must be is evident from this extraordinary disproportion, especially when one reflects that the labourers in Great Britain are living in the utmost distress. The consequence of this competition is that it is impossible for the tenants to live much better than the labourers, by reason of the high rents paid. The Irish people is thus held in crushing poverty, from which it cannot free itself under our present social conditions. These people live in the most wretched clay huts, scarcely good enough for cattle-pens, have scant food all winter long, or, as the report above quoted expresses it, they have potatoes half enough thirty weeks in the year, and the rest of the year nothing. When the time comes in the spring at which this provision reaches its end, or can no longer be used because of its sprouting, wife and children go forth to beg and tramp the country with their kettle in their hands. Meanwhile the husband, after planting potatoes for the next year, goes in search of work either in Ireland or England, and returns at the potato harvest to his family. This is the condition in which nine-tenths of the Irish country folks live. They are poor as church mice, wear the most wretched rags, and stand upon the lowest plane of intelligence possible in a half-civilised country. According to the report quoted, there are, in a population of $8^1/_2$ millions, 585,000 heads of families in a state of total destitution[b]; and according to other authorities, cited by Sheriff Alison,**

* Report of the Poor Law Commissioners for Ireland. Parliamentary Session of 1837.—*Note by Engels*.

** *Principles of Population*, vol. ii.—*Note by Engels*.

[a] The German editions of 1845 and 1892 have "annually produces".—*Ed*.

[b] In the German editions of 1845 and 1892 the word "destitution" is given in English in brackets after the German equivalent.—*Ed*.

there are in Ireland 2,300,000 persons who could not live without public or private assistance — or 27 per cent of the whole population paupers!

The cause of this poverty lies in the existing social conditions, especially in competition here found in the form of the subdivision of the soil. Much effort has been spent in finding other causes. It has been asserted that the relation of the tenant to the landlord who lets his estate in large lots to tenants, who again have their sub-tenants, and sub-sub-tenants, in turn, so that often ten middlemen come between the landlord and the actual cultivator — it has been asserted that the shameful law which gives the landlord the right of expropriating the cultivator who may have paid his rent duly, if the first tenant fails to pay the landlord, that this law is to blame for all this poverty. But all this determines only the form in which the poverty manifests itself. Make the small tenant a landowner himself and what follows? The majority could not live upon their holdings even if they had no rent to pay, and any slight improvement which might take place would be lost again in a few years in consequence of the rapid increase of population. The children would then live to grow up under the improved conditions who now die in consequence of poverty in early childhood. From another side comes the assertion that the shameless oppression inflicted by the English is the cause of the trouble. It is the cause of the somewhat earlier appearance of this poverty, but not of the poverty itself. Or the blame is laid on the Protestant Church forced upon a Catholic nation; but divide among the Irish what the Church takes from them, and it does not reach six shillings[a] a head. Besides, tithes are a tax upon landed property, not upon the tenant, though he may nominally pay them; now, since the Commutation Bill of 1838,[187] the landlord pays the tithes directly and reckons so much higher rent, so that the tenant is none the better off. And in the same way a hundred other causes of this poverty are brought forward, all proving as little as these. This poverty is the result of our social conditions; apart from these, causes may be found for the manner in which it manifests itself, but not for the fact of its existence. That poverty manifests itself in Ireland thus and not otherwise, is owing to the character of the people, and to their historical development. The Irish are a people related in their whole character to the Latin nations, to the French, and especially to the Italians. The bad features of their character we have already had

---

[a] The German editions of 1845 and 1892 have "two talers".—*Ed.*

depicted by Carlyle. Let us now hear an Irishman,[a] who at least comes nearer to the truth than Carlyle, with his prejudice in favour of the Teutonic character*:

"They are restless yet indolent, shrewd and indiscreet, impetuous, impatient and improvident, instinctively brave, thoughtlessly generous; quick to resent and forgive offences, to form and renounce friendships. With genius they are profusely gifted; with judgment sparingly."

With the Irish, feeling and passion predominate; reason must bow before them. Their sensuous, excitable nature prevents reflection and quiet, persevering activity from reaching development—such a nation is utterly unfit for manufacture as now conducted. Hence they held fast to agriculture, and remained upon the lowest plane even of that. With the small subdivisions of land, which were not here artificially created, as in France and on the Rhine, by the division of great estates,** but have existed from time immemorial, an improvement of the soil by the investment of capital was not to be thought of; and it would, according to Alison, require 120 million pounds sterling to bring the soil up to the not very high state of fertility already attained in England. The English immigration, which might have raised the standard of Irish civilisation, has contented itself with the most brutal plundering of the Irish people; and while the Irish, by their immigration into England, have furnished England a leaven which will produce its own results in the future, they have little for which to be thankful to the English immigration.

The attempts of the Irish to save themselves from their present ruin, on the one hand, take the form of crimes. These are the order of the day in the agricultural districts, and are nearly always directed against the most immediate enemies, the landlords' agents, or their obedient servants, the Protestant intruders, whose large farms are made up of the potato patches of hundreds of ejected families. Such crimes are especially frequent in the South and West. On the other hand, the Irish hope for relief by means of the agitation for the repeal of the Legislative Union with England.[188] From all the foregoing, it is clear that the uneducated

* *The State of Ireland*, London, 1807; 2nd ed., 1821. Pamphlet.—*Note by Engels.*
** (1892) Mistake. Small-scale agriculture had been the prevailing form of farming ever since the Middle Ages. Thus the small peasant farms existed even before the Revolution. The only thing the latter changed was their *ownership*; that it took away from the feudal lords and transferred, directly or indirectly, to the peasants.—*Note by Engels to the German edition of 1892.*

---

[a] John Wilson Croker.—*Ed.*

Irish must see in the English their worst enemies; and their first hope of improvement in the conquest of national independence. But quite as clear is it, too, that Irish distress cannot be removed by any Act of Repeal. Such an Act would, however, at once lay bare the fact that the cause of Irish misery, which now seems to come from abroad, is really to be found at home. Meanwhile, it is an open question whether the accomplishment of repeal will be necessary to make this clear to the Irish. Hitherto, neither Chartism nor Socialism has had marked success in Ireland.

I close my observations upon Ireland at this point the more readily, as the Repeal Agitation of 1843 and O'Connell's trial[189] have been the means of making the Irish distress more and more known in Germany.

We have now followed the proletariat of the British Islands through all branches of its activity, and found it everywhere living in want and misery under totally inhuman conditions. We have seen discontent arise with the rise of the proletariat, grow, develop, and organise; we have seen open bloodless and bloody battles of the proletariat against the bourgeoisie. We have investigated the principles according to which the fate, the hopes, and fears of the proletariat are determined, and we have found that there is no prospect of improvement in their condition.

We have had an opportunity, here and there, of observing the conduct of the bourgeoisie towards the proletariat, and we have found that it considers only itself, has only its own advantage in view. However, in order not to be unjust, let us investigate its mode of action somewhat more exactly.

THE ATTITUDE OF THE BOURGEOISIE
TOWARDS THE PROLETARIAT

In speaking of the bourgeoisie I include the so-called aristocracy, for this is a privileged class, an aristocracy, only in contrast with the bourgeoisie, not in contrast with the proletariat. The proletarian sees in both only the property-holder — i.e., the bourgeois. Before the privilege of property all other privileges vanish. The sole difference is this, that the bourgeois proper stands in active relations with the manufacturing, and, in a measure, with the mining proletarians, and, as farmer, with the agricultural labourers, whereas the so-called aristocrat comes into contact with the agricultural labourer only.[a]

I have never seen a class so deeply demoralised, so incurably debased by selfishness, so corroded within, so incapable of progress, as the English bourgeoisie; and I mean by this, especially the bourgeoisie proper, particularly the Liberal, Corn Law repealing bourgeoisie. For it nothing exists in this world, except for the sake of money, itself not excluded.[b] It knows no bliss save that of rapid gain, no pain save that of losing gold.* In the presence of this

---

* Carlyle gives in his *Past and Present* (London, 1843) a splendid description of the English bourgeoisie and its disgusting money-greed. Part of this description I translated for the *Deutsch-Französische Jahrbücher*, to which I refer the reader.—*Note by Engels*. (The last sentence is not given in the American edition of 1887 and the English edition of 1892.—*Ed.*)

---

[a] In the German editions of 1845 and 1892 the end of the sentence reads: "comes into contact with part of the mining and with the argicultural labourers only".— *Ed*.

[b] The German editions of 1845 and 1892 have here "for it lives only to make money".—*Ed*.

avarice and lust of gain, it is not possible for a single human sentiment or opinion to remain untainted. True, these English bourgeois are good husbands and family men, and have all sorts of other private virtues, and appear, in ordinary intercourse, as decent and respectable as all other bourgeois; even in business they are better to deal with than the Germans; they do not higgle and haggle so much as our own pettifogging merchants; but how does this help matters? Ultimately it is self-interest, and especially money gain, which alone determines them. I once went into Manchester with such a bourgeois, and spoke to him of the bad, unwholesome method of building, the frightful condition of the working-people's quarters, and asserted that I had never seen so ill-built a city. The man listened quietly to the end, and said at the corner where we parted: "And yet there is a great deal of money made here[a]; good morning, sir." It is utterly indifferent to the English bourgeois whether his working-men starve or not, if only he makes money. All the conditions of life are measured by money, and what brings no money is nonsense, unpractical, idealistic bosh. Hence, Political Economy, the Science of Wealth, is the favourite study of these bartering Jews. Every one of them is a Political Economist. The relation of the manufacturer to his operatives has nothing human in it; it is purely economic. The manufacturer is Capital, the operative Labour. And if the operative will not be forced into this abstraction, if he insists that he is not Labour, but a man, who possesses, among other things, the attribute of labour-force,[b] if he takes it into his head that he need not allow himself to be sold and bought in the market, as the commodity "Labour", the bourgeois reason comes to a standstill. He cannot comprehend that he holds any other relation to the operatives than that of purchase and sale; he sees in them not human beings, but hands, as he constantly calls them to their faces; he insists, as Carlyle says, that "Cash Payment is the only nexus between man and man." Even the relation between himself and his wife is, in ninety-nine cases out of a hundred, mere "Cash Payment".[c] Money determines the worth of the man; he is "worth

---

[a] In the German editions of 1845 and 1892 this remark is given in English followed by the German translation.—*Ed.*

[b] The German editions of 1845 and 1892 have "the ability to work" instead of "the attribute of labour-force".—*Ed.*

[c] In the German editions of 1845 and 1892 the sentence follows: "The shameful slavery in which money holds the bourgeoisie is imprinted even on the language through the rule of the bourgeoisie."—*Ed.*

ten thousand pounds".[a] He who has money is of "the better sort of people", is "influential", and what *he* does counts for something in his social circle. The huckstering spirit penetrates the whole language, all relations are expressed in business terms, in economic categories. Supply and demand are the formulas according to which the logic of the English bourgeois judges all human life. Hence free competition in every respect, hence the *régime* of *laissez-faire, laissez-aller*[190] in government, in medicine, in education, and soon to be in religion, too, as the State Church collapses more and more. Free competition will suffer no limitation, no State supervision; the whole State is but a burden to it. It would reach its highest perfection in a wholly ungoverned anarchic society, where each might exploit the other to his heart's content.[b] Since, however, the bourgeoisie cannot dispense with government, but must have it to hold the equally indispensable proletariat in check, it turns the power of government against the proletariat and keeps out of its way as far as possible.

Let no one believe, however, that the "cultivated" Englishman openly brags with his egotism. On the contrary, he conceals it under the vilest hypocrisy. What? The wealthy English fail to remember the poor? They who have founded philanthropic institutions, such as no other country can boast of! Philanthropic institutions forsooth! As though you rendered the proletarians a service in first sucking out their very life-blood and then practising your self-complacent, Pharisaic philanthropy upon them, placing yourselves before the world as mighty benefactors of humanity when you give back to the plundered victims the hundredth part of what belongs to them! Charity which degrades him who gives more than him who takes; charity which treads the downtrodden still deeper in the dust, which demands that the degraded, the pariah cast out by society, shall first surrender the last that remains to him, his very claim to manhood, shall first beg for mercy before your mercy deigns to press, in the shape of an alms, the brand of degradation upon his brow. But let us hear the English bourgeoisie's own words. It is not yet a year since I read in the *Manchester Guardian* the following letter to the editor, which

---

[a] The German edition of 1845 and 1892 have here "i.e., he owns that much". The expressions "he is worth ten thousand pounds", "the better sort of people", and "influential", are given in English with their German equivalents.—*Ed.*

[b] The German editions of 1845 and 1892 have here "as, e.g., in friend Stirner's 'society'".—*Ed.*

was published without comment as a perfectly natural, reasonable thing:

"MR. EDITOR,— For some time past our main streets are haunted by swarms of beggars, who try to awaken the pity of the passers-by in a most shameless and annoying manner, by exposing their tattered clothing, sickly aspect, and disgusting wounds and deformities. I should think that when one not only pays the poor-rate, but also contributes largely to the charitable institutions, one had done enough to earn a right to be spared such disagreeable and impertinent molestations. And why else do we pay such high rates for the maintenance of the municipal police, if they do not even protect us so far as to make it possible to go to or out of town in peace? I hope the publication of these lines in your widely-circulated paper may induce the authorities to remove this nuisance; and I remain,— Your obedient servant,

"A Lady."

There you have it! The English bourgeoisie is charitable out of self-interest; it gives nothing outright, but regards its gifts as a business matter, makes a bargain with the poor, saying: "If I spend this much upon benevolent institutions, I thereby purchase the right not to be troubled any further, and you are bound thereby to stay in your dusky holes and not to irritate my tender nerves by exposing your misery. You shall despair as before, but you shall despair unseen, this I require, this I purchase with my subscription of twenty pounds for the infirmary!" It is infamous, this charity of a Christian bourgeois! And so writes "A Lady"; she does well to sign herself such, well that she has lost the courage to call herself a woman! But if the "Ladies" are such as this, what must the "Gentlemen" be? It will be said that this is a single case; but no, the foregoing letter expresses the temper of the great majority of the English bourgeoisie, or the editor would not have accepted it, and some reply would have been made to it, which I watched for in vain in the succeeding numbers. And as to the efficiency of this philanthropy, Canon Parkinson himself says[a] that the poor are relieved much more by the poor than by the bourgeoisie; and such relief given by an honest proletarian who knows himself what it is to be hungry, for whom sharing his scanty meal is really a sacrifice, but a sacrifice borne with pleasure, such help has a wholly different ring to it from the carelessly-tossed alms of the luxurious bourgeois.

In other respects, too, the bourgeoisie assumes a hypocritical, boundless philanthropy, but only when its own interests require it; as in its Politics and Political Economy. It has been at work now

---

[a] R. Parkinson, *On the Present Condition of the Labouring Poor in Manchester.*—*Ed.*

well on towards five years to prove to the working-men that it strives to abolish the Corn Laws solely in their interest. But the long and short of the matter is this: the Corn Laws keep the price of bread higher than in other countries, and thus raise wages; but these high wages render difficult competition of the manufacturers against other nations in which bread, and consequently wages, are cheaper. The Corn Laws being repealed, the price of bread falls, and wages gradually approach those of other European countries, as must be clear to every one from our previous exposition of the principles according to which wages are determined. The manufacturer can compete more readily, the demand for English goods increases, and, with it, the demand for labour. In consequence of this increased demand wages would actually rise somewhat, and the unemployed workers be re-employed; but for how long? The "surplus population" of England, and especially of Ireland, is sufficient to supply English manufacture with the necessary operatives, even if it were doubled; and, in a few years, the small advantage of the repeal of the Corn Laws would be balanced, a new crisis would follow, and we should be back at the point from which we started, while the first stimulus to manufacture would have increased population meanwhile. All this the proletarians understand very well, and have told the manufacturers to their faces; but, in spite of that, the manufacturers have in view solely the immediate advantage which the repeal of the Corn Laws would bring them. They are too narrow-minded to see that, even for themselves, no permanent advantage can arise from this measure, because their competition with each other would soon force the profit of the individual back to its old level; and thus they continue to shriek to the working-men that it is purely for the sake of the starving millions that the rich members of the Liberal party pour hundreds and thousands of·pounds into the treasury of the Anti-Corn Law League, while every one knows that they are only sending the butter after the cheese, that they calculate upon earning it all back in the first ten years after the repeal of the Corn Laws.[a] But the workers are no longer to be misled by the bourgeoisie, especially since the insurrection of 1842. They demand of every one who presents himself as interested in their welfare, that he should declare himself in favour of the People's Charter as proof of the sincerity of his professions, and in so

---

[a] In the German editions of 1845 and 1892 the end of the sentence reads: "upon earning it all back ten- and a hundredfold in the first years after the repeal of the Corn Laws".—*Ed*.

doing, they protest against all outside help, for the Charter is a demand for the power to help themselves. Whoever declines so to declare himself they pronounce their enemy, and are perfectly right in so doing, whether he be a declared foe or a false friend. Besides, the Anti-Corn Law League has used the most despicable falsehoods and tricks to win the support of the workers. It has tried to prove to them that the money price of labour is in inverse proportion to the price of corn; that wages are high when grain is cheap, and vice versa, an assertion which it pretends to prove with the most ridiculous arguments, and one which is, in itself, more ridiculous than any other that has proceeded from the mouth of an Economist. When this failed to help matters, the workers were promised bliss supreme in consequence of the increased demand in the labour market; indeed, men went so far as to carry through the streets two models of loaves of bread, on one of which, by far the larger, was written: "American Eightpenny Loaf, Wages Four Shillings per Day", and upon the much smaller one: "English Eightpenny Loaf, Wages Two Shillings a Day". But the workers have not allowed themselves to be misled. They know their lords and masters too well.

But rightly to measure the hypocrisy of these promises, the practice of the bourgeoisie must be taken into account. We have seen in the course of our report how the bourgeoisie exploits the proletariat in every conceivable way for its own benefit! We have, however, hitherto seen only how the single bourgeois maltreats the proletariat upon his own account. Let us turn now to the manner in which the bourgeoisie as a party, as the power of the State, conducts itself towards the proletariat.[a] Laws are necessary only because there are persons in existence who own nothing; and although this is directly expressed in but few laws, as, for instance, those against vagabonds and tramps, in which the proletariat as such is outlawed, yet enmity to the proletariat is so emphatically the basis of the law that the judges, and especially the Justices of the Peace, who are bourgeois themselves, and with whom the proletariat comes most in contact, find this meaning in the laws without further consideration. If a rich man is brought up, or rather summoned, to appear before the court, the judge regrets that he is obliged to impose so much trouble, treats the matter as favourably as possible, and, if he is forced to condemn the

---

[a] In the German editions of 1845 and 1892 the sentence follows "It is quite obvious that all legislation is calculated to protect those who possess property against those who do not."—*Ed.*

accused, does so with extreme regret, etc., etc., and the end of it all is a miserable fine, which the bourgeois throws upon the table with contempt and then departs. But if a poor devil gets into such a position as involves appearing before the Justice of the Peace — he has almost always spent the night in the station-house with a crowd of his peers — he is regarded from the beginning as guilty; his defence is set aside with a contemptuous "Oh! we know the excuse", and a fine imposed which he cannot pay and must work out with several months on the treadmill. And if nothing can be proved against him, he is sent to the treadmill, none the less, "as a rogue and a vagabond".[a] The partisanship of the Justices of the Peace, especially in the country, surpasses all description, and it is so much the order of the day that all cases which are not too utterly flagrant are quietly reported by the newspapers, without comment. Nor is anything else to be expected. For on the one hand, these Dogberries do merely construe the law according to the intent of the farmers,[b] and, on the other, they are themselves bourgeois, who see the foundation of all true order in the interests of their class. And the conduct of the police corresponds to that of the Justices of the Peace. The bourgeois may do what he will and the police remain ever polite, adhering strictly to the law, but the proletarian is roughly, brutally treated; his poverty both casts the suspicion of every sort of crime upon him and cuts him off from legal redress against any caprice of the administrators of the law; for him, therefore, the protecting forms of the law do not exist, the police force their way into his house without further ceremony, arrest and abuse him; and only when a working-men's association, such as the miners, engages a Roberts, does it become evident how little the protective side of the law exists for the working-man, how frequently he has to bear all the burdens of the law without enjoying its benefits.

Down to the present hour, the property-holding class in Parliament still struggles against the better feelings of those not yet fallen a prey to egotism, and seeks to subjugate the proletariat still further. One piece of common land after another is appropriated and placed under cultivation, a process by which the general cultivation is furthered, but the proletariat greatly injured. Where there were still commons, the poor could pasture an ass, a pig, or

---

[a] The German editions of 1845 and 1892 give "a rogue and a vagabond" in English in brackets followed by the remark: "these words almost always go together". —Ed.

[b] The German editions of 1845 and 1892 have "construe the law according to its original meaning".—Ed.

geese, the children and young people had a place where they could play and live out of doors; but this is gradually coming to an end. The earnings of the worker are less, and the young people, deprived of their play-ground, go to the beer-shops. A mass of acts for enclosing and cultivating commons is passed at every session of Parliament. When the Government determined during the session of 1844 to force the all monopolising railways to make travelling possible for the workers by means of charges proportionate to their means, a penny a mile,[a] and proposed therefore to introduce such a third class train upon every railway daily, the "Reverend Father in God", the Bishop of London, proposed that Sunday, the only day upon which working-men in work *can* travel, be exempted from this rule, and travelling thus be left open to the rich and shut off from the poor. This proposition was, however, too direct, too undisguised to pass through Parliament, and was dropped. I have no room to enumerate the many concealed attacks of even one single session upon the proletariat. One from the session of 1844 must suffice. An obscure member of Parliament, a Mr. Miles, proposed a bill regulating the relation of master and servant which seemed comparatively unobjectionable. The Government became interested in the bill, and it was referred to a committee. Meanwhile the strike among the miners in the North broke out, and Roberts made his triumphal passage through England with his acquitted working-men. When the bill was reported by the committee, it was discovered that certain most despotic provisions had been interpolated in it, especially one conferring upon the employer the power to bring before any[b] Justice of the Peace every working-man who had contracted verbally or in writing to do any work whatsoever, in case of refusal to work or other misbehaviour, and have him condemned to prison with hard labour for two months, upon the oath of the employer or his agent or overlooker, i.e., upon the oath of the accuser. This bill aroused the working-men to the utmost fury, the more so as the Ten Hours' Bill was before Parliament at the same time, and had called forth a considerable agitation. Hundreds of meetings were held, hundreds of working-men's petitions forwarded to London to Thomas Duncombe, the representative of the interests of the proletariat. This man was, except Ferrand, the

---

[a] The German editions of 1845 and 1892 have here "about 5 silver groschen a German mile".— *Ed.*

[b] In the German editions of 1845 and 1892 the words "any" here and "misbehaviour" below are given in English in brackets after the corresponding German words.— *Ed.*

representative of "Young England",[191] the only vigorous opponent of the bill; but when the other Radicals saw that the people were declaring against it, one after the other crept forward and took his place by Duncombe's side; and as the Liberal bourgeoisie had not the courage to defend the bill in the face of the excitement among the working-men,[a] it was ignominiously lost.

Meanwhile the most open declaration of war of the bourgeoisie upon the proletariat is Malthus' Law of Population and the New Poor Law framed in accordance with it. We have already alluded several times to the theory of Malthus. We may sum up its final result in these few words, that the earth is perennially over-populated, whence poverty, misery, distress, and immorality must prevail; that it is the lot, the eternal destiny of mankind, to exist in too great numbers, and therefore in diverse classes, of which some are rich, educated, and moral, and others more or less poor, distressed, ignorant, and immoral. Hence it follows in practice, and Malthus himself drew this conclusion, that charities and poor-rates are, properly speaking, nonsense, since they serve only to maintain, and stimulate the increase of, the surplus population whose competition crushes down wages for the employed; that the employment of the poor by the Poor Law Guardians is equally unreasonable, since only a fixed quantity of the products of labour can be consumed, and for every unemployed labourer thus furnished employment, another hitherto employed must be driven into enforced idleness, whence private undertakings suffer at cost of Poor Law industry; that, in other words, the whole problem is not how to support the surplus population, but how to restrain it as far as possible. Malthus declares in plain English that the right to live, a right previously asserted in favour of every man in the world, is nonsense. He quotes the words of a poet, that the poor man comes to the feast of Nature and finds no cover laid for him, and adds that "she bids him begone",[b] for he did not before his birth ask of society whether or not he is welcome.[c] This is now the pet theory of all genuine English bourgeois, and very naturally, since it is the most specious excuse for them, and has, moreover, a good deal of truth in it under existing conditions. If, then, the problem is not to make the "surplus population" useful, to

---

[a] The German editions of 1845 and 1892 have here "and as nobody had any lively interest in defending it against the people", etc.—*Ed.*

[b] In the German editions of 1845 and 1892 this English phrase is given in brackets after its German equivalent.—*Ed.*

[c] Th. R. Malthus, *An Essay on the Principle of Population.*—*Ed.*

transform it into available population, but merely to let it starve to death in the least objectionable way and to prevent its having too many children, this, of course, is simple enough, provided the surplus population perceives its own superfluousness and takes kindly to starvation. There is, however, in spite of the violent exertions of the humane bourgeoisie, no immediate prospect of its succeeding in bringing about such a disposition among the workers. The workers have taken it into their heads that they, with their busy hands, are the necessary, and the rich capitalists, who do nothing, the surplus population.

Since, however, the rich hold all the power, the proletarians must submit, if they will not good-temperedly perceive it for themselves, to have the law actually declare them superfluous. This has been done by the New Poor Law. The Old Poor Law which rested upon the Act of 1601 (the 43rd of Elizabeth), naively started from the notion that it is the duty of the parish to provide for the maintenance of the poor. Whoever had no work received relief, and the poor man regarded the parish as pledged to protect him from starvation. He demanded his weekly relief as his right, not as a favour, and this became, at last, too much for the bourgeoisie. In 1833, when the bourgeoisie had just come into power through the Reform Bill, and pauperism in the country districts had just reached its full development, the bourgeoisie began the reform of the Poor Law according to its own point of view. A commission was appointed, which investigated the administration of the Poor Laws, and revealed a multitude of abuses. It was discovered that the whole working-class in the country was pauperised and more or less dependent upon the rates, from which they received relief when wages were low; it was found that this system by which the unemployed were maintained, the ill-paid and the parents of large families relieved, fathers of illegitimate children required to pay alimony, and poverty, in general, recognised as needing protection, it was found that this system was ruining the nation, was—

"a check to industry, a reward for improvident marriages, a stimulant to population, and a blind to its effects on wages; a national institution for discountenancing the industrious and honest, and for protecting the idle, the improvident and the vicious; the destroyer" of the bonds of family life; "a system for preventing the accumulation of capital, for destroying that which exists, and for reducing the rate-payer to pauperism; and a premium for illegitimate children" in the provision of aliment. (Words of the Report of the Poor Law Commissioners.)*

* Extracts from Information received from the Poor Law Commissioners. Published by authority. London, 1833.—*Note by Engels.*

This description of the action of the Old Poor Law is certainly correct; relief fosters laziness and increase of "surplus population". Under present social conditions it is perfectly clear that the poor man is compelled to be an egotist, and when he can choose, living equally well in either case, he prefers doing nothing to working. But what follows therefrom? That our present social conditions are good for nothing, and not as the Malthusian Commissioners conclude, that poverty is a crime, and, as such, to be visited with heinous penalties which may serve as a warning to others.[a]

But these wise Malthusians were so thoroughly convinced of the infallibility of their theory that they did not for one moment hesitate to cast the poor into the Procrustean bed of their economic notions and treat them with the most revolting cruelty. Convinced with Malthus and the rest of the adherents of free competition that it is best to let each one take care of himself,[b] they would have preferred to abolish the Poor Laws altogether. Since, however, they had neither the courage nor the authority to do this, they proposed a Poor Law constructed as far as possible in harmony with the doctrine of Malthus, which is yet more barbarous than that of *laissez-faire*, because it interferes actively in cases in which the latter is passive. We have seen how Malthus characterises poverty, or rather the want of employment, as a crime under the title "superfluity", and recommends for it punishment by starvation. The commissioners were not quite so barbarous; death outright by starvation was something too terrible even for a Poor Law Commissioner. "Good," said they, "we grant you poor a right to exist, but only to exist; the right to multiply you have not, nor the right to exist as befits human beings. You are a pest, and if we cannot get rid of you as we do of other pests, you shall feel, at least, that you are a pest, and you shall at least be held in check, kept from bringing into the world other 'surplus', either directly or through inducing in others laziness and want of employment. Live you shall, but live as an awful warning to all those who might have inducements to become 'superfluous'."

They accordingly brought in the New Poor Law, which was passed by Parliament in 1834, and continues in force down to the present day. All relief in money and provisions was abolished; the

---

[a] The German editions of 1845 and 1892 word the end of the sentence as follows: "that poverty should be treated as a crime according to the theory of determent".— *Ed.*

[b] The German editions of 1845 and 1892 have here "to pursue a consistent *laissez-faire* policy".— *Ed.*

only relief allowed was admission to the workhouses immediately built. The regulations for these workhouses, or, as the people call them, Poor Law Bastilles,[a] is such as to frighten away every one who has the slightest prospect of life without this form of public charity. To make sure that relief be applied for only in the most extreme cases and after every other effort had failed, the workhouse has been made the most repulsive residence which the refined ingenuity of a Malthusian can invent. The food is worse than that of the most ill-paid working-man while employed, and the work harder, or they might prefer the workhouse to their wretched existence outside. Meat, especially fresh meat, is rarely furnished, chiefly potatoes, the worst possible bread and oatmeal porridge, little or no beer. The food of criminal prisoners is better, as a rule, so that the paupers frequently commit some offence for the purpose of getting into jail. For the workhouse is a jail too; he who does not finish his task gets nothing to eat; he who wishes to go out must ask permission, which is granted or not, according to his behaviour or the inspector's whim; tobacco is forbidden, also the receipt of gifts from relatives or friends outside the house; the paupers wear a workhouse uniform, and are handed over, helpless and without redress, to the caprice of the inspectors. To prevent their labour from competing with that of outside concerns, they are set to rather useless tasks: the men break stones, "as much as a strong man can accomplish with effort in a day"; the women, children, and aged men pick oakum, for I know not what insignificant use. To prevent the "superfluous" from multiplying, and "demoralised" parents from influencing their children, families are broken up; the husband is placed in one wing, the wife in another, the children in a third, and they are permitted to see one another only at stated times after long intervals, and then only when they have, in the opinion of the officials, behaved well. And in order to shut off the external world from contamination by pauperism within these bastilles, the inmates are permitted to receive visits only with the consent of the officials, and in the reception-rooms; to communicate in general with the world outside only by leave and under supervision.

Yet the food is supposed to be wholesome and the treatment humane with all this. But the intent of the law is too loudly outspoken for this requirement to be in any wise fulfilled. The Poor Law Commissioners and the whole English bourgeoisie

---

[a] In the German editions of 1845 and 1892 the words "workhouses" and "Poor Law Bastilles" are given in brackets following their German equivalents.—*Ed.*

deceive themselves if they believe the administration of the law possible without these results. The treatment, which the letter of the law prescribes, is in direct contradiction of its spirit. If the law in its essence proclaims the poor criminals, the workhouses prisons, their inmates beyond the pale of the law, beyond the pale of humanity, objects of disgust and repulsion, then all commands to the contrary are unavailing. In practice, the spirit and not the letter of the law is followed in the treatment of the poor, as in the following few examples [192]:

In the workhouse at Greenwich, in the summer of 1843, a boy five years old was punished by being shut into the dead-room,[a] where he had to sleep upon the lids of the coffins. In the workhouse at Herne, the same punishment was inflicted upon a little girl for wetting the bed at night, and this method of punishment seems to be a favourite one. This workhouse, which stands in one of the most beautiful regions of Kent, is peculiar, in so far as its windows open only upon the court, and but two, newly introduced, afford the inmates a glimpse of the outer world. The author who relates this in the *Illuminated Magazine*,[b] closes his description with the words:

"If God punished men for crimes as man punishes man for poverty, then woe to the sons of Adam!"[193]

In November, 1843, a man died at Leicester, who had been dismissed two days before from the workhouse at Coventry. The details of the treatment of the poor in this institution are revolting. The man, George Robson, had a wound upon the shoulder, the treatment of which was wholly neglected; he was set to work at the pump, using the sound arm; was given only the usual workhouse fare, which he was utterly unable to digest by reason of the unhealed wound and his general debility; he naturally grew weaker, and the more he complained, the more brutally he was treated. When his wife[c] tried to bring him her drop of beer, she was reprimanded, and forced to drink it herself in the presence of the female warder. He became ill, but received no better treatment. Finally, at his own request, and under the most insulting epithets, he was discharged, accompanied by his wife. Two days later he died at Leicester, in consequence of the

---

[a] The German editions of 1845 and 1892 have here "for three nights".—*Ed.*

[b] Douglas Jerrold.—*Ed.*

[c] The German editions of 1845 and 1892 have here "who was also in the workhouse".—*Ed.*

neglected wound and of the food given him, which was utterly indigestible for one in his condition, as the surgeon present at the inquest testified. When he was discharged, there were handed to him letters containing money, which had been kept back six weeks, and opened, according to a rule of the establishment, by the inspector! In Birmingham such scandalous occurrences took place, that finally, in 1843,[a] an official was sent to investigate the case. He found that four tramps[b] had been shut up naked under a stair-case in a black hole, eight to ten days, often deprived of food until noon, and that at the severest season of the year. A little boy had been passed through all grades of punishment known to the institution; first locked up in a damp, vaulted, narrow, lumber-room; then in the dog-hole twice, the second time three days and three nights; then the same length of time in the old dog-hole, which was still worse; then the tramp-room, a stinking, disgustingly filthy hole, with wooden sleeping stalls, where the official, in the course of his inspection, found two other tattered boys, shrivelled with cold, who had been spending three days there. In the dog-hole there were often seven, and in the tramp-room, twenty men huddled together. Women, also, were placed in the dog-hole, because they refused to go to church and one was shut four days into the tramp-room, with God knows what sort of company, and that while she was ill and receiving medicine! Another woman was placed in the insane department for punishment, though she was perfectly sane. In the workhouse at Bacton, in Suffolk, in January, 1844, a similar investigation revealed the fact that a feeble-minded woman was employed as nurse, and took care of the patients accordingly[c]; while sufferers, who were often restless at night, or tried to get up, were tied fast with cords passed over the covering and under the bedstead, to save the nurses the trouble of sitting up at night. One patient was found dead, bound in this way. In the St. Pancras workhouse in London (where the cheap shirts already mentioned are made[d]), an epileptic died of suffocation during an attack in bed, no one coming to his relief; in the same house, four to six, sometimes eight children, slept in one bed. In

---

[a] The German editions of 1845 and 1892 have "in December 1843".—Ed.

[b] The German editions of 1845 and 1892 note here in brackets that this word ("trampers" in the German original) was explained above. (See p. 504 of this volume.) The words "black hole" are also given in English in brackets after the German equivalent.—Ed.

[c] The German editions of 1845 and 1892 have "was employed as nurse and did all sorts of inconceivable things to the patients".—Ed.

[d] The German editions of 1845 and 1892 do not have the words: "already mentioned" (the reference is to p. 499 of this volume).—Ed.

Shoreditch workhouse a man was placed, together with a fever patient violently ill, in a bed teeming with vermin. In Bethnal Green workhouse, London, a woman in the sixth month of pregnancy was shut up in the reception-room with her two-year-old child, from February 28th to March 19th, without being admitted into the workhouse itself, and without a trace of a bed or the means of satisfying the most natural wants. Her husband, who was brought into the workhouse, begged to have his wife released from this imprisonment, whereupon he received twenty-four hours imprisonment, with bread and water, as the penalty of his insolence. In the workhouse at Slough, near Windsor, a man lay dying in September, 1844. His wife journeyed to him, arriving at midnight; and hastening to the workhouse, was refused admission. She was not permitted to see her husband until the next morning,[a] and then only in the presence of a female warder, who forced herself upon the wife at every succeeding visit, sending her away at the end of half-an-hour. In the workhouse at Middleton, in Lancashire, twelve, and at times eighteen, paupers, of both sexes, slept in one room. This institution is not embraced by the New Poor Law, but is administered under an old special act (Gilbert's Act[194]). The inspector had instituted a brewery in the house for his own benefit. In Stockport, July 31st, 1844, a man, seventy-two years old, was brought before the Justice of the Peace for refusing to break stones, and insisting that, by reason of his age and a stiff knee, he was unfit for this work. In vain did he offer to undertake any work adapted to his physical strength; he was sentenced to two weeks upon the treadmill. In the workhouse at Basford, an inspecting official found[b] that the sheets had not been changed in thirteen weeks, shirts in four weeks, stockings in two to ten months, so that of forty-five boys but three had stockings, and all their shirts were in tatters. The beds swarmed with vermin, and the tableware was washed in the slop-pails. In the west of London workhouse, a porter who had infected four girls with syphilis was not discharged, and another who had concealed a deaf and dumb girl four days and nights in his bed was also retained.

As in life, so in death. The poor are dumped into the earth like infected cattle. The pauper burial-ground of St. Brides, London, is a bare morass, in use as a cemetery since the time of Charles II., and filled with heaps of bones; every Wednesday the paupers are

---

[a] The German editions of 1845 and 1892 have here "and then only for half-an-hour".— Ed.

[b] The German editions of 1845 and 1892 have here "in February 1844".— Ed.

thrown into a ditch fourteen feet deep; a curate rattles through the Litany at the top of his speed; the ditch is loosely covered in, to be reopened the next Wednesday, and filled with corpses as long as one more can be forced in. The putrefaction thus engendered contaminates the whole neighbourhood. In Manchester, the pauper burial-ground lies opposite to the Old Town, along the Irk; this, too, is a rough, desolate place. About two years ago a railroad was carried through it. If it had been a respectable cemetery, how the bourgeoisie and the clergy would have shrieked over the desecration! But it was a pauper burial-ground, the resting-place of the outcast and superfluous, so no one concerned himself about the matter. It was not even thought worth while to convey the partially decayed bodies to the other side of the cemetery; they were heaped up just as it happened, and piles were driven into newly made graves, so that the water oozed out of the swampy ground, pregnant with putrefying matter, and filled the neighbourhood with the most revolting and injurious gases. The disgusting brutality which accompanied this work I cannot describe in further detail.

Can any one wonder that the poor decline to accept public relief under these conditions? That they starve rather than enter these bastilles? I have the reports of five cases in which persons actually starving, when the guardians refused them outdoor relief, went back to their miserable homes and died of starvation rather than enter these hells. Thus far have the Poor Law Commissioners attained their object. At the same time, however, the workhouses have intensified, more than any other measure of the party in power, the hatred of the working-class against the property-holders, who very generally admire the New Poor Law.

From Newcastle to Dover, there is but one voice among the workers — the voice of hatred against the new law. The bourgeoisie has formulated so clearly in this law its conception of its duties towards the proletariat, that it has been appreciated even by the dullest. So frankly, so boldly has the conception never yet been formulated, that the non-possessing class exists solely for the purpose of being exploited, and of starving when the property-holders can no longer make use of it. Hence it is that this New Poor Law has contributed so greatly to accelerate the labour movement, and especially to spread Chartism; and, as it is carried out most extensively in the country, it facilitates the development of the proletarian movement which is arising in the agricultural districts.

Let me add that a similar law in force in Ireland since 1838, affords a similar refuge for eighty thousand paupers. Here, too, it has made itself disliked, and would have been intensely hated if it had attained anything like the same importance as in England. But what difference does the ill-treatment of eighty thousand proletarians make in a country in which there are two and a half millions of them? In Scotland there are, with local exceptions, no Poor Laws.

I hope that after this picture of the New Poor Law and its results, no word which I have said of the English bourgeoisie will be thought too stern. In this public measure, in which it acts *in corpore* as the ruling power, it formulates its real intentions, reveals the animus of those smaller transactions with the proletariat, of which the blame apparently attaches to individuals. And that this measure did not originate with any one section of the bourgeoisie, but enjoys the approval of the whole class, is proved by the Parliamentary debates of 1844. The Liberal party had enacted the New Poor Law; the Conservative party, with its Prime Minister Peel at the head, defends it, and only alters some pettifogging trifles in the Poor Law Amendment Bill of 1844. A Liberal majority carried the bill, a Conservative majority approved it, and the "Noble Lords" gave their consent each time. Thus is the expulsion of the proletariat from State and society outspoken, thus is it publicly proclaimed that proletarians are not human beings, and do not deserve to be treated as such. Let us leave it to the proletarians of the British Empire to reconquer their human rights.*

* To prevent misconstructions and consequent objections, I would observe that I have spoken of the bourgeoisie as a *class*, and that all such facts as refer to individuals serve merely as evidence of the way of thinking and acting of a *class*. Hence I have not entered upon the distinctions between the diverse sections, subdivisions and parties of the bourgeoisie, which have a mere historical and theoretical significance. And I can, for the same reason, mention but casually the few members of the bourgeoisie who have shown themselves honourable exceptions. These are, on the one hand, the pronounced Radicals, who are almost Chartists, such as a few members of the House of Commons, the manufacturers Hindley of Ashton, and Fielden of Todmorden (Lancashire), and, on the other hand, the philanthropic Tories, who have recently constituted themselves "Young England", among whom are the Members of Parliament, Disraeli, Borthwick, Ferrand, Lord John Manners, etc., Lord Ashley, too, is in sympathy with them. The hope of "Young England" is a restoration of the old "merry England" with its brilliant features and its romantic feudalism. This object is of course unattainable and ridiculous, a satire upon all historic development; but the good intention, the courage to resist the existing state of things and prevalent prejudices, and to recognise the vileness of our present condition, is worth something anyhow. Wholly isolated is the half-German Englishman, Thomas Carlyle, who, originally a Tory, goes beyond all those hitherto mentioned. He has sounded the social disorder more deeply than any other English bourgeois, and demands the organisation of labour.

Such is the state of the British working-class as I have come to know it in the course of twenty-one months, through the medium of my own eyes, and through official and other trustworthy reports. And when I call this condition, as I have frequently enough done in the foregoing pages, an utterly unbearable one, I am not alone in so doing. As early as 1833, Gaskell declared that he despaired of a peaceful issue, and that a revolution can hardly fail to follow. In 1838, Carlyle explained Chartism and the revolutionary activity of the working-men as arising out of the misery in which they live, and only wondered that they have sat so quietly eight long years at the Barmecide feast,[195] at which they have been regaled by the Liberal bourgeoisie with empty promises. And in 1844 he declared that the work of organising labour must be begun at once

"if Europe, at any rate if England, is to continue inhabitable much longer."[a]

And the *Times*, the "first journal of Europe", said in June, 1844:

"War to the mansion, peace to the cottage—is a watchword of terror which may yet ring through the land. Let the wealthy beware!"[196]

Meanwhile, let us review once more the chances of the English bourgeoisie.[b] In the worst case, foreign manufacture, especially that of America, may succeed in withstanding English competition, even after the repeal of the Corn Laws, inevitable in the course of a few years. German manufacture is now making great efforts, and that of America has developed with giant strides. America, with its inexhaustible resources, with its unmeasured coal and iron fields, with its unexampled wealth of water-power and its navigable rivers, but especially with its energetic, active population, in comparison with which the English are phlegmatic dawdlers,— America has in less than ten years created a manufacture

I hope that Carlyle, who has found the right path, will be capable of following it. He has my best wishes and those of many other Germans.— *Note by Engels.* (The last two sentences were omitted in the American edition of 1887 and the English edition of 1892.— *Ed.*)

(1892) But the February Revolution made him an out-and-out reactionary. His righteous wrath against the Philistines turned into sullen Philistine grumbling at the tide of history that cast him ashore.— *Added by Engels to the German edition of 1892.*

---

[a] T. Carlyle, *Past and Present.*— *Ed.*

[b] In the German edition of 1845 the concluding section does not begin with this passage, but with the first paragraph on this page. In the German edition of 1892 it is not separated at all from the rest.— *Ed.*

which already competes with England in the coarser cotton
goods,[a] has excluded the English from the markets of North and
South America, and holds its own in China, side by side with
England.[b] If any country is adapted to holding a monopoly of
manufacture, it is America. Should English manufacture be thus
vanquished — and in the course of the next twenty years, if the
present conditions remain unchanged, this is inevitable — the
majority of the proletariat must become forever superfluous, and
has no other choice than to starve or to rebel. Does the English
bourgeoisie reflect upon this contingency? On the contrary; its
favourite economist, McCulloch, teaches from his student's desk,
that a country so young as America, which is not even properly
populated, cannot carry on manufacture successfully or dream of
competing with an old manufacturing country like England. It
were madness in the Americans to make the attempt, for they
could only lose by it; better far for them to stick to their
agriculture, and when they have brought their whole territory
under the plough, a time may perhaps come for carrying on
manufacture with a profit. So says the wise economist, and the
whole bourgeoisie worships him, while the Americans take possession of one market after another, while a daring American
speculator recently even sent a shipment of American cotton
goods to England, where they were sold for re-exportation!

But assuming that England retained the monopoly of manufactures, that its factories perpetually multiply, what must be the
result? The commercial crises would continue, and grow more
violent, more terrible, with the extension of industry and the
multiplication of the proletariat. The proletariat would increase in
geometrical proportion, in consequence of the progressive ruin of
the lower middle-class and the giant strides with which capital is
concentrating itself in the hands of the few; and the proletariat
would soon embrace the whole nation, with the exception of a few
millionaires. But in this development there comes a stage at which
the proletariat perceives how easily the existing power may be
overthrown, and then follows a revolution.

Neither of these supposed conditions may, however, be expected
to arise. The commercial crises, the mightiest levers for all
independent development of the proletariat, will probably shorten

---

[a] The German editions of 1845 and 1892 have here in brackets "the main
product of English industry".—*Ed.*

[b] In the German editions of 1845 and 1892 the sentence follows: "The position
is the same in other branches of industry."—*Ed.*

the process, acting in concert with foreign competition and the deepening ruin of the lower middle-class. I think the people will not endure more than one more crisis. The next one, in 1846 or 1847, will probably bring with it the repeal of the Corn Laws* and the enactment of the Charter. What revolutionary movements the Charter may give rise to remains to be seen. But, by the time of the next following crisis, which, according to the analogy of its predecessors, must break out in 1852 or 1853, unless delayed perhaps by the repeal of the Corn Laws or hastened by other influences, such as foreign competition — by the time this crisis arrives, the English people will have had enough of being plundered by the capitalists and left to starve when the capitalists no longer require their services. If, up to that time, the English bourgeoisie does not pause to reflect — and to all appearance it certainly will not do so — a revolution will follow with which none hitherto known can be compared. The proletarians, driven to despair, will seize the torch which Stephens has preached to them; the vengeance of the people will come down with a wrath of which the rage of 1793 gives no true idea. The war of the poor against the rich will be the bloodiest ever waged. Even the union of a part of the bourgeoisie with the proletariat, even a general reform of the bourgeoisie, would not help matters. Besides, the change of heart of the bourgeoisie could only go as far as a lukewarm *juste-milieu*; the more determined, uniting with the workers, would only form a new Gironde, and succumb in the course of the mighty development. The prejudices of a whole class cannot be laid aside like an old coat: least of all, those of the stable, narrow, selfish English bourgeoisie. These are all inferences which may be drawn with the greatest certainty: conclusions, the premises for which are undeniable facts, partly of historical development, partly facts inherent in human nature. Prophecy is nowhere so easy as in England, where all the component elements of society are clearly defined and sharply separated. The revolution must come; it is already too late to bring about a peaceful solution; but it can be made more gently than that prophesied in the foregoing pages. This depends, however, more upon the development of the proletariat than upon that of the bourgeoisie. In proportion, as the proletariat absorbs socialistic and communistic elements, will the revolution diminish in bloodshed, revenge, and savagery. Communism stands, in principle, above the breach between

---

* And it did.—*Note by Engels to the American edition of 1887* (reproduced in the English edition of 1892—*Ed.*).

bourgeoisie and proletariat, recognises only its historic significance
for the present, but not its justification for the future: wishes,
indeed, to bridge over this chasm, to do away with all class
antagonisms [a] Hence it recognises as justified, so long as the
struggle exists, the exasperation of the proletariat towards its
oppressors as a necessity, as the most important lever for a labour
movement just beginning; but it goes beyond this exasperation,
because Communism is a question of humanity and not of the
workers alone. Besides, it does not occur to any Communist to
wish to revenge himself upon individuals, or to believe that, in
general, the single bourgeois can act otherwise, under existing
circumstances, than he does act. English Socialism, i.e., Communism, rests directly upon the irresponsibility of the individual. Thus
the more the English workers absorb communistic ideas, the more
superfluous becomes their present bitterness, which, should it
continue so violent as at present, could accomplish nothing; and
the more their action against the bourgeoisie will lose its savage
cruelty. If, indeed, it were possible to make the whole proletariat
communistic before the war breaks out, the end would be very
peaceful; but that is no longer possible, the time has gone by.
Meanwhile, I think that before the outbreak of open, declared war
of the poor against the rich,[b] there will be enough intelligent
comprehension of the social question among the proletariat, to
enable the communistic party, with the help of events, to conquer
the brutal element of the revolution and prevent a "Ninth
Thermidor". In any case, the experience of the French will not
have been undergone in vain, and most of the Chartist leaders
are, moreover, already Communists. And as Communism stands
above the strife between bourgeoisie and proletariat, it will be
easier for the better elements of the bourgeoisie (which are,
however, deplorably few, and can look for recruits only among the
rising generation) to unite with it than with purely proletarian
Chartism.

If these conclusions have not been sufficiently established in the
course of the present work, there may be other opportunities for
demonstrating that they are necessary consequences of the historical development of England. But this I maintain, the war of the
poor against the rich now carried on in detail and indirectly will

---

[a] The German editions of 1845 and 1892 do not have the phrase "to do away
with all class antagonisms".—Ed.

[b] The German editions of 1845 and 1892 have here "which has now become
inevitable in England".—Ed.

become direct and universal. It is too late for a peaceful solution. The classes are divided more and more sharply, the spirit of resistance penetrates the workers, the bitterness intensifies, the guerilla skirmishes become concentrated in more important battles, and soon a slight impulse will suffice to set the avalanche in motion. Then, indeed, will the war-cry resound through the land: "War to the mansion, peace to the cottage!"—but then it will be too late for the rich to beware.

Frederick Engels

Postscript
to *THE CONDITION OF THE WORKING-CLASS IN ENGLAND*[197]

AN ENGLISH TURNOUT[a]

In my book on the above subject I was unable to give factual proof of individual points. In order not to make the book too thick and indigestible, I had to consider my statements sufficiently proven when I had confirmed them by quotations from official documents, impartial writers or the writings of the parties whose interests I was attacking. This sufficed to guard me against contradiction in those cases where I was unable to speak from personal observation when describing particular living conditions. But it was not sufficient to produce in the reader the incontestable certainty which can only be given by striking, irrefutable *facts*, and which, especially in an age in which we are obliged by the infinite "wisdom of the fathers" to be sceptical, can never be generated by mere reasoning, no matter how good the authorities. Above all when it is a question of important consequences, of facts coalescing into principles, when it is not the condition of separate, small sections of the people that has to be described, but the position of whole classes in relation to each other, then facts are absolutely essential. For the reasons just mentioned, I was unable to provide these in all cases in my book. I will now make good this unavoidable deficiency and, from time to time, will present facts as I find them in the sources available to me. In order, at the same time, to demonstrate that my account is still correct today, I will only use facts which have taken place since I left England last year, and have become known to me only since my book was published.

---

[a] The author gives this term in English.—*Ed*.

Readers of my book will remember that I was chiefly concerned to describe the position of the bourgeoisie and the proletariat in relation to each other and the necessity of struggle between these two classes; and that I attached especial importance to proving how completely justified the proletariat was in waging this struggle, and to rebutting the English bourgeoisie's fine phrases by means of their ugly deeds. From the first page to the last, I was writing a bill of indictment against the English bourgeoisie. I will now provide a few more choice pieces of evidence. However, since I have already displayed enough passion over these English bourgeois it is not my intention to work myself up over them once again and, so far as I can, I will keep my temper.

The first good citizen and worthy *paterfamilias* we are going to meet is an old friend, or rather there are two of them. By 1843 Messrs. Pauling & Henfrey had already had Lord knows how many conflicts with their workers, who, refusing to be dissuaded even by the best of arguments from their demand that they should receive increased wages for increased work, stopped work. Pauling & Henfrey, who are important building contractors and employ many brickmakers, carpenters, and so on, took on other workers; this led to a conflict and in the end to a bloody battle with guns and cudgels in Pauling & Henfrey's brickyard, which resulted in the transportation of half a dozen workers to Van Diemen's Land,[198] all of which is dealt with at length in my book.[a] But Messrs. Pauling & Henfrey have to try something on with their workers every year, otherwise they are not happy; so they began baiting them again in October 1844. This time it was the carpenters whose well-being the philanthropic building contractors were anxious to promote. From time immemorial the custom had prevailed among the carpenters of Manchester and the surrounding area of not "striking a light" from Candlemas[b] to November 17, i.e., of working from six in the morning till six in the evening during the long days, and of starting as soon as it was light and finishing as soon as it began to get dark during the short days. Then from November 17 onwards the lights were lit and work carried on for the full time. Pauling & Henfrey, who had long had enough of this "barbaric" custom, decided to put an end to this relic of the "Dark Ages" with the help of gas lighting, and when one evening before six o'clock the carpenters could not see any longer and put away their tools and went for their coats, the foreman lit the gas

---

[a] See pp. 513-14 of this volume.—*Ed.*

[b] February 2.—*Ed.*

and said that they had to work till six o'clock. The carpenters, whom this did not suit, called a general meeting of the workers in their trade. Mr. Pauling, much astonished, asked his workers if they were dissatisfied about something since they had called a meeting. Some of the workers said that it was not they who were directly responsible for calling the meeting, but the committee of the craft union, to which Mr. Pauling replied that he didn't care a fig for the craft union, but he would like to put a proposition to them: if they would agree to the lights being lit he would be prepared in return to give them three hours off on Saturdays, and — generous fellow — also to allow them to work an extra quarter of an hour every day for which they would get extra pay! They on their part should work half an hour longer when all other workshops began to put on their lights. The workers considered this proposal and calculated that as a result Messrs. Pauling & Henfrey would gain a whole working hour every day during the short days, that each worker would have to work altogether 92 hours, i.e., $9^1/_4$ days extra without getting a farthing in return, and that taking into account all the workers employed by the firm, the above-named gentlemen would save £400 (2,100 taler) in wages during the winter months. So the workers held their meeting and explained to their fellow-workers that if one firm succeeded in putting this through, all the other firms would follow suit and, as a result, there would be a general indirect reduction in wages which would rob the carpenters in the district of about £4,000 a year. It was decided that on the following Monday all the carpenters employed by Pauling & Henfrey should hand in their 3-months' notice and if their employers did not change their minds, should stop work when this notice expired. The union on its part promised to support them by a general levy in the event of a stoppage of work.

On Monday, October 14, the workers went and gave in their notice, whereupon they were told that they could leave right away, which of course they did. The same evening another meeting of all the building workers took place, at which all categories of building workers pledged their support to the strikers. On the Wednesday and Thursday following, all the carpenters in the vicinity employed by Pauling & Henfrey also stopped work and the *strike* was thus in full swing.

The building employers, left so suddenly high and dry, immediately sent people out in all directions, even as far as Scotland, to recruit workers since in the whole vicinity there was not a soul willing to work for them. In a few days thirteen men did arrive from Staffordshire. But as soon as the strikers found an opportunity of talking to them and explaining the dispute and the reasons why they had stopped work, several of the new arrivals refused to continue working. But the masters had an effective way of dealing with this: they had the recalcitrants, along with those who led them astray, brought before *Daniel Maude*, Esquire, Justice of the Peace. But before we follow them there, we must first put the virtues of Daniel Maude, Esq., in their proper light.

Daniel Maude, Esq., is the "stipendiary magistrate"[a] or paid Justice of the Peace in Manchester. The English magistrates are usually rich bourgeois or landowners, occasionally also clergymen, who are appointed by the Ministry. But since these Dogberries understand nothing about the law, they make the most flagrant blunders, bring the bourgeoisie into ridicule and do it harm, since, even when faced with a worker, they are frequently reduced to a state of confusion if he is defended by a skilful lawyer, and either neglect some legal form when sentencing him, which results in a successful appeal, or let themselves be misled into acquitting him. Besides, the rich manufacturers in the big towns and industrial areas have no time to spare for passing days of boredom in a court of law and prefer to instal a *remplacant*.[b] As a result in these towns, on the initiative of the towns themselves, paid magistrates are usually appointed, men versed in law, who are able to take advantage of all the twists and subtle distinctions of English law, and when necessary to supplement and improve it for the benefit of the bourgeoisie. Their efforts in this respect are illustrated by the following example.

Daniel Maude, Esq., is one of those liberal justices of the peace who were appointed in large numbers under the Whig Government. Among his heroic exploits, inside and outside the arena of the Manchester Borough Court,[c] we will mention two. When in 1842 the manufacturers succeeded in forcing the workers of South Lancashire into an insurrection, which broke out in Stalybridge and Ashton at the beginning of August, some 10,000 workers, with *Richard Pilling*, the Chartist, at their head, marched on August 9 from there to Manchester

"to meet their masters on the Exchange and to see how the Manchester market was".[199]

---

[a] "Stipendiary magistrate" is in English in the original.—*Ed*.
[b] Substitute.—*Ed*.
[c] "Borough Court" is in English in the original.—*Ed*.

When they reached the outskirts of the town, they were met by Daniel Maude, Esq., with the whole estimable police force, a detachment of cavalry and a company of riflemen. But this was all only for the sake of appearances since it was in the interest of the manufacturers and liberals that the insurrection should spread and force the repeal of the Corn Laws. In this Daniel Maude, Esq., was in complete agreement with his worthy colleagues, and he began to come to terms with the workers and allowed them to enter the town on their promise to "keep the peace" and follow a prescribed route. He knew very well that the insurgents would not do this nor did he in the least wish them to—he could have nipped the whole contrived insurrection in the bud with a little energy but, had he done so, he would not have been acting in the interest of his Anti-Corn Law friends but in the interest of Sir Robert Peel. So he withdrew the soldiers and allowed the workers to enter the town, where they immediately brought all the factories to a standstill. But as soon as the insurrection proved to be definitely directed *against* the liberal bourgeoisie and completely ignored the "hellish Corn Laws", Daniel Maude, Esq., once more assumed his judicial office and had workers arrested by the dozen and marched off to prison without mercy for "breach of the peace"—so that he first caused the breaches and then punished them. Another characteristic feature in the career of this Manchester Solomon is revealed by the following. Since the Anti-Corn Law League was several times beaten up in public in Manchester, it holds private meetings, admission to which is by ticket only—but the decisions and petitions of which are presented to the public as those of public meetings, and as manifestations of Manchester "public opinion". In order to put a stop to this fraudulent boasting by the liberal manufacturers, three or four Chartists, among them my good friend *James Leach*, secured tickets for themselves and went to one of these meetings. When Mr. *Cobden* rose to speak, James Leach asked the Chairman whether this was a public meeting. Instead of answering, the Chairman called the police and had Leach arrested without more ado. A second Chartist asked the question again, then a third, and a fourth, all were set upon one after the other by the "bluebottles" (police) who stood massed at the door, and packed off to the Town Hall. They appeared the next morning before Daniel Maude, Esq., who was already fully informed about everything. They were charged with having caused a disturbance at a meeting, were hardly allowed to say a word, and then had to listen to a solemn speech by Daniel Maude, Esq., who told them that he knew them, that they were political vagabonds who did nothing but cause uproar at meetings and disturb decent, law-abiding *citizens* and a stop must be put to this kind of thing. Therefore—and Daniel 'Maude, Esq., knew very well that he could not impose any real punishment on them—therefore, he would sentence them to pay the costs this time.

It was before this same Daniel Maude, Esq., whose bourgeois virtues we have just described, that the recalcitrant workers from Pauling & Henfrey's were hauled. But they had brought a lawyer with them as a precaution. First to be heard was the worker newly arrived from Staffordshire who had refused to continue working at a place where others had stopped work in self-defence. Messrs. Pauling & Henfrey had a written contract signed by the workers from Staffordshire, and this was submitted to the magistrate.* The defending lawyer interjected that this agreement had been signed on a Sunday and was therefore invalid. With much dignity Daniel Maude, Esq., admitted that "business transactions" concluded on a Sunday were not valid, but said that he could not believe that Messrs. Pauling & Henfrey regarded this as a "business transaction"! So without spending very much time asking the worker whether he "regarded" the document as a "business transaction", he told the poor devil that he must either continue working or amuse himself on the treadmill for three months.—O Solomon of Manchester!—After this case had been dealt with, Messrs. Pauling & Henfrey brought forward the second accused. His name was *Salmon,* and he was one of the firm's old workers who had stopped work. He was accused of having intimidated the new workers into taking part in the strike. The witness—one of these latter—stated that Salmon had taken him by the arm and spoken to him. Daniel Maude, Esq., asked whether the accused had perhaps used threats or beaten him?—No, said the witness. Daniel Maude, Esq., delighted at having found an opportunity to demonstrate his impartiality—after having just fulfilled his duty to the bourgeoisie—declared that there was nothing in the case incriminating the accused. He had every right to take a walk on the public highway and to talk to other people as long as he did not

---

* This contract contained the following: the worker pledged himself to work for Pauling & Henfrey for *six months* and *to be satisfied with the wages which they would give him*; but Pauling & Henfrey were not bound to keep him for six months and could dismiss him *at any moment* with a week's notice, and although Pauling & Henfrey would pay his travelling expenses from Staffordshire to Manchester, they were to recover them by a weekly deduction of 2 shillings (20 silver groschen) from his wages. How do you like that really marvellous contract?—*Note by Engels*.

indulge in intimidating words or actions — he was therefore acquitting him. But Messrs. Pauling & Henfrey had at least had the satisfaction, by paying the costs of the case, of having the said Salmon sent to the lock-up for a night — and that was something after all. Nor did Salmon's happiness last long. For after having been discharged on Thursday, October 31, he was up again before Daniel Maude, Esq., on Tuesday, November 5th, charged with having assaulted Messrs. Pauling & Henfrey in the street. On that same Thursday on which Salmon had been acquitted, a number of Scotsmen arrived in Manchester, decoyed by false statements that the disputes were over and that Pauling & Henfrey could not find enough workers in their district to cope with their extensive contracts. On the Friday a number of Scottish joiners who had been working for some time in Manchester, came to explain the cause of the stoppage to their countrymen. A large number of their fellow-workers — some 400 — gathered around the inn where the Scots were quartered. But these Scotsmen were kept there like prisoners with a foreman on guard at the door. After some time, Messrs. Pauling & Henfrey arrived in order to escort in person their new workers to their place of work. When the group came out, those gathered outside called to the Scots not to take work against the Manchester rules of the trade and not to disgrace their fellow-countrymen. Two of the Scots did in fact lag behind a little and Mr. Pauling himself ran back to drag them forward. The crowd remained quiet, only prevented the group from moving too quickly and called to the Scots not to interfere in other people's business, to go back home, etc. Mr. Henfrey finally lost his temper; he saw several of his old workers in the crowd, among them Salmon, and in order to put an end to the affair, he gripped the latter by the arm. Mr. Pauling seized him by the other arm and both shouted for the police with all their might. The police inspector came up and asked what charge was being made against the man, at which both partners were greatly embarrassed. But they said, "We know the man." "Oh," said the inspector, "that's enough then, we can let him go for the time being." Messrs. Pauling & Henfrey, needing to bring some kind of charge against Salmon, considered the matter for several days until finally, on the advice of their lawyer, they lodged the above charge. After all the witnesses against Salmon had been heard, *W. P. Roberts*, the "Miners' Attorney General", the terror of all magistrates, suddenly rose up on behalf of the accused and asked whether he should still call his witnesses, since nothing had been brought against Salmon. Daniel Maude, Esq., let him question his witnesses, who testified that Salmon had behaved calmly until Mr. Henfrey took hold of him. When the proceedings for and against had been concluded, Daniel Maude, Esq., said that he would pass sentence on Saturday. Clearly, the presence of "Attorney General" Roberts led him to think twice before he spoke once.

On Saturday, Messrs. Pauling & Henfrey brought an additional *criminal* charge of conspiracy and intimidation against three of their old workers — *Salmon, Scott* and *Mellor*. By this they hoped to deliver a mortal blow to the craft union and, in order to be secure against the dreaded Roberts, they called in a distinguished barrister from London, Mr. *Monk*. As his first witness, Mr. Monk produced *Gibson*, one of the newly engaged Scotsmen, who had also acted as witness against Salmon the previous Tuesday. He declared that on Friday, November 1, as he and his companions came out of the inn, they were surrounded by a crowd of people who pushed and pulled them and that the three accused were among the crowd. Roberts now began to cross-question this witness, confronted him with another worker, and asked whether he, Gibson, had not told this worker the previous night that he had not known *he was under oath* when he was giving his evidence the previous Tuesday and that he had not really understood what he was supposed to do and say in court. Gibson replied that he did not know the man, he had been with two men the previous evening but could not say whether this man was one of them as it had been dark. *It was possible that he said something of the sort* since the form of oath in Scotland was different from that in England; he couldn't quite remember. Mr. Monk then rose and declared that Mr. Roberts had no right to put questions like that, to which Mr. Roberts replied that objections of that kind were quite in place when one was representing a bad cause, but that he had the right to ask what he wanted, not only where the witness was born but also where he had stayed every day since that time, and what he had had to eat every day. Daniel Maude, Esq., confirmed that Mr. Roberts had this right but gave him the fatherly advice to keep to the point as much as possible. Then, after Mr. Roberts had obtained from the witness a statement that he only really began working for Pauling & Henfrey on the day after the incident on which the charge was based, that is, on November 2, he dismissed him. Then Mr. Henfrey himself appeared as a witness and repeated what Gibson had said about the incident. At this, Mr. Roberts asked him: Are you not looking for an unfair advantage over your competitors? Mr. Monk again objected to this question.

Very well, said Mr. Roberts, I will put it more clearly. Mr. Henfrey, do you know that the working hours of the carpenters in Manchester are fixed by certain rules?

Mr. Henfrey: I have nothing to do with those rules, I have the right to make my own rules.

Mr. Roberts: Quite so. On oath, Mr. Henfrey, do you not demand longer working hours from your workers than other building contractors and master carpenters?

Mr. Henfrey: Yes.

Mr. Roberts: How many hours, approximately?

Mr. Henfrey did not know exactly and took out his notebook in order to calculate.

Daniel Maude, Esq.: You need not spend a long time working it out, just tell us roughly how many.

Mr. Henfrey: Well, about an hour in the mornings and an hour in the evenings for six weeks before the time when the lights are usually turned on, and the same for six weeks after the day when it is usual to stop putting on the lights.

Daniel Maude, Esq.: So every one of your workers has to work an extra 72 hours before the lights are turned on and 72 hours after, that is, 144 hours in 12 weeks?

Mr. Henfrey: Yes.

This statement was received with signs of great indignation by the public. Mr. Monk looked angrily at Mr. Henfrey and Mr. Henfrey looked at his barrister in confusion and Mr. Pauling tugged at Mr. Henfrey's coat-tails — but it was too late; Daniel Maude, Esq., who obviously saw that he would have to play at being impartial again that day, had heard the admission and made it public.

After two unimportant witnesses had been heard, Mr. Monk said that his evidence against the accused was now concluded.

Daniel Maude, Esq., then said that the plaintiff had not made out any case for a criminal investigation against the accused, not having shown that the threatened Scots had been taken on by Pauling & Henfrey before November 1, since there was no proof of a hire contract or employment of the men concerned before November 2, while charge had been lodged on November *1st*. Thus on this date the men were not yet employed by Pauling & Henfrey and the accused had every right to try and deter them by every legal means from going to work for Pauling & Henfrey. In reply to this, Mr. Monk said that the defendants had been engaged from the moment they left Scotland and boarded the steamer. Daniel Maude, Esq., remarked that it had indeed been stated that such hire contract had been made out but this document had not been produced. Mr. Monk replied that the document was in Scotland and he asked Mr. Maude to adjourn the case until it could be laid before the court. Mr. Roberts intervened here to say: this was something new to him. Evidence for the plaintiff had been declared concluded and now the plaintiff was demanding that the case be adjourned in order to introduce new evidence. He insisted that the case proceed. Daniel Maude, Esq., decided that both pleas were superfluous since no substantiated charge was before the court—upon which the accused were dismissed.

Meanwhile the workers had likewise not been inactive. Week after week they held meetings in the Carpenters' Hall or the Socialist Hall, called for aid from the different craft unions, which was given in plenty, never ceased to make known everywhere the behaviour of Pauling & Henfrey and finally sent delegates in all directions in order to inform their fellow craftsmen in all the areas where Pauling & Henfrey were recruiting workers, of the reasons for this recruitment and to prevent them taking work with this firm. Only a few weeks after the strike began there were seven delegates on their way and posters on the street corners in all the big towns in the country warned unemployed carpenters about Pauling & Henfrey. On November 9 some of the delegates who had returned reported on their mission. One of these, named *Johnson,* who had been in Scotland, described how Pauling & Henfrey's representative had recruited thirty workers in Edinburgh but as soon as they heard from him the real facts of the case they decided they would sooner starve than go to Manchester in such circumstances. A second delegate had been in Liverpool keeping watch on the arriving steamers, but not a single man had arrived and so he found that he had nothing to do. A third man had been in Cheshire but wherever he went he found he had nothing more to do, for the *Northern Star*, the workers' paper, had broadcast the real state of affairs far and wide and had put an end to any desire people had of going to Manchester. Indeed in one town, Macclesfield, the carpenters had already taken a collection in support of the strikers and promised to contribute a further shilling per man should the necessity arise. In other places he was able to stimulate the local craftsmen to initiate such contributions.

In order to provide Messrs. Pauling & Henfrey with another opportunity of coming to an agreement with the workers, all the craftsmen employed in the building trade gathered at the Carpenters' Hall on Monday, November 18th, elected a deputation to present an address to these gentlemen and marched in procession

with flags and emblems to the premises of Pauling & Henfrey.
First came the deputation followed by the strike committee, then
the carpenters, the brick-moulders and kiln-workers, the day
labourers, bricklayers, sawyers, glaziers, plasterers, painters, a
band, stonemasons, cabinetmakers. They passed the hotel where
their "Attorney General", Roberts, was staying and greeted him with
loud hurrahs as they marched by. Arrived at the premises, the
deputation fell out while the crowd marched on to Stevenson
Square where they were to hold a public meeting. The deputation
was received by the police who demanded their names and
addresses before allowing them to proceed any further. When
they had entered the office, the partners *Sharps & Pauling* told
them that they would accept no written address from a crowd of
workers brought together merely for the purpose of intimidation.
The deputation denied that this was their aim, since the procession had not even stopped, but had at once gone on its way. While
this procession of 5,000 workers continued its march, the deputation was finally received and taken into a room in which were
present the Chief Constable, an officer and three newspaper
reporters. Mr. Sharps, a partner in Pauling & Henfrey, usurped the
Chairman's seat, remarking that the deputation should be careful
what it said as everything would be duly recorded and, in certain
circumstances, would be used against them in court.—They
now began to ask the deputation what they were complaining about,
etc., and said that they wanted to give the men work according
to the rules customary in Manchester. The deputation asked
if the men picked up in Staffordshire and Scotland were working
according to the regulations for craftsmen prevailing in Manchester.

No, was the answer, we have a special arrangement with these men. Then your
people are to be given work again, and on the usual conditions? Oh, we are not
going to negotiate with any deputation but just let the men come and they will find
out on what conditions we are willing to give them work.

Mr. Sharps added that all firms with which he was connected
had always treated their workers well and paid them the highest
wages. The deputation replied that if, as they had heard, he was
associated with the firm of Pauling & Henfrey, this firm had
fiercely opposed the best interests of the workers.— A brickmaker,
a member of the deputation, was asked what the members of his
craft had to complain about.—

Oh, nothing just now, but we've had enough.*

* See above—the bloody fight at Pauling & Henfrey's brickyard.— *Note by
Engels.*

Oh, you've had enough, have you? answered Mr. Pauling with a sneer, and then took the opportunity of delivering them a long lecture about craft unions, strikes, etc., and the misery to which they brought the workers — whereupon one of the deputation remarked they were not by any means disposed to allow their rights to be taken away from them bit by bit, and, for example, to work 144 hours a year for nothing, as was now being demanded.— Mr. Sharps remarked that they ought also to take into account the loss incurred by those taking part in the procession because they were not working that day, as well as the cost of the strike, the loss of wages suffered by the strikers, etc. One of the deputation said:

That's nobody's business but ours and we won't ask you to contribute a farthing from your pocket.

With that the deputation left and reported to the assembled workers in the Carpenters' Hall, where it was revealed that not only had all those in the area working for Pauling & Henfrey (those who were not carpenters and were therefore not on strike) come to take part in the procession, but that many of the newly imported Scotsmen had also struck that very morning. A painter also declared that Pauling & Henfrey had made the same unjust demands on the painters as they had on the joiners but that they too intended to resist. In order to simplify the whole business and shorten the struggle it was decided that all building workers employed by Pauling & Henfrey should stop work. This they did. The painters stopped work on the following Saturday and the glaziers on the Monday, and on the new theatre for which Pauling & Henfrey had received the contract only two bricklayers and four day labourers were working after a few days instead of 200 men. Some of the new arrivals also stopped work.

Pauling & Henfrey foamed with rage. When three more of the new arrivals stopped work they were hauled before Daniel Maude, Esq., on Friday, November 22. The previous reverses had had no effect. A worker called *Read* was the first to be dealt with, charged with breach of contract; a contract which the accused had signed in Derby was laid before the court. Roberts, who was again defending, stated at once that there was not the slightest connection between the contract and the charge, they were two quite different things. Daniel Maude, Esq., saw the point right away once the formidable Roberts had made it, but it took him a long, harassing time to make it clear to the Counsel for the other side. Finally, the latter asked permission to alter the charge and after a while he came back with one that was much worse than the first.

When he saw that this would not do either, he asked for a further adjournment of the case and Daniel Maude, Esq., gave him until Friday, November 29, that is, a whole week, to consider the matter. I have not been able to find out whether or not he succeeded because the one issue of the paper which must have contained a report of the verdict is missing from my files. Meanwhile, Roberts went over to the offensive and had several of the recruited workers and one of Pauling & Henfrey's foremen brought before the court for forcing their way into the house of one of the strikers and assaulting his wife; in two other cases some of the workers on strike had been attacked. To his great regret, Daniel Maude, Esq., had to find all the accused guilty but he dealt with them as leniently as he possibly could and only bound them over to keep the peace themselves in future.

Finally, at the end of December, Messrs. Pauling & Henfrey succeeded in getting sentence against two of their opponents, likewise on charges of assault against one of their workers. But this time the court was not so lenient. Without more ado, it sentenced them to a month's imprisonment and bound them over to keep the peace after their release.

From here on news about the strike becomes meagre. It was still in full swing on January 18. I have found no later reports.[200] It has probably come to an end like most others; in the course of time Pauling & Henfrey will have secured a sufficient number of workers from distant parts and from a few turncoats from the workers' side; after a longer or shorter strike and its accompanying misery, for which the strikers will have been consoled by the consciousness that they have nothing to reproach themselves with and that they have helped to maintain the level of wages of their fellow workers, the majority of them will have found jobs elsewhere. And as for the points in dispute, Messrs. Pauling & Henfrey will have learnt that they cannot impose their will so rigorously, since for them also the strike involved considerable loss, and the other employers, after such a fierce struggle, will not think of changing the old rules of the craftsmen carpenters so soon.

Brussels

Written in the summer   Printed according to the journal
and autumn 1845

First published in
Das Westphälische Dampfboot
Bielefeld, 1846. I and II

Signed: *F. Engels*

Karl Marx

PEUCHET: ON SUICIDE[201]

French criticism of *society* has, at least, in part the great merit of
having shown up the contradictions and unnaturalness of modern
life not only in the relationships of particular classes, but in all
circles and forms of modern intercourse. And it has done that in
accounts evincing the warmth of life itself, broadness of view,
refined subtlety, and bold originality of spirit, which one will seek
in vain in any other nation. Compare the critical writings of Owen
and Fourier, for example, so far as they concern the relationships
of life, to gain an idea of this superiority of the French. It is by no
means only to the French "socialist" writers proper that one must
look for the critical presentation of social conditions; but to writers
in every sphere of literature, and in particular of novels and
memoirs. In a few excerpts on *suicide* from the *"Mémoires tirés des
Archives de la Police etc." par Jacques Peuchet* I shall give an example
of this French criticism. It may at the same time show what
grounds there are for the idea of the philanthropic bourgeois that
it is only a question of providing a little bread and a little
education for the proletarians, and that only the worker is stunted
by the present state of society, but otherwise the existing world is
the best of all possible worlds.

With Jacques Peuchet, as with many of the older, now almost
extinct, French professional men, who have lived through the
numerous upheavals since 1789, the numerous disappointments,
enthusiasms, constitutions, rulers, defeats and victories, criticism of
the existing property, family, and other private relations, in a
word of *private life,* appears as the necessary outcome of their
political experiences.

Jacques Peuchet (born 1760) proceeded from belles lettres to medicine, from medicine to law, from law to administration and the police. Before the outbreak of the French Revolution he was working with Abbé Morellet on a *Dictionnaire du commerce*, of which, however, only the prospectus was published, and at that time he was occupied mainly with political economy and administration. Peuchet was an adherent of the French Revolution for only a very short time; he very soon turned to the royalist party, for a time held the editorship of the *Gazette de France* and later even took over the notorious royalist *Mercure* from *Mallet du Pan.* Nevertheless, he wound his way very cleverly through the revolution, sometimes persecuted, sometimes occupied in the Department of Administration and the Police. The *Géographie commerçante,* 5 vol. in folio, which he published in 1800, attracted the attention of *Bonaparte,* the First Consul, and he was appointed a member of the *Conseil de commerce et des arts.* Later he occupied a higher position in the administration under the ministry of François de Neufchâteau. In 1814 the Restoration appointed him censor. During the 100 days[202] he retired. At the restoration of the Bourbons he was given the post of keeper of archives in the Paris police prefecture, which he held until 1827. *Peuchet* was not without influence, both directly and as a writer, on the speakers in the Constituent Assembly, the Convention, the Tribunate,[203] and the Chambers of Deputies under the Restoration. The best known of his many, mostly economic, works apart from the *Geography of Commerce* already referred to, is his statistics of France[a] (1807).

Peuchet wrote his memoirs, the materials for which he gathered partly from the Paris police archives, partly from his long practical experience in police and administration, as an *old man* and had them published only *after his death,* so that in no circumstances can he be counted among the "*hasty*" Socialists and Communists, who are known to lack so completely the marvellous thoroughness and comprehensive knowledge of the general run of our writers, officials and professional citizens.

Let us listen to our archive-keeper of the Paris police prefecture on *suicide!*

"The annual number of suicides, which is, as it were, normal and recurrent among us, must be regarded as a symptom of the faulty organisation of our society; for at times when industry is at a standstill and in crisis, in periods of dear food and hard winters, this symptom is always more conspicuous and assumes an epidemic character. Prostitution and theft then increase in the same proportion. Although poverty is the greatest source of suicide, we find it in all classes, among

---

[a] J. Peuchet, *Statistique élémentaire de la France.—Ed.*

Deutsches

Bürgerbuch

für 1845.

Herausgegeben

von

H. Püttmann.

Darmstadt, 1845.
Druck und Verlag von C. W. Leske.

Cover of the journal *Deutsches Bürgerbuch*, to which Engels contributed

Das

Westphälische Dampfboot.

Eine Monatsschrift.

Redigirt

von

Dr. Otto Lüning.

Zweiter Jahrgang.

Bielefeld, 1846.

Verlag von A. Helmich. — Druck von J. D. Küster, Wittwe.

Cover of the journal *Das Westphälische Dampfboot*, to which Engels contributed

Cover of the journal *Gesellschaftsspiegel*, to which Engels contributed

the idle rich as well as among artists and politicians. The variety of the causes which give rise to it seems to mock the monotonous and callous condemnation of the moralists.

"Consumptive diseases, towards which science is at present indifferent and ineffectual, abused friendship, deceived love, frustrated ambition, family suffering, repressed rivalry, dissatisfaction with a monotonous life, suppressed enthusiasm, are indubitably the causes of suicide in more generously endowed natures, and the love of life itself, this energetic driving force of personality, very often leads to putting an end to a detestable existence.

"Madame *de Staël*,[a] whose greatest merit is to have expressed commonplaces in brilliant style, has attempted to show that suicide is an act contrary to nature, and that it cannot be regarded as a deed of courage; she claims in particular that to fight despair is more worthy than to succumb to it. Such arguments little affect souls which are overwhelmed by misfortune. If they are religious, they look forward to a better world; if, on the contrary, they do not believe in anything, they seek the calm of Nothing. Philosophical tirades have no value in their eyes and are a poor refuge from suffering. It is above all in bad taste to maintain that an act so frequently committed is contrary to nature; suicide is in no way contrary to nature, since we witness it daily. What is against nature does not happen. On the contrary, it is *in the nature of our society* to produce many suicides, while Tartars do not kill themselves. *Hence all societies do not have the same products.* That is what we must tell ourselves, so as to work for the reform of our society and make it rise to a higher stage. As for courage, if it is considered courageous to defy death in broad daylight on the battlefield, under the domination of every form of excitement, there is nothing to prove lack of courage in one who administers death to himself in dark solitude. Such a debatable question is not disposed of by insulting the dead.

"Everything that has been said against suicide goes round and round in the same circle of ideas. People cite against it the decrees of Providence, but the existence of suicide is itself an open protest against her indecipherable decrees. They talk to us of our duties to this society without explaining or implementing our own claims on society, and finally they exalt the thousand times greater merit of overcoming pain rather than succumbing to it, a merit as sad as the prospects it opens up. In short, they make of suicide an act of cowardice, a crime against the law, society and honour.[b]

"Why is it that in spite of so many anathemas people kill themselves? Because the blood of men in despair does not run through their veins in the same way as that of the cold beings who take the time to coin all those fruitless phrases. *Man seems to be a mystery to man; he can only be blamed, he is not known.* When we see how light-mindedly the institutions under whose domination Europe lives dispose of the blood and life of the nations, how civilised justice surrounds itself lavishly with prisons, chastisements and instruments of death so as to sanction its insecure decisions; when we see the numerical immensity of the classes which on all sides are left in misery, and the social pariahs who are battered by brutal contempt, meant to be preventive, perhaps to save the trouble of lifting them out of their squalor; when we see all this, we fail to understand what entitles us to command the individual to respect in himself an existence which our customs, our prejudices, our laws and our morals generally trample underfoot.

"It was thought that it would be possible to prevent suicide by degrading punishments and by branding the memory of the culprit with infamy. What can

---

[a] Marx's italics here and below.—*Ed*.

[b] The word "society" is added by Marx.—*Ed*.

one say of the unworthiness of such branding of people who are no longer there to plead their case? The unfortunates, by the way, are little worried by that; and if suicide accuses anybody, it accuses above all the people who are left behind, because there is not one in this multitude who deserves that anyone should stay alive for him. Have the childish and cruel means devised been victorious against the whisperings of despair? What does he who wants to flee the world care about the insults which the world promises to his corpse? He only sees in them yet another act of cowardice on the part of the living. *What kind of society is it, indeed, where one finds the profoundest solitude in the midst of millions; where one can be overwhelmed by an irrepressible desire to kill oneself without anybody being aware of it? This society is no society,* it is *as Rousseau says, a desert inhabited by wild animals* In the positions which I held in the police administration suicides were part of my responsibility; I wished to learn whether among the causes motivating them there were any whose effect could be obviated. I undertook extensive work on the subject." I found that any attempts short of a *total reform of the present order of society* would be in vain.[a]

"Among the causes of despair which induce nervous, very excitable persons, passionate beings with deep feelings, to seek death, I discovered as the predominant factor the maltreatment, the injustices, the secret punishments, which hard parents and superiors inflict on persons dependent on them. *The revolution has not overthrown all tyrannies; the evils of which the arbitrary authorities were accused persist in the family, where they cause crises analogous to those of revolutions.*

"The relations between interests and temperaments, the true relations among individuals, have first to be created among ourselves *from the very foundations* and *suicide is only one of the thousand and one symptoms of the universal social struggle which is for ever spurring on to fresh deeds* and from which so many fighters withdraw because they are tired of being counted among the victims, or because they rebel against the thought of occupying a place of honour among the hangmen. If you want a few examples, I will cull them from authentic protocols.

"In the month of July 1816 the daughter of a tailor became engaged to a butcher, a young man of good morals, thrifty and hardworking, very devoted to his beautiful bride, who in turn was very fond of him. The young girl was a seamstress; she enjoyed the respect of all who knew her, and the bridegroom's parents loved her dearly. These good people missed no opportunity to hasten the day when they would have her as their daughter-in-law; they gave parties at which she was the queen and idol.

"The time of the marriage approached; all arrangements between the two families had been made and the contracts concluded. On the eve of the day fixed for the visit to the registrar, the young daughter and her parents were to have supper with the family of the bridegroom; an insignificant incident unexpectedly prevented this. Orders which had to be met for rich customers kept the tailor and his wife at home. They sent their apologies; but the butcher's mother came herself to fetch her daughter-in-law, who was given permission to go with her.

"Despite the absence of two of the principal guests the meal was one of the gayest. Many family jokes were told, which the prospect of a marriage makes permissible. They drank, they sang; they spoke about the future. The joys of a good marriage were eagerly discussed. They were still at table very late at night. By an easily explained indulgence the parents of the young man closed their eyes to

---

[a] This conclusion from the arguments of the author of the *Mémoires* is formulated by Marx himself. Instead of this sentence Peuchet says: "Without engaging in any theoretical investigation, I shall try to adduce facts."—*Ed.*

the silent understanding of the engaged couple. Their hands sought each other, love and intimacy went to their heads. Besides, the marriage was considered as accomplished and these young people had been visiting each other for quite a long time without giving cause for the slightest reproach. The emotion of the bridegroom's parents, the advanced hour, the mutual longing desire, loosed by the indulgence of their mentors, the unrestrained gaiety which always prevails at such meals, all this combined with the opportunity which offered itself smilingly, and the wine which was effervescing in the head, everything favoured an outcome which may be imagined. The lovers met again in the dark, when the lights had gone out. Everyone pretended not to notice, to suspect nothing. Their happiness had only friends here, no enviers.

"The young daughter only returned to her parents the next morning. A proof of how little guilty she believed herself to be lies in the fact that she returned alone. She slipped into her room and prepared her toilette; but no sooner did her parents notice her, than with fury they heaped the most shameful names and abuses on their daughter. The neighbourhood witnessed it, the scandal had no bounds. Imagine the shock which this child suffered from her modesty and the outrageous violation of her secret. In vain did the bewildered girl put it to her parents that they themselves were bringing her into disrepute, that she admitted her wrong, her folly, her disobedience, but that everything could be put right again. Her arguments and her grief failed to disarm the tailor couple."

The most cowardly, unresisting people become implacable as soon as they *can exercise their absolute parental authority. The abuse of this authority* is, as it were, *a crude compensation* for all the submissiveness and dependence to which they abase themselves willy-nilly in bourgeois society.

"Busybodies of both sexes came running to the scene and joined in the clamour. The feeling of shame caused by this abominable scene brought the child to the decision to take her own life. She hurried downstairs, through the crowd of the abusive and swearing neighbours; her eyes clouded with madness," she rushed to the Seine "and threw herself into the river. Boatmen brought her out of the water, dead, still in her wedding finery. Needless to say, those who at first had shouted against the daughter at once turned against her parents; this catastrophe frightened their empty souls.[a] A few days later the parents came to the police to claim a golden chain which the child had worn round her neck, a present from the future father-in-law, a silver watch and various other small pieces of jewelry, all of which had been deposited with the police. I did not fail to reproach these people energetically for their stupidity and barbarity. To say to these mad people that they would have to render account to God would have made very little impression on them in view of their egoistic prejudices and the peculiar kind of religiosity which prevails in the lower mercantile classes.

"Greed had brought them to me, not the desire to possess two or three keepsakes; I thought I could punish them through their greed. They were claiming their daughter's jewels; I refused these to them; I kept the certificates which they needed to reclaim these effects from the office where they had been deposited according to custom. So long as I held this post, their claims were in vain, and I found pleasure in defying their insults.

"In the same year there appeared in my office a young creole of attractive

---

[a] Peuchet has "this catastrophe struck fear into their souls".—*Ed.*

appearance from one of the richest families of Martinique. He objected most
emphatically to the handing over of the corpse of a young woman, his sister-in-law,
to the claimant, his own brother and her husband. She had drowned herself. This
kind of suicide is the commonest. Her body had been found not far from the
Grève d'Argenteuil by the officials employed to recover corpses. From one of the
well-known instincts of modesty which prevail in women even in the blindest
despair, the drowned woman had wound the seam of her skirt carefully round her
feet. This modest precaution proved her suicide beyond doubt. As soon as she had
been found she was taken to the morgue. Her beauty, her youth, her rich apparel
gave rise to a thousand speculations as to the cause of this catastrophe. The despair
of her husband, who was the first to identify her, was boundless; he did not fathom
this calamity, at least so I was told. I myself had not seen him before. I put it to the
creole that the claims of the husband had precedence over all others; he was
already having a magnificent marble tombstone erected for his unfortunate wife.
'After he has killed her, the monster!' shouted the creole, rushing to and fro in
his rage.

"From the excitement and despair of this young man, from his urgent pleading
to grant his request, from his tears, I believed I could conclude that he was in love
with her, and I told him so. He admitted his love; but with the most ardent
assurances that his sister-in-law had never known of it. He swore to that. He
wanted to bring to light the barbarities of his brother, even if it meant putting
himself in the dock, only to save the reputation of his sister-in-law, whose suicide
public opinion would, as usual, attribute to an intrigue. He begged me for my
support. What I could gather from his fragmentary, passionate declarations was
this: Monsieur de M..., his brother, rich and a connoisseur of the arts, a friend of
luxury and high society, had married this young woman about a year earlier,
apparently from mutual inclination; they were the most beautiful couple you could
see. After the marriage a blood defect, perhaps hereditary, in the constitution of
the young husband had broken out suddenly and violently. Formerly so proud of
his handsome appearance and his elegant figure, an excellence, a matchless
perfection of form, this man suddenly fell a prey to an unknown scourge against
whose devastations science was powerless; from head to foot he was most horribly
disfigured. He had lost all his hair, his spine had grown crooked. Day by day
emaciation and wrinkles changed him most strikingly, at least for others; for his
self-love tried to deny the obvious. Yet all this did not make him take to his bed; an
iron strength seemed to triumph over the attacks of the scourge. He vigorously
survived his own ruination. His body became a wreck, and his soul remained
buoyant. He continued to give banquets, to preside over hunting parties and to
lead the rich and magnificent way of life which seemed to be the law of his
character and his nature. But the insults, the jibes, the taunts of schoolboys and
street urchins when he exercised his horse in the promenades, the rude and
mocking laughter, solicitous warnings of friends about the countless occasions on
which he exposed himself to ridicule by insisting on gallant manners towards ladies,
eventually dispelled his illusion and made him cautious about himself. As soon as
he admitted to himself his ugliness and deformity, as soon as he was conscious of it,
his character became embittered; he became dejected. He seemed less keen on
taking his wife to parties, to balls, to concerts; he fled to his country residence; he
put an end to all invitations, avoided people under a thousand pretexts, and the
compliments his friends paid to his wife, which he had tolerated as long as his
pride gave him the certainty of his superiority, made him jealous, suspicious and
violent. He detected in all who insisted on visiting him the firm resolve to conquer
the heart of his wife, who was his last pride and his last consolation. At this time
the creole arrived from Martinique with business whose success seemed to be

favoured by the restoration of the Bourbons to the French throne. His sister-in-law received him with cordiality, and in the shipwreck of innumerable connections which she had contracted the newcomer preserved the advantage which his title of brother quite naturally gave him with Monsieur de M.... The creole foresaw the loneliness which would surround the household both as a result of the direct quarrels which his brother had with several of his friends and through a thousand indirect incidents which drove away and discouraged visitors. Without being clearly aware of the motives of love which made him jealous too, the creole approved these measures of isolation and encouraged them by his own advice. Monsieur de M... finished up by withdrawing entirely into a beautiful house in Passy, which in a short time became a desert. Jealousy feeds on the smallest things; when it does not know whereon to fasten, it turns against itself and becomes inventive; everything serves to sustain it. Perhaps the young woman longed for the pleasures of her age. Walls obstructed the view of neighbouring residences; the shutters were closed from morning to night."

The unfortunate wife was sentenced to the most intolerable slavery, and this slavery was only enforced by Monsieur de M... on the basis of the *Code civil* and the right of property, on the basis of social conditions which render love independent of the free sentiments of the lovers and allow the jealous husband to surround his wife with locks as the miser does his coffers; for she is only a part of his inventory.

"At night Monsieur de M... prowled round the house armed, making his rounds with dogs. He imagined he saw tracks in the sand and was misled into strange suspicions on the occasion of a ladder having been moved by a gardener. The gardener himself, a drunkard of almost 60, was placed as guard at the gate. The spirit of exclusion knows no bounds to its extravagances, it goes on to the absurd. The brother, innocent accomplice in all this, at last understood that he was assisting in making the misfortune of the young woman who, day by day kept under guard, insulted, bereft of everything which can divert a rich and happy imagination, became as gloomy and melancholy as she had been free and gay. She cried and concealed her tears, but their traces were visible. The creole was plagued by his conscience. Determined to declare himself openly to his sister-in-law and to make amends for his mistake, which had surely originated in his furtive feeling of love, he crept one morning into a small wooded pleasure garden where the prisoner went from time to time to get fresh air and look after her flowers. We must take it that availing herself of this very limited freedom she knew that she remained under the eyes of her jealous husband; for on seeing her brother-in-law, who for the first time had come face to face with her unexpectedly, the young woman displayed the greatest dismay. She wrung her hands. 'Go away, in heaven's name,' she cried to him in fright, 'go away!'

"And indeed, scarcely had he time to hide in a greenhouse, when Monsieur de M... suddenly appeared'. The creole heard cries, he tried to listen; the beating of his heart prevented him from understanding the least word of an explanation to which his concealment, should the husband discover it, could give a deplorable outcome. This event spurred on the brother-in-law; he saw the need henceforth to be the protector of a victim. He resolved to abandon all restraint of his love. Love can sacrifice everything but its right to protect, for this last sacrifice would be that of a coward. He continued to visit his brother, ready to speak to him openly, to reveal himself to him, to tell him everything. Monsieur de M... had as yet no suspicion of him, but his brother's insistence aroused it. Without being entirely clear on the causes of this interest, Monsieur de M... mistrusted them, anticipating where it might lead. The creole soon saw that his brother was not always absent, as he afterwards maintained, when people rang in vain at the gate of the house in Passy. A locksmith's apprentice made him keys after the models of those which his master had made for Monsieur de M.... After an interval of ten days, the creole, embittered by fear and tormented by the maddest imaginings, climbed the walls at night, smashed a railing in front of the main yard, reached the roof by a ladder and slid down the drain-pipe to below the window of a store-room. Violent cries caused him to creep unnoticed as far as a glass door. What he saw rent his heart. The light of a lamp shone in an alcove. Behind the bed-curtains, hair dishevelled and face purple with fury, Monsieur de M..., crouching half-naked near his wife on the bed which she dared not leave though half and half wresting herself from him, was heaping on her the most biting reproaches and seemed like a tiger ready to tear her to pieces. 'Yes,' he said to her, 'I am ugly, I am a monster and, I know it only too well, I inspire fear in you. You wish to be freed of me so that the sight of me may no longer be a burden to you. You are longing for the moment which will make you free. And don't tell me the opposite, I guess your thoughts in your fright and your resistance. You blush at the unworthy laughter which I arouse, you inwardly rebel against me! You no doubt count the minutes, one by one, which must elapse until I no longer beleaguer you with my weaknesses and my presence. Stop! I am seized with horrible desires, the frenzied wish to make you like myself, to disfigure - you, so that you can no longer hope to console yourself with lovers for the misfortune of having known me. I shall break all the mirrors in this house so that they shall not reproach me with the contrast, so that they cease to nurture your pride. Perhaps I should take you out into the world, or let you go there, to see how everybody encourages you to hate me? No, no, you shall not leave this house until you have killed me. Kill me, anticipate what I am tempted to do every day!' And the savage rolled on the bed with loud cries, gnashing his teeth, foaming at the mouth, with a thousand symptoms of madness, and striking himself in his fury, near this unfortunate woman who wasted on him the tenderest caresses and the most pathetic entreaties. At last she calmed him. No doubt, pity had replaced love, but that was not enough for this man who had become so terrible to look at, whose passion had retained so much energy. A long spell of depression was the sequel to this scene, which petrified the creole. He shuddered and did not know to whom to turn to save the unfortunate woman from this deadly martyrdom. This scene was apparently repeated every day, since for the convulsions which followed Madame de M. had recourse to bottles of medicine prepared for the purpose of restoring a little calm to her torturer.

"The creole was the only representative of the family of Monsieur de M. in Paris at the time. It is in such cases above all that one wants to curse the slowness of judicial procedure and the callousness of the laws which nothing can divert from their nicely arranged routine, particularly when it is a question only of a woman, a being whom the legislator surrounds with the least guarantees. A warrant for an arrest, some drastic measure, would alone have prevented the disaster which the witness of this madness foresaw too well. He decided, however, to risk everything, to take all consequences upon himself, since his wealth enabled him to make enormous sacrifices and not to fear responsibility for any risk involved. Already several doctors among his friends, determined like himself, were preparing to obtain entrance into Monsieur de M.'s house so as to diagnose these fits of madness and to separate the two spouses by direct force, when the occurrence of the suicide justified the belated preparations and put an end to the problem.

"Certainly, for anybody who does not limit the entire spirit of words to their letter, this suicide was a *treacherous murder* committed by the husband; but it was also the outcome of an extraordinary fit of jealousy. The jealous man needs a slave, the jealous man can love, but the love he feels is only a luxurious counterpart for jealousy; *the jealous man is above all a private property-owner.*[a] I prevented the creole from making a useless and dangerous scandal, dangerous above all to the memory of his loved one, for the idle public would have accused the victim of an adulterous connection with her husband's brother. I witnessed the funeral. Nobody but the brother and myself knew the truth. Around me I heard discreditable murmurings about this suicide and I despised them. One blushes for public opinion when one sees it close at hand with its cowardly embitterment and its dirty insinuations. Opinion is too much divided by people's isolation, too ignorant, too corrupt, because each is a stranger to himself and all are strangers to one another.[b]

"Incidentally, few weeks passed without bringing me more revelations of the same kind. In the same year I registered love liaisons caused by the parents' refusal to give their consent, and which ended with a double pistol shot.

"I also recorded suicides of men of the world reduced to impotence in the flowering of their age, whom the abuse of enjoyment had thrown into insuperable melancholy.

"Many people, after long and useless torture by harmful prescriptions, end their days dominated by the belief that medicine is incapable of freeing them from their ills.

"One could make a remarkable collection of quotations from famous authors and of poems written by despairing people preparing for their death with a certain ostentation. During the marvellously cold-blooded moment which follows the decision to die, a kind of infectious enthusiasm is exhaled from these souls and flows on to paper, even among classes which are bereft of all education. While they compose themselves for the sacrifice, whose depth they are pondering, all their strength is concentrated so as to gush out in a warm and characteristic expression.

"Some of these poems, which are buried in the archives, are masterpieces. A ponderous bourgeois, who puts his soul into his business and his god into commerce, may find all this very romantic and by his scornful laughter deny suffering which he does not understand: his disdain does not surprise us."

What else can one expect of three-percenters, who do not even suspect that daily, hourly, piece by piece, they are murdering themselves, their human nature!

"But what shall one say of the good people who pass for devout and educated, and who echo such filth? Without doubt it is of great importance that the poor devils should endure life, if only in the interests of the privileged classes of this world, which a general suicide of the trash would ruin; but is there no other means of making the existence of this class bearable than insults, sneers and fine words? Besides, there must exist a certain greatness of soul in these wretches who, determined as they are to die, destroy themselves and do not take the way of suicide by the detour of the scaffold. It is true that, the more our commercial

---

[a] This sentence was taken by Marx from the description of another case of suicide given by Peuchet below (cf. t. IV, p. 159).—*Ed.*

[b] The last sentence is taken by Marx from the description of another case of suicide given by Peuchet below (cf. t. IV, p. 167). Marx gave a free rendering and added the concluding words: "because each is a stranger to himself and all are strangers to one another."—*Ed.*

epoch[a] progresses, the rarer these noble suicides of misery become. Conscious hostility takes their place, and the miserable one inconsiderately runs the risk of theft and murder. It is easier to receive the death penalty than to get work.

"In rummaging through the police archives I have come across only one single case of cowardice in the list of suicides. That was a young American, Wilfrid Ramsay, who killed himself in order to escape a duel.

"The classification of the various causes of suicide would be the classification of the *very defects of our society*. One killed himself because he was robbed of an invention by intriguers, on which occasion the inventor, thrown into the direst poverty as a consequence of the lengthy scientific investigations to which he had to devote himself, was not even in a position to buy himself a patent. Another killed himself to avoid the enormous costs and the degrading legal prosecution consequent on monetary embarrassments which, by the way, are so common that men entrusted with the conduct of the general interest are not in the least concerned about them. Another again killed himself because he could not find work, after he had groaned for a long time under the insults and the stinginess of those in our midst who are the arbitrary distributors of work. [...][b]

"One day a doctor consulted me about a death of which he accused himself of having been the cause.

"One evening, returning to Belleville, where he lived, he was stopped by a veiled woman in the dark, in a narrow street from which his house stood off aside. She begged him in a tremulous voice to listen to her. At some distance whose features he could not distinguish was walking up and down. She was being watched by a man. 'Sir,' she told the doctor, 'I am pregnant, and when this is discovered I shall be disgraced. My family, public opinion, people of honour will not pardon me. The woman whose confidence I have betrayed would lose her reason, and without doubt would divorce her husband. I am not defending my case. I am the centre of a scandal which only my death could prevent from becoming public. I wanted to kill myself, people want me to live. I have been told that you have compassion, and this convinced me that you will not want to be an accomplice in the murder of a child, even if this child is not yet in the world. You see, it is a question of an abortion. I shall not debase myself by pleading extenuation for something I regard as the most reprehensible crime. In presenting myself to you I have merely yielded to the pleadings of others; for I shall know how to die. I shall summon death myself, and I need nobody for that. One can pretend to find pleasure in watering the garden; one can put on wooden clogs for it; one can choose a slippery place where one fetches water every day; one can arrange to disappear in the depth of the well; and people will say that it was an 'accident'. I have foreseen everything, Sir. I wish it could be the morning after, I would like to go with all my heart. Everything has been prepared so that it will happen just like that. I have been told to say this to you, and I have done so. You have to decide whether one murder shall occur or two. Because of my cowardice I had to swear that I would without reservation abide by your decision. Decide!'

"'This choice,' the doctor continued, 'horrified me. The voice of this woman had a pure and harmonious sound; her hand, which I held in mine, was fine and delicate; her frank and determined despair bespoke an excellent spirit. But the point at issue was one that really made me shudder; although in a thousand cases, in difficult deliveries, for example, when the surgeon's choice lies between saving

---

[a] Peuchet writes: "*les époques d'incrédulité*".—*Ed.*

[b] Marx omits the description of the case given by Peuchet in his *Mémoires*, t. IV, pp. 143-68; the text that follows is taken by Marx from the concluding part of the chapter, p. 169 *et seq.*—*Ed.*

the mother or the child, either politics or humaneness decides at will, without scruple.'

"'Flee abroad,' I said. 'Impossible,' she replied, 'it is not to be contemplated.'

"'Take the proper precautions.'

"'I can't, I sleep in the same alcove as the woman whose friendship I have betrayed.' 'She is your relative?' 'I must not tell you any more.'

"'I would have given my heart's blood,' the doctor continued, 'to save this woman from suicide or crime, or that she might escape this conflict without needing me. I charged myself with barbarism because I shrank from complicity in a murder. The struggle was terrible. Then a demon whispered to me that one does not kill oneself merely because one wishes to die; that compromised people can be forced to renounce their vices if their power to do evil is taken from them. I guessed luxury from the embroideries with which her fingers played, and the resources of wealth from the elegant diction of her speech. We believe that we owe less compassion to the rich; my self-esteem revolted against the thought of being tempted with gold, although up till then this matter had not been touched on, which was one more sign of delicacy and proof that my character was respected. My reply was a *refusal*; the lady went quickly away; the noise of a cabriolet convinced me that I would be unable to remedy what I had done.

"'A fortnight later the newspapers gave me the solution of the mystery. The young niece of a Paris *banker*, 18 years old at the most, the beloved ward of her aunt, who since the death of her mother had not let the girl out of her sight, had slipped and fallen into a brook on the estate of her guardians at Villemomble and had drowned. Her guardian was inconsolable; in his capacity of uncle the cowardly seducer could give way to his grief before the world.'

"One perceives that for want of something better, suicide is the extreme resort against the evils of private life.

"Among the causes of suicide I have very often found dismissal from office, refusal of work, or a sudden reduction in salary, as a consequence of which families can no longer procure the means of subsistence, the more so since most of them live from hand to mouth.

"At the time when the guards in the royal palace were being reduced, a good man was dismissed like the rest without more ado. His age and his lack of influence made it impossible for him to have himself transferred back into the army; industry was closed to him by his lack of knowledge. He tried to enter the civil service; competitors, numerous here as everywhere, stood in his way. He fell into gloomy distress and killed himself. In his pocket were found a letter and information about his circumstances. His wife was a poor seamstress; their two daughters, 16 and 18 years old, worked with her. *Tarnau*, our suicide, said in the papers he left behind that, 'since he could no longer be of use to his family and was compelled to be a burden on his wife and children, he considered it his duty to take his life so as to relieve them of this additional burden. He recommended his children to the Duchess of Angoulême; he hoped that in her goodness this princess would have compassion on so much misery.' I made a report to police prefect Anglès, and when the necessary formalities were completed the duchess had 600 francs sent to the unfortunate *Tarnau* family.

"Sad aid indeed, after such a loss. But how could one family[a] help all the unfortunate, since when everything is taken into account, the whole of France in its present state could not feed them. The charity of the rich would not suffice even if our whole nation were religious, which is far from the case. *Suicide solves the worst of the difficulty, the scaffold the rest. Sources of income and real wealth can be expected only*

---

[a] Peuchet writes "the royal family".—*Ed.*

from a recasting of our general system of agriculture and industry. It is easy to proclaim constitutions on paper, the right of every citizen to education, to work, and above all to a minimum of the means of subsistence. But it is not enough to write these generous wishes on paper, the proper task is to fructify these liberal ideas with material and intelligent social[a] institutions.

"The ancient world, paganism, has thrown up magnificent creations on the earth; will modern liberty lag behind her rival? Who will weld together these two splendid elements of might?"

———

Thus far *Peuchet*.

In conclusion we shall give one of his tables on the annual suicides in Paris.

From another of the tables given by *Peuchet* we learn that from 1817 to 1824 (inclusive) 2,808 suicides occurred in Paris.[b] Actually, of course, the figure was larger. In particular, as regards drowned persons whose bodies are exhibited in the morgue it is known in only very rare cases whether they were suicides or not.

Table of Suicides in Paris in the year 1824

Number	1st half year 198	Total 371
	2nd ,, ,, ... 173	

Of whom the attempt at suicide was survived by	125
,, ,, ,, ,, ,, ,, ,, not survived by	246
Of the male sex	239
,, ,, female sex	132
Unmarried	207
Married	164

	Voluntary heavy fall	47
	Strangulation	38
Manner of	By cutting instruments	40
death	,, firearms	42
	,, poisoning	28
	,, coal fumes	61
	Suffocation by voluntary plunge into water	115

	Passionate love, domestic quarrels and grief	71
	Illness, weariness of life, unsound mind	128
Motives	Misbehaviour, gaming, lotteries, fear of accusations and punishments	53
	Misery, poverty, loss of position, loss of job	59
	Unknown	60

Written in the second half of 1845

Published in 1846 in *Gesellschaftsspiegel*
Bd. II, Heft VII
Signed: *K. Marx*

Printed according to the journal
Published in English for the first
time

———

[a] The word "social" was added by Marx.—*Ed.*

[b] Peuchet writes "in the Seine Department".—*Ed.*

Frederick Engels

A FRAGMENT OF FOURIER'S ON TRADE[204]

The Germans are gradually beginning to spoil the communist movement too. Here also being as always the last and most inactive, they believe they can conceal their somnolence by contempt for their predecessors and empty philosophical boasting. Communism has hardly come into existence in Germany before it is being seized on by a whole host of speculative minds who imagine they have performed miracles by translating into the language of Hegelian logic propositions that long ago became commonplaces in France and England and now offering this new wisdom to the world as something unprecedented, as "true German theory", in order to be able to throw mud to their heart's content at the "bad practice" and "ridiculous" social systems of the narrow-minded French and English. This always ready German theory, which has had the boundless good fortune to get a whiff of Hegel's philosophy of history and to become embodied in the scheme of the eternal categories by some dried-up Berlin professor, and which then perhaps leafed through Feuerbach, a few German communist writings and Herr Stein's book on French socialism,[a] this German theory of the very worst sort has already, without the slightest difficulty, reconstrued French socialism and communism according to Herr Stein, has allotted it a subordinate position, has "*overcome*" it, and "*elevated*" it to the "higher stage of development" of the always ready "German theory".[205] It has never occurred to it, of course, to acquaint itself to any extent with

---

[a] Lorenz von Stein, *Der Socialismus und Communismus des heutigen Frankreichs. Ein Beitrag zur Zeitgeschichte.*—Ed.

the things to be elevated themselves, to take a look at Fourier, Saint-Simon, Owen and the French Communists—Herr Stein's meagre extracts are quite sufficient to bring about this brilliant victory of German theory over the wretched efforts of foreigners.

In contrast to this comical arrogance of German theory, which is incapable of dying, it is absolutely necessary to show the Germans what a lot they owe to foreigners since they became concerned with social questions. Among all the pompous phrases now loudly proclaimed in German literature as the basic principles of true, pure, German, theoretical communism and socialism, there has so far not been a single idea which has grown on German soil. What the French or the English said as long as ten, twenty and even forty years ago—and said very well, very clearly, in very fine language—the Germans have now at last during the past year become acquainted with in bits and have Hegelianised, or at best belatedly rediscovered it and published it in a much worse, more abstract form as a completely new discovery. I make no exception here of my own writings. What is peculiar to the Germans is only the bad, abstract, unintelligible and clumsy form in which they have expressed these ideas. And as befits genuine theoreticians, from what the French have produced—they still know almost nothing at all of the English—they have so far found worthy of their attention, apart from the *most general* principles, only what is worst and most theoretical: the schematic plans of future society, the *social systems*. The best aspect, the *criticism of existing society*, the real basis, the main task of any investigation of social questions, they have calmly pushed aside. Not to mention the fact that these wise theoreticians are accustomed also to speak contemptuously of, or to ignore altogether, the only German who has *really* achieved something, namely: *Weitling*.

I want to put before these wise gentlemen a short chapter from Fourier, which they could take as an example. It is true that Fourier did not start out from the Hegelian theory and for this reason unfortunately could not attain knowledge of absolute truth, not even of absolute socialism. It is true that owing to this shortcoming Fourier unfortunately allowed himself to be led astray and to substitute the method of series for the absolute method and thereby arrived at such speculative constructions as the conversion of the sea into lemonade, the *couronnes boréale* and *australe*,[a] the anti-lion, and the conjunction of the planets.[206] But, if it has to be, I shall prefer to believe with the cheerful Fourier in

---

[a] Northern and southern coronas.—*Ed*.

all these stories rather than in the realm of the absolute spirit, where there is no lemonade at all, in the identity of Being and Nothing and the conjunction of the eternal categories. French nonsense is at least cheerful, whereas German nonsense is gloomy and profound. And then, Fourier has criticised existing social relations so sharply, with such wit and humour that one readily forgives him for his cosmological fantasies, which are also based on a brilliant world outlook.

The fragment which I am reproducing here was found among Fourier's works after his death and was printed in the first number of the periodical *Phalange*,* published by the Fourierists from the beginning of 1845. I am omitting what relates to Fourier's positive system and what otherwise is of no interest, and in general am making such free use of the text as is absolutely necessary with the foreign Socialists in order to make the things they wrote with definite aims in view readable to a public which is alien to these aims. This fragment is by no means the most brilliant of Fourier's writings, nor is it the best of what he wrote about trade — and yet no German Socialist or Communist, with the exception of Weitling, has so far written anything remotely comparable to this rough sketch.

To save the German public the trouble of reading the *Phalange* itself, I should mention that this periodical is a purely monetary speculation on the part of the Fourierists, and Fourier's manuscripts published in it are of very unequal value. Messieurs the Fourierists who publish this review are germanised, pompous theoreticians who have replaced the humour with which their teacher unmasked the world of the bourgeoisie by a holy, thoroughgoing theoretical, learned seriousness, for which they are deservedly ridiculed in France and prized in Germany. The description of the imaginary triumphs of Fourierism which they present in the first issue of the *Phalange* could send a professor of the absolute method into raptures.

I begin my reproductions with a passage which has already been reprinted in the *Théorie des quatre mouvements*. This is the case with considerable sections of the present fragment of which, however, I shall give only what is most essential.

---

* *La Phalange.* Revue de la science sociale, XIVe année, 1re série in 8°, Paris, aux Bureaux de la Phalange, 1845.—Publication des Manuscrits de Fourier: "Section ébauchée des trois unités externes", pp. 1-42 of the January and February issue.—*Note by Engels.*

"We now touch on civilisation's most sensitive spot; it is an unpleasant task to raise one's voice against the folly of the day, against chimeras that are downright epidemical.

"To speak against the absurdities of trade today means to expose oneself to anathemas just as much as if one had spoken against the tyranny of the popes and the barons in the twelfth century. If it were a matter of choosing between two dangerous roles, I think it would be less dangerous to offend a sovereign with bitter truths than to offend the mercantile spirit which now rules as a despot over civilisation and even over sovereigns.

"And yet a superficial analysis will prove that our commercial systems debase and disorganise civilisation, and that in trade as in all other things we are going astray more and more under the guidance of the inexact sciences.

"The controversy on trade is hardly half a century old and has already produced thousands of volumes; and yet its originators have not seen that the trade mechanism is organised in such a way that it is a slap in the face for all common sense. It has subordinated the whole of society to one class of parasitical and unproductive people, the merchants. All the essential classes of society—the proprietor,* the farmer, the manufacturer, and even the government—find themselves dominated by an inessential, accessory class, the merchant, who should be their subordinate, their employed agent, removable and accountable, and who, nevertheless, directs and obstructs at will all the mainsprings of circulation.

"In respect of errors other than those of trade, public opinion and the learned bodies are, indeed, more tractable; it is pretty well agreed that the philosophical systems are dangerous illusions, that experience belies our boasting of perfection, that our theories of freedom do not square with civilisation, that our virtues are social comedies and our legislations labyrinths; there are even jokes about a fashionable controversy, ideology.[208] But tongue-wagging about commerce, with its theories of imports and exports, counterbalance, balance, and guarantee, has become the Ark of the Covenant before which everything bows down. This, then, is the illusion which we have to dispel.

"First of all we must show that our trade systems, which are now gaped at with stupid veneration, are the antipodes of truth, of justice, and therefore also of unity.

"It is difficult to make clear to a century that precisely that operation which it considers to be the masterpiece of all wisdom is nothing but the seal of ignorance stamped on its entire policy. Let us but look at the already known results: maritime monopoly, fiscal monopoly, growing national debts, bankruptcies in unbroken succession resulting from paper money, increasing villainy in all business relations. Already now we can stigmatise the mechanism of *free trade*, i.e., *of free lying*,[a] that veritable industrial anarchy, that monstrous power in society.

"How is it that the *most lying* class in the social body is most protected by the '*apostles of truth*'? How does it happen that today learned men who preach contempt of vile wealth praise only the class which pursues wealth *per fas et nefas*,[b] the class of stock exchange gamblers and corner-men? Formerly the philosophers were unanimous in censuring certain corporations which defended with flexibility of conscience the proposition that there is a difference between taking and stealing. How then have the same philosophers now become the apologists of a class which

---

* It must not be forgotten that Fourier was not a Communist.— *Note by Engels.*

---

[a] Engels' italics here and below.— *Ed.*

[b] By legal or illegal means.— *Ed.*

affirms, with still greater immorality, that haggling is not lying, that to dupe the buyer is not the same as robbing him, that stockjobbing and cornering are by no means plundering the productive class, in brief, that one must work only for money, not for fame;—for that is the refrain which the merchants sing in chorus: We don't pursue business *pour la gloire!** Is it then to be wondered at that the modern sciences went astray when they espoused the cause of those who openly profess such principles?"

Trade takes various forms according to the various social stages; for as it is the pivot of all social life, it exists as soon as there is any social condition in general. A people becomes social, forms a society, from the moment when it begins to carry out exchange. For this reason trade exists already among the *savages*, where it takes the form of direct barter. Under *patriarchy* it becomes indirect commerce; in *barbarism* the basis of the commercial method is formed by the monopolies, the fixing of maximums and prices and forcible government requisitions, and in *civilisation* by individual competition or lying and bewildering struggle.[a]

"There is no need for us to dwell on direct barter among the savages who have no knowledge of money. One man is lucky at the hunt and exchanges a piece of game for arrows made by another, who has not been hunting and needs eatables. This method is not even trade, it is barter."

The second method, indirect commerce, is "primitive trade. It is carried on through a go-between, who *becomes the owner of something which he did not produce and does not intend to consume*. This method, although it is bad and leaves room for arbitrariness, is nevertheless highly advantageous in the following three cases:

"1) in young countries, where only agriculture exists without industry; this is the state in which all colonies find themselves at the beginning;

"2) in harsh lands, as in Siberia and the African deserts; a merchant who defies heat and cold to carry objects of necessity to distant parts is a very useful man;

"3) in oppressed and constricted lands, where the Bedouin plunder caravans, exact ransom from merchants and often murder them—every kind of protection is due to him who braves these dangers in order to bring supplies to a distant land. When such a merchant becomes rich he certainly deserves it.

"In these three cases the merchants are neither Stock Exchange gamblers nor corner-men; they do not hawk, one speculator to another, the objects intended for consumption. On their arrival they offer them openly to the consumer in a bazaar or public market; they are the accelerators of industrial movement. They want to earn—nothing is more reasonable in the civilised world: he who has sown deserves to harvest. But it is very rare that the merchants content themselves with this function of theirs; singly or in alliance they scheme to obstruct the circulation of commodities in order to make prices immediately soar.

"*Trade becomes pernicious from the moment the go-betweens, due to their excessive number, become parasites* [on the social body][b] and are ready to conceal goods, to let them rise in price under the pretext of an artificially produced scarcity, in brief, to rob simultaneously the producer and the consumer through speculation tricks instead of serving both as simple, open go-betweens. We still see this openness at our small markets in villages and towns. The man who buys a hundred calves or

* This expression exists in literally the same form also among German merchants.—*Note by Engels*.

---

[a] In this paragraph Engels gives in his own words the content of Fourier's Table: *De l'echelle des méthodes commerciales appliquées aux diverses périodes.—Ed.*

[b] The words in brackets were added by Engels.—*Ed.*

sheep is a useful intermediary for twenty peasants, who would otherwise lose whole working days to bring them to market in town. When, on arriving at the market, he publicly offers his animals for sale, he thereby renders a service also to the consumers; but when by means of heaven knows what tricks he agrees with other 'friends of trade'[a] to hide three-quarters of the sheep, to tell the butchers that sheep are scarce, that he can only supply a few *friends,* to sell them half as dear again under this pretext, to alarm the buyers, and then to bring the hidden sheep out one after the other, to sell them at inflated prices in the atmosphere of alarm previously created and thus to extort a high ransom from the consumers—then this is no longer simple commerce, open offering of commodities free from any intrigue, it is compound commerce, whose endlessly changing tricks give birth to the thirty-six typical vices of our trade system and are tantamount to a legal monopoly. When one lays hands on the total product by ruse in order to make it dearer, that is robbing more by means of intrigues than the monopoly does by armed force.

"I shall not dwell any longer on the method of the barbarians. It comprises fixing of maximums, forcible requisitions and monopolies, which are still quite customary also in the civilised state. As I have already said elsewhere,[b] the various methods of individual periods overlap; one must not wonder, therefore, that civilisation borrows individual features from both higher and lower stages. Our civilised trade mechanism is thus an amalgamation of the characters of all periods, with those of the civilised stage, however, predominating—and these are much more despicable still than those of barbarism, because our trade is nothing but organised and legitimised robbery under the mask of legality. As a result, the racketeers and intermediaries can unite to cause artificial dearth of any foodstuffs and thus plunder both producers and consumers to heap up in a hurry scandalous fortunes of fifty millions, whose owners nevertheless complain that there is no protection of trade, that the merchants cannot subsist, that nothing is done, and that the state is being ruined if the merchant is reduced to the inability to make more than fifty millions!

"Meanwhile we are taught by a new[c] science that these people should be granted complete freedom. Let the merchants do their job, we are told; without this freedom the corner-man, who even so has earned only fifty million, would perhaps not even have made a single million, and his respectable family would have to manage on fifty thousand francs revenue—

"*Dii, talem avertite casum!*[d]

"... Contempt of commerce, a contempt inborn in all peoples, was prevalent in all nations considered to be honourable except for a few coastal clans of hucksters who derived benefit from commercial extortions and villainies. Athens, Tyre and Carthage, which profited by commerce, could not mock at it; everybody refrains from mocking at the ways in which he has enriched himself, and the financier least of all will mock at the art of adding ciphers to bills, or allowing the enemy to take away the ledgers and putting the cash in safety while reporting it also as having been taken by the enemy.

"In reality with ancient as well as with modern peoples commerce has always been an object of mockery on the part of all honourable classes. How can one have

---

[a] Quotes by Engels here and below.—*Ed.*

[b] Charles Fourier, *Théorie de l'unité universelle,* t. 2.—"Prolégomène".—*Ed.*

[c] The word "new" was added by Engels.—*Ed.*

[d] Ye gods, ward off such an occurrence! (A paraphrase from Virgil's poem *Aeneid,* Book III.)—*Ed.*

any esteem for an out-and-out rascally profession or a class of people who lie with every word they say and by means of this magic art earn millions while the honest landowner who cultivates his piece of land with great effort and exertion, using the best of his experience, barely achieves an insignificant increase in its yield?

"Meanwhile, for a century a new science called Economics has been exalting hucksters, stockjobbers, corner-men, usurers, bankrupts, monopolisers and commercial parasites to the peak of honours: the governments, daily deeper and deeper in debt, always intent on finding means of borrowing money, have found themselves forced to conceal their contempt and to spare this class of mercantile blood-suckers which keeps the money-coffers locked to civilisation and pumps out all the treasures of agricultural and industrial diligence under the pretext of serving it. It is not denied that trade ensures transportation, victualling, and distribution, but it does so like a servant who performs service actually worth a thousand francs annually and on the other hand robs his master of ten thousand francs, or ten times as much as he produces.

"As a young spendthrift secretly despises the Jew to whom he goes every week to get himself fleeced, but still always greets him very politely, so also the modern governments have, with obvious contempt, concluded an armistice with trade, which is doing all the better for the fact that it knows how to have itself lumped together with the very manufacturers whom it plunders. The economists, who have found in this merchants' hotch-potch a nursery of new dogmas, a mine of systems, have overthrown morality with all its high-sounding talk of truth in order to enthrone their favourites, the stockjobbers and bankrupts. Thereupon all the scholars rivalled in self-abasement; in the beginning science admitted those 'friends of trade' as its equals—Voltaire dedicated a tragedy to an English merchant.[a] Today these stockjobbers would have a good laugh if a scholar presumed to dedicate a tragedy to them! Stockjobbing has discarded the mask, it no longer needs the incense of the scholars; it wants secret—*and soon legal—participation in government*! And indeed we have seen the Aachen Congress unable to decide anything until two bankers arrived.[209]

"Despite the fact that the economic systems have exalted the Golden Calf of trade, they have been unable to put an end to the natural contempt which the nations feel towards it. It remains despised by the nobility, the clergy, the propertied classes, the officials, the lawyers, the scholars, despised by artists, soldiers, and every class worthy of respect. In vain has trade heaped sophism on sophism to prove to them that the stockjobbing blood-sucker should be respected—a natural disdain for this class of upstarts still prevails. Everybody yields to the upswing of a dogma favoured by fortune, but everybody continues in secret to despise the mercantile hydra, which takes no notice of this and pursues the course of its conquests.

"How is it that our century has made public the crimes of so many classes, even those of the Federates,[210] who only existed for a month in 1815, whence comes it that it has never occurred to this century, which has spared neither kings nor popes in its collections on crimes, to make public the crimes of the merchants? Yet writers are unanimous in complaining that they suffer from a lack of material. To show them how fruitful this material is, I shall make a methodical analysis of only a single one of the" (thirty-six) "crimes of civilised trade. These thirty-six reprehensible features of our trade under the domination of individual competition and of bewildering and lying struggle are the following:

---

[a] Voltaire, *Zaïre* (a tragedy dedicated to E. Falkner, an admirer and friend of the author).—*Ed*.

Synoptical Table of the Features of Civilised Trade[a]

Pivotal points: Intermediate ownership and the dismemberment of agriculture.

"1) The two-sidedness of trade.
2) Arbitrary determination of value.
3) Freedom of fraudulence.
4) Insolidarity, lack of mutual liability.[b]
5) Theft, removal of capital.
6) *Decrease in wages.*
7) *Artificial obstruction of supply sources.*
8) *Oppressive surpluses.*
9) Perverse interferences.
10) Destructive policy.
11) *Torpidness or general lack of credit* (recoil, repercussion).
12) *Fictitious money.*
13) Financial confusion.
14) *Epidemical crime.*
15) Obscurantism.
16) *Parasitism.*
17) *Cornering* (accaparement).
18) *Stockjobbing.*
19) *Usury.*
20) *Unfruitful work.*
21) Industrial lotteries (speculation on risk).
22) Indirect corporative monopoly.
23) *Fiscal monopoly, state administration enforced by falsification.*
24) The exotic, or *colonial monopoly.*
25) *Maritime monopoly.*
26) *Feudal,* caste *monopoly.*
27) Baseless provocation.
28) Loss.
29) *Falsification.*
30) Ruin of health.
31) *Bankruptcy.*
32) *Smuggling.*
33) Piracy.
34) Fixing of maximums and requisitions.
35) *Speculative slavery.*
36) *Universal egoism.*"

Of these thirty-six features we shall consider in detail only one, bankruptcy; before that I shall say a few words about some others.

II

FALSENESS OF THE ECONOMIC PRINCIPLES ON CIRCULATION
(Proved by three features of the Table, Nos. 7, 8 and 12: artificial obstruction of supply sources, oppressive surpluses and fictitious money)

"Our century, which has been so prolific of theories about the movement of industry, still cannot distinguish circulation from obstruction. It confuses circulation interrupted in places with that which is uninterrupted, simple circulation with

---

[a] In his work Fourier gives this table in the introductory section.—*Ed.*
[b] The words "lack of mutual liability" were added by Engels.—*Ed.*

compound. However, let us leave these dull distinctions; the facts may speak and serve us as a basis for principles which are directly opposed to those of economics.

"Both governments and peoples agree that forgers, both of money and of public securities, should be punished with death. Those who counterfeit coins and bank-notes are indeed condemned to death. A very wise precautionary measure. *But why does trade enjoy the right to forge money when this practice brings other people to the gallows?*

"Every bill of exchange made out by a merchant bears the seed of counterfeit, for it is extremely uncertain whether it will ever be paid. Everyone who steers a course towards bankruptcy floods circulation with his bills of exchange without intending ever to pay them. In this way he in fact makes and spreads counterfeit money.

"Will it be objected that everyone else enjoys the same privilege, that a property-owner, like a merchant, can put bills of exchange into circulation?

"That is not true. A property-owner cannot do that. A right is illusory when it cannot be exercised. Witness the constitutional right of the people to sovereignty, a pompous prerogative in spite of which the plebeian cannot even get his midday meal if he has not a sou in his pocket. And yet how far from the pretension to sovereignty is the claim to a midday meal. Many rights exist thus on paper, but not in reality, and their granting is an insult to him who cannot even ensure himself rights a hundred times less important.

"So it is with the property-owner as regards the issuing of bills of exchange. He has the right to issue them as the plebeian has the right to claim sovereignty; but to possess the right and to exercise it are two very different things. When the property-owner makes out a bill of exchange he will not find anybody who will accept it without a guarantee, and he will be treated as one who forges money. He will be required to hypothecate a completely debt-free immovable property and to pay a usurious rate of interest into the bargain. His bills of exchange would be accepted at this price, and with such a security they would be money with real value, not fictitious money like those of a second-hand dealer who, by virtue of his title as a 'friend of trade, finds means of putting into circulation 'good'[a] bills to the value of a million when he does not possess even the hundredth part of that sum, even 10,000 francs as guarantee for that million.

"How beautifully those governments let themselves be cheated who deprive themselves of this ability and guarantee it for the merchant! A merchant who has ten thousand francs security issues bills of exchange to the amount of a million when he pleases; he is protected and authorised to do so; he has the right to set this mass of paper in circulation without the law being entitled to investigate how he places his capital and what securities he has. The Treasury, offering a guarantee of say ten million, would have to be able, according to this ratio, to issue securities up to a thousand million. But if a government tries to do so without consulting public opinion, without informing it of the move, it will see its credit ruined and its country exposed to political disturbances; and yet it is only doing the same, only availing itself of the same privilege which is enjoyed by so many schemers, who often cannot offer the hundredth part of these guarantees and cannot run their business.

"It will be answered that these schemers know how to talk over the foolish and insinuate themselves into their confidence; it is therefore set up as a principle of commerce that the art of duping and plundering good-natured, credulous people deserves to be protected in every way and that this protection must be limited to the merchant and not be enjoyed by the government. I do not maintain that this fine art should be allowed to both, but on the contrary that it should be denied both to rulers and to merchants.

---

[a] The word "good" has been inserted by Engels.— *Ed.*

"From this it follows that the merchant enjoys the ability to *issue fictitious money in the form of bills of exchange* (twelfth feature)—a crime which is equivalent to forging money, for which the other categories of rascals are sent to the gallows—and that the trade system of civilised people legalises and protects *competition of fraudulence* (third feature).

"The accusation of forging money, like the other points of the accusation, will be answered as follows: there must be merchants in order to ensure circulation, and business would become impossible if these agents were placed under restraint; the state would disrupt the public credit and place the whole of its industry in jeopardy.

"It is true enough that a quality of trade is that it *forges our fetters still tighter whenever the social body shows any signs of resistance.* As soon as any administrative measure hampers the machinations of trade, trade restricts credit and paralyses circulation, while the state, which wanted to eliminate an old disorder, in the end adds new ones. This effect is called repercussion (eleventh feature) in the Table.

"This danger is used as the basis for establishing the principle: Let the merchants do their job, their complete freedom is the guarantee of circulation. An exceedingly false principle, for it is precisely this complete freedom which gives rise to all the tricks that are so obstructive to circulation: stockjobbing, cornering, bankruptcy, and so on, the consequences of which are the two features:

"7. Artificial obstruction of supply sources.

"8. Oppressive surpluses.

"Let us see what influence these two features have on circulation."

Trade does not content itself with delivering commodities from the producer to the consumer,[a] "it schemes by means of cornering and stockjobbing speculation to produce an artificial dearth of those food articles which are not exactly plentiful. In 1807 a stockjobbing manoeuvre suddenly raised the price of sugar to five francs in the month of May, and the same sugar dropped to two francs in July, although not the slightest new supplies had arrived. But the stockjobbing had been countered by means of false information and thus the sugar had been brought down to its value; the scheming and artificially aroused fears that there would be no supply had been disposed of. These schemes and artificial fears play their tricks every day with some food article and *make* it scarce without a real scarcity existing. In 1812, when the harvest was assured and the corner-men were disappointed in their hopes, enormous quantities of grain and flour were suddenly seen coming from their warehouses. So there had been no shortage at all and absolutely no danger of famine, if only these foodstuffs had been distributed rationally." But trade has the peculiarity that even *before* there is a danger, with an eye to its possibility, it diverts supplies, stops circulation, arouses panicky fears, produces artificial food shortage.

"The same effect is produced in times of surplus, when trade obstructs supplies out of affected fear of profusion. In the former case it operates positively, by buying up foodstuffs in anticipation; in the latter case negatively, by not buying and thus causing prices to drop so low that the peasant does not even get his production costs refunded. Hence arises the eighth feature, oppressive surpluses.

"Trade will retort that it does not need to buy when it foresees no profit, and that it will not be so insane as to overload itself with grain which offers no probability at all of a surcharge, while it, trade, can invest its capital far more usefully in such commodities as hold out profit for it because of their scarcity, which can easily be increased by cornering.

---

[a] Here Fourier refers to the third method (*le trafic ou négoce indirect intermédiaire*) quoted in his Table: *De l'echelle des méthodes commerciales appliquées aux diverses périodes.*—Ed.

"There you have convenient and pleasant principles in a social system in which people talk about nothing but mutual guarantees. Trade is therefore exempted whenever it pleases from serving the social body. It acts like an army which would be authorised to refuse to fight whenever danger were present, and to do service only in its own interest, without any consideration for the state interest. Such is our mercantile policy, so one-sidedly does it determine all obligations.

"In 1820 the price of grain dropped below three francs in various provinces in which a price of four francs hardly covered the costs. This would not have occurred had French trade bought in advance six months' food supplies for thirty million persons," as it would have had to do under a system of mutuality adapting itself to the interests of both parties.[a] "This reserve stock, withdrawn from circulation and locked up in granaries, would have kept up the price of the rest, and the peasant would not have suffered from the depreciation and the impossibility to market his products. But our trade system works exactly in the opposite direction: it aggravates the pressure of surplus and the evils of famine and thus has a destructive effect on both sides.[b]

"I have chosen the eighth feature, oppressive surplus, to show that the existing mode of trade has both negative and positive defects, and that it often sins by non-intervention, by omitting a service which it could easily render. For when in a time of famine the sum of five hundred million is required to buy up the corn, it is immediately available; but if this sum is needed for precautionary measures to increase stocks in times of surplus, not even five hundred talers[c] can be scraped together. There is neither mutuality nor guarantee in the contract concluded between the social body and the commercial body. The latter serves only its own interest, not that of society, and hence the abundant capital which it uses *is a robbery perpetrated against industry as a whole*. In the Table I have listed this robbery as the fifth feature: 'Removal of capital.'"

Thus, on both sides of trade "there is not the slightest sense of obligation towards the social body, which surrenders itself, bound hand and foot, to the Minotaur, to whom it guarantees despotic power over capitals and foodstuffs." Yes, indeed, despotic power! "After so many declamations against despotism we still have not discovered *the real one*, which is no other than *the despotism of trade*, that real satrap of the civilised world![d]

"To sum up, it follows from this that the civilised mechanism guarantees the merchants complete impunity for the crime of forging money, for which other classes are punished with death—and that this impunity is based on the pretence of help which they allegedly render to circulation but in reality refuse—positively by artificial obstruction of supply sources and negatively by oppressive profusion.

"To this falsity in the results must be added the lack of any principles. The economists admit that their science has absolutely no fixed principles; and it is indeed the height of unprincipledness to grant complete freedom to a class of so exceedingly depraved agents as the merchants.

"The consequence of all this is that the commercial movement proceeds by fits and starts, in spasms, surprises and excesses of all descriptions, as can be seen every day in the present trade mechanism, which can achieve only a periodically interrupted circulation, without regular graduation, without balance and guarantees.

---

[a] This summarises the ideas contained in the two preceding paragraphs of Fourier's work, which Engels omitted.—*Ed.*

[b] The last sentence is given by Engels abridged.—*Ed.*

[c] Fourier has "écus".—*Ed.*

[d] Engels gives the text of this paragraph in a somewhat abridged form.—*Ed.*

"An amusing result of this disorder is that people have the courage to reproach the government with financial abuses which they never dare to reproach trade with. Witness the two bankruptcies—that of Law's bank-notes and that of the assignats.[211] These were gradual bankruptcies, they were seen approaching from afar; with a timely partial sacrifice they could have been guarded against. Despite these extenuating circumstances the public gave no quarter. It rightly declared Law's notes and the assignats to be forgery, armed plunder.

"Why then does the same public good-naturedly tolerate the issue of counterfeit money by the merchants when it does not allow it for governments, even when these are cautious enough to prepare for the bankruptcy by a slow depreciation which affords the holders of the papers the possibility to evade it? This possibility does not exist for the holders of the securities issued by trade. Bankruptcy strikes them like a thunderclap. Many a man goes to sleep tonight in possession of 300,000 francs and wakes up tomorrow with no more than 100,000 as a result of a bankruptcy. The National Convention copied this manoeuvre in the operation of the Consolidated Third[212]; people did not tire of reproaching it with this as a fully established robbery. And yet every merchant is allowed the right to commit still more vexatious robberies and to steal by bankruptcy two-thirds of what he received, whereas the Convention withheld two-thirds of sums it had never received. How outrageous the crimes of trade become when compared with other, and even the biggest, political infamies![a]

"The following details will demonstrate that modern politics, by handing over trade to completely free merchants exempt from any kind of obligation, has set the wolf among the fold and provoked robberies of all kinds."

Let us now go on to bankruptcy to describe it in somewhat greater detail.

III
HIERARCHY OF BANKRUPTCY

"When a crime becomes very frequent, one gets accustomed to it and witnesses it with indifference.[213] In Italy or Spain people remain quite cool at the sight of a hired assassin stabbing his designated victim and taking refuge in a church, where he enjoys immunity. In Italy one sees fathers mutilate and murder their children to improve their voice, while the servants of 'the God of peace' encourage them to perpetrate these brutalities so as to obtain good singers for their choirs. Such abominations would arouse the indignation of all other civilised nations if they occurred amongst them," but on the other hand they "have other outrageous customs which would make the Italians' blood boil.

"If the customs and opinions within civilisation differ so much from nation to nation, how much more must they differ from one social epoch to another; how hateful would the vices which are tolerated in civilisation seem in less imperfect social stages! One can hardly believe that countries which call themselves well ordered can tolerate for a moment such abominations as bankruptcy.[b]

"Bankruptcy is the most ingenious and shameless villainy that has ever existed; it guarantees every merchant the ability to rob the public of a sum proportionate to his fortune or his credit, so that a rich man can say: 'I set up as a tradesman in 1808; on such and such a day in the year 1810 I will steal so and so many millions, whoever they may belong to.'

---

[a] Fourier has "such as the infamies of the Convention", which Engels omits.—*Ed.*

[b] The last sentence is given by Engels abridged.—*Ed.*

"Let us leave aside a present development, the new French code[214] and its intention to punish bankruptcy. There is no unanimity in respect of the success of this intention and means of evading the new laws are already being suggested. Therefore we shall first let practice decide and meanwhile base our arguments on already known facts; consider the disorders which result from the philosophical system and the principle: Leave the merchants complete freedom, without demanding any guarantee of the cleverness, the honesty or the solvency of each individual.

"From these arises, alongside other abuses, bankruptcy, a still more heinous robbery than highway robbery. However, people have become accustomed to it and put up with it so well that they even recognise *honest bankruptcies* — those in which the speculator steals only half.

"Let us go on to a detailed description of this kind of heroism, which was little known in antiquity. Since then it has experienced a brilliant upswing. It presents analysts with a series of developments which testify to our progress towards perfectibility.

Hierarchy of Bankruptcy.—Feature 31.—The Crimes of Trade.—A Free Series in Three Orders, Nine Genera, and Thirty-Six Species[215]

"*Right or ascending wing. Light hues.*

I. *The Innocent.*

    1) Child bankruptcy.
    2) Daredevil bankruptcy.
    3) Stealthy bankruptcy. .
    4) Posthumous bankruptcy.

II. *The Honourable.*

    5) Goose bankruptcy.
    6) Ecstatic bankruptcy.
    7) Unprincipled bankruptcy.

III. *The Seductive.*

    8) Amiability bankruptcy.
    9) Bankruptcy *de bon ton.*
    10) Amorous bankruptcy.
    11) Bankruptcy by favour.
    12) Sentimental bankruptcy.

"*Centre of the Series. Grandiose Hues.*

IV. *The Tacticians.*

    13) Fat bankruptcy.
    14) Cosmopolitan bankruptcy.
    15) Hopeful bankruptcy.
    16) Transcendent bankruptcy.
    17) Graded bankruptcy.

V. *The Manoeuvrers.*

    18) Running fire bankruptcy.
    19) Close-column bankruptcy.
    20) Marching-in-file bankruptcy.
    21) Skirmisher bankruptcy.

VI. *The Agitators.*

> 22) Bankruptcy in grand style.
> 23) Large-scale bankruptcy.
> 24) Attila bankruptcy.

"Left or Descending Wing. Dirty Hues.

VII. *The Cunning Sneakers.*

> 25) Compensation bankruptcy.
> 26) Bankruptcy out of rank.
> 27) Crescendo bankruptcy.
> 28) Godly bankruptcy.

VIII. *The Bunglers*

> 29) Fools' bankruptcy.
> 30) Invalids' bankruptcy.
> 31) Crushing bankruptcy.
> 32) Swinish bankruptcy.

IX. *The False Brothers.*

> 33) Villains' bankruptcy.
> 34) Gallows-bird bankruptcy.
> 35) Fugitive bankruptcy.
> 36) Bankruptcy for fun.

IV

ASCENDING WING OF BANKRUPTS

"In a very depraved, very grasping century one would be a general laughing-stock if one declaimed in a schoolmaster's tone against the accredited vices, against bankruptcy. It is much more sensible to chime in the dominant tone and to see the funny side of social crimes. So I shall try to prove that bankruptcy is an even much more laughable villainy than it is believed to be by its promoters and protectors, who see nothing but well-behaved trifles in its mercantile plunder.

"Everything is relative, in vice as in virtue. Even robbers have their standards of justice and honour. It is therefore no wonder that among themselves bankrupts admit principles and degrees in rascality. I have sought to use these as a basis for my division. I have divided them according to the custom in three corps, the first of which contains the light, graceful hues, the second the imposing, lofty characters, and the third the rather inconspicuous, trivial genera. The right wing will open the march-past."

The Innocent

"I. *Child bankruptcy* is that of the greenhorn who is making his debut in the career, and inconsiderately, without any preparatory tactics, indulges in the mad prank of going bankrupt. The notary easily puts the affair in order. He presents it as a folly of youth and says: 'Youth counts on your indulgence, Messieurs the Creditors.' The annoying business is wound up to the merriment of the public, for these greenhorn bankruptcies are always interlarded with amusing incidents: duped usurers, mystified skinflints,[a] etc.

"The bankrupt of this genus can risk masses of shabby affairs: appropriation of goods, scandalous loans, thefts from relatives, friends, neighbours—everything is washed away by the argument of a relative who says to the irate creditors: 'What can you expect—he is a child without any knowledge of business; one must close one's eyes where young people are concerned, he will improve with time.'

"These child bankrupts have a strong support on their side, namely mockery. One likes to mock in trade; one is inclined to mock at those who are duped rather than to censure the villains, and when a bankrupt has the laughers on his side he is sure to see the majority of his creditors capitulate immediately and to win his composition by assault.

"2. *Daredevil bankruptcy*; that of certain beginners who play double or quits, people who gallop off at full speed, speculate and manage their affairs like mad, make ducks and drakes with huge sums of money and play the grand gentleman to achieve by storm a temporary credit which they manage to secure by some secret sacrifice. When these daredevils once get going they heap blunder on blunder and usually end up in flight. The affair will be excused as botch work and easily arranged, for it provides material for mockery like the preceding one.

"These daredevils are extremely common in France and are here honoured with the title of speculators. They are very sure of their game if they hasten the discovery so that they can turn their somersault at the very moment when they are believed to have hardly got going, when everybody is ready to grant them credit for a first deal and thinks: 'he will certainly not come a cropper in the very first year.'

"3. *Stealthy bankruptcy*, the type carried out underhand, is one in which the embarrassed debtor proposes 'a small arrangement', a rebate of 25 per cent or coverage in goods to be over-assessed by 25 per cent. The mediator remarks to the creditors that this is very advantageous for them, for if they press the debtor and oblige him to go bankrupt they will lose at least 50 per cent.

"This kind of relative calculation is very much insisted upon in trade. One often comes across villains who, after they have robbed you of 30 per cent, try to prove that you are making an enormous profit because they are not fleecing you of 50 per cent. Others maintain that they have to bear heavy losses because they are earning no more than 40 per cent on you and actually should be earning 60 per cent. This apparently ridiculous way of reckoning is recognised everywhere in commerce; it has its greatest triumph in underhand bankruptcy. People insist that this small rebate of 25 per cent is a clear net profit compared with the 50 per cent that bankruptcy would cost. Shaken by the force of this argument, the creditors agree to the 'small arrangement'. He who was to receive 4,000 francs gets 3,000, and that is by no means called bankruptcy.

"4. *Posthumous bankruptcy*, which is adjudicated after the hero's death; it becomes a plea in defence of the deceased who hoped to set his business in order again and would certainly have been a credit to it if he had but lived. After that his excellent qualities are praised and his poor orphans sincerely pitied. Surely the creditors will not wish to worry a tearful widow! If she is beautiful that would be altogether barbaric! Meanwhile, the widow, with the help of a few persons of trust, has managed some sizable defalcations before the sealing. The deficiencies will be charged to the deceased, who did not have time to put his affairs in order and who will not come back to disprove this little fib. If there was a deficit of 25 per cent it will easily be increased to 50 per cent, it does not cost any more once one has made a beginning; besides, how stupid it would be to go bankrupt with a 25 per cent

---

[a] Here Fourier has "Harpagons" instead of "skinflints".—*Ed.*

deficit when people with one of 50 per cent are still considered honest—especially when the fault lies with a highly respectable deceased person, whose memory it would be abominable to discredit!"

The Honourable

"The four species mentioned are those of fictitious innocence. We now let those of real innocence pass in review. It would be unfair to brand bankrupts *en masse* because nine-tenths of them are scoundrels. I shall adduce three truly excusable classes. We shall have but too many guilty ones to accuse; so let us first seek some honest people among this confraternity, which has become so numerous since the revolution[a] that in some towns one no longer asks who has, but who has *not* gone bankrupt.

"5. *Goose bankruptcy* is that of an unfortunate one who does not peculate a mite, hands everything over to the creditors and throws himself on their mercy without any deception. The other bankrupts mock at him and declare him to be a simpleton[b] for not at least feathering his nest; and in fact such a loyal man is unworthy of our century of perfectibility.

"6. *Ecstatic bankruptcy* is the work of a man who is desperate, considers himself dishonoured and sometimes shoots himself or jumps into the water. It means one is well behind the times if one wishes to be an honest man in the 19th century, and moreover in trade!

"All the same it is a pleasure for me to have to say that one still comes across such people in trade, but they are few and far between—*rari nautes in gurgite vasto.*[c] Everybody foretells them their fate, so well known is the fact that out of ten villains that plunge into trade nine make their fortune, whereas out of ten honest people nine are ruined.

"7. *Unprincipled bankruptcy* is that of a booby who lets justice intervene and pronounce sentence branding him and stripping him naked instead of doing as so many clever people do, who manage to emerge from this predicament with honour and profit.—These three honest knights are so little worthy of the exalted confraternity that I pass over them quickly. We now come to a sort which is more capable of earning the applause of experts."

The Seductive

"Why should one not let oneself be seduced by bankrupts as one is by so many other wicked classes? We shall now inspect a clique which possesses every kind of charm and is made to conquer all hearts.

"8. *Amiability bankruptcy*, economical bankruptcy, is that of a little man as sweet as honey who desires nothing but the good of his creditors, would be desperate if he had to put them out of pocket, and presses them to negotiate for 50 per cent in order to avoid the intervention of justice which would devour the lot. He has the creditors notified that he wants to treat them as friends whose interests are dear to him. Full of gratitude for the friendly services they have rendered him, he trembles at the thought of having to cause them lawsuit costs. These smooth words and other guiles seduce some while others yield for fear of justice swallowing up the lot.

---

[a] Here Fourier has "*la régénération*". (He associated with the French Revolution a rebirth of the trade system which goes with civilisation.)—*Ed*.

[b] Fourier has "Jocrisse"—the simpleton in the popular French theatre and in Molière's comedy *Sganarelle.—Ed*.

[c] Rare swimmers in a vast gulf (Virgil, *Aeneid*).—*Ed*.

"9. *Bankruptcy de bon ton* is that of people who are very much liked in refined society and maintain their household on an excellent footing till the last moment. As they are *comme il faut* in all respects, they have abundant protection and when they are not at more than 60 per cent in deficit they easily get a composition; especially when the lady and the daughters of the house can be used as pleaders and avail themselves of the decision of a Sanchez[216] who allows them to wear a very transparent scarf when they go soliciting in important matters.

"10. *Amorous bankruptcy* is that of pretty ladies; it is not decent to complain about it, the fair sex is entitled to consideration. A pretty woman has a business, goes bankrupt,[a] robs you of a thousand talers[b]; if you pester her it only goes to show that you have no *savoir vivre*; she is right when she has no patience with the intractable. I heard one such lady say about a creditor: 'What a man! They even say he is still grumbling; I advise him, indeed, to complain about his fifty louis, I should have chalked him up for twice as much!' He had had certain intimacies with the lady, she had the right to treat him as ungrateful.

"11. *Bankruptcy by favour*, in the case of which it is obvious that the creditors derive profit—and how does that happen? When the bankrupt steals only a little, 40 per cent, and provides security, a very substantial caution, for the rest. This is considered so fortunate that the notary congratulates the assembled creditors, congratulates them on an excellent piece of business, a 'real favour'. To lose only four thousand francs out of ten thousand and to get six thousand paid back is a real advantage. Somebody not accustomed to commerce would be unable to appreciate this favour; he would want to have all of his ten thousand and would think he had been robbed of four thousand. What bad manners! To claim that a man robs you when he deducts 40 per cent discount and otherwise treats you in a friendly way!

"12. *Sentimental bankruptcy* occurs with certain people who deliver speeches to break your heart and pour out such floods of feeling and virtue over the creditor that he would be a barbarian if he did not instantly surrender, did not esteem himself happy to oblige such fine people who tenderly love all those whose money they cause to disappear. People of this kind pay with excellent excuses and very flattering eulogies, they catch the creditor by his feelings, converse with him only about his and their virtues; you feel so much improved when the conversation is over; you discover in yourself a multitude of virtues which amply outweigh the sum abstracted. You have a few thousand francs less but all the more virtues; it is a clear profit for beautiful souls.

"One of those actors[c] said to me one day: 'I was so sorry for the gentlemen, they are very fine, very respectable people'—and the good young man, as proof of his respect, robbed them[d] at once in the first deal with a bill of exchange which he gave them as a present and a token of welcome. He had drawn the sum in order to come into contact with them, and a month later he went bankrupt. What a joy for these gentlemen to have received his *respect* as a security for ten thousand francs!

"I have kept my word, I had promised a seductive company. There is nothing but friendship, favour, *bon ton*, and tender feelings in all bankruptcies of this truly amiable series. But if it is calculated to win hearts, others will command wonder, give rise to brilliant upswings, transcendent characters, and represent the heroes of their genus."

---

[a] The words "has a business, goes bankrupt" were added by Engels.—*Ed.*

[b] Fourier has "écus".—*Ed.*

[c] Fourier has "histrions"—literally actors in Ancient Rome; later it came to mean buffoons or comedians; figuratively—charlatans.—*Ed.*

[d] Fourier has "of 10,000 francs".—*Ed.*

V

CENTRE.—GRANDIOSE HUES

"We now come to the magnificent manifestations of the spirit of commerce, to the extensive operations which demonstrate the century's immense progress towards rebirth and perfectibility. Bankruptcy will here unfold its mastery and operate according to far-reaching plans, the exposition of which will prove the wisdom of the principle: Let the merchants do their job, leave them complete freedom for their lofty conceptions of deceit and plunder."

The Tacticians

"13. *Fat bankruptcy* is that of speculators of high standing who possess the genius of trade. Banker Dorante[217] has two million and wishes to achieve as soon as possible by some means a fortune of four to five million. By virtue of his known capital he receives credit amounting to eight million in bills of exchange, goods, etc., so he has a fund of ten million to play with. He plunges into grand speculation and deals in goods and state securities. At the end of the year he may have lost his two million instead of doubling them; you consider him as ruined—not at all, he will have the four million just as if he had transacted good business; for he still has the eight million that he has received and by means of an 'honest' bankruptcy he arranges to pay half of this over several years. So it happens that after losing his own two million he finds himself in possession of four million that he has abstracted from the public. What a wonderful thing, this free trade! Do you now grasp why one hears it said every day of a merchant: 'He is doing very well since his bankruptcy'?

"A further opportunity for the bankrupt: Dorante, after a peculation of four million, retains intact his honour and public respect, not as a lucky villain, but as an unlucky merchant. Let us explain this.

"Dorante obtained control over public opinion while he was pondering his bankruptcy: his fêtes in town, his country parties secured him warm supporters; the gilded youth is for him; the *belles* sympathise with his misfortune—misfortune today is a synonym for bankruptcy; there is praise for his noble character, which deserves a better lot. It almost seems, according to what his defenders say, that the bankrupt has come off worse than those whose fortune he has destroyed. It is all blamed on political events, the unfavourable conditions and other verbiage current among notaries who are adepts at holding off attacks by irate creditors. After the first storm Dorante brings in a few middlemen, a few opportunely distributed wads of money, and soon public opinion is so well hedged in that anybody who dares to speak against Dorante is declared to be a cannibal. And besides, those whom he robbed of the biggest sums are a hundred or two hundred miles[a] away, in Hamburg or in Amsterdam; they will cool down in time, they do not matter much, their distant yapping does not affect opinion in Paris. Moreover, Dorante only causes them to lose half of their money, and custom has it that he who steals only half is more unfortunate than guilty; so that in the public mind Dorante stands clean from the start. After a month public attention is diverted by other bankruptcies which create a bigger sensation and in which between two-thirds and three-quarters went west. New splendour for Dorante, who took only half, and then it is an old forgotten story. Dorante's house begins gradually to open to the public again, his cook recovers his old sway over hearts and minds and unheeded are the cries of

---

[a] Fourier has *"lieues"*.—*Ed.*

some black-galled creditors who have no sympathy for misfortune and have no regard for the consideration due to good society.

"Thus in less than six months ends the operation by which Dorante and those of his kind rob the public of millions, ruin families whose fortunes they hold in their hands, hurl honest merchants into bankruptcy which assimilates them to villains. Bankruptcy is the only social crime which spreads epidemically and plunges the honest man into the same disgrace as the rascal. The more honest merchant who has suffered from the bankruptcies of twenty knaves is himself forced in the end to cease his payments.

"Hence it comes that the villainous bankrupts, i.e., nine-tenths of the tribe, claim to be honest people who have been unfortunate and shout in chorus: We are to be pitied more than blamed. If you listen to them, they are all little saints, like galley-slaves, who all claim to have done nothing wrong.

"To this the supporters of free commerce will retort with talk of repressive laws, of tribunals; yes, indeed! Tribunals for people who steal several million at one go! Incidentally, the saying that petty thieves are hanged while the big ones go scot-free [a] is false as regards trade, for even the smallest bankruptcy evades justice under the protection of the merchants.

"14. *Cosmopolitan bankruptcy*. This is an alliance of the commercial mind with the philosophical. A bankrupt is a true cosmopolite if after exploiting one kingdom he goes through a series of bankruptcies in several others. This is a safe speculation. On arrival one is unknown, if necessary one changes one's name, as Jews do, and receives credit at once on the strength of the capital amassed as a result of an earlier bankruptcy. It is a delightful idea of modern politics to hand over the general administration of the industrial product to people who are not tied by any solid link, any big landed estate to their native country and who, as cosmopolites, can reckon on half a dozen successive bankruptcies in Paris, London, Hamburg, Trieste, Naples and Cadiz. I shall depict this bankruptcy under the heading of running fire, which has a cosmopolite as the pivotal point of its manoeuvre.

"15. *Hopeful bankruptcy*. This dates really from after the revolution [b] and is hardly half a century old. Young people formerly did not make their debut in commerce so early, they were never chiefs before their thirtieth year. Now at the age of eighteen they run a house and at twenty they can have their first bankruptcy, which justifies great hopes for the future. There are some who before they are thirty have already been bankrupt three times and more than once got through one hundred talers belonging to their sleeping partner. When one sees them one says: 'he is very young to have such fame, but we are living in the age of young people.'

"16. *Transcendent bankruptcy* requires a far-reaching plan, an immense upswing, an office with thirty to forty clerks, numerous ships, colossal interests in all countries, then a sudden crash, a terrible somersault the counterblasts of which echo in the four corners of the world, and a chaos of liquidations on the fat of which businessmen can thrive for ten years. It is an operation in which the mercantile genius is unfolded in all its brilliance; it must entail a loss of at least three-quarters, for in this mighty picture everything must be laid out magnificently.

"17. *Graded bankruptcy* is that of a speculator who, by wisely directing his operation, can achieve a career of seven or eight successive bankruptcies. In this case he must adopt a different course than the one who aims at only one or two.

"The principles are:

---

[a] The words "the big ones go scot-free" were added by Engels.— *Ed*.
[b] Fourier has "*la régénération*".— *Ed*.

"1) in the first bankruptcy to plunder only with measure; 50 per cent is sufficient, one must not make the people wild from the start, and the second bankruptcy would be too difficult if one discredited oneself at the first trial stroke through too great covetousness;

"2) in the second bankruptcy to plunder only very little, not more than 30 per cent, in order to prove that the bankrupt has learned something, that he already operates more skilfully and cautiously, and that he will become an accomplished merchant, a worthy 'friend of trade' , when he has recovered from this second blow;

"3) in the third to plunder abundantly, at least 80 per cent, claiming that it is no ordinary deficit, but one caused by extraordinary mischance; to see it through by pleading some critical circumstances, to draw attention to one's good behaviour in the second bankruptcy in order to prove that the blame lies entirely with events;

"4) in the fourth to plunder only 50 per cent in order to prove that one is a cautious man and knows how to remain within the appropriate bounds when not swept away by circumstances;

"5) in the fifth one can go as far as 60 per cent, because the public is accustomed to it; 10 per cent more or less spoils no speculation of this kind when public opinion has become accustomed to it; for it is known that whoever has had four bankruptcies will also have a fifth and a sixth. I have seen one bankrupt who was laughed at after his fourth bankruptcy because he wore a clerical hat as a sign of piety and good morals; he did not let himself be put off and prepared the fifth.

"The sixth and seventh are *ad libitum*, one has them only as age draws on and when one thinks of resting on one's laurels. Nothing is easier than to excuse a sixth bankruptcy; one is too old to change, nobody is surprised any longer. For the rest, it is argued that the government refuses to protect trade and is the cause of these little setbacks of honest businessmen.

"Let no one be surprised if I give here a few principles to be used in bankruptcy; it is a quite new art which, like economics, from which it sprang, has as yet no fixed principles, nor even a methodical nomenclature. For instance, titles have been given only to the first four stages in graded bankruptcy.

"The man who has had his first bankruptcy is simply a 'Knight',

"At the second he receives the title of 'Prince',

"At the third the title of 'King',

"At the fourth 'Emperor'.

"For the fifth, sixth and seventh grade there are not yet any names among the members of the trade. A true 'friend of trade' must rise to the full octave. In order to be a 'harmonious' bankrupt one must have had seven 'honest' bankruptcies with average losses of 50 per cent, and then a reinforced, a complete bankruptcy, as the pivotal point in the series; it is then allowed to plunder to the extent of at least 80 per cent as an indemnity for the moderation shown in the others; the fifty per cent of earlier bankruptcies is only the honest tariff, a quite small slice, giving nobody the right to censure, because it is the accepted rate for bankruptcies, a fixed price, exactly like the price of tartlets or coach fares."

The Manoeuvrers

"In this item we deal with the mass evolutions which require co-operation of different bankrupts for the good of trade and the triumph of lofty truth. These collective manoeuvres will show us four sorts of evolution artists.

"18. *Running fire bankruptcy*. This is generally caused by counterblasts, through a concatenation of bankruptcies, one caused by another. I shall describe one of the medium sort, the bourgeois kind, because they are most understandable for the bulk of readers. We shall take one of the cosmopolitan artists, whose definition I have postponed, as the pivotal point of the running fire manoeuvre.

"Judas Iscariot arrives in France[218] with 100,000 francs[a] capital, which he earned in his first bankruptcy; he establishes himself as a merchant in a town where he has six respected and accredited houses as rivals. In order to take away their clientele and their good reputation, Iscariot immediately begins to sell his wares at cost price, a sure way of attracting the multitude. Soon his rivals clamour in a most pitiful way about him; he laughs at their complaints and continues all the more to sell off everything at cost price.

"Thereupon the people shout so that it is a pleasure to hear them: Long live competition, long live the Jews, long live philosophy and fraternity! All commodities have become cheaper since Iscariot's arrival, and the public say to his rivals: You, Gentlemen, are the real Jews, you want to earn too much; Iscariot alone is an honest man, he is content with a moderate profit, because he runs no brilliant household as you do.—Vain are all the representations made by the old houses that Iscariot is a villain in disguise who sooner or later will come to grief; the public accuse them of jealousy and calumny and crowd more and more to the Jew.

"The calculation that this thief makes is as follows: By selling at cost price he loses only the interest on his capital, let it come to 10,000 francs annually, but ensures a good outlet for himself, makes a name for himself in the maritime towns as a good consumer and by prompt payment gets big credit. This trick is pursued for two years, after which Iscariot has earned nothing, though he has sold enormous quantities. His manoeuvre remains undetected, because Jews have only Jewish office staff, people who are the secret enemies of all nations and will never betray a villainy thought up by their 'own' people.

"When all is ripe for development, Iscariot puts in his whole credit, places giant orders in all maritime towns, buys goods on credit for the sum of 5-600,000 francs. He sends his wares abroad and sells his whole stock dirt cheap. When he has exchanged everything for money the good Iscariot vanishes with his briefcase and returns to Germany, where he has despatched the goods he bought on credit, sells them quickly and is four times as rich when he leaves France as he was on his arrival; he has 400,000 francs, and he goes to London or Leghorn to get a third bankruptcy under way.

"Now the veil suddenly falls and people come to their senses in the town where he struck his blow. People realise how dangerous it is to permit Jews to trade, those vagabonds who are not tied to anything. But this bankruptcy of Iscariot is only the first act of the farce; let us follow the running fire.

"The Jew has six rivals; we shall call them A, B, C, D, E, F.

"A had been in straits for a long time, he held out without capital, only by virtue of his good reputation; but through the arrival of the Jew he is robbed of all his clients, he could pursue the race only for a year, and, not mature for these new philosophical systems which protect vagabonds, he finds himself compelled to bow down before Iscariot's tactics and to *declare himself bankrupt*.

"B endured the blow longer; he already saw the Jew's villainy from afar and waited for the storm to pass in order to win back his clientele which the rascal Iscariot had taken away. But meanwhile he is involved in a bankruptcy abroad; that is enough to accelerate his fall; he thought he could hold out for two years but he is obliged to *go bankrupt* after only fifteen months.

"C was associated with a foreign house which is ruined by another Iscariot—for they are to be found in all towns; C is brought down by the fall of his associate,

---

[a] Here and elsewhere Fourier has "*livres*".—*Ed.*

and after making sacrifices for eighteen months to hold out against the competition from the Jewish blackguard, he finds himself forced to *go bankrupt.*

"*D* seems more honest than he is in reality. He still has the means to hold out, although he has been suffering from the Jew's competition for twenty months; but embittered by the losses which the latter has caused him, he lets himself be carried away by the vice of which he sees so many examples. He realises that three of his confraternity have opened up the march and that he will pass as a fourth in the alliance, pretexting real or fictitious misfortunes. Thus *D,* wearied by twenty months of struggle against Iscariot, sees that there is nothing cleverer for him than to *go bankrupt.*

"*E* had advanced considerable sums to his four successively bankrupt colleagues; he thought they were all solvent, and they were indeed, until Iscariot's manoeuvre spoilt their business for them. *E* finds himself stripped by the bankruptcies of these four houses; besides, he himself has no more clients; the entire public crowd to Iscariot, who sells off goods at cost price. *E* sees his funds annihilated, his credit destroyed, he is pressed, and as he can no more meet his commitments, he puts an end to it by *going bankrupt.*

"*F* has sufficient means, but as a result of the five previous bankruptcies, which warrant the conclusion that his will soon follow, he has lost his credit in all the maritime towns. Moreover, some of the bankrupts, having achieved a composition, are now selling at very low prices to be able to afford their payments when the first terms expire. In order to accelerate their sales, they lose one-tenth of the value and yet earn four-tenths, because they settled at 50 per cent. This entirely crushes *F,* and there is nothing left for him but to *go bankrupt* like his rivals.

"So the establishment of one vagabond or one Jew is sufficient to disorganise the whole merchant body of a large town and to draw the most honest people into crime; for every bankruptcy is more or less a crime, no matter how much it is extenuated by excellent pretexts such as those with which I have tinted these six bankruptcies, and there is hardly ever a word of truth in any of them. The truth of the matter is that everybody avidly seizes the opportunity to commit a theft if it remains unpunished.

"Occasionally running fire takes the form of ricochet fire, which is effective at a distance and involves a dozen houses in different countries simultaneously. They have common interests and the fall of the main house causes all the subsidiary houses concerned to crash, like a row of tin soldiers when the man at the end of the row is pushed.[a] This is a serious combination, worthy of figuring among the great manoeuvres, and in any case this ricochetting at a distance will have to form a special genus in a more accurate classification.

"19. *Close-column bankruptcy* requires favourable circumstances which serve as excuses, and prompt masses of merchants to risk the fateful leap. In this case they find support one in the other and are saved because of their number, like a regiment in close-column formation forces a way for itself with bayonets. Thus, when a favourable opportunity presents itself, bankrupts must close their ranks and post up a column of bankruptcies every day at the Stock Exchange; they must have them succeeding one another so quickly that public opinion is confused and compositions become easy to achieve in consideration of the difficult circumstances. These bankruptcies are seen occurring periodically in London; Paris too made a very beautiful attempt in close column in 1800, and it ended very happily for many 'friends of trade'.

"20. *Marching-in-file bankruptcy* is a series of bankruptcies which are linked

---

[a] Fourier has "*comme une file de capucins de carte*".—*Ed.*

together, but break out at suitable intervals of two to three months. Contrary to the close columns, which follow one another day after day, marching-in-file bankruptcies require mutual agreement so that one goes bankrupt when one's turn comes, at the very instant when the predecessor has squared his composition. For instance, A has achieved his composition three months after bankruptcy and B must instantaneously declare himself insolvent because the mediators now find the public well disposed and can say: it is the same story as in the case of A, one was bound to lead to the other, the same composition must be made. Just the same for C, who will go bankrupt three months later, then D, E, F, and G; if they maintain their co-operation properly and succeed in keeping to the interval, they achieve the same composition for all. Marching in file is a very safe manoeuvre when it is cleverly directed; but it does not fit all circumstances, and only the genius of the prospective bankrupt can determine in which cases it is applicable.

"21. *Skirmisher bankruptcy* involves at the start those starving wretches who initiate a great movement and here and there cause small bankruptcies in their retail trade. From this one concludes that business will be difficult and the campaign a fierce one. And indeed soon after that the heavy artillery is heard, bankruptcies involving millions break out and hold public attention for a long time. Then the movement ends with the rearguard skirmishers, the retailer bankrupts, the grocers in small towns, who bring the session to an end with their plunges."

The Agitators

"What! Is there not yet enough vexation and can you show us something still worse than the litany already described?

"I have only named the most honest. We are approaching the descending, despicable wing and can place here the bankrupts who operate according to far-reaching plans but disregard moral methods and compromise the lofty corporation.

"22. *Bankruptcy in grand style* affects all classes of society down to the smallest people, domestics and others, who deposit their modest savings with a hypocrite. Soon bankruptcy plunders landowners, the smaller middle class and the good-natured people in their hundreds. An entire town becomes involved. In general this type of bankruptcy affects particularly the non-trading classes of society and does significant harm to the corporation by arousing in the people and the petty bourgeoisie reflections which are hardly flattering for the respectable confraternity of the merchants.

"23. *Large-scale bankruptcy* is that of some obscure upstart who, without funds or backing, succeeds in breaking into big business and pulls off just as enormous a bankruptcy as the high and mighty bankers. It is generally wondered how this camp-follower could manage to strike up such acquaintances and to organise such a fat bankruptcy.

"This individual is the opposite of the preceding one; he takes a different road to attain the same goal, namely to excite public opinion against the tricks of the merchants and the preposterous laws which leave this scum complete freedom.

"24. *Attila bankruptcy* raises the fame of the bankrupts to the clouds and lays a country waste as if a whole army of vandals had swept across it. One can cite in this genus a brilliant bankruptcy pulled off in 1810 in Orleans by an amateur named T. He went bankrupt with a deficit of 16 million so excellently distributed over Orleans that the whole unfortunate town was laid low by it. All classes of citizens suffered from the devastation. Fugitives went as far as Lyons and spread the tidings: Orleans is destroyed, we are all ruined, T. is plunging everything into the abyss.

According to detailed reports, he had carried out his scheme so well that he had hoodwinked and plundered all classes, from rich capitalists to poor domestics who had saved a few talers[a] in their whole life and deposited them with the mercantile dealer and let themselves be robbed by him—under the protection of the fine principle: Let the merchants do their job, they know best what is in their interest.

"What robberies! What multiformity of crime in a single branch of commercial heroism! A single one, for let it be noted that bankruptcy is only the thirty-first feature of this lying trade for which science demands complete freedom under the pretext that the merchants know best what is in their interest—they know that indeed all too well, but they know only too little what is in the interest of the state and of industry, and so we are mystified by science and its theories on the absolute freedom of merchants.[b]"

VI

DESCENDING WING.—DIRTY HUES

"From the description of great feats of heroism we go on to more modest trophies. Not everything is great in bankruptcy like the three categories of the centre. Still, in the left wing too we shall bring together a remarkable collection, bankrupts in softened shades, people whose more burgherly virtues and failings will do good to the eye after the vivid brilliance of so many heroic deeds; we shall still find cohorts capable of cheering the reader—especially the last, that of the false brothers, who bring ill fame on the corps of bankrupts.—Let us begin with a more serious hue."

The Cunning Sneakers

"25. *Compensation bankruptcy* is declared to obtain compensation for some accident. For instance, a speculator loses a lawsuit today which costs him 100,000 francs. So tomorrow he declares himself bankrupt, and this brings him 200,000. Thus he wins the sum in litigation instead of losing it. This capacity of trade to compensate itself for the disfavour of circumstances is one of its finest qualities; it can find its interest in every mishap on land and sea.[c] If a shipowner experiences a shipwreck, he rehabilitates himself the next day by a good bankruptcy; and this type of bankruptcy is accepted without any contradiction because the notary says: 'It is not his fault, events forced him to it, he is more to be pitied than blamed.'

"To this a landowner whose deposit thus goes west will answer: 'I cannot get compensation when hail or a flood ruin my crops, I have nobody to fall back on.'—A fine argument! Should not landowners know that under the present order of things they are a dependent class, dependent on the unproductive people called merchants who dig their claws into every product of industry to get themselves paid at the expense of the masses like a volunteer corps which, for lack of an enemy to plunder, strips its own friends and the good people? Such is the merchant, a *veritable cossack of industry*[d] whose motto is: 'I do not work *pour la gloire*, I must have something to rake in.' Every merchant wants to rake in, and if somebody

---

[a] Fourier has "écus".—*Ed.*
[b] The last two sentences as given by Engels differ somewhat from the original.—*Ed.*
[c] The words "on land and sea" were added by Engels.—*Ed.*
[d] Fourier has "*cosaques industriels*".—*Ed.*

hopes to rake anything in from him by a lawsuit or otherwise, the merchant has his resources at hand and rakes in from others by means of a compensation bankruptcy.

"26. *Bankruptcy out of rank* is that of a wise man who has foreseen everything and put something aside with which he can face the storm and tame the intractable. If he wants to earn 200,000 francs by bankruptcy, he puts 300,000 aside, placing a third of it in useful hand-outs, presents, etc.; he knows how to quieten the most loud-mouthed, how to paralyse justice; a wad here, a wad there, and his case is briskly carried through. His bankruptcy brings him in the end a good number of friends, who get their piece of the cake and say that he is a man *comme il faut* who knows business inside out.

"27. *Crescendo bankruptcy* plays a farce in several acts which increase in interest as they develop. To start with, the affair is presented as a slight embarrassment, a case of shortage of disposable capital with a discount of 30 per cent necessary to prevent a crash. The creditors become worried and negotiate on the quiet, for they have been given to understand that things could take a bad turn and that the man in question must be supported. Meanwhile, in three months he is tottering again. Again the creditors are visited and made to fear his ruin; it is admitted that things are worse than was thought and that 50 per cent must be agreed to. Some of the creditors are vexed, the matter becomes entangled and bankruptcy is declared—and indeed on such terms that 80-90 per cent is lost instead of 50 per cent and the rest can be paid up only after some years. But the composition is still easy to bring about because the creditors, who have been skilfully handled and have successively become accustomed to a loss of 30, then 50, then 70 per cent, are weary of war; they sign and give the cursed business up as altogether lost, although it was said at the beginning that only 30 per cent was going to be lost. This method is not the worst and can be recommended to speculators who stick to principles.

"28. *Godly bankruptcy* is that of a holy man who belongs to all the confraternities and holds the cordon of the canopy at processions.[219] He easily finds credit and depositors and can prepare a far-reaching bankruptcy underhand. I have seen some bankruptcies of this type when the loss was 90 per cent. The advantage in such a case is that the bankrupt finds enough people who excuse him: 'Ah, he is a very pious man; if he has had no luck in business it is because he sets no store by the goods of this world.'—This piety is held up in order to hasten the composition, by which the pious apostle retains a good part of the goods of this world, together with the prospects of those of the other."

The Bunglers

"In every profession one finds ignoramuses who work without any principles and can produce only a bad job with the best material. So among bankrupts too there are dunces who can do nothing else but change gold into copper and ruin themselves in a very stupid manner where others would do splendid business. I want to adduce and deal briefly with four genera, for this really honest category has nothing entertaining. I only let them march past for the sake of completeness of our analysis.

"29. *Fools' bankruptcy* is that of those befooled people who, enticed by fashionable catchwords, venture into trade without knowing its tricks and naturally scorch their wings like moths in the candlelight. Since 1789 there have been many big property-owners who had no need whatever to get involved in this turmoil; they have been seen to lose a rich heritage and end up in bankruptcy by which they parted with their fortune and their honour. It must be noted incidentally that only the honest man loses his honour in bankruptcy, whereas the rascal, who knows the great principles of trade, can manage his bankruptcies in such a way that he acquires wealth and honour. But the great gentlemen who found themselves in this wasps' nest of trade wanted to negotiate honestly; they were surrounded by intriguers, played with like a ball and forced to end up with the bankruptcy of their illusions. Many small landowners have made the same mistake. Swept along by the mercantile race, they have abandoned their field, sold their small plot of land to set up a shop in town and meet their inevitable ruin.

"30. *Invalids' bankruptcy* is that of an incorrigible who wants to die with arms in hand. One sees many who ought to retire and who, weakened by age, can do nothing but bungle, are ignorant of the latest achievements and in their old age lose a slowly amassed fortune and obstinately hold out until repeated blunders make bankruptcy inevitable. How is one to describe a man of eighty who is a bachelor and has a fortune of two million, indeed sufficient for a single and aged man, and still obstinately continues huckstering at an age when he should retire and weep over his sins? When such a man gets himself ruined and loses his brilliant fortune in his eightieth year he is truly a mercantile fanatic. Such a man was the invalid bankrupt who is the prototype of this paragraph; for I have a prototype to show for all these species* so that I shall not be accused of exaggerating. Incidentally, many of these aged fanatics are to be found in every town; because they insist on continuing their trade, they deserve to be shamefully ruined, for today, when everything is raised to its quintessence, the need, in trade as in war, is for young people educated in modern tactics; and if bankruptcy is regarded as a harmless game for young people, it is indeed shameful for wealthy old men who should have thought of retiring twenty years ago.

"31. *Crushing bankruptcy* is that of enraged competitors who consciously rush towards ruin and indeed ruin themselves to dispute a small share of profit from a rival. One sees a great number of these who work at a loss in the hope that their rival will be ruined before they are, and that they themselves will remain masters of the battlefield. This disorder is prevalent particularly in the carrying trade and in the cloth markets such as Beaucaire,[220] and it leads to the 'crushed' being forced to go bankrupt.

"32. *Swinish bankruptcy* is that of a greenhorn who, instead of operating according to the principles, ruins himself, his wife and children and moreover exposes himself to the talons of justice and the contempt of the 'friends of trade', who respect only fat bankrupts who conform to the principles. In the jargon of commercial knaves they say of a bankrupt who thus ruins himself, his wife and children: That is indeed really swinish.—If he had had a fat bankruptcy, they would have called him a smart young man, a clever brain."

The False Brothers

"I give the name of false brothers to those who expose the honourable clan of the bankrupts to the contempt of the public. Some of them provoke indignation, others laughter. I do not include in this class the transcendents, who steal by the million—these are always respectable and never compromise the clan; a great thief has never been contemptible in civilisation, whereas the small ones are the people to be hanged, and when they excite public opinion against villains and small bankruptcies they are unworthy of admission to the corporation and deserve to be styled as false brothers.

* The names of these prototypes are given by Fourier in the original.—*Note by Engels*.

"33. *Villains' bankruptcy* is that of small-scale blackguards who commit such obnoxious petty thefts in their bankruptcy that the neighbourhood says they ought to be hanged. That would not be the case with thefts of 100,000 talers; but thefts of 100 talers[a] suggest the idea of the gallows. Incidentally these ideas are not dangerous for the knave, because the confraternity of the bankrupts[b] never allows its colleagues to be molested; otherwise justice would soon feel authorised to pass on from the petty thieves to the big ones, which would be very awkward for those who act according to great principles and have found a place in good society after an 'honest' bankruptcy.

"34. *Gallows-bird bankruptcy* is that by which besides dirty tricks, the man concerned commits also learned acts of perfidy, for instance, robs himself to provide an occasion for sentimental tactics.

"Scapin, a petty crook,[221] indulges in a scaramouch bankruptcy involving only 40,000 francs; he steals 30,000 francs, which constitutes the profit on the operation, and then offers the creditors the remainder, amounting to 10,000 francs. When he is asked about the deficit of 30,000 francs, he says that he does not know book-keeping like big merchants, and that he has been 'unlucky'. Perhaps you believe Scapin will be punished because he is a petty thief who steals only 30,000 francs—but do not the creditors know that if justice intervenes it will eat up the remaining 10,000 francs just for breakfast? And even when these 10,000 francs have disappeared, nothing will be settled; if they want to have Scapin hanged, it will cost them perhaps an additional 10,000 francs and it is still not known whether they will succeed. It is therefore better in any case to accept the moderate sum of 10,000 francs than to lose it and still have to pay just as much over and above. Through his notary Scapin puts forward this argument, *so that the bankrupt himself threatens his creditors with justice.* And why should Scapin's creditors be furious with him? Some of them think of following his noble example, the others are already ahead of him in their career. So, as wolf does not eat wolf, Scapin soon finds a number of signatories who declare themselves satisfied with his proposals; others sign for fear that justice may intervene; others again are intractable and speak of sacrificing all to have a blackguard sent to the galleys. Then Scapin sends them his wife and children, who implore his mercy with well-practised wailings, and so in a few days Scapin and his notary receive the majority of signatures. Thereupon the obstreperous, who are no longer needed, are made fun of. Their rage is laughed at. Scapin answers them with ingratiating words and profound bows, and immediately after the happy issue of the first bankruptcy, he starts to think of a new one.

"35. *Fugitive bankruptcy* is customary among small tenants in large towns. As the date of payment approaches they bolt and bring their wretched movables to safety 'under cover of the night.' It is very much in vogue among the silk weavers in Lyons; it is also resorted to by all elegant individuals of both sexes who order the very best things at restaurants, the tailor's and the shoemaker's, and are very accommodating as far as the price goes because they intend to pay with fine words and to bolt as soon as their creditors begin to get unpleasant.

"This kind of bankruptcy is droll and shows the corporation in a bad light. When one scoffs at a man who has cheated twenty petty shopkeepers, one easily becomes accustomed to scoffing at a man *comme il faut* whose bankruptcy ruins twenty families. These freedoms of criticism must be suppressed in order not to imperil the respect due to the honourable bankrupts among the 'friends of trade'.

---

[a] Here Fourier has "*écus*" and further on "*livres*", which Engels translates as "*francs*".—*Ed.*

[b] Fourier has "*la corporation des banqueroutiers*".—*Ed.*

"36. *Bankruptcy for fun* is that of a small retailer who goes bankrupt according to the very best form just like the high and mighty bankers and does not give his creditors more than five per cent. Among others, a Lyons actor, distinguished for his comical roles and therefore very much loved by the public, went bankrupt in this way. In all due form he offered his creditors the sum of *three per cent.* Some of them were vexed and wanted to send the bailiff to him; but he mystified justice as he mystified it on the stage in the *Avocat Patelin,* and all the public were on his side. His bankruptcy was a highly amusing comedy, which afforded many a priceless scene. The creditors could swear, the public only laughed at them as they did at Guillaume in the *Avocat Patelin.*

"I have now gone rapidly through all these definitions. However, my list is so incomplete that it can be considered as a mere outline to which everybody can supply the missing features.[a] There are masses of remarkable ones. Only a few days ago the Paris papers reported a brilliant bankruptcy, that of a certain Y., who established a pompously publicised agency with no more than 10,000 francs. I believe it was an office for the regeneration of trade or some other pompous title, by means of which he obtained a million from a few jackanapes, whom he paid as usual with a good bankruptcy. In a word, the number of bankruptcy genera which I have collected here can easily be doubled."

VII
CONCLUSION[b]

"When one reflects that bankruptcy is only a single one of the thirty-six features of trade, one finds difficulty in explaining why this so fearful mine of crimes, this mechanism of trade, has not yet been analysed; and that in this century, which is so uncompromising towards the crimes of all classes in society and has made public the crimes of kings and popes.

"When one reads this collection of merchants' filth, one cannot help wondering how it comes that a century which calls itself the friend of lofty truth has been able in all seriousness to grow enthusiastic over this lying trade, arguing that after all one cannot do without trade; as if for that reason one must accept fraud and theft such as those which we have listed in one single crime of trade, namely bankruptcy.

"However, let us finish what we have to say about this.

"The saying that justice sends only petty thieves to the gallows is proved false in trade. The bankrupt, even the smallest, evades prosecution, protected by the merchants themselves. We saw that under the last category (false brothers), which is that of miniature bankrupts.

"It would be vain to quote the punishment of a few fraudulent bankrupts; ninety-nine manage to get away with it, and if the hundredth fails he must be a stupid devil and not know how to pursue his intrigue. For the operation is so simple nowadays that the old precautionary measures have long ago been forgotten. Formerly a bankrupt used to flee to Trient, Liège or Carouge, but since the rebirth of 1789 this custom has been abandoned. Everybody now goes bankrupt *en famille.* The matter is quietly prepared, and when it explodes, one goes for a month to the country, to the intimacy of one's relatives and friends;

---

[a] At the beginning and the end of this paragraph Fourier's text is somewhat paraphrased by Engels.—*Ed.*

[b] Fourier has "Conclusion on Bankruptcy".—*Ed.*

the notary meanwhile puts everything in order. After a few weeks one reappears, and the public is so accustomed to this kind of story that it regards it as a pleasant joke; it is called 'being confined' and one says quite dispassionately: 'So-and-so is back, he has just had his confinement.'

"I have noted that bankruptcy is the only social crime which becomes epidemical and forcibly carries the honest man along the road of the scoundrel. If to bankruptcy we add stockjobbing and so many other infamies, we shall find that I was right when I affirmed that civilised people had never committed so many political follies as since they plunged into trade. Never have the philosophers, who dream of nothing but counterbalance and guarantees, thought of providing the social body with the guarantee which governments, judiciously enough, demand of their fiscal agents! A prince assures himself of the rectitude of his treasurer by means of a cash security and the prospect of inevitable punishment if he were to dare risk or squander the public monies deposited with him. Why does it not happen that the collectors of public monies appropriate the revenues from taxes and write letters of lamentation to the government saying: The misfortunes of the times, the critical circumstances, the deplorable accidents, etc., in a word, I have gone bankrupt, insolvent, or whatever you call it. Your treasury should contain ten million; I offer you half of that sum, five million, payable in five years. Allow yourself to be moved by the misfortune of a lamentable treasurer, maintain me in your confidence and the administration of your treasury, without which I am not even able to pay you the half which I now offer you; but if you leave me my position and my income, I shall endeavour to discharge my obligations towards you honourably, that is, to treat you to a second bankruptcy as soon as the treasury is full again.

"Such in brief is the content of all bankrupts' letters. If treasurers do not follow this example, it is because they know that no philosophical theory can save them from the punishment which the bankrupt evades—under the protection of the principle: 'Leave the merchants complete freedom without demanding any guarantee against their machinations.'"

* * *

So writes Fourier. The continuation of this article in the second issue of the *Phalange* contains three chapters on Stock Exchange operations, speculative purchase (*accaparement*) and parasitism, the greater part of which, however, has already been reprinted in the *Quatre mouvements*.[222] Partly for this reason, partly because the fragment given above is fully adequate for my purpose, I break it off here.

Let the learned German Herren, who so zealously sail the "stormy sea" of bottomless[a] theories, and above all fish for the "*principle*" of "socialism", follow the example of the *commis marchand*[b] Fourier. Fourier was no philosopher, he had a great hatred of philosophy and savagely ridiculed it in his writings and in this connection said a multitude of things which our German

---

[a] The German word "grundlos" can mean both "bottomless" and "without foundation".—*Ed.*

[b] Salesman.—*Ed.*

"philosophers of socialism" would do well to take to heart. True, they will object that Fourier, too, was abstract, that by means of his series he speculatively constructed God and the world in defiance of Hegel, but that will not save them. Fourier's eccentricities, which are, after all, products of genius, are no excuse for the boring so-called systematic expositions of arid German theory. Fourier speculatively constructs the future, after correctly understanding the past and the present; German theory first of all arranges past history according to its liking and then prescribes to the future, too, what direction it should take. Compare, for example, Fourier's epochs of social development (savagery, patriarchate, barbarism, civilisation) and his characterisation of them with Hegel's Absolute Idea, which laboriously makes its way through the labyrinth of history and despite the *four* world empires [223] at the end, but still grunting and groaning, achieves the semblance of a trichotomy—not to speak of the post-Hegelian speculative constructions. For, although Hegel's speculative construction still made some sense, even if it is turned upside-down, that of the post-Hegelian system manufacturers no longer makes any sense at all.

It is truly high time that the Germans at last stopped making such a fuss about their thoroughness. With a few meagre data they are capable not only of concocting any kind of theory, but also of linking it with world history. On the basis of the first fact that happens to reach them at third hand, concerning which they do not even know at all whether it occurred in such and such a way or some other, they will prove to you that it *must* have occurred in this particular way and no other. Has anyone in Germany written on social questions without also saying something about Fourier by which German thoroughness has most thoroughly exposed itself to ridicule! Among them is a Herr Kaiser,[a] who immediately used "L. Stein's excellent work" [b] for a world-historic speculative construction, the only pity about which is that all the facts it is based on are false. German theory has already at least twenty times allotted Fourier his "place in the development of the Absolute Idea"— each time a different place—and each time German theory relied for the facts on Herr Stein or other dubious sources. For this very reason, too, German "absolute socialism" is such terribly poor stuff. A little "humanitarianism", as the thing is called nowadays, a little "realisation" of this humanitarianism or, rather, monstrosity, a very little about property from Proudhon—at third or fourth

---

[a] H. W. Kaiser, *Die Persönlichkeit des Eigenthums.—Ed.*
[b] L. Stein, *Der Socialismus und Communismus des heutigen Frankreichs.—Ed.*

hand—a little moaning about the proletariat, and a little about the organisation of labour and wretched associations for raising the lower classes of the people [224]—together with boundless ignorance of political economy and the real character of society—that is the sum total of all this "socialism", which moreover loses its last drop of blood, the last trace of energy and strength through its non-partisanship in matters of theory, its "absolute tranquillity of thought". And with this tedious stuff they want to revolutionise Germany, set the proletariat in motion, and make the masses think and act!

If our German half or fully communist university lecturers had only taken the trouble to have a look at Fourier's main writings, which after all are as easy for them to obtain as any German book—what a treasure-trove of material for speculative construction and other uses they would have found in them! What a mass of new ideas—still new for Germany even today—would have offered itself to them there! Up to now these good people find nothing to reproach present-day society with except the condition of the proletariat, and even about that they are not capable of saying very much. Of course, the condition of the proletariat is the main point, but does that exhaust the criticism of present-day society? Fourier, who, except in his later works, hardly touches on this point at all, provides the proof that even without it existing society can be seen to be thoroughly reprehensible, and that by criticism of the bourgeoisie alone—namely of the bourgeoisie in its inner relationships, apart from its attitude to the proletariat—one can arrive at the necessity of a social reconstruction. For this aspect of criticism, Fourier up to now remains unique. Fourier inexorably exposes the hypocrisy of respectable society, the contradiction between its theory and its practice, the dullness of its entire mode of life; he ridicules its philosophy, its striving for *perfection de la perfectibilité perfectibilisante* [a] and *auguste vérité* [b]; he ridicules its "pure morality", its uniform social institutions, and contrasts all this with its practice, *le doux commerce*, which he criticises in a masterly manner, its dissolute delights which are no delights, its organisation of adultery in marriage, its general chaos. All these are aspects of contemporary society which have never yet been mentioned in Germany. True, there has been talk here and there about free love, about the position of woman and her emancipation; but what has been the result? A few confused

---

[a] Perfecting the perfectibility which is in process of becoming perfect.—*Ed.*

[b] August truth.—*Ed.*

phrases, a few blue-stockings, a little hysteria and a good deal of moaning about the German family — not even one bastard came out of it!

Let the Germans first acquaint themselves with the social movement abroad, both practical and literary—the practical movement includes the whole of English and French history during the last eighty years, English industry and the French Revolution—let them then do as much as their neighbours as regards practice and literature, and *only after that* will the time have come to raise such idle questions as that of the greater or lesser achievement of the various nations. But by then there will no longer be any audience for these sophistical disquisitions.

Until then it would be best for the Germans above all to acquaint themselves with what has been achieved abroad. All the books about this that have so far appeared are without exception *bad*. Anyhow, brief summaries of that kind can at best give only a criticism of those works, not the works themselves. The latter are partly rare and unobtainable in Germany, partly too voluminous, and in part mixed with matters which are now only of historical or literary interest and no longer interest the German public of 1845. To make available those works, the valuable contents of which are even now still new for Germany, requires a selection and editorial treatment such as the French, being in such matters also much more practical than we are, carry out in respect of all material coming to them from abroad. Such editions of the epoch-making socialist literature from abroad will shortly begin to be published. A number of German Communists, among them the best brains of the movement, who could just as easily produce works of their own, have joined in this undertaking,[225] which, it is to be hoped, will show the wise German theoreticians that all their wisdom is old stuff, the pros and cons of which have already been thoroughly discussed on the other side of the Rhine and the English Channel long ago. Only after they have seen what was done *before* them will they have an opportunity to show what *they themselves* can do.

Brussels

Written in the latter half of 1845

First published in the yearbook
Deutsches Bürgerbuch für 1846
Signed: *F. Engels*

Printed according to the yearbook

Published in English for the first time

The Northern Star,

AND NATIONAL TRADES' JOURNAL.

VOL. VIII. NO. 409.   LONDON, SATURDAY, SEPTEMBER 13. 1845.   PRICE FOURPENCE HALFPENNY
Five Shillings per Quarter.

Frederick Engels

THE LATE BUTCHERY AT LEIPZIG.— THE GERMAN WORKING MEN'S MOVEMENT[226]

The massacre at Leipzig,[227] which you commented on in your last number, and of which you gave a more detailed account some weeks ago, is continuing to occupy the attention of the German papers. This massacre,— surpassed in infamy by that of Peterloo[228] only,— is by far the most villainous act of scoundrelism that military despotism ever devised in this country. When the people were shouting, "Ronge for ever! down with Popery!" Prince John of Saxony, who, by-the-bye, is another of our many rhyming and book-writing princes, having published a very bad translation of the Italian poet Dante's "Hell"; this "hellish" translator tried to add military glory to his literary fame by planning a most dastardly campaign against the unarmed masses. He ordered the battalion of rifles, called in by the authorities, to divide into several detachments and to block up the passages to the hotel in which his literary "royal highness" had taken up his quarters. The soldiers obeyed, and pressed the people by enclosing them in a narrow circle, and advancing upon them into the gateway of the hotel; and from this unavoidable entering of the people into the sacred gateway of the royal residence, brought on by the military acting under Prince John's orders; from this very circumstance the pretext was taken to fire upon the people; by this very circumstance the firing has been tried to be justified by the Government papers! Nor is this all; the people were taken between the several detachments, and the plan of his royal highness was executed by a cross fire upon the defenceless masses; wherever they turned they met with a repeated volley from the rifles, and had not the soldiers, more humane than Prince John, fired mostly over the heads of the people, the slaughter would have been terrible. The indignation created by this piece of scoundrelism is general; the most loyal subjects, the warmest supporters of the present order of things, share in it, and pronounce their utter disgust at such proceedings. The affair will do a great deal of good in Saxony, a part of Germany that before all others, has always evinced an inclination for *talking*, and where action was sadly wanted. The Saxons, with their little constitutional government, their talking houses of parliament, their liberal deputies, liberal and enlightened parsons, etc., were, in Northern Germany, the representatives of moderate Liberalism, of German Whiggery; and yet, with all that, greater slaves of the King of Prussia than the Prussians themselves. Whatever the Prussian Government resolved, the Saxon ministry had to execute; nay, of late, the Prussian Government did not even take the trouble to apply to the Saxon ministry, but direct to the Saxon inferior authorities, as if they were not Saxon, but their own employees! Saxony is governed in Berlin, not in Dresden! and with all their talking and boasting the Saxons know very well that the leaden hand of Prussia presses hard enough upon them. To all this talking and boasting, to all this self-conceit and contentment which would make the Saxons a peculiar nation opposed to the Prussian, etc., this Leipzig massacre will put an end. The Saxons must see, now, that they are under the same military rule as all other Germans, and that, with all their constitution, liberal laws, liberal censorship, and liberal king's speeches,[a] martial law is the only one that has any practical existence in their little country. And there is another thing to aid this Leipzig affair in spreading the spirit of rebellion in Saxony; notwithstanding all the talking of the Saxon Liberals, the great majority of the Saxon people are only beginning to talk; Saxony is a manufacturing country, and among her linen-weavers, frame-work-knitters, cotton-spinners, pillow-lace-makers, coal and metal-miners, there has been, from time immemorial, an appalling amount of distress. The proletarian movement, which, from the Silesian riots, the weavers' battle as it is called, in June, 1844,[229] has spread all over Germany, has not left Saxony untouched. There have been movements at several places among the railway constructing workmen, and also among the calico-printers some time ago, and it is more than likely, though positive evidence cannot now be given, that communism is making

---

[a] Frederick Augustus II.— *Ed.*

its progress there as well as everywhere else, among the working people; and if the workers of Saxony enter the field, they are sure not to be satisfied with talking like their employers, the liberal "bourgeois".

Let me direct your attention somewhat more to the working class movement in Germany. In your paper of last week,[a] you predict a glorious revolution,—not such a one as that of 1688,[230]—to this country. In this you are perfectly right—I only would beg to correct, or rather to more clearly define your expression, that it is the youth of Germany that will bring about such a change. This youth is not to be looked for among the middle classes. It is from the very heart of our working people that revolutionary action in Germany will commence. It is true, there are among our middle classes a considerable number of Republicans and even Communists, and young men too, who, if a general outbreak occurred now, would be very useful in the movement, but these men are "bourgeois", profit-mongers, man-ufacturers by profession; and who will guarantee us that they will not be demoralised by their trade, by their social position, which forces them to live upon the toil of other people, to grow fat by being the leeches, the "exploiteurs" of the working classes? And if they remain proletarians in mind, though bourgeois in profession, their number will be infinitely small in comparison with the real number of the middle-class men, who stick to the existing order of things through interest, and care for nothing but the filling of their purses. Fortunately, we do not count on the middle classes at all. The movement of the proletarians has developed itself with such astonishing rapidity, that in another year or two we shall be able to muster a glorious array of working Democrats and Communists—for in this country Democracy and Communism are, as far as the working classes are concerned, quite synony-mous. The Silesian weavers, in 1844, gave the signal; the Bohemian and Saxon calico-printers and railway constructors, the Berlin calico-printers, and, indeed, the manufacturing classes of almost all parts of Germany, responded by turnouts and partial riots; the latter of which were almost always produced by the laws prohibit-ing combinations. The movement is now almost general through-out the country, and goes on quietly, but steadily, whilst the middle classes spend their time with agitating for "Constitutions", "Liberty of the Press", "Protective Duties", "German Catholicity", and "Protestant Church Reform". All these middle-class move-

---

[a] *The Northern Star* No. 408, September 6, 1845.— Ed.

ments, although not without some merit, do not touch the working classes at all, who have a movement of their own — a knife-and-fork movement. In my next letter more on this subject.[231]

Written September 8-11, 1845

First published in the newspaper
The Northern Star No. 409,
September 13, 1845
with an editorial note:
"From our own correspondent"

Printed according to the newspaper

Frederick Engels

VICTORIA'S VISIT.— THE "ROYALS" AT LOGGERHEADS.— ROW BETWIXT VIC AND THE GERMAN BOURGEOISIE.— THE CONDEMNATION OF THE PARIS CARPENTERS

Your little Queen has made a pretty mess of her visit to the Prussians. She treated the king[a] with such contempt, that he was glad to get rid of her, and showed that very plainly after her departure. The middle classes too are highly incensed at the contemptuous way she treated the daughters of the *"haute bourgeoisie"* of Cologne. The daughter of the Mayor of Cologne had to present "her Majesty" with a cup of tea, and Vic took not the cup, because touched by the hand of one not "noble". (!) She only took the spoon, and with it sipped the tea; at the same time turning her head aside, and treating the girl with the most marked contempt. The poor girl stood trembling awfully, not knowing whether to stand or to go away. Served her right; these purse-proud *bourgeois*, with all their cunning, are with their worship of kings and queens but *spoons* after all, and as such deserve to be treated. Your Queen carried her contempt so far as to rouse what little spirit they possess to show some resistance. She had subscribed 3,500 dollars (£500), to the building fund of the Cologne Cathedral, and the insulted Bourgeois of Cologne got up a meeting to discuss the propriety of returning her the money! The meeting was dispersed by the police and military. I hear, however, that they still contemplate subscribing the money amongst themselves, and sending it to England or Ireland, to relieve your starving poor. I hope they will do so. John Bull has been made to bleed pretty freely for bloodsucking German princes, and it is only fair that the German bourgeoisie should return a little of what poor John has been shamefully drained. The marked contempt with

---

[a] Frederick William IV.— *Ed.*

which your Queen treated our precious King and his court, arose,
I hear, from the fact of the limping Queen of Prussia[a] refusing the
arm of Prince Albert, and preferring that of Archduke Frederick
at Austria, as being of higher birth. It is very comical to see these
princes at loggerheads amongst themselves, and the bourgeoisie
at loggerheads with the princes; all the time not seeing the movement arising in the lowest depths around them—not seeing their
danger until too late.

You never gave in the *Star* the judgment of the Paris Tribunal
against the carpenters on strike, accused of combination—Vincent, the chief, was sentenced to three years, two others to a year,
some more to six months, I believe (imprisonment). However, they
are keeping out at least those whose masters won't give way.
Two-thirds of the masters have acceded to the workmen's demands, and in consequence of the above sentence, the sawyers
(*scieurs-à-long*) and other trades connected with building, have
turned out too. This affair does a tremendous deal of good.

Written between September 14 and 18,
1845

Printed according to the newspaper

Published in the newspaper
The Northern Star No. 410,
September 20, 1845
with an editorial note:
"From our own correspondent"

---

[a] Elisabeth.—*Ed.*

Frederick Engels

"YOUNG GERMANY" IN SWITZERLAND.[232]
(Conspiracy Against Church and State!)

The *Constitutionnel Neuchâtelois* gives a long, apparently official, report on a "vast conspiracy of atheists spread all over Switzerland". We take from it the following extracts:—

"After the discovery made some time ago of the Communist secret society, in the canton of Neuchâtel, another far more dangerous association has been discovered—an association extending its nets all over the Swiss confederacy, and purposing to overthrow, *by means of Atheism*, the fundamental principles of morality, and to revolutionize Germany by any means, *Regicide not excepted*. The members of this Association, which is known by the name of *Young Germany*, or the *Leman Confederacy*, are almost without exception German working men, with some of the old political refugees. In consequence of some information at the headquarters of the conspiracy, Lausanne, the chiefs of the great club of La Chaux-de-Fonds were apprehended, and a commission of inquiry appointed, the results of which are the following disclosures. This secret society exists since 1838, and has at its head Messrs. Standau and Döleke, professors of the German language, Wm. Marr, editor of their paper[a]; and Hoffmann, druggist. Dr. Fein and Dr. Rauschenplatt, German refugees; the first imprisoned at Lucerne on account of his having taken part in the late civil war[233]—the second at Strasburg, appear also to be connected with this society. The rules of the association contain the following articles:

The society is essentially and necessarily a secret one, its end being political propaganda. Every member obliges himself to remain within the association until forty years of age, to devote all his powers to the attainment of its aims, and not to stand in fear of any sacrifice. Every member engages himself to destroy all written documents, by which the association or its members might be traced. In Switzerland a central office is formed, corresponding with all those members that are returned to Germany, and leading the whole of the operations. None to be admitted as members who do not profess themselves *atheists and revolutionists*.

By the incredible activity of its members among the German working men—of whom there is a floating population of about 25,000 in Switzerland—this society

---

[a] *Blätter der Gegenwart für soziales Leben.—Ed.*

22**

has succeeded in establishing its branch-clubs in 26 towns in Switzerland, viz.: — Carouge, Nyon, Rolle, Aubonne, Morges, Lausanne, Aigle, Vevey, Yverdon, Moudon, Payerne, Chaux-de-Fonds, Fleurier, Berne, Biel, St. Imer, Porentruy, Burgdorf, Chur, Zug, Zurich, Winterthur, Basel, Lucerne, Friburg, and Geneva, besides two clubs in France, in Strasburg and Marseilles. Every six months the deputies of these clubs assemble in one of the localities, which for the next six months is then charged with the management of the general business. The incredible activity, and the really diabolic means brought into bearing by these propagandists for attracting the Germans, are frightful indeed. One of them, writing from Zurich to the central office, says:

"We are obliged to use great caution, on account of most of the newly arriving men being frightened by the ordinances and intimidations of the German governments. They will never enter a club unless they are told that it is not a political one. Thus we are obliged to treat them very cautiously, to bring them bit by bit into the right road, and the principal thing in this respect is to show them that religion is nothing but a pile of rubbish and dung. The only thing we can do is to prepare them here for the clubs in French Switzerland, and there we send those who intend leaving Zurich."

When the Morges club wanted to get into connection with the whitesmiths of that town, none of whom was a member, they instantly wrote to the central office, to send them a whitesmith who might be clever enough to bring those workmen into the society. The clubs were all in correspondence with each other, as well as with the central office. This correspondence has been partly seized, and shows by its contents how much the whole conspiracy was pervaded by a revolutionary spirit. Every club had a committee for preparing the subjects of discussion. The debates extended over all political, social, and religious questions. Some clubs were comparatively rich, and possessed libraries, newsrooms, pianos, &c; they were furnished with everything which might attract the workmen. The most powerful clubs were those of Geneva, Berne, Zurich, Lausanne, and La Chaux-de-Fonds; the last named club numbered (in a very small town) 200 members; and if we consider that in this same town, besides Young Germany, there existed a very numerous Communist club, we may think ourselves entitled to say, that Atheists and Communists in Switzerland are to be numbered by thousands. The association had a secret agitation committee, which was generally not known to the members at large; but every club contained one or two of those "Propagandists", whose business it was to keep up the steam, to direct the proceedings, and to develop the spirit of Atheism and revolutionism. Unfortunately, they succeeded but too well in this, as is proved by the fact, that the "infernal" periodical of Young Germany, published by Marr, numbered above 500 subscribers among the working people only. The paper openly proclaims Atheism as its principle.— "Germany," says this paper, "wants a political, religious, and social revolution; and if religion and politics should, during the course of this revolution, end in smoke, so much the better; socialised man will come forth purer and better from this purgatory."

Thus far the report, which is altogether written in an infamous and calumniatory style. Young Germany had existed in Switzerland since 1831, when, in consequence of the many insurrections in Germany, great numbers of young men, students, workmen, &c.; were obliged to leave their country. After a period of considerable activity this association collapsed towards 1837, when the general Bourgeoisie Government throughout Europe succeeded in suppressing the spirit of political agitation. Soon afterwards, however, the Communist clubs commenced to form themselves in the old home of Young Germany, on the shores of the Leman Lake, and to commence an animated debate with that merely political association. This debate ended in a settled quarrel, and decided enmity of the two parties; the main result, however, was, that Young Germany was obliged to extend its field of action, and not only to better define their political principles, as those of Radical, Republic, and Democratic, but also to take up social questions. While the middle classes of Germany kill their time; with "German Catholicity" and "Protestant Reforms" while they run after Ronge, and play the "Friends of Light"[234]; thus making it their chief business to effect some very little, almost invisible, good-for-nothing (but a Bourgeois) reform in religious matters, the working people of our country read and digest the writings of the greatest German philosophers such as Feuerbach, &c., and embrace the result of their inquiries, as radical as this result may appear. The people of Germany have no religion. How else would it have been possible to convert masses of them, not only in Switzerland, but in France, England, and at home, within the short space of a year? I refer to what I said last week but one on Bourgeoise movements and working-class movements[a]; I think these disclosures are a full confirmation of my statement.

Written between September 20 and 26, 1845

Published in the newspaper *The Northern Star* No. 411, September 27, 1845 with an editorial note "From our German correspondent"

Printed according to the newspaper

---

[a] See pp. 645-48 of this volume.—*Ed.*

Frederick Engels

PERSECUTION AND EXPULSION OF COMMUNISTS

Germany.—On the 11th instant, the authorities of the Grand Dukedom of Hesse, seized at Darmstadt, at the publisher's premises, the first number of a Communist Magazine, the *Rhenish Annals*,[a] edited by Püttmann. There were, however, only fifty-five copies found, the remainder of the edition having been previously sold. The publisher, Mr. Leske, was at the same time informed that the Magazine was placed under the control of the police, he having to produce every number before it was issued, to the police, and to procure a license for issuing the same, under a penalty, in case of non-compliance, of 500 florins (forty-five pounds sterling), or, according to the merits of the case, imprisonment. This blow aimed at the Communists, and at the same time at that little bit of a free press we have in Germany, will, however, prove useless. There are hundreds of means to elude this unconstitutional interference, which, no doubt, has been proceeded to at the instigation of the hated Prussian Government. This same Prussian Government has procured from the Saxon authorities the expulsion of several public authors from Leipsic, among whom is Mr. W. Marr, one of the heads of that Young German Conspiracy in Switzerland mentioned in my last.[b] In his case, as well as that of Weitling last year,[235] the authorities were afraid of imprisoning and bringing to judgment the party, although they had every legal pretence; they were satisfied with driving them away.

---

[a] *Rheinische Jahrbücher zur gesellschaftlichen Reform.*—*Ed.*

[b] See pp. 651-653 of this volume.—*Ed.*

Switzerland.— The Democratic Government of the Pays de Vaud has expelled from the canton Mr. A. Becker, a talented German Communist writer, as well as Mr. S. Schmidt and Dr. Kuhlmann, belonging to the same party, and dissolved the German Communist Club at Lausanne. The Radical Government of Zurich has likewise expelled Dr. Püttmann, editor of the above-named *Rhenish Annals*, and belonging, too, to the Communist party.[a]

Written in the middle of October 1845

Published in the newspaper
The Northern Star No. 415,
October 25, 1845
with an editorial note:
"From our own correspondent"

Printed according to the newspaper

---

[a] [A German friend informs us that the above announcement, as regards the expulsion of Mr. S. Schmidt, is premature. That, as yet, Mr. Schmidt has not been expelled from the Pays de Vaud.— *Ed. N. S.*]

Frederick Engels

HISTORY OF THE ENGLISH CORN LAWS[236]

[*Telegraph für Deutschland* No. 193, December 1845]

Until the middle of the last century England exported grain almost every year and very seldom needed to import this foodstuff from abroad. Since that time, however, the situation has been reversed. Under these circumstances the price of grain, on the one hand, was necessarily low and that of meat, on the other, was high, much arable land was converted into cattle pasture, while at the same time industry, and with it the population, owing to the invention of important machines, experienced an unprecedented growth. Hence England was first compelled to give up exporting corn and later had to import it from abroad. The twenty-five years' war against France during the revolution, which made imports difficult, compelled England more or less to restrict itself to its own soil. The obstacles which the war put in the way of imports had the same effect as a protective tariff. Grain prices rose, ground-rents likewise rose, in most cases to double the previous figure, and in some cases even fivefold. The result was that a large part of the area that had recently been converted into pasture was again used for corn. This increase in their incomes tempted the English landowners, who, incidentally, consist of a few hundred lords and some 60,000 baronets and squires not belonging to the nobility, to adopt an extravagant mode of living and a mutual emulation in luxury for which very soon even their increased rents no longer sufficed. Before long the estates were encumbered with a heavy burden of debt. When in 1814 peace removed the obstacles to import, the price of corn fell and the tenant-farmers, in view of the high rents, could no longer cover the cost of producing their corn. Only two ways out were possible: either that the landowners should reduce the rent or that a real

protective tariff should be imposed instead of the nominal one.
The landowners, who not only dominated the Upper House and the
Ministry but also (prior to the Reform Bill [237]) possessed fairly
unrestricted power in the Lower House, naturally chose the latter
course and in 1815 introduced the Corn Laws amid the furious
outcry of the middle classes and the people, at that time still
guided by the latter, and under the protection of bayonets. The
first Corn Law of 1815 prohibited import of corn altogether as
long as the price of corn in England remained under 80 shillings
a quarter. At this price or over,[a] foreign corn could be imported
freely. But this law was not in accord with the interests of either
the industrial or the agricultural population, and in 1822 it was
somewhat modified. However, this modification never came
into practical effect, for during the next few years prices always
remained low and never reached the level at which the import of
foreign corn was allowed. Despite all the improvements in the law
and despite the investigations of several parliamentary committees,
the tenant-farmers were unable to cover their production costs.
Finally, therefore, Huskisson and Canning invented their famous
sliding scale,[b] which their successors in the Ministry embodied in
the law.[238] By this scale, the import duty rose as the price of
home-produced corn fell and vice versa. By this means the English
farmer was to be ensured a high and constant price for his corn,
so that he could comfortably cope with his high ground-rent. But
this measure was of no avail either. The system became increasingly untenable; the middle classes, whose representatives were
predominant in the Lower House after the Reform Bill, became
more and more opposed to the Corn Laws, and within a year after
Sir Robert Peel's entry into the Ministry he found himself
compelled to lower the import tariff.

Meanwhile, opposition to the Corn Laws had become organised.
The industrial middle class, which had to pay its workers higher
wages because of the increase in the price of corn, resolved to do
its utmost to secure at any cost the abolition of these hated
laws — the last survivals of the old dominance of the agricultural
interests, which at the same time facilitated foreign competition
against English industry. Towards the end of 1838, some of the
leading Manchester manufacturers founded an anti-Corn Law
association, which soon spread in the neighbourhood and in other
factory districts, adopted the name of Anti-Corn Law League,

---

[a] The original has "under".— Ed.

[b] In the original the words "sliding scale" are given in English.—Ed.

started a subscription fund, founded a journal (the *Anti-Bread-Tax Circular*), sent paid speakers from place to place and set in motion all the means of agitation customary in England for achieving its aim. During its first years, which coincided with a four-years' slump in business, the Anti-Corn-Law League was extremely active. When, however, at the beginning of 1842, the business slump turned into a downright commercial crisis which threw the working class into the most atrocious poverty, the Anti-Corn-Law League became definitely revolutionary. It took as its motto the saying of Jeremiah: "They that be slain with the sword are better than they that be slain with hunger."[a] Its journal in clear language called on the people to revolt and threatened the landowners with the "pick-axe and the torch". Its itinerant agitators ranged the whole country and preached in a language no way less forceful than that of the journal. Meeting after meeting was held, petition after petition to Parliament was circulated, and when Parliament opened its session, a Congress of League representatives assembled simultaneously in the immediate neighbourhood of the Houses of Parliament. When, in spite of all this, Peel failed to abolish the Corn Laws, but only modified them, the Congress declared:

"The people has nothing more to expect from the government; it must rely only on itself; the wheels of the government machinery must be halted all at once and on the spot; the time for talking is over, the time has come for action. It is to be hoped that the people will no longer be willing to starve for the benefit of an aristocracy living in luxury; and if naught else avails, there is still a means by which the government can be compelled to give way: we must" (stated this Congress of leading manufacturers and municipal officials of the great factory towns) "we must throw the people on to the agricultural districts which have produced all the pauperism; but the people must not go there like a crowd of humble '*paupers*', but as if they had to 'quarter themselves on a mortal enemy'."[b]

This great means in the hands of the manufacturers, by which they wished in 24 hours to bring together a meeting of 500,000 persons on the Manchester racecourse and to raise an insurrection against the Corn Laws, consisted in *closing down their factories*.

[*Telegraph für Deutschland* No. 194, December 1845]

In July, business began to improve. The manufacturers received increased orders and they noted that the crisis was coming to an end. The people was still in a highly excited state and distress was

---

[a] *Lamentations of Jeremiah*, 4:9.—*Ed*.

[b] This passage has been retranslated from the German since it was not possible to trace the English original.—*Ed*.

universal; but if anything was to happen, it was high time for action. And so, when an increase in wages was to be expeeted owing to the improvement in business a manufacturer in Stalybridge suddenly reduced the wages of his workers, thereby compelling them to strike in order to maintain their wages at the previous level. The workers, to whom the signal for an insurrection was thus given, brought all the factories in the town and its environs to a standstill, which was easy for them to do since the manufacturers (all members of the Anti-Corn Law League), contrary to their custom, offered no resistance at all. The workers held meetings presided over by the manufacturers themselves, who tried to draw the people's attention to the Corn Laws. On August 9, 1842, four days after the outbreak of the insurrection, the workers marched to Manchester, where they met with no resistance at all, and brought all the factories to a standstill. The only manufacturer who opposed them was a conservative and hostile to the League. The insurrection spread to all the factory districts; nowhere did the urban authorities (on whom *everything* depends in England in such cases, as is well known), who were all members of the Anti-Corn [Law] League, offer any resistance. So far *everything* proceeded as the League wanted. But in one respect it had miscalculated. The people, whom it had driven into insurrection in order to force the abolition of the Corn Laws, did not care in the least about these laws. They demanded the wages of 1840 and the People's Charter.[239] As soon as the League noticed this, it turned against its allies. All its members were sworn in as special constables and formed a new army for the suppression of the insurrection, at the service of the government that was hostile to them. The involuntary insurrection of the people, who were not yet at all prepared for anything of the sort, was soon suppressed; the Corn Laws remained in force, and both the middle class and the people were given a profitable lesson. The Anti-Corn Law League, in order to furnish conspicuous proof that it had not been defeated by the failure of the insurrection, started a new large-scale campaign in 1843, with the demand for contributions from its members amounting to £50,000, and it amassed more than this sum in the course of a year. It began its agitation afresh, but it soon found itself compelled to seek a new audience. It always made a great boast that it found nothing more to do in the factory districts after 1843 and could therefore turn to the agricultural districts. But there was a snag to this. After the insurrection of 1842 it could no longer hold any public meetings in the factory districts without its representatives being most

ignominiously driven from the platform and literally beaten up by
the angry people whom it had so shamefully betrayed. Consequently, if it wanted to propagate its doctrines, it was compelled
to go to the agricultural districts. Here the League was of
some real service by arousing among the tenant-farmers a certain
feeling of shame at their dependence hitherto on the landowners,
and by making the agricultural class aware of more general
interests. In 1844, encouraged by its success with previous contributions, the League opened a new subscription list of £100,000.
On the following day the manufacturers in Manchester assembled
and within half an hour had subscribed £12,000. By November 1844, £82,000 had been collected, of which £57,000 had
already been spent. A few months later the League opened an
exhibition in London, which also must have brought in enormous
sums. If now one asks what has been the motive of this colossal
movement, which has spread from Manchester to the whole of
England and has carried with it the vast majority of the English
middle class, but which—we repeat—has not received an atom of
sympathy from the working class, it must be acknowledged that this
motive is the private interest of the industrial and commercial
middle class of Great Britain. For this class it is of the greatest
importance to have a system which, as it believes at least, ensures it
for all time a world monopoly of trade and industry by enabling it
to pay just as low wages as its competitors and to exploit all the
advantages that England possesses as a result of its 80 years' start
in the development of modern industry. From this point of view
the middle class alone, and not the people, benefits from the
abolition of the Corn Laws. Secondly, the middle class demands
this measure as a supplementary law to the Reform Bill. Through
the Reform Bill, which introduced suffrage based on a property
qualification and abolished the old electoral privileges of particular
individuals and corporations, the monied middle class had come, in
principle, to power. In reality, however, the landowning class still
retained a considerable preponderance in Parliament since it sends
there *directly* 143 members for the counties and *indirectly* almost all
the members representing small towns, and is represented in
addition by the Tory members from the towns. In 1841, this
majority of the agricultural interest brought *Peel* and the *Tories* into
the cabinet. The abolition of the Corn Laws would deal a fatal
blow to the political power of the landowners in the Lower House,
and hence in fact in the whole English legislature, since it would
make the tenant-farmers independent of the landowners. It would
proclaim capital to be the supreme power in England, but at the

same time it would shake the English Constitution to its foundations; it would rob an essential constituent of the legislative body, viz. the landed aristocracy, of all wealth and all power, and thereby exert a different and greater influence on the future of England than many other political measures. Once again, however, we find that from this aspect too the abolition of the Corn Laws' offers no advantage to the people.

Written in the autumn of 1845

First published in the journal
Telegraph für Deutschland Nos. 193
and 194, December 1845

The name of the author is given
in the editorial note

Printed according to the journal

Published in English for the first
time

FROM THE PREPARATORY
MATERIALS

Karl Marx

HEGEL'S CONSTRUCTION OF THE PHENOMENOLOGY [240]

1) Self-consciousness instead of man. Subject—object.

2) The *differences* of things are unimportant, because substance is conceived as self-distinction or because self-distinction, the distinguishing, the mental activity is regarded as the essential. Within the framework of speculation Hegel therefore makes distinctions that really grasp the vital point.

3) Abolition of *estrangement* is identified with abolition of *objectivity* (an aspect evolved by Feuerbach in particular).

4) Your *abolition* of the imagined object, of the object as object of consciousness, is identified with the *real objective* abolition, with sensuous *action*, *practice* and *real activity* as distinct from thinking. (Has still to be developed.)

Written presumably in November 1844

First published in: Marx/Engels, *Gesamtausgabe*, Abt. 1, Bd. 5, 1932

Printed according to the manuscript

Published in English for the first time

Karl Marx

DRAFT PLAN
FOR A WORK ON THE MODERN STATE [241]

1) The *history of the origin of the modern state* or the *French Revolution*.

The self-conceit of the political sphere—to mistake itself for the ancient state. The attitude of the revolutionaries towards civil society. All elements exist in duplicate form, as civic elements and [those of] the state.

2) The *proclamation* of the *rights of man* and the *constitution of the state*. Individual freedom and public authority.

Freedom, equality and unity. Sovereignty of the people.

3) *State* and *civil society*.

4) The *representative state* and the *charter*.

The constitutional representative state, the democratic representative state.

5) *Division of power*. Legislative and executive power.

6) *Legislative power* and the legislative bodies. Political clubs.

7) *Executive power*. Centralisation and hierarchy. Centralisation and political civilisation. Federal system and industrialism. *State administration* and *local government*.

8') *Judicial power* and *law*.

8") *Nationality* and the *people*.

9') The *political parties*.

9") *Suffrage*, the fight for the *abolition* of the state and of bourgeois society.

Written presumably in November 1844

First published in: Marx/Engels, *Gesamtausgabe*, Abt. 1, Bd. 5, 1932

Printed according to the manuscript

Published in English for the first time

Karl Marx

PLAN OF THE "LIBRARY OF THE BEST FOREIGN SOCIALIST WRITERS" [242]

Morelly	*Cercle soc[ial]* [243]	*Bentham*
Mably	*Hébert*	*Godwin*
Babeuf	*Jac. Roux* [a]	
Buonarroti	*Leclerc*	

Holbach	*Helvétius*
Fourier	*St. Simon*

Owen

(Lalande)

Considérant	*Writings* of the School

Producteur. Globe.

Cabet	*Dézamy. Gay.* and x

"Fraternité", l'égalitaire, etc.
l'humanitaire [244]

Proudhon

Written between March 7 and 17, 1845

First published in: Marx/Engels, *Gesamtausgabe*, Abt. 1, Bd. 5, 1932

Printed according to the manuscript

Published in English for the first time

---

[a] In the manuscript: Léroux. Presumably a slip of the pen.—*Ed.*

Karl Marx

FROM THE NOTEBOOK[245]

The divine egoist as opposed to egoistical man.

The delusion regarding the ancient state prevailing during the revolution.
"Concept" and "substance".

The revolution=history of the origin of the modern state.

Written presumably in April 1845

First published in: German
in Marx/Engels, *Gesamtausgabe*,
Abt. 1, Bd. 5, 1932

Printed according to the manuscript

Published in English for the first time

APPENDICES

1

TO THE READERS OF AND CONTRIBUTORS
TO THE *GESELLSCHAFTSSPIEGEL*[246]

The noble striving to hasten to the aid of suffering humanity, which, to the credit of the 19th century, manifests itself everywhere at the present time, has not yet in Germany a central press organ giving publicity on the one hand to the evils which must be remedied, and on the other to the proposed or already implemented measures for their redress, and casting light on their success or failure. We hereby submit to the public the first issue of such an organ, and hope that every friend of humanity will feel prompted to support the *Gesellschaftsspiegel* with appropriate reports.

In order to discover and apply the means for the radical and permanent elimination of the various and moreover artificially concealed evils in our social life, it is necessary first of all to find out what these evils are. For this reason the *Gesellschaftsspiegel* will cite before its forum all the maladies of the social body; it will publish general descriptions, monographs, statistical items, and individual typical cases serving to set the social relations of all the classes in their true light and to help the *associations* which are being formed to eliminate the social evils; it will stand exclusively on the ground of fact, and carry only facts and arguments based directly on facts, arguments the conclusions from which are also obvious facts.

The condition of the working classes will be first and foremost the object of our attention, for their condition is the most glaring of all evils in present-day civilised society. Descriptions, statistical data, individual striking facts from all parts of Germany, especially from those in which unusual distress prevails, will be welcome. Also reports on the numerical relation of the needy classes, the propertyless classes in general, to the propertied; on the growth of pauperism, and so on.

We shall include in the range of our survey the spiritual, intellectual and moral condition of the workers as well as their physical condition, and shall readily accept reports on the state of their health insofar as it is determined by the social conditions, and on the state of education and morality of the proletarians. Statistics on crime and prostitution, especially when accompanied by comparison of different periods of time, localities or living conditions, will also be given close attention.

The most fruitful fields for the purposes of the *Gesellschaftsspiegel* in this respect are:

1) *The large towns*, which cannot exist without a numerous propertyless class crowded together in a small area. Besides the usual consequences which the absence of property entails everywhere, we shall have to consider here the effect which this centralisation of the population has on the physical, intellectual, and moral condition of the working classes. Descriptions, statistical, medical, and other reports along with individual facts casting light on the "*disreputable areas*", mostly shrouded in darkness, of our towns, large and small, will be welcome.

2) *The industrial and factory districts*, whose existence also requires a numerous propertyless class. In this respect we wish to draw the attention of our contributors particularly to the following points:

(a) *The nature of work* in itself: individual kinds of work which owing to their character or to the unsuitable way in which they are carried out or to the excessively long working hours are injurious to health; child and woman labour in factories and its consequences; neglect of working and non-working children and wives of proletarians, breaking up of the family, supplanting of adult male labour by women and children, accidents caused by machinery, and so on.

(b) *Dependence of the workers on their employers*. In respect of this point we shall make it our duty to represent the interests of the defenceless working class against the power and especially against the unfortunately too frequent encroachments of the capitalists. We shall pitilessly hold up for public censure every single case of oppression of workers and shall be particularly grateful to our correspondents for most accurate reports on this subject giving names, places and dates. If in factories working hours are too long or night work is resorted to, if workers are obliged to clean machines in their spare time, if factory-owners are brutal or tyrannical towards their workers, lay down tyrannical working regulations, pay wages in goods instead of money—we shall especially fight this infamous truck system[a] wherever and in whatever forms or disguises it occurs—if workers are forced to work in unhealthy premises or to live in unsatisfactory lodgings belonging to the factory-owner—in a word, whenever any act of injustice is committed by the capitalists against the workers, we ask everybody who is in a position to do so to inform us on this score as soon and as exactly as possible. We want to make known to the public in the most exact and shameful details each and every violation of the laws that have been issued to protect the poor from the rich. Only in this way can the laws, which have so far existed mostly on paper, be made really effective.

(c) *Neglect of the workers* by society in general when, as a result of competition, the introduction of more efficient machinery, the employment of women and children, the fluctuations of trade and foreign competition the workers are deprived of employment, or when due to illness, injury or old age they are unable to work, as well as all deteriorations in the workers' living conditions due to lowering of wages.

Besides the *propertyless*, we shall also describe the *propertied class* in its outer and inner conditions. We shall have to prove with facts that *free competition between private businessmen without organisation of labour and commerce impoverishes the middle class*, concentrating property in the hands of a few and thus indirectly restoring the monopoly; that the parcelling out of landed property ruins the small landowner and indirectly restores big landed property; that the competitive struggle, in which we are all being involved, *undermines the foundations of society* and *demoralises the whole of society* by brutal self-interest.

The *Gesellschaftsspiegel* will not confine itself to describing material misery, or spiritual and moral misery only when it goes hand in hand with the former; on the contrary, it will describe misery in all its forms, and therefore also the misery of the higher classes; and in this description it will not confine itself to statistical articles and accounts of real facts taken from life; it will open its columns to fiction in prose and in verse, but only to such as depicts life *truly*. Descriptions *based on* life will be no less welcome than descriptions *taken from* life.

Let those to whom such a pitiless exposure of the condition of our industrial as well as agricultural and other population—a condition which has so far been for the most part hypocritically glossed

---

[a] The words "truck system" are in English in the original.—*Ed.*

over or concealed—those to whom so frank a presentation of our entire social condition as the one the *Gesellschaftsspiegel* intends to give causes too great head and heartache for them to be favourably disposed to our undertaking, let them reflect that in the long run the courage required to look an evil in the face and the calm derived from a clear knowledge of things have a more beneficial effect on mind and heart than the cowardly idealising sentimentality which seeks consolation from disconsolate reality in the falsehood of its ideal, which neither exists *nor can exist* because it is based on *illusions*! Such idealising sentimentality indeed displays hypocritical sympathy for the sufferings of humanity when these eventually develop into a *political scandal*—as we saw all the newspapers and journals overflowing with so-called socialism in connection with the Silesian disturbances[247]—but as soon as the *disturbances* are over, it *quietly* lets the poor go on starving.

Finally, the *Gesellschaftsspiegel* will carry reports on the efforts being made to remedy the social evils and the disorders of society, that is, on the one hand, *the work of the associations now being formed*,[248] and on the other, the coercive measures which hold some evils in check, but only to produce others. These include the pernicious effects of the degrading sentences which place a criminal for ever outside the pale of society, of intercourse with hardened criminals in ordinary prisons and of solitary confinement in Pennsylvania-type prisons, the numerous murders resulting from the laws against poaching; the state and operation of the poor laws and the sanitary police; the typical crimes, and so on.

In appealing to all who are in a position to send us reports on the above-mentioned and similar points to be laid before the forum of the *Gesellschaftsspiegel*, in particular to priests, school-teachers, doctors and officials, for friendly co-operation in the interest of the cause, we guarantee that whenever it is desired names will be kept secret and we shall hold our correspondents *responsible* only for the *correctness of the facts of which they inform us*. The editorial board assumes the responsibility for publication.

Written at the end of January 1845

Published in the annual *Gesellschaftsspiegel*, Bd. 1, 1845

Printed according to the journal

Published in English for the first time

2

CONTRACT
BETWEEN MARX AND THE LESKE PUBLISHERS
IN DARMSTADT ON THE PUBLICATION
OF *KRITIK DER POLITIK UND NATIONALÖKONOMIE*[249]

Between Herr Dr. Marx, at present residing in Paris, on the one hand, and the C.W. Leske Publishers in Darmstadt, on the other, the following Contract has been concluded today.

§ 1. Herr Dr. Marx gives the C.W. Leske Publishers the exclusive right to publish his work entitled *Kritik der Politik und Nationalökonomie*, which will comprise two volumes in octavo, each of more than twenty printed sheets.

§ 2. The Author, Dr. Marx, undertakes not to publish in another publishing house any work which could compete with the work named herein.

§ 3. In return, the Leske Publishers will pay Herr Dr. Marx the sum of francs 3,000 (three thousand francs) as royalties for the entire work, the first half of this sum to be paid when the complete Manuscript is handed in, and the second half on completion of the printing. The Publishers also undertake to deliver twelve copies free of charge to the Author.

§ 4. The Publishers will begin the printing of the work as soon as the Manuscript is handed in and will see to it that it appears in a suitable get-up.

§ 5. The edition of the *Kritik der Politik und Nationalökonomie* is fixed at 2,000 copies.

§ 6. This Contract is valid only for the first edition of the work. Should a second edition become necessary, a new contract will be concluded. It goes without saying, however, that in the event of a second edition the Leske Publishers retain a preferential right.

This Contract has been drawn up in duplicate and is signed by both contracting parties.

Paris, February 1, 1845   Dr. Karl Marx
                                                           C. Leske

First published in: K. Marx and F. Engels, *Works*, First Russ. ed., Vol. XXV, 1934

Printed according to the manuscript

Published in English for the first time

3

MARX TO LEOPOLD I, KING OF BELGIUM,
IN BRUSSELS [250]

Brussels, February 7, 1845
24, Place du petit sablon

Sire,

The undersigned, Charles Marx, Doctor of Philosophy, aged 26, from Trier, in the Kingdom of Prussia, intending to settle with his wife and child in Your Majesty's domains, respectfully takes the liberty of requesting Your Majesty to grant him permission to establish his residence in Belgium. He has the honour to be, with deepest respect,

Your Majesty's most humble and obedient servant,

Dr. Charles Marx

First published in *L'Europe Nouvelle* No. 346, 1924

Printed according to the manuscript

Translated from the French

Published in English for the first time

4

MARX'S UNDERTAKING NOT TO PUBLISH ANYTHING
IN BELGIUM ON CURRENT POLITICS [251]

To obtain permission to reside in Belgium I agree to pledge myself, on my word of honour, not to publish in Belgium any work on current politics.

March 22, 1845   *Dr. Karl Marx*

First published in *L'Europe Nouvelle*
No. 346, 1924

Printed according to the manuscript

Translated from the French

Published in English for the first time

5

MARX TO CHIEF BURGOMASTER GÖRTZ
IN TRIER [252]

Brussels, October 17 [1845]
Rue de l'Alliance 5, hors de la
Porte du Louvain

Your Excellency,

I most respectfully request you kindly to obtain for me from the esteemed royal government administration in Trier a certificate for emigration to the United States of North America. My discharge papers from royal Prussian military service [253] are to be found in the office of the Chief Burgomaster in Trier or of the royal government administration there.

Your Excellency's most obedient servant,

Dr. Karl Marx

First published in the pamphlet:
H. Schiel, *Die Umwelt des jungen
Karl Marx*, Trier, 1954

Printed according to the manuscript

Published in English for the first time

6

MARX TO CHIEF BURGOMASTER GÖRTZ
IN TRIER

*To His Excellency Herr Görtz, Royal Prussian Landrat
and Chief Burgomaster*

Your Excellency,

In reply to your esteemed letter of the 8th of this month I hereby state that my request of the 17th of the previous month for release from citizenship of the Kingdom of Prussia for the purpose of emigration to the United States of North America related solely to my own person, but, *if it should be necessary for granting consent,* I request that the release should be extended to my family as well.

Your Excellency's most obedient servant,

Dr. Karl Marx

Brussels, November 10, 1845

First published in the pamphlet:
H. Schiel, *Die Umwelt des jungen
Karl Marx*, Trier, 1954

Printed according to the manuscript

Published in English for the first time

NOTES
AND
INDEXES

NOTES

[1] The Holy Family, or Critique of Critical Criticism. Against Bruno Bauer and Co. is the first joint work of Karl Marx and Frederick Engels. At the end of August 1844, Engels, on his way back from Manchester to Barmen, stopped over in Paris, where he had his second meeting with Marx, a meeting which marked the beginning of their collaboration as authors.

During the ten days which Engels spent in Paris, he and Marx agreed to publish a criticism of the representatives of the Young Hegelian trend. They drew up the plan of a book which they at first called A Critique of Critical Criticism. Against Bruno Bauer and Co., divided the sections between themselves and wrote the Foreword. Engels wrote his sections before leaving Paris. Marx, whose share comprised the bigger part of the book, continued to work on it till the end of November 1844, considerably increasing the size of the book and drawing on his "Economic and Philosophic Manuscripts", on which he had been working during the spring and summer of 1844, as well as on his studies of the history of the French Revolution and his notes and summaries. During the printing of the book, Marx, on the advice of the publisher Löwenthal, added to the title the words "The Holy Family". The book was published in February 1845 in Frankfurt am Main by the Literarische Anstalt (J. Rütten) publishers. The table of contents (see contents of this volume, pp. v-xi) showed which sections had been written by Marx and which by Engels. The fact that the book, though of small format, exceeded twenty printed sheets in volume, exempted it from preliminary censorship in accordance with the regulations operating at the time in a number of German states.

"The Holy Family" is a sarcastic nickname for the Bauer brothers and their followers who supported the Allgemeine Literatur-Zeitung published in Charlottenburg from the end of 1843 to October 1844. While attacking the Bauers and other Young Hegelians, Marx and Engels at the same time critically analysed the idealist philosophy of Hegel himself.

Marx had shown his disagreement with the Young Hegelians already in the autumn of 1842 when, as an editor of the Rheinische Zeitung, he opposed the publication of superficial and pretentious articles submitted by the outwardly ultra-radical Berlin circle of "The Free" (Edgar Bauer, Max Stirner, Eduard Meyen and others). During the two years which had elapsed since Marx's clash with "The Free", Marx's and Engels' disagreement with the Young Hegelians on questions of theory and politics had deepened still more. This was accounted for not only by the transition of Marx and Engels to materialism and communism, but also by the evolution which had taken place during that time in the ideas of the Bauer brothers and their fellow-thinkers. In the *Allgemeine Literatur-Zeitung* Bauer and his group renounced the "radicalism of 1842" and, besides professing subjective idealist views, and counterposing chosen personalities, the bearers of "pure Criticism", to the allegedly sluggish and inert masses, they began spreading the ideas of moderate liberal philanthropy. Marx's draft of the Preface of his "Economic and Philosophic Manuscripts" shows that already in the summer of 1844 he saw in the evolution of the Young Hegelians' views a degeneration of that initially progressive trend, a deepening of the features of mysticism and transcendentalism peculiar to Hegel's idealism, the disintegration of the Hegelian school (see present edition, Vol. 3, p. 233).

It was to exposure of the Young Hegelians' views in the form which they had acquired in 1844 and to defence of their own new materialistic and communistic outlook that Marx and Engels decided to devote their first joint work.

The appearance of *The Holy Family* evoked a lively response in the German press. It was pointed out that this work was the most profound and the most forceful of all that Marx and Engels had recently written (*Mannheimer Abend-Zeitung*, March 25, 1845), that it expressed socialist views, since it criticised the "inadequacy of any half-measures directed at eliminating the social ailments of our time" (*Kölnische Zeitung*, March 21, 1845).

Reactionary circles immediately discerned the book's revolutionary trend. As early as December 1844, when the work was still printing, it was denounced in reports by Metternich's agents. The conservative *Allgemeine Zeitung*, polemising against the assessment of *The Holy Family* given by the *Kölnische Zeitung*, wrote with irritation on April 8, 1845, that in this book "every line preaches revolt ... against the state, the church, the family, legality, religion and property", that in it "prominence is given to the most radical and the most open communism, and this is all the more dangerous as Mr. Marx cannot be denied either extremely broad knowledge or the ability to make use of the polemical arsenal of Hegel's logic, what is customarily called 'iron logic'". A month and a half later, on May 23, 1845, the *Allgemeine Zeitung* again censured the *Kölnische Zeitung* for publishing a favourable opinion of *The Holy Family*.

Bruno Bauer's attempt to refute the criticism publicly (in the article "Charakteristik Ludwig Feuerbachs", published in *Wigand's Vierteljahrsschrift*, Leipzig, 1845, Bd. III) boiled down essentially to asserting that he had not been correctly understood. Marx replied to this "anti-criticism" of Bauer's with an article published in the journal *Gesellschaftsspiegel*, Elberfeld, January 1846 (see present edition, Vol. 5), which partly coincided in content with the section "Der Heilige Bruno gegen die Autoren der 'Heiligen Familie'" in Chapter 2 ("Der Heilige Bruno") of the first volume of *The German Ideology* (see present edition, Vol. 5).

During the lifetimes of Marx and Engels *The Holy Family* was not published in English. Only part of subsection d), "Critical Battle Against French Materialism", of Chapter VI, was reproduced by Engels in the Introduction to the 1892 English edition of *Socialism: Utopian and Scientific* (the German version of this introduction was published in *Die Neue Zeit* in 1895 under the title "Über den französischen Materialismus des XVIII. Jahrhunderts").

In the English language *The Holy Family, or Critique of Critical Criticism*, was published for the first time in 1956 by the Foreign Languages Publishing House, now Progress Publishers, Moscow, in the translation by Richard Dixon. The literary features of the work include the broad use of citations from French authors (Eugène

Sue, Pierre Joseph Proudhon, and others) in the language of the original, alongside citations translated into German, as well as the use of individual expressions in foreign languages, especially French. This feature is preserved in the present edition, the translations of the citations being given in footnotes. Emphasis in the citations (printed in clear-face italics or bold-face italics in cases of special emphasis) mostly belongs to Marx and Engels, who often translated the citations with abridgments.   Title-page

[2] The reference is to the review made by the bookbinder C. Reichardt of A. T Woeniger's *Publicistische Abhandlungen*, Berlin, 1843. The review was published in the *Allgemeine Literatur-Zeitung*, Heft I, December 1843 and Heft II, January 1844, under the general title "Schriften über den Pauperismus" and mentioned the author's profession. The short excerpts and individual expressions quoted by Engels below and at the end of Chapter I are taken from this review.   p. 9

[3] Here and elsewhere Engels quotes Reichardt's reviews of C. Brüggemann's book, *Preussens Beruf in der deutschen Staats-Entwickelung, und die nächsten Bedingungen zu seiner Erfüllung*, Berlin, 1843 and A. Benda's *Katechismus für wahlberechtigte Bürger in Preussen*, Berlin, 1843. Both reviews were published in the *Allgemeine Literatur-Zeitung*, Heft VI, May 1844.   p. 9

[4] The chapter contains a critical analysis of Julius Faucher's article, "Englische Tagesfragen", which was published in the *Allgemeine Literatur-Zeitung*, Heft VII, June 1844, Heft VIII, July 1844 (with the subtitle "Fortsetzung. Lord Ashley's Amendment") and Heft IX, August 1844 (with the subtitle "Fortsetzung. Ricardos Motion in Betreff der Einfuhrzölle"). The excerpts and expressions cited below were taken by Engels from this article.

The word *Mühleigner*, a literal translation of the English "mill-owner", does not exist in German. Engels here ridicules J. Faucher's way of using in his articles words which he himself coins after the English manner (see p. 16 of this volume). p. 12

[5] *The national Anti-Corn Law League* was founded in 1838 by the Manchester manufacturers Cobden and Bright. The English Corn Laws, first adopted in the 15th century, imposed high tariffs on agricultural imports in order to maintain high prices for them on the home market. In the first third of the 19th century, 1815, 1822, and later several laws were passed changing the conditions for corn imports, and in 1828 a sliding scale was introduced which raised import tariffs on corn when prices in the home market declined and, on the other hand, lowered tariffs when the home market prices rose.

The League widely exploited the popular discontent over the raising of corn prices. In its efforts to obtain the repeal of the Corn Laws and the establishment of complete freedom of trade, it aimed at weakening the economic and political positions of the landed aristocracy and lowering the cost of living thus making possible a lowering of the workers' wages.

The struggle between the industrial bourgeoisie and the landed aristocracy over the Corn Laws ended in 1846 with the repeal of these laws.   p. 13

[6] The struggle for legislation limiting the working day to ten hours started in England as early as the late 18th century and spread by the 1830s to the mass of the industrial workers. The representatives of the landed aristocracy saw their chance to use this popular slogan against the industrial bourgeoisie and supported the Ten Hour Bill in Parliament; the "Tory philanthropist" Lord Ashley headed the supporters of the Bill in Parliament from 1833. The Ten Hour Bill, applicable only to youths and women, was not passed until 1847.   p. 14

[7] When an important question is being discussed, the House of Commons sits in "Committee of the Whole House", which is tantamount to a closed sitting; in this case the function of committee chairman is performed by one of the Members named in the list of committee chairmen and appointed by the speaker.   p. 14

[8] The reference is to the speech made during the debate on the Ten Hour Bill in the House of Commons on March 15, 1844, by Sir James Graham, Home Secretary in Sir Robert Peel's Tory cabinet (*Hansard's Parliamentary Debates*. Third Series, Vol. LXXIII).   p. 15

[9] It was with the letter "J", the first letter of "Jungnitz", that the article "Herr Nauwerck und die philosophische Fakultät", published in the *Allgemeine Literatur-Zeitung*, Heft VI, May 1844, was signed. The publication of this article was preceded by E. Jungnitz's review of Karl Nauwerck's book *Über die Teilnahme am Staate*, Leipzig, 1844 (*Allgemeine Literatur-Zeitung*, Heft IV, March 1844). Engels took the short excerpts given below from this article.   p. 17

[10] The reference is to the dismissal of Bruno Bauer, whom the Prussian Government deprived, temporarily in October 1841 and permanently in March 1842, of the right to lecture in Bonn University because of his works criticising the Bible.

p. 17

[11] The excerpts cited in this paragraph are from the anonymous article "Proudhon" published in the *Allgemeine Literatur-Zeitung*, Heft V, April 1844. Its author was Edgar Bauer. Marx gives a detailed critical analysis of this article in section 4 of Chapter IV. E. Bauer's phrase "the tranquillity of knowledge" was ironically played up also in other sections of this chapter written by Marx and Engels.

p. 18

[12] In this section Engels analyses and cites a review by Edgar Bauer in the *Allgemeine Literatur-Zeitung*, Heft V, April 1844, of Flora Tristan's *Union ouvrière*, Paris, 1843.

p. 19

[13] In this section Engels deals with Edgar Bauer's review of F. F. A. Béraud's *Les filles publiques de Paris et la police qui les régit*, t. I-II, Paris et Leipzig, 1839. This review was published in the *Allgemeine Literatur-Zeitung*, Heft V, April 1844, under the title "Béraud über die Freudenmädchen".   p. 20

[14] In this section Marx criticised and cited Edgar Bauer's article "Die Romane der Verfasserin von Godwie Castle", published in the *Allgemeine Literatur-Zeitung*, Heft II, January 1844, and devoted to an analysis of the works of the German novelist Henriette von Paalzow.   p. 21

[15] Marx compares with Edgar Bauer's article "Proudhon" (*Allgemeine Literatur-Zeitung*, Heft V, April 1844), which he criticises and cites in this section, excerpts from the second, 1841, edition of Proudhon's *Qu'est-ce que la propriété? ou Recherches sur le principe du droit et du gouvernement. Premier mémoire* (the first edition appeared in 1840 in Paris). Marx quotes Proudhon's book sometimes from the French original, sometimes in his own German translation.

Marx later made a comprehensive critical appraisal of this work of Proudhon's in his article "Über Proudhon", which was published as a letter to Schweitzer, editor of the *Social-Demokrat*, in 1865.   p. 23

[16] The "Reformists" were a party of radical opponents of the July monarchy. The party consisted of democratic republicans and petty-bourgeois Socialists grouped

round the Paris newspaper *La Réforme*. The leaders of the Réforme party included Ledru-Rollin and Louis Blanc.   p. 25

¹⁷ *Digests* or *Pandects* were part of a compendium of Roman civil law (*Corpus iuris civilis*) compiled in 528-34 by Emperor Justinian I of the Eastern Roman Empire. They contained extracts from the works of prominent Roman jurists on civil law.
                                                                                              p. 30

¹⁸ Here and to the end of the subsection "Characterising Translation No. 4" Marx compared citations from Bauer's article with excerpts from another work by Proudhon, *Avertissement aux propriétaires, ou Lettre à M. Considérant, rédacteur de la Phalange, sur une défense de la propriété*. In content this book was close to Proudhon's *Qu'est-ce que la propriété?*, the closing section of which, "*Deuxième mémoire. Lettre à M. Blanqui, professeur d'économie politique au conservatoire des arts et métiers. Sur la propriété*", is quoted above.   p. 50

¹⁹ The quotations are from an anonymous review of Thiers' book *Geschichte der französischen Revolution* which was published in the *Allgemeine Literatur-Zeitung*, Heft VIII, July 1844. In "Critical Comment No. 5", Marx continues giving quotations from Edgar Bauer's article on Proudhon (*Allgemeine Literatur-Zeitung*, Heft V), comparing them with extracts from Proudhon's book *Qu'est-ce que la propriété?*   p. 51

²⁰ This chapter deals with and quotes from the review written by the Young Hegelian Szeliga (the pen-name of F. Z. Zychlinski) on the French writer Eugène Sue's novel *Les mystères de Paris*, which was published in 1843 and became well known as a sample of sentimental social fantasy woven into an adventure plot.
    Szeliga's review was printed in the *Allgemeine Literatur-Zeitung*, Heft VII, June 1844, under the title: "Eugen Sue: Die Geheimnisse von Paris. Kritik von Szeliga". Marx continues the critical analysis of this article in Chapter VIII.
    The excerpts from Sue's novel in the two chapters are given by Marx either in French or in German translation.   p. 55

²¹ The reference is to the *Charte constitutionnelle* which was adopted in France after the bourgeois revolution of 1830 and was the basic law of the July monarchy.
    In its fundamental principles the *Charte constitutionnelle* reproduced the constitutional charter of 1814, but the preamble of the 1814 charter, which spoke of the constitution being granted ("*octroyée*") by the king, was omitted and the rights of the upper and lower chambers were extended at the expense of certain royal prerogatives. According to the new constitution the king was considered only as the head of the executive authority and was deprived of the right to abrogate or suspend laws.
    The expression "*Charte vérité*" is an ironical allusion to the concluding words of Louis Philippe's proclamation of July 31, 1830: "henceforth the charter shall be the truth."   p. 56

²² Here and elsewhere quotations are made from Bruno Bauer's anonymous article, "Neueste Schriften über die Judenfrage", which was published in the *Allgemeine Literatur-Zeitung*, Heft I, December 1843. This article was Bruno Bauer's reply to criticism in the press of his book *Die Judenfrage*, Braunschweig, 1843, which was a reprint, with some additions, of his articles on the same subject published in the journal *Deutsche Jahrbücher für Wissenschaft und Kunst* in November 1842.
    Marx gave a critical analysis of this book in his article "On the Jewish Question", which was carried by the *Deutsch-Französische Jahrbücher* (see present edition, Vol.

23*

3). Later Bauer replied to criticism of his book in an article he published in the *Allgemeine Literatur-Zeitung*. In *The Holy Family* Marx ironically designates that article as "The Jewish Question No. 1", and the following articles as "The Jewish Question No. 2" and "The Jewish Question No. 3".   p. 79

[23] Ludwig Feuerbach's "Vorläufige Thesen zur Reformation der Philosophie" was written in January 1842 and prohibited by the censor in Germany. It was published in 1843 in Switzerland in the second volume of the collection, *Anekdota zur neuesten deutschen Philosophie und Publicistik*. This two-volume collection also contained articles by Karl Marx, Bruno Bauer, Friedrich Köppen, Arnold Ruge, and others.
                                                                                      p. 83

[24] *Doctrinaires*—a group of French bourgeois politicians during the Restoration (1815-1830). They were constitutional monarchists, enemies of the democratic and revolutionary movement and wished to unite the bourgeoisie and the nobility. Their ideal was a political system after the English model, formalising these two privileged classes' monopoly of governmental power in opposition to the broad "uneducated" and propertyless sections. The best known Doctrinaires were the historian François Guizot and the philosopher Pierre Paul Royer-Collard. p. 85

[25] Concerning Reply No. 1, Bruno Bauer's first article against critics of his *Die Judenfrage*, see Note 22. In this article Bauer polemises with the authors of a number of reviews on his book, as well as with the authors of books and pamphlets, including the following: *Die Judenfrage von Bruno Bauer näher beleuchtet*, by Dr. Gustav Philippson, Dessau, 1843; *Briefe zur Beleuchtung der Judenfrage von Bruno Bauer*, by Dr. Samuel Hirsch, Leipzig, 1843; *Literaturblatt des Orients*, 1843, No. 25 & ff. (Recension der Judenfrage von Bruno Bauer und der Briefe von Hirsch); *Der Israelit des neunzehnten Jahrhunderts*, published by Dr. M. Hess, 1843, and others.
                                                                                      p. 87

[26] This quotation is from Bruno Bauer's third article in reply to criticisms of his book *Die Judenfrage*. The article, a polemic against Marx and his work "Zur Judenfrage", published in the *Deutsch-Französische Jahrbücher*, was printed anonymously in the *Allgemeine Literatur-Zeitung*, Heft VIII, July 1844, under the title: "Was ist jetzt der Gegenstand der Kritik?" Below Marx resumes his quotations from and criticism of Bruno Bauer's first article, "Neueste Schriften über die Judenfrage" published in the *Allgemeine Literatur-Zeitung*, Heft I, December 1843.   p. 88

[27] The allusion here is to the five Napoleonic codes.   p. 90

[28] Here and elsewhere Marx criticises and quotes Bruno Bauer's review of the first volume of a course of lectures by the right Hegelian Hinrichs: *Politische Vorlesungen*, Bd. I-II, Halle, 1843. This review appeared anonymously in the *Allgemeine Literatur-Zeitung*, Heft I, December 1843. Subsequently the same monthly (Heft V, April 1844) carried Bauer's reviews of the second volume of lectures, which is analysed in the same chapter of *The Holy Family* under the title: "Hinrichs No. 2. 'Criticism' and 'Feuerbach'. Condemnation of Philosophy."
                                                                                      p. 90

[29] Here and elsewhere Engels quotes and analyses Bauer's anonymous review of the second volume of Hinrichs' lectures. The review was printed in the *Allgemeine Literatur-Zeitung*, Heft V, April 1844.   p. 92

[30] Here and elsewhere Marx quotes and analyses Bauer's second article in reply to criticism of his *Die Judenfrage*. It was printed anonymously under the same title as the first—"Neueste Schriften über die Judenfrage"—in the *Allgemeine Literatur-*

Zeitung, Heft IV, March 1844. The article analyses four polemical works, including *Die Judenfrage. Gegen Bruno Bauer,* by Dr. Gabriel Riesser in Hamburg, which appeared in Weil's *Konstitutionelle Jahrbücher*, 1843, Bd. 2 and 3.   p. 94

[31] The reference is to the measures taken by the Convention against speculators in foodstuffs. In September 1793 the Convention decreed the establishment of a general maximum — fixed prices for the main food products and consumer articles; the death penalty was introduced for speculation in and concealment of products.   p. 95

[32] "Was ist jetzt der Gegenstand der Kritik?" was the title of an article by Bruno Bauer printed anonymously in the *Allgemeine Literatur-Zeitung*, Heft VIII, July 1844. It was the third polemical article against critics of his *Die Judenfrage*, in this case primarily against Marx's article "Zur Judenfrage" in the *Deutsch-Französische Jahrbücher*. This article of Bauer's is quoted and analysed by Marx not only under the title "Absolute Criticism's Self-Apology. Its 'Political' Past" but also under the other titles in the section "Absolute Criticism's Third Campaign". p. 99

[33] In January 1843 the Young Hegelians' journal *Deutsche Jahrbücher für Wissenschaft und Kunst*, then appearing in Leipzig (up to July 1841 it had been published in the Prussian town of Halle under the title *Hallische Jahrbücher für Deutsche Wissenschaft und Kunst*), was closed down by the government of Saxony and prohibited throughout Germany by a decree of the Federal Diet. On January 19 of the same year the Prussian Government decided to forbid as of April 1, 1843, the publication of the *Rheinische Zeitung für Politik, Handel und Gewerbe,* which had been appearing in Cologne since January 1, 1842, and which, under the editorship of Marx (from October 1842), had acquired a revolutionary-democratic trend. Marx's resignation from the editorship on March 18, 1843, did not cause the government to rescind its decision, and the last issue appeared on March 31, 1843.   p. 100

[34] Concerning Bruno Bauer's dismissal from the chair of theology, see Note 10. Bauer replied to the Government's repressive measures by the publication in Zurich and Winterthur in 1842 of the pamphlet: *Die gute Sache der Freiheit und meine eigene Angelegenheit.*   p. 103

[35] The reference is to the review by Karl Christian Planck of Bauer's *Kritik der evangelischen Geschichte der Synoptiker*, Bd. 1-2, Leipzig, 1841, Bd. 3, Braunschweig, 1842. ("Synoptics" is the name given in the history of religion to the compilers of the first three Gospels.) The review was published in the *Jahrbücher für wissenschaftliche Kritik*, Berlin, June 1842, Nos. 107-114. Planck disputed Bauer's Young Hegelian theory on the origin of Christianity from the positions of the more moderate criticism of the Gospel sources given by Strauss.   p. 103

[36] Marx has in mind the section of Hegel's book *Phänomenologie des Geistes* entitled "Die Kampf der Aufklärung mit dem Aberglauben".   p. 103

[37] The article in question is Bruno Bauer's "Die Fähigkeit der heutigen Juden und Christen, frei zu werden", which was published in the collection *Einundzwanzig Bogen aus der Schweiz*, Zurich and Winterthur, 1843; along with the book *Die Judenfrage* (an enlarged edition of Bauer's articles on this subject first published in 1842), this article was subjected to a critical analysis by Marx in his article "Zur Judenfrage" in the *Deutsch-Französische Jahrbücher*.   p. 107

[38] The reference is to the attempt to unite the various Lutheran trends by means of the forced *Union of 1817*, when the Lutherans were united with the Reformed

(Calvinist) Church to form the Evangelical Church. The Old Lutherans, who opposed this union, seceded to form their own trend defending the "true" Lutheran Church.   p. 112

[39] The reference is to the policy of de-christianisation pursued in France by Hébert and his supporters in the autumn of 1793. Outwardly it was expressed in the closing of churches and the renunciation of Catholic rites. The forcible methods used to implement these measures outraged believers, especially among the peasants.   p. 114

[40] In their efforts to consolidate the Jacobin dictatorship, Robespierre and his supporters opposed the policy of de-christianisation. A decree of the Convention on December 6, 1793, prohibited "all violence or threats directed against the freedom of worship".   p. 114

[41] *Cercle social*— an organisation established by democratic intellectuals in Paris in the first years of the French Revolution. Its chief spokesman, Claude Fauchet, demanded an equalitarian division of the land, restrictions on large fortunes and employment for all able-bodied citizens. The criticism to which Fauchet and his supporters subjected the formal equality proclaimed in the documents of the French Revolution prepared the ground for bolder action in defence of the destitute by Jacques Roux, Théophile Leclerc and other members of the radical-plebeian *"Enragés".*   p. 119

[42] Marx has in mind the *Histoire parlementaire de la Révolution française,* t. 1-40, Paris, 1834-38, published by the French historian and publicist Ph. J. Buchez jointly with P. C. Roux-Lavergne. It consisted of numerous documents. The introductory articles by Buchez, a former Republican and pupil of Saint-Simon, who adopted the views of Christian Socialism in the 1830s, praised the Jacobins' activity and their revolutionary traditions but censured the steps taken by them against the Catholic clergy.   p. 119

[43] Robespierre's speech, "Rapport sur les principes de morale politique qui doivent guider la Convention nationale dans l'administration intérieure de la République, fait au nom du comité de salut public, à la séance du 5 février (17 Pluviôse) 1794", is quoted according to the German translation of the *Histoire parlementaire de la Révolution française,* by Buchez and Roux-Lavergne, t. 31, Paris, 1837.   p. 121

[44] The report made by Saint-Just in the name of the Committees of Public Safety and of General Security at the Convention's sitting of March 31 (11 Germinal), 1794, is quoted according to the German translation of the *Histoire parlementaire de la Révolution française,* by Buchez and Roux-Lavergne, t. 32, Paris, 1837.   p. 121

[45] The text of the report made by Saint-Just on the police at the Convention's sitting of April 15 (26 Germinal), 1794, was published in the *Histoire parlementaire de la Révolution française,* by Buchez and Roux-Lavergne, t. 32, Paris, 1837.   p. 121

[46] The *Directory*— the regime established in France as a result of the overthrow of the Jacobin government on July 27 (9 Thermidor), 1794, and the introduction on November 4, 1795, by the Thermidor Convention, of a new anti-democratic constitution. Supreme executive power was concentrated in the hands of five Directors. The Directory, whose rule was marked by the flowering of enterprise and speculation, remained in existence until the *coup d'état* of November 9 (18 Brumaire), 1799, which completed the bourgeois counter-revolution and led to the personal rule of General Napoleon Bonaparte.   p. 122

[47] The reference is apparently to the relevant articles in the *Staats-Lexikon, oder Encyklopädie der Staatswissenschaften*, Bd. 1-15, 1834-48, published by the German liberal historian C. Rotteck and the German liberal jurist C. Welcker. Rotteck was also the author of the four-volume *Allgemeine Weltgeschichte für alle Stände, von den frühesten Zeiten bis zum Jahre 1831*, Stuttgart, 1833.   p. 123

[48] The first complete edition of the work of P.J.G. Cabanis appeared in Paris in 1802. But a considerable part had been published in 1798 and 1799 in the Transactions of the French Academy, under the title: *Traité du physique et du moral de l'homme*.
                                                                                  p. 126

[49] The *Jansenists*—named after the Dutch theologian Cornelius Jansen—were an opposition trend among French Catholics in the 17th and early 18th centuries. Their views were vigorously resisted by official Catholicism.   p. 126

[50] A large excerpt from this subsection of *The Holy Family*, beginning with this sentence and ending with the words: "... deism is but an easy-going way of getting rid of religion'" (see p. 129 of this volume), was subsequently included with a few changes by Engels in his Introduction to the 1892 English edition of his *Socialism: Utopian and Scientific*. Accordingly the passage is here given in Engels' translation except for the changes which he made.   p. 127

[51] The *Nominalists* were adherents of a trend in medieval scholasticism, generally considered heretical and dangerous, which maintained that only individual things exist and that generality belongs only to *words*. They criticised the traditional "realist" doctrine, derived from Plato, that universals or "ideas" have real existence above and independent of individual things, and likewise the "conceptualist" view that while universals do not exist outside the mind they do exist in the mind as general conceptions. The doctrine of Nominalism was later forcefully taken up and developed by the English materialist philosopher Thomas Hobbes.
                                                                                  p. 127

[52] *Homoeomeriae*, according to the teaching of the ancient Greek philosopher Anaxagoras, are tiny qualitatively determined material particles which are infinite in number and variety and form the primary basis of all that exists; their combinations constitute all the variety of things.   p. 128

[52a] In his Introduction to the 1892 English edition of his *Socialism: Utopian and Scientific*, Engels gives the following explanation of this term: "'Qual' is a philosophical play upon words. Qual literally means torture, a pain which drives to action of some kind; at the same time the mystic Böhme puts into the German word something of the meaning of the Latin *qualitas*; his 'qual' was the activating principle arising from, and promoting in its turn, the spontaneous development of the thing, relation, or person subject to it, in contradistinction to a pain inflicted from without."   p. 128

[53] Claude Adrien Helvétius, *De l'homme, de ses facultés intellectuelles et de son éducation*, London, 1773. The first edition of this work, published after the author's death, appeared in London due to the efforts of the Russian ambassador in Holland, D.A. Golitsyn.   p. 130

[54] Many of the works by the philosophers mentioned were vigorously denounced by the Church and the Government authorities. La Mettrie's book, *L'homme machine*, published anonymously in Leyden in 1748, was burned and its author was banished

from Holland, where he had emigrated from France in 1745. When the first edition of Holbach's *Système de la Nature, ou des Loix du Monde physique et du Monde moral* was put out in 1770, the name of the author was given as J. B. Mirabeau, secretary of the French Academy who had died in 1760.   p. 130

[55] The first edition of Helvétius' book *De l'esprit* was published anonymously in Paris in 1758 and was burned by the public executioner in 1759.   p. 132

[56] The first edition of Holbach's *Système social, ou principes naturels de la morale et de la politique* was published anonymously in three volumes in 1773.   p. 133

[57] This is an allusion to the hostile campaign conducted for a number of years by the conservative Augsburg *Allgemeine Zeitung* against socialism and communism. In October 1842, this paper accused the *Rheinische Zeitung*, whose editor was Marx, of spreading communist views. In reply Marx published his article "Communism and the Augsburg *Allgemeine Zeitung*" (see present edition, Vol. 1). p. 134

[58] The reference is to members of a political grouping which formed in France around the newspaper *La Réforme* (see Note 16). One of the leaders of this grouping, the petty-bourgeois Socialist Louis Blanc, put out in 1839-40 a pamphlet entitled *L'organisation du travail*, which became widely known.   p. 135

[59] This is an ironic allusion to the ancient Roman tradition about the geese whose cackling saved Rome in 390 B.C. by waking the guards at the approach of the Gauls who had laid siege to the Capitol.   p. 135

[60] The quotation is taken from Bruno Bauer's review of the book *Leben und Wirken Friedrich von Sallet's, nebst Mittheilungen aus dem literarischen Nachlasse Desselben*, Breslau, 1844. The review was published anonymously in the *Allgemeine Literatur-Zeitung*, Heft VIII, July 1844.   p. 138

[61] Below Marx gives excerpts from the following reports: Zerrleder, "Correspondenz aus Bern" (*Allgemeine Literatur-Zeitung*, Heft III, February 1844, Heft VI, May 1844); E. Fleischhammer, "Correspondenz aus Breslau" (ibid., Heft IV, March 1844); Hirzel, "Correspondenz aus Zürich" (ibid., Heft IV, March 1844, Heft V, April 1844); "Correspondenz aus der Provinz" (ibid., Heft VI, May 1844). p. 145

[62] Bruno Bauer's reply (on behalf of the paper's editorial board) to the Tübingen correspondent was published in the *Allgemeine Literatur-Zeitung*, Heft VI, May 1844, under the heading "Correspondenz aus der Provinz". Excerpts from the reports published under this heading in the same issue are given below. p. 146

[63] *Berlin Couleur* was the name by which the correspondent of the *Allgemeine Literatur-Zeitung* mentioned above designated the Berlin Young Hegelians who did not belong to Bruno Bauer's group and criticised the *Allgemeine Literatur-Zeitung* on a number of petty points. Max Stirner was one of them.

The excerpts quoted in this and the concluding subsection of the chapter are from the anonymous letters published under the heading "Correspondenz aus der Provinz" in the *Allgemeine Literatur-Zeitung*, Heft VI, May 1844, as are also the editors' replies to these letters.   p. 149

[64] By the "philosophy of identity" is meant Schelling's early philosophical views which he expounded at the beginning of the 19th century. These views were based on the idea of the absolute identity of thinking and being, consciousness and matter as the root of everything which exists. These views represented a transitional stage in the

development of German classical philosophy, from the subjective idealism of Fichte to the absolute idealism of Hegel. But Schelling himself, in whose philosophical outlook religiosity and mysticism later came to dominate, not only condemned Hegel's philosophy in his subsequent pronouncements, and particularly in his lectures on the "Philosophy of Revelation" in Berlin University in 1841-42 (which were critically analysed by the young Engels in his pamphlet *Schelling and Revelation*); he even renounced the rational elements of his own "philosophy of identity" (see present edition, Vol. 2). p. 154

[65] The reference is to F. Gruppe's pamphlet *Bruno Bauer und die akademische Lehrfreiheit*, Berlin, 1842, directed against Bruno Bauer and the Young Hegelians. Marx had criticised this polemical pamphlet, which was written from a conservative standpoint (see present edition, Vol. 1, pp. 211-14). p. 157

[66] The reference is to the article "Emigranten und Märtyrer. Ein Beitrag zur Charakteristik der *Deutsch-Französischen Jahrbücher*", by H. L. Egidius, published in the journal *Konstitutionelle Jahrbücher*, 1844, Bd. II. p. 162

[67] The quotations from Fourier's works *Le nouveau monde industriel et sociétaire*, *Théorie des quatre mouvements et des destinées, générales* (the first edition was published in 1808) are given by Marx in his own translation and the quotation from *Théorie de l'unité universelle* is in French. p. 196

[68] Marx had in mind Théodore Dézamy, Jules Gay and their supporters, whose materialistic outlook he characterised in Chapter VI of *The Holy Family* (see p. 131 of this volume). The revolutionary and materialistic trend of French utopian communism included also the secret Babouvist societies of the 1840s influenced by Dézamy: the *"travailleurs égalitaires"*, which consisted mainly of workers and published the journal *l'Égalitaire*, and the *"humanitaires"*, supporters of the journal *l'Humanitaire*. In 1843 Engels wrote about the criticism of bourgeois marriage and family relations by representatives of these societies in his article "Progress of Social Reform on the Continent" (see present edition, Vol. 3, p. 392) p. 196

[69] This is an allusion to the leading role played by K. H. Sack, a professor of Bonn University, in the campaign waged by reactionary theological circles against the Young Hegelians, which began in connection with Bruno Bauer's transfer as a privat-dozent from Berlin to Bonn in 1839. Especially sharp attacks were made against Bauer's criticism of the Gospel sources and the atheistic conclusions following from his views on the origin of Christianity. In March 1842, Bauer was dismissed from Bonn University. The theological opponents of the Young Hegelians were ridiculed in Engels' satirical poem "The Insolently Threatened Yet Miraculously Rescued Bible", in which Sack figures under the ironical name of Beutel (in German, *Sack* means sack, *Beutel*—pouch) (see present edition, Vol. 2, pp. 313-51). p. 203

[70] The reference is to the petty German princes who lost their power and saw their possessions annexed by larger German states as a result of the reshaping of the political map of Germany during the Napoleonic wars and at the Vienna Congress (1814-15). p. 203

[71] *"Young England"* was a group of conservative writers and politicians, including Disraeli and Lord John Manners, who were close to the Tory philanthropists and formed a separate group in the House of Commons in 1841. Voicing the landed

aristocracy's dissatisfaction at the political and economic strengthening of the bourgeoisie, they criticised the capitalist system and supported half-hearted philanthropic measures for improving the condition of the workers. "Young England" disintegrated as a political group in 1845 and ceased to exist as a literary trend in 1848. In the *Manifesto of the Communist Party* Marx and Engels characterised the views of "Young England" as "feudal socialism" (see present edition, Vol. 6). See Engels' characterisation of it in the footnote on p. 578 of this volume.　　　　　　　　　　　　　　　　　　　　　　　　　　　　　　　p. 205

[72] Engels' article on "Continental Socialism" was written in the form of a private letter, which the addressee forwarded to the editorial office of the weekly *The New Moral World*, preceded and followed by accompanying texts (it appeared in this form in the paper). However, there are grounds for assuming that the introductory and concluding texts, written in the third person, were also written by Engels, who had his reasons for resorting to this indirect way of publishing his writings. This assumption is supported by the fact that the accompanying text is signed with the pen-name "Anglo-German", most probably pointing to Engels, who had lived some two years in England and had a good knowledge of conditions there. Apparently the note to the text of the letter was also by Engels.　　　　　　　　　　　　　　　　　　　　　　　　　　　　　p. 212

[73] *Ham Common folks*—a group of English Utopian Socialists who organised the Concordium Colony at Ham Common, near London, in 1842; followers of the English mystic James Pierrepont Greaves (1777-1842), the Ham Common Socialists preached moral perfection and an ascetic way of life; the colony broke up after only a short existence.　　　　　　　　　　　　　　　　　　　　　　p. 212

[74] The reference is to the attempt made by France during her conquest of Algeria to bring neighbouring Morocco also under her control. In August 1844, accusing the Sultan of Morocco of helping Abd-el-Kader, the chief of the Algerian tribes who were resisting French rule, the French started hostilities against Morocco. The Sultan was defeated and forced to cease his assistance to Abd-el-Kader and in 1845 sign a treaty advantageous to France.　　　　　　　　　　　　　　　　　　p. 212

[75] The "Description of Recently Founded Communist Colonies Still in Existence" was compiled by Engels on the basis of materials published in *The New Moral World*, *The Northern Star* and other publications. The main source was a series of 29 letters written by the Owenite John Finch and published in *The New Moral World* between January 13 and October 19, 1844, under the title "Notes of Travel in the United States". Engels gives some excerpts from Finch's letters in his own, rather free, German translation and italicises certain words and passages (the features of his method of quoting are taken into account in the present edition). In describing the communist colony of Harmony Hall in Hampshire, which was founded by Owen's followers in 1841 and existed until the beginning of 1846, Engels drew on Somerville's essay *A Journey to Harmony Hall, in Hampshire; with some particulars of the Socialist Community, to which the attention of the Nobility, Gentry and Clergy is earnestly requested*. This essay was published in *The Morning Chronicle* on December 13, 1842, and signed "One who has whistled at the Plough".

　　Engels' "Description" was published in the annual *Deutsches Bürgerbuch für 1845* without any signature. Engels' authorship is confirmed by his own reference to this material in a series of articles on the progress of communism in Germany published in the spring of 1845 in *The New Moral World* (see p. 240 of this volume).　　　　　　　　　　　　　　　　　　　　　　　　　　　　　　　p. 214

[76] The quotation is taken from the correspondence of Lawrence Pitkeithly of Huddersfield, "Where to, and how to proceed. Description of the Shaker Villages" (*The Northern Star* No. 286, May 6, 1843). p. 217

[77] The *Unitarians* (or *Anti-Trinitarians*) reject the dogma of the "Holy Trinity". The Unitarian Church first arose in England and America in the 17th century, and its teachings emphasise the moral and ethical side of the Christian religion in contrast to its external ritualist aspect. p. 223

[78] The series of articles "Rapid Progress of Communism in Germany" was Engels' last contribution to the London Owenite weekly *The New Moral World*. The series was written in the form of three letters to the editors, and printed in that form in the newspaper, only the first of them bearing a title. The numbering of the articles in the present edition is by the editors. p. 229

[79] The riot of the Silesian weavers took place on June 2-4, 1844, and was described by Marx in his article, "Critical Marginal Notes on the Article 'The King of Prussia and Social Reform. By a Prussian'", and by Engels in his reports "News from Prussia", and "Further Particulars of the Silesian Riots" (see present edition, Vol. 3). Soon after the Silesian events, in the second half of June 1844, there was a rising of textile workers in Prague, which led to workers' uprisings in a number of other Bohemian industrial areas, including Reichenberg (now called Liberec) and Böhmisch Leipa (now called Česka Lipa). The workers' movement, which was accompanied by the wrecking of factories and the destruction of machinery, was suppressed by government troops. p. 230

[80] The reference is to the article "Ein 'socialistischer' Spuk", which was published unsigned in a supplement to the *Kölnische Zeitung* No. 314, November 9, 1844. p. 231

[81] The translation was made by Engels after the earlier version of Heine's poem "Die Schlesischen Weber". Unlike the text first published in the newspaper *Vorwärts!* No. 55, July 10, 1844, the first stanza of this translation has an additional line, the third. A later version, edited by the author, with the additional, fifth stanza, was published in 1847. p. 232

[82] In *The New Moral World* the letter was dated February 22. But Engels reports on events which he witnessed or took part in between February 2 and 22, in particular the communist meeting at Elberfeld on February 8, not in this, but in the following article of the series (see pp. 237-38 of this volume). Hence either the dating is a misprint, or else was deliberately changed by the editors in order to disguise the time lag between the writing of the article and its publication. p. 234

[83] The reference is to the "*Associations for the Benefit of the Working Classes*" which were formed in a number of Prussian towns in 1844-45 on the initiative of the German liberal bourgeoisie, which had been alarmed by the *rising of the Silesian weavers*, in the summer of 1844 (see Note 79). They hoped by this means to divert the German workers from militant forms of struggle. But despite the efforts of the bourgeoisie and the governmental authorities to give these associations an innocent and philanthropical appearance, their establishment only gave fresh impetus to the urban masses' political activity and drew the attention of broad sections of German society to the social question. The scope of the movement to establish such associations was especially great in the towns of the industrial Rhine province, where the antagonisms between the bourgeoisie and the proletariat were acute and Prussian absolutism was faced with a radical-democratic opposition. The revolu-

tionary-democratic intelligentsia used meetings called to set up associations and discuss their statutes for the purpose of popularising radical ideas and counteracting the influence of the clergy and the liberal bourgeoisie. Seeing that the associations had taken so unlooked for a direction, the Prussian Government hastily cut short their activity in the spring of 1845 by refusing to approve their statutes and forbidding them to continue their work.

In *Elberfeld* in November 1844 an Educational Society was founded. From the very beginning its organisers had to fight attempts by the local clergy to bring it under their influence and give its activity a religious colouring. Engels and his friends wished to use the society's meetings and its committee to spread communist views. The statute of the society was not approved by the authorities and the society itself ceased to exist in the spring of 1845. p. 234

84 The reference is to the annual *Deutsches Bürgerbuch für 1845*, established in Darmstadt by the radical publicist H. Püttmann in December 1844. Besides several articles of the German or "true" socialist trend which was then emerging, the journal carried works by such revolutionary-democratic writers as W. Wolff and the poet G. Weerth. It also contained Engels' essay "Description of Recently Founded Communist Colonies Still in Existence" (see pp. 214-28 of this volume and Note 75). The next issue of the *Deutsches Bürgerbuch*, which appeared in Mannheim in the summer of 1846, contained Engels' translation of "A Fragment of Fourier's on Trade", which he made in summer and autumn 1845, with an introduction and a conclusion censuring for the first time the tendencies inherent in "true socialism" (see pp. 613, 642-43 of this volume). The "true Socialists" and the publications spreading their views, among them the *Deutsches Bürgerbuch*, were later criticised in detail by Marx and Engels in *The German Ideology* and other works (see present edition, Vol. 5). p. 235

85 What is meant is the prospectus of H. Püttmann's projected journal *Rheinische Jahrbücher zur gesellschaftlichen Reform*. Only two issues appeared, the first in Darmstadt in August 1845, the second in the small town of Bellevue, on the German-Swiss border, at the end of 1846. Marx and Engels used them to spread their communist views in Germany. The first issue carried the texts of Engels' speeches at meetings in Elberfeld on February 8 and 15, 1845 (see pp. 243-64 of this volume), and the second contained his article "Festival of Nations in London" (see present edition, Vol. 6). It was for this journal that Marx prepared in the spring of 1845 a long article on the German economist List (see pp. 265-93 of this volume). However, the journal was dominated by the "true Socialists", and Marx and Engels afterwards severely criticised it in *The German Ideology* (see present edition, Vol. 5). p. 235

86 The reference is to the monthly *Gesellschaftsspiegel*. Engels helped to organise this publication and compile its prospectus (see pp. 671-74 of this volume), but did not become one of its editors. The journal, which began to appear in 1845 in Elberfeld, edited by M. Hess, carried in January 1846 Marx's article "Peuchet: On Suicide" (see pp. 597-612 of this volume). But articles by "true Socialists" predominated. p. 235

87 On January 16, 1845, the French authorities decided to banish from France Marx, Heine, Bürgers, Bakunin and other contributors to *Vorwärts!* The Prussian Government had already made repeated attempts to persuade the Guizot cabinet to close down the paper, and had launched a campaign against it in the reactionary press. Under pressure from public opinion the French Government was forced to

annul its decision to expel Heine. But, on February 3, Marx was obliged to leave Paris and settle in Brussels.

Before his departure, on February 1, 1845, Marx concluded a contract with the Darmstadt publisher K.F.J. Leske for the publication of his two-volume work *Kritik der Politik und Nationalökonomie* (see the Appendices to this volume).   p. 235

[88] The reference is to the collection *Neue Anekdota*, which was published in Darmstadt in May 1845. It contained newspaper articles by M. Hess, K. Grün, O. Lüning and others, written mainly in the first half of 1844, which had been banned by the censor. Soon after the publication of the collection, Marx and Engels made a number of severely critical remarks about its contents, as can be seen from Grün's letters to Hess.   p. 241

[89] The reference is to the projected publication in German of the "Library of the Best Foreign Socialist Writers", which, as we learn from Engels' letters to Marx from Barmen in February and March 1845, was repeatedly discussed by the two friends.

A list, written by Marx, of authors whose works he proposed for inclusion in the "Library" is still extant (see p. 667 of this volume). But the project was not realised. The only work completed was "A Fragment of Fourier's on Trade" compiled by Engels with an introduction and a conclusion by him (see pp. 613-44 of this volume).   p. 241

[90] "*Secret offices*" or "black offices" were establishments under the postal departments in France, Prussia, Austria and a number of other countries to deal with the inspection of correspondence. They had been in existence since the time of the absolute monarchies in Europe.   p. 241

[91] On February 8, 15 and 22, 1845, meetings to discuss communism were held in Elberfeld and aroused considerable public interest. The second and third meetings attracted especially large attendances — from 130 to 200. Discussion of lectures and of readings from socialist literature, including poetry by Shelley and other authors, lasted many hours. As well as socialist-minded intellectuals, the audiences consisted largely of bourgeois from Barmen and Elberfeld with a sprinkling of visitors from other towns in the Rhine province of Prussia (Cologne and Düsseldorf). "All of Elberfeld and Barmen, from the monied aristocracy to small shopkeepers, were represented, the proletariat being the only exception," Engels wrote to Marx on February 22 about the third meeting, which had just taken place. He also described the two preceding ones. The meetings upset the local authorities, who took steps to put an end to public discussions on the subject.

Engels spoke on February 8 and 15. On February 22 excerpts were read from the essay on Communist Colonies which he had compiled and published about that time (see pp. 214-28 of this volume). An account of the meetings is included in the third report in his series on the progress of communism in Germany, published in *The New Moral World* (see pp. 237-39 of this volume).

The texts of Engels' speeches, prepared for publication by the author, were published together with excerpts from other speakers (M. Hess, G. A. Köttgen) in August 1845 in the first issue of *Rheinische Jahrbücher zur gesellschaftlichen Reform* (pp. 45-62 and 71-86). The title "Speeches in Elberfeld" has been taken from Engels' letter to Marx on March 17, 1845, in which he himself uses it.   p. 243

[92] In 1892 Engels returned, in the Preface to the English edition of *The Condition of the Working-Class in England*, to the problem of the cyclical character of economic crises in the early 19th century. "The recurring period of the great industrial crises

is stated in the text as five years," he wrote. "This was the period apparently indicated by the course of events from 1825 to 1842. But the industrial history from 1842 to 1868 has shown that the real period is one of ten years; that the intermediate revulsions were secondary, and tended more and more to disappear."
p. 245

93 See Note 79.   p. 254

94 *The Customs Union (Zollverein)* of the German states (initially they numbered 18), which established a common customs frontier, was founded in 1834 and headed by Prussia. By the 1840s the Union embraced most of the German states, with the exception of Austria, the Hansa cities (Bremen, Lubeck, Hamburg) and a few small states. Brought into being by the demand for an all-German market, the Customs Union contributed to Germany's eventual political unification.   p. 258

95 In 1842, as a result of the so-called first Opium War, which Britain had been waging against China since 1839, the unequal Nanking Treaty was imposed; one of the clauses envisaged the opening to English trade of five Chinese cities: Canton, Shanghai, Amoy, Ninbo and Fuchou.   p. 261

96 This work—a draft of an article against the German economist Friedrich List—was recently discovered among Marx's manuscripts which remained for a long time in the keeping of the grandchildren of his eldest daughter, Jenny Longuet. Marx and Engels had reacted critically to List's book (published in 1841) as early as February 1844 in the *Deutsch-Französische Jahrbücher* (see present edition, Vol. 3, 178, 421). Later they concluded that a full-scale criticism should be published of his views as typifying the attitudes of the German bourgeoisie—its striving for complete freedom of action to exploit the German workers without prejudice to the privileges of the nobility and its support of the feudal-monarchical political system while seeking to force the government to protect bourgeois interests against foreign competition. In a letter to Marx on November 19, 1844, Engels mentioned that he intended writing a pamphlet on List, and in another letter, on March 17, 1845, he greatly approved of Marx's own plans to publish in the journal *Rheinische Jahrbücher zur gesellschaftlichen Reform*, projected by Püttmann, a critical analysis of List's views. In his pamphlet Engels proposed to expand the critical remarks on List's practical suggestions (introduction of a protective system) which he had made in the second of his "Speeches in Elberfeld" (see pp. 258-62 of this volume). However, Engels did not write that pamphlet.

Neither did Marx's article on List appear in print. The extant drafts of the manuscript, abounding in abbreviations, erasures, corrections and insertions, are incomplete. The first sheet, apparently containing the author's title of the article and of the first chapter, is missing. Sheets 10-21 and 22 have also not been found. The extant part consists of large-size sheets numbered by Marx himself. Of these, numbers 2-5, containing four pages of text each, and sheet 6, containing text on the first three pages, belong to the first chapter. Following them is a small fragment on a separate unnumbered sheet. The second chapter, with the author's title, has reached us more complete and comprises sheets 7-9, containing four pages each. Of the third chapter only sheet 22 (two fragments filling two pages) and sheet 24 (four pages of text) are extant. The fourth chapter has the author's title and fills one unnumbered sheet (four pages).

In his manuscript Marx analyses and quotes the first volume of List's book according to the 1841 edition—Friedrich List, *Das nationale System der politischen Oekonomie. Erster Band. Der internationale Handel, die Handelspolitik und der deutsche*

Zollverein, Stuttgart and Tübingen, 1841. At the beginning of 1845 Marx made numerous excerpts from this edition which he used in his work. He quotes French sources in his own German translation, with the exception of one excerpt, from a work by Louis Say, which he purposely quotes in French to show List's deliberately inaccurate way of quoting. The emphasis in the quotations belongs for the most part to Marx.

In publishing the work in this edition, obvious slips of the pen in the manuscript have been corrected, editorial insertions have been made (in square brackets) where meaning might otherwise be obscure and some passages have been divided into paragraphs additional to those given by the author. Where the author's titles to chapters are missing, titles (in square brackets) have been supplied by the editors. The numbers of the sheets in the manuscript are given in Arab figures in square brackets. Words and phrases crossed out in the manuscript are not reproduced, although some of them have been taken into account in deciphering illegible passages. In the second chapter a number of paragraphs were crossed out by the author with a vertical line. Marx usually did that when he was using the crossed out passage in another place or in another variant of the work. Since the pages of the manuscript to which these passages could have been transferred are missing, the passages crossed out are reproduced in the context in question in angle brackets.

p. 265

[97] The word "obstacle" is written in the manuscript over the word "inconvenience". And later in the text Marx repeatedly uses this method of proposing variants. In the translation such words are given in brackets after the word over which the variant is written.   p. 265

[98] A *Molossus* in ancient prosody was a foot of three long syllables (———). Marx uses the term ironically to describe List's heavy style.   p. 266

[99] In numbering this point 3 Marx probably made a slip, since the preceding point is also numbered 3. The next point in the manuscript is numbered 4 (see below, p. 273).   p. 267

[100] The *Tribunate* was one of the four legislative institutions introduced in France by the Constitution of 1799 after the *coup d'état* of 18-19 Brumaire (9-10 November), 1799, which established the dictatorship of Napoleon Bonaparte. The Tribunate was abolished in 1807.   p. 270

[101] The *Notice historique sur la vie et les ouvrages de J.-B. Say* was prefaced to the seventh, supplementary, volume of Say's course in Political Economy, which was published soon after the author's death under the title: *Cours complet d'économie politique pratique. Volume complémentaire. Mélanges et correspondance d'économie politique; ouvrage posthume de J.-B. Say, publié par Charles Comte, son gendre*, Paris, 1833. Marx quotes with abridgments separate passages from pp. iii-xii of the "Notice historique" by Charles Comte.   p. 270

[102] *The Anti-Corn Law League*—see Note 5.

The movement for land reform, free allotment of plots to every worker and other democratic reforms arose in the 1840s in the United States of America and was headed by the National Reform Association.   p. 272

[103] Ironical allusions to List's arguments and use of words. The words enclosed in inverted commas by Marx — "freie, mächtige und reiche Bürger" — allude to List's expression "das Aufkommen eines freien, industriellen und reichen

Bürgertums" (the rise of a free, industrial and rich bourgeoisie) on page lxvi of his book. On page lxiv List claims credit for having shown the German gentry how profitable for them was the existence of an industrial bourgeoisie "zealously" working to increase the rents of their estates.   p. 272

[104] *"Confederation"* is one of List's favourite words. He speaks of "the confederation of various activities", "the confederation of various knowledge", "the confederation of various forces" (see List, op. cit., p. 223).   p. 275

[105] On page 208 of his book, List illustrates his teaching on productive forces and exchange values by the example of two fathers, each of whom has five sons and owns an estate bringing 1,000 talers net annual income in excess of what he expends to support his family. One of them places his 1,000 talers in a bank at interest and forces his sons to perform hard unskilled labour; the other uses his 1,000 talers to give his sons a higher education, so that they become highly skilled agronomists or engineers. According to List, the first father shows concern for the increase of exchange values, the second for the increase of productive forces. On page 209 List speaks of the Christian religion and monogamy as "rich sources of productive force".   p. 277

[106] List says: "Workshops and factories are the mothers and children of civic freedom, education, the arts and sciences...."   p. 277

[107] Below Marx makes clear that he understands "the abolition of labour" to mean the elimination of the existing forms of exploitation of labour, the enslavement and alienation of the working man, and emphasises the need to create social conditions under which industrial labour and industry would cease to be an object and instrument of oppression but would serve as a means for man to use his capacities and to master the forces of nature (see pp. 280-82 of this volume).   p. 279

[108] An allusion to the expression "industrial education", which is frequently used by List.   p. 282

[109] By *manufacturing force* ("die Manufakturkraft") List understands the productive power of factory industry. But he often uses this expression simply in the sense of factory industry.   p. 284

[110] An allusion to List's statement that his "theory of the productive forces" should be *worked out scientifically* ("wissenschaftlich auszubilden sei") side by side with "the theory of exchange values" developed by the "Smith-Say school" (List, op. cit., p. 187).   p. 284

[111] The reference is to List's argument, in Chapter 24 of his book, about the importance of "continuity" and "uninterruptedness of production" in the development of factory industry, the preservation and perfection of its technical means and the production skills of the workers. In comparing these arguments with those of J. F. Bray, Marx had in mind the latter's book, *Labour's Wrongs and Labour's Remedy; or the Age of Might and the Age of Right*, Leeds, 1839, which proved the injustice of the hereditary property of capitalists and landowners as non-productive and parasitic classes. In *The Poverty of Philosophy* (1847) Marx characterised Bray's views as communist (see present edition, Vol. 6).   p. 288

[112] The term *costs of production* ("Produktionskosten") is used by Marx in the sense of value of the product.   p. 288

113 See Note 5.   p. 289

114 The *Methuen Treaty* was a trade treaty concluded on December 27, 1703, between England and Portugal (by Lord Methuen for the English)—allies in the War of Spanish Succession (fought by the Anglo-Austro-Dutch coalition against France and Spain). The treaty opened wide access in Portugal for English woollens, in return for which Portugal received the right to export its wines to England on privileged terms. In his book List emphasised that this treaty was unfavourable to Portugal.   p. 293

115 Engels' plans to produce a big work on the social history of England were formed while he was still living in that country (from November 1842 to August 1844). Initially he intended to implement them in the form of a series of articles in the *Deutsch-Französische Jahrbücher* under the general title of *The Condition of England*. The February 1844 issue of the journal carried the first article in this series, and the other articles were published later in the Paris *Vorwärts!* (August-October, 1844—see present edition, Vol. 3) since the *Deutsch-Französische Jahrbücher* had ceased to be published. The series, however, remained incomplete. In the articles he wrote Engels was able merely to touch upon his main theme—the condition of the working class in England. He intended to amplify it later in one of the central chapters of his intended book on the social history of England, but in the end his realisation of the proletariat's special role in bourgeois society prompted him to make the condition of the English working class the object of a special study.

Upon his return to Barmen early in September 1844, Engels at once set about the accomplishment of his revised plan, using material he had collected while in England. "I am buried up to the neck in English newspapers and books from which I am compiling my book on the condition of English proletarians", he informed Marx on November 19, 1844. In January 1845 the work was appreciably advanced and, informing Marx of this on January 20, Engels told him of his intention to start, once it was finished, on a new work: *On the Historical Development of England and English Socialism*. In mid-March 1845 the manuscript was completed and sent to the Leipzig publisher Wigand. It appeared at the beginning of June 1845, when Engels had already moved to Brussels, where Marx, banished from France, had been since February of that year.

The response in the German press was lively. Many newspapers and journals, in particular the *Allgemeine Preussische Zeitung*, the *Allgemeine Literatur-Zeitung*, the *Janus. Jahrbücher deutscher Gesinnung, Bildung und That*, 1845, the *Gesellschaftsspiegel*, Jg. 1845, and a number of others carried reviews of the book. And in socialist circles it was received with great approval. Weydemeyer wrote that Engels' book was "without doubt one of the most important phenomena in our recent literature" ("Dies Buch gehört dem Volke", 1845). O. Lüning noted that the book instilled not only "hatred of and wrath against the oppressors", but also "a feeling of hope and faith in the final victory of reason and justice, in the eternal reason of mankind, which, despite all dangers and storms, will secure a beautiful future" (*Deutsches Bürgerbuch für 1846*). Revolutionary workers were educated on Engels' book. F. Lessner, a German worker who subsequently became an active member of the Communist League, recalled, for example, that it "was the first book I acquired and from which I first obtained an idea of the working-class movement".

Bourgeois critics, while acknowledging the accurate observation and the literary merit of the book, nevertheless deplored its revolutionary conclusions. Thus, in a review of recent literature published in the Berlin journal *Janus*.

Jahrbücher deutscher Gesinnung, in 1845 (Bd. 2, Heft 18), Professor F. A. H. Huber accused the author of making his work "a call for murder and arson written with bile, blood and passion". The polemic over Engels' book continued in the following years. For instance, the prominent German economist B. Hildebrand devoted to its analysis a considerable part of his work *Die Nationalökonomie oder Gegenwart und Zukunft*, Frankfurt am Main, 1848. Acknowledging the author's talent and the originality of his research, this critic took great exception to his communist ideas and declared his characterisation of English bourgeois society to be true in detail but incorrect as a whole.

Engels' book became well known also outside Germany. As early as July 1845, a few weeks after it was published, reviews appeared in Russia (*Literaturnaya Gazeta* No. 25, July 5, 1845). Engels' work was highly rated by revolutionary democrats. N. V. Shelgunov, in an article published in the journal *Sovremennik* in 1861, demonstrated the groundlessness of Hildebrand's attacks on Engels, whom he called "one of the best and noblest of Germans". The article summarised with approval the main content of Engels' work (*Sovremennik*, LXXXV, Sec. 1).

Marx, in his own economic researches, based himself in many respects on the material and conclusions of his friend's work, which he quoted in many passages of *Capital*. But later, Engels himself was very critical of his book. Acknowledging that it was written with genuinely youthful inspiration, "freshly and passionately, with bold anticipation" (see his letter to Marx of April 9, 1863), he at the same time found in it certain weaknesses typical of the initial stage in the development of scientific communism.

In later editions he took steps to warn the reader of its shortcomings. Thus, in the Appendix to the American edition (1887), which was included in the Preface to the English and German editions of 1892, Engels wrote: "... This book exhibits everywhere the traces of the descent of modern Socialism from one of its ancestors—the German philosophy. Thus great stress is laid on the dictum that Communism is not a mere party doctrine of the working class, but a theory compassing the emancipation of society at large, including the capitalist class, from its present narrow conditions. This is true enough in the abstract, but absolutely useless, and sometimes worse, in practice. So long as the wealthy classes not only do not feel the want of any emancipation, but strenuously oppose the self-emancipation of the working class, so long the social revolution will have to be prepared and fought out by the working class alone." Engels went on to explain why his assumption in 1845 that the social revolution in England was imminent had not been borne out. Among the causes for this he emphasised the decline of Chartism after 1848 and the temporary preponderance of reformist tendencies in the English working-class movement—bred out of England's industrial monopoly on the world market, which had turned out to be much more lasting than he had assumed.

The Condition of the Working-Class in England had several editions during the author's lifetime. As early as 1848, Wigand's publishing house in Leipzig put out a new impression of the work, marked "Second Edition" on the title page, although it was merely a reprint of the first.

The book was published in English for the first time in New York in 1887 in a translation made by the American Socialist Florence Kelley-Wischnewetzky. The American edition is the authorised one. Engels edited the translation, made a number of changes in the text, omitted the address "To the Working-Classes of Great-Britain" and the Preface to the first German edition of 1845, and provided the book with the new Preface of 1887 addressed to the American reader together with an Afterword (the Appendix written in 1886) dealing with changes that had since taken place in the condition of the English working class. He included in this Afterword the text of the article "England in 1845 and in 1885", which he had written in 1885. The title of the book was altered to *The Condition of the Working-Class in England in 1844*; in the table of contents only the titles of the chapters were preserved, without the enumeration of the questions discussed in them which had appeared in the German edition of 1845 (at the same time a short subject index was added); some drawings and the plan of Manchester were omitted, a number of references to sources in the text were given as footnotes, etc.

The text of the American edition was reproduced almost without change in the authorised English edition which was published in London in 1892. Engels wrote another special Preface, including in it almost without change the Afterword to the American edition of 1887, while the Preface for American readers was omitted. In the same year the Dietz publishing house in Stuttgart published the authorised second German edition, the text of which reproduced in the main that of 1845. Engels wrote for it a new Preface, identical on the whole with that of the 1892 English edition, but with additions in the concluding part and a number of new footnotes.

The present edition reproduces the English translation made by Florence Kelley-Wischnewetzky and edited by Engels himself. This text has also been collated with the original German edition and the major different readings affecting the meaning are given as footnotes. Some parts of the text which were omitted by Engels when he edited the English translation (for instance, the address to the English reader, the Preface to the first edition, the poem "The Steam King" by Edward Mead, the enumeration of subjects in the table of contents, etc.) have been restored according to the German edition, the relevant indications being given in footnotes or Notes at the end of the volume. The title of the book has also been given according to the first edition. Slips and omissions made by Florence Wischnewetzky have been corrected; in particular, she did not have at her disposal a number of English sources used by Engels and she gave quotations from them in retranslation from the German (in the American and English editions of 1887 and 1892 this was specially mentioned in the Translator's Note). In the present edition the texts of English sources quoted by Engels have been given according to the original, taking into account the author's method of quoting (abridgments, re-arrangement of the text, and so on). Errors in dates and in names of persons and places have been corrected, account being taken of the corrections introduced in the book: Engels, *The Condition of the Working Class in England*. Translated and edited by W. O. Henderson and W. H. Chaloner, New York, 1958. Use has been made of some original texts from rare sources quoted in the above-mentioned edition.

The author's prefaces to subsequent editions and the Afterword to the American edition of 1887 will be included in the relevant volumes of the present edition according to the dates of their writing.　　　　　　　　　　　p. 295

[116] The address "To the Working-Classes of Great-Britain" was written by Engels in English with the intention, as he informed Marx in his letter of November 19, 1844, of having it printed separately and sent to "English party leaders, literary men and Members of Parliament". In the 1845 and 1892 German editions of *The Condition of the Working-Class in England* the address was reproduced in English; it was not included in the American (1887) and English (1892) editions. In the present volume it is reproduced according to the German edition of 1892.　　　　　　　　　　　p. 297

[117] Engels' Preface to the first German edition of his book was not reproduced in the American (1887) or the English (1892) edition. However, it was included in the 1892 German edition. In the present volume it is given in translation from the German editions published in the author's lifetime. p. 302

[118] This intention was not carried out, although in the ensuing years, up to the beginning of the 1848 Revolution, Engels several times returned to it. During his stay in Brussels from April 1845 to August 1846, and in the following months, which he spent in Paris, Engels continued collecting material on England in addition to what he had collected in the preceding years. In July and August 1845, during trips to London and Manchester with Marx, he researched on this subject in the libraries of those cities. Three notebooks are extant, full of bibliographical notes and excerpts from originals (G. R. Porter, *The Progress of the Nation,* Vol. III, London, 1843; N. Godwin, *History of the Commonwealth of England,* Vol. I, London, 1824; T. Tooke, *A History of Prices,* Vol. II, London, 1838; F. M. Eden, *The State of the Poor,* Vols. I-III, London, 1797; [J. Aikin], *A Description of the Country from thirty to forty Miles round Manchester,* London, 1795; J. Butterworth, *The Antiquities of the Town, and a Complete History of the Trade of Manchester,* Manchester, 1822; J. W. Gilbart, *The History and Principles of Banking,* London, 1834, etc. For greater detail see Marx/Engels, *Gesamtausgabe,* Abt. 1, Bd. 4, S. 503-15). By the end of 1847 Engels' work had apparently made considerable headway; a short article printed on November 14 that year in the *Deutsche Brüsseler Zeitung,* with which Engels and Marx collaborated, mentioned his intention to put out a book under the title *On the History of the English Bourgeoise.* But this plan was not carried out. Nevertheless, in his articles and reports of those years Engels constantly touched upon various aspects of the social and political history of England. p. 302

[119] See Note 83. p. 303

[120] See Note 79. p. 304

[121] Actually, the first iron bridge in England was built in 1779 in Shropshire, over the Severn at Coalbrookdale. The bridge constructed according to Thomas Paine's design was cast near Rotherham in Yorkshire, but never erected by Paine. Its components, however, were used to build the second great iron bridge, over the river Wear (1796). p. 317

[122] This figure, taken from G. R. Porter's book *The Progress of the Nation,* Vol. I, London, 1836 (p. 345), applies to the mid-1830s. In Vol. III of his book, published in 1843 (op. cit., Vol. III, p. 86), Porter gives a higher figure 4,877,000 tons for the use of coal in iron-smelting in England in the forties. p. 318

[123] The *Reform Act* passed by the British Parliament in June 1832 was directed against the political monopoly of the landed and finance aristocracy, and reformed the basis of Parliamentary representation in favour of the industrial bourgeoisie and "middle classes". The proletariat and sections of the petty bourgeoisie, who had provided the main support in the preceding campaigns for reform, received no electoral rights. p. 322

[124] The data given were taken by Engels from the *Journal of the Statistical Society of London;* in particular, the description of working-class districts in Westminster is based on the "Report of the Committee of the Statistical Society of London, on the State of the Working Classes in the Parishes of St. Margaret and St. John"

(Vol. III, 1840) and the description of the district around Hanover Square on C. R. Weld's article: "On the condition of the working classes in the Inner Ward of St. George's Parish, Hanover Square" (Vol. VI, 1843). The number of inmates in the working-class houses in the parishes of St. John and St. Margaret is given according to the report by G. Alston quoted below. The *Journal of the Statistical Society of London*, Vol. III gives another figure—16,176 persons.   p. 333

[125] The report by the Rev. G. Alston, initially published in the radical paper *The Weekly Dispatch*, was reprinted in the Chartist newspaper *The Northern Star* No. 338, May 4, 1844. Engels quotes from this paper.   p. 334

[126] The description was given in *The Times*, November 17, 1843, and in *The Northern Star* No. 315, November 25, 1843.   p. 334

[127] The facts described in this and the preceding paragraph were apparently taken from a report published in *The Times*, January 16 and February 12, 1844.
                p. 335

[128] The data quoted were apparently taken from materials published in *The Times*, November 24 and December 22, 1843, February 5, 9, and 12, 1844, and *The Northern Star*, December 23 and 30, 1843.   p. 337

[129] The figures were apparently taken from C. B. Fripp's "Report of an Inquiry into the Condition of the Working Classes of the City of Bristol" published in the *Journal of the Statistical Society of London*, Vol. II (1839). They are somewhat inaccurately quoted: the 2,800 families constitute 46 per cent of the Bristol working-class families investigated who occupied only one room or part of one (the total number investigated was 5,981).   p. 340

[130] The quotation is from another work by J. C. Symons, namely the "Report from Assistant Hand-Loom Weavers' Commissioners", which he compiled and which was published in *Parliamentary Papers*, 1839, Vol. XLII, No. 159, p. 51. The following quotation is from the book quoted by Engels in his footnote: J. C. Symons, *Arts and Artisans at Home and Abroad*, the pages being those given in the footnote.
                p. 341

[131] The report, quoted by Engels, of the committee elected at Huddersfield on July 19, 1844, to investigate the town's sanitary conditions was printed in *The Northern Star* No. 352, August 10, 1844.   p. 344

[132] Engels gives this name to Kersall-moor—a hill near Manchester where the workers held meetings—by analogy with the Mons Sacer in ancient Rome, to which, tradition has it, the plebeians withdrew in 494 B.C. when they rose against the patricians.   p. 347

[133] The data given here were taken from the article "Wild beasts and rational beings", published in *The Weekly Dispatch*, May 5, 1844.   p. 366

[134] The case against the eleven butchers in Manchester was tried somewhat earlier than Engels reports from memory. A report on it was published in *The Manchester Guardian*, May 10, 1843. The session of the Court Leet (in the 1845 and 1892 German editions Engels calls it the "market court"), which heard cases of this kind, took place twice a year.   p. 369

[135] The *Liverpool Mercury* of February 9, 1844, is quoted with considerable abridgments, and in the 1845 and 1892 German editions in free translation.

In the present edition here, as in other cases, the abridgments have been preserved.   p. 370

[136] On the changes in the length of the crisis cycles see Note 92.   p. 382

[137] The report by the Rev. W. Champneys, quoted by Engels, on the condition of the East End poor employed by the day in the London docks, was first published in *The Weekly Dispatch* and then reprinted in *The Northern Star* No. 338, May 4, 1844.   p. 385

[138] The author presumably has in mind the *Report On the Sanitary Condition of the Labouring Population of Great Britain* (1842) by E. Chadwick or Dr. T. Southwood Smith's two reports to the Poor Law Commissioners on sanitary conditions in the East End of London in 1838 (see, for instance, p. 339).   p. 397

[139] The facts adduced here and below were apparently taken from the article "Frightful spread of Fever from Destitution", published in *The Northern Star* No. 328, February 24, 1844.   p. 397

[140] The information following is taken from the article "Quarterly Table of Mortality" (*The Manchester Guardian*, July 31, 1844), containing tables on the number of inhabitants (in 1841) and deaths (in 1843) in several towns.   p. 403

[141] R. Cowan's article "Vital Statistics of Glasgow" was published in the *Journal of the Statistical Society of London*, Vol. III, 1840.   p. 404

[142] The *Metropolitan Buildings Act*, a special law regulating building in London, was passed by Parliament in 1844.   p. 407

[143] Engels refers to the almost complete absence in the report under consideration of information on the textile industrial districts of Lancashire, Cheshire and the West Riding of Yorkshire.   p. 409

[144] The figures on crime quoted here and below were taken by Engels from G. R. Porter's book, *The Progress of the Nation*, Vol. III, London, 1843, Section VII, Chapter II, and from the *Journal of the Statistical Society of London*, Vol. VI, 1843 (J. Fletcher, "Progress of Crime in the United Kingdom").   p. 425

[145] The information was taken from materials submitted by a "Deputation of Master Manufacturers and Millowners in the County of Lancaster" and published in *The Manchester Guardian*, May 1, 1844. The figures concern 412 firms in the industrial county of Lancaster employing 116,281 workers.   p. 435

[146] Lord Ashley's speech was apparently quoted from *The Times* No. 18559, March 16, 1844, p. 4.   p. 437

[147] The letter quoted was printed in *The Fleet Papers*, a journal published by R. Oastler, Vol. IV, No. 35, August 31, 1844. Engels quotes an excerpt in German. This was re-translated from the German in the American (1887) and the English (1892) editions, and the beginning of the quotation was abridged and paraphrased. The beginning of the original excerpt reads as follows: "A shot time since a friend of mine that was out of work and who ust to work with me, at a former pearead, but who had being out of Wark for a Long time wor Compeld to go, on what we Labouring men Call, the tramp and having got to a place Calld Sant Hellins (I think it is in Lonckshire) and meeting with no sucsess, he thought that he would, bend is way towards Monchester, and just as he was Leaving the place,

he herd of one of his old mateys Leaving Close on the way — so he resolved that he would make him out if poseble — for he wishd to see him, thinking that he might perhaps help him to a job, and if not, he might give him a mouthful of something to Eat, and a nights Lodgings, has he said he was very heard-up."   . p. 439

[148] See Note 145.   p. 439

[149] *The Health and Morals of Apprentices' Act* (1802) limited the working time of child-apprentices to twelve hours and prohibited their employment at night. This law applied only to the cotton and wool industries; it made no provision for control by factory inspectors and was practically disregarded by the mill-owners. p. 442

[150] R. H. Greg's words were apparently reproduced by Engels from Lord Ashley's speech in the House of Commons on March 15, 1844, in support of the Ten Hour Bill. (See *The Times* No. 18559, March 16, 1844, p. 4.)   p. 450

[151] The article mentioned, J. Roberton's "An inquiry respecting the period of puberty in women", was printed in the *North of England Medical and Surgical Journal*, Vol. I (August 1830-May 1831). Engels possibly used the account of this article in P. Gaskell's book, *The Manufacturing Population of England*, London, 1833. p. 453

[152] The *Factory Act of 1819* forbade the employment of children under nine years of age in cotton spinning and weaving mills and also night work of children up to sixteen; for this category the working day was limited to twelve hours, not counting breaks for meals; since these were arranged by mill-owners as they thought fit, the working day often lasted fourteen hours or more.

The *Factory Act of 1825* ruled that breaks for meals were not to total more than $1^1/_2$ hours a day so that the working day would not come to more than $13^1/_2$ hours. Like the Act of 1819, that of 1825 did not provide for any control by the factory inspectors and was ignored by the mill-owners.   p. 459

[153] What is meant is the "Report from the Select Committee on the 'Bill to regulate the Labour of Children in the Mills and Factories of the United Kingdom'", 8th August, 1832 (*Parliamentary Papers*, Vol. XV, 1831-32).   p. 460

[154] The reference is to "Reports of the Inspectors of Factories for the half-year ending 31st December, 1843."   p. 463

[155] *Dissenters* were members of Protestant religious sects and trends in England who rejected to any extent the dogmas and rituals of the official Anglican Church.
                                                                                   p. 464

[156] The reference here is to the proposal made by the Peel cabinet to lower the customs duty on sugar imported from the West Indies in order to open the market for sugar imports from India and other countries.   p. 465

[157] Engels' prediction came true. On June 8, 1847, the Ten Hour Bill applicable to women and youths working in factories was passed by Parliament.   p. 465

[158] What is meant is the article entitled "The Truck System Extraordinary", which was published in the *Halifax Guardian*, November 4, 1843. It was reprinted in *The Sun*, from which it was reproduced in *The Northern Star* No. 315, November 25, 1843.   p. 472

[159] The poem by Edward P. Mead, "The Steam King" was printed in *The Northern Star* No. 274, February 11, 1843. The German translation of the poem was made

by Engels himself. The poem ends with the following two stanzas, which Engels omitted:

> The cheap bread crew will murder you
> By bludgeon, ball or brand;
> Then your Charter gain and the power will be vain
> Of the Steam King's bloody band.
>
> Then down with the King, the Moloch King
> And the satraps of his might:
> Let right prevail, then Freedom hail
> When might shall stoop to right.   p. 474

[160] The first letter, published in *The Morning Chronicle*, December 1, 1843, under the title "Distress at Hinckley", was reprinted in *The Northern Star* No. 317, December 9, 1843. Below Engels quotes also the second letter ("Letters to the Editor"), which was published in *The Morning Chronicle*, December 9, 1843.   p. 481

[161] The author refers to the series of articles by Léon Faucher published under various titles from October 1843 to July 1844, in the journal *Revue des deux Mondes*. Later they were published by the author in a collection under the title *Etudes sur l'Angleterre*, Vols. 1-2, Paris, 1845. The term "*démocratie industrielle*" quoted below occurs in Vol. 2, p. 147.   p. 488

[162] The quotation given above is from the article by A. Knight, "On the grinders' asthma", which was published in the *North of England Medical and Surgical Journal*, Vol. I, August 1830-May 1831. The second half of the preceding quotation is from the same source; the first half is from Knight's testimony to the Children's Employment Commission (Appendix to 2nd Report, Part I, 1842). The same publication contains extracts from his earlier mentioned article, which were possibly used by Engels.   p. 493

[163] See Note 118.   p. 502

[164] See Note 79.   p. 503

[165] The description of this event was taken by Engels from P. Gaskell's book, *The Manufacturing Population of England*, which appeared in 1833. The author pointed out that the murderers had not been found. But soon after the book's publication, the murderers of mill-owner Ashton's son — Joseph and William Mosley and William Garside — were apprehended, and in 1834 two of them were hanged in London.

The account of the following facts is based mainly on newspaper material (published in *The Northern Star*, *The Manchester Guardian*, *The Times*, and other papers).   p. 508

[166] Tradition has it that the Roman patrician Menenius Agrippa persuaded the plebeians who had rebelled and withdrawn to the Mons Sacer in 494 B.C. to submit by telling them the fable about the other parts of the human body revolting against the stomach because, they said, it consumed food and did no work, but afterwards becoming convinced that they could not exist without it.   p. 510

[167] The reference is to the rising of the Welsh miners organised by the Chartists in Newport and its environs in November 1839. The rising was caused by the miners' hard condition and the growing discontent among them over Parliament's rejection

of the Chartists' petition and the arrest of Chartist agitators. The Newport Rising, possibly intended to be the signal for a general armed struggle for the People's Charter, was put down by troops and used as a pretext for severe repressions. Later Engels again returned to this rising (see p. 519 of this volume).

The events of 1843 in Manchester were reported by Engels in his article "An English Turnout" (see pp. 584-96 of this volume). p. 513

[168] A detailed account of the strike at Birley's mill was given in *The Northern Star* No. 248, August 13, 1842, p. 5. p. 514

[169] This body, better known as the *London Working-men's Association*, the first Chartist organisation, was formally established on June 16, 1836. A project of parliamentary reform which became known as the People's Charter was published at the beginning of May 1838. (In all the editions of Engels' book which appeared during his lifetime, 1835 is given as the year when this document was drawn up; this was probably the result of a slip, and is corrected in the present edition.) At the Chartist meeting in Birmingham in August 1838 it was decided to fight for the People's Charter to be given the force of law. This demand was set forth in a petition to Parliament. p. 517

[170] Under a law of 1710 candidates to Parliament in borough seats had to own landed property yielding an income of at least £300 annually and in county seats £600 annually. p. 518

[171] The speech made by Stephens at the Chartist meeting of September 24, 1838, at Kersall-moor, near Manchester, was published in *The Northern Star* No. 46, September 29. Engels reproduced the relevant passage with abridgments. p. 519

[172] The author refers to the clashes between the Chartists and the police in Sheffield, Bradford and other towns. They were said to have been caused by provocateurs. p. 519

[173] The reference is to the *National Charter Association*, founded in July 1840, the first mass workers' party in the history of the working-class movement. In the years of upsurge it counted up to 50,000 members. The work of the Association was hindered by the absence of unity in ideas and tactics among its members and by the petty-bourgeois ideology of most of its leaders. After the defeat of the Chartists in 1848 the Association fell into decline and it ceased its activity in the fifties. p. 523

[174] Engels refers here to the agrarian plans of F. O'Connor and other Chartist leaders who shared the utopian view that the workers could be freed from exploitation and other social evils by returning them to the land. In 1845 the Chartist Land Co-operative Society was formed for this purpose on the initiative of F. O'Connor (later it operated under the name of National Land Company). It tried to buy up land with the contributions of workmen-shareholders and to rent it out to its members in small plots on easy terms. The scheme was not successful. p. 524

[175] *Home colonies* was the name given by Robert Owen and his supporters to their model communist colonies. For details about them see Engels' article "Description of Recently Founded Communist Colonies Still in Existence" (pp. 214-28 of this volume). p. 525

[176] *Mechanics' Institutes* were evening schools in which workers were taught general and technical subjects; such schools first appeared in Britain in 1823, in London and Glasgow. In the early 1840s there were over 200 of them, mainly in

the factory towns of Lancashire and Yorkshire. The bourgeoisie used these institutions to train skilled workers for industry and to bring them under the influence of bourgeois ideas, though initially this was resisted by the working-class activists. p. 527

[177] The following books were published in English: [Holbach], *Système de la nature* in 1817, Helvétius' *De l'esprit* in 1807, and *De l'homme* in 1777. Announcements of popular and inexpensive editions of the classics of French philosophy were carried by the Owenites' weekly *The New Moral World*. p. 528

[178] The English edition of Strauss' book *Das Leben Jesu* was published by Henry Hetherington in 1842 in a series of weekly instalments. p. 528

[179] It was apparently a question of Engels' intention to give a characterisation of English bourgeois political and economic writings in his planned work on the social history of England. (Concerning this intention see Note 118.) p. 528

[180] These data were given in *The Mining Journal*, Vol. 13, No. 420, September 9, 1843. p. 538

[181] The law forbidding the employment underground of women and of children under ten years of age was passed by Parliament on August 10, 1842, and came into force in March 1843. p. 539

[182] The *Court of Queen's Bench* is one of the oldest courts in England; in the 19th century (up to 1873) it was an independent supreme court for criminal and civil cases, competent to review the decisions of lower judicial bodies.

A *Writ of Habeas Corpus* is the name given in English judicial procedure to a document enjoining the relevant authorities to present an arrested person before a court on the demand of persons interested to check the legitimacy of the arrest. Having considered the reasons for the arrest, the court either frees the person arrested, sends him back to prison or releases him on bail or guarantee. This procedure, laid down by an Act of Parliament of 1679, does not apply to persons accused of high treason and can be suspended by decision of Parliament. p. 542

[183] The speech in question was made by Thomas Duncombe in the House of Commons on June 4, 1844. The report on it was first published in *The Times*, June 5, 1844, p. 2, and later reprinted in the Chartist *Northern Star* No. 343, June 8, 1844, p. 8. p. 546

[184] The reference is to the wars of the coalitions of European states against France under the Revolution and under Napoleon, wars which lasted from 1792 to 1815 with a short interruption in 1802-1803. Britain was an active member of these coalitions. p. 548

[185] The facts adduced are quoted from *The Times*, June 7, 10, and 21, 1844.

p. 552

[186] The quotations are from an essay by A. Somerville published in *The Morning Chronicle*, July 6, 1843. p. 556

[187] Before the Commutation Act of 1838 Irish peasants renting land paid tithes to the Established Church of Ireland. Under the Act of 1838 the tithe was

reduced by 25 per cent and commuted into a tax exacted from landlords and landowners. The latter in turn transferred this tax to the tenants, thus raising the rent.   p. 559

[188] The *Union of Ireland with Great Britain* was imposed on Ireland by the British Government after the suppression of the Irish rising of 1798. The Union, which entered into force on January 1, 1801, abolished the autonomy of the Irish Parliament and made the country still more dependent on England. The demand for the repeal of the Union became the most popular slogan in Ireland from the 1820s. Its leader, Daniel O'Connell, founder of the Repeal Association (1840), tried to steer the movement toward compromise with the British ruling classes. The agitation revived in the early 1840s.   p. 560

[189] The reference is to the trial of O'Connell and eight other leaders of the Repeal movement in 1844. The Tory government intended by this trial to deal it a decisive blow. O'Connell and his supporters were sentenced to up to twelve months imprisonment in February 1844, but the sentence was soon quashed by the House of Lords.   p. 561

[190] "*Laissez-faire, laissez-aller*" was the formula of the advocates of free trade and non-intervention of the state in economic relations.   p. 564

[191] See Note 71.   p. 570

[192] A considerable number of the facts adduced here were taken from *The Northern Star*. Engels made use, in particular, of the following articles and reports: "Brutality at a Workhouse", No. 295, July 8, 1843; "Inhuman Conduct of the Master of a Union Workhouse", No. 334, April 6, 1844; "Murder! Hellish Treatment of the Poor in the Coventry Bastille", No. 315, November 25, 1843; "Atrocities at the Birmingham Workhouse", No. 317, December 9, 1843; "Secrets of the Union Workhouse", No. 326, February 10, 1844; "St. Pancras Scoundrelism Again!", No. 328, February 24, 1844; "Infamous Treatment of an Englishman and his Family in Bethnal-Green Workhouse", No. 333, March 30, 1844; "Infernal Workhouse Cruelties", No. 359, September 28, 1844; "The Poor Laws.—Disgusting Treatment of the Poor", No. 328, February 24, 1844; "Horrible Profligacy in the West London Union Workhouse", No. 334, April 6, 1844.   p. 574

[193] The reference is to the article by Douglas Jerrold "The Two Windows", published in *The Illuminated Magazine*, Vol. III, May-October, 1844.   p. 574

[194] The *Gilbert Act of 1782* was one of the Poor Laws. It authorised the formation, on the demand of the rate-payers paying two-thirds of the value of rates, in any parish or group of parishes, of a Board of Guardians to control poor relief. However, unlike the workhouses of the New Poor Law of 1834, which were also administered by Boards of Guardians, the workhouses in "Gilbert Unions" contained only the impotent poor and pauper children. The Gilbert Act was not finally repealed until the early 1870s.   p. 576

[195] *Barmecide feast*—an expression taken from "The Arabian Nights". One of the Barmaks, a noble Persian family, derided a hungry beggar by telling him of an imaginary banquet. The expression was used by T. Carlyle in his *Chartism*, the first edition of which appeared in 1840, which is what Engels here alludes to. p. 579

[196] Quoted from *The Northern Star* No. 344, June 15, 1844. In an article headlined "Horrible Condition of the Agricultural Labourers" it reproduced with a commentary material on the occurrence which was published in *The Times*, June 7, 1844, under the title "Effect of the New Poor Law upon Wages".   p. 579

[197] This article was written by Engels in the spring and summer of 1845 after he had completed *The Condition of the Working-Class in England* and moved to Brussels. Judging by the title and subtitle, which is numbered I, and by the first paragraph, it was intended as the beginning of a series to supplement *The Condition of the Working-Class in England* with concrete illustrations. The article was published in the January and February issues of the journal *Das Westphälische Dampfboot* in 1846. However, the continuation did not follow and the article was not included by Engels in any of the editions of *The Condition of the Working-Class in England* published during his lifetime. It was first published in English in 1958 as an Appendix to the book: Engels, *The Condition of the Working Class in England*. Translated and edited by W. O. Henderson and W. H. Chaloner, New York, 1958. Engels wrote this article basing himself mainly on material published in *The Northern Star* Nos. 362-369, 371, 372, 375 from November 1844 to January 1845, which carried detailed reports on the strike described.   p. 584

[198] *Van Diemen's Land*—the name initially given by Europeans to the island of Tasmania, which was a British penal colony up to 1853.   p. 585

[199] These words were taken from a resolution passed by a meeting of workers at Ashton-under-Lyne on August 9, 1842, which decided on the action at Manchester.   p. 587

[200] According to a report published by *The Manchester Guardian* on December 24, 1844, the strike of the Pauling and Henfrey building workers ended the day before. The report admitted that the firm was forced to promise to observe the same working conditions as operated on the other building sites of the city.   p. 596

[201] This work was written by Marx to expose certain repulsive aspects of bourgeois society, its morals and customs, using documentary evidence provided by one of its representatives, the French jurist and economist, custodian of the Paris police archives, Jacques Peuchet. Marx carried out his intention by translating into German and publishing excerpts from *Mémoires tirés des archives de la police de Paris, pour servir à l'histoire de la morale et de la police, depuis Louis XIV jusqu'à nos jours. Par J. Peuchet, Archiviste de la Police*. T. I-IV, Paris, 1838, giving his own comments in an introductory section and occasional digressions. The excerpts were taken from Chapter LVIII "*Du suicide et de ses causes*" (t. IV, pp. 116-82). Marx gives the text with abridgments and sometimes in free rendering, without indicating by suspension periods the passages omitted. He left out altogether the material on pages 143-68, taking only a few phrases (see pp. 159 and 164), which he joined according to the sense to the excerpts from the beginning of the section. Some passages from Peuchet were given by Marx in his own formulation, emphasising their critical trend. The information on the author given by Marx in the introductory section was taken from the Introduction by A. Levasseur, the editor of the *Mémoires* (t. I, Introduction, pp. i-xx).

In the present edition Marx's own text (introductory and closing sections and the digressions in which he sums up) are printed in larger type and the excerpts from Peuchet's book in small type. Cases of substantial paraphrasing and other digressions from the original as well as re-arrangements made by Marx in quoting are pointed out in footnotes. The emphasis in the quotations is Marx's in all cases.

p. 597

[202] The *Hundred Days* is the second period of Napoleon's rule, from his restoration to the imperial throne on March 20 (after his return from the island of Elba) to his second abdication on June 22, 1815, four days after his defeat at Waterloo.

p. 598

[203] See Note 100.   p. 598

[204] The translation of the fragment from the manuscript of Charles Fourier was made by Engels as a first contribution to the plan which he and Marx had formed at the beginning of 1845 to publish in Germany a "Library of the Best Foreign Socialist Writers" with a general introduction and commentaries to each issue (see Engels' letters to Marx of February 22-26, March 7 and 17, 1845). The draft plan of this publication, drawn up by Marx (see p. 667 of this volume), shows that it was conceived as a representative series of works of French and English authors. But the plan was not carried out because of publishing difficulties. The translation of a few chapters of Fourier's *Des trois unités externes* was the only one carried out in the framework of the plan. It was begun by Engels evidently after he had moved from Barmen to Brussels in April 1845. The introduction and the conclusion were most probably written not before August, since they were a reply to the works of some of the "true Socialists" published at that time. Engels' translation and commentary were not printed until the middle of 1846 (in the annual *Deutsches Bürgerbuch für 1846*).

The fragment selected by Engels comprises the first seven chapters of Fourier's unfinished manuscript *Des trois unités externes* (written, apparently, between 1807 and 1821), most of which was published for the first time after the author's death in the Fourierist journal *La Phalange*, in the first two issues (January-February and March-April) of 1845. Some passages in the manuscript coincide with passages in the first, anonymous, publication (1808) of Fourier's work *Théorie des quatre mouvements et des destinées générales*. In the 1845 publication of *Des trois unités externes* they were replaced by suspension periods and references to pages of that work. In his translation Engels restored these passages according to the edition of the *Théorie des quatre mouvements* of 1841 (in the present edition all these cases are pointed out in the Notes).

The text of the seven chapters is given by Engels with abridgments, omissions not always being indicated by suspension periods, and in some cases fragments translated are joined by Engels' insertions. Some passages are translated with abridgments or in the form of a paraphrase, and sometimes the content is given in Engels' own words.

In the present edition the translation of Fourier's manuscript is reproduced in the form in which it was produced for publication by Engels. All his digressions from the original have been preserved. The whole of the translation — as distinct from Engels' introduction and conclusion — is printed in small type. The insertions made by Engels and the passages given in his rendering are printed without quotes. The most important cases of paraphrasing are pointed out in footnotes. The italics in the quoted text are mostly by Engels.   p. 613

[205] By "German theory of the very worst sort" Engels means "true socialism", which in 1844-45 was spreading among German intellectuals and craftsmen. It was a

mixture of the idealistic aspects of Feuerbachianism with French utopian socialism in an emasculated form. As a result, socialist teaching was turned into abstract sentimental moralising divorced from real needs. The vulgarisation of the French Utopian Socialists' views by "true socialism", combined with an arrogant and deprecatory attitude towards them, was especially marked in Grün's book *Die soziale Bewegung in Frankreich und Belgien* published in Darmstadt in August 1845.

This work of Engels reflects the intention which by then had matured in his and Marx's minds to dissociate themselves publicly from "true socialism" and to criticise its representatives. Marx and Engels gave a detailed criticism of "true socialism" in *The German Ideology*.   p. 613

[206] Here the author has in mind Fourier's fantastic descriptions of the changes which according to his vision of the future were destined to take place in nature: a change in the unpleasant taste of sea water, which would turn into lemonade, the appearance of heat-radiating coronas over the North and South Poles, the transformation of beasts of prey into animals useful to man, and so on.

The *method of series* is a method of classification typical of Fourier and applied by him in analysing various natural and social phenomena. By means of this method Fourier tried to develop a new social science according to which the social and psychological factor — the attraction and repulsion of passions — would be demonstrated as the main principle of social development (the passions, in turn, were divided into groups or series). In this method and its application by Fourier, unscientific and fantastic elements were combined with rational observations and spontaneous manifestations of dialectics.   p. 614

[207] Engels included in the first section material from the introduction ("Setting of the Question") and from the first chapter of Fourier's manuscript, to which the author gave the title "Successive Series of Trade Methods".

The beginning of the fragments from the words "We now touch on civilisation's most sensitive spot" to "the mainsprings of circulation" is taken from the *Théorie des quatre mouvements*, Paris, 1841, pp. 331-32. However, unlike the other passages which coincide textually with passages in *Théorie des quatre mouvements* and which were omitted in the journal *La Phalange*, the text of this passage was reproduced in the journal too.   p. 616

[208] By "*ideology*" and "*ideologists*" Fourier means a group of imitators of the French philosophy of the 18th century which was headed by the liberal thinker, economist and politician Antoine L. C. Destutt de Tracy (1754-1836), author of the five-volume *Eléments d'idéologie*, published in 1804.   p. 616

[209] At the Aachen Congress (1818) of the states of the Holy Alliance (Britain, Austria, Prussia and Russia) the heads of the biggest banking houses in Europe were enlisted to help work out the terms of France's payment of the contribution imposed on her after the defeat of Napoleon. It was decided to carry out the credit operations for the payment of this contribution through the English Baring Bank and the Anglo-Dutch Hope Bank. Apparently it was these two bankers that Fourier had in mind in this passage.   p. 619

[210] *The Federates of 1815* were volunteers who supported Napoleon during his short period of rule in 1815, from his return from Elba till his defeat at Waterloo (the Hundred Days).   p. 619

[211] The author has in mind the bank-notes issued in France in 1716 with the Government's permission by a special bank founded by the adventurer John Law,

who had decamped from England in 1720 after becoming bankrupt. As he had transferred his bank to the state beforehand, its ruin was a concealed form of state bankruptcy.

Assignats were paper money issued during the French Revolution from December 1789 and backed by the revenue from the sale of property confiscated from the feudal aristocracy and the church (national estates). As a result of emissions and speculation, which were particularly intensified after the counter-revolutionary coup in July 1794 (9 Thermidor), they quickly depreciated. In December 1796 their issue was stopped.   p. 624

[212] Fourier mistakenly attributes this operation to the Convention. It was carried out on September 30, 1797, by the Directory—the highest government body of the regime which replaced the Convention. The Directory reduced the value of all state bonds by two-thirds and recognised as payable only one-third, which received the name of Consolidated Third.   p. 624

[213] The text from the words "when a crime becomes very frequent, one gets accustomed to it and witnesses it with indifference" to "in which the speculator steals only half" was taken from the *Théorie des quatre mouvements*, pp. 341-43. Subsequently, Engels follows the text published in *La Phalange*.   p. 624

[214] By the new French code Fourier means the *Code civile* of Napoleon, which was introduced in 1804.   p. 625

[215] In the list of varieties of bankruptcy in Fourier's manuscript the names of bankrupt businessmen were given. But the publishers of the work in *La Phalange* omitted these, leaving in the subsequent description of each variety only names which were imaginary or borrowed from literary works. Engels himself points this out in a footnote (see p. 638 of this volume).   p. 625

[216] An allusion to the *Disputationes de sancto matrimonii sacramento*, by Tomas Sanchez, a Spanish Jesuit and theologian at the end of the 16th and the beginning of the 17th century. The book was notable for its refined casuistry and, at the same time, its freedom verging on pornography.   p. 629

[217] The text from the words "Banker Dorante has two million" to the end of point 13 ("for people who steal several millions at one go") was taken from the *Théorie des quatre mouvements*, pp. 343-46.   p. 630

[218] The text from the words "Judas Iscariot arrives in France" to "everybody avidly seizes the opportunity to commit a theft if it remains unpunished" was taken from the *Théorie des quatre mouvements*, pp. 348-51.   p. 633

[219] During certain Catholic services the *Blessed Sacrament* is solemnly carried under a portable canopy.   p. 637

[220] The small town of Beaucaire in the south of France became famous for its big annual fair.   p. 638

[221] The text from the words "Scapin, a petty crook" to the end of point 34 ("after the happy issue of the first bankruptcy, he starts to think of a new one") was taken from the *Théorie des quatre mouvements*, pp. 346-47.   p. 639

[222] The March-April issue of *La Phalange* carried, besides the three chapters of *Des trois unités externes* (Chapters VIII-X) mentioned by Engels, also Chapters

XI-XVIII ("Conclusions from What Has Been Proved About Trade", "The Tendency of the Trade System to Seven Monopolies", "On Sea Monopoly of Coarse or Destructive Hoisting", "On the Navigation Monopoly of a Simple United Structure", "On the Navigation Monopoly of a Complex United Structure", "Conclusion on Fraudulent Trade", "On the Trade Unity of People of Harmonic Structure", "On the Administrative Unity of People of Harmonic Structure"). The text coinciding with passages from the *Théorie des quatre mouvements* was omitted.   p. 641

[223] Engels ironically compares the picture of historic development given by Hegel in his *Philosophie der Geschichte* with the medieval Christian-feudal periodisation of world history according to the four empires: Assyrio-Babylonian, Medo-Persian, Greco-Macedonian, and Roman (the "Roman", in its various forms, including the Germanic Holy Roman Empire, was supposedly to last till the end of time). According to Hegel's conception, world history, the basis of which is the process of self-knowledge of the Absolute Idea or the world spirit, has gone through three main stages, namely, the history of Asia Minor and Ancient Egypt, the history of the Greco-Roman world, and the history of the German peoples. The nations whose history did not fit into this three-stage system were called "non-historical" by Hegel.   p. 642

[224] See Note 83.   p. 643

[225] The reference is to the project of a "Library of the Best Foreign Socialist Writers" (see Note 89). For this purpose Marx and Engels intended to enlist other members of the socialist movement, including M. Hess. But the fact that the latter had meanwhile embraced "true socialism" and become one of its spokesmen, made it practically impossible to collaborate with him, as also with a number of other editors and publishers of various German journals, and was one of the reasons why the "Library" did not materialise.   p. 644

[226] Engels' contributions to *The Northern Star* began late in 1843 and became regular from May 1844 (see present edition, Vol. 3). However, as a result of his departure from England in August 1844 and of his work on *The Condition of the Working-Class in England*, he discontinued his reports temporarily in the late summer of 1844. In July 1845, Marx and Engels left Brussels for England, where they spent about a month and a half (from July 12 to August 21) in Manchester and in London; they acquainted themselves with English social and political literature and expanded their contacts with the working-class movement. In London, on his way back from Manchester, Engels agreed with G. J. Harney, the editor of *The Northern Star*, to resume his work with the paper. From September 1845 up to the revolution of 1848 he regularly contributed articles and reports on the various Continental countries and the growth of the revolutionary, and above all, the working-class movement there. The article "The Late Butchery at Leipzig.— The German Working Men's Movement" was the first in this new series of reports.   p. 645

[227] The *massacre at Leipzig* was the shooting down of a popular demonstration by Saxon troops in Leipzig on August 12, 1845. The demonstration, on the occasion of a military parade welcoming the arrival of Crown Prince Johann, was in protest against the Saxon Government's persecution of the "German Catholics" movement and one of its leaders, the priest J. Ronge. The "German Catholics" movement, which arose in a number of German states in 1844, embraced a

considerable section of the middle and petty bourgeoisie; rejecting the supremacy of the Pope and many of the dogmas and rites of the Catholic Church, the "German Catholics" sought to adapt Catholicism to the needs of the developing German bourgeoisie.

The Northern Star took notice several times of the events in Leipzig. It carried information on them in Nos. 404 and 406, August 9 and 23, 1845, and in the report "Germany. The New Reformation", published in No. 408, September 6, 1845 (Engels refers to it at the beginning and the end of his article). The shooting in Leipzig was interpreted as a sign of the ripening of revolution in Germany.

p. 645

228 Peterloo was the name given, by analogy with the battle of Waterloo, to the massacre by troops on August 16, 1819, of unarmed participants in a mass meeting in support of electoral reform at St. Peter's Fields, near Manchester.

p. 645

229 See Note 79.   p. 646

230 The reference is to the revolution of 1688 (the overthrow of the Stuart dynasty and the enthronement of William III of Orange), after which constitutional monarchy was consolidated in England on the basis of a compromise between the landed aristocracy and the bourgeoisie.   p. 647

231 This theme was not developed in detail at the time in Engels' reports. He merely touched upon it in his article "'Young Germany' in Switzerland", which was published in The Northern Star two weeks later, on September 27, 1845 (see pp. 651-53 of this volume). Nevertheless Engels did not abandon his intention of describing the development of the German working-class movement in the 1840s in the columns of the Chartist newspaper, as is borne out by the series of articles on "The State of Germany" which he began in October 1845 but did not complete and carried only to the beginning of the 1840s (see present edition, Vol. 6).   p. 648

232 "Young Germany" was a revolutionary conspiratorial organisation of German émigrés in Switzerland in the 1830s and 1840s. Initially it comprised mainly petty-bourgeois intellectuals, whose object was to set up a democratic republic in Germany, but soon it came more under the influence of the trade unions and socialist clubs. In the mid-1830s, the Swiss Government, under pressure from Austria and Prussia, deported the German revolutionaries; the craftsmen's unions were closed. "Young Germany" virtually ceased to exist, though several groups of its followers still remained in the cantons of Geneva and Vaud. In the 1840s "Young Germany" was revived, when its members, under the influence of Ludwig Feuerbach's ideas, carried on mainly atheistic propaganda among the German émigrés, sharply opposing the communist trends, especially that of Weitling, although some of the members of "Young Germany" were more and more attracted by social questions. In 1845 "Young Germany" was again crushed.

The report "On the 'Discovery of the Conspiracy' of 'Young Germany'" which is quoted by Engels in abridged form in English was published in the Constitutionnel Neuchâtelois No. 109, September 11, 1845. The emphasis in the text is by Engels; in the newspaper only the words "Regicide not excepted" were stressed, and they were reproduced in italics by Engels.   p. 651

233 The reference is to the armed clash between clerical-patriarchal elements opposed to bourgeois reforms and the democratic forces of the Valais canton in March 1844. With the support of conservative circles in Lucerne and other cantons, the clericals temporarily gained the upper hand. Concerning these events see Engels' article "The Civil War in the Valais" (present edition, Vol. 3, p. 525). p. 651

234 On the "German Catholics" see Note 227.

"*Friends of Light*" was a religious trend directed against the pietism which, supported by Junker circles, was predominant in the official church and was distinguished by its extreme reactionary and hypocritical character. The "Friends of Light" movement was an expression of German bourgeois discontent with the reactionary order in Germany in the 1840s.   p. 653

235 Weitling and his supporters were arrested in June 1843 by the Zurich authorities and put on trial for communist activity considered dangerous to the state and public order. The trial took place in September, and the public prosecutor failed to secure conviction on the charge of high treason and conspiracy. Weitling was, however, condemned to six months imprisonment for inciting to crimes against property and insulting religion (the court of appeal, on the demand of the public prosecutor, increased the term to ten months) and to deportation from Switzerland; his followers were banished from the canton of Zurich. Weitling's trial was described by Engels in his article "Progress of Social Reform on the Continent" (see present edition, Vol. 3, pp. 392-408).   p. 654

236 The article was sent to the Hamburg journal *Telegraph für Deutschland* through Reichardt's Newspaper-Correspondence Bureau in Brussels, which provided the progressive German press with reports by German émigrés. Engels himself contributed to this paper only in his younger years, from 1839 to 1841 (see present edition, Vol. 2); he discontinued his collaboration because he was dissatisfied with the ideological and political stand and especially the liberal half-measures of the literary group of "Young Germany", whose press organ this journal was. In publishing the article the editors accompanied it with a note revealing its source. "As the author of this interesting article," the note said, "we can name the well-known Engels." In content the article coincides in part with the corresponding passages in the chapter on the labour movements in *The Condition of the Working-Class in England* (characterisation of the workers' unrest in Lancashire in summer 1842, see pp. 520-21 of this volume), and in part supplements some other sections of that book.   p. 656

237 What is meant is the Reform Act of 1832, see Note 123.   p. 657

238 The Bill introducing the sliding scale was drafted by Canning's Tory cabinet in 1827 and carried through Parliament the following year in a somewhat revised form by the Tory cabinet under Wellington.   p. 657

239 The *People's Charter*, containing the demands of the Chartists, was published on May 8, 1838, as a Bill to be submitted to Parliament. It consisted of six points: universal suffrage (for men on reaching the age of 21), annual elections to Parliament, secret ballot, equal electoral areas, abolition of the property qualification for Parliamentary candidates, a salary for Members of Parliament.   p. 659

240 Marx's note entitled "Hegel's Construction of the Phenomenology" is at the beginning of his Notebook for 1844-1847 (the first of his surviving Notebooks).

The basic ideas contained in the four points were developed in *The Holy Family*, in particular in the sections where, criticising the Young Hegelians' tendency to replace the revolutionary transformation of existing reality by abstract theoretical criticism of what exists, Marx showed that this tendency was based on Hegel's idealist conception developed in his *Phänomenologie des Geistes* (see pp. 85-86, 195-97 of this volume).   p. 665

241 This draft has no author's title and is near the beginning of Marx's Notebook for 1844-1847. The main points of the draft coincide with the points of the subject indexes compiled by Marx as early as the summer of 1843 for his "Kreuznach Notebooks" on world history, including the history of the French Revolution. In resuming his study of these problems after his arrival in Paris in the autumn of that year, Marx intended to write a *History of the Convention*. For this purpose he compiled a summary of the memoirs of the Jacobin Levasseur (see present edition, Vol. 3). The materials he collected, most of which have not come down to us, were used in part in *The Holy Family*. It was probably in connection with his plan to write a work on the French Revolution (he did not abandon this idea even in 1845 after his expulsion from Paris to Belgium, as is borne out by a report in the *Trier'sche Zeitung* of February 6, 1845) that he compiled this draft. In it Marx did not merely reproduce the text of the subject indexes to the "Kreuznach Notebooks", he made a substantial addition to point 9, adding the words "the fight for the abolition [*Aufhebung*] of the state and of bourgeois society", i.e., the fight to abolish the exploiter state and the whole existing system of social-economic relations.   p. 666

242 The Plan of the "Library of the Best Foreign Socialist Writers" is in Marx's Notebook for 1844-1847, among the notes relating to March 1845. (Concerning Marx and Engels' intention to put out such a publication and the causes which prevented its realisation see Note 89.) As is seen from further entries in his Notebook, Marx returned to this plan in the following months, recording the names of authors whose works should be added to the "Library" (in particular the names of Thompson, Campanella, Lamennais), and also the persons to be enlisted in the proposed publication (M. Hess was to translate the works of Buonarroti, Dézamy and others).

In listing the names of the Socialists Marx also mentions Lalande. This is probably a slip of the pen. He might have meant de Labord. True, further on in his Notebook Marx mentions Lalande's *De L'Association*, but in *Capital*, Vol. 1, he quotes Labord's book *De l'esprit d'association dans tous les intérêts de la Communauté*, Paris, 1818.   p. 667

243 See Note 41.   p. 667

244 The reference is to the *travailleurs égalitaires* and the *humanitaires*, see Note 68.   p. 667

245 These entries in Marx's Notebook for 1844-1847 immediately precede the famous "Theses on Feuerbach", written in April 1845 (see present edition, Vol. 5). In content the notes correspond to the first point of the "Draft Plan for a Work on the Modern State" given above—evidence that in the first months of his stay in Brussels Marx had not abandoned the plan of writing a work on the French Revolution, but still could not carry it out at that stage. The ideas briefly recorded in his notes have much in common with a number of those developed in *The Holy Family* (see pp. 122-28, 140-47 of this volume).   p. 668

[246] This address to the readers of and contributors to the Elberfeld journal *Gesellschaftsspiegel* was written by Engels and Hess. Engels took a part in preparing the publication of the journal, in drawing up its programme, and, as is seen from his letter to Marx of January 20, 1845, in compiling the prospectus published in the first issue in the form of this editorial address. As Engels wrote in one of his reports, "Rapid Progress of Communism in Germany", published in *The New Moral World* (see p. 234 of this volume), it was initially proposed that he should be one of the editors. The prospectus reflected Engels' intention that the journal would expose the evils of the capitalist system and defend the interests of the workers by criticising half-measures and advocating a radical transformation of the social system. Indeed, the concrete plan worked out by Engels for investigating the condition of the workers corresponded in many respects with the tasks he had set himself in writing *The Condition of the Working-Class in England*. But at the same time, not a few abstract philanthropic sentiments in the spirit of "true socialism", coming from Hess, had found a place in the prospectus. Dissatisfaction with the position adopted by Hess was apparently one of the causes of Engels' refusal to become one of the editors. In the third of the mentioned reports in *The New Moral World*, written in early April 1845, he named Hess alone as the publisher of the *Gesellschaftsspiegel* (see p. 240 of this volume). Under the editorship of Hess the journal very soon departed from the line envisaged by Engels in the prospectus and became a mouthpiece of the reformist and sentimental ideas of "true socialism".   p. 671

[247] The reference is to the riot of the Silesian weavers. See Note 79.   p. 674

[248] The reference is to the Associations for the Benefit of the Working Classes in Germany (see Note 83). These associations are characterised in Engels' article "Rapid Progress of Communism in Germany" (pp. 234, 237 of this volume).
                                                                                p. 674

[249] Marx studied political economy from the end of 1843, and by the spring of 1844 had set himself the task of writing a criticism of bourgeois political economy from the standpoint of materialism and communism; the draft "Economic and Philosophic Manuscripts of 1844" (see present edition, Vol. 3) written at this time have reached us incomplete. Work on *The Holy Family* in the autumn of 1844 forced Marx temporarily to interrupt his study of political economy; he returned to it only in December 1844; in February 1845, just before his expulsion from Paris, he concluded the publication contract with Leske. In Brussels Marx continued to study English, French, German, Italian and other economists and added to his Paris notebooks of quotations several more notebooks. In the autumn of 1845 he again turned to other work: he had concluded that a criticism of political economy should be preceded by an exposition of his new principles of general methodology and a critical review of current philosophical doctrines, and therefore concentrated on writing, jointly with Engels, *The German Ideology*. On the other hand, he firmly rejected (see his letter to Leske of August 1, 1846) the publisher's attempts to get him to adapt the projected work to the conditions of the reactionary censorship. On September 9, 1846, Leske informed Marx that, in view of rigorous censorship and police persecution, he would not be able to publish his work. In February 1847 the contract was cancelled.   p. 675

[250] This request was written four days after Marx's arrival in Brussels upon his expulsion from France by the French Government for taking part in editing *Vorwärts!* (see Note 87). Shortly after his arrival his wife joined him, with their eldest daughter, Jenny, who had been born in Paris.

Marx received no reply to his request. The Royal Belgian Government was reluctant to grant political asylum to revolutionary émigrés. Marx was immediately placed under secret surveillance as a "dangerous democrat and Communist".   p. 676

251 On March 22, 1845, Marx was summoned to the police administration in Brussels and asked to sign an undertaking as a condition for being allowed to stay in Brussels. Marx himself informed Heinrich Heine of this in a letter of March 24, 1845.   p. 677

252 Marx's two letters (October 17 and November 10, 1845) to Görtz, the Chief Burgomaster of Trier, were connected with his attempts to obtain the official documents required for emigration to the United States of America. As is clear from the second document, the request was motivated by the fact that after Marx's arrival in Brussels the Prussian Government, on whose insistence the French authorities had expelled him from Paris, began to try to get him deported from Belgium too. It was apparently in order to deprive the Prussian authorities of a formal pretext for interfering in his affairs, that Marx went to the trouble of requesting permission to emigrate to the U.S.A., the receipt of which would have been equivalent to release from his obligations as a Prussian citizen. There are no other documents to indicate that he had any intention at the time to emigrate with his family to North America. Regardless of the outcome of these steps, which most probably failed, Marx officially renounced Prussian citizenship in December 1845.   p. 678

253 In 1838 Marx was excused reporting for military service in Berlin because of a lung disease, and in 1841 he was pronounced unfit for military service.
                                                                                                  p. 678

NAME INDEX

A

Ainsworth and Crompton—textile manufacturers in Bolton—508

Albert, Prince Consort of Queen Victoria of Great Britain (1819-1861)—650

Alexander I (1777-1825)—Emperor of Russia (1801-25)—205

Alison, Sir Archibald (1792-1867)—Scottish historian and economist, Tory—14, 338, 389, 398, 412, 416, 417, 421, 424, 426, 558, 560

Alison, William Pulteney (1790-1859)—professor of medicine at Edinburgh University, Tory—338, 389, 398

Alston, G.—preacher of St. Philip's Church, Bethnal Green (London)—334

Anaxagoras (c. 500-428 B.C.)—Greek philosopher—128

Anglès, Jules Jean Baptiste (1778-1828)—police prefect in Paris—611

Angoulême, Marie Thérèse Charlotte, duchesse d' (1778-1851)—daughter of Louis XVI—611

Antonius, Marcus (83-30 B.C.)—Roman politician and general, supporter of Julius Caesar—122

Arch, Joseph—founder of the National Agricultural Labourers' Union—555

Aristides (c. 540-467 B.C.)—Athenian statesman and general during the Greco-Persian wars—121

Arkwright, Sir Richard (1732-1792)—English manufacturer, inventor of the spinning throstle, the carding engine and other spinning machines named after him—12, 812, 503

Arnauld, Antoine (1612-1694)—French philosopher, adherent of Descartes' theory of cognition—127

Ashley (Cooper Anthony Ashley, 7th Earl of Shaftesbury) (1801-1885)—English politician, Tory philanthropist—14, 423, 435, 437, 440, 451, 463, 464, 539, 578

Ashton, Thomas—manufacturer in Hyde (near Manchester)—477

Ashton, Thomas—son of Thomas Ashton, killed in 1831 during workers' disturbances in Hyde—508

Ashworth, Edmund (1801-1881)—English manufacturer, liberal—451, 477, 511

Attila (d. 453)—King of the Huns (433-453)—626, 635

B

Babeuf, François Noel (Gracchus) (1760-1797)—French revolutionary, advocate of utopian egalitarian communism, organiser of the "conspiracy of equals" —47, 119, 131, 667

Bacon, Francis, Baron Verulam, Viscount St. Albans (1561-1626)—English philosopher, naturalist and historian—128-29

Bailey, William—manufacturer in Stalybridge—520

Baines, Sir Edward (1800-1890)—English economist, liberal—429

Bakunin, Mikhail (1814-1876)—Russian revolutionary and writer, one of the ideologists of the Narodnik trend and of anarchism—212

Bardsley, Samuel Argent (1764-1851)—physician in Manchester (1790-1823), author of several works on medicine—420

Barham, Charles Foster (1804-1884)—English physician, member of the Children's Employment Commission in 1841—531

Barmecides—a noble Persian family which attained great power under the Abbasid caliphs—579

Barry, Sir David (1780-1835)—English physician and physiologist—445-48, 453-54

Bauer, Bruno (1809-1882)—German philosopher, Young Hegelian—7, 16, 39, 40, 78, 79, 81, 85-89, 91, 92, 94, 95, 99-104, 106-13, 115, 117-18, 131, 132, 134-44, 146-47, 149, 151, 152, 153-58, 166, 191-93, 211, 240

Bauer, Edgar (1820-1886)—German philosopher and writer, Young Hegelian, brother and fellow-thinker of Bruno Bauer—19-24, 33, 34, 37-43, 48, 50-53, 78, 87, 146, 147, 156-57, 188, 211, 213

Bäumler (Bimeler), Joseph Michael (c. 1778-1853)—German pastor, separatist; emigrated to America in 1817 and founded a communist colony at Zoar (Ohio)—220, 221

Bayle, Pierre (1647-1706)—French sceptic philosopher, critic of religious dogmatism—127

Beaumont de la Bonninière, Gustave Auguste de (1802-1866)—French liberal writer and politician, author of several works on slavery in the United States—186

Beaumont, Thomas B. (d. 1859)—English surgeon—445, 449

Becker, August (1814-1871)—German journalist, Utopian Communist; in the 1840s one of the leaders of the Weitling communities in Switzerland—242, 655

Benda, Daniel Alexander (1786-1870)—German liberal journalist—10

Benedix, Roderich (1811-1873)—German author and playwright, manager of a theatre in Elberfeld (1845)—238

Bentham, Jeremy (1748-1832)—English sociologist, theoretician of utilitarianism—131-34, 178, 188, 194, 528, 667

Bentley and White—owners of a sawmill at Bury (Lancashire)—509

Béraud, F.F.A.—police commissioner in Paris—20, 156

Birley, Hugh Hornby—Manchester manufacturer, Tory—514, 521

Bishop, Theresa—London working woman—335

Blackstone, Sir William (1723-1780)—English lawyer, advocate of constitutional monarchy—195

Blyth—manufacturer in Holmfirth (Yorkshire)—471

Böhme, Jakob (1575-1624)—German handicraftsman, pantheist philosopher—128

Borthwick, Peter (1804-1852)—English politician, Tory, editor of the Morning Post—578

Bourbons—French royal dynasty (1589-1792, 1814-15 and 1815-30)—81, 124, 598, 607

Bouverie, William Pleydell, 3rd Earl of Radnor (1779-1869)—English politician, Whig—555

Bowers—manufacturer at Holmfirth (Yorkshire)—471

Boz—see Dickens, Charles

Bray, John Francis (1809-1897)—English economist, Utopian Socialist, follower of Robert Owen, advocated the theory of "labour money"—288

Bridgewater, Francis Egerton, Duke of (1736-1803)—big English landowner, known as the "father of British inland navigation"—319

Brindley, James (1716-1772)—English engineer—319

Brocklehurst, John (1788-1870)—English manufacturer and financier, Member of Parliament for Macclesfield (1832-66), liberal—486-87

Brougham and Vaux, Henry Peter, 1st Baron (1778-1868)—English statesman, lawyer and writer, Whig—471

Brüggemann, Karl Heinrich (1810-1887)—German liberal journalist—10

Bruno—see Bauer, Bruno

Brutus, Marcus Junius (c. 85-42 B.C.)—Roman politician, republican, one of the initiators of the conspiracy against Julius Caesar—121-22

Buchez, Philippe Joseph Benjamin (1796-1865)—French politician, historian, Christian Socialist—119, 211

Buckingham, James Silk (1786-1855)—English writer and traveller, Member of Parliament for Sheffield (1832-37); in 1837-40 lived in America—222

Buonarroti, Filippo Michele (1761-1837)—Italian revolutionary, Utopian Communist; a leader of the French revolutionary movement in the late 18th and early 19th century, Babeuf's comrade-in-arms—119, 667

Bürgers, Heinrich (1820-1878)—German radical journalist—240

Burns, Major J. A.—member of the Children's Employment Commission in 1841—484

Bussey, Peter—delegate to the Chartist Convention of 1839; abandoned the Chartist movement after an unsuccessful attempt to raise a revolt in Yorkshire in 1839—519

Byron, George Gordon Noel, Lord (1788-1824)—English romantic poet—528

C

Cabanis, Pierre Jean Georges (1757-1808)—French physician and philosopher—125-26

Cabet, Étienne (1788-1856)—French writer, Utopian Communist, author of the book Voyage en Icarie—131, 667

Caesar, Gaius Julius (c. 100-44 B.C.)—Roman general and statesman—121-22

Canning, George (1770-1827)—English statesman, diplomat, Tory; Foreign Secretary (1807-09; 1822-27), Prime Minister (1827)—667

Carlyle, Thomas (1795-1881)—British writer, historian and philosopher, supported the Tories; preached views bordering on feudal socialism up to 1848; later a relentless opponent of the working-class movement—14, 368, 389, 390, 392, 414, 510, 560, 562, 563, 578-79

Carter—coroner for Surrey (London)—334

Cartwright, Edmund (1743-1823)—English parson, inventor of the power-loom—312

Cassius Longinus, Gaius (d. 42 B.C.)—Roman politician, republican, one of the organisers of the conspiracy against Julius Caesar—122

Catilina, Lucius Sergius (c. 108-62 B.C.)—Roman politician, organiser of the conspiracy against the aristocratic republic—121-22

Cato, Marcus Porcius (95-46 B.C.)—Roman statesman and philosopher, leader of the republicans—122

Chadwick, Sir Edwin (1800-1890)—English official, member of Parliamentary Factories Inquiry Commissions—339

Champneys, William Weldon (1807-1875)—English parson, philanthropist—385

Chaptal, Jean Antoine Claude (1756-1832)—French statesman and chemist—200

Charles I (1600-1649)—King of Great Britain and Ireland (1625-49), executed during the English revolution of the 17th century—262

Charles II (1630-1685)—King of Great Britain and Ireland (1660-85)—576

Cherbuliez, Antoine Élisée (1797-1869)—Swiss economist, wanted to combine Sismondi's doctrine with elements of the Ricardian theory—271, 287

Chevalier, Michel (1806-1879)—French engineer, economist and journalist, Saint-Simonist in the 1830s, later a free trader—283

Clavière, Étienne (1735-1793)—Swiss financier; during the French Revolution was a member of the Legislative Assembly, Minister for Finance in the Girondist Government—270

Clodius, Publius (c. 93-52 B.C.)—surnamed *Pulcher*—Roman politician, supporter of Julius Caesar—121

Cobden, Richard (1804-1865)—English manufacturer and politician, a leader of the free traders and founder of the Anti-Corn Law League—588

Collins, Anthony (1676-1729)—English philosopher—129

Collins, John Anderson (c. 1810-1879)—English Socialist; after his emigration to America became a follower of Fourier and an abolitionist, founded a communist colony in the state of New York (1813)—223

Comte, François Charles Louis (1782-1837) —French liberal writer and economist —24, 44-46, 270

Condillac, Étienne Bonnot de (1715-1780) —French philosopher, follower of Locke—127, 129

Considérant, Victor Prosper (1808-1893)— French writer, Utopian Socialist, disciple and follower of Fourier—667

Cowan, Robert—English physician, author of *Vital Statistics of Glasgow*—404

Coward, William (c. 1656-1725)—English physician and philosopher—129

Cowell, John W.—member of the Factories Inquiry Commission in 1833—441, 445, 450, 453, 454

Crémieux, Isaac Moïse, dit Adolphe (1796-1880)—French lawyer and politician, in the 1840s was a liberal—115

Croker, John Wilson (1780-1857)—British politician and writer—560

Crompton, Samuel (1753-1827)—English engineer, inventor of the spinning mule—12, 312

D

Dante, Alighieri (1265-1321)—Italian poet—645

Danton, Georges Jacques (1759-1794)— leading figure in the French Revolution; leader of the Right wing of the Jacobins—121

Davy, Sir Humphry (1778-1829)—English chemist and physicist—318, 537

Democritus (c. 460-c. 370 B.C.)—Greek philosopher, one of the founders of the atomistic theory—126, 128

Demosthenes (384-322 B.C.)—Greek orator and politician—121

Descartes (Cartesius), René (1596-1650)— French philosopher, mathematician and naturalist—125-26, 129, 130, 132

Destutt de Tracy, Antoine Louis Claude, Comte de (1754-1836)—French economist, philosopher, advocate of constitutional monarchy—33

Dézamy, Théodore (1803-1850)—French writer, advocate of utopian communism—131, 667

Dickens, Charles John Huffam (1812-1870) —English novelist—9, 327

Diderot, Denis (1713-1784)—French philosopher in the period of Enlightenment; atheist, leader of the Encyclopaedists—130, 528

Disraeli, Benjamin, Earl of Beaconsfield (1804-1881)—British author and statesman; in the 1840s adhered to the "Young England" group, subsequently became a Tory leader; Prime Minister (1868 and 1874-80)—420, 578

Dodwell, Henry, the younger (d. 1784)— English philosopher—129

Döleke, Hermann—teacher of German, one of the leaders of the "Young Germany" secret society in Switzerland—651

Douglas—manufacturer in Pendleton (Manchester)—446

Drinkwater J. E.—member of the Factories Inquiry Commission in 1833—445, 447, 469

Duncombe, Thomas Slingsby (1796-1861)—English radical politician, took part in the Chartist movement in the 1840s—322, 545, 569, 570

Dunoyer, Barthélemy Charles Pierre Joseph (1786-1862)—French economist and politician—283

Duns Scotus, John (c. 1265-1308)—medieval scholastic philosopher, Nominalist—127

Dupuis, Charles François (1742-1809)—French philosopher in the period of Enlightenment—130

Duveyrier, Charles (1803-1866)—French man of letters and lawyer, follower of Saint-Simon—283

E

Edgar—see *Bauer, Edgar*

Egidius, H. L.—see *Weil, Carl*

Elizabeth I (1533-1603)—Queen of England (1558-1603)—571

Elisabeth-Louise (1801-1873)—Queen of Prussia, wife of Frederick William IV —650

Engels, Frederick (1820-1895)—2, 4, 32, 212, 214, 229, 232, 235, 238-41, 295, 299, 304, 584, 613, 645, 651, 654, 656

Epicurus (c. 341-c. 270 B.C.)—Greek atomistic philosopher—126, 169

Estwood—manufacturer at Holmfirth (Yorkshire)—471

F

Faraday, Michael (1791-1867)—English physicist and chemist—546

Faucher, Julius (Jules) (1820-1878)—German writer, Young Hegelian; advocate of free trade—7, 12, 14, 38, 40, 78, 81, 87

Faucher, Léon (1803-1854)—French writer and politician of moderate liberal views—488

Fein, Georg (1803-1869)—took part in the democratic movement in Germany in the thirties and forties of the 19th century, member of the "Young Germany" secret society in Switzerland—651

Ferrand, William Bushfield—English landowner, Tory, member of the "Young England" group—569, 578

Ferrier, François Louis Auguste (1777-1861)—French economist and official, advocate of mercantilism—268, 269, 290-93

Feuerbach, Ludwig Andreas von (1804-1872)—German philosopher—39, 56, 83, 92-94, 125, 127, 139, 141, 147, 212, 235, 236, 613, 653, 665

Fichte, Johann Gottlieb (1762-1814)—German philosopher—120, 139

Fielden, John (1784-1849)—English manufacturer, philanthropist, proponent of factory legislation—578

Finch, John—English journalist, traveller, follower of Robert Owen, contributor to the newspaper *The New Moral World* —216, 217, 219-21, 240

Fleischhammer, Emil—correspondent of the *Allgemeine Literatur-Zeitung* in Breslau—145, 146

Fourier, François Marie Charles (1772-1837)—French Utopian Socialist—31, 50, 81, 84, 88, 131, 152, 194, 196, 201, 232, 263, 597, 613-16, 617, 618, 619, 620, 622, 641-43, 667

Foy, Maximilien Sébastien (1775-1825)—French general; liberal politician—74

François de Neufchâteau, Nicolas Louis, Comte (1750-1828)—French writer and politician, Minister for the Interior in the period of the Directory—598

Franks, R. H.—reporter in the Children's Employment Commission in England in 1841—497

Frederick Augustus II (1797-1854)—King of Saxony (1836-54)—646

Frederick William IV (1795-1861)—King of Prussia (1840-61)—649-50

Friedrich Ferdinand Leopold (1821-1847) —Archduke of Austria—650

Froment, M.—police official in Paris during the Restoration—74

Frost, John (1784-1877)—English radical, joined the Chartist movement in 1838; was sentenced to transportation to Australia for organising the miners' insurrection in Wales (1839); returned to England in 1856 after an amnesty—519

G

Galway, Ann—London working woman—334

Gans, Eduard (c. 1798-1839)—German philosopher, professor of law at Berlin University, follower of Hegel—179

Garnier, Germain, Marquis (1754-1821)—French economist and politician, monarchist; follower of the Physiocrats, translator and critic of Adam Smith—291

Gaskell, Peter—English physician and liberal journalist—14, 366, 401, 422, 426, 579

Gassendi, Pierre (1592-1655)—French philosopher, adherent of the atomistic theory propounded by Epicurus; physicist and mathematician—126

Gay, Jules (1807-after 1876)—French Utopian Communist—131, 667

Gibson—Scottish building worker—591

Gilbert, Thomas (1720-1798)—English lawyer and politician, one of the sponsors of the Poor Laws—576

Ginal—German pastor in Philadelphia, founder of a communist colony in Pennsylvania—222

Girard, Philippe Henri de (1775-1845)—French engineer, inventor of a flax-spinning machine—315

Godwin, William (1756-1836)—English writer and journalist, one of the founders of anarchism—528, 667

Goethe, Johann Wolfgang von (1749-1832) —German poet—63, 142, 175

Goldsmith, Oliver (1728-1774)—Anglo-Irish poet—552

Görtz—Prussian official, Chief Burgomaster of Trier in the 1840s—678, 679

Graham—Glasgow worker, strikebreaker —509

Graham, George—English official, Registrar-General of Births, Deaths, and Marriages—403

Graham, Sir James Robert George (1792-1861)—English statesman; a Whig at the beginning of his political career, later an adherent of Robert Peel; Home Secretary in Peel's Cabinet (1841-46); Tory—14, 16, 464-65

Grainger, Richard Dugard (1801-1865)—English physician and physiologist, member of the Children's Employment Commission in 1841—357, 402, 409, 480, 482, 483, 491

Greg, Robert Hyde (1795-1875)—big English manufacturer, liberal—450, 477

Grotius, Hugo (1583-1645)—Dutch scientist, lawyer, one of the founders of the theory of natural law—48

Grün, Karl Theodor Ferdinand (pen-name: *Ernst von der Haide*) (1817-1887)—German writer, in the mid-1840s a "true Socialist"—232

Gruppe, Otto Friedrich (1804-1876)—German writer and philosopher, opponent of the Young Hegelians; attacked Bruno Bauer in 1842—157

H

Hamilton, Alexander, Duke of (1767-1852) —big Scottish landowner, Whig—539

Hargreaves, James (d. 1778)—English spinner and weaver, inventor of the power-loom known as the jenny—12, 310

Hartley, David (1705-1757)—English physician and philosopher—129

Harun al-Rashid (763-809)—Caliph of Baghdad of the Abbasid dynasty (786-809)—179

Haslam, Messrs.—owners of the collieries in Belper—543

Hawkins, Francis Bisset (1796-1894)—English physician and journalist; member of the Factories Inquiry Commission in 1833—405, 436, 440, 441, 445, 446, 450, 451-53, 461, 466

Heathcoat, John (1783-1861)—English engineer, inventor of the bobbin-net machine—314

Hébert, Jacques René (1757-1794)—prominent figure in the French Revolution, leader of the Left wing of the Jacobins—114, 667

Hegel, Georg Wilhelm Friedrich (1770-1831)—German philosopher—12, 18, 20, 22, 23, 36, 40, 57, 60-61, 78, 79, 82, 85-87, 90-92, 103, 107, 114, 125, 130-31, 137-39, 141-42, 149, 167, 179, 192-93, 201, 613, 614, 641, 665

Heine, Heinrich (1797-1856)—German revolutionary poet—157, 232

Helvétius, Claude Adrien (1715-1771)—French philosopher, atheist, Enlightener—127, 129-33, 528, 667

Henfrey—manufacturer in Manchester—513, 585-86, 589-96

Hennen, John (1779-1828)—English army physician, author of several works on military medicine—339

Hess, Moses (1812-1875)—German radical journalist, one of the main exponents of "true socialism" in the mid-1840s—232, 235, 238-40

Hey, William (1772-1844)—English physician, member of the Factories Inquiry Commission in 1833—445, 446, 449

Higby (*Hizby*), *E. L.*—ironmaster in Pittsburg (Ohio), founder of a communist colony—223

Hilditch, Richard—English economist in the middle of the 19th century—287

Hindley, Charles—English manufacturer, philanthropist, supported Factory legislation—578

Hinrichs, Hermann Friedrich Wilhelm (1794-1861)—German professor of philosophy, Right-wing Hegelian—90-93, 97, 103, 108, 137, 138, 140, 141

Hirsch, Samuel (1809-1889)—Rabbi in Dessau, philosopher and writer of religious leanings—88, 89

Hirzel, Konrad Melchior (1793-1843)—Swiss politician and journalist, Zurich correspondent of the *Allgemeine Literatur-Zeitung*—145-47, 210

Hizby—see *Higby*

Hobbes, Thomas (1588-1679)—English philosopher—126, 129

Hobhouse, John Cam, Baron Broughton de Gyfford (1786-1869)—English liberal politician—459, 462

Hoffmann, Max—apothecary, one of the leaders of the "Young Germany" secret society in Switzerland—651

Holbach, Paul Henri Dietrich, Baron d' (1723-1789)—French philosopher, atheist, Enlightener—130, 132, 133, 528, 667

Holland, P. H.—physician in Manchester—404

Homer—epic poet of Ancient Greece, author of *Iliad* and *Odyssey*—47, 190

Hood, Thomas (1799-1845)—English realist poet, democrat—500

Horne, Richard Henry (1803-1884)—English writer, member of the Children's Employment Commission in 1841—409, 410, 492

Horner, Leonard (1785-1864)—English geologist and public figure; factory inspector (1833-56), member of the Factories Inquiry Commission in 1833 and of the Children's Employment Commission in 1841; took the side of the workers—435, 463

Hübner, Karl Wilhelm (1814-1879)—German realist artist of a democratic orientation—230

Hunt, Thomas—English Socialist, founder of the communist colony *Equality* in Wisconsin—223

Huntsman, Benjamin (1704-1776)—English inventor—317

Huskisson, William (1770-1830)—English statesman, Tory, Secretary of the Board of Trade (1823-27)—657

I

Ibbetson—manufacturer in Sheffield—508

J

Jerrold, Douglas William (1803-1857)—English journalist, correspondent of *The Illuminated Magazine* in the 1840s—574

Johann Nepomuk Marie Joseph (1801-1873)—Prince of Saxony; King of Saxony from 1854—645, 646

Johns, William—English physician, Registrar in Chief for Manchester—437

Johnson—worker at the factory of Pauling and Henfrey in Manchester—593

Jungnitz, Ernst (d. 1848)—German journalist, Young Hegelian, contributor to the *Allgemeine Literatur-Zeitung*—17

K

Kaiser, Heinrich Wilhelm—German writer of the 1840s, author of a work on French socialism and communism—642

Kant, Immanuel (1724-1804)—German philosopher—179

Kay-Shuttleworth, Sir James Phillips (1804-1877)—English physician and public figure.—351, 362, 364-66, 390, 467

Kennedy, John (1769-1855)—textile manufacturer in Manchester—468

Kitchen—manufacturer in Sheffield—508

Knight, Arnold—physician in Manchester—493

Köchlin—manufacturer in Württemberg—288

Köttgen (Koettgen), Gustav Adolf (1805-1882)—German artist and poet; took part in the working-class movement in the 1840s; his views were close to those of the "true Socialists"—238, 239

Krug, Wilhelm Traugott (1770-1842)—German philosopher—150

Kuhlmann, Georg—secret informer of the Austrian Government; in the 1840s preached the ideas of "true socialism" among the German artisans, followers of Weitling in Switzerland, using religious phraseology to pose as a prophet—655

L

Lamettrie (La Mettrie), Julien Offray de (1709-1751)—French physician and philosopher—125-26, 130

Law, John (1671-1729)—Scottish economist and financier, Director-General of Finance in France (1719-20)—126, 624

Leach, James—a spinner by profession, took an active part in the English labour movement, one of the leaders of Chartist organisations in Lancashire in the 1840s—429, 430, 469, 470, 485, 486, 488, 588

Leclerc, Théophile (b. 1771)—prominent figure in the French Revolution, one of the leaders of the revolutionary plebeian trend (*Enragés*)—119, 667

Lee, John (1779-1859)—Scottish pastor, rector of Edinburgh University from 1840—338

Lehon—Paris notary—70

Leibniz, Gottfried Wilhelm (1646-1716)—German philosopher and mathematician—99, 125, 126, 129, 130

Leifchild, John Roby—member of the Children's Employment Commission in 1841—497

Leon, Graf (Bernhard Müller)—German colonist in America, founder of the New Jerusalem communist colony in Philipsburgh—219

Leopold I (1790-1865)—King of Belgium (1831-65)—676

Leroux, Pierre (1797-1871)—French writer, Utopian Socialist—667

Le Roy (in Dutch—*De Roy*, in Latin, *Regius*), *Henry* (1598-1679)—Dutch physician and philosopher—125, 126

Leske, *Karl Friedrich Julius* (1821-1886)—German publisher; in the 1840s and 1850s was head of the publishing firm founded in 1821 in Darmstadt by his father Karl Wilhelm Leske, whose name he used to sign papers—654, 675, 676

Lessing, *Karl Friedrich* (1808-1880)—German artist of democratic tendencies—231

Lindley, *John*—inventor of the point-net machine—314

List, *Friedrich* (1789-1846)—German economist, advocated protectionism—258, 259, 265-78, 283-92

Locke, *John* (1632-1704)—English philosopher and economist—125, 127, 129-30, 131, 132

Londonderry, *Charles William Stewart (Vane), 3rd Marquess of* (1778-1854)—big English landowner, served in the army and in diplomacy—544

Loudon, *Charles* (1801-1844)—English physician, member of the Factories Inquiry Commission in 1833—445-46, 449, 452-54

Louis XIV (1638-1715)—King of France (1643-1715)—56

Louis Philippe I (1773-1850)—Duke of Orleans, King of France (1830-48)—213

Loustalot, *Elisée* (1762-1790)—French journalist, democrat, took part in the French Revolution, a Jacobin—82

Lovett, *William* (1800-1877)—English radical, participant in the Chartist movement; adherent of "moral force" and collaboration with the bourgeoisie—517-18

Lüning, *Otto* (1818-1868)—German physician and journalist, "true Socialist" in the mid-1840s—232, 240

Lyell, *Charles* (1797-1875)—British chemist and geologist—546

M

Mably, *Gabriel Bonnot de* (1709-1785)—French sociologist, proponent of utopian egalitarian communism—667

Mackellar—physician in Pencaitland (Scotland)—536

Mackintosh, *Robert*—member of the Factories Inquiry Commission in 1833—446, 451, 454, 461

Malebranche, *Nicolas de* (1638-1715)—French philosopher—125, 127, 129, 130

Mallet du Pan, *Jacques* (1749-1800)—Swiss journalist, monarchist, was connected with French counter-revolutionary émigrés, author of memoirs—598

Malthus, *Thomas Robert* (1766-1834)—English clergyman and economist, founder of the misanthropic theory of population—379, 380, 432, 570, 572

Mandeville, *Bernard de* (1670-1733)—English democratic writer, moralist and economist—131

Manners, *John James Robert, Lord*—see *Rutland, John*

Marat, *Jean Paul* (1743-1793)—leading figure in the French Revolution, prominent Jacobin—81

Marbach, *Oswald* (1810-1890)—German writer and poet, author of adaptations of German medieval epics and publisher of German *Volksbücher* (popular books)—163

Marmontel, *Jean François* (1723-1799)—French writer, representative of the moderate wing of the Enlighteners, member of the Paris Academy of Sciences from 1763—144

Marr, *Wilhelm* (1819-1904)—German journalist, one of the leaders of the "Young Germany" secret society in Switzerland, and editor of its paper *Blätter der Gegenwart für soziales Leben*—651, 652, 654

Martin du Nord, *Nicolas Ferdinand Marie Louis Joseph* (1790-1847)—French lawyer and politician, Minister of

Justice and Cults during the July monarchy (since 1840)—115, 117

Martineau, Harriet (1802-1876)—English writer, supporter of moderate social reforms—222

Marx, Jenny (née von Westphalen) (1814-1881)—Karl Marx's wife—676

Marx, Jenny (1844-1883)—Karl Marx's daughter—676

Marx, Karl (1818-1883)—2, 4, 8, 87, 106, 115, 117, 210, 232, 235-36, 240, 241, 256, 260, 287, 290, 597, 665, 666, 667, 668, 675-79

Mathew, Theobald (1790-1856)—Irish Catholic clergyman—423

Maude, Daniel—Justice of the Peace in Manchester—587-93, 595, 596

McAdam, John Loudon (1756-1836)—Scottish inventor, expert in highroad building—319

McCulloch, John Ramsay (1789-1864)—British economist who vulgarised David Ricardo's theories—269, 271, 287, 313, 380, 415, 580

McDurt, Thomas—worker at a cotton mill in Glasgow—453

Mead, Edward P.—English workers' poet; contributed to the Chartist newspaper The Northern Star—474

Melish, John (1771-1822)—English writer, geographer and traveller; he described communist colonies in America—222

Mellor—worker at the Pauling and Henfrey brick firm in Manchester—591

Menenius, Agrippa (d. 493 B.C.)—Roman patrician—510

Menzel, Wolfgang (1798-1873)—German conservative writer and literary critic—153

Miles, William (1797-1878)—English financier, Member of Parliament—569

Mill, James (1773-1836)—English philosopher and economist, adherent of Ricardo's theory—271, 287

Miller—Police Superintendent in Glasgow, Captain—342

Miltiades (c. 550 or 540-489 B.C.)—Athenian general and statesman during the Greco-Persian wars—121

Mirabeau, Honoré Gabriel Victor Riqueti, Comte de (1749-1791)—prominent figure in the French Revolution, constitutional monarchist—270

Mitchell, James (c. 1786-1844)—English public figure, author of several popular science works, member of the Children's Employment Commission in 1841—531, 532

Molière (real name: Jean Baptiste Poquelin) (1622-1673)—French dramatist—55, 627, 628

Monier de la Sizeranne, Paul Jean Ange Henri, Comte (1797-1878)—French journalist and dramatist—75

Monk—London barrister—591-93

Monteil (Montheil), Amans Alexis (1769-1850)—French historian—71

Montyon, Antoine Jean Baptiste Robert Auget, Baron de (1733-1820)—French philanthropist, one of the sponsors of "Virtue Prize"—190

Morellet, André (1727-1819)—French philosopher and economist, contributed to the Encyclopaedia—598

Morelly (18th cent.)—representative of utopian egalitarian communism in France—667

M'Quarry—Glasgow worker, strikebreaker—509

Müller, Wilhelm (literary pseudonym: Wolfgang Müller von Königswinter) (1816-1873)—German poet, physician in Düsseldorf (1845)—239

N

Napoleon I Bonaparte (1769-1821)—Emperor of the French (1804-14 and 1815)—10, 81, 123-24, 269, 270, 289, 290, 409, 598

Nauwerck, Karl Ludwig Theodor (1810-1891)—German journalist, Young Hegelian—16-18

Nelson, Horatio Nelson, Viscount (1758-1805)—English admiral—409

Newton, Sir Isaac (1642-1727)—English physicist, astronomer and mathematician—125

O

Oastler, Richard (1789-1861)—English politician, Tory philanthropist—438, 463, 464, 519

O'Connell, Daniel (1775-1847)—Irish lawyer and politician, leader of the liberal wing in the national liberation movement—561

O'Connor, Feargus Edward (1794-1855)—a leader of the Chartist Left, editor-in-chief of The Northern Star—367

Origen (Latin: Origenes) (c. 185-c. 254)—Christian theologian, one of the Fathers of the Church—158, 178

Owen, Robert (1771-1858)—British Utopian Socialist—84, 131, 188, 219, 223-24, 232, 252, 459, 525, 597, 614, 667

P

Paalzow, Henriette von (1788-1847)—German writer—21

Padgin—manufacturer in Sheffield—508

Paine, Thomas (1737-1809)—English writer, Republican, took part in the American War of Independence and in the French Revolution—317

Parkinson, Richard (1797-1858)—English clergyman, and journalist, philanthropist—420, 565

Parny, Evariste Désiré de Forges, Vicomte de (1753-1814)—French poet—69

Patteson, Sir John (1790-1861)—English jurist, member of the Queen's Bench (1830-52)—542

Pauling—manufacturer in Manchester—513, 585-86, 589-96

Pecchio, Giuseppe (1785-1835)—Italian man of letters and economist—269

Peel, Sir Robert (1750-1830)—English cotton manufacturer, Member of Parliament, Tory—442, 459

Peel, Sir Robert (1788-1850)—English statesman, Tory, Prime Minister (1841-46), repealed the Corn Laws in 1846—442, 465, 546, 578, 588, 657, 658, 660

Percival, Thomas (1740-1804)—English physician, philanthropist—442

Peuchet, Jacques (1758-1830)—French writer, economist, monarchist—597-98, 604, 609-12

Philippson, Gustav (1814-1880)—German pedagogue and writer—88

Pilling, Richard (b. 1800)—Chartist, cotton-mill worker, one of the leaders of a strike in Ashton and Stalybridge (1842)—587

Pindar (c. 522-443 B.C.)—Greek lyric poet, author of solemn odes—285

Piso, Lucius Calpurnius Carsoninus (b. 101 B.C.)—Roman consul in 58 B.C., supporter of Julius Caesar—122

Pitkeithly, Lawrence—English traveller, Chartist, visited and described the communist colony of Shakers in New Lebanon (New York state)—217

Planck, Karl Christian (1819-1880)—German Protestant theologian, philosopher—103

Plato (c. 427-c. 347 B.C.)—Greek philosopher—179

Porter, George Richardson (1792-1852)—English economist and statistician—313

Pounder, Robert—Leeds worker—438

Power A.—member of the Factories Inquiry Commission in England in 1833—437, 441, 445, 448, 454, 480

Priestley, Joseph (1733-1804)—English chemist and philosopher, public figure—129

Proudhon, Pierre Joseph (1809-1865)—French writer, economist and sociologist, one of the founders of anarchism—23-35, 38-53, 156, 528, 642, 667

Püttmann, Hermann (1811-1894)—German radical poet and journalist, in the mid-1840s representative of "true socialism"—232, 235, 240, 654, 655

R

Radnor, Earl of—see Bouverie, William Pleydell

Rapp, George (1757-1847)—German Socialist, founder of the sect of Christian Communists in the state of Ohio, North America—218-20

Rashleigh, William—English politician, Member of Parliament, publisher of the book Stubborn Facts from the Factories by a Manchester Operative—429

Rauschenplatt, Johann Ernst Hermann von (1807-1868)—German politician, emigrated to Switzerland, a member of the "Young Germany" secret society—651

Read—worker at the Pauling and Henfrey brick firm in Manchester—595

Reichardt, Carl Ernst—bookbinder in Berlin, follower of Bruno Bauer, contributor to the Allgemeine Literatur-Zeitung—9, 10, 38, 78

Ricardo, David (1772-1823)—English economist—31, 33, 271, 286, 290

Riesser, Gabriel (1806-1863)—German journalist of Jewish descent, advocate of equality for the Jews—95-98, 113

Ripley, George (1802-1880)—American Unitarian clergyman, in 1842 founded a communist colony in Brook Farm (Massachusetts)—223

Roberton, John (1797-1876)—English physician—405, 453

Roberts—owner of the machine-works in Manchester—511

Roberts, William Prowling (1806-1871)—English jurist connected with the Chartist and trade union movements—541-42, 544, 546, 547, 568, 569, 590-96

Robespierre, Maximilien François Marie Isidore de (1758-1794)—leading figure in the French Revolution, leader of the Jacobins, head of the revolutionary government (1793-94)—119, 121, 122

Robinet, Jean Baptiste René (1735-1820)—French philosopher—130

Robson, George—inmate of the workhouse in Coventry, died in 1843—574

Rohmer, Friedrich (1814-1856)—German philosopher—211

Rohmer, Theodor (1820-1856)—German journalist, F. Rohmer's brother—211

Ronge, Johannes (1813-1887)—German clergyman, one of the initiators of the "German Catholics" movement—645, 653

Rotteck, Carl Wenzeslaus Redecker von (1775-1840)—German historian and liberal politician—123

Rousseau, Jean Jacques (1712-1778)—French philosopher and writer of the Enlightenment—604

Roux, Jacques (1752-1794)—prominent figure in the French Revolution. One of the leaders of the revolutionary plebeian trend (Enragés)—119, 667

Roux-Lavergne, Pierre Célestin (1802-1874)—French historian and philosopher—211

Ruge, Arnold (1802-1880)—German radical journalist and philosopher, Young Hegelian—155

Russell, John Russell, 1st Earl of (1792-1878)—English statesman, Whig leader, Prime Minister (1846-52 and 1865-66), Foreign Secretary (1852-53 and 1859-65)—15

Rutland, John James Robert Manners, 7th Duke of (1818-1906)—English aristocrat, Tory, author of pamphlets on the condition of factory workers, member of the "Young England" group—578

Rymarkiewicz, Leon (born c. 1825)—participant in the revolutionary conspiracy of the Polish patriots in Posnan in 1844-45—241

Rymarkiewicz, Maximilian (born c. 1832)—participant in the revolutionary conspiracy of the Polish patriots in Posnan in 1844-45, brother of L. Rymarkiewicz—241

S

Sack, Karl Heinrich (1789-1875)—German Protestant theologian, professor in Bonn, advocate of religious orthodoxy—203

Sadler, Michael Thomas (1780-1835)—English economist and politician, philanthropic Tory—460-61, 463

Saint-Just, Antoine Louis Léon de Richebourg de (1767-1794)—prominent figure in the French Revolution, a Jacobin leader—121-22

Saint-Simon, Claude Henri de Rouvroy, Comte de (1760-1825)—French Utopian Socialist—31, 50, 282, 283, 614, 667

Salmon—worker at the Pauling and Henfrey brick firm in Manchester—589-91

Sanchez (Tomas) (1550-1610)—Spanish theologian—629

Saunders, Robert John—English factory inspector in the 1840s—463

Say, Jean Baptiste (1767-1832)—French economist, one of the founders of the "three production factors" theory (an apology of capitalist exploitation)—32, 43, 269, 270, 273

Say, Louis Auguste (1774-1840)—French economist, brother and follower of J.-B. Say—270, 291

Schelling, Friedrich Wilhelm Joseph von (1775-1854)—German philosopher—95, 154

Schiller, Johann Christoph Friedrich von (1759-1805)—German poet, dramatist, historian and philosopher—23, 202

Schlöffel, Friedrich Wilhelm (1800-1870)—Silesian manufacturer, democrat—242

Schmidt, Simon—German tanner, one of the organisers of the League of the Just in Switzerland, follower of Weitling—655

Scott—worker at the Pauling and Henfrey brick firm in Manchester—591

Scriven, Samuel S.—member of the Children's Employment Commission in England in 1841—496

Senior, Nassau William (1790-1864)—English economist, vulgarised Ricardo's theory, opposed shortening the working day—364

Serra, Antonio (16th-17th cent.)—Italian economist, one of the first representatives of mercantilism—269

Shakespeare, William (1564-1616)—English poet and dramatist—71, 542, 552

Sharp, Francis—member of the Royal Society of English Surgeons, physician in Leeds—445, 449

Sharp—owner of the machine-works in Manchester—511

Sharps—shareholder of the Pauling and Henfrey firm in Manchester—594-95

Shelley, Percy Bysshe (1792-1822)—English poet, revolutionary romantic—528

Sheppard, John (Jack) (1702-1724)—English thief, known for his escapes from prison, executed in London in 1724—409

Sieyès, Emmanuel Joseph (1748-1836)—leading figure in the French Revolution; abbot, deputy to the Convention, moderate constitutionalist (Feuillant)—32

Sismondi, Jean Charles Léonard Simonde de (1773-1842)—Swiss economist, representative of economic romanticism—33, 271-73

Smellie, James—Glasgow surgeon—451

Smith, Adam (1723-1790)—British economist—31, 33, 49, 267-69, 271, 273, 277, 287, 291-93, 380, 415

Smith, John—Glasgow worker, strike-breaker—509

Smith, Thomas Southwood (1788-1861)—English physician, member of the Children's Employment Commission in 1841—373, 397, 536

Solomon—King of the Hebrews (c. 974-c. 937 B.C.)—409, 588, 589

Somerville, Alexander (1811-1885)—English radical journalist, wrote under the pen-name of "One who has whistled at the Plough"—224, 240, 556

Spinoza (Baruch or *Benedictus) de* (1632-1677)—Dutch philosopher—124-25, 127, 129-32, 136-37, 139

Staël, Madame de (Anne Louise Germaine, born Necker, Baronne de Staël-Holstein) (1766-1817)—French romantic writer —603

Standau, Julius—teacher of German, took part in the democratic movement in Germany in the 1830s-1840s, one of the leaders of the "Young Germany" secret society in Switzerland—651

Stein, Heinrich Friedrich Karl, Baron vom und zum (1757-1831)—Prussian statesman, held various responsible posts in the government (1804-08), initiator of moderate reforms—10

Stein, Lorenz von (1815-1890)—German lawyer and historian, author of works on the socialist movement, supporter of "social monarchy"—134, 613, 614, 642

Stephens, Joseph Rayner (1805-1879)—English clergyman, took an active part in the Chartist movement in Lancashire (1837-39)—519, 524, 581

Stewart, Dugald (1753-1828)—Scottish philosopher, representative of what is known as "philosophy of common sense"—268

Stirner, Max (real name: *Johann Caspar Schmidt*) (1806-1856)—German philosopher, Young Hegelian, one of the ideologists of individualism and anarchism—240, 241, 329, 564

Strauss, David Friedrich (1808-1874)—German philosopher and writer, Young Hegelian—87, 103, 137-39, 142, 528

Stuart, James (1775-1849)—English physician and writer, Whig, factory inspector in 1833—444, 446, 451, 454, 457

Stumm-Halberg, Karl Ferdinand, Freiherr von (1836-1901)—German manufacturer and conservative politician—544

Sturge, Joseph (1793-1859)—English politician, free trader; joined the Chartists with a view to bringing the work-ing class under the influence of the radical bourgeoisie—523

Sue, Eugène Marie Joseph (1804-1857)—French writer, author of sentimental social novels—55-57, 62, 66-68, 70, 73-76, 162, 166, 168, 170, 171, 180-82, 185-88, 190-91, 197, 202-03

Symons, Jelinger Cookson (1809-1860)—English liberal journalist, member of the Children's Employment Commission in 1841—341-42, 410, 412, 432, 494, 503, 534

Szeliga—see Zychlinski, Franz

T

Tancred, Thomas—member of the Children's Employment Commission in England in 1841—497

Taylor, John (1804-1841)—English physician, member of the Left wing of the Chartist movement—519

Thomson, Charles Edward Poulett, Baron Sydenham (1799-1841)—English statesman, Whig—364

Thornhill, Thomas—English landowner, Whig—463

Tocqueville, Alexis Charles Henri Maurice Clérel de (1805-1859)—French liberal historian and politician—186

Tristan, Flora Célestine Thérèse Henriette (1803-1844)—French authoress, proponent of utopian socialism—19, 188

Tufnell, Edward Carlton—member of the Factories Inquiry Commission in England in 1833—437, 440, 444, 445, 450, 451

Turpin, Richard (Dick) (1706-1739)—English robber, executed in 1739—409

U

Ure, Andrew (1778-1857)—English chemist and economist, free trader—285, 310, 417, 429, 434, 457-59, 461, 462, 478, 510, 511

V

Vaughan, Robert (1795-1868)—English clergyman, historian and journalist—416

Victoria (1819-1901)—Queen of Great Britain and Ireland (1837-1901)—336, 518, 649, 650

Vidocq, François Eugène (1775-1857)—French secret police agent, presumed author of *Memoirs*; his name was used to denote a cunning sleuth and rogue—73, 163

Vincent—leader of a carpenters' strike in Paris (September 1845)—650

Virgil (Publius Vergilius Maro) (70-19 B.C.)—Roman poet—618, 628

Virgil, Polydore (c. 1470-1555)—English historian of Italian descent—71

Volney, Constantin François Chasseboeuf, Comte de (1757-1820)—French philosopher of the Enlightenment—130

Voltaire, François Marie Arouet de (1694-1778)—French philosopher, writer and historian of the Enlightenment—126, 268, 619

Voss, Johann Heinrich (1751-1826)—German poet, translator of works by Homer, Virgil and other ancient poets—190

W

Wade, John (1788-1875)—English writer, economist and historian—405

Wakefield, Edward Gibbon (1796-1862)—English writer, statesman, and economist; author of a colonisation theory—551

Watt, James (1736-1819)—Scottish engineer, inventor of the steam-engine—149, 312

Wedgwood, Josiah (1730-1795)—English pottery manufacturer, who devised improved pottery techniques—318

Weil, Carl (1806-1878)—German liberal journalist, editor of the *Konstitutionelle Jahrbücher* (1842-46); from 1851 official in Austria—162

Weill, Alexander (1811-1899)—German democratic journalist, in the 1840s emigrated to France, contributed to German and French newspapers—147

Weitling, Wilhelm Christian (1808-1871)—one of the early leaders of the working-class movement in Germany, tailor by trade, one of the theoreticians of utopian egalitarian communism—236, 614, 615, 654

Welcker, Carl Theodor (1790-1869)—German lawyer, liberal journalist, Landtag deputy in Baden—123

Wellington, Arthur Wellesley, 1st Duke of (1769-1852)—British general and statesman, Tory, Prime Minister (1828-30)—409

Wesley, John (1703-1791)—English clergyman, founder of Methodism—410

Wightman, Sir William (1784-1863)—English jurist, from 1841 member of the Queen's Bench—542

Wilhelm I (1781-1864)—King of Württemberg (1816-64)—288

Williams, Sir John (1777-1846)—English jurist, from 1834 member of the King's (later Queen's) Bench, liberal—542

Wolff, Christian, Freiherr von (1679-1754)—German philosopher, naturalist, economist and jurist—67

Wood, James and Francis—manufacturers in Bradford—449, 509-10

Wright, John—factory overseer in Macclesfield—446

Z

Zerrleder—presumed pseudonym of Bruno Bauer—145, 146

Zychlinski, Franz Zychlin von (1816-1900)—Prussian officer, Young Hegelian, contributed to periodicals published by B. Bauer under the pseudonym of Szeliga—7, 53-57, 60-67, 68, 69, 70, 71-77, 86, 162, 163, 165-68, 176-78, 180, 185, 190, 191, 194, 195-96, 202, 208, 209

INDEX OF LITERARY AND MYTHOLOGICAL NAMES

Aaron—the first high priest mentioned in the Bible.—410

Abraham (Bib.)—10, 101, 105, 107

Adam (Bib.)—410, 574

Badinot—character in Eugène Sue's novel *Les Mystères de Paris.*—203

Bradamanti. See Polidori

Bras rouge—character in Eugène Sue's novel *Les Mystères de Paris.*—73, 181

Cabrion—character in Eugène Sue's novel *Les Mystères de Paris.*—75, 76

Cecily—character in Eugène Sue's novel *Les Mystères de Paris.*—68-69

Chatelain—character in Eugène Sue's *Les Mystères de Paris.*—200

Chouette—character in Eugène Sue's *Les Mystères de Paris.*—180-85, 187

Chourineur—character in Eugène Sue's *Les Mystères de Paris.*—163-65, 168, 169, 180, 182, 206, 207

Christ, Jesus (Bib.)—65, 104, 154, 161, 410

Codrus—according to legend, the King of Athens, who lived in the 11th century B.C.—122

David—character in Eugène Sue's *Les Mystères de Paris.*—68, 164, 176-77, 205, 207

Don Quixote—hero of Cervantes' novel by the same name.—209

Dorante—character in Molière's play *Le bourgeois gentilhomme.*—630, 631

Eleonore—character in Parny's *Poésies érotiques.*—69

Ferrand, Jacques—character in Eugène Sue's *Les Mystères de Paris.*—69-71, 206, 209

Fleur de Marie—character in Eugène Sue's *Les Mystères de Paris.*—163, 166-76, 180-82, 186, 187, 204, 205, 208, 209

Fortunatus—hero of a German folk tale, who possessed a miraculous inexhaustible purse and a magic cap.—200

George, Madame—character in Eugène Sue's novel *Les Mystères de Paris.*—171-73, 205

Germain—character in Eugène Sue's *Les Mystères de Paris.*—165, 198, 205

Graun—character in Eugène Sue's *Les Mystères de Paris.*—202, 203, 205

Guillaume—character in the medieval French comedy *L'Avocat Patelin.*—640

Hahnemann—character in the German comic folk tale *Sieben Schwaben.*—163

Harpagon—a character in Molière's comedy *l'Avare.*—627

Harville, Clémence, Marquise d'—character in Eugène Sue's *Les Mystères de Paris.*—63, 64, 193-95, 205

Heracles (Hercules)—the most popular hero in Greek and Roman mythology, son of Zeus, celebrated for his great strength and valour.—135, 161, 176, 179, 201, 511

Jehovah (Bib.)—112

Jeremiah—biblical character, one of the Hebrew prophets, who wrote the Lamentations of Jeremiah on the occasion of the destruction of Jerusalem.—658

Jocrisse—the name of the simpleton in the French popular theatre, a character in Molière's comedy *Sganarelle.*—628

John, Saint, the Apostle—one of the twelve apostles to whom Christian tradition ascribes the authorship of the Book of Revelation, the Fourth Gospel and three Epistles actually written by different persons.—410

Judas Iscariot (Bib.)—one of the twelve apostles, the betrayer of Christ.—633-34

Laporte—character from Eugène Sue's *Les Mystères de Paris.*—171-73, 187

Lot—a character in the Old Testament (Genesis), who was rescued by God from the burning city of Sodom.—10

Zucenay, Duchesse de—character from Eugène Sue's *Les Mystères de Paris.*—64

Lycurgus—legendary Spartan legislator of the 9th-8th cent. B.C.—121-22

MacGregor, Sarah—character in Eugène Sue's *Les Mystères de Paris.*—63-66, 206, 209

Maître d'école—character in Eugène Sue's *Les Mystères de Paris.*—163, 165, 176-87, 202, 205-07

Mary (Bib.)—107

Micawber—character in Dickens' novel *David Copperfield.*—327

Minerva (Rom. Myth.)—the goddess of wisdom.—511

Minotaur (Gr. Myth.)—fabulous monster living on Crete, devouring youths and maidens sacrificed to it.—623

Moloch—the Sun-God in Carthage and Phoenicia, whose worship was accompanied by human sacrifices.—21, 266, 474

Morel—character in Eugène Sue's *Les Mystères de Paris.*—56

Morel, Louise—character in Eugène Sue's *Les Mystères de Paris.*—195

Moses (Bib.)—410

Murph—character in Eugène Sue's *Les Mystères de Paris.*—76, 165, 201-07

Paul, the Apostle (Bib.)—410

Peter, the Apostle (Bib.)—410

Pipelet, Alfred—character in Eugène Sue's *Les Mystères de Paris.*—72, 74-77

Pipelet, Anastasia—character in Eugène Sue's *Les Mystères de Paris.*—63, 72, 74, 75, 77

Polidori—character in Eugène Sue's *Les Mystères de Paris.*—71, 73, 201

Prometheus (Gr. Myth.)—a titan who stole fire from the gods and gave it to men.—511

Rigolette—character in Eugène Sue's *Les Mystères de Paris.*—74-76

Roland, Madame—character in Eugène Sue's *Les Mystères de Paris.*—71

Rudolph, Prince of Geroldstein (Gerolstein)—main character in Eugène Sue's *Les Mystères de Paris.*—62, 63, 74, 77, 162-88, 190, 193-98, 200-10

Samson—a biblical hero famous for his great physical strength and courage.—410

Sarah. See *MacGregor, Sarah*

Sarah (Sarai) (Bib.)—wife of Abraham.—101

Scapin—main character in Molière's comedy *Les Fourberies de Scapin.*—639

Schurimann. See *Chourineur*

Sisyphus (Gr. Myth.)—King of Corinth whom the gods condemned to eternal and exhausting labour.—467

Squelette—character in Eugène Sue's *Les Mystères de Paris.*—165

Swing—fictitious name used by farmworkers in the disturbances of 1830-31, a character in Wakefield's pamphlet *Swing Unmasked: or, the Causes of Rural Incendiarism.*—551, 554

Tortillard—character in Eugène Sue's *Les Mystères de Paris.*—180, 181, 187

Vishnu—in Hindu mythology the second god in the trinity (Brahma, Vishnu and Shiva), called the Preserver, the embodiment of eternally living nature.—54, 55

Willis—character in Eugène Sue's *Les Mystères de Paris.*—69, 205

INDEX OF QUOTED
AND MENTIONED LITERATURE

WORKS BY KARL MARX AND FREDERICK ENGELS

Marx, Karl. *Contribution to the Critique of Hegel's Philosophy of Law. Introduction* (present edition, Vol. 3)
— Zur Kritik der Hegelschen Rechtsphilosophie. Einleitung. In: *Deutsch-Französische Jahrbücher*, hg. von Arnold Ruge und Karl Marx, 1-ste und 2-te Lieferung, Paris, 1844.—236

Justification of the Correspondent from the Mosel (present edition, Vol. 1) ·
— Rechtfertigung des †† Korrespondenten von der Mosel. In: *Rheinische Zeitung* No. 15, January 15, 1843.—256

On the Jewish Question (present edition, Vol. 3)
— Zur Judenfrage. In: *Deutsch-Französische Jahrbücher*, hg. von Arnold Ruge und Karl Marx, 1-ste und 2-te Lieferung, Paris, 1844.—87, 88, 106, 108-10, 112-115, 117

Engels, Frederick. *The Condition of England. Past and Present by Thomas Carlyle, London, 1843* (present edition, Vol. 3)
— Die Lage Englands. *Past and Present* by Thomas Carlyle, London, 1843. In: *Deutsch-Französische Jahrbücher*, hg. von Arnold Ruge und Karl Marx, 1-ste and 2-te Lieferung, Paris, 1844.—562

The Condition of the Working-Class in England. From Personal Observation and Authentic Sources (this volume)
— Die Lage der arbeitenden Klasse in England. Nach eigner Anschauung und authentischen Quellen. Leipzig, 1845.—241, 584, 585
— (anon.) *Continental Movements* (present edition, Vol. 3). In: *The New Moral World* No. 32, February 3, 1844.—238
— (anon.) *Description of Recently Founded Communist Colonies Still in Existence* (this volume)
— Beschreibung der in neuerer Zeit entstandenen und noch bestehenden kommunistischen Ansiedlungen. In: *Deutsches Bürgerbuch für 1845*, Darmstadt, 1845.—239, 240
— *The Late Butchery at Leipzig.*—*The German Working Men's Movement* (this volume). In: *The Northern Star* No. 409, September 13, 1845.—653
— *Outlines of a Critique of Political Economy* (present edition, Vol. 3)

— Umrisse zu einer Kritik der Nationalökonomie. In: *Deutsch-Französische Jahrbücher*, hg. von Arnold Ruge und Karl Marx, 1-ste und 2-te Lieferung, Paris, 1844.—32, 325

— (anon.) *Progress of Social Reform on the Continent* (present edition, Vol. 3). In: *The New Moral World* No. 19, November 4, 1843 and No. 21, November 18, 1843.—238

— (anon.) *Speeches in Elberfeld* (this volume)

— [Zwei Reden in Elberfeld.] In: *Rheinische Jahrbücher zur gesellschaftlichen Reform*, Erster Band, Darmstadt, 1845.—238

— *"Young Germany" in Switzerland. Conspiracy Against Church and State* (this volume). In: *The Northern Star* No. 411, September 27, 1845.—654

Marx, K. and Engels, F.
The Holy Family, or Critique of Critical Criticism. Against Bruno Bauer and Company (this volume)

— *Die heilige Familie oder Kritik der kritischen Kritik. Gegen Bruno Bauer und Konsorten*, Frankfurt a. M., 1845.—240

WORKS BY DIFFERENT AUTHORS

Alison, A. *The Principles of Population, and their Connection with Human Happiness*, Vols. I-II, London, 1840.—389, 398, 412, 416, 417, 422, 424, 558, 560

Alison, W. P. *Notes on the Report of the Royal Commissioners on the Operation of the Poor Laws in Scotland*, 1844. In: *Journal of the Statistical Society of London*, Vol. VII, London, 1844.—398

— *Observations on the Management of the Poor in Scotland, and its Effects on the Health of the Great Towns*, Edinburgh, 1840.—338, 398

Baines, E. *History of the Cotton Manufacture in Great Britain...*, London [1835].— 312, 313, 429, 434, 446-47

Barry, D. See Documents: *Factory Inquiry Commission, Second Report*, 1833

Bauer, B. *Das entdeckte Christenthum. Eine Erinnerung an das achtzehnte Jahrhundert und ein Beitrag zur Krisis des neunzehnten*, Zürich und Winterthur, 1843.—101, 106, 107, 136, 139, 140, 152

— *Die evangelische Landeskirche Preussens und die Wissenschaft*, Leipzig, 1840.—112

— *Die Fähigkeit der heutigen Juden und Christen, frei zu werden.* In: *Einundzwanzig Bogen aus der Schweiz*, hg. von Georg Herwegh. Erster Theil, Zürich und Winterthur, 1843.—88, 107, 108, 110

— *Die gute Sache der Freiheit und meine eigene Angelegenheit*, Zürich und Winterthur, 1842.—16, 79, 93, 103, 112, 136

— (anon.) *Hinrichs, politische Vorlesungen, Band I, p. 332. Halle, 1843. Bei Schwetzschke und Sohn.* In: *Allgemeine Literatur-Zeitung*, Heft I, December 1843.—90-92

— (anon.) *Hinrichs, politische Vorlesungen, Zweiter Band, Halle, 1843. 489 S.* In: *Allgemeine Literatur-Zeitung*, Heft V, April 1844.—92-94

— *Die Judenfrage*, Braunschweig, 1843.—79, 87, 89, 90, 94, 95, 106-07, 111, 112, 115, 117, 118, 136

— *Kritik der evangelischen Geschichte der Synoptiker*, Bd. 1-2, Leipzig, 1841; Bd. 3, Braunschweig, 1842.—104, 107, 136-39, 166, 187

— (anon.) *Leben und Wirken Friedrich von Sallet's nebst Mittheilungen aus dem literarischen Nachlasse Desselben.* Herausgegeben von einigen Freunden des

Dichters. Mit Sallet's Bildniss. Breslau, 1844. Verlag von A. Schulz. P. 384.
In: *Allgemeine Literatur-Zeitung*, Heft VIII, July 1844.—138
— *Leiden und Freuden des theologischen Bewusstseins*. In: *Anekdota zur neuesten deutschen Philosophie und Publicistik*, hg. von A. Ruge, Bd. 2, Zürich und Winterthur, 1843.—152, 191-92
— (anon.) *Neueste Schriften über die Judenfrage*. In: *Allgemeine Literatur-Zeitung*, Heft I, December 1843; Heft IV, March 1844.—79-81, 82, 84, 87, 90, 95, 99
— *Staat, Religion und Parthei*, Leipzig, 1843.—91, 107, 112, 136
— (anon.) *Was ist jetzt der Gegenstand der Kritik?* In: *Allgemeine Literatur-Zeitung*, Heft VIII, July 1844.—26-27, 88, 99-102, 104-09, 111, 114, 117-22, 124, 133-37

Bauer, E. *Es leben feste Grundsätze!* In: *Berliner Novellen*, von A. Weill und Edgar Bauer, Berlin, 1843.—147
— (anon.) *Béraud über die Freudenmädchen*. In: *Allgemeine Literatur-Zeitung*, Heft V, April 1844.—20, 156-57
— (anon.) *Die drei Biedermänner. In drei Capiteln*. In: *Allgemeine Literatur-Zeitung*, Heft III-V, February-April 1844.—156
— (anon.) *Proudhon*. In: *Allgemeine Literatur-Zeitung*, Heft V, April 1844.—18, 23-31, 33, 34, 37-42, 43-48, 49-54
— (anon.) *Die Romane der Verfasserin von Godwie Castle*. In: *Allgemeine Literatur-Zeitung*, Heft II, January 1844.—21-23
— *Der Streit der Kritik mit Kirche und Staat*. Bern, 1844.—213
— (anon.) *Union ouvrière. Par Mme Flora Tristan. Edition Populaire.. Paris 1843*. In: *Allgemeine Literatur-Zeitung*, Heft V, April 1844.—19-21, 157, 188

Becker, A. *Was wollen die Kommunisten?* Lausanne, 1844.—242

Benda, D. A. *Katechismus für wahlberechtigte Bürger Preussens, oder Geist und Bedeutung der Städte-Ordnung vom 19. November 1808*. Berlin, 1843.—10

Bentham, J. *Théorie des peines et des récompenses...*, 3ième éd., T. II, Paris, 1826.—134, 178, 188

Béraud, F. F. A. *Les filles publiques de Paris et la police qui les régit*, T. I-II, Paris et Leipzig, 1839.—20, 156

Bible
  The Old Testament
    Lamentations of Jeremiah.—658
  The New Testament
    Matthew.—178, 203
    Romans.—203

Bischoff, J. *A Comprehensive History of the Woollen and Worsted Manufactures*, Vols. 1-2, London, 1842.—314

"*A boire, à boir, à boir!*" (A French drinking song).—211

Bray, J. Fr. *Labour's wrongs and labour's remedy; or, the age of might and the age of right*, Leeds, 1839.—288

Bruyes. *L'Avocat Patelin*, Paris, 1725.—640

Buchez, P. J. B., et P.C. Roux. *Histoire parlementaire de la Révolution française, ou Journal des Assemblées Nationales, depuis 1789 jusqu'en 1815*, ..., 40 vols. Paris, 1834-1838. (See Robespierre, M. and Saint-Just, L.)

Burns. See Documents: *Report of Commission of Inquiry into the Employment of Children and Young Persons in Mines and Collieries...*, First Report, 1842; Second Report, 1843

Cabanis, P.-J.-G. *Rapports du physique et du moral de l'homme*, T. I-II, Paris, 1843.—126

Carlyle, T. *Chartism*, London, 1840.—368, 389, 390, 414, 510, 579
— *Past and Present*, London, 1843.—386, 511-12, 562, 564, 579

Chaptal, J.-A.-C. *De l'industrie française*, T. I-II, Paris, 1819.—200

Comte, Ch. *Traité de la propriété*, T. I-II. Paris, 1834.—44-46

Condillac, E.-B. *Essai sur l'origine des connaissances humaines*, Amsterdam, 1746.—129

Cowan, R. *Vital Statistics of Glasgow, Illustrating the Sanatory Condition of the Population.* In: *Journal of the Statistical Society of London*, Vol. III, London, 1840.—404

Cowell, S. W. See Documents: *Factory Inquiry Commission*, Second Report, 1833

Croker, J. W. *Anti-Corn Law Agitation.* In: *The Quarterly Review*, Vol. 71, No. 141, London, 1843.—519-22, 588
— (anon.) *A Sketch of the State of Ireland, Past and Present*, 2-d ed., London, 1808.—560

Dante Alighieri's goettliche Comoedie. Metrisch übertragen und mit kritischen und historischen Erläuterungen versehen von Philalethes [Prinz Johann von Sachsen], Dresden, 1833; zweite Auflage, Dresden und Leipzig, 1839.—645

Dickens, Ch. *David Copperfield.*—327

Dies irae... (Requiem aeternam dona est).—211

Disraeli, B. *Sybil; or, the Two Nations*, Vols. 1-3, London, 1845.—420

Drinkwater. See Documents: *Factory Inquiry Commission*, Second Report, 1833

Egidius, H. L. *Emigranten und Märtyrer. Ein Beitrag zur Charakteristik der 'Deutsch-Französischen Jahrbücher'.* In: *Konstitutionelle Jahrbücher*, hg. von Dr. Karl Weil, Jahrgang 1844, Bd. II, Stuttgart, 1844.—162

Erlach, F. K. Freiherr von. *Die Volkslieder der Deutschen*, 5 Bände, Mannheim, 1834-1836; Bd. 4, 1835.—161

Faucher, J. *Englische Tagesfragen.* In: *Allgemeine Literatur-Zeitung*, Heft VII, June 1844.—12-14, 16, 81
— *Englische Tagesfragen. (Fortsetzung.) Lord Ashley's Amendment.* In: *Allgemeine Literatur-Zeitung*, Heft VIII, July 1844.—12, 14, 15, 16, 81
— *Englische Tagesfragen. (Fortsetzung.) Ricardos Motion in Betreff der Einfuhrzölle.* In: *Allgemeine Literatur-Zeitung*, Heft IX, August 1844.—12

Faucher, L. *Etudes sur l'Angleterre.* In: *Revue des deux Mondes*, T. 4, October 1, 1843 (*White-Chapel*); November 1, 1843 (*Saint-Giles*); December 1, 1843 (*Liverpool. Première partie*); December 15, 1843 (*Liverpool. Dernière partie*); T. 5, March 15, 1844 (*Manchester. Première partie*); T. 6, April 1, 1844 (*Manchester. Dernière partie*); May 15, 1844 (*La Ville de Leeds. Première partie*); June 15, 1844 (*La Ville de Leeds. Dernière partie*); T. 7, July 15, 1844 (*Birmingham*).—12-14, 16, 81, 488

Felkin, W. *Statistics of the Labouring Classes and Paupers in Nottingham.* In: *Journal of the Statistical Society of London*, Vol. II, London, 1839.—340

Ferrier, F. L. A. *Du gouvernement considéré dans ses rapports avec le commerce*, Paris, 1805.—268, 269, 290-292

Feuerbach, L. *Grundsätze der Philosophie der Zukunft*, Zürich und Winterthur, 1843.— 92, 141
— *Vorläufige Thesen zur Reformation der Philosophie*, January 1842. In: *Anekdota zur neuesten deutschen Philosophie und Publicistik*, hg. von Arnold Ruge, Bd. 2, Zürich und Winterthur, 1843.—83

Finch, J. *Notes of Travel in the United States*. In: *The New Moral World*, January 13-October 19, 1844.—216-17, 219-22, 240

Fleischhammer, E. *Correspondenz aus Breslau*. In: *Allgemeine Literatur-Zeitung*, Heft IV, March 1844.—145, 146

Fletcher, J. *Progress of Crime in the United Kingdom: Abstracted from the Criminal Returns for 1842* ... In: *Journal of the Statistical Society of London*, Vol. VI, London, 1843.—425, 426

Fourier, Ch. *Crime du commerce*. In: *La Phalange. Revue de la science sociale*, XIVe année, 1re Série, Tome II, Paris, 1845.—641
— *Le nouveau monde industriel et sociétaire...*, Paris, 1829.—196
— *Théorie des quatre mouvements et des destinées générales*. In: *Oeuvres complètes*, T. I, 2de éd., Paris, 1841.—196, 201, 615, 624-25, 630-31, 632-34, 639-42
— *Théorie de l'unité universelle*. In: *Oeuvres complètes*, T. IV, Vol. III, Paris, 1841.— 66, 196, 618
— *Des trois unités externes*. In: *La Phalange. Revue de la science sociale*, XIVe année, 1re Série, Tome 1er, Paris, 1845.—615-24, 625-29, 631-33, 634-41, 642

Franks. See Documents: *Report of Commission of Inquiry into the Employment of Children and Young Persons in Mines and Collieries...*, First Report, 1842; Second Report, 1843

Fripp, C. B. *Report of an Inquiry into the Condition of the Working Classes of the City of Bristol*. In: *Journal of the Statistical Society of London*, Vol. II, London, 1839.—340

Froment, M. *La police dévoilée, depuis la restauration et notamment sous messieurs Franchet et Delavau*, T. I-III, Paris, 1829.—74

Gaskell, P. *The Manufacturing Population of England, its Moral, Social, and Physical Conditions, and the Changes which have Arisen from the Use of Steam Machinery; with an Examination of Infant Labour*, London, 1833.—307-10, 365, 366, 368, 369, 401, 422, 425, 426, 508, 579

Geschichte von den sieben Schwaben. In: *Volksbücher*, hrsg. v. G. O. Marbach, Leipzig, 1838.—163

Goethe, J. W. von. *Faust. Der Tragödie erster Teil*.—63, 142
— *Zahme Xenien*, IX.—175

Goldsmith, O. *The Deserted Village*.—552

Graham, G. See Documents: *Fifth Annual Report of the Registrar General of Births...*

Grainger, R. D. See Documents: *Report of Commission of Inquiry into the Employment of Children and Young Persons in Mines and Collieries...*, First Report, 1842; Second Report, 1843

Gruppe, O. F. *Bruno Bauer und die akademische Lehrfreiheit*, Berlin, 1842.—157
— (anon.) *Die Winde oder ganz absolute Konstruktion der neuern Weltgeschichte durch Oberons Horn gedichtet von Absolutus von Hegelingen*, Leipzig, 1831.—157

Hawkins, F. B. See Documents: *Factory Inquiry Commission*, Second Report, 1833

Hegel, G. W. F. *Encyclopädie der philosophischen Wissenschaften im Grundrisse*, Dritte Ausgabe, Heidelberg, 1830.—78
— *Grundlinien der Philosophie des Rechts, oder Naturrecht und Staatswissenschaft im Grundrisse*, Bd. VIII, Berlin, 1833.—40, 87
— (anon.) *Phänomenologie des Geistes*, hg. von Johann Schulze. Zweite unveränderte Aufl., Berlin, 1841.—22, 23, 82, 103, 131, 138, 141, 192-93
— *Vorlesungen über die Geschichte der Philosophie*, Bd. XIII-XV, Berlin, 1833-1836. —131, 167-68
— *Werke*, Berlin, 1831-1845:
— *Wissenschaft der Logik*, 2-te Auflage, Bd. V, Berlin, 1841.—138

Heine, H. *Die Nordsee*, zweiter Zyklus, Gedicht *Fragen.*—157
— *Die schlesischen Weber*, Gedicht.—232

Helvétius, C. A. *De l'esprit*, T. I-II, Paris, 1822.—132, 133
— *De l'homme, de ses facultés intellectuelles et de son éducation*, T. I-II, Londres, 1775.—129

Hennen, J. *An account of the eruptive diseases which have lately appeared in the Military-Hospitals of Edinburgh*. In: *The Edinburgh Medical and Surgical Journal: Exhibiting a concise view of the latest and most Important Discoveries in Medicine, Surgery, and Pharmacy*, Vol. 14, Edinburgh, 1818.—339

Hess, M. *Die letzten Philosophen*, Darmstadt, 1845.—240
— *Ueber die Noth in unserer Gesellschaft und deren Abhülfe*. In: *Deutsches Bürgerbuch für 1845*, Darmstadt, 1845.—240

Hinrichs, H. F. W. *Hinrichs' politische Vorlesungen*, Bd. I-II, Halle, 1843.—90, 91

Hirzel, K. M. *Correspondenz aus Zürich*. In: *Allgemeine Literatur-Zeitung*, Heft IV, March 1844; Heft V, April 1844.—145-48, 210

d'Holbach, P.-H.-D. *Système social, ou principes naturels de la morale et de la politique...*, T. I-II, Paris, 1822.—133
— (anon.) *Système de la nature, ou des loix du monde physique et du monde moral, par M. Mirabaud*, Partie 1-2, Londres, 1770.—130, 133

Homer. *Iliad.*—47

[Hood, Thomas] *The Song of the Shirt*. In: *Punch, or the London Charivari*, Vol. V. London, 1843.—500

Horne, R. See Documents: *Report of Commission of Inquiry into the Employment of Children and Young Persons in Mines and Collieries...*, First Report, 1842; Second Report, 1843

Horner, L. See Documents: *Reports of the Inspectors of Factories...*

Jerrold, D. *The Two Windows*. In: *The Illuminated Magazine*, Vol. 3, May to October, London, 1844.—574

Johns, W. *Report upon the Working of the Registration and Marriage Acts, during the two years 1837-38 and 1838-39, in the registration district of Manchester*. In: *Journal of the Statistical Society of London*, Vol. III, London, 1840.—437

J[ungnitz, Ernst] *Herr Nauwerk und die philosophische Fakultät*. In: *Allgemeine Literatur-Zeitung*, Heft VI, May 1844.—17

Kaiser, H. W. *Die Persönlichkeit des Eigenthums in Bezug auf den Socialismus und Communismus im heutigen Frankreich*, Bremen, 1843.—642

Kay [Shuttleworth], J. Ph. *The Moral and Physical Condition of the Working Classes Employed in the Cotton Manufacture in Manchester*, Second Edition enlarged and containing an introductory Letter to the Rev. Thomas Chalmers, London, 1832.—351, 352, 362-66, 467

Knight, A. *On the grinders' asthma.* In: *North of England Medical and Surgical Journal*, August 1830-May 1831, Vol. I.—493, 494

La Mettrie, J. O. de. *L'homme machine*, London, 1751.—130

Leach, J. *Stubborn Facts from the Factories by a Manchester Operative.* Published and dedicated to the working classes by Wm. Rashleigh, M. P., London, 1844.—429, 430, 432, 468, 470, 485-88

Leifchild, J. R. See Documents: *Report of Commission of Inquiry into the Employment of Children and Young Persons in Mines and Collieries...*, First Report, 1842; Second Report, 1843

List, F. *Das nationale System der politischen Oekonomie.* Erster Band: *Der internationale Handel, die Handelspolitik und der deutsche Zollverein*, Stuttgart und Tübingen, 1841.—258, 259, 265, 268, 273, 277, 278, 284-88, 290

Livre (Le) noir de m-rs Delavau et Franchet, ou répertoire alphabétique de la police politique sous le ministère déplorable; ouvrage imprimé d'après les registres de l'administration, précédé d'une introduct. par M. Année, 2 éd, T. 1-4, Paris, 1829.—73

Locke, J. *An Essay Concerning Humane Understanding*, London, 1690.—127, 129

Loudon, Ch. See Documents: *Factory Inquiry Commission*, Second Report, 1833

Mackintosh. See Documents: *Factory Inquiry Commission*, Second Report, 1833

Malthus, Th. R. *An Essay on the Principle of Population; as it affects the Future Improvement of Society, with Remarks on the Speculations of W. Godwin, M. Condorcet and other Writers*, 1st ed., London, 1798.—380, 570-73

Mandeville, B. de. *The Fable of the Bees: or, Private Vices, Publick Benefits*, London, 1714.—131

Marmontel, J.-F. *Lucile.* In: *Oeuvres complètes*, T. IX, Paris, 1819.—144

McCulloch, J. R. *A Dictionary practical, theoretical and historical of commerce and commercial navigation.* A new ed., London, 1844.—313
— *A Statistical Account of the British Empire, exhibiting its Extent, Physical Capacities, Population, Industry and civil and religious Institutions*, 2 vols., London, 1837.—580

Mead, E. P. "The Steam-King". In: *The Northern Star* No. 274, February 11th, 1843.—474-77

Mirabaud, J. B. *Système de la nature....* See d'Holbach, P. H. D.

Mitchell, J. See Documents: *Report of Commission of Inquiry into the Employment of Children and Young Persons in Mines and Collieries...*, First Report, 1842; Second Report, 1843

Molière, J. B. *L'Avare.*—627
— *Le bourgeois gentilhomme.*—55
— *Sganarelle, ou Le cocu imaginaire.*—628

Monteil, A.-A. *Histoire des Français des divers états aux cinq derniers siècles*, T. I-X, Paris, 1828-1844.—71

Neue Anekdota. Hrsg. von Karl Grün, Darmstadt, 1845.—241

Oastler, R. *The Fleet Papers; being letters to Thomas Thornhill Esq. of Riddlesworth in the county of Norfolk, from Richard Oastler, his prisoner in the Fleet. With occasional communications from Friends*, 4 vols., London 1841-1844.—438, 439, 463

Owen, R. *Manifesto of Robert Owen, the Discoverer, Founder, and Promulgator of the Rational System of Society, and of the Rational Religion. Sixth Edition. To which are added a Preface and also an Appendix...*, London, 1840.—459
— *Observations on the Effect of the Manufacturing System: with hints for the improvement of those parts of it which are most injurious to health and morals*, 2nd ed., London, 1817.—459

Parkinson, R. *On the Present Condition of the Labouring Poor in Manchester...*, 3rd ed., London and Manchester, 1841.—420, 565

Parny, E. D. *Poésies érotiques*.—69

Pecchio, J. *Histoire de l'économie politique en Italie, ou Abrégé critique des économistes italiens; précédée d'une introduction. Traduite de l'italien par L. Gallois*, Paris, 1830.—269

Peuchet, J. *Dictionnaire universel de la géographie commerçante*, T. 1-5, Paris, 1799-1800.—598
— *Mémoires tirés des Archives de la Police de Paris, pour servir à l'histoire de la morale et de la police, depuis Louis XIV jusqu'à nos jours*, T. IV, Paris, 1838.—597, 598, 612
— *Statistique élémentaire de la France*, Paris, 1807.—598

Pitkeithly, L. *Emigration. Where to, and how to proceed. Description of the Shaker Villages*. In: *The Northern Star*, No. 286, May 6, 1843.—217

Polidori Vergilii Urbinatis, *De rerum inventoribus*, Lugduni Batavorum, 1644.—71

Porter, G. R. *The Progress of the Nation, in its various Social and Economical Relations from the Beginning of the Nineteenth Century to the Present Time*, 3 vols., London, 1836-1843.—313-19, 320, 425-27, 530

Power. See Documents: *Factory Inquiry Commission, Second Report*, 1833

Proudhon, P.-J. *Avertissement aux propriétaires, ou Lettre à M. Considérant, rédacteur de la Phalange, sur une défense de la propriété*, Paris, 1841.—50
— *Qu'est-ce que la propriété? Ou recherches sur le principe du droit et du gouvernement, Premier mémoire*, Paris, 1841.—23-32, 33-34, 37, 38, 40, 41, 43-49, 52, 528
— *Qu'est-ce que la propriété? Deuxième mémoire. Lettre à M. Blanqui, professeur d'économie politique au conservatoire des arts et métiers. Sur la propriété*, Paris, 1841—50, 135-36

R[eichardt], C[arl]. *Katechismus für wahlberechtigte Bürger in Preussen. Von Dr. A. Benda. Berlin, 1843 bei Springer*. In: *Allgemeine Literatur-Zeitung*, Heft VI, May 1844.—9
— *Preussens Beruf in der deutschen Staats-Entwickelung, und die nächsten Bedingungen zu seiner Erfüllung. Von C. Brüggemann*, Berlin, 1843, bei Besser. In: *Allgemeine Literatur-Zeitung*, Heft VI, May 1844.—9, 10
— *Schriften über den Pauperismus. Publicistische Abhandlungen: von Wöniger, Doctor beider Rechte und der Philosophie, 1843*. Berlin bei Hermes. In: *Allgemeine Literatur-Zeitung*, Heft I, December 1843.—9

— *Schriften über den Pauperismus. Die Gründe des wachsenden Pauperismus von A. T. Wöniger*. In: *Allgemeine Literatur-Zeitung*, Heft II, January 1844.—9

Ricardo, D. *Des principes de l'économie politique et de l'impôt. Traduit de l'anglais par Constancio avec des notes explicatives et critiques par J.-B. Say*, Seconde édition, Tome premier, Paris, 1835.—271, 387

Riesser, G. *Die Judenfrage. Gegen Bruno Bauer von Dr. Gabriel Riesser in Hamburg*. In: *Konstitutionelle Jahrbücher*, hg. von Dr. Karl Weil, Bd. 2-3, Stuttgart, 1843.—94-97, 113

Roberton, J. *An inquiry respecting the period of puberty in women*. In: *North of England Medical and Surgical Journal*, Vol. I, (August 1830-May 1831).—453

Robespierre, M. *Rapport sur les principes de morale politique qui doivent guider la Convention nationale dans l'administration intérieure de la République, fait au nom du comité de salut public, à la séance du 5 février (17 pluviôse) 1794*. In: P. J. B. Buchez et P. C. Roux, *Histoire parlementaire de la Révolution française, ou Journal des Assemblées Nationales depuis 1789 jusqu'en 1815...*, Tome 31, Paris, 1837.—119, 121

Robinet, J. B. *De la nature*, Nouv. éd., T. I-IV, Amsterdam, 1763-1766.—130

Rotteck, C. und Welcker, C. *Staats-Lexikon oder Encyklopädie der Staatswissenschaften*, Bd. 1-15; Supplemente Bd. 1-4, Altona, 1834-1848.—123

Sadler's Report. See Documents: *Report from the Select Committee on the 'Bill to regulate the Labour of Children in the Mills and Factories of the United Kingdom', 8th August, 1832*

Saint-Just, L. *Au nom des comités de salut public et de sûreté générale. Convention nationale. Séance du 31 mars (11 germinal) 1794*. In: P. J. B. Buchez et P. C. Roux, *Histoire parlementaire de la Révolution française...*, Tome 32, Paris, 1837.—120, 121
— *Rapport sur la police générale.—Du 26 germinal an 2 (15 avril 1794)*. In: P. J. B. Buchez et P. C. Roux, *Histoire parlementaire de la Révolution française...*, Tome 32, Paris, 1837.—120, 121

Saunders, R. J. See Documents: *Reports of the Inspectors of Factories...*

Say, J.-B. *Cours complet d'économie politique pratique. Volume complémentaire. Mélanges et correspondance d'économie politique; ouvrage posthume de J.-B. Say, publié par Charles Comte, son gendre*, Paris, 1833.—270
— *Traité d'économie politique, ou simple exposition de la manière dont se forment, se distribuent et se consomment les richesses*, T. I-II, Paris, 1803.—32, 43, 270

Say, L. A. *Études sur la richesse des nations et réfutation des principales erreurs en économie politique*, Paris, 1836.—271

Schiller, F. von. *Das Mädchen aus der Fremde*, Gedicht.—23
— *Die Räuber*.—202

Scriven, S. S. See Documents: *Report of Commission of Inquiry into the Employment of Children and Young Persons in Mines and Collieries...*, First Report, 1842; Second Report, 1843

Senior, N. W. *Letters on the Factory Act, as it affects the Cotton Manufacture, addressed to the Right Honourable the President of the Board of Trade, to which are appended, a Letter to Mr. Senior from Leonard Horner, Esq., and Minutes of a Conversation between Mr. Edmund Ashworth, Mr. Thomson and Mr. Senior*, London, 1837.—364

Serra, A. *Breve trattato delle cause, che possono far abbondare li regni, d'oro e d'argento, dove non sono miniere.* In: *Scrittori classici italiani di economia politica,* Ed. Pietro Custodi, Parte antica, T. I., Milano, 1803.—269

Shakespeare, W. *All's Well that Ends Well.*—71
— *Much Ado about Nothing.*—542

Sieyès, E. J. *Qu'est-ce que le tiers-état?,* Bordeaux, 1789.—32

Sismondi, J. C. L. Simonde de. *Études sur l'économie politique,* T. I-II, Bruxelles, 1837-1838.—273
— *Nouveaux principes d'économie politique ou de la richesse dans ses rapports avec la population,* Seconde édition, T. II, Paris, 1827.—272, 273

Smith, A. *An Inquiry into the Nature and Causes of the Wealth of Nations,* Vols. 1-2, London, 1776.—49
— *An Inquiry into the Nature and Causes of the Wealth of Nations.* With a Life of the Author, an introductory Discourse, Notes, and supplemental Dissertations. By J. R. McCulloch, 4 vols., Edinburgh, 1828.—49, 380, 415

Smith, T. S. See Documents: *Report of Commission of Inquiry into the Employment of Children and Young Persons in Mines and Collieries...,* First Report, 1842; Second Report, 1843

[Somerville, A.] (One who has whistled at the Plough.) *Notes from the Farming Districts, No. XVII. A journey to Harmony Hall, in Hampshire; with some particulars of the Socialist Community, to which the attention of the Nobility, Gentry and Clergy is earnestly requested.* In: *The Morning Chronicle,* December 13, 1842.—224-26, 240
— *The Farm Labourer. What is to be done?—More Churches or more Employment? (being a second notice of the Reports on the Employment of Women and Children in Agriculture, lately presented to Parliament by Command of Her Majesty).* In: *The Morning Chronicle,* July 6, 1843.—556

Southwood. See Documents: *Report of Commission of Inquiry into the Employment of Children and Young Persons in Mines and Collieries...,* First Report, 1842; Second Report, 1843

The State of Ireland. See [Croker, J. W.] *A sketch of the State of Ireland, Past and Present.*

Stein, L. *Der Socialismus und Communismus des heutigen Frankreichs.* Ein Beitrag zur Zeitgeschichte, Leipzig, 1842.—134, 613, 642

Stirner, M. *Der Einzige und sein Eigenthum,* Leipzig, 1845.—329, 564

Stockinger, A. *Distress at Hinckley.* In: *The Morning Chronicle,* December 1st, 1843.—480
— "To the editor of the *Morning Chronicle.*" In: *The Morning Chronicle,* December 9th, 1843.—480, 481

Strauss, D. F. *Das Leben Jesu,* 4. Aufl., Bd. 1-2., Tübingen, 1840.—528

Stuart, J. See Documents: *Factory Inquiry Commission,* Second Report, 1833

Stubborn Facts from the Factories. See Leach, J. *Stubborn Facts from the Factories by a Manchester Operative*

Sue, E. *Atar-Gull.*—57
— *Le Juif errant,* T. I-X, Paris, 1844-1845.—190
— *Les Mystères de Paris.* T I-XIV, Bruxelles, 1843.—55-57, 61-64, 66, 67, 69, 70, 73-75, 76, 77, 162-66, 168-76, 177, 179-88, 190, 194, 195, 201-09

— *Plick et Plock.*—57
— *La Salamandre.* Roman maritime, Bruxelles, 1832.—57

Symons, J. C. *Arts and Artisans at Home and Abroad: with Sketches of the Progress of Foreign Manufactures,* Edinburgh, 1839.—341, 412, 432, 503, 504

Symons, J. C. See Documents: *Report of Commission of Inquiry into the Employment of Children and Young Persons in Mines and Collieries...,* First Report, 1842; Second Report, 1843

Szeliga. *Eugen Sue: Die Geheimnisse von Paris, Kritik.* In: *Allgemeine Literatur-Zeitung,* Heft VII, June 1844.—54-57, 61-77, 162, 163, 166-68, 175, 176, 180, 186, 187, 190, 191, 194, 196, 197, 200-03, 209

Tancred, Th. See Documents: *Report of Commission of Inquiry into the Employment of Children and Young Persons in Mines and Collieries...,* First Report, 1842; Second Report, 1843

Thiers, *Geschichte der französischen Revolution.* In: *Allgemeine Literatur-Zeitung,* Heft VIII, July 1844.—52

Tufnell. See Documents: *Factory Inquiry Commission,* Second Report, 1833

Ure, A. *The Cotton Manufacture of Great Britain. Systematically investigated, and illustrated...,* 2 vols., London, 1836.—308, 310, 312, 429

— *The Philosophy of Manufactures: or, an Exposition of the Scientific, Moral and Commercial Economy of the Factory System of Great Britain,* Second Ed., London, 1835.—417, 434, 457-59, 461, 462, 477-78, 510

— *Philosophie des manufactures, ou Economie industrielle. Traduit sous les yeux de l'auteur,* Tome I, Bruxelles, 1836.—281

Vaughan, R. *The Age of Great Cities: or, Modern Society Viewed in its Relation to Intelligence, Morals, and Religion,* London, 1843.—416

Vidocq, F. E. *Mémoires de Vidocq, Chef de la Police de Sûreté, jusqu'en 1827, aujourd'hui propriétaire et fabricant de papiers à Saint-Mandé,* T. 1-2, Paris, 1828.—73

Virgil, *Aeneid,* Book III.—618, 628

Voltaire, F. M. *Zaïre.*—619

Wade, J. *History of the Middle and Working Classes; with a Popular Exposition of the Economical and Political Principles...,* Third Edition, London, 1835.—405, 406

Wakefield, E. G. *Swing Unmasked: or, the Causes of Rural Incendiarism,* London, 1831.—551

Weitling, W. *Garantien der Harmonie und Freiheit,* Vivis, 1842.—235-36

Weld, C. R. *On the Condition of the Working Classes in the Inner Ward of St. George's Parish, Hanover Square.* In: *Journal of the Statistical Society of London,* Vol. VI, London, 1843.—333

Zerrleder, *Correspondenz aus Bern.* In: *Allgemeine Literatur-Zeitung,* Heft III, February 1844; Heft VI, May 1844.—145, 146

DOCUMENTS

An Act for the further Amendment of the Laws relating to the Poor in England (7 & 8 Vict. cap. 101), 1844.—578

An Act for Regulating the Construction and the Use of Buildings in the Metropolis and its Neighbourhood (7 & 8 Vict. cap. 84), 1844.—407

An Act for the Reliefs of the Poor (43rd Elizabeth, Cap. 2), 1601.—571

Children's Employment Commission's Report. See *Report of Commission of Inquiry into the Employment of Children and Young Persons...*, First Report, 1842; Second Report, 1843

Code Napoléon, Paris und Leipzig, 1808.—90

Code pénal, ou code des délits et des peines, Cologne, 1810.—190

Corpus iuris civilis. Hrsg. von C. Otto, Bd. I, Leipzig, 1830.—30

Extracts from the Information received by His Majesty's Commissioners, as to the Administration and Operation of the Poor-Laws, Published by Authority, London, 1833.—571

Factories Inquiry Commission. First Report of the Central Board of His Majesty's Commissioners appointed to collect Information in the Manufacturing Districts, as to the Employment of Children in Factories, and as to the Propriety and Means of Curtailing the Hours of their Labour: with Minutes of Evidence, and Reports by the District commissioners, June 28, 1833 (No. 450).—366, 430, 431, 437, 441, 442, 443, 444, 446, 448-57, 469, 511

Factory Inquiry Commission. Second Report of the Central Board of His Majesty's Commissioners appointed to collect Information in the Manufacturing Districts, as to the Employment of Children in Factories, and as to the Propriety and Means of Curtailing the Hours of their Labour: with Minutes of Evidence, and Reports by the Medical Commissioners, 15th July, 1833 (No. 519).—366, 401, 405, 430, 431, 435-37, 439-41, 443-55, 457, 460-62, 466, 469, 480-83

Factories Inquiry Commission's Report. See *Factory Inquiry Commission. Second Report*, 1833

Fifth Annual Report of the Registrar General of Births, Deaths and Marriages in England, 2nd ed., London, 1843.—404

First Report of the Commissioners for inquiring into the State of Large Towns and Populous Districts, 2 vols., London, 1844.—404, 405

Gilbert's Act. *An Act for the Better Relief and Employment of the Poor* (22. George III. cap. 83), 1782.—576

Hansard's Parliamentary Debates: Third Series; Commencing with the Accession of William IV. Vol. LXVII. Comprising the Period from the twenty-eighth Day of February, to the twenty-fourth Day of March, 1843, London, 1843.—423, 465
— *...Vol. LXX. Comprising the Period from the sixteenth Day of June, to the twenty-eighth Day of July, 1843.*—463, 464
— *...Vol. LXXII. Comprising the Period from the first Day of February, to the twenty-first Day of February, 1844*, London, 1844.—464
— *...Vol. LXXIII. Comprising the Period from the twenty-second Day of February, to the second Day of April, 1844*, London, 1844.—433, 435-37, 440, 450, 451

— ...*Vol. LXXV. Comprising the Period from the thirtieth Day of May, to the twenty-sixth Day of June, 1844*, London, 1844.—540, 541, 545-46

Miles' Bill for Enlarging the powers of justices in determining complaints between masters, servants and artificers. Bill No. 58 of 1844. In: *Hansard's Parliamentary Debates*, Vols. LXXIII and LXXIV.—322, 569

Pauperism and Poor-Rates in the Parochial Year 1842; abstracted from the Ninth Annual Report of the Poor Law Commissioners, 1843. In: *Journal of the Statistical Society of London*, Vol. VI, London, 1843.—386

The People's Charter; being the Outline of an Act to provide for the Just Representation of the People of Great Britain in the Commons' House of Parliament. Embracing the principles of Universal Suffrage, No Property Qualification, Annual Parliaments, Equal Representation, Payment of Members, and Vote by Ballot. Prepared by a committee of twelve persons, six members of Parliament and six members of the London Working Men's Association, and addressed to the People of the United Kingdom, London, 1838.—517-18

Report from Assistant Hand-Loom Weavers' Commissioners. By J. C. Symons. In: *Parliamentary Papers*, Vol. XLII, 1839.—341

Report from the Select Committee on the 'Bill to regulate the Labour of Children in the Mills and Factories of the United Kingdom', 8th August 1832. In: *Parliamentary Papers*, Vol. XV, 1831-1832.—460

Report of Commission of Inquiry into the Employment of Children and Young Persons in Mines and Collieries and in the Trades and Manufactures in which Numbers of them work together, not being included under the terms of the Factories' Regulation Act, First Report, 1842; Second Report, 1843.—356, 402, 408-10, 445, 479, 480, 482-85, 489-99, 531-36, 538, 539, 545

Report of a Committee of the Manchester Statistical Society on the Condition of the Working Classes in an extensive manufacturing district in 1834, 1835 and 1836 (1838).—338

Report of the Committee of the Statistical Society of London, on the State of the Working Classes in the Parishes of St. Margaret and St. John, Westminster. In: *Journal of the Statistical Society of London*, Vol. III, London, 1840.—333

Reports of the Inspectors of Factories to Her Majesty's Principal Secretary of State for the Half-Year ending 31st December 1843. Presented to both Houses of Parliament by Command of Her Majesty, London, 1844.—435, 463

Report of the Poor Law Commissioners for Ireland. Parliamentary session of 1837. See *Third Report of the Commissioners appointed 'to inquire into the condition of the poorer classes in Ireland...'*

Report to Her Majesty's Principal Secretary of State for the Home Department, from the Poor Law Commissioners on an Inquiry into the Sanitary Condition of the Labouring Population of Great Britain; with Appendices. Presented to both Houses of Parliament, by Command of Her Majesty, July 1842, London, 1842.—339, 343, 365, 397, 405

Report to the Home Secretary... See *Report to Her Majesty's Principal Secretary of State for the Home Department.*

Report upon the Condition of the Town of Leeds and of its Inhabitants. By a Statistical Committee of the Town Council, October 1839. In *Journal of the Statistical Society of London,* Vol. II, London, 1840.—343, 396

Third Report of the Commissioners appointed 'to inquire into the condition of the poorer classes in Ireland, and into the various institutions at present established by law for their relief...' In: *Parliamentary Papers,* Vol. 34, 1836.—558

ANONYMOUS ARTICLES AND REPORTS
PUBLISHED IN PERIODIC EDITIONS

Allgemeine Literatur-Zeitung Heft VI, May 1844: *Correspondenz aus der Provinz.*—146-54, 156-61
— Heft VIII, July 1844: *1842.*—99

The Annual Register, or, a View of the history, politics and literature of the year 1838, London, 1839: *Chronicle.*—509
— *Evidence of James Moat.*—509
— *Evidence of James Murdoch.*—509

The Artizan. A Monthly Journal of the Operative Arts, London, 1844, Vol. 1, No. 10, October 31st, 1843: *On the Health of the Working Classes in Large Towns.*—339-43, 396, 405

Constitutionnel Neuchâtelois No. 109, September 11, 1845: *Neuchâtel.*—651-53

Daily Advocate and Advertiser, July 17th, 1843: [*Description of Bäumler's colony in Zoar, Ohio*].—221

Durham Chronicle No. 1286, June 28th, 1844: *The Coal Trade, Monopoly.*—318

Halifax Guardian No. 571, November 4th, 1843: *The Truck System Extraordinary.*—472

The Illuminated Magazine, Vol. 3, May-October, 1844: *The Dwellings of the Poor. From the note-book of an M. D.*—332

Kölnische Zeitung No. 314, November 9, 1844: *Ein 'socialistischer' Spuk.*—231

The Liverpool Mercury, and Lancashire General Advertiser, Supplement, February 9th, 1844: *Liverpool, Friday, February 9th, 1844.*—370

The Manchester Guardian
— February 4th, 1843: *Meetings of Deputies to receive reports of the Committees.*—387
— May 10th, 1843: *Manchester Court Leet.*—369
— December 20th, 1843: *Street Beggars. To the Editor of The Manchester Guardian.*—564, 565
— May 1st, 1844: *Statement of Facts, ... submitted by the Deputation of Master Manufacturers and Millowners in the County of Lancaster.*—435, 439
— June 15th, June 29th, July 24th, July 27th and August 3rd, 1844: [*Reports of serious accidents in factories*].—455
— July 3rd, July 31st, and August 10th, 1844: [*Reports of the cases of selling tainted meat to workers*].—369
— July 31st, 1844: *"Quarterly Table of Mortality" in 115 registrars' districts for the quarter ending, June 30th, 1844.*—403
— October 30th, 1844: *Turnout at Messrs. Kennedy's factory.*—468
[*Information on different incidents in factory towns*].—426

— November 2nd, 1844: *Messrs. Pauling and Co. and their Workmen.*—589
— November 27th, December 28th, 1844, and January 4th, 1845: [*Details about the strike of the Pauling and Henfrey workers*].—595, 596

The Mining Journal No. 420, T. 13, September 9th, 1843:
[*Statistics on accidents in mines*].—538

The Northern Star No. 46, September 29th, 1838: *Meeting at Kersal Moor, on Monday, Sept. 24th.*—519
— No. 295, July 8th, 1843: *Brutality at a Workhouse.*—574
— No. 315, November 25th, 1843: *Murder! Hellish treatment of the poor in the Coventry Bastille.*—574-75
— No. 317, December 9th, 1843: *Atrocities at the Birmingham Workhouse.*—575
— No. 318, December 16th, 1843: *The Important Investigation at the Birmingham Workhouse.*—575
— No. 319, December 23rd, 1843: *Continuation of the enquiry at the Birmingham Workhouse.*—575
— No. 326, February 10th, 1844: *Secrets of the Union Workhouse.*—575, 576
— No. 328, February 24th, 1844: *The Poor Laws.—Disgusting Treatment of the Poor.*—575, 576, 577
Record of Destitution. Frightful Spread of Fever from Destitution.—397
— No. 333, March 30th, 1844: *Infamous Treatment of an Englishman and his Family in Bethnal-Green Workhouse.*—576
— No. 334, April 6th, 1844: *Inhuman conduct of the master of a Union Workhouse.*—574
    Horrible Profligacy in the West London Union Workhouse.—576
— No. 336, April 20th, 1844: *The Miner's Monthly Magazine. Edited by W. P. Roberts Esq. Nos. I and II. London: Cleave, Shoe-lane.*—541
    Mr. Roberts.—Belper.—Messrs. Haslam. To prevent any mistake.—543
— No. 337, April 27th, 1844: *Truckism.*—471
— No. 338, May 4th, 1844: *Metropolitan Misery.—Religious Robbery.*—334, 385
    More Liberations of Miners.—542
— No. 344, June 15th, 1844: *Horrible Condition of the Agricultural Labourers.*—579
— No. 350, July 27th, 1844: *The Mad Marquis again. The Labour Struggle.*—544-45
— No. 352, August 10th, 1844: *Sanatory Condition of the town! Important proceedings.*—344
— No. 359, September 28th, 1844: *Infernal Workhouse Cruelties.*—576
— No. 362, October 19th, 1844: *Great Meeting of the Carpenters of Manchester and Salford.*—586
— No. 363, October 26th, 1844: *Manchester.—The Strike of Messrs. Pauling and Co.'s Carpenters and Joiners.*—586
— No. 365, November 9th, 1844: *Henfrey v. Salmon—Assault.*—589-91
    The Carpenters' and Joiners' Strike.—592-94
— No. 366, November 16th, 1844: *Another of Labour's Victories.—The Carpenters and Joiners of Manchester.*—592-94
— No. 367, November 23rd, 1844: *Manchester.—Great Aggregate Meeting of the Building Trades.*—595
— No. 368, November 30th, 1844: *Extension of the Strike.*—595
    More of Labour's Triumphs at Manchester and Wigan.—595-96
— No. 369, December 7th, 1844: *Another Victory for Labour. Manchester, Friday, Nov. 29th.*—595-96

— No. 375, January 18th, 1845: *Aggregate Meeting of the Manchester Building Trades.*—596

Sheffield and Rotherham Independent, February 3rd, 1844:
[*Note on the fire in the Soho Wheel Works in Sheffield*].— 509

The Times, October 12th, 1843: *London, Thursday, October 12, 1843.*—336-37
— November 17th, 1843: *Appalling Destitution.*—334
— December 22nd, 1843: *The Houseless poor.*—337
— January 16th, 1844: *Police. Worship-street.*—334
— February 12th, 1844: *Police. Marlborough-street.*—334, 335
To the editor of "The Times".—336-37
— June 7th, 1844: *The Incendiary Fires in Suffolk and Norfolk. (From our own correspondent).*—551, 552
— June 10th, 1844: *Incendiarism in Suffolk and Norfolk. (From our own correspondent).*—551, 552
— June 21st, 1844: *The Incendiary Fires in Suffolk and Norfolk. (From our own correspondent).*—551, 552

The Weekly Dispatch, No. 2212, March 17th, 1844: *Horrifying Conditions of the Staymakers and Stock-makers.*—449
— No. 2219, May 5th, 1844: *Wild beasts and rational beings.*—366, 372-73
— No. 2232, August 4th, 1844: *The Railway Bill.—More Oppression for the Poor.*—569
— No. 2251, December 15th, 1844: *Mortality in the Metropolis.*—406

INDEX OF PERIODICALS

Allgemeine Literatur-Zeitung—German monthly published in Charlottenburg from December 1843 to October 1844; organ of the Young Hegelians edited by Bruno Bauer—7, 12, 14, 20, 51, 77, 91, 99, 107, 117, 136, 138, 143, 147-48, 151, 153, 156-57, 210, 211

Allgemeine Zeitung—German conservative daily founded in 1798; from 1810 to 1882 was published in Augsburg—134

Allgemeines Volksblatt. Populärer Monatsbericht über die wichtigsten Zeitfragen—German democratic monthly published in Cologne from January 1845 to the beginning of 1846—240

Anekdota zur neuesten deutschen Philosophie und Publicistik—collection published in 1843 in Switzerland (Zurich and Winterthur) under the editorship of Arnold Ruge; Volumes I and II were printed; Marx's articles appeared in this collection —152, 192

The Anti-Bread-Tax-Circular—biweekly organ of the Anti-Corn Law League; initially its name was *The Anti-Corn-Law Circular*, published in Manchester from 1839 to 1843—658

The Artizan. A Monthly Journal of the Operative Arts—English monthly, organ of building engineers published in London from 1843 to 1873—339, 340, 342, 396, 405

Blätter der Gegenwart für soziales Leben—newspaper of German émigrés in Switzerland, founded by Wilhelm Marr and published in Lausanne from 1844 to 1845 as an organ of the radical secret society "Young Germany"—651, 652

Bürgerbuch. See *Deutsches Bürgerbuch*

Constitutionnel Neuchâtelois—Swiss newspaper of a conservative monarchist orientation, published in Neuchâtel three times a week from 1831 to February 1848—651

Le Courrier de Provence—French daily founded by H. G. Mirabeau, published in Paris from 1789 to 1791 with contributions by J.-B. Say—270

Daily Advocate and Advertiser—American daily originally founded under the name of *Pennsylvania Advocate*, but soon renamed; published in Pittsburgh (Ohio) from 1832 to 1843—221

Le Débat Social, organe de la démocratie—Belgian weekly, organ of radical-republican circles, published in Brussels from 1844 to 1849—213

La Décade philosophique, littéraire et politique—French republican newspaper published in Paris three times a month from 1794 to 1807 under the editorship of Jean Baptiste Say—270

La Démocratie pacifique—French daily published in Paris from 1843 to 1851 under the editorship of Victor Considérant; organ of the Fourierists—152, 213

Deutsch-Französische Jahrbücher—German annual journal published in Paris under the editorship of Karl Marx and Arnold Ruge. The only issue of the journal—a double number—appeared in February 1844—32, 87, 88, 106-09, 111, 113, 229, 325, 562

Deutsche Jahrbücher für Wissenschaft und Kunst—literary and philosophical journal of the Left Hegelians published in Leipzig under the editorship of Arnold Ruge from July 1841 to January 1843. It was closed down by the government of Saxony and forbidden all over Germany by decision of the Federal Diet—100, 107

Deutsches Bürgerbuch—German annual journal, organ of the "true Socialists"; altogether two volumes appeared: the first (for 1845) was published by Hermann Püttmann in Darmstadt in December 1844; the second (for 1846) was published in Mannheim in the summer of 1846. The *Deutsches Bürgerbuch* carried two articles by Frederick Engels—228, 235, 240, 644

Durham Chronicle—English liberal weekly published in Durham from 1820—318

The Edinburgh Medical and Surgical Journal—Scottish medical monthly, published in Edinburgh from 1805 to 1855—339

L'Égalitaire, Journal de l'organisation sociale—French monthly founded by Théodore Dézamy and published in Paris in 1840; expounded the ideas of utopian communism—667

The Examiner—English annual journal, organ of the liberal circles, published in London from 1808 to 1881—523

The Fleet Papers—weekly edition of letters and pamphlets published by Richard Oastler from 1841 to 1844 during his stay in the Fleet prison—464

La Fraternité de 1845. Organe du communisme—workers' monthly of the Babouvist trend, published in Paris from January 1845 to February 1848—667

La Gazette de France—French royalist daily published under this title in Paris from 1762 to 1792 and from 1797 to 1848—598

Gesellschaftsspiegel. Organ zur Vertretung der besitzlosen Volksklassen und zur Beleuchtung der gesellschaftlichen Zustände der Gegenwart—German monthly, organ of the "true Socialists", published under the editorship of Moses Hess in Elberfeld in 1845-46; altogether twelve issues appeared; Frederick Engels was one of its founders—235, 240, 601, 612, 671-74

Le Globe—French daily paper founded by Pierre Leroux and published in Paris from 1824 to 1832; in January 1831 it became the organ of the Saint-Simonists—667

Halifax Guardian—English conservative weekly published in Halifax from 1832—472

Hallische Jahrbücher für deutsche Wissenschaft und Kunst— German literary and philosophical journal of the Young Hegelians, published in Halle from 1838 to 1841, edited by Arnold Ruge— 132

The Illuminated Magazine—English liberal literary magazine published in London from 1843 to 1845— 332, 574

Journal des Débats politiques et littéraires— French daily newspaper founded in Paris in 1789; during the July monarchy it was published by the government— 190

Journal of the Statistical Society of London—English monthly statistical journal published in London from 1838—333, 343

Kölnische Zeitung—German daily published under this title from 1802 to 1945; organ of the liberal bourgeoisie— 231

Konstitutionelle Jahrbücher—German liberal journal published three times a year in Stuttgart from 1843 to 1847—162

The Leeds Mercury—English weekly (until 1861) founded in Leeds in 1718; in the 1840s became the organ of the Radicals—471

Literatur-Zeitung. See *Allgemeine Literatur-Zeitung*

Liverpool Mercury—English liberal daily published in Liverpool from 1811—370

The Manchester Guardian—English daily, organ of the free traders, from the middle of the 19th century organ of the Liberal Party; founded in Manchester in 1821—369-72, 403, 426, 436, 455, 468, 471, 538, 539, 564

Mercure de France—French monthly published in Paris in 1672-1820; from 1793 it was edited by Jacques Peuchet —598

The Miner's Advocate—English monthly, organ of the Miners' Union of Great Britain, published in Newcastle in the 1840s—541

The Mining Journal—English weekly journal dealing with commercial and technical problems, founded in London in 1835— 538

The Morning Chronicle—English daily published in London from 1770 to 1862; in the 1840s became the organ of the Whigs—224, 480, 556

The New Moral World: and Gazette of the Rational Society—English weekly founded by Robert Owen; organ of Utopian Socialists; published from 1834 to 1846, first in Leeds, then in London; Engels contributed to it from November 1843 to May 1845—212, 213, 217, 220, 221, 229, 234, 237, 242

The Northern Star—English weekly newspaper, central organ of the Chartists; published from 1837 to 1852, first in Leeds, then in London. Its founder and editor was Feargus O'Connor, George Harney being one of its co-editors. Engels contributed to the paper from 1843 to 1850— 471, 512, 554, 593, 647, 648, 650, 653, 655

North of England Medical and Surgical Journal—English journal published in London and Manchester from 1830 to 1831—453

Petites Affiches de Paris—French periodical founded in Paris in 1612; an information bulletin carrying various announcements and notices— 190

Das Pfennig-Magazin—German educational weekly of liberal tendencies published in Leipzig from 1833 to 1855—221

La Phalange. Revue de la science sociale—organ of the Fourierists, published in Paris from 1832 to 1849; it repeatedly changed its title, frequency of publication and size—615, 641

Pittsburg Daily Advocate and Advertiser. See *Daily Advocate and Advertiser*

Le Producteur, Journal philosophique de l'Industrie, des Sciences et des Beaux-Arts—French weekly published in Paris from 1825 to 1826; first printed organ of the Saint-Simonists—667

Punch, or the London Charivari—English comic weekly paper of a liberal trend, founded in London in 1841—500

Révolutions de Paris—French revolutionary and democratic weekly published in Paris from July 1789 to February 1794; till September 1790 the paper was edited by Elisée Loustalot—82

Revue des deux Mondes—French biweekly literary and political journal published in Paris since 1829—488

Rheinische Jahrbücher zur gesellschaftlichen Reform—German magazine, organ of the "true Socialists", published by Hermann Püttmann; altogether two issues appeared: the first in Darmstadt in August 1845, and the second in Bellevue, a place on the German-Swiss border, at the end of 1846; the magazine carried Engels' Elberfeld speeches—235, 240, 241, 264, 654, 655

Rheinische Zeitung für Politik, Handel und Gewerbe—German daily paper founded on January 1, 1842, as an organ of the oppositional circles of the Rhenish bourgeoisie, and published in Cologne till March 31, 1843; Marx was its editor from October 15, 1842, to March 17, 1843; under his influence the paper assumed a pronounced revolutionary and democratic character, which led to its suppression by the government—100, 107, 256

Le Satan—French satirical weekly of liberal tendencies, published in Paris from 1842 to 1844—191

Le Siècle—French daily published in Paris from 1836 to 1939. In the 1840s it was an oppositional organ which demanded electoral and other reforms—190

Der Sprecher oder: Rheinisch-Westphälischer Anzeiger—German democratic newspaper founded in Dortmund in 1798 and appearing until 1863; in the 1840s it was published in Wesel; Karl Grün, who later became a "true Socialist", was one of its editors from 1842 to November 1844—229-30

Statistical Journal. See *Journal of the Statistical Society of London*

The Sun—English liberal daily published in London from 1798 to 1876—472

Telegraph für Deutschland—German literary magazine founded by Karl Gutzkow; in 1837 it appeared in Frankfort on the Main, and from 1838 to 1848 in Hamburg. In the late thirties and early forties of the 19th century the magazine was the mouthpiece of the "Young Germany" group. Engels contributed to it from March 1839 to 1841—656, 658, 661

The Times—English daily founded in London in 1785—336, 337, 427, 552, 579

Trier'sche Zeitung—German daily founded in 1757 and published under this title until 1815; in the early forties of the 19th century it became a radical organ and later was influenced by the ideas of "true socialism"—229

Volksblatt. See *Allgemeines Volksblatt*

Vorwärts! Pariser deutsche Zeitschrift—German newspaper published in Paris twice a week from January to December 1844; organ of the moderate and from May 1844 of radical-democratic elements among German émigrés. Marx and Engels contributed to it, thus intensifying its revolutionary tendencies—212-13, 230

The Weekly Chronicle—English radical weekly published in London from 1836 to 1865—523

The Weekly Dispatch—English radical weekly published under this title in London from 1801 to 1928—366, 373, 406, 499, 523

Das Westphälische Dampfboot—German monthly, organ of the "true Socialists", published under the editorship of Otto Lüning in Bielefeld from January 1845 to December 1846 and in Paderborn from January 1847 to March 1848. Some of Marx and Engels' works were published in it—240, 596

Zeitschrift für spekulative Theologie—German theoretical journal of Hegelian tendencies, published in Berlin from 1836 to 1838 under the editorship of Bruno Bauer—143

SUBJECT INDEX

A

Absolute—see *Relative and absolute*

Abstraction—19, 20, 22, 23, 24, 35, 39, 40, 41, 53, 57-60, 66-67, 71, 72, 83, 97, 99, 110, 120, 128, 137, 141-42, 153, 155, 169, 178-80, 193, 205
— abstract and concrete—23, 40, 52, 53, 85, 166-67, 193

Aesthetics—55, 161, 167

Agitation—237, 525, 653

Agricultural proletariat—see *Working class*

Aim—37, 93-94, 123
— means to achieve it—93
— as an end in itself—123

Alchemy—27

Alienation—41, 50, 82, 116, 140, 141, 143, 160
— self-alienation—9, 21, 53, 82, 140
See also *Estrangement*

America—see *United States of America*

Analogy—10, 161, 166, 201, 206

Analysis and synthesis—114, 128

Anarchy—117, 122

Anti-Corn Law League, the—13, 15-16, 272, 289, 387, 417, 519, 520, 555, 566-67, 588, 657-60
See also *Corn Laws*

Antithesis—35-36
— between classes—35-37, 56, 244, 329, 411-12, 414, 418, 466, 497, 503, 528, 529, 556, 577-78, 581-82, 583
See also *Class struggle, Contradictions, Opposites, Working class*

Aristocracy—304, 520
See also *England—landed aristocracy, landlords*

Army—249-50

Artisans, handicraftsmen—116, 321, 325, 326, 488-89, 497

Asceticism—99, 128

Ashton—313, 345, 587

Astrology—27

Atheism, atheists—82, 89, 110, 127, 212-13, 412
— workers' atheism—421, 526, 538, 653

Atom—120-21, 128

B

Babouvism—47, 119

Barnsley—344

Basis and superstructure—109, 112

Being, existence
— and consciousness—36-38, 43, 53, 58, 59, 85-86, 125, 129, 141-42, 144, 191-93
See also *Consciousness*

Belfast—315

Belgium—213, 676, 677

Birmingham—318, 329, 340, 341, 488, 489, 491, 517, 529

Bohemia
— insurrection of cotton printers in 1844—230, 303-04, 503, 647

Bolton—12, 313, 345, 508

Bourgeoisie
— general characteristics—280-81, 285, 286, 325, 330-31, 375-80, 393, 409, 412-13, 416, 420, 421, 423, 424, 425, 427, 430, 431, 433, 434, 508, 525, 546-47, 673
— industrial (manufacturers)—409, 432, 435, 444, 457, 469, 473, 486, 509-10, 563
— liberal—416-17, 460, 517, 562, 570
— as a ruling class—298, 393
— and feudal monarchy—649-50
See also *Middle class*

Bourgeoisie in England
— general characteristics—212, 230, 267, 304, 323, 410-11, 413-14, 416-17, 419-21, 426, 458, 512, 555, 657, 660
— big—321, 325, 348, 497, 556-57
— petty—244, 321, 326, 371, 375, 488-89, 498, 520, 528, 548, 556, 580-81
— industrial (manufacturers)—322, 325, 326, 383, 409, 428, 430, 447, 456, 458, 459, 460, 461, 462, 469, 470, 486, 488-89, 510, 520, 538, 544, 555, 566, 587, 657, 658, 660
— commercial—660
— liberal—322, 416, 459, 460, 517, 520, 523, 528, 562, 570, 579
— as a ruling class—298, 393, 407, 409, 410, 412
— in Parliament—322, 323, 517
— its cultural level—528
— and working class (interrelations, exploitation)—349-50, 385-86, 413, 416, 418, 419, 423, 424, 425, 428, 434, 506-10, 520-21, 522, 523, 528, 538-40, 562-83, 585

Bourgeoisie in France—50, 56, 122-24, 212, 262-63, 267, 304
See also *French bourgeois revolution of the end of the 18th century*

Bourgeoisie in Germany—230, 237, 265-68, 274, 275, 292, 302-04, 393, 544, 563, 647-50, 652-53

Bourgeoisie, Prussian—649

Bourgeois political economy—31-32, 34, 42, 49-50, 198, 265-68, 271-72, 276, 284, 287, 290, 293, 598
See also *Malthusianism*

Bourgeois society—37, 69-70, 76, 123, 135, 267-68, 275-76, 280-81, 283, 303, 597, 671
— its organisation—275, 276
See also *Capitalist mode of production*

Bradford—315, 343, 519

Brain—22, 59, 66, 140

Bristol—340, 389

Bureaucracy—267

Bury—345

Byzantium—178

C

Capitalist mode of production—244, 245, 246, 247, 263-64, 330, 378, 456-58, 473, 479, 497-98, 508, 554-55, 564, 572

Cartesianism—126, 127
— Cartesian materialism—125, 130, 132

Casuistry
— moral—182, 185

Category—22, 30, 41, 42, 44, 53, 54, 57, 60, 67, 72, 73, 83, 93, 148, 153, 159-60, 191, 193
— abstract—67, 159-60
— logical—90
— philosophical—137

Catholicism—81, 346

Causality, cause and effect—13, 16, 46, 73, 134, 280, 285-86

Censorship—229

Charity, bourgeois—564-65, 570
See also *Humaneness, Philanthropy*
Chartism
— general characteristics—418, 477-78, 517-21, 577
— as an independent political movement of the working class—15, 517, 528-29, 545, 555

— People's Charter, political programme of Chartism—465, 517-19, 522, 566-67
— need for combining it with socialist theory—524-27
— and bourgeois and petty-bourgeois radicals—518, 522-23, 524, 528-29, 578
— General Working-men's Association of London (Lovett)—517-18
— National Charter Association—522-23
— and movement for the repeal of the Corn Laws (free traders)—13, 519-21
— and struggle for shorter working hours—13-15, 519, 523
— and Trade Unions—540-41
— and the agrarian question—523-24
— and the 1842 strike—512-17, 520-22, 566, 587, 588, 658-59

Chemistry—546
— chemical properties of substances—27

Cheshire—316, 403, 554

Children
— in England—399-401, 402, 405, 435-38, 440, 442-43, 496-97
See also *Child labour, Family, Mortality among children*

Child labour
— in factories—384, 408, 411, 441-44, 446-47, 450, 455-60, 463-64, 466, 468, 477-83, 485, 489-92, 494-97, 672, 673
— in mines and collieries—533, 534, 538-39
— in agriculture—550

China—261, 580

Christianity—56, 59, 85, 88-89, 94, 95, 109, 110, 169-81, 184
— and the state—88
— and the individual—178

Church—117, 653
— Anglican—409, 556
— in England—464, 477, 559, 564
See also *Religion*

Civilisation—251

Classes, the—197
— and their interrelations—584, 597, 671

— class prejudices—427
— propertied—13, 15, 16, 36, 526-27
— non-propertied—14, 36, 135
See also *Antithesis—between classes, Bourgeoisie, Class struggle, Peasantry, Working class*

Class contradictions—see *Antithesis—between classes*

Class solidarity—see *Working class—class solidarity*

Class struggle, the—243, 248, 329-30, 331, 375, 427, 429, 502, 508-09, 511, 512, 513, 554, 555, 580-83, 585
— between the proletariat and the bourgeoisie—323, 386, 413-14, 416, 427, 501, 506-08, 510, 511, 528-29, 561, 570, 582-83
— and social revolution—418
— and class-consciousness—417-18, 528-29
See also *Antithesis—between classes, Working class*

Clergy, the
— English—421
— German—235, 268
— French—213
— and secular education—408
See also *Church*

Communism (theory)—36-37, 52-53, 94-95, 130, 131, 136, 241, 263
— workers' communism (German, French, English)—124, 125, 302

Communism (economic formation)—246-52, 253, 254, 282
— public ownership of the means of production—254, 263
— productive forces—250-52
— abolition of class contradictions and class distinctions—246, 281-83
— ways of transition—253-55
— peaceful transition—253-54, 263, 465, 581-82
— and the state—248
— and labour—250-52
— policy of peace—249-50

Communist movement, Communists
— in England—242
— in Belgium—213
— in France—131, 152-53, 196, 212, 213, 242, 253, 526, 527, 582, 613, 614

— in Germany—213, 229-42, 256, 613, 644
— in Switzerland—242, 652-53, 655
Communist colonies—214-28
— in England—214, 215, 223-27, 235
— in the U.S.A.—214, 215, 217-18, 220-24, 232, 235, 238, 239
See also *Harmony, Rappites, Shakers*
Competition
— general characteristics—49, 122, 243-45, 251, 257-58, 261-62, 267, 275, 279, 280, 308, 326, 375-76, 379, 382, 427, 524, 555, 564, 566
— over land—556-59
— and monopoly—261-62
— between states—14, 259-61, 466, 480, 579-80, 657
— among workers—16, 251, 307-08, 372, 375-88, 433-34, 507-08
See also *Unemployment*
Concept, notion—70, 72, 78, 92, 93, 128, 132, 137, 138, 145, 668
Conception, idea—32, 33, 57, 60, 62, 81, 128, 137-39
Connection—120, 130
— interconnection—19
Consciousness—19, 31, 33, 39, 41, 53, 79, 85, 86, 104, 109, 119, 133, 141, 171, 174, 177, 178, 192, 665
— unconsciousness—33, 36, 39, 85, 113
See also *Reason, Self-consciousness, Thinking*
Contemplation—see *Perception*
Content—see *Form and content*
Contradictions—32, 33, 34, 36, 39, 41, 49, 58, 93, 99, 105, 107, 111, 114, 115, 116, 121, 128, 133, 139, 161, 166, 167, 168, 183
See also *Antithesis, Opposites*
Corn Laws—288, 289, 519-20, 522, 523, 549, 566, 588, 656-61
— repeal of—13, 15, 322, 411, 519-20, 521, 522, 555, 566, 579, 581, 588, 657-61
See also *Anti-Corn Law League*
Cost of production—16, 32, 49, 657
Court and legal procedure—467-68, 487, 541-42, 567-69, 587, 589-93, 650

Crime—234, 248, 249, 386, 412, 413, 422, 425-27, 494, 502, 508-09, 551, 553
— in England—412-13, 425-27, 508-09, 551
Crises, social—419
See also *Revolution*
Critical Criticism—see *Young Hegelianism*
Customs Union—259

D

Deduction—see *Induction and deduction*
Definitions—84, 95, 96, 97
Definition, determination—25, 28, 32, 45, 49-50, 52, 58, 60, 61, 84, 95, 97
Deism—129, 421
Derby—314, 340, 479, 481, 554
Development—23, 36, 76, 95, 96, 105, 128, 131, 138
— concrete—52
— spiritual—135
Dialectics—11, 23, 42, 61, 64, 73, 75, 78, 80, 93
— dialectical process of thinking—53, 78
— speculative dialectics—54, 103
Diseases, epidemics (engendered by the development of capitalism)—13, 364-65, 397-400
Dissenters—112, 464
Division of labour—325, 344-45, 381, 415-16
Dogmatism, dogma—20, 34, 83, 95, 96, 107, 158
Dublin—337, 338
Dundee—315

E

Economic crisis—382-84, 386-87, 388, 518
— development in cycles—383, 386
— commercial—245, 353, 381-83, 399, 429, 580-81, 658
— agrarian—548-49

— in 1837-39—245, 518
— in 1842—245, 386-88, 508, 520
— in 1847—386
Economic relationships—33, 53, 122, 197
Edinburgh—338, 339, 340, 341, 389, 397, 404
Education—235
— general education in communist society—253-54
— in England—407-12, 459, 462, 464, 477, 490-92, 494, .496, 527, 528
See also Schools in England
Egoism—120, 668
Elberfeld—237
Emancipation, political—see Revolution, bourgeois, Revolution, proletarian
Emigration
— political—229, 652-53
— Irish immigration to England— 321, 337, 355, 376-77, 389-92, 419-20, 560
Empiricism—39, 72, 80, 82, 85, 109, 155, 178
Energy—141
England
— general characteristics—307, 320, 328
— before the 19th cent.—307, 309, 312, 320
— as the leading capitalist country of the 19th cent.—245, 261, 318-19, 320, 328, 419, 465-66
— history of—309, 644
— population of—320, 321, 325, 326, 381, 416-18, 432-33, 548, 656
— agriculture, agrarian relations in— 289, 311, 318-19, 324, 358-60, 548-49, 550, 553, 554, 555-58, 568, 660, 661
— livestock breeding in—317, 557
— peasants, tenant farmers—288, 308, 311, 375, 548-52, 553-58, 559, 562, 657, 660
— landed aristocracy, landlords—288, 520, 548, 552, 553, 554, 555, 559, 562, 656-57, 660-61
— trade of—13, 245, 288-89, 312, 313, 317, 326, 381, 385, 480
— commercial crises—245, 360, 381-83, 398, 580-81

— communications—317-20, 569
— poor rates—386, 388, 549
— peasant movement in the 1830s and 1840s—553, 554, 557
— Constitution—14, 518, 661
— Parliament—14, 322, 503, 517-18, 546, 549, 569-70, 572, 578, 658, 660
— electoral system, Reform Bill of 1832—322, 503, 517-18, 571, 657, 660
— legislation of—322, 503, 514, 517-18, 567, 568, 569, 570, 660-61
— Poor Laws—322, 463, 464, 519, 523, 550, 553, 557, 568, 569, 570, 574, 577-78, 660-61
— laws against tramps and vagabonds —567-68
— Game Laws—552-53
— Factory Acts—13-14, 322, 428, 443, 459-66, 539, 569-70
— political parties in—13, 15, 304, 322, 381, 416, 517-18, 520, 555, 570, 646
— church of—464, 477, 559, 564
— prospects of proletarian revolution —260-61, 262, 546-47, 579-83
— and Ireland—560, 561
— temperance societies—423
— English, the—419, 560

See also Bourgeoisie in England, English bourgeois revolution of the 17th century, Industry in England, Industrial revolution in England, Ireland, Tories, Whigs, Workers' movement in England, Working class in England

English bourgeois revolution of the 17th century—262
English materialist philosophy—125, 126, 127-31
Enlighteners
— German—134-35
— French—124-25, 126
— and religion—124-25
Epicureanism—169
Epidemics—see Diseases, epidemics
Equality—38-39, 40, 41
— bourgeois—38-39
— and private property as its negation —41

Essence and phenomenon—21, 22, 27, 28, 33, 35, 41, 42, 52, 57-61, 64, 68, 72, 73, 84, 89, 93, 96, 97, 106, 107, 109-10, 114, 121, 123, 128, 138, 152, 174

Estrangement—41-43, 120, 192, 665
— self-estrangement—36, 41, 42

Ethics—see *Morality*

Europe (political characteristics)—652-53

Exchange value—266, 275-83, 284
See also *Value*

Existence—see *Being*

Experience—23, 79, 128, 129, 130

Exploitation
— of labour by capital—418-19, 461, 467, 469, 506-07
See also *Labour, Working class*

F

Factory legislation in England—13-14, 15, 322, 428, 443, 460, 462-66
— Apprentices' Act of 1802—459
— Factory Act of 1819—459
— Factory Act of 1825—459
— Factory Act of 1831—459-60
— 1833 (1834) Act—459, 461-62
— Lord Ashley's Act (1842) banning the employment of women and limiting the employment of children in mines and collieries—539
— Masters' and Servants' Act (1844)—322, 569-70
— Ten Hours' Bill (1844)—435, 460-61, 465-66

Factory legislation in Germany—672-73

Factory system—14, 284-85, 311-12, 434, 439, 445, 457-60, 466, 467, 472-73, 474-79, 485, 489, 497
See also *Child labour, Female labour, Labour*

Family
— of the worker—424-25, 437-38, 439-40, 497
— patriarchal—309

Fatherland—250

Female labour—406, 464
— female labour replacing male labour—384, 431, 434-36, 477, 672

— in factories—434-38, 440-42, 451-55, 464, 469, 481-82, 489, 497, 672, 673
— dress-makers, sewing-women—497-500
— in mines and collieries—533-35
— in agriculture—550
See also *Family, Women's question*

Feuerbach's philosophy—92-94, 139

Fichte's philosophy—139

Form and content—97, 107

Fourier's socialism—50, 84, 152, 263, 302, 613-15, 641-43

France—261, 309, 320, 644
— Directory—122
— during Consulate and Empire—74, 81, 123, 124, 270, 598
— restoration of the Bourbons—74, 81, 85, 124, 598
— the 100 days—598
— during the revolution of July 1830—124
— agriculture, agrarian relations—199, 200, 560
— home policy of—281
— police—598
— monarchist party—598
— radicals—135
— French, the—419, 512, 560
See also *Bourgeoisie in France, French bourgeois revolution of the end of the 18th century, Revolution of 1848-49 in France, Workers' movement in France, Working class in France*

Freedom—32, 33, 50, 94, 98, 111-16, 122, 129, 169, 170

French bourgeois revolution of the end of the 18th century—30-31, 81-82, 118-20, 122-24, 262, 320, 323, 517, 597, 598, 644, 666
— Declaration of the Rights of Man—113, 114, 122
— *Cercle social*—119
— *Enragés*—119
— Hébert's party—114
— Constituent Assembly—598
— Convention—598
— Thermidor—323
— revolutionary army, revolutionary wars—250

— Terror, revolutionary—74, 81, 95, 123-24
— constitutions—597
— and religion—111, 113-14
See also *Babouvism, Girondists, Jacobins*

French philosophy of the 18th cent.—124, 125, 126, 129-32, 139, 140

G

General—see *Individual, particular and general*

Geology—546

Geometry—128

Germany—256, 309, 320, 518, 549, 552, 645, 646
— agriculture, agrarian relations—549, 560
— trade, home and foreign—258, 259, 261-62, 275
— home policy and internal situation—229-42
— classes—671-72
— peasantry—413
— political system—111
— civil life—113, 120, 121
— court and law—672, 674
— poor laws—674
— army—249-50
— prospects of the revolution—238-39, 257, 259-62, 646-47
See also *Bourgeoisie in Germany, Customs Union, Industry in Germany, Socialism in Germany, Workers' movement in Germany, Working class in Germany*

German philosophy of the 18th and 19th cent.—7, 8, 17, 40, 41, 125, 153, 653
See also *Feuerbach's philosophy, Fichte's philosophy, Hegel's philosophy*

Girondists, the—581

Glasgow—314, 341, 489, 397, 421, 509

Grain
— prices of grain—286-87, 656
— export of grain—289
See also *Corn Laws*

Greece, ancient—120

Greek philosophy—126, 128

Guilds—116

H

Halifax—315, 344

Harmony (socialist colony)—223-27, 232, 235, 238

Hegel's philosophy—12, 20, 57, 60-61, 89, 100-01, 103, 131-32, 137-39, 141, 148-49, 167, 178, 192-93, 665
See also *Old Hegelianism, Young Hegelianism*

Heywood—345

History—12, 13, 32, 79-82, 86, 109, 114, 122, 124, 135, 150, 267, 671
— as activity of man pursuing his aims—93, 281
— Hegel's conception of history—85, 86, 114
— development of history—84
— historic progress—474
— role of masses in history—81, 82, 85, 94

"Holy Family"—see *Young Hegelianism*

Homoeomeriae—128

Housing question, the
— in capitalist society—331-66, 395-96, 470-72, 532, 539, 543-44
— in England—331-66, 373-74, 396-98, 434, 470-72, 491-92, 532, 539, 552, 559
See also *Lodging-houses*

Huddersfield—315, 344

Hull—13

Humanism, real—7, 125, 131

Humaneness—179
— bourgeois—462, 565, 571
— proletarian—420

I

Idea, thought—40-41, 49-50, 81-82, 94, 119, 125-26, 128, 129, 138, 168, 179, 184, 186, 203

Ideal—19, 82, 88, 140, 142, 170, 188

Idealism—16, 53, 80, 123, 137, 140, 153

Ideology—see *World outlook*

Idolatry—127

Individual, personality, the—22, 79, 85, 86, 113, 120, 122, 160

Individualism—276

Individual, particular and general—19, 52, 61, 62, 78, 85, 100, 114, 115, 124, 128-29, 142, 193

Induction and deduction—31, 128

Industry—116, 122, 130, 150, 244, 256, 260-61, 265, 280-81, 324-27, 354-56, 375, 381, 419, 433, 502, 659-60
See also *Industry in America, Industry in England, Industry in Germany*

Industry in America—579-80

Industry in England
— general characteristics—245, 259, 260-61, 275, 281, 283, 289, 324, 325-27, 344, 355-57, 379, 383-84, 389, 393, 419, 426, 433, 465-66, 497, 530, 548, 566, 579-80, 644, 656, 657-58, 660
— history from the middle of the 18th century to the beginning of the 19th century—311-21
— cotton—12, 313-14, 414, 428-29, 433-34, 580
— linen—315-16
— woollen—289, 314-15, 342
— silk—316
— lace—314, 481, 482-83
— textile—428-32, 479, 484
— iron and steel, machine-building, coal-mining, metal-working—316-18, 488-89, 491, 494, 532
— potteries—318, 495
— glass—496-97

Industry in Germany—245, 256, 258-61, 275

Industrial revolution in England—307, 309, 313, 320, 324, 325, 503

Infinity—129

Intellect, understanding—58, 128, 129
See also *Reason*

Intemperance (as a social category)—400, 401, 421-23, 444, 466, 467

Interdependence—113, 117

Interest, interests—41, 42, 81, 82, 120, 124, 126, 143, 174, 175
— material—123
— historic—41

— political—91, 123
— private, personal—113, 130-32, 206
— general, common—130, 132, 133, 134, 144

Internal and external—22, 23, 82, 83, 101, 108, 137-38, 174, 178

Internationalism, proletarian—298, 301

Inventions—12, 71, 289, 307, 310-13, 317, 344, 428, 429, 511, 656
See also *Industrial revolution in England*

Investigations—32, 83, 110, 112

Ireland—558, 559, 560
— population—321, 391
— history—321
— agrarian relations (tenant farmers)—391, 557-61
— English agrarian legislation for Ireland—559
— Poor Law of 1838, workhouses—577-78
— impoverishment and diseases of popular masses engendered by colonial oppression—397, 399, 533, 558-59, 649
— pauperism—558-59, 577-78
— Irish workers in England—322, 324, 376-77, 384, 390, 391, 392, 397, 399, 421, 577-78
— agricultural proletariat—558
— Irish, the—391-92, 421, 559, 560
See also *Working class in England—Irish workers, Repealers*

Italy—408

Italians—559

J

Jacobins—121-23

Jesuits, Jesuitism—126, 190

Jews, Jewish question—87, 88, 90, 95, 96, 98, 106-12, 113-14
See also *Judaism*

Judaism—90, 99, 110
See also *Jews*

K

Knowledge—53, 125, 129
See also *Conception, Senses*

L

Labour, work—278, 279 280, 672
— social—278, 279
— human—50
— conditions of labour under capitalism—414-16, 443-48, 450-52, 453-55, 462, 466-67, 468-69, 479-89, 530-39
— coerciveness of labour—415, 466, 468-69
— night work—444
— organisation of labour—19
— manual labour, its replacement by machines—312-13, 428-29, 433-35
— merging of industrial and agricultural labour—548
— system of fines—469-70, 486, 487, 488, 539-40
See also Child labour, Division of labour, Female labour, Working day
Labour time—48, 49
Lancashire—312, 313, 314, 315, 342, 344, 403, 410, 425, 445, 488, 494, 528, 554, 587
Landlords, landlordism—see England—landed aristocracy, landlords
Landed property—45-46, 116, 286-90, 318, 559, 673
See also England—agriculture, agrarian relations in
Language—319, 438
Law, right—31, 97, 116, 117
— Roman law—44
Law (juridical)—28, 29, 116, 117, 129, 179
Lease, tenant farmers—311, 319, 359-60, 548-49, 556-59
Leeds—315, 316, 329, 342, 343
Legislation, bourgeois—514-15, 567, 568
See also Bourgeois society, Court and legal procedure
Legislative acts regulating the working day in England—see Factory legislation in England
Leicester—314, 340, 470, 479, 480, 481
Leipzig butchery (1845)—see Workers' movement in Germany
Literature
— communist, utopian—235, 240

— socialist—56, 597, 644
— English—135, 289, 416-17, 420, 528
— German—229
— French—135
Liverpool—13, 313, 326, 340, 389, 403, 405, 593
Lodging-houses—336, 532
Logic—17, 24, 31, 45, 46-47, 62, 76, 90, 131, 137, 167
— Hegelian—18
— speculative—62, 157
See also Analogy, Definition, Subject and object, Tautology
London—320, 326-29, 331-37, 372, 389, 396, 397, 424, 498, 499, 517
Love—20-23, 439
Luddism—433, 503
See also Industrial revolution in England
Lumpenproletariat—see Working class in England—lumpenproletariat
Lyons—53
— revolt of Lyons weavers in 1834—512

M

Machine, machinery—13, 14, 308, 311, 317, 321, 325, 344, 482
— and appearance of the proletariat—321
— replacing manual labour—429-35, 482, 489, 548, 553
See also Inventions
Macclesfield—593
Malthusianism—379-80, 432, 570-73
Man, human being—7, 20, 22, 23, 27, 39, 40, 42, 43, 46, 49, 54, 65-66, 70-71, 82, 85, 87-88, 92, 93, 98-99, 107, 109, 111, 113, 114, 116, 120-21, 125, 127-34, 138, 139, 141-43, 150, 160, 165, 166, 167, 168, 169, 171-75, 178, 179, 181, 184, 185, 191-93, 201, 665
— his essence—21, 22, 39, 41, 106, 114, 115, 141-42, 174, 177, 194
— his activity—49, 50, 53, 54, 153, 176, 188
— his freedom and rights—87-88, 98-99, 111, 113, 114, 130-31

— his relationships—32, 42, 43
— his feelings—21, 22, 23, 35, 67, 84, 161, 174-75, 180-81
— needs of—52-53
— humanity, mankind—22, 26, 83, 84, 85, 88, 136, 139, 142, 144, 167, 177, 281, 671
— human and inhuman—33, 76, 110, 111, 113, 116, 195
See also *Alienation, Estrangement*

Manchester—12-13, 53, 313, 316, 326, 329, 344, 345, 347-66, 387-89, 396, 397, 403, 405, 406, 422, 423, 426, 455, 457, 464, 477, 478, 495, 512, 513, 517, 520, 521, 522, 564, 565, 587, 588, 592, 593, 657-60

Manifestation, sign—34-35, 123, 177

Masses—9, 11, 12, 78, 80, 81, 84, 85, 133-34, 135, 136, 154-56, 193, 244, 249-50, 514, 521-22
— their role in history—80-81, 84-85, 103

Materialism, material—22, 49, 80, 82, 85, 95, 113, 124-25, 126-31, 132, 136, 139-41, 150, 192, 196, 265-66
— material production—49, 150
— material conditions—95
— mechanical materialism—125

Mathematics—48
— mathematical motion—128

Matter—46, 83, 85, 93, 125, 128, 129, 132, 135, 136, 140-44, 194
— its forms—129, 140

Medicine—564

Metaphysics—17, 37, 62, 75, 79, 125, 126, 127, 130, 137-41, 166, 180
— Cartesian—126-27, 130
— of the 17th cent.—126, 127, 129, 132
— speculative—130

Middle class, the—244, 245, 321, 325, 349, 375, 388
See also *Bourgeoisie in England, Bourgeoisie in France, Bourgeoisie in Germany*

Middleton—345

Mind—60, 61

Mineralogy—58

Mode of production—150
See also *Social formation*

Monarchy—114, 115

Money, money system—53, 109
— as a form of private property—32
— power of money—412, 456-57, 562-64

Morality—130, 169-70, 180-85, 201, 308-09, 407, 411, 423-24, 483, 492, 496, 528, 643
— of the worker—343, 392, 408, 411, 412, 417, 419-20, 441, 442, 466-67, 483-84, 538, 539
See also *Crime, Family, Love*

Mortality—403, 404, 405-06, 532
— among children—405-06

Movement, motion—35, 125, 128, 140, 141, 142

Mysticism—11, 30, 39, 58, 60, 138, 167, 193

N

Napoleonic wars—289, 548, 656

Nation—153, 276, 281, 381
— national prejudices—298

Nationalism—120

Nature—129, 138, 139-41, 150, 167, 170, 172

Natural philosophy—22, 150

Natural science—57, 125, 128, 130, 149-50, 155

Necessity and chance—23, 25, 37, 61, 113, 130-31, 139

Needs, requirements—19, 38, 52, 113, 120, 278

Negation of the negation (law of)—22, 33-34, 160

Newcastle—543

Nobility—266
— the squire—656

Nominalism—127, 128

Norfolk—554

Nottingham—314, 340, 479, 481, 483

O

Oldham—313, 345

Old and new—103, 104, 106, 124

Old Hegelianism—142

Opium war (1842)—261

Opposites, opposition—14, 16, 34-48, 45, 54, 56, 58, 84, 85, 86, 94, 96, 98, 103, 105, 110, 112, 117, 130, 139, 141, 144, 148, 151, 154, 155, 158, 167, 168, 179, 193, 201, 203
See also *Antithesis, Contradictions*

Organisations and associations of workers—378, 418, 420, 459-60, 503-08, 509-10, 517, 540, 568
See also *Trade unions in England*

Orthography, English—409

Owen's socialism—84, 223-24, 232, 252-53, 459, 525-26, 614

P

Papism—268

Parcellation—116, 257

Paris—57, 597-612

Patriarchal relations—418, 550

Patriotic War of 1812 in Russia—124

Pauperism—12
— in England—549-50, 551, 571, 573
— in Ireland—558-59, 577
— in Germany—234, 671-72
See also *Charity, bourgeois, Humaneness, bourgeois, Philanthropy, Workhouses in England*

Peasantry—289, 375, 548, 550, 553
See also *Lease, tenant farmers*

Penalty
— penal theory—176-79, 186

Perception—58, 61, 129, 158
— sensory perception—58, 61

Person, individual—23, 79, 248, 253, 426, 514

Phenomenology—665

Philanthropy—237, 384-85, 459, 460, 474, 525-26, 578, 597, 649
See also *Charity, bourgeois, Humaneness, bourgeois*

Philistines
— German—267, 268, 280, 282, 283

Philosophy—7, 24, 39, 76-77, 85-93, 125, 129

See also *English materialist philosophy, German philosophy of the 18th and 19th cent., Scholasticism, Speculation*

Philosophers—17, 29, 59, 60, 146-47

Phraseology—266, 291

Physics—125, 126, 128, 130

Physiocrats—see *Bourgeois political economy*

Poaching—551-53

Police—73, 598

Political economy—see *Bourgeois political economy*

Poor relief—see *Philanthropy*

Population
— centralisation of; towns—325, 326, 394, 416-18, 441, 548
— in England—321, 326, 381, 432, 548

Practice—see *Theory and practice*

Pragmatism—41

Predicate—21

Premises, preconditions—31, 32, 35, 42, 45, 101
See also *Logic*

Press
— bourgeois—480, 523, 543
— socialist and communist—212-13, 654-55, 674
— in Germany—229, 231, 671
— in France—212-13

Preston—12, 313, 345, 522

Price—32, 50

Principles—7, 12, 14, 16, 17, 27, 28, 31, 39-41, 82, 89, 93, 105, 115, 121, 129, 130-31, 584
— basic—121, 129, 131-32

Private property—35, 36, 42-43, 49, 278
— its forms—32, 33, 53
— proletariat as its creation—35-36
— "drives itself to its own dissolution"—36
— its essence—33
— historical justification of its existence—41

Privileges—115-16

Production—49

Productive forces—266, 276, 277, 284-88

Profit
— on capital—32

Progress—29, 82-85
— historic—474
— social—26
— scientific and technical—32, 259-61, 480
See also *Industrial revolution in England*
Proof—25, 28, 45, 67, 79, 80, 81
Property—289, 325, 421, 497
— as the negation of equality (according to Proudhon)—40-41
— centralisation of property—14
— the right of property (according to Proudhon)—45
See also *Landed property, Private property*
Prostitution—251, 332, 422, 424, 441-42, 469, 494, 672
Protectionism—258-60, 261-62, 266-67, 274, 275, 282, 290, 656, 657
See also *Trade*
Protestantism—346-47
Proudhonism—23-35, 38, 39, 40-54, 156-57, 528, 642-43
Prussia—646, 649, 676
— internal policy—112, 234
— government—230, 234
— socialist movement—237, 238
Psychology—31, 99

R

Rappites—218-20
Rationalism—128
Reading-rooms (at factories) in England—477
— proletarian—527
See also *Education in England*
Reality—53
— objective reality—193
— as a criterion of truth—27-28
— abstraction from reality—19, 58, 59, 60, 141-42, 180
— real man—22, 39, 53, 85-86, 108-09, 120-21, 139, 153, 160, 175, 177, 192, 248
— Hegel's conception of—60-61, 79, 85-86, 90, 139, 191-92
— Young Hegelians' idealist conception of reality—7, 12-13, 19, 23, 24-25, 27-28, 53, 58-61, 77, 79, 83-84, 90, 95-96, 108-09, 125, 140-42, 145, 155, 157-60, 180
— and semblance—33, 58, 83, 101-02, 248
— and ideas, concepts, notions—19, 49-50, 53, 58-61, 77, 79, 82, 120-21, 145
— and thinking, consciousness—54, 58, 140-41, 190-93
— and its reflection in philosophy—7, 126-27
— and religion—108-09, 175, 177
— and possibility—126, 127
— and bourgeois political economy—32-33, 42, 54
Reason—32, 41, 58-61, 65, 85, 90, 128, 129, 141, 142, 143, 179
— abstract reason—59-60, 66-67
— common sense, common human reason—143, 147, 151
"Rebecca" (peasant revolt in 1843)—557
Reflection—110
Relative and absolute—114, 121
Religion—89, 97, 108, 109, 116, 166, 408-11, 421, 464, 526, 527, 564
— Christianity—59, 89, 109, 110
— freedom of conscience—111-12
— religious consciousness—166
— religious fanaticism—421
— religious sects—215-18, 408, 409
— and the state—111-12, 117
— in England—408, 411, 419-21, 464, 496, 526, 538
See also *Atheism, Catholicism, Christianity, Church, Judaism, Protestantism, Theology*
Repealers—560, 561
Rent of land—271-72, 287, 288, 289-90, 656
— as an economic expression of landed property—289
Revolution
— general characteristics (its essential features and tasks)—81, 82, 118-19
— and economic crises—580-81
— revolution of the minority—81, 82
See also *Masses—their role in history, Revolution, bourgeois, Revolution, proletarian*

Revolution, bourgeois, the
— general characteristics (its essential features and nature)—81, 82, 110-11, 122-23
— its limitations (incompleteness, half-heartedness)—81, 82, 261-62

Revolution, proletarian, the
— general characteristics (its essential features and tasks)—36, 37, 109-10, 257, 258, 260, 261-64, 266-67, 282, 283
— prerequisites for—261, 262
— historical inevitability of—418, 580-81
— its international character (revolutions breaking out simultaneously in a number of countries)—261
— fundamental difference from the bourgeois revolution—87, 88, 94, 95, 110-11, 261, 262
— and the role of the proletarian party—581-82
— and resort to revolutionary violence—546-47, 581-82
— possibility of a peaceful development and an objective necessity of transition to the armed struggle in the course of the revolution—263-64, 581-82
See also *Revolution—general characteristics*

Revolution, technical—see *Industrial revolution in England, Progress—scientific and technical*
Revolution of 1848-49 in France—579
Right—see *Law*
Rochdale—313, 315, 345, 430
Rome—120, 268, 510
— plebs—510
Russia—289

S

Saint-Simon's socialism—50, 282-83, 614
Salford—363, 464
Saxony—646, 647
Scepticism—127, 201-02, 584
Scholasticism—107, 127
Schools in England—407, 408, 411, 412, 459, 462, 464, 477, 490, 491, 494

— Sunday schools—408-09, 410, 492, 496
See also *Education*
Science—24-27, 28, 30, 31, 32, 41, 58, 89, 93, 127, 128, 129
See also *Mathematics, Natural science, Physics*
Scotland—319, 386, 404, 422, 484, 503, 530, 533, 534, 535, 578, 591
See also *Working class in England—Scottish workers*
Sects, religious—see *Religion*
Self-consciousness—7, 12, 39-41, 79, 80, 82, 85-86, 93, 104
See also *Consciousness*
Semblance, appearance—33, 36, 37, 58, 83, 84-85, 99-103, 108-09, 116, 138, 140, 141, 145, 196
Senses, sensuousness—19, 22, 58, 61, 65-69, 82, 83, 120, 128, 129, 150, 178, 181, 192
— sensations—130
— world of the senses—23, 58, 128, 178, 184, 192
— sensuous understanding—58
— experience of the senses—23, 128
See also *Perception*
Sensationalism—127, 128, 129
See also *Senses*
Serfdom—413, 472
Shakers and the foundation of communist colonies in the U.S.A.—215-18
Sheffield—317-18, 340, 488, 492-94, 508, 509, 519
Silesia
— riot of the weavers in 1844—230, 258, 303-04, 646, 674
Slavery—113, 122, 380, 413, 473, 474
Social estates—88-89
Social formation—150, 642
Social relations—158
Socialism (theory)—53, 94-95, 130, 136, 302, 418
— in England—14, 125, 153, 231, 302, 418, 524-27
— in Germany—229-31, 241, 303, 614, 642-43
— in France—125, 153, 614
See also *Communism (theory)*

Socialism, petty-bourgeois—24-25, 53, 94-95, 241

Socialism, scientific—94-95, 232

Socialism, utopian—84, 152-53, 232, 251-53, 263, 302, 459, 524-27, 613-14
See also Fourier's socialism, Owen's socialism, Saint-Simon's socialism

Socialist movement, Socialists
— in England—215, 524-27
— in France—19, 24, 25, 212-13, 598
See also Communist movement, Communists

Society—49-50, 131, 160, 251-52
— feudal—122-23, 243, 473, 550
See also Bourgeois society

Somersetshire—316

Sophistry—34, 61, 140, 174, 182, 185

Spain—408, 548

Speculation—7, 13, 23, 57, 125, 139, 143, 166, 167, 168, 178-79, 191
— German—7
— critical—35, 37

Spinoza school—124, 131, 137, 139

Spirit—7, 135, 141-42, 153
— Hegel's conception of—15-16, 77, 84-85, 139, 167
— Young Hegelians' conception of—7, 40, 77, 82-86, 94, 97, 104-05, 113, 134-36, 139-44, 145-46, 177-78, 186, 206

Spiritualism—7, 42, 82, 84, 94, 122, 128, 145, 150, 178

Staffordshire—488, 491

Stalybridge—313, 345, 346, 587

State—88, 95-96, 110-11, 115, 120-21, 124
— of antiquity—113, 122
— bourgeois—112-14, 116, 117, 274, 666, 668
— democratic representative—114, 115, 122, 123, 666
— and the national question—111
— and religion—111-12, 117

Statistics—247

Stockport—345, 346, 430, 464, 521

Stoicism—169

Strikebreakers—544, 586-87

Strikes and strike movement in England—458, 505, 506, 507, 508-12, 540-41, 584, 585
— in 1812—503
— in 1818—503-04
— in 1822—503
— in 1842-43 (Manchester)—387, 512-17, 521-23, 585, 587-96, 659, 660
— in 1844 (of coal-miners in the north of England)—426, 460, 541-47, 569, 585
See also Chartism, Workers' movement in England

Strikes and strike movement in France—512, 650

Subject and object—21, 22, 59, 60, 61, 71, 72, 75, 78, 79, 80, 82, 85, 129, 137, 138, 141, 142, 144-45, 159, 160, 167, 192, 193, 665

Substance—58-60, 125, 129, 131, 132, 137-41, 160, 668

Suffolk—554

Suicide—412, 597-612

Summary—128

Superstition—127

Sweden—532

Switzerland—242, 651, 652, 653

T

Tautology—20, 84, 153

Taxes—254-55
— general progressive tax—254

Teism—110

Teleology—79

Terror—74, 81, 95, 122-23, 124

Theology—17, 89, 94, 102, 109, 110, 112, 127, 143

Theory and practice—
— their dialectical correlation—53
— their unity—153, 235-36, 263
— discrepancy between them—613-15, 641-44
— their contradiction—115-16, 643-44
— criticism of the idealist interpretation of the correlation between theory and practice—39, 46, 82,

141-42, 192-93, 613-15, 641-44, 665
— the role of practice in transforming reality—53, 82, 94-95, 506-07
— revolutionary practice—12, 94-95, 263
— theory and practice of the working-class movement—84

Thermidor—see *French bourgeois revolution of the end of the 18th century*

Thinking, thought—13, 39, 53, 54, 82-83, 97, 126-29, 140-43, 151, 153, 158, 191-93, 665
— abstract—39-40
— absolute—159
— ability to think—21
— speculative—58
See also *Being and consciousness*

Time—48-49
See also *Labour time*

Tories—14, 15, 289, 381, 416, 463-64, 465, 503, 519, 520, 521, 555-56, 578
— philanthropic Tories—460, 473, 578
— Tory Cabinet of Robert Peel—660

Towns—292-93, 325-30, 339, 340, 373, 394-95, 416-19, 423, 441, 444, 460, 467, 498, 532, 556
— factory—12, 13, 325, 326, 327, 394-95, 416-19, 441, 444, 460, 498, 532
— in England—313-14, 317, 318, 319-21, 326, 328-74, 459, 660
— in Germany—672
See also *Birmingham, London, Manchester and other towns*

Trade—33, 116, 289, 292-93
— as a form of private property—33
— free trade—267
See also *Economic crisis, Protectionism*

Trade unions in England—13, 503-07, 509, 510, 526, 540-43, 544-47, 586, 591, 593
See also *Workers' movement in England*

Transcendentalism—7, 40

Truth—26, 27, 28, 79, 80, 138, 139, 140

U

Unemployment—250, 251, 261, 377, 381, 382, 384-88, 396, 429-31, 433, 553-54, 566

See also *Competition, Working class*

United States of America—116, 247, 272, 289
— position of Negroes—468-69
See also *Communist colonies in the U.S.A.*

Universe—140, 142

Usury—423

V

Value—32-33, 46, 47, 49-50
— exchange value—266, 275-83, 284

W

Wage-labour—36, 53

Wages—16, 32, 52, 53, 278, 279, 286, 287, 288, 307, 308, 330, 377-81, 387, 431-32, 504, 505, 507, 594, 596, 658, 659
— dependence on the introduction of machines—431-32
— in agriculture—549-51, 552
— truck system—470, 471, 473, 539, 542, 673
— in England—13, 307, 308, 376-79, 387, 426-27, 431, 432, 481, 505-07, 508, 523, 549, 550, 552, 571

Wars—249-50
See also *Napoleonic wars, Patriotic War of 1812 in Russia*

Weitling's communism—235-36, 614, 615

Whigs—14, 460, 463, 578
— German Whiggery—646

Will—13, 95, 98

Women's question—438-42
See also *Child labour, Family, Female labour*

Workers' associations—52-53, 503-04
See also *Trade unions in England*

Workers' movement—227, 263, 302, 321, 418, 419, 581-82, 653
See also *Class struggle, Communist movement, Strikes and strike movement in England, Strikes and strike movement in France*

Workers' movement in England
— general characteristics—242, 321, 324-25, 344, 418, 428, 433, 444,

488, 489, 494, 498, 501-22, 526,
529, 541-47, 553, 561, 566, 582-
83, 645
— movement for shorter working
hours—15, 459, 460, 465, 519, 523,
569
— struggle for higher wages—426,
505-07, 523, 586
— and peasantry—555
See also *Chartism, Luddism, Strikes and
strike movement in England, Trade
unions in England*

Workers' movement in France—263, 512,
650

Workers' movement in Germany—227-28,
230, 236, 253-54, 256-57, 646-48
— "Leipzig butchery" (1845)—645-46

Workhouses in England —521, 573-77

Working class
— general   characteristics — 36-37,
265, 302-04, 330-31, 376, 379,
419-20, 421
— its rise and development—257,
259, 260, 261, 309-11, 320-21, 324-
27, 354-56, 375
— its world-historic role — 36-37, 257,
421
— its condition in capitalist society—
302-03, 322-23, 329-32, 373-74,
423-25, 473-74, 671
— antithesis and struggle between the
proletariat and the bourgeoisie—
35, 323, 329-30, 375-76, 379,
385-86, 413-16, 419-20, 427, 506-
08, 510, 529, 561-63, 570
— need for its organisation—376
— its class-consciousness—36-37, 53,
253-54, 418, 419, 501, 529, 546-47
— its internationalism—212, 303-04
— class solidarity—565
— its living conditions—36, 37, 373-
74, 394-95
— dwellings—331-42, 355-57, 395-96
— food—368-74, 399-400, 434, 491
— similar conditions of workers' life
in various countries—302-04
— conditions   of   labour—415-16,
443-46, 447-48, 450-52, 453-56,
462, 468-69, 479-89, 530-39
— competition among workers—16,
250-51,   307-08,   372,   375-88,
433-34, 507-08

— humaneness—420
— agricultural   proletariat—257,
310-11, 548-62
See also *Revolution, proletarian, Unemployment, Workers' movement, Working
class in England, Working class in
France, Working class in Germany,
Working class in Ireland*

Working class in England
— general   characteristics — 36-37,
262-63, 297, 302-03, 321, 322, 326-
27, 354-56, 373-74, 413, 418-19,
421, 428, 435, 436, 470, 473-74,
500, 501-02, 584
— its rise and development—307-08,
310-11, 312, 317, 320-21, 324, 325,
326, 344-45, 375, 548
— world-historic role—36-37
— workers doing their work at home,
handicraftsmen—308, 310, 311,
321, 488-89
— antithesis between the proletariat
and the bourgeoisie; class antagonism and class struggle—36, 323,
375-76, 379-80, 413-14, 415-16,
497-98, 501, 506-07, 512-13, 562-
83, 585, 660
— labour aristocracy—461, 477
— class-consciousness of—36-37, 84,
134-36, 418, 419, 529, 546-47
— internationalism of—298-99
— humaneness—420
— class solidarity—546-47, 565
— its living conditions—303, 331-32,
348-49, 373-74, 392-95, 398, 400,
403-04, 405-07, 658
— dwellings—331-66, 373-74, 396-99,
407, 434, 470-72, 491-92, 532,
539, 543, 558
— conditions   of   labour—415-16,
443-48, 450, 451-52, 453-56, 462,
468-69, 479-89, 530-39, 585-86
— enmity   towards   Irish   workers—
376-77, 392
— Irish workers—322, 324, 376-77,
390, 392, 399, 421, 534, 544
— Scottish workers—590, 591, 593
— agricultural   proletariat—13, 257,
284-85, 310-11, 548-62
— weavers—308, 310, 311
— lumpenproletariat—251, 552
— moral principles—308-09, 343, 392,

411, 412, 419, 420, 441, 442, 483, 484, 496, 538
— its atheism—412, 421, 526, 538
— education and upbringing—407-12, 421, 490-92, 494, 496, 526-28, 538
See also *Chartism, Factory system, Industry in England, Trade unions in England, Wages, Workers' movement in England*

Working class in France—212, 213, 262-63
— its theoretical consciousness—36-37, 84
— Proudhon's standpoint—41

Working class in Germany—230, 236, 237, 256, 257, 259, 260, 261, 303, 304, 647, 652-53, 671-73
See also *Workers' movement in Germany*

Working class in Ireland—390, 392
— agricultural proletariat—558-59

Working day
— in England—13, 14, 15, 382, 384, 408, 428, 435-36, 443, 444, 461-66, 479, 481-82, 491-92, 499-500, 533, 592-93, 672

— movement for the Ten Hours' Bill —15, 459, 460, 461, 463, 464, 465, 519, 569
See also *Factory legislation*

World outlook—170

Writers
— socialist and communist—36, 84
— and censorship—82-83

Y

Yeomen—see *England—peasants, tenant farmers*

Yorkshire—342, 403

"Young England"—205, 570, 578

"Young Germany"—651-53, 654

Young Hegelianism—7-9, 10-11, 20, 39-42, 47-51, 52-54, 78-79, 82, 94, 95, 96, 97, 99-103, 105-15, 131-34, 136-61, 191, 197-200, 211
See also *Reality—Young Hegelians' idealist conception of reality*